NINTH EDITION

A HISTORY OF THE MODERN WORLD

MODERN WORLD

Since 1815

R. R. Palmer   Joel Colton   Lloyd Kramer

Boston   Burr Ridge, IL   Dubuque, IA   Madison, WI   New York
San Francisco   St. Louis   Bangkok   Bogotá   Caracas   Kuala Lumpur
Lisbon   London   Madrid   Mexico City   Milan   Montreal   New Delhi
Santiago   Seoul   Singapore   Sydney   Taipei   Toronto

McGraw-Hill Higher Education

*A Division of The **McGraw-Hill** Companies*

A HISTORY OF THE MODERN WORLD: SINCE 1815
Published by McGraw-Hill, an imprint of The McGraw-Hill Companies, Inc. 1221
Avenue of the Americas, New York, NY, 10020. Copyright © 2002, 1995, 1992, 1984,
1978, 1971, 1965, 1956, 1950 by The McGraw-Hill Companies, Inc. All rights reserved.
No part of this publication may be reproduced or distributed in any form or by any
means, or stored in a database or retrieval system, without the prior written consent of
The McGraw-Hill Companies, Inc., including, but not limited to, in any network or other
electronic storage or transmission, or broadcast for distance learning.
Some ancillaries, including electronic and print components, may not be available to
customers outside the United States.

This book is printed on acid-free paper.

domestic   3 4 5 6 7 8 9 0 DOC/DOC 0 9 8 7 6 5 4 3
international   1 2 3 4 5 6 7 8 9 0 DOC/DOC 0 9 8 7 6 5 4 3 2 1

ISBN 0-07-241790-0

Editorial director: *Jane Karpacz*
Executive editor: *Lyn Uhl*
Developmental editor: *Anne Sachs*
Marketing manager: *Janise Fry*
Project manager: *Laura Ward Majersky*
Production supervisor: *Susanne Riedell*
Media producer: *Dave Edwards*
Senior designer: *Pam Verros*
Associate supplement producer: *Vicki Laird*
Photo research coordinator: *Judy Kausal*
Photo researcher: *Photosearch, Inc., New York*
Cover and interior designer: *Michael Warrell*
Cover art: *Historical Picture Archives / ©Corbis; View from the Transept of Crystal Exhibition Palace
    during Great Exhibition, London, 1851*
Typeface: *10/12 Times Roman*
Compositor: *ElectraGraphics, Inc.*
Printer: *R. R. Donnelley & Sons Company*

Library of Congress Control Number: 2001091414

INTERNATIONAL EDITION ISBN 0-07-112137-4
Copyright © 2002. Exclusive rights by The McGraw-Hill Companies, Inc.
for manufacture and export.
This book cannot be re-exported from the country to which it is sold by McGraw-Hill.
The International Edition is not available in North America.

www.mhhe.com

R. R. PALMER was born in Chicago in 1909. After graduating from the University of Chicago he received his PhD from Cornell University in 1934. From 1936 to 1963 he taught at Princeton University, taking leave during the Second World War to work on historical projects in Washington, D.C. In 1963 he went to Washington University in St. Louis as dean of arts and sciences, but in 1969 he resumed his teaching, this time at Yale. After his retirement in 1977, he returned to live in Princeton, where he was affiliated with the Institute for Advanced Study. In recent years he and his wife have resided in a retirement community in Newtown, Pennsylvania. His most important books include *Catholics and Unbelievers in Eighteenth Century France* (1939); *Twelve who Ruled: The Year of the Terror in the French Revolution* (1941, 1989); and the two-volume *Age of the Democratic Revolution* (1959, 1964), for the first volume of which he won the Bancroft Prize. He has also written, translated, and edited a number of other books. He was president of the American Historical Association in 1970 and has received honorary degrees from universities in the United States as well as abroad. He was awarded the Antonio Feltrinelli International Prize for History in Rome in 1990.

JOEL COLTON graduated from the City College of New York, served as a military intelligence officer in Europe in World War II, and in 1950 received his PhD from Columbia University. From 1947 to 1989 he taught at Duke University, where he chaired the department of history from 1967 to 1974. He received a Distinguished Teaching Award in 1986. From 1974 to 1981, on leave from Duke University, he served with the Rockefeller Foundation in New York as director of its research and fellowship program in the humanities. In 1979 he was elected a fellow of the American Academy of Arts and Sciences and was named a national Phi Beta Kappa lecturer in 1983–1984. He has received Guggenheim, Rockefeller Foundation, and National Endowment for the Humanities fellowships. He has served on the editorial boards of the *Journal of Modern History, French Historical Studies,* and *Historical Abstracts.* He has been co-president of the International Commission on the History of Social Movements and Social Structures. His writings include *Compulsory Labor Arbitration in France, 1936–1939* (1951); *Léon Blum: Humanist in Politics* (1966, 1987), for which he received a Mayflower Award; *Twentieth Century* (1968, 1980), in the *Time-Life Great Ages of Man* series; and numerous contributions to journals, encyclopedias, and collaborative volumes. He has co-authored with R. R. Palmer the successive editions since 1956 of *A History of the Modern World.*

LLOYD KRAMER was born in Maryville, Tennessee. He graduated from Maryville College and received his PhD from Cornell University in 1983. Before entering Cornell, he was a teacher in Hong Kong and traveled widely in Asia. After completing his graduate studies, he taught at Stanford University and Northwestern University. Since 1986 he has been a professor in the history department at the University of North Carolina, Chapel Hill, where he has received two awards for distinguished undergraduate teaching. His writings include *Threshold of a New World: Intellectuals and the Exile Experience in Paris, 1830–1848* (1988); *Lafayette in Two Worlds: Public Cultures and Personal Identities in an Age of Revolutions* (1996), which won the Gilbert Chinard Prize from the Society for French Historical Studies and the Annibel Jenkins Biography Prize from the American Society for Eighteenth-Century Studies; and *Nationalism: Political Cultures in Europe and America, 1775–1865* (1998). He has also edited several books, including a collection of essays on historical education in America. He has been a member of the School of Historical Studies at the Institute for Advanced Study in Princeton and served as president of the Society for French Historical Studies.

Brief Contents

Contents

Chapter **11**   REACTION VERSUS PROGRESS,
1815–1848   *427*

Chapter **12**   REVOLUTION AND THE REIMPOSITION
OF ORDER, 1848–1870   *475*

Chapter **13**   THE CONSOLIDATION OF LARGE
NATION-STATES, 1859–1871   *509*

List of Illustrations

List of Maps, Charts, and Tables

Preface

Continuing changes in the contemporary world often obscure the long historical processes that have created the modern societies in which we live. Bombarded by the mass media's images of conflict or innovation or cultural diversity or globalization, most of us hear little about the broad historical patterns and contexts that give wider meaning to the cascading events that flash across our newspapers, televisions, and computer screens. This new edition of *A History of the Modern World* may therefore be seen as the most recent version of a constant search for historical perspectives on the complex, often bewildering events of modern life. It provides a narrative of the people, events, ideas, institutions, and social changes that have created modern societies and that will continue to influence people around the world in the twenty-first century.

We have designed this book for readers who will live in a new century of worldwide economic, political, and cultural interactions, but we have begun with the assumption that contemporary global systems must be understood as the latest stages in a long history of transnational exchanges, conflicts, and social transformations. The book thus goes beyond the histories of specific nations and people to describe broad historical trends that have affected people throughout the modern world. We have sought to explain the rise of nation-states and the global conflicts that have molded the world's diverse societies over the last several centuries, but we have also emphasized the evolving global economy, the importance of science and technology, the significance of religious traditions, the international diffusion of new ideas, the changing mores of social life, and the complex relations between Western cultures and other cultures around the world.

The term *modern,* as we use it in this book, refers very broadly to the historical evolution of societies and cultures over the last five centuries, but we devote more chapters to the recent past than to the early modern era. We also focus primarily on developments in the West until the global character of modernity in recent times leads toward an increasingly global narrative of recent history. Although the book stresses the crucial influence of European societies and traditions on the emergence of what we now call modern world history, it also discusses past global exchanges and conflicts that have created the international characteristics of modern social, economic, and cultural life.

ORGANIZATION OF THE BOOK

The book is organized in chapters that carry the narrative across specific chronological eras, moving steadily toward the present. Yet the clearly defined sections within each chapter typically deal with themes, events, or issues that do not develop in simple chronological order. Each chapter focuses on a specific time frame, but each historical period is approached through discussions of themes and problems as well as through accounts of similarities and differences in various nations and regions of the world. Chronology thus offers an overall structure and organizing framework for the book's analytical arguments about the historical origins and evolution of modern societies.

These chronological and thematic components of the book's organization represent some of the important continuities that link this new edition to its predecessors. At the same time, however, the book has been substantially altered to make it more accessible for a new generation of readers. A new author has joined in the writing and revising of the text, and there have been significant changes in the book's content and design.

✒ NEW FEATURES OF THE BOOK

Reflecting trends in contemporary historical scholarship, the book includes new information from recent research in social and cultural history. There are new sections on the role of women in various historical contexts; new descriptions of cultural and intellectual movements in the early modern, modern, and contemporary periods; more attention to the historical significance of cultural institutions, rituals, and symbols; and new analysis of global economic and political interactions.

Readers will find, for example, concise new discussions of family life during the Renaissance and Reformation; new descriptions of literary debates, salon culture, and the evolving public sphere in the early and late Enlightenment; and new information on the cultural dimensions of the French Revolution. Later chapters of the book (in volume 2 of the paperback edition) include new sections on the emergence of feminism, new accounts of European cultural debates about science and the idea of progress, and new material on modernist cultural movements that gained influence after World War I. All of the chapters on the world since 1945 have been extensively revised to include new information on recent international conflicts and also to provide historical perspectives on the increasing globalization of contemporary economic and cultural life. Although the history of political conflicts and institutions remains an important theme throughout the book, some of the complex details of national political histories have been reduced to expand the discussion of social and cultural history.

The pages of the book have also been redesigned to help readers more easily follow the argument through each chapter. The section and subsection titles now appear in color rather than in black, the maps have sharper color shadings and contrasts, and new marginal notes have been added to show readers the key subjects on almost every page and suggest themes that they can more easily identify as they make their way through the book. We have also removed almost all of the footnotes and thematic cross-references to other chapters, but important themes can still be traced through the detailed index.

The visual component of this edition has been extended through the addition of many new illustrations. Like other kinds of documents and sources, visual information is important to historical understanding; indeed, knowing how to read and critically evaluate an image, painting, or photograph is an essential form of analytical thought and an important aspect of cross-cultural comparisons. To that end, this edition includes over 200 new illustrations. Unlike previous editions, which presented most of its illustrations in clustered photo essays, this edition integrates text with images from the historical periods that are discussed in the chapters where they appear, and they contribute important evidence to support the overall themes of the book.

In addition to the many illustrations in each chapter, we have also added new four-color inserts that convey both the artistic creativity and cultural or social preoccupations of different historical eras. The color gives more clarity to the themes of the artists' work and to a visual history that (like the written text) shows the gradual emergence of a modern social and cultural world. Brief captions also accompany all of the illustrations, pointing to connections between events or issues in the book's narrative and the themes in the images.

✑ CONTINUITIES IN THE NEW EDITION

The changes in this latest version of *A History of the Modern World* have been introduced to enhance the book's accessibility, but not to replace or weaken the style, content, narrative, and analytical qualities that have appealed to teachers and students who have used this book in its earlier editions. Readers will still find informative, concise accounts of major events, political transformations, and influential leaders in many different societies and national traditions. They will also find an updated, comprehensive bibliography that describes books for further reading and research on every subject in this book. And they will find a wide range of helpful maps and charts that summarize the changing boundaries, populations, and economies of nations and social groups in the modern world.

More generally, however, readers of this new edition of a well-established book will find that it expresses again a strong belief in the value of historical knowledge and historical perspectives for anyone who wishes to understand as well as to live in the evolving modern world. This book achieves its purpose whenever it helps or provokes readers of any age or background to understand themselves and their world with new knowledge and new insights.

✑ SUPPLEMENTS FOR THE INSTRUCTOR

Instructor's Manual/Test Bank   The first half of this unique manual offers a chapter-by-chapter guide to some of the best documentaries, educational films, feature films, videos, and audio recordings to enhance classroom discussion. Brief overviews help instructors select the films best suited to each course topic. In this new edition, the manual also provides instructors with chapter objectives and points for discussion for each chapter, followed by a test bank containing multiple choice, essay, and identification test questions.

Computerized Test Bank   This on-disk version of the test bank is available for both Macintosh and IBM-compatible computers to allow instructors to customize each test.

Overhead Transparencies   This set of over 150 overhead transparencies containing a variety of fine art and maps—many taken directly from the text—can be used to illuminate classroom lectures.

Slide Set   Available through your local McGraw-Hill sales representative, instructors can choose from a list of hundreds of fine art slides to create a customized slide set that will complement the text and enhance classroom lectures.

Instructor's Online Learning Center   At the homepage to the text-specific website, instructors will find a downloadable version of the Instructor's Manual. Instructors can also create web-based homework assignments or classroom activities by linking to the Student Online Learning Center and can create an interactive course syllabus using McGraw-Hill's PageOut site at www.mhhe.com/pageout.

PageOut (www.mhhe.com/pageout)   On the PageOut website, instructors can create their own course websites. PageOut requires no prior knowledge of HTML, no long hours of coding, and no design skills on the instructor's part. Instructors need simply to plug the course information into a template and click on one of the 16 designs. The process takes little time and provides a professionally designed website. Powerful features include an interactive course syllabus that lets instructors post content and links, an online gradebook, lecture notes, bookmarks, and even a discussion board where instructors and students can discuss course-related topics.

Videos   A wide range of videos on classic and contemporary topics in history is available through the Films for the Humanities and Sciences collection. Instructors can illustrate and enhance lectures by selection from a series of videos that are correlated to the course. Contact your local McGraw-Hill sales representative for further information.

SUPPLEMENTS FOR THE STUDENT

Student Study Guide   Written by two of the text authors, this volume helps students to process and master important concepts covered in the text, stimulating reflection and interpretation rather than rote memorization. For each section, the study guide provides study questions, key discussion sentences, and identifications. For each chapter, there are general essay questions and general discussion passages. Wherever possible, map exercises are also included.

Student Online Learning Center   At the homepage to the text-specific website, students can link to an interactive study guide, including online essay questions, interactive mapping exercises, Internet exercises, chronology activities, and links to online primary source documents. Links to trusted history search engines also make the Online Learning Center an ideal place to begin web-based research.

ACKNOWLEDGMENTS

We gratefully acknowledge the help of the many people who have helped with the production of this book. We owe a particular debt to the editors and staff of McGraw-Hill, Inc., which has published this book since its seventh edition. We are grateful also to Alfred A. Knopf, Inc., the earlier publisher of this book, for having continued to make it available in a trade edition for the general public. The assistance at McGraw-Hill of Lyn Uhl, Anne Sachs, Judy Kausal, Laura Majersky, Megan McLean, and others has been invaluable and essential for the completion of the book. We have relied also on the expert advice and research skills of Deborah Bull and Jullie Chung, who have helped us find numerous new illustrations.

We have benefited from the expert advice of reviewers who offered suggestions for the variety of ways in which a new edition of this book might be revised; and we have drawn many other ideas from colleagues and students who have used earlier editions of the book in their courses. We mention specifically Judah Adelson, State University of New York, New Paltz; Stephanie Mooers Christelow, Idaho State University; Marvin R. Cox, University of Connecticut; Gary B. Ferngren, Oregon State University; Elizabeth C. George, Southern Illinois University; Mary Louise Loe, James Madison University; Richard A. Oehling, Assumption College; Thomas W. Perry, Boston College; Don Reid, University of North Carolina, Chapel Hill; Roger Schlesinger, Washington State University; John F. Sweets, University of Kansas; and K. Steven Vincent, North Carolina State University. None of these people are in any way responsible for the book's shortcomings, but all have contributed to its strengths.

Regrettably, because of problems that often accompany advanced age, R. R. Palmer was unable to take an active role in the preparation of this new edition, but he remains the guiding influence and inspiration behind this book. Finally, we wish to acknowledge the exceptional support and contributions of our colleagues and our families, who have helped us carry this book through a new phase of authorial transition and into a new century of historical scholarship. They are a vital part of this ongoing intellectual collaboration, and we have drawn often on their insights and wisdom.

R. R. Palmer
Joel Colton
Lloyd Kramer

Geography and History

History is the experience of human beings in time, but that experience takes place also in geographic space. Geography describes and maps the earth, but it also studies the changing relationships between human activities and the surrounding environment.

The universe, of which our planet earth and our solar system form but a small part, is now thought to be at least 12 billion years old. The earth is thought to be about 4.6 billion years old. Yet the entire history (and prehistory) of humankind goes back only 3.5 to 5 million years, or perhaps only 2 million years, depending on how humans are defined. What we call history—the recorded cultures and actions of human beings—began with the invention of early forms of writing only about 5,500 years ago.

Oceans and continents have moved about over the span of time, changing in size, shape, and location. The continents as we know them took on their distinctive forms less than 100 million years ago. There was a time when dinosaurs, which became extinct some 60 million years before the first humans even emerged, could walk from North America to Europe (as we now call these continents) on solid land in a warm climate. It is only a few thousand years since the end of the most recent glacial age, which may not be the last. That Ice Age, which began about 2 million years ago and reached its coldest point only 20,000 years ago, was caused by a slight shift in the earth's orbit around the sun. Water froze into ice 1–2 inches thick and covered the northern parts of the planet (in North America as far south as present-day Chicago and in Europe across large parts of the British Isles and the nearby mainland). The melting of this ice produced the coastlines, offshore islands, inland seas, straits, bays, and harbors that we know today, as well as some of the large river systems and lakes. The process of change in the earth's surface continues. Niagara Falls, on the border between the United States and Canada, has been receding because the ongoing cascade of water has been eroding the underlying rock. The ocean's tides and human construction erode our shorelines as well, and many scientists believe current patterns of global warming may eventually change the oceans and coasts in much of the world.

Ice Age

The oceans presently cover more than two-thirds of the earth's surface, and many large land areas in the remaining third are poorly suited for habitation by human beings or most other animal and plant organisms. One-tenth of the land remains under ice, as in Antarctica and Greenland, much is tundra, much is desert, as in the Sahara, and much land lies along the windswept ridges of high mountains. Like the oceans, these regions have been important in human history, often acting as barriers to movement and settlement. Human history has therefore evolved in relatively small, scattered sections of the earth's total surface.

Origins of human beings

Researchers have found persuasive material evidence to show that human beings originated in Africa. Humans belonging to the species *Homo erectus,* the Latin term used by anthropologists and others to denote the upright, walking predecessors of modern humans, seem to have migrated from Africa about 1.8 million years ago, perhaps because of environmental pressures or perhaps because of simple curiosity. Our own species *Homo sapiens,* the Latin term connoting increased cognitive and judgmental abilities, emerged no more than about 100,000 years ago. When humans went beyond merely utilitarian accomplishments and demonstrated aesthetic and artistic interests as well as advanced toolmaking, say 35,000 years ago, we refer to them as the subspecies *Homo sapiens sapiens,* the remaining survivors of a very complex human family tree.

The great Ice Age lowered the seas by hundreds of feet and froze huge quantities of water. The English Channel became dry. Land bridges opened up between Siberia and North America over what we now call the Bering Strait. Hunters seeking game walked from one continent to the other. When the glaciers melted, forests sprang up, and many of the open areas in which humans had hunted disappeared, providing added motivation for movement.

Our human ancestors spread eventually to every continent except Antarctica. In doing so, human groups became isolated from each other for millennia, separated by oceans, deserts, or mountains. Wherever they wandered, they evolved slightly over time, developing superficial physical differences that modern cultures have defined as the characteristics of various racial groups. But "race" is a cultural idea rather than a mark of biologically significant differences. All human beings belong to the *Homo sapiens* species, all derive from the same biological ancestry, and all are mutually fertile. Only a very few human genes are responsible for physical differences such as skin pigmentation, in comparison to the vast number of genes that are shared by all members of the human species.

Race: a cultural concept

The basic anatomy and genetic makeup of modern humans has not changed over the last 100,000 years. Geographic separation accounts for the emergence over shorter time periods of distinctive cultures, which can be seen, for example, in the different historical and cultural development of the pre-Columbian Americas, Africa, China, India, the Middle East, and Europe. On a still smaller time scale, geographic separation also explains differences in languages and dialects.

Geography and culture

Geographic distances and diversity of climate have also produced differences in flora and fauna, and hence in the plants and animals upon which humans are dependent. Wheat became the most usual cereal in the Middle East and Europe, millet and rice in East Asia, sorghum in tropical Africa, maize in pre-Columbian America. The horse, first domesticated in north-central Asia about 4,500 years ago, was for centuries a mainstay of Europe and Asia for muscle power, transportation, and fighting. The somewhat less versatile camel was adopted later and more slowly in the Middle East, and the Americans long had no beasts of burden except the llama. Such differences did not begin to diminish until early modern travelers crossed the oceans, taking plants and animals with them and bringing others back to environments where they had never lived before.

Although much remains obscure about the origins of life, and new discoveries and calculations are always displacing older hypotheses, paleontologists studying plant and animal fossils (including human ones) have used techniques such as radiocarbon dating to transform our knowledge of the earth and of the earliest human beings. In geography, aerial and satellite photography and computer technology have enabled us to refine older conceptions of continents and oceans. And astrophysicists are now studying vast amounts of new data about the universe, which have been sent to them from powerful telescopes mounted on unmanned spaceships.

Cartography, the art and science of mapmaking, has evolved rapidly, but we tend to forget how our maps often remain conventional and even parochial. It was Europeans and descendants of Europeans who designed our most commonly used maps, which are oriented North-South and West-East from fixed points in their horizons, and which therefore reflect their own European cultural assumptions. Similar biases can be found in the maps of other cultures too. The Chinese for centuries defined and visualized their country as the

"Middle Kingdom." In the early modern centuries maps drawn in India typically represented South Asia as forming the major part of the world. One such map depicted the European continent as a few marginal areas labeled England, France, and "other hat-wearing islands."

Changing conceptualizations of the globe continue in our day. A map drawn and published in the 1990s in Australia, demonstrating the Australian perspective from "down under," shows South Africa at the top of the map and Capetown at the very tip, the large expanse of contemporary African nations in the middle, and the various European countries crowded at the bottom, the latter appearing quite insignificant. The European-invented term "Middle East" has been called into question, and this region of the world is now often designated as Western Asia. Even our traditional concept of Europe as one of the seven continents (Africa, Asia, Europe, North America, South America, Australia, and Antarctica) is now questioned. Why, for example, should the Indian peninsula be a "subcontinent" when it roughly matches the size and exceeds the population and diversity of the European "continent" (at least that part of the "continent" that lies west of the former Soviet Union)? Europe itself is, of course, actually a peninsula, in a way that the other continents are not. Some geographers ask us to consider it more properly as part of Asia, the western part of a great "Eurasian landmass." Defined in these terms, Europe becomes more of a cultural conception, arising out of perceived differences from Asia and Africa, than a continent in a strictly geographical sense.

Europe and history

However we define its place on the globe, Europe has undoubtedly shaped much of modern world history—partly because of its overseas expansion, partly because of what it borrowed from other parts of the world, and partly because of its decisive economic and cultural influence on the emergence of an increasingly global civilization. Europe is of course only one of many important cultural spheres in human history, but its contributions to what we call modern world history give it crucial importance to the themes of this book. Because Europe will be so important in the chapters that follow, the reader, like a traveler about to embark on a trip, is invited to study the accompanying topographical map. The physical features of Europe and its surrounding territories have remained virtually unchanged over historic time, despite the constant political and cultural transformations in European societies.

Europe is not large. Even with European Russia, it contains hardly more than 6 percent of the earth's land surface, occupying about the same area as the United States mainland plus Alaska. It is only a little larger than Australia. It is physically separated from Africa by the Mediterranean Sea, although the Mediterranean historically has been as much a passageway as a barrier. A truer barrier emerged when the Sahara Desert dried up only a few thousand years ago, so that northern Africa might be said to belong as much to southern Europe, or culturally to the Middle East, as it does to sub-Saharan Africa. The physical separation of Europe from Asia is even less clear. The conventional boundary has been the Ural Mountains in Russia, but they are low and wide, are not an impressive chain, and do not stretch far enough to make an adequate boundary. The Russians themselves do not recognize any official distinction between European and Asian Russia.

The Mediterranean Sea

Europe is indeed one of several peninsulas jutting off from Asia, like the Arabian and Indian peninsulas. But there are differences. For one thing, the Mediterranean Sea is unique among the world's bodies of water. Closed in by the Strait of Gibraltar, which is only 8 miles wide, it is more shielded than other seas from the open ocean and is protected from the most violent ocean storms. Though over 2,000 miles long, it is subdivided by islands and peninsulas into lesser seas with identities of their own, such as the Aegean and the Adriatic, and it provides access also to the Black Sea. Because it is possible to travel great distances without being far from land, navigation developed on the Mediterranean from early times and one of the first civilizations appeared on the island of Crete. It is possible also to cross between Europe and Asia at the Bosporus and between Europe and Africa at Gibraltar. Populations became mixed by migration, and various historic empires—the Carthaginian, Roman, Byzantine, Arabic, Spanish, Venetian, and Ottoman—have effectively used the Mediterranean to govern their component parts. After the Suez Canal was built in the nineteenth century, the Mediterranean became an important segment in the "lifeline of empire" for the British Empire in its heyday.

In southern Europe, north of the Mediterranean and running for its whole length, is a series of mountains, produced over the geological ages by the pushing of the gigantic mass of Africa against the small Eurasian peninsula. The Pyrenees close off Spain from the north, as the Alps do Italy; the Balkan Mountains are difficult to penetrate. The only place where one can travel at water level from the Mediterranean to the north is by the valley of the Rhone River, so that France is the only country that belongs both to the Mediterranean and northern Europe. North of the mountains is a great plain extending from western France all the way into Russia and on into Asia, passing south of the Urals. If one were to draw a straight line from Amsterdam east through what is called the Caspian Gate, north of the Caspian Sea, as far as western China, one would never in traveling these 3,500 miles be higher than 2,000 feet above sea level. This plain has at various times opened Europe to Mongol and other invasions, enabled the Russians to move east and create a huge empire, and made Poland a troubled battleground.

Mountains

The European rivers are worth particular attention. Most are navigable, and they also give access to the sea. With their valleys, they provided areas where intensive local development could take place. Thus the most important older cities of Europe are on rivers—London on the Thames, Paris on the Seine, Vienna and Budapest on the Danube, Warsaw on the Vistula. In northern Europe it was often possible to move goods from one river to another, and then in the eighteenth century to connect them by canals. The importance of water is shown again by the location of Copenhagen, Stockholm, and St. Petersburg on the Baltic and of Amsterdam and Lisbon, which grew rapidly after Europeans began traversing the Atlantic Ocean.

Rivers

There are important geographical conditions such as climate that a topographical map cannot show. Climate depends on latitude, ocean currents, and winds that bring or withhold rainfall. Europe lies as far north as the northern United States and southern Canada; Madrid and Rome are in the latitude of New York, and Stockholm and St. Petersburg are as far north as the middle of Hudson Bay. Europe is thus within what is called the temperate zone—somewhat misleadingly, since the temperate zone by definition is the region of pronounced difference between winter and summer seasons. But the parts of Europe near the sea have less extreme temperatures than the corresponding northerly regions of America, and the Mediterranean countries have more sunshine and less severe winters than either northern Europe or the northern United States. Everywhere the winters are cold enough to suppress infectious pathogens and pests and keep out certain diseases that afflict warmer countries. These winters also obliged Europeans to expend more effort on clothing, housing, and heating. The warm summers with their growing seasons have produced an annual cycle of agriculture, and rainfall has been adequate but not excessive. Europe is the only continent that has no actual desert. It is also for the most part a region of fertile soil. In short, since the end of the Ice Age, or since humans learned to survive winters, Europe has been one of the most favored places on the globe for human habitation.

Climate

Climate itself, we know, can change. Studies of tree rings, fossil plants, and alpine glaciers show that average temperatures were warmer from the end of the Ice Age throughout ancient and medieval times, and then fell from about 1400 to 1850, when the winters

White
Sea

N. Dvina R.

URAL MOUNTAINS

0   100   200   300 miles

L. Onega

L. Ladoga

NORTH RUSSIAN PLAIN

St. Petersburg

L. Peipus

Volga R.   Kama R.

Dvina R.   Moscow

Oka R.

Ural R.

KIRGHIZ STEPPE

CENTRAL RUSSIAN HIGHLANDS

VOLGA HEIGHTS

B L A C K   E A R T H   R E G I O N

Syr Darya

Pripet R.

PRIPET
MARSHES

Aral
Sea

TURANIAN PLAIN

Kiev

Dnieper R.

Donets R.

Volga R.   CASPIAN DEPRESSION

Bug R.

Dniester R.

Prut R.

DONETS HEIGHTS   Don R.

Amu Darya

Sea of
Azov

Odessa

CRIMEA

Caspian Sea

IAN ALPS

Bucharest

OF
CHIA

Danube R.

Black Sea

CAUCASUS MOUNTAINS

MTS.

Sinop

ARMENIAN
HIGHLANDS

Araxes R.

Maritsa R.

RHODOPE
MTS.

Istanbul

Sea of
Marmara

Bosporus

Kizilirmak R.

L. Van

L. Urmia

ELBURZ MTS.

Tehran

Ankara

Dardanelles

ASIA MINOR
(ANATOLIAN PENINSULA)

Aegean Sea

Meander R.

TAURUS MOUNTAINS

MESOPOTAMIAN PLAINS

Tigris R.

DODECANESE IS.

Rhodes   CYPRUS

Euphrates R.   Baghdad

ZAGROS MTS.

CRETE

Jerusalem   Jordan R.

Dead Sea

SYRIAN
DESERT

Persian Gulf

Alexandria   NILE DELTA

Suez Canal

Cairo   SINAI
PENINSULA

Nile R.   Gulf of
Aqaba

NEFUD DESERT

lengthened and the growing season shortened. By that time Europeans could simply wear more wool, which suggests why sheep raising and the woolen trade became a main staple of European commerce.

If we say that climate and the environment not only set limits but also provide opportunities for what human beings can do, then there is no such thing as geographical determinism. Geography is not destiny. What happens depends on the application of knowledge and abilities in any particular time and place and in any particular culture. What constitutes a natural resource varies with the state of technology and the possibilities of economic exchange. Even the disadvantages of distance can be overcome by developing new means of transportation. The oceans that long divided human beings became a highway for the Portuguese, Spanish, Dutch, French, and English, and later for others. Chinese sailors also used the oceans for trade until their rulers made a conscious decision to insulate their populations from outside contact. For most of human history, neither persons, information, nor commands could travel much more than 30 miles a day. Localism prevailed, and large-scale commercial or governmental organizations were hard to create and maintain. Like most other regions of the world, therefore, Europe was long made up of small local units, pockets of territory each with its own customs, way of life, and manner of speech, largely unknown to or ignorant of others, and looking inward upon itself. A "foreigner" might come from a thousand miles away, or from only 10.

Geographical determinism

Agriculture

Agriculture, like commerce and industry, depends on human invention and decision making. The state of agriculture obviously depends on natural conditions, but it has also depended historically on the invention of the plow, the planting of appropriate crops, the rotation of fields to prevent soil exhaustion, and the availability of livestock from which manure could be obtained as fertilizer. It benefits from stability and is affected by demographic changes. If population grows, new and less fertile or more distant areas must be brought under cultivation. Nor can agriculture be improved without the building of roads and a division of labor between town and country, in which agrarian workers produce surpluses for those not engaged in agriculture. And for agriculture, as for other productive enterprises, elementary security is essential. Farming cannot proceed, nor food be stored over the winter, unless the men and women who work the fields can be protected from attack. Such protection was for several centuries imposed by the Roman Empire, in more recent times (barring wars) by the national state, and in between by barons who at the least protected the peasants who worked for them and by kings seeking peace in their kingdoms.

The maps in the present volume cannot show in detail all of the waterways, mountains, and geographical barriers that have helped to shape the course of human history, but they do point to the role of geography in the evolution of political and economic power, or what has become known as geopolitics. Human beings have always developed their institutions, their cultures, and their histories through interactions with the natural world, and maps remind us that all human activities take place in geographical space. Readers can also use their imaginations and the scale of maps to convert space into time, remembering that until the invention of the railroad both people and news traveled far more slowly than today. At a rate of 30 miles a day it would take three weeks to travel from London to Venice, and at least six weeks for an exchange of letters. Over the centuries Europe in human terms has not been such a small place after all. Communication to places outside Europe took even longer. In our own day, when we travel at supersonic speeds and measure electronic communication in nanoseconds, or one-billionth of a second, the barriers of geographic space have virtually disappeared. Yet human beings remain profoundly dependent on their natural environments, and human history remains firmly embedded in the geography of the planet earth.

PROLOGUE:

A REVOLUTIONARY HALF-CENTURY
AND THE EXPANSION OF EUROPEAN POWER

The reader will see, if only by looking at the page numbers, that this book is the second half of a larger work. It begins quite abruptly with Europe in the year 1815. It may be asked why it should begin with 1815, and why an account of the modern world should seem to be mainly about Europe.

There is no spectacular date to signify the emergence of modern times. The year 1815 is convenient because it was in that year that Napoleon Bonaparte was finally defeated at Waterloo, and his attempt at building a European empire ended. A long period of revolutionary turmoil and profound change came to a close in 1815. It had lasted for almost half a century if we count from the American Revolution, which had broken up the old British Empire, weakened France's monarchy, and established the United States of America. The new American republic aroused great interest in Europe, for it gave new meaning and new force to ideas of constitutional government, republicanism, political rights, and civil liberties. These ideas were magnified and geographically disseminated by the French Revolution of 1789. For 20 years, from 1794 to 1814, a reformed and renovated France dominated the European continent. The early stages of movements for Latin American independence also began in this revolutionary era.

The changes that resulted from the American and French revolutions appeared mainly in new conceptions of liberty and equality, as reflected in constitutions, law, and personal status. The Americans gave reality to ideas that were well known in Europe and so had an influence there. In France the Revolution in some ways only accelerated long-continuing trends. It "abolished feudalism," but feudalism had been declining for centuries. It consolidated the modern state by professionalizing its civil service, army, law courts, schools, and tax-collecting machinery, but kings had long worked in these directions. It improved the national trading area by overcoming provincial barriers and introducing uniform law codes, as well as uniform weights and measures in the metric system. Monarchies had made similar efforts. In general, a middle class that had been growing for centuries achieved a victory over older vested interests.

But the French Revolution was also innovative. Liberty and the possession of rights were not new in Europe, but hitherto they had depended on one's social class or religion, or on agreements between a ruler and a particular group to which one belonged. Now liberty meant liberty for the individual, not for this or that group. Equality meant equality of civil rights irrespective of social class or religion and in France, even of race. Civil rights included freedom from abuse by government, freedom of speech, religion, and association, and the right to own property. Property itself became more "private," that is, disentangled from the remnants of feudalism. Representative government, which had long meant merely consultation by monarchs with social estates (such as church, nobility, and towns), now meant a system in which individual voters elected legislators and officials for limited terms of office. The word "citizen" became a hallmark of the new era. Where formerly it had meant someone sharing in the liberties of a town, it now meant someone participating in the sovereignty of the nation, which protected individual rights. The two most famous documents of the era were the American Declaration of Independence of 1776 and the French Declaration of the Rights of Man and Citizen of 1789, which proclaimed both national sovereignty and what are now called civil and human rights.

The French Revolution aroused exceptional political and personal passions among its supporters and opponents throughout Europe, even during its more moderate early phases. After 1792, when France went to war with the leading European powers, the leaders of the Revolution adopted increasingly radical policies to defend their revolutionary reforms and to spread the new political principles in Europe. A French Republic was established in September 1792, the deposed King Louis XVI was executed early in the following year, and a systematic repression and execution of suspected counterrevolutionaries (known as the Terror) spread across France in 1793–1794. Meanwhile, the revolutionary regime raised a large army, whose inspired soldiers and new commanders soon triumphed over all other military forces on the continent and ensured the survival of France's new political order. The Terror came to an end. But there was little stability in the French Republic, and the continuing political conflicts ultimately gave Napoleon Bonaparte the opportunity to seize power through a coup in 1799.

Governing France as First Consul and then as Emperor until 1814, Napoleon suppressed democratic institutions and kept the French state under his own authoritarian control. At the same time, however, he codified numerous legal reforms of the revolutionary era, and through his military triumphs he promoted these new legal principles in the other nations of Europe. His armies, wars, and strategic alliances made him for a time the most powerful ruler in the Western world, but his uncontrolled ambitions led finally to military failures and the collapse of his empire. After Napoleon's final defeat and the postwar diplomatic settlement at the Congress of Vienna in 1815, European nations fought no major or prolonged wars for almost a century. It was during this era that Europe exerted its greatest influence on the course of modern world history.

The century from 1815 to 1914, or from the collapse of Napoleon's empire to the First World War, was precisely the period when the modernization of Europe proceeded most rapidly. These hundred years saw the increasing use of power machinery in the Industrial Revolution, the revolution in transportation by railroad and steamship, the rise of almost instant communications with the telegraph and ocean cables, the development of world markets, modern science, and huge manufacturing and commercial cities. Social classes were restructured; where formerly the difference between aristocrat and commoner had been important, the big difference now was between those who possessed capital and those who depended wholly on their own labor. Politically, the century after 1815 was a time when national consciousness was acutely heightened and various peoples were consolidated into national states. Democracy advanced and socialism appeared. The idea of revolution, derived in its modern form from the French Revolution, aroused hopeful expectations in some and pessimistic fears in others. Meanwhile a vast emigration from

EUROPE, 1815

Boundaries are those set by the Congress of Vienna. France was reduced to the borders it had in 1789. Prussia was firmly installed on both banks of the Rhine, but South Germany remained as reorganized by Napoleon. Poland was again partitioned, with a larger share than in 1795 going to Russia—which also acquired Finland and Bessarabia. The Austrians added Venetia to what they had held before 1796. The union of the Dutch and Belgian Netherlands lasted only until 1831, when the kingdom of Belgium was established. Otherwise, the boundaries of 1815 lasted until the Italian war of 1859, which led to the unification of Italy.

KINGDOM OF NORWAY
AND SWEDEN

FINLAND
(Russia, 1808)

St. Petersburg

Oslo

Stockholm

Reval

SCOTLAND

Edinburgh

Riga

UNITED KINGDOM
OF GREAT BRITAIN AND IRELAND

*North
Sea*

DENMARK   Copenhagen

Baltic Sea

HELIGOLAND
(Britain)

EAST
PRUSSIA

LITHUANIA

IRELAND   Dublin

SCHLESWIG

Danzig

Niemen R.

ENGLAND

HOLSTEIN

Hamburg

Vistula R.

RUSSIAN
EMPIRE

KINGDOM OF THE
NETHERLANDS

HANOVER

Elbe

London

Berlin

Warsaw

*ATLANTIC
OCEAN*

English Channel

Rhine R.

BELGIUM
(Ind. 1831)

Cologne

KINGDOM OF
POLAND
(1815–1831)

Rouen

Seine R.

LUX.

HESSE

SAXON
STATES

SAXONY

Breslau

Cracow

GALICIA

Paris

Prague

BAVARIA

Metz

LORRAINE

Austerlitz

Loire R.

Strasbourg

ALSACE

BADEN

WÜRT-
TEMBERG

Munich

Vienna

Pressburg

*BESSARABIA
(Russia 1812)*

FRANCE

Bern

AUSTRIA

AUSTRIAN EMPIRE

SWITZERLAND

TYROL

Budapest

HUNGARY

MOLDAVIA
(Autonomous 1829)

Bordeaux

Garonne R.

Lyon

SAVOY

LOM-
BARDY

ILLYRIAN

VENETIA

Burgos

Rhône R.

PIEDMONT

Milan

CROATIA

Douro R.

Ebro R.

Toulouse

PARMA

Nice

MODENA

DALMATIA

Belgrade

WALLACHIA
(Autonomous 1829)

Danube R.

PYRENEES

Marseille

Genoa

BOSNIA

SERBIA
*(Autonomous
1829)*

OTTOMAN EMPIRE

PORTUGAL

SPAIN

Madrid

Toulon

LUCCA

TUSCANY

PAPAL
STATES

Adriatic Sea

MONTENEGRO

Sofia

BULGARIA

Tagus R.

Lisbon

Guadiana R.

Barcelona

Elba

Po R.

Rome

KINGDOM OF SARDINIA

Salonica

Seville

Valencia

CORSICA
(France)

*Aegean
Sea*

Cadiz

Gibraltar *(Britain)*

*BALEARIC IS.
(Spain)*

Naples

KINGDOM OF THE
TWO SICILIES

IONIAN I.
(Britain)

Athens

MOROCCO

Algiers

Palermo

GREECE
(Independent 1829)

SICILY

ALGERIA
(France, 1830)

TUNISIA
(Turkish)

MALTA
(Britain)

CRETE

Mediterranean Sea

	Ottoman Empire		Prussia
	Austrian Empire		Kingdom of Sardinia
	Bavaria		

OTTOMAN EMPIRE

TRIPOLI

TRIPOLI

0   100   200   300 miles

Europe built up communities of European type overseas, notably in the United States, whose population rose between 1820 and 1910 from about 9 to 90 million. The population of Europe itself more than doubled in these same years, exceeding 400 million at the close of the nineteenth century.

Europe thus created a combination of political and economic power such as had never yet been seen in the world's history. Able now to reach other parts of the earth more speedily and effectively than ever before, Europeans had an enormous impact on the ancient cultures of Asia, Africa, and the Americas, though these regions of the world also influenced Europe as their commodities, cultural traditions, and people streamed increasingly into European societies. The European ascendancy reached its height about the year 1900, with the penetration of China, the transformation of Japan, and the reduction of most of the rest of Asia and of Africa to the status of colonies within a half-dozen European empires. In the twentieth century the position of Europe relatively declined, partly because of bloody conflicts within Europe itself, but mainly because the apparatus which had made Europe so dominant can now be found in other parts of the world. Some, like the United States, are essentially offshoots of Europe. Others have neither had nor wanted connections with Europe until recent times. But all peoples have become caught up in a process of modernization or "development," which has usually meant acquiring some of the technical, scientific, and organizational skills first exhibited by Europeans.

The modern world consists of an expanding global economy and a shared global civilization that overlies many traditional cultures. Each region has its own familiar and underlying, deeper level of life, Europe and the United States as well as India or Bolivia, but above them all is an interconnected world of science, fast transportation, computerized communications, radio and television, industry and machines, trade and finance, loans and debts, investments and banking systems. In most countries, as they become modern, pressures have mounted for increased democracy, and all modern governments, democratic or not, must seek to arouse the energies and support of their populations. In a modern society old customs loosen, and ancestral religions are questioned. There is a demand for individual liberation, and an expectation of a higher standard of living. Everywhere there is a drive for more equality—between sexes and among races, between high and low incomes, between adherents of different religions, or between different parts of the same country. Movements for social change may be slow and gradual, or revolutionary and catastrophic, but movement of some kind is universal.

Such are a few of the indexes of modernity. Since they appeared first in the history of Europe, or of the European world in the extended sense in which the United States is included, the present book deals mainly with Europe, while emphasizing the points of economic and social contact with the larger world. In the later chapters it devotes increasing attention to the earth as a whole. Its framework is intended to help the reader view the history of the modern world as a steadily growing system of global connections in the economic, political, social, and cultural lives of all modern peoples.

Chapter 11

REACTION VERSUS PROGRESS, 1815–1848

In the period of some 30 years preceding 1815 two "revolutions" had been taking place. One was the upheaval associated with the French Revolution and the Napoleonic empire. Basically, it was mainly political, having to do with the organization of government, public power and authority, public finance, taxation, administration, law, individual rights, and the legal position of social classes. The other "revolution," a revolution in a more metaphorical sense, was primarily economic, having to do with the production of wealth, the techniques of manufacture, the exploitation of natural resources, the formation of capital, and the distribution of products to consumers. The political and the economic revolutions, in these years, to a surprising degree, went on independently of each other. Until 1815 the political revolution affected mainly the Continent, while the economic revolution was most active in England. The Continent, while renewing itself politically, remained economically less advanced than England. England, transformed economically, remained conservative in other respects. Hence it has been possible, in the preceding chapters, to deal with the French Revolution and its Napoleonic sequel without attending to the Industrial Revolution, as the economic changes then occurring in England are always called.

It may be (the matter is arguable) that the Industrial Revolution was more important than the French Revolution or any other. In a telescopic view of world history the two biggest changes experienced by the human race in the past 10,000 years may have been the agricultural or Neolithic revolution, which ushered in the first civilizations, and the Industrial Revolution, which ushered in the civilization of the last two centuries. However that may be, it proves on closer examination that the economic and the political, the Industrial Revolution (or industrialization) and the other institutions of a society, cannot long be kept apart in the historical study of modern times. The Industrial Revolution

Chapter emblem: Detail from an engraving, *Young Saint-Simonienne* (1832), by Malreuve.

427

Political and economic factors

occurred first in England, becoming evident about 1780, because of certain political characteristics of English society, because access to world markets had been gained by earlier commercial and naval successes, and because English life offered rewards to the individual for a spirit of risk-taking and innovation. Nor can the effects of political and economic revolution, in England or elsewhere, be kept apart for the years after 1815.

With the defeat of Napoleon and signing of the peace treaty at Vienna in 1815, it seemed that the French Revolution was at last over. European conservatism had triumphed; since it frankly opposed the new "French ideas," it can appropriately be called "reaction." But the processes of industrialization, as they accelerated in England and spread to the Continent, worked against the politically conservative settlement. They greatly enlarged both the business and wage-earning classes, and so made it harder for monarchs and landed aristocrats to maintain their control over public power. Industrial development in the nineteenth century was often called "progress," and progress proved stronger than reaction.

Industrial society arose in England, Western Europe, and the United States, in the nineteenth century, within the system known as capitalism. In the twentieth century, after the Russian Revolution, industrial societies were created in which capitalism was vehemently rejected. Industrialism and capitalism are therefore by no means the same. Yet all industrial societies use capital, which is defined as wealth that is not consumed but is used to produce more wealth, or future wealth. An automobile is a consumer's good; the automobile factory is the capital. What distinguishes a capitalist from a noncapitalist society is not the existence of capital but the kinds of people who control it. The distinctions sometimes become blurred. But in one form of society the control of capital is through private ownership, or institutions of private property, by which capital is owned by individuals, families, or corporations that are in turn owned by shareholders; in any case not by the state. In such societies, though ownership may be widespread, most capital is controlled by relatively few people, responding to market forces. In the other form of society productive capital in principle belongs to the public, and is in effect owned and controlled by the state or its agencies; such societies usually call themselves socialist, because the first socialists rejected the principle of private ownership of the means of production, that is, of capital. In these societies the control of capital, or decisions on saving, investment, and production, are also in the hands of relatively few under some form of central plan.

Industrialism versus capitalism

In Europe the institutions of secure private property had been developed since the Middle Ages, and much that happened in the French Revolution was designed to protect property from the demands of the state. Possession of property was held to be the basis of personal independence and political liberty, and the expectation of keeping future profits inspired, in some, a willingness to commit their capital to new and uncertain ventures. It made possible an entrepreneurial spirit. There had been a commercial capitalism in Europe at least since the sixteenth century. Industrialization in Europe was therefore capitalist. Countries outside the West-European orbit, and industrializing later, faced a different problem. A country in which little capital had accumulated from the trade and agriculture of previous generations, and which had few owners of capital or enterprising individuals, could hardly industrialize by European methods. If it lacked the European background, in which various political, social, legal, and intellectual features were as important as the economic, it would have to achieve industrialization by other methods. This usually meant that innovation, planning, decision making, control, and even domination rested with the state.

In the short run, within a few years, the Industrial Revolution in Western Europe favored the liberal and modernizing principles proclaimed in the French Revolution. In the middle run, or in half a century, it made Europe overwhelmingly more powerful than other parts of the world, leading to a worldwide European ascendancy in the form of imperialism. In the still longer run, by the twentieth century, it provoked a retaliation, in which other countries tried hastily to industrialize in self-protection, or to improve the condition of their peoples, desperately hoping to catch up with the West while loudly denouncing it as imperialist and capitalist. Of these newer industrial societies the Soviet Union and the People's Republic of China would be the most prominent.

52. THE INDUSTRIAL REVOLUTION IN BRITAIN

On the whole, from the beginning of history until about 1800, the work of the world was done with hand tools. Since then it has been increasingly done by machines. Before about 1800 power was supplied by human or animal muscle, reinforced by levers or pulleys, and supplemented by the force of running water or moving air. Since then power has been supplied by the human manipulation of more recondite forms of energy found in steam, electricity, the combustion of gases, and most recently within the atom. The process of shifting from hand tools to power machinery is what is meant by the Industrial Revolution. Its beginning cannot be dated exactly. It grew gradually out of the technical practices of earlier times. It is still going on, for in some countries industrialization has barely begun, and even in the most highly developed it is still making advances. But the first country to be profoundly affected by industrialization was Great Britain, where its effects became manifest in the half-century following 1780.

It seems likely, despite the emphasis placed on revolutionary upheavals by historians, that people are habitually quite conservative. Working people do not put off their old way of life, move to strange and overcrowded towns, or enter the deadly rounds of mine and factory except under strong incentive. Well-to-do people, living in comfort on assured incomes, do not risk their wealth in new and untried ventures except for good reason. The shifting to modern machine production requires in any country a certain mobility of people and of wealth. Such mobility may be produced by state pressure, as in the twentieth-century industrialization of the Soviet Union. In England a high degree of social mobility existed in the eighteenth century in consequence of a long historical development.

The Agricultural Revolution in Britain

The English Revolution of 1688, confirming the ascendancy of Parliament over the king, meant in economic terms the ascendancy of the more well-to-do property-owning classes. Among these the landowners were by far the most important, though they counted the great London merchants among their allies. For a century and a half, from 1688 to 1832, the British government was substantially in the hands of these landowners—the "squirearchy" or "gentlemen of England." The result was a thorough transformation of farming, an Agricultural Revolution without which the Industrial Revolution could not have occurred.

Many landowners, seeking to increase their money incomes, began experimenting with improved methods of cultivation and stock raising. They made more use of fertilizers (mainly animal manure); they introduced new implements (such as the drill seeder and horse-hoe); they brought in new

Agricultural experimentation

crops, such as turnips, and a more scientific system of crop rotation; they attempted to breed larger sheep and fatter cattle. An improving landlord, to introduce such changes successfully, needed full control over his land. He saw a mere barrier to progress in the old village system of open fields, common lands, and semicollective methods of cultivation. Improvement also required an investment of capital, which was impossible so long as the soil was tilled by numerous poor and custom-bound small farmers.

The old common rights of the villagers were part of the common law. Only an act of Parliament could modify or extinguish them. It was the great landowners who controlled Parliament, which therefore passed hundreds of "enclosure acts," authorizing the enclosure, by fences, walls, or hedges, of the old common lands and unfenced open fields. Land thus came under a strict regime of private ownership and individual management. At the same time small owners sold out or were excluded in various ways, the more easily since the larger owners had so much local authority as justices of the peace. Ownership of land in England, more than anywhere else in central or western Europe, became concentrated in the hands of a relatively small class of wealthy landlords, who let it out in large blocks to a relatively small class of substantial farmers. This development, though in progress throughout the eighteenth century, reached its height during the Napoleonic wars.

The enclosure acts

One result was greatly to raise the productivity of land and of farm labor. Fatter cattle yielded more meat, more assiduous cultivation yielded more cereals. The food supply of England was increased, while a smaller percentage of the population was needed to produce it. Labor was thus released for other pursuits. The greater number of the English country people became wage earners, working for the farmers and landlords, or spinning or weaving in their cottages for merchants in the towns. English working men and women were therefore dependent on daily wages long before the coming of the factory and the machine. Working people became mobile; they would go where the jobs were, or where the wages were slightly higher. They also became available for new kinds of work because fewer of them were needed on the land to produce food. Such conditions hardly obtained except in Great Britain. On the Continent agricultural methods were less productive, and the rural workers were more established on the soil, whether by institutions of serfdom as in eastern Europe or by the possession of property or firm leaseholds as in France.

Industrialism in Britain: Incentives and Inventions

Meanwhile, as the Agricultural Revolution ran its course in the eighteenth century and into the nineteenth, the British had conquered a colonial empire, staked out markets all over the Americas and Europe, built up a huge mercantile marine, and won command of the sea. The British merchant could sell more, if only more could be produced. He had the customers, he had the ships, and moreover he could obtain the capital with which to finance new ideas. The profit motive prompted the search for more rapid methods of production. The old English staple export, woolen cloth, could be marketed indefinitely if only more of it could be woven. The possibilities in cotton cloth were enormous. The taste of Europeans for cottons had been already formed by imports from Asia. By hand methods Europeans could not produce cotton in competition with the East. But the market was endless if cotton could be spun, woven, and printed with less labor, that is, by machines. Capital was available, mobile, and fluid because of the rise of banking, credit, and stock companies. Funds could be shifted from one enterprise to another. Wealthy landowners and merchants could divert some of their profits to industry. If an invention proved a total loss, as sometimes happened, or if it required years of development before producing any income, still the investment could be afforded. Only a country already wealthy from commerce and agriculture could have been the first to initiate the machine age. England was such a country.

These conditions induced a series of successful inventions in the textile industry. In 1733 a man named John Kay invented the fly shuttle, by which only one person instead of two was needed to weave cloth on a loom. The resulting increase in the output of weaving set up a strong demand for yarn. This was met in the 1760s by the invention of the spinning jenny, a kind of mechanized spinning wheel that enabled workers to increase their production of yarn. The new shuttles and jennies were first operated by hand and used by domestic workers in their homes. But in 1769 Richard Arkwright patented the water frame, a device for the multiple spinning of many threads. At first it was operated by water power, but in the 1780s Arkwright introduced the steam engine to drive his spinning machinery. Thus requiring a considerable installation of heavy equipment, he gathered his engines, frames, and workers into large and usually dismal buildings, called mills by the English, or factories in subsequent American usage. Mechanical spinning now for a time overwhelmed the hand weavers with yarn. This led to the development of the power loom, which became economically practicable shortly after 1800. Weaving as well as spinning was therefore done increasingly in factories. These improvements in the finishing process put a heavy strain on the production of raw cotton. An ingenious Connecticut Yankee, Eli Whitney, while acting as a tutor on a plantation in Georgia, in 10 days produced a cotton gin, which by speeding up the removal of seeds greatly increased the output of cotton. The gin soon spread through the American South, where the almost decaying plantation economy was abruptly revived, becoming an adjunct to the Industrial Revolution in England. British imports of raw cotton multiplied fivefold in the 30 years following 1790. In value of manufactures, cotton rose from ninth to first place among British industries in the same years. By 1820 it made up almost half of all British exports.

Inventions in the textile industry

The steam engine, applied to the cotton mills in the 1780s, had for a century been going through a development of its own. Scientific and technical experiments with steam pressures had been fairly common in the seventeenth century, but what gave the economic impetus to invention was the gradual dwindling away of Europe's primeval stocks of timber. The wood shortage became acute in England about 1700, so that it was more difficult to obtain the charcoal needed in smelting iron, and smelters turned increasingly to coal. Deeper coal shafts could not be sunk until someone devised better methods of pumping out water. About 1702 Thomas Newcomen built the first economically significant steam engine, which was soon widely used to drive pumps in the coal mines. It consumed so much fuel in proportion to power delivered that it could generally be used only in the coal fields themselves. In 1763 James Watt, a technician at the University of Glasgow, began to make improvements on Newcomen's engine. He formed a business partnership with Matthew Boulton. Boulton, originally a manufacturer of toys, buttons, and shoe buckles, provided the funds to finance Watt's rather costly experiments, handmade equipment, and slowly germinating ideas. By the 1780s the firm of Boulton and Watt was eminently successful, manufacturing steam engines both for British use and for the export trade.

The steam engine

At first, until further refinements and greater precision could be obtained in the working of iron, the engines were so cumbersome that they could be used as stationary engines only, as in the new spinning mills of Arkwright and others. Soon after 1800 the steam engine was successfully used to propel river boats, notably on the Hudson River in 1807, by Robert Fulton, who employed an imported Boulton and Watt engine. Experiments with steam power for land transportation began at the same time. As it was in the coal fields of England a century before that Newcomen's engine had been put to practical uses, so now it was in the coal fields that Watt's engine first became a locomotive. Well before 1800 the mines had taken to using railways, on which wagons with flanged wheels, drawn by horses, carried coal to canals or to the sea. In the 1820s steam engines were successfully placed on moving vehicles. The first fully satisfactory locomotive was George Stephenson's *Rocket,* which in 1829, on the newly built Liverpool and Manchester Railway, not only reached an impressive speed of 16 miles per hour but met more important safety tests as well. By the 1840s the era of railroad construction was under way in both Europe and the United States.

The Industrial Revolution in Great Britain in its early phase, down to 1830 or 1840, took place principally in the manufacture of textiles, with accompanying developments in the exploitation of iron and coal. The early factories were principally textile factories, and indeed mainly cotton mills; for cotton was an entirely new industry to Europe and hence easily mechanized, whereas the long established woolen trade, in which both employers and workers hesitated to abandon their customary ways, was mechanized more slowly. The suddenness of the change must not be exaggerated. It is often said that the Industrial Revolution was not a revolution at all. As late as the 1830s only a small fraction of the British working people were employed in factories. But the factory and the factory system were even then regarded as the coming mode of production, destined to grow and expand, mighty symbols of the irresistible march of progress.

Some Social Consequences of Industrialism in Britain

The Britain that emerged fundamentally unscathed and in fact strengthened from the wars with Napoleon was no longer the "merrie England" of days of yore. The island was becoming crowded with people, as was the lesser island of Ireland. The combined population of Great Britain and Ireland tripled in the century from 1750 to 1850, rising from about 10 million in 1750 to about 30 million in 1850. The growth was distributed very unevenly. Formerly, in England, most people had lived in the south. But the coal and iron, and hence the steam power, lay in the Midlands and the north. Here whole new cities rose seemingly out of nowhere. In 1785 it was estimated that in England and Scotland, outside of London, there were only three cities with more than 50,000 people. Seventy years later, the span of one lifetime, there were 31 British cities of this size.

Preeminent among them was Manchester in Lancashire, the first and most famous of industrial cities of modern type. Manchester, before the coming of the cotton mills, was a rather large market town. Though very ancient, it had not been significant enough to be recognized as a borough for representation in Parliament. Locally it was organized as a manor. Not until 1845 did the inhabitants extinguish the manorial rights, buying them out at that time from the last lord, Sir Oswald Mosley, for £200,000, or about $1 million. In population Manchester grew from 25,000 in 1772 to 455,000 in 1851. But until 1835 there was no regular procedure in England for the incorporation of cities. Urban organization was more backward than in Prussia or France. Unless inherited from the Middle Ages, a city had no legal existence. It lacked proper officials and adequate tax-raising and lawmaking powers. It was therefore difficult for Manchester, and the other new factory towns, to deal with problems of rapid

The invention of the steam locomotive and railways contributed decisively to early nineteenth-century industrialization. These primitive trains, about 1840, are running on wooden rails with "guidance wheels" at a strange angle to keep them on the track.

(Mansell Collection/Time Pix)

urbanization, such as provision for police protection, water and sewers, or the disposal of garbage.

The new urban agglomerations were drab places, blackened with the heavy soot of the early coal age, settling alike on the mills and the workers' quarters, which were dark at best, for the climate of the Midlands is not sunny. Housing for workers was hastily built, closely packed, and always in short supply, as in all rapidly growing communities. Entire families lived in single rooms, and family life tended to disintegrate. A police officer in Glasgow observed that there were whole blocks of tenements in the city, each swarming with a thousand ragged children who had first names only, usually nicknames—like animals, as he put it.

Unskilled labor

The distressing feature of the new factories was that for the most part they required unskilled labor only. Skilled workers found themselves degraded in status. Hand weavers and spinners, thrown out of work by the new machines, either languished in a misery that was the deepest of that of any class in the Industrial Revolution or else went off to a factory to find a job. The factories paid good wages by the standards for unskilled labor at the time. But these standards were very low, too low to allow a man to support his wife and children. This had generally been true for unskilled labor, in England and elsewhere, under earlier economic systems also. In the new factories the work was so mechanical that children as young as six years old were often preferred. Women, too, worked for less and were often more adept at handling a bobbin, which brought many women spinners from the older, displaced "cottage industries" into the new industrial working class.

Hours in the factories were long, 14 a day or occasionally more; and though such hours were familiar to persons who had worked on farms, or at domestic industry in rural households, they were more tedious and oppressive in the more regimented conditions that were necessary in the mills. Holidays were few, except for the unwelcome leisure of unemployment, which was a common scourge, because the short-run ups and downs of business were very erratic. A day without work was a day producing nothing to live on, so that even where the daily wage was relatively attractive the worker's real income was chronically insufficient. Workers in the factories, as in the mines, were almost entirely unorganized. They were a mass of recently assembled humanity without traditions or common

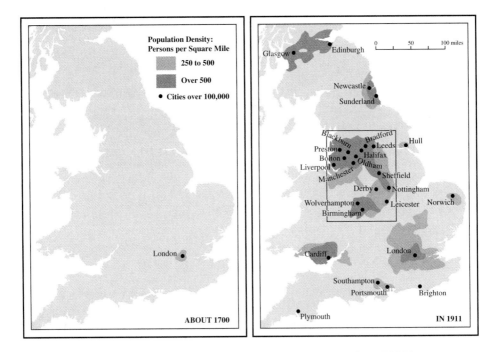

BRITAIN BEFORE AND AFTER THE INDUSTRIAL REVOLUTION
In 1700 England, Scotland, and Wales had only one city with a population of more than 100,000. In 1911 they had nearly 30, most of which were located in the industrialized Midlands (the area within the small rectangle).

ties. They bargained individually with their employers who, usually small business people themselves, facing ferocious competition with others, often in debt for the equipment in their own factories, or determined to save money in order to purchase more, held their wages bill to the lowest possible figure.

The factory owners, the new "cotton lords," were the first industrial capitalists. They were often self-made men, who owed their position to their own intelligence, persistence, and foresight. They lived in comfort without ostentation or luxury, saving from each year's income to build up their factories and their machines. Hard-working themselves, they thought that landed gentlemen were usually idlers and that the poor tended to be lazy. They were usually honest, in a hard and exacting way; they would make money by any means the law allowed, but not beyond it. They were neither brutal nor knowingly hard-hearted. They gave to charitable and philanthropic causes. They believed that they did the poor a favor by furnishing them with work and by seeing to it that they worked diligently and productively. Most of them disapproved of public regulation of their business, though a few, driven by competition to expedients that they did not like, such as the employment of small children, would have accepted some regulation that fell on all competitors equally. It was a cotton magnate, the elder Robert Peel, who in 1802 pushed the first Factory Act through Parliament. This act purported to regulate the conditions in which pauper children were employed in the textile mills, but it was a dead letter from the beginning, since it provided no adequate body of factory inspectors. The English at this time, alone among the leading European peoples, had no class of trained, paid, and professional government administrators; nor did they yet want such a class, preferring self-government and local initiative. To have inspectors for one's affairs smacked of Continental bureaucracy. The fact that the older methods of economic regulation were obsolescent, actually unsuited to the new age, had the effect of discrediting the idea of regulation itself. The new industrialists wanted to be left alone. They considered it unnatural to interfere with business and believed that, if allowed to follow their own judgment, they would assure the future prosperity and progress of the country.

The cotton lords

Classical Economics: "Laissez-Faire"

The industrialists were strengthened in these beliefs by the emerging science of political economy. In 1776 Adam Smith published his epochal *Wealth of Nations,* which criticized the older mercantilism, with its regulatory and monopolistic practices, and urged, though with moderation, that certain "natural laws" of production and exchange be allowed to work freely in economic markets. Smith was followed by Thomas R. Malthus, David Ricardo, and the so-called Manchester School. Their doctrine was dubbed (by its opponents) laissez-faire and in its elaborated form is still called classical economics. It held, basically, that there is a world of economic relationships autonomous and separable from government or politics. It is the world of the free market and is regulated within itself by certain "natural laws," such as the law of supply and demand or the law of diminishing returns. All person should follow their own enlightened self-interest; all know their own interests better than anyone else; and the sum total of individual interests will add up to the general welfare and liberty of all. Government should do as little as possible; it should confine itself to preserving security of life and property, providing reasonable laws and reliable courts, and so ensuring the discharge of private contracts, debts, and obligations. Not only business, but education, charity, and personal matters generally should be left to

Self-interest and free trade

private initiative. There should be no tariffs; free trade should reign everywhere, for the economic system is worldwide, unaffected by political barriers or national differences. As for workers, according to classical economists before about 1850, they should not expect to make more than a bare minimum living; an "iron law of wages" brings it about that as soon as workers receive more than a subsistence wage they breed more children, who eat up the excess, so that they reduce themselves, and the working class generally, again to a subsistence level. Workers, if discontented, should see the folly of changing the system, for this *is* the system, the natural system—there is no other. Political economy as taught in grim Manchester was not without reason called the "dismal science."

Working people's experiences

For working people in England the Industrial Revolution was a hard experience. It should be remembered, however, that neither low wages, nor the 14-hour day, nor the labor of women and children, nor the ravages of unemployment were anything new. All had existed for centuries, in England and western Europe, as agricultural and commercial capitalism replaced the more self-sufficient economies of the Middle Ages. The factory towns were in some ways better places to live in than the rural slums from which many of their people came. Factory routine was psychologically deadening, but the textile mills were in some ways not worse than the domestic sweatshops in which manufacturing processes had previously been carried on. The concentration of working people in city and factory opened the way to improvement in their condition. It made their misery apparent; philanthropic sentiment was gradually aroused among the more fortunate. Gathered in cities, workers obtained more knowledge of the world. Mingling and talking together they developed a sense of solidarity, class interest, and common political aims; and in time they became organized, establishing labor unions by which to obtain a larger share of the national income.

Britain after the fall of Napoleon became the workshop of the world. Though factories using steam power sprang up in France, Belgium, New England, and elsewhere, it was really not until after 1870 that Great Britain faced industrial competition from abroad. The British had a virtual monopoly in textiles and machine tools. The English Midlands and Scottish Lowlands shipped cotton thread and steam engines to all the world. British capital was exported to all countries, there to call new enterprises into being. London became the world's clearinghouse and financial center. Progressive people in other lands looked to Britain as their model, hoping to learn from its advanced industrial methods, and to imitate its parliamentary political system.

53.   THE ADVENT OF THE "ISMS"

The combined forces of industrialization and of the French Revolution led after 1815 to the proliferation of doctrines and movements of many sorts. These broke out in a general European revolution in 1848. As for the 33 years from 1815 to 1848, there is no better way of grasping their long-run meaning than to reflect on the number of still living "isms" that arose at that time.

So far as is known the word "liberalism" first appeared in the English language in 1819, "radicalism" in 1820, "socialism" in 1832, "conservatism" in 1835. The 1830s first saw "individualism," "constitutionalism," "humanitarianism," "feminism," and "monarchism." "Nationalism" and "communism" date from the 1840s. Not until the 1850s did the English-speaking world use the world "capitalism" (French *capitalisme* is much older); and not until even later had it heard of "Marxism," though the doctrines of Marx grew out of and reflected the troubled times of the 1840s.

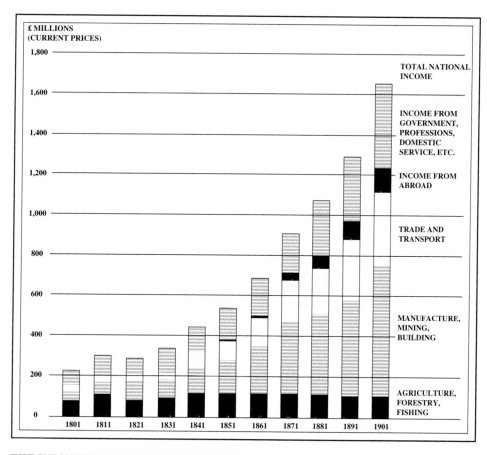

THE INDUSTRIAL REVOLUTION IN BRITAIN (AS SHOWN BY SOURCES OF INCOME)

British national income grew about eightfold in the nineteenth century. Income derived from agriculture, forestry, and the like remained about the same, but the income from these activities sank from one-third to one-sixteenth of all income. By 1851 half the national income came from manufacturing, trade, and transportation, and by 1901 three-quarters came from these sources. The category "income from abroad" refers to interest and dividends on loans and investments outside Great Britain, which grew rapidly after the 1850s.

Source: P. Deane and W. A. Cole, *British Economic Growth* (Cambridge, England: Cambridge University Press, 1962), pp. 166–167.

The rapid coinage of new "isms" does not in every case mean that the ideas they conveyed were new. Many of them had their origin in the Enlightenment, if not before. People had loved liberty before talking of liberalism and been conservative without knowing conservatism as such. The appearance of so many "isms" shows rather that people were making their ideas more systematic. To the "philosophy" of the Enlightenment were now added an intense activism and a partisanship generated during the French Revolution. People were obliged to reconsider and analyze society as a whole. The social sciences were taking form. An "ism" (excluding such words as "hypnotism" or "favoritism") may be defined as the conscious espousal of a doctrine in competition with other doctrines. Without the "isms" created in the 30-odd years after the peace of Vienna it is impossible to understand or even talk about the history of the world since that event, so that a brief characterization of some of the most important is in order.

Romanticism

One of the "isms" was not political. It was called "romanticism," a word first used in English in the 1840s to describe a movement then half a century old. Romanticism was primarily a theory of literature and the arts. Its great exponents included William Wordsworth, Lord Byron, Percy Bysshe Shelley, and Mary Shelley in England; Victor Hugo, René Chateaubriand, and George Sand in France; and Friedrich von Schiller, Friedrich Schlegel, and many others in Germany. As a theory of art it raised basic questions on the nature of significant truth, on the importance of various human faculties, on the relation of thought and feeling, on the meaning of the past and of time itself. Romanticism rejected the emphasis on classical rules and rational order that had shaped aesthetic theory during much of the eighteenth century. Romantics celebrated the idiosyncratic visions of creative individuals rather than the symmetries of classical art and literature. They helped produce the modern image of defiant artistic rebels. Representing a new way of sensing all human experience, romanticism affected much thinking on social and public questions.

Love of the unclassifiable

Possibly the most fundamental romantic attitude was a love of the unclassifiable—of moods or impressions, scenes or stories, sights or sounds or things concretely experienced, personal idiosyncrasies or peculiar customs which the intellect could never classify, box up, explain away, or reduce to an abstract generalization. The romantics, characteristically, insisted on the value of feeling as well as of reason. They were aware of the importance of the subconscious. They were likely to suspect a perfectly lucid idea as somehow superficial. They loved the mysterious, the unknown, the half-seen figures on the far horizon. Hence romanticism contributed to a new interest in strange and distant societies and in strange and distant historical epochs. Where the philosophes of the Enlightenment had deplored the Middle Ages as a time of intellectual error, the romantic generation looked back upon them with respect and even nostalgia, finding in them a fascination, a colorfulness, or a spiritual depth which they missed in their own time. The "Gothic," which rationalists thought barbarous, had a strong appeal for romantics. A Gothic Revival emerged in the arts, of which one example was the British Parliament buildings, built in the 1830s.

Creative genius

In medieval art and institutions, as in the art and institutions of every age and people, the romantics saw the expression of an inner genius. The idea of original or creative genius was in fact another of the most fundamental romantic beliefs. A genius was a dynamic spirit that no rules could hem in, one that no analysis or classification could ever fully explain. Genius, it was thought, made its own rules and laws. The genius might be that of the individual person, such as the artist, writer, or Napoleonic mover of the world. It might be the genius or spirit of an age. Or it might be the genius of a people or nation, the *Volksgeist* of Herder, an inherent national character making each people grow in its own distinctive way, which could be known only by a study of its history; romanticism thus merged in many places with new forms of nationalism. Here again romanticism gave a new impetus to study of the past. Politically, romantics could be found in all camps, conservative, liberal, and radical. Let us turn to the more political "isms."

NEW HOUSES OF PARLIAMENT.

The new British Houses of Parliament were built during the 1830s. They became a prominent example of the Gothic revival in architecture and of the early nineteenth-century romantic fascination with the Middle Ages.

(Hulton Getty)

Classical Liberalism

The first Liberals, calling themselves by that name (though Napoleon used that word for his own system), arose in Spain among certain opponents of the Napoleonic occupation. The word then passed to France, where it denoted opposition to royalism after the restoration of the Bourbons in 1814 and where it gained intellectual influence through the work of liberal writers such as Benjamin Constant. In England, many Whigs became increasingly liberal, as did even a few Tories. Liberal political theorists also had influence in England, most notably in the writings of John Stuart Mill, and a new Liberal Party became an important force in British politics during the 1850s. Nineteenth-century, or "classical," liberalism varied from country to country, but it showed many basic similarities, including an emphasis on the rights and liberties that individuals should possess in every well-ordered, modern society.

Liberals were generally persons of the business and professional classes, together with enterprising landowners wishing to improve their estates. They believed in what was modern, enlightened, efficient, reasonable, and fair. They had confidence in the human capacity for self-government and self-control.

Liberal beliefs

They set a high value on parliamentary or representative government, working through reasonable discussion and legislation, with responsible ministries and an impartial and law-abiding administration. They demanded full publicity for all actions of government, and to ensure such publicity they insisted on freedom of the press and free rights of assembly. All these political advantages they thought most likely to be realized under a good constitutional monarchy. Outside England they favored explicit written constitutions. They were not democrats; they generally opposed giving every man the vote, fearing the excesses of mob rule or of irrational political action. Only as the nineteenth century progressed did liberals gradually and reluctantly come to accept the idea of universal male suffrage. Many continued to oppose female suffrage, though some liberals such as John Stuart Mill argued that women should have the same voting rights as men. Liberals subscribed to the doctrines of the "rights of man" as set forth in the American and French revolutions, but with a clear emphasis on the right of property, and in their economic views they typically followed the British Manchester School or the French economist J. B. Say. They favored laissez-faire, were suspicious of the ability of government to regulate business, wanted to get rid of the guild system where it still existed, and disapproved of attempts on the part of the new industrial laborers to organize unions.

Internationally they advocated freedom of trade, to be accomplished by the lowering or abolition of tariffs, so that all countries might exchange their products easily with each other and with industrial England. In this way, they thought, each country would produce what it was most fitted for, and so best increase its wealth and standards of living. From the growth of wealth, production, invention, and scientific progress they believed that the general progress of humanity would ensue. They generally frowned upon the established churches and landed aristocracies as obstacles to advancement. They believed in the spread of tolerance and education. They were also profoundly civilian in attitude, disliking wars, conquerors, army officers, standing armies, military expenditures. They wanted orderly change by processes of legislation. They shrank before the idea of revolution. Liberals on the Continent usually admired Great Britain.

Radicalism, Republicanism, Socialism

Radicalism, at least as a word, originated in England, where about 1820 the Philosophical Radicals proudly applied the term to themselves. These Radicals in the 1820s included not only the few working-class leaders who were beginning to emerge but also many of the new industrial capitalists, who were still unrepresented in Parliament. They took up where such English "Jacobins" as Thomas Paine had left off a generation earlier, before the long crisis of the French wars had discredited all radicalism as pro-French.

The Philosophical Radicals were a good deal like the French philosophes before the Revolution. They were followers of an elderly sage, Jeremy Bentham, who in prolific writings from 1776 to 1832 undertook to reform the English criminal and civil law, church, Parliament, and constitution. The English Radicals professed to deduce the right form of institutions from the fundamental traits of human nature and psychology. They impatiently waved aside all arguments based on history, usage, or custom. They went to the roots of things. ("Radical" is from the Latin word for "root.") They wanted a total reconstruction of laws, courts, prisons, poor relief, municipal organization, rotten boroughs, and fox-hunting clergy. Their demand for the reform of Parliament was vehement and insistent. They detested the Church of England, the peerage, and the squirearchy. Many radicals would just as soon abolish royalty also; not until the long reign of Queen Victoria (1837–1901) did the British monarchy become undeniably popular in all quarters. Above all, radicalism was democratic; it demanded a vote for every adult Englishman. After the Reform Bill of 1832 the industrial capitalists generally turned into liberals, but the working-class leaders remained radical democrats, as will be seen.

Demands for radical reforms

On the Continent radicalism was represented by militant republicanism. The years of the First French Republic, which to liberals and conservatives signified horrors associated with the Reign of Terror, were for the republicans years of hope and progress, cut short by forces of reaction. Republicans were a minority even in France; elsewhere, as in Italy and Germany, they were fewer still, though they existed. Mostly the republicans were drawn from intelligentsia such as students and writers, from working-class leaders protesting social injustice, and from elderly veterans, or the sons and nephews of veterans, to whom the Republic of '93, with its wars and its glory, was a living thing. Because of police repression, republicans often joined together in secret societies. They looked with equanimity on the prospect of further revolutionary upheaval, by which they felt that the cause of liberty, equality, and fraternity would be advanced. Strong believers in political equality, they were democrats demanding universal male suffrage. They favored parliamentary government but were much less primarily concerned with its successful operation than were the liberals. Most republicans were bitterly anticlerical. Remembering the internecine struggle between the church and the republic during the French Revolution, and still facing the political activity of the Catholic clergy (for republicanism was most common in Catholic countries), they regarded the Catholic church as the implacable enemy of reason and liberty. Opposed to monarchy of any kind, even to constitutional monarchy, intensely hostile to church and aristocracy, conscious heirs of the great French Revolution, organized in national and international secret societies, not averse to overthrowing existing regimes by force, the more militant republicans were considered by most people, including the liberals, to be little better than anarchists.

Republican ideals

Republicanism shaded off into socialism. Socialists generally shared the political attitudes of republicanism but added other views besides. The early socialists, those before the Revolution of 1848, were of many kinds, but all had certain ideas in common. All of them regarded the existing economic system as aimless, chaotic, and outrageously unjust. All thought it improper for owners of wealth to have so much economic power—to give or deny work to the worker, to set wages and hours in their own interests, to guide all the labors of society in the interests of private profit. All therefore questioned the value of private enterprise, favoring some degree of communal ownership of productive assets—banks, factories, machines, land, and transportation. All disliked competition as a governing principle and set forth principles of harmony, coordination, organization, or association instead. All flatly

Socialist views

and absolutely rejected the laissez-faire of the liberals and the political economists. Where the latter thought mainly of increasing production, without much concern over distribution, the early socialists thought mainly of a fairer or more equal distribution of income among all useful members of society. They believed that beyond the civil and legal equality brought in by the French Revolution a further step toward social and economic equality had yet to be taken.

One of the first socialists was also one of the first cotton lords, Robert Owen (1771–1858) of Manchester and the Scottish Lowlands. Appalled at the condition of the mill-hands, he created a kind of model community for his own employees, paying high wages, reducing hours, sternly correcting vice and drunkenness, building schools and housing and company stores for the cheap sale of workers' necessities. From such paternalistic capitalism in his early years he passed on to a long lifetime spent in crusading for social reforms, in which he was somewhat handicapped, not only by the opposition of industrialists, but also by his unpopular radicalism in matters of religion.

Most of the early socialists were French, spurred onward by the sense of an uncompleted revolution. One was a nobleman, the Count de Saint-Simon (1760–1825), who had fought in the War of American Independence, accepted the French Revolution, and in his later years wrote many books on social problems. He and his followers,

Saint-Simonians and Fourier

who called themselves not socialists but Saint-Simonians, were among the first clear exponents of a planned society. They advocated the public ownership of industrial equipment and other capital, with control vested in the hands of great captains of industry or social engineers, who should plan vast projects like the digging of a canal at Suez, and in general coordinate the labor and resources of society to productive ends. Of a different type was Charles Fourier (1772–1837), a somewhat doctrinaire thinker who subjected all known institutions to a sweeping condemnation. His positive program took the form of proposing that society be organized in small units which he termed "phalansteries." Each of these he conceived to contain 1,620 persons, each doing the work suited to his natural inclination. Among the practical French no phalanstery was ever successfully organized. A number were established in the United States, still the land of Europe's utopian dream; the best known, since it was operated by literary people, was the Brook Farm "movement" in Massachusetts, which ran through a troubled existence of five years from 1842 to 1847. Robert Owen also, in 1825, had founded an experimental colony in America, at New Harmony, Indiana, on the then remote and unspoiled banks of the Wabash; it, too, lasted only about five years. Such schemes, presupposing the withdrawal of select spirits to live by themselves, really had little to say about the problems of society as a whole in an industrial age.

The French working classes

Politically the most significant form of socialism before 1848 was the movement stirring among the working classes of France, a compound of revolutionary republicanism and socialism. The politically minded Paris workers had been republican since 1792. For them the Revolution, in the 1820s, 1830s, 1840s, was not finished but only momentarily interrupted. Reduced to political impotence, discriminated against in their rights in the law courts, obliged to carry identity papers signed by their employers, goaded by the pressures of industrialization as it spread to France, they developed a deep hostility to the owning classes of the bourgeoisie. They found a spokesman in the Paris journalist Louis Blanc, editor of the *Revue de progrès* and author of the *Organization of Work* (1839), one of the most constructive of the early socialist writings. He proposed a system of "social workshops," or state-supported manufacturing centers, in which the workers should labor by and for themselves without the intervention of private capitalists. Of this kind of socialism we shall hear more.

As for "communism," it was at this time an uncertain synonym for socialism. A small group of German revolutionaries, mainly exiles in France, took the name for themselves in the 1840s. They would have been historically forgotten had they not included Karl Marx and Friedrich Engels among their members. Marx and Engels consciously used the word in 1848 to differentiate their variety of socialism from that of such utopians as Saint-Simon, Fourier, and Owen. But the word *communism* went out of general use after 1848, to be revived after the Russian Revolution of 1917, at which time it received a somewhat new meaning.

Feminism

Feminism emerged as a new political and cultural movement in the early nineteenth century, though the term itself did not appear until some women in France began to refer to themselves as "feminists" during the 1830s. There were several strands of feminism, as there were several strands of all significant "isms," but most feminists shared various ideas with liberals, radicals, or socialists. Feminism sought to expand the rights of women in both public and private life. Drawing on the legacy of the French Revolution and its conceptions of human rights, feminists argued that the "rights of man" existed also for women (much as republicans and socialists claimed that such rights must also exist for poor people and workers). Some feminists, extending the arguments of Mary Wollstonecraft's influential book, *A Vindication of the Rights of Women* (1792), worked mainly to secure new voting and civil rights for women. Other feminists, though they might also support the quest for voting rights, worked mainly to reform the laws that regulated family life or to advance the rights of women in education, cultural life, and the economy. Both of these tendencies in early nineteenth-century feminism drew on Enlightenment ideas about human rights, reform, education, and progress, so that feminism resembled republicanism, radicalism, and socialism in its links to eighteenth-century predecessors, including French writers such as Condorcet and Olympe de Gouges.

The writers and activists who sought new political rights for women tended to be "egalitarian" feminists; that is, they stressed the ways in which women and men shared the use of reason and universal human rights. Despite the obvious connection to themes of the French Revolution, the campaign for women's political rights developed more rapidly in early nineteenth-century England and America. These national differences may have reflected the fact that voting rights generally became more widespread in England and America in the decades before 1848; or the different feminisms may have developed because French republicanism had become hostile to female political activities during the later stages of the French Revolution, and because the Napoleonic Code had given French women a subordinate position in the patriarchical legal system that regulated family relations. In any case, French feminists in the nineteenth century tended to focus on the social, cultural, or legal rights of women rather than on campaigns to win the vote.

Egalitarian feminism

The first nineteenth-century advocates for women's rights in England were Philosophical Radicals and followers of the socialist leader Robert Owen. The socialists Anne Wheeler and William Thompson, for example, published an important statement of the new feminist themes in their *Appeal on Behalf of Women* (1825), which traced the inferior status of women to flaws in the

English feminists

economic system. Similar arguments appeared also in the writings of Owen himself and in the publications of his feminist friend, the Scottish writer Frances Wright. But the most influential English argument for women's political rights emerged in the works of the liberal writers Harriet Taylor and John Stuart Mill, who worked together as close intellectual partners for more than 20 years (they ultimately married after the death of her first husband). Beginning in the 1830s, Taylor and Mill produced important works on the social, legal, and political inequalities that women faced in even the most advanced modern societies. Their collaboration led finally to Mill's famous book, *The Subjection of Women* (1869), in which Mill referred to the decisive influence of Taylor's ideas, though she had died before its publication. Mill built his case for women's political and social rights on the claim that women were inherently equal to men (hence entitled to the same rights) and on the utilitarian argument that society could only benefit from the increased participation of women in public life. Translated into all the major European languages, his book had much subsequent influence on feminist campaigns for the political and legal rights of women in other nations as well as in England. Meanwhile, American women launched their own campaign for voting rights at a convention in Seneca Falls, New York, where leaders such as Elizabeth Cady Stanton declared, in 1848, that women were entitled to vote because they were "created equal" with men.

Feminists also entered public life on the Continent during the 1830s and 1840s, especially in France. Socialists such as Saint-Simon and Fourier gave critical attention to the history of the family, thereby encouraging their followers to develop a social analysis of traditional restrictions on the rights of women. Women activists in the Saint-Simonian groups of the 1830s established journals whose titles asserted new feminist identities: *The Free Woman* and *The New Woman*. A new generation of women writers also began to extend the earlier work of Germaine de Staël, who had argued that "it is useful to society's enlightenment and happiness that women should carefully develop their intelligence and their reason." All feminists advocated better education for young women, reforms in property and divorce laws to enhance women's independence, and the right of women to participate in public debates. Many feminists in France, however, moved away from the egalitarian arguments for women's rights by stressing certain differences between men and women. The special responsibilities of motherhood, for example, gave women a distinctive, essential task in educating the rising generation, but only well-educated, competent women could raise intelligent, well-educated children. Feminists thus strongly supported the creation of new schools for girls and began seeking women's access to higher education (public secondary schools for girls were not established in France until the 1880s).

French feminism

In addition to the campaigns for education and legal reforms, many feminists became writers in order to describe the social lives of women or to assert their claims for a place in public life. The travel writings of Flora Tristan, for instance, examined the social constraints that women faced in both South America and Europe. Another French writer of Tristan's generation, George Sand, became the most influential literary woman of the 1840s. Her many novels and essays often portrayed independent women, but her own life was almost as famous and controversial as her books. Critics mocked her for wearing male clothing, smoking cigars, and living with men outside marriage, yet Sand also won the admiring support of readers throughout Europe, many of whom saw her as a model for new forms of female cultural and political expression. She therefore became a famous symbol for both supporters and enemies of the new feminism; indeed, the term "George Sandism" was used to condemn women whose behavior seemed radical or unconventional. Such hos-

The Saint-Simonian movement in France produced early feminist publications and also helped to launch a new social analysis of the restrictions on women's rights. This engraving by the artist Malreuve in 1832 suggests the unconventional behavior of the Saint-Simonian feminists; the woman is wearing a short dress and pants and standing beside a document that says simply "Doctrine of St. Simon. The Free Woman?"

(Bibliothèque Nationale de France, Paris)

tility indicates how feminism had become one of the postrevolutionary "isms," though the political campaign for women's voting rights and other legal reforms would not achieve its main objectives until the twentieth century.

Nationalism: Western Europe

Nationalism, since it arose so largely in reaction against the international Napoleonic system, has already been introduced in the preceding chapter. It was the most pervasive and the least crystallized of the new "isms," in part because it usually overlapped with various forms of romanticism, republicanism, or liberalism. In western Europe—Britain, France, or Spain—where national unity already existed, nationalism was not a doctrine for nation-building so much as a set of political and cultural beliefs, easily aroused when national interests were questioned but normally taken for granted. Elsewhere—in Italy, Germany, Poland, the Austrian and Turkish empires—where peoples of the same nationality were politically divided or subject to foreign rule, nationalism was becoming a deliberate and conscious program for political action. It was undoubtedly the example of the West, of Great Britain and France, successful and flourishing because they were unified nations, that stimulated the ambitions of other peoples to become unified nations too. The period

This caricature of George Sand, which appeared in a lithograph by Alcide Lorentz in 1842, mocks the famous author for her apparently "masculine" actions. Dressed in pants, holding a cigarette, and surrounded by her writings and political concerns, Sand is ridiculed in both the image and in a sarcastic caption—which alludes to her claim that genius "has no sex."

(Bibliothèque Nationale de France, Paris)

after 1815 was in Germany a time of rising agitation over the national question, in Italy of the Risorgimento or "resurgence," in eastern Europe of the Slavic Revival.

    The movement was led by intellectuals, who often found it necessary to instill in their compatriots the very idea of nationality itself. They seized upon Herder's conception of the *Volksgeist,* or national spirit, each applying it to his own people. Usually they began with a cultural nationalism, holding that each people had a language, history, world view, and culture of its own, which must be preserved and perfected. They then usually passed on to a political nationalism, holding that to preserve this national culture, and to ensure liberty and justice for its individual members, each nation should create for itself a sovereign state. Governing authorities, they held, should be of the same nationality, that is, language, as those they governed. All persons of the same nationality, that is, language, should be encompassed within the same state.

Volksgeist

    Since such ideas could not be fully realized without the overthrow of every government in Europe east of France, thoroughgoing nationalism was inherently revolutionary. Outspoken nationalists were discountenanced or persecuted by the authorities and consequently formed secret societies in large numbers. The Carbonari, organized in Italy in the time of Napoleon, was the best known, but there were many others—like the *Veri Italiani,* the Apophasimenes, and the Sublime and Perfect Masters. In some regions Masonic lodges might serve the same purpose. In many of the societies nationalism was mixed with liberalism, socialism, or revolutionary republicanism in an undifferentiated way. Members were initiated by a complex ritual intended to impress upon them the dire consequences of betraying the society's se-

Secret societies

crets. They used special grips and passwords and adopted revolutionary names to conceal their identity and baffle the police. They were usually so organized that the ordinary member knew the identity of only a few others, and never of the higher-ups, so that those arrested could reveal nothing important. The societies kept busy, circulating forbidden literature and generally maintaining a revolutionary ferment. Conservatives dreaded them, but they were not really dangerous to any government that enjoyed the support of its people.

Best known of the nationalist philosophers in western Europe was the Italian Joseph Mazzini (1805–1872), who spent most of his adult life in exile in France and England. In his youth he joined the Carbonari, but in 1831 *Mazzini* he founded a society of his own, called Young Italy, and he edited and smuggled into Italy copies of a journal of the same name. Young Italy was soon imitated by other societies of similar aim, such as Young Germany. In 1834 Mazzini organized a filibustering expedition against the kingdom of Sardinia, hoping that all Italy would rise and join him. Undeterred by its total failure, he continued to organize, to conspire, and to write. For Mazzini nationality and revolution were a holy cause in which the most generous and humane qualities were to find expression. He was a moral philosopher, as may be judged from the title of his most widely read book, *The Duties of Man,* in which he placed a pure duty to the nation intermediate between duty to family and to God.

To the Germans, divided and frustrated, nationality became almost an obsession. It affected everything from folklore to metaphysics. *Grimm's Fairy Tales,* for example, was first published in 1812. It was the work of the two Grimm brothers, founders of the modern science of comparative linguistics, who traveled about Germany to study the popular dialects and in doing so collected the folktales that for generations had been current among the common people. They hoped in this way to find the ancient, native, indigenous "spirit" of Germany, deep and unspoiled in the bosom of the *Volk.* The same preoccupation with nationhood revealed itself in the philosophy of Hegel (1770–1831), possibly the most extraordinary of all nineteenth-century thinkers.

To Hegel, witnessing the spectacle of the Napoleonic years, it was evident that for a people to enjoy freedom, order, or dignity it must possess a potent and independent state. The state, for him, became the institutional embodiment of reason and liberty—the "march of God through the world," as he put it, meaning not *Hegel's* an expansion in space through vulgar conquest, but a march through time *philosophy* and through the processes of history. Hegel conceived of reality itself as a process of endless change, a development having an inner logic and necessary sequence of its own. He thus broke with the more static and mechanical philosophy of the eighteenth century, with its fixed categories of unchangeable right and wrong. He became a philosopher of history, in which he saw the unfolding of a "Universal Spirit" or "Idea" across time, and linked it in complex ways to reason and freedom. He held that change came about through a historical "dialectic," or irresistible tendency of the Universal Spirit and the human mind to move forward by the creation of opposites. A given state of affairs (the *thesis*) would in this view inevitably produce the conception of an opposite state of affairs (the *antithesis*), which would equally inevitably be followed by a reconciliation and fusion of the two (the *synthesis*). Thus, for example, the very disunity of Germany, by producing the opposing idea of unity, would ultimately bring about the creation of a German state.

The Hegelian dialectic was soon to be appropriated by Karl Marx to new uses, but meanwhile Hegel's philosophy, with other currents in Germany, made the study of history more philosophically meaningful than it had ever been before. History, the study of time

LANGUAGES OF EUROPE

National movements in modern Europe often referred to the distinctive languages of various national groups, but there are only three main European language families: Germanic, Latin, and Slav. The map shows language areas in the early twentieth century. It does not show the overlap of adjoining languages, bilingual areas, or the existence of small language "pockets" such as Turkish in the Balkans, Greek in Asia Minor, Yiddish in Poland, or German in scattered parts of eastern Europe. In the extreme northwest is the "Celtic fringe," to which the Breton, Welsh, and Gaelic languages were pushed back in the early Middle Ages. For the area within the diamond-shaped zone no map on this scale can give a realistic idea of the overlapping languages. During the Second World War and its aftermath, however, many language pockets in eastern Europe were wiped out through exchange, transportation, or destruction of peoples.

process, seemed to be the very key with which to unlock the true significance of the world. Historical studies were stimulated, and the German universities became centers of historical learning, attracting scholars from many countries. Most eminent of the German historians was Leopold von Ranke (1795–1886), founder of the "scientific" school of historical writing. Ranke, too, though intellectually scrupulous to the last degree, owed much of his incentive to his national feeling. His first youthful work was a study of the *Latin and Teutonic Peoples;* and one of his main ideas, throughout his long life, was that Europe owed its unique greatness to the coexistence and interplay of several distinct nations, which had always resisted the attempts of any one nation to control the whole. By the latter Ranke really meant France—the France of Louis XIV and Napoleon. The Germans, said Ranke in 1830, had a mission from God to develop a culture and a political system entirely different from those of the French. They were destined to "create the pure German state corresponding to the genius of the nation." Whether Western constitutional, parliamentary, and individualist principles were suited to the national character of Germany seemed to Ranke very doubtful.

In economics Friedrich List, in his *National System of Political Economy* (1840), held that political economy as taught in England was suited only to England. It was not an abstract truth but a body of ideas developed in a certain historical stage in a certain country. List thus became a founder of the historical or institutional school of economics. The doctrine of free trade, he said, was designed to make England the world's industrial center by keeping other countries in the status of suppliers of raw material and food. But any country, he held, if it was to be civilized and develop its own national culture, must have cities, factories, industries, and capital of its own. It must therefore put up high tariffs (at least temporarily, in theory) for protection. List, it should be remarked, had developed his ideas during a sojourn in the United States, where Henry Clay's "American system" was in fact a national system of political economy.

List's economics

Nationalism: Eastern Europe

In eastern Europe the Poles and the Magyars had long been active political nationalists, the Poles wishing to undo the partitions of Polish territories and reestablish their Polish state, the Magyars insisting on autonomy for their kingdom of Hungary within the Habsburg empire. But for the most part nationalism in eastern Europe long remained more cultural than political. Centuries of development had tended to submerge the Czechs, Slovaks, Ruthenians, Romanians, Serbs, Croats, Slovenes—and even the Poles and Magyars in lesser degree. Their upper classes spoke German or French and looked to Vienna or to Paris for their ideas. The native languages had remained peasant languages, barely known outside the isolated peasant cultures in which they were spoken. It seemed that many of these languages would disappear.

But early in the nineteenth century the process began to reverse itself. Patriots began to demand the preservation of their historic cultures. They collected folktales and ballads; they studied the languages, composing grammars and dictionaries, often for the first time; and they took to writing books in their mother tongues. They urged their own educated classes to give up foreign ways. They wrote histories showing the famous exploits of their several peoples in the Middle Ages. A new nationalism stirred the Magyars; in 1837 a national Hungarian theater was established at Budapest. In what was to become Romania a former Transylvanian peasant youth named George Lazar began as early as 1816 to teach at Bucharest. He lectured in Romanian (to the surprise of the upper classes, who preferred Greek), telling how Romania had a distinguished history back to the Roman emperor Trajan. As for the Greeks, they entertained visions of restoring the medieval Greek empire (known to Westerners as the Byzantine Empire) in which persons of Greek language or Greek Orthodox religion should become the predominant people of the Balkans.

Preservation of historic cultures

The most far-reaching of the East European movements was the Slavic Revival. The Slavs included the Russians, Poles, Ukrainians, Byelorussians, and Ruthenians; the Czechs and Slovaks; and the South Slavs, consisting of the Slovenes, Croats, Serbs, and Bulgars. All branches of the Slavs began to develop new nationalisms. In 1814 the Serb Vuk Karajich published a grammar of his native tongue and a collection of *Popular Songs and Epics of the Serbs;* he worked out a Serbian alphabet, translated the New Testament, and declared that the dialect of Ragusa (now Dubrovnik) should become the literary language of all South Slavs. In

The Slavic Revival

1836 the Czech historian Francis Palacky published the first volume of his *History of Bohemia*, designed to give the Czechs a new pride in their national past. He first wrote his book in German, the common reading language of educated Czechs. But he soon recast it into Czech, significantly reentitling it a *History of the Czech People.* Among Poles the poet and revolutionary Adam Mickiewicz may be mentioned. Arrested by the Russians in 1823 for membership in a secret society, he was soon allowed by the tsarist government to pass into western Europe. From 1840 to 1844 he taught Slavic literature at the Collège de France, using his lecture platform as a rostrum to deliver eloquent pleas for the liberation of all peoples and overthrow of autocracy. He wrote epic poems on Polish historical themes and continued to be active among the revolutionary Polish exiles settled in France.

Russia itself, which Poles and Czechs regarded as very backward, was slower to develop a pronounced national sense. Under Tsar Alexander I a Western or European orientation prevailed, but in Alexander's last years and after his death in 1825 the doctrines of Slavophilism began to spread. Russian Slavophilism, or the idea that Russia possessed a way of life of its own, different from and not to be corrupted by that of Europe, was simply the application to Russia of the fundamental idea of the *Volksgeist.* Such views in Russia were at least as old as the opposition to the reforms of Peter the Great. In the nationalistic nineteenth century they crystallized more systematically into an "ism," and they tended to merge into Pan-Slavism, which made substantially the same assertions for the Slavic peoples as a whole. But Pan-Slavism, before 1848, was no more than embryonic.

Russian Slavophilism

Other "Isms"

Romanticism, liberalism, radical republicanism, socialism, feminism, and nationalism were after 1815 the political and cultural forces driving Europe onward toward a future still unknown. Of other "isms" less need be said. Conservatism remained strong. Politically, on the Continent, conservatism upheld the institutions of absolute monarchy, aristocracy, and church and opposed the constitutional and representative government sought by liberals. As a political philosophy, conservatism built upon the ideas of Edmund Burke, who had held that every people must change its institutions by gradual adaptation and that no people could suddenly realize in the present any freedoms not already well prepared for in the past. This doctrine lacked appeal for those to whom the past had been a series of misfortunes. Conservatism sometimes passed into nationalism, since it stressed the firmness and continuity of national character. But nationalists at this time were more often liberals or republicans. Monarchism was conservative and even reactionary. Gone was the enlightened despotism of the last century, when kings had boldly irritated their nobles and defied their churches. After the thunders of the French Revolution aristocracy and monarchy huddled together, and their new watchword was to maintain "the throne and the altar."

Conservatism

Deeper than other "isms," a feeling shared in varying ways by people of all parties, was the profound current of humanitarianism. It consisted in a heightened sense of the reality of cruelty inflicted upon others. Here the thought of the Age of Enlightenment suffered no reversal. Torture was gone, and even conservative monarchical governments showed no inclination to restore it. Conditions in prisons, hospitals, insane asylums, and orphanages improved. People became more concerned about the misery of pauper children, chimney sweeps, women in the mines, and black slaves. Russian serf owners and American slave

Humanitarianism

owners began to show psychological signs of moral doubt. To degrade human beings, use them as work animals, torture them, confine them unjustly, hold them as hostages for others, tear apart their families, and punish their relatives were regarded by Europeans as foreign to true civilization, something distant, "Turkish" or "Asiatic," like the castration of eunuchs, the impressment of janissaries, or the burning of widows. The Christian sense of the inviolability of the human person was now again, in a more secular, mundane way, beginning to relieve the sufferings of humanity.

54.   THE DIKE AND THE FLOOD: DOMESTIC

It is now time to resume the narrative of political events, broken off at the close of the last chapter with the peace settlement of 1814–1815. The governments that defeated Napoleon wanted to assure themselves above all else that the disturbances of the past 25 years would not be renewed. In France the restored Bourbon king, Louis XVIII, aspired to keep his throne for himself and his successors. In Great Britain the Tory governing class hoped to preserve the old England that they had so valiantly saved from the clutches of Bonaparte. In Germany, Austria, Italy, and central Europe the chief aim of Metternich, who for another 33 years remained the mastermind of these regions, was to maintain a system in which the prestige of the Habsburg dynasty should be supreme. The aims of the tsar, Alexander, were less clear. He was feared by representatives of the other powers as a dreamer, a self-chosen world savior, a man who said he wanted to bring Christianity into politics, a crowned Jacobin, and even a liberal. It became one of Metternich's chief hopes to convert Alexander to conservatism.

The arrangements made by the victorious powers were in some ways moderate, at least when the provocations they had undergone in the Napoleonic wars are considered. Partly by the tsar's insistence written constitutions existed after 1814 in France and in Russian or "Congress" Poland. Some of the rulers of south German states allowed a measure of representative government. Even the king of Prussia promised a representative assembly for his kingdom, though the promise was not kept. But it was difficult to maintain any kind of stability. The forces of the political right, the privileged classes (or in France the former privileged classes) denounced all signs of liberalism as dangerous concessions to revolution. Those of the political left—liberals, nationalists, republicans—regarded the newly installed regimes as hopelessly reactionary and inadequate. Statesmen were jittery on the subject of revolution, so that they met every sign of agitation with attempts at repression, which though they might drive agitation temporarily underground really only made it worse by creating additional grievances. A vicious circle was set endlessly revolving.

Reaction after 1815: France, Poland

In France Louis XVIII in 1814 granted an amnesty to the regicides of 1793. But the regicides, like all republicans, found the France of 1814 an uncomfortable place to live in, exposed as they were to the unofficial vengeance of counterrevolutionaries, and in 1815 most of them rallied to Napoleon when he returned from Elba. This exasperated the royalist counterrevolutionaries beyond all measure. A brutal "white terror" broke out. Upper-class youths murdered Bonapartists and republicans; Catholic mobs seized and killed Protestants at Marseilles and Toulouse. The Chamber of Deputies chosen in 1815 (by the tiny electorate of 100,000

The "white terror"

well-to-do landowners) proved to be more royalist than the king—*plus royaliste que le roi.* The king himself could not control the mounting frenzy of reaction, which he was sensible enough to realize would only infuriate the revolutionary element still further, as in fact happened. In 1820 a fanatical workingman assassinated the king's nephew, the Duke de Berry. Those who said that all partisans of the French Revolution were criminal extremists seemed to be justified. The reaction deepened, until in 1824 Louis XVIII died and was succeeded by his brother Charles X. Not only was Charles X the father of the recently murdered Duke de Berry, but for over 30 years he had also been the acknowledged leader of implacable counterrevolution. As the Count of Artois, youngest brother of Louis XVI, he had been among the first to emigrate in 1789. He was the favorite Bourbon among the most obstinate ex-seigneurs, nobles, and churchmen. Regarding himself as hereditary absolute monarch by the grace of God, he had himself crowned at Reims with all the romantic pomp of ages past, and proceeded to stamp out not only revolutionary republicanism but liberalism and constitutionalism as well.

In Poland, it will be recalled, the Vienna settlement created a constitutional kingdom, with Alexander as king, joined in merely personal union with the Russian empire. The new machinery did not work very well. The Polish constitution provided for an elected diet, a very wide suffrage by the standards of the day, the Napoleonic civil code, freedom of press and religion, and exclusive use of the Polish language. But the Poles discovered that Alexander, though favoring liberty, did not like to have anyone disagree with him. They could make little use of their much touted freedom in any actual legislation. The elected diet could not get along with the viceroy, who was a Russian. In Russia the serf-owning aristocracy viewed Alexander's idea of a constitutional kingdom in Poland with a jaundiced eye. They wanted no experimentation with liberty on the very borders of Russia.

The Poles themselves played into the hands of their enemies. For the Poles were nationalist at least as much as they were liberal. They were dissatisfied with the boundaries accorded to Congress Poland. They dreamed of the vast kingdom that had existed before the First Partition in 1772 and so agitated the interminable question of the Eastern Border, laying claim to huge territories in the Ukraine and Byelorussia. At the University of Vilna professors and students began to join secret societies. Some members of these societies were revolutionaries aiming at driving out Alexander, reuniting with Prussian and Austrian Poland, and reconstituting an independent Polish state. It was in the discovery and breaking up of one such society that Adam Mickiewicz was arrested in 1823. Reaction and repression now struck the University of Vilna.

Polish ambitions

Reaction after 1815: The German States, Britain

In Germany those who had felt national stirrings during the Wars of Liberation were disillusioned by the peace treaty, which maintained the several German principalities about as Napoleon had left them and purposely united them only in a loose federation, or Bund. National ideas were most common in the numerous universities, where students and professors were more susceptible than most people to the doctrines of an eternal *Volksgeist* and a far-flung *Deutschtum.* National ideas, being a glorification of the German common people, carried with them a kind of democratic opposition to aristocrats, princes, and kings. Students in many of the universities in 1815 formed college clubs, called collectively the *Burschenschaft,* which, as centers of serious political discussion, were to replace the older clubs devoted to drinking and dueling. The *Burschenschaft,* a kind of German youth movement, held a nationwide congress at Wartburg in 1817. Students listened to rousing speeches by patriotic professors, marched about in "Teutonic" costume, and burned a few reactionary books. This undergraduate performance was no immediate threat to any established state, but the nervous governments took alarm. In 1819 a theology student assassinated the German writer Kotzebue, known as an informer in the service of the tsar. The assassin received hundreds of letters of congratulation, and at Nassau the head of the local government barely escaped the same fate at the hands of a pharmacy student.

Metternich now chose to intervene. He had no authority in Germany except in that Austria was a member of the Germanic federation. He regarded all these manifestations of German national spirit, or of any demand for a more solidly unified Germany, as a threat to the favorable position of the Austrian Empire and to the whole balance of Europe. He called a conference of the principal German states at Carlsbad in Bohemia; the frightened conferees adopted certain resolutions, proposed by Metternich, which were soon enacted by the diet of the Bund. These Carlsbad Decrees (1819) dissolved the *Burschenschaft* and the equally nationalistic gymnastic clubs (some of whose members thereupon joined secret societies). They provided for government officials to be placed in the universities and for censors to control the contents of books and the periodical and newspaper press. The Carlsbad Decrees remained in force for many years, and they imposed an effective check on the growth of liberal and nationalist ideas in Germany.

Metternich intervenes

Metternich was unable to persuade the south German rulers to retract the constitutions they had granted. The rulers here, in Bavaria, Württemberg, and elsewhere, found that with representative government they could rally popular support as well as assimilate the numerous new territories that they had obtained from Napoleon. But in general, throughout Germany, after 1820, repression of new or unsettling ideas was the rule. Still more so was this true of the Austrian Empire, which Metternich could more directly control.

Nor did Great Britain escape the dreary rounds of agitation and repression. As elsewhere, radicalism produced reaction and vice versa. Britain after Waterloo was a country devoted to its old traditions but also afflicted by the most advanced social evils. In 1815, at the close of the wars, the landed classes feared an inrush of imported agricultural products and consequent collapse of farm prices and rentals. The gentry who controlled Parliament enacted a new Corn Law, raising the protective tariff to the point where import of grain became impossible unless prices were very high. Landlords and their farmers benefited, but wage earners found the price of breadstuffs soaring out of reach. At the same time there was a postwar depression in industry. Wages fell and many were thrown out of work. These conditions naturally contributed to the spread of political radicalism, which looked first of all to a drastic reform of the House of Commons, in order that thereafter a radical program of social and economic legislation might be enacted.

Economic crisis spurs radicalism

A riot broke out in London in December 1816. In the following February the Prince Regent was attacked in his carriage. The government suspended habeas corpus and employed *agents provocateurs* to obtain evidence against the agitators. Industrialists of Manchester and the new factory towns, determined to force through the reform of parliamentary representation, took the chance offered by the distress of the working classes to organize mass meetings of protest. At Birmingham a crowd elected a mock member of Parliament. At sprawling Manchester 80,000 people staged an enormous demonstration at St. Peter's Fields in 1819; they demanded universal male suffrage, annual election of the House of Commons, and the repeal of the Corn Laws. Although perfectly orderly they were fired upon by soldiers; 11 persons were killed and about 400 were wounded, including 113 women. Radicals called this episode the Peterloo massacre in derisive comparison with the battle of Waterloo.

The Peterloo massacre

The frightened government thanked the soldiers for their brave upholding of the social order. Parliament rushed through the Six Acts (1819), which outlawed "seditious and blasphemous" literature, put a heavy stamp tax on newspapers, authorized the search of private houses for arms, and rigidly restricted the right of public meeting. A group of revolutionaries thereupon plotted to assassinate the whole cabinet at a dinner; they were caught in Cato Street in London in 1820—whence the name "Cato Street Conspiracy." Five of them were hanged. Meanwhile, for publishing the writings of Thomas Paine, Richard Carlisle spent seven years in prison.

"Our example," wrote the Duke of Wellington to a Continental correspondent in 1819, "will be of value in France and Germany, and it is to be hoped that the world will escape from the general revolution with which we all seem to be threatened."

In summary, reactionary policies entrenched themselves everywhere in the years following the peace. The reaction was due only in part to memories of the French Revolution. It was due even more to the living fear of revolution in the present. This fear, though exaggerated, was no mere hallucination. Sensing the rising flood, the established interests desperately built dikes against it in every country. The same is true of international politics at the time.

55.   THE DIKE AND THE FLOOD: INTERNATIONAL

At the Congress of Vienna in 1814–1815 the powers agreed to hold meetings in the future to enforce the treaty and take up new issues as they arose. A number of congresses of the Great Powers resulted, which are of significance as an experimental step toward international regulation of the affairs of Europe. The congresses resembled, in a tentative and partial way, the League of Nations that arose after the First World War of 1914–1918, or the United Nations that followed during and after the war of 1939–1945. The powers had also, in 1815, in alarm after the return of Napoleon, subscribed to Alexander I's Holy Alliance, which became the popular term for the collaboration of the European states in the congresses. The Holy Alliance, on the face of it a statement of Christian purpose and international concord, gradually became an alliance for the suppression of revolutionary and even liberal activity, following in that respect the trend of the governments which made it up.

The Congress of Aix-la-Chapelle, 1818

The first general postwar assemblage of the powers took place at the congress of Aix-la-Chapelle (or Aachen) in 1818. The principal item on the agenda was to withdraw the allied army of occupation from France. The French argued that Louis XVIII would never be popular in France so long as he was supported by a foreign army. The other powers, since they all desired the French to forget the past and accept the Bourbons, withdrew their military forces without disagreement. They arranged also to have private bankers take over the French reparations debt (the 700 million francs imposed by the second Treaty of Paris); the bankers paid the allied governments, and the French in due time paid the bankers.

Alexander's internationalism

Tsar Alexander was still the most advanced internationalist of the day. He suggested at Aix-la-Chapelle a kind of permanent European union and even proposed the maintenance of international military forces to safeguard

The "Peterloo Massacre" of 1819 was condemned in this caricature by the English artist George Cruikshank. A peaceable crowd gathered in St. Peter's Fields, Manchester, to demand political reforms and repeal of the Corn Laws (which placed high tariffs on imported grains), but a militia of part-time soldiers opened fire on the protestors, causing numerous casualties. The British government responded by commending the soldiers and passing new restrictions on public meetings.

(Mansell Collection/Time Pix)

recognized states against changes by violence. Governments if thus reassured against revolution, he argued, would more willingly grant constitutional and liberal reforms. But the others demurred, especially the British foreign minister Lord Castlereagh. The British declared themselves willing to make international commitments against specified contingencies, such as a revival of aggression on the part of France. But they would assume no obligations to act upon indefinite and unforeseeable future events. They reserved the right of independent judgment in foreign policy.

Concretely, the congress addressed itself to the problems of the Atlantic slave trade and of the recurring nuisance of the Barbary pirates. It was unanimously agreed that both should be suppressed. To suppress them required naval forces, which only the British possessed in adequate amount, and it meant also that naval captains must be authorized to stop and search vessels at sea. The continental states, always touchy on the subject of British sea power, refused to countenance any such uses of the British fleet. They feared for the freedom of the seas. As for the British, they would not even discuss placing British warships in an international naval pool or putting British squadrons under the authority of an international body. Nothing therefore was done; the slave trade continued, booming illicitly with the endless demand for cotton; and the Barbary pirates were not disposed of until the French occupied and annexed Algeria some years later. The growth of international institutions was blocked by the separate interests of the sovereign states.

Revolution in Southern Europe: The Congress of Troppau, 1820

Scarcely had the Congress of Aix-la-Chapelle disbanded when revolutionary agitation came to a crisis in southern Europe. It was not that revolutionary or liberal sentiment was stronger here than in the north, in the sense of having more followers, but rather that the governments in question, those of Spain, Naples, and the Ottoman Empire, were inefficient, ignorant, flimsy, and corrupt. Many of the revolutionaries were hardly more than middle-class liberals; indeed, the Spaniards at this time were the first to use the word "liberal" in this modern political sense. Many of them had at first accepted the Napoleonic occupation of Spain as a progressive development but had then turned against it and proclaimed a new constitution in 1812, modeled on the French revolutionary constitution of 1789–1791. After Napoleon's final defeat they attempted to force the restored Bourbon kings of Spain and Naples to adopt this constitution of 1812.

Revolution in Spain and Naples

In 1820 the governments of both Spain and Naples collapsed with remarkable ease before the demonstrations of revolutionaries. The kings of both countries reluctantly took oaths to the Spanish constitution of 1812. But Metternich saw the insurrections as the first symptoms of a revolutionary seizure against which Europe should be quarantined. It was a fact that revolutionary agitation was international, easily leaping across frontiers, because of the operations of secret societies and of political exiles and because in any case the same ideas had been aroused in all countries by the French Revolution. Metternich considered Italy in particular to be within the legitimate sphere of influence of the Austrian Empire. He therefore called a meeting of the Great Powers at Troppau, hoping to use the authority of an international congress to put down the revolution in Naples. The governments of Great Britain and France, not eager to play Austria's game, sent only observers to the congress. Metternich's main problem was, as usual, Alexander. What would be the attitude of the liberal tsar, the friend and patron of constitutions, toward the idea of a constitutional monarchy in Naples? At an inn in Troppau Metternich and Alexander met alone, and there held a momentous interview over the teacups. Metternich reviewed the horrors of revolutionism, the unwisdom of granting any concessions lest revolutionaries be encouraged. Alexander was already somewhat disillusioned by the ungrateful feelings of the Poles. He was troubled by rumors of disaffection among officers in his own army. He had always believed that constitutions should be granted by legitimate sovereigns, not extorted from them by revolutionaries, as had happened in Naples. He allowed himself to be persuaded by Metternich. He declared that he had always been wrong and that Metternich had always been right; and he announced himself ready to follow Metternich's political judgment.

Thus fortified, Metternich drew up a document, the protocol of Troppau, for consideration and acceptance by the five Great Powers. It held that all recognized European states should be protected by collective international action, in the interests of general peace and stability, from internal changes brought about by force. It was a statement of collective security against revolution. Neither France nor Great Britain accepted it. Castlereagh wrote to Metternich that if Austria felt its interests to be threatened in Naples it should intervene in its own name only. It was not the repression of the Neapolitan revolution that the Tories of 1820 objected to, so much as the principle of a binding international collaboration.

A gap opens between East and West

Metternich could get only Russia and Prussia to endorse his protocol, in addition to Austria. These three, acting as the Congress of Troppau, authorized Metternich to dispatch an Austrian army into Naples. He did so; the Neapolitan revolutionaries were arrested or put to flight; the incompetent and brutal Ferdinand I was restored as "absolute" king; the demon of revolution was seemingly exorcised. Reaction won out. But the Congress of Troppau, ostensibly a Europewide international body, had in effect functioned as an antirevolutionary alliance of Austria, Russia, and Prussia. A gap opened between the three Eastern autocracies and the two Western powers—even when the latter consisted of Tories and Bourbons.

Spain and the Near East: The Congress of Verona, 1822

Thousands of revolutionaries and liberals fled from the terror raging in Italy. Many went to Spain, now dreaded by conservatives as the main seat of revolutionary infection. The Middle East also seemed about to ignite in conflagration. Alexander Ypsilanti, a Greek who had spent his adult life in the military service of Russia, in 1821 led a band of armed followers from Russia into Romania (still a part of Turkey), hoping that all Greeks and pro-Greeks in the Turkish empire would join him. He expected Russian support, since the penetration of Turkey by the use of Greek Christians had long been a pet project of Russian foreign policy. The possibility of a Turkish empire converted into a "Greek" empire and dependent on Russia was naturally unpleasant to Metternich. To deal with all these matters an international congress met at Verona in 1822.

Alexander, in shifting from liberal to reactionary views, had not changed his belief in the need for concerted international action. Had pure power politics determined his decisions, he would doubtless have favored Ypsilanti's Grecophile revolution. But he stood by the principle of international solidarity against revolutionary violence. He refused to support Ypsilanti, who found less enthusiasm for Greek culture among the Romanians and Balkan peoples than he had expected and was soon defeated by the Turks. As for intervention to repress the uprising in Greece itself, the question did not arise since the Turkish government proved quite able for a time to handle the matter without assistance.

Ypsilanti refused support

The question of the revolution in Spain was settled by foreign intervention. The Bourbon regime in France had no taste for a Spain in which revolutionaries, republicans, political exiles, and members of secret societies might be harbored. The French government proposed to the Congress of Verona that it be authorized to dispatch an army across the Pyrenees. The Congress welcomed the offer, and despite many dire predictions of ruin, arising from memories of Napoleon's disaster, a French army of 200,000 men moved into Spain in 1823. The campaign proved to be a military promenade through a cheering country. Spanish liberals,

The French invade Spain

constitutionalists, or revolutionaries were a helpless minority. The mass of the people saw the invasion as a deliverance from Masons, Carbonari, and heretics and shouted with satisfaction at the restoration of church and king. Ferdinand VII, unscrupulous and narrowminded, repudiated his constitutional oath and let the vindictive ecclesiastics, grandees, and hidalgos have their way. The revolutionaries were savagely persecuted, exiled, or jailed.

Latin American Independence

The disturbances in Europe had their repercussions in all parts of America. While Great Britain was engaged against Napoleon, the United States fought its inconclusive War of 1812 against the former mother country, and a few years later, after minor military operations, obtained the cession of Florida from Spain. Latin America was affected more positively. The Portuguese royal family, to escape Napoleon, had taken refuge in its Brazilian empire, but when the dynasty was restored at Lisbon one of its members refused to leave Brazil, which remained as an "empire" independent of Portugal until succeeded by a republican regime in 1889.

Spanish America reached over the enormous area from San Francisco to Buenos Aires. Here, too, the thought of the Enlightenment, the news of the American and French revolutions, the Napoleonic occupation of Spain, and the restoration in 1814 of the Bourbon Ferdinand VII to the Spanish throne all had their effects. The British had been penetrating Spanish America commercially for over a century, and during the Napoleonic wars they had increased their exports to it twentyfold. There were thus business interests in Spanish America that resisted any return to the old Spanish imperial system of trade controls. More fundamental was the resentment, growing up over several generations, felt by the creoles for the peninsulars, the creoles being the whites of Spanish descent born in America and the peninsulars those born in Spain who were sent out to occupy the highest offices in the empire. In many places most of the people were native Indians or mestizos of mixed Spanish and Indian origin, often living in depressed conditions and far from the capital cities, so that the movement for independence never took on the widespread popular character that it did in the British colonies that became the United States. It was mainly led by creoles who were active in municipal governments in the towns. At times, as when the revolt was against the Napoleonic government in Spain or against the ephemeral liberal regime in Spain in 1820, the movement for independence recruited some very conservative elements among large landowners and high churchmen. But the important leaders, such as Simón Bolívar and José de San Martín, were men who had spent years in Europe and preferred the new constitutional principles but were in the end frustrated in their aspirations for their own country. The dissensions that long continued to afflict Spanish America were all present within the independence movement itself.

Motives for revolt

Because of its vast extent, over 6,000 miles interrupted by mountain barriers, there could be less unity in the liberation of Spanish America than had been possible, however difficult, in the North American rebellion against England. There could be no Continental Congress such as had met in Philadelphia in 1774. Revolts took place separately within the great vice-royalties: New Spain (Mexico), New Granada (Colombia and Venezuela), Peru (including Ecuador and most of Bolivia and Chile), and La Plata (Argentina, with claims over what are now Uruguay and Paraguay).

The first revolts were against Joseph Bonaparte after Napoleon made him king of Spain in 1808. The rebels proclaimed their loyalty to the deposed Ferdinand VII, who,

Simón Bolívar (1783–1830) was known as "The Liberator" for his leadership of the South American revolutionary movements. He had lived in Europe, where he was strongly influenced by the political ideas of the French Revolution. Although his revolutionary campaigns secured the independence of several new nations, Bolívar's attempts to establish stable, constitutional governments were generally stymied during the 1820s.

(Hulton Getty)

however, when restored in 1814, refused to make any concessions to American demands, so that revolutionary sentiment turned against him also. There followed a series of disconnected struggles between those fighting for independence (with or without much internal change) and combinations of officials, army officers, landowners, and churchmen who remained loyal to the Spanish crown. Bolívar became the liberator of Venezuela and Colombia. San Martín became the liberator of Argentina and Chile, and both combined in the liberation of Peru. In Mexico, by way of exception, there was a true mass rising of Indians and mestizos, which was put down by the middle- and upper-class leaders, so that independent Mexico entered upon a long period of chronic turmoil. All Spanish America was troubled by disputes over boundaries, federations formed only to dissolve, and attempted conquests and secessions, so that it was only later in the nineteenth century that the map of South and Central America took form as we know it today.

Let us return to the congress of European powers meeting in Verona in 1822. At the very time when a French army suppressed the revolution in Spain the revolutionaries in Spanish America were declaring their independence. At Verona, the tsar Alexander urged the Congress to mediate between Spain and its colonies. This was a euphemistic way of suggesting military intervention in Spanish America, following the principle of the protocol of Troppau. The British objected. Even the Tory government favored revolutions that might break up the Spanish empire into independent states, with which free trade treaties might be negotiated. Without at least benevolent neutrality from the British fleet no armed force could sail to America. The Spanish Americans therefore maintained their

British favor Spanish American independence

independence, thanks in part to the use made by the British of their sea power on this occasion.

The new republics received strong moral support from the United States also. In December 1823 President James Monroe, in a message to Congress, announced the "Monroe Doctrine." It stated that attempts by European powers to return parts of America to colonial status would be viewed as an unfriendly act by the United States. The British foreign minister George Canning (who had just succeeded Castlereagh) had at first proposed a joint statement by Great Britain and the United States against the East European powers on the Spanish-American question. President Monroe, at the advice of his secretary of state, John Quincy Adams, decided instead to make a unilateral statement in the form of a message to Congress. They intended to aim their "doctrine" at Great Britain as well as the Continental states, since the British, with their command of the sea, were in fact the only power by which the independence of American states could in practice be threatened. Canning, having no such threats in mind, and concerned more with the Congress of Verona, accepted the line taken by the United States. Indeed, he declared with a flourish that he had "called the New World into existence to redress the balance of the Old." The Monroe Doctrine, at its inception, was a kind of counterblast to the Metternich doctrine of the protocol of Troppau. Where the latter announced the principle of intervention against revolution, the Monroe Doctrine announced that revolutions in America, if they resulted in regimes recognized by the United States, were outside the pale of attention of European powers. In any case the efficacy of the Monroe Doctrine long depended on the tacit cooperation of the British fleet.

The Monroe Doctrine

Over 300 years of European colonial empires in America now came to an end, with few exceptions, in the half-century following the United States declaration of independence. One exception was Canada, where membership in the British empire was voluntary, at least for the English-speaking inhabitants, and where both the English and French Canadians resisted threats of annexation by the United States. The other exceptions were in the West Indies, where Haiti was independent, the smaller islands remained British, French, or Dutch, and the large islands of Cuba and Puerto Rico remained Spanish until the Spanish-American War of 1898.

The End of the Congress System

After the Congress of Verona no more such meetings were held. The attempt at a formal international regulation of European affairs was given up. In the broadest retrospect, the congresses failed to make progress toward an international order because, especially after Alexander's conversion to Metternich's conservatism, they came to stand for nothing except preservation of the status quo. They made no attempt at accommodation with the new forces that were shaping Europe. It was not the policy of the congresses to forestall revolution by demanding that governments institute reforms. They simply repressed or punished all revolutionary agitation. They propped up governments that could not stand on their own feet.

Liberalism advances

In any case the congresses never succeeded in subordinating the separate interests of the Great Powers. Perhaps Alexander's repudiation of Ypsilanti was a sacrifice of Russian advantage to international principle; but when the Austrian government intervened to crush the revolution in Naples, and when the French government crushed the revolution in Spain, though in both cases they acted with an international mandate, each was really promoting what it conceived to be its own interests. The interest of Great Britain was to pull away from the system entirely. As defined by Castlereagh and by Canning after him, it was to stand aloof from permanent international commitments, to preserve a free exercise of sea power and foreign policy, and to take a benevolent view toward revolution in other countries. Since France eventually pulled away also, the Holy Alliance ceased to be even ostensibly a European system and became no more than a counterrevolutionary league between the three East European autocracies. With a majority of the five Great Powers highly liberal, the cause of liberalism in Europe was advanced by the collapse of the international system. At the same time the collapse of the system opened the way to the uncontrolled nationalism of the sovereign states. "Things are getting back to a wholesome state again," wrote George Canning in 1822. "Every nation for itself and God for us all!"

Russia: The Decembrist Revolt, 1825

Alexander I, "the man who defeated Napoleon," the ruler who had led his armies from Moscow to Paris, who had frightened the diplomats by the Russian shadow that he threw over the Continent, and who yet in his way had been the great pillar of constitutional liberalism and international order, died in 1825. His death was the signal for revolution in Russia. Officers of the Russian army, during the campaigns of 1812–1815 in Europe, had become acquainted with many unsettling ideas. Secret societies were formed even in the Russian officer corps; their members held all sorts of conflicting ideas, some wanting a constitutional tsardom in Russia, some demanding a republic, some even dreaming of an emancipation of the serfs. When Alexander died it was for a time uncertain which of his two brothers, Constantine or Nicholas, should succeed him. The restless coteries in the army preferred Constantine, who was thought to be more favorable to innovations in the state. In December 1825 they proclaimed Constantine at St. Petersburg, having their soldiers shout "Constantine and Constitution!" The soldiers, it is said, thought that Constitution was Constantine's wife.

But the fact was that Constantine had already renounced his claims in favor of Nicholas, who was the rightful heir. The uprising, known as the Decembrist revolt, was soon put down. Five of the mutinous officers were hanged; many others were condemned to forced labor or interned in Siberia. The Decembrist revolt was the first manifestation of the modern revolutionary movement in Russia—of a revolutionary movement inspired by an ideological program, as distinguished from the elemental mass upheavals of Pugachev or Stephen Razin. But the immediate effect of the Decembrist revolt was to clamp repression upon Russia more firmly. Nicholas I (1825–1855) maintained an unconditional and despotic autocracy.

Constantine and Nicholas

Ten years after the defeat of Napoleon the new forces issuing from the French Revolution seemed to be routed, and reaction, repression, and political immobility seemed to prevail everywhere in Europe. The dike—a massive dike—seemed to be containing the flood.

56. THE BREAKTHROUGH OF LIBERALISM IN THE WEST: REVOLUTIONS OF 1830–1832

The dike broke in 1830, and in western Europe the stream thereafter never stopped. The seepage, indeed, had already begun. By 1825 Spanish America was independent. The British and the French had pulled away from the congress system. The Greek nationalist movement against the Turks had broken out in the early 1820s.

With the defeat of Ypsilanti in 1821 the Greek nationalists turned somewhat away from the idea of a neo-Greek empire and more toward the idea of independence for Greece proper, the islands and peninsulas where Greek was the predominant language. Tsar Nicholas was more willing than Alexander to assist this movement. The governments of Great Britain and France were not inclined to let Russia stand as the only champion of Balkan peoples. Moreover, liberals in the West thought of the embattled Greeks as ancient Athenians fighting the modern oriental despotism of the Turkish empire.

The result was a joint Anglo-French-Russian naval intervention, which destroyed the Turkish fleet at Navarino Bay in 1827. Russia again, as often in the past, sent armies into the Balkans. A Russo-Turkish war and a great Middle Eastern crisis followed, in the course of which the rival powers agreed in 1829 to recognize Greece as an independent kingdom. The Balkan states of Serbia, Wallachia, and Moldavia were also recognized as autonomous principalities within the badly shaken Ottoman Empire (see maps: v2 p. xxvii/combined edition p. 424, and p. 632). From the same crisis Egypt emerged as an autonomous region under Mehemet Ali. Egypt in time became a center of Arabic nationalism, which cut down Ottoman power in the south just as Balkan nationalism did in the north.

France, 1824–1830: The July Revolution, 1830

It was in 1830, and first of all in France, that the wall of reaction really collapsed. Charles X became king in 1824. In the next year the legislative chambers voted an indemnity, in the form of perpetual annuities totaling 30 million francs a year, to those who as émigrés thirty-odd years before had had their property confiscated by the revolutionary state. Catholic clergy began to take over classrooms in the schools. A law pronounced the death penalty for sacrilege committed in church buildings. But the France of the restored Bourbons was still a free country, and against these apparent efforts to revive the Old Regime a strong opposition developed in the newspapers and in the chambers. In March 1830 the Chamber of Deputies, in which the bankers Laffitte and Casimier-Périer led the "leftist" opposition, passed a vote of no confidence in the government. The king, as was his legal right, dissolved the Chamber and called for new elections. The elections repudiated the king's policies. He replied on July 26, 1830, with four ordinances issued on his own authority. One dissolved the newly elected Chamber before it had ever met; another imposed censorship on the press; the third so amended the suffrage as to reduce the voting power of bankers, merchants, and industrialists and to concentrate it in the hands of the old-fashioned aristocracy; the fourth called for an election on the new basis.

These July Ordinances produced on the very next day the July Revolution. The upper bourgeois class was of course desperate at being thus brazenly ousted from political life.

Charles X abdicates

But it was the republicans—the nucleus of revolutionary workers, students, and intelligentsia in Paris—that actually moved. For three days, from July 27 to 29, barricades were erected in the city, behind which a swarming populace defied the army and the police. Most of the army refused to fire. Charles X, in no mood to be made captive by a revolution like his long-dead brother Louis XVI, precipitately abdicated and headed for England.

Some of the leaders wished to proclaim a democratic republic. Working people hoped for better conditions of employment. The political liberals, supported by bankers, industrialists, various journalists, and intellectuals, had other aims. They had been satisfied in general with the constitutional charter of 1814; it was only to the policies and personnel of the government that they had objected, and they wished now to continue with constitutional monarchy, somewhat liberalized, and with a king whom they could trust. A solution to the deadlock was found by Lafayette, the aging hero of the American and the French revolutions, who became commander of the reorganized National Guard and a popular symbol of national unity. Lafayette produced the Duke of Orleans on the balcony of the Paris Hôtel de Ville, embraced him before a great concourse of people, and offered him as the answer to France's need. The duke was a collateral relative of the Bourbons; he had also, as a young man, served in the republican army of 1792. The militant republicans accepted him, willing to see what would develop; and the Chamber of Deputies on August 7 offered him the throne, on condition that he observe faithfully the constitutional charter of 1814. He reigned, until 1848, under the title of Louis Philippe.

The regime of Louis Philippe, called the Orléanist, bourgeois, or July Monarchy, was viewed very differently by different groups in France and in Europe. To the other states of Europe and to the clergy and legitimists within France, it seemed shockingly revolutionary. The new king owed his throne to an insurrection, to a bargain made with republicans, and to promises made to parliament. He called himself not king of France but king of the French, and he flew not the Bourbon lily but the tricolor flag of the Revolution. The latter produced an effect on the established classes not unlike that of the hammer and sickle after the Russian Revolution. He cultivated a popular manner, wore sober dark clothing (the ancestor of the modern business suit), and carried an umbrella. Though in private he worked stubbornly to maintain his royal position, in public he adhered scrupulously to the constitution.

The July Monarchy

The constitution remained substantially what it had been in 1814. The main political change was one of tone; there would be no more absolutism, with its notion that constitutional guarantees could be abrogated by a reigning prince. Legally the main change was that the Chamber of Peers ceased to be hereditary, to the chagrin of the old nobility, and that the Chamber of Deputies was to be elected by a somewhat enlarged body of voters. Where before 1830 there had been 100,000 voters, there were now about 200,000. The right to vote was still based on the ownership of a considerable quantity of real estate. About one-thirtieth of the adult male population (the top thirtieth in the possession of real property) now elected the Chamber of Deputies. The beneficiaries of the new system were the upper bourgeoisie—the bankers, merchants, and industrialists. The big property owners constituted the *pays légal*, the "legal country," and to them the July Monarchy was the consummation and stopping place of political progress. To others, and especially to the radical democrats, it proved as the years passed to be a disillusionment and an annoyance.

Revolutions of 1830: Belgium and Poland

The immediate effect of the three-day Paris revolution of 1830 was to set off a series of similar explosions throughout Europe, most notably in Belgium and Poland. These in turn, coming after the collapse of the Bourbons in France, brought the whole peace settlement of 1815 into jeopardy. It will be recalled that the Congress of Vienna had joined Belgium with the Dutch Netherlands to create a strong buffer state against a resurgent France and had also done what it could to prevent direct pressure of Russian power upon central Europe by way of Poland. Both these arrangements were now undone.

The Dutch-Belgium union proved economically beneficial, for Belgian industry complemented the commercial and shipping activity of the Dutch, but politically it worked poorly, especially since the Dutch king had absolutist and centralizing ideas. The Belgians, though they had never been

The benefits of the Dutch-Belgian union

LIBERTY LEADING THE PEOPLE

by Eugène Delacroix (French, 1798–1863)

Delacroix, a founder of the romantic school in nineteenth-century French art, painted this picture soon after the July Revolution in Paris in 1830. It well illustrates the idealistic conception of revolution that prevailed among revolutionaries before 1848. Revolution is shown as a noble and moral act on behalf of the abstract ideals of liberty. The figures express determination and courage but show no sign of hatred or even anger. They are not a class; they are the people, affirming the rights of man. Liberty, holding the tricolor aloft, is a composed and even rational goddess.

(Art Resource, NY)

independent, had always stood stiffly for their local liberties under former Austrian rulers (and Spanish before them); now they did the same against the Dutch. The Catholic Belgians disliked Dutch Protestantism; those Belgians who spoke French (the Walloons) objected to regulations requiring the use of Dutch. About a month after the July Revolution in Paris disturbances broke out in Brussels. The leaders asked only for local Belgian self-government, but when the king took arms against them they went on to proclaim independence. A national assembly met and drafted a constitution.

Revolution in Poland

Nicholas of Russia wished to send troops to stamp out the Belgian uprising. But he could not get his forces safely through Poland. In Poland, too, in 1830, a revolution broke out. The Polish nationalists saw in the fall of the French Bourbons a timely moment for them to strike. They objected also to the appearance of Russian troops bound presumably to suppress freedom in western Europe. One incident led to another, until in January 1831 the Polish diet proclaimed the dethronement of the Polish king (i.e., Nicholas), who thereupon sent in a large army. The Poles, outnumbered and divided among themselves, could put up no successful resistance. They obtained no support from the West. The British government was unsettled by agitation at home. The French government, newly installed under Louis Philippe, had no wish to appear disturbingly revolutionary, and in any case feared the Polish agents who sought its backing as international firebrands and republicans. The Polish revolution was therefore crushed. Congress Poland disappeared; its constitution was abrogated, and it was merged into the Russian empire. Thousands of Poles settled in western Europe, where they became familiar figures in republican circles. In Poland the engines of repression rolled. The tsar's government exiled some thousands to Siberia, began to Russify the Eastern Border, and closed the universities of Warsaw and Vilna. Since meanwhile it was too late for the tsar any longer to contemplate intervention in Belgium, it may be said that the sacrifice of the Poles contributed to the success of the West European revolution of 1830, as it had to that of the great French Revolution of 1789–1795.

It was true enough, as Nicholas maintained, that an independent Belgium presented great international problems. Belgium for 20 years before 1815 had been part of France. A few Belgians now favored reunion with it, and in France the republican left, which regarded the Vienna treaty as an insult to the French nation, saw an opportunity to win back this first and dearest conquest of the First Republic. In 1831, by a small majority, the Belgian national assembly elected as their king the son of Louis Philippe, who, however, not wishing trouble with the British, forbade his son to accept it. The Belgians thereupon elected Leopold of Saxe-Coburg, a German princeling who had married into the British royal family and became a British subject. He was in fact the uncle of a 12-year-old girl who was to be Queen Victoria. The British negotiated with Talleyrand, sent over by the French government (it was his last public service); and the result was a treaty of 1831 (confirmed in 1839) setting up Belgium as a perpetually neutral state, incapable of forming alliances and guaranteed against invasion by all five of the Great Powers. The aim intended by the Treaty of Vienna, to prevent the annexation of Belgium to France, was thus again realized in a new way. Internally Belgium presently settled down to a stable parliamentary system, somewhat more democratic than the July Monarchy in France but fundamentally offering the same type of bourgeois and liberal rule.

Reform in Great Britain

The three-day Paris revolution of 1830 had direct repercussions across the Channel. The quick results following on working-class insurrection gave radical leaders in England the idea that threats of violence might be useful. On the other hand, the ease and speed with which the French bourgeoisie gained the upper hand reassured the British middle classes, who concluded that they might unsparingly embarrass the government without courting a mass upheaval.

The Tory regime in England had in fact already begun to loosen up. A group of younger men came forward in the 1820s in the Tory party, notably George Canning, the foreign minister, and Robert Peel, son of one of the first cotton manufacturers. This group was sensitive to the needs of British business and to the liberal doctrines of free trade. They reduced tariffs and liberalized the old Navigation Acts, permitting British colonies to trade with countries other

The Tory regime

than Britain. The Liberal Tories also undermined the legal position of the Church of England, forwarding the conception of a secular state, though such was hardly their purpose. They repealed the old laws (which dated from the seventeenth century) forbidding dissenting Protestants to hold public office except through a legal fiction by which they pretended to be Anglicans. They even allowed the Test Act of 1673 to be repealed and Catholic Emancipation to be adopted. Catholics in Great Britain and Ireland received the same rights as others. Capital punishment was abolished for about a hundred offenses. A professional police force was introduced, in place of the old-fashioned and ineffectual local constables. (It is after Robert Peel that London policemen came to be called "bobbies.") The new police were expected to handle protest meetings, angry crowds, or occasional riots without having to call for military assistance.

There were two things that the Liberal Tories could not do. They could not question the Corn Laws, and they could not reform the House of Commons. By the Corn Laws, which set the tariff on imported grain, a tariff raised to new heights in 1815, the gentlemen of England protected their rent rolls; and by the existing structure of the House of Commons they governed the country, expecting the working class and the business interests to look to them as natural leaders.

Problems of representation

Never in 500 hundred years of its history had the Commons been so unrepresentative. No new borough had been created since the Revolution of 1688. The boroughs, or urban centers having the right to elect members of Parliament, were heavily concentrated in southern England. With the Industrial Revolution, population was shifting noticeably to the north. The new factory towns were unrepresented. Of the boroughs, many had decayed over the centuries; some were quite uninhabited, and one was under the waters of the North Sea. In a few boroughs real elections took place, but in some of them it was the town corporation, and in others the owners of certain pieces of real estate, that had the right to name members of Parliament. Each borough was different, carrying over the local liberties of the Middle Ages. Many boroughs were entirely dominated by influential persons called borough-mongers by their critics. As for the rural districts, the "forty-shilling freeholders" chose two members of Parliament for each county, in a convivial assembly much influenced by the gentlefolk. It was estimated about 1820 that fewer than 500 men, most of them members of the House of Lords, really selected a majority of the House of Commons.

Some two dozen bills to reform the House of Commons had been introduced in the half-century preceding 1830. They had all failed to pass. In 1830, after the Paris revolution, the issue was again raised by the minority party, the Whigs. The Tory prime minister, the Duke of Wellington, the victor of Waterloo and a most extreme conservative, so immoderately defended the existing system that he lost the confidence even of some of his own followers. The existing methods of election in England, he declared, were more perfect than any that human intelligence could contrive at a single stroke. After this outburst a Whig ministry took over the government. It introduced a reform bill. The House of Commons rejected it. The Whig ministry thereupon resigned. The Tories, fearing popular violence, refused to take the responsibility for forming a cabinet. The Whigs resumed office and again introduced their reform bill. This time it passed the Commons but failed in the House of Lords. An angry roar went up over the country. Crowds milled in the London streets, rioters for several days were in control at Bristol, the jail at Derby was sacked, and Nottingham castle was burned. Only the passage of the bill, it seemed, could prevent an actual revolution. Using this argument the Whigs got the king to promise to create enough new peers to change the majority in the House of Lords. The Lords yielded rather than be swamped, and in April 1832 the bill became law.

The Reform Bill of 1832 was a very English measure. It adapted the English or medieval system rather than following new ideas unleashed by the French Revolution. On the Continent, constitutional political systems in

The Reform Bill of 1832

countries such as France rested on the idea that each representative should represent roughly the same number of voters and that voters should qualify to vote by a flat uniform qualification, usually the payment of a stated amount of property taxes. The British held to the idea that members of the House of Commons represented boroughs and counties, in general without regard to size of population (with exceptions). In other words, no attempt was made to create equal electoral districts, and the vote was still distributed in the reformed boroughs and counties on the basis of economic status, reliability, and permanence. The total effect on the size of the electorate was to raise the number of voters in the British Isles from about 500,000 to about 813,000. Some persons actually lost their votes, namely, the poorer elements in the handful of old boroughs which had been fairly democratic, like the borough of Westminster in greater London.

The most important change was not the increased size of the electorate but its redistribution by region and by class. The Reform Bill reallocated the seats in the House of Commons. Fifty-six of the smallest older boroughs were abolished, their inhabitants thereafter voting as residents of their counties. Thirty other small boroughs kept the right to send only one burgess to Parliament instead of the historic two. The 143 seats thus made available were given to the new industrial towns, where the middle classes now gained the right to vote—factory owners and businessmen and their principal employees; doctors, lawyers, brokers, merchants, and newspaper people; relatives and connections of the well-to-do.

The Reform Bill of 1832 was more sweeping than the Whigs would have favored except for their fear or revolution. It was more conservative than the democratic radicals would have accepted, except for their belief that the suffrage might be widened in the future. Whether Great Britain in 1830 was in danger of any real revolution can never be known. In any case a distressed mass of workers was led by an irate manufacturing interest that was unwilling to tolerate any longer its exclusion from political life. Had these elements consented to general violence a real revolution might have occurred. Yet there was no violent revolution in Britain. The

The ambiguous impact of reform

reason probably lies first of all in the existence of the historic institution of Parliament, which, erratic though it was before the Reform Bill, provided the means by which social changes could be legally accomplished and continued, in principle, to enjoy universal respect. Conservatives, driven to the wall, would yield; they could allow a revision of the suffrage because they could expect to remain themselves in public life. Radicals, using enough violence to scare the established interest, did not thereafter face a blank wall; they could expect, once the breach was made, to carry some day a further democratization of Parliament and with it their social and economic program by orderly legislation.

Britain after 1832

But the Reform Bill of 1832 was in its way a revolution. The new business interests, created by industrialization, took their place alongside the old aristocracy in the governing elite of the country. The aristocratic Whigs who had carried the Reform Bill gradually merged with formerly radical

Liberals and Conservatives

industrialists and with a few Liberal Tories to form the Liberal party. The main body of the Tories, joined by a few old Whigs and even a few former radicals, gradually turned into the Conservative party. The two parties alternated in power at short intervals from 1832 to the First World War, this being the classic period in Great Britain of the Liberal-Conservative two-party system.

In 1833 slavery was abolished in the British Empire. In 1834 a new Poor Law was adopted. In 1835 the Municipal Corporations Act, second only to the Reform Bill in basic importance, modernized the local government of English cities; it broke up the old local oligarchies and brought in uniform electoral and administrative machinery, enabling city dwellers to grapple more effectively with the problems of urban life. In 1836 the House of Commons allowed the newspapers to report how its members voted—a long step toward publicity of government proceedings was thus taken. Meanwhile an ecclesiastical commission reviewed the affairs of the Church of England; financial and administrative irregularities were corrected, together with the grosser inequalities between the income of upper and lower clergy, all of which had made the church formerly a kind of closed preserve for the landed gentry.

The Tory counteroffensive

The Tories, thus assaulted in their immemorial strongholds of local government and the established church, carried a counteroffensive into the strongholds of the new liberal manufacturing class, namely, the factories and the mines. Tories became champions of the industrial workers. Landed gentlemen, of whom the most famous was Lord Ashley, later seventh Earl of Shaftesbury, took the lead in publicizing the social evils of a rapid and indeed ruthless industrialization. They received some support from a few humanitarian industrialists; indeed, the early legislation tended to follow practices already established by the best or strongest business firms. A Factory Act of 1833 forbade the labor of children less than nine years old in the textile mills. It was the first effective piece of legislation on the subject because it provided for paid inspectors and procedures for enforcement. An act of 1842 initiated significant regulation in the coal mines; the employment underground of women and girls, and of boys under 10, was forbidden.

The greatest victory of the working classes came in 1847 with the Ten Hours Act, which limited the labor of women and children in all industrial establishments to 10 hours a day. Thereafter men commonly worked only 10 hours also, since the work of men, women, and young people was too closely coordinated for the men to work alone. The Liberal John Bright, Quaker and cotton magnate, called the Ten Hours Act "a delusion practiced on the working classes." To regulate the hours of labor was contrary to the accepted principles of laissez-faire, economic law, the free market, freedom of trade, and individual liberty for employer and worker. Yet the Ten Hours Act stood, and British industry continued to prosper.

The Anti–Corn Law League

Gathering their strength, the Whig-liberal-radical combination established in 1838 an Anti-Corn Law League. Wage earners objected to the Corn Laws because the tariff on grain imports kept up the price of food. Industrial employers objected to them because, in keeping up food prices, they also kept up wages and cost of production in England, thus working to England's disadvantage in the export trade. Defenders of the Corn Laws argued that protection of agriculture was necessary to maintain the natural aristocracy of the country (most land being owned by peers and gentry, as has been seen), but they also sometimes used more widely framed economic arguments, affirming that Britain should preserve a balanced economy as between industry and farming, and avoid becoming too exclusively dependent on imported food. The issue became a straight contest between the industrialists, acting with working-class support, and the aristocratic and predominantly Tory landowning interest. The Anti–Corn Law League, whose headquarters were at Manchester, operated like a modern political party. It had plenty of money, supplied by large donations from manufacturers and small ones from laboring people. It sent lecturers on tour, agitated in the newspapers, and issued a stream of polemical pamphlets and educational books. It held political teas, torchlight processions, and open-air mass meetings. The pressure proved irresistible and received a final impetus from a famine in Ireland. It was a Tory government, headed by Sir Robert Peel, which in 1846 yielded before so vociferous a demand.

The repeal of the Corn Laws in 1846 stands as a symbol of the change that had come over England. It reaffirmed the revolutionary consequences of the Reform Bill of 1832. Industry was now a governing element in the country. Free trade was henceforth the rule. Great Britain, in return for the export of manufacturers, became deliberately dependent on imports for its very life. It was committed henceforth to an international and even worldwide economic system. The first to undergo the Industrial Revolution, possessing mechanical power and methods of mass production, the British could produce yarn and cloth, machine tools and railroad equipment, more efficiently and more cheaply than any other people. In Britain, the workshop of the world, people would pour increasingly into mine, factory, and city; live by selling manufactures, coal, shipping, and financial services to the other peoples of the earth; and obtain raw cotton, rare ores, meat, cereals, and thousands of lesser but still vital necessities from the rest of the earth in exchange. The welfare of Britain depended on the maintenance of a freely exchanging worldwide economic system and, as always, on the British navy's control of the sea.

57. TRIUMPH OF THE WEST EUROPEAN BOURGEOISIE

In general, the decades following 1830 may be thought of as a kind of golden age of the West-European bourgeoisie, or what in English would be called the upper middle class. In the older meaning, in French, a *bourgeois* had been someone who was not of the nobility but enjoyed an income from business, a profession, or the ownership of property. After the French Revolution, and even more after 1830, the word took on new meanings, not all of them consistent. Artists, literary people, and old-line aristocrats might disdain the bourgeois as a person of uncultivated tastes, supposedly interested only in making money. From another point of view, shared by social theorists and working-class leaders, the bourgeois was someone who could hire the labor of other people for business enterprises, recreational activities, or household service. In a word, the bourgeois was the employer. In any case, the bourgeoisie and the aristocracy tended to become more alike in the nineteenth century in their daily pursuits and style of life, and to draw income from the possession of income-producing property or capital. The bourgeoisie, formerly identified in contrast to the nobility, was now identified in contrast to the working class, that is, those whose whole income depended on daily labor in shops, offices, farms, or factories.

The reigning liberal doctrine was the "stake in society" theory; those should govern who have something to lose. In the France of the July Monarchy (1830–1848), only about one adult male in 30 had the vote. In the Britain of the first Reform Bill (1832–1867), one man in eight could vote for a member of the House of Commons. In France only the most well-to-do were enfranchised; in Britain, virtually the whole middle class, which, however, long supported

"Stake in society" theory

BIG INVESTMENTS

by Honoré Daumier (French, 1808–1879)

The Revolution of 1830, romanticized at first by Delacroix and most European liberals, was in fact followed by a period of moneymaking and business ferment (as well as rapid economic development), made famous by the novels of Balzac and the graphic art of Daumier. This lithograph of 1837 shows a financier with bundles of stock certificates piled beside him, offering to sell shares in factories, foundries, and breweries to a skeptical client. Daumier's satirical images provided vivid, memorable critiques of the corruptions and hypocrisies in nineteenth-century political and economic life.

(Bibliothèque Nationale de France, Paris)

members of the aristocracy for the highest public positions. In Britain the continuation of the Tory landed interest in politics somewhat blunted the edge of capitalist and managerial rule, resulting in the passage of significant legislation for the protection of industrial labor. In France the aristocratic landed interest, weaker and less public spirited than in England, lost much of its influence by the Revolution of 1830, and less was done to relieve the condition of labor.

The bourgeois age left its mark on Europe in many ways. For one thing, western Europe continued to accumulate capital and build up its industrial plant. National income was constantly rising, but a relatively small share went to the laboring class and a relatively large share went to owners of capital. This meant that less was spent on consumers' goods—housing, clothing, food, recreation—and that more was saved and available for reinvestment. New stock companies were constantly formed, and the law of corporations was amended, allowing for the extension of corporate enterprise to new fields. The factory system spread from Britain to the Continent and within Britain from the textile industry to other lines of production. The output of iron, a good index to economic advancement in this phase of industrialism, rose about 300 percent in Great Britain between 1830 and 1848 and about 65 percent in France between 1830 and 1845. (All the German states combined, at the latter date, produced about a tenth as much iron as Great Britain and less than half as much as France.) Railroad building began in earnest after 1840. In 1840 Samuel Cunard put four steamships into regular transatlantic service. Much capital was exported; as early as 1839 an American estimated that Europeans (mainly British) owned $200,000,000 worth of stocks in American companies. Such investments financed the purchase of British and other goods and helped to rivet together a world economic system, in which western Europe and especially England took the lead, with other regions remaining in a somewhat subordinate status.

The Frustration and Challenge of Labor

The bourgeois age had the effect also of estranging the world of labor. The state in Britain and France was as near as it has ever been to what Karl Marx was soon to call it—a committee of the bourgeois class. Already in France people spoke worriedly of the *prolétaires,* those at the bottom of society, who had nothing to lose. Republicans in France, radical democrats in Britain, felt cheated and imposed upon in the 1830s and 1840s. They had in each country forced through a virtual revolution by their insurrections and demonstrations and then in each country had been left without the vote. Some lost interest in representative institutions. Excluded from government, they were tempted to seek political ends through extragovernmental, which is to say revolutionary or utopian, channels. Social and economic reforms seemed to the average worker far more important, as a final aim, than mere governmental innovations. Workers were told by respected economists that they could not hope to change the system in their own favor. They were tempted, therefore, to destroy the system, to replace it utterly with some new system conceived mainly in the minds of thinkers. They were told by the Manchester School, and by its equivalent in France, that the income of labor was set by ineluctable natural laws, that it was best and indeed necessary for wages to remain low, and that the way to rise in the world was to get out of the laboring class altogether, by becoming the owner of a profitable business and leaving working people about where they were.

The reigning doctrine emphasized the conception of a labor market. **The labor market** The worker sold labor, the employer bought it. The price of labor, or wage, was to be agreed upon by the two individual parties. The price would naturally fluctuate according to changes in supply and demand. When a great deal of a certain kind of labor was required the wage would go up, until new persons moved into the market offering more labor of this type, with the result that something like the old wage would again be established. When no labor was needed none should be bought, and persons who could not sell labor might then subsist for a time by poor relief.

**The Poor Law
of 1834**

The new Poor Law of 1834 was especially repugnant to the British working class. It corrected crying evils of the old poor laws that had left millions of people in habitual poverty but did nothing constructive to relieve productive workers suffering from occasional or cyclical unemployment. The new law followed the stern precepts of the dismal science; its main principle was to safeguard the labor market by making relief more unpleasant than any job. It granted relief only to persons willing to enter a workhouse, or poorhouse; and in these establishments the sexes were segregated and life was in other ways made noticeably less attractive than in the outside world. The workers considered the new law an abomination. They called the workhouses "bastilles." They resented the whole conception of a labor market, in which labor was to be bought and sold (or remain unsold) like any other commodity. The fluctuating, cyclical labor market contributed to the social instability of working-class families and may also have created new tensions between women and men. Court records from early nineteenth-century England suggest that violent family disputes became more common when women earned significant portions of the working family's household income or found work more readily than their unemployed husbands; such situations challenged the traditional relations in English family life, though women almost always received lower wages than men.

In the long run it would be the increase in productivity that would improve the condition of the workers. Meanwhile the friends of the working class offered two means of escape. One was to improve the position of labor in the market. This led to the formation of labor unions for control of the labor supply and collective bargaining with employers. Such unions, illegal in France, were barely legal in Great Britain after 1825, though it was still illegal in both countries to strike. The other means of escape was to repudiate the whole idea of a market economy and of the capitalist system. It was to conceive of a system in which goods were to be produced for use, not for sale; and in which working people should be compensated according to need, not according to the requirements of an employer. This was the basis of most forms of nineteenth-century socialism.

Socialism and Chartism

Socialism spread rapidly among the working classes after 1830. In France it blended with revolutionary republicanism. There was a revival of interest in the great Revolution and the democratic Republic of 1793. Cheap reprints of the writings of Robespierre began to circulate in the working-class quarters of Paris. Robespierre was now seen as a people's hero. The socialist Louis Blanc, for example, who in 1839 published his *Organization of Work* recommending the formation of "social workshops," also wrote a long history of the French Revolution, in which he pointed out the egalitarian ideals that had inspired the National Convention in 1793. In Britain, as befitted the different background of the country, socialistic ideas blended in with the movement for further parliamentary reform. This was advanced by the working-class group known as the Chartists, from the People's Charter which they drafted in 1838.

Chartism was far more of a mass movement than the French socialism of the day. Only a few Chartists were clearly socialists in their own minds. But all were anticapitalistic. All could agree that the first step must be to win working-class representation in Parliament. The Charter of 1838 consisted of six points. It demanded (1) the annual election of the House of Commons by (2) universal suffrage for all adult males, through (3) a secret ballot and (4) equal electoral districts; and it called for (5) the abolition of property qualifications for membership in the House of Commons, which perpetuated the old idea that Parliament should be composed of gentlemen of independent income, and urged instead (6) the payment of salaries to the elected members of Parliament, in order that people of small means might serve. A convention composed of delegates sent by labor unions, mass meetings, and radical societies all over the country met in London in 1839. Convention was an ominous word, with French revolutionary and even terrorist overtones; some members of this British convention regarded it as the body really representing the people and favored armed violence and a general strike, while others stood only for moral pressure upon Parliament.

The Charter of 1838

A petition bearing over a million signatures, urging acceptance of the Charter, was submitted to the House of Commons. The violent and revolutionary wing, or "physical force" Chartists, precipitated a wave of riots which were effectively quelled by the authorities. In 1842 the petition was again submitted. This time, according to the best estimate, it was signed by 3,317,702 persons. Since the entire population of Great Britain was about 19 million it is clear that the Charter, whatever the exact number of signatures, commanded the explicit adherence of half the adult males of the country. The House of Commons nevertheless rejected the petition by 287 votes to 49. It was feared that political democracy would threaten property rights and the whole economic system as they then existed. The Chartist movement gradually died down in the face of firm opposition by the government and the business classes and was weakened by mutual fears and disagreements among its own supporters. It had not been entirely fruitless; for without popular agitation and the publicizing of working-class grievances, the Mines Act of 1842 and the Ten Hours Act of 1847 might not have been enacted. These measures in turn alleviated the distress of industrial workers and kept alive a degree of confidence in the future of the economic system. Chartism revived briefly in 1848, as will be seen in the next chapter; but in general, in the 1840s, British working people turned from political agitation to the forming and strengthening of labor unions by which they could deal directly with employers without having to appeal to the government. Not until 1867 was the suffrage extended in Great Britain, and it took about 80 years to realize the full program of the Charter of 1838, except for the annual election of Parliament, for which there soon ceased to be any demand.

Petitions and the defeat of the Chartists

It is not easy to summarize the history of Europe between 1815 and 1848. Among all the forces set free by the French and Industrial revolutions—liberalism, conservatism, nationalism, republicanism, socialism, feminism, democracy—no stabilization had been achieved. No international system had been created; Europe had instead fallen increasingly into two political camps, composed of a West in which liberal conceptions moved forward and an East in which three autocratic monarchies held sway. Western Europe favored the principles of nationality; governments in central and eastern Europe still opposed them. The West was growing collectively richer, more liberal, more bourgeois. Middle-class people in Germany, central Europe, and Italy (as well as in Spain and Portugal) did not usually enjoy the dignities and emoluments that they enjoyed in Great Britain or France. But

The newly organized London police await the arrival of a Chartist procession in the 1840s. The British government introduced a more disciplined police force to avoid incidents such as the Peterloo Massacre and to manage the mass demonstrations of groups such as the Chartists, who campaigned (unsuccessfully) for more democratic electoral laws.

(Mansell Collection/Time Pix)

the West had not solved its social problem; its whole material civilization rested upon a restless and sorely tried working class. Everywhere there was repression, in varying degree, and everywhere apprehension, more in some places than in others; but there was also hope, confidence in the progress of an industrial and scientific society, and faith in the unfinished program of the rights of individuals. The result was the general Revolution of 1848.

Chapter 12

REVOLUTION AND THE REIMPOSITION OF ORDER, 1848–1870

Fears haunting the established classes of Europe for 30 years came true in 1848. Governments collapsed all over the Continent. Remembered horrors appeared again, as in a recurring dream, in much the same sequence as after 1789 only at a much faster rate of speed. Revolutionaries milled in the streets, kings fled, republics were declared, and within four years there was another Napoleon. Soon thereafter came a series of short wars.

Never before or since has Europe seen so truly universal an upheaval as in 1848. While the French Revolution of 1789 and the Russian Revolution of 1917 both had immediate international repercussions, in each of these cases a single country took the lead. In 1848 the revolutionary movement broke out spontaneously from native sources from Copenhagen to Palermo and from Paris to Budapest. Contemporaries sometimes attributed the universality of the phenomenon to the machinations of secret societies, and it is true that the faint beginnings of an international revolutionary movement existed before 1848; but the fact is that revolutionary plotters had little influence upon what actually happened, and the nearly simultaneous fall of governments is quite understandable from other causes. Many people in Europe sought substantially the same goals—constitutional government, the independence and unification of national groups, an end to serfdom and manorial restraints where they still existed. With some variation, there was a common body of ideas among politically conscious elements of all countries. Some of the powers that the new forces had to combat were themselves international, notably the Catholic church and the far-spreading influence of the Habsburgs, so that resistance to them arose independently in many places.

Chapter emblem: Detail from a nineteenth-century illustration of the crowd marching on the Tuileries in Paris during the Revolution of 1848.

In any case, only the Russian empire and Great Britain escaped the European revolutionary contagion of 1848, and the British received a very bad scare.

But the Revolution of 1848, though it shook the whole Continent, lacked basic driving strength. It failed almost as rapidly as it succeeded. Its main consequence, in fact, was to strengthen the more conservative forces that viewed all revolution with alarm. Revolutionary ideals succumbed to military repression. To some extent the governments of the 1850s and 1860s, while hostile to revolution, satisfied some of the aims of 1848, notably in national unification and constitutional government with limited representation, but they did so in a mood of calculated realism, and while reasserting their own authority. The repressed Revolution of 1848 also left a legacy of class fears and class conflict, in which prophets of a new society also became more realistic, as when Karl Marx, branding earlier forms of socialism as "utopian," offered his own views as hard-headed and "scientific."

58.   PARIS: THE SPECTER OF SOCIAL REVOLUTION IN THE WEST

The July Monarchy in France was a platform of boards built over a volcano. Under it burned the repressed fires of the republicanism put down in 1830, which since 1830 had become steadily more socialistic.

Politics in the July Monarchy became increasingly separated from the evolving social classes in French society. So few interests were represented in the Chamber of Deputies that the most basic issues were seldom debated. Even most of the bourgeois class had no representation. Graft and corruption were more common than they should have been, as economic expansion favored stockjobbing and fraud by business promoters and politicians in combination. A strong movement set in to give the vote to more people instead of to only one man in 30. Radicals wanted universal male suffrage and a republic, but liberals asked only for a broadening of voting rights within the existing constitutional monarchy. The king, Louis Philippe, and his prime minister, Guizot, instead of allying with the liberals against the radicals, resolutely and obtusely opposed any change whatsoever.

The "February" Revolution in France

Reformers, against the king's expressed wishes, planned a great banquet in Paris for February 22, 1848, to be accompanied by demonstrations in the streets. The government on February 21 forbade all such meetings. That night barricades were built in the working-class quarters. These consisted of paving blocks, building stones, or large pieces of furniture thrown together across the narrow streets and intersections of the old city and constituting a maze within which insurgents prepared to resist the authorities. The government called out the National Guard, which refused to move. The king now promised electoral reform, but republican firebrands took charge of the semimobilized working-class elements, which held a demonstration outside the house of Guizot. Someone shot at the guards placed around the house; the guards replied, killing 20 persons. The republican organizers put some of the corpses on a torch-lit cart and paraded them through the city, which, armed and barricaded, soon began to swarm in an enormous riot. On February 24 Louis Philippe, like Charles X before him, abdicated and made for England. The February Revolution of 1848, like the July Revolution of 1830, had unseated a monarch in three days.

The constitutional reformers hoped to carry on with Louis Philippe's young grandson as king, but the republicans, now aroused and armed, poured into the Chamber of Deputies and forced the proclamation of the Republic. Republican leaders set up a provisional government of 10 men, pending election by all France of a Constituent Assembly. Seven of the 10 were "political" republicans, the most notable being the poet Lamartine. Three were "social" republicans, the most notable being Louis Blanc. A huge crowd of workers appeared before the Hôtel de Ville, or city hall, demanding that France adopt the new socialist emblem—the red flag. They were dissuaded by the eloquence of Lamartine, and the tricolor remained the republican standard.

Proclamation of the Republic

Louis Blanc urged the Provisional Government to push through a bold economic and social program without delay. But since the "social" republicans were in a minority in the Provisional Government (though probably not among Paris republicans generally), Louis Blanc's ideas were very much watered down in the application. He wanted a Ministry of Progress to organize a network of "social workshops," the state-supported and collectivist manufacturing establishments that he had projected in his writings. All that was created was a Labor Commission, with limited powers, and a system of shops significantly entitled "national" rather than "social." The National Workshops, as they are always called in English (though "workshop" suggests something more insignificant than Louis Blanc had in mind), were agreed to by the Provisional Government only as a political concession, and no significant work was ever assigned them for fear of competition with private enterprise and dislocation of the economic system. Indeed, the man placed in charge of them admitted that his purpose was to prove the fallacies of socialism. Meanwhile the Labor Commission was unable to win public acceptance for the 10-hour day, which the British Parliament had enacted the year before. One action of the Provisional Government, however, had permanent effect, the final abolition of slavery in the French colonies.

Louis Blanc

The National Workshops became in practice only an extensive project in unemployment relief. Women were excluded from the workshops, but men of all trades, skilled and unskilled, were set to work digging on the roads and fortifications outside Paris. They were paid two francs a day. The number of legitimate unemployed increased rapidly, for 1847 had been a year of depression and the revolution prevented the return of business confidence. Other needy persons also presented themselves for remuneration, and soon there were too many men for the amount of work made available. From 25,000 enrolled in the workshops by the middle of March, the number climbed to 120,000 by mid-June, by which time there were also in Paris another 50,000 whom the bulging workshops could no longer accommodate. In June there were probably almost 200,000 essentially idle but able-bodied men in a city of about a million people.

The National Workshops

The Constituent Assembly, elected in April by universal male suffrage throughout France, met on May 4. It immediately replaced the Provisional Government with a temporary executive board of its own. The main body of France, a land of provincial bourgeois and peasant landowners, was not socialist in the least. The temporary executive board, chosen by the Constituent Assembly in May, included no "social" republicans. All five of its members, of whom Lamartine was the head, were known as outspoken enemies of Louis Blanc. Blanc and the socialists could no longer expect even the grudging and insincere concessions that they had so far obtained.

The battle lines were now drawn, after only three months of revolution, somewhat as they had been drawn in 1792 after three years. Paris again stood for a degree of revolutionary action in which the rest of the country was not prepared to share. Revolutionary leaders in Paris, in 1848 as in 1792, were unwilling to accept the processes of majority rule

There was in Paris a well-established tradition of revolutionary agitation, so that a conflict between political activists and the police in February 1848 could lead quickly toward the well-known patterns of radical political upheaval: crowds and barricades in the streets, publications calling for revolutionary change, and emotional responses to popular national symbols such as the tricolor flag. This nineteenth-century illustration depicts part of the Parisian crowd that marched on the Tuileries, forcing King Louis-Philippe to abdicate power and leave the country.

(Snark/Art Resource, NY)

or slow parliamentary deliberation. But the crisis in 1848 was more acute than in 1792. A larger proportion of the population were wage earners. Under a system of predominantly merchant capitalism, in which machine industry and factory concentration were only beginning, the workers were tormented by the same evils as the more industrialized working classes of England. Hours were if anything longer, and pay was less, in France than in Great Britain; insecurity and unemployment were at least as great; and the feeling that a capitalist economy held no future for the laborer was the same. In addition, where the English worker shrank from the actual violation of Parliament, the French worker saw nothing very sacrilegious in the violation of elected assemblies. Too many regimes in France since 1789, including those preferred by the comfortable classes, had been based on insurrectionary violence for the French workers to feel much compunction over using it for their own ends.

The "June Days" of 1848

On the one hand stood the nationally elected Constituent Assembly. On the other, the National Workshops had mobilized in Paris the most distressed elements of the working class. Tens of thousands had been brought together where they could talk, read journals, listen to speeches, and concert common action. Agitators and organizers naturally made use of the opportunity thus presented to them. Men in the workshops began to feel desperate, to sense that the social republic was slipping from them perhaps forever. On May 15 they attacked the Constituent Assembly, drove its members out of the hall, declared it dissolved, and set up a new provisional government of their own. They announced that a social revolution must follow the purely political revolution of February. But the National Guard, a kind of civilian militia, turned against the insurgents and restored the Constituent Assembly. The Assembly, to root out socialism, prepared to get rid of the National Workshops. It offered those enrolled in them the alternatives of enlistment in the army, transfer to provincial workshops, or expulsion from Paris by force. The whole laboring class in the city began to resist. The government proclaimed martial law, the civilian executive board resigned, and all power was given to General Cavaignac and the regular army.

Paris on the verge of revolution

There followed the "Bloody June Days"—June 24 to 26, 1848—three days during which a terrifying class war raged in Paris. Over 20,000 men from the workshops took to arms (more would doubtless have done so had not the government continued to pay wages in the workshops during the insurrection), and they were joined by other unnumbered thousands of men and women from the working-class districts of the city. Half or more of Paris became a labyrinth of barricades defended by determined men and equally resolute women. Military methods of the time made it possible for civilians to shoot it out openly with soldiers; small arms were the main weapons, and armies had no armored vehicles or even any very devastating artillery. The soldiers found it a difficult operation, even several generals being killed, but after three days the outcome was in doubt no longer. Ten thousand persons had been killed or wounded. Eleven thousand insurgents were taken prisoner. The Assembly, refusing all clemency, decreed their immediate deportation to the colonies.

Class war

The June Days sent a shudder throughout France and Europe. Whether the battle in Paris had been a true class struggle, how large a portion of the laboring class had really participated (it was large in any case), how much they had fought for permanent objectives, and how much over the temporary issue of the workshops—all these were secondary questions. It was widely understood that a class war had in fact broken out. Militant workers were confirmed in a hatred and loathing of the bourgeois class, in a belief that capitalism existed in the last analysis by the callous shooting of working-class men and women in the streets. People above the laboring class were thrown into a panic. They were sure that they had narrowly escaped a ghastly upheaval. The very ground of civilized living seemed to have quaked. After June 1848, wrote a Frenchwoman of the time, society was "a prey to a feeling of terror incomparable to anything since the invasion of Rome by the barbarians."

Nor were the signs in England much more reassuring. There the Chartist agitation was revived by the February Revolution in Paris. "France is a Republic!" cried the Charist Ernest Jones; the Chartist petition was again circulated and was soon said to have 6 million signatures. Another Chartist convention met, considered by its leaders to be the forerunner of a Constituent Assembly as in France. The violent minority was the most

The revival of Chartist agitation

active; it began to gather arms and to drill. The old Duke of Wellington swore in 70,000 special constables to uphold the social order. Clashes occurred at Liverpool and elsewhere; in London the revolutionary committee laid plans for systematic arson and organized men with pickaxes to break up the pavements for barricades. Meanwhile the petition, weighing 584 pounds, was carried in three cabs to the House of Commons, which estimated that it contained "only" 2 million signatures and again summarily rejected it. The revolutionary menace passed. One of the secret organizers in London proved to be a government spy; he revealed the whole plan at the critical moment, and the revolutionary committee was arrested on the day set for insurrection. Most Chartists had in any case refused to support the militants, but the truculent minority of radical workers and journalists had a deeper sense of envenomed class consciousness. The word "proletarian" was imported from France. "Every proletarian," wrote the Chartist editor of *Red Revolution,* "who does not see and feel that he belongs to an enslaved and degraded class is a *fool."*

The specter of social revolution thus hung over western Europe in the summer of 1848. Doubtless it was unreal; in all probability there could have been no successful socialist revolution at the time. But the specter was there, and it spread a sinking fear among all who had something to lose. This fear shaped the whole subsequent course of the Second Republic in France and of the revolutionary movements that had by this time begun in other countries as well.

The Emergence of Louis Napoleon Bonaparte

In France, after the June Days, the Constituent Assembly (keeping General Cavaignac as a virtual dictator) set about drafting a republican constitution. It was decided, in view of the disturbances just passed, to create a strong executive power in the hands of a president to be elected by universal male suffrage. It was decided also to have this president elected immediately, even before the rest of the constitution was finished. Four candidates presented themselves: Lamartine, Cavaignac, Ledru-Rollin—and Louis Napoleon Bonaparte. Lamartine stood for a somewhat vaguely moral and idealistic republic; Cavaignac, for a republic of disciplined order; Ledru-Rollin, for somewhat chastened social ideas. What Bonaparte stood for was not so clear. He was, however, elected by an avalanche of votes in December 1848, receiving over 5,400,000, compared to only 1,500,000 for Cavaignac, 370,000 for Ledru-Rollin, and a mere 18,000 for Lamartine.

Bonaparte's background

Thus entered upon the European stage the second Napoleon. Born in 1808, Louis Napoleon Bonaparte was the nephew of the great Napoleon. His father, Louis Bonaparte, was at the time of his birth the king of Holland. When Napoleon's own son died in 1832 Louis Napoleon assumed the headship of the Bonaparte family. He resolved to restore the glories of the empire. With a handful of followers he tried to seize power at Strasbourg in 1836 and at Boulogne in 1840, leading what the following century would know as *Putsches.* Both failed ridiculously. Sentenced to life imprisonment in the fortress of Ham, he had escaped from it as recently as 1846 by simply walking off the grounds dressed as a stonemason. He expressed advanced social and political ideas, had probably joined the Carbonari in his youth, and had taken part in the Italian revolutionary uprising of 1830. He wrote two books, one called *Napoleonic Ideas,* claiming that his famous uncle had been misunderstood and checkmated by reactionary forces, and one called the *Extinction of Poverty,* a somewhat anticapitalist tract like so many others of its time. But he was no friend of "anarchists," and in the spring of 1848, while still a refugee in England, he enrolled as one of

Wellington's special constables to oppose the Charitst agitation. He soon returned to France. Compromised neither by the June Days nor by their repression, he was supposed to be a friend of the common people and at the same time a believer in order; and his name was Napoleon Bonaparte.

For 20 years a groundswell had been stirring the popular mind. It is known as the Napoleonic Legend. Peasants put up pictures of the emperor in their cottages, fondly imagining that it had been Napoleon who gave them the free ownership of their land. The completion of the Arch of Triumph in 1836 drove home the memory of imperial glories, and in 1840 the remains of the emperor were brought from St. Helena and majestically interred at the Invalides on the banks of the Seine. All this happened in a country where, government being in the hands of a few, most people had no political experience or political sense except what they had gained in revolution. When millions were suddenly, for the first time in their lives, asked to vote for a president in 1848, the name of Bonaparte was the only one they had ever heard of. "How should I not vote for this gentleman," said an old peasant, "I whose nose was frozen at Moscow?"

So Prince Louis Napoleon became president of the republic, by an overwhelming and indubitable popular mandate, in which an army officer was his only even faintly successful rival. He soon saw the way the wind was blowing. The Constituent Assembly dissolved itself in May 1849 and was replaced by the Legislative Assembly provided for in the new constitution. It was a strange assembly for a republic. It may be recalled that in 1797 the first normal election in the First Republic had produced a royalist majority. Now in the Second Republic, under universal male suffrage, the result was the same. Five hundred of the deputies, or two-thirds, were really monarchists, but they were divided into irreconcilable factions—the Legitimists, who favored the line of Charles X, and the Orléanists, who favored that of Louis Philippe. One-third of the deputies called themselves republicans. Of these, in turn, about 180 were socialists of one kind of another; and only about 70 were political or old-fashioned republicans to whom the main issue was the form of government rather than the form of society itself.

President by popular mandate

The president and the Assembly at first combined to conjure away the specter of socialism, with which republicanism itself was now clearly associated. An abortive insurrection of June 1849 provided the chance. The Assembly, backed by the president, ousted 33 socialist deputies, suppressed public meetings, and imposed controls on the press. In 1850 it went so far as to rescind universal male suffrage, taking the vote away from about a third of the electorate—naturally the poorest and hence most socialistic third. The Falloux Law of 1850 put the schools at all levels of the education system under supervision of the Catholic clergy; for, as M. Falloux said in the Assembly, "lay teachers have made the principles of social revolution popular in the most distant villages" and it was necessary "to rally around religion to strengthen the foundations of society against those who want to divide up property." The French Republic, now actually an antirepublican government, likewise intervened against the revolutionary republic established by Mazzini in the city of Rome. French military forces were sent to Rome to protect the pope; they remained there 20 years.

Antirepublican government

To the conservatives Bonaparte knew that he was virtually indispensable. They were so sharply divided between two sets of monarchists—Legitimist and Orléanist—that each would accept any antisocialist regime rather than yield to the other. Bonaparte's problem was to win over the radicals. He did so by urging in 1851 the restoration of universal suffrage, which he had himself helped repeal in 1850. He now posed as the people's friend, the one man in public life who trusted the common man. He let it be thought that greedy plutocrats controlled the Assembly and hoodwinked France. He put his lieutenants in as ministers of war and of the interior, thus controlling the army, the bureaucracy, and the police. On December 2, 1851, the anniversary of Austerlitz, he sprang his coup d'état. Placards appeared all over Paris. They declared the Assembly dissolved and the vote for every adult Frenchman reinstated. When members of the Assembly tried to meet, they were attacked, dispersed, or arrested by the soldiers. The country did not submit without fighting. One hundred and fifty persons were killed in Paris, and throughout France probably 100,000 were put under arrest. But on December 20 the voters elected Louis Napoleon president for a term of 10 years, by a vote officially stated as 7,439,216 to 646,737. A year later the new Bonaparte proclaimed the empire, with himself as Emperor of the French. Remembering Napoleon's son, he called himself Napoleon III.

How the empire functioned will be seen below. Not only the republic was dead. The republic as republicans understood it, an egalitarian, anticlerical regime with social-

The demise of parliamentary government

ist or at least antibourgeois tendencies, had been dead since June 1848. Feeble anyway, it was killed by its reputation for radicalism. Liberalism and constitutionalism were dead also, at least in the political institutions by which the new Napoleon now governed France. Bourgeois and property-owning monarchists were greater sticklers for constitutional liberalism than were the republicans or the Bonapartists or than town laborers or rural peasants. But the monarchists, hopelessly divided among themselves, were now pushed aside. For the first time since 1815 France ceased to have any significant parliamentary life.

59. VIENNA: THE NATIONALIST REVOLUTION IN CENTRAL EUROPE AND ITALY

The Austrian Empire in 1848

The Austrian Empire of the Habsburgs, with its capital at Vienna, was in 1848 the most populous European state except Russia. Its peoples, living principally in the three major geographical divisions of the empire (Austria, Bohemia, and Hungary) were of about a dozen recognizably different nationalities or language groups—Germans, Czechs, Magyars, Poles, Ruthenians, Slovaks, Serbs, Croats, Slovenes, Dalmatians, Romanians, and Italians (see maps: v2 p. xxvii/combined edition p. 424, and p. 448). In some parts of the empire the nationalities lived in solid blocks, but in many regions two or more were interlaced together, the language changing from village to village, or even from house to house, in a way quite unknown in western Europe.

The diversity of the empire

Germans, the leading people, occupied all of Austria proper and considerable parts of Bohemia and were scattered also in small pockets throughout Hungary. The Czechs occupied Bohemia and the adjoining Moravia. The Magyars were the dominant group in the historic kingdom of Hungary, which contained a mixture of nationalities with a considerable number of Slavic peoples. Two of the most advanced parts of Italy also belonged to the empire—Venetia, with its capital at Venice, and Lombardy, whose chief city was Milan.

The Czechs, Poles, Ruthenians, Slovaks, Serbs, Croats, Slovenes, and Dalmatians in the empire were all Slavs; that is, their languages were all related to one another and to the several forms of Russian. Neither the Magyars nor the Romanians were Slavs. The Magyars, as national sentiment grew, prided themselves on the uniqueness of their language in Europe and the Romanians prided themselves on their linguistic affiliations with the Latin peoples of the West. Romanians, Magyars, and Germans formed a thick belt separating the South Slavs from those of the north. Germans and Italians within the empire were in continual touch with Germans and Italians outside. The peoples of the empire represented every cultural level known to Europe. Vienna, where the Waltz King Johann Strauss was reigning, recognized no peer except Paris itself. Milan was a great center of trade. Bohemia had long had a textile industry of importance, which was beginning to be mechanized in the 1840s; but 200 miles to the south a Croatian intellectual remarked, about the same time, that the first steam engine he ever saw was in a picture printed on a cotton handkerchief imported from Manchester.

Thus the empire ruled from Vienna included, according to political frontiers established 70 years later, in 1918, all of Austria, Hungary, and Czechoslovakia, with adjoining portions of Poland, Romania, Yugoslavia, and Italy. But the political authority of Vienna reached far beyond the borders of the empire. *Vienna's authority and leadership* Austria since 1815 had been the most influential member of the German confederation, for Prussia in these years was content to look with deference upon the Habsburgs. The influence of Vienna was felt throughout Germany in many ways, as in the enactment and enforcement of Metternich's Carlsbad Decrees mentioned in the last chapter. It reached also through the length of Italy. Lombardy and Venetia were part of the Austrian Empire. Tuscany, ostensibly independent, was governed by a Habsburg grand duke. The kingdom of Naples or the Two Sicilies, comprising all Italy south of Rome, was virtually a protectorate of Vienna. The papal states looked politically to Vienna for leadership, at least until 1846, when the College of Cardinals elected a liberal-minded pope, Pius IX—the one contingency upon which Metternich confessed he had failed to reckon. In all Italy there was only one state ruled by a native Italian dynasty and attempting any consistent independence of policy—the kingdom of Sardinia (called also Savoy or Piedmont) tucked away in the northwest corner around Turin. Italy, said Metternich blandly, was only a "geographical expression," a mere regional name. He might have said the same of Poland, or even of Germany, though Germany was tenuously joined in the Bund, or loose confederation, of 1815.

These peoples since the turn of the century had all felt the flutters of the *Volksgeist*, persistent stirrings of a cultural nationalism, and among Germans, Italians, Poles, and Hungarians a good deal of political agitation and liberal reformism had been at work. Metternich, in Vienna, had discouraged such manifestations for over 30 years, ominously predicting that if allowed to break out they would produce the *bellum omnium contra omnes*—"the war of all against all." As a prophet he was not wholly mistaken, but if it is the business of statesmanship not merely to prophesy events but to control them it cannot be said that the regime of Metternich was very successful. The whole nationalities question was evaded. The fundamental problem of the century, the bringing of peoples into some kind of mutual and moral relationship with their governments—the problem of which nationalism, liberalism, constitutionalism, and democracy were diverse aspects—remained unconsidered by the responsible authorities of central Europe. All that Metternich offered was the idea that a reigning house, with an official bureaucracy, should rule benevolently over peoples with whom it need have no connection and who need have no connection with each other. They were the ideas of the eighteenth century, dating from before the French Revolution and best suited to an agricultural and localistic society.

The March Days

In March 1848 everything collapsed with incredible swiftness. At that time the diet of Hungary had been sitting for some months, considering constitutional reforms and, as usual, debating further means of keeping German influence out of Hungary. Then came news of the February Revolution in Paris. The radical party in the Hungarian diet was aroused. Its leader, Louis Kossuth, on March 3 made an impassioned speech on the virtues of liberty. This speech was immediately printed in German and read in Vienna, where restlessness was also heightened by the news from Paris. On March 13 workers and students rose in insurrection in Vienna, erected barricades, fought off soldiers, and invaded the imperial palace. So flabbergasted and terrified was the government that Metternich, to the amazement of Europe, resigned and fled in disguise to England.

Metternich's fall

The fall of Metternich proved that the Vienna government was entirely disoriented. Revolution swept through the empire and through all Italy and Germany. On March 15 rioting began in Berlin; the king of Prussia promised a constitution. The lesser German governments collapsed in sequence. On the last day of March a pre-Parliament met to arrange the calling of an all-German national assembly. In Hungary, aroused by Kossuth's national party, the diet on March 15 enacted the March Laws, by which Hungary assumed a position of complete constitutional separatism within the empire, while still recognizing the Habsburg house. The harassed Emperor Ferdinand a few days later granted substantially the same status to Bohemia. At Milan between March 18 and 22 the populace drove out the Austrian garrison. Venice proclaimed itself an

The Revolution of 1848 spread rapidly across the European continent, provoking an uprising in Vienna by mid-March. Workers, students, and even soldiers joined together to erect barricades and resist the king's loyal troops. This nineteenth-century image of the Viennese crowd, however, suggests the tensions within a movement that rallied behind a banner for "King, Freedom, and Fatherland."

(Snark/Art Resource, NY)

independent republic. Tuscany drove out its grand duke and also set up as a republic. Charles Albert was king of Sardinia, a kingdom that came also to be called Piedmont because its capital Turin and much of its territory apart from the island of Sardinia lay in northwest Italy at the foot of the Alps. Stimulated by events in Paris, Charles Albert had granted a constitution to his small country. He now declared war on Austria on March 23 and invaded Lombardy-Venetia, hoping to bring that area under his house of Savoy. Italian troops streamed up from Tuscany, from Naples (where revolution had broken out as early as January), and even from the papal states (the new pope being in some sympathy with national and liberal aims) to join in an all-Italian war against the seemingly helpless Austrian government.

Thus in the brief span of these phenomenal March Days the whole structure based on Vienna went to pieces. The Austrian Empire had fallen into its main components, Prussia had yielded to revolutionaries, all Germany was preparing to unify itself, and war raged in Italy. Everywhere constitutions had been widely promised by stupefied governments, constitutional assemblies were meeting, and independent or autonomous nations struggled into existence. Patriots everywhere demanded liberal government and national freedom—written constitutions, representative assemblies, responsible ministries, a more or less extended suffrage, restrictions upon police action, jury trial, civil liberty, freedom of press and assembly. And where it still existed—in Prussia, Galicia, Bohemia, Hungary—serfdom was declared abolished and the peasant masses became legally free from control by their local lords.

The Turning of the Tide after June

The revolution, as in France, surged forward until the month of June, and then began to ebb. For its steady reflux there are many reasons. The old governments had been only stunned in the March Days, not really broken. They merely awaited the opportunity to take back promises extorted by force. The force originally imposed by the revolutionaries could not be sustained. The revolutionary leaders were not really very strong. Middle-class, bourgeois, property-owning, and commercial interests were nowhere nearly as highly developed as in western Europe. The revolutionary leaders were to a large extent writers, editors, professors, and students: intellectuals rather than the representatives of powerful social and economic interests. In Vienna, Milan, and a few other cities the working class was numerous and socialist ideas were fairly common, but the workers were not as literate, organized, politically conscious, or irritated as in Paris or Great Britain. They were strong enough, however, to disquiet the middle classes; and especially after the specter of social revolution rose over western Europe, the middle-class and lower-class revolutionaries began to be afraid of each other. The liberated nationalities also began to disagree. The peasants, once emancipated, had no further interest in revolution. Nor were the peasants at this time conscious of nationality; nationalism was primarily a doctrine of the educated middle classes or of the landowning classes in Poland and Hungary. Since the old internationally minded aristocracy furnished the bulk of officers in the armies, and the peasants the bulk of the soldiers, the armies remained almost immune to nationalist aspirations. This attitude of the armies was decisive.

The tide first turned in Prague. The all-German national assembly met at Frankfurt-on-the-Main in May. Representatives from Bohemia had been invited to come to Frankfurt, since many Germans had always lived in Bohemia and since Bohemia formed part of the confederation of 1815 as it had of the Holy Roman Empire before it. But the idea of belonging to a national

The first Pan-Slav assembly

EUROPEAN REVOLUTIONS, 1848

The map shows cities in which notable revolutionary upheavals occurred during 1848. Although opponents of the revolutionary agitation suspected an international conspiracy, the revolutions erupted more or less spontaneously as urban populations took to the streets with demands for constitutional government, national independence, or new civil rights. It should be noted that the revolutions of 1848 took place mainly in central and eastern Europe—a pattern that suggests the spreading influence of ideas that had appeared earlier in the American and French revolutions. But the failure of these revolutions led to a resurgence of conservatism and delayed or prevented the development of liberal, constitutional governments in most of central and eastern Europe.

German state, a Germany based on the principle that the inhabitants were Germans (which had not been the principle of the Holy Roman Empire or of the confederation of 1815) did not appeal to the Czechs in Bohemia. They refused to go to the all-German congress at Frankfurt. Instead, they called an all-Slav congress of their own. At Prague, in June 1848, this first Pan-Slav assembly met. Most of the delegates were from Slav communities within the Austrian Empire, but a few came from the Balkans and non-Austrian Poland.

The spirit of the Prague congress was that of the Slavic Revival described in the last chapter; the Czech historian Palacky was in fact one of its most active figures. The congress was profoundly anti-German, since the essence of the Slavic Revival was resistance to Germanization. But it was not profoundly anti-Austrian or anti-Habsburg. A few extremists, indeed, maintained that Slavdom should be the basis of political regeneration, and that the world therefore had no place for an Austrian Empire. But the great majority at the Prague congress were Austroslavs. Austroslavism held that the many Slavic peoples, pressed on two sides by the population masses of Russians and Germans, needed the Austrian Empire as a political frame within which to develop their own national life. It demanded that the Slavic peoples be admitted as equals with the other nationalities in the Austrian Empire, enjoying local autonomy and constitutional guarantees.

The Germans of Bohemia, the Sudeten Germans, were of course attracted to the Frankfurt Assembly. They were eager to be included in the unified Germany about to be formed. As the Bohemian Czechs would be a minority in a German Germany, so the Bohemian Germans would be a minority in a Czech Bohemia. There was therefore friction among the mixed people of Bohemia and in Prague, a bilingual city.

Victories of the Counterrevolution, June–December, 1848

But the Emperor Ferdinand, and the advisers on whom he chose to rely, would have nothing to do with national movements, since they were also liberal, bristling with restrictions upon the powers of the state. All therefore were to be resisted. The first victory of the old government came at Prague. In that city a Czech insurrection broke out on June 12, at the time when the Slav congress was sitting, and was made worse by local animosities between Czechs and Germans. Windischgrätz, the local army commander, bombarded and subdued the city, thereby reasserting Habsburg military control. The Slav congress dispersed.

The next victory of the counterrevolution came in north Italy in the following month. Only Lombardy-Venetia, of all parts of the empire, had declared independence from the Habsburgs during the upheavals of March. The diminutive kingdom of Sardinia had lent support and had declared war on Austria. Italians from all over the peninsula had flocked in to fight; and until after the June Days in Paris it seemed not impossible that republican France might intervene, to befriend fellow revolutionaries, as in 1796. But in France no radical or expansionist revolution succeeded. The Italians were left to themselves. Radetsky, the Austrian commander in Italy, overwhelmingly defeated the king of Sardinia at Custozza on July 25. The Sardinian king, Charles Albert, retreated into his own country. Lombardy and Venetia were restored with savage vengeance to the Austrian Empire.

The Italians defeated

The third victory of the counterrevolution came in September and October. The Hungarian radical party of Louis Kossuth was liberal and even democratic in many of its principles, but it was a Magyar nationalist party above all else. Triumphant in the March Days, it completely shook off the German connection. It moved the capital from Pressburg near the Austrian border to Budapest in the center of Hungary. It changed the official language of Hungary from Latin to Magyar. Less than half the people of Hungary were Magyars, and Magyar is an extremely difficult language, quit alien to the Indo-European tongues of Europe. It soon became clear that one must be a Magyar to benefit from the new liberal constitution and that the Magyars intended to denationalize and Magyarize all others with whom they shared the country. Slovaks, Romanians, Germans, Serbs, and Croats violently resisted, each group determined to keep its own national identity unimpaired. The Croats, who had enjoyed certain Croatian liberties before the Magyar revolution, took the lead under Count Jellachich, the "ban," or provincial governor, of Croatia. In September Jellachich raised a civil war in Hungary, leading a force of Serbo-Croatians, supported by the whole non-Magyar half of the population. Half of Hungary, alarmed by Magyar nationalism, now looked to the Habsburgs and the empire to protect them. Emperor Ferdinand made Jellachich his military commander against the Magyars. Hungary dissolved into the war of all against all.

Magyar nationalism

At Vienna the more clear-sighted revolutionaries, who had led the March rising, now saw that Jellachich's army, if successful against the Magyars, would soon be turned against them. They therefore rose in a second mass insurrection in October 1848. The emperor fled; never had the Viennese revolution gone so far. But it was already too late. The Austrian military leader Windischgrätz brought his intact forces down from Bohemia. He besieged Vienna for five days and forced its surrender on October 31.

Vienna recaptured

With the recapture of Vienna the upholders of the old order took heart. Counterrevolutionary leaders—large estate holders, Catholic clergy, high-ranking army men—decided to clear the way by getting rid of the Emperor Ferdinand, considering that promises made in March by Ferdinand might be more easily repudiated by his successor. Ferdinand abdicated and on December 2, 1848, was succeeded by Francis Joseph, a boy of 18, destined to live until 1916 and to end his reign in a crisis even more shattering than that in which he began it.

Final Outburst and Repression, 1849

For a time in the first part of 1849 the revolution in many places seemed to blaze more fiercely than ever. Republican riots broke out in parts of Germany. In Rome someone assassinated the reforming minister of Pius IX. The pope fled from the city, and a radical Roman Republic was proclaimed under three Triumvirs, one of whom was Mazzini, who hastened from England to take part in the republican upheaval. In north Italy Charles Albert of Sardinia again invaded Lombardy. In Hungary, after the revived Habsburg authorities repudiated the new Magyar constitution, the Magyars, led by the flaming Kossuth, went on to declare absolute independence. But all these manifestations proved short-lived. German republicanism flickered out. Mazzini and his republicans were driven from Rome, and Pius IX was restored, by intervention of the French army. The Sardinian king was again defeated by an Austrian army on March 23, 1849. In Hungary the Magyars put up a terrific resistance, which the imperial army and the anti-Magyar native irregulars could not overcome. The Habsburg authorities now renewed the procedures of the Holy Alliance. The new Emperor Francis Joseph invited the Tsar Nicholas to intervene. Over 100,000 Russian troops poured over the mountains into Hungary, soon defeated the Magyars, and laid the prostrate country at the feet of the court of Vienna. This was in August 1849.

The nationalist upheaval of 1848 in central Europe and Italy was now over. The Habsburg authority had been reasserted over Czech nationalists in Prague, Magyars in Hungary, Italian patriots in north Italy, and liberal revolutionists in Vienna itself.

Antirevolutionism

Reaction, or antirevolutionism, became the order of the day. Pius IX, the "liberal pope" of 1846, resumed the papal throne, disillusioned in his liberal ideas. The breach between liberalism and Roman Catholicism, which had opened wide in the first French Revolution, was made a yawning chasm by the revolutionary violence of Mazzini's Roman Republic and by the measures taken to repress it. Pius IX now reiterated the anathemas of his predecessors. He codified them in 1864 in the *Syllabus of Errors,* which warned all Catholics, on the authority of the Vatican, against everything that went under the names of liberalism, progress, and modern civilization. As for the nationalists in Italy, many were disillusioned with the firecracker methods of romantic republicans and inclined to conclude that Italy would be liberated from Austrian influence only by an old-fashioned war between established powers.

In the Austrian Empire, under Prince Schwarzenberg, the emperor's chief minister, the main policy was now to oppose all forms of popular self-expression, with a sophistication, in view of the events of 1848, that Metternich had never known, and with a candid reliance on military force. Constitutionalism was to be rooted out, as well as all forms of nationalism—Slavism, Magyarism, Italianism, and also Germanism, which would draw the sentiments of Austrian Germans from the Habsburg empire to the great kindred body of the

Joseph Mazzini (1805–1872) led the short-lived Republic in Rome during the Italian upheavals of 1849, but his new regime was soon suppressed by foreign powers and he retreated to the life of an exile in England. Although Mazzini's Romantic nationalism lost favor in Italy after about 1850, his writings and political activities gave him a prominent place in the intellectual life of London, where this photograph was taken in the early 1860s.

(The Granger Collection, NY)

German people. The regime came to be called the Bach system, after Alexander Bach, the minister of the interior. Under it, the government was rigidly centralized. Hungary lost the separate rights it had had before 1848.

The Bach system

The ideal was to create a perfectly solid and unitary political system. Bach insisted on maintaining the emancipation of the peasants, which had converted the mass of the people from subjects of their landlords into subjects of the state. He drove through a reform of the legal system and law courts, created a free trading area of the whole empire with only a common external tariff, and subsidized and encouraged the building of highways and railroads. The aim, as in France at the same time under Louis Napoleon, was to make people forget liberty in an overwhelming demonstration of administrative efficiency and material progress. But some, at that time, would not forget. A liberal said of the Bach system that it consisted of "a standing army of soldiers, a sitting army of officials, a kneeling army of priests, and a creeping army of informers."

60. FRANKFURT AND BERLIN: THE QUESTION OF A LIBERAL GERMANY

The German States

Meanwhile, from May 1848 to May 1849, the Frankfurt Assembly was sitting at the historic city on the Main. It was attempting to bring a unified German state into being, one which should also be liberal and constitutional, assuring civil rights to its citizens and possessing a government responsive to popular will as manifested in free elections and open parliamentary debate. The mid-nineteenth-century failure to produce a democratic Germany was long one of the overshadowing facts of modern times.

Obstacles to unification

The convocation of the Frankfurt Assembly was made possible by the collapse of the existing German governments in the March Days of 1848. These governments, the 39 states recognized after the Congress of Vienna, were the main obstacles in the way of unification. The reigning princes and their ministers enjoyed a heightened political stature from political independence. The German states resisted the surrender of sovereignty to a united Germany just as national states in later eras were to resist the surrender of sovereignty to a United Nations. In another way Germany was a miniature of the political world. It consisted of both great and small powers. Its great powers were Prussia and Austria. Austria was the miscellaneous empire described earlier. Prussia after 1815 included the Rhineland, the central regions around Berlin, West Prussia and Posen (acquired in the partitions of Poland), and historic East Prussia. The former Polish areas were inhabited by a mixture of Germans and Poles (see map, v2 p. xxvii/combined edition pp. 206–207, 424). Neither of these great powers could submit to the other or allow the other to dominate its lesser German neighbors. The small German powers, in turn, upheld their own independence in the balance between the two great ones.

German dualism

This German "dualism," or polarity between Berlin and Vienna, had been somewhat abated under the common menace of the Napoleonic empire. The whole German question had lain dormant, so far as the governments were concerned, nor did it agitate the old aristocracies. In Prussia the Junkers, the owners of great landed estates east of the Elbe, were singularly indifferent to the all-German dream. Their political feeling was not German but Prussian. They were making a good thing of Prussia for themselves and could expect only to lose by absorption into Germany as a whole, for in Germany west of the Elbe the small peasant holding was the basis of society, and there was no landowning element corresponding to the Junkers. The rest of Germany looked upon Prussia as somewhat uncouth and eastern; but this feeling, too, had been abated in the time of Napoleon, when patriots from all over Germany enlisted in the Prussian service.

Berlin: Failure of the Revolution in Prussia

Prussia was illiberal but not backward. Frederick William III repeatedly evaded his promise to grant a modern constitution. His successor, Frederick William IV, who inherited the throne in 1840 and from whom much was at first hoped by liberals, proved to be a somewhat cloudy and neomedieval romantic, equally determined not to share his authority with his subjects. At the same time the government, administratively speaking, was efficient, progressive, and fair. The universities and elementary school system surpassed those of western Europe. Literacy was higher than in England or France. The government followed in mercantilist traditions of evoking, planning, and supporting economic life. In 1818 it initiated a tariff union, at first with tiny states (or enclaves) wholly enclosed within Prussia. This tariff union, or *Zollverein,* was extended in the following decades to include almost all Germany.

On March 15, 1848, as noted above, rioting and street fighting broke out in Berlin. For a time it seemed as if the army would master the situation. But the king, Frederick William IV, a man of notions and projects and erratically conscientious, called off the soldiers and allowed his subjects to elect the first all-Prussian legislative assembly. Thus though the army remained intact, and its Junker officers remained unconvinced, revolution proceeded superficially on its way. The Prussian Assembly proved surprisingly radical, since it was dominated by anti-Junker lower-class extremists from East Prussia. These men were supporting Polish revolutionaries and exiles who sought the restoration of Polish freedom. Their main belief was that the fortress of reaction was tsarist Russia—that the whole structure of Junkerdom, landlordism, serf-owning, and repression of national freedom depended ultimately on the armed might of the tsarist empire. (The subsequent intervention of Russia in Hungary indicated the truth of this diagnosis.) Prussian radicals, like many elsewhere, hoped to smash the Holy Alliance by raising an all-German or even European revolutionary war against Russia, to precipitate which they supported the claims of the Poles.

Radical assemblies

Meanwhile the radical-dominated Berlin Assembly granted local self-government to the Poles of West Prussia and Posen. But in those areas Germans and Slavs had long lived side by side. The Germans in Posen refused to respect the authority of Polish officials. Prussian army units stationed in Posen supported the German element. As early as April 1848, a month after the "revolution," the army crushed the new pro-Polish institutions set up in Posen by the Berlin Assembly. It was clear where the only real power lay. By the end of 1848, in Prussia as in Austria, the revolution was over. The king again changed his mind; and the old authorities, acting through the army, were again in control.

The Frankfurt Assembly

Meanwhile a similar story was enacted on the larger stage of Germany as a whole. The disabling of the old governments left a power vacuum. A self-appointed committee convoked a preliminary parliament, which in turn arranged for the election of an all-German assembly. Bypassing the existing sovereignties, voters throughout Germany sent delegates to Frankfurt to create a federated superstate. The strength and weakness of the resulting Frankfurt Assembly originated in this manner of its election. The Assembly represented the moral sentiment of people at large, the liberal and national aspirations of many Germans. It stood for an idea. Politically it represented nothing. The delegates had no power to issue orders or expect compliance. Superficially resembling the National Assembly which met in France in 1789, the German National Assembly at Frankfurt was really in a very different position. There was no preexisting national structure for it to work with. There was no all-German army or civil service for the Assembly to take over. The Frankfurt Assembly, having no power of its own, became dependent on the power of the very sovereign states that it was attempting to supersede.

The Assembly met in May 1848. Its members with a handful of exceptions were not at all revolutionary. They were overwhelmingly professional people—professors, judges, lawyers, government administrators, clergy both Protestant and Catholic, and prominent businessmen. They wanted a liberal, self-governing, federally unified, and "democratic" though not egalitarian Germany. Their outlook was earnest, peaceable, and legalistic; they hoped to succeed by persuasion. Violence was abhorrent to them. They wanted no armed conflict with the existing German states. They wanted no war with Russia. They wanted no general international upheaval of the working classes. The example of the June Days in Paris, and the Chartist agitation in Great Britain, coinciding with the early weeks of the Frankfurt Assembly, increased the dread of that body for radicalism and republicanism in Germany. The tragedy of Germany (and hence of Europe) lies in the fact that this German revolution came too late, at a

An untimely revolution

time when social revolutionaries had already begun to declare war on the bourgeoisie, and the bourgeoisie was already afraid of the lower classes. It is the worker or artisan, not the professor or respectable merchant, who in unsettled times actually seizes firearms and rushes to shout revolutionary utterances in the streets. Without lower-class insurrection not even middle-class revolutions have been successful. The combination effected in France between 1789 and 1794, an unwilling and divergent combination of bourgeois and lower-class revolutionaries, was not and could not be effected in Germany in 1848. One form of revolutionary power—controlled popular turbulence—the Germans of the Frankfurt Assembly would not or could not use. Quite the contrary: when radical riots broke out in Frankfurt itself in September 1848 the Assembly undertook to repress them. Having no force of its own, it appealed to the Prussian army. The Prussian army put down the riots, and thereafter the Assembly met under its protection.

Questions of territory

But the most troublesome question facing the Frankfurt Assembly was not social but national. What, after all, was this "Germany" which so far existed only in the mind? Where was the line really to be drawn in space? Did Germany include Austria and Bohemia, which belonged to the Bund of 1815 and had in former days belonged to the Holy Roman Empire (see map, p. 522)? Did it include all Prussia, although eastern Prussia had lain outside the empire and did not now belong to the Bund? On the side toward Denmark, did it include the duchies of Schleswig and Holstein, which belonged to the Danish king, who was therefore himself, as ruler of Holstein, a member of the 1815 confederation? And if, as poets said, the Fatherland existed wherever the German tongue was spoken, what of the German communities in Hungary and Moravia, or along the upper Baltic and in the city of Riga, or in some of the Swiss cantons and the city of Zurich, or for that matter in Holland, which had left the Holy Roman Empire only 200 years before—not long as time is measured in Europe.

These last and most soaring speculations, though they had already been launched by a few bold spirits, were put out of mind by the men of the Frankfurt Assembly. The other questions remained. The assembly at Frankfurt, eager to create a real Germany, naturally could not offer one smaller than the shadow Germany that they so much deplored. Most therefore were Great Germans; they thought that the Germany for which they were writing a constitution should include the Austrian lands, except Hungary. This would mean that the federal crown must be offered to the Habsburgs. Others, at first a minority, were Little Germans; they thought that Austria should be excluded and that the new Germany should comprise the smaller states and the entire kingdom of Prussia. In that case the king of Prussia would become the federal emperor.

Dependence on Austrian and Prussian armies

The desire of the Frankfurt Assembly to retain non-German peoples in the new Germany, at a time when these peoples also were feeling national ambitions, was another reason for its fatal dependency upon the Austrian and Prussian armies. The Frankfurt Assembly applauded when Windischgrätz broke the Czech revolution. It expressed its satisfaction when Prussian forces put down the Poles in Posen. On this matter the National Assembly at Frankfurt and the Prussian Assembly at Berlin did not agree. The men of Frankfurt, thinking the Prussian revolutionary assembly too radical and pro-Polish and wanting no war with Russia, in effect supported the Prussian army and the Junkers against the Berlin revolution, without which the Frankfurt Assembly itself could never have existed.

A still clearer case arose over Schleswig-Holstein. These duchies belonged to the Danish king. Schleswig, the northern of the two, had a mixed population of Danes and

The Frankfurt Assembly that convened in May 1848 (as depicted in this nineteenth-century illustration) consisted mostly of professional people who feared the working classes almost as much as or more than they feared the political powers of kings and Prussian aristocrats. The members of the Assembly wrote a constitution and sought to create a constitutional monarchy for all Germany outside Austria. But the Prussian king would not accept this kind of constitutional appointment to royal power and the Frankfurt Assembly's national, democratic aspirations were destroyed when the Assembly was dissolved in 1849.

(AKG London)

Germans. The Germans in Schleswig rebelled in March 1848; and the Danes, who also had a constitutional upheaval at the time, proceeded to incorporate Schleswig integrally into their modernized Danish state. When the Frankfurt Assembly met, it found that the preliminary parliament had already declared an all-German war upon Denmark in defense of fellow Germans in Schleswig. Having no army of its own, the Frankfurt Assembly invited Prussia to fight the war; and the revolutionary Prussian government in Berlin was at first able to persuade the Prussian generals to initiate a campaign. Great Britain and Russia prepared to intervene to keep control of the mouth of the Baltic out of German hands. The Prussian army simply withdrew from the war. Its officers had no desire to antagonize Russia or to advance the interests of nationalist revolutionaries in Germany. The Frankfurt Assembly, humiliated and helpless, was obliged to accept the armistice concluded by the Prussian generals. Radical socionationalistic riots broke out against the Junkers, the tsar, and the Frankfurt Assembly; and it was at this time that the Assembly called in Prussian forces for its own protection.

The Failure of the Frankfurt Assembly

By the end of 1848 the debacle was approaching. The nationalists had checkmated each other. Everywhere in central Europe, from Denmark to Naples and from the Rhineland to the Transylvanian forests, the awakening nationalities had failed to respect each other's aspirations, had delighted in each other's defeats, and by quarreling with each other had hastened the return of the old absolutist and nonnational order. At Berlin and at Vienna the counterrevolution, backed by the army, was in the saddle. At this very time, in December, the Frankfurt Assembly at last issued a Declaration of the Rights of the German People. It was a humane and high-minded document, announcing numerous individual rights, civil liberties, and constitutional guarantees, much along the line of the French and American declarations of the eighteenth century, but with one significant difference—the French and Americans spoke of the rights of man, while the Germans spoke of the rights of Germans. In April 1849 the Frankfurt Assembly completed its constitution. It was now clear that Austria must be excluded, for the simple reason that the restored Habsburg government refused to come in. The Danubian empire, as already seen, was as profoundly opposed to Germanism as to any other nationalistic movement. The Little Germans in the Assembly therefore had their way. The hereditary headship of a new German empire, a constitutional and federal union of German states minus Austria, was now offered to Frederick William IV, the king of Prussia.

Frederick William tempted

Frederick William was tempted. The Prussian army officers and East Elbian landlords were not. They had no wish to lose Prussia in Germany. The king himself had his scruples. If he took the proffered crown he would still have to impose himself by force on the lesser states, which the Frankfurt Assembly did not represent and could not bind and which were in fact still the actual powers in the country. He could also expect trouble with Austria. He did not wish war. Nor was it proper for an heir to the Hohenzollerns to accept a throne circumscribed with constitutional limitations and representing the revolutionary conception of the sovereignty of the people. Declaring that he could not "pick up a crown from the gutter," he turned it down. It would have to be offered freely by his equals, the sovereign princes of Germany.

The failure of liberal nationalism

Thus all the work of the Frankfurt Assembly went for nothing. Most members of the Assembly, having never dreamed of using violence in the first place, concluded that they were beaten and went home. A handful of extremists remained at Frankfurt, promulgated the constitution on their own authority, urged revolutionary outbreaks, and called for elections. Riots broke out in various places. The Prussian army put them down—in Saxony, in Bavaria, in Baden. The same army drove the rump Assembly out of Frankfurt, and that was the end of it.

In summary, Germany in 1848 failed to solve the problem of its unification in a liberal and constitutional way. Liberal nationalism failed, and a less gentle kind of nationalism soon replaced it. The weakness and failures of German lib-eralism in 1848–1849 in the long run contributed to a fateful estrangement between Ger-many and western Europe. Thousands of disappointed German liberals and revolutionar-ies migrated to the United States, which came to know them as the "forty-eighters." They brought to the new country, besides a ripple of revolutionary agitation, a stream of people trained in science, medicine, and music, and of highly skilled craftsmen like silversmiths and engravers.

The Prussian Constitution of 1850

In Prussia itself the ingenious monarch undertook to placate everybody by issuing a con-stitution of his own, one that should be peculiarly Prussian. It remained in effect from 1850 to 1918. It granted a single parliament for all the miscellaneous regions of Prussia. The parliament met in two chambers. The lower chamber was elected by universal male suf-frage, not along the individualist or egalitarian principles of the West but by a system that in effect divided the population into three estates—the wealthy, the less wealthy, and the general run of the people. Division was made according to payment of taxes. Those few big taxpayers who together contributed a third of the tax returns chose a third of the mem-bers of district electoral colleges, which in turn chose deputies to the Prus-sian lower house. In this way one large property owner had as much voting power as hundreds of working people. Large property in Prussia in 1850 still meant mainly the landed estates of the East Elbian Junkers, but as time went on it came to include industrial property in the Rhineland also. The Junkers likewise were not harmed by the final liquidation of serfdom. They increased the acreage of their holdings, as after the reforms of Stein in the early nineteenth century; and the former servile agricultural workers turned into free wage earners economically de-pendent on the great landowners.

Voting power of landowners

For 1850 the Prussian constitution was fairly progressive. If the mass of the people could elect very few deputies under the indirect system described, the mass of the British people, until 1867 or even 1884, could elect no deputies to Parliament at all. But the Prus-sian constitution remained in force until 1918. By the close of the nineteenth century, with democratic advances making their appearance elsewhere, the electoral system in Prussia, remaining unchanged, came to be reactionary and illiberal, giving the great landowners and industrialists an unusual position of special privilege within the state.

61. THE NEW TOUGHNESS OF MIND: REALISM, POSITIVISM, MARXISM

The Revolution of 1848 failed not only in Germany but also in Hungary, in Italy, and in France. The "springtime of peoples," as it was called, was followed by chilling blasts of winter. The dreams of half a century, visions of a humane nationalism, aspirations for lib-eralism without violence, ideals of a peaceful and democratic republican commonwealth, were all exploded. Everywhere the cry had been for constitutional government, but only in a few small states—Denmark, Holland, Belgium, Switzerland, Piedmont—was constitu-tional liberty more firmly secured by the Revolution of 1848. Everywhere the cry had been for the freedom of nations, to unify national groups or rid them of foreign rule; but nowhere was national liberty more advanced in 1850 than it had been two years before. France obtained universal male suffrage in 1848 and kept it permanently thereafter (except for a brief reversion to a restricted suffrage in 1850–1851); but it did not obtain democracy; it obtained a kind of popular dictatorship under Louis Napoleon Bonaparte. One accomplishment, however, was real enough. The peasantry was emancipated in the German states and the Austrian Empire. Serfdom and manorial restraints were abolished, nor were they reimposed after the failure of the revolution. This was the most fundamental accomplishment of the whole movement. The peasant masses of central Europe were thereafter free to move about, find new jobs, enter a labor market, take part in a money economy, receive and spend wages, migrate to growing cities—or even go to the United States. But the peasants, once freed, showed little concern for constitutional or bourgeois ideas. Peasant emancipation, in fact, strengthened the forces of political counterrevolution.

New freedoms for peasants

The most immediate and far-reaching consequence of the 1848 revolutions, or of their failure, was a new toughness of mind. Idealism and romanticism were discredited in European culture and politics. Revolutionaries became less optimistic; conservatives, more willing to exercise repression. It was now a point of pride to be realistic, emancipated from illusions, willing to face facts as they were. The future, it was thought, would be determined by present realities rather than by imaginings of what ought to be. Industrialization went forward, with England still far in the lead, but spreading to the Continent and initiating the momentous transformation of Germany. The 1850s were a period of rising prices and wages, thanks in part to the gold rush in California. There was more prosperity than in the 1840s; the propertied classes felt secure, and spokesmen for labor turned from theories of society to the organizing of viable unions, especially in the skilled trades.

Materialism, Realism, Positivism

In basic philosophy the new mental toughness appeared as materialism, holding that everything mental, spiritual, or ideal was an outgrowth of physical or physiological forces. In literature and the arts it was called realism. Writers and painters broke away from romanticism, which they said colored things out of all relation to the real facts. They attempted to describe and reproduce life as they found it, without intimation of a better or more noble world. The French writer Gustave Flaubert, for example, wrote meticulous descriptions of a provincial woman's tedious, unhappy marriage in his famous novel *Madame Bovary* (1857), a book that both mocked the illusions of romantic literature and showed the new artistic desire for a precise, unsentimental literary language. More and more people came to trust science, not merely for an understanding of nature, but for insights into the true meaning of human life and social relations. In religion the movement was toward skepticism, renewing the skeptical trend of the eighteenth century, which had been somewhat interrupted during the intervening period of romanticism. It was variously held, not by all but by many, that religion was unscientific and hence not to be taken seriously; or that it was a mere historical growth among peoples in certain stages of development and hence irrelevant to modern civilization; or that one ought to go to church and lead a decent life, without taking the priest or clergyman too seriously, because religion was necessary to preserve the social order against radicalism and anarchy. To this idea the radical counterpart was of course that religion was a bourgeois invention to delude the people.

"Positivism" was another term used to describe the new attitude. It originated with the French philosopher Auguste Comte, who had begun to publish his numerous volumes on *Positive Philosophy* as long ago as 1830 and was still writing in the 1850s. He saw human history as a series of three

Auguste Comte

stages, the theological, the metaphysical, and the scientific. The revolutions in France, he thought, both of 1789 and of 1848, suffered from an excess of metaphysical abstractions, empty words, and unverifiable high-flying principles. Those who worked for the improvement of society must adopt a strictly scientific outlook, and Comte produced an elaborate classification of the sciences, of which the highest would be the science of society, for which he coined the word "sociology." This new science would build upon observation of actual facts to develop broad scientific laws of social progress. Comte himself, and his closest disciples, envisaged a final scientific Religion of Humanity, which, stripped of archaic theological and metaphysical concerns, would serve as the basis for a better world of the future. More generally, however, positivism came to mean an insistence on verifiable facts, an avoidance of wishful thinking, a questioning of all assumptions, and a dislike of unprovable generalizations. Positivism in a broad sense, both in its demand for observation of facts and testing of ideas, and in its aspiration to be humanly useful, contributed to the growth of the social sciences as a branch of learning.

In politics the new toughness of mind was called by the Germans *Realpolitik*. This simply meant a "politics of reality." In domestic affairs it meant that people should give up utopian dreams, such as had caused the debacle of 1848, and content themselves with the blessings of an orderly, honest, hard-working government. For radicals it meant that people should stop imagining that the new society would result from goodness or the love of justice and that social reformers must resort to the methods of politics—power and calculation. In international affairs *Realpolitik* meant that governments should not be guided by ideology, or by any system of "natural" enemies or "natural" allies, or by any desire to defend or promote any particular view of the world; but that they should follow their own practical interests, meet facts and situations as they arose, make any alliances that seemed useful, disregard ethical theories and scruples, and use any practical means to achieve their ends. The same persons who, before 1848, had been not ashamed to express pacifist and cosmopolitan hopes now dismissed such ideas as a little softheaded. War, which governments since the overthrow of Napoleon had successfully tried to prevent, was accepted in the 1850s as a strategic option that was sometimes needed to achieve a political purpose. It was not especially glorious; it was not an end in itself; it was simply one of the tools of realistic statesmanship. *Realpolitik* was by no means confined to Germany, despite its German name and despite the fact that the famous German chancellor Bismarck became its most famous practitioner. Two other tough-minded thinkers, each in his own way, were Karl Marx and Louis Napoleon Bonaparte.

Realpolitik

Early Marxism

Karl Marx and Friedrich Engels were among the disappointed revolutionaries of 1848. Marx (1818–1883) was the son of a lawyer in the Prussian Rhineland. He studied law and philosophy at several German universities and received a doctoral degree in 1841. Unable to find an academic job, Marx associated with radical German intellectuals, began writing for left-wing journals, and soon moved to Paris with other Germans who wanted to produce philosophical publications in the historic birthplace of modern revolutions. Engels (1820–1893), the son of a well-to-do German textile manufacturer, was sent as a young man to Manchester in England where his father owned a factory, to learn the business and then manage it. Marx and Engels met in Paris in 1844. There they began a collaboration in thinking and writing that lasted for 40 years.

A BURIAL AT ORNANS

by Gustave Courbet (French, 1819–1877)

A new "realism" emerged in many spheres of European culture after the failure of the revolutions in 1848. The artist Courbet in fact began to use the term realism in this period to describe his work, which frequently depicted ordinary people and peasants on monumental canvasses. Paintings such as this portrayal of a funeral in the French countryside disturbed many nineteenth-century critics because Courbet painted images of the lower classes and also because he refused to romanticize his subjects or to portray common people in sentimental poses.

(Giraudon/Art Resource, NY)

The Communist League

In 1847 they joined the Communist League, a tiny secret group of revolutionaries, mainly Germans in exile in the more liberal Western Europe. The word "communist" then had only a vague and uncertain meaning, and the League, as Engels later recalled, was at first "not actually much more than the German branch of the French secret societies." It agitated like other societies during the Revolution of 1848 and issued a set of "Demands of the Communist Party in Germany," which urged a unified indivisible German republic, democratic suffrage, universal free education, arming of the people, a progressive income tax, limitations upon inheritance, state ownership of banks, railroads, canals, mines, and the like, and a degree of large-scale, scientific, collectivized agriculture. It was such obscurely voiced radicalism that alarmed the Frankfurt Assembly. With the triumph of counterrevolution in Germany the Communist League was crushed.

It was for this League that Marx and Engels wrote their *Communist Manifesto,* which was published in January 1848. But there was as yet no Marxism, and Marxism played no role in the Revolution of 1848. As a historical force Marxism set in during the 1870s. Meanwhile, with the failure of the revolution, Engels returned to his factory at Manchester. Marx also settled in England, spending the rest of his life in London, where, after long labors in the library of the British Museum, he finally produced his huge work called *Capital,* of which the first volume was published in German in 1867. The final two volumes were edited by Engels and published after Marx's death.

Sources and Content of Marxism

Marxism may be said to have had three sources or to have merged three national streams of early nineteenth-century European history: German philosophy, French revolutionism, and the British Industrial Revolution. As a student in Germany, and for a while thereafter, Marx mingled with a group known as Young Hegelians, who were actually critics of Hegel in that they expected the course of history to lead to a free and democratic society, instead of to the existing Prussian state as Hegel had maintained. They joined with liberals in resisting the repressive measures that prevailed in Germany after the defeat of Napoleon. Like democrats and republicans, they believed that the promise of the French Revolution had not yet been fulfilled, since social and economic equality should follow the civil and legal equality already won. In keeping with the general movement of romanticism, they hoped for a more personal emancipation from the trammels of society, government, and religion. In the mid 1840s, elaborating on Hegel, Marx developed the idea of the *alienation of labor,* a social experience and state of mind produced when human beings in the historic process of mechanization become estranged from the objects on which they work. This alienation, as Marx described it, was a distinctive feature of modern capitalist societies. The economic system of wage labor and private ownership of the means of production kept workers from identifying with or benefiting from the products of their labor.

The Young Hegelians

It followed that true freedom would become possible only when private property in capital goods was abolished. Some of the writings in which these youthful ideas were worked out in the 1840s were not published until a century later. They then led to a reconsideration of Marxism, in which the early Marx was seen more as a social analyst than as a revolutionary. But they had little impact on the growth of Marxism as a program for revolutionary socialism in the nineteenth century.

Engels, engaged in the Manchester cotton industry, possessed a personal knowledge of the new industrial and factory system in England. He was in touch with some of the most radical Chartists, though he had no confidence in Chartism as a constructive movement. In 1844 he published a revealing book, *The Condition of the Working Classes in England.* He drew from his observations much the same conclusions that Marx drew from philosophical analysis and historical study. The depressed condition of labor was an actual fact. It was a fact that labor received a relatively small portion of the national income and that much of the product of society was being reinvested in capital goods, which belonged as private property to private persons. Government and parliamentary institutions, also as a matter of fact, were in the hands of the well-to-do in both Great Britain and France. Religion was commonly held to be necessary to keep the lower classes in order. The churches at the time actually took little interest in problems of the workers. The family, as an institution, was indeed disintegrating among laboring people in the cities, through exploitation of women and children and the overcrowding in inadequate and unsanitary living quarters.

Engels and British industrialism

All these facts were seized upon and dramatized in the *Communist Manifesto,* as a summons to revolution. The outbreak of revolution in France in February, and its rapid spread to other countries, naturally confirmed Marx and Engels in their beliefs. The actual class war that shook Paris in the June Days was taken by them as a manifestation of a universal class struggle, in which the workers or proletariat would rise against the owners of capital, the bourgeoisie.

As a call to action, the *Communist Manifesto* was meant to be inflammatory. It went beyond facts to denunciation and exhortation. It said that

The Communist Manifesto

workers were deprived of the wealth they had themselves created. It called the state a committee of the bourgeoisie for the exploitation of the people. Religion was a drug to keep the worker quietly dreaming upon imaginary heavenly rewards. The women and children in working-class families had been prostituted and brutalized by the bourgeoisie. It seemed to Marx and Engels that uprooted workers should be loyal to nothing—except their own class. Even country had become meaningless. The proletarian had no country. Workers everywhere had the same problems and faced everywhere the same enemy. Therefore "let the ruling classes tremble at a communist revolution. The proletarians have nothing to lose but their chains. They have a world to win. Workingmen of all countries, unite!" So closed the *Manifesto*.

But Marx was no mere revolutionary schemer, like the "revolution-makers," as he later scornfully called them. His mature thought was a system for producing revolution, but it showed how revolution would necessarily come by operation of vast historical forces.

It was from English sources that Marx developed much of his economic theory, as expounded at length in *Capital*. From British political economy he adopted the subsistence theory of wages, or Iron Law (which orthodox economists presently abandoned since wages did in fact begin to rise). It held that the average worker could never obtain more than a minimum living standard—of which the corollary, for those who wished to draw it, was that the existing economic system held out no better future for the laboring class as a class. Marx likewise took over from orthodox economists the labor theory of value, holding that the value of any human-made object depended ultimately on the amount of labor put into it—capital being regarded as the stored up labor of former times. Orthodox economists soon discarded the theory that economic value is produced by the input of labor alone. Marx, from the labor theory, developed his doctrine of surplus value. This was very intricate; but surplus value meant in effect that workers were being robbed. They received in wages only a fraction of the value of the products which their labor produced. The difference was expropriated by the bourgeois capitalists—the private owners of the factories and the machines. And since workers never received in wages the equivalent of what they produced, capitalism was constantly menaced by overproduction, the accumulation of goods that people could not afford to buy. Hence it ran repeatedly into crises and depressions and was obliged also to be constantly expanding in search of new markets. It was the depression of 1847, according to Marx, that had precipitated the Revolution of 1848; and with every such depression during the rest of his lifetime Marx hoped that the day of the great social revolution was drawing nearer.

British political economy

What brought all these observations together in a unified and compelling doctrine was the philosophy of dialectical materialism. By dialectic, Marx meant what the German philosopher Hegel had meant, that all things are in movement and in evolution and that all change comes through the clash of antagonistic elements. The word itself, coming from the Greek, meant originally a way of arriving at a higher conclusion through a series of propositions, as in a logical argument. The implications of the dialectic, for both Hegel and Marx, were that all history, and indeed all reality, is a process of development through time, a single and meaningful unfolding of events in a clear historical direction; that every event happens for good and sufficient reasons; and that history—though not exactly predetermined—is always shaped by impersonal forces and deep structural changes rather than by individuals or chance events.

Dialectical materialism

Marx differed from Hegel in one vital respect. Whereas Hegel emphasized the primacy of ideas in social change, Marx gave emphasis to the primacy of material conditions,

Karl Marx as he appeared near the end of his life. By the time he sat for this photograph in the early 1880s, he had been living in London for about 30 years, but he had developed many of his social and historical theories while living on the European continent in the political, economic, and revolutionary context of the 1840s.

(Hulton Getty)

or the relations of production, which included technology, inventions, natural resources, and property systems. It is these that create the social world in which people live. It is the relations of production that determine what kind of religions, philosophies, governments, laws, and moral values are accepted. To believe that ideas precede and generate actualities was, according to Marx, the error of Hegel. Hegel had thought, for example, that the mind conceives the idea of freedom, which it then realizes in the Greek city-state, in Christianity, in the French Revolution, and in the kingdom of Prussia. Not at all, according to Marx: the idea of freedom, or any other idea, is generated by the actual economic and social conditions. Conditions are the roots; ideas, the trees. Hegel had held the ideas to be the roots and the resulting actual conditions to be the trees. Or as Marx and Engels said, they found Hegel standing on his head and set him on his feet again.

The picture of historical development offered by Marx was somewhat as follows. Material conditions, or the relations of production, give rise to economic classes. Agrarian conditions produce a landholding or feudal class, but with changes in trade routes, money, and productive techniques a new commercial or bourgeois class arises. Each class, feudal and bour-

Historical development

geois, develops an ideology suited to its needs. Prevailing religions, governments, laws, and morals reflect the outlook of these classes. The two classes inevitably clash. Bourgeois revolutions against feudal interests break out—in England in 1642, in France in 1789, in Germany in 1848, though the bourgeois revolution in Germany proved abortive.

Meanwhile, as the bourgeois class develops, it inevitably calls another class into being, its dialectical antithesis, the proletariat. The bourgeois is defined as the private owner of capital, the proletarian as the wage worker who possesses nothing but his own hands. The more a country becomes bourgeois, the more it becomes proletarian. The more production is concentrated in factories, that more the revolutionary laboring class is built up. Under competitive conditions the bourgeois tend to devour and absorb each other; ownership of the factories, mines, machines, and railroads (capital) becomes concentrated into very few hands. Others sink into the proletariat. In the end the proletarianized mass simply takes over from the remaining bourgeois. It "expropriates the expropriators," and abolishes private property in the means of production.

The social revolution is thus accomplished. A classless society results, because class arises from economic differences which have been done away with. The state and religion, being outgrowths of bourgeois interests, also disappear. For a time, until all vestiges of bourgeois interests have been rooted out, or until the danger of counterrevolution against socialism has been overcome, there will be a "dictatorship of the proletariat." After that the state will "wither away," since there is no longer an exploiting class to require it.

Meanwhile the call is to war. Bourgeois and proletarian are locked in a universal struggle. It is really war, and as in all war all other considerations must be subordinated to it.

Class war between bourgeois and proletariat

Periods of social calm are not peace; they are merely interludes between battles. Workers and labor unions must be kept in a belligerent and revolutionary mood. They must never forget that the employer is their class enemy and that government, law, morality, and religion are merely so much artillery directed against them. Morals are "bourgeois morals" law is "bourgeois law," government is an instrument of class power, and religion is a form of psychological warfare, a means of providing "opium" for the masses. Workers must not let themselves be fooled; they must learn how to detect the class interest underlying the most exalted institutions and beliefs. In this piece of military intelligence, ferreting out the ways of the enemy, they will be helped by intellectuals especially trained in explaining it to them.

Worker solidarity

Like all fighting forces, the workers need a disciplined solidarity. Individuals must lose themselves in the whole—in their class. It is a betrayal of their class for workers to rise above the proletariat, to "improve themselves," as the bourgeois says. It is dangerous for labor unions merely to obtain better wages or hours by negotiation with employers, for by such little gains the war itself may be forgotten. It is likewise dangerous, and even treasonous, for workers to put faith in democratic machinery or "social legislation," for the state, an engine of repression, can never be made into an instrument of welfare. Law is the will of the stronger (i.e., the stronger class); "right" and "justice" are thin emanations of class interest. We must hold, wrote Marx in 1875 to "the realistic outlook which has cost so much effort to instill into the party, but which has now taken root in it"; and we must not let this outlook be perverted "by means of ideological nonsense about 'right' and other trash common among the democrats and French Socialists."

The Appeal of Marxism: Its Strength and Weaknesses

The original Marxism was a hard doctrine, with both advantages and handicaps in the winning of adherents. One of its advantages was its claim to be scientific. Marx classified earlier and rival forms of socialism as utopian: they rested on moral indignation, and their formula for reforming society was for human beings to become more just, or for the upper classes to be converted to sympathy for the lower. His own doctrine, Marx insisted, had nothing to do with ethical ideas; it was purely scientific, resting upon the study of actual facts and real processes, and it showed that socialism would be not a miraculous reversal but a historical continuation of what was already taking place. He also considered it utopian and unscientific to describe the future socialist society in any detail. It would be classless, with neither bourgeois nor proletarian; but to lay any specific plans would be idle dreaming. Let the revolution come, and socialism would take care of itself.

Marxism was a strong compound of the scientific, the historical, the metaphysical, and the apocalyptic. But some elements of Marxism stood in the way of its natural propagation. The working people of Europe were not really in the frame of mind of an army in battle. They hesitated to subordinate all else to the distant prospect of a class revolution. They were not exclusively class-people, nor did they behave as such. Enough of religion was still alive in them, and of older natural-law ideas, to inhibit the belief that morality was a class weapon, or right and justice "trash." They had national loyalties to country. Only with great difficulty could they associate themselves emotionally with a world proletariat in an unrelenting struggle against their own neighbors.

Conflicting working-class values

The cure for the revolutionism of 1848 proved in time to be the admission of the laboring classes to a fuller membership in society. Wages generally rose after 1850, labor unions were organized, and by 1870 in the principal European countries the workingman very generally had a vote. Through their unions, workers were often able to get better wages and working conditions by direct pressure upon employers. Having the vote, they gradually formed working-class parties, and as they proceeded to act through the state they had less inclination to destroy it. Marx's word for such maneuvers was "opportunism." Opportunism, the tendency of working people to better themselves by dealing with employers and by obtaining legislation through existing government channels, was the most dangerous of all dangers to the Revolution. For in war people do not negotiate or pass laws; they fight. From Marxism the working class absorbed much, including a watchful hostility to employers and a sense of working-class solidarity; but on the whole, as Marxism spread at the close of the nineteenth century it ceased to be really revolutionary. Had the old Europe not gone to pieces in the twentieth-century wars, and had Marxism not been revived by Lenin and transplanted to Russia, it is probable that Marx's ideas would have been domesticated into the general body of European thought and that much less would have been said about them in later years.

Opportunism

62.   BONAPARTISM: THE SECOND FRENCH EMPIRE, 1852–1870

We have seen how Louis Napoleon Bonaparte, elected president of the republic in 1848, in 1852 made himself Emperor of the French with the title of Napoleon III. Those willing to fight for the parliamentary and liberal institutions which he crushed were silenced. He became chief of state on a wave of popular acclaim.

Political Institutions of the Second Empire

Napoleon III, like Napoleon I, came to power because of the fear of radicalism in a discredited republic. Otherwise he bore little resemblance to his famous uncle. He was not a professional soldier or a great organizer. When he became president of the republic at the age of 40 he had been an adventurer and a conspirator, but he had also written two books on the "social question," and he undoubtedly felt more concern than Napoleon I for the plight of the working classes. Where Napoleon I had been disdainful of public opinion, his nephew recognized it as an opportunity, not a nuisance. Though journalists and intellectuals generally distrusted him, he drew some of them to his side; he tried to placate the Catholic interests; and he appealed to the masses by giving them the vote (however useless), by promises of prosperity, and by pageantry. He understood perfectly that a single leader exerts more magnetism than an elected assembly. And he knew that a Europe still shuddering over the June Days was hoping desperately for order in France.

He gloried in modern progress. Toward the changes coming over Europe the monarchs of the old school usually showed an attitude of timidity and doubt if not positive opposition. Napoleon III boldly offered himself as the leader in a brave new world.

Modern progress   Like his uncle, he announced that he embodied the sovereignty of the people. He said that he had found a solution to the problem of mass democracy.

In all the other great Continental states and in Great Britain, in 1852, universal suffrage was thought to be incompatible with intelligent government and economic prosperity. Napoleon III claimed to put them together. Like Marx and other "realists" after 1848 he held that elected parliamentary bodies, far from representing an abstract "people," only accentuated class divisions within a country. He declared that the regime of the restored Bourbons and the July Monarchy had been dominated by special interests, that the Republic of 1848 had first been violent and anarchic and then had fallen into the hands of a distrustful assembly that robbed the laboring man of his vote, and that France would find in the empire the permanent, popular, and modern system for which it had been vainly searching since 1789. He affirmed that he stood above classes and would govern equally in the interests of all. In any case, like many others after 1848, he held that forms of government were less important than economic and social realities.

Authoritarian political institutions   The political institutions of the Second Empire were therefore authoritarian, modeled on those of the Consulate of the first Bonaparte. There was a Council of State, composed of experts who drafted legislation and advised on technical matters. There was an appointive Senate with few significant functions. There was a Legislative Body elected by universal male suffrage.

The elections were carefully managed, so that the government's official candidates rarely faced any kind of political opposition. The Legislative Body had no independent powers of its own. It could not initiate legislation but only consider what was submitted to it by the emperor. It had no control over the budget, for the emperor was legally free to borrow money as he saw fit. It had no power over the army or the foreign office or the making of war and peace. To publish speeches made in the legislative chamber was against the law. Any five members, by requesting a secret session, could exclude the public from the galleries. Parliamentary life sank toward absolute zero.

To captivate public attention and glorify the Napoleonic name the new emperor set up a sumptuous court at the Tuileries. Balked in the ambition to marry into one of the great dynasties, Napoleon III chose as his empress a young Spanish noblewoman, Eugénie, who was destined to outlive the empire by 50 years, dying in 1920. It was said to be a love match—a sure sign of popularized royalty. The court life of the empire was brilliant and showy beyond anything known at the time in St. Petersburg or Vienna. The note of pageantry was further struck in the embellishment of the city of Paris. Baron Haussmann, one of the most creative of city planners, gave Paris much of the appearance that it has today. He built roomy railway stations with broad approaches, and he constructed a system of boulevards and public squares offering long vistas ending in fine buildings or monuments, as at the Place de l'Opéra. He also modernized the sewers and the water supply. The building program, like the expensive court, had the additional advantage of stimulating business and employment. And the cutting of wide avenues through the crooked streets and congested old houses would permit easier military operations against insurrectionists entrenched behind barricades, should the events of 1848 ever be repeated.

Economic Developments under the Empire

It was as a great social engineer that Napoleon III preferred to be known. In his youth he had tried to read the riddle of modern industrialism, and now, as emperor, he found some of his main backers in former Saint-Simonians, who called him their "socialist emperor." Saint-Simon, it may be recalled, had been among the first to conceive of a centrally planned industrial system. But the Saint-Simonians of the 1850s shared in the new sense of being realistic, and their most signal triumph was the invention of investment banking, by which they hoped to guide economic growth through the concentration of financial resources. They founded a novel kind of banking institution, the *Crédit Mobilier,* which raised funds by selling its shares to the public, and with the funds thus obtained bought stock in such new industrial enterprises as it wished to develop. A land bank, or *Crédit Foncier,* was likewise established to lend funds to landowners for the improvement of agriculture.

The times were exceedingly favorable for expansion, for the discovery of gold in California in 1849, and in Australia soon afterward, together with the newly organized credit facilities, brought a substantial increase in the *Expansion* European money supply, which had a mildly inflationary effect. The steady rise of prices and all money values encouraged company promotion and investment of capital. Railway mileage, increasing everywhere in the Western world, increased in France from 3,000 to 16,000 kilometers in the 1850s. The demand for rolling stock, iron rails, auxiliary equipment, and building materials for stations and freight houses kept the mines and factories busy. The railway network was rationalized, 55 small lines in France being merged into six big regional trunks. Iron steamboats replaced wooden sailing ships. Between 1859 and 1869 a French company built the Suez Canal, which it continued to own for almost a century, though the British government after 1875 was the principal stockholder.

Large corporations made their appearance, in railroads and banking first of all. In 1863 the law granted the right of "limited liability," by which a stockholder could not lose more than the par value of the stock, however insolvent or debt-burdened the corporation might become. This encouraged investment by persons of small means, and by capitalists large and small in enterprises of which they knew very little; thus the wealth and savings of the country were more effectively mobilized and put to work. Stocks and shares became more numerous and diversified. The Stock Exchange boomed. Financiers—those whose business was to handle money, credit, and securities—assumed a new eminence in the capitalistic world. A good many people became very rich, richer perhaps than anyone had ever been in France before.

The emperor aspired also to do something for the working class, within the limits of the existing system. The land bank was of some use to the more substantial peasants. Jobs were plentiful and wages were good, by the ideas of the day, at least until the temporary depression of 1857. The emperor had a plan, as did some of the Saint-Simonians, for organizing forces of workers in military fashion and setting them to clear and develop

Napoleon III's ambitious plan to rebuild the city of Paris became one of the great urban projects of modern times. Organized by the strong-willed Baron Haussmann, the systematic, controversial reconstruction of Parisian streets, parks, buildings, sewers, and monuments transformed the city and produced an aesthetic grandeur that has drawn visitors ever since. This photograph shows some of the construction workers and the tools they used to build the new streets.

(Giraudon/Art Resource/NY)

Napoleon's "socialistic" initiatives

uncultivated land. Not much was done in this direction. More was accomplished in the humanitarian relief of suffering. Hospitals and asylums were established, and free medicines were distributed. The outlines of a social-welfare state began somewhat vaguely to appear. Meanwhile the workers were building up unions. All combinations of workers had been prohibited during the French Revolution, a prohibition that was deemed to be still in force until the ambiguous legal position of labor unions began to change. In 1864 it even became legal for organized workers to go on strike. Large labor units, or unions, and large business units, or corporations, were thus legalized at the same time. Napoleon III hardly did enough for labor to rank as a working-class hero, but he did enough to be suspected as "socialistic" by many middle-class people of the day.

Later authoritarian regimes, bent like the Second Empire on a program of economic development, were usually highly protectionist, unwilling to face open competition with the rest of the world. Napoleon III believed in freedom of international trade. He had a project for a tariff union with Belgium, which some Belgians also supported. Belgium was already well industrialized, and a Franco-Belgium union, especially since Belgium had the coal that France lacked, would have formed a trading area of very great strength. But the plan was blocked by private interests in both countries and strongly opposed by both Great

Britain and the German *Zollverein*. The emperor then turned to an all-around reduction of import duties. Since the repeal of the Corn Laws in 1846 the free traders were in power in England. They were eager to abolish trade barriers between Britain and France. Napoleon III, overriding unusual opposition in his Legislative Body, concluded a free trade treaty with Great Britain in 1860. He set aside 40 million francs of government funds to assist French manufacturers in making adjustments to British competition; but this sum was never spent in full, and it has hence been concluded that French industry was able to compete successfully with the more intensively mechanized industry of Britain. The Anglo-French treaty was accompanied by lesser trade agreements with other countries. It looked, in the 1860s, as if Europe might actually be about to enter the promised land of freedom of trade.

Free trade treaty with Britain

Internal Difficulties and War

But by 1860 the empire was running into trouble. It took a few years to overcome the depression of 1857. By his free trade policy the emperor made enemies among certain industrialists. The Catholics objected to his intervention in Italy, where he briefly joined an anti-Austrian military campaign in 1859. After 1860 opposition mounted. The emperor granted more leeway to the Legislative Body. The 1860s are called the decade of the Liberal Empire—all such terms being relative. How the empire would have fared had purely internal causes been left free scope we shall never know. Louis Napoleon actually ruined himself by war. His empire evaporated on the battlefield in 1870. But he was at war long before that.

"The empire means peace," he had assured his audiences in 1852: *l'Empire, c' est la paix.* But war is after all the supreme pageantry (or was then); France was the strongest country of Europe, and the emperor's name was Napoleon. Less than a year and a half after the proclamation of the empire France was at war with a European state for the first time since Waterloo. The enemy was Russia, and the war was the Crimean War. Napoleon III did not alone instigate the Crimean War. Many forces in Europe after 1848 made for war; but Napoleon III was one of these forces. In 1859 the new Napoleon was fighting in Italy, from 1862 to 1867 in Mexico, and in 1870 in France itself, in a war with Prussia which he could easily have avoided. These wars form part of the story of the following chapter.

"The Empire means peace"

It is enough to say here that in 1870 the Second Empire went the way of the First, into the limbo of governments tried and discarded by the French. It had lasted 18 years, exactly as long as the July Monarchy, and longer than any other regime known in France, up to that time, since the fall of the Bastille. Not until the 1920s and 1930s, when dictators sprouted all over Europe, did the world begin to think that Louis Napoleon had been an omen of the future rather than a bizarre reincarnation of the past.

Chapter 13

THE CONSOLIDATION OF LARGE NATION-STATES, 1859–1871

Only a dozen years, from 1859 to 1871, were enough to see the formation of a new German empire, a unified kingdom of Italy, a Dual Monarchy of Austria-Hungary, drastic internal changes in tsarist Russia, the triumph of central authority in the United States, the creation of a united Dominion of Canada, and the modernizing or "Europeanization" of the empire of Japan. All these disparate events reflected profound changes brought in by the railroad, steamship, and telegraph, which made the communication of ideas, exchange of goods, and movement of people over wide areas more frequent and easier than ever before. New technologies and the rapid development of new industries strengthened the political power of nation-states, which became dynamic, shaping forces in the evolving social and economic life of all modern societies.

63. BACKGROUNDS: THE IDEA OF THE NATION-STATE

Before 1860 there were two prominent nation-states in Europe—Great Britain and France. Spain, united on the map, was internally so miscellaneous as to belong to a different category. Portugal, Switzerland, the Netherlands, and the Scandinavian countries were nation-states, but small and peripheral. The characteristic political organizations were small states comprising fragments of a nation, such as were strewn across the middle of Europe—

Chapter emblem: Detail from a photograph of Giuseppe Garibaldi, a leader of the Italian movement for national unification in the early 1860s.

Hanover, Baden, Sardinia, Tuscany, or the Two Sicilies—and large sprawling empires made up of all sorts of peoples, distantly ruled from above by dynasties and bureaucracies, such as the Romanov, Habsburg, and Ottoman domains. Except for recent developments in the Americas the same mixture of small nonnational states and of large nonnational empires was to be found in most of the rest of the world.

Since 1860 or 1870 a nation-state system has prevailed. The consolidation of large nations became a model for other peoples large and small. In time, in the following century, other large groups of people undertook to establish nation-states in India, Pakistan, Indonesia, Iran, and Nigeria. Small and middle-sized populations increasingly thought of themselves as nations, entitled to their own sovereignty and independence. Some of these

Unity and disunity

sovereignties that emerged after 1945 comprise fewer people than a large modern city. The idea of the nation-state has served both to bring people together into larger units and to break them apart into smaller ones. In the nineteenth century, outside the disintegrating Ottoman Empire, from which Greece, Serbia, Bulgaria, and Romania became independent, and in which an Arab national movement also began to stir, the national idea served mainly to create larger units in place of small ones. The map of Europe, from 1871 to 1918, was the simplest it has ever been before or since (see map, pp. 528–529).

About the idea of the nation-state and the movement of nationalism much has been said already in this book. Earlier chapters have described the ferment of national ideas and movements stirred up by the French Revolution and by the Napoleonic domination of Europe, the nationalist agitation and repression of the years after 1815, and the frustration and failure of patriotic aspirations in Germany, Italy, and central Europe in the Revolution of 1848. For many in the nineteenth century, nationalism, the winning of national unity and independence and the creation of the nation-state, became a kind of secular faith.

A nation-state may be thought of as one in which supreme political authority somehow rests upon and represents the will and feeling of its inhabitants. There

Characteristics of nation-states

must be a people, not merely a swarm of human beings. The people must basically will and feel something in common. They must sense that they belong—that they are members of a community, participating somehow in a common social and cultural life, that the government is their government, and that outsiders are "foreign." The outsiders or foreigners are usually (though not always) those who speak a different language. The nation is usually (though not always) composed of all persons sharing the same speech. A nation may also possess a belief in common descent or racial origin (however mistaken), or a sense of a common history, a common future, a common religion, a common geographical home, or a common external menace. Nations take form in many ways. But all are alike in feeling or imagining themselves to be communities, permanent communities in which individual persons, together with their children and their children's children, are committed to a collective destiny on earth.

In the nineteenth century governments found that they could not effectively rule, or develop the full powers of state, except by enlisting this sense of membership and

Consolidation and constitutionalism

support among their subjects. The consolidation of large nation-states had two distinguishable phases. Territorially, it meant the union of preexisting smaller states. Morally and psychologically it meant the creation of new ties between government and governed, the admission of new segments of the population to political life, through the creation or extension of liberal and representative institutions. This happened even in Japan and in tsarist Russia. National consolidation in the nineteenth century favored constitutional progress. Although there was considerable variation in the real power of the new political institutions and in the extent of self-government actually realized, parliaments were set up for the new Italy, the new Germany, the new Japan, the new Canada; and the movement in Russia was in the same direction. In Europe, some of the aims which the revolutionists of 1848 had failed to achieve were now realized by the established authorities.

They were realized, however, only in a series of wars. To create an all-German or an all-Italian state, as the revolutions of 1848 had already shown, it was necessary to break the power of Austria, render Russia at least temporarily ineffective, and overthrow or intimidate those German and Italian governments which refused to surrender their sovereignty. In the United States, to maintain national unity as understood by President Lincoln, it was necessary to repress the movement for Southern independence by force of arms. For 40 years after 1814 there had been no war between established powers of Europe. Then in 1854 came the Crimean War, in 1859 the Italian War, in 1864 the Danish War, in 1866 the Austro-Prussian War, and in 1870 the Franco-Prussian War. Concurrently the Civil War raged in the United States. After 1871, for 43 years there was again no war between the major European powers.

The Crimean War, 1854–1856

Before moving on to the first of the national consolidation movements, the Italian, we must examine the Crimean War which, though seemingly remote and unconnected, helped to make possible the success of the European national movements. Its chief significance for Europe is that it seriously weakened both Austria and Russia, the two powers most bent on preserving the peace settlement of 1815 and on preventing national changes. It was also the first war covered by newspaper correspondents, and the first in which women, led by Florence Nightingale, established their position as army nurses.

The pressure of Russia upon Turkey was an old story. Every generation saw its Russo-Turkish war. In the last Russo-Turkish war, to go back no further, that of 1828–1829, the Tsar Nicholas I protected the independence newly won by Greece and annexed the left bank of the mouth of the Danube. Now, in 1853, Nicholas again made demands upon the still large but decaying Ottoman Empire, *Russian pressure* moving in on the two Danubian principalities, Wallachia and Moldavia (later to be known as Romania), with military forces (see map, p. 632). The dispute this time ostensibly involved the protection of Christians in the Ottoman Empire, including the foreign Christians at Jerusalem and in Palestine. Over these Christians the French also claimed a certain protective jurisdiction. The French had for centuries been the principal Western people in the Middle East. They had often furnished money and advisers to the sultan, they carried on a huge volume of trade, they staffed and financed Christian missions, and they were continually talking of building a Suez canal. Napoleon III had especial reason to resent the tsar Nicholas, who regarded him as a revolutionary adventurer. Napoleon III encouraged the Turkish government to resist Russian claims to protect Christians within Turkey. War between Russia and Turkey broke out late in 1853. In 1854 France joined the side of the Turks, as did Great Britain, whose settled policy was to uphold Turkey and the Middle East against penetration by Russia. The two Western powers were soon joined by a small ally, the kingdom of Sardinia, better known because of its Italian mainland territory and seat of government as Piedmont, which had no visible interest in the issues in the Middle East and entered the war mainly for the purpose of advancing the Italian question.

The British fleet successfully blockaded Russia in both its Baltic and Black Sea outlets. French and British armies invaded Russia itself, landing in the Crimean peninsula, to which all the important fighting was confined. The Austrian Empire had its own reasons not to wish Russia to conquer the Balkans and Constantinople, or to see Britain and France master the situation alone; Austria therefore, though not yet recovered from the upheaval of 1848–1849, mobilized its armed forces at a great effort to itself and occupied Wallachia and Moldavia, which the Russians evacuated under this threat of attack by a new enemy.

Tsar Nicholas died in 1855, and his successor, Alexander II, sued for peace.

Peace in 1856

A congress of all the great powers made peace at Paris in 1856. By the treaty the powers pledged themselves jointly to maintain the "integrity of the Ottoman Empire." The Russian tide ebbed a little. Russia ceded the left bank of the mouth of the Danube to Moldavia and gave up its claim to the special protection of Christians in the Turkish empire. Moldavia and Wallachia (united as Romania in 1858), together with Serbia, were recognized as self-governing principalities under protection of the European powers. At the Congress of Paris all seemed harmonious. There seemed to be such a thing as Europe, undertaking collective obligations, protecting small states, rationally and peaceably conducting its affairs.

The Crimean War weakened the international position of Austria and Russia, but its most enduring effect on nations such as Britain may have come in the ways that wars were described in the popular press and in the new role of women nurses. Florence Nightingale arrived in the Crimea with 36 nurses and was at first opposed by army doctors. She is pictured here in one of the hospitals where she began to create the new military and social identity of the female nurse.

(Hulton Getty)

But trouble was in the making. Napoleon III needed glory. The Italians wanted some kind of unified Italy. The Prussians, who had done nothing in the Crimean War, and were only tardily invited to the Congress of Paris, feared that their status as a great power might be slipping away. Napoleon III, the Italian nationalists, the Prussians, all stood to gain by change. Change in central Europe and Italy meant a tearing up of the Treaty of Vienna of 1815, long guarded by Metternich and unsuccessfully challenged by the revolutionaries of 1848. Now, after the Crimean War, the forces opposing change were very weak. It was the Russian and Austrian empires that had stood firmly for the status quo. But these two powers, which had most seriously attempted to uphold the Vienna settlement, could do so no longer. The first proof came in Italy.

64. CAVOUR AND THE ITALIAN WAR OF 1859: THE UNIFICATION OF ITALY

Italian Nationalism: The Program of Cavour

In Italy there had long been about a dozen sizable states, together with a few very small ones. Several of them had dissolved in the Italian movements that accompanied the wars of the French Revolution. All had been reorganized, first by Napoleon and then by the Congress of Vienna. The governments of these states were generally content with their separate independence. But the governments were remote from their peoples.

There was a widespread disgust in Italy with the existing authorities, and a growing desire for a liberal national state in which all Italy might be embodied and which might resurrect the Italian grandeur of ancient times and of the Renaissance. This sentiment, the dream of an Italian Risorgimento, or resurgence, had become very heated at the time of the French Revolution and Napoleon, then had been transformed into a moral purpose by the writings of Mazzini. Mazzini, who had invested the cause of Italian unity with almost a holy character, had seen his hopes for a unified republican Italy elevated for a brief moment and then blasted in the general debacle of 1848. In the stormy events of 1848 the papacy had been frightened off by the radical romantic republicanism of Mazzini, Garibaldi, and other firebrands and could no longer be expected to support the cause of Italian nationalism. And the same events had shown that Austria could not be ousted from the Italian peninsula without the aid of an outside power.

Italian Risorgimento

These lessons were not lost on the prime minister of Piedmont, which was ruled since 1848 as a constitutional monarchy and was now under King Victor Emmanuel. This prime minister after 1852 was Camillo di Cavour, one of the shrewdest political tacticians of that or any age. Cavour was a liberal of Western type. He tried to make the state a model of progress, efficiency, and fair government that other Italians would admire. He worked hard to plant constitutional and parliamentary practices. He favored the building of railroads and docks, the improvement of agriculture, and emancipation of trade. He followed a strongly anticlerical policy, cutting down the number of religious holidays, limiting the right of church bodies to own real estate, abolishing the church courts—all without negotiation with the Holy See. A liberal and constitutional monarchist, a wealthy landowner in his own right, he had no sympathy for the revolutionary, romantic, and republican nationalism of Mazzini.

Cavour shared in that new toughness of mind described in the last chapter. He embraced a politics of reality. He did not approve of republicans but

Cavour's "politics of reality"

was willing to work with them surreptitiously. He did not idealize war but was willing to make war to unify Italy under the house of Savoy. With unruffled calculation he took Piedmont into the Crimean War, sending troops to Russia, in the hope of winning a place at the peace table and raising the Italian question at the Congress of Paris. It was evident to him that against one great power one must pit another and that the only way to get Austria out of Italy was to use the French army. It became his master plan deliberately to provoke war with Austria, after having assured himself of French military support.

It was not difficult to persuade Napoleon III to collaborate. The Bonapartes looked upon Italy as their ancestral country, and Napoleon III, in his adventurous youth, had traveled in conspiratorial Italian circles and even participated in an Italian insurrection in 1831. Now, as emperor, in his role of apostle of modernity, he entertained a "doctrine of nationalities" which held the consolidation of nations to be a forward step at the existing stage of history. To fight reactionary Austria for the freedom of Italy would also mollify liberal opinion in France, which in other ways Napoleon was engaged in suppressing. The last note in persuasion was furnished by an Italian republican named Orsini, who in 1858, finding the French emperor too slow to make up his mind, attempted to assassinate him with a bomb. Napoleon III reached a secret agreement with Cavour. In April 1859, Cavour tricked Austria into a declaration of war. The French army poured over the Alps.

There were two battles, Magenta and Solferino, both won by the French and Piedmontese. But Napoleon III was now in a quandary. The Prussians began to mobilize on the Rhine, not wishing France to create an Italian sphere of influence for itself. In Italy, with the defeat of the Austrians, revolutionary agitation broke out all over the peninsula, as it had a decade before—and the French emperor was no patron of popular revolution. The revolutionaries overthrew or denounced the existing governments and clamored for annexation to Piedmont. In France, as elsewhere, the Catholics, fearful that the pope's temporal power would be lost, upbraided the emperor for his godless and unnecessary war. The French position was indeed odd, for while the bulk of the French army fought Austria in the north, a detachment of it was still stationed in Rome, sent there in 1849 to protect the pope against Italian republicanism. Napoleon III, in July 1859, at the height of his victories, stupefied Cavour. He made a separate peace with the Austrians.

Franco-Austrian agreement

The Franco-Austrian agreement gave Lombardy to Piedmont but left Venetia within the Austrian Empire. It offered a compromise solution to the Italian question, in the form of a federal union of the existing Italian governments, to be presided over by the pope. This was not what Cavour, or the Piedmontese, or the more fiery Italian patriots wanted. Revolution continued to spread across the northern Italian states. Tuscany, Modena, Parma, and Romagna drove out their old rulers. They were annexed to Piedmont, after plebiscites or general elections in these regions had shown an overwhelming popular favor for this step. Since Romagna belonged to the papal states, the pope excommunicated the organizers of the new Italy. Undeterred, representatives of all north Italy except Venetia met at the Piedmontese capital of Turin in 1860 in the first parliament of the enlarged kingdom. The British government hailed these events with enthusiasm, and Napoleon III also recognized the expanded Piedmontese state, in return for the transfer to France of Nice and Savoy, where plebiscites disclosed enormous majorities for annexation to France.

The Completion of Italian Unity

There were now, in 1860, a north Italian kingdom, the papal states in the middle, and the kingdom of the Two Sicilies, ruled by a Bourbon king in Naples and still standing in the south. The latter was being undermined by revolutionary agitation, as often in the past. A Piedmontese republican, Giuseppe Garibaldi, brought matters to a head. Somewhat like Lafayette, Garibaldi was a "hero of two worlds," who had fought for the independence of Uruguay, lived in the United States, and been one of the Triumvirs in the short-lived Roman Republic of 1849. He now organized a group of about 1,150 personal followers—Garibaldi's Thousand, or the Red Shirts—for an armed expedition to the south. Cavour, unable openly to favor such filibustering against a neighboring state, connived at Garibaldi's preparations and departure. Garibaldi landed in Sicily and soon crossed to the mainland. Revolutionists hastened to join him, and the government of the Two Sicilies, backward and corrupt, commanding little loyalty from its population, collapsed before this picturesque intrusion.

Garibaldi now prepared to push from Naples up to Rome. Here, of course, he would meet not only the pope but also the French army, and the international scandal would reverberate throughout the globe. Cavour decided that so extreme a step must be averted, but that Garibaldi's successes must at the same time be used. Anticipating Garibaldi, a Piedmontese army entered the papal states, carefully avoiding Rome, and proceeded onward into Naples. Garibaldi, though not all his followers, was now ready to accept a monarchy as the best solution to the problem of Italian unification. The chief of the Red Shirts, the one-time foe of kings, consented to ride in an open carriage with Victor Emmanuel through the streets of Naples amid

Garibaldi's compromise

cheering thousands. Plebiscites held in the Two Sicilies showed an almost unanimous willingness to join with Piedmont. In the remainder of the papal states, except for Rome and its environs, plebiscites were held also, with the same result. A parliament representing all Italy except Rome and Venetia met in 1861, and the Kingdom of Italy was formally proclaimed, with Victor Emmanuel II as king "by grace of God and the will of the nation." Venetia was added in 1866, as a prize for Italian aid to Prussia in a war against Austria, and Rome was annexed in 1870 after the withdrawal of French troops in the Franco-Prussian War of 1870.

So Italy was "made," as the phrase of the time expressed it. It had been made by the long high-minded apostolate of Mazzini, the audacity of Garibaldi, the cold policy of Cavour, by war and insurrection, by armed violence endorsed by popular vote.

Persistent Problems after Unification

Very little was settled or ended by unification. Even territorially, the more pronounced nationalists refused to believe that Italian unity was completed. They looked beyond, to regions of mixed population where Italians were numerous or preponderant—to the Trentino, to Trieste, to certain Dalmatian islands, or to Nice and Savoy. They saw in these regions an *Italia irredenta,* "an unredeemed Italy," awaiting in its turn the day of incorporation. Irredentism even passed into the English language as a word signifying a vociferous demand, on nationalist grounds, for annexation of regions beyond one's own frontiers.

The occupation of Rome in 1870 by the Italian government opened the rift between church and state still wider. The pope, deprived of territories he had held for a thousand years, renewed his condemnations and chose to remain in lifelong seclusion in the Vatican. His successors followed the

Occupation of Rome

same policy until 1929. Hence good Italian patriots were bound to be anticlerical, and good Catholics were bound to look upon the Italian state with unfriendly eyes. The regional differences between northern and southern Italy did not disappear with unification. The north looked upon the agrarian south—the land of priest, landlord, and impoverished peasant—as disgracefully backward.

UNIFICATION OF ITALY, 1859–1870

PIEDMONT
LOMBARDY VENETIA
Milan Venice
Turin
PARMA
MODENA
Florence
TUSCANY PAPAL STATES
KINGDOM OF SARDINIA
ROME
NAPLES
SARDINIA
SICILY

FORMATION OF DUAL MONARCHY OF AUSTRIA-HUNGARY, 1867

AUSTRIA
Vienna
Budapest
HUNGARY

FORMATION OF DOMINION OF CANADA, 1867

NORTHWEST TERRITORIES
LABRADOR 1949
NEWFOUND-LAND 1949
BRITISH COLUMBIA 1871
ALBERTA 1905
SASKATCHEWAN 1905
MANITOBA 1870
QUEBEC 1867
MARITIME PROVINCES 1867
ONTARIO 1867
Ottawa

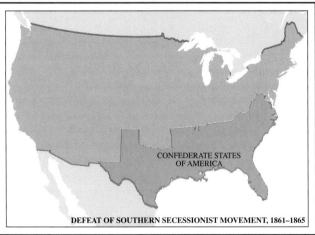

CONFEDERATE STATES
OF AMERICA

DEFEAT OF SOUTHERN SECESSIONIST MOVEMENT, 1861–1865

This photograph of Giuseppe Garibaldi suggests the confident, charismatic personal style that enabled him to lead a spirited group of Italian nationalists or "Red Shirts" into southern Italy, to form an alliance with King Victor Emmanuel of Piedmont, and to help establish a unified Italian nation-state.

(Hulton Getty)

The new Italy was parliamentary but not democratic. At first the vote was only given to some 600,000 persons out of more than 20 million. Not until 1913 was the suffrage significantly broadened. Meanwhile parliamentary life, confined to a few, was somewhat unrealistic and frequently corrupt. With the mass of the population excluded from the vote, the revolutionary agitation continued unabated after the unification. Garibaldi himself, in the 1860s, made two more attempts to seize Rome by violence. In general, the revolutionary movement shifted from the older republican nationalism to the newer forms of Marxian socialism, anarchism, or syndicalism.

But the dream of ages was realized. Italy was one. The period that seemed so shameful to patriots, the long centuries that had elapsed since the Renaissance, were now terminated in the glories of a successful Risorgimento.

65.   BISMARCK: THE FOUNDING OF A GERMAN EMPIRE

To play upon the divisions among the Germans, keeping them in rivalry with each other and dependent upon outside powers, had been the policy of France ever since the Reformation and of Russia since it began to take part in the affairs of Europe. The pulverization of the Germanic world was in fact a kind of negative prerequisite to the development of modern history as we know it, for without it the economic and cultural leadership of Europe would hardly have become concentrated along the Atlantic seaboard, or a great military empire have arisen in Russia and spread along the Baltic and into Poland.

NATION BUILDING, 1859–1867

In the eight years after 1859 Italy was unified (except for the city of Rome, annexed in 1870), the Habsburg government tried to solve its nationalities problem by creating the Dual Monarchy of Austria-Hungary, the United States affirmed its unity by defeating a Southern secessionist movement, and the Dominion of Canada was formed to include all of British North America (dates show the accession of provinces) except Newfoundland and Labrador, which were added in 1949.

Gradually, as we have seen, the Germans became dissatisfied with their position. They became nationalistic during and after the Napoleonic wars. Many German thinkers held that Germany was different from the West, destined someday to work out a peculiarly German way of life and political system of its own. To the Slavs the Germans felt immeasurably superior. German philosophy, as shown most clearly in Hegel, took on a certain characteristic tone. It pronounced individualism to be Western; it skipped lightly over individual liberty; it tended to glorify group loyalties, collectivist principles, and the state. It emphasized the progressive evolution of history, which in the thought of Hegel, and after him Marx, became a vast impersonal force almost independent of human beings. History was said to ordain, require, necessitate, condemn, justify, or excuse. What one did not like could be dismissed as a mere historical phase, opening into a quite different and more attractive future. What one wanted, in the present or future, could be described as historically necessary and bound to come.

The German States after 1848

In 1848 a series of revolutions unseated the several governments of Germany. At the Frankfurt Assembly a group composed essentially of private citizens undertook to organize a united Germany by constitutional methods. They failed because they had no power. Hence after 1848 the Germans began to think in terms of power, developing a somewhat extreme admiration for *die Macht*. The men of Frankfurt failed also, perhaps, because they were insufficiently revolutionary. The Germans were a sober, orderly, and respectful people. They were still attached emotionally to their several states. What happened in Italy, a revolutionary destruction of all the old governments except that of Piedmont, could not happen in Germany.

After the failure of the 1848 revolution German nationalists and liberals were confused. By 1850 the old states were restored—Austria and Prussia, the kingdoms of Hanover, Saxony, Bavaria, and Württemberg, together with about 30 other states ranging in size down to the free cities of Hamburg and Frankfurt. The loose confederation of 1815, linking all these states together, was restored also (see map, p. 522). But within this framework great economic and social changes were occurring. Between 1850 and 1870 the output of both coal and iron in Germany multiplied sixfold. In 1850 Germany produced less iron than France; in 1870, more. Germany was overcoming the economic and social lag which had characterized it for 300 years. A *Zollverein,* formed by Prussia in 1834, included almost all Germany outside Austria and Bohemia and provided a large measure of economic unity. The German cities were growing, bound together by railroad and telegraph, requiring larger supporting areas on which to live. Industrial capitalists and industrial workers were becoming more numerous. With the advantages of unity more obvious than ever, with the ideals of 1848 badly compromised, with an exaggerated respect for the state and for power, and with a habit of accepting the successful event as the "judgment of history," the Germans were ripe for what happened. They did not unify themselves by their own exertions. They fell into the arms of Prussia.

Advantages of unity

Prussia in the 1860s: Bismarck

Prussia had always been the smallest and most precarious of the great powers. Ruined by Napoleon, it had risen again. It owed its international influence and internal character to its army. Actually it had fought rather fewer wars than other great powers, but its army enabled Prussia to expand by conquest or diplomacy. The taking of Silesia in 1740, of parts of Poland in the 1770s and 1790s, of the Rhineland in 1815 by an international bargain were the highlights of Prussian growth. After 1850 those who controlled the destinies of Prussia were apprehensive. Their state had been shaken by revolution. In the Crimean War and at the Congress of Paris they were hardly more than spectators. Italy was unified without any Prussian saying yes or no. It seemed as if the hard-won and still relatively recent position of Prussia might be waning.

Since 1815 the population of Prussia had grown from 11 to 18 million, but the size of the army had not changed. Merely to enforce existing principles of conscription would therefore almost double the army. But this would require increased financial appropriations. After 1850 Prussia had a parliament. It was a parliament, to be sure, dominated by men of wealth; but some of the wealthy Prussians, notably the capital owners of the Rhineland, were liberals who wished the parliament to have control over government policies. These men did not like professional armies and considered the Prussian Junkers, from whom the officer corps was recruited, as their main rivals in the state. The parliament refused the necessary appropriations. The king at this juncture, in 1862, appointed a new chief minister, Otto von Bismarck.

Parliamentary politics

Bismarck was a Junker from old Brandenburg east of the Elbe. He cultivated the gruff manner of an honest country squire, though he was in fact an accomplished man of the world. Intellectually he was far superior to the rather unsophisticated landlord class from which he sprang and for which he often felt an impatient contempt. He shared in many Junker ideas. He advocated, and even felt, a kind of stout Protestant piety. Although he cared for the world's opinion, it never deterred him in his actions; criticism and denunciation left him untouched. He was in fact obstinate. He was not a nationalist. He did not look upon all Germany as his Fatherland. He was a Prussian. His social affinities, as with the Junkers generally, lay to the East with corresponding landowning elements of the Baltic provinces and Russia. The West, including the bulk of Germany, he neither understood nor trusted; it seemed to him revolutionary, turbulent, free-thinking, materialistic. Parliamentary bodies he considered ignorant and irresponsible as organs of government. Individual liberty seemed to him disorderly selfishness. Liberalism, democracy, socialism were repugnant to him. He preferred to stress duty, service, order, and the fear of God. The idea of forming a new German union developed only gradually in his mind and then as an adjunct to the strengthening of Prussia.

Bismarck

Bismarck thus had his predilections and even his principles. But no principle bound him, no ideology seemed to him an end in itself. He became the classic practitioner of *Realpolitik*. The time came when the Junkers thought him a traitor to his class, when even the king was afraid of him, when he outraged and then mollified the august house of Habsburg, when he made friends with liberals, democrats, and even socialists, and in turn made enemies of them. First he made wars, then he insisted upon peace. Enmities and alliances were to him only matters of passing convenience. The enemy of today might be the friend of tomorrow. Far from planning out a long train of events, then following it step by step to a grand consummation, he seems to have been practical and opportunistic, taking advantage of situations as they emerged and prepared to act in any one of several directions as events might suggest.

In 1862, as minister president, it was his job, or duty, to outface the liberals in the Prussian parliament. For four years, from 1862 to 1866, Bismarck waged this constitutional struggle. The parliament refused to vote

Constitutional struggle

Otto von Bismarck's pragmatic use of power and his successful campaign to create a unified German nation-state made him the most successful practitioner of *Realpolitik* in late nineteenth-century Europe. This photograph suggests the talent for well-focused observation that enabled Bismarck to see clearly what was at stake in the many political and diplomatic conflicts of his generation.

(Hulton Getty)

the proposed taxes. The government collected them anyway. The taxpayers paid them without protest—it was the orderly thing to do, and the collectors represented public authority. The limitations of Prussian liberalism, the docility of the population, the respect for officialdom, the belief that the king and his ministers were wiser than the elected deputies, all clearly revealed themselves in this triumph of military policy over the theory of government by consent. The army was enlarged, reorganized, retrained, and reequipped. Bismarck fended off the showers of abuse from the liberal majority in the chamber. The liberals declared that the government's policy was flagrantly unconstitutional. The constitution, said Bismarck, could not have been meant to undermine the state. The government, said the liberals, was itself undermining Prussia, for the rest of Germany hoped to find in Prussia, as Italy had found in Piedmont, a model of political freedom. What the Germans admired in Prussia, replied Bismarck coldly, was not its liberalism but its power. He declared that the Prussian boundaries as set in 1815 were unsound, that Prussia must be prepared to seize favorable opportunities for further growth. And he added one of his most memorable utterances: "Not by speeches and majority votes are the great questions of the day decided—that was the great error of 1848 and 1849—but by blood and iron."

Bismarck's Wars: The North German Confederation, 1867

A favorable opportunity was not long in presenting itself. The Danes, engaged in a process of national consolidation of their own, wished to make the duchy of Schleswig an integral part of Denmark. The population of Schleswig was part Dane and part German. The diet of the German confederation, unwilling to see Germans thus annexed outright to Denmark, called for an all-German war upon the Danes, just as the revolutionary Frankfurt Assembly had done during a similar conflict in 1848. Bismarck had no desire to support or strengthen the existing German confederation. He wanted not an all-German war but a Prussian war. To disguise his aims he acted jointly with Austria. In 1864 Prussia and Austria together went to war with Denmark, which they soon defeated. It was Bismarck's intention to annex both Schleswig and the duchy of Holstein to Prussia, gaining whatever other advantages might present themselves from future trouble with Austria. He arranged a provisional occupation of Schleswig by Prussia and of Holstein by Austria. Disputes soon arose over rights of passage, the keeping of internal order, and other problems with which occupying forces are commonly afflicted. While pretending to try to regulate these disputes he allowed them to ripen.

He now proceeded to discredit and isolate Austria. The British government was at the time following a policy of nonintervention in the affairs of the Continent. The Russian empire was in no position for action; it was divided internally by a reform program then at its height; it was in a mood of hostility to Austria, because of events of the Crimean War, and well disposed toward Prussia and Bismarck, because Bismarck in 1863 took care to support it against an uprising of the Poles. To win over the new kingdom of Italy Bismarck held out the lure of Venetia. As for France, Napoleon III was embarrassed by domestic discontents and had his army committed to adventures in Mexico. In addition, Bismarck charmed him at a confidential interview at Biarritz, where vague oral intimations of French expansion were exchanged, and the two men seemed to agree to a needed modernization of the map of Europe. To weaken Austria within Germany, Bismarck presented himself as a democrat. He proposed a reform of the German confederation, recommending that it have a popular chamber elected by universal male suffrage. He calculated that the mass of the German people were wedded neither to the well-to-do capitalistic liberals, nor to the existing government structures of the German states, nor to the house of Habsburg. He would use "democracy" to undermine all established interests that stood in his way.

Bismarck as democrat

Meanwhile the occupying powers continued to quarrel over Schleswig-Holstein. Austria finally raised the matter formally in the German federal diet, one of whose functions was to prevent war between its members. Bismarck declared that the diet had no authority, accused the Austrians of aggression, and ordered the Prussian army to enter Holstein. The Austrians called for federal sanctions in the form of an all-German force to be sent against Prussia. The result was that Prussia, in 1866, was at war not only with Austria but also with most of the other German states. The Prussian army soon proved its superiority. Trained to an unprecedented precision, equipped with the new needle-gun, by which the infantryman could deliver five rounds a minute, brought into the zone of combat by an imaginative strategy that made use of the new railroads, commanded by the skill of von Moltke, the Prussian army overthrew the Austrians at the battle of Sadowa (or Königgrätz) and defeated the other German states soon thereafter. The Austro-Prussian, or Seven Weeks' War, was amazing in its brevity. Bismarck hastened to make peace before the other European powers could realize what had happened.

Seven Weeks' War

Prussia annexed outright, together with Schleswig-Holstein, the whole kingdom of Hanover, the duchies of Nassau and Hesse-Cassel, and the free city of Frankfurt. Here the old governments simply disappeared before the axe of the "red reactionary." The German federal union disappeared likewise. In its place, in 1867, Bismarck organized a North German Confederation, in which the newly enlarged Prussia joined with 21 other states, all of which combined it greatly outweighed. The German states south of the river Main—Austria, Bavaria, Baden, Württemberg, and Hesse-Darmstadt—remained outside the new organization, with no kind of union among themselves. Meanwhile the kingdom of Italy annexed Venetia.

For the North German Confederation Bismarck produced a constitution. The new structure, though a federal one, was much stronger than the now defunct Confederation of 1815. The king of Prussia became its hereditary head. Ministers were responsible to him. There was a parliament with two chambers. The upper chamber, as in the United States, represented the states as such, though not equally. The lower chamber, or Reichstag, was deemed to represent the people and was elected by universal male suffrage. Such flirting with democracy

A new constitution

THE GERMAN QUESTION, 1815–1871

From 1815 to 1866 there were 39 German states joined in the German Confederation (the largest states are shown here). The movement to create a unified Germany gave rise in this era to opposing nationalist groups: the Great Germans, who favored an all-German union that would include Austria; and the Little Germans, who were willing to exclude Austria and its empire from a new German nation-state. Bismarck was a Little German but a Great Prussian. He (1) enlarged Prussia by conquest in 1866; (2) joined Mecklenburg, Saxony, and other regions with Prussia in the North German Confederation of 1867; and (3) combined this Confederation with Bavaria, Württemberg, and other southern states to form the German Empire in 1871. He also (4) conquered Alsace-Lorraine from France and (5) excluded Austria from the new German empire. These boundaries remained unchanged until 1918.

seemed madness to both conservative Junker and liberal bourgeois. It was indeed a bold step, for only France at the time illustrated universal suffrage in Europe on a large scale, and in the France of Napoleon III neither old-fashioned conservatives nor genuine liberals could take much satisfaction. As for Great Britain, where voting rights were extended in this same year, 1867, they were still given to less than half the adult male population. Bismarck sensed in the "masses" an ally of strong government against private interests. He negotiated even with the socialists, who had arisen with the industrialization of the past decade, and who, in Germany at this time, were mainly followers of Ferdinand Lassalle. The Lassallean socialists, unlike the Marxian, believed it theoretically possible to improve working-class conditions through the action of existing governments. To the great annoyance of Marx, then in England (his *Capital* first appeared in 1867), the bulk of the German socialists reached an understanding with Bismarck. In return for a democratic suffrage they agreed to accept the North German Confederation. Bismarck, for his part, by making use of democratic and socialist sentiment, won popular approval for his emerging empire.

The Franco-Prussian War

It was clear that the situation was not yet stable. The small south German states were left floating in empty space; they would sooner or later have to gravitate into some orbit or other, whether Austrian, Prussian, or French. In France there were angry criticisms of Napoleon III's foreign policy. French intervention in Mexico had proved a fiasco. A united Italy had been allowed to rise on France's borders. And now, contrary to all principles of French national interest observed by French governments for hundreds of years, a strong and independent power was being allowed to spread over virtually the whole of Germany. Everywhere people began to feel that war was coming between France and Prussia. Bismarck played on the fears of France felt in the south German states. South Germany, though in former times often a willing satellite to France, was now sufficiently nationalistic to consider such subservience to a foreign people disgraceful. To Bismarck it seemed that a war between Prussia and France would frighten the small south German states into a union with Prussia, leaving only Austria outside—which was what he wanted. To Napoleon III, or at least to some of his advisers, it seemed that such a war, if successful, would restore public approval of the Bonapartist empire. In this inflammable situation the responsible persons of neither country worked for peace.

Meanwhile a revolution in Spain had driven the reigning queen into exile, and a Spanish provisional government invited Prince Leopold of Hohenzollern, the king of Prussia's cousin, to be constitutional king of Spain. To entrench the Prussian royal house in Spain would naturally be distasteful to France. Three times the Hohenzollern family refused the Spanish offer. Bismarck, who could not control such family decisions but who foresaw the possibility of a usable incident, deviously persuaded the Spanish to issue the invitation still a fourth time. On July 2, 1870, Paris heard that Prince Leopold had accepted. The French ambassador to Prussia, Benedetti, at the direction of his government, met the king of Prussia at the bathing resort of Ems, where he formally demanded that Prince Leopold's acceptance be withdrawn. It was withdrawn on July 12. The French seemed to have their way. Bismarck was disappointed.

France thwarts new Spanish king

The French government went still further. It instructed Benedetti to approach the king again at Ems and demand that at no time in the future would any Hohenzollern ever become a candidate for the Spanish throne. The king politely declined any such commitment and telegraphed a full report of the conversation to Bismarck at Berlin. Bismarck, receiving the telegram, which became famous as the "Ems dispatch," saw a new opportunity, as he put it, to wave a red flag before the Gallic bull. He condensed the Ems telegram for publication, so reducing and abridging it that it seemed to newspaper readers as if a curt exchange had occurred at Ems, in which the Prussians believed that their king had been insulted and the French believed that their ambassador had been snubbed. In both countries the war party demanded satisfaction. On July 19, 1870, on these trivial grounds, and with the ostensible issue of the Spanish throne already settled, the irresponsible and decaying government of Napoleon III declared war on Prussia.

A short war

Again the war was short. Again Bismarck had taken care to isolate his enemy in advance. The British generally felt France to be in the wrong. They had been alarmed by French operations in Mexico, which suggested an ambition to re-create a French American empire. The Italians had long been awaiting the chance to seize Rome; they did so in 1870, when the French withdrew their troops from Rome for use against Prussia. The Russians had been awaiting the chance to upset a clause of the Peace of 1856 that forbade them to keep naval vessels in the Black Sea. They did so in 1870.

The War of 1870, like the others of the time, failed to become a general European struggle. Prussia was supported by the south German states. France had no allies. The French army proved to be technically backward compared with the Prussian. War began on July 19; on September 2, after the battle of Sedan, the principal French army surrendered to the Germans. Napoleon III was himself taken prisoner. On September 4 an insurrection in Paris proclaimed the Third Republic. The Prussian and German forces moved into France and laid siege to the capital. Though the French armies dissolved, Paris refused to capitulate. For four months it was surrounded and besieged.

The German Empire, 1871

With their guns encircling Paris, the German rulers or their representatives assembled at Versailles. The château and gardens of Versailles, since Louis XVI's unceremonious departure in October 1789, had been little more than a vacant monument to a society long since dead. Here, in the most sumptuous room of the palace, the resplendent Hall of Mirrors, where the Sun King had once received the deferential approaches of German princes, Bismarck on January 18, 1871, caused the German Empire to be proclaimed. The king of Prussia received the hereditary title of German emperor. The other German rulers (excepting, to be sure, the ruler of Austria, and those whom Bismarck had himself dethroned) accepted his imperial authority. Ten days later the people of Paris, shivering, hungry, and helpless, opened their gates to the enemy. France had no government with which Bismarck could make peace. It was not at all clear what kind of government the country wanted.

Bismarck's demands

Bismarck insisted on the election of a Constituent Assembly by universal suffrage. He demanded that France pay the German Empire a war indemnity of five billion gold francs (then an enormous and unprecedented sum) and cede to it the border region of Alsace and most of Lorraine. Though the Alsatians spoke German, most of them felt themselves to be French, having shared in the general history of France since the seventeenth century. There was strong local protest at the transfer to Germany, and the French never reconciled themselves to this cold-blooded amputation of their frontier. The peace dictated by Bismarck was embodied in the treaty of Frankfurt of May 10, 1871. Thereafter, as will be seen, the French Constituent Assembly gradually proceeded to construct the Third Republic.

The new German Empire was officially proclaimed in January 1871 at the historic French palace in Versailles. King Wilhelm of Prussia became the German Emperor. This picture shows how Bismarck assembled his military officers and representatives from all of the constituent German states in the famous "Hall of Mirrors"—a symbolic site of past French grandeur that made the German celebration all the more humiliating for the French.

(Bismarck Museum/Bildarchiv Preussischer Kulturbesitz)

The consolidation of Germany transformed the face of Europe. It reversed the dictum not only of the Peace of Vienna but even of the Peace of Westphalia. The German Empire, no sooner born, was the strongest state on the continent of Europe. Rapidly industrialized after 1870, it became more potent still. Bismarck, by consummate astuteness, by exploiting the opportunities offered by a Europe in flux and with no more fighting than that involved in a few weeks in three short wars, had brought about what European statesmen of many nationalities had long said should at all costs be prevented. He outwitted everybody in turn, including the Germans. The united all-German state that issued from the nationalist movement was a Germany conquered by Prussia. Prussia, with its annexations of 1866, embraced almost all Germany north of the Main River. Within the empire it had about two-thirds of the area. Before such unanswerable success the Prussian liberals capitulated, and the Prussian parliament passed an indemnity act; the gist of it was that Bismarck admitted to a certain high-handedness during the constitutional struggle but that the parliament

The strength of the German state

legalized the disputed tax collections *ex post facto,* agreeing to forgive and forget, in view of the victory over Austria and its consequences. Thus liberalism withered away before nationalism.

The German Empire received substantially the constitution of the North German Confederation. It was a federation of monarchies, each based in theory on divine or hereditary right. At the same time, in the Reichstag elected by universal male suffrage, it rested on a kind of mass appeal and was in a sense democratic. Yet the country's ministers were responsible to the emperor and not to the elected chamber. Moreover, it was the rulers who joined the empire, not the peoples. There were no popular plebiscites as in Italy. Each state kept its own laws, government, and constitution. The people of Prussia, for example, remained for Prussian affairs under the rather illiberal constitution of 1850, while in affairs of the Reich, or empire, they enjoyed an equal vote by universal suffrage. The emperor, who was also the king of Prussia, had legal control over the foreign and military policy of the empire. The German Empire in effect served as a mechanism to magnify the role of Prussia, the Prussian army, and the East Elbian Prussian aristocracy in world affairs.

66.   THE DUAL MONARCHY OF AUSTRIA-HUNGARY

The Habsburg Empire after 1848

Bismarck united Germany, but he also divided it, for he left about a sixth of the Germans outside his German Empire. These Germans of Austria and Bohemia had now to work out a common future with the dozen other nationalities in the Danubian domain.

Habsburg resilience

The clumsiness of the old Habsburg multinational empire is clear enough, but more impressive is its astonishing capacity to live and to survive. Prussia and France, in the 1740s, had tried unsuccessfully to dismember it. Smashed four different times by the French between 1796 and 1809, it outlived this crisis, and after 1815, under Metternich, it guided the counsels of Europe. Broken up in 1848, restored by the intervention of Russia in 1849, dislocated by its effort at mobilization in 1855, attacked by Napoleon III in 1859 and by Bismarck in 1866, it still continued to hold together and disappeared finally only in 1918 in the cataclysm of the First World War. But the events of the 1850s and 1860s greatly altered its character.

The essential question, in a nationalist age, was how the Habsburg government would react to the problems raised by national self-expression. By Habsburg, in this period, one means primarily Francis Joseph, who as emperor from 1848 to 1916 reigned even longer than his famous contemporary, Queen Victoria. Francis Joseph, like many others, could never shake off his own tradition. His thoughts turned on his house and on its rights. Buffeted unmercifully by the waves of change and by central European nationalisms, he cordially disliked everything liberal, progressive, or modern. Personally, Francis Joseph was incapable of enlarged views, ambitious projects, bold decisions, or persevering action. And he lived in a pompous dream world, surrounded in the imperial court by great noblemen, high churchmen, and bespangled personages of the army.

Germanic centralization

Yet the government was not idle; it was, if anything, too fertile in devising new deals and new dispensations. Various expedients were tried after 1849, but none was tried long enough to see if it would work. For several years the ruling idea was centralization—to govern the empire through the German language and with German efficiency, maintaining the abolition of serfdom as accomplished in 1848 (and which required a strong official control over the landlords if it was to work in practice) and favoring the building of railroads and other apparatus of material progress. This Germanic and bureaucratic centralization was distasteful to the non-German nationalities, and especially to the Magyars. It is important to say Magyars, not Hungarians, because the Magyars composed less than half the very mixed population of Hungary within its then existing borders. Nevertheless the Magyars, as the strongest of the non-German groups, and hence the most able to maintain a political system of their own, felt the Germanic influence as most oppressive. In the war of 1859 the Magyars sympathized with the Italians.

The Compromise of 1867

In 1867 a compromise was made, known as the *Ausgleich*. It was essentially a bargain between the Germans of Austria-Bohemia and the Magyars of Hungary. It worked to the common disadvantage of the Slavs, who were viewed as a backward, less civilized people by both the Germans and the Magyars. The compromise created a Dual Monarchy, of a kind unparalleled in Europe. West of the river Leith was the Empire of Austria; east of it was the Kingdom of Hungary. The two were now judged exactly equal. Each had its own constitution and its own parliament, to which in each country the governing ministry was henceforth to be responsible. The administrative language of Austria would be German; of Hungary, Magyar. Neither state might intervene in the other's affairs. The two were joined by the fact that the same Habsburg ruler should always be emperor in Austria and king in Hungary. Yet the union was not personal only; for, though there was no common parliament, delegates of the two parliaments were to meet together alternately in Vienna and Budapest, and there was to be a common ministry for finance, foreign affairs, and war. To this common ministry of Austria-Hungary both Austrians and Hungarians were to be appointed.

A dual monarchy

In effect, the compromise treated Austria as a kind of German nation-state and Hungary as a Magyar nation-state. But the Germans formed less than half the people of Austria, as did the Magyars of Hungary. Austria included the Slovenes, Czechs, Poles, and Ruthenians (and a few Italians); Hungary included the Slovaks, the Croats, the Serbs, and the Transylvanians, who were essentially Romanians. All these people felt aggrieved.

Both Austria and Hungary, under the Dual Monarchy, were in form constitutional parliamentary states, although the principle of ministerial responsibility was not consistently honored. Neither was democratic. In Austria, after much juggling with voting systems, a true universal male suffrage was instituted in 1907. In Hungary, when the First World War came in 1914, still only a quarter of the adult male population had the vote. Socially, the great reform of 1848, the abolition of serfdom, was not allowed to lead on to upsetting conclusions. The owners of great landed estates, especially in Hungary (but also in parts of the Austrian Empire) remained the unquestionably dominant class. They were surrounded by landless peasants, an agrarian proletariat, composed partly of lower classes of their own nationality and partly of entire peasant peoples, like the Slovaks and Serbs, who had no educated or wealthy class of their own. National and social questions therefore came together. For some nationalities, especially the Magyars, not only a national but also a social and economic ascendancy was at stake. Landlordism became the basic social issue. A landowning class, educated and civilized, faced a depressed peasant mass that was generally left out of the advancing civilization of the day.

National and social questions

̃agoda

St. Petersburg

• Moscow

Orenburg •

U S S I A N   E M P I R E

Don R.

Ural R.

Kiev •

Volga R.

Dnieper R.

Astrakhan •

• Rostov

Dniester R.

BESSARABIA

• Odessa

Sea of Azov

CRIMEA

Caspian Sea

DOBRUJA

Stevastopol •

Black Sea

C A U C A S I A

Baku •

• Sinope

O T T O M A N   E M P I R E

Constantinople •

Tabriz •

Dardanelles

Tigris R.

Smyrna •

PERSIA

Euphrates R.

M E S O P O T A M I A

CYPRUS
(Turkish)

SYRIA

Baghdad •

ETE (Turkish)

ARABIA

0   100   200   300 miles

EUROPE, 1871

This map shows the existence of the newly unified German Empire and a unified Kingdom of Italy. The German domain was enlarged by the incorporation of Schleswig (in the neck of the Danish peninsula) and the annexation from France of Alsace and parts of Lorraine (the regions around Strassburg and Metz on the map). From 1871 to 1914, Europe had fewer separate states than at any other time in its history. There were no further changes in national borders during this period except for the voluntary separation of Norway and Sweden in 1905 and various realignments in southeastern Europe as the Ottoman Empire withdrew from the Balkans.

67.   LIBERALIZATION IN TSARIST RUSSIA: ALEXANDER II

Tsarist Russia after 1856

For Russia also the Crimean War set off a series of changes. The ungainly empire, an "enormous village" as it has been called, stretching from Poland to the Pacific, had proved unable to repel a localized attack by France and Great Britain, into which neither of the Western powers had put anything like its full resources. Alexander II (1855–1881), who became tsar during the war, was no liberal by nature or conviction. But he saw that something drastic must be done. The prestige of western Europe was at its height. There the most successful and even enviable nations were to be found. The reforms in Russia therefore followed, at some distance, the European model.

Imperial Russia was a political organization very difficult to describe. Its own subjects did not know what to make of it. Some, called Westernizers in the mid–nineteenth century, believed Russia destined to become more like Europe. Others, the Slavophiles, believed Russia to be entrusted with a special destiny of its own, which imitation of Europe would only weaken or pervert.

Autocracy of the tsar

That Russia differed from Europe at least in degree was doubted by nobody. The leading institution was the autocracy of the tsar. This was not exactly the absolutism known in the West. In Russia certain very old European conceptions were missing, such as the idea that spiritual authority is independent of even the mightiest prince or the old feudal idea of reciprocal duties between king and subject. The notion that people have certain rights or claims for justice at the hands of power, which no one in Europe had ever expressly repudiated, was in Russia a somewhat doctrinaire importation from the West. The tsardom did not rule by law; it ran the country by ukase, police action, and the army. The tsars, since Peter and before, had built up their state very largely by importing European technical methods and technical experts, often against strong objection by native Russians of all classes, upon whom the new methods were, when necessary, simply forced. More than any state in Europe, the Russian empire was a machine superimposed upon its people without organic connection—bureaucracy pure and simple. But as the contacts with Europe were joined, many Russians acquired European ideas in which the autocracy was not interested—ideas of liberty and fraternity, of a just and classless society, of individual personality enriched by humane culture and moral freedom. Many people with such sentiments found themselves chronically critical of the government and of Russia itself. The government, massive though it seemed, was afraid of such people. Any idea arising outside official circles seemed pernicious, and the press and the universities were as a rule severely censored.

The severity of Russian serfdom

A second fundamental institution, which had grown up with the tsardom, was legalized bondage or serfdom. The bulk of the population were serfs dependent upon masters. Russian serfdom was more onerous than that found in east-central Europe until 1848. It resembled the slavery of the Americas in that serfs were "owned"; they could be bought and sold and used in occupations other than agriculture. Some serfs worked the soil, rendering unpaid labor service to the gentry. Others could be used by their owners in factories or mines or rented out for such purposes. Others were more independent, working as artisans or mechanics, and even traveling about or residing in the cities, but from their earnings they had to remit certain fees to the lord or return home when he called them. The owners had a certain paternalistic responsibility for their serfs, and in the villages the gentry constituted a kind of personal local government. The law, as in the American South, did little or nothing to interfere between gentry and servile mass, so that the serfs' day-to-day fortunes depended on the personality or economic circumstances of their owners.

By the mid–nineteenth century both conservative and liberal Russians were agreeing that serfdom must someday end. Serfdom was in any case ceasing to be profitable; some two-thirds of all the privately owned serfs (that is, those not belonging to the tsar or state) were mortgaged as security for loans at the time of Alexander II's accession. Increasingly serfdom was recognized as a bad system of labor relations, making the muzhiks into illiterate and stolid drudges, without incentive, initiative, self-respect, or pride of workmanship, and also very poor soldiers for the army.

Educated Russians, full of Western ideas, were estranged from the government, from the Orthodox church, which was an arm of the tsar, and from the common people of their own country. They felt ill at ease in a nation of uneducated peasants and a pang of guilt at the virtual slavery on which their own position rested. Hence arose, at about the time under discussion, another distinctive feature of Russian life, the intelligentsia. In Russia it was thought so exciting to be educated, to have ideas, to subscribe to magazines, or engage in critical conversation that the intelligentsia sensed themselves as a class apart. They were made up of students, university graduates, and persons who had a good deal of leisure to read. Such people, while not very free to think, were more free to think than to do almost anything else. The Russian intelligentsia tended to sweeping and all-embracing philosophies. They believed that intellectuals should play a large role in society. They formed an exaggerated idea of the direct influence of thinkers upon the course of historical change. Their characteristic attitude was one of opposition. Some, overwhelmed by the mammoth immobility of the tsardom and of serfdom, turned to revolutionary and even terroristic philosophies. This only made the bureaucrats more anxious and fearful, and the government more fitfully repressive.

Western ideas and education

The Emancipation Act of 1861 and Other Reforms

Alexander II, on becoming tsar in 1855, attempted to enlist the support of the liberals among the intelligentsia. He gave permission to travel outside Russia, eased the controls on the universities, and allowed the censorship to go relatively unenforced. Newspapers and journals were founded, and those written by Russian revolutionaries abroad, like the *Polar Star* of Alexander Herzen in London, penetrated more freely into the country. The result was a great outburst of public opinion, which was agreed at least on one point, the necessity of emancipating the peasants. This was in principle hardly a party question. Alexander's father, Nicholas I, had been a noted reactionary, who abhorred Western liberalism and is memorable for having organized, as the "Third Section" of his chancellory, a system of secret political police until then unparalleled in Europe for its arbitrary and inquisitorial methods. Yet Nicholas I had taken serious measures to alleviate serfdom. Alexander II, basically conservative on Russian affairs, proceeded to set up a special branch of the government to study the question. The government did not wish to throw the whole labor system and economy of the country into chaos, nor to ruin the gentry class without which it could not govern at all. After many discussions, proposals, and memoranda, an imperial ukase of 1861 declared serfdom abolished and the peasants free.

By this great decree the peasants became legally free in the Western sense. They were henceforth subjects of the government, not subjects of their owners. It was hoped that they would be stirred by a new sense of human dignity. As one enthusiastic official put it shortly after emancipation: "The people are erect and transformed; the look, the walk, the speech, everything is changed." The gentry lost their old quasi-manorial jurisdiction over the villages. They could no longer exact forced and unpaid labor or receive fees arising from servitude.

Land allocation

It is important to realize what the Act of Emancipation did and did not do. Roughly (with great differences from region to region) it allocated about half the cultivated land to the gentry and half to the former serfs. The latter had to pay redemption money for the land they received and for the fees which the gentry lost. The Russian aristocracy was far from weakened; in place of a kind of human property largely mortgaged anyway, they now had clear possession of some half the land, they received the redemption money, and were rid of obligations to the peasants.

The peasants, on the other hand, now owned some half the arable land in their own right—a considerable amount by the standards of almost any European country. They did not, however, possess it according to the principles of private property or independent farming that had become prevalent in Europe. The peasant land, when redeemed, became the collective property of the ancient peasant village assembly, or *mir.* The village, as a unit, was responsible to the government for payment of the redemption and for collection of the necessary sums from its individual members. The village assembly, in default of collection, might require forced labor from the defaulter or a member of his family; and it could prevent peasants from moving away from the village, lest those remaining bear the whole burden of payment. It could (as in the past) assign and reassign certain lands to its members for tillage and otherwise supervise cultivation as a joint concern. To keep the village community intact, the government presently forbade the selling or mortgaging of land to persons outside the village. This tended to preserve the peasant society but also to discourage the investment of outside capital, with which equipment might be purchased, and so to retard agricultural improvement and the growth of wealth.

Inequality among peasants

Not all peasants within the village unit were equal. As in France before the Revolution, some had the right to work more land than others. Some were only day laborers. Others had rights of inheritance in the soil (for not all land was subject to reassignment by the commune) or rented additional parcels of land belonging to the gentry. These lands they worked by hiring other peasants for wages. These more substantial peasants, as agricultural entrepreneurs, resembled farmers of the type found in France or the United States. None of the Russian peasants, however, after the emancipation, possessed full individual freedom of action. In their movements and obligations, as in their thoughts, they were restricted by their villages as they had once been restricted by their lords.

Alexander II proceeded to overhaul and westernize the legal system of the country. With the disappearance of the lord's jurisdiction over his peasants a new system of local courts was needed in any case, but the opportunity was taken to reform the courts from bottom to top. The arbitrariness of authority and defenselessness of the subject were the inveterate evils. They were greatly mitigated by the edict of 1864. Trials were made public, and private persons received the right to be represented in court by lawyers of their own choosing. All class distinctions in judicial matters were abolished, although in practice

The emancipation of the peasants in Russia transformed the legal status of the former serfs and opened opportunities for the development of more prosperous peasant communities. There was still much poverty in the Russian countryside after 1861, but the people who are drinking and playing music outside this rural Russian house seem to be part of the prospering post-emancipation peasant class.

(Library of Congress)

peasants continued to be subject to harsh disadvantages. A clear sequence of lower and higher courts was established. Requirements were laid down for the professional training of judges, who henceforth received stated salaries and were protected from administrative pressure. A system of juries on the English model was introduced.

A system of self-government

While thus attempting to establish a rule of law, the tsar also moved in the direction of allowing self-government. He hoped to win over the liberals and to shoulder the upper and middle classes with some degree of public responsibility. He created, again by an edict of 1864, a system of provincial and district councils called zemstvos. Elected by various elements, including the peasants, the zemstvos gradually went into operation and took up matters of education, medical relief, public welfare, food supply, and road maintenance in their localities. Their great value was in developing civic sentiment among those who took part in them. Many liberals urged a representative body for all Russia, a Zemsky Sobor or Duma, which, however, Alexander II refused to concede. After 1864 his policy became more cautious. A rebellion in Poland in 1863 inclined him to take advice from those who favored repression. He began to mollify the vested interests that had been disgruntled by the reforms and to whittle down some of the concessions already granted. But the essence of the reforms remained unaffected.

Revolutionism in Russia

The autocrat who thus undertook to liberalize Russia barely escaped assassination in 1866, had five shots fired at him in 1873, missed death by half an hour in 1880 when his imperial dining room was dynamited, and in 1881 was to be killed by a bomb. The revolutionaries were not pleased with the reforms, which if successful would merely strengthen the existing order. Dissatisfied intelligentsia in the 1860s began to call themselves "nihilists": they believed in "nothing"—except science—and took a cynical view of the reforming tsar and his zemstvos. The peasants, saddled with heavy redemption payments, remained basically unsatisfied, and intellectuals toured the villages fanning this discontent. Revolutionaries developed a mystic conception of the revolutionary role of the Russian masses. Socialists, after the failure of socialism in Europe in the Revolution of 1848, came in many cases to believe, as Alexander Herzen wrote, that the true and natural future of socialism lay in Russia, because of the very weakness of capitalism in Russia and the existence of a kind of collectivism already established in the village assemblies or communes.

Bakunin and anarchism

More radical than Herzen were the anarchist Bakunin and his disciple Nechaiev. In their *People's Justice* these two called for terrorism not only against tsarist officials but against liberals also. As they wrote in the *Catechism of a Revolutionist,* the true revolutionary "is devoured by one purpose, one thought, one passion—the revolution. . . . He has severed every link with the social order and with the entire civilized world. . . . Everything which promotes the success of the revolution is moral, everything which hinders it is immoral." Terrorism (which is really to say assassination) was rejected by many of the revolutionaries, especially by those who in the 1870s took up the scientific socialism of Karl Marx. To Marx it did not seem that frantic violence would advance an inevitable social process. But other groups, recognizing the inspiration of men like Bakunin and Nechaiev, organized secret terroristic societies. One of these, the People's Will, determined to assassinate the tsar. In an autocratic state, they held, there was no other road to justice and freedom.

Alexander II, alarmed by this underground menace, which of course did not escape the attention of the police, again turned for support to the liberals. The liberals, who were themselves threatened by the revolutionaries, had become estranged from the government by its failure to follow through with the reforms of the early 1860s. Now, in 1880, to rally support, the tsar again relaxed the autocratic system. He abolished the dreaded Third Section or secret police set up by his father, allowed the press to discuss most political subjects freely, and encouraged the zemstvos to do the same. Further to associate representatives of the public with the government, he proposed, not exactly a parliament, but two nationally elected commissions to sit with the council of state. He signed the edict to this effect on March 13, 1881, and on the same day was assassinated, not by a demented individual acting wildly and alone, but by the joint efforts of the highly trained members of the People's Will.

Alexander III, upon his father's death, abandoned the project for elected commissions and during his whole reign, from 1881 to 1894, reverted to a program of brutal resistance to liberals and revolutionaries alike. The new regime established by peasant emancipation, judicial reform, and the zemstvos was nevertheless allowed to continue. How Russia finally received a parliament in 1905 is explained below in the chapter on the Russian Revolution. At present it is enough to have seen how even tsarist Russia, under Alexander II, shared in a liberal movement that was then at its height. The abolition of serfdom, putting both aristocrat and peasant more fully on a money economy, opened the way for capitalistic development within the empire. And between the two confining walls of autocracy and revolutionism—equally hard and unyielding—European ideas of law, liberty, and humanity began to spread in a tentative way.

Between autocracy and revolutionism

68.   THE UNITED STATES: THE AMERICAN CIVIL WAR

The history of Europe, long interconnected with that of the rest of the world, by the early twentieth century became merged with it entirely. Similarly the development of non-European regions, long a collection of separate stories, was to fuse into a single worldwide theme, to which later chapters of this book are largely devoted. It is no great leap at this point to pass to a treatment of areas outside Europe, some of which underwent in the 1860s the same process of national consolidation, or attempted consolidation, already traced in Italy and Germany, Austria, Hungary, and the Russian empire. In particular, foundations were laid for two new powerful nation-states like those of Europe—the United States of America and the Empire of Japan. The huge Dominion of Canada was also established.

Growth of the United States

As in the time of the American Revolution and Napoleon, the history of the United States in the nineteenth century reflected that of the European world of which it formed a part. The most basic fact, besides territorial expansion, was rapid growth. This was so obvious as to lead a French observer in the 1830s, Alexis de Tocqueville, to make a famous prediction: that within a century the United States would have 100 million people and would, along with Russia, be one of the two leading powers of the world. By 1860, with 31 million, the United States was almost as populous as France and more so than Great Britain.

The growth in numbers was due to a prolific birth rate, but also to the arrival of immigrants, who became prolific in their turn. The immigrants in

Immigration

this era—except for an uncounted, because illegal, importation of slaves—came almost entirely from Europe, and before 1860 almost entirely from Great Britain, Ireland, and Germany. The immigrants did not desire to surrender their native ways. Some brought skills that the new country greatly needed, but immigration also presented a true social problem, obliging peoples to live together without common tradition. On the whole, it appears that the older Americans accepted the reshaping of their country rather calmly, with antiforeign movements occasionally surfacing but then quickly subsiding. Few concessions were made to the immigrant populations. English was the language of the public schools, the police, law courts, local government, and public notices and announcements. Usually the immigrant had to know some English to hold a job. On the other hand no one was exactly forced to become "Americanized"—the new arrivals were free to maintain churches, newspapers, and social gatherings in their own tongues. The fact that the English, Scots, and Irish already spoke English, and that the Germans readily learned it, alleviated the language issue. The immigrants did not constitute minorities in the European sense. They were more than willing to embrace American national attitudes as formed in the eighteenth century—the national traditions of republicanism and self-government, of individual liberty, free enterprise, and unbounded opportunity for self-improvement. The old America impressed itself on the new, being somewhat impressed itself in the process. In this sense a new nationality was being consolidated.

The Estrangement of North and South

But at the same time the nation was falling to pieces. North and South became completely estranged. The Industrial Revolution had contrary effects on the two regions. It turned the South into an economic associate of Great Britain. The South became the world's chief producer of raw cotton for the Lancashire mills. The Southerners, living by the export of a cash crop, and producing virtually no manufactures, wished to purchase manufactured goods as cheaply as possible. Hence they favored free trade, especially with Great Britain. In the North, the Industrial Revolution led to the building of factories. Northern factory owners, usually backed by their workers, demanded protection from the inflow of British goods, with which no other country at the time could easily compete. The North therefore favored a high tariff, which the South declared to be ruinous.

More fundamental was the difference in the status of labor. As the demand for raw cotton reached unprecedented magnitudes the South fell more deeply under the hereditary curse of the Americas—the slave and plantation system. In the nineteenth century slavery increasingly revolted the moral conscience of thoughtful people on both sides of the Atlantic. It was abolished in the British colonies in 1833, in the French colonies in 1848, and in the Spanish American republics at different dates in the first half of the century. Similarly, serfdom was abolished in the Habsburg possessions in 1848 and in Russia in 1861. The American South could not, and after about 1830 no longer even wished to, shake the system off. The South was the Cotton Kingdom whose "peculiar institution" controlled the unfree labor of blacks. Whites were hurt by the system as well as blacks. Few free workers could prosper alongside a mass of subservient and virtually uncompensated labor. The incoming Europeans settled overwhelmingly in the North, the South remaining more purely "Anglo-Saxon"—except that in its most densely peopled areas some half of the people were of African descent.

Slave labor and the plantation system

In the movement westward, common in North and South, the pressure in the South came mainly from planters wishing to establish new plantations and in the North from persons hoping to set up small farms and from businessmen bent on founding new towns, building railroads, and creating markets. As once France and Great Britain had fought for control beyond the Alleghenies, so now North and South fought for control beyond the Mississippi. In 1846 the United States made war upon Mexico by methods at which Bismarck would not have blushed. The North widely denounced the war as an act of Southern aggression but was willing enough to take the ensuing territorial conquests, which comprised the region from Texas to the Pacific. The first new state created in this region, California, prohibited slavery. Since 1820 the United States had held together precariously by the Missouri Compromise, under which new states, as set up in the West, were admitted to the Union in pairs, one slave and one free, so that a rough equality was maintained in the Senate and in the presidential electoral vote.

With the creation of California this balance of power was upset in favor of the North, so that in return, by the "compromise of 1850," the North agreed to enforce the laws on runaway slaves to the satisfaction of the South. But the new strictness toward fugitive slaves ran against mounting sentiment in the North. Attempts to arrest blacks in free states and return

The compromise of 1850

them to slavery aroused abolitionist sentiment to a higher pitch. The abolitionists, a branch of the humanitarian movement then sweeping the European world, and somewhat resembling the radical democrats who came forward in Europe in 1848, demanded the immediate and total elimination of slavery, without concession, compromise, or compensation for the property interests of the slave owners. Abolitionists denounced the Union itself as the unholy accomplice in a social abomination.

By 1860 a sense of sectionalism had developed in the South not different in principle from the nationalism felt by many peoples in Europe. In their proud insistence on states' rights and constitutional liberties, their aristocratic and warlike codes of ethics, their demand for independence from outside influence and for freedom in ruling their own subject people, the Southern whites suggested nothing in Europe so much as the Magyars of the Austrian Empire. They now wondered whether their way of life could be safely maintained within the Union which they had helped to create. They viewed Northerners as outsiders, unsympathetic, foreign, hostile, and the South as potentially an independent and distinct nation. They were aware that within the Union they were increasingly a minority; for where in 1790 North and South had been approximately equal, by 1860 the North had outrun the South in population, mainly because of the stream of migration from Europe. The incipient nationalism of the South resembled the nationalist sentiments of a small nation struggling against a great empire. In the North, nationalism favored maintaining the whole existing territory of the United States. Northerners by 1860, with a few exceptions, refused to admit that any state of the Union could withdraw, or secede, for any reason.

In 1860 the new Republican party elected Abraham Lincoln president. It advanced a program of free Western lands for small farmers, a higher tariff, transcontinental railroad building, and economic and capitalistic development on a national scale. The new party's radical wing, to which Lincoln himself did not belong, was vehemently abolitionist and anti-Southern in

Lincoln and the secession of the South

sentiment. Southern leaders, after the election of Lincoln, brought about the formal withdrawal of their states from the United States of America and the creation of the Confederate States of America reaching from Virginia to Texas. Lincoln ordered the armed forces to defend the territory of the United States, and the resulting Civil War, or war of Southern independence, lasting four years and involving battles as great as those of Napoleon, was the most harrowing struggle of the nineteenth century with the exception of the Taiping rebellion in China.

European governments, while never recognizing the Confederacy, were partial to the South. The United States stood for principles still considered revolutionary in Europe, so that while the European working classes generally favored the North, the upper classes were willing enough to see the North American republic end in collapse and failure. In addition, Great Britain and France saw in the breakup of the United States the same advantages that they had formerly seen in the breakup of the Spanish empire. In the Confederate States the British, and the French to a lesser degree, expected to find another free trade country, supplying western Europe with raw materials and buying its manufactures; in short, they saw not a competitor like the North, but a complementary partner to the industry of the Old World. It was likewise during the American Civil War that a French army sent by Napoleon III invaded Mexico to create a puppet empire under an Austrian archduke. Thus the only serious attempt to ignore the Monroe Doctrine, violate the independence of Latin America, and revive European colonialism in the Americas occurred at the time when the United States was in dissolution.

The Union upheld

But the North won the war and the Union was upheld. The Mexicans rid themselves of their unwanted emperor. Tsar Alexander II sold Alaska to the United States. The war ended the idea of the Union as a confederation of member states from which members might withdraw at will. In its place triumphed the idea that the United States was a national state, composed not of member states but of a unitary people irrevocably bound together. This doctrine was written explicitly into the Fourteenth Amendment to the Constitution, which pronounced all Americans to be citizens not only of their several states but of the United States and forbade any state to "deprive any person of life, liberty or property without due process of law"—"due process" to be determined by authority of the national government. The new force of central authority was felt first of all in the South. President Lincoln, using his war powers, issued the Emancipation Proclamation in 1863, abolishing slavery in areas engaged in hostilities against the United States. The Thirteenth Amendment in 1865 abolished slavery everywhere in the country. No compensation was paid to the slave owners, who were therefore financially ruined. The abolitionist campaign for the human rights of black Americans prevailed over the historic American deference to the rights of property. The legal authority of the United States was thus used for an annihilation of individual property rights without parallel (outside modern communism) in the history of the Western world; for neither the nobility in the French Revolution, nor the Russian serf owners in 1861, nor the slave owners of the West Indies in the nineteenth century, nor the owners of businesses nationalized by twentieth-century socialists in western Europe had to face such a total and overwhelming loss of property values as the slave owners of the American South.

After the Civil War: Reconstruction; Industrial Growth

The assassination of Lincoln in 1865 by a fanatical Southern patriot strengthened those radical Republicans who said that the South must be drastically reformed. With the old Southern upper class completely ruined, Northerners of many types poured into the defeated country. Some came to represent the federal government, some to dabble in local politics, some to make money, and a great many out of democratic and humanitarian impulses, to teach the distressed ex-slaves the elements of reading and writing or of useful trades. Blacks in the South voted, sat in legislatures, occupied public office. This period, called Reconstruction, may be compared to the most advanced phase of the French Revolution, in that "radical republicans" undertook to press liberty and equality upon a recalci-

Les nègres affranchis colportant le décret d'affranchissement du président Lincoln.

The victories of Union armies during the American Civil War preserved the unity of the United States and also gave the national government the power to abolish slavery. This illustration from a French journal in 1863 provides a European image of newly freed people celebrating President Lincoln's Emancipation Proclamation and leaving the places where they had been enslaved. Lincoln's proclamation is posted on the side of the coach.

trant country, under conditions of emergency rule and under the auspices of a highly centralized national government with a mobilized army. The Southern whites strenuously objected, and the Northern radicals discredited themselves and gradually lost their zeal. Reconstruction was abandoned in the 1870s, and, by what Europeans would call a counterrevolution, the Southern whites and even members of the old planter class gradually regained control.

The Northern business interests—financiers, bankers, company promoters, railway builders, manufacturers—expanded greatly with the wartime demand for munitions and military provisioning. They received protection by the Morrill tariff of 1861. In the next year, partly as a war

The dominance of business and finance

measure, the Union Pacific Railroad was incorporated, and in 1869, at a remote spot in Utah, the last spike was driven in the first railroad to span the American continent. The Homestead Act, providing farms to settlers on easy conditions, and the granting of public lands to certain colleges (ever since called land-grant colleges), largely for the promotion of agricultural sciences, encouraged the push of population and civilization into the West. Vast tracts of land were given by the government to subsidize railway building. With the destruction of the Southern slaveholders, who before the war had counterbalanced the rising industrialists, it was now industry and finance that dominated national politics in the increasingly centralized United States. The Fourteenth Amendment, for many years, was mainly interpreted not to protect the civil rights of individual persons but the property rights of business corporations against restrictive legislation by the states. The shift of political power from the states to the federal government accompanied and protected the shift of economic enterprise from local businesses to far-flung and continent-embracing corporations. As in France under Napoleon III, there was a good deal of corruption, fraud, speculation, and dishonestly or rapaciously acquired wealth; but industry boomed, the cities grew, and the American mass market was created. On Fifth Avenue in New York, and in other Northern cities, rose the pretentious and gaudy mansions of the excessively rich.

In short, the American Civil War, which might have reduced English-speaking America to a scramble of jealously competing minor republics, resulted instead in the economic and political consolidation of a large nation-state, liberal and democratic in its political principles, and committed enthusiastically to private enterprise in its economic system.

69.   THE DOMINION OF CANADA, 1867

North of the United States, at the time of the Civil War, lay a number of British provinces unconnected with one another and each in varying degree dependent on Great Britain. The population had originated in three great streams. One part was French, settled in the St. Lawrence valley since the seventeenth century. A second part was made up of descendants of United Empire Loyalists, old seaboard colonists who, remaining faithful to Britain, had fled from the United States during the American Revolution. They were numerous in the Maritime Provinces and in Upper Canada, as Ontario was then called (see map, p. 516). A third part consisted of recent immigrants from Great Britain, men and women of the working classes who had left the home country to improve themselves in America.

French resistance to assimilation

The French firmly resisted assimilation to the English-speaking world around them. Their statute of freedom was the Quebec Act of 1774, which had been denounced as "intolerable" by the aroused inhabitants of the thirteen colonies, but which put the French civil law, French language, and French Catholic church under the protection of the British Crown. The French looked with apprehension upon the stream of immigrants, English-speaking and Protestant, which began to flow into Canada about 1780 and thereafter never stopped. There was constant irritation between the two nationalities.

Upper and Lower Canada

The British government tried various expedients. In 1791 it created two provinces in the St. Lawrence and Great Lakes region—a Lower Canada to remain French, and an Upper Canada to be English. They received the same form of government as that enjoyed by the thirteen colonies before their break from the empire. Each colony, that is, had a locally elected assembly with certain powers of taxation and lawmaking, subject to veto by the British authorities, as represented either by the governor or by the London government itself. For many years there was no objection to these arrangements. The War of 1812, in which the United States embarked on the conquest of Canada, aroused a national sentiment among both French and English in that country, together with a willingness to depend politically upon Great Britain for military security. But the internal political differences continued. In Lower Canada the French feared the English-speaking minority. In Upper Canada the old aristocracy of United Empire Loyalists, who had carved the province from the wilderness, hesitated to share control with the new immigrants from Great Britain. Between the provinces there were grievances also, since Lower Canada stood in the way of Upper Canada's outlet to the sea. In 1837 a superficial rebellion broke out in both provinces. It was put down virtually without bloodshed.

Lord Durham's Report

In Great Britain at this time the reforming Whigs were busily renovating many ancient English institutions. Some of them had definite views on the administration of colonies. In general, they held that it was not necessary to control a region politically to trade with it. This was an aspect of the free trade doctrine, separating economics from politics, business from power. The Whig reformers were rather indifferent to empire, unconcerned with military, naval, or strategic considerations. A few even thought it natural for colonies, when mature, to drop away entirely from the mother country. Whigs, liberals, and radicals all wished to economize on military expenditure, to relieve British taxpayers by cutting down British garrisons overseas.

After the Canadian insurrection of 1837 the Whig government sent out the Earl of Durham as governor. Durham, one of the framers of the parliamentary Reform Bill of 1832, published his views on Canadian affairs in 1839. Durham's Report was long regarded as one of the classic documents in the rise of the British Commonwealth of Nations. He held that in the long run French separatist feeling in Canada should be extinguished and all Canadians should be brought to feel a common citizenship and national character. He therefore called for the reuniting of the two Canadas into one province. To consolidate this province he *Call for reuniting the provinces* proposed an intensive development of railways and canals. In political matters he urged the granting of virtual self-government for Canada and the introduction of the British system of "responsible government," in which the elected assembly should control the executive ministers in the province, the governor becoming a kind of legal and ceremonial figure like the sovereign in Great Britain.

Most of Durham's Report was accepted immediately. Upper and Lower Canada were combined into one province, with the machinery of self-government, in 1840. The British army was withdrawn. The Canadians undertook to maintain their own military establishment, still regarded as necessary, since the era of the famous undefended frontier between Canada and the United States had not yet dawned. The principle of responsible government was established in the late 1840s, the governors of Canada allowing the elected assembly to adopt policies and appoint or remove ministers as it chose. Responsible government, still confined to internal matters, worked satisfactorily from the beginning. But one feature of the new plan, the union of the two Canadas, began to produce friction as the English-speaking immigration continued. The *The appeal of a federation* French were afraid of being outnumbered in their own country. Many Canadians therefore turned to the idea of a federation, in which the French and English areas might each conduct its own local affairs, while remaining joined for larger purposes in a central government.

Founding of the Dominion of Canada

Federalism in Canada was thus partly a decentralizing idea, aimed at satisfying the French element by a redivision into two provinces, and in part a plan for a new centralization or unification, because it contemplated bringing all the provinces of British North America into union with the St. Lawrence and Great Lakes region, to which alone the term Canada had hitherto been applied. While the people of British North America discussed federation the Civil War was disrupting the United States. In the face of this unpleasant example, the Canadians formed a strong union in which all powers were to rest in the central government except those specifically assigned to the provinces. The federal constitution, drafted in Canada by Canadians, was passed through the British Parliament in 1867 as the British North America Act, which constitutionally established the Dominion of Canada. The eastern maritime provinces (Nova Scotia, New Brunswick, and Prince Edward Island) joined Quebec and Ontario in the Dominion, and the new political arrangements facilitated Canada's rapid westward expansion to the Pacific coast. In 1982 the British North America Act was replaced by a new agreement, which explicitly recognized the sovereign independence of Canada and its power to frame a constitution for itself. By the 1980s, however, the French speakers of Quebec had become more determined to defend the autonomy of their own province and culture, so it was again necessary to recognize a special status for Quebec. The western provinces had also grown and become more protective of their interests. The relationship between the central and provincial governments, along with bilingualism, or the equal recognition of the French and English languages, again became serious problems.

By the legislation of 1867 the new dominion received a common federal parliament, in which a ministry responsible to the majority in parliament governed according to British principles of "responsible," or cabinet, government. The Dominion of Canada, though at first not large in population, possessed from the beginning a significance beyond the mere number of its people. It was the first example of successful devolution, or granting of political liberty, within one of the European colonial empires. It embodied principles which Edmund Burke and Benjamin Franklin had vainly recommended a century before to keep the thirteen colonies loyal to Great Britain. The dominion after 1867 moved forward from independence in internal matters to independence in such external affairs as tariffs, diplomacy, and the decisions of war and peace. It thus pioneered in the development of "dominion status," working out precedents later applied in Australia (1901), New Zealand (1907), the Union of South Africa (1910), and in the 1920s, temporarily, in Ireland. By the middle of the twentieth century the same idea, or what may be called the Canadian idea, was also applied to the worldwide process of decolonization as it affected non-European peoples, notably in India, Pakistan, Sri Lanka, and the former British colonies in Africa, until all these peoples chose to become republics, though still loosely and voluntarily joined together and to Great Britain in a Commonwealth of Nations.

Pioneering dominion status

More immediately, in America, the founding of the dominion, a solid band of self-governing territory stretching from ocean to ocean, stabilized the relations between British North America and the United States. The United States regarded its northern borders as final. The withdrawal of British control from Canadian affairs furthered the United States conception of an American continent entirely free from European political influence.

✒ 70. JAPAN AND THE WEST

The Japanese, when they allowed the Westerners to discover them, were a highly civilized people living in a complex society. They had many large cities, they enjoyed the contemplation of natural scenery, they went to the theater, and they read novels. With their stylized manners, their fans and their wooden temples, their lacquer work and their painting on screens, their tiny rice fields and their curious and ineffectual firearms, they seemed to Europeans to be the very acme of everything quaint. This European view of Japan is immortalized in *The Mikado* of Gilbert and Sullivan, first performed in 1885. Not long thereafter the idea of Japanese quaintness, like the idea of the Germans as an impractical people given mainly to music and metaphysics, had to be revised. The Europeans, in "opening" Japan, opened up more than they knew.

In 1853, the American Commodore Perry forced his way with a fleet of naval vessels into Yedo Bay, insisted upon landing, and demanded of the Japanese government that it engage in commercial relations with the United States and other Western powers. In the next year the Japanese began to comply, and in 1867 an internal revolution took place, of which the most conspicuous consequence was a rapid westernizing of Japanese life and institutions. But if it looked as if the country had been "opened" by Westerners, actually Japan had exploded from within.

Background: Two Centuries of Isolation, 1640–1854

For over two centuries Japan had followed a program of self-imposed isolation. No Japanese was allowed to leave the islands or even to build a ship large enough to navigate the high seas. No foreigner, except for handfuls of Dutch and Chinese, was allowed to enter. Japan remained a sealed book to the West. The contrary is not quite so true, for the Japanese knew rather more about Europe than Europeans did about Japan. The Japanese policy of seclusion was not merely based upon ignorance. Initially, at least, it was based on experience.

The first Europeans—three Portuguese in a Chinese junk—are thought to have arrived in Japan in 1542. For about a century thereafter there was considerable coming and going. The Japanese showed a strong desire to trade with the foreigners, from whom they obtained clocks and maps, learned about printing and shipbuilding, and took over the use of tobacco

Early contact with Europeans

and potatoes. Thousands also adopted the Christian religion as preached to them by Spanish and Portuguese Jesuits. Japanese traveled to the Dutch Indies and even to Europe. The Japanese in fact proved more receptive to European ideas than other Asian peoples. But shortly after 1600 the government began to drive Christianity underground; in 1624 it expelled the Spaniards, in 1639 it expelled the Portuguese, and in 1640 it expelled all Europeans except for a few Dutch merchants who were allowed to remain at Nagasaki under strict control. From 1640 to 1854 these few Dutch at Nagasaki were the only channel of communication with the West.

The reasons for self-seclusion, as for its abandonment later, arose from the course of political events in Japan. The history of Japan showed an odd parallel to that of Europe. In Japan, as in Europe, a period of feudal warfare was followed by a period of government absolutism, during which civil peace was kept by a bureaucracy, an obsolescent warrior class was maintained as a privileged element in society, and a commercial class of native merchants grew wealthier, stronger, and more insistent upon its position.

When the first Europeans arrived, the islands were still torn by the wars and rivalries of the numerous clans into which the Japanese were organized. Gradually one clan, the Tokugawa, gained control, taking over the office of "shogun." The shogun was a kind of military head who governed in the name of the emperor, and the hereditary Tokugawa shogunate, founded in 1603, lasted until 1867. The early Tokugawa shoguns concluded from a good deal of evidence that the Europeans in Japan, both merchants and missionaries, were engaging in feudal or interclan politics and even aspiring to dominate Japan by helping Christian or pro-European Japanese to get into power. The first three Tokugawa shoguns, to establish their own dynasty, to pacify and stabilize the country, and to keep Japan free from European penetration, undertook to eliminate Christianity and adopted the rigid policy of nonintercourse with the rest of the world.

The Tokugawa shoguns

Under the Tokugawa Japan enjoyed peace, a long peace, for the first time in centuries. The Tokugawa shoguns completed the detachment of the emperor from politics, building him up as a divine and legendary being, too august and too remote for the hurly-burly of the world. The emperor remained shut in at Kyoto on a modest allowance furnished by the shoguns. The shoguns established their own court and government at Yedo (later called Tokyo); and as Louis XIV brought nobles to Versailles, or Peter the Great forced his uncouth lords to build town houses in St. Petersburg, so the shoguns required the great feudal chieftains and their men-at-arms to reside at least part of the year in Yedo.

Military dictatorship

The shoguns administered the country through a kind of military bureaucracy or dictatorship. This formidable instrument of state watched over the great lords (called daimyo), who, however, retained a good deal of feudal authority over their subjects in the regions most distant from Yedo. The great lords and their armed retainers (the samurai), having no further fighting to occupy them, turned into a landed aristocracy which spent a good deal of its time in Yedo and other cities. As a leisure class, they developed new tastes and standards of living and hence needed more income, which they obtained by squeezing the peasants, and which they spent by buying from the merchants.

The merchant class greatly expanded by catering to the government and the gentry. Japan in the seventeenth century passed on to a money economy. Many lords fell seriously into debt to the merchants. Many samurai, like lesser nobles in France or Poland at the time, were almost ridiculously impoverished, hard-pressed to keep up appearances, with nothing except social status to distinguish them from commoners.

Class divisions

The law, as in Europe under the Old Regime, drew a sharp line between classes. Nobles, merchants, and peasants were subject to different taxes and were differently punished for different offenses. What was a crime for a commoner would be excusable for a samurai; or what in a samurai would be a punishable breach of honor would be accepted in a common person. The samurai had the right to carry two swords as a mark of class and could in theory cut down an impudent commoner without arousing further inquiry. In practice the shoguns repressed violence of this kind, but there was much less development of law and justice than in the European monarchies of the Old Regime. Economically the merchants and artisans prospered. By 1723 Yedo was a city with 500,000 people; by 1800 with over 1,000,000, it was larger than London or Paris, and 20 times as large as the largest city in the United States. After 1800 some merchants were able to purchase the rank of samurai for money. The old class lines were beginning to blur.

Though deliberately secluded, the economic and social life of Japan was thus by no means static. The same is true of its intellectual life. Buddhism, the historic religion, lost its hold on many people during the Tokugawa period, so that Japan in its way underwent, like the West, a secularization of ideas. As a code of personal conduct there was a new emphasis on Bushido, the "way of the warrior," a kind of nonreligious moral teaching which exalted the samurai virtues of honor and loyalty. With the decline of Buddhism went also a revival of the cult of Shinto, the "way of the gods," the ancient indigenous religion of Japan, which held, among much else, that the emperor was veritably the Son of Heaven. There was much activity in the study and writing of history, arousing, as in Europe, an acute interest in the national past. History, like Shinto, led to a feeling that shoguns were usurpers and that the emperor, obscurely relegated to Kyoto, was the true representative of everything highest and most lasting in the life of Japan.

Secularization and Shinto

Meanwhile, through the crack left open at Nagasaki, Western ideas trickled in. The shogun Yoshimune in the mid–eighteenth century permitted the importation of Occidental books, except those relating to Christianity. A few Japanese learned Dutch and began to decipher Dutch books on anatomy, surgery, astronomy, and other subjects. In 1745 a Dutch-Japanese dictionary was completed. For European manufactures also—watches, glassware, velvets, woolens, telescopes, barometers—there came to be an eager demand, satisfied as much as possible by the methodical Dutch. Nor were the Japanese wholly uninformed about politics in the West. While the most assiduous Westerner could learn nothing of the internal affairs of Japan, an educated Japanese could, if he wished, arrive at some idea of the French Revolution, or know who was president of the United States.

The Opening of Japan

When Perry in 1853 made his unwanted visit he therefore had many potential allies within Japan. There were nobles, heavily in debt, unable to draw more income from agriculture, willing to embark upon foreign trade and to exploit their property by introducing new enterprises. There were penurious samurai, with no future in the old system, ready and willing to enter upon new careers as army officers or civil officials. There were merchants hoping to add to their business by dealing in Western goods. There were scholars eager to learn more of Western science and medicine. There were patriots fearful that Japan was becoming defenseless against Western guns. Spiritually the country was already adrift from its moorings, already set toward a course of national self-assertion, restlessly susceptible to hazily understood new ideas. Under such pressures, and from downright fear of a bombardment of Yedo by the Americans, which if it would not subdue Japan would at least ruin the declining prestige of the shogunate, the shogun Iesada in 1854 signed a commercial treaty with the United States. Similar treaties were soon signed with the Europeans.

In the following years were sown the seeds of much later misunderstanding between Japan and the West. The Europeans and Americans tended to be trigger-happy in the discharge of naval ordnance against less well-armed peoples. The Japanese, a proud and elaborately civilized nation, soon found that the whites considered them backward. They found, for example, as soon as they learned more of the West by reading and travel, that the treaties they signed in the 1850s were not treaties between equals as understood in the West. These first treaties provided that Japan should maintain a low tariff on imports and not change it except with the consent of the foreign powers. To give outsiders a voice in determining

The seeds of conflict

JAPAN IN THE LATE TOKUGAWA PERIOD

The Tokugawa regime lasted from 1603 to 1867. The map shows the divisions and power rivalries within Japan around the time that Western nations began to enter the region in the mid-nineteenth century. The Tokugawa shogunate controlled the territory around Yedo (later called Tokyo), but independent nobles in Choshu, Satsuma, and other parts of the country controlled large areas that the shogun at Yedo could not bring under his authority. As the Western powers entered Japan after 1854, a strong demand for reforms emerged in Choshu and Satsuma, leading to the overthrow of the Tokugawa shogun in 1867, the establishment of a new national ("Meiji") government, and the rapid development of a new industrial economy.

tariff policy was not the custom among sovereign states of the West. The early treaties also provided for extraterritoriality. This meant that Europeans and Americans residing in Japan were not subject to Japanese law but remained under the jurisdiction of their respective homelands as represented by consular officials. Such extraterritorial provisions had long been established in Turkey and were currently taking root in China. Europeans insisted upon them in countries where European principles of property, debt, or security of life and person did not prevail. At the same time, of course, no European state ever permitted a foreign power to exercise jurisdiction within its borders. Extraterritoriality was a mark of inferiority, as the Japanese soon discovered.

Antiforeign reaction

A strong antiforeign reaction developed after 1854. It was at first led by certain nobles of the western islands, the lords of Choshu and Satsuma, who had never been fully subordinated to the shogun at Yedo, and who now dreamed of overturning the Tokugawa shogunate and leading a national revival with the emperor as its rallying point. Their first idea was to check Western penetration (as two and a half centuries before) by driving the Westerners out. But in 1862 some Englishmen unintentionally violated a small point of Japanese etiquette. One of them was killed. The British government demanded punishment for the offending Japanese, who were followers of the lord of Satsuma. The shogun proved unable to arrange this, and the

British navy thereupon bombarded the capital of Satsuma. In the same year the lord of Choshu, who commanded the straits of Shimonoseki with some ancient artillery, ordered it to fire on passing vessels. The British, French, Dutch, and United States governments immediately protested, and, when the embarrassed shogun proved unable to discipline Choshu, they dispatched an allied naval force to Shimonoseki. The forts and shipping of Choshu were destroyed, and an indemnity of $3,000,000 was imposed. These incidents were remembered in Japan long after they were forgotten in Europe and the United States. It was likewise remembered that the Western powers, discovering that the shogun was not the supreme ruler of the country, sent a naval expedition to Kyoto itself and required the emperor to confirm the treaties signed by the shogun and to reduce import duties, under threat of naval bombardment.

The Meiji Era (1868–1912): The Westernization of Japan

The lords of Choshu and Satsuma now concluded that the only way to deal with the West was to adopt the military and technical equipment of the West itself. They would save Japan for the Japanese by learning the secrets of the Western power. First they forced the resignation of the shogun, whose prestige had long been undermined anyway and who had now discredited himself first by signing undesirable treaties with the West and then failing to protect the country from outrage. The last shogun abdicated in 1867. The reformers declared the emperor restored to his full authority. It was their intention to use the plenitude of imperial power to consolidate and fortify Japan for its new position in the world. In 1868 a new emperor inherited the throne; his name was Mutsuhito, but according to Japanese custom a name was given to his reign also, which was called Meiji ("enlightened peace"). The Meiji era (1868–1912) was the great era of the westernization of Japan.

Japan turned into a modern nation-state. Feudalism was abolished, most of the great lords voluntarily surrendering into the emperor's hands their control over samurai and common people. "We abolish the clans and convert them into prefectures," declared one imperial decree. The legal system was reorganized and equality before the law was introduced, in the sense that all persons became subject to the same rules regardless of class. In part with the hope of getting rid of extraterritoriality, the reformers recast the criminal law along Western lines, deleting the bizarre and cruel punishments which Europeans considered barbaric. A new army was established, modeled mainly on the Prussian. The samurai in 1871 lost his historic right to carry two swords; he now served as an army officer, not as the retainer of a clannish chief. A navy, modeled on the British, followed somewhat later. Control of money and currency passed to the central government, and a national currency, with decimal units, was adopted. A national postal service began to function, and above all the government developed a national school system, which soon brought a high rate of literacy to Japan. Buddhism was discouraged, and the property of Buddhist monasteries was confiscated. Shinto was the cult favored by the government. Shinto gave a religious tincture to national sentiment and led to a renewed veneration of the imperial family.

A modern nation-state

In 1889 a constitution was promulgated. It confirmed the civil liberties then common in the West and provided for a parliament in two chambers, but it stressed also the supreme and eternal authority of the emperor, to whom the ministers were legally responsible. In practice, in the new Japan, the emperor never actively governed. He remained aloof, as in the past; and political leaders, never fully responsible to the parliament, tended to govern freely in what they conceived to be the interests of the state.

Distinctive characteristics of Japan's new industrial economy appear in this illustration of a silk reeling factory by the artist Ichiyosai. Working in a Western-style brick building under the supervision of factory foremen, women produce silk within the structures of a modern industrial system, but they continue to wear Japanese clothing (in contrast to the visitors in the left foreground), thereby expressing the cultural mixtures of an older society and a new economic order.

(Laurie Platt Winfrey, Inc.)

Industrial and financial modernization

Industrial and financial modernization went along with and even preceded the political revolution. In 1858 the first steamship was purchased from the Dutch. In 1859 Japan placed its first foreign loan, borrowing five million yen by a bond issue floated in England. In 1869 the first telegraph connected Yokohama and Tokyo. The first railroad, between the same two cities, was completed in 1872. In 1870 appeared the first spinning machinery. Foreign trade, almost literally zero in 1854, was valued at $200 million a year by the end of the century. The population rose from 33 million in 1872 to 46 million in 1902. The island empire, like Great Britain, became dependent on exports and imports to sustain its dense population at the level of living to which it aspired.

The westernization of Japan still stands as the most remarkable transformation ever undergone by any people in so short a time. It recalls the westernizing of Russia under Peter over a century before, though conducted somewhat less brutally, more rapidly, and with a wider consent among the population. For Japan, as formerly for Russia, the motive was in large measure defense against Western penetration, together with an admiration for Western statecraft and an ambition to become an international power. The new government institutions helped to produce a more unified nation-state of the type then developing throughout Europe and the Americas. What the Japanese wanted from the West was primarily science, technology, and organization. They were content enough with the innermost substance of their culture, their moral ideas, their family life, their arts and amusements, their religious conceptions, though even in these they showed an uncommon adaptability. Essentially it was to protect their internal substance, their Japanese culture, that they took over the external apparatus of Western civilization. This apparatus—science, technology, machinery, arms, political and legal organization—was the part of Western civilization for which other peoples generally felt a need, which they hoped to adopt without losing their own spiritual independence, and which therefore, though sometimes rather scornfully dismissed as materialistic, became the common ground for the interdependent worldwide civilization that emerged at the close of the nineteenth century.

In brief, the world between 1850 and 1870, revolutionized economically by the railroad and steamship, was revolutionized politically by the formation of large and consolidated nation-states. These states at the time all embodied certain liberal and constitutional principles, or at least the machinery of parliamentary and representative government. But the whole earth had also become an arena in which certain nations or powers sought to promote their economic and political interests. The Great Powers in 1871 were Great Britain, Germany, France, Austria-Hungary, and Russia. Britain had produced a daughter nation in Canada. Whether Italy was to be called a Great Power was not yet clear. No one knew what Japan would do. All agreed that the United States would one day play a large role in international politics, but the time was not yet.

Chapter **14**

EUROPEAN

CIVILIZATION,

1871–1914:

ECONOMY AND POLITICS

Half a century elapsed between the period of national consolidation described in the last chapter and the outbreak of the First World War in 1914. In this half-century Europe in many ways reached the climax of the modern phase of its civilization and also exerted its maximum influence upon peoples outside Europe.

For Europe and the European world the years 1871 to 1914 were marked by hitherto unparalleled material and industrial growth, international peace, domestic stability, the advance of constitutional, representative, and democratic government, and continued faith in science, reason, and progress. But in these very years, in politics, economics, philosophy, and the arts, there were forces operating to undermine the liberal premises and tenets of this European civilization. At the same time, a new wave of European imperialism spread across Africa and Asia, creating new colonial empires, new global economic connections, and new international and cross-cultural conflicts. All of these developments contributed to and reflected the European ascendancy before 1914, and all produced a legacy that has decisively influenced the modern world down to our own time. For purposes of historical analysis, we must separate this complex era into different thematic strands. This chapter therefore examines economic and political trends in Europe after 1871, the next describes European social and cultural movements in this era, and the following one discusses the worldwide impact of European imperialism. By 1914, the institutions and ideas of modern European civilization were spreading across most of the world, but these same institutions and ideas were also facing new critical challenges from within Europe and from people on other continents who resented the European domination of their economies, governments, and cultures.

Chapter emblem: Detail from a photograph of Italian immigrants arriving in New York about 1900.

71.   THE "CIVILIZED WORLD"

Materialistic and Nonmaterialistic Ideals

With the extension of the nation-state system Europe was politically more divided than ever. Its unity lay in the sharing by all Europeans of a similar way of life and outlook, which existed also in such "European" countries as the United States, Canada, Australia, and New Zealand. Europe and its offshoots constituted what Europeans called the "civilized world." Other regions—mostly in Asia, Africa, and Latin America—were said to be "backward." (They are in our day often referred to as "developing" or "less developed.") Europeans were extremely conscious and inordinately proud of their civilization in the half-century before 1914. They believed it to be the well-deserved outcome of centuries of progress. Believing themselves to be the most advanced branch of mankind in the most important areas of human endeavor, they assumed that all peoples should respect the same social ideals—that so far as they were unwilling or unable to adopt them they were backward, and that so far as they did adopt them they became civilized in their turn. Such ideas shaped the ideology and practice of European imperialism, which entered a dynamic new phase in the late nineteenth century.

The ideals of European civilization were in part materialistic. If Europeans considered their civilization to be better in 1900 than in 1800, or better in 1900 than the ways of non-Europeans at the same time, it was because they had a higher standard of living, ate and dressed more adequately, slept in softer beds, and had more satisfactory sanitary facilities.

The ideal of civilization

It was because they possessed ocean liners, railroads, and streetcars, and after about 1880 telephones and electric lights. But the ideal of civilization was by no means exclusively materialistic. Knowledge as such, correct or truthful knowledge, was held to be a civilized attainment—scientific knowledge of nature, in place of superstition or demonology; geographical knowledge, by which civilized people were aware of the earth as a whole with its general contours and diverse inhabitants. The ideal was also profoundly moral, derived from Christianity, but now secularized and detached from religion. An Englishman, Isaac Taylor, in his *Ultimate Civilization* published in 1860, defined this moral ideal by listing the contrasting "relics of barbarism" which he thought were due to disappear—"Polygamy, Infanticide, Legalized Prostitution, Capricious Divorce, Sanguinary and Immoral Games, Infliction of Torture, Caste and Slavery." The first four of these had been unknown to the approved customs of Europe at least since the coming of Christianity (though prostitution was more or less tolerated in almost all European societies). Torture went out of use about 1800, even in the illiberal European states; and legalized caste and slavery, in the course of the nineteenth century. But there were few non-European peoples, in 1860, among whom two or three of Taylor's "relics" could not be found.

Indices of advancement

There are certain other indices, more purely quantitative, worked out by sociologists to show the level of advancement of a given society. One of these is the death rate, or number of persons per thousand of population who die each year. In England, France, and Sweden the "true" death rate (or death rate regardless of the proportion of infants and old people, who are most susceptible to death) is known to have fallen from about 25 (per 1,000 per year) before 1850, to 19 in 1914 and 18 in the 1930s. Indeed, before the Second World War, it stood seemingly stabilized at about 18 in all countries of northwestern Europe, the United States, and the British dominions. Death rates in countries not "modern" run over

40 even in favorable times. A closely related index is infant mortality, which fell rapidly after 1870 in all countries affected by medical science. Thus a woman under more modern conditions had to go through pregnancy and childbirth less often to produce the same number of surviving children. Another index is life expectancy, or the age that a person has an even chance of attaining. In England life expectancy at birth rose from 40 years in the 1840s to 59 in 1933 and to 76 in the 1990s. In India in 1931 it was less than 27 years. It had risen to about 60 in the 1990s. Still another index is the literacy rate, or proportion of persons above a certain age (such as 10) able to read and write. In northwestern Europe by 1900 the literacy rate approached 100, whereas in some countries of the world it had still not risen very far above zero. A further basic index is the productivity of labor, or amount produced by one worker in a given expenditure of time. This is difficult to compute, especially for earlier periods for which statistical data are lacking. In the 1930s, however, the productivity of a farmer in Denmark was over ten times that of a farmer in Albania. All northwestern Europe was above the European average in this respect with the exception of Ireland, whereas Ireland, Spain, Portugal, Italy and all eastern Europe were below it.

The essence of civilized living doubtless is in the intangibles, in the way in which people use their minds, and in the attitudes they form toward others or toward the conditions and planning of their own lives. The intangibles, however, are not always agreed upon by persons of different culture or ideology. On the quantitative criteria there is less disagreement; all, with few exceptions, wish to lower the death rate, raise the literacy rate, and increase the productivity of human exertion. Whatever we might say about the intangible qualities of a civilized society, if we apply quantitative or sociological indices alone, we can say that for about four decades after 1870 there was in fact, and not merely in the opinion of Europeans, a modern, civilized world of which Europe was the center.

The "Zones" of Civilization

Or rather, a certain region of Europe was the center. For there were really two Europes, an inner zone and an outer. A Frenchman writing in the 1920s describing the two Europes that had risen since 1870, called the inner zone the "Europe of steam," and bounded it by an imaginary line joining Glasgow, Stockholm, Danzig, Trieste, Florence, and Barcelona. It included not only Great Britain but Belgium, Germany, France, northern Italy, and the western portions of the Austrian Empire. Virtually all heavy European industry was located in this zone. Here the railway network was thickest. Here the wealth of Europe was concentrated, in the form both of a high living standard and of accumulations of capital. Here likewise were almost all the laboratories and all the scientific activity of Europe. Here, in the same zone, lay the strength of constitutional and parliamentary government and of liberal, humanitarian, socialist, and reformist movements of many kinds. In this zone the death rate was low, life expectancy was high, conditions of health and sanitation were at their best, literacy was almost universal, productivity of labor was impressive. To the same zone, for practical purposes, belonged certain regions of European settlement overseas, especially the northeastern part of the United States.

The outer zone included most of Ireland, most of the Iberian and Italian peninsulas, and all Europe east of what was then Germany, Bohemia, and Austria proper. The outer zone was agricultural, though the productivity of agriculture, per farm worker or per acre, was far less than in the inner zone. The people were poorer, more illiterate, and more likely to die young. The wealthy were landlords, often absentees. The outer zone lived increasingly after 1870 by selling grain, livestock,

The outer zone

TRAIN IN THE SNOW

by Claude Monet (French, 1840–1926)

Trains became one of the new symbols of modernity during the nineteenth century, but few artists saw them as appropriate subjects for paintings. Monet and other Impressionists, however, wanted to apply their artistic techniques to the familiar objects of everyday life, including the iron shapes of a passing locomotive. In this typical Impressionist rendering of modern technology, the solid mass of the train melts into the play of light and the indeterminate grays of a dull winter day.

(Giraudon/Art Resource, NY)

wool, or lumber to the more industrialized inner zone but was too poor to purchase many manufactured products in return. To obtain capital it borrowed in London or Paris. Its social and political philosophies were characteristically imported from Germany and the West. It borrowed engineers and technicians from the first zone to build its bridges and install its telegraph systems and sent its youth to universities in the first zone to study medicine or other professions. Many areas of European settlement overseas, for example in Latin America and the southern part of the United States, may also be thought of at that time as belonging to this outer zone.

Beyond the European world lay a third zone, the immense reaches of Asia and Africa, all viewed as "backward" by the standards or cultural assumptions of Europe, with the exception of the recently Europeanized Japan, and all destined, with the exception of Japan, to become heavily dependent upon Europe in the half-century after 1870. Much of the world's history since 1870 could be written as the story of relations among these three zones; but it is necessary in all human matters to guard against formulas that are too simple. And there are always changes as well as continuities in the histories of all human societies.

72.   BASIC DEMOGRAPHY: THE INCREASE OF THE EUROPEANS

European and World Population Growth since 1650

All continents except Africa gained enormously in population in the three centuries following 1650, but it was Europe that grew the most. There is little doubt that the proportion of Europeans in the world's total, including those of European origin in other continents, reached its maximum for all time between 1850 and the Second World War. Estimates are given in the table on page 556, beginning with 1650.

The causes of the rise in population after 1650 cannot be positively known. Some of them obviously operated in Asia as well as Europe. In Europe the organized sovereign states, as established in the seventeenth century, put an end to a long period of civil wars, stopping the chronic violence and marauding, with the accompanying insecurity of agriculture and family life, which were more deadly than wars fought between governments. Similarly, the Tokugawa kept peace in Japan, and the Manchu or Qing dynasty brought a long period of order in China. The British rule in India and the Dutch in Java, by curbing famine and violence, allowed populations to grow very rapidly. All such factors, which allowed more people to remain alive longer, also favored the stability of families and the birth and raising of children. Death rates could fall and birth rates could rise from similar causes. The great exception to the swelling rise of population was Africa, where the slave trade removed over 10 million people (and what would have been an even larger number of their descendants) in three or four centuries, and where slave raiding led to the disruption of African cultures. In the Americas the native Indians were devastated by diseases brought from Europe to which at first they had no immunity.

Causes of demographic growth

In Europe, sooner than elsewhere, other causes of growth were at work beyond the maintenance of civil peace. They included liberation from certain endemic afflictions, beginning with the subsiding of bubonic plague in the seventeenth century and the use of vaccination against smallpox in the eighteenth. Agricultural improvement produced more food, notably in England about 1750. The improvement of transportation, by road, canal, and railroad, made localized famine a thing of the past, since food could be moved into areas of temporary shortage. With the Industrial Revolution larger populations could subsist in Europe by importing food from overseas. In the cities of Europe and North America, by 1900, the supply of pure drinking water and facilities for the disposal of garbage and sewage were better than in the past.

Improved living conditions

Hence population grew for several generations more substantially in Europe and its offshoots than elsewhere. Approximate percentages are given in the table. Asia, by these estimates, increased less than threefold between 1650 and 1900, but Europe increased

ESTIMATED POPULATION OF THE WORLD BY CONTINENTAL AREAS

	Millions					
	1650	**1750**	**1850**	**1900**	**1950**	**2000**
Europe	100	150	263	396	532	729
United States and Canada	1	2	26	82	166	304
Australasia-Oceania	2	2	2	6	13	53
Predominantly "European"	103	154	291	484	711	1086
Latin America	12	16	38	74	162	519
Africa	100	106	111	133	217	785
Asia	330	515	822	959	1396	3683
Predominantly "Non-European"	442	637	971	1166	1775	4987
World Total	545	791	1262	1650	2486	6073

	Percentages					
Europe	18.3%	19.1%	20.8%	24.0%	21.5%	12.0%
United States and Canada	.2	.2	2.1	5.0	6.7	5.0
Australasia-Oceania	.4	.2	.2	.3	.5	1.0
Predominantly "European"	18.9	19.5	23.1	29.3	28.7	18.0
Latin America	2.2	2.0	3.0	4.5	6.5	8.5
Africa	18.3	13.0	8.8	8.1	8.7	12.9
Asia	60.6	65.0	65.1	58.1	56.1	60.6
Predominantly "Non-European"	81.1	80.0	76.9	70.7	71.3	82.0
World Total	100.0	100.0	100.0	100.0	100.0	100.0

*This table is designed to show only the numbers and proportion of people living in predominantly "European" cultures (that is, descended from societies with European languages and traditions) and "non-European" cultures over the modern period. It reveals the rapid increase in the proportion of "Europeans" in this sense from 1750 to 1900, and a steady decline in the "European" proportion during the twentieth century. The table is subject to serious reservations. The population of the former Soviet Union is divided between Europe and Asia, but millions of Russian "Europeans" have long lived in the Asian parts of the former U.S.S.R. It must also be remembered that the population of the United States consists of Africans and Asians as well as Europeans, that the people in Latin American countries now generally speak a European language and differ widely in their racial composition, and that there are well over four million persons of European origin in southern Africa. In short, the table has nothing to do with race, for there are many whites who do not live in "European" cultural zones and many "nonwhite" people in the Americas and elsewhere (including Europe) who participate fully in institutions and languages derived from Europe.

Source: For 1650 to 1900, A. N. Carr-Sanders, *World Population* (Oxford: Oxford University Press, 1936); for 1750, 1850, and 1900, John D. Durand, "The Modern Expansion of World Population," in *Proceedings of the American Philosophical Society,* vol. 111 (1967); and for 1950 and 2000, *United Nations Demographic Yearbook and World Population Prospects* (United Nations: New York, 1989) and *The New York Times 2001 Almanac* (New York, 2000).

fourfold, and the total number of Europeans, including the descendants of those who migrated to other continents, multiplied fivefold. The ascendancy of European civilization in the two and a half centuries after 1650 was due in some measure to merely demographic growth. But while in 1900 the proportion of "Europeans" in all continents was approaching a third of the human race, after 1900 this proportion began to fall. By the beginning of the twenty-first century it could be projected that "Europeans" would constitute only a tenth of the human beings on the planet in the year 2100.

Stabilization of European Population

Stabilization and relative decline of European population followed from a fall in the birth rate. As early as 1830 the birth rate began noticeably to drop in France, with the result that France, long the most populous European state, was surpassed in population by Germany about 1870, by the British Isles about 1895, and by Italy about 1930. France, once thought to be decadent for this reason, was in fact only the leading country in a population cycle through which the European countries seemed to pass. The birth rate, which had fallen below 30 per hundred in France in the 1830s, fell to that level in Sweden in the 1880s, in England in the 1890s, and in Germany, Bohemia, and the Netherlands between 1900 and 1910. After the Second World War there was a temporary rise, but by 2000 the birth rate was only 15 per 1,000 or less in Europe and North America, hardly sufficient to maintain existing population levels. In much of the rest of the world, except China, it was still well over 30.

The reduced birth rate is not a mere dry statistical item, nor does it affect populations merely in the mass. It is one of the indices of modern civilization, first appearing in that inner European zone in which the other indices were also highest, and thence spreading outward in a kind of wave. Concretely, a low birth rate in the nineteenth century meant that families averaged from two to four children, where in former times, or today under conditions not "modern," families may be found to consist of 10 children or even more. The low birth rate reflects the small family system, than which few institutions were more fundamental to modern life. The principal means used to hold down the birth rate, or to limit the family, is the practice of contraception. But the true causes, or reasons why parents wish to limit their families are deeply embedded in the codes of modern society.

Historical demographers have detected a "European family pattern" as far back as the seventeenth century. It was a pattern in which, in comparison to other societies, Europeans married later, and a larger number never married at all. Late marriage shortened the number of years during which a woman bore children and enabled young people to acquire skills or accumulate savings (as in tools and household goods) before setting up new families. The effect was a less explosive population growth, and less extreme poverty, than occurred in some other parts of the world. Evidence indicating the practice of contraception can he found in the eighteenth century among the upper classes, by study of the number and spacing of their children. The practice seems to have spread to other social classes during the French Revolution. The Code Napoleon that followed required that inheritances be divided among all sons and daughters. The French peasants, many of them owners of land, began to limit themselves to two or three children, in order that all children (by inheritance, marriage, and dowries) might remain in as high an economic and social position as their parents. It was thus economic security and the possession of a social standard that led to the reduced birth rate in France.

A European family pattern

In the great cities of the nineteenth century, in which standards of life for the working classes often collapsed, the effect might at first be a proliferation of offspring. But life in the city, under crowded conditions of housing, also set a premium on the small family. There were many activities in the city that people with many children could only with difficulty enjoy. After about

Life in the city

1880 child labor became much less frequent among the working classes. When children ceased to earn part of the family income parents tended to have fewer of them. About the same time governments in the advanced countries began to require universal compulsory schooling. The number of years spent in education, and hence in economic dependency upon parents, grew longer and longer, until it became common even for young adults to be still engaged in study. Each child represented many years of expense for its parents. The ever rising idea of what it was necessary to do for one's children, and the desire of parents to give them every possible advantage in a competitive world, were probably the most basic causes of voluntary limitation of the family. Hardly less basic was the desire to lighten the burdens upon mothers. The small family system, together with the decline of infant mortality, since they combined to free women from the interminable bearing and tending of infants, probably did more than anything else to improve the position of women in modern societies. Freed at least in part from the traditional cycles of pregnancy and child care, middle-class women were eventually able to pursue advanced education, new professions, and new kinds of social or political activities. The use of contraception also spread widely among the working class during the early twentieth century; demographic research in England, for example, suggests that almost 70 percent of working-class couples were using contraception by the 1930s (compared to fewer than 20 percent in 1900).

But the effects of the small family system upon total population became manifest more slowly. More people lived on into the middle and older age groups, and the fall of the birth rate was gradual, so that in all the leading countries total numbers continued to rise, except in France, which hardly grew between 1900 and 1945. The persistent note was one of superabundant increase. In five generations, between 1800 and 1950, some 200 million "Europeans" grew into 700 million "Europeans" around the globe. Since productivity increased even more rapidly, the standard of living for most of these "Europeans" rose in spite of the increase of numbers, and there was no general problem of overpopulation.

Growth of Cities and Urban Life

Where did so many people go? Some stayed in the rural areas where most people had always lived. Rural populations in the inner zone became more dense, turning to the more intensive agriculture of truck gardening or dairy farming, leaving products like wool and cereal grains to be raised elsewhere and then imported. But it is estimated that of every seven persons added to the western European population only one stayed on the land. Of the other six, one left Europe altogether and five went to the growing cities.

The nineteenth-century city was mostly the child of the railroad, for with the railroads it became possible for the first time to concentrate manufacturing in large towns, to which bulky goods such as foods and fuel could now be moved in great volume. The growth of cities between 1850 and 1914 was phenomenal. In England two-thirds of the people lived in places of 20,000 or less in 1830, in 1914 two-thirds lived in places of 20,000 or more. Germany, the historic land of archaic towns carried over from the Middle Ages, rivaled England after 1870 in modern industrial urbanization. Whereas in 1840 only London and Paris had a million people, the same could be said by 1914 of Berlin, Vienna, St. Petersburg, and Moscow.[1] Some places, like the English Midlands and the Ruhr valley in Ger-

---

[1]And, outside Europe, of New York, Chicago, Philadelphia, Rio de Janeiro, Buenos Aires, Calcutta, Tokyo, and Osaka.

The evolving demographic pattern in nineteenth-century European bourgeois families may be seen in this portrait of a Victorian-era English family sitting in their garden. The declining number of children eventually gave women more time and freedom for diverse activities because they were less tied to long cycles of pregnancies and childrearing.
(Hulton Getty)

many, became a mass of contiguous smaller cities, vast urban agglomerations divided only by municipal lines.

The great city set the tone of modern society. City life was impersonal and anonymous; people were uprooted, less tied to home or church than in the country. They lacked the country person's feeling of deference for aristocratic families. They lacked the sense of self-help characteristic of older rural communities. It was in the city that the daily newspaper press, which spread rapidly in the wake of the telegraph after 1850, found its most habitual readers. The so-called yellow or sensational press appeared about 1900. Articulate public opinion was formed in the cities, and city people were on the whole disrespectful of tradition, receptive to new ideas,

Impact of urban life

having in many cases deliberately altered their own lives by moving from the country or from smaller towns. That socialism spread among the industrial masses of European cities is hardly surprising. It is less often realized that some of the more blatant nationalism that arose after 1870 was stimulated by city life, for people felt increasingly detached from all institutions except the state. At the same time city life, by its greater facilities for schooling, reading, and discussion, made for a more alert and informed public opinion of an enlightened kind.

Migration from Europe, 1850–1940

During the same period in which cities were growing, almost 60 million people left Europe altogether, of whom possibly a fifth sooner or later returned. The Atlantic Migration—aptly so called, because all crossed the ocean except those who moved from European to Asian Russia—towers above all others in magnitude, and possibly also in significance, for it was by this means that earlier colonial offshoots of Europe were transformed into new Europes alongside the old. All parts of Europe contributed, as shown in the table below, which comprises the years from 1850 to 1940. Before 1850 the mass movement had scarcely begun, though at that time over a million immigrants had entered the United States since the close of the Napoleonic wars. After 1940 the character of intercontinental migration was greatly transformed. In recent decades, since the Second World War, there have been large migrations into Europe from Africa and Asia, and into the Americas from places outside Europe. But in the century before 1940 the migration of European peoples was a key force in the dissemination of European institutions and cultures.

The Atlantic Migration

It is hard to give satisfactory figures for emigration from Europe. In the statistical sources the English, Scots, Welsh, and Irish are mixed, and until the First World War, that

EMIGRATION FROM EUROPE, 1850–1940

From:	British Isles	18,300,000
	Italy	10,200,000
	Russia	9,000,000
	Germany	5,000,000
	Spain	4,500,000
	Austria-Hungary	4,200,000
	Portugal	2,500,000
	Sweden	1,200,000
	Norway	750,000
	Denmark	470,000
	Finland	390,000
	France	390,000
	Switzerland	340,000
	Netherlands	210,000
	Belgium	150,000
		57,600,000

Source: William Woodruff, *The Impact of Western Man* (New York: St. Martin's Press, 1966), p. 106.

is until 1914, the Poles, Czechs, other Slavic peoples, Hungarians, East European Jews, and others were included among emigrants from the Russian, Austro-Hungarian, and German empires. Millions of Jews, Irish, Poles, and many thousands of others are therefore invisible in the figures below, which also include several million Russians who moved from European to Asian parts of what became the Soviet Union. It must be remembered also that some intercontinental migration did not involve Europeans. For a few years after 1850 black slaves were still brought illegally to the United States and Brazil. Workers went from India to the West Indies and South Africa, and many Chinese settled in the United States and southeast Asia. With these reservations, the following table reflects European emigration in the 90 years preceding the Second World War.

The British and Irish went to the British dominions and the United States. The Italians divided between the United States and Latin America. Spaniards settled overwhelmingly in the Spanish American republics, and the Portuguese settled in Brazil. The Germans moved overwhelmingly to the United States, though some went to Argentina and Brazil. The new countries received the following influxes of people:

IMMIGRATION INTO VARIOUS COUNTRIES, 1850–1940

To:		
	United States	32,300,000
	Asian Russia	7,000,000
	Argentina	6,600,000
	Brazil	4,700,000
	Canada	4,300,000
	Australia	2,900,000
	New Zealand	650,000
	Uruguay	600,000
	Cuba	600,000
	South Africa	250,000
	Mexico	250,000

Source: Woodruff, *Impact of Western Man,* p. 108.

The extraordinary preponderance of the United States is apparent. At the same time, it is well to rectify the impressions of most Americans on the subject. Almost half the European migration was directed elsewhere than to the United States. Asian Russia was second only to the United States in the receipt of new settlers. Canada received fewer immigrants than Argentina, and New Zealand was closely followed by Cuba and Uruguay.

The exodus from Europe was due to a remarkable and temporary juxtaposition of causes. One fundamental cause, or precondition, was that before 1914 the new countries welcomed immigration. Hands were wanted to farm the land, build houses, dig in the mines. This was least true of Australia and New Zealand, which preferred to limit themselves to English-speaking settlers and which also pioneered as social democracies, becoming models, even before 1900, of legislation to protect the working classes. One result was that no inrush of outsiders to compete for jobs at low wages was desired. A similar combination of national preferences and labor protectionism led to laws restricting immigration in the United

Causes of the exodus

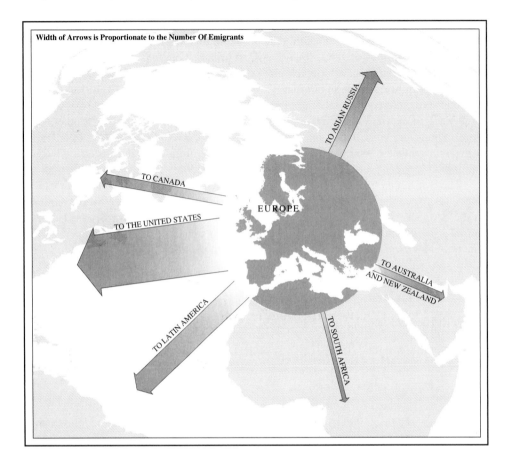

Width of Arrows is Proportionate to the Number Of Emigrants

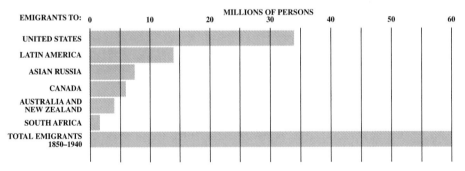

MIGRATION FROM EUROPE, 1850–1940

About 60 million people left Europe in the century preceding the Second World War, distributing themselves as shown in the diagram above. (See figures on p. 561.) About half went to the United States, but the migration of European peoples also built up "European" societies in other regions of the world. These overseas "European" societies produced food and raw materials for Europe and borrowed capital or bought manufactured goods from Europe, thus helping to support European economic development and to expand the modern, worldwide economic system.

The mass migration of people is one of the distinctive social patterns of the modern world. This Italian woman and her children, who arrived in New York about 1900, were part of a vast emigration out of Europe that affected societies and economies on every continent.

(Snark/Art Resource, NY)

States in 1921 and 1924. Thereafter immigrants could enter only under quotas, and the quotas were lowest for eastern and southern Europe from which most emigration was then forthcoming.

In Europe there were many conditions propelling emigrants outward. Physically, the steamship made it easier and cheaper to cross the sea, and the railroad helped people to get to the ports as well as to distribute themselves after landing in the new countries. Economically, people in the mass could for the first time afford a long journey. People migrated to improve their material circumstances; but some crests in the wave of emigration coincided with crests in the business cycle in Europe, when jobs in Europe were plentiful and wages were at their highest. Of the opposite case, of actual flight from economic ruin or starvation, the emigration from Ireland after 1846 is the best example. In the "great potato famine" of 1845–1849 nearly 1 million Irish died of starvation and disease, and more than 1.5 million emigrated to the United States in the next few years. After the revolutions of 1848 a certain number of Europeans left Europe for political reasons, and, later on, to avoid compulsory military service. The best example of flight from actual persecution is that of the Jews of Russia and Russian Poland, of whom a million and a half moved to the United States in the 15 years preceding the First World War.

But perhaps most basic in the whole European exodus was the underlying liberalism of the age. Never before (nor since) had people been legally so free to move. Old laws requiring skilled workmen to stay in their own countries were repealed, as in England in 1824. The old semicommunal agricultural villages, with collective rights and obligations, holding individuals to their native groups, fell into disuse except in Russia. The disappearance of

Freedom of movement

serfdom allowed the peasants of eastern Europe to change residences without obtaining a lord's permission. Governments permitted their subjects to emigrate, to take with them their savings of shillings, marks, kronen, or lire, and to change nationality by becoming naturalized in their new homes. The rise of liberty in Europe, as well as the hope of enjoying it in America, made possible the great emigration. For so huge a mass movement the most remarkable fact is that it took place by private initiative and at private expense. Individuals, families, and small local groups (to borrow the metaphor of one authority) detached themselves atom by atom from the mass of Europe, crossed the seas on their own, and reattached themselves atom by atom to the accumulating mass of the New World. The mass migrations of the late nineteenth century thus launched a worldwide movement of people that continues to the present day and remains one of the most characteristic social patterns of modern world history.

73.   THE WORLD ECONOMY OF THE NINETEENTH CENTURY

How did the swelling population of Europeans manage to feed itself? How, in fact, did it not merely feed itself but enjoy an incomparably higher standard of living in 1900 than in 1800? By science, industry, transportation, communications, and the expansion of global trading systems. And by organization—in business, finance, and labor.

The "New Industrial Revolution"

The Industrial Revolution entered upon a new phase. The use of steam power, the growth of the textile and metallurgical industries and the advent of the railroad had characterized the early part of the century. Now, after 1870, new sources of power were tapped, the already mechanized industries expanded, new industries appeared, and industry spread geographically.

Industrial advances

The steam engine itself was refined and improved. By 1914 it still predominated over other power machinery, but electricity with its incomparable advantages came into use. The invention of the internal combustion (or gasoline) engine and the diesel engine gave the world automobiles, airplanes, and submarines in the two decades before 1914; the advent of the automotive and aviation industries made oil one of the most coveted of natural resources. In the new chemical industries industrial research laboratories were replacing the individual inventor. Chemists discovered new fertilizers and from coal tar alone produced a bewildering array of new products ranging from artificial food flavors to high explosives. With the latter the first great tunnels were built, the Mount Cenis in 1873, the Simplon in 1906—both in the Alps; and great new canals, the Suez in 1869, the Kiel in 1895, the Panama in 1914. Chemistry made possible the production of synthetic fabrics like rayon, which revolutionized the textile industry. Electricity transformed all indoor and outdoor lighting. There was a communications revolution too. The telephone appeared in the 1870s. Marconi brought the continents closer together, successfully transmitting wireless signals across the Atlantic in 1901. The moving picture and the radio modestly presented themselves before 1914. Medicine ran a tongue-twisting alphabetical gamut from anesthetics to X-rays; yellow fever was overcome. Vastly improved processes for refining iron ore made possible a great expansion in the production of steel, the key product of the new industrial age; aluminum and other metal alloys were also produced through new industrial processes. Railroad mileage multiplied; the European network, including the Russian, increased from 140,000 miles in 1890 to 213,000 in 1914.

In the new phase of the Industrial Revolution machine industry spread geographically from Britain and Belgium, the only truly industrial countries in 1870, to France, Italy, Russia, Japan, and, most markedly, to Germany and the United States. In Europe industrial production was concentrated in the "inner zone." Three powers alone—Britain Germany, and France—accounted in 1914 for more than seven-tenths of all European manufactures and produced over four-fifths of all European coal, steel, and machinery. Of the major European powers Germany was now forging ahead. To use steel alone as a criterion, in 1871 Germany was producing annually three-fifths as much steel as Britain; by 1900 it was producing more, and by 1914 it was producing twice as much as Britain—but only half as much as the new industrial giant, the United States. By 1914 American steel output was greater than that of Germany, Britain, and France combined. Britain, the pioneer in mechanization, was being outstripped in both the Old World and the New. The three European powers increased their industrial production by about 50 percent in the two decades before 1914, but the United States had a far higher annual growth rate from 1870 to 1913, 4.3 percent as compared to the next leading powers, Germany with 2.9 percent, Britain with 2.2 percent, and France with 1.6 percent. By 1914 the United States had moved ahead of Europe in the mechanization of agriculture, in manufactures, and in coal and steel production, in which it was producing over two-fifths of the world's output. The Americans were pioneering also in assembly-line, conveyor-belt techniques for the mass production of automobiles and all kinds of consumer goods.

The industrial powers

Free Trade and the European "Balance of Payments"

It was Britain in the mid-nineteenth century, then the workshop of the world, that had inaugurated the movement toward free trade. It will be recalled that in 1846, by the repeal of the Corn Laws, the British embarked upon a systematic free trade policy, deliberately choosing to become dependent upon overseas imports for their food. France adopted free trade in 1860. Other countries soon followed. It is true that by 1880 there was a movement back to protective tariffs, except in Britain, Holland, and Belgium. But the tariffs were impediments rather than barriers, and until 1914 the characteristic of the economic system was the extreme mobility of goods across political frontiers. Politically, Europe was more than ever nationalistic; but economic activity, under generally liberal conditions in which business was supposed to be free from the political state, remained predominantly international and globe-encircling.

Broadly speaking, the great economic accomplishment of Europe before 1914 was to create a system by which the huge imports used by industrial Europe could be acquired and paid for. All European countries except Russia, Austria-Hungary, and the Balkan states imported more than they exported. It was the British again who led in this direction. Britain had been a predominantly importing country since the close of the eighteenth century. That is to say, despite the expanding export of cotton manufactures and other products of the Industrial Revolution, Britain consumed more goods from abroad than it sent out. Industrialization and urbanization in the nineteenth century confirmed the same situation. Between 1800 and 1900 the value of British exports multiplied eightfold, but the value of imports into Great Britain multiplied tenfold, and in the decade before 1914 the British had an import surplus of about three-quarters of a billion dollars a year. Great Britain and the industrial

Imports versus exports

The Bessemer steel-making process enhanced the production of steel and rapidly became an important component of industrial expansion during the later decades of the nineteenth century. Its importance for Britain is suggested by this illustration of the future King Edward VII and his wife, who are observing the new methods of steel production from box seats at a factory in Sheffield in 1875.

(The Mansell Collection/Time Pix)

countries of Europe together (roughly Europe's "inner zone"), at the beginning of the twentieth century, were drawing in an import surplus, measured in dollars, of almost $2 billion every year (the dollar then representing far more goods than it came to represent later). The imports into Europe's inner zone consisted of raw materials for its industries and of food and amenities for its people.

How were the imports paid for? How did Europe enjoy a favorable "balance of payments" despite an unfavorable balance of trade in commodities? Export of European manufactures paid for some imports, and even most, but not all. It was the so-called invisible exports that made up the difference, that is, shipping and insurance services rendered to foreigners, and interest on money lent out or invested, all bringing in foreign exchange. Shipping and insurance were important. An Argentine merchant in Buenos Aires, to ship hides to Germany, might employ a British vessel; he would pay the freight charges in Argentine pesos, which might be credited to the account of the British shipowner in an Argentine bank; the British shipowner would sell the pesos to someone, in England or elsewhere in Europe, who needed them to buy Argentine meat. The far-flung British merchant marine thus earned a considerable amount of the food and raw materials needed by Britain. To insure themselves against risks of every conceivable kind people all over the world turned to Lloyds

Invisible exports

CLASSIC LANDSCAPE

by Charles Sheeler (American, 1883–1965)

This landscape depicts an American plant of the Ford Motor Company in 1931, but it also symbolizes what has been called the Second Industrial Revolution. In this phase of industrialization, electricity, the internal combustion engine, and the automobile were especially important, and industry spread far beyond its early centers in Britain and western Europe. The picture is "classic" in its clear delineation, its array of familiar mathematical forms, and the universality of its message. The plant seems rational and precise, but there are no human beings. It is as if the machine had a life of its own and could do without human hands.

(Collection of Mr. and Mrs. Barney A. Ebsworth, National Gallery of Art, Washington)

of London. With the profits drawn from selling insurance the British could buy what they wished. Governments or business enterprises borrowed money in Europe, mainly in England; the interest payments, putting foreign currencies into European and British hands, constituted another invisible export by which an excess of imports could be financed. But the lending of money to foreigners is only part of a larger phenomenon, the export of capital.

The Export of European Capital

The migration of millions of Europeans had the effect of creating new societies, basically European in character, which both purchased manufactures from Europe and produced the food, wool, cotton, and minerals that Europe needed. It could not have had this effect if Europe had exported people only, especially people of such small means as most emigrants were. Europe also exported the capital necessary to get the new settlers and the new worlds into production.

The export of capital meant that an older and wealthier country, instead of using its whole annual income to raise its own standard of living, or to add to its own capital by expanding or improving its houses, factories, machinery, mines, and transportation, diverted some of its income to expanding or improving the houses, factories, machinery, mines, and transportation of foreign countries. It meant that British, French, Dutch, Belgian, Swiss, and eventually German investors in the desire to increase their income bought the stocks of foreign business enterprises and the bonds of foreign businesses and governments; or they organized companies of their own to operate in foreign countries; or their banks granted loans to banks in New York or Tokyo, which then lent the funds to local users.

Capital arose in Europe to some extent from the savings of quite small people, especially in France, where peasants and modest bourgeois families were notably thrifty. But most capital accumulated from savings by the well-to-do. The owners of a business concern, for example, instead of spending the concern's income by paying higher wages, took a portion of it in profits or dividends, and instead of spending all this on their own living, reinvested part of it in domestic or foreign enterprises. The gap between rich and poor was thus one cause of the rapid accumulation of capital, though the accumulation of capital, in the nineteenth century, produced in turn a steady rise of living standards for the working classes. In a sense, however, the common people of western Europe, by forgoing the better housing, diet, education, or pleasures that a more democratic or consumer-oriented society might have planned for them, made possible the export of capital and hence the financing and building up of other regions of the world.

Capital accumulation

The British were the chief exporters of capital, followed at some distance by the French, and at the close of the century by the Germans. As early as the 1840s half the annual increase of wealth in Great Britain was going into foreign investments. By 1914 the British had $20 billion in foreign investments, the French had about $8.7 billion, and the Germans had about $6 billion. A quarter of all the wealth owned by the inhabitants of Great Britain consisted in 1914 of holdings outside the country. Almost a sixth of the French national wealth lay in investments outside France. All three countries had given hostages to fortune, and fortune proved unkind, for in the First World War the British lost about a quarter of their foreign investments, the French lost about a third, and the Germans lost all.

These huge sums, pouring out from Europe's inner zone for a century before 1914, at first went mainly to finance the Americas and the less affluent regions of Europe. European capital was also invested in Asia and Africa, especially after the rapid expansion of Europe's colonial empires in the 1890s. No country except Great Britain completely built its railways with its own resources. In the United States the railway system was built very largely with capital obtained from England. In central and eastern Europe British companies often constructed the first railways, then sold out to native operating companies

The recipients of European capital

or to governments which subsequently ran them. In the Argentine Republic the British not merely financed and built the railways, but long continued to operate and own them. In addition, up to 1914 the British sold about 75 million tons of coal a year to South America to keep the railways going, not to mention items for replacement and upkeep of equipment. Docks, warehouses, mines, plantations, processing and manufacturing establishments all over the world were similarly built up with capital drawn from Europe. European capital also helped emigrants in the new countries to develop new public services and institutions that required major financial investments. In the United States, for example, state and local governments very commonly sold their bonds in Europe to build roads, pave streets, or construct school systems for the westward-moving population. A few of these American bonds proved a partial or total loss to European investors. On the whole, by 1914, the United States had paid back a good deal of its indebtedness. Even so, in 1914, Americans still owed about $4 billion to Europeans—a sum three times as large as the national debt of the United States at the time.

An International Money System: The Gold Standard

The international economy rested upon an international money system, based in turn upon the almost universal acceptance of the gold standard. England had adopted the gold standard in 1821, when the pound sterling was legally defined as the equivalent of 113 grains of fine gold. Western Europe and the United States adopted an exclusively gold standard in the 1870s. A person holding any "civilized" money—pounds, francs, dollars, marks, and the like—could turn it into gold at will, and a person holding gold could turn it into any money. The currencies were like so many different languages all expressing the same thing. All had substantially the same value, and until 1914 the exchange rates between currencies remained highly stable. It was assumed that no modern, civilized country's currency ever "fell"; such things might happen in Turkey or China, or in the French Revolution, but not in the world of modern progress and civilized affairs.

The important currencies were all freely exchangeable. A French merchant selling silks to a German, and hence receiving German marks, could turn the marks into francs, pounds sterling, or dollars. That is, he was not obliged to buy from Germany or spend his money in Germany but could use the proceeds of his German sale to buy French, British, or American goods or services as he chose. Trade was multilateral. A country needing imports from another country, such as American cotton, did not have to sell to that country to obtain them; it could sell its own goods anywhere and then import according to its needs.

Currency exchange

It was the acceptance of the gold standard, and the fact that all important countries possessed a sufficient share of gold to support their currencies, that made possible so fluid an interchange. At the same time the gold standard had less wholesome effects. It was hard on countries that lacked gold. And it produced a gradual fall of prices, especially between 1870 and 1900, because (until the gold discoveries in South Africa, Australia, and Alaska in the 1890s) the world's production of gold lagged behind the expanding production of industrial and agricultural goods. Persistently declining prices were a hardship to those who habitually worked with borrowed money—many farmers, many businessmen, and debtor nations as a whole. A famous speech of William Jennings Bryan in the United States in 1896, declaring that mankind should not be crucified "upon this cross of gold," expressed a common, worldwide anger about a financial system that worked against the interests of

Effects of the gold standard

indebted persons and indebted nations. But falling prices were an advantage to the wage-earning class, which generally improved its position in these years, and also to the wealthy, the owners and lenders of capital, the bankers and financiers, who so long as prices were falling were repaid in money of more value than that which they had lent.

*London
at the center*

The center of the global economic and financial system was London. The London banks came forward in consequence of the defeat of Napoleon, the older financial centers in Amsterdam having been ruined in the Revolutionary and Napoleonic wars. It may be recalled also that the victors in 1815 imposed upon France an indemnity of 700 million francs, which in 1818 was taken over by a syndicate of private bankers; the London banks played a leading part in this affair and so developed their connections with many government treasuries. In the Crimean War of 1854–1856, with England at war with Russia, the London banks floated loans for the Russian government—so independent were business and politics at the time. The early adoption of the gold standard in England meant that many people, British and foreign, kept their funds in the form of sterling on deposit in London, where quantities of available capital therefore accumulated.

The banks, too, grew up in the financing of the British export trade, itself borne on the tide of the Industrial Revolution. A small Lancashire manufacturer, for example, might receive an order for a gross of scissors from an unknown merchant in Trieste. He would draw a bill or "sight draft" against the Trieste merchant, and take this bill to a financial institution known as an acceptance house. The acceptance house, which in the course of its business had acquired a microscopic knowledge of the credit of thousands of individuals and firms in all parts of the world, would then "discount" the bill, giving cash to the Lancashire manufacturer and collecting from the Trieste merchant through international banking channels. In this way the bank took a burden off the British manufacturer and extended short-term credit to foreigners for the purchase of British goods. Many acceptance houses gradually went into the business of long-term foreign lending also. London became the apex of a pyramid which had the world for its base. It was the main center of exchange of currencies, the clearinghouse of the world's debts, the depository from which all the world borrowed, the banker's bank, the insurance agency's resort for reinsurance, as well as the world's shipping center and the headquarters of many international corporations.

A World Market: Unity, Competition—and Insecurity

Never had the earth been so unified economically, with each region playing specific roles in a global specialization. Western Europe, and in 1870 mainly Great Britain, was the world's industrial workshop. Other parts of the earth supplied its many needs. An English economist marveled in 1866 that Britain now had its granaries in Chicago and Odessa, its forests in Canada and the Baltic, its sheep farms in Australia, and its gold and silver mines in California and Peru, while drinking tea brought from China and coffee from East Indian plantations. The same could have been said of most of Europe's inner zone by the time of the First World War.

*A true world
market*

A true world market had been created. Goods, services, commodities, money, capital, people moved back and forth almost without regard to national boundaries. Articles were bought and sold at uniform world prices. Dealers in wheat, for example, followed prices in Minneapolis, Liverpool, Buenos Aires, and Danzig as reported by telegraph and cable from day to day. They bought

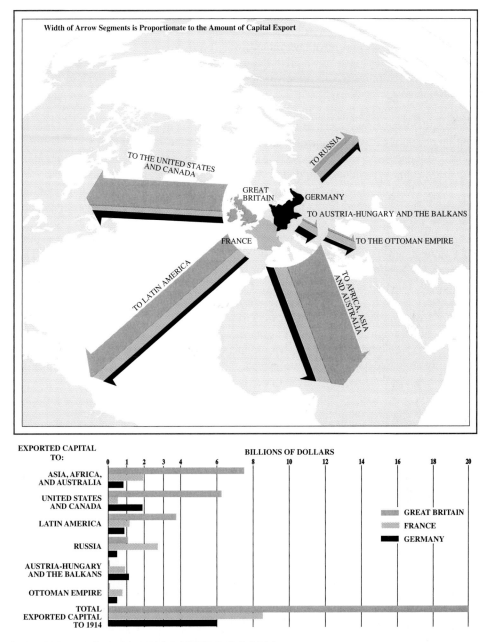

Width of Arrow Segments is Proportionate to the Amount of Capital Export

EXPORT OF EUROPEAN CAPITAL TO 1914

In 1914 the British, French, and Germans held upwards of $30 billion in foreign and colonial loans and investments, distributed as shown on the map. Dutch investments, especially in the West Indies, together with Swiss, Belgian, and Scandinavian holdings would add several billion dollars more. Proceeds from such investments helped Europeans to pay for the excess of their imports over exports. British capital predominated in the overseas world, while the less developed regions of eastern Europe and the Middle East were financed mainly from Germany and France. Much of the investment shown here was lost or expended in the First World War.

where it was cheapest, and sold where it was dearest. In this way the world's wheat supply was distributed roughly according to need or ability to pay. The worker of Milan, if the Italian crop was poor and prices were high, was fed from another source. On the other hand, the Italian wheat grower would in this case feel the pinch of world competition. The world market, while it organized the world into a unified economic system, at the same time brought distant regions into competition for the first time. The producers of goods and commodities—whether businessman, factory employee, farmer, or coffee planter—had no secure outlet for their products, as had generally been true in the past. They were in competition not only with persons across the street or down the road but also with other producers throughout the world; this worldwide system of production and consumption established the modern economic foundation for what is now called "globalization."

The creation of an integrated world market, the financing and building up of countries outside of Europe, and the consequent feeding and support of Europe's increasing population were the great triumphs of the nineteenth-century system of unregulated capitalism. The system was intricate, with thousands and even millions of individuals and business firms supplying each other's wants without central planning. But it was extremely precarious, and the position of most people in this network of global economic exchanges was exceedingly vulnerable. Region competed against region, and person against person. A fall of grain prices in the American Middle West, besides ruining a few speculators, might oblige Prussian or Argentine wheat growers to sell at a price at which they could not live. Factory owners might be driven out of business if competitors successfully undersold them or if a new commodity made their own product obsolete. The workers, hired only when needed by an employer, faced unemployment when business slackened or the permanent disappearance of their jobs by the next labor-saving invention.

Cycles of boom and depression

The system went through cycles of boom and depression, the most notable example of the latter being the "long depression" that set in about 1873 and lasted to about 1893. The new global economy depended on expansion and on credit; but sometimes people could not pay their debts, so that credit collapsed, and sometimes expansion failed to keep pace with expectations, and anticipated profits proved to be losses. To combat the essential insecurity of private capitalism, all manner of devices were resorted to. Governments adopted protective tariffs on the one hand and social insurance and welfare legislation on the other; trade unionism and socialist movements grew; business mergers took place. These and other measures, to which we shall return, signaled the gradual decline in the years after 1880 of nineteenth-century unregulated, laissez-faire capitalism.

Changes in Organization: Big Business

A great change came over capitalism itself about 1880 or 1890. Formerly characterized by a very large number of very small units, small businesses run by individuals, partnerships, or small companies, it was increasingly characterized by large and impersonal corporations. The attractions of the "limited liability" corporation as a form of business organization and as a means of encouraging investment arose from laws, enacted by most countries in the nineteenth century, which limited the individual investor's personal loss in the event of a bankruptcy to the amount of his or her shares of stock in the enterprise. The corporation, in its modern form appearing first with the railroads, became the usual form of organization for industry and commerce. As machinery grew more complicated, only a

The "limited liability" corporation

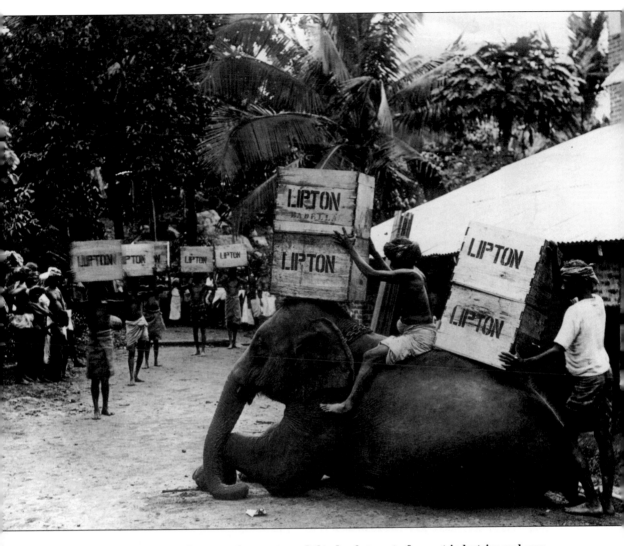

The new world market strongly encouraged the development of export industries and commodity production in agrarian societies that mainly produced food in earlier times. During the decades before 1914, the colonized areas of Asia, Africa, and the Americas rapidly increased their production of commodities such as tea, coffee, sugar, and cocoa, most of which flowed into the more industrialized, capitalist economies of Europe and North America. These workers in India collected tea for export and thus participated, though with low wages, in a global trading system that transformed agriculture and daily life in almost every part of the world.

(The Art Archive)

large pool of capital could finance it. And as corporations grew in size and number, relying on the sale of stock and the issue of bonds, the influence of banking and financial circles was enhanced. Financiers, using not so much their own money as the savings of others, had a new power to create or to extinguish, to stimulate, discourage, or combine corporate enterprises in various industries. Industrial capitalism brought finance capitalism with it.

Corporate organization made it possible to concentrate diverse economic processes under unified management. In retail commerce, large department stores appeared after about 1870 in the United States and France, selling all kinds of goods that were formerly sold only in small shops and establishing a fixed price for each piece of merchandise. In

Vertical integration

industry, steel offers a good example. Steel became in any case a big business when heavy blast furnaces were introduced. It was not safe for the steel business, or for the blast furnaces, to rely for iron and coal on independent producers who might sell it to whomsoever they pleased. The steel works therefore began to operate mines of their own or to buy out or otherwise reduce coal and iron mines to subsidiary status. Some, to assure their markets, began to produce not merely steel but steel manufactures as well—steel ships, railway equipment, naval and military ordnance. Thus entire processes from mining to finished product became concentrated in a "vertical" integration.

By "horizontal" integration concerns at the same level combined with each other to reduce competition and to protect themselves against fluctuations in prices and in markets. Some fixed prices, some agreed to restrict production, some divided up markets among themselves. They were called trusts in the United States, cartels in Europe. They were common in many of the new industries at the close of the century, such as chemicals, aluminum, and oil. In steel such combinations produced the great interests of Krupp in Germany, Schneider-Creusot in France, Vickers-Armstrong in Great Britain. It

"Captains" of industry, "titans" of finance

was in the United States that such big business developed furthest, headed by "captains" of industry and "titans" of finance. Andrew Carnegie, by origin a poor Scottish immigrant boy, produced more steel than all England; in 1901 he sold out to an even more colossal organization, the United States Steel Corporation, formed by the financier J. P. Morgan. It was in the United States, too, that concern over monopoly and the power of big business in general was felt most strongly; antitrust legislation, beginning with the Sherman Act of 1890, was enacted but never with any substantial effect.

Many of the new combinations were beneficial in making the ups and downs of business less erratic, and so providing more stable prices and more continuous and secure employment. Generally they reduced the costs of production; but whether the savings went into higher profits, higher wages, or lower prices depended on numerous factors. Some trusts were more greedy than others or confronted with only weakly organized or unorganized labor. In any case, for good or ill, decisions rested with management and finance. A new kind of private power had arisen, which its critics like to call "feudal." Since no economic system had ever been so centralized up to that time, never in fact had so few people exercised so much economic power over so many. The middle class, with the rise of great corporations, came typically to consist of salaried employees; the salaried person might spend a lifetime with the same company, and feel toward it, in its disputes with labor or government, a loyalty not unlike that of a lord's retainer in feudal times. The laboring class was less amenable; labor attempted to organize unions capable of dealing with increasingly gigantic employers. It also after about 1880 played an increasingly decisive role in the politics of all advanced nations.

74.   THE ADVANCE OF DEMOCRACY: THIRD FRENCH REPUBLIC, UNITED KINGDOM, GERMAN EMPIRE

In the years from 1815 to 1870 European political life had been marked by liberal agitation for constitutional government, representative assemblies, responsible ministries, and guarantees of individual liberties. In the years from 1871 to 1914, even where these liberal objectives were not fully achieved but remained as goals, the most notable political development was the democratic extension of the vote to the working class—the adoption of universal male suffrage, which in turn meant for the first time the creation of mass political parties and the need for political leaders to appeal to a wide electorate. Although there was growing agitation for female voting rights in the decades before 1914, the extension of male suffrage in these years did not generally take place because of protest movements, as in the days of the Chartists or of the radical reformers in France. Governments for a variety of reasons extended the suffrage on their own. Often democratization took place in a continuing monarchical and aristocratic framework, but almost everywhere by 1914 the machinery at least of democratic self-government was being introduced. In addition, to counter the growing strength of socialism after 1871, and for humanitarian reasons, governments were also assuming responsibility for the social and economic problems arising from industrialism. The welfare state in its modern form was taking shape.

France: The Establishment of the Third Republic

In France the democratic republic was not easily established, and its troubled early years left deep cleavages within the country. It will be recalled that in September 1870, when the empire of Napoleon III revealed its helplessness in the Franco-Prussian War, insurrectionaries in Paris, as in 1792 and 1848, again proclaimed the Republic. A provisional government of national defense sought desperately to continue the war, but the cause was hopeless. By January 1871, a bitter siege of Paris came to an end and an armistice was signed. Bismarck, insisting that only a properly constituted government could make peace, permitted the election, by universal male suffrage, of a National Assembly which was to consider his peace terms and draft a constitution for the new French state. When the elections were held in February, it was found, as in 1848 (and, indeed, 1797), that republicanism was so distrusted by the French people as a whole, and most especially in the provinces and rural areas, that a free election brought monarchist elements into power. Republicanism was still thought to be violent—bellicose in its foreign policy, turbulent in its political workings, unfriendly to the church, and socialistic or at least egalitarian in its views of property and private wealth. The new Assembly contained only about 200 republicans out of more than 600 deputies.

But the Paris republicans, who had defended France when Napoleon III failed to do so, who for four months had been besieged, starved, and frozen by the Germans, and who still refused to make peace on the harsh terms imposed by Bismarck and about to be accepted by the Assembly, refused to recognize the latter's authority. A civil war broke out between the National Assembly, now sitting at Versailles, and the city of Paris, where a revolutionary municipal council or "Commune" was set up. Paris, so lately attacked by German soldiers, was now attacked by French.

The Paris Commune, which lasted from March to May 1871, seemed to be another explosion of social revolution. Actually, it was in essence a revival of the Jacobinism of 1793. It was fiercely patriotic and republican, anti-German, opposed to wealthy bourgeois, aristocrats, and clergy, in favor of government controls upon prices, wages, and working conditions, *The Paris Commune* but still not socialist in any sweeping or systematic way. Among its leaders, however, there were a few of the new international revolutionary socialists, who saw in a Jacobin or democratic republic a step toward their new order. Marx in England, and others elsewhere, hopefully read into the Commune the impending doom of the bourgeoisie. This was precisely what more conservative elements feared. To many of the French middle and

The Bon Marché department store in Paris became a well-known example of the new, large stores that began to displace smaller shops and independent merchants. The new era is evident in this late nineteenth-century illustration of the store's vast expanse, proliferation of merchandise, and affluent shoppers. Department stores provided a safe meeting place for women as well as lower prices for the many new products of the industrial era.

(Picture Collection, The New York Public Library, Astor, Lenox, and Tilden Foundations) peasant class, and to people like them all over Europe, it seemed that the Communards were wild and savage destroyers of nineteenth-century civilization. The fighting in Paris was atrocious beyond anything known in any preceding French revolution. The Communards, in final desperation, burned a number of public buildings and put to death the archbishop of Paris, whom they held as a hostage. The forces of the National Assembly, when finally triumphant, were determined to root out the inveterate revolutionism of Paris. Some 330,000 persons were denounced, 38,000 were arrested, 20,000 were put to death, and 7,500 were deported to New Caledonia. The Third Republic was born in an atmosphere of class hate and social terror.

The form of government for the new regime still had to be established. The monarchist majority in the Assembly was itself evenly divided between those who favored a restoration of the Bourbon family and those who favored the Orléanist. In the end, even after they were reconciled, the Bourbon candidate alienated everyone by his stiff insistence on a return to the white flag of the Bourbons. The monarchists checkmated each other. Meanwhile, after extended discussion of various constitutional projects, the Assembly adopted in 1875 not a constitution, but certain constitutive laws. By a margin of one vote, a resolution indirectly amounting to the establishment of a republic was passed. The new laws provided for a president, a parliament in two chambers, and a council of ministers, or cabinet, headed by a premier. The Senate was to be elected by a complicated and indirect system of election; the Chamber of Deputies, by universal, direct, male suffrage.

Within two years, in 1877, the role of the president, the ministers, and the parliament was further clarified as a result of an unsuccessful attempt by an early president, Marshal MacMahon, to dismiss a premier of whom he did not approve but who had the backing of the Chamber. MacMahon proceeded to dissolve the Chamber and to hold new elections, but the example of Napoleon III's transformation of the Second Republic into an authoritarian regime was still fresh. The elections vindicated the principle of parliamentary primacy and of the responsibility of the premier and his cabinet to the legislature, a responsibility which in France meant generally but not exclusively to the lower house. The true executive in republican France for a long time was to be the premier and his cabinet, themselves held strictly to account by a majority of the legislature. Unfortunately, that majority, in a parliament where a dozen or so parties were represented, was always difficult to form and could be created only by unstable, temporary, shifting party alliances, coalitions, or blocs. No president, and indeed no premier, could henceforth dissolve the Chamber in order to hold new elections and consult the country as could be done in Britain. Actually, under the Third Republic the substantial machinery of state—ministries, prefectures, law courts, police, army, all under highly centralized control—was carried over virtually untouched as in all upheavals since the time of Napoleon I. France in the nineteenth century, so volatile in appearance, in effect underwent less extensive reorganization than any other leading country in Europe.

Parliamentary primacy

Troubles of the Third French Republic

Yet the Third Republic was precarious. The government had changed so often since 1789 that all forms of government seemed to be transitory. Questions that in other countries were questions about specific government policies or party programs became in France fundamental questions of "regime"—monarchy versus republic. Many people, especially those influenced by the upper classes, the Catholic clergy, and the professional army

This barricade and its defenders suggest the revolutionary fervor of the Paris Commune, which controlled the French capital in the spring of 1871. The Commune was in many respects a revival of revolutionary Jacobinism rather than a precursor of social revolution, but it provoked intense fear and brutal repression from more conservative forces in French society. Revolutionary images of Parisian radicals in the streets—as seen in this photograph—made the Paris Commune a symbol of political idealism and martyrdom for many socialists and a symbol of dreadful social dangers for the middle and upper classes.

(AKG London)

officers, continued to feel a positive aversion to the republic. On the other hand, the unmerciful and vindictive repression of the Commune made many middle-class people sympathetic to the republicans. Many turned republican simply because no other form of government established itself or because it was the form of government that divided the country the least. As republicanism took in wider elements of society, it became less revolutionary and less fearsome. In 1879, for the first time, republicans won control of both houses of the government. In the 1880s their radicalism hardly went further than the founding of a democratic and compulsory school system at government expense and the passage of anticlerical legislation intended to curb church influence in education.

The Dreyfus Affair

For over a quarter of a century, however, republican energies had to be expended in defense of republican institutions in order to ensure the survival of the regime. An initial crisis arose in 1886–1889, when General

Boulanger gathered around him an incongruous following that included not only Bonapartists, monarchists, and aristocrats but also extreme radical republicans who wished a war of revenge against Germany, and workers disgruntled over their unhappy lot. Boulanger became a popular figure and seemed for a moment about to seize power. But the menace collapsed in a comical failure as the general lost heart at the crucial hour and fled into exile. Meanwhile, in the 1880s and 1890s scandals and revelations of corruption in high republican circles provided ammunition for the antirepublicans. Moreover, the hope that unsympathetic French Catholics would rally to the republic, as urged by French prelates and by Pope Leo XIII in 1892, was shattered by the Dreyfus Affair, which in the late 1890s rocked the country and indeed the world.

In 1894 Captain Dreyfus, a Jewish army officer, was found guilty of treason by a military court and deported to Devil's Island. Evidence accumulated showing his innocence and pointing to the guilt of another officer, a Major Esterhazy, an adventurer known to be riddled with gambling debts. But the army refused to reopen the case, unwilling to admit it had erred; a staff officer, Major Henry, even forged documents to confirm Dreyfus's guilt. Meanwhile anti-Semites, royalists, traditionalists, militarists, and most of the "best" people fought the reopening of the case, deeming it unpatriotic to shake the nation's confidence in the army and wishing also to disgrace the republican regime. The partisans of Dreyfus stubbornly upheld him, both because they believed in justice and because they wished to discredit their antirepublican adversaries. The country was deeply split. Finally, in 1899, Dreyfus was pardoned, and in 1906 he was fully exonerated. In the aftermath of the affair, leftist republicans and socialists revenged themselves by blocking the promotions of antirepublican officers and by anticlerical legislation. In 1905, in a series of laic laws, they "separated" church and state, ending the close relationship established under Napoleon's concordat a century earlier.

The Strength and Weakness of the Republic

The Third Republic, when the First World War came in 1914, a test which it was successfully to meet, had lasted over twice as long as any French regime since 1789. Born unwanted and accidentally, though it still had opponents, it now commanded the loyalty of the overwhelming mass of the French people. What it had done, since 1871, was to domesticate democratic republicanism in Europe. Republicanism, one of the most militant of revolutionary movements down to 1870, had been shown in France to be compatible with order, law, parliamentary government, economic prosperity, and a mutual tolerance between classes, to the extent at least that they no longer butchered each other in the streets. Industrial workers were in many ways less well off than in England or Germany, but there were fewer of them; and for most people France in these years was a pleasant country, full of painters, writers, scholars, and scientists, full of bankers, bourgeois and well-established farmers, a country living comfortably and unhurriedly on the savings of generations, and one in which, in a close-knit family group, average men and women could plan securely for their own and their children's future.

Domesticating republicanism

But the very comforts and values of bourgeois France were not those that would equip it for leadership in the modern age of technology and industrial power. Though substantial economic progress was made, the country lagged behind Germany in industrial development; the French entrepreneur showed little inclination to take the business risks needed for industrial growth. Politically, the fragmentation of political parties, itself a democratic reflection of a divided public opinion, and the distrust for historic reasons of a strong executive power led to the rise and fall of numerous short-lived ministries—no fewer than 50 in the years between 1871 and 1914. Ministerial instability was to be a chronic symptom of the Third Republic both before and after 1914; continuity of government policy was, however, generally maintained because of stability in certain key ministries and because of the permanent civil service.

French labor remained a steady source of discontent. Although French workers benefited from some labor legislation in the two decades after 1890, they continued to feel frustrated at the failure to establish a "social republic." Socialist representation in the Chamber grew, thus strengthening the antiroyalist factions in the French government.

The Radical Socialists

However, the most important single party of the republic, the Radicals, or Radical Socialists, were in actuality radical republicans—patriotic, anticlerical, spokesmen for the small shopkeepers and the lesser propertied interests; they drew the line at the advanced social legislation that labor expected from them, and on occasion their leaders even took positive steps to prevent unionization and to suppress strikes. Since some of these Radicals had started out as socialists, the distrust of French workers for all politicians and even for political processes was intensified. But the difficulties of the republic went deeper. The political energies of the republican statesmen had gone into liquidating the past, into curbing the political strength of the monarchists, the church, and the army; by the turn of the century, even before these older issues were fully resolved, the republic was compelled to meet the challenge of labor and to face other domestic and international pressures that were to try it sorely. The Third Republic was to weather the crisis of the First World War but not that of the Second.

The British Constitutional Monarchy

The British constitutional monarchy in the half-century before 1914 was the great exemplar of reasonable, orderly, and peaceable self-government through parliamentary methods. For over 60 years, spanning two-thirds of the nineteenth century, Victoria reigned (1837–1901) and gave her name to a distinguished era of material progress, literary accomplishment, and political stability. The two great parties, Liberal and Conservative, the heirs roughly of the Whigs and Tories, took form in the 1850s, the former producing its great leader in William E. Gladstone, the latter, a series of leaders of whom the most colorful was Benjamin Disraeli.

The advance toward an egalitarian political democracy in Britain was more cautious and slower than in France. The Reform Bill of 1832 had granted the vote to about an eighth of the adult male population. The democratic Chartist agitation of the 1830s and 1840s attracted wide popular support but failed to produce further reforms in the electoral system. In 1867, however, in response to continued demand for a wider suffrage, the Second Reform Bill was passed, Conservatives as well as Liberals outdoing one another in an effort to satisfy the country and to win new political strength for their own party.

The extension of suffrage

The bill, adopted under Disraeli's Conservative ministry, extended the suffrage from about 1 million eligible voters to about 2 million, or over a third of the adult males in the United Kingdom, reaching down far enough to include most workers in the cities. Disraeli's colleague Lord Derby called it a "leap in the dark." In 1884, under Liberal auspices, the suffrage was again broadened, this time in the rural areas, adding some 2 million additional voters and enfranchising over three-fourths of all adult males in the country. Not until 1918 did Great Britain adopt universal male suffrage, as generally understood; and at that time the long campaign for women's political rights gained at least a partial victory when women over the age of 30 received the right to vote.

Despite the extension of the suffrage, the leadership of the country at the turn of the century was still in the hands of the upper and wealthier classes. Until 1911 the government paid no salaries to members of the House of Commons, who therefore, in both great parties, were usually gentlemen with private incomes, possessing the same family background and education. An attitude of sportsmanship and good feeling was characteristic of British politics. The two parties alternated in power at regular intervals, each indulgent toward the other, carrying over and developing rather than reversing the policies of its predecessor in office. Both parties sought support where they could find it, the Liberals leaning somewhat more on the industrial and commercial interests, the Conservatives on the landed aristocracy; both sought and succeeded in winning their share of the new working-class vote.

The Liberals were usually the more willing to pioneer, the first of the four ministries of Gladstone being especially notable in this respect. Gladstone in this first ministry (1868–1874) developed the principle of state-supported public education under the Forster Education Act of 1870, introduced the secret ballot, formally legalized labor unions, promoted competitive examinations for civil service posts, reorganized the upper judiciary, eliminated the purchase and sale of commissions in the army (a form of property in office), and by abolishing religious tests enabled persons not members of the Church of England to graduate from Oxford and Cambridge. The Conservative party, less sensitive to pressure from business interests for a laissez-faire policy in economic matters, and continuing the tradition of early Tory reformers, took the initiative in further labor legislation. Under Disraeli's second ministry (1874–1880), the existing acts regulating public sanitation and conditions in mines and factories were extended and codified, safety measures were enacted to protect sailors, and the first attempt to regulate housing conditions for the poorer classes was initiated. But the Liberals, it must be added, protected the workers' interests too. In Gladstone's second ministry (1880–1885) workers were assured of compensation for injuries not of their own responsibility, and in 1892, before the formation of his fourth ministry (1892–1894), Gladstone campaigned to shorten labor hours and to extend employers' liability in accidents.

Liberals and Conservatives

British Political Changes after 1900

At the turn of the century important changes were discernible on the British political scene. Labor emerged as an independent political force, the Labour party itself being organized shortly after 1900. The rise of labor had a deep impact upon the Liberal party and indeed upon liberalism itself. With many persons insisting that protective measures be taken to counteract the poor health, low income, and economic insecurity of British workers, the Liberals abandoned their traditional position of laissez-faire and sponsored a policy of government intervention and social legislation in behalf of working people. The Liberals, though they acted in part for humanitarian reasons, were aware that with the emergence of the Labour party workers who customarily had voted for them might readily transfer their allegiance.

Rise of British labor

SUNDAY AFTERNOON ON THE ISLAND OF LA GRANDE JATTE
by Georges Seurat (French, 1859–1891)

This picture of sunny calm, painted in 1886, conveys the well-being that many Europeans enjoyed in the late nineteenth century. The people portrayed here seem to live in a peaceable world that is far removed from a later age of speed and mechanical amusements. Technically, this is one of the most remarkable pictures ever painted. The artist created it without the use of lines by filling the canvas with thousands of minute dots of the primary colors, which blur and mix in the eye to produce the forms, hues, light, and shadows of nature.

(The Art Institute of Chicago)

In control of the government from 1906 to 1916, with Herbert Asquith as prime minister and David Lloyd George as chancellor of the exchequer during most of this time, the Liberals put through a spectacular program of social welfare. Sickness, accident, old-age, and a degree of unemployment insurance were adopted, and a moderate minimum wage law was enacted. Labor exchanges, or employment bureaus, were set up over the country. Restrictions on strikes and other trade union activities were removed. To meet the costs of the new program as well as of other government expenditures, Lloyd George's budget of

1909 called for progressive income and inheritance taxes: wealthier taxpayers would be taxed at progressively higher rates. He was in effect advancing the then novel idea of using taxation to modify the social extremes of wealth and poverty. It was a "war budget," he said, intended "to wage war against poverty." Its fiscal measures were directed primarily at the landed aristocracy, and it aroused great opposition, especially in the House of Lords, where the contest over the budget led to a further constitutional curtailment of the power of the upper house. The Parliament Act of 1911 deprived the Lords of all veto power in money matters and of all but a two-year delaying veto on action of the Commons in other legislation. At this time, too, the government voted to pay salaries to members of the House of Commons, making it possible for workers and others without independent incomes to take seats in Parliament.

A war against poverty

The Liberal party was embracing a program of positive state intervention in social and economic matters that the older liberalism, nurtured on the doctrines of laissez-faire and the Manchester School, would not have accepted. With the Liberals actively seeking the support of labor and altering much in their traditional program, the Conservatives in the twentieth century tended to become the party of industry as well as of landed wealth and to replace the Liberals as the champions of economic liberalism and laissez-faire. In the next generation, after the First World War, the Conservatives were to remain one of the two major parties of the country; the Liberals were to be far outstripped by the Labour party.

State intervention

Meanwhile, despite its gains, labor was not pacified. Real wages showed a tendency to fall after 1900, and great coal and railway strikes broke out in 1911 and 1912. The British capacity to survive crises without violence, while still conspicuous, was being strained. An even more serious threat came from Ireland.

The Irish Question

Britain suffered from one of the most bitter minorities conflicts in Europe—what the British called the Irish question. After 1801 Britain was known as the United Kingdom of Great Britain and Ireland, Ireland having been incorporated into the United Kingdom as a defensive measure against pro-French sympathies in Ireland during the wars of the French Revolution. The Irish representatives who sat in Parliament were generally obstructionist in their tactics. The Irish had many substantial grievances, among which two were conspicuous. The Irish peasants were defenseless against their landlords, far more so, for example, than the French peasants before 1789; and the Irish people, though predominantly Catholic, were obliged to pay tithes to the established Church of Ireland (an Anglican sister church to the Church of England), which also owned a good deal of the land.

Gladstone, in his first ministry, disestablished the Church of Ireland. He also initiated measures to protect the Irish farm tenant. By 1900, under Conservative auspices, Irish tenants were being assisted by the British government to buy out their landlords—often English or Anglicized and absentee Irish landowners. The Irish also wanted home rule, or a parliament of their own. Gladstone, in trying to give it to them in 1886, split his Liberal party, part of which went along with the Conservatives in opposing a political division of the British Isles. Home rule was finally granted to Ireland in 1914. But the Ulstermen, Protestants of northern Ireland, objected vehemently to inclusion in an autonomous Ireland, in which they would be outnumbered by the Catholics of the south. The latter, however, insisted with equal vehemence on the inclusion of Ulster, not wishing a political division of Ireland.

Home rule

The Ulstermen, backed by British Conservatives, started arming and drilling to resist the act of Parliament that authorized home rule. Great Britain, in 1914, was about to see a civil war on its own doorstep. It suffered from something like the insoluble nationalist disputes that afflicted Austria-Hungary. During the First World War home rule was suspended, and after considerable violence on both sides Catholic Ireland (Eire) received dominion status in 1922, but eventually dissolved all ties with Britain. Northern Ireland remained in the United Kingdom and was dominated by Protestants, so that its Catholic minority continued to be an alienated, discontented population within the British state. The "Irish question" remained an unresolved issue, generating bitter resentments and violent conflicts during all of the twentieth century.

Bismarck and the German Empire, 1871–1890

The German Empire, as put together by Bismarck in 1871 with William I, king of Prussia, as Kaiser, was a federation of monarchies, a union of 25 German states, in which the weight of monarchical Prussia, the Prussian army, and the Prussian landed aristocracy was preponderant. It developed neither the strong constitutionalism of England nor the democratic equality that was characteristic of France. To win popular support for his projects, Bismarck exploited existing democratic and socialist sentiment and provided that members of the Reichstag, the lower chamber, be elected by universal male suffrage. Remaining chancellor of the united empire for some 20 years, from 1871 to 1890, he usually tried to have a majority in the Reichstag on his side, but he recognized no dependence on a majority in principle, holding to the doctrine that it was the emperor and his chancellor who were to govern the country. Moreover, in practice, the legislative powers of the lower house were severely restricted, and the upper chamber, representing the princes and not the people, and favored by the government, tended to be more important. Despite the nature of the empire, the Prussian conservatives, the East Elbian Junker landlords, were at first by no means enthusiastic over Bismarck's unified Germany. They opposed his democratic concessions and were left horrified when in 1872 he undertook to extinguish what was left of their manorial jurisdiction over their peasants.

Bismarck in the 1870s therefore leaned not on the Conservatives but on the National Liberals. With their aid he put through a number of economic and legal measures designed to consolidate the unity of the new empire. Bismarck's first serious conflict developed with the Catholic church. At the very time that he was bent on subordinating all groups within the state to the sovereign power of the new empire, the church had spoken out. In 1864 in the *Syllabus of Errors,* it denounced the encroachment of all governments on educational and church affairs; in 1870 the new dogma of papal infallibility made it incumbent on Catholics to accept unreservedly the pope's pronouncements in matters of faith and morals. To many, the implication was that the new empire could not count on the undivided loyalty of its Catholic citizens. To defend Catholic interests and those of the south German states where Catholicism predominated, Catholic elements had organized the strong Center party, which now upheld the church pronouncements. In 1871 Bismarck launched the *Kulturkampf,* or "battle for modern civilization." The Liberals joined in eagerly. Like nineteenth-century liberals elsewhere (Gladstone's campaign against Anglican privilege and the French laic laws have just been mentioned), they were strongly anticlerical and disapproved of the influence of organized churches in public and private life. Laws were put through imposing restrictions upon Catholic worship and education, the Jesuits were ex-

The Catholic church

pelled, and many Catholic bishops throughout Germany were arrested or went into exile. But Bismarck gradually concluded that the anti-Catholic legislation was fruitless, that he had overestimated the danger to the state of organized Catholicism, and that he needed the support of the Center party for other parts of his program.

In 1879, with the support of the Center and Conservative parties but to the dismay of many of his erstwhile Liberal allies, Bismarck abandoned free trade and adopted a protective tariff that provided needed revenues for the government and gave satisfaction both to agricultural and industrial interests. Meanwhile, the country's rapid and spectacular industrial expansion had stimulated the growth of the German working class, and to Bismarck's alarm, socialism was spreading.

The German Social Democratic party had been founded in 1875 by a fusion of Marxian socialists and the reformist followers of Ferdinand Lassalle on an essentially moderate program which Marx had denounced. But even a moderate socialism was mistrusted by Bismarck. He shared in the European horror at the recent Paris Commune, he feared socialism as anarchy, and he knew that socialism was in any case republican, which made it a potentially revolutionary movement in an empire of monarchies. Two radical attempts on the emperor's life (in neither case by Social Democrats) provided him with all the excuse he needed. In 1878, having already made peace with the Catholics, he set out to eradicate socialism. Antisocialist laws from 1878 to 1890 prohibited socialist meetings and socialist newspapers. For 12 years socialism was driven underground. But repression was not his only weapon; he turned also to another tactic. Bismarck sought to persuade the workers to place

Repression of socialism

their faith in him and the German Empire rather than in Marx and the prophets of socialism. To that end, in the 1880s, he initiated an extensive program of social legislation. Workers were insured by the state against sickness, accident, and incapacity in old age. "Our democratic friends," said Bismarck, "will pipe in vain when the people see princes concerned with their well-being." In social insurance imperial Germany was, from whatever motives, years ahead of more democratic England, France, and the United States.

Bismarck failed to kill socialism. The number of socialists elected to the Reichstag was greater in 1890 than in 1878—for Bismarck's antisocialist campaign, in deference to the then current standards of civilized government, never suppressed the voter's freedom to vote as he chose. It seems, however, that Bismarck by the later 1880s was more apprehensive than ever of social revolution that would destroy his empire and contemplated some kind of coup d'état in which the Reichstag would be throttled. He never reached this point because in 1890, at the age of 75, he was obliged by the new emperor, William II, to retire.

The German Empire after 1890: William II

William I died in 1888 and was succeeded by his son Frederick III, who had been married for many years to Victoria, the eldest daughter of England's Queen Victoria. Incurably ill of cancer, he died some three months after his accession. Frederick's son, William II, the last king of Prussia and the last German Kaiser,

William II

began his reign (1888–1918) as a young man of 29, full of startling ideas about his personal power and privileges, somewhat in contrast to his father. He was also uncomfortable in the presence of an elder statesman who had made the German Empire, who had been his grandfather's aide and adviser, and whom he regarded partly with veneration and partly as an old fogy. William soon quarreled with Bismarck over continuation of the antisocialist laws and over matters of foreign affairs. When Bismarck forbade his ministers to meet with the emperor on policy matters unless he was present, William resolved that he, and not Bismarck, would rule the empire, and in 1890 he ordered Bismarck to resign, "dropping the pilot," in the celebrated phrase. Under the four chancellors who succeeded Bismarck, it was William who dominated policy.

A "new course"

After 1890 Germany embarked upon what was termed a "new course." In foreign affairs this meant a more aggressive and ambitious colonial, naval, and diplomatic policy. In domestic affairs it meant a more conciliatory attitude toward the masses. The antisocialist laws were dropped, and the system of social security legislation was enlarged and codified. But no democratic adjustment seemed possible. William II believed in the divinely ordained prerogatives of the house of Hohenzollern, and the empire still rested on the power of the federated princes, the Junkers, the army, and the new industrial magnates. But the Social Democrats, the Progressive party, and other democratic forces were growing in strength. They demanded, for Prussia, a reform of the illiberal constitution of 1850, and for the Reich, real control over the federal chancellor by the majority party in the Reichstag. In the election of 1912 the Social Democrats reached a new high by polling four and a quarter million votes, about one-third of the total, and by electing 110 members to the Reichstag, in which they now formed the largest single party; yet they were excluded from the highest posts of government. Even had war not come in 1914, it is clear that the imperial Germany created by Bismarck was moving toward a constitutional crisis in which political democracy would be the issue.

Developments Elsewhere; General Observations

Political scene in Italy

Of political developments in other European states before 1914, something has already been said in the preceding chapter. Italy had become a constitutional monarchy in the 1860s and completed its unification by the forceful seizure of Rome in 1870. Despite parliamentary reforms, Italian political life in substance was characterized by unstable majorities and by opportunistic maneuvering and manipulation by moderate liberal political leaders, who maintained themselves in office for long periods of time by shuffling and reshuffling political coalitions. Deputies, in a form of parliamentary politics that was baptized *trasformismo* (or a kind of "crossing over") moved readily from one party group to another—for favors granted. The liberal leaders were anticlerical, and the quarrel with the papacy over the seizure of the papal territories remained unsettled. The popes refused to recognize the Italian kingdom and forbade Catholics to participate in its affairs or even to vote in elections. Catholics voted nonetheless and in 1907 bishops in each diocese were permitted to relax the ban, as they increasingly did.

Industry had begun to make an appearance in the northern cities like Milan. More as a matter of expediency than out of any democratic impulse, the government moved to extend the franchise to the working classes. The narrow suffrage of 1861 was broadened, first in 1882, and then in 1912, when the new reform increased the number of eligible voters from 3 to 8 million, or virtually universal male suffrage. Because of illiteracy and political inertia not all of the newly enfranchised hastened to exercise their voting privilege. The social problem remained serious, too, despite some modest labor legislation. Poverty and illiteracy, especially in the agrarian south, were grievous problems, and radical unrest appeared in the industrial cities. The first manifestations of an antiparliamentary ideology, chauvinistic nationalism, and explosive irrationalism appeared in the writings and political activism of literary men like Gabriele d'Annunzio and Filippo Marinetti, the latter publishing in 1909 the manifesto of a violently nihilistic movement he called "futurism." The machinery of political democracy was established in Italy, but there could be no assurance about the direction Italian parliamentary democracy was taking.

In the Dual Monarchy of Austria-Hungary, created by the compromise of 1867, Austria and Hungary were each in form constitutional parliamentary states. In theory, the Emperor-King Francis Joseph ruled through ministries responsible to the legislature in each state. However, in the important sphere of matters affecting the empire as a whole, such as foreign affairs and military questions, there was little parliamentary restraint on the emperor. Here he had virtually final authority; moreover, in all matters he still had broad powers to govern by decree, which he exercised. As in Germany, the tide of socialism was held back both by repressive laws and by social insurance and benevolent legislation. The most serious problem in the empire remained not socialism but agitation by the various subject nationalities, the Czechs and other Slavic peoples. Political democracy took a different course in Austria than in Hungary. In the former, partly as an effort to placate nationalist sentiment, universal male suffrage was introduced in 1907. In the latter it was bitterly and successfully resisted by the Magyars, who saw in it a weapon that could be employed by the Slavs to contest and destroy the Magyar preponderance. Austria itself, despite the democratic suffrage, was ruled very much like the German Empire, with the legislature able to debate and criticize but not control policy.

Austria-Hungary

Of other countries it can be said that the political forms of democracy showed signs of advancing everywhere. Universal male suffrage was adopted in Switzerland in 1874, in Belgium in 1893, in the Netherlands in 1896; and in the next few years in Norway and Sweden (Norway was peacefully separated in 1905 from Sweden). In southern Europe, besides Italy, universal male suffrage was introduced in Spain, Greece, Bulgaria, Serbia, and after the revolt of 1908, in Turkey. Although both Spain and Portugal were beset by civil wars, constitutional forms were eventually adopted in both countries, universal male suffrage being introduced in Spain in 1890 and a liberal suffrage in Portugal under a republic in 1911. Even tsarist Russia, after the Revolution of 1905, received a Duma, or national parliament, elected on a wide franchise but on an indirect and undemocratic class basis, and with narrow powers. Among states west of the Russian empire, only Hungary and Romania had a highly restricted suffrage on the eve of the First World War. The vote for women progressed more slowly. Women voted before 1914 only in certain western states of the United States, in Australia, New Zealand, Finland, and Norway. Not until after the First World War did female suffrage begin to make significant advances, and women did not have the right to vote in France and Italy until after the Second World War.

Democratic advances

The progress of representative and democratic institutions did not mean an end to the rule of monarchs, landed aristocrats, and other minority interests. For one thing, with the exception of France and Switzerland, Europe remained monarchical. Second, despite the growing importance of parliaments, parliamentary control over political life was far from guaranteed; emperors and kings still ruled through their chancellors and prime ministers. Of the major world powers it was mainly in the United States (at least for white males), Britain, and France that democratic and popular control was something of a reality. But the extension of the suffrage, by the relaxation of property qualifications, had a dynamic of its own and was altering the

Expansion of the suffrage

framework of politics everywhere; mass political parties, including socialist parties and confessional, or religious-oriented parties, were replacing the older, narrow oligarchic political organizations, and support now had to be sought on a wider electoral basis. In almost all Europe, and in many of the outlying areas peopled by European descendants, democracy was advancing, even within the older framework. By 1871, most European nations, with the notable exception of Russia, had already won written constitutions, guarantees of personal freedom, parliamentary and representative institutions, and limitations on absolutism; in the years between 1871 and 1914 the most significant new political factor was the advance of male suffrage.

The growing populations and economies of European nations thus created a social stability in which political institutions gradually became more democratic and more responsive to public opinion. Wealth and resources flowed into Europe from all parts of the world, so that the middle classes and even workers had more comforts and material goods than ever before—and more opportunities to participate in the political institutions of their various nations. Europe's dominant role in the global economy, the massive migration of European people, and the military power of European nation-states gave European civilization its extraordinary world influence in the decades before 1914.

During these same years, however, the power of industrial corporations, capitalist financial institutions, and European ideas and attitudes also provoked opposition, which appeared in popular political movements, as in socialism, and in criticisms of imperialism. The critics eventually influenced many people outside Europe, gaining a following wherever European economic and cultural institutions had appeared. European criticisms of Western capitalism, traditions, and ideas became another aspect of Europe's influence around the world.

Chapter 15

EUROPEAN
CIVILIZATION,
1871–1914:

SOCIETY AND CULTURE

The belief in progress has been at the center of modern thought since the Scientific Revolution of the seventeenth century. Although some romantic poets, conservatives, and socialists questioned the consequences of modern technologies and industry, most people in the nineteenth century assumed that progress was both inevitable and beneficial. Liberals were especially optimistic about progressive developments in all the main spheres of modern life: scientific knowledge, new inventions, economic expansion, constitutional government, and protection for fundamental human rights. But the liberals were by no means alone in seeing the late nineteenth-century European ascendancy as the historical confirmation of human progress.

There were also many Europeans, however, who believed that whole groups of human beings were denied the benefits of modern civilization, that workers were not receiving their rightful share of modern wealth, or that women were not entering their rightful place in modern political life. The popular new political movements in these decades thus presumed that they were on the side of progress, and in fact they often gained new rights or benefits for the groups they represented.

Meanwhile, science itself continued to produce advances in both the theoretical understanding of nature and the technological inventions that transformed modern societies. Yet it was also at this time that various advanced thinkers began to question the certitudes of scientific knowledge and to stress the limits of human reason, thus challenging cultural assumptions that sustained the popular belief in human progress. These new trends in European intellectual life before 1914 began to erode some of the confidence in the progressive evolution of human history (at least among certain philosophers or artists) and to

Chapter emblem: Albert Einstein as he appeared after he had published scientific papers on the theory of relativity in 1905 and 1916.

undermine the optimism of classical liberalism. The idea of progress remained a powerful theme in all modern cultures, but by the early twentieth century the limits and consequences of progress were also becoming subjects for historical reflection and cultural debate.

75.   THE ADVANCE OF DEMOCRACY: SOCIALISM, LABOR UNIONS, AND FEMINISM

Opponents
of liberalism

The artisan and laboring classes had never viewed with much favor the rise of capitalism or of "bourgeois" liberalism. They had always been suspicious of free competition, unrestrained private enterprise, the Manchester School, laissez-faire, the laws of supply and demand, the free market for goods and labor, the idea of an economy independent of states and governments. These were the ideas of middle-class liberals, not of radical democrats. Popular leaders had opposed them in the French Revolution in 1793. The English Chartists had been outspokenly anticapitalistic, and on the Continent the ideas of socialism had been spreading. In 1848 there was a strong movement among the working classes for a "social" republic, and, though the social revolution failed in 1848, the force of it was enough to terrify the possessing classes and shape the philosophy of Karl Marx. With the advent of the ballot, workers pressed for social legislation and used their political power to gain a greater measure of social democracy.

But in addition, before and after obtaining the ballot, working people resorted to other devices for the improvement of their position. Against the owners of capital, who controlled the giving of jobs, there were two principal lines of action. One was to abolish the capitalists; the other, to bargain with them. The former led to socialism; the latter, to the formation of labor unions. Socialism, in logic, meant the extinction of the private employer as such. Trade unionism, in logic, meant that the workers had every reason to keep their employers prospering in business in order that bargaining with them might produce more results. The working-class movement thus contained an internal contradiction which was never completely resolved.

Workers and
intellectuals

Middle-class and educated people who took up the workers' cause, the "intellectuals" of the movement—Karl Marx, Friedrich Engels, Louis Blanc, Ferdinand Lassalle, and thousands of less famous names—tended more to socialism than to unionism. They thought of society as a whole, they saw the economy as a complex social system, they thought of the future in long-run terms, and their time scale allowed generously for whole historical epochs to come and go. The actual workers, put to work at an early age, barely educated if at all, with the waking hours of their adult lives spent on manual jobs, were inclined to keep their attention more on unionism than on socialism. To earn a shilling more every week beginning next week, to be spared the nervous strain and physical danger of constant exposure to unprotected machinery, to have 15 minutes more every day for lunch, were likely to seem more tangible and important than far-reaching but distant plans for a reconstructed society. The worker looked on the intellectual as an outsider, however welcome; the intellectual looked on the worker as shortsighted and timid, however much in need of help.

After the failures of 1848 the socialist and trade union movements diverged for a generation. The 1850s, compared with the hungry '40s, were a time of full employment, rising wages, and increasing prosperity for all classes. Workers set to organizing unions, socialist thinkers to perfecting their doctrines.

The Trade Union Movement and Rise of British Labor

Organizations of wage workers, or labor unions in the modern sense (as distinguished from medieval craft guilds), had long maintained a shadowy and sporadic existence. But they had always been extralegal, frowned upon or actually prohibited by governments. French revolutionaries in the Le Chapelier Act of 1791, British Tories in the Combination Act of 1799, had been as one in forbidding workers to unite. It was the rise of "bourgeois" liberalism, so insensitive to the worker in most ways, that first gave legal freedom to labor unions. The British unions received a tacit recognition from the Liberal Tories in 1825 and explicit recognition from Gladstone's Liberal ministry in 1871. French unions were recognized by Napoleon III in 1864, then restrained in the reaction caused by the Commune, then fully legalized in 1884. In Germany Bismarck negotiated with labor leaders to find support against the vested interests that stood in his way.

The prosperity of the 1850s favored the formation of unions, for workers can always organize most easily when employers are most in need of their services. The craft union— or union of skilled workers in the same trade, such as carpenters—was at first the typical organization. It was most fully developed in England, where a "new model" unionism was introduced by the Amalgamated Society of Engineers (i.e., machinists) in 1851. It was the policy of the "new model" union officials to take the unions out of politics, to forget the semisocialism of the Chartists, to abandon Robert Owen's grandiose idea of "one big union" for all workers, and to concentrate on advancing the interests of each separate trade. The new leaders proposed to be reasonable with employers, avoid strikes, accumulate union funds, and build up their membership. In this they were very successful; the unions took root; and the two governing parties in England, reassured by the unexpected moderation of working-class representatives, combined to give the town worker the vote in 1867.

"New model" unionism

In the 1880s, and especially with the great London dock strike of 1889, which closed the port of London for the first time since the French Revolution, unions of unskilled workers began to form. Industrial unionism, or the joining in one union of all workers in one industry, such as coal or transportation, regardless of the skill or job of the individual worker, began to take shape at the same time. In some cases the older skilled unionists joined with unskilled laborers who worked beside them. By 1900 there were about 2,000,000 union members in Great Britain, compared with only 850,000 in Germany and 250,000 in France.

It was largely because British workers were so far advanced in trade unionism, and so successful in forcing collective bargaining upon their employers, that they were much slower than their Continental counterparts in forming a workers' political party. By the 1880s, when avowed socialists were already sitting in French, Belgian, and German parliaments, the only corresponding persons in Britain were a half-dozen "Lib-Labs," as they were called, laboring men elected on the Liberal ticket. The British Labour party was formed at the turn of the century by the joint efforts of trade union officials and middle-class intellectuals. Where on the Continent the labor unions were often led, and even brought into being, by the socialist political parties, in Britain it was the labor unions that brought into being, and subsequently led, the Labour party. Hence for a long time the Labour party was less socialistic than working-class parties on the Continent. Its origin and rapid growth were due in large measure to a desire to defend the unions as established and respectable institutions.

The British Labour party

The unions were threatened in their very existence by a ruling of the British courts in 1901, the Taff Vale decision, which held a union financially responsible for business losses incurred by an employer during a strike. The shortest and most orderly strike, by exhausting a union's funds, might ruin the union. The year before, steps had been taken to bring together the unions and all other existing labor and socialist organizations into a labor representation committee, in preparation for the elections of 1900; the effort was not very successful and only 2 of the 15 labor candidates were returned. But the Taff Vale decision unified all ranks and precipitated the formation of the modern Labour party. In the election of 1906 the new Labour party sent 29 members to Parliament, which thereupon overruled the Taff Vale decision by new legislation. The social legislation put through Parliament by the Liberal party government in the next few years, in good part under pressure from labor, has been described in the last chapter.

The Taff Vale decision

European Socialism after 1850

As for socialism, which had so frightened the middle and upper classes in 1848, it seemed in the 1850s to go into abeyance. Karl Marx, after issuing the *Communist Manifesto* with Engels in 1848, and agitating as a journalist in the German revolution of that year, withdrew to the secure haven offered by England, where, after years of painstaking research, he published the first volume of his *Capital* in 1867. This work, of which the succeeding two volumes were published after his death, gave body, substance, and argument to the principles announced earlier in the *Communist Manifesto*. Marx, during more than 30 years in London, scarcely mixed with the labor leaders then building up the English unions. Hardly known to the English, he associated mainly with political exiles and temporary visitors of numerous nationalities. The first volume of *Capital* was not published in English until 1886.

The First International

In 1864 there took place in London the first meeting of the International Working Men's Association, commonly known as the First International. It was sponsored by a heterogeneous group, including the secretary of the British carpenters' union, Robert Applegarth; the aging Italian revolutionary, Mazzini; and Karl Marx. With the union officials absorbed in union business, leadership in the Association gradually passed to Marx, who used it as a means of publicizing the ideas about to appear in his *Capital*. At subsequent annual congresses, at Geneva, Lausanne, Brussels, and Basel, Marx built up his position. He made the Mazzinians unwelcome, and he denounced the German Lassalleans for their willingness to cooperate with Bismarck, arguing that it was not the business of socialists to cooperate with the state but to seize it. His sharpest struggle was with the Russian Bakunin. With his background in tsarist Russia, Bakunin believed the state to be the cause of the common man's afflictions; he was hence an "anarchist," holding that the state should be attacked and abolished. To Marx anarchism was abhorrent; the correct doctrine was that the state—tsarist or bourgeois—was only a product of economic conditions, a tool in the class struggle, a weapon of the propertied interests, so that the true target for revolutionary action must be not the state but the capitalist economic system. Marx drove Bakunin from the International in 1872.

The Paris Commune

Meanwhile members of the First International watched with great excitement the Paris Commune of 1871, which they hoped might be the opening act of a European working-class upheaval. Members of the International infiltrated the Commune, and the connection between the two, though rather incidental, was one reason why the French Provisional Government repressed the Commune with such terrified ferocity. But the Commune actually destroyed the First International. The Commune had been bloody and violent, an armed rebellion against the democratically elected National Assembly of France. Marx praised it as a stage in the international class war. He even saw in it a foretaste of what he was coming to call the "dictatorship of the proletariat." He thus frightened many possible followers away. Certainly British trade unionists, sober and steady individuals, could have nothing to do with such doings or such doctrines. The First International faded out of existence after 1872.

But in 1875, at the Gotha conference, Marxian and Lassallean socialists effected enough of a union to found the German Social Democratic party, whose growth thereafter, against Bismarck's attempts to stop it, has already been noted. About 1880 socialist parties sprouted in many countries. In Belgium, highly industrialized, a Belgian Socialist party appeared in 1879. In the industrial regions of France some workers were attracted to Jules Guesde, a self-taught worker, former Communard, and now a rigid Marxist, who held it impossible to emancipate the working class by compromise of any sort; others followed the "possiblist" Dr. Paul Brousse, who thought it possible for workers to arrive at socialism through parliamentary methods; still others supported Jean Jaurès, who eloquently linked social reform to the French revolutionary tradition and the defense of republican institutions. Not until 1905 did the socialist groups in France form a unified Socialist party. In England, in 1881, H. M. Hyndman founded a Social Democratic Federation on the German model and with a Marxist program; it never had more than a handful of members. In 1883 two Russian exiles in Switzerland, Plekhanov and Axelrod, recent converts to Marxism, founded the Russian Social Democratic party, from which the communism of the following century was eventually to be derived. The socialist parties all came together to establish an international league in 1889, known as the Second International, which thereafter met every three years and lasted until 1914.

*The Second
International*

Revisionist and Revolutionary Socialism, 1880–1914

The new socialist parties of the 1880s were all Marxist in inspiration. Marx died in 1883. Marxism or "scientific socialism," by the force of its social analysis, the mass of Marx's writings over 40 years, and an attitude of unyielding hostility to competing socialist doctrines, had become the only widely current form of systematic socialism. Strongest in Germany and France, Marxism was relatively unsuccessful in Italy and Spain, where the working class, less industrialized anyway, more illiterate, unable to place its hopes in the ballot, and habituated to insurrectionism in the manner of Garibaldi, turned more frequently to the anarchism preached by Bakunin.

Nor was Marxism at all successful in England; workers stood by their trade unions, and middle-class critics of capitalism followed the Fabian Society, established in 1883. The Fabians (so called from the ancient Roman general Fabius Cunctator, the "delayer," or strategist of gradual methods) were very English and very un-Marxist. George Bernard Shaw, H. G. Wells, and Sidney and Beatrice Webb were among early members of the Society. For them socialism was the social and economic counterpart to political democracy, as well as its inevitable outcome. They held that no class conflict was necessary or even existed, that gradual and reasonable and conciliatory measures would in due time bring about a socialist state, and that improvement of local government, or municipal ownership of such things as waterworks and electric lighting, were steps toward this consummation. The Fabians, like the trade union

*Fabian socialism
in England*

The French painter Jean Béraud depicted the leaders and audience at this well-attended workers' meeting in 1884. The labor movement was becoming a more organized, influential political force at this time, and Béraud's picture suggests both the political passions and organization that were giving workers a new role in European societies.

(Staatsbibliothek, Berlin)

officials, were content with small and immediate satisfactions. They joined with the unions to form the Labour party. At the same time, by patient and detailed research into economic realities, they provided a mass of practical information on which a legislative program could be based.

The Marxist or Social Democratic parties on the Continent grew very rapidly. Marxism turned into a less revolutionary "parliamentary social-

Parliamentary socialism on the Continent

ism"—except indeed for the Russian Social Democratic party, since Russia had no parliamentary government. For the growth of socialist parties meant that true workers, and not merely intellectuals, were voting for socialist candidates for the Reichstag, Chamber of Deputies, or whatever the lower house of parliament might be called; and this in turn meant that the psychology and influence of labor unions within the parties were increased. The workers, and their union officials, might in theory consider themselves locked in an enormous struggle with capital; but in practice their aim was to get more for themselves out of their employers' business. They might believe in the internationalism of the workers' interests; but in practice, acting through the parliaments of national states, they would work for orderly legislation benefiting the workers of their own country only—social insurance, factory regulation, minimum wages, or maximum hours.

Nor was it possible to deny, by the close of the century, that Marx's anticipations (based initially on conditions of the 1840s) had not come true, at least not yet; the bourgeois was getting richer, but the proletarian was not getting poorer. Real wages—or what the wage earner's income would actually buy, even allowing for the losses due to unemployment—are estimated to have risen about 50 percent in the industrialized countries between 1870 and 1900. The increase was due to the greater productivity of labor through mechanization, the growth of the world economy, the accumulation of capital wealth, and the gradual fall in prices of food and other items that the workers had to buy.

Repeatedly, but in vain, the Second International had to warn its component socialist parties against collaboration with the bourgeoisie. Marxism began in the 1890s to undergo a movement of revisionism, led in France by Jean Jaurès, Socialist leader in the Chamber of Deputies, and in Germany by Eduard Bernstein, Social Democratic member of the Reichstag and author in 1898 of *Evolutionary Socialism,* an important tract setting forth the new views. The revisionists held that the class conflict might not be absolutely inevitable, that capitalism might be gradually transformed in the workers' interest, and that now that the workers had not only the vote but also a political party of their own, they could obtain their ends through democratic channels, without revolution and without any dictatorship of the proletariat. Most socialists or social democrats followed the revisionists.

The revisionists

This tendency to "opportunism" among Marxists drove the really revolutionary spirits into new directions. Thus there arose revolutionary syndicalism, of which the main intellectual exponent was a Frenchman, Georges Sorel. "Syndicalism" is simply the French word for trade unionism (*syndicat,* a union), and the idea was that the workers' unions might themselves become the supreme authoritative institutions in society, replacing not only property and the market economy, but also government itself. The means to this end was to be a stupendous general strike, in which all workers in all industries would simultaneously stop work, thus paralyzing society and forcing acceptance of their will. Syndicalism made most headway where the unions were weakest, as in Italy, Spain, and France, since here the unions had the least to lose and were most in need of sensational doctrines to attract members. Its strongest base was in the French General Confederation of Labor, founded in 1895.

Syndicalism

Among orthodox Marxists there was also a revival of Marxist fundamentals in protest against revisionism. In Germany Karl Kautsky arraigned the revisionists as compromisers who betrayed Marxism for petty-bourgeois ends. In 1904 he and other rigorists prevailed upon the Second International to condemn the political behavior of the French socialist Alexandre Millerand who in 1899 had accepted a ministerial post in a French cabinet. Socialists might use parliaments as a forum, the International ruled, but socialists who entered the government itself were unpardonably identifying themselves with the enemy bourgeois state. Not until the First World War did socialists henceforth join the cabinet of any European country. In the Russian Social Democratic party the issue of revisionism came to a head in 1903, at a party congress held in London—for the most prominent Russian Marxists were mainly exiles. Here a group led by the committed revolutionist V. I. Lenin demanded that revisionism be stamped out. Lenin won a majority, at the moment at least, and hence the uncompromising Marxists were called Bolsheviks (from the Russian word for majority), while the revisionist or conciliatory Russian Marxists, those willing to work with bourgeois liberals and democrats, were subsequently known as Mensheviks or the "minority" group. But in 1903 the Russian Marxists were considered very unimportant.

Orthodoxy vs. Revisionism

In general, in Europe's inner zone, by the turn of the century, most people who called themselves Marxists were no longer actively revolutionary.

Marxism transformed

As revolutionary republicanism had quieted down in the Third French Republic, so revolutionary Marxism seemed to have quieted down into the milder doctrines of social democracy. What would have happened except for the coming of war in 1914 cannot be known; possibly social revolutionism would have revived, since real wages no longer generally rose between 1900 and 1914, and considerable restlessness developed in labor circles, punctuated by great strikes. But in 1914 the working class as a whole was in no revolutionary mood. Workers still sought a greater measure of social justice, but the social agitation so feared or hoped for in 1848 had subsided. There seem to have been three principal reasons. Capitalism had worked well enough to raise the workers' living standard above what they could remember of their parents' or grandparents'; workers had the vote and so felt that they participated in the state, could expect to benefit from the government, and had little to gain by its overthrow; and they had their interests watched over by organized and increasingly powerful unions, by which a larger share in the national income could be demanded and passed on to them.

Feminism, 1880–1914

The campaign for women's rights also became more international and better organized during the same decades that the new workers' parties were spreading across Europe. Women received less pay than men for the work they performed in the new industrial economy, and in most places they still faced numerous restrictions on their rights to own property, participate in political meetings, vote in elections, and attend universities. The movement for women's rights therefore continued to promote the kind of reforms that feminists had been advocating since the early nineteenth century, including more access to education and the right to vote. Women's groups on the Continent tended to emphasize legal and social reforms rather than voting rights, whereas British and American feminists gave more attention to the campaign for women's suffrage. But activists in all industrialized societies were increasingly drawn to national and international organizations, in part because such groups created useful networks for spreading information and political ideas. American women such as Susan B. Anthony and Elizabeth Cady Stanton joined with European feminists to establish an International Council of Women in 1888, and the growing demand for women's rights could be heard across the borders of all modern nations.

Suffragettes seek the vote

Although some feminists worked to make birth control available to more women or to improve the conditions of women workers, the quest for voting rights attracted the most public attention, especially in the United States and Britain. New organizations such as the National American Woman Suffrage Association and, in Britain, the Women's Social and Political Union sponsored petitions, mass meetings, and protests that demanded equal voting rights in both local and national elections. The suffrage movement in Britain became especially militant after the British Parliament rejected every legislative proposal to grant women the vote—a pattern of official opposition that had become part of British politics since the 1860s. Frustrated by the stubborn resistance of male politicians, the energetic leader of the Women's Social and Political Union, Emmeline Pankhurst, led a radical wing of the suffrage movement into a campaign of violent protests. Pankhurst's supporters and allies disrupted sessions of Parliament, broke store windows, destroyed mailboxes, and damaged government buildings to protest the exclusion of women from British elections and political institutions. When arrested, the "suffragettes" went on hunger strikes, to which the police responded by painful forcible feedings through tubes lowered into their stomachs.

The British campaign for women's voting rights often mobilized women for marches in the streets, public demonstrations, and confrontations with government officials. The protestors at this march in 1913 were following a woman who had been arrested at an early suffragist demonstration, and the presence of the police is an example of the close government surveillance that was part of every such event.

(Hulton Getty)

Pankhurst and other suffragettes were widely ridiculed in the British press and Parliament, but their campaign attracted growing support during the First World War (when the militant protests were suspended), and, as noted earlier, British women over the age of 30 finally received the right to vote in 1918. Women also gained the right to vote in Germany, the United States, and other Western nations in this same postwar era. The campaign for voting rights was only one component of modern feminism, however, and the movement to enhance women's rights in the economy, legal system, family, and education would develop new themes and new political strategies throughout the twentieth century.

76.   SCIENCE, PHILOSOPHY, THE ARTS, AND RELIGION

Faith in the powers of natural science has been characteristic of modern society for over three centuries, but never was there a time when this faith spread to so many people, or was held so firmly, so opportunistically, and with so few qualms or mental reservations as in the half-century preceding the First World War. Science lay at the bottom of the whole movement of industrialization; and if science gained wide popularity after about 1870, in that persons ignorant of science came to look upon it as an oracle, it was because it manifested itself to everybody in the new wonders of daily life. Hardly had the world's more industrialized regions digested the railroad, the steamship, and the telegraph when a whole series of new inventions began to appear. In the 30 years following 1875 the number of patents tripled in the United States, quadrupled in Germany, and multiplied in all modern countries. The scientific and technical advance was as completely international (though confined mainly to the "inner zone") as any movement the world has ever seen. Never had the rush of scientific invention been so fundamentally useful, so helpful to the constructive labors and serious problems of mankind, and in that sense human.

Changing conceptions in science

In more basic scientific thinking important changes set in about 1860 or 1870. Up to that time, generally speaking, the underlying ideas had been those set forth by Isaac Newton almost two centuries before. The law of universal gravitation reigned unquestioned, and with it, hardly less so, the geometry of Euclid and a physics that was basically mechanics. The ultimate nature of the universe was thought to be regular, orderly, predictable, and harmonious; it was also timeless, in that the passage of ages brought no change or development. By the end of the epoch considered here, that is, by 1914, the old conceptions had begun to yield on every side.

The Impact of Evolution

In impact upon general thinking the greatest change came in the new emphasis upon biology and the life sciences. Here the great symbolic date is the publication by Charles Darwin of the *Origin of Species* in 1859. Evolution, after Darwin, became the order of the day. Evolutionary philosophies, holding that the way to understand anything was to understand its development, were not new in 1859. Hegel had introduced the evolutionary conception into metaphysics; and he and Marx, into historical theories of human society. The idea of progress, taken over from the Age of Enlightenment, was a kind of evolutionary philosophy; and the great activity in historical studies, under romantic and nationalist auspices, had made people think of human affairs in terms of a time process. In the world of nature, the rise of geology after 1800 had opened the way to evolutionary ideas, and venturesome biologists had allowed themselves to speculate on an evolutionary development of living forms. What Darwin did was to stamp evolution with the seal of science, marshaling the evidence for it and offering an explanation of how it worked. In 1871, in *The Descent of Man,* he applied the same hypotheses to human beings.

By evolution, Darwin meant that species are mutable; that no species is created to remain unchanged once and for all; and that all species of living organisms, plant and animal, microscopic or elephantine in dimensions, living or extinct, have developed by successive small changes from other species that went before them. An important corollary was that all life was interrelated and subject to the same laws. Another corollary was that the whole history of living things on earth, generally held by scientists in Darwin's time to be many millions of years, was a unified history unfolding continuously in a single meaningful process of evolution.

Darwin thought that species changed, not by any intelligent or purposeful activity in the organism, but essentially by a kind of chance. Individual organisms, through the play of heredity, inherited slightly different characteristics, some more useful than others in food getting, fighting, or mating; and the organisms that had the most useful characteristics tended to survive, so that their characteristics were passed on to offspring, until the whole species gradually changed. Certain phrases, not all of them invented by Darwin, summed up the theory. There was a "struggle for existence" resulting in the "survival of the fittest" through "natural selection" of the "most favored races"—races meaning not human races but the strains within a species. The struggle for existence referred to the fact that, in nature, more individuals were born in each species than could live out a normal life span; the "fittest" were those individual specimens of a species having the most useful characteristics, such as fleetness in deer or ferocity in tigers; "natural" selection meant that the fittest survived without purpose in themselves or in a Creator; the "favored races" were the strains within a species having good survival powers.

"Survival of the fittest"

Darwin's ideas precipitated a great outcry. Scientists rushed to defend and churchmen to attack him. The biologist T. H. Huxley became the chief spokesman for Darwin—"Darwin's bulldog." He debated with, among others, the bishop of Oxford. Darwin was denounced, with less than fairness, for saying that human beings came from monkeys. It was feared that all grounds of human dignity, morality, and religion would collapse. Darwin himself remained complacent on this score. Under civilized conditions, he said, the social and cooperative virtues were useful characteristics assisting in survival, so that "we may expect that virtuous habits will grow stronger, becoming perhaps fixed by inheritance." Much of the outburst against Darwin was somewhat trivial, nor were those who attacked him generally noted for spiritual insight; yet they were not mistaken in sensing a profound danger.

That Darwinism said nothing of God, Providence, creative design, or salvation was not surprising; no science ever did. That evolution did not exactly square with the first chapter of Genesis was disturbing but not fatal; much of the Old Testament was already regarded as symbolic, at least outside certain fundamentalist circles. Even the idea that humans and animals were of one piece was not ruinous; the animal side of human nature had not escaped the notice of theologians. The novel and upsetting effect of evolutionary biology was to change the conception of nature. Nature was no longer a harmony, it was a scene of struggle, "nature red in tooth and claw." Struggle and elimination of the weak were natural, and as means toward evolutionary development they might even be considered good. Such conceptions of what was good or beneficial for evolutionary progress profoundly challenged traditional religious ideas about morality and virtue. There were no fixed species or perfected forms, but only an unending flux. Change was everlasting; and everything seemed merely relative to time, place, and environment. There were no norms of good and bad; a good organism was one that survived where others perished; adaptation replaced virtue; outside it there was nothing "right." The test was, in short, success; the "fit" were the successful; and here Darwinism merged with that toughness of mind, or *Realpolitik*, which was appearing in Europe at the same time from other causes.

Changing views of nature

Such at least were the implications if one generalized from science, carrying over scientific findings into human affairs, and the prestige of science was so great that this is precisely what many people wished to do. With the popularization of biological evolution, a school known as Social Darwinists actively applied the ideas of the struggle for existence and survival of the fittest to human society. Social Darwinists were found all over Europe and the United States. Their doctrines were put to various political and cultural uses, to show that some peoples were naturally superior to others, such as whites to blacks, or Nordics to Latins, or Germans to Slavs (or vice versa), or non-Jews to Jews; or that the upper and

Social Darwinism

middle classes, comfortable and contented, deserved these blessings because they had proved themselves "fitter" than the shiftless poor; or that big business in the nature of things had to take over smaller concerns; or that some states, such as the British or German Empires, were bound to rise, or that war was morally a fine thing, proving the virility and survival value of those who fought.

Genetics, Anthropology, and Psychology

Gregor Mendel

Meanwhile Gregor Mendel (1822–1884), an Austrian monk patiently experimenting with the cross-pollination of garden peas in his Augustinian monastery, arrived at an explanation of how heredity operates and how hybridization can take place. Unlike Darwin, his findings, published in 1866, were ignored until 1900, when they were rediscovered and became the basis for the new science of genetics. Mendel's ideas foreshadowed the amazing breakthroughs in the scientific study of heredity and control over genetic materials in the second half of the twentieth century.

Anthropologists began to study the physical and cultural characteristics of all branches of humankind. Physical anthropologists became interested in the several human "races," some of which they considered might be "favored" in the Darwinian sense, that is, superior in inheritance and survival value. Some European scientists and intellectuals in this era argued that the whites were the most competent race, and among the whites the Nordics, or Germans and Anglo-Saxons. The public became more race conscious than Europeans had ever been before. On the other hand the cultural anthropologists, surveying all manner of primitive or complex societies with scientific disinterest, seemed sometimes to teach a more deflating doctrine. Scientifically, it seemed, no culture or society was "better" than any other, all being adaptations to an environment, or merely a matter of custom—of the *mores,* as people said in careful distinction from "morals." The effect was again a kind of relativism or skepticism—a negation of values, a belief that right and wrong were matters of social convention, psychological conditioning, mere opinion, or point of view. We are describing, let it be emphasized, not the history of science itself but the effects of science upon European civilization at the time.

Anthropology and religion

The impact of anthropology was felt keenly in religion too. Sir James Frazer (1854–1941) in his multivolumed *The Golden Bough* could demonstrate that some of the most sacred practices, rites, and ideas of Christianity were not unique but could be found among numerous premodern societies and that, moreover, only the thinnest of lines divided magic from religion. Anthropology, like Darwinian evolution, undermined traditional religious beliefs.

Psychology, as a science of human behavior, led to thoroughly upsetting implications about the very nature of human freedom and rationality. It was launched in the 1870s as a natural science by the German physiologist Wilhelm Wundt (1832–1920), who developed various new experimental techniques. The Russian Ivan Pavlov (1849–1936) conducted a famous series of experiments in which he "conditioned" dogs to salivate automatically at the ringing of a bell once they had become accustomed over a period of time to associate the sound with the serving of their food. Pavlov's observations were important. They implied that a great part of animal behavior, and presumably human behavior, could be explained on the basis of conditioned responses. In the case of human beings these are responses which humans make automatically by virtue of their earlier environment and training and not through choice or conscious reasoning.

Sigmund Freud

Most significant of all the developments in the study of human behavior was the work of Sigmund Freud (1856–1939) and those influenced by him. Freud, a Viennese physician, founded psychoanalysis at the turn of the century. He came to believe that certain forms of emotional disturbance like hysteria were traceable to earlier forgotten episodes of patients' lives. After first trying various techniques such as hypnosis, which he soon abandoned, he employed free association, or free recall. If patients could be helped to bring these suppressed experiences into conscious recall, the symptoms of illness would often disappear. From these beginnings Freud and his followers explored the role that the unconscious played in all human behavior, he himself stressing the sexual drive. In one of his most famous books, *The Interpretation of Dreams* (1900), he stressed dreams as a key to understanding the unconscious; elsewhere he related his findings to religion, war, education, art, and literature. Freud and Freudian ideas had great influence on the social and behavioral sciences, and a good deal of the Freudian vocabulary later entered into everyday modern language and popular culture. In its deepest significance psychoanalysis, by revealing the wide areas of human behavior outside conscious control, suggested that human beings were not essentially rational creatures at all. Although Freud identified with the scientific traditions of the Enlightenment, his theory of the unconscious called into question the classical liberal and Enlightenment assumptions about how reasonable persons developed, explained, and acted upon their individual interests or beliefs.

The New Physics

The revolution in biology of the nineteenth century, together with the developments in psychology and anthropology, were soon to be matched and surpassed by the revolution in physics. In the late 1890s physics was on the threshold of a revolutionary transformation. Like Newtonian mechanics in the seventeenth century and Darwinian evolution in the nineteenth, the new physics represented one of the great scientific revolutions of all time. There was no single work comparable to Newton's *Principia* or Darwin's *Origin of Species* unless Albert Einstein's theory

Einstein's theory of relativity

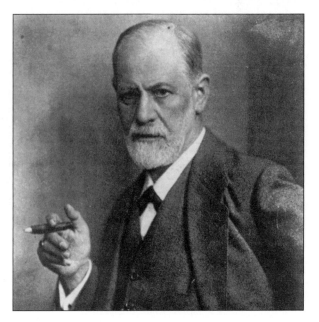

Sigmund Freud's description of the unconscious mind reshaped modern conceptions of human psychology and influenced the arts, literature, and social theories as well as the medical treatment of mental illnesses. As this photograph suggests, however, the "revolutionary" Dr. Freud was also a typical member of his own cultural milieu—the professional class in early twentieth-century Vienna.

(Culver Pictures, Inc.)

of relativity, propounded in a series of scientific papers in 1905 and 1916, might be considered as such. Instead there were a series of discoveries and findings, partly mathematical and then increasingly empirical, that threw new light on the nature of matter and energy. In Newtonian physics the atom, the basic unit of all matter, which the Greeks had hypothesized in ancient times, was like a hard, solid, unstructured billiard ball, permanent and unchanging; and matter and energy were separate and distinct.

But a series of discoveries from 1896 on profoundly altered this view. In 1896 the French scientist Antoine Henri Becquerel discovered radioactivity, observing that uranium emitted particles or rays of energy. In the years immediately following, from the observations and discoveries of the French scientists Pierre and Marie Curie and the Englishmen J. J. Thomson and Lord Rutherford, there emerged the notion that atoms were not simple but complex and, moreover, that various radioactive atoms were by nature unstable, releasing energy as they disintegrated. The German physicist Max Planck demonstrated in 1900 that energy was emitted or absorbed in specific and discrete units or bundles, each called a quantum; moreover, energy was not emitted smoothly and continuously as previously thought, nor was it as distinguishable from matter as once supposed. In 1913, the Danish physicist Niels Bohr postulated an atom consisting of a nucleus of protons surrounded by electrically charged units, called electrons, rotating around the nucleus, each in its orbit, like a minuscule solar system.

With radioactivity scientists were being brought back to the idea long rejected, the favored view of the alchemists, that matter was transmutable; in a way undreamed of even by the alchemists, it was convertible into energy. This the German-born Jewish scientific genius Albert Einstein (1879–1955) expressed in a famous formula $e = mc^2$. From his theory of relativity emerged also the profoundly revolutionary notion that time, space, and motion were not absolute in character but were relative to the observer and the observer's own movement in space. In later years, in 1929 and in 1954, Einstein brought together into one common set of laws, as Newton formerly had done, a unified field theory, an explanation of gravitation, electromagnetism, and subatomic behavior. Difficult as it was for even the serious-minded to grasp, and a great deal was still the subject of scientific controversy, it modified much that had been taken for granted since Newton. The Newtonian world was being replaced

$$e = mc^2$$

The new theories that emerged in physics after 1900 transformed earlier Newtonian science and gave the young Albert Einstein an international reputation. This picture shows Einstein standing next to his personal books and papers in the 1920s, several years before he moved to the United States to escape the intolerance and repression in Nazi Germany.

(Hulton Getty)

by a four-dimensional world, a kind of space-time continuum; and in mathematics, non-Euclidian geometries were being developed.

It turned out, too, that neither cause and effect nor time and space nor Newton's law of universal gravitation meant very much in the subatomic world nor indeed in the cosmos when objects moved with the speed of light. It was impossible, as the German scientist Werner Heisenberg demonstrated a little later, in 1927, by his principle of uncertainty, or indeterminacy, to ascertain simultaneously both the position and the velocity of the individual electron. On these foundations established before the First World War there developed the new science of nuclear physics and the tapping of the atom's energy. The atom and its world of subatomic particles were discovered to be even more complex than conceived of before 1914.

Trends in Philosophy and the Arts

Although some writers and artists resembled earlier Romantic thinkers in criticizing Enlightenment ideas or modern science, most European intellectuals in this period viewed science as the model for all forms of knowledge. They were drawn to positivism or to the belief that scientific methods provided the only "positive" knowledge of the world. Anything unknowable to science must therefore remain unknowable forever—a doctrine called agnosticism, or the acknowledgment of ignorance. Herbert Spencer (1820–1903) in England and Ernst Haeckel (1834–1919) in Germany were widely read popularizers of agnosticism; both also pictured a universe governed by Darwinian evolution. For Spencer especially, all philosophy could be unified, organized, and coordinated through the doctrine of evolution; this doctrine he applied not only to all living things but also to sociology, government, and economics as well. The evolution of society, he felt, was toward the increasing freedom of the individual, the role of governments being merely to maintain freedom and justice; they were not to interfere with natural social and economic processes, nor to coddle the weak and unfit. Yet, like Darwin himself, Spencer believed that altruism, charity, and goodwill as individual ethical virtues were themselves useful and laudable products of evolutionary development.

Agnosticism

These latter views were not shared by another of the serious writers of the age, also much influenced by evolutionary ideas, the German philosopher Friedrich Nietzsche (1844–1900). More a philosopher of art than of science, and drawing upon many intellectual currents of the century, Nietzsche was an unsystematic, radical thinker to whom it is easy to do less than justice. It is evident, however, that he held a low opinion of modern, democratic societies. From a background of evolutionary thinking he developed the concept of a Superman, a new kind of noble being who would create new ethical values and philosophical truths that would enable him to dominate and dazzle the multitude. Qualities of humility, patience, helpfulness, hope, and love, in short the specifically Christian virtues, Nietzsche described as a slave morality concocted by the weak to disarm the strong. Qualities of courage, love of danger, intellectual excellence, and beauty of character, he prized more highly. Indeed he argued that all humans, even philosophers, were driven more by their instincts and a "will to power" than by reason or rational thought. His views were in essence a new form of classical paganism. Nietzsche was neither much read nor much respected by his contemporaries, who considered him unbalanced or even insane; but he nevertheless expressed with unshrinking frankness many implications of the new evolutionary

Friedrich Nietzsche

ideas. And his critique of reason and rationality had wide influence among anti-Enlightenment thinkers both before and after the First World War.

As in the sciences and philosophy, so in works of creative imagination—literature, drama and the fine arts—the changes at the dawn of the twentieth century ushered in the contemporary age. Some writers, like Emile Zola in France or Henrik Ibsen in Scandinavia, turned to the portrayal of social problems, producing a realistic literature that dealt with industrial strife, strikes, prostitution, divorce, or insanity. New psychological theories appeared in fictional portraits of troubled characters and irrational human behavior. The new literature was indeed often truer to life than the older. In a sense the arts followed the intellectual developments of the age, reflecting, as they do today, attitudes of relativism, irrationalism, social determinism, and interest in the operations of the unconscious mind. On the other hand, never had artist and society been so far apart. The painter Paul Gaugin, an extreme case, fled to the South Seas, abandoned his family and modern European life, and reveled in the stark violence of tropical colors. Others became absorbed in technicalities or mere capricious self-expression. Art at its extreme fringe became incomprehensible and the average person was deprived of a visual means (as old as the cave paintings of the Stone Age) of perceiving and enjoying the world. After the First World War, and on into the present, the same trends of subjectivism in the arts attracted a wider, less skeptical, audience. People read books without punctuation (or with peculiar punctuation); listened to music called atonal, composed for effects of discord and dissonance; and studied intently abstract or "nonobjective" paintings and sculpture to which the artists themselves often refused to give titles.

Increasingly remote from modern industrial society, artists and their art exemplified the specialization of the modern world. Artists were no longer speaking for society or creating art for common use or enjoyment but were specialists plying their trade and pursuing their own concerns—like other specialists whose work was often incomprehensible to outsiders.

The Churches and the Modern Age

Religion, too, was displaced. It was now a long time since almost everyone had looked to religion for guidance. But religion was more threatened after 1860 or 1870 than ever in the past, because never before had science, or philosophies drawing upon science, addressed themselves so directly to the nature of life and of human existence. Never before had so many of the fundamental premises of traditional religion been questioned or denied. Darwinian evolution challenged the value of Christian ethics as well as the traditional picture of Creation, and anthropologists questioned the uniqueness of the most sacred Christian tenets. There developed also the "higher" criticism of the Bible, an effort to apply to the Scriptures the techniques of scholarship long applied to secular documents, to incorporate archeological discoveries, and to reconstruct a naturalistic, historical account of ancient religious times. This form of critical, textual analysis, going back at least to the seventeenth century, now took on significant proportions and was applied both to the Old Testament and the New. In the case of the Old Testament the patient scrutiny of style and language cast doubt on the validity of certain prophecies; and in the New the inconsistencies of the several Gospel sources were made patent. The German theologian David Friedrich Strauss (1808–1874), one such critical scholar, was the author of a widely discussed *Life of Jesus,* in which many miraculous and supernatural episodes were reverently but firmly explained away as myth.

*Threats
to religion*

The sensitive French historian and man of letters Ernest Renan (1823–1892) in a some-what similar vein wrote on Jesus and the origins of Christianity and on the life of ancient Israel, giving secular explanations for the oldest religious stories and beliefs. Moreover, the whole tenor of the time, its absorption in material progress, likewise kept people away from church; and the wholesale uprooting, the movement from country to city, often broke religious ties.

The Protestant churches were less successful than the Catholic in pro-tecting their membership from the disintegrating effects of the age. Church attendance among Protestants became increasingly casual, and the doc-trines set forth in sermons seemed increasingly remote. Protestants tradi-tionally trusted their own private judgment and regarded their clergy as their own agents, not as authoritative teachers placed above them. Protestants also had al-ways set special emphasis on the Bible as the source of religious belief; and as doubts ac-cumulated on the literal truth of Biblical narratives there seemed no other authoritative source on which to rely.

Challenges to Protestantism

Protestants tended to divide between modernists and fundamentalists. The fundamen-talists, as they were called in the United States, in an effort to defend the literal word of Scripture, were often obliged to deny the most indubitable findings of science. The mod-ernists were willing enough to be scientific and to interpret much of the Bible as allegory, but only with difficulty could they recapture any spirituality or urgent feeling of Christian truth. Most Protestant churches were slow to face the social problems and wholesale in-justices produced by the economic system, though a group of "Christian socialists" had emerged by the early twentieth century in some Protestant denominations. Because edu-cation itself and care for orphans, sick, and mentally disturbed persons passed to the state, Protestant groups had less to do in the relief of suffering and the upbringing of the young. Protestantism, to the regret of many Protestants, became increasingly a customary obser-vance by people whose minds were elsewhere. Not until after the First World War could a strong Protestant revival be discerned, with a reaffirmation of basic doctrines by theolo-gians such as Karl Barth, and a movement on the part of divergent Protestant churches to combine.

The Roman Catholic church proved more resistant to the trends of the age. We have seen how Pope Pius IX (1846–1878), after being driven from Rome by republicans in 1848, gave up his inclinations to liberalism. In 1864, in the *Syllabus of Errors,* he denounced as erroneous a long list of widely current ideas, including the faith in rationalism and science, and he vigorously de-nied that the head of the church "should reconcile and align himself with progress, liber-alism, and modern civilization." The *Syllabus* was in form a warning to Catholics, not a matter of dogma incumbent upon them to believe. In dogma, the Immaculate Conception of the Virgin Mary was announced as dogmatic truth in 1854; a century later, in 1950, the bodily assumption of Mary into heaven was proclaimed. Thus the Catholic church reaf-firmed in a skeptical age, and against Christian modernists, its faith in the supernatural and miraculous.

Catholicism resists

Pius IX also convened an ecumenical church council which met at the Vatican in 1870. It was the first such council since the Council of Trent some 300 years before. The Vatican Council proclaimed the dogma of papal infallibility, which holds that the pope, when speaking *ex cathedra* on matters of faith and morals, speaks with a final and supernatural authority that no Catholic may question or reject. The Vatican Council, and the acceptance of papal infallibility by Catholics, was the climax of centuries of development within the church. In brief, as the world grew more national, Catholicism became more international. As state sovereignty and secularism grew, Catholic clergy looked increasingly to the spiritual powers of Rome for protection against alien forces. Much in the past 300 years had made Catholics distrustful of their own governments or of non-Catholics in their midst— the Protestantism and the state churches of the sixteenth century, the Jansenist movement of the seventeenth, the anticlericalism of enlightened despotism in the eighteenth, the hostility to the church shown by the French Revolution, and by liberalism, republicanism, and socialism in the nineteenth century. By 1870 the net effect was to throw Catholics into the arms of the Holy See. Ultramontanism, the unconditional acceptance of papal jurisdiction, prevailed over the old Gallican and other national tendencies that had long existed within the Catholic church.

Vatican City

In 1870, while the 600 prelates of the Vatican Council were sitting, the new Italian state unceremoniously entered and annexed the city of Rome. The pope's temporal power thus disappeared. It is now widely agreed that with the loss of local temporal interests the spiritual hold of the papacy on Catholics throughout the world was ultimately enhanced. The popes long refused, however, to recognize the loss of Rome; and each pope in turn, from 1870 to 1929, adopted a policy of self-imprisonment in the Vatican grounds. By the Lateran treaty of 1929 the papacy finally recognized the Italian state, and Italy conceded, along with much else, the existence of a Vatican City about a square mile in area, as an independent state not legally within Italy at all. The papacy thus gained the independence from national or secular authority deemed necessary by Catholics to the performance of its role.

Pius IX's successor, Leo XIII (1878–1903), carried on the counteroffensive against irreligion and instituted a revival of medieval philosophy as represented by Thomas Aquinas. But Leo XIII is chiefly remembered for formulating Catholic social doctrine, especially in the encyclical *Rerum Novarum* ("of modern things") of 1891, to which subsequent pontiffs have adhered, and from which various movements of Catholic socialism are derived. *Rerum Novarum* upheld private property as a natural right, within the limits of justice; but it found fault with capitalism for the poverty, insecurity, and even degradation in which many of the laboring classes were left. It declared that much in socialism was Christian in principle; but it criticized socialism insofar as (like Marxism) it was materialistic and antireligious. The pope therefore recommended that Catholics, if they wished, form socialist parties of their own and that Catholic workers form labor unions under Catholic auspices.

Rerum Novarum

Jewish emancipation

As for Judaism, the Jews were a small minority, but their condition had always been a kind of barometer reflecting changes in the atmosphere of tolerance as a whole. In the nineteenth century the basic trend was toward emancipation and assimilation. Science and secularism had the same dissolving effect upon Orthodox Judaism as upon traditional Christianity. Reform Judaism grew up as the Jewish counterpart to modernism in other faiths. Individual Jews increasingly gave up their old distinctive Jewish way of life. In society at large, the prevalence of liberalism allowed them to act as citizens and to enter business or the professions like everybody else. Jews were thus freed from old legal discriminations that had been imposed on them for centuries.

Toward the end of the century two tendencies counter to assimilation became evident. One, a cultural and political nationalism, originated with Jews themselves, some of whom feared an assimilation that would lead to a loss of Jewish identity and perhaps even the disappearance of Judaism itself. The other countertendency, or barrier to assimilation,

This is a photograph of the Jewish journalist Theodor Herzl (1860–1904), who responded to anti-Semitic ideologies in central Europe and the anti-Semitism of the Dreyfus Affair in France by launching a new Zionist movement in late nineteenth-century Europe. Herzl organized the first international Zionist conference and called for the creation of a new Jewish state in Palestine, which was at this time part of the Ottoman Empire and occupied by a predominantly Arab population.

(Zionist Archives and Library)

was the rise of anti-Semitism, noticeable in many quarters by 1900. Racist theories, dislike for Jewish competitors in business and the professions, socialist scorn for Jewish capitalists like the Rothschilds, upper-class fears of Jewish revolutionists and Marxists, together with a growth of ethnic nationalism, which held that France should be purely French and Latin, Germany purely German and Nordic, or Russia purely Russian and Slav, all combined to raise an anti-Semitic hue and cry. In Russia there were actual pogroms, or massacres of Jews. In France the Dreyfus case, which dragged on from 1894 to 1906, revealed unsuspected depths of anti-Semitic fury. Many Jews were forced by such hostility into a new sense of Jewish identity. The Hungarian-born Jewish journalist Theodor Herzl was one. Appalled by the turbulence of the Dreyfus affair in civilized France, which he observed firsthand as a reporter for a Vienna newspaper, he founded modern, or political, Zionism when he organized the first international Zionist congress at Basel in 1897. Zionists hoped to establish a Jewish state in Palestine, in which Jews from all the world might find refuge, although there had been no independent Jewish state there since ancient times.

The rise of anti-Semitism

Many Jews, wishing civic assimilation yet despairing of obtaining it, began to sympathize with the Jewish nationalist movement, looking to Zionism and a Jewish renascence as a way to maintain their own dignity. Others insisted that Judaism was a religious faith, not a nationality by itself; that Jews and non-Jews within the same country shared in exactly the same nationality, citizenship, and political or social outlook. Liberals and democrats were of the same opinion. On the integration of Jews into the larger community the traditions of the Enlightenment, the American and French revolutions, the empire of Napoleon I, and the liberalism of the nineteenth century all agreed.

77. THE WANING OF CLASSICAL LIBERALISM

The net effect of the political, economic, and intellectual trends described above was twofold. There was a continued advance of much that was basic to liberalism and at the same time a weakening of the grounds on which

Liberalism changed

liberalism had firmly rested ever since the seventeenth and eighteenth centuries. A third effect might be noted too. Even where the essentials of liberalism persisted, in program and doctrine it underwent important changes; liberalism persisted but the classical type of liberalism was in eclipse.

Classical liberalism, the liberalism in its heyday in the nineteenth century, went back at least as far as John Locke in the seventeenth century and the philosophes of the eighteenth. It found its highest nineteenth-century expression in political philosophers like John Stuart Mill and in the outlook of political leaders like William Gladstone. Classical liberalism had as its deepest principle the liberty of the individual. Man, or each specimen of mankind, according to liberals, was or could become a freestanding human being. "Man" meant for them any member of the human race, *homo sapiens,* though in practice, except for a few like Mill, they were usually thinking of adult males. The very principle of liberalism, however, with its stress on the autonomy of the individual, also contributed to the growing movement for women's rights.

The individual, in this view, was not simply formed by race, class, church, nation, or state but was ultimately independent of all such things. Individuals did not have such and such ideas because they belonged to such and such a group, but were capable of the free use of reason or of thinking matters out independently, apart from their own interests, prejudices, or unconscious drives. And, since this was so, people of different interests could reasonably and profitably discuss their differences, make compromises, and reach solutions by peaceable agreement. It was because they thought all persons potentially reasonable that liberals favored education. They opposed all imposition of force upon the individual, from physical torture to mental indoctrination.

The rational individual

In religion, liberals thought each individual should adopt any faith or no faith as he or she chose and that churches and clergy should play little or no part in public affairs. In politics, they thought that governments should be constitutional and limited in power, with individuals governing themselves through their chosen representatives, with issues presented, discussed, and decided by the use of intelligence, both by the voters in election campaigns and by elected deputies in parliamentary debate. The will of a majority, or larger number of individuals, was taken as decisive, with the understanding that the minority might become a majority in its turn as individuals changed opinions. At first distrustful of democracy, fearing the excesses of popular rule, and eager to limit political power and the suffrage to the propertied classes, in the course of the nineteenth century liberals had accepted the democratic principle of universal male suffrage, if not yet the vote for women. In economics, liberals thought of the whole world as peopled by individuals doing business with one another—buying and selling, borrowing and lending, hiring and firing—without interference from governments and without regard to religion or politics, both of which were thought to impose superficial differences upon the underlying uniformity of mankind. The practical consequences of liberalism were toleration, constitutionalism, laissez-faire, free trade, and an international or nonnational economic system. It was thought that all peoples would progress to these same ends.

There never was a time, even in one country, when all liberal ideas were simultaneously triumphant. Pure liberalism, like most other cultural and political ideologies, has never existed except as a doctrine. Advancing in one way, liberalism would be blocked or reversed in another. On the whole, Europe before 1914 was predominantly liberal. But signs of the wane of liberalism set in clearly about 1880; some, like the changing conceptions of human behavior and the new interest in the irrational, have already been mentioned.

The Decline of Nineteenth-Century Liberalism: Economic Trends

The free economy produced many hardships. The worker tossed by the ups and downs of a labor market, the producer tossed by those of a world commodity market, alike clamored for protection against exposure. A severe depression in 1873 sent prices and wages into collapse, and the economy did not fully recover until 1893. European farmers, both small French farm owners and big Junker landlords of East Germany, demanded tariff protection; they could not compete with the American Middle West or the steppes of South Russia, both opened up by rail and steamship and both of which after 1870 poured their cereals at low prices into Europe. The revival of tariffs and decline of free trade, very marked in Europe about 1880, thus began with the protection of agricultural interests. Industry soon demanded the same favors. In Germany the Junkers and the rising Rhineland industrialists joined forces in 1879 to extort a tariff from Bismarck. The French in 1892 adopted a high tariff to shelter both manufacturing and agricultural interests. The United States, rapidly industrializing, also adopted protective tariffs beginning in the 1860s, the earliest of all.

The Industrial Revolution was now definitely at work in countries other than Great Britain. There was an increasing resistance to buying manufactures from England, selling only raw materials and foodstuffs in return. Everywhere there was a revival of the arguments of the German economist Friedrich List, who a half-century before, in his *National System of Political Economy* (1840), had branded free trade as a system mainly advantageous to the *A revival of List* British and declared that no country could become strong, independent, or even fully civilized if it remained an agrarian supplier of unfinished goods. With Germany, the United States, and Japan manufacturing for export, a nationalist competition for world markets set in, contributing also to the drive for colonies and the phenomena of imperialism described in the next chapter. The new imperialism itself was another sign of the waning of liberalism, which had been largely indifferent to colonies.

In all these respects the division between politics and economics, postulated by liberals, began to fade. A kind of neomercantilism arose, recalling the attempts of governments in the seventeenth and eighteenth centuries to subordinate economic activity to political ends. A better term is economic nationalism, which became *Economic* noticeable by 1900. Nations struggled to strengthen themselves by tariffs, *nationalism* by trade rivalries, and by internal regulation, without regard to the effect upon other nations. And for individual workers or business entrepreneurs, in purely economic matters, it now made a great difference to what nation they belonged, by what government they were backed, and under what laws they lived.

It was of course to protect themselves against insecurity and abuse as individuals that workers formed labor unions. It was likewise to protect themselves against the uncertainties of uncontrolled markets that business interests began to merge, to concentrate in large corporations, or to form monopolies, trusts, or cartels. The rise of big business and organized labor undermined the theory and practice of individual competition to which classical liberalism had been attached. Organized labor, socialist parties, universal male suffrage, and a sensitivity to social distress all obliged political leaders to intervene increasingly in economic matters. Factory codes became more detailed and better enforced. Social insurance, initiated by Bismarck, spread to other countries. Governments regulated the purity of foods and drugs. The social service *The "new" liber-* state developed, a state assuming responsibility for the social and economic *alism and the* welfare of the mass of its own subjects. The "new" liberalism, that of *welfare state* the Liberals in England of the David Lloyd George era, of the Republican

President Theodore Roosevelt and the Democratic President Woodrow Wilson in the United States, accepted the enlarged role of the government in social and economic matters. Both Theodore Roosevelt and Wilson, and others, sought also to reestablish economic competition by government action against monopolies and trusts. The new liberals were generally more favorably disposed toward workers and the disadvantaged classes than toward business; the improvement of the workers' lot would vindicate the old humanitarian concern of liberalism with the dignity and worth of the individual person. The welfare state with an enlarged role for government, remote as it was from the older liberalism, was the direction taken by the new liberals. Others, liberal and otherwise, viewed with concern the growing power of governments and centralized authority and were apprehensive for individual liberties.

Intellectual and Other Currents

Liberalism, both old and new, was undermined also by many developments in the field of thought described earlier in this chapter—Darwinian evolution, the new psychology, trends in philosophy and the arts. Paradoxically, this great age of science found that the human being was not a rational animal. Darwinian theory implied that the human species was merely a highly evolved organism whose faculties were merely adaptations to an environment. Psychology seemed to teach that what was called reason was often only rationalization, or a finding of alleged "reasons" to justify material wants or emotional and unconscious needs, and that conscious reflection dominated only a narrow part of human behavior. Ideas themselves were said to be the products of cultural conditioning or of social power. There were English ideas or Anglo-Saxon ideas, or bourgeois or progressive or reactionary ideas. In politics, some believed that parties or nations with conflicting interests could never reasonably agree on a program common to both, since neither could ever get beyond the limitations of its own outlook. It became common to dismiss the arguments of an adversary without further thought and without any expectation that thought could overcome difficulties. This insidious "anti-intellectualism" was destructive to liberal principles. If, because of prior conditioning, it was impossible to change one's mind, then there was no hope of settling matters by persuasion.

Challenges to Liberalism

From the view that the human being was not essentially a rational creature, which in itself was only a scientific attempt at a better understanding of human behavior, it was but a short step deliberately to reject reason and to emphasize and cultivate the irrational; to stress the will, intuition, impulse, and emotion; and to place a new value on violence and conflict. A philosophy of "realism," a kind of unrealistic faith in the constructive value of struggle and a tough-minded rejection of ideas and ideals, spread. It was not new. Marxism, since the 1840s, had taught that class war, latent or open, was the motivating power of history. Now Nietzsche rejected the ordinary ethical virtues in favor of personal courage and daring; and the Social Darwinists glorified the successful and the dominant in all phases of human activity as the "fit" in the perpetual struggle for existence. Other thinkers embraced a frank irrationalism. Georges Sorel, the philosopher of syndicalism, in his *Reflections on Violence* in 1908, declared that violence was good irrespective of the end accomplished (so much did he hate existing society) and that workers should be kept alert in the class war through believing in the "myth" of a future general strike. They should believe in such a strike, with its attendant debacle of bourgeois civilization, even though it was known to be only a "myth." The function of thought, in this philosophy of the social

These miners, who were on strike at a coal mine in northern France in 1906, represent the militancy of the early twentieth-century European labor movement. Demanding better wages, better working conditions, and a greater role in public life, labor became an important force in the political cultures of all major European states during this era.

(Roger-Viollet)

myth, was to keep people agitated and excited and ready for action, not to achieve any correspondence with rational or objective truth. Such ideas passed into the fascism and other activist movements of the twentieth century.

Thus, the end of the nineteenth century, the greatest age of peace in Europe's history, abounded in philosophies glorifying struggle. People who had never heard a shot fired in anger solemnly announced that world history moved forward by violence and antagonism. They said not merely that struggle existed (which would have been a purely factual statement) but that struggle was a positive good through which progress was to be accomplished. The popularity of struggle was due not only to the intellectuals but also in part to actual

The popularity of struggle

historical events. People remembered that before 1871 certain weighty questions had been settled by force, that the movements of social revolution in 1848 and in the Paris Commune of 1871 had been put down by the military, and that the unity of Italy and Germany, as well as of the United States, had been confirmed by war. In addition, after 1871, all continental European states maintained large standing armies, the largest ever maintained until then in time of peace.

In economic and political matters, even in England, the homeland of liberalism, there were numerous signs between 1900 and 1914 that the older liberalism was on the wane. Joseph Chamberlain led a movement to return to tariff protection (to repeal, so to speak, the repeal of the Corn Laws); it failed at the time, but was strong enough to disorient the Conservative party in 1906. The Liberal party abandoned its traditional laissez-faire policy in sponsoring the labor legislation of the years following 1906. The new Labour party required its members in Parliament to vote as directed by the party, thus initiating a system of party solidarity, eventually copied by others, that hardened the lines of opposition, denied that individuals should freely change sides, and hence reduced the practical significance of parliamentary discussion. The Irish nationalists had long used unparliamentary methods; in 1914, when Parliament at last enacted Irish home rule, the anti-Irish and conservative interests prepared to resist parliamentary action by force. The English suffragettes, despairing of ever getting the men to listen to reason, resorted to the amazingly "un-English," violent political actions that have been noted earlier in the discussion of feminism. And in 1911 and 1912 great railway and coal strikes disclosed the sheer power of organized labor.

The persistence of liberalism

Still, it is the persistence of liberalism rather than its wane that should be emphasized at the close of two chapters on European history in the half-century before 1914. Tariffs existed, but goods still circulated freely in world trade. Nationalism was heightened, but there was nothing like totalitarianism. Racist ideas were in the air, but they still had little political importance. Anti-Semitism was sometimes vocal; but all governments except the Russian protected the rights of Jews, and the years from 1848 to 1914 were in fact the great period of Jewish integration into general society. The laissez-faire state was disappearing, but social legislation continued the humanitarian strain that had always been an essential part of liberalism. A few advanced revolutionaries preached social catastrophism, but social democrats and working people were overwhelmingly revisionist, loyal to parliamentary procedures and to their existing states. Doctrinaires exalted the grim beauty of war, but all governments down to 1914 tried to prevent war among the great powers. And despite the skepticism of some radical philosophers and intellectuals, there was still a supreme popular faith in progress.

Chapter 16

EUROPE'S WORLD SUPREMACY, 1871–1914

European civilization, as described in the last two chapters, spread to the whole earth after about 1870. The large European nation-states, which were now equipped with the overwhelming new powers of science and industry, gained empires for themselves throughout the globe. The history of Europe—as of Asia, Africa, and the Americas—became more closely involved in the history of the world.

For a while the most active of the imperial nation-states were located in Europe, and the 40 years preceding the First World War were the years of Europe's world supremacy. With the rise of the United States the term "Western" came into use, signifying European in an expanded sense. The arrival of Japan made the term "Western" inappropriate in some ways, as did other later developments. By the mid–twentieth century it was customary to speak of "developed" parts of the world, in comparison with which others were seen as "less developed," or "developing." There even came to be a "Third World," with no specific geographic identity of its own, but which came to mean the developing countries. These terms represented efforts to deal with the same basic reality, namely, a bifurcation between modern and traditional societies, rich countries and poor ones, or between the powerful and the weak.

The Third World

For the first time in human history, by 1900, it was possible to speak of a world civilization. Although retaining important differences in languages, culture, and social practices, all countries were drawn into a world economy and a world market. The attributes of political and economic modernity were much the same everywhere—modern science,

Chapter emblem: Detail from a Chinese illustration of an attack on Europeans during China's anticolonial "Boxer Uprising" in 1899.

modern weapons of warfare, machine industry, fast communications, industrial organization, efficient taxation and law enforcement, and modern public health, sanitation, and medicine.

But not all peoples participated in this global evolution on equal terms. It was the Europeans, or "Westerners," who reaped the greatest rewards. Elsewhere, tribal societies and massive old civilizations alike began to come apart, reacting to the pressures of modern economic and social changes. Scientific ideas changed ways of thinking everywhere, as they had in Europe. In India, China, or Africa local industries often suffered, and many people found it harder than ever to subsist even at a low level. The building of railways in China, for example, threw boatmen, carters, and innkeepers out of work. In India, the hand spinners and weavers of cotton could not compete in their own villages with the machine-made products of Lancashire. In parts of Africa, tribal groups that had lived by owning herds of cattle, moving from place to place to obtain grazing lands, found white farmers or plantation or mine owners occupying their country and were often forced by the white man's law to give up their migratory habits. Peoples of all races began to produce for export—rubber, raw cotton, jute, petroleum, tin, gold—and hence were exposed to the rise and fall of world prices. A depression tended to become a world depression, dragging all down alike.

Imperialism

Imperialism, or the colonialism of the late nineteenth century, may be briefly defined as the government of one people by another. European imperialism proved to be transitory. It was a phase in the worldwide spread of the industrial and scientific civilization which had originated in Europe's "inner zone." That it was not the last phase became clear as the twentieth century unfolded. The subordinated peoples, forcibly introduced to the West by imperialism, came to sense a need for modernizing and industrializing their own countries and for the aid of Western science, skill, and capital; but they wished to get rid of imperialists, govern themselves, and control the conditions under which modernization and borrowing should take place. In opposition to European empires, subject peoples began to assert ideas learned from Europe—ideas of liberty and democracy, and of an anticapitalism that passed easily into socialism. Many such ideas were derived from the French and American revolutions, or from Marxism, or from the whole modern history of Europe itself, but these ideas were transformed or challenged as they entered into the political and cultural traditions of other civilizations.

The present chapter deals only with the imperialist phase of this global transformation. By one of the ironies of history, the imperialist rivalries of the European powers, while representing Europe's world supremacy, also contributed to the disaster of the First World War, and so to the collapse of such supremacy as Europe had enjoyed.

78.   IMPERIALISM: ITS NATURE AND CAUSES

European civilization had always shown a tendency to expand. In the Middle Ages Latin Christendom spread by conquest and conversion to include the whole area from Spain to Finland. Then came the age of overseas discoveries and the founding of colonial empires, whose struggles filled the seventeenth and eighteenth centuries and of which the Europeanization of the Americas was the most far-reaching consequence. At the same time European culture spread among the upper classes of Russia. The defeat of Napoleon left only one of the old colonial empires standing in any strength, namely, the British. For 60 years after 1815 there were no significant colonial rivalries. In many circles there was an indifference to overseas empire. Under principles of free trade, it was thought unnecessary to exercise political influence in areas in which one did business. Actually, in these years, the French moved into Algeria, the British strengthened their Indian empire, the Dutch developed Java and the neighboring islands more intensively, and the Western powers "opened" Japan and began to penetrate China. But there was no overt conflict among Europeans, and no systematic program, doctrine, or "ism."

Rather suddenly, about 1870 or 1880, colonial questions came again to the fore. In the short space of two decades, by 1900, the advanced industrial countries partitioned most of the earth among themselves. A world map by 1900 showed their possessions in some nine or ten colors.

The New Imperialism

The new imperialism differed both economically and politically from the colonialism of earlier times. The older empires had been maritime and mercantile. European traders, in India, Java, or Canton, had simply purchased the wares brought to them by local merchants as produced by local methods. They operated on a kind of cash-and-carry basis. European governments had had no territorial ambitions beyond the protection of way stations and trading centers. To these generalizations America had been an exception. It had neither native states which Europeans respected, nor native industries in which Europeans were interested. Europeans therefore developed territorial claims, and invested capital and brought in their own methods of production and management, especially in the then booming sugar islands of the West Indies.

New imperialism versus old colonialism

Under the new imperialism Europeans were by no means content simply to purchase what local merchants provided. They wanted goods of a kind or in a quantity that preindustrial handicraft methods could not supply. They moved into the so-called "backward" countries more thoroughly. They invested capital in them, setting up mines, plantations, docks, warehouses, factories, refineries, railroads, river steamships, and banks. They built offices, homes, hotels, clubs, and cool mountain resorts for European officials and visitors. Taking over the productive life of the country, they transformed large elements of the local population into the wage employees of foreign owners and so introduced the class problems of industrial Europe in a form accentuated by racial difference. Or they lent money to non-European rulers—the khedive of Egypt, the shah of Persia, the emperor of China—to enable them to hold up their tottering thrones or simply to live with more pleasure and magnificence than they could pay for from their usual revenues. Europeans thus developed a huge financial stake in governments and economic enterprises outside the West.

To secure these investments, and for other reasons, in contrast to what had happened under the older colonialism, the Europeans now aspired to political and territorial domination. Some areas became outright colonies, directly governed by white men. Others became protectorates: here the native chief, sultan, bey, rajah, or prince was maintained and guaranteed against internal upheaval or external conquest. A European "resident" or "commissioner" usually told him what to do. In other regions, as in China or Persia, where no single European state could make good its claims against the others, they arranged to divide the country into "spheres of influence," each European power having advisory privileges and investment and trade opportunities within its own sphere. The sphere of influence was the vaguest of all forms of imperial control; supposedly, it left the country independent.

Political and territorial domination

European access to colonial territories in the period of the "new imperialism" often depended on the construction of new railroads, which carried both people and goods into and out of the interior districts of the European colonies. This picture portrays the arrival of a locomotive that a team of elephants pulled into central India when a new railroad track was built in the region of Indore.

(Picture Collection, The New York Public Library, Astor, Lenox, and Tilden Foundations)

An enormous differential opened up, about 1875, between the power of European and non-European states. Queen Elizabeth had dealt with the Great Mogul of the Indian subcontinent with genuine respect, at least in part because his revenues in the early seventeenth century were some twenty times greater than those of the English monarchy. Even Napoleon had pretended to regard the shah of Persia as an equal. Then came the Industrial Revolution in Europe, iron and steel ships, heavier naval guns, more accurate rifles. Democratic and nationalist movements produced large and unified European peoples, united in the service and financial support of their governments. Seemingly endless wealth, with modern administration, allowed European governments to tax, borrow, and spend without apparent limit. The modern nation-states loomed as enormous power complexes without precedent in the world's history. At the same time it so happened that all the principal non-European empires were in decay. They were receiving a minimum of support from their own subjects. As in the eighteenth century when the disintegration of the Mogul empire had enabled the British to take over India, so in the nineteenth century the decrepitude of the sultan of Turkey, the sultan of Zanzibar, the shah of Persia, the emperor of China, and the shogun of Japan made European intervention remarkably easy. Only the Japanese were able to revolutionize their government in time to ward off imperialist penetration. Even the Japanese, however, were restricted by early treaties that controlled their tariff policies until after 1900.

So great was the difference in the sheer mechanics of power that usually a mere show of force allowed the Europeans to impose their will. A garrison of only 75,000 white troops long held India for the British. Numerous sporadic little wars were constantly fought—Afghan wars, Burmese wars, Zulu wars—which passed unnoticed by Europeans in the home country and were no more like a true national war than the operations of the United States army against the Indians of the western plains. The Spanish-American War of 1898 and the Boer War of 1899 were also wars of colonial type, fought between entirely unequal parties. Often a show of naval strength was enough. It was the classic age of the punitive or minatory bombardment. We have seen how the American Commodore Perry threatened to bombard Tokyo in 1854. In 1856 the British consul at Canton, to punish acts of violence against Europeans, called upon the local British admiral to bombard that Chinese city. In 1863 the British bombarded Satsuma, and in 1864 an allied force including Americans bombarded Choshu—precipitating revolution in Japan. Similarly, Alexandria was bombarded in 1882 and Zanzibar in 1896. The usual consequence was that the local ruler signed a treaty, reorganized the government, or accepted a European (usually British) adviser.

Europeans impose their will

Incentives and Motives

Behind the aggressiveness lay many pressures. The Europeans could not maintain for themselves the style of life to which they had become accustomed except by bringing the rest of the world within their orbit. But many other needs felt in Europe drove people into distant, unknown places. Catholic and Protestant groups sent growing numbers of missionaries to regions increasingly remote and wild. The missionaries sometimes got into trouble with the local people, and some were even killed. Public opinion in the home countries, soon learning of such events by ocean cable, might clamor for political action to suppress such outbreaks of anti-Christian violence. Similarly, science required scientific expeditions for geographical exploration, or for botanical, zoological, or mineral discoveries, or for astronomical or meteorological observations. Wealthy persons traveled more, now that travel was so easy; they hunted tigers or elephants, or simply went to see the sights. It seemed only reasonable, at the close of the nineteenth century, that all Europeans wherever they might choose to go should enjoy the personal security and the orderly legal procedures that European governments sought to provide for the Western people who visited or lived in their overseas empires.

Economically, European life required material goods, many of which only tropical regions could supply. Even the working classes now drank tea or coffee every day. After the American Civil War Europe relied for its cotton increasingly on Africa and the East. Rubber and petroleum became staple needs. The lowly jute, which grew only in India, was used to make burlap, twine, carpets, and the millions of jute bags employed in commerce. The lordly coconut tree had innumerable common uses, which led to its intensive cultivation in the Dutch Indies. Various parts of it could be eaten, or manufactured into bags, brushes, cables, rope, sails, or doormats or converted into coconut oil, which in turn went into the making of candles, soap, margarine, and many other products.

Raw materials

Industrial countries also attempted to sell their own products, and one of the reasons given by imperialists, in support of imperialism, was the urgent necessity of finding new markets. The industrialization of Germany, the United States, Japan, and other countries, after about 1870, meant that they competed with each other and with Great Britain for

Europe's overseas colonies gave European travelers new places to visit and new forms of "exotic" adventure that developed within the social and legal hierarchies of imperial political systems. The Englishwomen depicted here are going into an Asian forest for a picnic, accompanied by servants who carry their food and handle their horses and by escorts whose pith helmets symbolize the heyday of the British Empire.

(Hulton Getty)

Neomercantilism

foreign trade. The slowly declining price level after 1873 meant that a business firm had to sell more goods to turn over the same amount of money. Competition was more intense. The advanced industrial countries raised tariffs to keep out each other's products. It was therefore argued that each industrialized nation must develop a colonial empire dependent on itself, an area of "sheltered markets," as the phrase went in England, in which the home country would supply manufactured goods in return for raw materials. The idea was to create a large self-sufficient trading unit, embracing various climates and types of resources, protected if necessary from outside competition by tariffs, guaranteeing a market for all its members and wealth and prosperity for the home country. This phase of imperialism is often called neomercantilism, since it revived in substance the mercantilism of the sixteenth to the eighteenth centuries.

The profit motive

Purely financial considerations also characterized the new imperialism. Money invested in the so-called "backward" countries, by the close of the nineteenth century, brought a higher rate of return than if invested in the more industrialized ones. For this there were many reasons, including the cheap labor of non-European regions, the heavy and unsatisfied demand for non-European products, and the greater risk of losses in half-unknown areas where European ideas of law and order did not prevail. By 1900 western Europe and the northeastern United States were equipped with their basic industrial apparatus. Their railway networks and first factories were built. Opportunities for investment in these countries became stabilized. At the same time, these countries themselves accumulated capital seeking an outlet. In the mid-century most exported capital was British-owned. By the close of the century more French, German, American, Dutch, Belgian, and Swiss investors were investing or lending outside their own borders. In 1850, most exported capital went to build up Europe, the United States, Canada, Australia, or Argentina. By 1900 more of it was going to undeveloped regions in other parts of the world. This capital was the property of individual small savers or of large banking combinations. Investors preferred "civilized" political control over the parts of Asia, Africa, or Latin America in which their railroads, mines, plantations, government loans, or other investments were situated. Hence the profit motive, or desire to invest "surplus" capital, promoted imperialism.

This analysis was put forward by critics like the English socialist J. A. Hobson, who wrote an influential book on imperialism in 1903, and later by Lenin, in his *Imperialism, the Highest Stage of World Capitalism,* written in 1916. They ascribed imperialism primarily to the accumulation of surplus capital and condemned it on socialist grounds. Argued Hobson especially, if more of the national income *Socialist critics* went to workers as wages, and less of it to capitalists as interest and dividends, or if wealthy people were more heavily taxed and the money used for social welfare, there would be no surplus of capital and no real imperialism. Since the working class, if this were done, would also have more purchasing power, it would be less necessary to look endlessly for new markets outside the country. But the surplus capital explanation of imperialism was not entirely convincing. That investors and exporters were instrumental in the rise of imperialism was of course very true. That imperialism arose essentially from the capitalists' pressure to invest abroad was more doubtful. Perhaps even more basic was Europe's need for imports—only by enormous imports could Europe sustain its dense population, complex industry, and high standard of living. It was the demand for such imports—cotton, cocoa, coffee, copper, copra, and the like drawn from the colonies—that made investment in the colonies financially profitable. Moreover, non-Europeans themselves often asked for the capital, glad though the European lenders were to lend it at high rates. In 1890 this might mean merely that a shah or sultan wanted to build himself a new palace, but the need of non-Europeans for Western capital was basic, nor was it to decline in later times. Lastly, the imperialism of some countries, notably Russia and Italy, which had little capital and few modern-type capitalists of their own, could not reasonably be attributed to pressure for lucrative foreign investments.

For the British, however, the capitalistic incentive was of great importance. We have seen how the British, in 1914, had $20 billion invested outside Great Britain, a quarter of all their wealth. About half, or $10 billion, was invested in the British Empire. Only a tenth of French foreign investments was in French colonies. French investment in the colonial world in general, however, including Egypt, Suez, South Africa, and Asia in addition to the French colonies, amounted to about a fifth of all French foreign investments. Only an infinitesimal fraction of German foreign investment in 1914 was in German colonies, which were of slight value. A fifth of German foreign investments, however, was placed in Africa, Asia, and the Ottoman Empire. These sums are enough to suggest the pressures upon the European governments to assert political influence in Africa, Turkey, or China.

Foreign economic interests in Russia

In addition, French investors (including small bourgeois and even affluent peasants) had in 1914 a huge stake in the Russian empire. Russia, an imperial power with respect to adjoining countries in the Balkans and Asia, occupied an almost semicolonial status with respect to western Europe. The tsardom in its last 20 years, not unlike the Ottoman sultanate or the Qing dynasty in China, was kept going by foreign loans, predominantly French. The French in 1914 had lent over $2 billion to Russia, more than to all colonial regions combined. For these huge outlays the motivation was at least as much political as economic. The French government often urged French banks to buy Russian bonds. The aim was not merely to make a profit for bankers and small investors but to build up and hold together a military ally against Germany.

Politics went along with economics in the whole process of imperialist expansion. National security, both political and economic, was as important an aim as the accumulation of private wealth. So, too, was the growing concern in many quarters over the economic security and welfare of the working classes. The ideas of the British statesman Joseph Chamberlain (1836–1914) illustrated how these motives entered into imperialist thinking.

Joseph Chamberlain

Chamberlain, father of Neville Chamberlain, who was to be prime minister of Britain in the years just prior to the Second World War, began as a Birmingham manufacturer, the type of man who a generation before would have been a staunch free trader and upholder of laissez-faire. Discarding the old individualism, he came to believe that the community should and could take better care of its members, and, in particular, that the British community (or empire) could advance the welfare of Britons. As mayor of Birmingham he introduced a kind of municipal socialism, including public ownership of utilities. As colonial secretary from 1895 to 1903, he preached Britain's need for "a great self-sustaining and self-protecting empire" in an age of rising international competition—a worldwide British trading area, developed by British capital, which would give a secure source of raw materials and food, markets for exports, and a steady level of profits, wages, and employment.

Chamberlain saw with misgivings the tendencies toward independence in Canada, New Zealand, and the Australian Commonwealth. For these dominions he favored complete self-government, but he hoped that, once assured of virtual independence, they would reknit their ties with each other and with Great Britain. Such a reintegration of the empire he called "imperial federation." Britain and its dominions, in Chamberlain's view, should pool their resources not only for military defense but also for economic well-being. The dominions had already levied tariffs against British manufacturers in order to build up their own. Chamberlain, to favor British exports, urged the dominions to charge a lower duty on British wares than on the same wares coming from foreign countries. In return, he even proposed that Great Britain adopt a protective tariff, so that it might then favor Canadian or Australian goods by imposing on them a lower rate. His plan was to bind the empire together by economic bonds, making it a kind of tariff union, or system of "imperial preference." Since Britain imported mainly meat and cereals from the dominions, Chamberlain was obliged to recommend a tariff even upon these—to "tax the people's food," repudiating the very ark of the covenant of Free Trade upon which the British economy had rested for half a century. The proposal was rejected. Chamberlain died in 1914, his goal unaccomplished. But after the First World War the British Empire, or Commonwealth of Nations, followed closely along the lines he had mapped out.

Working classes and imperialism

Whether the economic welfare and security of the European working classes was advanced by imperialism is still debated. It is probable that the worker in western Europe did benefit from imperialism. Socially conservative imperialists were joined in this belief by thinkers of the extreme Left. Marx himself, followed by Lenin, thought that the European worker obtained higher real wages through the inflow of low-priced colonial goods. To Marxists this was unfortunate, for it gave European workers a vested interest in imperialism, made the European proletariat "opportunistic" (i.e., unrevolutionary), and blocked the formation of a true international world proletariat of all races.

Another imperialist argument much heard at the time held that European countries must acquire colonies to which surplus population could migrate without altogether abandoning the native land. It seemed unfortunate, for example, that so many Germans or Italians emigrating to the United States should be lost to the fatherland. This argument was purely specious. No European country after 1870 acquired any colony to which European families in any numbers wished to move. The millions who still left Europe, up to 1914, persisted in heading for the Americas, where in the circumstances no European colony could be founded.

The competitive nature of the European state system introduced other almost exclusively political elements. The European states had to guard their security against each other. They had to keep some kind of balance among themselves, in the overseas world as in Europe. Hence, as in the scramble for Africa, one government often hurriedly annexed territory simply for fear that another might do so first. Or again, colonies came to have an intangible but momentous value in symbolism and prestige. To have colonies was a normal criterion of greatness. It was the sign of having arrived as a Great Power.

Diplomacy and imperialism

A belief in the cultural or religious mission of European civilization led to the establishment of European schools, churches, and hospitals in much of Africa and Asia. The Englishwoman in this photograph, Elizabeth Mort, was a Protestant deaconess at a Christian mission in Fukien, China; the man standing behind her suggests the important presence of local workers and assistants in all overseas European institutions.

(Church Mission Society Archives, London)

Britain and France had had colonies for centuries. Therefore the new powers formed in the 1860s—Germany, Italy, Japan, and in a sense the United States—had to have colonies also.

Imperialism as Crusade

Imperialism arose from the commercial, industrial, financial, scientific, political, journalistic, intellectual, religious, and humanitarian impulses of Europe compounded together. It was an outthrust of modern Western civilization, and its advocates claimed that it would bring civilization and enlightenment to those who still sat in darkness. Faith in "modern civilization" had become a kind of substitute religion. Imperialism was its crusade.

So the British spoke of the White Man's Burden; the French, of their *mission civilisatrice;* the Germans, of diffusing *Kultur;* the Americans, of the "blessings of Anglo-Saxon protection." Social Darwinism and popular anthropology taught the racist doctrine that the white races were "fitter" or more gifted than the peoples of other races. Some imperialists argued, more reasonably, that the backwardness of non-Europeans was due to historic, and hence temporary, causes but that for a long period into the future the civilized whites must keep a guardianship over their darker protégés. The psychology of imperialism contained strands of idealism and humanitarianism as well as greed, and numerous Europeans went to the colonies to build schools or hospitals rather than railroads or mines. Young people of good family left the pleasant lands of Devonshire or Poitou to spend long and lonely years in hot, isolated places, sustained by the thought that they were advancing the work of humanity. It was a good thing to put down slave raiding, torture, and famine; to combat degrading superstitions; to fight the diseases of neglect and filth; and to promote the ideas and institutions of legal justice (even though colonial legal systems did not treat the colonizers and native people in the same way). But these accomplishments, however real, went along all too obviously with European self-interest and were expressed with unbearable complacency and gross condescension to the larger part of the human race. As Rudyard Kipling wrote in 1899 (in his exhortation to Americans after their taking over of the Philippines):

Trade missions

> *Take up the White Man's burden—*
> *Send out the best ye breed—*
> *Go bind your sons to exile,*
> *To serve your captives' need;*
> *To wait in heavy harness,*
> *On fluttered folk and wild—*
> *Your new-caught sullen peoples,*
> *Half devil and half child.*

79.   THE AMERICAS

After the general considerations above, let us examine each of the earth's great regions in turn, and first the Americas, where we must begin our discussion earlier in the century, before the age of the "new imperialism."

In America the breakup of the Spanish and Portuguese empires in the first quarter of the nineteenth century, during and after the Napoleonic wars, left the vast tract from Colorado to Cape Horn very unsettled. Most of the people were Indian or a mixture of Indian and white *(mestizo)*, with clusters here and there of pure European stock, which the nineteenth-century immigration was greatly to increase. In the former Spanish empire, except in inaccessible spots, the Spanish culture and language predominated. In Brazil, in the former Portuguese empire, the culture was Portuguese, and the country, though independent after 1822, remained a monarchy (or "empire") until 1889, when it became a republic. In the former Spanish domains the disappearance of royal control left a large number of flaccid and shifting republics, chronically engaged in border disputes with one another. Fortunately for these republics, at the time of independence in the 1820s, European imperialism was at a low ebb. We have seen how the Congress of Verona considered ways of returning them to Spain but was opposed by Great Britain and how the United States, in 1823, supplemented the British action by announcing the Monroe Doctrine. But it was by the United States that one of the new republics was first threatened from the outside.

The United States and Mexico

Mexico, on becoming independent of Spain, reached almost to the Mississippi and the Rocky Mountains. Hardly was it independent when land seekers from the United States swarmed over its northeastern borders. They brought with them their slaves, to grow the cotton so voraciously demanded in industrial England. The Mexican Republic did not allow slavery. The newcomers proclaimed their own republic, which they called Texas. Agitation developed for annexation to the United States. Mexico objected, but in 1845 the United States annexed Texas. A war followed, in which Mexico lost to the United States not only *The Mexican-American War* Texas but the whole region from Texas to the California coast. As is usual in such affairs, the loser preserved a longer memory than the winner. It soon seemed only natural in the United States to possess these regions; in Mexico many decades had to pass before the wound was healed. Mexico had lost half its territory to an aggressive neighbor within the first generation of its independence. Meanwhile, though some Americans condemned the war, most people in the United States justified this vast annexation of Mexican territory by arguing that their nation had far better facilities than Mexico for civilizing the region.

The next threat to Mexico came from Europe. Mexico, at a time of internal disorders, contracted large loans on exorbitant terms, the European lenders rightly estimating Mexican credit to be highly unsound. When the liberal president Benito Juárez (a pure-blooded Indian, at least racially "non-European") repudiated the loans, the European bondholders demanded satisfaction from their governments. The United States was paralyzed by the Civil War. Great Britain, France, and Spain, which had never recognized the Monroe Doctrine, in 1861 sent combined military forces to Veracruz. The British proposed seizure of the customs houses in Mexican ports and appropriation of the custom revenues to pay off the debt (an expedient introduced in China three years before); but the French had more ambitious designs. Unknown both to the British, who wanted only to collect debts, and *European intervention in Mexico* to the Spanish, who dreamed of setting up a new Bourbon monarchy in Mexico, the Emperor Napoleon III had a secret project for establishing a French satellite state in Mexico, which French capital and exports might subsequently develop. He planned to create a Mexican empire with the Austrian archduke Maximilian as its figurehead emperor. The British and Spanish disapprovingly withdrew their forces. The French army proceeded into the interior. Maximilian reigned for some years, but Napoleon III gradually concluded that conquest of Mexico was impossible or too expensive. It further appeared, by 1865, that the

United States was not going to collapse after all, as expected and even hoped for by the European governing classes. The United States protested strongly to the French government. The French withdrew, Maximilian was captured and shot, and Juárez and the Mexican liberals came back to power.

The United States, before 1870, had thus in turn both despoiled and protected the adjoining part of Latin America. This ambivalent situation became characteristic of the New World. As the United States became a great power, the Monroe Doctrine became an effective barrier to European territorial ambitions. Latin America never became subject to imperialism as completely as did Asia and Africa. On the other hand, the United States became the imperialist power feared above all others south of the border. It was the *Yanqui* menace, the Colossus of the North.

The Monroe Doctrine

In the 1870s in the course of its turbulent politics, both citizens of Mexico and foreign residents were obliged to pay forced loans to rival leaders. The State Department at Washington demanded that American citizens be reimbursed by the Mexican government. The double standard characteristic of imperialism—one standard for "civilized" and one for "uncivilized" states—became clear in the exchange of notes. The Mexican government, now under Porfirio Díaz, attempted to lay down the principle that "foreigners locating in a country accepted the mode of life of the people . . . and participated not only in the benefits of such residence but also in the adversities. Foreigners should enjoy the same guarantees and the same legal protection as natives, but no more." The Mexicans observed that the United States had never recognized the claims of foreigners for losses sustained in its Civil War. The United States, under President Hayes, held on the other hand that citizens of advanced states, operating in more primitive regions, should continue to enjoy the security of property characteristic of their home countries. When on another occasion the United States sent troops to the border, and the Mexicans objected, the secretary of state remarked on "the volatile and childish character of these people and their incapacity to treat a general question with calmness and without prejudice." Mexico retorted that the United States had "disregarded all the rules of international law and practice of civilized nations and treated the Mexicans as savages, as Kaffirs of Africa."

Imperialism's double standard

It was, in fact, a principle of international law in the nineteenth century that civilized states might not intervene in each other's affairs but had the right of intervention in so-called "backward" countries. In the dispute of 1877 the United States classified Mexico as backward, "volatile and childish." The Mexicans objected to being treated like "savages and Kaffirs," and not like a civilized nation. The leaders of both nations thus agreed that there were different legal standards for "civilized" and "uncivilized" nations, but they strongly disagreed on which of the two standards should apply in Mexico.

United States Imperialism in the 1890s

The 1890s saw a crescendo of imperialism both in Europe and in the United States. In 1895, in a resounding restatement of the Monroe Doctrine, President Cleveland forbade the British to deal directly with Venezuela in a boundary dispute affecting British Guiana. The British were obliged to accept international arbitration. When, however, the adjacent Colombia faced a revolution in the Isthmus of Panama, the United States supported the revolutionaries and, consulting nobody, recognized Panama as an independent republic. Here the United States leased and fortified a Canal Zone, over which it long kept control, and proceeded to build the

The Panama Canal

Panama Canal. Panama became in effect what Europeans would call a protectorate of the United States.

Meanwhile what was left of the old Spanish American empire, confined to Cuba and Puerto Rico, was agitated by revolutionary movements that were fighting for national independence. Sympathies in the United States lay with the revolutionaries. Every sign of the new imperialism showed itself unmistakably. Americans had $50 million invested in Cuba. They bought the bonds issued by Cuban revolutionaries in New York. Cuban sugar, whose production was disrupted by political troubles, was necessary to the famed American standard of living. An orderly and amenable Cuba was vital to American strategic interests in the Caribbean, in the soon to be built canal, and in the Pacific. The barbarity of the Spanish authorities was deplored as an outrage to modern civilization. The newspapers, especially the new "yellow" press, roused the American public to a fury of moral indignation and imperial self-assertion. The climax came when an American warship, the *Maine,* sank under mysterious circumstances in Havana harbor. (Most historians now believe the ship exploded because of a mechanical flaw.)

The Spanish-American War

The United States easily won the ensuing war with Spain in 1898. Puerto Rico was annexed outright, as were the Philippine Islands on the other side of the world. Cuba was set up as an independent republic, subject to the Platt Amendment, a series of provisions by which the United States obtained the right to oversee Cuba's relations with foreign powers and to intervene in Cuba in matters of "life, property, individual liberty," and "Cuban independence." Thus the United States obtained another protectorate in the Caribbean. The American government proceeded to intervene directly in Cuba on several occasions during the following two decades—interventions that were remembered much longer in Cuba than in the United States. The growth of Cuban nationalism and the subsiding of American imperialism led to abrogation of the Platt Amendment in 1934. Later, after the Second World War, the Philippines formally received independence in 1946 and Puerto Rico became a self-governing commonwealth in 1952.

It was under President Theodore Roosevelt, the peppery "hero of San Juan hill," that the imperial power of the United States was most emphatically trumpeted. He announced in 1904 that weakness or misbehavior "which results in a general loosening of the ties of civilized society may . . . require intervention by some civilized nation," and that the Monroe Doctrine might force the United States "to the exercise of an international police power." In the following year Santo Domingo fell into such financial disorder that European creditors were alarmed. To forestall any pretext for European intervention, the United States sent a financial administrator to Santo Domingo, reformed the economy of the country, and impounded half the customs receipts to pay its debts. Roosevelt declared—in what came to be known as the "Roosevelt Corollary" to the Monroe Doctrine—that, since the United States would not permit European states to intervene in America to collect debts, it must itself assume the duty of intervention to safeguard the investments of the civilized world. The Monroe Doctrine, initially a negative warning to Europe, now stood with the new corollary as a positive notice of supervision of all the Americas by the United States. A quarter of a century of "dollar diplomacy" followed, in which the United States repeatedly intervened, by military or other means, in the Caribbean and Mexico. But the Roosevelt Corollary, like the Platt Amendment, created so much anger and hostility in Latin America that the Washington government finally repudiated it.

The Roosevelt corollary

The story of the Hawaiian Islands was as typical of the new imperialism as any episode in the history of any of the European empires. Known originally to outsiders as the Sandwich Islands, these spots of land long enjoyed

The Hawaiian Islands

These American soldiers in a trench near Manila were part of the armed force that drove Spain out of the Philippines, repressed the Filipino independence movement, and transformed the Philippine islands into a colony of the United States. The annexation of the Philippines and Hawaii in the 1890s made the United States an influential imperial power in the Pacific and East Asia.

(Hulton Getty)

isolation in the vastness of the mid-Pacific. The growth of navigation in the nineteenth century introduced them to the world. Sailors, whalers, missionaries, and vendors of rum and cloth filled Honolulu by 1840. The native ruler, lacking the power to control this new situation, almost accepted a British protectorate in 1843 and in 1875 did accept a virtual protectorate by the United States, which guaranteed Hawaiian independence against any third party, obtained trading privileges, and acquired Pearl Harbor as a naval base. American capital and management entered the island. They created huge sugar and pineapple industries, entirely dependent on export to, and investment by, the United States. In 1891, when Queen Liliuokalani came to the throne, she tried to check westernization and Americanization. The American interests, endangered by her nativist policies, overthrew the queen and set up an independent republic, which soon sought annexation to the United States. It was the story of Texas reenacted. For several years the issue hung in the balance because of lingering disapproval in the United States for such strong-arm methods. But with Japan revealing imperial designs in 1895, the rush of the other powers into China, the Spanish-American War, acquisition of the Philippines, and plans for the Panama Canal, the United States "accepted its destiny" in the Pacific, and annexed the Hawaiian Republic by joint resolution of Congress in 1898. Hawaii became a state in the American union in 1959.

80. THE DISSOLUTION OF THE OTTOMAN EMPIRE

The Ottoman Empire in the 1850s

Of all parts of the non-European world, the Ottoman, or Turkish, Empire was the nearest to Europe, and with it Europeans had for centuries had close relations. It had for long extended from Hungary and the Balkan peninsula to the south Russian steppes and from Algeria to the Persian Gulf. The empire was not at all like a European state. Immense in extent, it was a congeries of religious communities. Most of its people were Muslim, including both orthodox Muslims and such reform sects as Druses and Wahabis; some were Jews who had always lived in the Middle East; many were Christian, principally Greek Orthodox and Armenian, who had also always lived there. The Turks were the ruling class and Islam was the dominant religion. Only Muslims, for example, could serve in the army; non-Muslims were known as *raya*, the "flock" or "herd"—they paid the taxes. Persons of different religion lived side by side, each under the laws, courts, and customs of his or her own religious group. Religious officials—patriarchs, bishops, rabbis, imams, ulemas—were responsible to the Turkish government for their own people, over whom therefore they had a great deal of authority.

Western Europeans had their own special rights. Roman Catholic clergy, living mainly in Palestine, looked to the pope in religion and to France for a mundane protector. Western merchants enjoyed the regime of the "capitulations," or special rights granted by the Ottoman government in numerous treaties going back to the sixteenth century. By the capitulations Turkey could not levy a tariff of more than 8 percent on imported goods. Europeans were exempt from most taxes. Cases involving two Europeans, civil or criminal, could be settled only in a court held by a European consul under European law. Disputes between a European and an Ottoman subject were settled in Turkish courts, but in the presence of a European observer.

The capitulations

The Ottoman Empire, in short, completely lacked the European idea of nationalism or national unity. The European idea of sovereignty and a uniform law for all its peoples were also absent, as was the idea of the secular state, or of law and citizenship separated from religion. The empire had fallen behind Europe in scientific, mechanical, material, humanitarian, and administrative achievements.

Turkey was called the "sick man of Europe," and its long decline constituted the Eastern Question. Since the loss of Hungary in 1699 the Ottoman Empire had entered on a long process of territorial disintegration (see map, p. 632). That the empire lasted another two centuries was due to the European balance of power. But by the 1850s the empire was falling away at the edges. Russia had advanced in the Crimea and the Caucasus. Serbia was autonomous, Greece was independent, and Romania was recognized as a self-governing principality. The French occupied Algeria. A native Arab dynasty, the Sauds, of the Wahabi reform sect, ruled over much of Arabia. A former Turkish governor of Egypt, Mehemet Ali, had established his family as hereditary rulers or "khedives" in the Nile valley. Notwithstanding these changes, the Ottoman Empire in the 1850s was still huge. It encompassed not only the Turkish or Anatolian peninsula (including Armenia and territory south of the Caucasus) but also the central portion of the Balkan peninsula from Constantinople to the Adriatic where many Christians of Slavic nationality lived, Tripoli (Libya) in North Africa, and the islands of Crete and Cyprus. Egypt and Arabia, though autonomous, were still under the nominal suzerainty of the sultan.

The "sick man of Europe"

The Crimean War of 1854–1856 opened a new phase in Ottoman history as in that of Europe. We have seen how this war was followed by the consolidation of great nation-states in Europe and how the United States, Canada, and Japan consolidated or modernized themselves at the same time. The Turks tried to do the same between 1856 and 1876.

The Crimean War

In the Crimean War the Turks were on the winning side, but the war affected them as it affected Russia, the loser. Exposing their military and political weakness, it pointed up the need of better organization. The outcome of the war was taken to prove the superiority of the political systems of England and France. It was therefore on Western lines that Turkish reformers wished to remodel. It was not merely that they wished to defend themselves against another of the periodic wars with Russia. They wished also to avoid being periodically saved from Russia by the West, a process which if continued could lead only to French or British control of Turkey.

Attempts at Reform and Revival, 1856–1876

In 1856 the Ottoman government issued the Hatt-i Humayun, the most far-reaching Turkish reform edict of the century. Its purpose was to create an Ottoman national citizenship for all persons in the empire. It abolished the civil authority of religious hierarchs. Equality before the law was guaranteed, as was eligibility to public office without regard to religion. The army was opened to Christians and Muslims alike, and steps were even taken to include both in nonsegregated military units. The edict announced a reform of taxes, security of property for all, abolition of torture, and reform of prisons. It promised to combat the chronic evils of graft, bribery, and extortion by public officials.

For 20 years there were serious efforts to make the reform decree of 1856 a reality. Western and liberal ideas circulated freely. Newspapers were founded. Writers called for a national Turkish revival, threw off the old Persian style in literature, composed histories of the Ottomans, translated Montesquieu and Rousseau. Foreign loans entered the country. Railroads joined the Black Sea and the Danube. Abdul Aziz (1861–1876), the first sultan to travel to Europe, visited Vienna, London, and the great Paris world's fair of 1867. But powerful resistance developed against such radical changes. Also, the best efforts of the Turkish reformers miscarried. There were too few Turks with skill or experience in the work required. Abdul Aziz took to spending his borrowed money somewhat too freely for purposes of the harem. In 1874 the Ottoman government, having recklessly overborrowed, repudiated half its debt.

A new and more determined reforming minister, Midhat Pasha, goaded by opposition and desperate at the weight of inertia, deposed Abdul Aziz in 1876, deposed the latter's nephew three months later, and set up Abdul Hamid II as sultan.

Abdul Hamid II

The new sultan at first briskly went along with the reform movement, proclaiming a new constitution in 1876. It declared the Ottoman Empire to be indivisible, and promised personal liberty, freedom of conscience, freedom of education and the press, and parliamentary government. The first Turkish parliament met in 1877. Its members earnestly addressed themselves to reform. But they reckoned without Abdul Hamid, who in 1877 revealed his true intentions. He got rid of Midhat, packed off the parliament, and threw away the constitution.

Repression after 1876

Abdul Hamid reigned for 33 years, from 1876 to 1909. For all this time he lived in terror, fighting back blindly and ferociously against forces that he could not understand. Once when a consignment of dynamos reached the Turkish customs it was held up by fearful officials, because the contents were declared to make several hundred revolutions per minute. Again, chemistry books for use in the new American college were pronounced seditious, because their chemical symbols might be a secret cipher. The sultan sensed that tempering with the old Ottoman way would lead to ruin. He dreaded any moves to check his own whim or power. He was thrown into a panic by Turkish reformers and westernizers, who became increasingly terroristic in the face of his opposition. Driven away by Abdul Hamid, some tens of thousands of Young Turks, the activists of the reform era before 1876, or their children and successors, lived in exile in Paris, London, or Geneva, plotting their return to Turkey and vengeance upon Abdul the Damned. The sultan was frightened also by agitation among his non-Turkish subjects. Nationalist Armenians, Bulgars, Macedonians, and Cretans defied and taunted the Ottoman authorities, which responded with the Bulgarian massacres of 1876 and the Armenian massacres of 1894. These horrible butcheries of thousands of peasants by Ottoman troops came as a shock to Europeans, who were no longer accustomed to such violence within their own nation-states. Last, and with good reason, Abdul Hamid lived in a creeping fear of the designs of the imperialist European powers upon his dissolving empire.

Abdul Hamid's fears

A thoroughly reformed, consolidated, and modernized Ottoman Empire was far from what the European governments desired. They might wish for humanitarian reforms in Turkey, for more efficiency and honesty in Turkish government and finance, and even for a Turkish parliamentary system. Such demands were eloquently expressed by liberals like Gladstone in England. But no one wanted what Turkish reformers wanted, a reinvigorated Ottoman Empire that could deal with Europe politically as an equal.

The Russo-Turkish War of 1877–1878: The Congress of Berlin

In Russia, since the time of Catherine II in the eighteenth century, many had dreamed of installing Russia on the shores of the Bosporus. Constantinople they called Tsarigrad, the Imperial City, which Orthodoxy was to liberate from the infidel. Crusading motives, in a nationalist and imperialist age, reappeared anew in the form of Pan-Slavism. This was now a doctrine preached by leading Russians, including the novelist Dostoevski, the poet Tyutchev, and the publicist Danilevsky. Danilevsky's *Russia and Europe,* published in 1871, predicted a long war between Europe and Russia, to be followed by a grand federation of the East, in which not only Slavs, but Greeks, Hungarians, and parts of Asian Turkey would be included under Russian control. This type of Pan-Slavism was favored and patronized by the Russian government because it diverted attention from internal and revolutionary troubles. As for the Slav peoples of the Ottoman Empire, they were willing to use Russian Pan-Slavism as a means of combating their Turkish rulers. Insurrection against the Turks broke out in Bosnia in 1875, in Bulgaria in 1876. In 1877 Russia declared war on Turkey. Russia was again on the move against the Ottoman Empire for the sixth time in a hundred years.

Pan-Slavism

The British, who had fought Russia over Turkey in 1854, were prepared to do so again. A number of recent developments added to their apprehension. The Suez Canal was completed in 1869. It was within the territory of the Ottoman Empire. It restored the Middle East to its ancient position as a crossroads of world trade. The British also took alarm when Russia, in 1870, in the confusion of the Franco-Prussian War, repudiated a clause in the treaty of 1856 and began to build a fleet on the Black Sea. In 1874 Benjamin Disraeli, a Conservative and an imperialist, became prime minister of Great Britain. By a sudden coup in the following year he was able to buy up, from the almost bankrupt ruling khedive of Egypt, 44 percent of the shares of the Suez Canal Company. In 1876, in a dramatic affirmation of imperial splendor, he had Queen Victoria take the title of empress of India. British commercial and financial interests in India and the Far East were growing, and the Suez Canal, of which the British government was now the principal stockholder, was becoming the lifeline of empire. But the Ottoman state, and hence the whole Middle East, was now collapsing before the Russians, whose armies advanced rapidly through the Balkans, reached Constantinople, and forced the Turks to sign a treaty in 1878, the treaty of San Stefano. By this treaty Turkey ceded to Russia Batum and Kars on the south side of the Caucasus Mountains, gave full independence to Serbia and Romania, promised reforms in Bosnia, and granted autonomy to a new Bulgarian state, whose boundaries were to be very generously drawn and which everyone expected to be dominated by Russia. England seethed with a popular clamor for war against Russia. The outcry gave the word "jingoism" to the language:

*The treaty
of San Stefano*

> We don't want to fight, but by jingo, if we do,
> We've got the men, we've got the ships, we've
>   got the money too.

*Weakness
of Turkey*

It now appeared that the weakness of Turkey, its inability to fend off foreigners from its borders, would precipitate at least an Anglo-Russian and possibly a general European war. But war was averted by diplomacy. Bismarck assembled a congress of all the European great powers at Berlin in 1878. Once again Europe attempted to assert itself as a unity, to restore life to the much-battered Concert of Europe by dealing collectively with the common problem presented by the Eastern Question. The congress in effect initiated a partition of the Ottoman domain, thereby keeping peace in Europe at the expense of Turkey. The European balance now both protected and dismembered Turkey at the same time.

The Russians were persuaded at Berlin to give up the treaty of San Stefano that they had imposed on the Turks, but they still obtained Batum and Kars and won independence for the Serbs and Romanians. Montenegro, too, was recognized as an independent state. They compromised on Bulgaria, which was divided into three zones with varying degrees of autonomy, all still nominally within the Ottoman Empire. Austria-Hungary was authorized by the congress to "occupy and administer" Bosnia (but not annex it) in the interests of civilization and in compensation for the spread of Russian influence in the Balkans. To the British the Turks ceded Cyprus, a large island not far from the Suez Canal. The French were told that they might expand from Algeria into Tunisia. To the Italians (who counted least) it was more vaguely hinted that someday, somehow, they might expand across the Adriatic into Albania. As Bismarck put it, "the Italians have such a large appetite and such poor teeth." Germany took nothing. Bismarck said he was the "honest broker," with no interest except in European peace.

The Suez Canal, which was completed in 1869, quickly became Britain's all-important lifeline to its Asian empire and a busy crossing point for the expanding global economy. This picture shows the ship of Edward, Prince of Wales, entering the canal in 1875, when the prince was en route to India.

(Hulton Getty)

The treaty of Berlin in 1878 dispelled the immediate threat of war. But it left many continuing problems which, because they were not dealt with successfully, became a principal cause of the First World War 36 years later. Neither the Balkan nationalists nor the Russian Pan-Slavs were satisfied. The Turks, both reactionaries like Abdul Hamid and the revolutionary Young Turks in exile, were indignant that peace had been made by further dismemberment of their territory. The demonstrated weakness of Turkey was a constant temptation to all concerned. In the years before 1914 German influence grew. Germans and German capital entered Turkey, projecting, and partially completing, a great Berlin to Bagdad railway to be accompanied by the exploitation of Middle Eastern resources. The railroad was all but completed before 1914 despite the protests and representations of the Russians, the French, and particularly the British, who saw in it a direct threat to their empire in India.

The continuing Turkish problem

Egypt and North Africa

For Egypt, technically autonomous within the Ottoman Empire, the 1850s and 1860s were a time of progress in the Western sense as they had been for the empire as a whole. The Egyptian government modernized its administration, court system, and property law, cooperated with the French in building the Suez Canal, encouraged shipping on the Red Sea, and let British and French interests construct railroads. Between 1861 and 1865, while the American South was unable to export raw cotton, the annual export of Egyptian cotton rose from 60 million to 250 million pounds. Egypt more than Turkey was drawn into the world market, and the khedive of Egypt became a Westernized ruler. The khedive Ismail built himself a fine new opera house in Cairo, where, in 1871, two years after the opening of the Suez Canal, Verdi's *Aïda*, written at the khedive's request, was resoundingly performed for the first time.

Such improvements cost a good deal of money, borrowed in England and France. The Egyptian government was soon in financial straits, only temporarily relieved by the sale of canal shares to Disraeli. By 1879 matters reached the point where Western banking interests forced the abdication of

British intervention

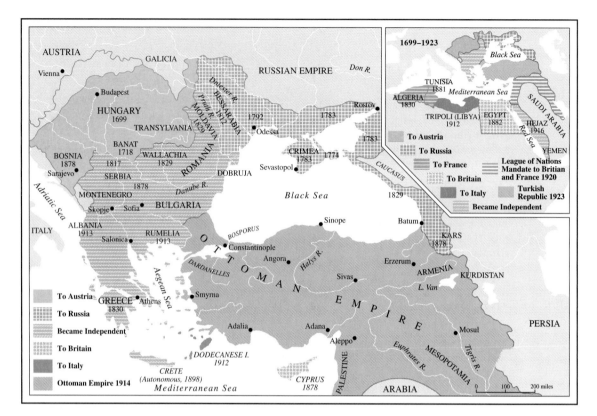

THE DISSOLUTION OF THE OTTOMAN EMPIRE, 1699–1914

Beginning in 1699, with the loss of Hungary to the Austrian Habsburgs, the Ottoman Empire entered upon a long process of territorial disintegration. Dates shown are those at which territories dropped away. In general, regions lost before 1815 were annexed directly by Austria and Russia. European territories lost in the nineteenth century emerged as independent states, owing to the rise of nationalism and rivalries among the great European powers. In the Arab world, reaching from Algeria to the Persian Gulf, regions lost before the First World War were absorbed into European colonial empires; those lost at the end of the First World War were mostly assigned to France and Britain as mandates, but after the Second World War these regions became independent Arab states and the Republic of Israel. A Turkish nationalist movement blocked European attempts to partition Turkey after the First World War, and in 1923 the Turks established the Turkish Republic.

Ismail and his replacement by Tewfik, who, fascinated by the new Western technological marvels, soon let himself become thoroughly enmeshed by his creditors. This led to nationalistic protests within Egypt, headed by Colonel Arabi. In a pattern repeated in many parts of the colonial world, especially in nineteenth-century China, the nationalists opposed both the foreigners and their own government, charging it with being a mere front for foreign interests. Arabi's movement, an early expression of Arab nationalism, led to riots in Alexandria, where Europeans had to flee aboard British and French shipping in the harbor. A British squadron then unceremoniously bombarded Alexandria. British troops (the French, though invited to take part, refused) disembarked in 1882 at Suez and Alexandria, defeated Arabi, and took Tewfik under their protection. The military intervention of 1882 was said by the British to be temporary, but British troops remained there for a long time, through two world wars and well into the twentieth century, not leaving until 1956.

Egypt thus became a British protectorate. The British protected the khedive from discontent within his own country, from the claims of the Ottoman court, and from the rival attentions of other European powers. The British resident from 1883 to 1907, an exceptionally capable administrator named Evelyn Baring, the first Earl of Cromer, did much to reconstruct the economy of the country, reform its taxation, ease the burdens on the peasants and raise their productivity, while encouraging the growth of raw materials wanted by England and assuring regular payment of interest to British, French, and other holders of Egyptian bonds.

Egypt as protectorate

The French strenuously objected when the British stayed on so long in Egypt. It had long been the French who had the greatest investments in the Middle East, and persons in that region who were at all westernized—Egyptians, Syrians, Turks—overwhelmingly preferred the French language and culture to the English. The French, harboring deep suspicion of British designs in Egypt, compensated themselves by building a North African empire farther west. They developed Algeria, assumed a protectorate over Tunisia, and began to penetrate Morocco. Upon these French advances the British, and soon the Germans, looked with unmitigated disfavor. Rivalry for the spoils of the Ottoman Empire thus created enmity among the Great Powers and constituted a fertile source of the war scares, fears, and diplomatic maneuvers that preceded the First World War.

The dissolution of the Ottoman Empire became indistinguishable from the whole chronic international crisis before 1914. It is enough to say here, to keep the fate of the Ottoman Empire in focus, that Abdul Hamid's frantic defensive policies came to nothing and that the Young Turks won control of the Ottoman government in 1908. They forced the restoration of the constitution of 1876 and introduced many reforms. Finally, when all Europe became involved in war in 1914, Russia again declared war on Turkey, and the Turks came into the war on the side of Germany, whose political and economic influence in the empire had been steadily growing. During the war, with British aid, the Arabs detached themselves from the empire, becoming eventually independent Arab states. Egypt, too, ended all connections with the empire. In 1923 a Turkish republic was proclaimed. It was confined to Constantinople and the Anatolian peninsula, where the bulk of the Turkish people lived. The new republic proceeded to undergo a thorough nationalist and secular revolution.

Young Turks

81.   THE PARTITION OF AFRICA

South of Mediterranean Africa lay the Sahara desert, and south of that lay sub-Saharan Africa, of which Europeans knew so little that they called it the Dark Continent. Africa is so gigantic that even the part south of the Sahara is almost as large as the whole continent of North America. For centuries Europeans knew only its coasts—the Gold Coast, Ivory Coast, Slave Coast—to which from an inexhaustible interior had come shackled processions of captive slaves, as well as the swelling waters of enormous rivers, like the Nile, Niger, and Congo, whose sources in the dim hinterland were a subject of romantic speculation. The people were black, but diverse both in physique and in culture, and speaking almost a thousand languages. They had learned to work iron as long ago as the third century before Christ, and they were adept in many arts, such as bronze sculpture, gold artifacts, weaving, basketry, and the making of ceremonial masks with strikingly symbolic or abstract patterns. Along the northern fringe some had been won to Islam, but mostly they adhered to their traditional religions.

The "Dark Continent"

They lived mainly in villages in tribal communities, engaged in agriculture or moving herds of cattle from place to place. But great cities or agglomerations had also arisen, from Timbuktu in the north with its old caravan trade across the Sahara, to the vast complex of buildings at Zimbabwe in the south, which was already in ruins when the Europeans first saw it. There had also been extensive kingdoms whose memory was preserved, in the absence of writing, by specially trained narrators from one generation to the next. But these kingdoms had disappeared or declined. They had been weakened by intertribal wars, or by the slave trade which set Africans against one another to satisfy the demand of outsiders, or by demographic causes that are now hard to trace. Hence Africa, somewhat like the Ottoman Empire and China, met the assault of the Europeans at a time when its powers of resistance were reduced. Before the mid–nineteenth century there were no permanently resident whites south of the Sahara except for a few Arabs who had been on the east coast since the seventh century and the Europeans who had been at the Cape of Good Hope since 1652. In the Union of South Africa, when it was established in 1910, some 1.1 million whites lived along with about 5 million blacks.

The Opening of Africa

Livingstone and Stanley

Missionaries, explorers, and individual adventurers first opened this world to Europe. The historic pair, Livingstone and Stanley, well illustrate the drift of Europe. Long before the imperialist age, in 1841, the Scot David Livingstone arrived in southeast Africa as a medical missionary. He gave himself to humanitarian and religious work, with a little occasional trading and much travel and exploration, but without political or true economic aims. Exploring the Zambesi River, he was the first white man to look upon the Victoria Falls. Fully at home in inner Africa, safe and on friendly terms with its native people, he was quite content to be let alone. But the hectic forces of modern civilization sought him out. Word spread in Europe and America that Dr. Livingstone was lost. The New York *Herald,* to manufacture news, sent the roving journalist H. M. Stanley to find him, which he did in 1871. Livingstone soon died, deeply honored by the Africans among whom he worked. Stanley was a man of the new era. Seeing vast economic possibilities in Africa, he went to Europe to solicit backers. In 1878 he found a man with the same ideas, who happened to be a king, Leopold II, king of the Belgians.

Leopold, for all his royalty, was at heart a promoter. China, Formosa, the Philippines, and Morocco had in turn attracted his fancy, but it was the central African basin of the Congo that he decided to develop. Stanley was exactly the man he was looking for, and the two founded at Brussels, with a few financiers, an International Congo Association in 1878. It was a purely private enterprise; the Belgian government and people had nothing to do with it. Europeans considered all Africa inland from the coasts to be, like America in the time of Columbus, a *terra nullius,* without government and claimed by nobody, wide open to the first Western persons who might arrive. Stanley, returning to the Congo in 1882, in a year or two concluded treaties with over 500 chiefs, who in return for a few trinkets or a few yards of cloth put their marks on his mysterious European papers and accepted the blue-and-gold flag of the Association.

Since the Dark Continent was still innocent of internal frontiers, no one could tell how much ground the Association might soon cover by these methods. The German explorer Karl Peters, working inland from Zanzibar, was signing treaties with the chiefs of East Africa. The Frenchman Brazza, departing from the west coast and distributing the tricolor in every village, was claiming on the Congo River itself a territory larger than France. The Portuguese aspired to join their ancient colonies of Angola and Mozambique into a trans-African empire, for which they required a generous portion of the interior. Britain supported Portugal. In every case the home governments in Europe were still hesitant over involvement in an Africa of which they knew little. But they were pushed on by small organized minorities of colonizing enthusiasts, and they faced the probability that if they missed the moment it would be too late.

Bismarck, who personally thought African colonies an absurdity but was sensitive to the new pressures, called another conference at Berlin in 1885, this time to submit the African question to international regulation. Most European states, as well as the United States, attended. The Berlin conference had two goals: to set up the territories of the Congo Association as an international state, under international auspices and restrictions; and to draft a code governing the way in which European powers wishing to acquire African territory should proceed.

The Berlin conference of 1885

The Congo Free State, which in 1885 took the place of the International Congo Association, was not only an international creation but also embodied in some ways what became known after the First World War as international mandates or international trusteeships for "backward" peoples. The Berlin conference specified that the new state should not be the colony of any power, including Belgium, but delegated its administration to Leopold. It drew the boundaries, making the Congo Free State almost as large as the United States east of the Mississippi, and it added certain specific provisions: the Congo River was internationalized, persons of all nationalities should be free to do business in the Congo state, there should be no tariff levied on imports, and the slave trade should be suppressed. Leopold in 1889 reassembled the signatory powers in a second conference, held at Brussels. The Brussels conference took further steps to root out the slave trade, which remained a stubborn though declining evil, because the Muslim world was several generations behind the Christian in abolishing slavery. The Brussels conference also undertook to protect the rights of the local people, correct certain glaring abuses, and reduce the traffic in liquor and firearms.

But all this effort at internationalism failed because Europe had no international machinery by which the hard daily work of enforcing general agreements could be carried out. Although slavery was banned, Leopold went his own way in the Congo. His determination to make it commercially profitable for his own benefit led him to unconscionable abuses. Europe and America demanded rubber and the Congo was at the time one of the world's few sources of supply. The Congo people, already afflicted by the diseases and enervation of a lowland equatorial climate, could be made to tap enough rubber trees for assigned quotas of rubber sap only by inhumanly severe coercion. Leopold and his agents, some of whom were African, and the managers of the concessions he leased out extorted forced labor from the native population, compelling them to meet impossible quotas under brutal conditions, with the resulting deaths of thousands. The rubber trees meanwhile were destroyed without any plans for replacement.

The Belgian Congo

Leopold, by ravaging its resources and virtually enslaving its people, was able to draw from the Congo a handsome income and to amass a personal fortune. He nevertheless could not make the entire enterprise profitable and needed investment capital for further development. He therefore borrowed from his own government in 1889 and 1895 in return for giving the government the right to annex the Congo in 1901. The parliament turned down the opportunity that year, but beginning in 1904 public outrage mounted after European press revelations of the scandalous atrocities in the Congo. A concerted campaign compelled the Belgian government in 1908 to take the Congo over from Leopold, who died the following year. The Congo Free State became the Belgian Congo, a Belgian colony. Under the government's administration the worst excesses of forced labor and other abuses were ended, even though the Congo remained a continuing enticement for enrichment and investment for Europeans and other outsiders.

The Berlin conference of 1885 had also laid down, for expansion in Africa, certain rules of the game—a European power with holdings on the coast had prior rights in the hinterland; occupation must not be on paper only, through drawing lines on a map, but must consist in real occupation by administrators or troops; and each power must give proper notice to the others as to what territories it considered its own. A wild scramble for "real occupation" quickly followed. In 15 years the entire continent was parceled out. The sole exceptions were Ethiopia, and, technically, Liberia, founded in 1822 as a colony for emancipated American slaves and virtually a protectorate of the United States.

Everywhere a variant of the same process was repeated. First would appear a handful of white men, bringing their inevitable treaties—sometimes printed forms. To get what they wanted, the Europeans commonly had to ascribe powers to the chief that by the customs of the tribe he did not possess—powers to convey sovereignty, sell land, or grant mining concessions. Thus the Africans were baffled at the outset by foreign legal conceptions. Then the Europeans would build up the position of the chief, since they themselves had no influence over the people. This led to the widespread system of "indirect rule," by which colonial authorities acted through the existing chiefs and tribal forms. There were many things that only the chief could arrange, such as security for isolated Europeans, porter services, or gangs of workmen to build roads or railroads.

"Indirect rule"

Labor was the overwhelming problem. For pure slavery Europeans now had an abhorrence, and they abolished it wherever they could. But the Africans, so long as they lived in their traditional way, did not react like the free wage earner postulated in European business and economics. They had little expectation of individual gain and almost no use for money. They thus seemed to work only sporadically by European standards, disdaining the continuous and tedious labor that Europeans wanted them to perform. The result was that Europeans all over Africa resorted to forced labor. For road building, systems like the French *corvée* before the Revolution reappeared. Or the chief would be required to supply a quota of able-bodied men for a certain length of time, and frequently he did so gladly to raise his own importance in the eyes of the Europeans. More indirect methods were also used. The colonial government might levy a hut tax or a poll tax, payable only in money, to obtain which the African would have to seek a job. Or the new government, once installed, might allocate so much land to Europeans as private property (another foreign conception) that the local tribe could no longer subsist on the lands that remained to it. Or the whole tribe might be moved to a reservation, like Indians in the United States. In any case, while the women tilled the fields or tended the stock at home, the men would move off to take jobs under the whites for infinitesimal pay. The men then lived in compounds, away from family and tribal kindred; they became demoralized; and the labor they gave, untrained and unwilling, would scarcely have been tolerated in more industrialized societies. In these circumstances everything was done to uproot the Africans, and little was done to benefit them or to protect the social systems in which they had lived before the Europeans arrived.

The labor problem

PRECOLONIAL AFRICA: SITES AND PEOPLES

This map shows Africa before colonization by the Europeans in the nineteenth century. It does not refer to a particular date or to particular kingdoms that the Europeans displaced. Names in burgundy designate important ancient or medieval centers, such as the Ghana and Mali empires, which no longer existed in modern times. Even the most extensive African kingdoms had indefinite and shifting boundaries, which cannot be readily indicated on a map. "Bantu," as used in the phrase "Bantu peoples," refers to a large group of languages spoken from north of the Congo River to the southern African coast. Concentrations of other language groups and peoples are also shown.

Conditions improved with the twentieth century, as traditions of enlightened colonial administration were built up. Some colonial officials even came to serve as buffers or protectors of the local peoples against the intruding white man's economic interests. Throughout, it was part of the ethos of imperialism to put down slavery, tribal warfare, superstition, disease, and illiteracy. Slowly a westernized class of Africans grew—chiefs and the sons of chiefs, Catholic priests and Protestant ministers, warehouse clerks and government

African workers built the new European-owned mines that began sending valuable minerals around the world. The laborers in this picture are digging a new gold mine in southern Africa in the late 1880s.

(Hulton Getty)

employees. Young men from Nigeria or Uganda appeared as students at Oxford, the University of Paris, or universities in the United States. Westernized Africans usually resented both exploitation and paternalism. They showed signs of turning nationalistic, like their counterparts in the Ottoman Empire and Asia. If they wanted westernization, it was at a pace and for a purpose of their own. As the twentieth century progressed, nationalism in Africa grew more vocal, more intense, and more forceful in challenging the European powers.

Friction and Rivalry between the Powers

The colonial race in Africa

Meanwhile, in the 15 years from 1885 to 1900, the Europeans in Africa came dangerously near to open blows. The Portuguese annexed huge domains in Angola and Mozambique. The Italians took over two barren tracts, Italian Somaliland and Eritrea on the Red Sea. They then moved inland, in quest of more imposing possessions, to conquer Ethiopia and the headwaters of the Nile. Some 80,000 Ethiopians, however, defeated and routed 20,000 Italians in pitched battle at Adowa in 1896. It was the first time that Africans successfully defended themselves against the forces of a European imperialist nation, and it discouraged invasion of Ethiopia by the Italians (or other Europeans) for 40 years. Italy and Portugal, like the Congo Free State and Spain (which retained a few vestiges of former days), were able to enjoy sizable holdings in Africa because of mutual fears among the principal contenders. The principal contenders were Great Britain, France, and Germany. Each preferred to have territory held by a minor power rather than by one of its significant rivals.

The Germans were latecomers in the colonial race, which Bismarck entered with re-luctance. By the 1880s all the usual imperialist arguments were heard in Germany, though most of them, such as the need for new markets, for emigration to overseas territories, or for the investment of capital, had little or no application in tropical Africa. The Germans established colonies in German East Africa and in the Cameroons and Togo on the west coast, along with a desert area that came to be called German Southwest Africa (where they ruthlessly suppressed the rebellious Herero people). It did not escape the notice of German imperial planners that someday the Congo and the Portuguese colonies might be joined with their colonies in a solid German belt across the African heartland. The French controlled most of West Africa, from Algeria across the Sahara and the Sudan to various points on the Guinea coast. They also occupied Obok on the Red Sea, and after the Italian defeat in 1896 their influence in Ethiopia grew. French planners therefore dreamed of a solid French belt across Africa from Dakar to the Gulf of Aden. The French government in 1898 dispatched Captain J. B. Marchand with a small party eastward from Lake Chad to hoist the tricolor far away on the upper Nile, in the southern part of the Sudan, which no European power as yet "effectively" occupied.

The two presumptive east-and-west belts, German and French, were cut (presumptively) by a north-and-south belt, projected in the British imperial imagination as an "Africa British from the Cape to Cairo." From the Cape of Good Hope Cecil Rhodes pushed northward into what was later called Rhodesia (now Zimbabwe). Kenya and Uganda in the mid-continent were already under British control. In Egypt, a British protectorate since 1882, the British began to support old Egyptian claims to the upper Nile. The first venture proved a disaster when in 1885 a British general popularly known as "Chinese Gordon" for previous military successes in China, leading an Egyptian force, was killed by Muslim troops at Khartoum. In the following decade British opinion turned imperialist in earnest. Another British officer, General Kitchener (with a young man named Winston Churchill under his command), again started southward up the Nile and defeated the local Muslims in 1898 at Omdurman. He then pushed on further upstream. At Fashoda he met Marchand.

The ensuing Fashoda crisis brought Britain and France to the verge of war. Already at odds over Egypt and Morocco, the two governments used the encounter at Fashoda to force a showdown. It was a test of strength, not only *The Fashoda crisis* for their respective plans for all Africa but also for their relative position in all imperialist and international issues. Both at first refused to yield. The British virtually threatened to fight. The French, fearful of their insecurity against Germany in Europe, at last decided not to take the risk. They backed down and recalled Marchand from Fashoda. A wave of hatred for the British swept over France.

The British no sooner won this Pyrrhic victory than they became involved in more unpleasantness at the other end of the African continent. In 1890 Cecil Rhodes had become prime minister of the Cape Colony. He was a principal sponsor of the Cape-to-Cairo dream. Two small independent neighboring republics, the Transvaal and the Orange Free State, stood in his way. Their people were Afrikaners—descendants of the Dutch who had originally settled the Cape in the seventeenth century and, after 1815, when England annexed the Cape of Good Hope, had made the "great trek" to escape from British rule. The Boers, as the English called them (from the Dutch word for farmer), were simple, obstinate, and old-fashioned. They thought slavery not ungodly and disliked promoters, fortune hunters, footloose adventurers, mining-camp people, and other uitlanders, or outsiders.

The discovery of diamonds and gold in the Transvaal brought the issue to a head. British capital and British people poured in. The Transvaal refused to pass legislation needed by the mining corporations and their employees. In 1895 Rhodes, attempting to

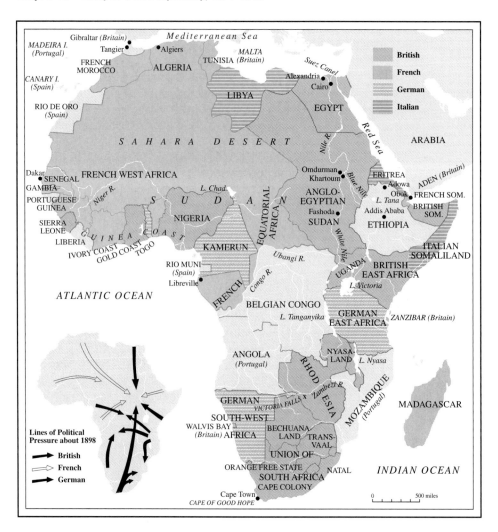

AFRICA, 1914

The map shows the recognized colonial holdings of European nations in 1914. The insert suggests the general directions of European expansion about 1898. These expansionary pressures led to the Fashoda crisis in 1898 and the Boer War in 1899. In 1898 the British and German governments held secret discussions on the possible partitioning of the Portuguese colonies, but no such partitioning took place because the British greatly preferred to have the Portuguese colonies remain in the hands of Portugal.

The South African War

precipitate revolution in the Transvaal, sent a party of armed irregulars, under Dr. Jameson, a physician-turned-colonial administrator, over its borders. This Jameson Raid was a failure, but in Europe a great cry went up against British bullying of a small inoffensive republic. The German emperor, William II, dispatched a famous telegram to Paul Kruger, president of the Transvaal, congratulating him on his driving off the invaders "without having to call for the support of friendly powers," that is, Germany. Three years later, in 1899, the British Empire went to

The British military campaign against the Transvaal and the Orange Free State between 1899 and 1902 was widely condemned, in part because it was waged against descendants of seventeenth-century Dutch settlers (the Afrikaners or Boers) in South Africa. This picture of British soldiers crossing a river suggests the scale and costs of the Boer War, which became especially notorious when the British interned Afrikaner women and children in concentration camps, where thousands perished.

(Hulton Getty)

war with the two small republics. The South African (or Boer) War lasted until 1902; the British sent in 300,000 troops, and to combat an elusive and irregular adversary they felt obliged to ravage the country and intern about 120,000 women and children in concentration camps, where about 20,000 died. But once subdued and brought within the British system the two republics were left with their self-governing institutions. In 1910 the Transvaal and the Orange Free State were combined with Cape Colony and Natal to form the Union of South Africa, which received semi-independent status along the lines of the Dominion of Canada.

The Fashoda crisis and the Boer War, coming in rapid succession, revealed to the British the bottomless depths of their unpopularity in Europe. All European governments and peoples were pro-Boer; only the United States, involved at the time in a similar military conquest of the Philippines, showed any sympathy for the British. The British, after the Boer War, began to rethink their international position, as will soon be seen.

As in the case of the Ottoman Empire, rivalry between the Great Powers over the spoils of Africa embittered international relations and helped prepare the way for the First World War. In Africa as a whole, there was little territorial change after the Boer War, although in 1911 Italy took Libya from the Turks. In 1914 the Germans were excluded from their short-lived empire. Had the Germans won the First World War, the map of Africa would probably have been greatly revised, but since they lost it the only change was to assign the German colonies, under international mandate, to the French, British, and Belgians. With this change, and except for Italy's ephemeral conquest of Ethiopia in 1935, the

Embittered international relations

map of Africa remained what the brief years of partition had made it until the spectacular end of the European empires after the Second World War.

🎕 82.   IMPERIALISM IN ASIA: THE DUTCH, THE BRITISH, AND THE RUSSIANS

The Dutch East Indies and British India

British India and the Dutch East Indies, in the half-century before the First World War, were the Europeans' ideal colonies. They illustrated the kind of empire that all imperialists would have wished to have, and a glance at them suggests the goal toward which imperialism was logically moving.

Whereas all countries of western Europe showed a surplus of imports, receiving more goods from the rest of the world than they sent out, India and Indonesia invariably, year after year and decade after decade, showed a surplus of exports, sending out far more goods than they took in. This export surplus was the hallmark of the profitable colonial area, geared closely into the world market, with low purchasing power for the native population and kept going by foreign investment and management. Both regions, in addition, were so large as to have a good deal of internal business—commerce, insurance, banking, transportation—which never appeared in the statistics for world trade, but which, being dominated by Europeans, added immeasurably to their profits. Both had rich and varied natural resources, tropical in character, so that they never competed with the products of Europe—though India even before 1914 showed tendencies to industrialization. In both regions the people were adept and quick to learn. But they were divided by religion and language, so that, once conquered, they were relatively easy for Europeans to govern.

Export surplus

Neither region before the First World War had any self-government at the highest levels. Both were ruled by a civil service, honest and high-minded by its own lights, in which the most illustrious, most influential, and best-paying positions were reserved for Europeans. Hence upper-class families in England and the Netherlands valued their empires as fields of opportunity for their sons—somewhat as they had formerly valued an established church. In both India and Indonesia the governments were more or less benevolent despotisms, which, by curbing warfare, plague, and famine, at least allowed the population to grow in numbers. Java, with 5 million people in 1815, had 48 million in 1942. India's population in the same years grew from less than 200 million to almost 400 million. Finally, as the last virtue of a perfect colony, no foreign power directly challenged the British in India or the Dutch in their islands.

European colonial rule

The Dutch in 1815 occupied little more than the island of Java itself. In the following decades the British moved into Singapore, the Malay peninsula, and north Borneo, and made claims to Sumatra. The French in the 1860s appeared in Indochina. The Germans in the 1880s annexed eastern New Guinea and the Marshall and Solomon islands. Ultimately it was the mutual jealousy of these three that preserved the Dutch position.

The Dutch took the initiative themselves. To forestall occupation by other Europeans, and to put down native pirates and find raw materials that the world demanded, the Dutch spread their rule over the whole 3,000-mile extent of the archipelago. They created an empire in place of the old chain of trading posts concerned only with buying and selling. Revolts were suppressed in 1830, 1849, and 1888; not till the twentieth century was northern

Sumatra or the interior of Celebes brought under control. For some decades the Dutch exploited their huge empire by a kind of forced labor, the "culture system," in which the authorities required farmers to deliver, as a kind of tax, stated amounts of stated crops, such as sugar or coffee. After 1870 a freer system was introduced. The Dutch also, as an important matter of policy, favored instruction in the Malay and Javanese languages, not in Dutch. This preserved the native cultures from westernizing disintegration but at the same time meant that Western ideas of nationalism and democracy entered more slowly.

The "culture system"

In India, in 1857, the British faced a dangerous rebellion, commonly called the Indian Mutiny, as if it had been a revolt of undisciplined soldiers only. The British army in India, with its "sepoys" (native Indian troops), was the only organization through which Indians could exert any collective pressure. The proportion of sepoys in the army was high in 1857 (about five-sixths) because British units had been withdrawn for the Crimean War and for action in China. Many Indians, outside the army, had been unhappy with British policies for decades. Rulers had been conquered and dethroned. Landowners had lost their property and been replaced by new ones more friendly to the British. Religious sentiments were inflamed. The British too obviously regarded Indian beliefs as repulsive; they had outlawed suttee, or widow burning, the ancient Hindu practice of a widow burning herself to death on the funeral pyre of her deceased husband; suppressed the Thugs, a small sect of holy assassins; and one British officer even declared that in ten years the government would abolish caste. Many Hindus therefore saw the British as dangerous opponents of their ancient religious traditions. Meanwhile, the Muslims were mobilized by Wahabi fundamentalism, a popular reform movement that sought to purify and defend the religious practices of Islam. Mysterious propaganda circulated over India. It infiltrated the sepoys, announcing to Muslim soldiers that certain newly issued cartridges were greased with the fat of a pig and to Hindus that the same cartridges were greased with the fat of a cow. Since for Hindus the cow was sacred, and for Muslims to touch pork was profane, much agitation was produced. The sepoys mutinied in the Ganges valley; and with them the other injured interests, including the fading Great Mogul and his court, rose against the British.

The Indian Mutiny

The British put down the rebellion with much brutality, aided by the fact that western and southern India took no part in it. But the uprising persuaded the British to a radically new course of policy, pursued basically until the end of the Indian empire almost a century later. The British East India Company and the Mogul empire were both finally and forever done away with. British authorities ruled directly, but the British concluded that they must rule India with and through the Indians themselves, not against them. This in practice meant a collaboration between the imperial power and the Indian upper classes. The British began to shelter Indian vested interests. They supported the Indian landlords and became more indulgent toward Indian "superstition." Where before 1857, when they conquered an Indian state, they had simply abolished it and incorporated its territories, after the Mutiny they kept the remaining Indian states as protectorates. States existing in 1857, such as Hyderabad and Kashmir and over 200 others, with their galaxy of rajahs and maharajahs, carried on to the end of British rule in 1947. It was largely to provide a fitting summit for this mountain of Indian royalty that Queen Victoria was proclaimed empress of India in 1877.

British rule in India

India had been a considerable manufacturing country by preindustrial standards, Indian merchants had once been important throughout the Indian Ocean, and before 1800 Indian exports to Europe had included many textiles and other finished goods. The native

The great Sepoy Rebellion in 1857 among local troops in India shook the British Empire more profoundly than any other event of the nineteenth century. Although the Indian Mutiny (as the British called it) was eventually suppressed, this illustration suggests why the violence and brutality left bitter memories on all sides and why the British soon restructured the whole system by which they governed Indian society.

(Hulton Getty)

crafts collapsed before modern industrialism reinforced by political power. "India," observed a British expert in 1837, "can never again be a great manufacturing country, but by cultivating her connection with England she may be one of the greatest agricultural countries in the world." Free trade (made possible by military superiority, usually overlooked by the economists) turned Britain into the world's workshop and India into a supplier of raw materials. Indian exports, in the latter part of the nineteenth century, consisted increasingly of raw cotton, tea, jute, oilseeds, indigo, and wheat. The British shipped their manufactures in return. Business in India boomed; India came to have the densest railway network outside of Europe and North America. It is important to note, however, as a commentary on European trade with poor countries, that Britain in 1914 did far more trading with the 6 million people of Australia and New Zealand than with the 315 million impoverished people of India.

The British, in contrast to the Dutch, decided in 1835 to favor instruction in English, not in the native languages. The historian T. B. Macaulay, one of the commission to make this recommendation, branded the Indian languages as vehicles of barbarous and unenlight-

This photograph of the future Indian national leader Jawaharlal Nehru indicates the kind of British education that many young Indians received during the imperial era. Nehru studied at Harrow School (where this picture was taken about 1905) and at Cambridge University before joining Gandhi in the independence movement during the 1920s. He later served as the first prime minister of independent India from 1947 until his death in 1964.

(Hulton Getty)

ened ideas—a bar to progress. The British also, after the Mutiny, admitted Indians to the civil service and to governors' councils—sparingly indeed, but more than the Dutch in Indonesia. There were also many Indian businessmen. A class of westernized Indians grew up speaking perfect English and often educated in England. They demanded more of a role in the affairs of their country. In 1885 the predominantly Hindu Indian National Congress was organized; in 1906, the All-India Muslim League. Muslim separatism, while favored by the British and sometimes even blamed upon them, was natural to India and exploited by some Indian leaders. Nationalism spread. It became increasingly anti-British, and radical nationalism turned also against the Indian princes, capitalists, and businessmen, as accomplices in imperialism, and so took on the color of socialism. In the period of the First World War, under nationalist pressure, the British granted more representation to Indians, especially in provincial affairs. But the movement toward self-rule was never fast enough to overcome the basic anti-British feeling of the Indian peoples, and Indian nationalism grew rapidly after the First World War.

Indian nationalism

Conflict of Russian and British Interests

While no outsider yet threatened the British in India, British statecraft discerned in the northern sky a large cloud which was clearly approaching. The Russian empire had occupied northern Asia since the seventeenth century. About 1850 Russian pressure on inner Asia resumed. It was a type of imperialism in which neither the demand for markets nor for raw materials, nor for the investment of capital, counted for much. In these matters

0   200   400   600   800   1,000 miles

ARCTIC   OCEAN

St. Petersburg
Archangel

Moscow

R U S S I A N   E M P I R E

S   I   B   E

Yenisey R.

Ob R.

Mediterranean Sea

Black Sea

Constantinople

Samara

Tobolsk

Tomsk

TRANS-SIBERIAN RAILROAD

Omsk

Irkutsk

OTTOMAN

Astrakhan

EUROPE
ASIA

Aral
Sea

L. Balkhash

Urga

OUTER MONGO
(Autonomous, 1912 Russia)

EMPIRE   Mosul

Cairo
Suez Canal   Jerusalem

Baku

Caspian Sea

1846

1873

1873   1881

1854

1884   1864   Tashkent   1860-65

Baghdad   Tehran

Basra

RUSSIAN SPHERE,
1907

Mecca

Mery   1876
BOKHARA
1885   1868

PERSIA

AFGHANISTAN
Kabul

BRITISH
SPHERE,
1907

1895

Kashgar

SINKIANG

KASHMIR
1846

C H I

HEJAZ   ARABIA

Red Sea

Persian Gulf

AFRICA

YEMEN

OMAN

Aden (Britain, 1839)

BALUCHISTAN
1883

PUNJAB

Karachi

Delhi

Indus R.

T I B E T

H I M A L A Y A S

NEPAL

Lhasa

BHUTAN

Chu

YÜNNA

Brahmaputra R.

Diu
(Portugal)

Bombay

INDIA

Ganges R.

Calcutta

BURMA
(Britain, 1852, 1885)

BRITISH   INDIA

1852

Hyderabad
Goa
(Portugal)
Madras

Yanaon
(France)

Bay of Bengal

Rangoon

1826

SIA

Bangkok

Pondicherry (France)

Karikal (France)

ANDAMAN
IS. (Britain)

CEYLON

INDIAN   OCEAN

JEHOL

GREAT WALL

Peking

Tientsin   Taku

Grand Canal

Tsinan

Kiao-chow
(Germany, 1898)

SHANTUNG

Kinchow

MANCHURIA

Mukden

KOREA

Gulf of
Chili

Dairen
Port Arthur

(Lease to
Russia, 1898;
Japan, 1905)

Chifu   Wei-hai-wei
(Britain, 1898)

Tsingtao

Yellow Sea

CRITICAL AREA, 1895–1905

0   100   200 miles

ALASKA
(Purchased by U.S.A.
from Russia, 1867)

ALEUTIAN IS. (U.S.A., 1867)

*Bering
Sea*

KAMCHATKA

*Sea of
Okhotsk*

Yakutsk

SAKHALIN

KURIL IS.
(Japan, 1875)

KARAFUTO
(Japan, 1905)

AMUR PROVINCE
1858

Amur R.

Khabarovsk

MANCHURIA

MARITIME
PROVINCE
(Russia, 1868)

Vladivostok
1860

Harbin

*Sea of
Japan*

JAPANESE EMPIRE

ONGOLIA

Mukden

Tokyo

JEHOL

KOREA
(Japan, 1905, 1910)

PACIFIC OCEAN

Peking

Port Arthur
(Japan, 1905)

Tientsin

Kiao-chow
(Germany, 1898)

Shanghai
(Britain, 1842)

Nanking

*East
China
Sea*

MARIANA IS.
(Germany, 1899)

Hankow

Ningpo
1842

RYUKYU IS.

Foochow

Amoy

FORMOSA (Japan, 1895)
PESCADORES (Japan, 1895)

GUAM
(U.S.A., 1898)

ANGSI
ch Sphere)

Canton (Britain, 1842)
Hong Kong (Britain, 1842)

Maçao (Portugal, 1557)

Kwang-chow
(Lease to France, 1898)

CAROLINE IS.
(Germany, 1899)

HAINAN

Manila

PHILIPPINES IS.
(U.S.A., 1898, 1899)

YAP

FRENCH
INDOCHINA
1884, 1907

PELAU

*South
China Sea*

NEW GUINEA

KAISER WILHELMSLAND
(Germany, 1884)

Saigon

BRITISH
NORTH BORNEO
1888

TATES
0, 1824)

SARAWAK
1888

ingapore
itain, 1819)

BORNEO

CELEBES

EAST INDIES

UTCH

(Portugal, 1859)

Darwin

TIMOR

AUSTRALIA

atavia

JAVA

IMPERIALISM IN ASIA, 1840–1914

The map shows boundaries and possessions as they appeared in 1914. During these years the British and Dutch filled out their holdings in India and the East Indies. The Russians pressed southward from Siberia into Central Asia, founded Vladivostok in 1860, and entered Manchuria at the close of the century. The French built their empire in Indochina and the United States took control of the Philippines. The Germans, as latecomers, were confined to miscellaneous parts of the western Pacific. The Japanese won control of Korea and the island of Formosa (now Taiwan). Meanwhile all of the imperial powers obtained special rights and concessions in China.

Russia was itself semicolonial with respect to the West. The Russians had, like the Westerners, a sense of spreading their type of civilization; but Russian expansion was distinctively political in that most of the initiative came from the government. Russia was an icebound empire, craving warm-water ports. It was a landlocked empire, so that whichever way it turned it moved toward one ocean or another. The ocean was the domain of the Westerners, and in particular the British.

In the large picture, Russia pushed by land against the Ottoman Empire, Persia, India, and China, all of which the British (and others) reached by sea. In 1860, on the shores of the Sea of Japan, the Russians founded Vladivostok, the farthest-flung of all Slavic cities, whose name meant Lord of the East. But their advance in the mid-century was mainly in the arid and thinly settled regions of western Asia. The British had already fought two Afghan wars to keep Afghanistan as a no-man's land between Russia and India. In 1864 the Russians took Tashkent, in Turkestan. A decade later they touched India itself but were kept away by an Anglo-Russian agreement, which allotted a long tongue of land to Afghanistan and so separated the Indian and Russian empires by 20 miles—the new frontier, in the high Pamirs, on the roof of the world, was to be sure, scarcely adapted to military operations.

Foreign interests in Persia

Russian advances in Turkestan, east of the Caspian, increased the pressure on Persia, which had long felt the same pressure west of the Caspian, where cities like Tiflis and Baku, now Russian, had once been Persian. If Tiflis and Turkestan could fall to the Russian empire, there was no reason why Persia should not do so next—except that Persia had a seacoast and so might also be available for occupancy by the British. In 1864 a British company completed the first Persian telegraph as part of the line from Europe to India. Other British investments and interests followed. Oil became important about 1900. In 1890, to bolster the Persian government against Russia, the British granted it a loan—taking the customs in Persian Gulf ports as collateral. In 1900 the Russian government granted the same favor, making its own loan to Persia, and appropriating as security all Persian customs except those of the Gulf. Russian ships appeared in the Persian Gulf in 1900, a demonstration soon countered by a state visit to Persia by the Viceroy of India, Lord Curzon. Clearly Persia was losing control of its own affairs, falling into zones, turning ripe for partition. A Persian nationalist revolution, directed against all foreigners and against the subservient government of the shah, broke out in 1905 and led to the assembly of the first parliament but hardly settled the question of Persian independence. In 1907 the British recognized a Russian "sphere of influence" in northern Persia; the Russians, a British sphere in the south (see map, pp. 646–647).

Spheres of influence

Imperial ambitions had deepened the hostility between Great Britain and Russia, with disputes over Persia and the Indian borderlands adding fuel to the quarrel they had long waged over the Ottoman Empire. We have seen how the struggle for Africa had at the same time estranged Britain from France and indeed from all Europe.

83.   IMPERIALISM IN ASIA: CHINA AND THE WEST

China before Western Penetration

But the biggest bone of imperialist contention was offered by China. On this bone every Great Power without exception tried to bite. The Manchu, or Ch'ing (now transliterated as Qing), dynasty (1644–1912) held a suzerainty over the whole area affected by Chinese civilization, from the mouth of the Amur River (as far north as Labrador) to Burma and In-

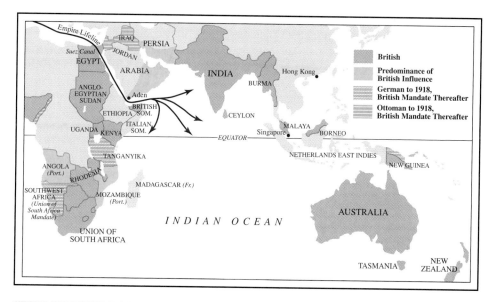

"THE BRITISH LAKE," 1918

This map shows the most important parts of the British Empire except for Canada, the Caribbean islands, and the United Kingdom itself. All shores of the Indian Ocean are shown to be British, except for French Madagascar, the politically weak Portuguese, Italian, and Dutch colonies, and the Arabian and Persian coasts, in which British influence was strong. It is easy to see why the Mediterranean and Suez Canal, leading from Europe into the Indian Ocean, were called the lifeline of the British Empire.

dochina (as far south as Panama), and from the ocean westward into Mongolia and Tibet. In the old Chinese view China was the Middle Kingdom, the civilized center of the world surrounded by less enlightened peoples. The Europeans were outlandish barbarians. A few had trickled through to China since the European Middle Ages. But the Chinese people persistently wanted nothing to do with them.

China was moving into an upheaval of its own even before Western influence became of any importance. For about 4,000 years the country had seen dynasties come and go in a kind of cycle. The Qing dynasty in the nineteenth century was clearly nearing its end. It was failing to preserve order or to curb extortion. About 1800 a White Lotus Society revolted and was suppressed. In 1813 a Heavenly Reason Society attempted to seize Peking (Beijing). In the 1850s a Muslim rebellion set up a temporary independent state in the southwest. Greatest of all the upheavals was the Taiping Rebellion of 1850, in which as many as 20 million people, approximately the population of Great Britain at the time, are thought to have perished. Except that some fragmentary Christian ideas, obtained from missionaries,

The Taiping Rebellion

were expressed by some of the Taipings (and its leader claimed to be the younger brother of Jesus), the rebellion was due entirely to Chinese causes. The rebels attacked the Manchus, who had come from Manchuria two centuries before, as corrupt foreigners ruling over China. Their grievances were poverty, extortion, rack-renting, and absentee landlords.

The Taipings set up a state in south China, and their armies were at first disciplined, but the fighting lasted so long that both the Taiping leaders and the Manchu commanders sent against them got out of control, and much of the country sank into chronic banditry and disorder. It was in this period that China's war lords, men controlling armed forces but obeying no government, appeared. The Manchus managed to put down organized Taiping resistance after 14 years, with some European assistance, led by the British General Gordon, the "Chinese Gordon" who later died at Khartoum. But it is clear that Chinese social confusion, agrarianism, and nationalism (the latter at first only anti-Manchu) antedated the impact of European imperialism.

Into this distracted China the Europeans began to penetrate about 1840. It became their policy to extort concessions from the Manchu empire but at the same time to defend the Qing dynasty against internal opposition, as was shown by the exploits of Gordon. This was because they needed some kind of government in China with which they could make treaties, legalizing their claims and binding upon the whole country.

The Opening of China to the West

The modern phase of Chinese relations with the West was inauspiciously opened by the Opium War of 1839–1841. We have already observed how, though Europeans wanted Chinese products, the Chinese had no interest in buying European products in return. Trade therefore was difficult, and the British East India Company had for decades solved the problem of getting Chinese tea for Europe by shipping Indian-grown opium in return, since opium was one available commodity for which a Chinese demand existed. When the Chinese government attempted to control the inflow of opium the British government went to war. Fifteen years later, in 1857, Britain and France combined in a second war upon China to force the Chinese to receive their diplomats and deal with their traders. The Chinese proving contumacious, 17,000 French and British soldiers entered Beijing and deliberately burned the emperor's very extensive Summer Palace, an appalling act of vandalism from which soldiers brought back enough stolen cultural objects—vases, tapestries, porcelain, enamels, jades, wood carvings—to set a fashion in Europe and America for Chinese art.

From the first of these wars arose the treaty of Nanking (1842); from the second, the treaties of Tientsin (1857), whose terms were soon duplicated in still other treaties signed by China with other European powers and with the United States. The resulting complex of interlocking agreements imposed certain restrictions on China, or conferred certain rights upon foreigners, which came to be known as the "treaty system." To the British in 1842 the Chinese ceded the island of Hong Kong outright, and somewhat later granted adjoining territories on a long lease. They opened over a dozen cities, including Shanghai and Canton (now called Guangzhou), to Europeans as "treaty ports." In these cities Europeans were allowed to make settlements of their own, immune to all Chinese law. Europeans traveling in the Chinese empire remained subject only to their own governments, and European and American gunboats began to police the Yangtse River. The Chinese likewise paid large war indemnities, though it was they themselves who suffered most of the damages. They agreed to levy no import duty over 5 percent and so became a free trade market for European products. To administer and collect the customs a staff of European experts was introduced. Money from the customs, collected with a new efficiency, on a swelling volume of imports, went in part to the British and French in payment of the indemnities, but part remained with the Qing government, which, as noted, the Europeans had no desire to overthrow.

The treaty system

Annexations and Concessions

While China was thus permeated at the center like an aging cheese, by extraterritorial and other insidious privileges for Europeans, whole slabs of it were cut away at the outer rim. The Russians moved down the Amur River, established their Maritime Province, and founded Vladivostok in 1860. The Japanese, now sufficiently westernized to behave like Europeans in such matters, in 1876 recognized the independence of Korea. The British annexed Burma in 1886. The French in 1883 assumed a protectorate over Annam despite Chinese protests; they soon combined five areas—Annam, Cochin China, Tonkin, Laos, and Cambodia—into French Indochina. (The first three were known also as Vietnam, a word not familiar in the West until after the Second World War.) These outlying territories had never, it is true, been integral parts of China proper; but it was with China that they had had their most important political and cultural relations and to the Chinese emperor that they had paid tribute.

Japan, whose modernization has been described, lost little time in developing an imperialistic urge. An expansionist party already looked to the Chinese mainland and to the south. Japanese imperialism first revealed itself to the rest of the world in 1894, when Japan went to war with China over disputes in Korea. The Japanese soon won, equipped as they were with *Japanese imperialism* modern weapons, training, and organization. They obliged the Chinese to sign the treaty of Shimonoseki in 1895, by which China ceded Formosa and the Liaotung peninsula to Japan and recognized Korea as an independent state. The Liaotung was a tongue of land reaching down from Manchuria to the sea; at its tip was Port Arthur. Manchuria was the northeastern part of China itself.

This sudden Japanese triumph precipitated a crisis in east Asia. No one had realized how strong Japan had become. Europeans were astounded that a people who were not "European," that is, white, in their culture or race should show such aptitude for modern war and diplomacy. It was to be supposed that Japan had designs on Manchuria.

Now it so happened that Russia, not long before, in 1891, had begun to build the Trans-Siberian Railway, whose eastern terminus was to be Vladivostok, the "Lord of the East." Manchuria extended northward in a great *"Lord of the East"* hump between central Siberia and Vladivostok. The Russians, whether or not they ever dominated Manchuria themselves, could not allow its domination by another Great Power. It happened also that Germany was at this time looking for a chance to enter the Far Eastern arena, and that France had formed an alliance with Russia, whose goodwill it was eager to retain.

Russia, Germany, and France therefore registered an immediate joint demurrer with the Tokyo Foreign Office. They demanded that Japan give up the Liaotung peninsula. The Japanese hesitated; they were indignant, but they yielded. The Liaotung went back to China.

In China many alert people were humiliated at the defeat by the Japanese whom they had despised. The Chinese government, at last facing the inevitable, began madly to plan westernization. Huge loans were obtained from Europe—the customs being pawned as security, following the pattern well established in Turkey, Persia, and Santo Domingo. But the European powers did not wish China to become consolidated too soon. Nor had they forgotten the sudden apparition of Japan. The result was a frantic scramble for further concessions in 1898.

It seemed in 1898 as if the Chinese empire in its turn would be partitioned. The Germans extorted a 99-year lease on Kiaochow Bay, plus exclusive rights in the Shantung

NORTHEAST CHINA AND ADJOINING REGIONS

Manchuria became an object of dispute among China, to which it belonged historically, Russia, and Japan. It was dominated by the Russians from 1898 to 1905, by the Japanese from 1905 to 1945, and again by the Russians from 1945 to 1950, when they transferred it to the People's Republic of China. Korea was dominated by Japan from about 1895 (and formally annexed by Japan in 1910) until the end of the Second World War. It was then divided into Russian and American occupation zones. After the Korean War (1950–1953) it remained divided into two independent states, North Korea under a Communist regime and a Western-supported South Korea.

peninsula. The Russians took a lease on the Liaotung peninsula from which they had just excluded Japan; they thus obtained Port Arthur and rights to build railroads in Manchuria to interlock with their Trans-Siberian system. The French took Kwangchow and the British Wei-hai-wei, in addition to confirming their sphere of influence in the Yangtse valley. The Italians demanded a share but were refused. The United States, fearing that all China might soon be parceled out into exclusive spheres, announced its policy of the Open Door. The idea of the Open Door was that China should remain territorially intact and independent and that powers having special concessions or spheres of influence should maintain the 5 percent Chinese tariff and allow businessmen of all nations to trade without discrimination. The British supported the Open Door, as a means of discouraging actual annexations by Japan or Russia, which, as the only Great Powers adjacent to China, were the only ones that could dispatch real armies into its territory. The Open Door was a program not so much of leaving China to the Chinese, as of assuring that all outsiders should find it literally "open."

The Open Door

If readers will imagine what the United States would be like if foreign warships patrolled the Mississippi as far as St. Louis; if foreigners came and went throughout the country without being under its laws; if New York, New Orleans, and other cities contained foreign settlements outside its jurisdiction but in which all banking and management were concentrated; if foreigners determined the tariff policy, collected the proceeds, and remitted much of the money to their own governments; if the western part of the city of Washington had been burned (the Summer Palace), Long Island and California had been annexed to distant empires (Hong Kong and Indochina), and all New England was coveted by two immediate neighbors (Manchuria); if the national authorities were half in collusion with these foreigners and half victimized by them; and if large areas of the country were prey to bandits, guerrillas, and revolutionary secret societies conspiring against the helpless government and occasionally murdering some of the foreigners—then they can understand how observant Chinese felt at the end of the nineteenth century, and why the term "imperialism" came to be held by so many of the world's peoples in abomination.

One Chinese secret society, its name somewhat literally translated as the Order of Literary Patriotic Harmonious Fists, and so dubbed the Boxers by hostile Westerners, broke out in insurrection in 1899. The Boxers pulled up railway tracks, fell upon Chinese Christians, besieged the foreign legations, and killed about 300 foreigners. The European powers, joined by Japan and the United States, sent a combined international force against the insurgents, who were put down. The victors imposed still more severe controls on the Chinese government and inflicted an indemnity of $330 million. Of this the United States received $24 million, of which, in 1924, it canceled the balance that was still due. On the other hand, as a consequence of the Boxer Uprising, the Qing officials strove desperately to strengthen themselves by westernization, while at the same time the revolutionary movement in China, aiming at expulsion of Manchus and foreigners alike, spread rapidly throughout the country, especially in the south, under the leadership of Sun Yat-sen.

The Boxer Uprising

84. THE RUSSO-JAPANESE WAR AND ITS CONSEQUENCES

Meanwhile Russia and Japan opposed each other's intrigues in Manchuria and Korea. The Japanese felt a need for supplying their new factories with raw materials and markets on the Asian mainland, for employment for their newly westernized army and navy, and for recognized status as a Great

Russo-Japanese rivalry

Chinese resentments against their government's concessions to Western imperialist powers erupted in the violence of the so-called Boxer Uprising in 1899. This Chinese illustration of an attack on a group of Europeans conveys the anger that fueled the movement and the new national identity that was spreading across China.

(British Museum)

Power in the Western sense. The Russian government needed an atmosphere of crisis and expansion to stifle criticism of tsarism at home; it could not abide the presence of a strong power directly on its East Asian frontier; it could use Manchuria and Korea to strengthen the exposed outpost of Vladivostok, which was somewhat squeezed against the sea and landlocked by Japanese waters. The Russians had obtained a concession from China to build the Chinese Eastern Railway to Vladivostok across the heart of Manchuria. A railway, in Manchuria, implied special zones, railway guards, mining and timber rights, and other auxiliary activities. The Japanese saw the fruits of their successful war of 1895 against China greedily enjoyed by their rival. In 1902 Japan signed a military alliance with Great Britain. We have seen how the British were alarmed by their diplomatic isolation after Fashoda and the Boer War, and how for many years they had been expecting to have trouble with Russia. The Anglo-Japanese military alliance lasted 20 years.

War broke out in 1904, undeclared, by Japanese naval attack on Russian installations at Port Arthur. Both sides sent large armies into Manchuria. The battle of Mukden, in the number of men engaged, which was 624,000, was the largest battle that human experience had thus far witnessed. Military observers were present from all the major powers, anxiously trying to learn what the next war in Europe would be like. The Russians sent their Baltic fleet around three continents to the Far East, but to the world's amazement the Russian fleet was met and destroyed at Tsushima Strait by the new and untested navy of Japan. Russian communications by sea were thereby broken, and since the Trans-Siberian Railway was unfinished and since the Japanese also won the battle of Mukden, Russia was beaten.

At this point the president of the United States, Theodore Roosevelt, stepped upon the scene. With an outpost in the Philippines and growing interest in China, it was to the American advantage to have neither side win too overwhelming a victory in the Far East. The most imperially minded of all American presidents offered his mediation, and plenipotentiaries of the two powers met at Portsmouth, New Hampshire. By the treaty of Portsmouth, in 1905, Japan recovered from Russia what it had won and lost in 1895, namely, Port Arthur and the Liaotung peninsula, a preferred position in Manchuria, which remained nominally Chinese, and a protectorate in Korea, which remained nominally independent, although a few years later in 1910 it was annexed by Japan. Japan also received from Russia the southern half of the island of Sakhalin. Much of what Russia lost to Japan in 1905 was regained 40 years later at the end of the Second World War.

The treaty of Portsmouth

The Russo-Japanese War was the first war between Great Powers since 1870. It was the first war fought under conditions of developed industrialism. It was the first actual war between westernized powers to be caused by competition in the exploitation of undeveloped countries. Most significant of all (except for the Ethiopian rout of the Italians), it was the first time that a nation of nonwhite people had defeated a nation of white people in modern times. Asians had shown that they could learn and play, in less than half a century, the game of the Europeans.

The Japanese victory set off long chains of repercussions in at least three different directions. First, the Russian government, frustrated in its foreign policy in East Asia, shifted its attention back to Europe, where it resumed an active role in the affairs of the Balkans. This contributed to a series of international crises in Europe, of which the result was the First World War. Second, the tsarist government was so weakened by the war, both in prestige and in actual military strength, and opinion in Russia was so disgusted at the clumsiness and incompetency with which the war had been handled, that the various underground movements were able to come to the surface, producing the Revolution of 1905. This in turn was a prelude to the great Russian Revolution 12 years later, of which Soviet communism was the outcome. Third, news of Japan's victory over Russia electrified those who heard of it throughout the non-European world. The fact that Japan was itself an imperialist power was overlooked in the excited realization that the Japanese were not a European power. Only half a century ago the Japanese, too, had been "backward"— defenseless, bombarded, and bulldozed by the Europeans.

Consequences of Japanese victory

The moral was clear. Everywhere leaders of subjugated peoples concluded, from the Japanese precedent, that they must bring Western science and industry to their own countries, but that they must do it, as the Japanese had done, by getting rid of control by the Europeans, supervising the process of modernization themselves, and preserving their own native national character. New "hybrid elites" in colonized societies thus combined their growing knowledge of Western culture with a growing pride in their own cultures and traditions, thereby creating the new nationalisms that would become a major, worldwide legacy of modern European imperialism. Nationalist revolutions began in Persia in 1905, in Turkey in 1908, in China in 1911. In India and Indonesia many were stirred by the Japanese achievement. In the face of rising agitation, the British admitted an Indian to the Viceroy's Council in 1909, and in 1916 the Dutch created a People's Council, to include Indonesian members, in the Dutch East Indies. The self-assertion of Asians was to grow in intensity after the First World War.

Asian self-assertion and nationalism

The Japanese victory and Russian defeat can therefore be seen as steps in three mighty developments: the First World War, the Russian Revolution, and the Revolt of Asia. These three together put an end to Europe's world supremacy and to confident ideas about the inevitable progress and expansion of European civilization; or at least they so transmuted them as to make the world of the twentieth century far different from that of the nineteenth.

Chapter 17

THE FIRST WORLD WAR

Somewhere before 1914 Europe went off its course. Europeans believed themselves to be heading for a kind of high plateau, full of a benign progress and more abundant civilization, in which the benefits of modern science and invention would be more widely diffused and even competitive struggle worked out somehow for the best. Instead, Europe stumbled in 1914 into disaster. It is not easy to see exactly where Europe went astray, at what point, that is, the First World War became inevitable, or (since the human mind does not know what is truly inevitable) so overwhelmingly probable that only the most Olympian statesmanship could have avoided it. But no such statesmanship appeared, and Europe fell into a deadly, grinding war that consumed much of its wealth, killed millions of its young men, and ultimately weakened or even destroyed much of its power and influence around the world.

85. THE INTERNATIONAL ANARCHY

After 1870 Europe lived in a repressed fear of itself. The great questions of the mid-century had been settled by force. The German Empire was only the strongest and most obvious of the new structures which armed power had reared. Never had the European states maintained such huge armies in peacetime as at the beginning of the twentieth century. One, two, or even three years of compulsory military service for all young men became the rule. In 1914 each of the Continental Great Powers had not only a huge standing army but millions

The inevitability of war?

Chapter emblem: Soldier in the trenches near Passchendaele, Belgium, in 1917.

of trained reserves among the civilian population. Few people wanted war; all but a few sensational writers preferred peace in Europe, but many took it for granted that war would come someday. In the last years before 1914 the idea that war was bound to break out sooner or later probably made some statesmen, in some countries, more willing to unleash it.

Rival Alliances: Triple Alliance versus Triple Entente

Political diagnosticians, from Richelieu to Metternich, had long thought that an effective union of Germany would revolutionize the relationships of Europe's peoples. After 1870 their anticipations were more than confirmed. Once united (or almost united), the Germans entered upon their industrial revolution. Manufacturing, finance, shipping, population grew phenomenally. By 1900, for example, Germany produced more steel than France and Britain combined, though in 1865 the French alone had produced more than the Germans. People in Germany felt that they needed and deserved a "place in the sun," by which they vaguely meant some kind of acknowledged supremacy like that of the British. Neither the British nor the French, the leaders of modern Europe since the seventeenth century, could share wholeheartedly in such German aspirations. The French nursed the chronic grievance of Alsace and Lorraine, annexed to Germany in 1871. The British as the years passed saw German salesmen appear in their foreign markets, selling goods often at lower prices and by what seemed ungentlemanly methods; they saw Germans turn up as colonial rivals in Africa, the Middle East, and the Far East; and they watched other European states gravitate into the Berlin orbit, looking to the mighty German Empire as a friend and protector to secure or advance their interests.

A "place in the sun"

Bismarck after 1871 feared that in another European war his new German Empire might be torn to pieces. He therefore followed, until his retirement in 1890, a policy of peace. We have seen him as the "honest broker" at the Berlin Congress of 1878, helping to adjudicate the Eastern Question, and again offering the facilities of Berlin in 1885 to regulate African affairs. To isolate France, divert it from Europe, and keep it embroiled with Britain, he looked with satisfaction on French colonial expansion. He took no chances, however; in 1879 he formed a military alliance with Austria-Hungary, to which Italy was added in 1882. Thus was formed the Triple Alliance, which lasted until the First World War. Its terms were, briefly, that if any member became involved in war with two or more powers its allies should come to its aid by force of arms. To be on the safe side, Bismarck signed a "reinsurance" treaty with Russia also. Since Russia and Austria were enemies (because of the Balkans), to be allied to both at the same time took considerable diplomatic finesse. After Bismarck's retirement his system proved too intricate, or too lacking in candor, for his successors to manage. The Russo-German agreement lapsed. The French, faced by the Triple Alliance, soon seized the opportunity to form their own alliance with Russia, the Franco-Russian Alliance signed in 1894. In its time this was regarded as politically almost impossible. The French Republic stood for everything radical; the Russian empire, for everything reactionary and autocratic. But ideology was thrown to the winds, French capital poured into Russia, and the tsar bared his head to the *Marseillaise.*

The Triple Alliance

The Continent was thus divided by 1894 into two opposed camps, the German-Austrian-Italian against the Franco-Russian. For a time it seemed that this rigid division might soften. Germany, France, and Russia cooperated in the Far Eastern crisis of 1895 to stem the expanding power of Japan. All were anti-British at the time of Fashoda and the Boer War. The Kaiser, William II, outlined tempting pictures of a Continental league against the global hegemony of England and her empire.

Much depended on what the British would do. They had long prided themselves on a "splendid isolation," going their own way, disdaining the kind of dependency that alliance with others always brings. Fashoda and the Boer War came as a shock. British relations with France and Russia were very bad. Some in England, including Joseph Chamberlain, therefore thought that a better understanding with Germany was to be sought. Arguments of race, in this race-conscious age, made the English and Germans feel akin. But politically it was hard to cooperate. The Kaiser's Kruger Telegram of 1896, expressing support for the South African Boers in their conflict with Britain, was a studied insult. Then in 1898 the Germans decided to build a navy.

"Splendid isolation"

A new kind of race now entered the picture, the naval competition between Germany and Great Britain. British sea power for two centuries had been all too successful. The American Admiral Mahan, teaching at the Naval War College, and taking his examples largely from British history, argued that sea power had always been the foundation of Britain's greatness and that in the long run sea power must always choke off and ruin a power operating on land. Nowhere were Mahan's books read with more interest than in Germany. The German naval program, mounting rapidly after 1898, in a few years became a source of concern to the British, and by 1912 was felt as a positive menace. The Germans insisted that they must have a navy to protect their colonies, secure their foreign trade, and "for the general purposes of their greatness." The British held with equal resolution that England, as a densely populated industrial island, dependent even for food upon imports, must at all costs control the sea in both peace and war. They adhered stubbornly to their traditional policy of maintaining a navy as large as the next two combined. The naval race led both sides to enormous and increasing expenditures. In the British it produced a sense of profound insecurity, driving them as the years passed ever more inescapably into the arms of Russia and France.

Naval race

Slowly and cautiously the British emerged from their diplomatic isolation. In 1902 they formed a military alliance with Japan against their common enemy, Russia. The decisive break came in 1904, from which may be dated the immediate series of crises issuing 10 years later in the First World War.

In 1904 the British and French governments agreed to forget Fashoda and the accumulated bad feeling of the preceding 25 years. The French recognized the British occupation of Egypt, and the British recognized the French penetration of Morocco. They also cleared up a few lesser colonial differences and agreed to support each other against protests by third parties. There was no specific alliance; neither side said what it would do in the event of war; it was only a close understanding, an *entente cordiale.* The French immediately tried to reconcile their new friend to their ally, Russia. After defeat by Japan the Russians proved amenable. The British, increasingly uncertain of German aims, proved likewise willing. In 1907 Britain and Russia, the inveterate adversaries, settled their differences in an Anglo-Russian Convention. In Persia, the British recognized a Russian sphere of influence in the north, while the Russians recognized a British sphere in the south and east. By 1907 England, France, and Russia were acting together. The older Triple Alliance faced a newer Triple Entente, the latter somewhat the looser, since the British refused to make any formal military commitments.

Triple Entente

The Crises in Morocco and the Balkans

The Germans, who already felt encircled by the alliance of France and Russia, naturally watched with concern the drift of England into the Franco-Russian camp.

**Testing
the Entente**

The entente cordiale was barely concluded when the German government decided to test it, to find out how strong it really was or how far the British would go in support of France. The French, now enjoying British backing, were taking over more police powers, concessions, and loans in Morocco. In March 1905 Kaiser William II disembarked from a German warship at Tangier, where he made a startling speech in favor of Moroccan independence. To diplomats everywhere this carefully staged performance was a signal: Germany was attempting not primarily to keep France out of Morocco, nor even to reserve Morocco for itself, but to break up the new understanding between France and England. The Germans demanded and obtained an international conference at Algeciras (at which the United States was represented), but the conference, which met in 1906, supported the French claims in Morocco, only Austria voting with Germany. The German government had thus created an incident and been rebuffed. The British, disturbed by German diplomatic tactics, stood by the French all the more firmly. French and British army and naval officers now began to discuss common plans. Distrust of Germany also inclined the British to bury the hatchet with Russia in the next year. The German attempt to break the Entente simply made it more solid.

In 1911 came a second Morocco crisis. A German gunboat, the *Panther,* arrived at Agadir "to protect German interests." It soon developed that the move was a holdup; the Germans offered to make no further trouble in Morocco if they could have the French Congo. The crisis passed, the Germans obtaining some trifling accessions in Africa. But a member of the British cabinet, David Lloyd George, made a rather inflammatory speech on the German menace.

**Crises in the
Balkans**

Meanwhile a series of crises rocked the Balkans. The Ottoman Empire, in an advanced state of dissolution, still held a band of territory from Constantinople westward to the Adriatic (see map, p. 665). South of this band lay an independent Greece. North of it, on the Black Sea side, lay an autonomous Bulgaria and an independent Romania. In the center and west of the peninsula, north of the Turkish belt, was the small, landlocked, independent kingdom of Serbia, adjoined by Bosnia-Herzegovina, which belonged legally to Turkey but had been "occupied and administered" by Austria since 1878. Within the Austro-Hungarian Empire, adjoining Bosnia on the north and west, lay Croatia and Slovenia.

Serbs, Bosnians, Croats, and Slovenes all spoke basically the same language, Serbo-Croatian, the main difference being that Serbs and Bosnians wrote with the eastern or

ANGLO-GERMAN INDUSTRIAL COMPETITION, 1898 AND 1913

This diagram shows the huge increase in world trade in the years before the First World War and also the fact that German exports grew in these years more rapidly than British exports. The exports of both countries together multiplied no less than threefold in these 15 years. The increase reflected a small rise in prices, but it was mainly due to a real increase in volume of business. In 1913, total German exports about equaled the British, but German exports to the United States and Russia greatly exceeded the British. Note how the Germans even gained exports in British India, where the liberalism of British trade policy freely admitted competitive goods. In merchant marine, though the Germans doubled their tonnage, the British continued to enjoy an overwhelming lead.

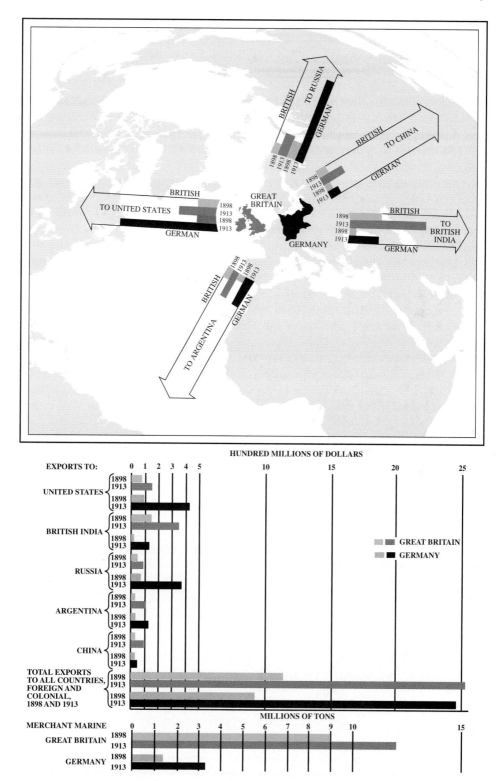

Ethnic and religious divisions

Cyrillic alphabet while the Croats and Slovenes wrote with the western or Roman alphabet. The difference reflected deep differences in religion. The Slovenes and Croats had long been Roman Catholic, and hence affiliated with Western Europe; the Serbs and many Bosnians were Eastern Orthodox and so closer to Russia; and there were also, especially in Bosnia, large numbers of Slavs who were Muslims, converted during the Ottoman domination. With the Slavic Revival, which emphasized language, many of these peoples came to feel that they were really one people, for which they took the name South Slavs, or Yugoslavs. After the Dual Monarchy was formed in 1867, as we have seen, the Slavs of the Habsburg empire were kept subordinate to the German Austrians and the Hungarian Magyars. By 1900 radical Slav nationalists within the empire had concluded that the Dual Monarchy would never grant them equal status, that it must be broken up, and that all South Slavs should form an independent state of their own. Concretely, this meant that an element of the Austro-Hungarian population, namely, the Croatian and Slovenian nationalists, wished to get out of the empire and join with Serbia across the border. Serbia became the center of South Slav agitation.

This brew was brought to a boil in 1908 by two events. First, the Young Turks, whose long agitation against Abdul Hamid has been noted, managed in that year to carry through a revolution. They obliged the sultan to restore the liberal parliamentary constitution of 1876. They showed, too, that they meant to stop the dissolution of the Ottoman Empire by taking steps to have delegates from Bulgaria and Bosnia sit in the new Ottoman parliament. Second, Russia, its foreign policy in the Far East ruined by the Japanese war, turned actively to the Balkan and Turkish scene. Russia, as always, wanted control at Constantinople. Austria wanted full annexation of Bosnia, the better to discourage Pan-Yugoslav ideas. But if the young Turks really modernized and strengthened the Ottoman Empire, Austria would never get Bosnia nor the Russians, Constantinople.

The first Balkan crisis

The Russian and Austrian foreign ministers, Alexander Isvolsky and Alois von Aehrenthal, at a conference at Buchlau in 1908 came to a secret agreement. They would call an international conference, at which Russia would favor Austrian annexation of Bosnia, and Austria would support the opening of the Straits to Russian warships. Austria, without waiting for a conference, proclaimed the annexation of Bosnia without more ado. This infuriated the Serbs, who had marked Bosnia for their own. Meanwhile, that same year, the Bulgarians and the Cretans broke finally with the Ottoman Empire, Bulgaria becoming fully independent, Crete uniting with Greece. Isvolsky was never able to realize his plans for Constantinople. His partners in the Triple Entente, Britain and France, refused to back him; the British in particular were evasive on plans for opening the Straits to the Russian fleet. The projected international conference was never called. In Russia itself public opinion knew nothing of Isvolsky's secret deal. The known fact in Russia was that the Serbs, the little Slav brothers of Russia, had their toes rudely stepped on by the Austrians by the annexation of Bosnia.

This "first Balkan crisis" presently passed. The Russians, weakened by the Japanese war and by the revolutionary turmoil of 1905, accepted the Austrian *fait accompli*. Austrian influence in the Balkans seemed to be growing. And South Slav nationalism was frustrated and inflamed.

Two Balkan wars

In 1911 Italy declared war on Turkey, from which it soon conquered Tripoli and the Dodecanese Islands. With the Ottomans thus embarrassed, Bulgaria, Serbia, and Greece joined forces in their own war against Turkey, hoping to annex certain Balkan territories to which they believed they had a right. Turkey was soon defeated, but the Bulgarians claimed more of Macedonia than the Serbs would yield, so that the first Balkan war of 1912 was followed in 1913 by a second, in which Albania also, a mountainous region on the Adriatic, mainly Muslim, was the subject of angry discord. The Serbs occupied part of it in the two Balkan wars, but Greeks also claimed a part, and it had also on several occasions been vaguely promised to Italy. Russia supported the Serbian claim. Austria was determined to shut off the Serbs from access to the sea, which they would obtain by annexation of Albanian territory. An agreement of the great powers, to keep the peace, conjured up an independent kingdom in Albania. This confirmed the Austrian policy, kept Serbia from the sea, and aroused vehement outcries in both Serbia and Russia. But Russia again backed down. Serbian expansionism was again frustrated and inflamed.

The third Balkan crisis proved to be the fatal one. It was fatal because two others had gone before it, leaving feelings of exasperation in Austria, desperation in Serbia, and humiliation in Russia.

The Sarajevo Crisis and the Outbreak of War

On June 28, 1914, a young Bosnian revolutionary, a member of the Serbian secret society called "Union of Death" and commonly known as the Black Hand, acting with the knowledge of certain Serbian officials, assassinated the heir to the Habsburg empire, the Archduke Francis Ferdinand, in the streets of Sarajevo, the Bosnian capital, in the Austrian Empire. The world was shocked at this terrorist outrage and at first sympathized with the protests of the Austrian government. Francis Ferdinand, who would soon have become emperor, was known to favor some kind of transformation of Austria-Hungary, in which a more equal place might be given to the Slavs; but the reformer who makes a system work is the most dangerous of all enemies to the implacable revolutionary, and it is perhaps for this reason that the archduke was killed by the Black Hand.

The assassination at Sarajevo

The Austrian government was determined to end the South Slav separatism that was gnawing its empire to pieces. It decided to crush the independence of Serbia, the nucleus of South Slav agitation, though not to annex it, since there were now thought to be too many Slavs within the empire already. The Austrian government consulted the German to see how far it might go with the support of its ally. The Germans, issuing their famous "blank check," encouraged the Austrians to be firm. The Austrians, thus reassured, dispatched a drastic ultimatum to Serbia, demanding among other things that Austrian officials be permitted to collaborate in investigating and punishing the perpetrators of the assassination. The Serbs counted on Russian support, even to the point of war, judging that Russia could not yield in a Balkan crisis, for the third time in six years, without losing its influence in the Balkans altogether. The Russians in turn counted on France; and France, terrified at the possibility of being some day caught alone in a war with Germany and determined to keep Russia as an ally at any cost, in effect gave a blank check to Russia.

The German "blank check"

The Serbs rejected the critical item in the Austrian ultimatum as an infringement on Serbian sovereignty, and Austria thereupon declared war upon Serbia. Russia prepared to defend Serbia and hence to fight Austria. Expecting that Austria would be joined by Germany, Russia rashly mobilized its army on the German as well as the Austrian frontier. Since the power which first mobilized had all the advantages of a rapid offensive, the German government demanded an end to the Russian mobilization on its border and, receiving no answer, declared war on Russia on August 1, 1914. Convinced that France would in any case enter the war on the side of Russia, Germany also declared war on France on August 3.

The German decisions were posited on a reckless hope that Great Britain might not enter the war at all. England was bound by no formal military alliance. Even the French

Archduke Francis Ferdinand of Austria meets here with leaders of the Catholic church during his visit to Sarajevo on June 28, 1914. Shortly after this meeting, the Archduke (the tall man with a moustache) and his wife were assassinated by a Serbian nationalist. The ensuing diplomatic crisis mobilized all of the nations in the European alliance system and led to the First World War of 1914–1918.

(Hulton Getty)

English isolation

did not know for certain, as late as August 3, whether the British would join them in war. The British clung to scraps of their old proud isolation; they hesitated to make a final choice of sides; and as the foreign secretary Sir Edward Grey repeatedly explained, in England only parliament could declare war, so that the foreign office could make no binding promise of war in advance. It has often been said that had the German government known as a positive fact that England would fight, the war might not have come. Hence the evasiveness of British policy is made a contributing cause of the war. In reality, the probability that England would fight was so great that to underestimate it, as the Germans did, was an act of supreme folly. The British government was deeply committed to France, especially through naval agreements, but what swept the British public toward the French was the German invasion of Belgium. The German plan to crush France quickly was such that it could succeed only by crossing Belgium. When the Belgians protested, the Germans invaded anyway, violating the treaty of 1839 which had guaranteed Belgian neutrality. England declared war on Germany on August 4.

Causes of the First World War

The mere narration of successive crises does not explain why the chief nations of Europe within a few days became locked in combat over the murder of an imperial personage. Among more obvious general causes, the alliance system may be singled out. Europe was divided into two camps.

THE BALKANS, 1878 AND 1914

Austria and Russia had gradually pushed the Ottoman Empire out of Europe since 1699. The Congress of Berlin in 1878 attempted to stabilize the situation by recognizing Romania, Serbia, and Montenegro as independent monarchies, and northern Bulgaria as an autonomous principality within the Ottoman Empire. The ambitions and discontents of these new states, of Greece, and of non-Turkish people remaining within the Ottoman Empire culminated in the Balkan Wars of 1912–1913. Albania then became independent, and Serbia, Bulgaria, and Greece became contiguous. Austrian and Russian pressures meanwhile continued; in 1908 Austria annexed Bosnia, where the South Slav population, like the Serbs, was hostile to the Austrian annexation.

Every incident tended to become a test of strength between the two. A given incident, such as German intervention in Morocco, or the assassination of Francis Ferdinand, could not be settled on its own merits, merely by the parties concerned. However it was dealt with, one of the two camps was deemed to have lost or gained and hence to have lost or gained in influence in other incidents, of perhaps greater purport, that would arise in the future. Each power felt that it must stand by its allies whatever the specific issue. This was because all lived in the fear of war, of some nameless future war in which allies would be necessary.

The Germans complained of being "encircled" by France and Russia. They dreaded the day when they might have to face a war on two fronts. Willing to accept even a Europeanwide war to break their threatened "encirclement" by the Entente powers, they were obliged to hold to their one ally, Austria-Hungary, which was in turn able to sell its support at its own price. The French dreaded a coming conflict with Germany, which in 40 years had far surpassed France in population and industrial strength; they were obliged to cling to their ally Russia, which therefore could oblige the French to yield to Russian wishes. As for Russia and Austria, they were both tottering empires. Especially after 1900, the tsarist regime suffered from endemic revolutionism; and the Habsburg empire, from chronic nationalistic agitation. Authorities in both empires became desperate.

Like the Serbs, they had little to lose and were therefore reckless. It was Russia that drew France and hence England into war in 1914, and Austria that drew Germany. Seen in this light, the tragedy of 1914 is that the most backward or politically bankrupt parts of Europe, through the alliance system, dragged the more advanced parts automatically into ruin.

The German Empire, too, faced an internal crisis. The Social Democrats became the largest party in the Reichstag in 1912. Their sentiments for the most part were antimilitarist and antiwar. But the German imperial government recognized no responsibility to a majority in the chamber. Policy was determined by men of the old unreconstructed upper class, in which army and navy interests, now reinforced by new business interests, were very strong; and even moderates and liberals shared in the ambition to make Germany a world power, the equal of any. The perplexities the ruling groups faced at home, the feeling that their position was being undermined by the Social Democrats, may have made them more willing to view war as a way out. And while it is not true that Germany started the war, as its enemies in 1914 popularly believed, it must be granted that its policies had for some years been rather peremptory, arrogant, devious, and obstinate. In a broad sense, the emergence of a consolidated industrial Germany after 1870, making its bid for world-power status relatively late, was a distant and basic cause of war.

The alliance system was only a symptom of deeper trouble. In a word, the world had an international economy but a national polity. Economically, each European people now required habitual contact with the world as a whole. Each people was to that extent dependent and insecure. Industrial countries were especially vulnerable, relying as they did on import of raw materials and food and on export of goods, services, or capital in return. There was, however, no world state to police the worldwide system, assuring participation in the world economy to all nations under all conditions. Each nation had to take care of itself. Hence came much of the drive for imperialism, in which each Great Power tried to stake out part of the world system for itself. And hence also came the quest for allies and for binding alliances. The alliances, in a world that was in the strict sense anarchic (and seemed likely to remain so), were a means by which each nation attempted to bolster up its security; to assure that it would not be cut off, conquered, or subjected to another's will; to obtain some hope of economic success in the competitive struggle for use of the world's goods.

86.   THE ARMED STALEMATE

The First World War lasted over four years, from 1914 to the end of 1918, the United States entering with effective result in the last year. Germany and its allies were called the Central Powers, while the Entente governments were termed the Allies. The war was appalling in its human costs; on the western front, more men were used and killed in the First World War than in the Second.

The Schlieffen Plan

At first a short war, as in 1870, was universally expected. The German General Staff had its plans ready for a two-front struggle against France and Russia. The disadvantage of fighting on two fronts was offset by the possession of good rail lines, which allowed the rapid shuttling of troops from one front to the other. The German war plan, known as the Schlieffen Plan, rested upon this fact. The idea was first to defeat France by the rapid wheeling motion of a tremendous army through Belgium and then to turn at more leisure against Russia, whose great size and less developed railways would make its deployment much slower.

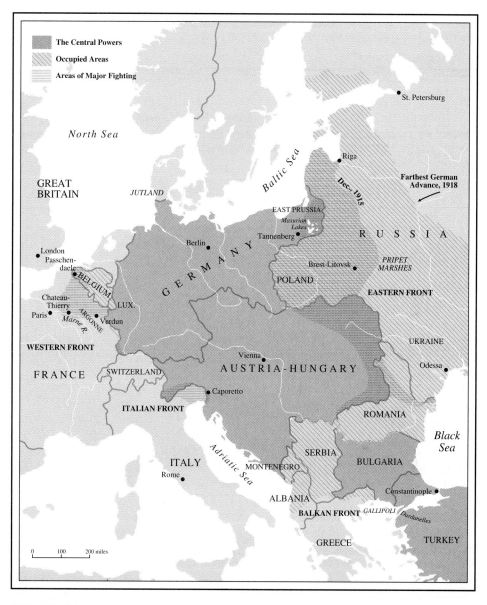

The Central Powers

Occupied Areas

Areas of Major Fighting

THE FIRST WORLD WAR

Land fighting in the First World War was mainly confined to the areas shown by the darker horizontal shading. The huge battles on the western front, which produced more casualties than all of the battles in the West during the Second World War, swayed back and forth over an area less than 100 miles wide.

The War on Land, 1914–1916

On August 3, 1914, the Germans launched 78 infantry divisions in the West. They were opposed by 72 French divisions, 5 British, and 6 Belgian. The Germans swept irresistibly forward. The Schlieffen Plan seemed to be moving like clockwork. The civilian authorities made plans for the conquest and annexation of large parts of Europe. Then a

Almost everyone in 1914 expected a short war and a quick resolution of the international crisis. These German soldiers at the Berlin railway station were preparing to board trains that would take them to the front. Accompanied by their wives or girlfriends and carrying flowers, they departed Berlin amid the optimistic fanfare that spread across all Europe in the early days of the war.

(AKG London)

hitch occurred: the Russians were fulfilling the terms of their alliance; the 10 billion francs invested by the French in Russia now paid their most significant dividend. The Russians pushed two armies into Germany, penetrating into East Prussia. Moltke withdrew forces from the German right wing in France, on August 26, for service in the East. The Germans moved on, but their striking arm was weakened and their lines of communication were already overextended. Joffre, the French commander, regrouping his forces, with strong support from the relatively small British contingent and at exactly the right moment, ordered a counterattack.

The battle of the Marne

The ensuing battle of the Marne, fought from September 5 to 12, changed the whole character of the war. The Germans were obliged to retreat. The hope of felling France at a single blow was ended. Each side now tried to outflank and destroy the other until the battle lines extended to the sea. The Germans failed to win control of the Channel ports; French and British communications remained uninterrupted. For these reverses the great victories meanwhile won by the Germans on the eastern front, though of gigantic proportions (the battles of Tannenberg and the Masurian Lakes, at which 225,000 Russians were captured), were in the long run small consolation.

In the West the war of movement now settled into a war of position. The armies on the western front became almost immobile. The units of horse cavalry—the uhlans, hussars, and lancers that had pranced off to war in high spirits—disappeared from the field. Since aviation was barely beginning, and motor transport was still new (the armies had trucks, but no self-propelled guns, and no tanks until very late in the war), the basic soldier more than ever was the man on foot. The most deadly new weapon was the machine gun, which made it impossible for foot soldiers to advance across open fields without overwhelming artillery preparation. The result was a long stalemate of war in the trenches in which the indispensable infantry sought protection.

War in the trenches

In 1915 the Germans and Austro-Hungarians put their main effort into an attempt to knock out Russia. They pressed far into the tsarist empire. The Russian losses were enormous—2 million killed, wounded, or captured in 1915 alone. But at the end of the year the Russian army was still fighting. Meanwhile the British and French, hoping to open up communications with Russia, launched a naval attack on Turkey, aiming at Constantinople by way of the Dardanelles. They poured 450,000 men into the narrow peninsula of Gallipoli, of whom 145,000 were killed or wounded. After almost a year the enterprise was given up as a failure.

In 1916 both sides turned again to northern France in an attempt to break the deadlock. The Allies planned a great offensive along the river Somme, while the Germans prepared one in the neighborhood of Verdun. The Germans attacked Verdun in February. The French commander Joffre put in General Pétain to defend it but resisted committing his main reserves, holding them for the coming offensive on the Somme. Pétain and his troops, held to minimum numbers, thus had to take the full weight of the German army. The battle of Verdun lasted six months, it drew the horrified admiration of the world, and it became a legend of determined resistance ("they shall not pass"), until the Germans finally abandoned the attack because they sustained almost as many casualties as the French—330,000 to 350,000.

The battle of Verdun

While the inferno still raged at Verdun the Allies opened their offensive on the Somme in July. They brought up unheard of amounts of artillery, and the newly raised British army was present in force. The idea was to break through the German line simply by stupendous pressure; on both sides, Allied and German, the art of generalship had sunk to an all-time low. Despite a weeklong artillery bombardment the British lost 60,000 men on the first day of the attack. In a week they had advanced only one mile along a six-mile front. In a month they had advanced only $2^{1}/_{2}$ miles. The battle of the Somme, lasting from July to October, cost the Germans about 500,000 men, the British 400,000, and the French 200,000. Nothing of any value had been gained. It was, indeed, at the Somme that the British first used the tank, an armored vehicle with caterpillar tracks that could crash through barbed wire, lunge over trenches, and smash into machine gun nests; but the tanks were introduced in such small numbers, and with such skepticism on the part of many commanders, that they had no effect on the battle.

The battle of the Somme

The miseries and dangers of the muddy trenches on the western front are conveyed in this photograph of soldiers in the battle of Passchendaele in 1917. Human life in such conditions became a raw struggle for survival; most soldiers reported that the grinding, daily experience on a battlefield seemed very far removed from the nationalism or political concerns of civilians and government leaders.

(Imperial War Museum, London)

The War at Sea

With land armies thus helpless, both sides looked to the sea. The long preponderance of British sea power, and the more recent Anglo-German naval race, would now be tested.

Naval blockade The British, with French aid, imposed a strict naval blockade. International law at the time placed goods headed for a country at war into two classes. One class was called contraband; it included munitions and certain specified raw materials which might be used in the manufacture of military equipment. The other class, including foodstuffs and raw cotton, was defined as noncontraband. A country was supposed, by international law, to be able to import noncontraband goods even in wartime. These terms of wartime law had been set forth as recently as 1909 at an international conference held in London. The purpose was to make it impossible for a sea power (that is, the British) to starve out an enemy in wartime or even to interfere with normal civilian production. The jealousy of Continental Europe for British sea power was an old story.

Such law, if observed, would make the blockade of Germany entirely ineffective, and the Allies did not observe it. To starve out the enemy and ruin his economy was precisely their purpose. Economic warfare took its place alongside armed attack as a military weapon, as in the days of Napoleon. The Allies announced a new international law. The distinction between contraband and noncontraband was gradually abolished. The British navy (aided by the French) proceeded to stop all goods of whatever character destined for

Germany or its allies. Neutrals, among whom the Americans, Dutch, and Scandinavians were the ones mainly affected, were not allowed to make for German ports at all.

The United States protested vehemently against these regulations. It defended the rights of neutrals. It reasserted the distinction between contraband and noncontraband, claimed the right to trade with other neutrals, and upheld the "freedom of the seas." Much mutual bad feeling resulted between the American and British governments in 1915 and 1916. But when the United States entered the war it adopted the Allied position, and its navy joined in enforcing exactly the same regulations. International law was in fact changed. In the Second World War the very words "contraband" and "freedom of the seas" were never heard.

The Germans countered with an attempt to blockade England. A few isolated German cruisers were able for some time to destroy British shipping in the several oceans of the world. But the Germans relied mainly on the submarine, against which the British naval power at first seemed helpless. The submarine was an unrefined weapon; a submarine commander could not always tell what kind of ship he was attacking, nor could he remove passengers, confiscate cargo, escort the vessel, or indeed do much except sink it. Citing British abuses of international law in justification, the German government in February 1915 declared the waters surrounding the British Isles to be a war zone, in which Allied vessels would be torpedoed and neutral vessels would be in grave danger.

Submarine warfare

Three months later the liner *Lusitania* was torpedoed off the Irish coast. About 1,200 persons were drowned, of whom 118 were American citizens. The *Lusitania* was a British ship; it carried munitions of war manufactured in the United States for Allied use; and the Germans had published ominous warnings in the New York papers that Americans should not take passage on it. Americans then believed that they should be able to sail safely, on peaceable errands, on the ship of a belligerent power in wartime. The loss of life shocked the country. President Wilson informed the Germans that another such act would be considered "deliberately unfriendly." The Germans, to avoid trouble, refrained for two years from making full use of their submarines. For two years the Allied use of the sea was only partly impeded.

The Lusitania

Allied access to the sea was confirmed by the one great naval engagement of the war, the battle of Jutland. The German admirals became restless at seeing their newly built navy skulking behind minefields on the German shores, yet they could not presume to challenge the superior British Grand Fleet, posted watchfully at Scapa Flow. They hoped, however, to decoy smaller formations of British ships, destroy them one by one, and perhaps eventually obtain enough of a naval balance in the North Sea to loosen the British blockade, by which Germany was slowly being strangled. They were themselves, however, trapped into a major engagement in which the British Grand Fleet of 151 ships took them by surprise. After a few hours of furious combat the Germans were able to withdraw into mined waters. They had lost less tonnage and fewer men than the British. They had proved themselves to be dangerously proficient in naval combat. But they had failed to undermine the British preponderance at sea.

Diplomatic Maneuvers and Secret Agreements

With no military solution in sight, both sides looked about for new allies. The Ottoman Empire, fearing Russia, had joined Germany and Austria-Hungary as early as October 1914. Bulgaria, being anti-Serb, had done the same in 1915.

*Italy joins
the Allies*

The leading new prospect was Italy, which, though formally a member of the Triple Alliance, had long ago drifted away from it. Both sides solicited the Italian government, which bargained imperturbably with both. The Italian public was divided. Both Catholic and socialist leaders recommended staying at peace, but extreme nationalists saw a chance to obtain their *irredenta,* the border regions in which Italians lived but which had not been incorporated at the time of national unification. The Italian government cast its lot with the Allies in the secret treaty of London of 1915. It was agreed that if the Allies won the war Italy would receive (from Austria) the Trentino, the south Tyrol, Istria and the city of Trieste, and some of the Dalmatian Islands. If Britain and France took over Germany's African colonies, Italy should receive territorial increases in Libya and Somaliland. The treaty of London, in short, carried on the most brazen prewar practices of territorial expansionism. It must be remembered that the Allies were desperate. Italy, thus bought, and probably against the will of most Italians, opened up a front against Austria-Hungary in May 1915.

The Allies likewise made plans for a final partition of the Ottoman Empire, which still reached from Constantinople through the Middle East into Arabia and into Mesopotamia (modern Iraq). By a secret treaty they agreed that, upon an Allied victory, Mesopotamia was to go to Britain, Syria and southeastern Asia Minor to France, small portions to Italy, and Kurdistan and Armenia to Russia.

Each side tampered with minorities and discontented groups living within the domains of the other. The Germans promised an independent Poland, to embarrass Russia. They stirred up local nationalism in the Ukraine. They raised up a pro-German Flemish movement in Belgium. They persuaded the Ottoman sultan, as caliph, to proclaim a holy war in North Africa, hoping that irate Muslims would drive the British from Egypt and the French from Algeria. This had no success. German agents worked in Ireland and one Irish nationalist, Sir Roger Casement, landed in Ireland from a German submarine, precipitating the Easter Rebellion of 1916, which was suppressed by the British.

*The Zimmer-
mann telegram*

To Americans the most amazing of similar activities was the Zimmermann telegram. In 1916 an American military force had crossed the Mexican border in pursuit of bandits, against protests by the Mexican government. Relations between the United States and Germany were also deteriorating. In January 1917 the German state secretary for foreign affairs, Arthur Zimmermann, dispatched a telegram to the German minister at Mexico City, telling him what to say to the Mexican president. He was to say that if the United States went to war with Germany, Germany would form an alliance with Mexico and if possible Japan, enabling Mexico to get back its "lost territories." These latter referred to the region conquered by the United States from Mexico in the 1840s—Texas, New Mexico, and Arizona (California was not mentioned by Zimmermann, who was no doubt somewhat vague on the exact history and location of these Alsace-Lorraines of America). Zimmermann's telegram was intercepted and decoded by the British, and passed on to them to Washington. Printed in the newspapers, it shocked public opinion in the United States.

The Allies were more successful in appealing to nationalist discontent, for the obvious reason that the most active national minorities were within the lands of their enemies. They were able to promise restoration of Alsace-Lorraine to France without difficulty. They promised independence to the Poles, though anticipating some difficulty as long as the Russian monarchy stood. It was easier for them to favor national independence for Czechs, Slovaks, and South Slavs, since an Allied victory would dissolve the Austro-Hungarian empire.

Within the Ottoman Empire the British aroused Arab hopes for independence. The British Colonel T. E. Lawrence led an insurrection in the Hejaz against the Turks; and the emir Hussein of Hejaz, with British support, in 1916 took the title of king of the Arabs, with a kingdom reaching from the Red Sea to the Persian Gulf. Zionists saw in the impending Ottoman collapse the opportunity to realize their dream for a Jewish state in Palestine. Since Palestine was peopled by Arabs (and had been for over 1,000 years) the Zionist program conflicted with British plans to sponsor Arab nationalism. Nevertheless, in the Balfour note of 1917, the British government promised support for the idea of a "Jewish home-land" in Palestine. For the Armenians these years were especially disastrous. They were a Christian people living in the eastern part of the Anatolian peninsula where it abuts on Russia, and like other peoples in the Ottoman Empire, including the Turks themselves, they had developed aspirations for a national state of their own, which conflicted with the plans of Turkish reformers to Turkify the empire. It was only 20 years since such clashes had produced the Armenian massacres of 1894 which had horrified Europe. Now in 1915 the Turkish government, as the Russian army threatened its eastern frontier, ordered the deportation of Armenians from the war zone as potential sympathizers with Russia and the Western Allies. Supposedly they were to be resettled in Syria and Palestine. In fact, in the atmosphere of military crisis, political hatred, bureaucratic contempt, and wartime scarcities hundreds of thousands of Armenians perished in what many in later years defined as a genocidal massacre. Virtually no Armenians remained within what became the Turkish republic a few years later. The surviving Armenians became another of the world's scattered peoples with no state of their own except for a small Armenian republic, briefly independent after 1918, then part of the Soviet Union for 70 years, and finally independent again after 1991.

Disruption in the Ottoman Empire

Meanwhile during the war the British and French easily moved into the German colonies in Africa. The British foreign secretary, Sir Edward Grey, revealed to Colonel House, President Wilson's personal emissary, that the Allies did not intend that Germany should ever get its colonies back.

In China, too, the third important area of imperialist competition, the war accelerated the tendencies of preceding years. The Japanese saw their own opportunity in the self-slaughter of the Europeans. Japan had also been allied to Britain since 1902. In August 1914 Japan declared war on Germany. It soon overran the German concessions in China and the German islands in the Pacific, the Marshalls and Carolines. In January 1915 Japan presented its Twenty-One Demands on China, a secret ultimatum for further concessions, most of which the Chinese were obliged to accept. Japan thereby proceeded to turn Manchuria and north China into an exclusive protectorate.

Japan in China

As for the Germans, their war aims were even more expansionist and more menacing to existing boundaries in Europe itself. Early in September 1914, when a quick victory seemed within their grasp, Bethmann-Hollweg, who remained chancellor until the summer of 1917, drew up a list of German war aims which stayed unaltered until the end of hostilities. The plans called for an enlarged German Empire dominating all central Europe and annexations or satellites in both western and eastern Europe. In the east, Lithuania and other parts of the Baltic coast were to become German dependencies, large sections of Poland were to be directly annexed, and the remainder was to be joined with Austrian Galicia to form a German-dominated Polish state. In the west, Belgium was to become a German dependency to provide more direct

German expansionism

access to the Atlantic, and French Lorraine with its rich iron ore was to be added to the already German parts of Alsace-Lorraine. Colonial adjustments, including the acquisition of most of central Africa from coast to coast, were also projected. The political map of Europe and of colonial Africa would thus be transformed.

All these developments, especially the Allied negotiations, whether accomplished facts or secret agreements, affecting Europe, Asia, or Africa, became very troublesome later at the peace conference. They continued some of the most unsettling tendencies of European politics before the war. It does not appear that the Allies, until driven by Woodrow Wilson, gave any thought to means of controlling anarchic nationalism or of preventing war in the future. As president of the United States, Wilson for a long time could see little to choose between the warring alliances, though his personal sympathies were with England and France. In 1916 he attempted to mediate, entering into confidential discussions with both sides; but both still hoped to win on their own terms, so that negotiation was fruitless. Wilson judged that most Americans wished to remain uninvolved, and in November 1916 he was reelected to a second term, on the popular cry, "he kept us out of war." Wilson urged a true neutrality of thought and feeling, or a settlement, as he said, that should be a "peace without victory."

A "peace without victory"

As of the end of 1916, it is hard to see how the First World War would have turned out, had not two new sets of forces been brought in.

87.   THE COLLAPSE OF RUSSIA AND THE INTERVENTION OF THE UNITED STATES

The Withdrawal of Russia: Revolution and the Treaty of Brest-Litovsk

The first victim of the First World War, among governments, was the Russian empire. As the Russo-Japanese War had led to the Revolution of 1905 in Russia, so the more ruinous conflict in Europe led to the far greater Revolution of 1917. The story of the Russian Revolution is told in the following chapter. It is enough to say here that war offered a test that the tsarist government could not meet. Bungling, dishonest, and secretive, incapable of supplying the materiel required for modern fighting, driving hordes of peasants into battle in some cases even without rifles, losing men by the millions yet offering no goal to inspire sacrifice, the tsarist regime lost the loyalty of all elements of its people.

In March 1917 the troops in St. Petersburg mutinied, while strikes and riots desolated the city. The Duma, or Russian parliament, used the occasion to press its demands for reform. On March 15 Nicholas II abdicated. A Provisional Government took over, made up of liberal noblemen and middle-class leaders, generally democrats and constitutionalists, with at first only one socialist. The Provisional Government remained in office from March to November 1917. Its members, who shared in the liberalism of western Europe, believed that a liberal and parliamentary regime could not succeed in Russia unless the German Empire were defeated. They took steps, therefore, to prosecute the war with a new vigor. In July 1917 an offensive was opened in Galicia, but the demoralized Russian armies again collapsed.

The Provisional Government

The mass of the Russian people were wearied of a war in which they were asked to suffer so much for so little. Nor did Russian peasants or workers feel any enthusiasm for the westernized intellectuals and professional men who headed the Provisional Government. Ordinary Russians, so far as they had any politics, were drawn to one or another of numerous forms of socialism, Marxist and non-Marxist. The Russian Marxist party, the Social Democrats, was divided between Menshevik and Bolshevik factions, the latter being the more extreme. The Bolshevik leaders had for some time lived as exiles in western Europe. Their principal spokesman, V. I. Lenin, with a few others, had spent the war years in Switzerland. In April 1917 the German government offered safe passage to Lenin through Germany to Russia. A railway car full of Bolsheviks, carefully "sealed" to prevent infection of Germany, was thus hauled by a German train to the frontier, whence it passed on to St. Petersburg, or Petrograd, as the city was renamed during the war. The aim of the Germans in this affair, as in the sending of Roger Casement to Ireland in a submarine, was of course to use a kind of psychological warfare against the enemy's home front. It was to promote rebellion against the Provisional Government and thus at last to eliminate Russia.

The Bolsheviks return from exile

The position of the Provisional Government became rapidly more untenable, from many causes, until by November 1917 the situation was so confused that Lenin and the Bolsheviks were able to seize power. The Bolsheviks stood for peace with Germany, partly to win popular favor in Russia and partly because they regarded the war impartially, as a struggle between capitalist and imperialist powers which should be left to exhaust and destroy each other for the benefit of socialism. On December 3, 1917, a peace conference opened between the Bolsheviks and the Germans at Brest-Litovsk. Meanwhile the peoples within the western border of the old Russia—Poles, Ukrainians, Bessarabians, Estonians, Latvians, Finns—with German backing, proclaimed their national independence. The Bolsheviks, since they would not or could not fight, were obliged to sign with Germany a treaty to which they vehemently objected, the treaty of Brest-Litovsk of March 3, 1918. By this treaty they acknowledged the "independence," or at least the loss to Russia, of Poland, the Ukraine, Finland, and the Baltic provinces.

The treaty of Brest-Litovsk

For the Germans the treaty of Brest-Litovsk represented their maximum success during the First World War; it accomplished some of the war aims formulated at the beginning of hostilities. Not only had they neutralized Russia, but they also now dominated eastern Europe through puppets placed at the head of the new independent states. They relieved the effects of the naval blockade by drawing considerable quantities of foodstuffs from the Ukraine, though less than they expected. A certain number of German troops remained in the East to preserve the new arrangements. But it was no longer a two-front war. Masses of the German army were shifted from east to west. The High Command, under Hindenburg and Ludendorff since August 1916, prepared to concentrate for a last blow in France to end the war in 1918.

The year 1918 was essentially a race to see whether American aid could reach Europe soon enough, in sufficient amount, to offset the added strength which Germany drew from the collapse of Russia. In March of that year the Germans, beginning with gas attacks and a bombardment by 6,000 artillery pieces, opened a formidable offensive before which the French and British both recoiled. On May 30, 1918, the Germans again stood at the Marne, 37 miles from Paris. At this time there were only two American divisions in action, though the United States had been at war for over a year. At this point in the story there are therefore two open questions: how the United States entered the war, and the length of time required for the buildup of its forces overseas.

American intervention

The United States and the War

We have seen how President Wilson clung persistently to neutrality. The American people were divided. Many had been born in Europe or were the children of immigrants. Those of Irish origin were anti-British; those of German origin were often sympathetic to Germany. On the other hand, since the time of the Spanish-American and Boer wars, a noticeable current of friendliness to the English had been running, more than ever before in American history. The sale of war materiel to the Allies, and the purchase of the bonds of Allied governments, had given certain limited though influential circles a material interest in an Allied victory. The idealism of the country was on the side of England and France, so far as it was not isolationist. An Allied victory would clearly advance the cause of democracy, freedom, and progress far more than a victory of the German Empire. On the other hand, England and France were suspected of somewhat impure motives, and they were allied with the Russian autocracy, the reactionary and brutal tsardom.

The fall of tsarism made a great impression. Democrats and progressives now came forward even in Russia. No one had ever heard of Lenin or foresaw the Bolshevik Revolution. It seemed in the spring of 1917 that Russia was struggling along the path that England, France, and America had already taken. An ideological barrier had dropped away, and the demand for American intervention to safeguard democracy became more insistent.

The Germans gave up the attempt to keep the United States out. Constricted ever more tightly by the blockade, and failing to get a decision on land, the German government and High Command listened more readily to the submarine experts, who declared that if given a free hand they could force British surrender in six months. It was the chief example in the First World War of the claim that one branch of the service could win the war alone. Civilian and diplomatic members of the government objected, fearing the consequences of war with the United States. They were overruled; it was a good example of the way in which, in Germany, the army and navy had taken the highest policy into their hands. Unrestricted submarine warfare was to be resumed on February 1, 1917. It was foreseen that the United States would declare war, but the German High Command believed that this would make no immediate difference. They estimated in 1917 (correctly) that between the time when the United States entered a European war and the time when it could take part with its own army about a year must intervene. Meanwhile, the planners said, in six months they could force Britain to accept defeat.

On January 31, 1917, the Germans notified Wilson of the resumption of unrestricted submarine attacks. They announced that they would sink on sight all merchant vessels found in a zone around the British Isles or in the Mediterranean. Wilson broke off diplomatic relations and ordered the arming of American freighters. Meanwhile, the publication of the Zimmermann telegram convinced many Americans of German aggressiveness. German secret agents also had been at work in America, fomenting strikes and causing explosions in factories engaged in the manufacture of munitions for the Allies. In February and March several American ships were sunk. Americans regarded all these activities as an interference with their rights as neutrals. Wilson at last concluded that Germany was a menace. Having made his decision, Wilson saw a clear-cut issue between right and wrong, and he obtained a rousing declaration of war from Congress, on April 6, 1917. The United States went to war "to make the world safe for democracy."

At first the German campaign realized and even exceeded the predictions of its sponsors. In February 1917 the Germans sank 540,000 tons of shipping, in March 578,000 tons, in April, as the days grew longer, 874,000 tons. Something akin to terror, with difficulty concealed from the public, seized on the government in London. Britain was reduced to a mere six-week reserve of food. Gradually countermeasures were developed—mine barges, hydrophones, depth charges, airplane reconnaissance, and most of all the convoy. It was found that a hundred or more freighters together, though all had to steam at the pace of the slowest, could be protected by a sufficient concentration of warships to keep submarines away. The United States navy, which, unlike the army, was of considerable size and ready for combat, supplied enough additional force to the Allies to make convoying and other antisubmarine measures highly effective. By the end of 1917 the submarine was no more than a nuisance. For the Germans the great plan produced the anticipated penalty without the reward—its net result was only to add America to their enemies.

On the western front in 1917, while the Americans desperately got themselves ready for the war they had entered, the French and British continued to hold the line. The French, finding in General Nivelle a commander who still believed in the breakthrough, launched an offensive so unsuccessful and so bloody that mutiny spread through the French army. Pétain then replaced Nivelle and restored discipline to the exhausted and disillusioned soldiers, but he had no thought of further attack. "I am waiting for the Americans and the tanks," he said. The British then assumed the main burden. For three months late in 1917 they fought the dismal battle of Passchendaele. They advanced five miles, near Ypres, at a cost of 400,000 men. At the very end of 1917 the British surprised the Germans with a raid by 380 tanks, which penetrated deep into the German lines, but were obliged to withdraw, since no reserve of fresh infantry was at hand to exploit their success.

The French and British hold the line

Meanwhile the Austro-Hungarians, strongly reinforced by German troops, overwhelmed the Italians at the disastrous battle of Caporetto. The Central Powers streamed into northern Italy, but the Italians, with British and French reinforcements, were able to hold the line. The net effect of the campaigns of 1917, and of the repulse of the submarine at the same time, was to reemphasize the stalemate in Europe, incline the weary Allies to await the Americans, and give the Americans what they most needed—time.

The Americans made good use of the time given them. Conscription, democratically entitled selective service, was adopted immediately after the declaration of war. The United States army, whose professionals in 1916 numbered only 130,000, performed the mammoth feat of turning over 3.5 million civilians into soldiers. With the navy, the United States came to have over 4 million in its armed services (which may be compared with over 12 million in the Second World War). Aid flowed to the Allies. To the loans already made through private bankers were added some $10 billion lent by the American government itself. The Allies used the money mainly to buy food and munitions in the United States. American farms and factories, which had already prospered by selling to the Allies during the period of neutrality, now broke all records for production. Civilian industry was converted to war uses; radiator factories turned out guns, and piano factories manufactured airplane wings. Every possible means was employed to build up ocean shipping, without which neither American supplies nor American armies could reach the theater of war. Available shipping was increased from 1 million to 10 million tons.

America mobilizes for war

Civilian consumption was drastically cut. Eight thousand tons of steel were saved in the manufacture of women's corsets and 75,000 tons of tin were spared in the making of children's toy wagons. Every week people observed meatless Tuesday, and sugar was rationed. Daylight-saving time, invented in Europe during the war, was introduced to save coal. By such means the United States made enormous stocks available for its Allies as well as itself, though for some items, notably airplanes and artillery ammunition, the American armies, when they reached France, drew heavily on British and French manufactures.

The Final Phase of the War

The Germans, as we have seen, victorious in the east, opened a great final offensive in the west in the spring of 1918, hoping to force a decision before American participation turned the balance forever. To oppose it, a unity of command was achieved for the first time when a French general, Ferdinand Foch, was made commander in chief of all Allied forces in France, with the national commanders subordinate to him, including Pershing for the Americans. In June the Germans first made contact with American troops in significant force, meeting the Second Division at Château-Thierry. The German position was so favorable that civilians in the German government thought it opportune to make a last effort at a compromise peace. The military, headed by Hindenburg and Ludendorff, successfully blocked any such attempts; they preferred to gamble on one final throw. The German armies reached their farthest advance on July 15 along the Marne.

The armistice

There were now nine American divisions in the Allied line. Foch used them to spearhead his counterattack on July 18. The badly overstrained Germans began to falter. Over 250,000 American troops were now landing in France every month. The final Allied offensive which opened in September, with American troops in the Argonne occupying an eastern sector, proved more than the Germans could withstand. The German High Command notified its government that it could not win the war. The German foreign office made peace overtures to President Wilson. An armistice was arranged, and on November 11, 1918, firing ceased on the western front.

Since Germany's allies had surrendered during the preceding weeks, the war, or at least the shooting war in western Europe, was now over. The horror it brought to individual lives cannot be told by statistics, which dryly report that almost 10 million men had been killed and 20 million had been wounded. Each of the European Great Powers (except Italy) lost from 1 million to 2 million in killed alone. The United States, with some 330,000 casualties of all types (of whom 115,000 died) lost in the entire war fewer men than the main combatants had lost in such a single battle as Verdun or Passchendaele.[1] American assistance was decisive in the defeat of Germany. But it came so late, when the others had been struggling for so long, that the mere beginnings of it were enough to turn the scale. On the date of the armistice there were 2 million American soldiers in France, and another 1 million were on the way. But the American army had really been in combat only four months. During the whole year 1918, out of every hundred artillery shells that were fired by the three armies, the French fired 51, the British fired 43, and the Americans fired only 6.

---

[1] Of the 115,000 American deaths only 50,000 represented men killed in battle, the remainder representing mainly deaths by disease. The great influenza epidemic of 1918, which brought death to over 20 million people, civilians and military alike, in all parts of the world, probably accounted for 25,000 deaths in the American army.

These American soldiers were part of the divisions that began to arrive in France during 1917, but the American military presence did not become significant until the following year. The steady arrival of fresh troops from the United States enabled the Allied commanders to launch a decisive final offensive and forced the German high command to recognize that Germany could not win the war.

(Hulton Getty)

88.   THE COLLAPSE OF THE AUSTRIAN AND GERMAN EMPIRES

The war proved fatal to the German and Austro-Hungarian empires, as to the Russian. The subject Habsburg nationalities, or the "national councils" representing them in the Western capitals, obtained recognition from the Allies, and in October 1918 declared their independence. The last Austrian emperor, Charles I, abdicated on November 12, and on the next day Austria was proclaimed a republic, as was Hungary in the following week. Before any peace conference could convene, the new states of Czechoslovakia, Yugoslavia, an enlarged Romania, a republican Hungary, and a miniature republican Austria were in existence by their own action.

Habsburg "national councils"

The German Empire stood solid until the closing weeks. Liberals, democrats, and socialists had lately begun to press for peace and democratization. Yet it was the High Command itself that precipitated the debacle. In the last years of the war dictatorial powers had become concentrated in the hands of General Ludendorff, and in September 1918 only he and his closest military associates realized that the German cause was hopeless. On September 29, at supreme headquarters at Spa in Belgium, Ludendorff informed the Kaiser that Germany must ask for peace. He urged that a new government be formed in Berlin, reflecting the majority in the Reichstag, on democratic parliamentary principles.

In calling for immediate peace negotiations, he seems to have had two ideas in mind. First, he might win time to regroup his armies and prepare a new offensive. Or if collapse became unavoidable, then the civilian or democratic elements in Germany would be the ones to sue for peace.

Democracy in Germany

The liberal Prince Max of Baden was found to head a cabinet in which even socialists were included. In October various reforms were enacted, the Bismarckian system was ended, and Germany became a liberal constitutional monarchy. For Ludendorff the changes were not fast enough. What was happening was essentially simple. The German military caste, at the moment of Germany's crisis, was more eager to save the army than to save the empire. The army must never admit surrender; that was an affair for small men in business suits. Emperor, High Command, officers, and aristocrats were unloading frantically upon civilians.

President Wilson unwittingly played into their hands. Speaking now as the chief of the Allied coalition, the one to whom peace overtures were first made, he insisted that the German government must become more democratic. It may be recalled how Bismarck, after defeating France in 1871, demanded a general election in France before making peace. Wilson, unlike Bismarck, really believed in democracy; but in a practical way his position was the same. He wanted to be sure that he was dealing with the German people itself, not with a discredited elite. He wanted it to be the real Germany that applied for and accepted the Allied terms. In Germany, as realization of the military disaster spread, many people began to regard the Kaiser as an obstacle to peace. Or they felt that Germany would obtain better terms if it appeared before the Allies as a republic. Even the officer corps, to halt the fighting before the army disintegrated, began to talk of abdication. Sailors mutinied at Kiel on November 3, and councils of workers and soldiers were formed in various cities. The socialists threatened to withdraw from the newly formed cabinet (that is, go into opposition and end the representative nature of the new government) unless William II abdicated. A general strike, led by minority socialists and syndicalists, began on November 9. "Abdication," Prince Max told the emperor, "is a dreadful thing, but a government without the socialists would be a worse danger for the country." William II abdicated on November 9, and slipped across the frontier into Holland, where despite cries to try him as a "war criminal" he lived quietly until his death in 1941. Germany was proclaimed a republic on the day he abdicated. Two days later the war stopped.

The Weimar Republic

The fall of the empire in Germany, with the consequent adoption of the republic, did not arise from any basic discontent, deep revolutionary action, or change of sentiment in the German people. It was an episode of the war. The republic (soon called the Weimar Republic) arose because the victorious enemy demanded it, because the German people craved peace, because they wished to avoid forcible revolution, and because the old German military class, to save its face and its future strength, wished at least temporarily to be excused. When the war ended, the German army was still in France, its discipline and organization still apparently unimpaired.

No hostile shot had been fired on German soil. It was said later, by some, that the army had not been defeated, that it had been "stabbed in the back" by a dissolving civilian home front. This was untrue; it was the panic-stricken Ludendorff who first cried for "democracy." But the circumstances in which the German republic originated made its later history, and hence all later history, very troubled.

89. THE ECONOMIC, SOCIAL, AND CULTURAL IMPACT OF THE WAR

Effects on Capitalism: Government-Regulated Economies

European society was forced by the First World War into many basic changes that were to prove more lasting than the war itself. First of all, the war profoundly affected capitalism as previously known. Essential to the older capitalism (or economic liberalism, or free private enterprise) had been the idea that government should leave business alone, or at the most regulate certain general conditions under which businesses went about their affairs. Before 1914 governments had increasingly entered the economic field. They had put up tariffs, protected national industries, sought for markets or raw materials by imperialist expansion, or passed protective social legislation to benefit the wage-earning classes. During the war all belligerent governments controlled the economic system far more minutely. Indeed, the idea of the "planned economy" was first applied in the First World War. For the first time (with such rare and archaic precedents as France's revolutionary dictatorship of 1793) the state attempted to direct all the wealth, resources, and moral purpose of society to a single end.

The "planned economy"

Since no one had expected a long war, no one had made any plans for industrial mobilization. Everything had to be improvised. By 1916 each government had set up a system of boards, bureaus, councils, and commissions to coordinate its war effort. The aim was to see that all labor was effectively utilized and that all natural resources within the country, and all that could possibly be imported, were employed where they would do the most good. In the stress of war free competition was found to be wasteful and undirected private enterprise was found to be too uncertain and too slow. The profit motive came into disrepute. Those who exploited shortages to make big profits were stigmatized as profiteers. Production for civilian use, or for mere luxury purposes, was cut to a minimum. Businesses were not allowed to set up or close down factories as they chose. It was impossible to start a new business without government approval, because the flotation of stocks and bonds was controlled and raw materials were made available only as the government wished. It was equally impossible to shut down a business engaged in war production; if a factory was inefficient or unprofitable the government kept it going anyway, making up the losses, so that in some cases management came to expect government support. Here too the tests of competition and profitability were abandoned.

The new goal was coordination or "rationalization" of production in the interests of the country as a whole. Labor was discouraged from protesting against hours or wage rates, and the big unions generally agreed to refrain from strikes. For the upper and middle classes it became embarrassing to show their comforts too openly. It was patriotic to eat meagerly and to wear old clothes. War gave a new impetus even to the idea of economic equality, if only to enlist rich and poor alike in a common cause.

The "rationalization" of production

Military conscription was the first step in the allocation of manpower. Draft boards told some men to report to the army, granting exemptions to others to work safely in war industries. Given the casualty rates at the front, state determination over individual life could hardly go farther. With the insatiable need for troops, drawing in men originally exempted or at first rejected as physically inadequate, great numbers of women poured into factories and offices, and in Britain even into newly organized women's branches of the armed forces. Women took over many jobs which it had been thought only men could do. Women did not remain in the labor force after the war in such large numbers, most making way for the returning veterans, but the wartime experience in this and the Second World War was part of the process by which the labor force in all countries was enlarged, women's place in modern society was revolutionized, and the lives and outlook of millions of individual women were turned more actively toward participation in national economies. The First World War thus contributed to the redefinition or reorganization of women's work—a social process that had begun in the early Industrial Revolution and that would be intensified during the Second World War and in the years that followed.

During the war governments did not directly force men or women to drop one job and take another. There was no systematic labor conscription except in Germany. But by influencing wage scales, granting draft exemptions, forcing some industries to expand and others to contract or stand still, and propagandizing the idea that work in an arms factory was patriotic, the state shifted vast numbers of workers to war production. Impressed or "slave" labor was not used in the First World War, nor were prisoners of war obliged to give labor service, though there were some abuses of these rules of international law by the Germans, who were possibly the least scrupulous and certainly the most hard-pressed.

Governments controlled all foreign trade. It was intolerable to let private citizens ship off the country's resources at their own whim. It was equally intolerable to let them use up foreign exchange by importing unneeded goods or to drive up prices of necessities by competing with one another. Foreign trade became a state monopoly, in which private firms operated under strict licenses and quotas. The greatest of the exporting countries was the United States, whose annual exports rose from $2 billion to $6 billion between 1914 and 1918. The endless demand for American farm and factory products naturally drove up prices, which, however, were fixed by law in 1917, for the most important items.

As for the European Allies, which even before the war had exported less than they imported and were now exporting as little as possible, they could make purchases in the United States only by enormous loans from the American government. British and French citizens, under pressure from their own governments, sold off their American stocks and bonds, which were bought up by Americans. The former owners received pounds sterling or francs from their own governments, which in return took and spent the dollars paid by the new American owners. In this way the United States ceased to be a debtor country (owing some $4 billion to Europeans in 1914), and became the world's leading creditor country. By 1919 Europeans were in debt to the United States by about $10 billion.

The Allies controlled the sea, but they never had enough shipping to meet rising demands, especially with German submarines taking a steady though fluctuating toll. Each government set up a shipping board to expand shipbuilding at any cost and to assign available shipping space to whatever purposes— troop movements, rubber imports, foodstuffs—the government considered most urgent in view of overall plans. Control and allocation eventually became international under the Interallied Shipping Council, of which the United States was a member after entering the war. In England and France, where all manufactures depended on imports, government control of shipping and hence of imports was itself enough to give control over the whole economy.

Germany, denied access to the sea and also to Russia and western Europe, was obliged to adopt unprecedented measures of self-sufficiency. The oil of Romania and the grain of Ukraine, which became available late in the war, were poor substitutes for the world trade on which Germany had formerly depended. The Germans went with less food than other belligerents. Their government controls became more thorough and more efficient, producing what they called "war socialism." In Walter Rathenau they found a man with the necessary ideas. He was a Jewish industrialist, son of the head of the German electrical trust. One of the first to foresee a long war, he launched a program for the mobilization of raw materials. Early in the war it seemed that Germany might be soon defeated by lack of nitrogen, necessary to make explosives. Rathenau sweepingly requisitioned every conceivable natural source, including the very manure from the farmers' barnyards, until German chemists succeeded in extracting nitrogen from the air. The German chemical industry developed many other substitute products, such as synthetic rubber. German production was organized into war companies, one for each line of industry, with private business firms working under close government supervision.

German "war socialism"

The other belligerent governments also replaced competition between individual firms and factories with coordination. Consortiums of industrialists in France allocated raw

The need for workers during the First World War opened opportunities for women in jobs that were traditionally open only to men. These German women, who were working in an armaments factory in 1917, exemplified this trend in the workforce and also the general mobilization of an entire population to serve the demands of modern warfare.

(AKG London)

materials and government orders within each industry. The War Industries Board did the same in the United States. In Britain, similar methods became so efficient that by 1918, for example, the country produced every two weeks as many shells as in the whole first year of the war and turned out 70 times as much heavy artillery.

Inflation, Industrial Changes, Control of Ideas

No government, even by heavy taxes, could raise all the funds it needed except by printing paper money, selling huge bond issues, or obliging banks to grant it credit. The result, given heavy demand and acute shortages, was rapid inflation of prices. Prices and wages were regulated but were never again so low as before 1914. The hardest hit by this development were those whose money income could not easily be augmented—people living on supposedly safe investments, those drawing annual salaries, professional people, government employees. These classes had been one of the most stabilizing influences in Europe before the war. Everywhere the war threatened their status, prestige, and standard of living. The huge national debts meant higher taxes for years to come. The debt was most serious when it was owed to a foreign country. During the war the Continental Allies borrowed from Britain, and they and the British both borrowed from the United States. They thereby mortgaged their future. To pay the debt, they were bound for years to export more than they imported—or, roughly, to produce more than they consumed. It may be recalled that in 1914 every advanced European country habitually imported more than it exported. That fact, basic to the European standard of life, was now threatened with reversal.

Mortgaging the future

Moreover, with Europe torn by war for four years, the rest of the world accelerated its own industrialization. The productive capacity of the United States increased immensely. The Japanese began to sell in China, in India, in South America the cotton textiles and other civilian goods which these countries for the time being could not obtain from Europe. Argentina and Brazil, unable to get locomotive parts or mining machinery from England, began to manufacture them themselves. In India the Tata family, a group of wealthy Parsees controlling $250 million of native Indian capital, developed numerous manufacturing enterprises, one of which became the largest iron and steel works in the British Empire. With Germany entirely out of the world market, with Britain and France producing desperately for themselves, and with the world's shipping commandeered for war uses, the position of western Europe as the world's workshop was undermined. After the war Europe had new competitors. The economic foundations of the nineteenth century had slipped away. The age of European supremacy was in its twilight.

Industry spreads

All the belligerent governments during the war attempted to control ideas as they did economic production. Freedom of thought, respected everywhere in Europe for half a century, was discarded. Propaganda and censorship became more effective than any government, however despotic, had ever been able to devise. No one was allowed to sow doubt by raising any basic questions.

It must be remembered that the facts of the prewar crises, as related above, were then largely unknown. People were trapped in a nightmare whose causes they could not comprehend. Each side wildly charged the other with having started the war from pure malevolence. The long attrition, the fruitless fighting, the unchanging battle lines, the appalling casualties were a severe ordeal to morale. Civilians, deprived of their usual liberties, working

Propaganda and public opinion

Every nation in the First World War used propaganda posters to rally public support, recruit soldiers, and show the evil actions of the enemy. The picture on the left is an Austrian postcard with the typical image of a soldier defending the "Fatherland, Family, and Future." The child represents the nation's future. The poster on the right portrays the female symbol of the French Republic, Marianne, who is calling on the French to buy war bonds "for the flag and for victory." This money will support the soldiers who stand behind Marianne and defend the French nation.

(AKG London and Corbis)

harder, eating dull food, seeing no victory, had to be kept emotionally at a high pitch. Placards, posters, diplomatic white papers, schoolbooks, public lectures, solemn editorials, and slanted news reports conveyed the message. The new universal literacy, the mass press, the new motion pictures, proved to be ideal media for the direction of popular thinking. Intellectuals and professors advanced complicated reasons, usually historical, for loathing and crushing the enemy. In Allied countries the Kaiser was portrayed as a demon, with glaring eyes and abnormally bristling mustaches, bent on the mad project of conquest of the world. In Germany people were taught to dread the day when Cossacks and Senegalese should rape German women and to hate England as the inveterate enemy which inhumanly starved little children with its blockade. Each side convinced itself that all right was on its side and all wrong, wickedness, and barbarity were on the other. An inflamed opinion helped to sustain men and women in such a fearsome struggle. But when it came time to make peace the rooted convictions, fixed ideas, profound aversions, hates, and fears became an obstacle to political judgment.

Cultural Pessimism

We have seen how many European intellectuals in the decades before 1914 began to question the theories of classical liberalism and to celebrate the social value of human struggle and violence. Such ideas, widely disseminated by popular writers and intellectuals, contributed to the public enthusiasm that accompanied each nation's entry into the Great War. Indeed, some of the best-known younger writers, including Charles Péguy in France and Rupert Brooke in England, went off to die in the early battles, leaving literary testaments about the spiritual nobility of sacrifices for the nation. But as the war dragged on through more than four murderous years, much of the early literary patriotism turned into cynicism, pessimism, and despair. By 1918, famous war poets such as Siegfried Sassoon and Wilfred Owen were condemning the horrors of a senseless war and mocking the propaganda that flowed from every national government. Irony and bitterness became pervasive themes in the creative works of post–World War I European culture.

War poets

The war's most widespread cultural consequence thus emerged in new forms of cultural pessimism. The psychological studies of Sigmund Freud, for example, increasingly emphasized the raw power of human aggression—what Freud began to call the death instinct—which could never be completely tamed in even the most advanced modern societies. His famous postwar book, *Civilization and its Discontents,* offered pessimistic descriptions of the endless struggle between humanity's deep irrational drives and civilized moral standards, a

Freud and Spengler

Wilfred Owen, pictured here in his army uniform, was one of the English war poets who described the horrors of the First World War. He was killed in France, one week before the armistice in November 1918.

(Imperial War Museum, Q79045)

struggle in which the instincts of both individuals and whole social groups seemed constantly to overwhelm the precarious defenses of civilization. A different kind of pessimism appeared in the influential work of Oswald Spengler, the German philosopher-historian whose book *The Decline of the West* (1918) became a best-selling account of how Western civilization had fallen into crisis and decay. Drawing on cyclical theories of life and death, Spengler traced the history of the West from its energetic youth (the Renaissance) to a creative middle passage (the eighteenth century) to a declining old age (the twentieth century). Spengler's historical theories, so alien to the nineteenth-century liberal confidence in Western progress and expansion, attracted attention far beyond Germany because they offered explanations for events that seemed otherwise to be simply chaotic and absurd.

This sense of a crisis in Western culture spread also through new literary and artistic movements, most notably, perhaps, in the nonsensical productions of Dadaism. The Dada movement, developing in Switzerland after 1915 and promoted by the poet Tristan Tzara, rejected the structures of traditional literature and generated nihilistic criticisms of Western rationality, aesthetic ideals, and social conventions. After a brief moment of postwar popularity in Paris, Dadaism vanished from the scene, but its fascination with irrational impulses, "spontaneous" writing, and strange dreams passed into the more enduring ideas of Surrealism. Meanwhile, even the most sober-minded European authors believed that the war had exposed a sickness in the heart of European civilization. The great German writer Thomas Mann, for example, set his postwar novel *The Magic Mountain* within a Swiss sanatorium, where everyone is ill and where tubercular characters from all parts of Europe debate the flawed traditions of Western civilization. And the Irish poet W. B. Yeats, also seeing that something in Europe had gone terribly wrong, summarized the anxiety of a whole generation in his famous poem "The Second Coming" (1919):

Tzara, Mann, Yeats

> *Mere anarchy is loosed upon the World,*
> *The blood-dimmed tide is loosed, and everywhere*
> *The ceremony of innocence is drowned;*
> *The best lack all conviction, while the worst*
> *Are full of passionate intensity.*

90.   THE PEACE OF PARIS, 1919

The late ally, Russia, was in the hands of the Bolsheviks by 1919, ostracized like a leper colony, and taking no part in international relations. The late German and Austro-Hungarian empires were already defunct, and more or less revolutionary regimes struggled to replace them. New republics already existed along the Baltic coast, in Poland, and in the Danube basin but without effective governments or acknowledged frontiers. Europe east of France and Italy was in a state approaching chaos, with revolution on the Russian style threatening. Western Europe was wrenched out of all resemblance to its former self. The Allied blockade of Germany continued. In these circumstances the victors assembled in Paris, in the bleak winter of 1919, to reconstruct the world. During 1919 they signed five treaties, all named after Paris suburbs—St.-Germain with Austria, Trianon with Hungary, Neuilly with Bulgaria, Sèvres with Turkey (1920), and most especially, with Germany the Treaty of Versailles.

The world looked with awe and expectation to one man—the president of the United States. Wilson occupied a lone eminence, enjoyed a universal

Woodrow Wilson

prestige. Victors, vanquished, and neutrals admitted that American intervention had decided the conflict. Everywhere people who had been long tried, confused, bereaved, were stirred by Wilson's thrilling language in favor of a higher cause, of a great concert of right in which peace would be forever secure and the world itself would be at last free. Wilson reached Europe in January 1919, visiting several Allied capitals. He was wildly acclaimed, and almost mobbed, greeted as the man who would lead civilization out of its wasteland.

The Fourteen Points and the Treaty of Versailles

Wilson's views were well known. He had stated them in January 1918 in his Fourteen Points—principles upon which, after victory, peace was to be established. The Fourteen Points demanded an end to secret treaties and secret diplomacy (or in Wilsonian language, "open covenants openly arrived at"); freedom of the seas "alike in peace and in war"; removal of barriers and inequalities in international trade; reduction of armaments by all powers; colonial readjustments; evacuation of occupied territory; self-determination of nationalities and a redrawing of European boundaries along national lines; and, last but not least, an international political organization to prevent war. On the whole, Wilson stood for the fruition of the democratic, liberal, progressive, and nationalistic movements of the century past, for the ideals of the Enlightenment, the French Revolution, and the revolutions of 1848. As Wilson saw it, and as many believed, the World War should end in a new type of treaty. There was thought to be something sinister about peace conferences of the past, for example, the Congress of Vienna of 1815. The old diplomacy was blamed for leading to war. Lenin in his own way and for his own purposes was saying this in Russia too. It was felt that treaties had too long been wrongly based on a politics of power or on unprincipled deals and bargains made without regard to the people concerned. Democracy having defeated the Central Powers, people hoped that a new settlement, made in a democratic age, might be reached by general agreement in an atmosphere of mutual confidence. There was a real sense of a new era.

A new era

Wilson had had some difficulty, however, in persuading the Allied governments to accept his Fourteen Points. The French demanded a guarantee of German payment for war damages. The British vetoed the freedom of the seas "in peace and war"; it was naval rivalry that had estranged them from Germany, and they had fought the war to preserve British command of the sea. But with these two reservations the Allies expressed their willingness to follow Wilson's lead. The Germans who asked for the armistice believed that peace would be made along the lines of the Fourteen Points with only the two modifications described. In addition, the socialists and democrats now trying to rule Germany thought that having overthrown the Kaiser and the war lords, they would be treated by the victors with moderation and that a new democratic Germany would reemerge to take its rightful place in the world.

Twenty-seven nations assembled at Paris in January 1919, but the full or plenary sessions were unimportant. Matters were decided by conferences among the Big Four—Wilson himself, Lloyd George for England, Clemenceau for France, Orlando for Italy. The conjunction of personalities was not a happy one. Wilson was stern and stubbornly righteous; Lloyd George, a fiery and changeable Welshman; Clemenceau, an aged patriot, the "tiger of France," who had been politically active since the Franco-Prussian War of 1870; Orlando, a passing phenomenon of Italian politics. None of them was especially equipped for the task in hand. Clemenceau was a pronounced nationalist, Lloyd George had always been concerned with domestic reforms, Orlando was by training a professor like Wilson, and Wilson, a former college president, imbued with a sense of mission, lacked concrete knowledge or intimate feeling for peoples other than his own. However, they democratically represented the governments and peoples of their respective countries, and thus spoke with an authority denied to professional diplomats of the old school.

Wilson first fought a hard battle for a League of Nations, a permanent international body in which all nations, without sacrificing their sovereignty, should meet together to discuss and settle disputes, each promising not to resort to war. Few European statesmen had any confidence in such a League. But they yielded to Wilson, and the covenant of the League of Nations was written into the treaty with Germany. In return, Wilson had to make concessions to Lloyd George, Clemenceau, Orlando, and the Japanese. He was thus obliged to compromise the idealism of the Fourteen Points. Probably compromise and bargaining would have been necessary anyway, for such general principles as national self-determination and colonial readjustment invariably led to differences of opinion in concrete cases. Wilson allowed himself to believe that, if a League of Nations were established and operating, faults in the treaty could later be corrected at leisure by international discussion.

A League of Nations

A special kind of disagreement arose over the covenant of the League. Wilson wished to include a clause endorsing religious freedom. The Japanese insisted that it be broadened to condemn racial discrimination as well. The Americans and British were opposed for fear that an international authority might interfere with their immigration practices. In the end both proposals were abandoned.

The great demand of the French at the peace conference was for security against Germany. On this subject the French were almost rabid. The war in the West had been fought almost entirely on their soil. To trim Germany down more nearly to French size, they proposed that the part of Germany west of the Rhine be set up as an independent state under Allied auspices. Wilson and Lloyd George objected, sagely observing that the resulting German resentment would only lead to another war. The French yielded, but only on condition that they obtain their security in another way, namely, by a promise from both Britain and the United States to join them immediately if they were again attacked by the Germans. An Anglo-French-American guarantee treaty, with these provisions, was in fact signed at Paris. France obtained control over the Saar coal mines for 15 years; during that time, a League commission would administer the Saar territory and in 1935 a plebiscite would be held. Lorraine and Alsace were returned to France. German fortifications and troops were banned from a wide belt in the Rhineland. Allied troops would occupy the Rhineland for 15 years to ensure German compliance with the treaty.

Alsace and Lorraine

In eastern Europe the Allies wished to set up strong buffer states against Bolshevism in Russia. Sympathies with Poland ran high. Those parts of the former German Empire that were inhabited by Poles, or by mixed populations of Poles and Germans—Posen and West Prussia—were assigned to the new Polish state. This gave Poland a corridor to the sea, but at the same time cut off the bulk of Germany from East Prussia. Danzig, an old German town, became a free city, belonging to no country. Upper Silesia, a rich mining country, went to Poland after a disputed plebiscite. In Austria and among the Sudeten Germans of Bohemia, now that there was no longer a Habsburg empire (whose existence had blocked an all-German union in 1848 and also a few years later in the time of Bismarck), a feeling developed for annexation to the new German republic. But the feeling was unorganized, and in any case the Allies naturally refused to make Germany bigger than it had been in 1914. Austria remained a dwarf republic; and Vienna, a former imperial capital cut off from its empire—a head severed from its body and scarcely more capable of sustaining life. The Bohemian Germans became disgruntled citizens of the new state of Czechoslovakia.

Germany loses its colonies

Germany lost all its colonies. Wilson and the South African General Smuts, to preserve the principle of internationalism against any imputation of raw conquest, saw to it that the colonies were actually awarded to the League of Nations. The League, under "mandates," assigned them to various powers for administration. In this way France and Great Britain divided the best of the African colonies; the Belgian Congo was slightly enlarged; and the Union of South Africa took over German Southwest Africa. In the colonial world, Italy got nothing. Japan received the mandate for the German Pacific islands, north of the equator; Australia, for German New Guinea and the Solomon Islands; New Zealand, for German Samoa. The Japanese claimed rights over the German concessions in China. The Chinese at the Paris conference tried to get all special concessions and extraterritorial rights in China abolished. No one listened to such proposals. By a compromise, Japan received about half the former German rights. The Japanese were dissatisfied. The Chinese walked out of the conference.

The Allies took over the German fleet, but the German crews, rather than surrender it, solemnly scuttled it at Scapa Flow. The German army was limited to 100,000. Since the Allies forbade conscription, or the annual training of successive groups of young civilians, the army became exclusively professional, the officer class retained political influence in it, and the means used by the Allies to demilitarize Germany served if anything the contrary purpose. The treaty forbade Germany to have any heavy artillery, aviation, or submarines. Wilson saw his plan for universal disarmament applied to Germany alone.

War damages

The French, even before the armistice, had stipulated that Germany must pay for war damages. The other Allies made the same demand. Wilson, at the conference, was stupefied at the size of the bills presented. The Belgians suggested, for their own share, a sum larger than the entire wealth of all Belgium according to officially published Belgian statistics. The French and British proposed to charge Germany with the entire expenses, including war pensions, incurred by them during the war. Wilson observed that "total" reparation, while not strictly unjust, was absolutely impossible, and even Clemenceau noted that "to ask for over a trillion francs would lead to nothing practical." The insistence on enormous reparations was in fact largely emotional. No one knew or considered how Germany would pay, though all dimly realized that such sums could only be made up by German exports, which would then compete with the Allies' own economic interests. The Germans, to avoid worse, even offered to repair physical damages in Belgium and France, but were brusquely refused on the ground that the Belgians and French would thereby lose jobs and business. No total at all was set for reparations in the treaty; it was made clear that the sum would be very large, but it was left for a future commission to determine. The Allies, maddened by the war and themselves loaded with fantastic debts to the United States, had no desire in the matter of reparations to listen to economic reason and regarded the reparations as simply another means of righting a wrong and of putting off the dangers of a German revival. As a first payment on the reparations account the treaty required Germany to surrender most of its merchant marine, make coal deliveries, and give up all property owned by German private citizens abroad. This last proviso ended Germany's prewar career as an exporter of capital.

These four men represented the leading Allied powers at the Versailles peace conference in 1918: (from left to right) Vittorio Emanuele Orlando of Italy, David Lloyd George of Great Britain, Georges Clemenceau of France, and Woodrow Wilson of the United States. Neither the Germans nor the Russians were represented at Versailles. The decisions of the peace conference, including a "war guilt" clause that blamed Germany for the recent war, produced deep resentments among the excluded peoples.

(Corbis)

It was with the specific purpose of justifying the reparations that the famous "war guilt" clause was written into the treaty. By this clause Germany explicitly "accepted the responsibility" for all loss and damage resulting from the war "imposed upon them (the Allies) by the aggression of Germany and her allies." The Germans themselves felt no such responsibility as

The "war guilt" clause

they were now obliged formally to accept. They considered their honor as a people to be impugned. The war guilt clause gave a ready opening to agitators in Germany and made even moderate Germans regard the treaty as something to be escaped from as a matter of self-respect.

**The Treaty
of Versailles**

The Treaty of Versailles was completed in three months. The absence of the Russians, the decision not to give the Germans a hearing, and the willingness of Wilson to make concessions in return for obtaining the League of Nations, made it possible to dispose of intricate matters with considerable facility. The Germans, when presented with the completed document in May 1919, refused to sign. The Allies threatened a renewal of hostilities. A government crisis ensued in Berlin. No German wished to damn himself, his party, or his principles, in German eyes, by putting his name to a document which all Germans regarded as outrageous. A combination drawn from the Social Democratic and Catholic parties finally consented to shoulder the hateful burden. Two abashed and virtually unknown representatives appeared at the Hall of Mirrors at Versailles and signed the treaty for Germany in the presence of a large concourse of Allied dignitaries.

The other treaties drafted by the Paris conference, in conjunction with the Versailles treaty, laid out a new map for eastern Europe and registered the recession of the Russian, Austrian, and Turkish empires. Seven new independent states now existed: Finland, Estonia, Latvia, Lithuania, Poland, Czechoslovakia, and Yugoslavia. Romania was enlarged by adding areas formerly Hungarian and Russian; Greece was enlarged at the expense of Turkey. Austria and Hungary were now small states, and there was no connection between them. The Ottoman Empire presently disappeared: Turkey emerged as a republic confined to Constantinople and Asia Minor: Syria and Lebanon went to France as mandates of the League of Nations; Palestine and Iraq went to Great Britain on the same basis. The belt of states from Finland to Romania was regarded as a *cordon sanitaire* (a quarantine zone) to prevent the infection of Europe by communism. The creation of Yugoslavia (or the Kingdom of the Serbs, Croats, and Slovenes, as it was called until 1929), although dominated by the Serbs and under the Serbian monarchy, seemed to fulfill the aims of the South Slav movement which had set off the fatal crisis of 1914. The fact, however, that Italy received Trieste and some of the Dalmatian Islands (in keeping with the secret treaty of 1915) left the more ambitious South Slavs discontented.

Significance of the Paris Peace Settlement

**National self-
determination**

The most general principle of the Paris settlement was to recognize the right of national self-determination, at least in Europe. Each people or nation, as defined by language, was in principle set up with its own sovereign and independent national state. Czechoslovakia, a special case, had two national components, as its originally hyphenated name Czecho-Slovakia made clear. Nationalism triumphed in the belief that it went along naturally with liberalism and democracy. It must be added that the peacemakers at Paris had little choice in this matter, for the new states had already declared their independence. Since in eastern Europe the nationalities were in many places intermixed, and since the peacemakers did not contemplate the actual movement and exchange of populations to sort them out, each new state found alien minorities living within its borders or could claim that people of its own kind still lived in neighboring states under foreign rule. There were Hungarians and Germans in Czechoslovakia, Ruthenians in Poland, Poles in Lithuania, Bulgarians in

Romania—to cite only a few examples. Hence minority problems and irredentism troubled eastern Europe, as they had before 1914. Eventually it was the complaint of Germans in Czechoslovakia that they were an oppressed minority, together with the irredentist demand of Germany to join these outlying Germans to the fatherland, that produced the Munich crisis preceding the Second World War.

The Treaty of Versailles was designed to put an end to the German menace. It was not a successful treaty. The wisdom of it has been discussed without end, but a few comments can safely be made. For practical purposes, with respect to Germany, the treaty was either too severe or too lenient. It was too severe to conciliate and not severe enough to destroy. Possibly the victors should have dealt more moderately with the new German republic, which professed their own ideals, as the monarchical victors over Napoleon, in 1814, had dealt moderately with the France of the restored Bourbons, regarding it as a regime akin to their own. As it was, the Allies imposed upon the German Republic about the same terms that they might have imposed upon the German Empire. They innocently played the game of Ludendorff and the German reactionaries; it was the Social Democrats and liberals who bore the "shame" of Versailles. The Germans from the beginning showed no real intention to live up to the treaty. On the other hand, the treaty was not sufficiently disabling to Germany to destroy its economic and political strength. Even the degree of severity that it incorporated soon proved to be more than the Allies were willing to enforce.

The failure of Versailles

The treaty makers at Paris in 1919, working hastily and still in the heat of war, under pressure from press and propaganda in their own countries, drafted a set of terms which the test of time showed that they themselves did not in the long run wish to impose. As the years passed, many people in Allied countries declared various provisions of the Versailles treaty to be unfair or unworkable. The loss of faith by the Allies in their own treaty only made easier the task of those German agitators who demanded its repudiation. The door was opened for Adolf Hitler.

Even at the beginning the Allies showed doubts. Lloyd George, in the last weeks before the signing, tardily called for certain amendments, though in vain; for in 1919 British opinion shifted somewhat from fear of Germany to the fear of Bolshevism, and already the idea of using Germany as a bulwark against communism was expressed. The Italians disliked the whole settlement from the beginning; they observed that the spoils of Africa and the Middle East went only to France and Great Britain. The Chinese were also dissatisfied. The Russians, when they reentered the international arena some years later, found a situation that they did not like and had had no part in making. They objected to being faced with a *cordon sanitaire* from Finland to Romania and soon remembered that most of this territory had once belonged to the Russian empire.

Victors' uneasiness

The United States never ratified the Treaty of Versailles at all. A wave of isolationism and disgust with Europe spread over the country; and this feeling, together with some rational criticism of the terms and a good deal of party politics, caused the Senate to repudiate Wilson's work. The Senate likewise refused to make any advance promises of military intervention in a future war between Germany and France and hence also declined to ratify the Anglo-French-American guarantee treaty on which Wilson had persuaded Clemenceau to rely. The French considered themselves duped, deprived both of the Rhineland and of the Anglo-American guarantee. They raised more anguished cries over their insecurity. This led them to try to hold Germany down while it was still weak, in turn raising many further complications.

Areas Lost by Germany

Areas Lost by Russia

Areas Lost by Ottoman Empire

Austria and Hungary plus areas lost by
Austro-Hungarian Empire

EUROPE, 1923

The map shows European boundaries between the two World Wars, after the Peace of Versailles and certain other agreements. Germany returned Alsace-Lorraine to France and lost the region around Danzig (the "Polish corridor") to Poland. In place of the Austro-Hungarian empire we find the "succession states"—Austria, Hungary, Czechoslovakia, Yugoslavia, and Romania. Poland regained its independence, and Finland and the three Baltic states, Estonia, Latvia, and Lithuania, emerged from the tsarist empire. Most of Ireland became a "free state" in the British Commonwealth of Nations, only Ulster remaining in the United Kingdom. These boundaries lasted until 1938, when Germany annexed Austria and the Sudeten part of Czechoslovakia.

*The League
of Nations*
The League of Nations was established at Geneva. Its mere existence marked a great step beyond the international anarchy before 1914. Wilson's vision did not die. But the United States never joined; Germany was not admitted until 1926, or Russia until 1934. The League could handle and dispatch only such business as the Great Powers were willing to allow. It was associated with a West European ascendancy that no longer corresponded to the facts of the world situation. Its covenant was part of the Versailles treaty, and many people in many countries, on both sides in the late war, saw in it not so much a system for international adjudication as a means for maintaining a new status quo in favor of Britain and France.

The First World War dealt a last blow to the ancient institutions of monarchy and aristocratic feudalism. Thrones toppled in Turkey, in Russia, in Austria-Hungary, in the German Empire and the individual German states; and with the kings went the courtly retainers and all the social preeminence and special advantage of the old landed aristocracies. The war was indeed a victory for democracy, though a bitter one. It carried further a process as old as the French and American revolutions. But for the basic problems of modern civilization, industrialism and nationalism, economic security and international stability, it gave no answer. And it left the major European nations much weaker than before to face the rising economic power of America; the revolutionary government of the newly established Soviet Union; and the emerging anticolonial movements of Africa and Asia.

Chapter **18**

THE RUSSIAN REVOLUTION AND THE SOVIET UNION

No less powerful than the First World War as a force shaping the twentieth century was the revolution in Russia, of which the decisive step was the seizure of power by the Bolshevik party in November 1917. The Russian Revolution of 1917 can be compared in its historical magnitude with the French Revolution of 1789. Both originated in deeply-lying and distant causes, and both made their repercussions felt in many countries for many years. The present chapter will set forth the revolutionary process in Russia over half a century. We shall begin with the old regime before 1900, pass through the two revolutions of 1905 and 1917, and survey the Union of Soviet Socialist Republics down to 1939, at which time a new order had been consolidated under Joseph Stalin, a form of "planned economy" had been realized, and the last of the original revolutionaries, or Old Bolsheviks, either had been silenced or put to death.

The comparison of the Russian Revolution to the French is enlightening in many ways. Both were movements of liberation, the one against "feudalism" and "despotism," the other against "capitalism" and "imperialism." Neither was a strictly national movement dealing with merely domestic troubles; both addressed their message to all the world. Both attracted followers in all countries. Both aroused a strong reaction on the part of those whose view of life was endangered. And both showed the same pattern of revolutionary politics: a relative unity of opinion so long as the problem was to overthrow the old regime, followed by disunity and conflict over the founding of the new, so that one set of revolutionaries eliminated others, until a small, organized, and determined minority

French and Russian revolutions

Chapter emblem: Families of soldiers marching in St. Petersburg in 1917 to demand more rations for Russian troops.

(Jacobin democrats in 1793, Bolshevik communists in 1918) suppressed all opposition in order to defend or advance the revolutionary cause; and in short order (within a matter of months in France, years in Russia), many of the most intensely revolutionary leaders were themselves suppressed or liquidated.

The differences are equally deserving of notice. Relatively speaking, or compared by many criteria with other European countries, Russia in 1900 was in the rear, and France in 1780 in many ways was in the lead. The main strength of the French Revolution lay in the middle classes, who soon managed to prevail over more extreme pressures. In the Russian Revolution middle-class people were also active, especially at first, but they proved unable to cope with mass discontents and succumbed to a more radical party which appealed to workers and peasants. In France the Revolution just "happened," so to speak, in that ordinary people from many walks of life unexpectedly found themselves in a revolutionary situation, and even the Jacobin dictatorship was improvised by individuals who had spent their lives thinking of other things. In Russia professional revolutionaries worked for the revolution long in advance, and the dictatorship of the Bolsheviks realized the plans and preparations of 20 years.

In France the revolution was followed by a reaction in which émigrés returned, dispossessed classes reappeared in politics, and even the Bourbons were restored. The French Revolution was followed by a century of uneasy compromise. The Russian Revolution effectively wiped out its opposition; few émigrés returned; no Romanovs regained their throne. The Russian Revolution was in this sense more immediately successful. But in the long run the differences reemerged. By the 1990s the ideas proclaimed in Russia in 1917 were in ruins, while those proclaimed in France in 1789 were widely accepted, such as representative constitutional government, with equal civil rights under national sovereignty and legal safeguards for persons and property.

Repercussions of the revolution in Russia

The repercussions of the Russian Revolution were the more far-reaching because of the very ambivalence of Russia itself. Since the days of Peter the Great and before, it had always faced toward both Europe and Asia. It was European, yet it was also outside Europe and even opposed to it. If about 1900 it was the least developed of the major European countries, it was at the same time one of the most developed, industrialized, or modernized parts of the non-European world. Its revolution could win sympathy on the left in Europe because it reinforced the old European socialist objections to capitalism. It aroused the interests of submerged peoples in other continents because it also denounced imperialism (that is, the possession of colonies by Europeans), affirming that imperialism was merely the "highest stage" of capitalism and that both must be overthrown together. The Soviet Union, once established, came to occupy an intermediate position between the West and the colonial world (or what later came to be called the Third World). In the West it could long be feared or admired as the last word in social revolution. In the colonial, or formerly colonial, world it suggested new beginnings, a new way to become modern without being capitalistic or European, a step in a worldwide rebellion against European supremacy. The Russian Revolution thus not only produced communism and hence fascism in Europe but also added strength to the anticolonial movements in Asia, as explained in the following chapters.

Although professional revolutionaries worked for revolution in Russia, they did not "cause" it. Lenin and the Bolsheviks did not bring about the Russian Revolution. They captured it after it had begun. They boarded the ship in midstream. The Russian Revolution, like all great revolutions, originated in a totality of previous history, in diverse local causes, and in the prolonged dissatisfaction of many kinds of people.

91.   BACKGROUNDS

Russia after 1881: Reaction and Progress

We have seen in earlier chapters how the tsarist autocracy arose, how it ruled as a machine superimposed upon its subjects, how the upper class became westernized while the masses sank further into serfdom, and how an intelligentsia developed, divorced both from the work of government and the activities of the people. It has been explained in Chapter 13 how Alexander II freed the serfs in 1861 and created provincial and district councils or zemstvos, elected mainly by landowners, which attended to such matters as roads, schools, and hospitals.

In 1881 Alexander II was assassinated by members of the People's Will. His son, Alexander III (1881–1894), tried to stamp out revolutionism and to silence even peaceable criticism of the government. Revolutionaries and terrorists were driven into exile. The People's Will as an organized group became extinct. Jews were subjected to pogroms, by far the worst of any (until then) in modern times. For the first time the empire adopted a program of systematic Russification. Poles, Ukrainians, Lithuanians, the peoples of the Caucasus, the scattered German communities, the Muslim groups in central Asia, all faced the prospect of forcible assimilation to Russian culture. The philosopher and chief official of this movement was Pobiedonostsev, procurator of the Holy Synod, or layman head, under the tsar, of the Russian Orthodox church. Pobiedonostsev saw in the West something alien and doomed. Drawing on such old enemies of the French Revolution as Edmund Burke, he attacked Western rationalism and liberalism in his writings, declared that Slavs had a peculiar national character of their own, and dreamed of turning Holy Russia into a kind of churchly community, in which a disciplined clergy should protect the faithful from the insidious influence of the West.

Russification in the old regime

This is not, however, what happened. In the closing decades of the nineteenth century Russia became more than ever before a part of European civilization. Almost overnight it presented Europe with great works of literature and music that Europeans could appreciate. The Russian novel became known throughout the Western world. All could read the novels of Tolstoy (1828–1910) without a feeling of strangeness; and if the characters of Turgenev (1818–1883) and of Dostoevski (1821–1881) behaved more strangely, the authors themselves were obviously within the great European cultural family. The melodies of Tchaikovsky (1840–1893) and of Rimsky-Korsakov (1844–1908) became very familiar throughout Europe and America; if they sometimes seemed hauntingly wild, distant, or sad, they still betrayed no more than the usual amount of national idiosyncrasy. Russians also contributed to the sciences, notably chemistry. They were considered to be especially talented in the more abstruse intellectual exercises, such as higher mathematics, physics, or chess.

Russia also, from the 1880s, began to pass through the Industrial Revolution and take its place as an integral part of the world economic system. European capital entered the country, financing railways, mines, and factories (as well as government and the army) until by 1914 Europeans had about the same amount invested in Russia as in the United

*Industrialization
before 1914*

States, some $4 billion in each case. In 1897, under the reforming ministry of Count Witte, Russia adopted the gold standard, making its currency readily convertible with all others. In the quarter-century between 1888 and 1913 the Russian railway mileage more than doubled, the miles of telegraph wires multiplied fivefold, the number of post offices trebled, and the number of letters carried by the mails multiplied seven times.

Although still industrially undeveloped by Western standards, without, for example, any machine tool industry or chemical plants, Russia was industrializing rapidly. Exports rose in value from 400 million rubles in 1880 to 1.6 billion in 1913. Imports, though smaller, grew more rapidly, quintupling in the same period. They consisted of such items as tea and coffee and of the machines and industrial goods made in western Europe. For a long time after the revolution, the Soviet Union conducted less foreign trade than did the Russian empire on the eve of the First World War. The Soviet regime, to keep control over its own economic system, tried to depend as little as possible on outside markets and sources of supply.

Industrialization, in Russia as in all countries, brought an increase both of the business and of the wage-earning classes, or, in socialist terminology, of the bourgeoisie and of the proletariat. Though growing, they were still not numerous by standards of the West. Factory workers, laboring for 11 or more hours a day, for low wages under hard conditions, were in somewhat the same position as in England or France before 1850. Unions were illegal and strikes were prohibited. Nevertheless, great strikes in the 1890s called attention to the misery of the new industrial workers. There was one distinctive feature to the Russian proletariat. Russian industry was heavily concentrated; half of Russia's industrial workers were employed in factories employing over 500 persons. It was easier for workers under such circumstances to be organized economically and at the proper time to be mobilized politically. As for the Russian business and capitalist class, it was relatively the weaker because of several features in the situation. Ownership of much of Russia's new industrial plant was in foreign hands. Much was owned by the tsarist government itself; Russia already had the largest state-operated economic system in the world. Moreover, in Russia (unlike the United States at the time) the government itself was a heavy borrower from Europe; hence it was less dependent financially on its own people and more able to maintain an absolutist regime.

The "Cadets"

Nevertheless, the rising business and professional classes, reinforced by enterprising landowners, were strong enough to form a liberal segment of public opinion, which emerged in 1905 as the Constitutional Democratic party (or "Cadets"). Many of those who were active in the provincial zemstvos also became Constitutional Democrats. They were liberals, progressives, or constitutionalists in the Western sense, thinking less about the troubles of factory workers and peasants than about the need for a nationally elected parliament to control the policies of state.

Russia remained predominantly agricultural. Its huge exports were mainly farm and forest products. The peasants formed four-fifths of the population. Free from their former lords since 1861, they lived in village communes called *mirs*. In most communes much of the land was divided and redivided among peasant households by agreement of the village community, nor could anyone leave without communal permission. The peasants still carried a considerable burden. Until 1906 they paid redemption money arising from the Emancipation of 1861, and even after that, other forms of onerous payments. They also paid high taxes, for the government defrayed the interest on its foreign loans from taxes raised at home. The constantly rising export of cereals (also used to pay off debts contracted by Russia in the West) tended to keep food from the farmer's table; many peasants raised the best wheat for sale and ate black bread themselves. The farm population, in short (as in other countries in similar stages of their development), bore a considerable share of the costs of industrialization.

Under such pressures, and because of their crude methods of cultivation, the peasants were forever demanding more land. "Land hunger" was felt both by individual families and by the *mirs*. The Emancipation had turned over roughly half the land to peasant ownership, individual and collective; and in the following half-century the peasants added to their share by buying from nonpeasant owners. The *mirs* were by no means obsolescent. They were in fact flourishing; they acquired far more land by purchase than did individual buyers, and perhaps half or more of the peasants valued communal security above the uncertain pleasures of private property. The exceptions were the minority of more enterprising and wealthier peasants, later called the kulaks. Such a one was Leon Trotsky's father, who, a hard-working, plain, and illiterate man, owned or leased the equivalent of a square mile of land, employed scores of field hands at harvest time, and permanently maintained a large domestic staff. That such a "big farmer" could afford so many employees suggests the poverty in which the bulk of the peasants lived. Not all of the well-to-do peasants were as affluent as Trotsky's father, but the big farmers stood out conspicuously from the mass, by whom they were not liked.

Peasant demands

The Emergence of Revolutionary Parties

The peasants were the ancient source of revolutionary disturbance in Russia. Fables about famous rebels such as Pugachev and Stephen Razin circulated in peasant legend. After the Emancipation the peasants continued to believe that they had some kind of rights in *all* the land of former estates on which they had formerly been serfs—not merely in the portion that had been allotted to peasant possession. They demanded (and obtained) credit from the government to buy from the big landowners or former masters. Their land hunger could not be appeased. They remained jealous of the landed aristocrat's very existence. In Russia, as elsewhere in Europe, and unlike the United States, the rural population was divided into two sharply distinct classes, on the one hand the peasants of all types who worked the soil, and on the other the gentry who resided upon it. The two never intermarried. They differed not merely economically but in speech, dress, and manners, and even in the looks of their faces and hands. But in the last three decades of the nineteenth century the Russian peasants were notably quiet. Insurrectionism seemingly subsided.

The other traditional source of revolutionary disturbance lay among the intelligentsia. In the conditions in which the Russian empire had grown up, many of the best and purest spirits were attracted to violence. Revolutionary intelligentsia (as distinguished from those who were simply liberal or progressive) yearned for a catastrophic overthrow of the tsardom. Since the days of the Decembrists in 1825 they had formed secret organizations, comprising a few hundred or thousands of members, engaged in outwitting the tsarist police, by whom they were bafflingly interpenetrated. At a Bolshevik party congress held in 1913, out of 22 delegates present, no fewer than five, unknown to the others, were government spies.

The intelligentsia

The revolutionary intelligentsia, since there was normally little that they could do, spent their time in vehement discussion and interminable refinement of doctrine. By 1890 the terrorism and nihilism of the 1870s were somewhat passé. The great question was

Although new industries began to develop in Russia during the early twentieth century, most people continued to live and work in the countryside. This picture of peasants harvesting hay before the First World War shows that women performed much of the labor and that modern machinery had not yet reached Russian farms.

(Library of Congress)

where these willing officers of a revolutionary movement could find an army. Disputation turned upon such topics as whether the peasants or the new factory workers were the true revolutionary class, whether the peasants were potentially proletarian or incurably petty bourgeois, whether Russia was bound to experience the same historical process as the

West, or whether it was different; and, specifically, whether Russia had to go through capitalism or might simply skip the capitalist stage in reaching the socialist society.

Most of the revolutionary intelligentsia were "populists." Some had once belonged to the now broken People's Will. Some continued to approve of terrorism and assassination as morally necessary in an autocratic country. They generally had a mystical faith in the vast inchoate might of the Russian people, and since most Russians were peasants, the populists were interested in peasant problems and peasant welfare. They believed that a great native revolutionary tradition existed in Russia, of which the peasant rebellion of Pugachev, in 1773, was the chief example. The populists admired the *mir,* in which they saw the European socialist idea of a "commune" represented. They read and respected Marx and Engels (indeed, a populist first translated the *Communist Manifesto* into Russian); but they did not believe that an urban proletariat was the only true revolutionary class. They did not believe that capitalism, by creating such a proletariat, had inevitably and logically to precede socialism. They said that, in Russia, the horrors of capitalism could be skipped. They addressed themselves to the plight of the farmer and the evils of landlordism, favored strengthening the *mir* and equalizing the shares of all peasants in it, and, since they did not have to wait for the prior triumph of capitalism in Russia, they thought that revolution might come quite soon. This populist sentiment crystallized in the founding in 1901 of the Social Revolutionary party.

Populism

Two populists, Plekhanov and Axelrod, fleeing to Switzerland in the 1870s, there became converted to Marxism. In 1883 they founded in exile the organization from which the Russian Social Democratic or Marxist party was to grow. A few Marxists began to declare themselves (though not publicly) in Russia itself. When the youthful Lenin met his future wife Krupskaya in 1894, she already belonged to a circle of argumentative Marxists. The fact that the peasants in the 1890s were disappointingly quiescent, while machine industry, factor labor, and strikes were developing rapidly, turned many of the revolutionary intelligentsia, though only a minority, from populism to Marxism. To Plekhanov and Axelrod were added, as young leaders, Vladimir Ilyich Lenin (1870–1924), Leon Trotsky (1879–1940), Joseph V. Stalin (1879–1953), and others.

Marxism

Of these it was Lenin who, after Marx, was to be claimed by communism as a father. Lenin was a short almost rotund man, with a bounding quickness and intense, penetrating gaze. High cheekbones and somewhat slanting eyes showed an Asian strain on the paternal side; Russian friends at first said that he looked "like a Kalmuck." His hair receded in early youth, leaving a massive forehead, behind which a restless mind was inexhaustibly at work. Even in his twenties he was called the Old One. He was of upper-middle-class origin, son of an inspector of schools who rose in the civilian bureaucracy to a rank equivalent to major general. His boyhood was comfortable and even happy, until the age of 17, when his elder brother, a student at St. Petersburg, became somewhat incidentally involved in a plot to assassinate Alexander III, for which he was put to death by order of the tsar himself. Because of the blot on the family record it became impossible for Lenin to continue with his law studies. He soon joined the ranks of professional revolutionaries, having no other occupation and living precariously from the party funds, which came mainly from the donations of well-to-do sympathizers.

Lenin

Arrested as a revolutionary, he spent three years of exile in Siberia. Here the tsarist government treated educated political prisoners with an indulgence not later shown by the Soviet regime. Lenin and most of the others lived in cottages of their own or boarded with local residents. No labor was required of them. They borrowed books from Europe; met and visited with one another; debated, played chess, went hunting, meditated, and wrote. They chafed, however, at being cut off from the mainstream of Russian political life back home. Lenin, his term over, proceeded in 1900 to western Europe, where except for short secret trips to Russia he remained until 1917. His intellectual vigor, irresistible drive, and shrewdness as a tactician soon made him a force in the party. Genius has been called the faculty for everlasting concentration upon one thing. Lenin, said his one-time close associate Axelrod, "for twenty-four hours of the day is taken up with the revolution, has no thoughts but thoughts of revolution, and even in his sleep dreams of nothing but revolution."

The Social Democrats

In 1898 the Marxists in Russia, spurred on by émigrés, founded the Social Democratic Labor party. They were not more revolutionary than the larger group of Social Revolutionaries. They simply had a different conception of the revolution. First of all, as good Marxists, they were more inclined to see the revolution as an international movement, part of the dialectical process of world history in which all countries were involved. Russia for them was no different from other countries except that is was less advanced. They expected the world revolution to break out first in western Europe. They particularly admired the German Social Democratic party, the largest and most flourishing of all the parties that acknowledged the fatherhood of Marx.

If the Social Democrats were more oriented to Europe than the Social Revolutionaries, it was because so many of their spokesmen lived there in exile. They tended to think that Russia must develop capitalism, an industrialist proletariat, and the modern form of class struggle before there could be any revolution. Seeing in the urban proletariat the true revolutionary class, they looked upon the peasantry with suspicion, ridiculed the *mir,* and abhorred the Social Revolutionaries. Like Marx himself, the Russian Marxists disapproved of sporadic terrorism and assassination. For this reason, and because their doctrine seemed somewhat academic and their revolution seemed rather conditional and far in the future, the Marxists were for a time actually favored by the tsarist police, who regarded them as less dangerous than the Social Revolutionaries.

Split in the Social Democrats: Bolsheviks and Mensheviks

The Russian Marxists held a second party congress in Brussels and London in 1903, attended by émigrés like Lenin and delegates from the underground in Russia, and by Social Democrats and members of lesser organizations. The purpose of the congress was to unify all Russian Marxism, but in fact it split it forever. The two resulting factions called themselves Bolshevik, or majority, and Menshevik, or minority. Lenin was the main author of the split and hence the founder of Bolshevism. Although he obtained his majority after one participating organization, the Jewish Bund, had seceded in indignation, and by calling for surprise votes on tactical issues, and although after 1903 it was usually the Mensheviks who had the majority, Lenin clung proudly and stubbornly to the term Bolshevism, with its favorable connotation of a majority in his support. For a number of years after 1903 the Social Democrats remained at least formally a single Marxist party, but they were now irreconcilably divided into two wings. In 1912 the Bolshevik wing organized itself as a separate party.

Leninism

Bolshevism, or Leninism, originally differed from Menshevism mainly on matters of organization and tactics. Russian Marxists referred to each other as "hards" and "softs." The "hards" were attracted to Lenin; the "softs" repelled by him. Lenin believed that the party should be a small revolutionary elite, a hard core of reliable and zealous workers. Those who wished a larger and more open party, with membership for mere sympathizers, became Mensheviks. Lenin insisted upon a strongly centralized party, without autonomy for national or other component groups. He demanded strong authority at the top, by which the central committee would determine the doctrine (or party line) and control personnel at all levels of the organization. The Mensheviks favored a greater degree of influence by the membership as a whole. Lenin thought that the party would strengthen itself by purges, expelling all who developed deviations of opinion. The Mensheviks favored covering up or bridging over all but the most fundamental disagreements. The Mensheviks came to recommend cooperation with liberals, progressives, and bourgeois democrats. Lenin regarded such cooperation as purely tactical and temporary, never concealing that in the end the Bolsheviks must impose their views through a dictatorship of the proletariat. The Mensheviks, in short, came to resemble the Marxists of western Europe, so far as that was possible under Russian conditions. Lenin stood for the rigid reaffirmation of Marxian fundamentals—dialectical materialism and irreconcilable class struggle.

If we ask what Leninism added to the original Marxism, the answer is not easy to find. Lenin accepted Marx's governing ideas: that capitalism exploited the workers; that history was shaped by economic forces and was moving toward socialism; that class struggle was the law of society; and that existing forms of religion, government, philosophy, and morals were weapons of the ruling class. He did, however, develop and transform into a first-rank element of Marxism certain theories of imperialism and of the "uneven development of capitalism" that had been propounded in only general terms by Marx and Engels. In the Marxist-Leninist view, "imperialism" was exclusively a product of monopoly capitalism, that is, capitalism in its big business, "highest," and "final" stage, which develops differently and at different times in each country. Monopoly capitalism is bent on exporting surplus capital and investing it in underdeveloped areas for greater profits. The unceasing drive for colonies and markets in a world already almost completely partitioned leads inevitably to international imperialist wars for the redistribution of colonies, as well as to intensified national colonial struggles for independence; both provide new revolutionary opportunities for the proletariat.

Imperialism and development

In other respects, Lenin roundly denounced all who attempted to "add" anything to the fundamental principles of Marx. Nothing infuriated him so much as revisionist efforts to tone down the class struggle or hints that Marxism might in the last analysis perhaps find room for some kind of religion. As he wrote in 1908: "From the philosophy of Marxism, cast of one piece of steel, it is impossible to expunge a single basic premise, a single essential part, without deviating from objective truth, without falling into the arms of bourgeois-reactionary falsehood." Lenin was a convert. He discovered Marxism; he did not invent it. He found in it a theory of revolution which he accepted without reservation as scientific and on which he was more outspokenly dogmatic even than Marx himself. His powers of mind, which were very great, were spent in demonstrating how the unfolding events of the twentieth century confirmed the analysis of the master.

But it was by his powers of will that Lenin was most distinguished, and if Leninism contributed little to Marxism as a theory, it contributed a great deal to it as a movement. Lenin was an activist. He was the supreme agitator, a field commander in the class war, who could dash off a polemical pamphlet,

Lenin as activist

Lenin built the Russian Bolshevik party into a disciplined revolutionary movement by insisting that a small, centralized elite should make all of the party's key strategic decisions. When the opportunity for revolutionary action finally arrived during the First World War, the Bolsheviks had an effective, centralized political organization, a well-defined Marxist conception of class conflict, and the strong-willed leadership of Lenin—who is shown here addressing a crowd in the spring of 1920.

(SOVFOTO)

dominate a party congress, or address throngs of workers with equal ease. Beside him, Marx and Engels seem almost to be mere recluses or sociologists. Marx and Engels had preferred to believe that the dictatorship of the proletariat, when it came, would represent the wishes of the great majority in a society in which most people had become proletarians. Lenin more frankly foresaw the possibility that the proletarian dictatorship might represent the conscious wishes of a small vanguard and might have to impose itself on great masses by an unshrinking use of force.

Above all, Lenin developed Marx's idea of the role of the party. He drew on the rich experience of pre-Marxist revolutionaries in Russia—the mysterious use of false names, invisible ink, secret ciphers, forged passports, and hidden rendezvous—the whole conspiratorial wonderland which, when it existed to a lesser degree in the West before 1848, drew Marx's scorn and laughter. Lenin's conception of the party was basically Marx's, reinforced by his own experience as a Russian. The party was an organization in which intellectuals provided leadership and understanding for workers, who could not see for themselves. For trade unionism, concerned only with the day-to-day demands of workers, Lenin had even less patience than Marx. "The unconscious growth of the labor movement," he wrote, "takes the form of trade unionism, and trade unionism signifies the mental enslavement of the workers to the bourgeoisie." The task of intellectuals in the party, the elite, or experts, was to make the trade unions and the workers class-conscious and hence revolutionary. Armed with "objective" knowledge, known to be correct, the party leadership naturally could not listen to the subjective opinions of others—the passing ideas of laborers, of peasants, of mistaken party subordinates, or of other parties pretending to know more than Marx himself. The idea that intellectuals supply the brains and workers the brawn, that an elite leads while the toilers meekly follow, is understandable enough in view of the Russian back-

The party

ground, which had created on the one hand a painfully self-conscious intelligentsia and on the other a repressed working class and peasantry deprived of all opportunity for political experience of their own. It was one of the most distinctive traits of Leninism and one of the most foreign to the democratic movement of the West.

Leninism accomplished the marriage of Russian revolutionary traditions with the Western doctrine of Marxism. It was an improbable marriage, whose momentous offspring was to be communism. But at the time, when Bolshevism first appeared in 1903, it had little or no effect. A real revolution broke out in Russia in 1905. It took the revolutionary émigrés almost entirely by surprise.

92. THE REVOLUTION OF 1905

Background and Revolutionary Events

The almost simultaneous founding at the turn of the century of the Constitutional Democratic, Social Revolutionary, and Social Democratic parties was clearly a sign of mounting discontent. None of these was as yet a party in the Western sense, organized to get candidates elected to office, for there were no elections in Russia above the provincial zemstvo level. All three parties were propaganda agencies, made up of leaders without followers, intellectuals who followed various lines of thought. All, even those who became Constitutional Democrats, were watched by the police and obliged to do most of their work underground. At the same time, after 1900, there were signs of growing popular unrest. Peasants were trespassing on lands of the gentry and even rising in local insurrections against landlords and tax collectors. Factory workers sporadically refused to work. But with these popular movements none of the new parties had formed any solid links.

Growing discontent

The government refused to make concessions of any kind. The tsar, Nicholas II, who had mounted the throne in 1894, was a man of narrow outlook. To the Little Father all criticism seemed merely childish. Tutored in his youth by Pobiedonostsev, the lay leader of the Russian Orthodox church, he regarded all ideas questioning autocracy, Orthodoxy, and Great Russian nationalism as un-Russian. That persons in the government should be controlled by interests outside the government—the mildest liberalism or most orderly democracy—seemed to the tsar, the tsarina, and the leading officials to be a monstrous aberration. Autocracy, for them, was the best and only, as it was the God-given, form of government for Russia.

The chief minister, Plehve, and the circles at court, hoped that a short successful war with Japan would create more attachment to the government. The war went so badly that its effect was the reverse. Critics of the regime (except for the handful of the most internationalist Marxists) were sufficiently patriotic to be ashamed at the ease with which Russia was defeated by an upstart, Asian power. As after the Crimean War, there was a general feeling that the government had exposed its incompetence to all the world. Liberals believed that its secret methods, its immunity to criticism or control, had made it sluggish, torpid, obstinate, and inefficient, unable either to win a war or to lead the economic modernization that was taking place in Russia. But there was little that the liberals could do.

Response to military defeat

The police had recently allowed a priest, Father Gapon, to go among the St. Petersburg factory workers and organize them, hoping thus to counter the propaganda of revolutionaries. Father Gapon took up their grievances in all seriousness. They believed, as uneducated peasants only recently transplanted to the city, that if only they could reach the ear of the Little Father, the august being high above all hard capitalists and stony officials, he would hear their complaints with shocked surprise and rectify the evils that afflicted Russia. They drew up a petition, asking for an 8-hour day, a minimum daily wage of one ruble (50 cents), a repudiation of bungling bureaucrats, and a democratically elected Constituent Assembly to introduce representative government into the empire. Unarmed, peaceable, respectful, singing "God save the Tsar," a crowd of 200,000—men, women, and children—gathered before the tsar's Winter Palace one Sunday in January 1905. But the tsar was not in the city, and his officials were afraid. Troops marched up and shot down the demonstrators in cold blood, killing several hundred.

Reactions to "Bloody Sunday"

"Bloody Sunday" in St. Petersburg snapped the moral bond upon which all stable government rests. The horrified workers saw that the tsar was not their friend. The autocracy stood revealed as the force behind the hated officials, the tax collectors, the landlords, and the owners of the industrial plants. A wave of political strikes broke out. Social Democrats (more Mensheviks than Bolsheviks) appeared from the underground or from exile to give revolutionary direction to these movements. Councils or "soviets" of workers were formed in Moscow and St. Petersburg. The peasants, too, in many parts of the country spontaneously began to erupt, overrunning the lands of the gentry, burning manor houses and doing violence to their owners. Social Revolutionaries naturally tried to take over this movement. The liberal Constitutional Democrats, professors, engineers, business people, lawyers, leaders in the provincial zemstvos founded 40 years before, tried also to seize leadership or at least use the crisis to force the government's hand. All agreed on one demand—that there should be more democratic representation in the government.

The tsar yielded grudgingly and as little as possible. In March 1905 he promised to call to office men "enjoying the confidence of the nation." In August (after the ruinous battle of Tsushima) he agreed to call a kind of Estates General, for which peasants, landowners, and city people should vote as separate classes. Still the revolution raged unchecked. The St. Petersburg Soviet, or workers' council, led mainly by Mensheviks (Lenin had not yet reached Russia), declared a great general strike in October. Railroads stopped, banks closed, newspapers ceased to appear, and even lawyers refused to go to their offices. The strike spread to other cities and to the peasants. With the government paralyzed, the tsar issued his October Manifesto. It promised a constitution, civil liberties, and a Duma to be elected by all classes alike, with powers to enact laws and control the administration.

The October Manifesto

The tsar and his advisers intended to divide the opposition by releasing the October Manifesto, and in this they succeeded. The Constitutional Democrats, with a Duma promised, allowed themselves to hope that social problems could henceforth be dealt with by parliamentary methods. Liberals were now afraid of revolutionaries, industrialists feared the strength shown by labor in the general strike, and landowners demanded a restoration of order among the peasants. Aroused peasants and workers were not yet satisfied: the former still wanted more land and less taxation; the latter, a shorter working day and a living wage. The several branches of revolutionary intellectuals worked upon the continuing popular agitation, hoping to carry matters forward until the tsarist monarchy was abolished and a socialist republic was established with themselves at its head. They believed also (and correctly) that the October Manifesto was in any case a deception, which the tsar would refuse to adhere to as soon as revolutionary pressure was removed. The soviets continued to seethe, local strikes went on, and there were mutinies among soldiers at Kronstadt and sailors in the Black Sea fleet.

The angry response to "Bloody Sunday" in early 1905 erupted in a wave of strikes, demands for political reform, and militant demonstrations, including this protest march in St. Petersburg. Most of the protestors in this photograph were students, and they were marching behind red flags that had become a modern symbol for revolutionary political movements.
(SOVFOTO)

But the government was able to maintain itself. With the middle-class liberals now inactive or demanding order, the authorities arrested the members of the St. Petersburg Soviet. Peace was hastily made with Japan, and reliable troop units were recalled from the Far East. The revolutionary leaders fled back to Europe, or again went underground, or were caught and sent to prison or to Siberia; executions were carried out in the countryside.

The Results of 1905: The Duma

The chief apparent result of the Revolution of 1905 was to make Russia, at least ostensibly, into a parliamentary type of state, like the rest of Europe. The promised Duma was convoked. For ten years, from 1906 to 1916, Russia had at least the superficial attributes of a semiconstitutional monarchy.

But Nicholas II soon showed that he did not intend to yield much. He drew the teeth of the new Duma before the assembly could even be born, by announcing in advance, in 1906, that it would have no power over foreign policy, the budget, or government personnel. His attitude toward constitutional monarchy continued until 1917 to be entirely negative; the one thing that tsarism would not allow was any real participation in government by the public. Within this "public" the two extreme fringes were equally impervious to liberal constitutionalism. On the Right, stubborn upholders of pure autocracy and the Orthodox church organized the Black Hundreds, terrorizing the peasantry and urging them to boycott the Duma. On the Left, in 1906, the Social Revolutionaries and both the Bolshevik and Menshevik wings of the Social Democrats likewise refused to recognize the Duma, urged workers to boycott it, and refused to put up any candidates for election.

The first Duma

The short-lived first Duma was elected in 1906 by a system of indirect and unequal voting, in which peasants and workers voted as separate classes, and with proportionately far less representation than was granted to the landlords. In the absence of socialist candidates, workers and peasants voted for all sorts of people, including the liberal Constitutional Democrats (the Cadets), who obtained a sweeping majority. The Cadets, when the Duma met, found themselves still fighting for the bare principle of constitutional government. They demanded true universal male suffrage and the responsibility of ministers to a parliamentary majority. The tsar's response was to dismiss the Duma after two months. The Cadets fled to Viborg in autonomous Finland, which the tsarist police generally let alone. It is significant that these constitutional liberals and democrats, in council at Viborg, again appealed for a general strike and nonpayment of taxes—that is, for mass revolution. But real revolutions are not easy to start, and nothing happened.

The second Duma

A second Duma was elected in 1907, with the government trying to control the elections through suppression of party meetings and newspapers, but since Social Revolutionaries and Mensheviks now consented to take part, some 83 socialists were elected. The Cadets, becoming fearful of the revolutionary Left, concluded that constitutional progress must be gradual and showed a willingness to cooperate with the government. But the Duma came to an abrupt end when the government denounced and arrested some 50 socialists as revolutionaries bent only on destruction. A third Duma, elected after an electoral change that gave increased representation to the landed propertied class and guaranteed a conservative majority, managed to hold several sessions between 1907 and 1912, as did a fourth Duma from 1912 to 1916. The deputies, by following the lead of the government, by addressing themselves only to concrete issues, by losing themselves in committee work, and by avoiding the basic question of where supreme power lay, kept precariously alive a modicum of parliamentary institutions in the tsarist empire.

The Stolypin Reforms

Some officials believed that the way to checkmate the revolutionaries, and strengthen the hold of the monarchy, was for the government, while keeping all controls in its own hands, to attract the support of reasonable and moderate people by a program of reforms. One of these was Peter Stolypin, whom the tsar retained as his principal minister from 1906 to 1911. It was Stolypin who dissolved the first two Dumas. But it was not his policy merely to stand still. His aim was to build up the propertied classes as friends of the state. He believed, perhaps rightly, that a state actively supported by widespread private property had little to fear from doctrinaire intellectuals, conspirators, and émigrés. He therefore favored and broadened the powers of the provincial zemstvos, in which the larger landowners took part in administering local affairs. For the peasantry he put through legislation more sweeping than any since the Emancipation, allowing peasants to sell their shares in the communal land of the *mirs* and leave their villages. Peasants also gained the right to acquire private control over land and to buy property from the communes or the gentry.

The Stolypin policy was successful. Between 1907 and 1916, 6.2 million families out of 16 million who were eligible applied for legal separation from the *mir*. There was no mistaking the trend toward individual property and independent farming. But the results of the Stolypin program must not be exaggerated. The *mir* was far from broken. A vast majority of peasants were still involved in the old system of common rights and communal restrictions. The land shortage was still acute in the agricultural areas where yields were highest. Land hunger and poverty continued in the countryside. There were new big farmers—called *kulaks*—to be resented and envied, but the largest landed proprietors were still the gentry. About 30,000 landlords owned nearly 200 million acres of land, and another 200 million acres made up other large landed estates.

Success of the Stolypin program

Stolypin was not left long to carry on his program. The tsar gave him only an unwilling support. Reactionary circles disliked his tampering ways and his Western orientation. Social Revolutionaries naturally cried out against dissolution of the communes. Even Marxists, who should in theory have applauded the advance of capitalism in Russia, feared that Stolypin's reforms might do away with agrarian discontent. "I do not expect to live to see the revolution," said Lenin in these years. Stolypin was shot dead while attending the theater in Kiev, in the presence of the tsar and tsarina, in 1911. The assassin, a member of the terrorist wing of the Social Revolutionaries, is thought also to have been a secret agent of the reactionary tsarist police. It may be added that Stolypin's predecessor, Plehve, and about a dozen other high officials within the past few years had similarly died at the hands of assassins.

But all in all, despite its violence and repression, the Russian empire on the eve of the First World War was moving in a Western direction. Its industries were growing, its railways were expanding, and its exports were almost half as great in value as those of the United States. It had a parliament, if not a parliamentary government. Private property and individualist capitalism were spreading to new layers of the people. There was a guarded freedom of the press, illustrated, for example, by the legal and open establishment of the Bolshevik party paper, *Pravda*, in St. Petersburg in 1912. It is not possible to say how far this development might have gone, for it was menaced on both the Right and the Left by obstinate and obscurantist reactionaries upholding the absolute tsardom and by revolutionaries whom nothing but the end of tsardom and wholesale transformation of society could appease. But both extremes were discouraged. The desperation of extreme reactionaries in the government, the feeling that they might in any case soon lose their position, perhaps made them the more willing to precipitate a European war by armed support of Serbian nationalists. As for the revolutionary parties, and especially the Bolsheviks, they were losing in membership on the eve of the war, their leaders lived year after year in exile, dreaming of the great days of 1905 which stubbornly failed to repeat themselves and sometimes pessimistically admitting, as Lenin did, that there might be no revolution in their time.

Westernization

93.   THE REVOLUTION OF 1917

End of the Tsardom: The Revolution of March 1917

War again put the tsarist regime to a test that it could not meet. In this war, more total than any had ever been, willing cooperation between government and people was indispensable to success. This essential prerequisite the tsarist empire did not have. National minorities, Poles, Ukrainians, the peoples of the Caucasus, Jews, and others, were disaffected. As for the socialists, who in every other European parliament voted for funds to finance the war, the dozen otherwise disunited socialists in the Duma refused to do so and were promptly jailed. The ordinary worker and peasant marched off with the army, but without the sense of personal conviction felt by common people in Germany and the West. More decisive was the attitude of the middle class. Because they patriotically wished Russia to win, the glaring mismanagement of the government was the more intolerable to them. The Russian disasters at the battles of Tannenberg and the Masurian Lakes, with which the war opened in 1914, were followed by the advance of the Central Powers into Russia in 1915, at the cost of 2 million Russian soldiers killed, wounded, or captured.

Middle-class support

At the war's outbreak middle-class people, as in all countries, offered their assistance to the government. The provincial zemstvos formed a union of all zemstvos in the empire to facilitate the mobilization of agriculture and industry. Business groups at Petrograd (as St. Petersburg was briefly renamed) formed a Commercial and Industrial Committee to get the factories into maximum production. The government distrusted these signs of public activity arising outside official circles. On the other hand, organized in this way, middle-class people became conscious of their own strength and more critical of the bureaucracy. Rumors spread that some officials in the war ministry itself were pro-German, reactionaries who feared the liberalism of England and France, with which Russia was allied.

Life at court was bizarre even for Russia. The tsarina Alexandra, German by origin, looked upon all Russians outside her own circle with contempt, incited her husband to play the proud and pitiless autocrat, and took advice from a self-appointed holy man, the mysterious Rasputin. She was convinced that Rasputin possessed supernatural and prophetic powers, because he had apparently cured her young son of hemophilia. Rasputin, by his influence over her, had a voice in appointments to high office. All who wished an audience with the imperial pair had to go through him. Patriotic and enlightened persons of all classes vainly protested. In these circumstances, and given the military defeats, the union of zemstvos and other such war-born bodies complained not merely of faults of administration but of fundamental conditions in the state. The government responded by holding them at arm's length. The tsarist regime, caught in a total war, was afraid of the help offered by its own people.

Deepening of political divisions

During the war, in September 1915, the Duma was suspended. It was known that reactionaries—inspired by the tsarina, Rasputin, and other sinister forces—expected that a victory in the war would make it possible to kill liberalism and constitutionalism in Russia. The war thus revived all the basic political issues that had been latent since the Revolution of 1905. The union of zemstvos demanded the assembly of the Duma. The Duma reassembled in November 1916 and, conservative though it had always been, expressed loud indignation at the way affairs were conducted. Among all elements of the population, dissatisfaction with the course of the war and with the government's ineptitude mounted. In December Rasputin was assassinated by nobles at the court. The tsar began to consider repression and again adjourned the Duma. Machine guns were issued to the police. Members of the Duma, and of the new extragovernmental bodies, concluded that the situation could be saved only by force. It is when moderate persons, normally concerned with their own business, come to such conclusions that revolution becomes a political possibility. The shift of moderates and liberals, their need of a coup d'état to save themselves from reactionaries, likewise raised the long-failing prospects of the minority of professional revolutionaries.

Again it was the workers of Petrograd who precipitated the crisis. Food had become scarce, as in all the belligerent countries. But the tsarist administration was too clumsy and too demoralized by graft to institute the controls that had become usual elsewhere, such as maximum prices and ration cards. It was the poorest who felt the food shortage most keenly. On March 8, 1917, food riots broke out, which soon developed, doubtless with the help of revolutionary intellectuals, into political insurrection. Crowds shouted, "Down with the tsar!" Troops within the city refused to fire on the insurgents; mutiny and insubordination spread from unit to unit. Within a few days a Soviet of Workers' and Soldiers' Deputies, on the model of 1905, had been organized in Petrograd.

Middle-class leaders, with the government now helpless, demanded dismissal of the ministry and formation of a new one commanding the confidence of a majority of the Duma. The tsar retaliated by disbanding the Duma. The Duma set up an executive committee to take charge until the situation clarified. There were now two new authorities in the city: one, the Duma committee, essentially moderate, constitutionalist, and relatively legal; the other, the Petrograd Soviet, representing revolutionary forces arising by spontaneous upsurge from below. The Petrograd Soviet (or workers' "council") was to play in 1917 a role like that of the Paris Commune of 1792, constantly pushing the supposedly higher and more nationwide authority to the left. The Soviet became the public auditorium and administrative center of the working-class upheaval. Since it was generally socialist in its outlook, all the factions of doctrinaire socialists—Social Revolutionaries, Mensheviks, Bolsheviks—tried to win it over and utilize it for their own ends.

The Petrograd Soviet

The Duma committee, under pressure from the Petrograd Soviet, on March 14 set up a Provisional Government under Prince Lvov. The Duma liberals, as a concession to the Soviet, admitted one socialist to the new government, Alexander Kerensky, a moderate, legal-minded Social Revolutionary, and they furthermore consented to demand the abdication of Nicholas II. The tsar was then at the front. He tried to return to his palace near Petrograd, but the imperial train was stopped and turned back by troops. The army, fatefully, was taking the side of the revolution. The very generals in the field, unable to vouch for the loyalty of their men, advised abdication. Nicholas yielded; his brother the grand duke declined to succeed him; and on March 17, 1917, Russia became a republic.

The Bolshevik Revolution: November 1917

The Provisional Government, following the best precedents of European revolutions, called for elections by universal male suffrage to a Constituent Assembly, which was to meet late in the year and prepare a constitution for the new regime. It tried also to continue the war against Germany. In July an offensive was mounted, but the demoralized armies were quickly routed. Pending final decision by the Constituent Assembly, the Provisional Government promised wholesale redistribution of land to the peasants but took no action. Meanwhile, the peasants, driven by the old land hunger, were already overrunning the

Russia's costly military defeats and the food shortages that developed because of the long war contributed decisively to the revolutionary uprising that overthrew Tsar Nicholas II. Similar discontents soon undermined popular support for the Provisional Government, which tried to continue the war. These women in St. Petersburg were demanding increased food rations for Russian soldiers, but their demonstration in 1917 is an example of the wider political mobilization that swept across Russia during that revolutionary year.
(SOVFOTO)

rural districts, burning and looting. At the front the armies melted away; many high officers refused to serve the republic, and masses of peasant soldiers simply turned their backs and went home, unwilling to be absent while land was being handed out. The Petrograd Soviet, opposing the Provisional Government, called for speedy termination of the war. Fearing reactionary officers, it issued on March 14 its Order No. 1, entrusting command within the army to committees elected by both officers and soldiers. Discipline collapsed.

Revolution advancing

The revolution was thus already well advanced when Lenin and the other Bolsheviks arrived in Petrograd in the middle of April. They immediately took sides with the Petrograd Soviet against the Provisional Government, and with similar soviets that had sprung up in other parts of the country. In July an armed uprising of soldiers and sailors, which the Bolshevik central committee disapproved of as premature, was put down. The Bolsheviks were blamed, and Lenin had to flee to Finland. But as a bid for popular support the Provisional Government named the socialist Kerensky as its head in place of Prince Lvov in an uneasy coalition of moderate socialists and liberals. Kerensky's middle position was next threatened from the

Right. The newly appointed military commander, General Kornilov, dispatched a force of cavalry to restore order. Not only conservatives but liberals wished him success in the hope that he would suppress the soviets. Kornilov's movement was defeated, but with the aid of the Bolsheviks, who rallied with other socialists, and of revolutionary-minded soldiers in the city who offered armed resistance. Radicals denounced liberals as accomplices in Kornilov's attempt at counterrevolution, and both camps blamed Kerensky for having allowed the plot to be hatched under his government. Both liberals and moderate socialists abandoned Kerensky, and he had to form a government of uncertain political support. Meanwhile the food shortage worsened, with transport disarranged and the farm population in turmoil, so that workers in the city listened more willingly to the most extreme speakers.

The Bolsheviks adapted their program to what the most aroused elements in a revolutionary people seemed to want. Lenin concentrated on four points: first, immediate peace with the Central Powers; second, redistribution of land to the peasants; third, transfer of factories, mines, and other industrial plants from the capitalists to committees of workers in each plant; and, fourth, recognition of the soviets as the supreme power instead of the Provisional Government. Lenin, though a rigid dogmatist on abstract questions, was a flexible and bold tactician, and his program in 1917 was dictated more by the immediate situation in Russia than by considerations of theoretical Marxism. What was needed was to win over soldiers, peasants, and workers by promising them "peace, land, and bread." With this program, and by infiltration and parliamentary stratagems, as well as by their accuracy as political prophets—predicting the Kornilov counterrevolution and "unmasking" the trend of middle-way liberals to support it—the Bolsheviks won a majority in the Petrograd Soviet and in soviets all over the country.

Lenin thereupon raised the cry, "All power to the Soviets!" to crush Kerensky and forestall the coming Constituent Assembly. Kerensky, to broaden the base on which he stood, and unable to wait for the Constituent Assembly, convoked a kind of preparliament representing all parties, labor unions, and zemstvos. Lenin and the Bolsheviks boycotted his preparliament. Instead they called an all-Russian Congress of Soviets.

"All power to the Soviets!"

Lenin now judged that the hour had come for the seizure of power. The Bolsheviks themselves were divided, many like Zinoviev and Kamenev opposing the move, but Lenin was backed by Trotsky, Stalin, and a majority of the party Central Committee. Troops garrisoned in Petrograd voted to support the soviets, which the Bolsheviks now controlled. On the night of November 6–7, 1917, the Bolsheviks took over telephone exchanges, railway stations, and electric power plants in the city. A warship turned its guns on the Winter Palace, where Kerensky's government sat. The latter could find almost no one to defend it. The hastily assembled Congress of Soviets pronounced the Provisional Government defunct and named in its place a Council of People's Commissars, of which Lenin became the head. Trotsky was named commissar for foreign affairs; Stalin, commissar for nationalities. Kerensky fled, eventually arriving in the United States, where he died in 1970.

At the Congress of Soviets Lenin introduced two resolutions. One called upon the belligerent governments to negotiate a "just democratic peace," without annexations and without indemnities; the second "abolished all landlord property" immediately and without compensation. Although determined to establish a proletarian dictatorship, the Bolsheviks knew the importance of the Russian peasants. The millions of acres belonging to the large estates that were now expropriated provided a base of support for the new regime without which it could hardly have survived.

Resolutions on peace and property

Thus was accomplished the Bolshevik or November Revolution.[1] But the long awaited Constituent Assembly remained to be dealt with. It met in January 1918. Thirty-six million persons had voted for it. Of these, 9 million had voted for Bolshevik deputies, showing that the Bolshevik program, launched less than a year before by a small band of émigrés, had a widespread mass appeal. But almost 21 million had voted for Kerensky's party, the agrarian, populist, peasant-oriented Social Revolutionaries. However, said Lenin, "to hand over power to the Constituent Assembly would again be compromising with the malignant bourgeoisie." The Assembly was broken up on the second day of its sessions; armed sailors dispatched by the people's commissars simply surrounded it. The dissolution of the Constituent Assembly was a frank repudiation of majority rule in favor of "class rule"—to be exercised for the proletariat by the Bolsheviks. The dictatorship of the proletariat was now established. Two months later, in March 1918, the Bolsheviks renamed themselves the Communist party.

The New Regime: The Civil War, 1918–1922

In these same months, the Communists, or Bolsheviks, signed the peace of Brest-Litovsk with Germany, surrendering to Germany control over the Baltic provinces, Poland, and the Ukraine. The conquests of two centuries were thus abandoned; not since the days of Peter the Great had the Russian frontier been so far from central Europe. To Lenin it made no difference. He was convinced that the events that he had just mastered in Russia were the prelude to a general upheaval; that the war, still raging in the West, would bring all Europe to the inevitable proletarian or Marxist revolution; that Imperial Germany was therefore doomed; and that Poles, Ukrainians, and others would soon emerge, like the Germans themselves, as free socialist peoples. In any case, it was largely by promising peace that Lenin had won enough backing to overthrow Kerensky, who on this deep popular demand had delayed too long, waiting for England and France to release Russia from its treaty obligations as an ally. But real peace did not come, for the country sank immediately into civil war.

Not only old tsarist reactionaries, and not only liberals, bourgeois, zemstvo members, and Constitutional Democrats, but all types of anti-Leninist socialists as well, Mensheviks and Social Revolutionaries, scattered in all directions to organize resistance against the regime of soviets and people's commissars, and they obtained aid from the Western Allies. Both sides competed for the support of the peasants.

As for the new regime, the oldest of its institutions was the party, founded as a wing of the Social Democrats in 1903; the next oldest were the soviets, dating from 1905 and 1917; and then came the Council of People's Commissars set up on the day of the coup d'état. The first institution founded under the new order was a political police, an Extraordinary All-Russian Commission of Struggle Against Counterrevolution, Speculation, and Sabotage, commonly known from its Russian initials as the Cheka and in later years, without basic change of methods or purpose, under such successive names as the OGPU, the NKVD, the MVD, and the KGB. It was established on December 7, 1917. In January 1918 the Red Army was founded, with Leon Trotsky as war commissar and virtually its creator. In July a constitution was promulgated.

---

[1]Also known as the October Revolution, since according to the Julian calendar, used in Russia until 1918, the events described took place in October.

In social policy the Bolsheviks at first adopted no long-range plans, contenting themselves with a mixture of principle and expediency known as "war communism." They nationalized some of the largest industrial enterprises but left the bulk under the control of workers' committees. The pressing problem was to find food, which had ceased to move through any normal channels. The peasants, very much as in the French Revolution under similar conditions—worthless money, insecure property titles, unruly hired hands, armed marauding, and a doubtful future—were producing less food than usual, consuming it themselves, or hoarding it on their own farms. The response of the government and city workers was also much as in 1793. The new government levied requisitions, required the peasants to make stated "deliveries," and invited labor unions to send armed detachments into the country to procure food by force. Since it was naturally the big farmers who had the surplus, they came into disrepute as starvers of the people. Class war broke out, rabid, ferocious, and elemental, between farmers who feared that their very subsistence as well as their property would be taken away and city people, often supported by hungry agricultural laborers, who were driven to desperation by famine. Many peasants, especially the larger farmers, therefore rallied to anti-Bolshevik political leaders.

"War communism"

Centers of resistance developed on every side. In the Don valley a small force assembled under Generals Kornilov and Denikin, with many army officers, gentry landowners, and expropriated business people taking part in it. The Social Revolutionaries gathered followers on the middle Volga. Their most significant military support came from a force of some 45,000 Czechs, who had deserted or been captured from the Austro-Hungarian armies and had then been organized as a Czech Legion to fight on the side of Russia and the Allies. After the November Revolution and the peace of Brest-Litovsk, these Czechs decided to leave Russia by way of the Trans-Siberian Railroad, return to Europe by sea, and resume fighting on the western front. When Bolshevik officials undertook to disarm them they allied with the Social Revolutionaries on the Volga.

The Allied governments believed that Bolshevism was a temporary madness that with little effort could be stopped. They wished above all to bring Russia back into the war against Germany, an objective they sought to achieve by launching a military intervention in East Asia, through Vladivostok. The Japanese, who had declined military aid to their allies in any other theater, viewed this action favorably, seeing in the ruin of the Russian empire a rare opportunity to develop their sphere of influence in East Asia. It was agreed that an interallied military force should land at Vladivostok, cross Siberia, join with the Czechs, break up Bolshevism, and fall upon the Germans in eastern Europe. For this ambitious scheme Britain and France could supply no soldiers, engaged as they were on the western front; the force turned out to be American and Japanese, but predominantly Japanese, since Japan contributed 72,000 men and the United States only 8,000. They landed at Vladivostok in August 1918.

Allied responses

The civil war lasted until 1920, or even later in some places. It became a confused melee in which the Bolsheviks struggled against Russian opponents, independence-minded nationalities, and foreign intervention. The Red Army fought in Ukraine first against the Germans and then against the French, who occupied Odessa as soon as the war ended in Europe. It reconquered Ukraine, Armenia, Georgia, and Azerbaijan, all of which had declared their independence in 1918; put to flight a hundred thousand "Whites," as the counterrevolutionaries were called, under Wrangel in the south; and fought off Admiral Kolchak, who in Siberia proclaimed himself ruler of all Russia. In 1920, the Bolsheviks carried on a war with the new republic of Poland, which was scarcely organized when it set out to recover the huge Ukrainian and Byelorussian territories that had been Polish before 1772. A small force of British, French, and American troops occupied the northern Russian city of Archangel until the end of 1919, and the Japanese remained at Vladivostok until the end of 1922.

Disunity among anti-Bolshevik forces

But the anti-Bolshevik forces could never unite. The anti-Communist Russians represented every hue of the political spectrum from unregenerate tsarists to left-wing Social Revolutionaries. Many of the rightist anti-Bolsheviks openly antagonized the peasants by proceeding to restore expropriated landed estates in areas they occupied; many engaged in vindictive reprisals in a kind of "white terror." The Allies themselves could not agree; the French sent troops to Ukraine and gave aid to the Poles, but the British and Americans wanted to end all military entanglements as soon as the armistice with Germany was signed. Leon Trotsky, on the other hand, forged in the crucible of the civil wars the hard and solid metal of the Red Army, recruiting it, organizing it, restoring its discipline, equipping it as best he could, assigning political commissars to watch it, and assuring that trustworthy officers occupied its high command. The Bolsheviks could denounce the foreign intervention and appeal to national patriotism; and they could win peasant support by the distribution of land.

By 1922 the Bolsheviks, or Communists, had established themselves up to the frontiers of the former tsarist empire in every direction except on the European side. There the band of Baltic states—Finland, Estonia, Latvia, and Lithuania—remained independent; Romania had acquired Bessarabia, the new Romanian frontier reaching now almost to Odessa; and Poland, as a result of the war of 1920, retained a frontier farther east than the Allies themselves had intended. Russia had lost thousands of square miles of territory and buffer areas acquired over the centuries by the tsars. They remained lost until the Second World War. But peace was won and the regime stood.

The Red Terror

It was during these civil wars that the Red Terror broke out in Russia. Like the famous Terror in France in 1793, it was in part a response to civil and foreign war. Before the Bolshevik Terror, the old Jacobin Terror paled. They differed as the cruelty and violence endemic in the old Russia differed from the more humane or law-abiding habits of western Europe. Thousands were shot merely as hostages (a practice unknown to Europe for some centuries); and other thousands were killed without even the summary formalities of revolutionary tribunals. The Cheka was the most formidable political police that had yet appeared. The Bolshevik Terror was aimed at the physical extermination of all who opposed the new regime. A bourgeois class background would go far to confirm the guilt of the person charged with conspiring against the Soviet state. As a chief of the Cheka said: "The first questions you should put to the accused person are, To what class does he belong, what is his origin, what was his education, and what is his profession? These should determine the fate of the accused. This is the essence of the Red Terror."

But a working-class background for a man or a woman made little difference. In 1918 a young woman named Fanny Kaplan shot at Lenin and wounded him. She deposed that she had favored the Constituent Assembly, that her parents had emigrated to America in 1911, that she had six working-class brothers and sisters; and she admitted that she had intended to kill Lenin. She was of course executed, as were others in Petrograd. When the sailors at Kronstadt, who were among the first adherents of the Bolsheviks, rose in 1921, objecting to domination of the soviets by the party (threatening a kind of leftist renewal of the revolution, like the Hébertists who had opposed Robespierre), they were branded as petty bourgeois and shot down by the thousands. The Terror struck at the revolutionists

The Bolsheviks' consolidation of power and victory in the civil war of 1918–1920 depended on the powerful, carefully controlled Red Army, which Leon Trotsky organized in the first years of the revolution. This is a Red Army artillery battalion that was engaged in the suppression of the Kronstadt sailors' uprising in 1921.

(ITAR-TASS/SOVFOTO)

themselves quite as much as it did the bourgeoisie; it was to continue to do so long after the revolution was secure.

The Terror succeeded in its purpose. Together with the victories of the Red Army, it established the new regime. Those "bourgeois" who survived took on the protective coloration of "toilers." No bourgeois as such presumed to take part in the politics of Russia. Mensheviks and other socialists fleeing to Europe told appalling stories of the human toll taken by Lenin. Horrified European socialists repudiated communism as an atrocious, Russian perversion of Marxism. But, at whatever cost, Lenin and his followers were now able to start building the socialist society as they understood it.

A new regime

94.   THE UNION OF SOVIET SOCIALIST REPUBLICS

Government: The Nationalities and Federalism

With the end of the civil wars and foreign intervention, and with the termination of the war with Poland, it became possible in 1922 to establish the Union of Soviet Socialist Republics. There were at first four such republics in the Union, but political reorganization and the occupation of new territories at the beginning of the Second World War increased the number to 15. Although many of these new republics were established in central Asia, most of the Soviet Union's population lived in three large Slavic regions: the Russian Soviet Federated Socialist Republic (since 1991, the Russian Federation), the Ukrainian Soviet Socialist Republic (since 1991, Ukraine), and the Byelorussian Soviet Socialist Republic (since 1991, Belarus). In the new Union, which geographically replaced the old Russian empire, the name Russia was not officially used. The guiding conception was a blend of the national and the international: to recognize nationality by granting autonomy to national groups, while holding these groups together in a higher union and allowing new groups to enter regardless of historic frontiers. In 1922 the expectation of world revolution was still alive. The constitution, formally adopted in 1924, pronounced the founding of the U.S.S.R. to be "a decisive step by way of uniting the workers of all countries into one World Soviet Socialist Republic." It made the Union, in principle, fluid and expansible, declared that any member republic might secede (none did so until 1991) and that newly formed soviet socialist republics might join (none ever did voluntarily). When the U.S.S.R. occupied contiguous territories (once part of the tsarist empire) after the outbreak of the Second World War, these territories were also transformed into Soviet Socialist republics—the three Baltic states, Estonia, Latvia, and Lithuania, after two decades of independence; Bessarabia, detached from Romania; and Karelia, taken from Finland after the Russo-Finnish War. Bessarabia became the Moldavian S.S.R. (since 1991, Moldova), and Karelia temporarily, from 1940 to 1956, had the status of a Karelo-Finnish S.S.R., a 16th Soviet Socialist republic.

An answer to the problem of nationalism

The federal principle in the U.S.S.R. was designed to answer the problem of nationalism. The tsardom, in its last decades, had tried to deal with this problem by systematic Russification. The nationalities had resisted, and nationalist discontent had been one of the forces fatally weakening the empire. Nationalism, or the demand that national groups should have their own political sovereignty, had not only broken up the Austro-Hungarian empire but "Balkanized" central and eastern Europe. This might have happened after 1917 in Russia except for the fact that the Red Army during the civil wars occupied large parts of the tsarist empire which had broken away and declared their independence. As it turned out, in 1922 the U.S.S.R. occupied a sixth of the world's land area and was adjoined on the west by a Europe which in one twenty-seventh of the world's land surface contained 27 independent states.

A hundred languages were spoken in the Soviet Union, and 50 distinct nationalities were recognized within its borders. Many of these were extremely small, splinter groups or isolated communities left by the ebb and flow of humanity in inner Asia over thousands of years. All recognized nationalities received a cultural autonomy, or the right to use their own language, have their own schools, wear their own dress, and follow their own folkways without interference. Indeed, the Soviet authorities favored the growth of cultural nationalism. Some 50 languages were reduced to writing for the first time, and the new regime encouraged the singing of national songs, performance of dances, and collection of folklore.

The Soviet republics

Administratively the nationalities were put on various levels, with varying degrees of separate identity according to their size and importance. The most important were the soviet republics themselves. Within the soviet republics were autonomous republics, autonomous regions, and cultural districts, all having some representation in the upper legislative house, the Soviet of Nationalities, created by the constitution of 1936. But in practice the Russian

A good example of early "socialist realism" in Soviet art, this Soviet political poster from 1918 celebrates "One Year of Proletarian Dictatorship," and portrays the early achievements of the revolution. A worker and a peasant stand on the symbols and chains of the old regime. The happy people in the background are celebrating their triumph and moving confidently toward a prosperous, industrialized future.

(SOVFOTO)

S.F.S.R., with over half the population and three-fourths of the territory of the Union, predominated over the others. When to the Russian were added the Ukrainian and the Byelorussian republics, the overwhelmingly Russian and Slavic character of the Union was marked. Moreover all political and economic rights were severely limited by the concentration of authority in the hands of the central government. There was little substance in the formal claim that each constituent republic was sovereign and had the right to conduct its own foreign affairs (like the British Dominions). During the Second World War there was evidence that separatism had not wholly died down, remaining especially alive in Ukraine, and several autonomous areas were officially dissolved for separatist activities or even for collusion with the German invaders. By the late 1980s it became increasingly apparent that the Soviets could not prevent the disintegration of the multinational empire that they had inherited from the tsars.

Government: State and Party

Government in the Union, and in each component republic, followed a pattern worked out during the revolution and written into the constitutions of 1924 and 1936. In theory, a principle of parallelism was adopted. On the one hand was the state: on the other, paralleling the state but technically not part of it, was the party. But the close interlocking relationship between the two made the parallelism virtually meaningless.

Elections

On the side of the state, the distinctive institution was the council or soviet. Here elections took place, and authority proceeded from the bottom upward to the top through an ascending hierarchy of local, provincial, and national Soviets. Under the constitution of 1924 only "toilers" had the right to vote. Surviving bourgeois, private traders, "persons using the labor of others to make a profit," as well as priests, were excluded from the suffrage. In the constitution of 1936 a more direct democratic procedure was introduced. Voters henceforth directly elected members of the higher soviets, a secret ballot was adopted, no class was any longer denied the vote, and a bicameral parliament was created. On the state side, as set forth in the constitution of 1936, the government embodied many seemingly democratic features.

The Central Committee of the party

Yet alongside the state, at all levels and in all localities, was the party. Only one party was allowed, the Communist, though nonparty members might be elected to the soviets or to other official positions. In the party, authority began at the top and proceeded downward. At its apex stood the Central Committee, whose membership varied from about 70 in the 1930s to more than double that in later years. Within the Central Committee a powerful Politburo, or political bureau, of about a dozen members dominated discussions of policy and personnel. An even more powerful general secretary, the office that Stalin virtually fashioned, dominated the entire structure and apparatus with authority over appointments and assignments at all levels. Although a party congress was held every few years and issues were debated, ultimately the congress simply registered policies already laid out by the higher bodies. Thus power and authority flowed downward and outward, as in an army, or as in a highly centralized government agency or large private corporation in the West, except that the party was not subject to any outside control. Discipline was likewise enforced in ways not used in liberal countries, the fearsome machinery of the secret police being available for use against party members as well as those outside.

Growth and nature of the party

The number of party members, men and women, which could not have been more than 70,000 at the time of the revolution, rose to about 2 million by 1930, 3 million by 1940, and to 19 million in the late 1980s. The Leninist ideal of a highly disciplined party, made up of faithful and zealous workers who willingly carried out orders, the ideal on which the Bolsheviks had separated from the Mensheviks in 1903, continued to characterize the Communist party in the Soviet Union. A party of 2 million members, though small in contrast to the population of the U.S.S.R., still represented an enormous growth for the party itself, in which for each old member (who had joined before 1917) there were thousands of new ones. To preserve party unity under the new conditions strict uniformity was enforced. Members intensively studied the principles of Marxism-Leninism, embraced dialectical materialism as a philosophy and even as a kind of religion, learned to take orders without question or compunction and to give authoritative leadership to the mass of nonparty members among whom they worked. The base of the party structure consisted of small nuclei or cells. In each factory, in each mine, in each office, in each class at the universities and technical schools, in each labor union, in each at least of the larger villages, one, two, or a dozen of the local people (factory workers, miners, office workers, students, etc., as the case might be) belonged to the party and imparted party views and party momentum to the whole.

The function of the party, in Marxist terms, was to carry out the dictatorship of the proletariat. It was to lead the people as a whole to the realization of socialism and, in day-to-day affairs, to coordinate the ponderous mechanism of government and make it work. Party members were present at all levels of the government. Throughout the whole structure, the party decided what the state should do.

The party in the U.S.S.R., by the 1930s, functioned as a tightly knit, highly disciplined leadership group. Those who joined it were willing to work hard, devote themselves to party matters day and night, absorb and communicate the party policy (or "line"), go where they were sent, attend meetings, speak up, perceive and explain the significance of small passing events for the Soviet Union or the world revolution, and master intricate technical details of farming, manufacturing, or the care of machinery, so that others would look to them willingly for advice. The party was a specially trained elite whose members were in constant touch with each other. It was the thin stream of lifeblood which, by circulating through all the diverse tissues of the U.S.S.R.—the multitudinous republics, soviets, bureaus, army, industrial, and other enterprises owned under socialism by the state—kept the whole complex body unified, organic, functioning, and alive.

The party's leadership role

If the party was a leadership group, the corollary was that more than 95 out of 100 persons were condemned to be followers, and while it is perhaps true (as apologists for the system maintained) that under any system true leadership is exercised by a tiny fraction of people, the difference between Communist and non-Communist in the U.S.S.R. became a clear matter of social status. As the years passed, many Communists in the U.S.S.R. were less the revolutionary firebrand type than the successful and efficient man or woman in any social system. They represented the satisfied, not the dissatisfied. They enjoyed extensive material privileges, not only for themselves but also for their children. They became a new vested interest. Within the party, members had to be not so much leaders as followers. A homogeneous and monolithic organization had to present a solid front to the far more numerous but unorganized outsiders. Within the party, from time to time, a great deal of difference of opinion and open discussion was tolerated (indeed, since there was only one party all political questions were intraparty disputes), but in the end the entire membership had to conform. The party favored a certain fertility of mind in inventing ways to get things done, but it did not favor, and in fact repressed, originality, boldness, risk-taking, or freedom of thought or action. The dangers of stagnation in such a system became apparent within the Soviet Union itself in later times.

The New Economic Policy, 1921–1927

By 1920 "war communism" as we have seen, had hopelessly antagonized the peasants, who, it was estimated, were cultivating only 62 percent as much land as in 1914. This fact, together with a severe drought and the breakdown of transportation, produced a great famine. Millions of people died. The ravages of eight years, of the First World War, the revolution, the civil wars, the Terror, had left the country in ruins, its productive facilities thrown back by decades as compared with 1914. The mutiny of the Kronstadt sailors in 1921 revealed profound disillusionment in the revolutionary ranks themselves. Lenin concluded that socialization had advanced too fast. He openly advocated a compromise with capitalism, a strategic retreat. The New Economic Policy, or NEP, adopted in 1921, lasted until 1927. Most of the decade of the 1920s saw a relaxation of tempo (and of terror) for most people in the U.S.S.R.

Private enterprise under the NEP

Under the NEP, while the state controlled the "commanding heights" of the economy, maintaining state ownership of the basic productive industries,

THE UNION OF SOVIET SOCIALIST REPUBLICS, 1922–1991

The U.S.S.R. was over 5,000 miles long and covered one-sixth of the land area of the globe. It was the only state that immediately adjoined so many important political areas—Europe in the west, the Middle East in the south, China along a long frontier, Japan across a narrow sea, and the United States on the coast near Alaska. The Union had 15 member republics, of which the

Russian was by far the largest. Most of it lay farther north than the Great Lakes of North America, but around Tashkent, in the latitude of New York and Chicago, cotton and citrus fruits were grown by irrigation. The diversion of rivers for this purpose led to environmental disasters such as the spread of deserts and the gradual drying up of the Aral Sea.

it allowed a great deal of private trading for private profit. The basic problem was to restore trade between town and country. The peasants would produce nothing beyond the needs of their own subsistence unless they could exchange their surplus for city-made wares such as clothing or tools. The city people had to be fed from the country if they were to turn out factory products or even continue to live in the city. Under the NEP, peasants were allowed to sell their farm products freely. Middlemen were allowed to buy and sell farm products and manufactured articles at will, selling to whom they pleased, at market prices, and at a profit to themselves. The NEP thus favored the big individualist farmer or kulak. Indeed, rural changes initiated before 1914 were still at work; peasant families consolidated millions of acres as private property in 1922, 1923, and 1924. Correspondingly, other peasants became "proletarians," wage-earning hired hands. The NEP also favored the sprouting of a new-rich commercial class, neobourgeois who ate expensive dinners in the restaurants of Moscow, and whose very existence seemed to explode the dream of a classless society. Under the NEP the worst damages of war and revolution were repaired. But there was no real progress, for in 1928 Russia was producing only about as much grain, raw cotton, cattle, coal, and oil as in 1913, and far less than it presumably would have produced (given the rate of growth before 1913) had there been no revolution.

Social and Cultural Changes after the Revolution

Most Bolsheviks wanted their revolution to accomplish much more than the reconstruction of the state and economy; they wanted to revolutionize the daily lives of the workers, peasants, and "toilers," whom they now expected to construct a new classless society. The new Soviet society was supposed to destroy traditional gender hierarchies as well as the hierarchies of class and wealth. Under the legal reforms of the revolutionary regime, women received equal voting rights, the right to divorce, and new access to birth control and abortion—which was legalized in 1920. The new theoretical rights, however, did not have much immediate effect on the social or economic lives of most women in the Soviet Union. Some of the new rights soon lost significance (for example, the right to vote) or disappeared (for example, abortion became illegal again in the 1930s and 1940s), and traditional social relations among the rural masses could not simply be transformed by revolutionary decrees. But it is also true that many girls and young women, like the boys from the working classes, began to receive more education, especially after the turmoil of the Civil War subsided in the early 1920s.

Women's rights

The campaign to improve prerevolutionary literacy rates was only one example of the early Bolshevik aspirations for radical cultural changes. Writers and artists rallied to the revolutionary cause, seeing the social upheaval as part of a wider rejection of traditional ideas and artistic forms. The creative film director, Sergei Eisenstein, joined with avant-garde theatrical groups to create imaginative new techniques for editing films, portraying dramatic action, and representing political themes. Using his new techniques, Eisenstein produced a famous film about the Russian Revolution of 1905, *Potemkin* (1925), which was commissioned by the Soviet government and which is still regarded by many critics as one of the most innovative films in the early history of cinema. Meanwhile, some radical artists sought to combine "futurist" art with the socialist revolution, and a young Russian poet named Vladimir Mayakovsky moved on from a famous "Ode to Revolution" to innovative

Art, literature, and film

experiments with a new poetic language. In the end, though, Mayakovsky fell into despair and committed suicide as Soviet society entered into the Stalinist era of rigid social control. By the late 1920s the period of experimental art was over, and the new cultural orthodoxy of "socialist realism" was celebrating the beauty of large factories and tractors rather than the abstract mysteries of the artistic avant-garde. Like all other spheres of Soviet life, art fell under the strict control of the Communist party and government institutions.

Stalin and Trotsky

Lenin died in 1924 prematurely at the age of 54 after a series of paralyzing strokes that left him incapacitated in the last two years of his life. His embalmed remains were put permanently on view in the Kremlin; Petrograd was renamed Leningrad; a leader cult was built up around his name and image. The party presented him as a deified equal of Marx himself, and it became necessary for all schools of communist thought to claim unflinching fidelity to the Leninist tradition. Actually, in his own lifetime, the Old Bolsheviks had never regarded Lenin as infallible. They had often differed with him and with each other. As he lay dying, and after his death, his old companions and contemporaries, carrying on the feuding habits of the émigré days, fought with each other for control of the party in Lenin's name. They disputed over Lenin's intentions. Had he secretly thought of the NEP as a permanent policy, as Bukharin maintained? If not, how would he have modified it, and, most especially, how soon? Quietly, behind the scenes, as general secretary of the party, without much attention to broader problems, a hitherto relatively modest member named Joseph Stalin, whom Lenin had warned against, was drawing all the strings of party control into his own hands. More openly and vociferously, Leon Trotsky, who as war commissar in the critical years had been only less conspicuous than Lenin himself, raised the basic issues of the whole nature and future of the movement.

Trotsky, in 1925 and 1926, inveighed against the lassitude that had descended upon socialism.[2] The NEP with its tolerance of bourgeois and kulaks excited his contempt. He developed his doctrine of "permanent revolution," an incessant drive for proletarian objectives on all fronts in all parts of the world. He championed world revolution, which many in the party were beginning to discard in favor of first building socialism in one country. He denounced the tendency to bureaucratic ossification in the party and urged a new movement of the masses to give it life. He called for more forceful development of industry and for the collectivization of agriculture, which had figured in Communist manifestos ever since 1848. Above all, he demanded immediate adoption of an overall plan, a central control and operation of the whole economic life of the country.

Permanent revolution

Trotsky failed to carry the party with him. He was charged with leftist deviationism, machinations against the Central Committee, and inciting to public discussion of issues outside the party. Stalin wove his web. At a party congress in1927, 95 percent of the delegates dutifully voted for Stalin and the Central Committee and fewer than 5 percent voted for Trotsky. Trotsky was first exiled to Siberia, then banished from the U.S.S.R.; he lived

---

[2]For communists, though not for socialists, the terms "communism" and "socialism" were almost interchangeable, since Russian Communists regarded their own system as true socialism and all other socialism as opportunistic, reactionary, or false. Communism was also defined, in the U.S.S.R., as a future state of society toward which socialism, that is, Soviet socialism, was the intermediate stage.

first in Turkey, then France, then Mexico, writing and propagandizing for the "permanent revolution," stigmatizing developments in the U.S.S.R. as "Stalinism," a monstrous betrayal of Marxism-Leninism, organizing an underground against Stalin as he had done in former days against the tsar. He was murdered in Mexico in 1940 under mysterious circumstances, presumably by a Soviet agent or sympathizer. Not until the late 1980s was anyone in the U.S.S.R. permitted to talk or write about him and his contributions to the revolution.

95.   STALIN: THE FIVE-YEAR PLANS AND THE PURGES

Economic Planning

Hardly had Trotsky been expelled when Stalin and the party appropriated certain fragments of his program. In 1928 the party launched the First Five-Year Plan, aimed at rapid industrialization and the collectivization of agriculture. "Planning," or the central planning of a country's whole economic life by government officials, was to become the distinctive feature of Soviet economics and the one that, for a time, was to have the greatest influence on the rest of the world.

In retrospect, it seems strange that the Communists waited ten years before adopting a plan. The truth seems to be that the Bolsheviks had only confused ideas of what to do after their seizure of power. Marxism for the most part gave only general hints. Marxism was primarily an analysis of existing or bourgeois society. It was also a theory of class war. But to portray any details of a future society, or specify what should be done after the class war had been won by the proletariat, was according to Marx and Engels sheer utopian fantasy. The bourgeoisie, to be sure, would be destroyed; there would be "social ownership of the means of production," and no "exploitation of man by man"; everyone would work, and there would be neither leisure class nor unemployment. This was not much to go on in the operation of a modern industrial system.

One great constructive idea had been mapped out, most clearly by Engels. *Within* each private enterprise, Engels had observed, harmony and order reigned; it was only *between* private enterprises that capitalism was chaotic. In the individual factory, he noted, the various departments did not compete with each other; the output of all departments was planned and coordinated by management. In a larger way, the great capitalist mergers and trusts, controlling many factories, prevented blind competition between them, assigned specific quotas to each, anticipated, coordinated, and stabilized the work of each plant and each person by an overall policy. With the growth of large corporate enterprise, observed Engels, the area of economic life under free competition was constantly reduced,

Engels' centralized economy

and the area brought under rational planning was constantly enlarged. The obvious next step, according to Engels and other socialists, was to treat *all* the economic life of a country as a single factory with many departments, or a single enormous monopoly with many members, under one unified, far-seeing management.

Wartime conditions and economic planning

During the First World War the governments of belligerent countries had in fact adopted such centralized controls, not because they were socialistic but because in time of war people were willing to subordinate their usual liberties to a single undisputed social purpose—victory. The "planned society" therefore made its first actual (though incomplete) appearance in the First World War. It was partly from socialist doctrine as exemplified by Engels, partly from experience of the war, and in even larger measure from the pressure to meet the continuing chronic problems of the country by raising its productive level that Stalin and the party in Russia gradually developed the idea of a plan. The war experience was especially valuable for the help it gave on technical questions of economic planning, such as the kind of bureaus to set up, the kind of forecasts to make, and the kind of statistics to collect.

The U.S.S.R. decided to plan for five years into the future, beginning with 1928. The aim of the plan was to strengthen and enrich the country, make it militarily and industrially self-sufficient, lay the groundwork for a true workers' society, and overcome the Russian reputation for backwardness. As Stalin said in a speech in 1929: "We are becoming a country of metal, a country of automobiles, a country of tractors. And when we have put the U.S.S.R. in a motor car and the *muzhik* in a tractor. . . . we shall see which countries may then be 'classified' as backward and which as advanced."

The First Five-Year Plan was declared fulfilled in 1932, and a Second Five-Year Plan was launched, lasting until 1937. The Third, inaugurated in 1938, was interrupted by the war with Germany in 1941. New plans were introduced after 1945.

The First Five-Year Plan

The First Five-Year Plan (like its successors) listed the economic goals to be achieved. It was administered by an agency called the Gosplan. Within the frame of general policy set by the party, the Gosplan determined how much of every article the country should produce, how much of the national effort should go into the formation of capital and how much should go into producing articles for daily consumption, what wages all classes of workers should receive, and at what prices all goods should be exchanged. Because all decisions were made at the top, it was as much a command economy as a planned economy. At the bottom level, in the individual factory, the local management drew up its requirements, or estimates of what it would need, in raw material, machinery, trained workers, plant facilities, and fuel, if it was to deliver the planned quantity of its product at a stated date. Thousands of estimates were passed up the planning ladder until they reached the Gosplan, which, balancing them against each other and against other needs as seen at the top, determined how much steel, coal, and so on, should be produced, and in what qualities and grades; how many workers should be trained in technical schools and in what particular skills; how many machines should be manufactured and how many spare parts; how many new freight cars should be constructed and which lines of railway track needed repair; and how, where, when, and to whom the steel, coal, technicians, machines, and rolling stock should be made available. The plan, in short, undertook to control, by conscious management, the flow of resources and workforce which was regulated in capitalist economies by shifts in demand and supply, and through changes in prices, wage levels, profits, interest rates, or rent.

The system was exceedingly intricate. It was not easy to have the right number of ball bearings, for example, arrive at the right place at the right time, in exact correspondence to the amounts of other materials or to the number of workers waiting to use them. Sometimes there was overproduction; sometimes, underproduction. The plan was often amended as it was applied in action. Countless reports, checkups, and exchanges of information were necessary. A huge class of bureaucrats came into existence to handle the paperwork. The plan achieved some of its goals, exceeded a few, and failed in some. The criteria for fulfillment were almost always quantitative.

Building capital wealth

The primary objective of the First Five-Year Plan was to build up the heavy industry, or capital wealth, of the U.S.S.R. The aim was to industrialize without the use of foreign loans.[3] Russia in 1928 was still chiefly an agricultural country. The world offered hardly any case of a country shifting from agriculture to industry without borrowing capital from abroad. Britain, the original home of the Industrial Revolution, was the best example, although even there, in the eighteenth century, a great deal of capital invested in England was owned by the Dutch. An agricultural country could industrialize from its own resources only by drawing upon agriculture itself. An agricultural revolution had been prerequisite to an industrial revolution in England. By enclosure of land, the squeezing out of small independent farmers, and the introduction of scientific cultivation, under the auspices of a growing class of wealthy landowners, England had both increased its production of food and released many of the rural population to find employment in industry. The First Five-Year Plan called for a similar agricultural revolution in Russia, without benefit to landlords and under the auspices of the state.

The Collectivization of Agriculture

The plan, as originally conceived, called for the collectivization of only one-fifth of the farm population, but Stalin suddenly revised the plan in the winter of 1929 to include the immediate collectivization of the greater part of the peasantry. The plan set up collective farms, averaging a few thousand acres apiece, which were considered to be the property not of the state but of the peasants collectively who resided on them. (A few state-operated collective farms were also established, as models for the others.) Individual peasants were to pool their privately owned fields and livestock in these collectives. Those peasants who possessed fields or stock in considerable amount, the prosperous peasants or kulaks, resisted surrendering them to the new collectives. The kulaks were therefore liquidated as a class. Zealous detachments of Communists from the cities used violence; poor peasants turned upon rich ones; hundreds of thousands of kulaks and their families were killed and many more were transported to labor camps in remote parts of the Soviet Union. The trend that had gone on since Stolypin and indeed since the Emancipation, building up a class of property-owning, labor-hiring, and "bourgeois" peasants, was now abruptly reversed. Collectivization was intended to convert the peasantry into a class more nearly resembling the proletariat of Marxian doctrine, a class of people who as individuals owned no capital and employed no labor, and so would better fit into a proletarian, or socialist, state. The year 1929, not 1917, was the great revolutionary year for most people in Russia.

The human costs of collectivization

Collectivization was accomplished at the cost of village class war in which many of the most capable farmers perished and at the cost also of a wholesale destruction of livestock. The big farmers slaughtered their horses, cattle, pigs, and poultry rather than give them up. Even middling and small farmers did the same, caring nothing about animals that were no longer their own. The ruinous loss of animals was the worst unforeseen calamity of the First Five-Year Plan. The agricultural disorders led to a deadly famine in southeast Russia

---

[3]The Bolsheviks had repudiated the entire debt of the tsarist empire. Their credit in capitalist countries was therefore not good, so that, in addition to fearing dependence upon foreign lenders, they were in any case for a long time unable to borrow large sums.

The creation of collective farms during Stalin's First Five-Year Plan was one of the most radical and most resented economic actions of the new Communist regime. Millions of farm animals were destroyed by angry peasants and millions of people died in the subsequent period of repression and famine. But the creation of large-scale agriculture and tractor stations gradually made it possible for farmers to use new machinery in Russian fields. These farmers were heading for work on new tractors in the early 1930s.

(SOVFOTO)

and the Ukraine in 1932 that cost millions of lives. Despite the famine Stalin refused to cut back on cereal and other food exports because they were needed to pay for industrial imports under the Five-Year Plan.

By introducing thousand-acre units in place of very small ones, collectivization made it possible to apply capital to the soil. Formerly the average peasant had been far too poor to buy a tractor and his fields had been too tiny and dispersed for him to use one, so that only a few rare kulaks had employed any machinery. In the course of the First Five-Year Plan hundreds of Machine Tractor Stations were organized throughout the country. Each, in its region, maintained a force of tractors, harvesting combines, and expert agronomists, which could be dispatched from one collective farm to another by local arrangement. The application of capital was intended to increase the output per peasant. It was also much easier administratively for higher authorities to control the agricultural surplus (products not consumed

Mechanization of agriculture

by the village itself) from a single collective farm than from numerous small and unorganized peasants. Each collective was assigned a quota. Members of the collective could sell in a free market any products they raised beyond this quota; but meanwhile the government knew the quantity of agricultural produce it could count on, either to feed the cities and other regions that did not produce their own food or for export in the world market to pay for imports of machinery from the West. By 1939 all but a negligible fraction of the peasantry was collectivized, but collectivization failed to increase agricultural output. The new collectives denied peasants the freedom to make their own economic decisions, destroyed their incentive to improve the land they worked, and prevented them from passing land on to their heirs. Agriculture therefore remained a troubled sector of the economy. Collectivization made possible, however, the success of industrialization by augmenting the supply of industrial workers. Since the villages needed less labor, 20 million people moved from country to city between the years 1926 and 1939 and were available for jobs in the new industries.

The Growth of Industry

While the agricultural base was being revolutionized, industrialization went rapidly forward. At first there was considerable dependence on the capitalist countries. Engineers and other technicians from western Europe and the United States went to work in the Soviet Union. Much machinery was imported. But the worldwide depression that set in about 1931, bringing a catastrophic fall of agricultural prices, made foreign-made machines more costly in terms of the cereals that were the chief Soviet export. The international situation also deteriorated. While the U.S.S.R. always considered the whole outside world hostile to it, both Japan and Germany in the 1930s showed overt hostility. From the beginning the Five-Year Plans had as one of their objectives the military self-sufficiency of the country. The Second Five-Year Plan, launched in 1933, though in some ways less ambitious than the first, showed an even greater determination to cut down imports and achieve national self-sufficiency, especially in the heavy industry basic to war production.

Rates of industrial growth

No ten years in the history of any Western country ever showed such a rate of industrial growth as the decade of the first two plans in the Soviet Union. In Great Britain industrialization had been gradual; in Germany and the United States it had been more rapid, and in each country there had been decades in which output of coal or iron doubled; but in the U.S.S.R., from 1928 to 1938, production of iron and steel expanded four times and that of coal expanded three and a half times. In 1938 the U.S.S.R. was the world's largest producer of farm tractors and railway locomotives. Four-fifths of all its industrial output came from plants built in the preceding ten years. Two plants alone, at the new cities of Magnitogorsk in the Urals and Stalinsk 1,000 miles farther east, produced as much iron and steel as the whole Russian empire in 1914. In 1939 the U.S.S.R., as measured by purely quantitative standards, was surpassed in gross industrial output only by the United States and Germany.

The plans called for a marked development of industry east of the Urals, and so brought a modernization of life for the first time to inner Asia. New industrial cities rose in the old Turkestan (divided into the five Asian Soviet socialist republics) and in Siberia. Copper mines were opened in the Urals and around Lake Balkhash; lead mines, in eastern Asia and in the Altai Mountains. New grain-producing regions were developed in Siberia and in the Kazakh S.S.R. The capital of the Uzbek S.S.R., Tashkent, formerly a remote town of bazaars and caravans, grew to be a city of over half a million, a center of cotton culture, copper mining, and electrical industries, connected with the north by the newly built Turksib Railway. The Kuznetsk basin, in the south, 2,000 miles inland from every ocean, was found to possess coal deposits of high grade. Kuznetsk coal and the iron ores of the Urals became complementary, though separated by a thousand miles. The opening of all these new areas, requiring the movement of food to the Uzbek S.S.R. in exchange for cotton or of Ural iron to the new Kuznetsk cities, demanded a revolution in transportation. The railroads in 1938 carried five times as much freight as in 1913.

These astounding developments were enough to change the relative economic strength of the world's peoples with respect to one another. It was significant that inner Asia was for the first time turning industrial. It was significant, too, that although the U.S.S.R. conducted less foreign trade than the Russian empire had, it carried on more trade than the old Russia with its Asian neighbors, with which it formed new and close connections. In part because of these developments in Asia, the Russia that went to war with Germany in 1941 proved to be a different antagonist from the Russia of 1914. Industrialization in the Urals and in Asia enabled the U.S.S.R. (with a good deal of Allied assistance) to survive the German occupation and destruction of the older industrial areas in the Don valley. The new "socialist fatherland" proved able to absorb terrible losses and strike back. A great deal of the increased industrial output had gone to equip and modernize the Red Army.

Changes brought by modernization

At the same time, the degree of industrialization of the U.S.S.R. can easily be exaggerated. It was phenomenal because it started from so little. Qualitatively, by Western criteria, standards of production were low. Many of the hastily constructed new plants were shoddy and suffered from rapid depreciation. In efficiency, as shown by output per worker employed, the U.S.S.R. continued to lag behind the West. In intensity of modernization, as shown by output of certain items in proportion to the whole population, it also lagged. Per capita of its huge population, in 1937, the U.S.S.R. produced less coal, electricity, cottons, woolens, leather shoes, or soap than did the United States, Britain, Germany, France, or Japan, and less iron and steel than any of them except Japan. Production of paper is revealing because paper is used in so many "civilized" activities—in books, newspapers, magazines, schools, correspondence, placards, maps, pictures, charts, business and government records, and household articles and amenities. Where the United States about 1937 produced 103 pounds of paper per person, Germany and Great Britain each produced 92, France produced 51, and Japan produced 17, the U.S.S.R. produced only 11.

Social Costs and Social Effects of the Plans

Industrialization in Russia demanded a huge and continuing sacrifice on the part of the people. It was not merely that kulaks lost their lives, or that millions of others, whose exact numbers have never been known, were found to be enemies of the system and sent off to correctional labor camps. All were required to accept a program of austerity and self-denial, going without the better food, housing, and other consumer goods that might have been produced, in order that the capital wealth and heavy industry of the country might be built up. As much as a third of the national income was reinvested in industry every year—twice as much as in the England of 1914, though probably not more than in the England of 1840. The plan required hard work and low wages. Better housing, better food, better clothing, and more leisure would follow once the basic industries had been built. Morale was sustained by propaganda. One of the chief functions of party members was to explain why

Sacrifices and rewards

sacrifices were necessary. In the late 1930s life began to ease; food rationing was abolished in 1935, and a few more products of light industry, such as dishes and fountain pens, began to appear in Soviet retail stores. Living standards were at least up to those of 1927 with prospects brighter for raising them. But the need for war preparations, as the world again approached chaos, again drove back the vision of the Promised Land.

Socialism, as realized in the plans, did away with some of the evils of unrestrained free enterprise. There was no acknowledged unemployment. There was no cycle of boom and depression. There was less misuse of women and children than in the early days of industrialism in the West. There was a minimum below which no one was supposed to fall. On the other hand, there was no economic equality. Marxism, indeed, had never seen complete equality of income as a principal objective. While there was no handful of very rich people, as in the West (where the income of the very rich usually came from inherited property), the differences in income were nevertheless great. High government officials, managers, engineers, and favored artists and intellectuals received the highest rewards. People with large incomes could build up precarious little fortunes for themselves and their children. They could not, however, under socialism, own any industrial capital, that is, buy shares of stock or other equities. There was, of course, no stock exchange.

Competition

Competition persisted. In 1935 a miner named Stakhanov greatly increased his daily output of coal by devising improvements in his methods of work. He also greatly increased his wages, since Soviet workers were paid at piece rates. His example proved contagious; workers all over the country began to break records of all kinds. The government publicized their achievements, called them Stakhanovites and "labor heroes," and pronounced the movement to be "a new and higher stage of socialist competition." In labor circles in the United States such straining to increase output would be called a speed-up, and piecework wages had long been anathema to the organized labor of all countries. Nor was management free from competitive pressure. A factory manager who failed to show the net income (or "profit") upon which the plan counted, or who failed to meet his quota of output, might lose not only his job but also his social status—or even his life. Poor management was often construed as sabotage. Insufficient use of the workers and resources allocated to a factory was considered a betrayal of Soviet society and a waste of the property of the nation. The press, not otherwise free, freely denounced whole industries or individual executives for failures to meet the plan.

Foreign observers often found the distinctive feature of the new system to lie in this kind of competition or emulation, or in a feeling that everybody was busily toiling and struggling to create a socialist fatherland. Workers in the 1930s, it seemed, had a real belief that the new industrial wonders were their own. It became a national pastime to watch the mounting statistics, the fulfilling of quotas or targets. Instead of sports pages, newspaper readers read eagerly about the latest doings (or misdoings) on the economic front.

The price of solidarity

Solidarity was purchased at the price of totalitarianism. The government supervised everything. There was no room for skepticism, independence of thought, or any criticism that weakened the will to achieve. As in tsarist times, no one could leave the country without special permission, which was given far more rarely than before 1914. There was, of course, only one party. There were no free labor unions, no free press, no freedom of association, and at best only an irritable tolerance for religion. Soviet Jews faced widespread suspicion, distrust, and harassment. Art, literature, and even science became vehicles of political propaganda; creative, experimental works—and the people who promoted them—disappeared from Soviet cultural life. Dialectical materialism was the official philosophy. Conformity was the ideal, and the very passion for solidarity made for fear and suspicion of all who might go astray. As for the

The rapid industrialization of the Soviet Union emphasized heavy machinery rather than consumer goods, but the Soviets also began to produce their own cars. This automobile factory in the city of Gorky (a city renamed by the Soviets for the Russian writer) represented the new industrial economy and also expressed the requisite political loyalty to Stalin.

(SOVFOTO)

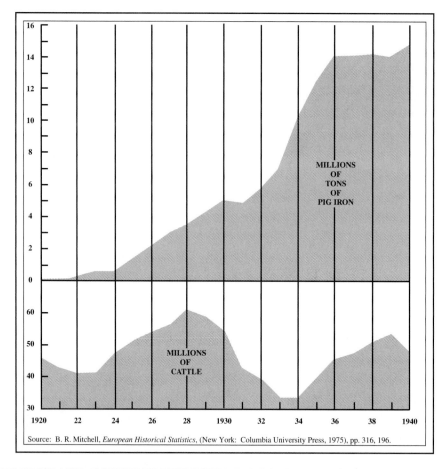

Source: B. R. Mitchell, *European Historical Statistics*, (New York: Columbia University Press, 1975), pp. 316, 196.

PIG IRON AND CATTLE IN THE SOVIET UNION, 1920–1940

This chart reveals clearly what happened in the Soviet economy during the 20 years after the revolution—an enormous buildup of heavy industry at the expense of food supplies. In the disorganization of the revolution and civil war, iron mines and forges were producing almost nothing in 1920. By the late 1920s, output of pig iron regained the pre-revolutionary level, but the great upsurge came with the Second Five-Year Plan. By 1940 Russia was producing more pig iron than Germany, and far more than Britain or France. Numbers of cattle, by contrast, grew in the 1920s, but fell catastrophically during the collectivization of agriculture and by 1940 hardly exceeded the figure for 1920.

number of people sacrificed to Stalin's Juggernaut—liquidated bourgeois, liquidated peasants, purged party members, disaffected persons sentenced to long terms in labor camps—a precise figure is difficult to arrive at, but it certainly reached many millions over the years, which many suspected at the time, and which a later generation of Soviet leaders confirmed.

The Purge Trials of the 1930s

In 1936 socialism was judged to have proved so successful that a new constitution for the U.S.S.R. was proclaimed. It enumerated, as rights of Soviet citizens, not merely the usual civil liberties of Western democracy but the rights to steady employment, rest, leisure, economic security, and a comfortable old age. All forms of racism were condemned. It reorganized the Soviet republics and granted equal and direct universal suffrage, as explained above. The constitution of 1936 received favorable comment in the West, where it was hoped that the Russian Revolution, like former revolutions, had at last turned into more peaceable and quiet channels. It was nonetheless apparent that the Communist party remained the sole governing group in the country, that Stalin was tightening his dictatorship, and that the party was racked by internal troubles.

It was natural that the rapid changes of the 1930s should provide divergences of opinion among the party leaders. Because open disagreement with Stalin's policies was not possible, many may have turned to conspiracy. A moderate group, led by Bukharin, had urged more gradual methods in collectivizing the peasants and greater latitude for small private business, as in the days of the NEP. On the left, the mastermind was the exiled Trotsky. Whether there were conspiracies or not, Stalin acted preemptorily. As early as 1933, the party underwent a drastic purge, in which a third of its members were expelled. Even the faithful were appalled at Stalin's growing ruthlessness. Serge Kirov, an old friend and revolutionary companion of Stalin since 1909, head of the Leningrad party apparatus, and member of the Politburo since 1930, showed signs of leading the disaffected. In 1934 he was assassinated in his office, very probably by a police agent of Stalin's. Stalin used the assassination to strike out at his opponents, imagined or real, by a revival of terror, immediately executing over a hundred persons and launching the extraordinary purges of the next four years.

Diverging opinions

A series of sensational trials took place. In 1936 sixteen Old Bolsheviks were brought to trial. Some, like Zinoviev and Kamenev, had been expelled from the party in 1927 for supporting Trotsky and subsequently, after the proper recantations, had been readmitted. Now they were charged with the murder of Kirov, with plotting the murder of Stalin, and with having organized, in 1932, under Trotsky's inspiration, a secret group to disrupt and terrorize the Central Committee. To the amazement of the world, all the accused made full confession to the charges in open court. All blamed themselves as unworthy and erring reprobates. All were put to death. In 1937, after similar trials, 17 other Old Bolsheviks met the same fate or received long prison sentences. In 1938 Bukharin and others, denounced as "rightists," were charged with wanting to restore bourgeois capitalism and were executed. The same confessions and self-accusations followed in almost every case, with no other verifiable evidence adduced. How these confessions were obtained in open court from hardened revolutionaries apparently in full possession of their faculties and bearing no sign of physical harm mystified the outside world. Only later did it become clear that psychological torture had broken the will of those accused and that threats against their families (or promises to spare them) had played a part.

Trials of the Old Bolsheviks

In addition to these public trials there were other arrests, private inquisitions, and executions. In 1937, in a secret court martial, Marshal Tukhachevski and seven other top generals were accused of Trotskyism and conspiring with the Germans and Japanese and were summarily shot. The purges embraced the highest levels of the party, government, military, intellectual, and scientific circles, and reached down to the lesser echelons as well. In later years the KGB itself disclosed that in the years 1930–1953 (the year of Stalin's death) 3,778,334 persons had been tried and sentenced for "counterrevolutionary" activity and crimes against the state, most of them in the Great Terror of 1934–1938, and

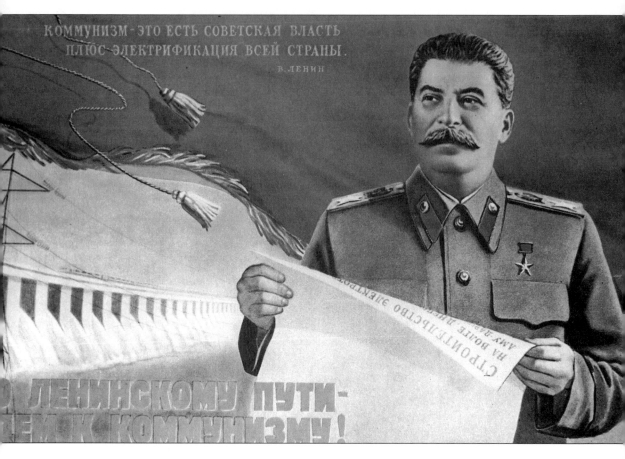

Soviet propaganda depicted Stalin as the benevolent national leader and as the worthy successor to Lenin. This typical poster shows a thoughtful, visionary Stalin with a new hydroelectric plant in the background. The artist, Konstantin Ivanov, quoted Lenin on the poster and gave this work a straightforward political title: "To communism—along the path laid by Lenin."
(SOVFOTO)

that 786,098 were executed; unknown others died in prison camps. The innocence of many of Stalin's victims was officially confirmed and their reputations were posthumously restored.

Reinforcing the dictatorship

By these purges Stalin's dictatorship was reinforced. It may be that a real danger of renewed revolution was averted. Had the tsarist government dealt as summarily with Bolsheviks as Bolsheviks dealt with one another there could have been no November Revolution. Above all, Stalin rid himself by the purges of all possible rivals for his own position. He disposed of the embarrassment of having colleagues about him who could remember the old days, who could quote Lenin as a former friend, or belittle the reality of 1937 by recalling the dreams of 1917. After 1938 there were virtually no Old Bolsheviks left. The aging but still explosive professional revolutionaries were now dead. A younger group, products of the new order, practical, constructive, impatient of "agitators," and acquiescing in Stalin's dictatorship, were operating what was now an established system.

96. THE INTERNATIONAL IMPACT OF COMMUNISM, 1919–1939

Socialism and the First World War

Marxism had always been international in its outlook. To Marx, and the early Marxists, existing states (like other institutions) owed their character to the class struggle. They were no more than committees of the bourgeoisie to govern the proletariat, destined to be dismantled and pass away in the course of inevitable historic processes. After Marx's death, as Marxist parties grew in numbers, and as states of western Europe became more democratic, most people who called themselves Marxists accepted the national state, seeing in it a means by which the workers' lot could be gradually improved. This view was part of the movement of revisionism, or what more rigorous Marxists called "opportunism." In the First World War national loyalty proved its strength. The socialist parties in the Reichstag, the French Chamber, and other parliamentary bodies voted for war credits without hesitation. Socialist workers reported for mobilization like everyone else. In Germany socialists said that the reactionary Russian tsardom must be resisted; in France, that the Germans menaced the entire French nation. In general, all political parties, including the socialists, declared a moratorium on party politics during the war.

Small minorities of socialists in every country, however, refused to accept the war. Marxian socialism had long taught that workers of all nations were bound by the supreme loyalty of class, that their real enemies were the capitalists of their own countries, that international wars were capitalist and imperialist quarrels, and that class struggle was the only kind of warfare that the proletarian should accept. These socialists denounced the action of the socialist majorities as a sellout to capitalism and imperialism. They met in international conferences with each other and with socialists from the neutral countries. Active among them were Lenin and other Russian Social Democrats then in Switzerland. "The only task for socialists," wrote Lenin in 1914, "is to convert the war of peoples into a civil war." The minority or antiwar socialists met at the small Swiss town of Zimmerwald in 1915, where they drew up a "Zimmerwald program," calling for immediate peace without annexations or indemnities. This had no effect on most socialists in the belligerent countries. The Zimmerwald group itself soon began to split. Most Zimmerwalders regarded peace, or the repudiation of the war, as their aim. But a "Zimmerwald Left" began to develop, inspired mainly by Lenin and the Russian émigrés. This faction made its aim not peace but revolution. It hoped that the war would go on until it caused social revolution in the belligerent countries.

Class solidarity versus nationalism

Then in April 1917, with the German imperial government arranging their trip and wishing them bon voyage, Lenin and the other Bolsheviks went back to Russia and accomplished the November Revolution. Lenin, until his death in 1924, believed that the Russian Revolution was only a local phase of a world revolution—of *the* revolution of strict Marxian doctrine. Russia, for him, was the theater of currently most active operations in the international class war. Because he expected proletarian upheaval in Germany, Poland, the Danube valley, and the Baltic regions, he accepted without compunction the treaty of Brest-Litovsk. He took no pride in Russia; he was no patriot or "social-chauvinist," to use his own term. In the founding of the U.S.S.R. in 1922 he saw a nucleus around which other and greater soviet republics of any nationality might coalesce.

The First World War was in fact followed by attempted revolutions in Germany and eastern Europe. With the German and Austro-Hungarian empires wrecked,

Attempted revolutions in Europe

socialists and liberals of all descriptions strove to establish new regimes. Among socialists the old differences persisted, between socialists or social democrats favoring gradual, nonviolent, and parliamentary methods and a more extreme group who saw in postwar disintegration a chance to realize the international proletarian revolution. The first group looked upon the Bolshevik Revolution with horror; the second looked upon it with admiration. The first group included not only trade union officials and practical socialist politicians but also such prewar giants of Marxian exegesis as Karl Kautsky and Eduard Bernstein. Even Kautsky, who had upheld pure Marxism against the revisionism of Bernstein, could not stomach the methods of Lenin. The mass of European socialists, with their fiercest leaders removed, were to remain characterized by relative moderation. Marxist in principle, they were in fact more than ever wedded to gradual, peaceable, and parliamentary methods. The second group, radical Leninists, continued to agitate for the forcible overthrow of European capitalism and European political institutions.

Lenin and the Bolsheviks, though absorbed in their own revolution, gave all possible aid to the radical fringe of left socialists in Europe. They sent large sums of money to Germany, to Sweden, to Italy. When the Bolshevik Karl Radek was arrested in Berlin he was said to have a secret plan for proletarian revolution in all central Europe in his possession. But the chief instrument of world revolution, created in March 1919, was the Third or Communist International.

The Founding of the Third International

The Second International, which since its foundation in 1889 had met every two or three years until 1914, held its first postwar meeting at Berne in 1919. It represented socialist parties and labor organizations of all countries. The Berne meeting was stormy, for a small minority vehemently demanded "revolution as in Russia, socialization of property as in Russia, application of Marxism as in Russia." Overruled at Berne, they repaired to Moscow and there founded a new International in conjunction with the Russian Communist party, and with Lenin and the Russians dominating it completely. It was Lenin's hope, by founding a new International of his own, to discredit moderate socialism and to claim for the Communists the true line of succession from the First International of Karl Marx.

The Third International

The first congress of the Third International in 1919 was somewhat haphazard, but at the second, in 1920, the extreme left parties of 37 countries were represented. The Russian party was supposedly only one component. Actually, it supplied most of the personnel and most of the funds; the Bolshevik Zinoviev was its first president, remaining in this office until his disgrace as a Trotskyist in 1927. The Third or Communist International—the Comintern—was in part a spontaneous rallying of Marxists from all countries who accepted the Bolshevik Revolution as the true fruition of Marxism and so were willing to follow the Russian lead; but, even more, it was the creation and weapon of the Bolsheviks themselves, by which they wished to discredit and isolate the moderate socialists and bring about world revolution. Of all enemies the Communists hated the socialists most, reserving for them even stronger epithets than they bestowed upon capitalists and imperialists, because Communists and socialists were competing for the same objective, the leadership of the world's working class.

Parties adhering to the Comintern were obliged to drop the old name "socialist" and call themselves Communist. They were obliged to accept strong international centralization. Where the Second International had been a loose federation and its congresses were hardly more than forums, the Third International put strong powers in the hands of its Executive Committee, whose orders the Communist parties of all countries had to obey. Since there was a kind of interlocking directorate by which members of the Central Committee of the party in Russia sat also as members of the Executive Committee of the Third International, the top Communists in Russia had, in the Comintern, an "apparatus" by which they could produce desired effects in many countries—the use of party members to penetrate labor unions, foment strikes, propagandize ideas, or interfere in elections.

The second congress of the International, in 1920, endorsed a program of Twenty-One Points, written by Lenin. These included the requirements that each national party must call itself Communist, repudiate "reformist" socialism, propagandize labor unions and get Communists into the important union offices, infiltrate the army, impose an iron discipline upon members, require submission to the orders of the international Executive, use both legal channels and secret underground methods, and expel promptly any member not hewing to the party line. Making no pretense of respect for parliamentary democracy, the second congress ruled that "the only question can be that of utilizing bourgeois state institutions for their own destruction." The Comintern was not an assemblage of humanitarians engaged in welfare work; it was a weapon for revolution, organized by revolutionaries who knew what revolution was.

Lenin's Twenty-One Points

For several years the U.S.S.R., using the Comintern or more conventional diplomatic channels, promoted world revolution as best it could. Communists from many countries went to Russia for indoctrination. Native-born or Russian agents proceeded to the Dutch Indies, to China, to Europe, to America. Until 1927 the Chinese revolutionists welcomed assistance from Moscow; the Russian Borodin became an adviser in their affairs. In 1924, in England, publication of the "Zinoviev letter," in which, at least allegedly, the Comintern urged British workers to provoke revolution, let to a great electoral victory for the Conservative party. The Bolshevik menace, real and imagined, produced everywhere a strong reaction. It was basic to the rise of fascism described in the following chapters.

Promoting world revolution

In 1927, with the suppression of Trotskyism and world revolutionism in Russia, and with the concentration under Stalin on a program of building socialism in one country, the Comintern moderated its activities. In 1935, as fascist dictators became noisily bellicose and threatened the Soviet Union, the U.S.S.R. through the Comintern instructed all Communist parties, each in its own country, to enter into coalitions with socialists and advanced liberals in what were called "popular fronts," to combat fascism and reaction and so support the national defense of their own countries. During the Second World War (in 1943), as a gesture of goodwill to Great Britain and the United States, the U.S.S.R. abolished the Comintern entirely. It reappeared for a few years from 1947 to 1956 under a new name, the Communist Information Bureau or Cominform, and was then disbanded.

It was not through the Comintern that the U.S.S.R. exerted its greatest influence on the world in the years after 1917. It exerted its influence by the massive fact of its very existence. By 1939 it was clear that a new type of economic system had appeared. Before 1917 no one in Europe or Asia had thought that anything was to be learned from Russia. Twenty years later even critics of the U.S.S.R. feared that it might represent the wave of the future. Its sheer

The U.S.S.R.'s impact

power was soon demonstrated in the Second World War. Marxism was no longer merely a theory; there was an actual society, embracing a sixth of the globe, which called itself Marxist.

In every country those who were most critical of capitalist institutions compared them unfavorably to those of the Soviet Union. Most of those who in the 1930s hoped to profit from the Soviet experience were not actually Communist. Some believed that something like Soviet results might be obtained without the use of Soviet methods, which were dismissed as typically Russian, a deplorable heritage from the tsars. With the appearance of Communism and Communist parties, socialism and socialist ideas seemed in contrast to be middling and respectable. Everywhere in the 1930s the idea of planning began to find favor. Workers obtained more security against the fluctuations of capitalism. The so-called "backward" peoples, especially in Asia, were particularly impressed by the achievement of the U.S.S.R., which had shown how a traditional society could modernize without falling under the influence of foreign capital or foreign guidance.

For a long time the Communist party in the Soviet Union presented itself as the leader of world revolution and tried to exert control over Communist parties in all other countries. This became increasingly difficult. Over the years the U.S.S.R. pursued diplomatic and military policies and engaged in acts of aggression and territorial expansion, such as the tsarist state might have done. By the late 1980s the U.S.S.R. was no longer an innovative, or some would say, a viable society. Its economic system was in a shambles; the component republics demanded autonomy or independence. The revelation from within the Soviet Union itself of the persecution and deaths of millions of innocent victims, along with the restiveness of its own nationalities, undermined its role as leader of oppressed peoples elsewhere. European Communist parties proclaimed their independence from Moscow and a new form of communism emerged in 1949 in the People's Republic of China. Yet all Communist parties, including the Chinese, are derived from Marxism and from the Russian Revolution of 1917, once hailed as the first great victory over capitalism and imperialism. It was thus a revolution that profoundly influenced fervent supporters and passionate opponents throughout much of the twentieth century. But the repressive political system, stifling cultural policies, and economic failures of the Soviet state ultimately produced a widespread hostility to Communism, even among many of its former advocates and supporters.

Waning Soviet influence in later years

Chapter 19

THE APPARENT
VICTORY
OF DEMOCRACY

We have followed events in the Soviet Union to about the year 1939 but have left the story of Europe and the rest of the world at the signing of the peace treaties of 1919. We must deal now with the period of just 20 years that elapsed between the formal close of the First World War in 1919 and the outbreak of the Second World War in 1939. In these 20 years the world made a dizzy passage from confidence to disillusionment and from hope to fear. It went through a few years of superficial prosperity, abruptly followed by unparalleled economic disaster. For a time, in the 1920s, democracy seemed to be advancing almost everywhere; then, in the 1930s, dictatorship began to spread. Let us first examine the apparent triumphs of democracy in the 1920s, turn next to the devastating worldwide effects of the Great Depression that began in 1929, and then, in the following chapter, trace the painful decade of the 1930s.

97. THE ADVANCE OF DEMOCRACY AFTER 1919

The first years following the war were troubled. Even the victors faced serious difficulties in reconversion from war to peace. Veterans demobilized from the huge armies found themselves unemployed and psychologically restless. Farms and factories geared to maximum production during the war faced a sudden disappearance of markets. They produced more than could now be sold, so that the war was followed by a sharp postwar depression, which, however, had run its course by 1922. Basically, the economic position even of the victors was seriously damaged, for the war had disjointed the world of 1914, in which industrial western Europe had lived by exchange with eastern Europe and with overseas countries.

Chapter emblem: Mahatma Gandhi leading a group of nonviolent protestors in 1930 during the political campaign for India's national independence.

Gains of Democracy and Social Democracy

The war, President Wilson had said, was fought to make the world safe for democracy. Political democracy now made advances everywhere. The new states that emerged from the war all adopted written constitutions and universal suffrage. Democracy made advances even in countries that had long been in large measure democratic. Great Britain dropped the last barriers to universal male suffrage in 1918. The most conspicuous innovation was the growing enfranchisement of women. We have seen how the women's suffrage movement in Great Britain achieved an important breakthrough in 1918, when women received a somewhat restricted right to vote; in 1928 the restrictions were dropped and the vote was granted on an equal basis with men. In 1920, through an amendment to the constitution, female suffrage became general in the United States. Women voted also in Germany and in most of the new states of Europe. In the Soviet Union women received the vote on an equal basis with men after the revolution in 1917.

In most European countries the successors of the old prewar socialists gained in strength. With the left wings of the old socialists generally seceding, calling themselves

The 19th amendment to the Constitution gave American women the right to vote in all elections. This poster, which was published by the League of Women Voters shortly after the amendment was approved in 1920, urged women to use their new voting rights by going to the polls.

(Hulton Getty)

Communists, and affiliated with each other and with Moscow in the Communist International, the European socialists or social democrats were preponderantly parties of peaceable or revisionist Marxism, entirely willing to carry on the class conflict by parliamentary and legislative methods. Labor unions, with new self-confidence gained from the role they had played in the war, grew in membership, prestige, and importance.

Social legislation that before the war would have seemed radical was now enacted in many places. An eight-hour legal working day became common, and government-sponsored insurance programs against sickness, accident, and old age were either adopted or extended; an act of 1930, in France, insured almost 10 million workers. An air of progressive democracy pervaded Europe and the European world. The social service, or welfare, state, already under way in the late nineteenth century, was becoming more firmly established.

Social legislation enacted

Only in Italy in the early postwar years, of the states that might have been expected to continue their prewar democratic gains, did democracy receive a sharp setback. Italy had been a parliamentary state since 1861 and had introduced a democratic male suffrage in the elections of 1913. In 1919 the Italians held their second such elections. But Italian democracy soon abruptly ended. In 1922 an agitator named Benito Mussolini, leading a movement which he called Fascism (thereby adding a new word to the world's political vocabulary), ended Italian parliamentary government and founded his Fascist regime. Lenin had already created the first single-party state; Mussolini became the first of the dictators of postwar Europe outside the Soviet Union. Fascist Italy, in the 1920s, was the chief exception in what seemed to be a rising tide of democracy.

Mussolini

The New States of Central and East-Central Europe

In central and east-central Europe—in Germany, in the territory of the former Austro-Hungarian empire, and in the western fringe of former tsarist Russia—new states and new governments struggled to establish themselves. The new postwar states included, besides republican Germany, the four successor states to the Habsburg empire—Austria, Hungary, Czechoslovakia, and Yugoslavia; and the five states that had broken away from the Russian empire—Poland, Finland, Estonia, Latvia, and Lithuania (see map, pp. 694–695). The other small states in eastern Europe, Romania, Bulgaria, Greece, and Albania, had already been independent before 1914; their boundaries underwent some modification and their governments underwent considerable reorganization after the war. Turkey, the successor to the Ottoman Empire, was also a new republic.

The new states were to a large extent accidents of the war. Nowhere, except possibly in Poland, did they represent a deeply felt, long-maturing, or widespread revolutionary sentiment. Only an infinitesimal number of Germans in 1914 would have voted for a republic. Even among the nationalities of Austria-Hungary in 1914 few persons would have chosen the complete breakup of the Habsburg empire. The republicans, moderate socialists, agrarians, or nationalists who now found themselves in power had to improvise governments for which there had been little preparation. They had to contend with reactionaries, monarchists, and members of the old aristocracy. They had also to deal with the real revolutionaries, who, inspired by Lenin's success, hoped to bring about the dictatorship of the proletariat. A Communist revolt broke out in Germany in 1919 but was quickly suppressed; Soviet regimes were actually set up but were soon crushed in Hungary and in the German state of Bavaria; and as late as 1923 there was a Communist uprising in the German state of Saxony.

Accidents of war

The new states all embodied the principle of national self-determination, which held that each nationality should enjoy political sovereignty—one nation, one government. But people in this region were and always had been locally intermixed. Each of the new states therefore included minority nationalities; for, with the exception of an exchange of populations between Greece and Turkey, arranged in 1923, there was no thought of the actual physical removal of "alien" groups. Poland, Czechoslovakia, and Yugoslavia were the most composite of the new states. Poland and Czechoslovakia each had many disaffected Germans. In Czechoslovakia the Slovaks resented Czech domination and in Yugoslavia Croatian and other separatist movements opposed Serb domination of the new Yugoslav state.

Self-determination

Nevertheless, despite economic and nationalist troubles, the new states and governments attempted at the outset to make themselves democratic. Except for the German republic they were all relatively small. All the newly created states were republics except Yugoslavia, which was under the older Serbian dynasty. Hungary started out in 1918 as a republic, but the attempt of the Communist leader Béla Kun to found a Hungarian Soviet Republic in 1919 brought back the counterrevolutionaries who restored the Habsburg monarchy in principle, though they were prevented by foreign pressure from restoring the king in person. Hungary emerged in 1920 as a monarchy with a perennially vacant throne, under an authoritarian regency exercised by Admiral Horthy. All smaller states of Europe, including Hungary, possessed at least the machinery of democracy until the 1930s; that is, they had constitutions, parliaments, elections, and a diversity of political parties. If civil liberty was sometimes violated, the right to civil liberty was not denied; and if elections were sometimes rigged, they were at least in principle supposed to be free.

Economic Problems of Eastern Europe; Land Reform

Eastern Europe for centuries had been an agrarian region of large landed estates, which supported on the one hand a wealthy landowning aristocracy of almost feudal outlook, and on the other an impoverished mass of agricultural workers with little or no property of their own. The landed aristocracy had been the chief support of the Austro-Hungarian empire and an important pillar of the old order in the tsarist empire and in eastern Prussia. The mass of the rural population, through all this region, had been free from serfdom, or released from subjection to manorial landlords, only since the middle of the preceding century. The middle class of business and professional people was small except in Austria and Bohemia, the western portion of Czechoslovakia. In general, the whole region was conscious of lagging behind western Europe, not only in industry, factories, railroads, and great cities, but also in literacy, schooling, reading habits, health, death rates, length of life, and material standard of living.

The new states set out to modernize themselves, generally on the model of the West. They introduced democratic and constitutional ideas. They put up protective tariffs, behind which they tried to develop factories and industries of their own. But the new national boundaries created difficulties. Where Europe in 1913 had had 6,000 miles of frontiers, after the war it had almost 10,000, and all the increase was in eastern Europe. Goods circulated much less easily. Protected industries in the old agricultural regions produced inefficiently and at high cost. Old and established industries, in Austria, Czechoslovakia, and western Poland, cut off by the new frontiers and new tariffs from their former markets, fell upon hard times.

Obstacles to modernization

The working class of Vienna lived in misery. Vienna, a city of 2 million persons, formerly the capital of an empire of 50 million, was now the capital of a republic of 6 million. In Czechoslovakia the German minority living in the Sudetenland complained that in hard times the German businesspeople and workers, because of government policies, always suffered more than their Czech counterparts. Economically, the carving up of eastern Europe into a dozen independent states was self-defeating.

The greatest of reforms undertaken by the new east-European states was the reform of landownership. Although it far from solved basic economic problems in the area, it did have substantial effect on the pattern of land distribution. The whole traditional agrarian base of society was overturned. The work of the revolutions of 1848, which, in the Habsburg lands, had liberated the peasants but left them landless, was now carried a step further. The example of the Russian Revolution gave a powerful stimulus, for in Russia in 1917 peasants had driven off landlords, and Communists won a hearing among discontented and propertyless peasants from Finland to the Balkans. Not until 1929, it should be recalled, did the Soviet Union embark on the collectivization of agriculture; until then, communism appeared to favor the small individual farmer. But it may be said with equal truth that the model for agrarian reform lay in the West, especially in France, the historic land of the small peasant proprietor.

Land reform

Land reform worked out differently in different countries. In the Baltic states the big properties belonged almost entirely to German families, the "Baltic barons," descendants of the medieval Teutonic Knights. In Estonia, Latvia, and Lithuania the nationalist dislike for Germans made it easier to liquidate landlords. Small farms here became the rule. In Czechoslovakia over half the arable land was transferred from large to small owners; here again, the fact that many great landowners had been German, in some cases since the days of the Thirty Years' War in the seventeenth century, made the operation more palatable, though it inflamed the German minority in Bohemia. In Romania and Yugoslavia the breakup of large estates, though considerable, was less thorough. In Finland, Bulgaria, and Greece the issue hardly arose, since small landownership was already common. Land reform had least success in Poland and Hungary, where the landed magnates were exceptionally strong and well rooted.

After the land reforms, political parties of peasants or small landholders became the chief democratic force within the various states on the western border of Russia. Often they inclined to socialism, especially since capitalism was associated in their minds with foreign investors and outsiders. On the other hand, the great landowners, the former aristocrats of the prewar empires, whether already expropriated or merely threatened with expropriation, were confirmed in a reactionary outlook. The land reforms did not solve basic economic problems. The new small farms were very small, frequently no more than ten acres. The peasant owners lacked capital, agricultural skill, and knowledge of the market. Farm productivity did not rise. In place of old differences between landlord and tenant there developed new differences between the more comfortable peasants and the proletarian hired hands. The continuance of relative poverty, the obstinacy of reactionary upper classes, the new stresses and strains among the peasants themselves, the economic distortions produced by numerous tariff walls, and the lack of any sustained tradition of self-government all helped to frustrate the democratic experiments launched in the 1920s.

Peasant and smallholder parties

98.   THE GERMAN REPUBLIC AND THE SPIRIT OF LOCARNO

The keystone of Europe was Germany. Germany, too, had its revolution in 1918. But it was a revolution without revolutionaries, a negative revolution caused more by the disappearance of the old than by any vehement arrival of the new. The emperor and the High Command of the army, in the last weeks of the war, had bowed out of the picture, leaving it to others to face defeat and humiliation. For a time, after November 1918, the men in charge of affairs were mainly Social Democrats. The Social Democrats were Marxists, but their Marxism was the tamed, toned down, and revisionist Marxism that had prevailed for 20 years before the advent of Lenin. They were trade union officials and party managers. They could look back, in 1918, on decades spent in developing labor organizations and building up the Social Democratic party, which in 1912 had become the largest single party in the Reichstag. Now, in 1918, they were a cautious and prudent group, essentially conservative, more anxious to preserve what they had already achieved than to launch audacious new social experiments. Before 1917 the Social Democrats considered themselves well to the Left. But the Bolshevik Revolution in Russia, and the emergence of a pro-Bolshevik or Communist element in Germany, put the Social Democrats in the middle. The middle is an awkward spot, especially in disturbed times; the Communists regarded the Social Democrats as reactionaries, despicable traitors to the working-class movement; whereas the true reactionaries, recruited from old monarchists, army officers, Junker landowners, and big business groups, saw in social democracy, or professed to see in it, a dangerous flirtation with Bolshevism.

The middle group in Germany, the Social Democrats reinforced by the Catholic Center party and others, was more afraid of the Left than of the Right. They were appalled, in 1918 and 1919, by the stories brought out of Russia, not merely by fugitive bourgeois or tsarist aristocrats, but by refugee Social Democrats, Mensheviks, and anti-Leninist Bolsheviks, many of whom the socialists had long known and trusted in the Second International. In January 1919 the Spartacists,[1] led by Karl Liebknecht and Rosa Luxemburg, attempted to bring about a proletarian revolution in Germany, like that in Russia. Lenin and the Russian Bolsheviks aided them. For a time, there seemed to be a possibility that Germany might go communist, that the Spartacists might succeed in imposing a dictatorship of the proletariat. But the Social Democratic Provisional Government crushed the Spartacist uprising, turning for that purpose to demobilized army officers and volunteer vigilantes recruited from the disbanding army. The Spartacist leaders Liebknecht and Luxemburg were arrested and shot while in police custody. The events of "Spartacus Week" widened a chasm between Social Democrats and Communists.

The Spartacists

Shortly after, elections were held for a National Constituent Assembly. No single party received a majority, but the Social Democrats were the leading party. A coalition of Social Democrats, Center party, and liberal democrats dominated the Assembly. After several months of deliberations at the city of Weimar, in July 1919, a constitution was adopted establishing a democratic republic. The Weimar Republic (as the regime in Germany from 1919 to the advent of Hitler in 1933 is called) was soon threatened ominously from the

---

[1]So named from Spartacus, a Roman slave who led a slave revolt in south Italy in 72 B.C.

The Spartacists in Germany tried to provoke a Soviet-style, Communist revolution in early 1919, but their uprising was suppressed by the Social Democratic Provisional Government. These people are burning political pamphlets that they had seized from Spartacist newspaper offices.

(Hulton Getty)

Right. In 1920 a group of disaffected army officers staged a *putsch,* or armed revolt, put the republican government to flight, and attempted to place a puppet of their own, one Dr. Kapp, at the head of the state. The Berlin workers, by turning off public utilities, stopped the Kapp *putsch* and saved the republic. But the Weimar government never took sufficiently firm measures to put down private armed bands led by reactionary or outspokenly antidemocratic agitators. One of these was soon to be Adolf Hitler, who as early as 1923 staged an abortive revolt in Munich. Nor, being democratic and liberal, did it ever deny the rights of election to the Reichstag, and of free speech in the Reichstag and in public, either to Communists or to antidemocratic reactionaries.

The Weimar Republic was in principle highly democratic. The constitution embodied all the devices then favored by the most advanced democrats, not only universal suffrage, including the vote for women, but also proportional representation and the initiative, referendum, and recall. But

The Weimar Republic

except for the legal eight-hour day and a few other such safeguards to the workers' welfare (and traditional demands of organized labor) the republic of which the Social Democrats were the main architects in its formative years was remote from anything socialistic. No industries were nationalized. No property changed hands. No land laws or agrarian reforms were undertaken, as in the new states of eastern Europe; the East Elbian Junkers remained untouched in their landed estates. There was almost no confiscation even of the property of the former Kaiser and other ruling dynasties of Bismarck's federal empire. The very statues of emperors, kings, princes, and grand dukes were left standing in the streets and squares. Officials, civil servants, police agents, professors, schoolteachers of old imperial Germany remained at their respective duties. The army, though limited by the Versailles treaty to 100,000 men, remained the old army in miniature, with all its essential organs intact, and lacking only in mass. The soldiers were peasant youths enlisted for long terms and soon formed to German and Prussian military traditions. In the officer corps the old professional and aristocratic influences remained strong.

Never had there been a revolution so mild, so reasonable, so tolerant. There was no terror, no fanaticism, no stirring faith, no expropriation, no émigrés. There had in truth been no revolution at all, in the sense in which England, France, the United States, Russia, and other countries, either recently or in the more distant past, had experienced revolutions.

The German Democracy and Versailles

The supreme question for Europe and the world was how Germany would adjust to the postwar conditions. How would the Germans accept the new internal regime of democracy? How would they accept the new German frontiers and other provisions of the Treaty of Versailles? The two questions were unfortunately interconnected. The Weimar Republic and the Treaty of Versailles were both products of the defeat of Germany in the war. There were many in Germany who favored democracy, notably the numerous Social Democrats, and many more possibly could have been won over to it, given time and favorable conditions. But no one, not even the Social Democrats, accepted the Treaty of Versailles or the new German frontiers as either just or final. If democracy in Germany meant the perpetual acceptance of the treaty without amendment, or if it meant economic distress or hardship which could either reasonably or unreasonably be explained as consequences of the treaty, then democracy would lose such appeal as it had for the Germans.

The German republicans, we have seen, protested against the Versailles treaty before signing, and signed only under pressure. The Allies continued the wartime naval blockade after the armistice; this confirmed, in German eyes, the argument that the Treaty of Versailles was a *diktat,* a dictated peace, Carthaginian, ruthless, and vengeful. The "war guilt" clause, while it perhaps on the one hand satisfied a peculiar Anglo-American sense of morality, on the other hand offended a peculiar German sense of honor. Neither the reparations demanded of them, nor the new frontiers, were accepted by the Germans as settled. Reparations they regarded as a perpetual mortgage on their future. They generally expected, some day, to revise their eastern frontier, recover at least the Polish corridor, and merge with German-speaking Austria.

The Versailles treaty as "diktat"

The French lived in fear of the day when Germany would recover. Their plans for their own security and for the collective security of Europe against a German revival had been disappointed. They had been unable to detach the Rhineland from Germany. The United States Senate had refused to ratify the treaty, signed at Paris by Wilson, by which the United States was to guarantee France against German invasion in the future. Both Britain and the United States showed a tendency to isolation, to pull away from the Continent, to get back to "normalcy," to work mainly for a restored trade in which a strong Germany would be a large customer. The League of Nations, of which the United States was not a member and in which every member nation had a veto, offered little assurance of safety to the French. The French began to form alliances against a potentially resurgent Germany with Poland, Czechoslovakia, and other East European states. They insisted also on German payment of reparations. The amount of reparations, left unstated in the treaty, was fixed by a Reparations Commission in 1921 at 132 billion gold marks (the equivalent of $35 billion), a sum that even non-German economists said was more than Germany could possibly pay.

French fear

The Weimar government in these circumstances looked to the Soviet Union, which had been no party to the Versailles treaty and claimed no reparations. The Soviet government meanwhile, concluding from the failure of proletarian revolution in Germany and Hungary that the time was not ripe for the sovietizing of Europe, prepared to enter into normal diplomatic relations with established governments. Germany and the Soviet Union, despite ideological repugnance, thus signed the treaty of Rapallo in 1922. In the following years the Soviet Union obtained needed manufactures from Germany, and German factories and workers

Soviet-German relations

Le Moulin de La Galette
by **Pierre-Auguste Renoir** (French, 1841–1919)
Renoir helped create the impressionist style of painting, which used contrasting colors to convey subtle variations of sunlight and shadows. This painting of dancers and friends at a popular Parisian dancehall is an example of the impressionists' interest in the everyday life and leisure of late nineteenth-century French society.
(Scala/Art Resource, NY)

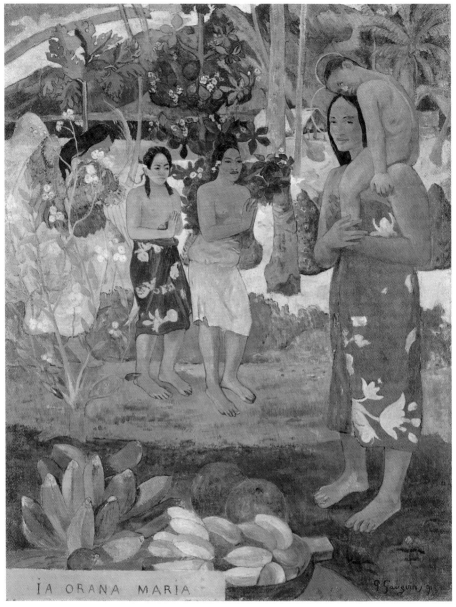

Ia Orana Maria
by **Paul Gauguin** (French, 1848–1903)
Gauguin moved to Tahiti in the early 1890s, searching for non-European alternatives
to the culture and art he had known in France. His use of color and his portrayal of
Tahitians influenced avant-garde European artists, but Gauguin also continued to
draw on (classical) Western artistic themes. The title of this painting means "Hail
Mary," an allusion to the Biblical Annunciation in which the angel Gabriel told the
Virgin Mary that she would give birth to a child.

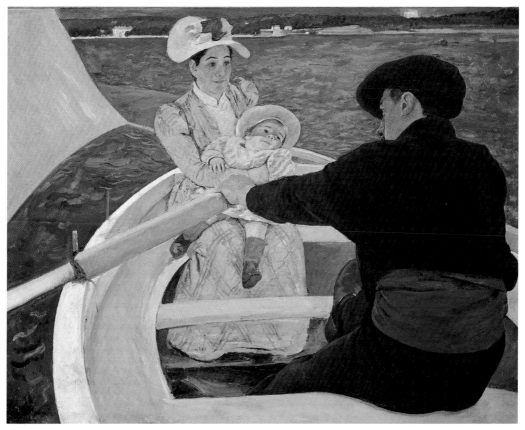

The Boating Party, 1893
by **Mary Cassatt** (American, then in France, 1844–1926)
Cassatt developed her most distinctive works under the influence of both Impressionism and the traditions of Japanese art. She painted many pictures of mothers with their children, including this colorful and slightly mysterious image of a man rowing two people across a European lake.

Self-Portrait with Beret, 1898-1899
by **Paul Cézanne** (French, 1839–1906)
Cézanne went beyond early Impressionist art to develop a new emphasis on the shapes or contours of natural objects, buildings, and people. He also applied his innovative techniques to portraits of himself, striving to depict his identity as a painter through both the style and the content of such works.

2-4

Panel for Edwin R. Campbell No. 1, 1914
by **Vasily Kandinsky** (Russian, then in Germany and France, 1866–1944)
Kandinsky was one of the first artists to paint purely abstract works. This painting,
which Kandinsky completed in 1914, conveys an early twentieth-century artistic
desire to use shapes and colors without reference to physical objects. Modernist
artists wanted their colors to represent a personal vision rather than objective,
external realities.

(Vasily Kandinsky, *Panel for Edwin R. Campbell No. 1.* 1914. Oil on canvas, 64 x 31 1/2" [162.5 x 80
cm]. The Museum of Modern Art, New York. Mrs. Simon Guggenheim Fund. Photograph ©2001 The
Museum of Modern Art, New York/©2001 Artists Rights Society [ARS], New York/ADAGP, Paris)

Composition With The Ace of Clubs
by **Georges Braque** (French, 1883–1963)
This painting is an example of the Cubist movement in the early twentieth century. Braque and
the Cubists broke up the visual world into lines and planes, stressing almost mathematical
patterns and multiple perspectives rather than the bursts of color or pure abstractions that
appeared in other works of modern art.

The Assembly Line
by **Diego Rivera** (Mexican, 1886–1957)

Twentieth-century artists have often depicted modern social realities as well as personal visions or abstract uses of color. This detail from a mural, Detroit Industry, that Diego Rivera painted in Detroit during the 1930s emphasizes stark social divisions between the workers on an automobile assembly line and the visitors who are watching them work.

(Mural: Detroit Industry, South Wall [detail], 1932-1933. Diego M. Rivera, Gift of Edsel B. Ford. Photograph © 2001 The Detroit Institute of Arts. Photograph: Cenidiap/INBA, Mexico. Reproduction authorized by Nacional de Bellas Artes y Literatura/© 2001 Banco de México, Diego Rivera & Frida Kahlo Museums Trust. Av. Cinco de Mayo No. 2, Col. Centro, Del. Cuauhtémoc 06059. México, D.F.)

The Survivor
by **George Grosz** (German, then American, 1893–1959)
Grosz was a refugee from Nazi Germany. This picture, which he painted in 1945, vividly portrays the horrors of modern warfare, the brutal collapse of civilization, and the terrified emotions of an isolated, filthy survivor. Note the symbolism of a broken swastika in the arrangement of the man's body and the debris.

were kept busy by orders from the Soviets. The German army dispatched officers and technicians to give instruction to the Red Army. Obliged by the Treaty of Versailles to restrict its activities, the German army was in fact able, through its work in Russia and through a number of subterfuges at home, to maintain a high standard of training, planning, technical knowledge, and familiarity with new weapons and equipment.

Reparations, the German Inflation of 1923, Recovery

The French, blocked in the attempt to collect reparations and assisted by the Belgians, in 1923 sent units of the French army to occupy the industrial sites of the Ruhr valley. The Germans responded by general strikes and passive resistance. To sustain the workers the Weimar government paid them benefits, grinding paper money off the printing presses for this purpose. Germany, like other belligerent countries, had suffered from inflation during and after the war; neither the imperial nor the Weimar government had been willing to impose heavier taxes to offset it. But what now swept Germany was different from ordinary inflation. It was of catastrophic and utterly ruinous proportions. Paper money became literally worthless. By the end of 1923 it took over 4 trillion paper marks to equal a dollar.

This inflation brought far more of a social revolution than the fall of the Hohenzollern empire had ever done. Debtors paid off debts in worthless money. Creditors received baskets full of meaningless paper. Salaries even when raised lagged behind the soaring cost of living. Annuities, pensions, *A social revolution* proceeds of insurance policies, savings accounts in the banks, income from bonds and mortgages—every form of revenue which had been arranged for at some time in the past, and which often represented the economy, foresight, and personal planning of many years—now turned to nothing. The middle class was pauperized and demoralized. Middle-class people were now materially in much the position of workers and proletarians. Their whole view of life, however, made it impossible for them to identify themselves with the laboring class or to accept its Marxist or socialist ideologies. They had lost faith in society itself, in the future, in the old burgher codes of self-reliance and rational planning of their own lives in an understandable world. A kind of moral void was created, with nothing for them to believe in, hope for, or respect.

The inflation, however, by wiping out all outstanding indebtedness within the country, made it possible, once the losses were written off and accepted, to start up economic production afresh. The United States was persuaded to play a reluctant role. The United States, in these years, demanded payment of the huge war debts owed to it by the Allies. The Allies—Britain, France, Belgium—insisted that they could not pay debts to the United States unless they collected reparations from Germany. In 1924 the Dawes Plan, named for the American Charles G. Dawes, was instituted in *The Dawes Plan* Germany to assure the flow of reparations. By the Dawes Plan the French evacuated the Ruhr, the reparations payments were cut down, and arrangements were made for the German republic to borrow abroad. A good deal of American private capital was invested in Germany in the following years, both in German government bonds and in German industrial enterprises. Gradually, so at least it seemed, Germany was put on its feet. For four or five years the Weimar Republic even enjoyed a bustling prosperity, and there was a good deal of new construction in roads, housing, factories, and ocean liners. But the prosperity rested in good measure on foreign loans, and the Great Depression that began in 1929 reopened all the old questions.

The Spirit of Locarno

These years of economic prosperity were years also of relative international calm. Yet none of the fundamental international issues were addressed or resolved. The universal German hatred for the Treaty of Versailles elicited no concessions from the Allies. Conceivably, had the Allies been willing at this time to amend the treaty by international agreement, they might have taken wind from the sails of nationalistic rabble-rousers in Germany and so spared themselves much later grief. It may be, however, that no possible concession would have sufficed. The great problem was to prevent a German overthrow of the treaty structure by violence, especially in eastern Europe where the Germans regarded the new frontiers as basically subject to reconsideration. After the Ruhr incident, and adoption of the Dawes Plan, a group of moderate and peace-loving men shaped the foreign policy of the principal countries—Gustav Stresemann in Germany, Édouard Herriot and Aristide Briand in France, Ramsay MacDonald in England.

The charter of the League of Nations provided for international sanctions against potential aggressors. Like the system of congresses after the Peace of Vienna, the League was supposed to assure peaceable compliance with the peace treaties, or their modification without resort to force. No one expected the League, by any authority of its own, to prevent war between Great Powers, but the League achieved various minor pacifications in the 1920s, and in any case its headquarters at Geneva offered a convenient meeting place in which statesmen could talk.

The Locarno treaties

As a further assurance against war, in 1925 at Locarno, the European powers signed a number of treaties. These marked the highest point in international goodwill reached between the two World Wars. Germany signed a treaty with France and Belgium guaranteeing their respective frontiers unconditionally. It signed arbitration treaties with Poland and Czechoslovakia—not guaranteeing these frontiers as they stood, but undertaking to attempt changes in them only by international discussion, agreement, or arbitration. France signed treaties with Poland and Czechoslovakia promising military aid if they were attacked by Germany. France thus fortified its policy of balancing German power in the East by its own diplomatic alliances and by supporting the Little Entente, as the alliance of Czechoslovakia, Yugoslavia, and Romania was called. Great Britain "guaranteed"—that is, promised military aid in the event of violation—the frontiers of Belgium and France against Germany. It did not give an equivalent guarantee with respect to Czechoslovakia or Poland. The British took the view, in 1925, that their own security would be threatened by German expansion westward, but not by German expansion to the east. It was on the borders of Czechoslovakia and Poland, 14 years later, that the Second World War began. Had Britain gone along with France in 1925 in guaranteeing these two countries, then abided by the guarantee, the Second World War might possibly have been prevented. On the other hand, no war ever depends on any single decision; it is the accumulation of many decisions that matters.

In 1925 people talked with relief of the "spirit of Locarno." In 1928 international harmony was again strengthened when the French foreign minister Briand and the United States Secretary of State Frank B. Kellogg arranged for the Pact of Paris. Ultimately signed by 65 nations, it condemned recourse to war for the solution of international controversies. Although no measures of enforcement were provided and a number of reservations were added before certain countries signed, the pact solemnly affirmed the will of the nations to renounce war as an instrument of national policy.

In the mid-1920s the outlook was indeed full of hope. At Locarno, Germany had of its own volition (and not by the *diktat* of Versailles) accepted its borders both east and west, to the extent of abjuring violence and unilateral action even in the east. In 1926 Germany joined the League of Nations. Germany appeared to be a going concern as a democratic republic. Democracy seemed to work, as well as could be expected, in most of the new states of eastern Europe, and Communist Russia itself had halted its postwar revolutionary offensive. The world was again prosperous, or seemed to be so. World production was at or above the prewar level. In 1925 the world's production of raw materials, it was estimated, was 17 percent greater than in 1913. World trade, by 1929, measured in hard money— gold—had almost doubled since 1913. The war and the postwar troubles were remembered as a nightmare from which Europe had finally escaped. It seemed that, after all, the world had been made safe for democracy.

A hopeful outlook

But complacency was shattered by the great world depression, by the growth of a malignant nationalism in Germany, due in part to the depression, and by the assertion of a new militancy in Japan, which also was not unrelated to the depression. But let us turn first to the postwar years in Asia.

99. ANTI-IMPERIALIST MOVEMENTS IN ASIA

Resentments in Asia

The peoples of Asia had never been satisfied with the position in which the great European expansion of the nineteenth century had placed them. Increasingly they condemned everything associated with "imperialism." In this respect there was little difference between countries actually governed by Europeans as parts of European empires in the nineteenth century, such as British India, the Netherlands Indies, French Indochina (or the American Philippines), and countries that remained nominally independent under their own government, such as China, Persia, and the Ottoman Empire. In the former, as political consciousness awakened, there was objection to the monopoly of Europeans in the important offices of government. In the latter, there was objection to the special rights and privileges enjoyed by Europeans, the widespread impounding of customs revenues to pay foreign debts, the capitulations in Turkey, the extraterritorial rights in China, the spheres of influence in Persia which divided the country between British and Russians.

By imperialism, in either case, aroused Asians meant a system whereby the affairs of their own country were conducted, its resources were exploited, its people were employed, for the benefit of foreigners, Europeans, or white people. They meant the system of absentee capitalism, by which the plantations, docks, or factories before their eyes, and on which they themselves labored, were the property of owners thousands of miles away whose main interest in them was a regular flow of profits. They meant the constant threat that an alien civilization would disintegrate and eat away their own ancient cultures. They meant the burden of having to speak a European language or the calamity of having to fight in wars originated by Europeans. And they meant the airs of superiority assumed by whites, the race consciousness exhibited by all Westerners, though perhaps most of all by the British and Americans, the color line that was everywhere drawn, the attitudes varying between contempt and condescension, the relation of native "boy" and European "sahib." Imperialism to them signified the gentlemen's clubs in Calcutta to which no Indian was ever admitted, the

Imperialism in Asia

hotels in Shanghai from which Chinese were carefully kept out, the park benches in various cities on which no "native" could ever sit. In deeper psychology, as well as in economics and in politics, the revolt of self-conscious Asians was a rebellion against an imperial system that reduced them to social inferiority and humiliation in their own societies.

The revolt against the West was generally ambivalent or two-sided. It was a revolt against Western supremacy, but at the same time, in most cases, those who revolted meant to learn from and imitate the West, in order that, by taking over Western science, industry, organization, and other sources of Western power, they might preserve their own identity and achieve political and economic equality with the Western nation-states. Anti-imperialist movements and intellectuals thus borrowed from Western culture, even as they vehemently rejected Western ideologies that assumed the superiority of European institutions or races.

Anti-imperialist revolts

The crisis in Asia had broken out with the Russo-Japanese War, when an Asian people, in 1905, defeated a great European power for the first time. In 1906 revolution began in Persia, leading to the assembly of the first *majlis,* or parliament. In 1908 the Young Turks staged a successful revolution in Constantinople and summoned a parliamentary assembly to represent all regions then in the Ottoman Empire. In 1911 the revolutionists in China, led by Sun Yat-sen, overthrew the Manchu (or Qing) dynasty and proclaimed the Chinese Republic. In each case the rebels charged their old monarchs—shah, sultan, emperor—with subservience to Western imperialists. In each case they summoned national assemblies on the prevailing democratic model of Europe, and they proposed to revive, modernize, and westernize their countries to the degree necessary to avoid domination by the West.

First World War and Russian Revolution

In the First World War almost all the Asian peoples were somehow involved. The Ottoman Empire, allied with Germany, immediately repudiated all the capitulations, or special legal rights of Europeans. Persia attempted to remain neutral and to get rid of the partition made in 1907 between British and Russian spheres, but it became a battleground of British, Russian, and Turkish forces. China, which joined the Allies, attempted at the peace conference to have the extraterritorial rights in China abolished. We have seen how this request of the Chinese Republic was refused, and how the Allies instead transferred many of the prewar German concessions to the Japanese. The dependent regions of Asia, the Dutch, French, and British possessions, were stimulated economically by the war. The Netherlands Indies, though remaining neutral, increased its output of foodstuffs, oil, and raw materials. India developed its steel industry and textile manufactures and contributed over a million soldiers, combat and service troops, to the British cause. All the dependent regions were stirred by Woodrow Wilson's call to make the world safe for democracy.

The home governments made concessions. They were naturally afraid to go too far; they insisted that their subject peoples were not yet capable of self-government. Huge investments were at stake, and the whole world economy depended on the continuing flow of raw materials from tropical and subtropical countries. But they did compromise. In 1916 the Dutch created a legislative assembly to advise the governor general of the Indies; half its members were Indonesians. In 1917 the British agreed to a measure of self-government in India; an Indian legislative assembly was set up with 140 members, of whom 100 were elected, and in the provinces of British India the number of elected representatives and of local Indian offi-

Home government concessions

cials was increased. The French in 1922 provided for a somewhat similar assembly in Indochina. Thus all three imperial powers, at about the same time, began to experiment with
consultative bodies whose membership was partly elective, partly appointive, and partly
non-European, partly European. The United States introduced an elected assembly in the
Philippine Islands in 1916.

The Russian Revolution added a new stimulus to unrest in Asia. The
Bolsheviks denounced not only capitalism but also imperialism. In Marxist-
Leninist ideology imperialism was an aspect of capitalism, which Lenin
had called the "highest" or "final" phase of capitalist economies. Colonial
peoples also tended to identify the two, not so much for Marxist reasons as

*Bolshevik anti-
imperialism*

because modern capitalism was a foreign or "imperialist" phenomenon in colonial countries, where the ownership and the management of large enterprises were both foreign. Nationalism in Asia, the movement for independence or for more equality with the West, thus
easily shaded off into socialism and the denunciation of capitalistic exploitation. The Bolsheviks were quick to see the advantages for themselves in this situation. As it became clear
that the world revolution, as expected by Lenin, would not soon come to pass in Europe, the
Russian Communists turned to Asia as the theater in which world capitalism might be attacked by a great flanking movement. In September 1920 a "congress of oppressed Eastern
peoples" assembled at Baku, on the coast of the Caspian Sea. Zinoviev, head of the Communist International, called for war upon "the wild beasts of British capitalism." Not much
was accomplished at the conference. But a few radicals from Asian countries in the following years sojourned in Moscow, and a few Communists dispatched from Moscow stirred up
the discontents which existed, quite without Russian instigation, all over Asia.

The postwar situation in Asia was thus extremely fluid. People who were not Communists hailed communism as a liberating force. Anti-Westerners declared that their countries must westernize, at least in certain spheres of science, technology, and social organization. Nationalism overshadowed all other "isms." In the Indian National Congress rich
Indian capitalists worked together with socialist leaders in relative harmony so long as the
common enemy was the British.

The Turkish Revolution: Kemal Atatürk

The most immediately successful of the revolutionary movements was the one in Turkey.
The Young Turks at first, in 1908, had meant to prevent the further dissolution of the Ottoman Empire. This proved to be impossible. In the Balkan wars of 1912–1913 the Ottoman power was almost totally excluded from the Balkan peninsula. In the World War, in
which the Turks were on the losing side, the Arabs with a great deal of British assistance
broke away. After the war, in 1921, the Greeks invaded the Anatolian peninsula. They
dreamed of a greater Greece embracing both sides of the Aegean. Europeans still regarded
Turkey as the sick man of Europe, the Ottoman state as doomed to extinction, and the
Turkish people as barbarous and incompetent. The Allies had agreed in 1915 to partition
Turkey; and after the war the Western powers favored the Greek invasion. Italian and
French forces occupied parts of Anatolia, and Italians, French, and British undertook to
take Constantinople from Turkish rule, though its disposition remained uncertain. In these
circumstances a powerful army officer named Mustapha Kemal rallied Turkish national resistance. Within two years, and with aid from the Soviet Union, the Turks drove the Greeks
and the Western Allies away. They affirmed their hold on the Anatolian peninsula, and on
both shores of the Straits, including Constantinople, which was renamed Istanbul.

*The Turkish
Republic*

The Nationalists, under the energetic drive of Mustapha Kemal, now put through a sweeping revolution. They abolished the sultanate and the caliphate, since the sultan had somewhat compromised himself with foreigners, and was also, as caliph or commander of the faithful, a religious functionary for all Islam and hence a conservative influence. The Turkish Republic was promulgated in 1923.

Where the Ottoman Empire had been a composite organization made up of diverse religious communities, among which the Muslims were the ruling group, the Turkish Republic was conceived as a national state in which the "people," that is, the Turkish people, were sovereign. Universal suffrage was introduced, along with a parliament, a ministry, and a president with strong powers. Non-Turks in Asia Minor now became "foreign" in a way they had not been before. We have seen that the Armenians were deported or massacred during the First World War. The other large non-Turkish and Christian people were the Greeks. After the war about 1.4 million Greeks either fled or were officially transported from Asia Minor to Greece, and, in exchange, some 400,000 Turks residing in northern Greece were transported to Turkey. The exchange of populations caused great hardship, it uprooted most of the Greek element that had lived in Asia Minor since 1000 B.C., and it overwhelmed the impoverished Greek kingdom by obliging it suddenly to absorb a mass of destitute refugees, who were a quarter as numerous as the population of Greece itself. But it enabled the Turkish Republic to acquire a relatively homogeneous population (except for a Kurdish minority in eastern Turkey), and it ended minority disputes between Greece and Turkey until new problems arose after the Second World War.

*Separation
of church
and state*

For the first time in any Muslim country the spheres of government and religion were sharply distinguished. The Turkish Republic affirmed the total separation of church and state. It declared religion to be a private belief, and it tolerated all religions. Government was reorganized on secular and nonreligious principles stemming from the French Revolution. The law of the Koran was thrust aside. The new law was modeled on the Swiss Code, the most recently codified European legislation, itself derived from the Code Napoleon.

Mustapha Kemal urged women to put aside the veil, to come out of the harem, to vote, and to occupy public office. He made polygamy a crime. Men he required by law to discard the fez. He fought against the fez as Peter the Great had fought against the beard, and for the same reason, seeing in it the symbol of conservative and backward habits. The hat, "headgear of civilization," correspondingly became the symbol of progress. The people shifted to Western dress. The Western alphabet became mandatory; literate Turks had to learn to read again, and illiteracy was reduced. The Western calendar and the metric system were adopted. Turks were required to assume hereditary family surnames, like Westerners; Kemal himself took the name Atatürk, or Great Turk. The capital was moved from Istanbul to Ankara. The republic put up a high tariff. In 1933 it adopted a five-year plan for economic development. The Turks, having shaken off foreign influence, were determined not to become again dependent on Western capital or capitalism. The five-year plan provided for mines, railroads, and factories, mainly under government ownership. At the same time, while willing to accept Russian aid against the Western powers, the republic had no patience with communism, which it suppressed. The Turks wanted a modern Turkey—by and for the Turks.

*Persia's
revolution*

Persia experienced a similar revolution, somewhat less drastic. In 1921 Reza Khan, an army officer, overthrew the older ruling dynasty and in 1925 became shah. The old concessions, capitulations, and spheres were done

The president of the new Turkish Republic, Mustapha Kemal Atatürk, sought to reduce the influence of Islam. In this photograph from about 1925, he shows his support for Westernizing policies by wearing European-style clothes and by dancing at his daughter's wedding.

(Hulton Getty)

away with, and the Persian government renegotiated its oil contracts, asserting more control over foreign corporations and receiving a larger return from them in taxes and royalties. In 1935, to emphasize its break with the past, Persia took the name of Iran.

The National Movement in India: Gandhi and Nehru

India at the close of the First World War was on the verge of revolution against British rule. Discontented Indians looked for leadership to Mohandas K. Gandhi, the Mahatma, or Holy One, who in the following decades, though hardly typical of modern Asia, attained a worldwide eminence as the champion of subjected peoples. Gandhi had been educated in England in the 1890s and had practiced law in South Africa, where he became aware of racial discrimination as a worldwide problem. In India, after 1919, he led a movement for self-government, for economic and spiritual independence from Great Britain, and for greater tolerance within India itself both between Hindus and Muslims and between upper-caste Hindus and the depressed outcastes and untouchables. The weapons he favored were those of the spirit only; he preached nonviolence, passive resistance, civil disobedience, and the boycott. He took to self-imposed fasts and hunger strikes to cope with his British jailers and later with the Indians themselves.

Gandhi and his most loyal followers, as the troubles mounted, refused to be elected to or take part in the partially representative institutions that the British cautiously introduced and also boycotted the British economic position in India, by refusing to buy or use goods imported from England.

Gandhi's campaign

The latter touched the British in a sensitive spot. Before the World War half of all exports of British cotton cloth had gone to India. By 1932 this proportion fell to a quarter. Gandhi turned against all industrialism, even the mechanized industry that was growing up in India itself. He put aside Western costume, took to using a spinning wheel and living on goat's milk, urged Indian peasants to revive their old handicrafts, and appeared on solemn occasions clad in no more than a homespun loincloth. By the high level of his principles Gandhi made himself an inspiration to many groups that differed on more mundane matters. Even in the West he was regarded as one of the great religious teachers of all time.

India was very much divided within, and the British maintained that because of these divisions the ending of British rule would precipitate anarchy.

Divisions in society and politics

There were Hindus and Muslims, between whom clashes and terrorist outrages were chronic. (Gandhi was himself assassinated in 1948 by an anti-Muslim Hindu fanatic.) There were the hundreds of minor potentates of the native states. There were Indian capitalists and wealthy industrialists, like the Tata family, and growing masses of proletarians produced by Indian industrialization. There were the higher castes and the outcastes, and there were hundreds of millions of peasants living in rural poverty. In politics, there were those who demanded full independence, boycotted the British, and spent years in jail, as did Gandhi and his more practical-minded but devoted follower, Jawaharlal Nehru; and there were the moderates who believed that they might best advance the welfare of India by accepting government office, cooperating with the British, and working for dominion status within the British Empire. Marxism exerted a strong appeal, not indeed on the spiritual and pacific Gandhi, but on Nehru and even many of the less radical leaders. In the 1920s the Soviet Union stood in their eyes for the overthrow of imperialism; in the 1930s it pointed the way toward economic development by its adoption of five-year plans. For a people wishing to raise itself by its own bootstraps, to move from poverty to industrial strength and higher living standards without loss of time, and without dependence on foreign capital and capitalism, the Soviet Union with its economic planning seemed to offer a more appropriate model and more practical lessons than the rich democracies of the West, with their centuries of gradual progress behind them.

The 20 years between world wars were years of repeated disturbance, of rioting and repression, of sporadic violence despite the exhortations of

Continuing struggle for independence

Gandhi, of conferences and round tables, reforms and promises of reform, with a drift in the 1930s toward more participation of Indians in the affairs of the Indian empire. Independence was not won until after the Second World War; with it took place a partition of the Indian subcontinent into two new nations, a predominantly Hindu India and a predominantly Muslim Pakistan.

In the Netherlands Indies, where the nationalist movement was less developed than in India, the interwar years were more quiet. A serious rebellion, in which communists took part, broke out in 1922 but was suppressed by the Dutch. The peoples of the archipelago were almost as diverse as those of India. Only the Dutch empire had brought them politically together. Opposition to the Dutch gave them a common program. In 1937 the legislative council petitioned for the grant of dominion status. But not until after the Second World War and the failure of a military effort to repress the nationalists did the Dutch, in 1949, concede independence.

The Chinese Revolution: The Three People's Principles

The Chinese Revolution had opened in 1911 with the overthrow of the Manchu (Qing) dynasty, which itself had belatedly begun to introduce westernizing reforms. The Chinese Republic was proclaimed, but the first immediate result was the establishment in Peking

The religious commitments and nonviolent principles of Mohandas Gandhi profoundly shaped the Indian movement for national independence after the First World War. He is shown here in typically simple clothing as he led his followers on a "walk to the sea" to collect salt and to promote his nonviolent campaign for Indian national independence.

(Corbis)

(now Beijing) of a military dictatorship exercised by General Yüan Shih-kai, who had been a close adviser to the Manchus and who, until his death in 1916, never ceased to cast covetous eyes on the now empty imperial throne itself. In the south the veteran revolutionary Dr. Sun Yat-sen reorganized the Guomindang (National People's, or Nationalist party), successor to the prerevolutionary network of underground societies of which he had been the chief architect.[2] Sun, elected the first president of the republic by a revolutionary provisional assembly, resigned within a few months in favor of General Yüan, who he mistakenly believed would unite the country under a parliamentary regime. Subsequently, in the confusion that followed the struggle for power in Peking after Yüan's death in 1916, Sun was proclaimed president of a rival government in the south at Canton (now Guangzhou), which exercised a nominal power over the southern provinces. Not until 1928 could any government have any basis for claiming actual rule over China—and even then, there were important exceptions. For most of these years the country was virtually in the hands of contending war lords, each of whom pocketed the customary taxes in his own locality, maintained his own army, and recognized no superior authority.

Sun Yat-sen and the Nationalists

It was Sun Yat-sen who best expressed the ideas of the Chinese Revolution. Born in 1867 and educated under American influence in the Hawaiian Islands, he had received a medical degree at Hong Kong, had traveled extensively about the world, studied Western ideas, lectured to Chinese audiences in America, collected money for his conspiracies against the Manchus, and had returned from Europe to take part in the revolution. Shortly before his death in 1925 Sun gathered the lectures which he had been expounding for years into a book, *The Three People's Principles.* The book sheds much light on the revolt of China, and of all Asia, against the supremacy of the West.

Democracy, nationalism, livelihood

The three people's principles, according to Sun Yat-sen, were democracy, nationalism, and livelihood. Livelihood meant social welfare and economic reform—a more equitable distribution of wealth and land, a gradual end to poverty and unjust economic exploitation. By nationalism Dr. Sun meant that the Chinese who had always lived mainly in the clan and family had now to learn the importance of the nation and the state. They were in fact a great nation, he thought, the world's most cultured, and had once prevailed from the mouth of the Amur to the East Indies. But they had never been cohesive. The Chinese had been "a sheet of loose sand"; they must now "break down individual liberty and become pressed together into an unyielding body like the firm rock which is formed by the addition of cement to sand."

By democracy Sun Yat-sen meant the sovereignty of the people. Like Rousseau, he gave little attention to voting, elections, or parliamentary processes. He believed that while the people were sovereign, the able should govern. Government should be conducted by experts, a principle he criticized the West for neglecting. Dr. Sun felt a warm sympathy for Lenin. Yet he was by no means a doctrinaire Marxist. Marxism he thought inapplicable to China, arguing that the Chinese must take Marxism as they took all other Western ideas, avoiding slavish imitation, using, adapting, amending, rejecting as they saw fit. China had no native capitalism in any Marxist or Western sense. The "capitalists" in China, he said,

---

[2]The Pinyin system is now widely used for the transliteration of Chinese names and words into languages like English that use the Latin alphabet, replacing the older Wade-Giles spelling in 1979. Kuomintang is now rendered as Guomindang, Mao Tse-tung as Mao Zedong, Peking as Beijing, Chou En-lai as Zhou Enlai, Teng Hsiaop'ing as Deng Xiaoping, and so on. For a few names like Sun Yat-sen or Chiang Kai-shek the original spellings are often retained.

were owners of land, especially in the cities, such as Shanghai, where the coming of Westerners had raised land values to dizzy heights. Hence if China could get rid of imperialism it would take a long step toward getting rid of capitalism also; it could begin to equalize landowning and confiscate unearned rents. Since China, he observed, had no true capitalists the state itself must undertake capitalist and industrial development. This would require loans of foreign capital and the services of foreign managers and technicians, adding another reason why the Chinese state, to maintain control, must be strong.

With Sun Yat-sen, in short, democracy easily shaded off into a theory of benevolent and constructive dictatorship. Marxism, communism, socialism, "livelihood," the planned society, welfare economics, and antiforeign and anti-imperialist sentiment were all mixed together—in some ways as the ideas of the Chinese Communists would later be.

The first aim of Sun Yat-sen and of the revolutionists in China was to shake off the "treaty system" that had bound China to outside interests since 1842. In this respect the Paris peace conference had been disappointing; the Chinese not only failed to obtain the abolition of Western privileges and extraterritorial rights but also could not win back the former German concessions that the Japanese had taken over during the war. Widespread student and worker demonstrations directed against the Western powers took place on May 4, 1919. The May Fourth movement heightened the antiforeign consciousness.

Antiforeign sentiments

As the Western powers proved obdurate, Sun and the Guomindang turned to Russia. They declared the Russian and Chinese revolutions to be two aspects of the same worldwide movement of liberation. The Chinese Communist party, organized in 1921, became allied with the Guomindang in 1923. The latter accepted Russian Communist advisers, notably the veteran revolutionist Borodin, whom Sun Yat-sen had known years before in the United States. The Soviet Union, following its strategy of outflanking world capitalism by penetrating Asia, sent military equipment, army instructors, and party organizers into China. It also surrendered the Russian concessions and extraterritorial rights acquired in China by the tsars. The Chinese policy of friendliness to Russia began to produce the hoped for effects; the British, to draw China from Russia, gave up a few of their lesser concessions at Hankow and other cities.

Alliances with Russia

China: Nationalists and Communists

The Guomindang, its armies reorganized and strengthened, now displayed a fresh vitality and after 1924 launched a military and political offensive, planned by the ever active Russian advisers, supported by the Chinese Communists, and headed by Chiang Kai-shek, who succeeded to the leadership of the Nationalist party upon Sun's death in 1925. Chiang's main objectives were to compel the independent war lords and the regime still holding office in Beijing to accept the authority of a single Nationalist government. By the end of 1928 Chiang's armies had swept northward, occupied Beijing, and transferred the seat of government to Nanjing. Chiang now exercised at least nominal control over most of China, although effective control was still limited by the recalcitrance of many provincial war lords. The outside powers, acknowledging the accomplishments of the Guomindang, extended diplomatic recognition to the Nanjing government and conceded its right to organize and run the country's tariff and customs affairs. They also partially surrendered their extraterritorial privileges and pledged to abolish them completely in the near future.

Communists purged from the Kuomindang

In 1927, while a measure of national unity was being forged in the country, an open break occurred between the Guomindang and its left wing. In the course of the northern military campaign, and particularly in the seizure of Nanjing, popular disturbance and excesses, including the killing of a number of foreigners, had taken place, allegedly fomented by the Communists. These radical disturbances frightened and alienated the wealthier and more conservative element in the Guomindang and so jeopardized Chiang's chief source of financial assistance for his government and army. Chiang himself, also, had never apparently considered the alliance with either the Communists or the Russians as anything more than one of convenience. Chiang took decisive action, purging Communists and Russian advisers from the party, and executing many. Borodin and others fled to Moscow, and a Communist-led uprising in Guangzhou was forcefully suppressed. A number of armed Communist groups fled to the safety of the mountain regions in the south and joined other guerrilla contingents. In that way the Chinese Red Army was formed; among its leaders were Mao Zedong, a former librarian, teacher, newspaper editor, and union organizer, who had been one of the founding members of the party.

Chiang, with the renewed financial and moral support of the Guomindang bankers, resumed the northern offensive whose success by 1928 has been described. But the original revolutionary impulse of the Guomindang was now dissipated. Made up of men who feared social upheaval and who often regarded their own maintenance in power as their chief goal, it exercised a kind of one-party dictatorship over most of China under Chiang's leadership. Chiang himself recognized mounting popular dissatisfaction with the reluctance or inability of the party to initiate reforms, but he was still busy consolidating the regime and after 1931 he had to contend with Japanese aggression. During these years he conceived a deadly hatred for Communists and those who actively agitated for revolutionary reform.

A united front against Japan

The Communists, operating now in southeast China, fed on popular discontent and drew support from the peasantry by a systematic policy of expropriation and distribution of large landed estates as well as by intensive propaganda. They succeeded in fighting off Chiang's armies and even in winning over part of his troops. Organizing a network of local soviets, in 1931 they proclaimed a Chinese Soviet Republic in the southeast. When the Nationalist armies succeeded in dislodging them, the Communists, under Mao's leadership, undertook in 1934–1935 an amazing 6,000-mile march over near-insuperable terrain to north-central Yenan, closer, it was said, to Soviet supply lines. About 90,000 began the Long March, of which only half survived. They entrenched themselves again, fought off the Nationalist armies, and built up a strong popular following among the rural masses. With the Japanese invasion of north China well under way they abandoned their revolutionary offensive and pressed Chiang to end the civil war and to create a united front against the Japanese aggressor. Chiang reluctantly consented, so that by 1937 an alliance was formed between the Nationalists and the Communists; the Chinese Red Army was placed under Nationalist control; a united China would face the Japanese. But the uneasy alliance was not to last even until the defeat of Japan in the Second World War. Guomindang and Communists would soon engage in a deadly struggle for power.

Japan: Militarism and Aggression

The Nationalist movement in China caused apprehension in Japan, whose rise as a modern power has already been traced. The Japanese, at least since the Sino-Japanese War of 1895, had looked upon the huge disintegrating area of China as a field for expansion of

Mao Zedong and Zhou Enlai led nearly 100,000 Communists on the famous "Long March" from southeast China to the northwest province of Yenan in 1934–1935. They were escaping the armies of the Nationalist Guomindang and seeking to establish new bases near the Soviet Union. This picture shows Mao and Zhou as they appeared at the time of the march, which crossed almost 6,000 miles of remote terrain and became a legendary event in the history of the Chinese Communist party.

(Hulton Getty)

their own interests, in this scarcely differing from Europeans, except that they were closer to the scene. During the World War they had presented their Twenty-One Demands on China, taken over the German concessions in Shantung, and sent troops into eastern Siberia. During the war the industrialization of Japan proceeded apace; Japan captured many markets while the Europeans were locked in the struggle; and after the war the Japanese remained one of the chief suppliers of textiles for the rest of Asia. The Japanese could produce at lower prices than the Europeans, prices at which the penniless masses of Asia were more able to buy. They themselves sustained their standard of living in their mountainous islands by importing raw materials and selling manufactures. But the Chinese Nationalists hoped to erect a protective tariff; it was for this reason, among others, that they denounced the treaty system, which for almost a century had bound China to international free trade. The Chinese, like the Turks, hoped to industrialize and westernize their own country behind a high tariff wall, which would shut out Japanese manufactures as well as others.

During the 1920s the civilian, liberal, Western-oriented element in Japan remained in control of the government. In 1925 universal male suffrage was adopted. Europeans and Americans generally viewed the Japanese with sympathetic approval, as the most progressive of all non-Europeans, the one Asian people who had ably learned to play its part in the advancing worldwide civilization. But there was another facet to Japan. The constitution of 1889 and parliamentary operations were but a façade that concealed political realities. Only in Japan of all modern countries did a constitutional law prescribe that the war and navy ministers must be active generals or admirals. The diet itself had sharply restricted powers. Ministers governed in the name of the supreme and sacred authority of the emperor, to whom they were alone responsible. Economically, the government's sponsorship of industrial growth had resulted in a tremendous concentration of economic power in the hands of four family trusts known collectively as the Zaibatsu. The business interests and the civilian political leaders all looked to an expanding empire and growing markets, but the most restless group in Japan drew its strength from the nationalist revival which, even before the "opening" of Japan in 1854, had cultivated Shinto, emperor worship, and the way of the warrior as a new and modern way of life. This element was recruited in large part from the old clansmen and samurai, whom the "abolition of feudalism" had uprooted from their accustomed ways and who in many cases found no outlet for their energies in the new regime. Many of these men now served as officers in the army. Often they regarded the West as decadent. They dreamed of the day when Japan would dominate all East Asia.

Nationalist revival

About 1927 this group began to hold ministries in the Japanese government and to turn Japanese policy into increasingly aggressive and militaristic attitudes toward China. In 1931 Japanese army units stationed in southern Manchuria (where the Japanese had been since defeat of the Russians in 1905), alleging the mysterious murder of a Japanese officer at Mukden, seized Chinese arsenals and spread northward over all Manchuria. In 1932, charging the Chinese with economic warfare against Japan (Chinese boycotts were in fact damaging the Japanese export trade), the Japanese landed 70,000 troops at Shanghai. They soon withdrew, preferring to concentrate at this stage on the occupation of the northern part of China. They declared Manchuria to be an independent state under an emperor they themselves selected (they chose the last Chinese emperor, the "boy-emperor" Pu Yi, who had been deposed in 1911) and renamed the state Manchukuo.

The invasion of Manchuria

After the Manchurian invasion the Chinese appealed to the League of Nations. The League sent a commission of inquiry, which, under Lord Lytton, found Japan at fault for disturbing the peace. Japan defiantly withdrew from the League. The small powers in the League generally cried for military sanctions, but the Great Powers, knowing that they would be the ones to bear the burden of military intervention against Japan, and in any case inclined to see no threat to their own immediate security, refused to take any stronger measures, so that, in effect, the Japanese remained in occupation of Manchuria and northeast China. With the Japanese conquest of Manchuria one tributary of the coming torrent had begun to flow. But the world at this time was also stunned by economic depression. Each government was preoccupied with its own internal social problems.

100. THE GREAT DEPRESSION: COLLAPSE OF THE WORLD ECONOMY

The capitalist economic system was a delicate and interlocking mechanism in which any disturbance was rapidly transmitted with accelerating impact through all the parts. For many basic commodities prices were determined by the free play of supply and demand in a worldwide market. There was much regional division of labor; large areas lived by producing a few specialized articles for sale to the world as a whole. A great deal of production, both local and international, especially in the 1920s, was financed by credit, which is to say by promises of repayment in the future. The system rested upon mutual confidence and mutual exchange—on the belief of lenders, creditors, or investors that they would get their money back, on the belief of borrowers that they could pay their debts, on the ability of farms and factories to market their products at prices high enough to bring a net return, so that farmers and factory people might purchase the output of other factories and farms, and so on round and round in countless circles of mutual interdependence, and throughout the world as a whole.

The Prosperity of the 1920s and Its Weaknesses

The five years after 1924 were a period of prosperity, in that there was a good deal of international trade, building, and development of new industries. The automobile, for example, still an oddity in 1914, became an article of mass production after the war; and its widespread use increased the demand for oil, steel, rubber, and electrical equipment, caused the building or rebuilding of tens of thousands of miles of roads, and created whole new secondary occupations for thousands as truckdrivers, garage mechanics, or filling-station attendants. Similarly the mass popularity of radios and moving pictures had repercussions in all directions. The ensuing expansion was most phenomenal in the United States, but almost all countries enjoyed it in greater or lesser degree. "Prosperity" became a mystic term, and some thought that it would last indefinitely, that the secret of human plenty and of progress had been found, and that science and invention were at last realizing the hopes of ages.

But there were weaknesses in this prosperity, various imperfections in this or that gear or valve of the mechanism, flaws which, under stress, were to bring the whole intricate structure to a halt. The expansion was largely financed by credit, or borrowing. Laboring people received less than a proportionate share; wages lagged behind profits and dividends, so that mass purchasing power, even when inflated by installment buying (another form of credit), could not absorb the vast output that it was technically possible to produce. *A prosperity financed by credit*
And throughout the world the whole decade of the 1920s was a time of chronic agricultural depression, so that farmers could neither pay their debts nor purchase manufactures to the degree required for the smooth functioning of the system.

Military operations in the First World War had reduced wheat fields under cultivation in Europe by a fifth. The world price of wheat went up, and farmers in the United States, Canada, and elsewhere increased their acreage. Often, to acquire land at high prices, they assumed mortgages which in later years they were unable to repay. After the war Europe restored its own wheat production, and eastern Europe reentered the world market. Agriculture was increasingly mechanized, and farmers rapidly increased their output of wheat *Worldwide agricultural depression*
by using a tractor-drawn harvester-thresher combine. At the same time dry farming opened up new land, and agronomic science increased the yield per acre. The result of all these numerous developments was a superabundant output of wheat. But the demand for wheat was what economists call "inelastic." By and large, within the area of the Western world, people already ate as much bread as they wanted and would buy no more; and the undernourished masses of Asia, who in pure theory could have consumed the excess, could not pay even low costs of production or transportation. The world price of wheat fell incredibly. In 1930 a bushel of wheat, in terms of gold, sold for the lowest price in 400 years.

Wheat growers in all continents were faced with ruin. Growers of many other crops faced the same dismal prospect. Cotton and corn, coffee and cocoa all collapsed. Brazilian and African planters were caught by overproduction and falling prices. In Java, where not only had the acreage in sugar been extended, but also the unit yield of sugar from the cane had multiplied ten times under scientific cultivation over the past century, the bottom dropped out of prices in the world market. There were indeed other and more profitable forms of agricultural production—for example, in oranges and eggs, of which world consumption was steadily growing. But the coffee planter could not shift to eggs, nor the Iowa farmer to oranges. Not to mention the requirements of climate, the ordinary farmer or peasant lacked the capital, the special knowledge, or the access to refrigerated transportation that these newer branches of agriculture demanded. For the one thing that the average farmer or peasant knew how to do—grow wheat and other cereals—the new wonderful world of science and machinery had too little place.

The acute phase of the Great Depression, which began in 1929, was made worse by this chronic background of agricultural distress, since there was no reserve of purchasing power on the farms. The farmer's plight became even worse when the city people, struck by depression in industry, cut down their expenditures for food. Agricultural depression, rather than industrial depression, was at the bottom of widespread troubles in the inter-war years throughout eastern Europe and the colonial world.

The Crash of 1929 and the Spread of Economic Crisis

The depression, in the strict sense, began as a stock market and financial crisis. Prices of stocks had been pushed upward by years of continuing expansion and high dividends. At the beginning of 1929 prices on the European stock exchanges began to weaken. But the real crisis, or turning point, came with the crash on the New York Stock Exchange in October 1929. Here values had been driven to fantastic heights by excessive speculation. Not only professional speculators, but quite ordinary people, in the United States, as an easy way to make a good deal of money, bought stock with borrowed funds. Sometimes, trading on "margin," they "owned" five or ten times as much stock as the amount of their own money put into it; the rest they borrowed from brokers, and the brokers borrowed from banks, the purchased stock in each case serving as collateral. With money so easy to obtain, people pushed up stock prices by bidding against each other and enjoyed huge fortunes on paper; but if prices fell, even a little, the hapless owners would be obliged to sell their stock to pay off the money they had borrowed. Hence the weakening of values on the New York Stock Exchange set off uncontrollable tidal waves of selling, which drove stock prices down irresistibly and disastrously. In a month stock values dropped by 40 percent, and in three years, from 1929 to 1932, the average value of 50 industrial stocks traded on the New York Stock Exchange dropped from 252 to 61. In these same three years 5,000 American banks closed their doors.

Crisis reaches the rest of the world

The crisis passed from finance to industry and from the United States to the rest of the world. The export of American capital came to an end. Americans not only ceased to invest in Europe but sold the foreign securities that they had. This pulled the foundations from under the postwar revival of Germany and hence indirectly of much of Europe. Americans, their incomes falling, ceased to buy foreign goods; from Belgium to Borneo people saw their American markets slip away, and prices tumbled. In 1931 the failure of a leading Vienna bank, the *Creditanstalt,* sent a wave of shivers, bankruptcies, and business calamities over Europe. Everywhere business firms and private people could not collect what was owed them or even draw on money that they thought they had in the bank. They could not buy, and so the factories could not sell. Factories slowed down or closed entirely. Between 1929 and 1932, the latter year representing the depth of the depression, world production is estimated to have declined by 38 percent, and the world's international trade fell by two-thirds. In the United States the national income fell from $85 billion to $37 billion.

Unemployment, a chronic disease ever since the war, assumed the proportion of pestilence. In 1932 there were 30 million unemployed persons statistically reported in the world; and this figure did not include the further

Unemployment

millions who could find work only for a few hours in the week, or the masses in Asia or Africa for whom no statistics were to be had. The worker's wages were gone, the farmer's income now touched bottom; and the decline of mass purchasing power forced more idleness of machinery and more unemployment. People in the prime of life spent years out of work. Young people could not find jobs or establish themselves in an occupation. Skills and talents of older people grew rusty. Millions were reduced to living, and supporting their families, on the pittances of charity, doles, or relief. Great modern cities saw an outburst of sidewalk art, in which, at busy street corners, jobless able-bodied men drew pictures on the pavement with colored chalk, in the hope of attracting a few sixpence or dimes. People were crushed in spirit by a feeling of uselessness; months and years of fruitless job hunting left them demoralized, bored, discouraged, embittered, frustrated, and resentful. Never had there been such waste, not merely of machinery which now stood idle but also of the trained and disciplined labor force on which all modern societies were built. And people chronically out of work naturally turned to new and disturbing political ideas.

Political and Economic Reactions to the Crisis

Optimists at the time, of whom President Herbert Hoover in the United States was one, declared that this depression, though a severe one, was basically only another periodic low point in the business cycle, or alternation of expansion and contraction, which had ebbed and flowed in the Western world for over a century. Prosperity, they blithely said, was "just around the corner." Others felt that the crisis represented the breakdown of the whole system of capitalism and free private enterprise. These people, in many cases, looked for signs of the future in the planned economy then being introduced in the U.S.S.R. There was something in both views. After 1932, in part for purely cyclical reasons—because the depression cut down indebtedness and reduced the costs of doing business—it again became possible to produce and sell. World steel production, for example, which had stood at 121 million tons in 1929, and then collapsed to 50 million in 1932, by 1936 again reached 122 million. To a considerable degree, to be sure, revival was due to rearmament. On the other hand, the Great Depression did put an end to the old economic system in the old sense. Even if such a stricken economy had internal powers of full recuperation after a few years, people would not stand for such terrifying insecurity in their personal lives. The horrors of mass unemployment were long remembered.

All governments took steps to provide work and incomes for their people. All, in one way or another, strove to free themselves from dependency on the uncertainties of the world market. The interlocking world economy

Economic nationalism

collapsed both from the depression itself and from the measures adopted to cure it. The most marked economic consequence of the depression was a strong movement toward economic nationalism—toward greater self-sufficiency within the sphere which each government could hope to control.

The internationalism of money, the gold standard, and the free convertibility of currencies one into the other were gradually abandoned. Countries specializing in agricultural exports were among the first to be pinched. Agricultural prices were so low that even a

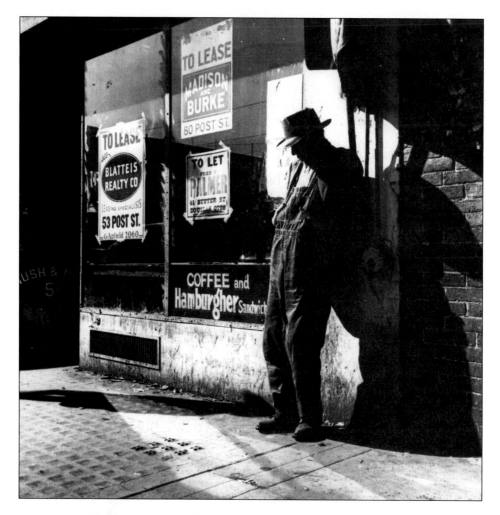

This picture by the American photographer Dorthea Lange conveys some of the personal dimensions of the social and economic crisis of the 1930s. An idle, unemployed man stands outside a vacant store on an empty street in San Francisco. The photograph suggests the sense of failure and social disorientation that spread across much of the industrialized world during the decade of the Great Depression.

(Photo by D. Lange. Public domain. Courtesy of Franklin D. Roosevelt Library.)

large quantity of exports failed to produce enough foreign currency to pay for needed imports; hence the exporting country's currency fell in value. The currencies of Argentina, Uruguay, Chile, Australia, and New Zealand all depreciated in 1929 and 1930. Then came the turn of the industrial countries. England, as the depression went on, could not sell enough exports to pay for imports. It had to pay for imports in part by sending gold out of the country; thus the gold reserve supporting the pound sterling declined, and people who had pounds sterling began to convert their pounds into dollars or other currencies for which they thought the gold basis was more secure. This was known, in the poetic language of economics, as the "flight from the pound." In 1931 Great Britain went off the gold standard, which is to say that it devalued the pound. But after Britain devalued, some 20 odd other countries, to protect their own exports and their own industries, did the same. Hence somewhat the same relative position reappeared. Even the United States, which possessed most of the world's gold supply, abjured the gold standard and devalued the dollar in 1934. The purpose was mainly to help American farmers, for with dollars cheaper in terms of foreign currencies, foreigners could afford to buy more American agricultural products. But it became harder for foreigners to sell to the United States.

Hence the depression, adding its effects to those of the World War and postwar inflation, led to chaos in the international monetary exchanges. Governments manipulated their currencies to uphold their sagging exports. Or they imposed exchange controls: they required that foreigners from whom their own people purchased, and to whom they thus gave their own currency, should use this currency to buy from them in return. Trade, which had been multilateral, became increasingly bilateral. That is, where Brazilian importers of steel, for example, had formerly bought steel wherever they wished, at the prices or quality they preferred, they now had to obtain steel, often regardless of price or precise quality, from a country to which Brazil had sold enough of its own products to make payment possible. Sometimes, notably in the relations between Germany and East European countries in the 1930s, bilateralism degenerated into actual barter. The Germans would exchange a certain number of cameras with Yugoslavia in return for a certain number of pigs. In such cases the very conception of a market disappeared.

International monetary exchanges in chaos

Currency control was one means of keeping one's own factories from idleness, by holding or capturing export markets in time of depression. Another way of keeping one's own factories going (or farms, or mines, or quarries) was to shut out competitive imports by the old device of protective tariffs. The United States, hit by depression in 1929, enacted the unprecedentedly high Hawley-Smoot tariff in 1930, which soon contributed to the further decline of international trade. Other countries, equally or more distressed, now could sell less to America and hence buy fewer American goods. Other countries likewise raised their own tariffs, in the desperate hope of reserving national markets for their own people. Even Great Britain, citadel of free trade in the nineteenth century, turned to protectionism. It also revived and adopted Joseph Chamberlain's old idea of an imperial tariff union, when in 1932, by the Ottawa agreements, Britain and the British dominions adopted a policy of having lower tariffs against one another than against the world outside.

Even tariffs were not always enough for economic nationalists. Quotas or quantitative restrictions were adopted in many nations. By this system a government said in effect not merely that goods brought into the country must pay a high tariff duty, but that above a certain amount no goods could be brought in at all. Increasingly both importers and exporters worked under government licenses, in order that a country's entire foreign trade could be centrally planned and managed. Such methods approached those of the Soviet Union, which asserted a government monopoly over all foreign trade, exported only to finance imports, and determined, without the bother of tariffs, the exact quantity of imported commodities that it would take.

Quotas

Thus the world economy disintegrated into fiercely competing national economic systems. In the oceanic wreckage of the Great Depression, each state tried to create an island of economic security for its own people. Some efforts were made to break down the rising barriers. An International Monetary and Economic Conference, meeting in London in 1933, attempted to open the clogged channels of world trade; it ended in failure, as did attempts to stabilize the exchange rates of various currencies. Soon thereafter, the wartime Allies defaulted on their debt payments to the United States. Legislation in Congress then denied them the right to float bonds, or obtain new loans, in the American securities market. American actions thus reinforced economic nationalism. The era that had opened with Woodrow Wilson's dream of international economic cooperation was ending with an unprecedented intensification of economic rivalry and national self-centeredness; it was only one of the promises of the postwar world to be blasted by the Great Depression.

Cultural Reactions to the Crisis

The effects of the economic crisis spread to the cultural and intellectual life of the 1930s. Responding to the despair and social dislocation of the masses of unemployed, artists and writers turned to describing painful social realities and committed themselves to political activism.

All this was in contrast to the 1920s. The postwar decade had been a period of great achievement in what is generally called "modernist" art and literature, in which painters projected disjointed dreamlike scenes evoking their personal memories or disorienting personal experiences and writers emphasized their own personal vision and the interior lives of the characters whom they depicted.

Modernism

These writers were responsible for remarkable explorations of memory, time, and the internal workings of the human mind. The Irish writer James Joyce published his famous novel *Ulysses* portraying the life and thoughts of its leading character during a single day in Dublin, contributing with it to a new literary fascination with interior monologues and "stream of consciousness" writing, which was soon followed by the dramas of the American playwright Eugene O'Neill. The French novelist Marcel Proust developed lengthy descriptions of personal and emotional experiences in his multivolume *Remembrance of Things Past,* and the English writer Virginia Woolf examined the complex passage of time through the characters she created in novels such as *To the Lighthouse.* A generation of American writers, including Ernest Hemingway, had even settled in Paris after the First World War to pursue experimental forms of literature and art. The political and social world by no means disappeared from "modernist" literature, but these writers were more concerned with exploring the inner complexities of human psychology.

Now, under the harsh economic conditions of the 1930s, it became common to reject the literary exploration of psychological anxieties as inadequate or even as self-indulgent. A new kind of "realist" literature and literature of political engagement won support from intellectuals in all industrial societies, especially among those who believed that the Great Depression had grown out of fundamental flaws and injustices in the capitalist economy. Some writers, like the French novelist André Gide for a time, as well as other writers, artists, and film-makers embraced communism and praised the social experiments of the

Realism

Soviet Union. Others simply decided that they should set aside the arcane language of the literary avant-garde and write about the social suffering of the day. A new genre of proletarian literature came into being. Many who had settled in Paris returned to the United States in the early 1930s. As the American critic Malcolm Cowley noted in his *Exile's Return,* the new social problems called for new kinds of writing. Where *Ulysses* was a classic modernist work of the 1920s, John Steinbeck's *The Grapes of Wrath* may be seen as a classic "social novel" of the 1930s. Steinbeck wrote about the social miseries of America's impoverished, displaced farmers rather than the personal memories of an alienated intellectual. His

AUTOUR D'ELLE

by Marc Chagall (Russian, then French, 1887–1984)

Although this painting clearly does not represent the social realism that emerged in the 1930s, it exemplifies the diversity of twentieth-century art. It was painted by Chagall in 1945 in memory of his wife. At the center is the Russian city of Smolensk, where they had been married 30 years before. The surrounding faces and figures are individually quite distinct, but they float disconnectedly like the vivid images in a dream. Past and present, memory and perception, fantastic and real objects flow together in a free play of the unconscious mind. These qualities characterized surrealism, of which the younger Chagall had been a forerunner.

(Scala/Art Resource, NY/© 2001 Artists Rights Society (ARS), New York/ADAGP, Paris) themes and those elaborated by others exemplified the cultural anxiety that spread across the globe in the wake of the unprecedented economic crisis—an anxiety that fostered a new literary and artistic "realism" as well as angry political extremism, which, as we shall see, was now attracting new support in Europe, the United States, and other parts of the world.

Chapter **20**

DEMOCRACY
AND DICTATORSHIP

In the 1920s, people in a general way believed that despite the horrors of the World War the twentieth century was realizing the material and political goals summed up in the idea of progress. In the 1930s, they began to fear that "progress" was a phantom, to speak the word self-consciously with mental quotation marks, and to be content if only they could prevent a relapse into positive barbarism and a new world war.

The Great Depression ushered in the nightmare of the 1930s. Everywhere the demand was for security. Each nation tried to live, so far as possible, within itself. Each regulated, controlled, guided, planned, and tried to rescue its own economic system, attempting to be as little influenced as possible by the unpredictable behavior of other countries. Within each country the same search for security encouraged the advancement of the welfare state and social democracy.

Where democratic institutions were strong and resilient, governments took steps to protect individuals against the ravages of unemployment and destitution and to help guard against future catastrophes. On the other hand, where democratic governments were not well established or taken for granted, which was the case in many countries after the First World War, dictatorship spread alarmingly in the 1930s with the coming of the depression. Democracy was said to be suited only to wealthy or prosperous countries. Unemployed people generally cared far more for economic help, or for promises of economic help, than for any theory of how persons wielding public power should be selected. The cry was for a leader, someone who would act, make decisions, assume responsibilities, get results, inspire confidence, and restore national pride. The Great Depression opened the way for unscrupulous and ambitious political adventurers, for dictators like Adolf Hitler in Germany, whose solution to all problems, economic, political, and international, it turned out, was war.

Chapter emblem: Benito Mussolini addressing a Fascist meeting in Italy in 1932.

101. THE UNITED STATES: DEPRESSION AND NEW DEAL

Profound changes took place in the United States, where the stock market crash of 1929 had precipitated the great economic collapse. In 1932 national income had dropped to less than half of what it had been in 1929; 12 million to 14 million were unemployed. The Republican President Herbert Hoover, elected in 1928 at the floodtide of prosperity, was identified in the public mind with the hard times. Hoover viewed with disfavor any large-scale government intervention, convinced that the business cycle that had brought the depression would in turn bring prosperity and that once business confidence was restored recovery would begin. His administration did act, proposing for the world economy a one-year suspension of payments on all intergovernmental debts and at home giving financial assistance to banks and railroads, expanding credit facilities, and helping to save the mortgages of some farmers and small home owners.

But Hoover would go no further; he opposed immediate direct federal relief to the jobless; veterans seeking payment of their wartime bonuses to tide them over the bad times were ejected from Washington; unemployment, business failures, and farm foreclosures continued. In the election of 1932 the millions of unemployed workers, disheartened urban lower middle classes, and distressed farmers swept the Republican administration from office and elected the first Democratic president since Woodrow Wilson. The new president was Franklin Delano Roosevelt. The combination of recovery, relief, and reform legislation that he inaugurated is known as the New Deal.

FDR's recovery, relief, and reform legislation

The new president embarked on a program of improvisation and experimentation, but with such dispatch and vigor as to generate at once an electric enthusiasm. Within a short time an impressive array of legislation was put through Congress. The program of assistance to farmers, small home owners, and industry initiated under the Hoover administration was expanded so that it was no longer recognizable.

The government provided financial assistance for the relief of the unemployed and sponsored a broad public works program to absorb the jobless, first by loans to the states for the construction of housing, roads, bridges, and schools, later by a direct federal works program. To meet the financial crisis, the banks were temporarily closed and then reopened under stricter supervision. The dollar was taken off the gold standard and devalued, principally to help the farmers compete in foreign markets. In agriculture, the government offered subsidies to farmers who agreed to curtail farm production, even subsidizing the destruction of crops and livestock, so that ruinous surpluses which had been one cause of the agricultural distress might be eliminated. It was a paradox, to be sure, for the government to reduce acreage and destroy agricultural products while city populations were in want. But the administration sought to meet the deep-seated agricultural crisis that antedated the depression as well as to cope with the immediate situation. Subsequently, farmers received subsidies for devoting part of their land to soil-conserving crops. A Civilian Conservation Corps promoted conservation and reforestation, and relieved unemployment by giving jobs to almost 3 million young people. For industry a National Recovery Administration (the NRA) for a time encouraged business firms to set up voluntary "codes of fair competition," which helped to regulate prices and production.

All these measures were designed to set the ailing capitalist system on its feet again by creating purchasing power and stimulating industrial activity. The major innovation was government spending, or "deficit financing." Although never following any consistent economic philosophy, the New Deal policies indirectly reflected the theories of the British economist John Maynard Keynes. In his

earlier writings and in his most famous book *The General Theory of Employment, Interest, and Money* published in 1936, he argued that if private investment funds were idle, government funds must be employed to encourage economic activity and to increase purchasing power until such time as private funds flowed again. In order to get money into circulation and to "prime the pump" of industrial production, the government undertook a huge borrowing and spending program. Unorthodox as deficit financing was, it seemed to many at the time the only direct and rapid method of preventing economic collapse in a capitalist system. In all these recovery and reform activities the federal government assumed a role that it had hitherto played only in wartime. New government agencies proliferated; the federal payroll grew; the government debt more than doubled between 1932 and 1940.

From the beginning, some longer-range reform measures were adopted in addition to the recovery measures. To prevent overspeculation and the recurrence of a crash such as that of 1929, a Securities and Exchange Commission was created to regulate the issuance of stock and to supervise the operations of the stock exchange. Bank deposits were guaranteed by federal insurance so that depositors would not lose their lifetime savings. A Tennessee Valley Authority served as a pilot program in flood control, regional economic development, and cheap public power production.

After 1935 the focus shifted to regulation and reform. Sound economic recovery had not been achieved; there were still at least 5 million persons who could not find jobs in private industry. Business leaders who at first had been responsive to the government's new role in the economy now resisted the government's regulation of finance and industry. The Supreme Court declared the NRA and other New Deal measures unconstitutional.

The major New Deal reforms after 1935 were designed to improve the condition of labor and to moderate economic insecurity. A broad national Social Security Act in 1935 provided for unemployment, old-age, and disability insurance. Here the United States was a latecomer. Germany, Britain, and other European countries had had such legislation since before the First World War. A Fair Labor Standards Act established 40 hours as a maximum normal workweek and set a minimum hourly wage; child labor was curtailed. A third measure, the National Labor Relations (or Wagner) Act, virtually transformed the American industrial scene. For the first time the federal govern-

ment and the law were solidly aligned on the side of the unions. The new act guaranteed the right of workers to set up and bargain through unions of their choice, outlawed company unions, and prohibited employers from interfering with union organizing or discriminating against union members. Under its aegis the older American Federation of Labor (AFL) was revitalized and a new vigorous Congress of Industrial Organizations (CIO) came into being, which organized workers on an industrywide basis and reached down to unskilled workers in such industries as automobile, steel, textile, maritime, and rubber. Millions never before organized, including women and African-American workers, became part of powerful labor unions with expanding treasuries. Total union membership rose from about 4 million in 1929 to 9 million by 1940. Militant and conscious of its new strength but hardly touched by revolutionary ideology, American labor chose not to create a third party but to operate within the traditional two-party system, generally supporting Roosevelt's Democratic party.

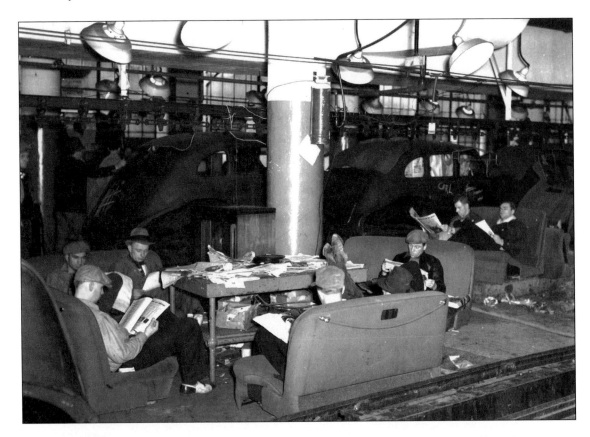

**The economic crisis of the 1930s and changes in the laws governing labor relations contributed
to the rapid growth and new militancy of labor unions in the United States. This picture of an
automobile factory in Flint, Michigan, in the late 1930s shows workers engaged in a sit-down
strike. Such strikes became one of the strategies that workers used to express their grievances
about wages, working conditions, or restrictions on the organizing of labor unions.**

(Library of Congress)

Other social measures were undertaken to aid tenant farmers and sharecroppers. For
the cities programs of slum clearance and low-cost housing were initiated. These steps
reached out to help that "one-third of a nation ill-nourished, ill-clad, ill-housed" described
by the president in 1937. If the New Deal did not strike at the deeper roots of American
poverty, it demonstrated the nation's humanitarian concern.

Slow and gradual recovery

Government spending and renewed confidence in the soundness of the
country's institutions created a slow, gradual, and partial recovery. In mid-
1937 a recession occurred. Business activity slid backward when government spending slowed down; the recession did not end until 1938 when
government spending was resumed. By 1939 national income had risen to
double what it had been at the depth of the depression but still short of June 1929. Resistance from the business community itself may have played a part in the failure to achieve
full recovery. The rising public debt, antibusiness pronouncements by the government,
heavier corporate and income taxes, and the many concessions to labor undoubtedly fright-

ened off business investments and led to what was called a "sit-down strike" of capital. Some claimed that wage rates had risen too sharply, adding to production costs and therefore discouraging business expansion. The New Deal did much to help economic recovery, but it did not end the depression. Complete recovery, the elimination of unemployment, the full use (and expansion) of the nation's productive capacity had to wait upon the huge war expenditures, by which depression spending was to be dwarfed. By 1938 or so the New Deal was over; the administration turned its attention from domestic reform to the gathering storm in Europe and the Far East.

The changes were substantial under what some called the "Roosevelt Revolution." Enlarging the role of the federal government as no previous administration had done, the New Deal transformed the noninterventionist state into a social service or welfare state. The government imposed controls on business, used its powers to redistribute wealth, and introduced a broad social security system. Labor's power and political influence grew. The responsibility of public authority for the social and economic welfare of the people was clearly established. When the Republican party later returned to power, it opposed in principle the further growth of the welfare state and the expanding role of the federal government, but it retained the New Deal reforms, a tacit admission that the New Deal had not intended to destroy capitalism but to preserve and revive it.

The New Deal, however, engendered violent feelings, which lingered on. Roosevelt, himself of patrician and well-to-do background, denounced the "economic royalists"; in turn he was called a "traitor to his class." When the Supreme Court declared some New Deal measures unconstitutional, he made plans to reorganize and enlarge the Court, which aroused more political hostility. Despite vociferous opposition, in the election of 1936 Roosevelt won all but two states, and he was subsequently reelected in 1940 and 1944 (during the war, to be sure), for unprecedented third and fourth terms. A constitutional amendment, adopted in 1951, limited a president to two terms.

Reelection of FDR

Roosevelt's opponents, at the time and later, argued that the New Deal had created an enormous regulatory bureaucracy, expensive and cumbersome, a threat to the freedom and self-reliance of the citizenry. But others contended that despite its waste and inconsistencies, unorthodox financial policies, enlargement of the executive power, and expansion of the bureaucracy, it represented a bold and humanitarian way of meeting the economic crisis; it preserved and reaffirmed American faith in its democratic system at a time when democracy was succumbing or was threatened elsewhere.

102. TRIALS AND ADJUSTMENTS OF DEMOCRACY IN BRITAIN AND FRANCE

British Politics: The 1920s and the Depression

Britain, like the United States, even in the troubles of the depression, remained firmly attached to representative institutions and democratic principles. The Great Depression aggravated and intensified Britain's older economic difficulties. More dependent on overseas markets than any other people, the British until 1914 had managed to hold their lead, exporting industrial products and capital, selling insurance and other services, and importing foodstuffs. But in the years before 1914 the British were increasingly losing their markets because of the emergence of other economically aggressive industrial nations, the growth of tariff barriers, the development of indigenous textile and other industries in India and elsewhere in the East, the competition of new textile products with British cottons and woolens, and the substitution of new sources of fuel for British coal. The losses were accelerated by the economic disruption of the First World War, the disappearance of many overseas investments, and the postwar disorganization and impoverishment of markets. The rise in tariffs after the war and the customs barriers raised in the new small states of Europe also hurt British exports. After 1918 Britain lived in a world no longer dependent on, or eager for, its manufactures. Britain's very historical primacy as the pioneer industrial country was also a handicap. Both labor and management had become adjusted to older conditions, and the more recently industrialized countries had less antiquated techniques and machinery.

The net result of all this was that in the interwar years, even in times of relative prosperity for the rest of the world, Britain was in depression and suffered severely from unemployment. The unemployment insurance adopted in 1911 was called heavily into play. By 1921 over 2 million unemployed were receiving benefit payments, contemptuously called the "dole" by those who disliked it. Unemployment insurance, an expanded old-age pension system, medical aid, government-subsidized housing, and other social welfare measures helped to relieve economic distress and to prevent any drastic decline in the living standards of British workers. The welfare state was well under way in Britain before the Labour party took office after the Second World War.

Unemployment insurance

The labor unions made a strenuous effort to retain wage gains and other concessions won in wartime. Industry, hard-pressed itself, resisted. This situation reached a climax in 1926 in the coal-mining industry, which was in a particularly bad plight; government subsidies had not helped and even conservative investigators had recommended some form of amalgamation and public management. A strike by the coal miners led to a "general strike" supported by the other British unions; about half of the 6 million organized workers in Britain left their jobs as a token of sympathy and solidarity. But the government declared a state of emergency and made use of army and navy personnel and middle-class volunteers to take over essential services. The strike ended in failure, and even in a setback for the trade unions, which were put under stricter control by the Trades Disputes Act of 1927, a measure that declared all general or sympathy strikes illegal and even forbade the unions from raising money for political purposes.

After the election of 1922, the Labour party displaced the Liberal party as the second of the two great parties of the country and faced the Conservatives as the official opposition. The Labour party could more consistently and more actively champion both labor legislation and bolder measures to deal with Britain's troubled economic state. The Labour party, moreover, which had been no more than a loose federation of trade union and socialist organizations before the war, tightened its organizational structure and, bridging the gap between the trade unionists and the socialists, committed itself in 1918 to a program of socialism. But it was a program of gradualist, democratic socialism operating through customary British parliamentary procedures and hence able to gain the goodwill of large sections of the middle classes.

The Labour party

Twice, in 1924 and in 1929, Labour governed the country with Ramsay MacDonald as prime minister, in each case as a coalition government. In 1924 Labour proved its moderation. It did no more than extend unemployment relief and inaugurate housing and public works projects; indeed it acted firmly in the face of strikes that broke out. But it aroused opposition when it gave diplomatic recognition to the Soviet Union and pledged a loan to the Soviets for the purchase of British goods. Meanwhile newspapers published the so-called Red (or Zinoviev) letter purporting to be secret instructions for British Labour groups from the head of the Communist International urging preparations for a Communist uprising in Britain. The document's authenticity has never been established, but the Conservatives successfully exploited it and won the election of 1924.

In the election of May 1929, however, Labour's representation almost doubled, and the Conservative representation dropped proportionately. MacDonald again became prime minister. Thus the Wall Street crash and the worldwide depression came while the Labour party government was in office. The effects of the depression were quickly felt. Unemployment, which had hovered about the 1 million mark in 1929, soon approached the 3 million figure. The government expended large sums to supplement the unemployment insurance payments. Gold flowed out of the country, tax receipts declined, the public debt grew. Alarmed by the mounting deficit, MacDonald made plans to introduce a severe retrenchment policy, even to the extent of reducing the "dole" payments. The Labour party was outraged; some of the Labour ministers in his cabinet refused to support him. He was read out of the party, along with those ministers who had gone along with him. MacDonald thereupon formed an all-party coalition cabinet known as the National government, which in an election of 1931 won an overwhelming victory, but it was the Conservative members of the coalition who took a majority of the seats in Parliament.

The formation of the National government

The National government coped with the depression chiefly along retrenchment lines, under Ramsay MacDonald from 1931 to 1935, Stanley Baldwin to 1937, and Neville Chamberlain after 1937. In addition to retrenchment and budget balancing, the government encouraged industry to reorganize and rationalize production by providing low-interest loans. Mainly, the government concentrated on economic nationalist measures rather than on fundamental changes in the capitalist economic system. As in the United States, despite some recovery from the depths of the depression, none of the steps taken brought full recovery or full employment. Unemployment persisted until military conscription and an expanded armament program absorbed the jobless. The Labour party, partially recovering its strength in the election of 1935, denounced the timid expedients of the Conservatives, whom it held responsible for the apathy and gloom gripping the country.

Britain and the Commonwealth: Imperial Relations

To the older British Empire—India, the crown colonies, protectorates, and spheres of influence—the postwar settlement added a number of League of Nations mandates. British rule in its various forms extended to almost 500 million people, a fourth of the earth's population and land surface. It was principally in Ireland, Egypt, India, and Palestine that the British faced complex imperial problems after the First World War. In Palestine, where the British exercised a League of Nations mandate, Arabs and Jews fought with each other and with Britain. In Egypt, in 1922, Britain, although retaining the right to station some troops there, formally ended the protectorate it had established 40 years earlier; but many questions, especially the status of the Sudan, remained unresolved. In India the agitation for national independence, as we have seen, grew more intense. In these areas nothing resembling a solution was arrived at until after the Second World War. In Ireland the independence movement managed to establish a separate republic.

The Irish question had disoriented English politics for 40 years. Home rule, authorized by Parliament in 1914, had been deferred for the duration

The Irish question

of the war. During the hostilities the Irish nationalists even accepted German support and rose in rebellion against the British in 1916. The rebellion was suppressed, but after the war the Irish nationalists, led by the Sinn Fein party, fought a small but savage war of independence against the British. In 1922 the British finally recognized the Irish Free State, granting it dominion status within the British Commonwealth. But to the vehement dissatisfaction of the Irish Nationalists the Protestants in Ulster, the northern counties where Presbyterians of Scottish origin had lived for three centuries and where they comprised a majority of the population, insisted on remaining outside the new state; they continued to be part of what was now called the United Kingdom of Great Britain and Northern Ireland. In 1937 the Irish Free State affirmed its full sovereignty and took the name Eire. In 1949 it broke all ties with the British Commonwealth and renamed itself the Republic of Ireland. The Irish question, however, remained unsettled throughout the rest of the century because the Irish agitated for the annexation of Ulster, conducted a tariff war with Britain, tried for a time to revive Gaelic as a substitute for the English language, and fell into violent disputes. These conflicts pitted Irish moderates against Irish extremists, the latter perpetrating assassinations and continuing disturbances to further their cause of uniting all Ireland with the Irish Republic. The Protestants in Ulster meanwhile remained obdurate about retaining their own religious and cultural identity and maintaining their political affiliation with Britain.

The dominions

As for the dominions, the political status of these areas of European settlement overseas was now more clearly defined than ever before. The dominions—Canada, Australia, New Zealand, and the Union of South Africa—had long pursued their own policies, even levying tariffs against British goods. They had all joined loyally with Great Britain in the First World War, but all were stirred by a nationalism of their own and desired their independence to be regularized and promulgated to the world. An imperial conference in 1926 defined "dominion status," which was corroborated by the Statute of Westminster of 1931. The dominions became legally equal with each other and with Great Britain. No act passed by the British Parliament would apply to a dominion save by the dominion's own consent. Despite independent policies in economic matters and even in foreign affairs, the bonds between the dominions and Britain remained firm; the support of the dominions in the Second World War was to be vital in Britain's survival. In the postwar world, with decolonization, the Commonwealth became a larger and even more flexible institution.

France: The 1920s and the Coming of the Depression

When the depression came to France, agitation of fascist type made more headway than in Britain or the United States. Earlier, in the 1920s, France was preoccupied with recovery from the physical destruction of the war, the instability of public finances, and the fear of a resurgent Germany. Immediately after 1919, and for most of the 1920s, the government was run by coalitions of parties of the conservative Right, that is, parties supported by business and financial interests, well disposed toward the army and church, and determined to maintain stability in domestic affairs. For about two years, from 1924 to 1926, the Radical Socialists were in control; this party of the moderate left, whose leader was Edouard Herriot, served as spokesman for the lower classes, small business, and farmers; it advocated progressive social legislation so long as increased taxes were not necessary. Despite its name, a carryover from an earlier era, it was firmly committed to private enterprise and private property; it was staunch in its defense of individual liberties and fervently anti-

Britain repeatedly used its armed forces to suppress the movement for Irish independence during and after the First World War. The British army thus operated in Ireland's cities as a kind of special police force. These troops were holding back the crowd in a Dublin street while other soldiers conducted a raid on Irish nationalists in 1921.

(Hulton Getty)

clerical; sometimes, it seemed, its anticlericalism was a substitute for any more positive program.

Although the Radical Socialists cooperated in parliamentary elections with the Socialists, the other major party of the Left, the two parties differed too profoundly on economic policies to preserve stable coalitions. In the 1920s the Socialists were still recovering from the secession of the more orthodox Marxists who had formed a French Communist party. Both Left and Right

Hostility to the republic

in France shaded off into antidemocratic groups that were hostile to the parliamentary republic. These included the Communists on the Left, who sat in Parliament and took part in elections; and on the extreme Right, royalists of the *Action Française* and other antirepublican organizations, which operated principally outside the Chamber as militant and noisy pressure groups.

The outstanding figure of the moderate conservative right was Raymond Poincaré, who sent troops into the Ruhr in 1923 when the Germans failed to pay reparations, and who also "saved" the franc. The reparations question was extremely important for French finances. The country had undertaken a large-scale reconstruction program to repair the wartime devastation of northern and eastern France, and had counted upon the defeated enemy to pay. When German reparations were not paid as anticipated, the public debt mounted, a balanced budget became impossible, and the franc declined precipitously. The huge war expenditures, heavy loss of foreign investments, notably in Russia, and an out-

Poincaré's measures

moded taxation program which invited widespread evasion added to French difficulties. After 1926, when the financial crisis reached a climax, a "national union" ministry under Poincaré inaugurated new taxes, tightened tax collection, cut down drastically on government expenditures to balance the budget, and eventually stabilized the franc—at about one-fifth its prewar value. The internal debt was thus in effect largely repudiated, to the despair of many bondholders, but the threat of a runaway inflation like that of the Weimar Republic was avoided. From 1926 to 1929 the country prospered. New factories, replacing those destroyed in the war, were modern and up to date. The index of industrial production rose; tourists flocked in. As in many other countries, however, workers did not share proportionately in the prosperity of the 1920s. The unions received a sharp setback when immediately following the war a series of major strikes ended in failure. Collective bargaining in the country was also virtually unknown, nor were workers mollified by a social insurance program adopted by a reluctant parliament, which went into effect in 1930.

The Great Depression came later to France and was less severe than in the United States or Germany. Trade declined. Unemployment increased; in 1935, close to 1 million workers were unemployed, and half of those employed worked part-time. Industrial production, which in 1930 was 40 percent above the prewar level, sank by 1932 to 1913 figures. The government displayed its older pattern of unstable, shifting, short-lived ministries; in 1933 five ministries rapidly succeeded one another (there were some 40 in the 20 interwar years). The depression cabinets followed a policy of retrenchment and economy, clung to the gold standard, and faced the threat of an aggressive new government in Germany, where Adolf Hitler had become chancellor in 1933.

Depression Ferment and the Popular Front

In the uneasy years of the depression, the latent right-wing hostility to the republic came to the surface. Fascist-type "leagues" appeared in open imitation of Italian and German fascist organizations, many obtaining funds from wealthy industrialists; the older *Action Française* and right-wing veterans' associations like Colonel de le Rocque's *Croix de Feu* were also active. The same elements that had been antirepublican, antidemocratic, or monarchist since the French Revolution, and which had rallied behind Boulanger and denounced Dreyfus, now grew more strident in their attacks on the parliamentary republic.

Scandals

In 1934 it seemed for a moment that the opportunity awaited by the antirepublican elements had come. A political and financial scandal shook the country. A financial manipulator and adventurer with important political connections, Stavisky by name, induced the municipal authorities at Bayonne to launch a flotation of worthless bonds. Faced with exposure, he fled and apparently committed suicide; the sensationalist press encouraged the rumor that he had been shot by the police to prevent the implication of high-ranking politicians. A clamor went up accusing the government of involvement in the financial scandal. Where elsewhere such an affair would have called only for turning the incumbents out of office, in France it supplied ammunition for those who demanded the end of the republic itself, which was now equated with corruption and venality.

The agitation reached a climax in the riots of February 1934. A mob of fascist tendency assembled in the Place de la Concorde, threatened the Chamber, and battled with the police; several were killed and hundreds were injured. French liberals and democrats, organized labor, and socialists were outraged by the threat to the republic. The Communists, hostile to the fascist groups, were unfriendly to the government too, but soon, guided by the Comintern, they sensed the danger to the Soviet Union in the event of a French fascist triumph and joined with the antifascists. As elsewhere, in the 1930s the Communists emerged from their sectarian revolutionary isolation, became patriotic, and widened their prestige, influence, and appeal. An impressive labor-sponsored general strike was held a week after the riots. Shortly thereafter, Radical Socialists, Socialists, and Communists drew together in a political coalition that came to be known as the Popular Front, of the kind that was being organized, or advocated, in many countries in the 1930s. It campaigned on a pledge to defend the republic against fascism, to take measures against the depression, and to introduce labor reforms. In the spring of 1936 it won a decisive victory at the polls. The French Socialists for the first time in their history became the leading party in the Chamber; their chief, Léon Blum, long a spokesman for democratic and reformist socialism, became premier of a coalition cabinet of Socialists and Radical Socialists; the Communists, who had increased their representation in the Chamber from 10 to 72 seats, did not join the cabinet but pledged their support.

The emergence of the French Socialists

The Popular Front and After

Blum's Popular Front ministry, although it lasted little more than a year, put through a program of far-reaching legislation. In part, this was due to the Popular Front election program, in part to unforeseen events, for the tremendous enthusiasm generated by the victory led to a spontaneous nationwide wave of "sit-down strikes," in which the striking workers refused to leave their factories or shops until Blum pledged a number of immediate reforms.

Parliament in short order passed laws providing for a 40-hour week, vacations with pay, and a collective bargaining law. As in the case of the Wagner Act in the United States, the encouragement given to collective bargaining led to the nationwide signing of collective contracts for the first time in the country's history and to enormous growth in trade union membership, from about 1 million to 5 million in a year's time. Labor's strength grew also when the Communist and non-Communist labor confederations reunited. Other legislation was important too. Steps were taken to nationalize the armaments and aviation industry; the fascist armed leagues were, at least in theory, dissolved; the Bank of France was reorganized and placed under government control to break the power of the nation's close-knit

Overdue measures for reform and recovery

The French Popular Front brought the leftist, anti-fascist political parties together in a governing coalition that held power for about a year in 1936–1937. Despite its brevity, the Popular Front government introduced numerous reforms that became permanent features of French social and economic life. This photograph shows Premier Léon Blum addressing supporters of the Popular Front on Bastille Day in 1936.

(AKG London)

economic elite, the so-called "two hundred families." Machinery was established for the arbitration of labor disputes. Aid was given to farmers through price fixing and government purchases of wheat. As in the United States all these measures aimed at both recovery and reform; Blum spoke openly of his program as a "French New Deal." But French conservatives, and the quasi-fascists to their Right, cried revolution; they uttered dark predictions that a French Lenin would follow Blum. They did not conceal their sullen resentment at what had come to pass: the fate of Catholic France in the hands of a leftist, a Socialist, and a Jew. Even salvation by a warrior from outside the country, one who had demonstrated his anti-Bolshevism, would be preferable. They envied the protection given to established interests by Mussolini, and there were those who even muttered "better Hitler than Léon Blum."

The Popular Front reforms, long overdue though they were, came to France at a time when the sands were rapidly running out. While France had a 40-hour week, German arms plants were operating at full capacity. In the shadow of Nazi remilitarization a rearmament program had to be undertaken at the very same time as reform; even moderates argued that the country could not afford both. Opposition from many quarters hindered success. French employers balked at cooperating in the new labor reforms and tried to pass on rising production costs to the consumer. Labor was disgruntled at the price rises that canceled out its wage gains. Both employers and labor applied the 40-hour week in such a manner that plants were shut down for two days a week instead of operating in shifts, as the law had intended. Nothing could check the flight of gold from the country. Industrial production hardly rose; even in 1938, when it had shown substantial recovery in other countries, it was only 5 percent higher in France than at the depth of the depression.

The overthrow of Blum's government

In July 1936 the Spanish Civil War had broken out. The Communists attacked the Blum government for refusing aid to the hard-pressed Spanish Popular Front government, which was fighting fascist forces across the Pyrenees; Blum, following the lead of Britain and fearing involvement, resisted. In 1937, after a year in office, the Blum government was overthrown by the Senate, which refused to grant it emergency financial powers. The Popular Front coalition rapidly disintegrated. By mid-1938 the Radical Socialists had abandoned their allies on the Left, and under Edouard Daladier formed a conservative ministry, whose attention was increasingly occupied by the international crisis. Little remained of the Popular Front, or indeed of the strength of labor, which declined rapidly and exhausted itself further by an unsuccessful general strike in 1938 in protest against nullification of the 40-hour week. For the French worker, 1936 had gone the way of other "great years"; the comfortable classes had been thrown into panic by the social turmoil; internal division and class hatreds had grown sharper. Yet the French democracy, the Third Republic itself, had been successfully preserved and its domestic enemies repulsed, at least for a time.

Western Europe and the Depression

Britain and France, and indeed all western Europe, Europe's inner zone, never fully recovered from the Great Depression before the Second World War. When economic expansion resumed after the war, the interwar years seemed like a deep trough in Europe's economic history. Western Europe barely maintained its old industrial equipment in the depression and was unable to utilize even its existing machinery to capacity. Moreover, as the events of 1929 had clearly shown, Europe's economic dependence on the United States was pronounced, and the U.S.S.R. was becoming an industrial giant. The economic destiny of Europeans in the 1930s was very much in doubt.

There were other signs of decline. The birth rate in western Europe in the 1930s fell to its lowest recorded levels as people postponed marriage or limited the size of their families because of economic and psychological stresses. Birth rates did not run significantly higher than death rates; the population was stagnating and growing older. There was a scarcity of middle-age men because of the casualties of the First World War. Politically neither British nor French democratic political leaders were able to cope with the economic dilemmas of the depression era. Nor could the Socialists, who found little practical guidance in the ideas of Marxian economics or class struggle, but failed to renew or reinvigorate their own doctrines in any significant way.

Other signs of decline

103. ITALIAN FASCISM

Though they shade into each other imperceptibly, it is possible to distinguish dictatorship from totalitarianism. Dictatorship, an old phenomenon in history, has commonly been regarded as a mere expedient, designed for emergencies and believed to be temporary; at most, it is a theory of government. Totalitarianism, as it arose after the First World War, was not merely a theory of government but a theory of life and of human nature. It claimed to be no expedient but a permanent form of society and civilization, and so far as it appealed to emergency for justification, it regarded life itself as an everlasting emergency. Let us first review the pertinent events in Italy and Germany and then return to the idea of totalitarianism.

The belief widely held in the 1920s that democracy was generally advancing was not deeply disturbed by the failure of Russia or Turkey or China to develop effective parliaments or liberal institutions. These were regarded as "backward" countries, in the throes of revolution; someday, when conditions quieted down, it could be supposed, they would move forward to democracy as known in the West. The first jarring exception to the apparent victory of democracy was furnished by Italy, a country that was an integral part of Europe and European history, a nation that since 1861 had accepted parliamentary liberalism, but where, in 1922, Benito Mussolini seized control of the government and proclaimed *Fascismo*.

Mussolini, born in 1883, the son of a blacksmith, was a fiery and pugnacious character, who before the war had followed the career of professional revolutionary, left-wing socialist, and radical journalist. He had read and digested works such as Sorel's *Reflections on Violence* and the writings of Nietzsche. During the war he turned intensely nationalist, clamored for Italian intervention on the side of the Allies, and demanded the conquest from Austria of *Italia irredenta,* the "unredeemed" Italian lands to the north and across the Adriatic. In the war he rose to the modest rank of corporal. In March 1919 he organized, mainly from demobilized and restless ex-soldiers, his first fighting band, or *fascio di combattimento. Fascio* meant a bunch or bundle, as of sticks; it called to mind the Latin *fasces,* or bundle of rods, carried by the lictors in ancient Rome as a symbol of state power—for Mussolini loved to conjure up ancient glories.

In 1919 Italian glories were dim. Italy had entered the war on the side of the Allies quite frankly for territorial and colonial spoils; the secret treaty of London in 1915 had promised the Italians certain Austrian lands and a share in German and Turkish possessions. During the war Italian arms did not especially shine; Italian troops were routed at Caporetto in 1917. Yet Italy lost over 600,000 lives in the war, and the Italian delegates came to the peace conference confident that their sacrifices would be recognized and their territorial aspirations would be satisfied. They were rapidly disappointed. Wilson refused to honor the provisions of the London secret treaty and other demands of the Italians. Britain and France displayed no eagerness to side with Italy. The Italians received some of the Austrian territories promised to them, but they were given no part of the former German or Turkish possessions as mandates.

After the war Italy, like other countries, suffered from the burden of wartime debt and from acute postwar depression and unemployment. Social unrest spread. In the countryside land seizures took place, not in any significant proportions but enough to spread concern among landowners; tenant farmers refused to pay rents; peasants burned crops and destroyed livestock. In the cities great strikes broke out in heavy industry and in transportation. Some of the strikes turned into sit-down strikes, the workers refusing to leave the plants; demands were raised even for worker control of the factories. Moderate socialist and labor leaders disavowed all such extremism, but left-wing socialists who, as elsewhere, had turned communist and joined the Third International, fanned the existing discontents. Meanwhile, armed bands of young men, most prominent of whom were the Blackshirts or Fascists, brawled with Communists and ordinary workers in the streets. By the late summer of 1920 the strikes and the agrarian unrest had subsided, although violence in the streets persisted.

During the months of turmoil the government refrained from any bold action. The Italian parliamentary system in the prewar years had never functioned impressively nor commanded widespread esteem; now respect for parliament and the weak, shifting, coalition ministries sank even lower. In 1919 the first postwar election was held, under a law that added proportional representation to the universal male suffrage introduced in 1913. The Socialists and a new Catholic Popular, or Christian Socialist, party made an impressive showing. In 1921, in the wake of the postwar disturbances, new elections were held. Liberals and democrats, moderate socialists, and the Catholic Popular party were all returned in large numbers. Mussolini's Fascist movement won 35 of the 500-odd seats. Despite this less than impressive showing (the best ever made by the Fascists in a free election), the Fascist ranks were swelling, in the backwash, as it were, of the postwar unrest.

Mussolini and the Fascists at first went along with the radical tide; they did not disapprove the factory seizures; they inveighed against plutocracy and war
profiteers and called for a high levy on capital and profits. But Mussolini,
never one to sacrifice opportunity for principles or doctrine, soon came forward with his Fascists as the upholders of national law and order, and hence
property; he now pledged battle "against the forces dissolving victory and
nation." Although the social agitation subsided, burning itself out on its

Mussolini:
upholding order
and property

own, and there had never been any real threat of a Soviet-style revolution, the propertied
classes had gone through a great fright; they found comfort in the Fascist movement and
were willing to lend it financial support. Patriots and nationalists of all classes rallied to it,
as well as the lower middle class, which was pinched by economic inflation and, as elsewhere, was unable to find protection or solace in labor unions or socialist movements. The
black-shirted upholders of national order proceeded methodically to administer beatings
(and doses of castor oil) to Communists and alleged Communists, to Socialists and Christian Socialists, and to ordinary persons who did not support them; nor did they refrain from
arson and murder. Vigilante fascist squadrons, the *squadristi,* broke up strikes, demolished
labor union headquarters, and drove from office duly elected Socialist and Communist
mayors and town officials. Mussolini nevertheless reinforced his claim as paladin of law,
authority, and order by declaring his loyalty to king and church; a few years earlier he had
been a rabid republican and anticlerical.

In October 1922 the "March on Rome" took place. The Blackshirts
mobilized for a threatened coup and began to converge from various directions on the capital; Mussolini remained at a safe distance in Milan. The lib-
eral-democratic coalition cabinet had viewed the events of the past two

The "March
on Rome"

years with disapproval but at the same time with satisfaction that the Blackshirts were
serving a useful national purpose by suppressing troublemakers on the Left. Now they
made belated but ineffectual gestures to save the situation by an effort to have martial law
declared; the king refused to approve. The cabinet resigned and Mussolini was named premier. It was all quite legal, or almost so. Indeed Italy was still in form a constitutional and
parliamentary government. Mussolini headed only a coalition ministry and received from
parliament no more than a year's grant of full emergency powers to restore order and introduce reforms.

But soon it was clear in whose hands power rested. Before the expiration of his emergency powers Mussolini forced through parliament a law providing that any party secur-
ing the largest number of votes in an election should automatically receive two-thirds of
the seats in the legislature. This was Mussolini's solution to the instability of coalitions and
blocs in parliamentary governments like those of Italy and France (and indeed of most
other Continental democracies), where a single party hardly ever enjoyed a majority. The
two-thirds law was not even necessary. In the 1924 elections, although seven opposition
slates appeared, the Fascists, aided by government control of the electoral machinery and
the use of *squadristi,* received well over three-fifths of the total vote.

After the elections of 1924 the highly respected Socialist deputy Matteotti publicly exposed hundreds of cases of armed Fascist violence and of fraud and chi-
canery. He was murdered by Fascists. There was widespread indignation in
the country, and the press clamored for Mussolini's resignation. The opposition parties even seceded from the Chamber, wanting to have nothing to

Matteotti's
murder

do with such a government. Mussolini, not directly involved in the assassination, expressed a willingness to punish the perpetrators, but he eventually took full

Benito Mussolini liked to portray his Fascist regime in Italy as a restoration of the power and grandeur of ancient Rome. Speaking here at a Fascist rally in 1932 and surrounded by uniformed followers as well as symbols of the Roman Empire, Mussolini struck a characteristic stance to convey a public image of decisive, powerful leadership in the authoritarian Italian state.

(Hulton Getty)

responsibility, and moved to consolidate his dictatorship. Within a few years he reduced the Italian parliament to a nonentity, put the press under censorship, destroyed the labor unions, deprived labor of the right to strike, and abolished all political parties except the Fascist party.

Fascism in the 1920s was an innovation which the rest of the world was slow to understand. In his more flamboyant moments Mussolini strutted, stuck out his jaw, and glared ferociously; he jumped through flaming hoops to show his virility and had his chief subordinates do likewise; to the outside world this seemed an odd way of demonstrating fitness for public office. He denounced democracy as historically outmoded and declared that it accentuated class struggle, split people into countless minority parties, and led to selfishness, futility, evasion, and empty talk. In place of democracy he preached the need of vigorous action, under a strong leader; he himself took the title of Leader, or *Duce*. He denounced liberalism, free trade, laissez-faire, and capitalism, along with Marxism, materialism, socialism, and class consciousness, which he said were the evil offspring of liberal and capitalistic society. In their place he preached national solidarity and state management of economic affairs, under the same Leader's farseeing and audacious vision. And in fact Mussolini seemed to bring a kind of efficiency; as the saying went, he at least made the trains run on time.

The corporative state

Mussolini introduced, at least in theory, the syndical, or corporative state, which had been discussed in both left- and right-wing circles for many years. Left-wing syndicalism, especially before the First World War, looked to revolutionary labor unions to expropriate the owners of industry and then to assume the direction of political and economic life. A more conservative syn-dicalism was endorsed and encouraged by the Catholic church, with which Mussolini had made his peace when he signed the Lateran accord in 1929 recognizing the independence and sovereignty of Vatican City. The conservative type of syndicalism looked nostalgically toward a revival of the medieval guilds, or "corporations," in which master and journey-men, employer and employees, had labored side by side in a supposedly golden age of so-cial peace.

The Fascist corporative system really resembled neither syndicalist theory because in Italy the hand of the state was writ large, something that none of the older corporative doc-trines had anticipated. It went through a number of complicated stages, but as it finally emerged in the 1930s, it provided for the division of all economic life into 22 major areas, for each of which a "corporation" was established. In each corporation representatives of the Fascist-organized labor groups, the employers, and the government determined work-ing conditions, wages, prices, and industrial policies; and in a national council these rep-resentatives were supposed jointly to devise plans for Italy's economic self-sufficiency. In each case the role of government was decisive and the whole structure was under the ju-risdiction of the minister of corporations. As a final step, these corporative economic chambers were integrated into the government proper so that in 1938 the old Chamber of Deputies was superseded by a Chamber of Fasces and Corporations representing the cor-porations and the Fascist party, its members selected by the government and not subject to popular ratification.

None of this was democratic, but this was an improvement over democracy, the Fas-cists asserted. A legislature in an advanced economic society, they said, should be an economic parliament; it should represent not political parties and geographical constituencies but economic occupations. Organization *State control of economic life* along such lines would do away with the anarchy and class conflict engen-dered by free capitalism, which only sap the strength of the national state.

Real authority in any event rested with the government—the head of the government, who settled most matters by decree. In point of fact, social unrest and class conflict were "ended," not by the corporative system as such, but by the prohibition of strikes and lock-outs and the abolition of independent labor unions. The corporative system represented the most extreme form of state control over economic life within a framework of private en-terprise and a relatively capitalistic economy, that is, one in which ownership continued to rest in private hands. It was the Fascist answer to Western-style democracy and to Soviet proletarian dictatorship. Fascism, said Mussolini, is the "dictatorship of the state over many classes cooperating."

When the depression struck, none of Italy's economic controls availed very much. Mussolini was eager to lay upon the world depression the blame for Italy's continuing eco-nomic ills. He turned to a vigorous program of public works and to increasing economic self-sufficiency. A "battle of wheat" was launched to increase food production; progress was made in reclaiming swamp areas in central Italy and in developing hydroelectric power as a substitute for the coal that Italy lacked. Throughout the Fascist era no fundamental reform changed the status of the peasants. The existing structure of society, which in Italy meant social extremes of wealth and poverty, remained unaltered. Fascism failed to provide either the economic security or the material well-being for which it had demanded the sacrifice of individual freedom. But it undeniably substituted a widespread psychological exhilaration, a feeling that Italy was undergoing a heroic national revival; and after 1935 to support that feeling Mussolini turned increasingly to military and imperialist adventures.

**The appeal
of fascism**

Fascism came to be regarded in other countries as a possible alternative to democratic or parliamentary government, as an actual corrective to troubles whose reality no one could deny. All Communists hated it, and so did all Socialists, labor leaders, moderate leftists, and idealistic liberals. Wealthier or established people, because of fear of Bolshevism, made more allowances in its favor. In East European countries, often highly nationalistic, or influenced by disgruntled landowners, or simply unused to settling questions by majority vote, fascism made a considerable appeal. In the Latin countries, in Spain, Portugal, and France, Mussolini's corporative state found champions and admirers. Sometimes, in Europe and elsewhere, intellectuals spun refined, sophisticated theories about the new order of discipline and authority, forgetting how Mussolini himself with unusual candor had written, "Fascism was not the nursling of a doctrine worked out beforehand with detailed elaboration; it was born of the need for action."

104. TOTALITARIANISM: GERMANY'S THIRD REICH

The Rise of Adolf Hitler

It was in Germany that Mussolini found his aptest pupil. Born in Austria in 1889, Adolf Hitler did little before the war. He was not an intellectual, like the prewar journalist Mussolini. He was never a socialist, but he fell into a restless and somewhat ignorant type of radicalism. Son of an Austrian customs official, he lost his father at 14 and his mother a few years later. He dropped out of high school at 16 and at 19 came to the great metropolis of Vienna as an art student but was never accepted into the academy to which he sought admission. When the small inheritance left by his parents ran out and a government grant for orphan students ended, he drifted into various menial jobs, occasionally selling a few of his postcard and poster paintings but mainly eking out a marginal existence with hardly any friends, money, or livelihood.

Hitler's dislikes

The young Hitler did not like what he saw in Vienna: neither the trappings of the Habsburg court, nor the nobility of eastern Europe who rode by in their carriages, nor the mixed nationalities of the Danubian empire, nor the Vienna worker's attachment to international Marxism, nor above all the Jews, who thanks to a century of liberal influences had become assimilated into the German culture and now occupied many distinguished positions in business, law, medicine, and journalism in the city. He became exceedingly race conscious, like many others in many countries at the time; the youthful Hitler took a special satisfaction in thinking of himself as a pure German of the good old German stock. He became violently anti-Semitic, and he also disliked aristocracy, capitalism, socialism, cosmopolitanism, internationalism, and "hybridization."

His aversion to Austria led him in 1913 to move to Munich, capital of the South German state of Bavaria. Once again he drifted without livelihood except by occasionally selling a few of his watercolors. When the war broke out, he volunteered for the German army. He served as a dispatch runner to the front line, and at one point was the victim of a gas attack that temporarily blinded him and injured his vocal cords. Although he rose in rank only to the rough equivalent of corporal, he received important military decorations. For Hitler, as for Mussolini and others, the war was a thrilling, noble, and liberating experience. The average individual, in modern society, led a pretty dull existence. Peace, for many, was a drab routine from which war was an exciting emancipation. Human atoms, floating in an impersonal and unfriendly world, they were stirred by the nationalism which the war aroused into a sense of belonging to, believing in, fighting for something greater than themselves, but which was yet their own. When peace returned, they felt a letdown.

When the war ended, Hitler remained for a time on active duty and was transferred to Munich. Bavaria in 1919 was a principal focus of the Communist offensive in central Europe; a Bavarian Soviet Republic even existed for about three weeks until crushed by the federal government in Berlin. The Communist threat made Bavaria a busy center for anticommunist, antisocialist, antirepublican, and antidemocratic agitation of all kinds, and the seat of a disgruntled illiberalism. It swarmed with secret societies and paramilitary organizations led by discontented army officers or others who fitted with difficulty into the new Weimar democracy. Hitler, working with the army's political instruction program which had been created to combat socialist and democratic propaganda among the demobilized veterans and workers and *Nazi origins*
to keep alive a patriotic and military spirit, joined at the army's behest a tiny party called the German Workers' party and soon became its leader. Early in 1920 he proclaimed its 25-point program, the party now calling itself the National Socialist German Workers' party. Thus were born the Nazis, so called from the German way of pronouncing the first two syllables of "National." Now demobilized, Hitler was fully launched on a career of radical politics.

In earlier pages we have noted the beginnings of the Weimar Republic and the burdens it was compelled to bear from the start—the Versailles peace, reparations, the catastrophic inflation of 1923. Something has been said also of the failure of the republicans to inaugurate the kind of deep social changes that might have democratized the political and social structure of German society and thereby strengthened republican forces. For five years after the war, violence remained sporadic in Germany. Communist agitation continued; but more dangerous, because they attracted more sympathy among the Germans, were the maneuvers of monarchist and antirepublican organizations, which maintained armed bands and threatened uprisings like the unsuccessful Kapp *putsch* of 1920. (One such private "army" was the Brownshirts or Storm Troopers maintained by the Nazis.) Such bands even resorted to assassination. Thus Walter Rathenau was murdered in 1922; he had organized German production during the war, and in 1922 he was foreign minister, but he had democratic and internationalist inclinations—and was a Jew. Another victim was Matthias Erzberger, a leading moderate politician of the Catholic Center party—he had helped "betray" the army by signing the armistice.

In 1923, when reparations payments were not forthcoming, the French army occupied the Ruhr. A clamor of national indignation swept over Germany. Hitler and the National Socialists, who since 1919 had obtained a considerable following, denounced the Weimar government for shameful submission to the French. They judged the moment opportune for seizing power, and at the end of 1923, in imitation of Mussolini's march on Rome the year before, the Brownshirts staged the "beer hall *putsch*" in Munich. Hitler jumped on the platform, fired a revolver at the ceiling, and shouted that the "national revolution has broken out." But the police suppressed the disturbance, and Hitler was sentenced to five years in prison. He was released in less than a year; the Weimar democracy dealt mildly with its enemies. *The "beer hall putsch"*

In prison Hitler wrote his book, *Mein Kampf (My Struggle)*, a turbid stream of personal recollection, racism, nationalism, collectivism, theories of history, Jew baiting, and political comment. *Mein Kampf* sold widely. The book and the publicity that had accompanied the five-week trial converted Hitler into *Mein Kampf* a political figure of national prominence. The former soldier was not alone in his ideas; no less a person than General Ludendorff, who had distinguished himself in the war, and after the war became one of the most grotesquely unbalanced of the old officer class, gave his warm support to Hitler and even took part in the beer hall *putsch.*

Beginning in 1924, with the French out of the Ruhr, reparations adjusted, a new and stable currency adopted, and loans from foreign countries, mainly the United States, Germany began to enjoy an amazing economic revival. National Socialism lost its appeal; the party lost members, Hitler was regarded as a charlatan, and his followers, as a lunatic fringe. All seemed quiet. Then came the Great Depression in 1929. Adolf Hitler, who might have faded out of history, was transformed by the circumstances attending the depression in Germany into a figure of Napoleonic proportions.

The crisis confronting Germany

No country suffered more than Germany from the worldwide economic collapse. Foreign loans abruptly ceased or were recalled. Factories ground to a halt. There were 6 million unemployed. The middle class had not really recovered from the great inflation of 1923; struck again, after so brief a respite, they lost all faith in the economic system and in its future.

The Communist vote steadily mounted; the great middling masses, who saw in communism their own death warrant, and who are extremely numerous in any highly developed society, looked about desperately for someone to save them from Bolshevism. The depression also stirred up the universal German loathing for the Treaty of Versailles. Many Germans explained the ruin of Germany by the postwar treatment it had received from the Allies—the constriction of its frontiers, the loss of its colonies, markets, shipping, and foreign investments, the colossal demand for reparations, the occupation of the Ruhr, the inflation, and much else.

Any people in such a trap would have been bewildered and resentful. But the way out chosen by the Germans was perhaps a product of deeper attitudes formed by German experience in the past centuries. Democracy—the agreement to obtain and accept majority verdicts, to discuss and compromise, to adjust conflicting interests without wholly satisfying or wholly crushing either side—was hard enough to maintain in any country in a true crisis. In Germany democracy was itself an innovation, which had yet to prove its value, which could easily be called un-German, an artificial and imported doctrine, or even a foreign system foisted upon Germany by the victors in the late war.

Hitler's propaganda

Hitler inflamed all such feelings by his propaganda. He denounced the Treaty of Versailles as a national humiliation. He denounced the Weimar democracy for producing class struggle, division, weakness, and wordy futility. He called for "true" democracy in a vast and vital stirring of the people, or *Volk,* behind a Leader who was a man of action. He declared that Germans, pure Germans, must rely only on themselves. He inveighed against Marxists, Bolsheviks, communists, and socialists, throwing them all together in a deliberate beclouding of the issues; but he claimed to favor the right kind of socialism for the little man, that is, the doctrine of the National Socialist German Workers' party. He ranted against unearned incomes, war profits, the power of the great trusts and chain stores, land speculators, interest slavery, and unfair taxes. Above all, he denounced the Jews. Jews, like others, were found in all political camps. To the Left, Jewish capitalists were anathema. To the Right, Jewish revolutionaries were a horror. In anti-Semitism Hitler found a lowest common denominator upon which to appeal to all parties and classes. At the same time the Jews were a small minority (only 600,000 in all Germany), so that in an age of mass politics it was safe enough to attack them.

In the election of 1930 the Nazis won 107 seats in the Reichstag; in 1928 they had won only 12; their popular vote went up from 800,000 to 6.5 million. The Communist representation rose from 54 to 77. By July 1932 the Nazis more than doubled their popular vote, won 230 seats, and were now by far the largest single party though because of the multiplicity of parties they fell well short of a majority. In another election, in November 1932, the Nazis, though still well out in front, showed some loss of strength, losing 2 million votes, and dropping to 196 seats. The Communist vote had risen progressively to a peak of 100 in November 1932.

After the relative setback of November 1932 Hitler feared that his movement was passing. But certain conservative, nationalist, and antirepublican elements—old aristocrats, Junker landowners, army officers, Rhineland steel magnates, and other industrialists—had conceived the idea that Hitler could be useful to them. From such sources, which supported other reactionary causes as well, came a portion of Nazi funds. This influential group, mainly from the small Nationalist party, imagined that they would be able to control Hitler and hence control the wave of mass discontent of which in such large measure he had made himself the leader; they were little disturbed by his anticapitalist program.

After Bruening's resignation in June 1932, Franz von Papen headed a Nationalist cabinet with the backing of the influential army leader General Kurt von Schleicher. In December 1932 Schleicher forced Papen's downfall and succeeded him. When he, too, was compelled to resign a month later, both men, intriguing separately, prevailed upon President Hindenburg to name Hitler chancellor of a coalition cabinet. On January 30, 1933, by entirely legal means, Adolf Hitler became chancellor of the German Republic; other positions in the new cabinet were occupied by the Nationalists, with whom the Nazis were to share power.

Hitler named chancellor

But to share power was not the Nazis' aim. Hitler called for another election. A week before election day the Reichstag building caught fire. The Nazis, without any real evidence, blamed it on the Communists. They frightened the population with a Red scare, suspended freedom of speech and press, and set loose the Brownshirts to bully the voters. Even so, in the election, the Nazis won only 44 percent of the vote; with their Nationalist allies, they had 52 percent. Hitler, trumpeting a national emergency, was voted dictatorial powers by a pliant Reichstag from which the Communist deputies had been excluded. The Nazi revolution now began.

The Nazi State

Hitler called his new order the Third Reich. He declared that, following on the First Reich, or Holy Roman Empire, and the Second Reich, or empire founded by Bismarck, the Third Reich carried on the process of true German history, of which, he said, it was the organic outgrowth and natural culmination. The Third Reich, he prophesied, would last a thousand years.

Like Mussolini, Hitler took the title of Leader, or, in German, the *Führer.* He claimed to represent the absolute sovereignty of the German people. Jews were considered un-German. Democracy, parliamentarianism, and liberalism were stigmatized as "Western" and together with communism were labeled as "Jewish." The new "racial science" classified Jews as non-Aryans and included as Jewish anyone who had one Jewish grandparent. Almost at once Jews were driven from public office, the civil service, teaching, and other professions. The Nuremberg laws of 1935 deprived Jews of all citizenship rights and forbade intermarriage

Anti-Semitism

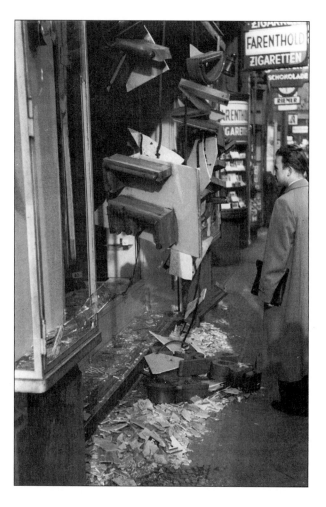

The Nazi-orchestrated attack on Jewish shops and businesses in November 1938 carried the official anti-Semitism of the Nazi state to a new level of violence in German cities. The shattered windows and signs at this Jewish store in Berlin convey the meaning of *Kristallnacht*—the night of broken glass.

(AKG London)

or even sexual relations between Jews and non-Jews. On November 9, 1938, *Kristallnacht,* the "night of broken glass," the anti-Semitism of Nazi Germany turned to fierce violence. When a 17-year-old Polish-Jewish student, distraught by the mistreatment of his parents, shot and killed a German diplomatic official in the German Embassy in Paris, Nazi storm troopers in a savage orgy of vandalism, looting, and incendiarism smashed Jewish shops, businesses, and synagogues in German cities, beat up thousands of Jews, and rounded up 30,000 to be sent to concentration camps. Party and government leaders moved in to control the storm troopers and to use anti-Semitism for their own purposes. The government levied a billion-mark fine on the Jewish community for provoking the assault and collected the insurance payments for the shattered glass and other property damage. Jews who in the wake of these events belatedly tried to flee the country discovered that neither they nor their families could readily find places of refuge; the doors in Europe and the United States were for the most part closed to them. The events of 1938 in Germany still resembled an older-style pogrom, but they foreshadowed the state-organized systematic destruction, in the Holocaust, of six million European (and German) Jews in the grisly death camps.

The new totalitarian order was thought of as absolutely solid, or monolithic, like one huge single slab of rock in which no particle had any separate structure. Germany ceased to be federal; all the old states such as Prussia and Bavaria were abolished. All political parties except the National Socialists were destroyed. The Nazi party was itself violently purged on the night of June 30, 1934, when many of the old Brownshirt leaders, those who represented the more social revolutionary wing of the movement, were accused of plotting against Hitler and were summarily shot. A secret political police, the Gestapo *(Geheime Staatspolizei),* together with People's Courts, and a system of permanent concentration camps in which thousands were detained without trial or sentence, suppressed all ideas at variance with the Leader's.

Law itself was defined as the will of the German people operating in the interests of the Nazi state. Churches, both Protestant and Catholic, were "coordinated" with the new regime; their clergy were forbidden to criticize its activities, international religious ties were discouraged, and efforts were made to keep children out of religious schools. The government encouraged anti-Christian pagan movements, in worship of the old Teutonic gods, but nothing was sponsored so much as worship of Nazism and its *Führer.* A Nazi Youth Movement, and schools and universities, indoctrinated the rising generation in the new concepts. The total, all-encompassing repression thwarted the efforts of a few dedicated Germans to develop a broad resistance movement.

"Coordinating" German society

Labor unions also were "coordinated"; they were replaced by a National Labor Front. Strikes were forbidden. Under the "leadership principle" employers were set up as small-scale *Führers* in their factories and industries and given extensive control, subject to close government supervision. An extensive public works program was launched, reforestation and swamp drainage projects were organized, housing and superhighways were built. A vast rearmament program absorbed the unemployed and within a short time unemployment disappeared. Even under Nazi statistics labor's share in the national income was reduced, but workers had jobs; and an organization called Strength Through Joy attended to the needs of people with small incomes, providing entertainment, vacations, and travel for many who could never otherwise afford them.

The government assumed increasing controls over industry, while leaving ownership in private hands. In 1936 it adopted a Four-Year Plan of economic development. All countries after the Great Depression tended to economic nationalism, but Nazi Germany set up the goal of autarky and self-sufficiency—absolute independence from foreign trade. German chemists developed artificial rubber, plastics, synthetic textiles, and many other substitute products to enable the country to do without raw materials imported from overseas.

Economic autarky and self-sufficiency

For Europe as a whole one of the basic economic problems, especially after the World War, was that while the Continent was economically a unit dependent on exchange between diverse regions, politically it was cut to pieces by tariff restrictions, currency differences, and hothouse industries artificially nurtured by nationalist ambition. The Nazis claimed to have a solution for this problem in a network of bilateral trade agreements assuring all neighboring peoples an outlet for their products. But it was a solution in which Germans were to be the most industrial, most advanced, most powerful, and most wealthy, and other Europeans were to be relegated to permanently inferior status. And what could not be accomplished under trade agreements and economic penetration could be accomplished by conquest and war. Within a few years after 1933, although the regime had its share of bureaucratic confusion and personal rivalries, the Nazi revolution had turned Germany into a huge disciplined war machine, its internal foes liquidated or silenced, its mesmerized masses roaring their approval in giant demonstrations, ready to follow the Führer in storming new Valkyrian heights. "Today Germany," went an ominous phrase, "tomorrow the whole world."

Totalitarianism: Some Origins and Consequences

Totalitarianism was a many-sided thing. It had appeared first with the Bolshevik Revolution, for in the denial of individual liberty the Soviet regime did not differ from the most extreme anti-Soviet totalitarianism as manifested in Germany. (Although Mussolini was the first to use the term "totalitarian," and advance it as an ideology, the Fascist regime that he established was not sufficiently all-encompassing to merit that term.) There were important differences in principle. Theoretically, the proletarian dictatorship was temporary; it did not at first glorify the individual Leader-Hero; and it was not nationalistic, for it rested on a principle of worldwide class struggle in all nations alike. It adopted a democratic-sounding constitution and paid at least lip service to individual rights. Its constitution officially condemned racism, and it did not deliberately and consciously cultivate an ethics of war and violence. But as time passed, Soviet totalitarianism became harder to distinguish from others. The Soviet dictatorship and one-party state seemed as permanent as any political system; the hollowness of the constitution and the guarantee of individual rights became more apparent; a cult developed around the person of Stalin; the emphasis became more nationalistic, falling less on the workers of the world and more on the glories of the Soviet motherland; and it sent untold numbers to harsh labor camps to perish.

The evolution of totalitarianism

Totalitarianism, as distinct from mere dictatorship, though it appeared rather suddenly after the First World War, was no historic freak. It was an outgrowth of a good deal of development in the past. The state was an institution that had continuously acquired new powers ever since the Middle Ages; step by step, since feudal times, it had assumed jurisdiction over law courts and men at arms, imposed taxes, regulated churches, guided economic policy, operated school systems, and devised schemes of public welfare. The First World War had continued and advanced the process. The twentieth-century totalitarian state, mammoth and monolithic, claiming absolute dominion over every department of life, now carried this old development of state sovereignty to a new extreme. For centuries, for example, the state had clashed with the church. The twentieth-century dictators did the same. In addition, however, they were in most cases not merely anticlerical but explicitly anti-Christian, offering, or rather imposing, a "total" philosophy of life.

Reliance on historic nationalism

This new philosophy drew heavily upon a historic nationalism which it greatly exaggerated. It rejected classical liberalism, which stressed the autonomy of rational individuals, and promoted instead an organic theory of society. It held that society (or the nation or state) was a kind of living organism within which the individual person was but a single cell. Individuals, in this theory, had no independent existence; they received life itself, and all their ideas, from the society, people, nation, or culture into which they were born and by which they were nurtured. In Marxism, the absolute subordination of individuals to their class came to much the same thing. Individuals were a microscopic cell, meaningless outside the social body. They were but clay to be molded by the imprint of their groups. It made little sense, given such theories, to speak of the individual's "reason" or "freedom," or to allow individuals to have their own opinions, or to count up individual opinions to obtain a merely numerical majority. Valid ideas were those of the group as a whole, of the people or nation (or, in Marxism, the class) as a solid block. Even science was a product of specific societies; there was a "Nazi science" which was bound to differ in its conclusions from democratic bourgeois, Western, or "Jewish" science; and for the Soviets there was a Soviet science, consistent with dialectical materialism and better equipped to see the truth than the decadent bourgeois, capitalistic, or "fascist" science of the non-Soviet world. All art, too—music, painting, poetry, fiction, architecture, sculpture—was good art insofar as it expressed the society or nationality in which it appeared.

The avowed philosophy of totalitarian regimes was subjective. Whether an idea was held to be true depended on whose idea it was. Ideas of truth, or beauty, or right were not supposed to correspond to any outer or objective reality; they had only to correspond to the inner nature, interests, or point of view of the people, nation, society, or class that entertained such ideas. The older Enlightenment concepts of reason, natural law, natural right, and the ultimate alikeness of all mankind, or of a common path of all mankind in one course of progress, disappeared.

The totalitarian regimes did not simply declare, as a dry finding of social science, that peoples' ideas were shaped by environment. They set about shaping them actively. Propaganda became a principal branch of government. Propaganda was hardly new, but in the past, and still in the democratic countries, it had been a piecemeal affair, urging the public to accept this or that political party, or rally to this or that campaign. Now, like all else, it became "total." Propaganda was monopolized by the state, and it demanded faith in a whole view of life and in every detail of this coordinated whole. Formerly the control of books and newspapers had been mainly negative; under Napoleon or Metternich, for example, censors had forbidden statements on particular subjects, events, or persons. Now, in totalitarian countries, control of the press became frighteningly positive. The government manufactured thought. It manipulated opinion. It rewrote history. Writers were required to present whole ideologies, and books, newspapers, magazines, and the radio diffused an endless and overwhelming cloud of words. Loudspeakers blared in the streets, gigantic blown-up photographs of the Leader looked down in public places. The propaganda experts were sometimes fanatics, but often they were cynics like Dr. Goebbels in Germany, too intelligent to be duped by the rubbish with which they duped their country.

Propaganda

The very idea of truth evaporated. No norm of human utterance remained except political expediency—the wishes and self-interest of those in power. No one could learn anything except what the government wanted people to know. No one could escape the omnipresent official doctrine, the insidious penetration of the very recesses of the mind by ideas planted by outsiders for their own purposes. People came to accept, and even to believe, the most extravagant statements when they were endlessly repeated, year after year. Barred from all independent sources of information, having no means by which any official allegation could be tested, the peoples of totalitarian countries became increasingly in fact, and not merely in sociological theory, incapable of the use of reason.

Racism, more characteristic of Nazi Germany than of totalitarianism in general, was a further exaggeration, or degradation, of older ideas of nationalism and national solidarity. It defined the nation in a tribal sense, as a biological entity, a group of persons possessing the same physical ancestry and the same or similar physical characteristics. Anti-Semitism was the most venomous form of racism in Europe. While a latent hostility to Jews had always been present in the Christian world, modern anti-Semitism had little to do with Christianity. It arose in part from the fact that, in the nineteenth century, with the general removal of religious disabilities, the Jews entered into general society and many of them achieved positions of prominence, and especially so in Germany, so that from the point of view of any individual non-Jew they could be represented as dangerous competitors in business or the professions. But most of all, anti-Semitism was inflamed by propagandists who wished people to feel their

Racism

The Nazi regime used public spectacles to send a message of irresistible national power to both the German people and foreign observers. The annual Nazi rallies at Nuremberg became the most carefully organized expressions of allegiance to the Third Reich and the Nazi ideology. The salute to Hitler, as shown in this photograph of the Führer leading his officers between rows of soldiers at Nuremberg in 1938, was a typical example of the fervent loyalty and emotion that such events were designed to evoke.

(Corbis)

supposed racial purity more keenly or to forget the deeper problems of society, including poverty, unemployment, and economic inequities.

Totalitarianism "resolves" class conflict

For totalitarianism was an escape from the realities of class conflict. It was a way of pretending that differences between rich and poor were of minor importance. Typically, a totalitarian regime came into power by stirring up class fears, then remained in power, and represented itself as indispensable, by declaring that it had settled the class problem. Thus Mussolini, Hitler, and certain lesser dictators, before seizing office, pointed alarmingly to the dark menace of Bolshevism; and, once in power, declared that all classes stood shoulder to shoulder in slablike solidarity behind the Leader.

Nor were events in Russia (or in China after the Second World War) altogether different. The Bolsheviks in 1917, armed with the ideas of Karl Marx, aroused the workers against capitalists, landlords, middle-class people, and rich peasants; once in power and after extensive liquidations, they declared that the classless society had arrived, that no true social classes any longer existed, and that all citizens stood solidly behind a regime from which, they said, all good citizens benefited equally. Only the democracies admitted that they suffered from internal class problems, from maladjustments between rich and poor or between favored and unfavored groups in society.

The dictatorships blamed their troubles on forces outside the country. They accused dissatisfied persons of conspiring with foreigners or refugees—with being the tools of Trotskyism, imperialism, or international Jewry. Or they talked of the struggle between rich nations and poor nations, the "have" and the "have not" countries, and thus transformed the problem of poverty into an international struggle. In the distinction between "have" and "have not" countries there was, of course, more than a grain of truth; in more old-fashioned language some countries (in fact the European democracies, as well as the United States and the British dominions of the 1930s) had progressed farther than others in their economic productivity and accumulation of wealth. It is probable that any propaganda is more effective if partly true. But when the totalitarians blamed their troubles on other countries and transformed the conflict between "have" and "have not" into a struggle between nations, they gave the impression that war might be a solution for social ills.

Violence, the acceptance and even glorification of violence, was indeed the characteristic most clearly distinguishing the totalitarian from the democratic systems. We have seen how a cult of violence, or belief that struggle was beneficial, had arisen before the First World War. The war itself habituated people to violence and direct action. Lenin and his followers showed how a small group could seize the helm of state under revolutionary or chaotic conditions. Mussolini in 1922 taught the same lesson, with further refinements; for the Italy in which he seized power was not at war, and it was merely the threat or possibility of revolution, not revolution itself, that provided him with his opportunity. In the 1920s, for the first time since the seventeenth century, some of the most civilized parts of Europe, in time of peace, saw private armies marching about the country, bands of uniformed and organized ruffians, Blackshirts or Brownshirts, who manhandled, abused, and even killed law-abiding citizens with impunity. Nor would anyone in the 1920s have believed that, by the 1930s, Europe would see the reintroduction of torture.

The glorification of violence

The very ethics of totalitarianism was violent and neopagan. It borrowed from and distorted Nietzsche and other prewar theoreticians, who, safe and civilized, had declared that people should live dangerously, avoid the flabby weakness of too much thought, throw themselves with red-blooded vigor into a life of action. The new regimes all instituted youth movements. They appealed to a kind of juvenile idealism, in which young people believed that by joining some kind of squad, donning some kind of uniform, and getting into the fresh air they contributed to a great moral resurgence of their country. Young men were taught to value their bodies but not their minds, to be tough and hard, and to regard mass gymnastics as patriotic demonstrations. Young women were taught to breed large families without complaint, to be content in the kitchen, and to look with awe upon their virile mates.

The body cult flourished while the mind decayed. Especially in National Socialism the ideal was to turn the German people into a race of splendid animals, pink-cheeked, Nordic, and upstanding. Contrariwise, euthanasia was adopted for the chronically ill and the insane and was proposed for the aged. Nazi ideologists produced pseudoscientific racist theories to explain and justify their actions. Later, in the Second World War, when the Nazis overran eastern Europe, they committed Jews and others to the gas chambers, destroying over six million human beings by the most scientific methods. Human beings were animals; one bred the kind one wanted and killed the kind one did not.

The Spread of Dictatorship

The trend toward dictatorship spread in Europe in the 1930s. By 1938 only 10 out of 27 European countries remained democratic, in the sense that different political parties honestly competed for office and that citizens within generous limits thought and acted as they pleased. They were Great Britain and France; Holland, Belgium, and Switzerland; Czechoslovakia and Finland; and the three Scandinavian countries Denmark, Norway, and Sweden.

The collapse of democratic governments

The promise of the early 1920s that constitutional and democratic government would flourish was thwarted. The weakness or absence of a parliamentary or democratic tradition, low education and literacy standards, the hostility of reactionary elements, the fear of Bolshevism, and the dissatisfaction of existing national minorities, all coupled with the economic strains resulting from the Great Depression, contributed to the collapse of the new representative institutions. Apart from the avowedly totalitarian or fascist regimes of Germany and Italy, the new dictatorships and authoritarian systems generally rested on a combination of personal and military power, but several reflected or absorbed some of the ideological features of a generic fascism. In Portugal, Salazar inaugurated a clerical-corporative dictatorship in 1932 that lasted for over four decades. In Austria, Dollfuss fused various right-wing political and military elements into a clerical-fascist "Christian" dictatorship which violently suppressed the Socialists and sought in vain to counter the German threat. In Spain General Franco established a right-wing authoritarian government after a bloody civil war (described in the next chapter). In many respects the dictatorships of Latin America under their caudillos and military juntas resembled the European military dictatorships; similar repressive one-party regimes have reappeared in other parts of the world down to the present.

The authoritarian regimes were alike in repressing individual liberties, banning opposition parties, and abolishing or nullifying parliamentary institutions. Many borrowed features of fascism, establishing a corporative state, outlawing independent labor organizations, and forbidding strikes; many, like Hungary, Romania, and Poland, instituted anti-Semitic legislation. None went so far as Hitler's Third Reich in the total coordination of all political, economic, intellectual, and biological activities in a revolutionary mass-based dictatorship.

The acceptance and glorification of violence, it has been noted, was the feature most clearly distinguishing the totalitarian from the democratic systems. War in the Nazi and Fascist ethics was a noble thing, and the love of peace a sign of decadence. (The Soviet regime by its own theory regarded war with non-Soviet powers as inevitable some day, but did not preach it as a positive moral good.) The exaltation of war and struggle, the need for maintaining national solidarity, the habit of blaming foreign countries for social troubles, together with the considerable armaments programs on which the dictatorships embarked, plus the personal ambition and egotistical mania of individual dictators, made the decade of the 1930s a time not only of domestic reaction but of recurrent international crises, of which the last, in 1939, led to war.

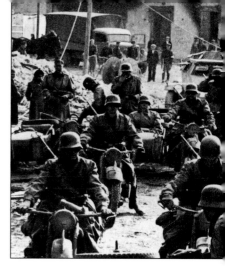

Chapter 21

THE SECOND
WORLD WAR

Peace in the abstract, the peace that is the mere absence of war, does not exist in international relations. Peace is never found apart from certain conditions; it means peaceable acceptance of given conditions, or peaceable and orderly transformation of conditions by negotiation and agreement. The conditions, in the 1930s, were basically those laid down by the Paris peace conference of 1919—the states recognized, the frontiers drawn, the terms agreed to, at the close of the First World War. In the 1930s neither Germany, Italy, Japan, nor the U.S.S.R. was content with these conditions; they were "revisionist" or dissatisfied powers; and the first three were willing to undertake war itself to make a change. Great Britain, France, and the United States were satisfied powers, expecting no benefit from change in the conditions; but on the other hand they had lost faith in the conditions and were unwilling to risk war for the sake of upholding them. They had made a treaty in 1919 which a dozen years later they were unwilling to enforce. They stood idly by, as long as they could, while the dissatisfied powers tore to pieces the states recognized, the frontiers drawn, and the terms agreed to at the Peace of Paris. From the Japanese invasion of Manchuria in 1931 to the outbreak of European war in 1939, force was used by those who wished to upset international order, but never by those who wished to maintain it. A new world war was therefore launched by nations that had never accepted the outcome of the last one.

The war that raged across the world from 1939 to 1945 was the most destructive conflict in human history. It was also the most widely dispersed, global war that has ever been fought. The Second World War affected nations on every continent; caused the deaths of almost 60 million people (at least two-thirds of whom were civilians); produced vast physical damage in cities, factories, and countrysides; generated new forms of genocidal mass murder as well as new military weapons of mass destruction; and contributed decisively to

Chapter emblem: German troops entering a destroyed Polish village in September 1939.

the new global influence of two superpower nations—the United States and the Soviet Union.

Historians often disagree about the social or political consequences of warfare, but the Second World War was unquestionably one of the definitive, shaping events in modern world history. Both the haunting memories and complex legacy of the Second World War still influence modern cultures and people everywhere at the beginning of the twenty-first century.

105. THE WEAKNESS OF THE DEMOCRACIES: AGAIN TO WAR

The Pacifism and Disunity of the West

While dictators stormed in the 1930s, the Western democracies were swayed by a profound pacifism, which may be defined as an insistence on peace regardless of consequences. Many people, especially in England and the United States, believed that the First World War had been a mistake, that little or nothing had been gained by it, that they had been deluded by wartime propaganda, that wars were really started by armaments manufacturers, that Germany had not really caused the war of 1914, that the Treaty of Versailles was too hard on the Germans, that vigorous peoples like the Germans or Italians needed room for expansion, that democracy was after all not suited to all nations, that it took two to make a quarrel, and that there need be no war if one side resolutely refused to be provoked—a whole system of pacific and tolerant ideas in which there was perhaps the usual mixture of truth and misunderstanding.

The pacifism of the West had other roots, most evident in France. About 1.4 million Frenchmen had died in the First World War; half of all French males between the ages of 20 and 32 in 1914 had been killed. To the French it was

The pacifism of the West

inconceivable that such a holocaust should be repeated. French strategy was therefore defensive and sparing of manpower. If war came, the French expected to fight it mainly in the elaborate fortifications, called the Maginot Line, which they built on their eastern frontier facing Germany, from the Swiss to the Belgian border; to its north the Ardennes forest was to be a barrier to any invader. During the depression France was torn by internal class conflict and by fascist and quasi-fascist agitation. Many French on the Right, historically unsympathetic to the republic and seeing, or claiming to see, in such movements as the Popular Front the threat of social revolution, did not conceal their admiration for Mussolini or even for Hitler. Abandoning their traditional role as ardent nationalists, they would do nothing to oppose the dictators. On the other hand, many on the Left looked with sympathy upon the Soviet Union. France was ideologically too divided in the 1930s to possess any firm foreign policy, and all elements took false comfort from the supposed impregnability of the French Chinese Wall.

A similar situation, in lesser degree, prevailed in Great Britain and the United States. The loss and bloodshed of the First World War were remembered. It was well known that another world war would be even more horrible; there was an unspeakable dread of the bombing of cities. Typical of the time was a resolution adopted by students at Oxford in 1933 that they would never take up arms for their country under any conditions; peace movements appeared among American college students too. The pull between Left and Right was felt in England and America. In the 1930s, when any international action seemed to favor either the U.S.S.R. on the one hand, or Hitler and Mussolini on the other, it was hard to establish any foreign policy on a firm basis of national unity. In Britain some members of the upper classes were overtly sympathetic to the fascist dictators, or saw in them a bulwark against communism. The government itself tried to be noncommittal; it believed that some means of satisfying or appeasing the more legitimate demands of the dictators might be found. Neville Chamberlain, prime minister after 1937, became the principal architect of the appeasement policy.

The United States government, despite President Roosevelt's repeated denunciation of the aggressors, followed in practice a policy of rigid isolation. Neutrality legislation, enacted by a strong isolationist bloc in Congress in the years 1935 to 1937, forbade loans, export of munitions, and use of American shipping facilities to any belligerent once the president had recognized a state of war in a given area. Many believed that the United States had been drawn into the First World War by such economic involvement. From this American neutrality legislation the aggressors of the 1930s derived great benefit, but not the victims of aggression.

As for the rulers of the U.S.S.R., they were revisionist and dissatisfied in that they did not accept the new frontiers of eastern Europe nor the territorial losses incurred by Russia in the First World War. They resented the *cordon sanitaire* created in 1919 against the spread of Bolshevism, the ring of small states on their borders from Finland to Romania, which were almost without exception vehemently anti-Soviet. They had no fondness for the international

Russian resentment

status quo, nor had they abandoned their long-range revolutionary objectives. But, as Communists and as Russians, they were obsessed by fear of attack and invasion. Their Marxist doctrine taught the inherent hostility of the entire capitalist world; the intervention of the Western Allies in the revolution and civil wars confirmed their Marxist theory. And long before the Bolshevik Revolution, in the days of Napoleon and earlier, the fertile Russian plains had tempted ambitious conquerors. Resentful and suspicious of the outside world, in the 1930s the men in the Kremlin were alarmed primarily by Germany. Hitler, in *Mein Kampf* and elsewhere, had declared that he meant to obliterate Bolshevism and subordinate large stretches of eastern Europe to Germany.

The Soviets became interested in collective security, in international action against aggression. In 1934 they joined the League of Nations. They instructed Communist parties to work with socialists and liberals in popular fronts. They offered assistance in checking fascist aggressors, signing mutual assistance pacts with France and Czechoslovakia in 1935. But many people fled from the Soviet embrace with a shudder. They distrusted Soviet motives, or they were convinced that the purges and trials of the 1930s had left the Soviets weak and undependable as allies, or they felt that the fascist dictators might be diverted eastward against the Soviets and so spare the Western democracies. Here again, though the Soviet Union was ostensibly willing, no effective coalition against aggression could be formed.

The March of Nazi and Fascist Aggression

Adolf Hitler perceived these weaknesses with uncanny genius. Determined to wreck the whole treaty system, which most Germans, to be sure, found humiliating, he employed tactics of gradual encroachment that played on the hopes and fears of the democratic peoples. He inspired in them alternating tremors of apprehension and sighs of relief. He would rage and rant, arouse the fear of war, take just a little, declare that it was all he wanted, let the former Allies naïvely hope that he was now satisfied and that peace was secure; then rage again, take a little more, and proceed through the same cycle.

Each year he precipitated some kind of emergency, and each time the French and British saw no alternative except to let him have his way. In 1933, soon after seizing power, he took Germany out of the League and out of the Disarmament Conference then taking place. He successfully wooed Poland, long France's ally, and in 1934 the two countries signed a nonaggression treaty. That same year the Nazis of Austria attempted a *putsch,* assassinated the Austrian chancellor, Dollfuss, and demanded the union of Austria with Germany. The Western powers did nothing. It was Mussolini who acted. Not desiring to see Germany installed at the Brenner Pass, he mobilized large Italian forces on the frontier, discouraged Hitler from intervening openly in Austria, and so preserved the independence of Austria for four more years. In January 1935 a plebiscite was conducted in the Saar by the League of Nations as stipulated under the Versailles treaty. Amidst intense Nazi agitation, the Saar voted for reunion with the Reich. Two months later, in March 1935, Hitler dramatically repudiated those clauses in the Versailles treaty intended to keep Germany disarmed; he now openly built up the German armed forces. France, England, and Italy protested such arbitrary and one-sided denunciation of an international treaty but did nothing about it. Indeed, Great Britain entered into a naval agreement with Germany, to the consternation of the French.

Hitler's triumphs

On March 7, 1936, using as his justification the new Franco-Soviet pact, Hitler repudiated the Locarno agreements (which had confirmed post–World War I national borders) and reoccupied the Rhineland; that is, he sent German troops into the German territory west of the Rhine, which by the Treaty of Versailles was supposed to be a demilitarized zone. There was talk in the French government of action, and at this time Hitler might have been checked, for German military strength was still weak and the German army was prepared to withdraw, or at least consult, at signs of resistance. But the French government was divided and unwilling to act without Britain; and the British would not risk war to keep German troops from occupying German soil. The next year, 1937, was a quiet one, but Nazi agitation flared up in Danzig, which the Treaty of Versailles had set up as a free city. In March 1938 German forces moved into Austria, and the union of Austria and Germany, the *Anschluss,* was at last consummated. In September 1938 came the turn of Czechoslovakia and the Munich crisis. To understand it we must first pick up other threads in the story.

Mussolini's ambitions

Mussolini, too, had his ambitions and required sensational foreign triumphs to magnetize the Italian people. Since 1919 the Italians had been dissatisfied with the peace arrangements. They had received nothing of the former Turkish territories and German colonies that had been liberally parceled out, as mandates, to Great Britain, France, Belgium, Japan, South Africa, Australia, and New Zealand. They had never forgotten the humiliating defeat of Italian forces by Ethiopia at Adowa in 1896, which had blocked Italy's imperial ambitions in northeast Africa. Ethiopia remained the only part of black Africa (with the exception of Liberia) that was still independent.

In 1935 Italy invaded Ethiopia. The League of Nations, of which Ethiopia was a member, pronounced the Italian action an unwarranted aggression and imposed sanctions on Italy, by which members of the League were to refrain from selling Italy either arms or raw materials—oil was excepted. The British even gathered large naval forces in the Mediterranean in a show of strength. In France, however, there was considerable sympathy for Mussolini in important quarters, and in England there was the fear that if sanctions became too effective, by refusal of oil or by closure of the Suez Canal, Italy might be provoked into a general war. Mussolini was thus able to defeat Ethiopia in 1936 and to combine it with Italian Somaliland and Eritrea in an Italian East African empire. Haile Selassie, the Ethiopian emperor, made futile pleas for further action at Geneva. The League of Nations again failed, as in the earlier occupation of Manchuria by Japan, to provide machinery for disciplinary action against a wayward Great Power.

The Spanish Civil War, 1936–1939

Hardly had the Ethiopian crisis been disposed of, to the entire satisfaction of the aggressor, when another serious crisis broke out in Spain. In 1931, after a decade of political disturbance, a rather mild revolution had driven out Alfonso XIII, of the Bourbon family, and brought about the establishment of a democratic Spanish Republic. Old hostilities within the country came to a head. The new republican government undertook a program of social and economic reform. To combat the old entrenched power of the church, anticlerical legislation was enacted: church and state were separated, the Jesuit order was dissolved and its property was confiscated, and the schools were removed from clerical control. The old movement for Catalan independence was somewhat mollified by the grant of considerable local autonomy. To placate the peasantry the government began to break up some of the larger landed estates and to redistribute the land. The government's program was never pushed vigorously enough to satisfy extremist elements, who manifested their dissatisfaction in strikes and uprisings, particularly in industrial Barcelona, the Catalan capital, and the mining areas of the Asturias, but it was radical enough to antagonize the great property owners and the church. After 1933 the government fell into the hands of rightist and conservative parties, who ruled through ineffective and unpopular ministries. An insurrection of the miners in the Asturias was put down with much brutality. Agitation for Catalan independence was repressed.

In February 1936 new elections were held. All groups of the Left—republicans, socialists, syndicalists, anarchists, communists—joined in a Popular Front against monarchists, clericals, army officers, other adherents of the old regime, and Falangists, or Spanish fascists. The Left won a victory at the polls, and pressed forward with a reform program. In July 1936, a group of military men led an insurrection against the Republican government; General Francisco Franco emerged as leader. The parties of the Left united in resistance and the whole country fell into civil war. It was the most devastating war in all Spanish history; over 600,000 human beings lost their lives, and it was accompanied by extreme cruelties on both sides. For nearly three years the republican or loyalist forces held their own before finally succumbing to the insurgents led by Franco, who in March 1939 established an authoritarian, fascist-type rule over the exhausted country.

Francisco Franco

Spain provided a rehearsal for the greater struggle soon to come. The republican government could legitimately have looked forward to the purchase of arms abroad to suppress the rebellion, but Britain and France were resolved not to let the war expand into a general conflict. They forbade the shipment of war materials to the republican government; even the French Popular Front government put obstacles in the way of aid to the hard-pressed Spanish Popular Front. The United States extended its neutrality legislation to cover civil wars and placed an embargo on the export of arms to Spain. At British and French instigation 27 nations, including all the major European powers, agreed not to intervene or take sides. But the nonintervention policy proved a fiasco. Germany, Italy, and the Soviet Union

Spain splits the world

intervened anyway. The former two supported Franco and denounced the republicans as the tools of Bolshevism, while the U.S.S.R. supported the republic, reinforced the growing strength of the Spanish Communists, and stigmatized the rebels under Franco as the agents of international fascism. Germans, Italians, and Russians sent military equipment to Spain, testing their tanks and planes in battle. The fascist bombings of Guernica, Madrid, and Barcelona horrified the democratic world. The Germans and Italians sent troops (the Italians over 50,000); the Soviets if only for geographical reasons did not send troops but sent technicians and political advisers. Thousands of volunteers of leftist or liberal sympathy, from the United States and Europe, went to Spain to serve with the republican forces. Spain became the battlefield of contending ideologies. The Spanish Civil War split the world into fascist and antifascist camps.

As in the case of Ethiopia, the war in Spain helped bring Germany and Italy together. Mussolini had at first, like others, feared the revival of a militant Germany. He had outfaced Hitler when the latter threatened to absorb Austria in 1934. The Ethiopian war, Italian ambitions in Africa, and a clamorous Italian demand for ascendancy in the Mediterranean, the *mare nostrum* of the ancient Romans, estranged Italy from France and Britain. In 1936, soon after the outbreak of the Spanish Civil War, Mussolini and Hitler came to an understanding, which they called the Rome-Berlin Axis—the diplomatic axis around which they hoped the world might turn. That year Japan signed with Germany an Anti-Comintern Pact, soon ratified by Italy too; ostensibly an agreement to oppose communism, it was actually the foundation for a diplomatic alliance. Each, thus furnished with allies, was able to push its demands with more success. In 1938 Mussolini accepted what he had denied to Hitler in 1934—the German absorption of Austria.

GUERNICA

by Pablo Picasso (Spanish, 1881–1973)

Picasso painted this famous picture shortly after the fascist bombing of the Spanish city of Guernica in 1937. Although it expressed Picasso's response to a specific event in the Spanish Civil War, its disjointed images of the death, suffering, and destruction in modern warfare quickly gave this work a haunting, universal, cultural and historical meaning.

(Art Resource, NY/© 2001 The Estate of Pablo Picasso/Artists Rights Society (ARS), New York)

Meanwhile, in 1937, Japan, using as a pretext the firing upon Japanese troops at the Marco Polo Bridge near Beijing, launched a brutal full-scale invasion of eastern China and within a short time controlled most of the country. The Japanese occupation of Nanjing in 1937, then the Chinese capital, was accompanied by such violence and atrocities on the part of the Japanese military that it came to be known and long remembered as the "rape of Nanjing." The Chinese could fight on only from the hinterland. The League again ineffectually condemned Japan. The United States refrained from applying its neutrality legislation since no war was officially declared. This made possible the extension of loans to China, the victim of aggression, but also made possible the purchase by the Japanese of vitally needed scrap iron, steel, oil, and machinery from American industry. The Japanese were left free to pursue their expansionist ambitions in Asia, in part because the Western nations were distracted and divided by the mounting tensions in Europe.

The "rape of Nanjing"

The Munich Crisis: Climax of Appeasement

By annexing Austria in March 1938 Hitler added about 6 million Germans to the Reich. Another 3 million Germans lived in Czechoslovakia (see maps, pp. 448, 694–695). All those who were adults in 1938 had been born under the Habsburg empire. They had never, since 1918, been content with their new position as a minority in a Slavic state and had long complained about various forms of subtle discrimination. There were Polish, Ruthenian, and Hungarian minorities also, and since even the Slovaks had a strong sense of separate identity, there was in actuality no preponderant national majority of any kind. The fact that Czechoslovakia had one of the most enlightened minorities policies in Europe, enjoyed the highest living standard east of Germany, and was the only country in central Europe in 1938 that was still democratic only demonstrated the difficulty of maintaining a multinational state even under the most favorable of conditions.

Czechs divided

Czechoslovakia was strategically the keystone of Europe. It had a firm alliance with France, which had repeatedly guaranteed to defend it against German attack, and an alliance with the Soviet Union, which was contingent on the functioning of the French alliance. With Romania and Yugoslavia it formed the Little Entente, upon which France relied to maintain the existing boundaries in that part of Europe. It had a well-trained army, important munitions industries, and strong fortifications against Germany, which, however, were located in precisely the Sudeten border area where the population was almost all German. When Hitler annexed Austria—since Vienna is further east than Prague—he enclosed Czechoslovakia in a vise. From the German point of view it could now be said that Bohemia-Moravia, which was almost a third German anyway, formed a bulge protruding into the German Reich.

The Sudeten Germans of Czechoslovakia, whether Nazis or not, fell under the influence of agitators whose aim was less to relieve their grievances than to promote National Socialism. Hitler fomented their demands for union with Germany. In May 1938 rumors of an imminent German invasion caused the Czechs to mobilize; Russia, France, and England issued warnings. Hitler issued assurances but was nevertheless determined to smash the Czechs in the autumn. France and England were appalled by their narrow escape from war. The nervous French acquiesced in the leadership of Britain, which in the following months strove to avoid any firm stand that might precipitate war. The Czechs, under pressure from Britain and France, accepted British mediation on the Sudeten issue and in the summer of 1938 offered wide concessions to the Sudeten Germans amounting to regional autonomy, but this was not enough to satisfy Hitler, who loudly proclaimed that the plight of the Germans in Czechoslovakia was intolerable and must be corrected. The Soviets urged a firm stand, but the Western powers had little confidence in Soviet military strength and, given the Soviet geographical situation, their ability to render assistance to Czechoslovakia; moreover, they feared that firmness might mean war. They could not be sure whether Hitler was bluffing. He might, if opposed, back down; but it seemed equally likely, or indeed more so, that he was entirely willing to fight.

As the crisis grew in September 1938, the British prime minister, Neville Chamberlain, who had never flown in his life before, flew to Germany twice to sound out Hitler on his terms. The second time Hitler raised his demands so that even the British and French could not accept them. Mobilization began; war seemed imminent. Suddenly, in the midst of the unbearable tension, Hitler invited Chamberlain and Edouard Daladier, the French premier, to a four-power conference at Munich, to be attended by his ally, Mussolini. The Soviet Union and Czechoslovakia itself were excluded. At Munich Chamberlain and Daladier accepted Hitler's terms and then put enormous pressure on the Czech government to yield—to sign its own death warrant. France, urged on by England in an appeasement course that it was only too willing to follow, repudiated its treaty obligation to protect Czechoslovakia, ignored the Soviets who reaffirmed their willingness to aid the Czechs if the French acted, and abandoned its whole system of a Little Entente in the East. The Munich agreement permitted Germany to annex the adjoining fringe of Bohemia in which the majority of the people were Germans. This fringe contained the mountainous approaches and the fortifications, so that its loss left Czechoslovakia militarily defenseless. After promises to guarantee the integrity of what remained of Czechoslovakia, the conference disbanded. Chamberlain and Daladier were welcomed home with cheers. Chamberlain reported that he had brought "peace in our time." Again the democracies sighed with relief, hoped that Hitler had made his last demand, and told themselves that, with wise concessions, there need be no war.

Appeasement: the Munich agreement

The Munich crisis, with its death sentence to Czechoslovakia, revealed the helpless weakness into which the Western democracies had fallen by 1938. It may be that there was in fact little that the French and British could do at Munich to save Czechoslovakia. Their countries lagged behind Germany in military preparedness. They were impressed by the might of the German army and air force. Bolder leaders than Daladier and Chamberlain, knowing the state of their own armed forces, would have declined to risk a quarrel. They desperately wanted peace and would buy it at a high price, not daring to believe that they were dealing with a blackmailer whose price would always be raised.

Western democratic weakness

They suffered, too, from another moral uncertainty. By the very principle of national self-determination, accepted by the victors after the First World War, Germany could argue that it had a right to all that it had hitherto demanded. Hitler, in sending German troops into the German Rhineland, annexing Austria, stirring up Danzig, and incorporating the Bohemian Germans, had only asserted the right of the German people to have a sovereign German state. Moreover, if Hitler could be diverted eastward, enmeshed in a war with Russia, then communism and fascism might destroy each other—so one might hope. Possibly it was one of Hitler's motives, in the Munich crisis, to isolate Russia from the West and the West from Russia. If so, he succeeded well enough.

In the weeks following Munich the international commission set up to arrange the new boundaries worked further injustices on Czechoslovakia, dispensing even with the plebiscites which had been agreed to for disputed areas. Meanwhile the Poles and Hungarians brought forth their demands on the hapless Czechs. The Poles seized the Teschen district; and Hungary, under a German and Italian award, took 7,500 square miles of Slovakia. France and Britain were not consulted and did not seriously protest.

End of Appeasement

The final disillusionment came in March 1939. Hitler marched into Bohemia-Moravia, the really Czech part of Czechoslovakia, which he transformed into a German protectorate. Exploiting Slovak nationalism, he declared Slovakia "independent." Czechoslovakia, merely trimmed down at Munich, now disappeared from the map. Having promised to take only a bite, Hitler swallowed the whole. He then seized Memel from Lithuania and raised demands for Danzig and the Polish Corridor. A horrible realization now spread in France and Britain. It was clear that Hitler's most solemn guarantees were worthless, that his designs were not limited to Germans, but reached out to all eastern Europe and beyond, that he was essentially insatiable, that he could not be appeased. In April 1939 his partner in aggression, Mussolini, took over Albania.

The Western powers belatedly began to make preparations for a military stand. Britain, changing its East European policy at the eleventh hour, gave a guarantee to Poland and followed that with guarantees to Romania and Greece. That spring and summer the British tried to form an anti-German alliance with the U.S.S.R. But Poland and the Baltic states were unwilling to allow Soviet armies within their borders, even for the purpose of defending themselves against the Germans. The Anglo-French negotiators refused to put pressure on them. Since the Poles, in 1920, had conquered more territory than the Allies had meant them to have, pushing their eastern border well into Byelorussia, almost to Minsk, the Anglo-French scruples seemed to the Soviets unnecessarily delicate. They did not wish the Germans to launch an attack on them from a point as far east as Minsk. They may have thought also that what the French and British really wanted was for the Soviet Union to take the brunt of the Nazi attack. They considered it an affront that the British sent lesser officials as negotiators to Moscow when the prime minister himself had three times flown personally to deal with Hitler.

The Soviets, having quietly undertaken negotiations earlier that spring, on August 23, 1939, openly signed a treaty of nonaggression and friendship with Nazi Germany. In a provision kept secret at the time, it was agreed that in any future territorial rearrangement the Soviet Union and Germany would divide Poland between them, that the Soviet Union would enjoy a preponderant influence in the Baltic states and have its claim to Bessarabia, lost to Romania in 1918, recognized. In return the Soviets pledged to stay out of any war between Germany and Poland or between Germany and the Western democracies.

The Nazi-Soviet Pact

The Nazi-Soviet Pact stupefied the world. Communism and Nazism, supposed to be ideological opposites, had come together. A generation more versed in ideology than in power politics was dumbfounded. The pact was recognized as the signal for war; all last-minute negotiations failed. The Germans invaded Poland on September 1. On September 3 Great Britain and France declared war on Germany. The second European war in a generation, soon to be the Second World War, began.

106. THE YEARS OF AXIS TRIUMPH

Nazi Europe, 1939–1940: Poland and the Fall of France

The Second World War opened with an assault on Poland. German forces totaling over 1 million men, spearheaded by armored divisions and supported by the massed air power of the *Luftwaffe*, rapidly overran western Poland and subdued the ill-equipped Polish armies.

**German
Blitzkrieg**

The outcome of the campaign, a spectacular example of *Blitzkrieg,* or light-
ning warfare, was clear within the first few days; organized resistance
ended within a month. The Germans set about to integrate their Polish conquest into the Reich.

Simultaneously, the Soviet Union, acting under the secret clauses of the Nazi-Soviet
Pact, moved into the eastern half of Poland two weeks after the German invasion; the territory occupied was roughly equivalent to that lost to Poland in 1920. The Soviets proceeded also to establish fortified bases in the Baltic states—Estonia, Latvia, and Lithuania.
Finland resisted Soviet demands. It refused to cede border territories sought by the Russians or to yield military rights within their country. The Soviets insisted; Leningrad, the
second major city of the U.S.S.R., lay only 20 miles from the Finnish frontier. When negotiations foundered, the Soviets attacked in November 1939. Finnish resistance was
valiant and at first effective, but the small country was no match for the U.S.S.R. Western
democratic sympathies were with the Finns; the British and French sent equipment and
supplies and planned an expeditionary force. The Soviet Union was expelled from the
League of Nations for the act of aggression—the only power ever to be expelled. By
March 1940 the fighting was over. Finland had to yield somewhat more territory to the
U.S.S.R. than originally demanded but retained its independence.

The German army launched the
brutal violence of the Second
World War with its motorized
assault on Poland.   The new
term *Blitzkrieg* was used to describe this kind of rapid military
advance, which is represented
here by the arrival of German
troops in a bombed-out Polish
village.   Closely supported by
air power and moving quickly
on motorcycles, trucks, and armored vehicles, the Germans
showed how the new tactics of
offensive warfare could overwhelm the defensive strategies
that had stopped advancing
armies in the First World War.

(AKG London)

Meanwhile all was deceptively quiet in the West. The pattern of 1914, when the Germans reached the Marne in the first month of hostilities, failed to repeat itself. The French sat behind their Maginot Line; the British had few troops; the Germans did not stir from behind their Siegfried Line, or West Wall, in the Rhineland. Hardly any air action took place. It was called the "phony war." The Western democracies rejected Hitler's peace overtures after the conquest of Poland but clung to their peacetime outlook. The hope still lingered that somehow a real clash might even yet be averted. During this same strange winter, a cold and bitter one, the Germans put their forces through special training, whose purpose became apparent in the spring.

The "phony war"

On April 9, 1940, the Germans suddenly attacked and overran Norway, ostensibly because the British were laying mines in Norwegian waters in an endeavor to cut off German sources of Swedish iron ore. Denmark, too, was overrun, and an Allied expeditionary force with inadequate air strength had to withdraw. Then on May 10, the Germans delivered their main blow, striking at the Netherlands, Belgium, Luxembourg, and France itself. Nothing could stand against the German armored divisions and dive bombers. The Nazi use of massed tanks, though already demonstrated in Poland, took the French and British by surprise. Strategically, the Allies expected the main advance to be in central Belgium, as in 1914, and indeed as in the original German plan, which had been altered only a few months earlier. Hence the French and British sent into Belgium the best-equipped troops they had.

But the Germans delivered their main armored thrust, seven divisions, through Luxembourg and the Ardennes forest, long considered by the French General Staff impassable to tanks. In France, skirting the northwestern end of the Maginot Line, which had never been extended to the sea, the German armored divisions crossed the Meuse, drove deep into northern France against confused and ineffective resistance and, racing westward toward the Channel ports, cut off the Allied armies in Belgium. The Dutch, fearful of further air attack on their crowded cities, capitulated. The Belgian king sued for an armistice, and a large part of the French armies surrendered. The British fell back upon Dunkirk and could hope only to salvage their broken forces before the trap closed completely. Fortunately Hitler had halted the advance of his overextended armored divisions. In the week ending June 4 an epic evacuation of over 330,000 British and French troops was successfully executed from the beaches of Dunkirk, under air cover, with the help of all kinds of British vessels, manned in part by civilian volunteers, even though the precious equipment of the shattered army was almost totally abandoned.

In June the German forces drove relentlessly southward. Paris itself was occupied on June 13, and Verdun was occupied two days later; by June 22 France sued for peace and an armistice was signed. Hitler danced with glee.

Fall of France

France, obsessed by a defensive military psychology at the outset of the war, its armies unprepared for mechanized warfare, its government divided, its people split into hostile and suspicious factions, had fallen into the hands of an openly defeatist group of leaders. The fall of France left the world aghast. Everyone knew that France was no longer its former self, but it had still been considered a Great Power, and its collapse in one month seemed inconceivable. Some French, fleeing to England, established a Free French movement under General Charles de Gaulle; others formed a resistance movement in France. The British made the bitter decision to destroy a part of the French fleet anchored in the Algerian harbor of Oran to prevent its falling into enemy hands.

France itself under the terms of the armistice was occupied in its northern two-thirds by the Germans. The Third Republic, its capital now at Vichy

Vichy France

in the unoccupied southern third, was transformed by vote of a confused and stunned parliament into an authoritarian regime headed by the 84-year-old Marshal Pétain and the cynical and unscrupulous Pierre Laval. The republic was dead; the very slogan "Liberty, Equality, Fraternity" was banned from official use. French fascist groups, long frustrated in their campaigns to destabilize or destroy the Third Republic, now saw their opportunity to undermine republican traditions in French politics and society. Pétain, Laval, and others, claiming that they were acting to shield France from further suffering, proceeded to collaborate with the Nazis and to integrate Vichy France into the "new order" in Europe (see map, p. 818). The Vichy government cooperated in sending hundreds of thousands of French workers as slave laborers to Germany and even took the initiative in identifying and deporting thousands of French Jews to what were eventually Nazi death camps. The French people themselves had hard choices to make. Some chose to cooperate with the collaborators and the victorious Germans; others chose in a variety of ways to resist, some even joining the underground Resistance; most went about their daily lives waiting out the trying times until the fortunes of war might change. Not for many years after the war did the French admit responsibility as a nation for the misdeeds of the Vichy era.

Mussolini attacked France in June 1940, as soon as it was clear that Hitler had defeated it. Shortly thereafter, he invaded Greece and moved against the British in Africa. The *Duce* tied his own destinies, for good or ill, to those of the *Führer*. Since the Germans were emphatically the senior partner in this combination, since they were on good terms with Franco in Spain, and since the U.S.S.R. was benevolently neutral, they now dominated the European continent.

History seemed to repeat itself, in the distant and unreal way in which it ever repeats. The Germans controlled almost exactly the same geographical area as Napoleon. Organizing a new "continental system," they made plans to govern, exploit, and coordinate the resources, industry, and labor of Europe. Not having planned for a long war, and only belatedly mobilizing their resources for a sustained military effort, they intensified the exploitation of their conquered subjects. They impressed millions, prisoners of war or civilians, as slave labor, to work under close control in the German war industries. They garrisoned Europe with their soldiers, creating what they called *Festung Europa,* the Fortress of Europe. In every country they found sympathizers, collaborators, or "quislings"—the prototype was Vidkun Quisling, who had organized a Norwegian Fascist party in 1933 and was Norwegian premier from 1942 to 1945. Once Hitler was at war with the Soviet Union, some Europeans joined Hitler in the crusade against Bolshevism; 500,000 non-Germans fought in the divisions of the Waffen SS.

Festung Europa

The Battle of Britain and American Aid

In 1940, as in 1807, only Great Britain remained at war with the conqueror of Europe. After Dunkirk the British awaited the worst, momentarily expecting invasion. Winston Churchill, who replaced Chamberlain as prime minister in May 1940 during the military debacle, rose to the summit of leadership in adversity. To Parliament and the British people he promised nothing but "blood, toil, tears, and sweat." He pledged implacable war against "a monstrous tyranny, never surpassed in the dark, lamentable catalogue of human crime." To the American democracy across the Atlantic he appealed "Give us the tools, and we will finish the job." The United States began to respond. Since 1939, and even before, the American government had been anything but neutral. Opinion was excitedly divided. One group, called isola-

American "neutrality"

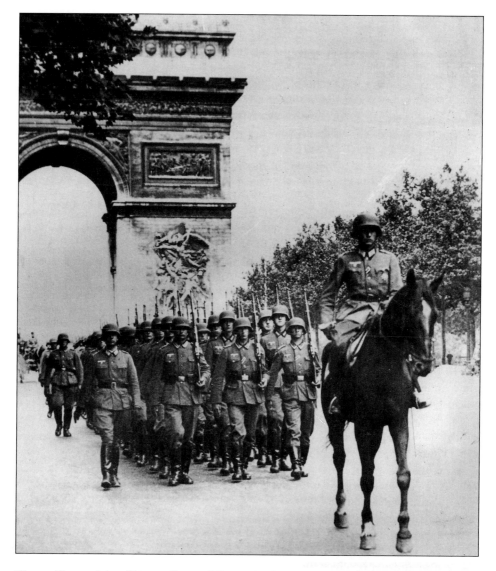

The rapid, complete military collapse of France in 1940 stunned the French people and indeed the entire world. Parisians faced this humiliating sight of German troops marching through the great symbol of French nationalism, the Arc de Triomphe, as they began to cope with an oppressive German military occupation that would last more than four years.

(Corbis)

tionist, opposed involvement in the European war, believing that Europe was hopeless, or that the United States could not save it, or that the Germans would win anyway before America could act, or that Hitler, even if victorious in Europe, constituted no danger to the United States. Another group, the interventionists, urged immediate aid to the Allies, believing that Hitler was a menace, that fascism must be destroyed, or that the Nazis, if they subjugated all Europe, would soon tamper with the Latin American republics. President Roosevelt was an interventionist, convinced that American security was endangered; he tried to unite national opinion by declaring that the United States might openly assist the Allies without itself fighting, by using "measures short of war."

The neutrality legislation of the mid-1930s was amended in November 1939, when the ban on the sale of arms was repealed. Roosevelt described Britain as "the spearhead of resistance to world conquest"; the United States was to be "the great arsenal of democracy." Both were fighting for a world, he said, in which the Four Freedoms were to be secure—freedom of speech, freedom of worship, freedom from want, and freedom from fear. In June 1940, immediately after Dunkirk, the United States sent a small initial shipment of arms to Britain. A few months later the United States gave the British 50 overage destroyers in return for the right to maintain American bases in Newfoundland, the Bermudas, and the British Caribbean islands. In 1941 it adopted Lend-Lease, a policy of providing arms, raw materials, and food to powers at war with the Axis. At the same time, in 1940 and 1941, the United States introduced conscription, built up its army and air force, and projected a two-ocean navy. Plans for joint hemisphere defense were developed with the Latin American republics. To protect its shipping it secured bases in Greenland and Iceland and convoyed Allied shipping as far as Iceland.

"The great arsenal of democracy"

After the fall of France, the Germans stood poised for an invasion of Britain. But they had not calculated on such rapid and easy successes in Europe, they had no immediately practical plan for an invasion, and they needed to win control of the air before a sea invasion could take place. Moreover, there was always the hope, in Hitler's mind at least, that the British might sue for peace, or even become an ally of Germany. The air assault on Britain began that summer and reached its climax in the autumn of 1940. Never until then had any bombing been so severe. But the Germans were unable to win control over the air in the battle of Britain.

Air war over Britain

Gradually the British Royal Air Force fought off the bombers with more success; new radar devices helped detect the approach of enemy planes, as did a remarkable British intelligence operation called Ultra, by which the British (with the help of the Poles) early in the war broke the code of an important German communications device, called Enigma, used for military conversations at the highest level. This crucial intelligence operation was not revealed until many years after the war's end. Although Coventry was wiped out, the life and industry of other cities were badly disrupted, and thousands of people were killed, 20,000 in London alone, still the productive activity of the country carried on. Nor, contrary to the predictions of air power theorists, did the bombings break the morale of the civilian population.

In the winter of 1940–1941 the Germans began to shift their weight to the east. Hitler set aside the planned invasion of Britain, for which he seems never to have had much enthusiasm anyway. He had already decided, like Napoleon before him, that before committing his resources to an invasion of England he must dispose of the U.S.S.R., a project much closer to his ideology and his illusions.

The Nazi Invasion of Russia: The Russian Front, 1941–1942

The Nazi-Soviet Pact of 1939 which had precipitated the war, like the alliance between Napoleon and Alexander I, was never a warm or harmonious understanding. Both parties probably entered it mainly to gain time. The Soviets gained space as well, pushing their borders westward. Stalin, incredibly, seems to have convinced himself that he could remain uninvolved in the war going on. But he and the Nazis soon began to dispute over eastern Europe. The Soviets, with the Nazis preoccupied by the war, hoped to win complete control over the Baltic and to gain influence in the Balkans as well. They had already occupied eastern Poland and the three Baltic states and won territory from Finland. In June 1940, to the chagrin of the Germans, they quietly sovietized and converted the three Baltic states into member republics of the U.S.S.R. The old German landowning class, the famous "Baltic barons," who had lived there for centuries, were uprooted and were returned to German soil. At the same time, the Soviets seized from Romania the Bessarabian province that they had lost in the First World War and incorporated it, too, as a Soviet republic. The Russians were expanding toward the Balkans, another area of historic Russian interest, and seemed bent on winning control over eastern Europe.

This the Germans viewed with dismay. They wished to reserve eastern Europe for themselves as a counterpart to industrial Germany. Hitler moved to bring the Balkans under German control. By early 1941 he blackmailed or, by territorial concessions, cajoled Romania, Bulgaria, and Hungary into joining the Axis; they became Axis lesser partners and were occupied by German troops; Yugoslavia also was occupied despite resistance by the army and population. Greece, too, was subjugated, the Germans coming to the rescue of Mussolini's hard-pressed troops. Hitler thus barred Soviet expansion in the Balkans and made the Balkan states part of the Nazi new order. The Balkan campaigns delayed his plans, but now, to crush the Soviets, and to gain the wheat harvests of the Ukraine and the oil wells of the Caucasus, the core of the Eurasian "heartland," Hitler struck, and on June 22, 1941, invaded the U.S.S.R. Stalin, ignoring warnings he had received, was caught completely by surprise and momentarily seemed incapable of mounting any kind of defense.

Hitler takes the Balkans

The German army threw 3 million men into Russia along a vast 2,000-mile front. The Russians gave way. One swift moving battle melted into another. By the autumn of 1941 the Germans had overrun Byelorussia and most of the Ukraine. In the north, Leningrad was in a state of siege; in the south, the Germans had entered the Crimean peninsula and were besieging Sebastopol. And toward the center of the vast front, the Germans stood, exhausted, but apparently victorious, within 25 miles of Moscow. But the overconfident German forces had not calculated on the stubbornness of Soviet resistance as Stalin recovered from his initial shock, replaced some of his military commanders, and rallied the country to the defense of the Russian motherland. Nor were the Germans prepared to fight in an early and extraordinarily bitter Russian winter, which suddenly descended upon them. A counteroffensive, launched by the Red Army that winter, saved Moscow.

The Nazi invasion of Russia

Hitler, disgusted and impatient with his subordinates, took over direct command of military operations; he shifted the main attack to the south and began a great offensive in the summer of 1942 directed toward the oil fields of the Caucasus. Sebastopol soon fell; the siege of Stalingrad began. After the failure to take Moscow, Hitler, aware now that the war would not be brief, took steps to mobilize the German economy on a full wartime basis. Germany had been ready for war in 1939 as no other major power had been, but lacked preparation in depth for a protracted conflict. In the early months of 1942 Hitler found in Albert Speer an organizing genius who, despite all kinds of obstacles from party leaders and government functionaries, coordinated labor and resources in the next two years and tripled armaments production.

1942, the Year of Dismay: Russia, North Africa, the Pacific

A year after the invasion, in the fateful summer of 1942, the German line reached from beleaguered Leningrad in the north, past the western outskirts of Moscow, past Stalingrad on the Volga southward to the Caucasus Mountains; the Germans were within a hundred miles of the Caspian Sea. But the Russians had traded space for time. Though the industrial Don basin and the food-producing Ukraine were overrun, the deliveries of Caucasus oil rendered hazardous and uncertain, the Russians continued to fight; industries were shifted to the new Ural and Siberian cities; and neither the Soviet economy nor the Soviet government was yet struck in a vital spot. A "scorched earth" policy, in which the retreating Russians destroyed crops and livestock, and guerrilla units wrecked industrial and transportation facilities, guaranteed that Russian resources would not fall into the hands of the advancing conqueror.

The desert campaigns

Simultaneously, late in 1942 the Axis also moved forward in North Africa. Here the desert campaigns started in September 1940 with an Italian eastward offensive from Libya, which succeeded in crossing over into Egypt. The stakes were high—control over Suez and the Mediterranean. At the height of the battle of Britain, Churchill made the decision to send troops and supplies, much needed at home, to North Africa. A British counteroffensive against vastly superior numbers swept the Italians out of Egypt and by early 1941 the British moved deep into Libya. Shortly thereafter the British overran Ethiopia and ended Mussolini's short-lived East African empire. But in North Africa fortunes were fickle. A German elite force, the Afrika Korps under General Rommel, in the spring of 1941 attacked in Libya and drove the British back to the Egyptian frontier. A few months later, once more on the offensive, the British advanced into Libya. Again fortunes shifted. By mid-1942 Rommel had repulsed the British and penetrated Egypt. The British took up a stand at El Alamein, 70 miles from Alexandria, their backs to the Suez Canal. Here they held the Germans.

But it seemed in 1942 that the Axis armies, breaking through the Soviet Caucasus and across the isthmus of Suez in North Africa, might enclose the whole Mediterranean and Middle East in a gigantic vise, and even, moving farther east, make contact with their allies the Japanese, who were at this time penetrating into the Indian Ocean. For the Pacific situation in the latter half of 1941 had also exploded. It was Japan that finally drew the United States into war.

Japan and the Pacific

The Japanese, in 1941, had conducted a war against China for ten years. With the war raging in Europe, Japanese expansionists saw a propitious moment to assert themselves throughout east Asia. In 1940 they cemented their alliance with Germany and Italy in a new three-power pact; the following year they concluded a neutrality treaty with the Soviet Union. From the Vichy French the Japanese obtained a number of military bases and other concessions in Indochina. The United States belatedly placed an embargo on the export of such materials as scrap iron and steel to Japan. Hesitating to precipitate any all-out drive of the Japanese toward the Dutch East Indies and elsewhere, the United States still sought some definition of Japanese ambitions in southeast Asia. The new Japanese prime minister, General Hideki Tojo, a staunch champion of the Axis, publicly proclaimed that the influence of Britain and the United States was to be totally eliminated from Asia, but he agreed to send representatives to Washington for negotiations.

Pearl Harbor

At the very time that the Japanese representatives in Washington were carrying on conversations with the Americans, on December 7, 1941, without warning, the Japanese launched a heavy air raid on the American naval base at Pearl Harbor in Hawaii and began to invade the Philippines. Simultaneously, they launched attacks on Guam, Midway, Hong Kong, and Malaya. The Americans were caught off guard at Pearl Harbor; close to 2,500 were killed, the fleet was crippled, and the temporary disablement of the American naval forces allowed the Japanese to roam at will in the western Pacific. The United States and Great Britain declared war on Japan on December 8. Three days later Germany and Italy declared war on the United States, as did the Axis puppet states; the war had become a global struggle.

The Japanese, working overland through Malaya, two months later captured Singapore, a British naval base long famous for its supposed impregnability, the veritable Gibraltar of the East. The sinking by air of the British battleship *Prince of Wales,* a feat often pronounced by naval experts to be impossible, added to the general consternation. In 1942 the Japanese conquered the Philippines, Malaya, and the Netherlands Indies. They invaded New Guinea and threatened Australia; they moved into the Aleutians. They streamed into the Indian Ocean, occupied Burma, and seemed about to invade India. Everywhere they found ready collaborators among enemies of European imperialism. They held up the idea of a Greater East Asia Co-Prosperity Sphere under Japanese leadership, in which the one clear element was that the Europeans should be ejected.

Meanwhile, as noted, the Germans stood at the Caucasus and almost at the Nile. And in the Atlantic, even to the shores of the United States and the American republics, German submarines were sinking Allied ships at a disastrous rate. The Mediterranean was unusable. For the Soviet-Western alliance, 1942 was the year of dismay. Despite Allied naval and air victories in the Pacific, the late summer and autumn of 1942 was the worst period of the war. Few realized, wrote the United States Chief of Staff General George C. Marshall some years later, how "close to complete domination of the world" were Germany and Japan and "how thin the thread of Allied survival had been stretched." That Germany and Japan had no plans to concert their strategy and operations was no small factor in the eventual Allied victory.

The year of dismay

107. THE WESTERN-SOVIET VICTORY

Plans and Preparations, 1942–1943

By January 1942 twenty-six nations, including the three Great Powers—Britain, the United States, and the U.S.S.R.—and representing every continent, were aligned against the Axis, a combination to which President Roosevelt gave the name the United Nations. Each pledged to use all its resources to defeat the Axis and never to make a separate peace. The Grand Alliance against the Axis aggressors, which could not be created in the 1930s, had at last been consummated.

The two Atlantic democracies, the United States and Great Britain, pooled their resources under a Combined Chiefs of Staff. Never had any two sovereign states formed so close a coalition. In contrast with the First World War an overall strategy was in effect from an early date. It was decided that Germany was the main enemy, against which it was necessary to concentrate first. For the time being the Pacific war was relegated to the background. Australia became the chief base for operations against the Japanese. The American navy and air force soon brought Japanese southward expansion to a halt and frustrated Japanese efforts to cut off supply lines to Australia; naval and air victories were won in the spring of 1942 in the battle of the Coral Sea and at Midway, the only relief to the overall gloom of that period. In the summer American forces landed at Guadalcanal in the Solomon Islands. A long ordeal of "island hopping" began.

A unified strategy

EUROPE 1942

The map shows Europe at the height of Axis military success during the Second World War. Austria, the Sudetenland, Bohemia-Moravia, Poland, and Alsace-Lorraine were all joined to Hitler's Reich. The Atlantic coast from southern France to northern Norway was under German military occupation, as was much of Russia. Southern Europe from Vichy France to Romania was also occupied or allied with Germany.

In Europe the first point of concentration was an air bombardment of Germany. The Soviet Union, dissatisfied, called for a true "second front," an immediate invasion by ground forces that would relieve the pressure of the German divisions that were devastating their country. Suspicious of the West as ever, they regarded the failure to establish a second front as new evidence of anti-Soviet feeling.

But neither the United States nor Britain, in 1942, was ready to undertake land action by a direct assault on *Festung Europa*. Although in the Second World War, as in the First, more than two years elapsed between the outbreak of war in Europe and the intervention of the United States, and although in the second war American military preparations be-

gan much sooner, the United States in 1942 was still involved in the cumbersome processes of mobilization, converting industry to the production of
war materials for itself and its Allies, imposing controls on its economy to
prevent a runaway inflation, and giving military training to its profoundly civilian-minded
people, of whom over 12 million men and women eventually served in the armed forces—
over three times as many as in the First World War. Large numbers of women, as in Britain,
and more so than in the First World War, took wartime jobs in defense and other industries.
In contrast, almost to the end, Nazi ideology placed obstacles in the way of utilizing
women in German factories. In any case, for a year after the United States entered the war,
German submarines enjoyed enough control of the Atlantic to make large shipments of
troops too risky. In effect, they blockaded the American army in the United States.

War preparations

   The American and British navies, however, gradually won the battle of the Atlantic;
the submarine menace was reduced to tolerable proportions by the first part of 1943. The
Americans and British decided to begin the assault upon Germany, from Great Britain as
a base, with a massive and prolonged air bombardment. Because precision bombardment
of factories and other military targets proved difficult either by day or by night, the air assaults became area bombings; German cities were bombed mercilessly and civilians were
the largest casualties. In Hamburg in 1943 fires raged on and destroyed most of the city after several days of incessant bombing. Since not everything could be shipped across the
Atlantic at the same time, and since the United States and Britain were engaged in war
with Japan as well, land invasion had to be deferred until 1944. The embattled Russians
questioned whether the Western Allies ever really meant to face the German army at all.

The Turning of the Tide, 1942–1943: Stalingrad, North Africa, Sicily

Meanwhile, at the end of 1942 the tide had begun to turn. In November an Anglo-
American force under the command of General Dwight D. Eisenhower effected a surprise
invasion of Algeria and Morocco in an amphibious operation of unprecedented proportions. The Allies, failing to win the cooperation of the French in North Africa as they had
hoped to do, turned to the Vichy French political leader Admiral Darlan in a calculated act
of expediency that brought protest in many quarters. Darlan assisted the Allies in assuming control but was soon assassinated. In the competition that developed in the succeeding
months for leadership of the French liberation committee, newly established in Algiers,
General de Gaulle, though virtually ignored by President Roosevelt, easily pushed aside
all rivals and moved forward with plans for France's revival.

   On the Continent, after the North African landings, the Germans took over control of
unoccupied France as well; they were frustrated, however, in the effort to seize the remainder of the French fleet when French crews scuttled their ships at Toulon. In North
Africa the invading forces fought their way eastward into Tunisia. Meanwhile British
forces under General Montgomery, having held the Germans at El Alamein
in June 1942, had already launched their third (and final) counteroffensive
in October, even before the invasion; they now pushed the Germans westward from Egypt until a large German force was crushed between the two
Allied armies and destroyed in Tunisia. By May 1943 Africa was cleared of

*Africa cleared
of Axis forces*

Axis forces. Mussolini's dream of an African empire had been thwarted; the Mediterranean
was open; the threat to Egypt and the Suez Canal was ended.

   At the same time it became clear, in the winter of 1942–1943, that the
Germans had suffered a catastrophic reversal in the Soviet Union in the titanic

Stalingrad

The destruction of cities and loss of life on the eastern front during the Second World War went far beyond the destruction and losses in all other theaters of the war. This photograph of Stalingrad at the time of the huge, extended battle for that city suggests the incredible desolation and losses that resulted from the fighting and the vast movement of armies across the Soviet Union and all of eastern Europe.

(AKG London)

battle of Stalingrad. In August 1942 massive German forces, an army of over a quarter million, began an all-out assault on Stalingrad, the vital key to all transport on the lower Volga; by September they had penetrated the city itself. Stalin ordered his namesake city held at all costs; Russian soldiery and the civilian population took a desperate stand. Hitler, still gambling on one big victory, was as obstinate in ordering the city taken. After weeks of fighting, the Germans occupied most of the city when suddenly a great Red Army counterattack, led by General Zhukov, trapped the German army and took a terrible toll; fewer than 100,000 were left to surrender in February 1943. The Soviets followed up their victory with a new counteroffensive, a great westward drive that regained for them what they had initially lost in the first year of the war. After Stalingrad, despite some setbacks, the Soviet Union was on the offensive for the remainder of the war. Stalingrad (or Volgograd as it was later renamed) was a turning point not only in the history of the war but in the history of central and eastern Europe as well.

American equipment meanwhile all through 1943 arrived in the Soviet Union in prodigious quantities. The terms of Lend-Lease were liberally extended to the Soviets; a stream of American vehicles, clothing, food, and supplies of all kinds made its way laboriously to the U.S.S.R. through the Arctic Ocean and through the Persian Gulf. Machinery and equipment were sent for the Soviet arms plants, which were themselves tremendously increasing their output. Anglo-American bombing meanwhile was cutting into German airplane production at home. The Allied contribution to the Soviet war effort was indispensable, but Russian human losses were tremendous. Between 20 and 25 million people in the Soviet Union died from war-related causes. More than two-thirds of these casualties were civilians; many had been killed early in the war by Nazi murder squads whose assignment was to eliminate all so-called "undesirable" persons from territories occupied by the German army. But the number of battle deaths alone went far beyond Allied losses in other military theaters of the war. The Soviet Union lost more men in the battle of Stalingrad, for example, than the United States lost in combat during the entire war in all theaters combined.

With contemporary American successes in the Solomon Islands at the end of 1942 and the slow throttling of German submarines in the Atlantic, the beginning of the year 1943 brought new hope for the Allies in all quarters. In a spectacular campaign in July–August 1943, the British, Canadians, and Americans conquered the island of Sicily. Mussolini fell; the 21-year-old Fascist regime came to an end. Mussolini set up an "Italian Social Republic" in the north, but it was no more than a German puppet government. Some months later, in April 1945, the Duce, as he attempted to flee the country, was seized and shot by anti-Fascist Italians. When the new Italian government under Marshal Badoglio, in August 1943, tried to make peace, the German army occupied Italy. The Allies, having crossed to the Italian mainland from Sicily, attacked from the south. In October the Badoglio government declared war on Germany, and Italy was recognized by the Allies as a "cobelligerent." But the Germans stubbornly blocked the advance of the Allies to Rome despite new Allied landings and beachheads. The Italian campaign turned into a long and disheartening stalemate because the Western Allies, concentrating troops in Britain for the approaching cross-Channel invasion, could never spare enough for the Italian front.

New hope for the Allies

The Allied Offensive, 1944–1945: Europe and the Pacific

Festung Europa, especially along its western approaches, the coasts of Holland, Belgium, and France, bristled with every kind of fortification that German scientific and military ingenuity could devise. A seaborne attack upon Europe was an operation of wholly unprecedented kind. It differed from the earlier amphibious attacks on Algeria, Sicily, or the Pacific islands in that the defender in Europe, in the very part of Europe where the road and railway network was thickest, could immediately rush overwhelming reserves to the spot attacked—except insofar as feinting tactics kept him uncertain, air power destroyed his transport, or the Russians held the bulk of his forces in the East. Precise and elaborate plans had been worked out. Ten thousand aircraft were to provide aerial protection, scores of warships were to bombard the coast, 4,000 ships were to carry the invading troops and their supplies across the Channel, artificial harbors were to be created where none existed.

The invasion of Europe began before dawn on June 6, 1944. The spot selected was the coast of Normandy directly across the Channel from England; false intelligence reports, planted by the Allies, led the Germans to expect the main thrust at Calais. An unparalleled combination of forces, British, Canadian, and American, land, sea, and air, backed up by huge accumulations of supplies and troops assembled in Great Britain, and the whole under the unified command of General Eisenhower, assaulted the French coast, established a beachhead, and maintained a front. The Allies poured in their strength, over 130,000 men the first day, 1 million within a month. The Germans were at first thrown back more easily than had been expected. By August Paris was liberated, by September the Allies crossed the frontier of Germany itself. In France, Italy, and Belgium the Resistance movements, which had grown up in secret during the years of German occupation, came into the open and drove out Germans and pro-German collaborators. In Germany itself no widespread or deeply rooted Resistance movement ever developed, but a small group of Germans, military and civilian, formed an underground. On July 20, 1944, after the failure of earlier efforts, it attempted to assassinate Hitler by exploding a bomb at his military headquarters in East Prussia; Hitler was only injured and took a fearsome revenge on the conspirators.

The invasion of Europe

In August, in another amphibious operation, the Allies landed on the French Mediterranean coast and swept up from southern France to join the Allied forces advancing against stiffening resistance. At one point, momentarily, the Allied offensive suffered a serious reversal. A sudden German drive under Hitler's direct personal orders in December 1944, unleashed under radio silence to thwart Allied intelligence, was launched against thinly held American lines on the Belgian sector in the Ardennes, created a "bulge" in the advancing armies, and caused heavy losses and confusion. But the Allies rallied, and Hitler used up his armored reserves in the effort. Neither the Ardennes counteroffensive nor the new destructive weapons rained on Britain, jet-propelled flying bombs and rockets, opening up the missile age, availed the Germans. All this time the Americans and British kept up their massive air bombardments, killing over 50,000 civilians in the fire-bombing of Dresden in February 1945. On the ground they pushed on and smashed through the heavily fortified Siegfried Line. The last natural obstacle, the Rhine, was crossed when in March 1945 American forces by a stroke of luck discovered an undestroyed bridge at Remagen; they poured troops over it and established a bridgehead—the first troops to cross the Rhine in combat since the armies of Napoleon. The main crossing, under the British, subsequently took place farther to the north. Soon the Allies were accepting wholesale surrenders in the Ruhr valley.

The eastern front

Meanwhile in 1944 the Russian armies swept the Germans from the Ukraine, Byelorussia, the Baltic states, and eastern Poland. By August they reached the suburbs of Warsaw. The Polish underground rose against the Germans but the Soviets, determined that Poland not be liberated by non-Communist Polish leadership, refused to permit aid to the rising, and it was crushed, with a heavy loss of Polish lives. Earlier, in 1943, the mass graves of thousands of Polish prisoners of war, mainly officers, had been found by the Germans in the Katyn Forest. Despite continuing Soviet denials at the time, the Russian archives years later revealed that they had been shot by the Red Army on Stalin's orders in 1940, after the Soviet Union had joined with Germany in partitioning Poland. The Russians, their lines now overextended, and checked for several months by German strength in Poland, pushed southward into Romania and Bulgaria; both countries changed sides and declared war against Germany. Early in 1945 the Soviets, reopening their offensive, forced their way into East Prussia and Silesia and by February reached the Oder, 40 miles from Berlin, where Zhukov paused to regroup his forces. In March and April Russian forces occupied Budapest and Vienna.

The final drive on Germany

The final drive on Germany began. Hitler moved troops from the collapsing western front to reinforce the stand on the Oder and to protect his capital. In April the Americans reached the Elbe, about 60 miles from Berlin, with hardly any obstacles before them; but here they halted, by decision of General Eisenhower. The Americans, whose supply lines were already overextended, wanted a clear line of demarcation from the Russians; they also believed it necessary to divert forces southward against a possible German last stand in the Alps. But mainly the decision was made as a gesture of goodwill toward the Russians, who were to be permitted to take Berlin as compensation for their heavy sacrifices in the common cause, and to preserve the Western-Soviet coalition until final victory. Similarly, the American troops that moved southward were held back from taking Prague and the Soviets were permitted to take the Czech capital too. At the end of the war the Soviets were in control of all the major capitals of central and eastern Europe.

The Western Allies and the Soviets offered no terms to Hitler, nor to any Germans. They demanded unconditional surrender, and the Germans fought on in the very streets of Berlin. On the last day of April Hitler perished by his own hand in the ruins of his capital after denouncing some of his closest party subordinates as traitors. Admiral Doenitz, designated by Hitler as his successor, went through the formalities of surrender on May 8, 1945. Since fighting had already ceased on the Italian front a few days earlier, the war in Europe was over.

Meanwhile a generation reared to mistrust the fabricated atrocity tales of the First World War painfully, and belatedly, became aware of the real German horrors of the Second—hostages rounded up and shot in reprisal for resistance; whole villages like Lidice in Czechoslovakia or Oradour-sur-Glane in France razed to the ground and their inhabitants slain or deported; concentration camps like Dachau and Buchenwald, where the prisoners were given minimal rations and worked to death, and where Allied troops found only pitifully emaciated survivors; above all, the mass death camps with gas chambers and crematory ovens at Auschwitz (where at its peak 12,000 victims a day were gassed to death), Treblinka, Belzéc, Sobibor, and others, where peoples whom the Nazis deemed "inferior" could be systematically liquidated. In the areas of Nazi domination in eastern Europe, the Nazis first used special firing squads and mobile gas units to kill "undesirables," but as the war went on they transported millions of men, women, and children in railroad cattle cars to the mass death camps where some were worked to death and others were put to death at once. By far the largest proportion killed were some 6 million Jews, but Poles, Russians, other Slavic peoples, Gypsies, and others were slain as well.

For the Jews in what came to be known as the Holocaust, the annihilation policy, decided upon at a high-level Nazi meeting at Wannsee in January 1942, was to be the "Final Solution" to the "Jewish problem" which Hitler had agitated, with maniacal fury, for so many years. Genocide, the planned, systematic effort to destroy a whole people, was the greatest of the Nazi sins against humanity. Although there have been mass murders in many other places and eras of human history, the genocidal attack on European Jews had a uniquely modern scale and scientific organization, which explains in part why it has produced such painful memories and questions for later generations. How could such murderous events occur in the heart of modern European civilization? The fact that the Holocaust was carried out by ordinary people and bureaucrats raises pointed questions about individual and collective responsibilities for deadly government policies, about the danger of misused, modern technologies, and about the destructive consequences of racist ideologies. Survivors have described extraordinary acts of courage and human will among the prisoners in Nazi death camps, but the Holocaust has become the modern world's most terrifying example and memory of systematic murder and human brutality.

The "final solution"

In the Pacific, American operations against Japan had dragged on for three years, hampered by the strategic decision to concentrate against Germany first. Slowly, from points in the Solomon Islands, the easternmost fringe of the Indonesian archipelago, American forces, at first very small, worked their way in a northwesterly direction toward faraway Japan. They had to fight in turn for Guadalcanal, for New Guinea, for the reconquest of the Philippines, all against stubborn entrenched Japanese resistance and at heavy cost. They had to fight for the Japanese islands in the mid-Pacific taken by Japan from the Germans after the First World War and converted into powerful naval bases—the Gilbert Islands, the Marshalls, the Carolines, the Marianas. In October 1944 they won an impressive naval

**4. Greatest Axis Expansion,
December 1941–November 1941**

**1. Hitler Invades Poland
September 1, 1939**

**6. Germany Surrenders
May 8, 1945**

**2. France Surrenders
June 22, 1940**

**5. Allies Invade:
North Africa, November 8, 1942
Normandy Coast, June 6, 1944**

**3. United States:
Bases-Destroyer Deal, September 2, 1940
Enacts Lend-Lease, March 11, 1941
Enters the War December 8, 1941**

← Allied Thrusts

← Lend-Lease Supply Lines

Hitler's "Empire"

Allied with Germany

Occupied by the Axis

At War Against the Axis

THE SECOND WORLD WAR

These two maps show the global character of the war and the central position of the United
States with respect to the European and Pacific theaters. The numbered legends summarize the
successive stages of the war in both the Eastern and Western hemispheres. In 1942, with the
Germans reaching as far east as Egypt and Stalingrad, and the Japanese as far west as Burma,
the great danger to the Soviet-Western alliance was that these two might join forces, dominate
southern Asia, control the oil resources of the Persian Gulf, and stop the flow of Western supplies to the Soviet Union from this direction. The almost simultaneous Soviet-Western successes, late in 1942, at Stalingrad and El Alamein, and in the invasion of Morocco-Algeria and
of Guadalcanal, proved to be the turning point of the war. In 1943 the German submarine campaign in the Atlantic was defeated, so that American troops and supplies could move more

freely to Europe. The invasion of Normandy in June 1944, with continuing pressure from the east, brought about the German surrender in May 1945. Meanwhile, in the Pacific, American occupation of the islands and reoccupation of the Philippines prepared the way for the surrender of Japan, which followed the dropping of two atomic bombs in August 1945.

victory over the Japanese in the battle of Leyte Gulf. In March 1945 they fought with heavy casualties to take the eight-square-mile strategic island of Iwo Jima. Finally, in a protracted and bloody battle lasting over 2 1/2 months, in the spring of 1945 they won the island of Okinawa, only 300 miles from Japan itself. Okinawa was captured just as the Germans collapsed in Europe. From the new Allied bases that had been won, from Saipan in the Marianas, from Iwo Jima, from Okinawa, and from aircraft carriers at sea, a crushing air offensive was launched against Japan, shattering Japanese industry, destroying the

THE HOLOCAUST

This map shows the loss of life that resulted from what the Nazis called their "Final Solution"—that is, their systematic program of destroying the Jews and Judaism. Before the Second World War most European Jews lived in Poland and the adjoining parts of the Soviet Union. The Germans occupied all of these areas during the war, so that most deaths occurred in these territories. The map shows both the number killed in each country and the percentage of its Jewish population that were victims of this deliberate genocide. The numbers add up to about 6 million men, women, and children, or an estimated two-thirds of the Jewish population of Europe as a whole. Although word of this annihilation policy reached the outside world through the Vatican and other sources, the Allied leaders at first disbelieved the reports, and then, giving priority to their military objectives, did nothing to stop the systematic slaughter.

remnants of the Japanese navy, and compelling the Japanese government to give serious thought to suing for peace. The Allied leaders refused to believe that Japanese defenses were ready to crumble or that the Japanese were ready to negotiate. The American army prepared to shift combat troops from the European theater to Asia. The stage was being set for a full-scale invasion of Japan itself.

The atomic bomb

Then, on August 6, 1945, an American aircraft dropped an atomic bomb, built in the United States in utmost secrecy by European refugee and American scientists, on the city of Hiroshima, with a population of 200,000 people. The city was destroyed in this single explosion, and 78,000 lives

The human consequences of Nazi brutalities appear in this picture of a Nazi concentration camp near the German city of Ohrdruf in early May 1945. American soldiers were making their way through the camp, where the Nazis had subjected Poles, Czechs, German Jews, and German political prisoners to forced labor and then shot or flogged to death the internees who could no longer work.

(Corbis)

were lost; thousands of others were injured or suffered the long-term effects of radiation. Two days later, the Soviet Union, which had pledged to enter the conflict in the East within three months after the surrender of Germany, declared war on Japan and invaded Manchuria. On August 9 a second American atomic bomb struck Nagasaki and killed tens of thousands more. The Japanese made peace at once. On September 2, 1945, the formal surrender was signed. The emperor was permitted to remain as head of state, but Japan was placed under a United States army of occupation. Meanwhile, the atomic bomb, like the death camps of the Holocaust, soon became another haunting memory and symbol of the new forms of violence and mass destruction that a staggeringly costly global war had bequeathed to humanity.

The Second World War of the twentieth century was over, the greatest conflict in human history. The same cold impersonal statistics that had recorded 10 million killed in the First World War reported 15 million military deaths and (unlike the First World War) more than twice as many civilian fatalities. Soviet military deaths were estimated at over 6 million, German at 3.5 million, Chinese at 2.2 million, Japanese at 1.3 million, Polish at 700,000. British and Commonwealth losses were over 400,000, American about 300,000, French about 200,000. Over 25 million suffered battle wounds. The military death figures would have been higher except that one of every two of those wounded was saved by new sulfa and penicillin drugs and blood plasma transfusions. None of these statistics could be more than approximate, and no one could estimate the complete toll of human lives lost from Allied and Axis bombings, Nazi mass slayings of Jews in the Holocaust and of other people in all the German-occupied nations, Nazi and Soviet deportation policies, and postwar famines and epidemics. Some estimates place the total at 60 million men, women, and children, but at such figures the human mind retreats and human sensitivities are dulled.

108. THE FOUNDATIONS OF THE PEACE

Whereas the First World War had been concluded by a peace conference a few months after the close of hostilities, the Second World War ended in no such clear-cut settlement. Nothing like the Treaty of Versailles of 1919 followed the defeat of Germany in 1945. The terms of peace, as they gradually developed, left no such single symbol of humiliation as the Versailles treaty had represented. The peace terms emerged episodically, at first during a series of conferences among the Allied nations during the war, and then in a series of de facto arrangements in the years after 1945.

The foundations of a peaceable postwar world were being laid, it was thought, at a number of meetings where the strategy of the war itself was being planned. As early as August 1941 Roosevelt and Churchill met at sea off the coast of Newfoundland and drew up the Atlantic Charter. There were meetings in 1943 at Casablanca, at Cairo, and at Teheran (which was close enough to the Soviet Union for Stalin to participate); and in the final phase of the war, in February 1945, at Yalta (a Crimean resort city in the Soviet Union), and in July 1945 at Potsdam, in the environs of shattered Berlin.

The Atlantic Charter, issued jointly by Roosevelt and Churchill at their first meeting, resembled in spirit the Fourteen Points of Woodrow Wilson. It pledged that sovereign rights and self-government would be restored to all who had been forcibly deprived of them, that all nations would have equal access to world trade and world resources, that all peoples would work together to achieve improved living standards and economic security. The postwar peace, it promised, would assure people of all lands freedom from fear and want, and end force and aggression in international affairs. Here, and in the Four Freedoms enunciated by President Roosevelt, the ideological basis of the peace was proclaimed. At the 1943 conferences, and through other consultations, the Allies endeavored to concert their military plans. At Casablanca, in January 1943, they resolved to accept nothing less than the "unconditional surrender" of the Axis powers. This vague formula, adopted somewhat cavalierly at American initiative, and without much thought to possible political implications, was intended mainly to prevent a recurrence of anything like the ambiguity surrounding the armistice of 1918.

"Unconditional surrender"

At Teheran, in December 1943, Roosevelt and Churchill met with Stalin for the first of two wartime meetings. They discussed the postwar occupation and demilitarization of Germany, laid plans for a postwar international organization, and debated strategy for winning the war. Throughout the war Roosevelt, unwilling to disturb the unity of the Western-Soviet coalition in the global struggle in which America was engaged, followed a policy of postponing controversial territorial and political decisions until victory was assured. Churchill was more apprehensive. Steeped in traditional balance-of-power politics, he sensed that without prior diplomatic bargaining and political arrangements, the victory over the Nazis would leave Russia dominant over all central and eastern Europe. At Teheran he proposed operations in the Mediterranean and an invasion through the Balkans, for political reasons but mainly out of concern for the casualties that a cross-Channel invasion would involve. But Roosevelt persuaded him otherwise. It was agreed that a landing in France would take place in the spring of 1944; thus the major second front that Stalin had been promised would finally be opened. Stalin pledged that he would launch a simultaneous offensive on the eastern front.

The strategy that would win the war in the next 18 months was decided upon at Teheran, but that strategy, without political agreements, all but guaranteed the Soviet domination of eastern Europe. Later, in October 1944, as the Russian armies advanced westward, Churchill visited Stalin and sketched out a demarcation of spheres of influence for the Western powers and the Soviets in the Balkan states (a Soviet preponderance in Romania and Bulgaria, a Western preponderance in Greece, and an even division of influence in Hungary and Yugoslavia). Soviet control over the Baltic states had virtually been conceded by the British earlier. But Roosevelt would not agree to any such arrangement, which he considered old-fashioned and a dangerous revival of the worst features of pre-1914 diplomacy.

Soon, however, political decisions had to be made. The two conferences that arrived at the most important political decisions were the meetings at Yalta and at Potsdam in 1945. The Yalta meeting in February 1945 took place when the Allies were close to final victory—closer, events disclosed, than anyone at the time realized. The three Allied statesmen met at an old tsarist Crimean summer resort on the Black Sea, toasted their common triumphs, and, as at Teheran, took the measure of each other. Roosevelt thought of himself as a mediator between Churchill and Stalin where European issues were involved. He took pains to avoid giving Stalin the impression that he and Churchill were in any sense united against him; in point of fact, Roosevelt was suspicious of Churchill's devotion to empire and colonial ties, which he considered anachronistic for the postwar world. Despite differences, the Big Three reached agreements, at least formally, on Poland and eastern Europe, the future of Germany, the war in Asia, and the projected postwar international organization—the United Nations.

The agreements at Yalta

The discussion of Poland and eastern Europe raised the most serious difficulties. Stalin's armies, having driven the Nazi forces to within 40

Poland and eastern Europe

miles of Berlin, were in control of Poland and almost all eastern and central Europe. The Russians remembered these areas as anti-Soviet, and Poland particularly as the perpetrator of aggression against Soviet territory in 1920 and as the ancient corridor of attack upon Russia. Stalin had already taken steps to establish a "friendly" government in Poland, that is, a government subservient to the Soviets. Neither Roosevelt nor Churchill had fought the war against the Nazis to leave the Soviet Union the undisputed master of central and eastern Europe and in a position to impose a totalitarian political system on all this vast area. At Yalta, Roosevelt and Churchill extracted from Stalin a number of promises for the areas he controlled. In accordance with the Atlantic Charter, the liberated states were to be permitted provisional governments "broadly representative of all democratic elements in the population," that is, not consisting merely, as in the case of the provisional government of Poland already established, of authorities subservient to the Soviets. They pressed Stalin to pledge also the "earliest possible establishment through free elections of governments responsive to the will of the people." The pledge was a verbal concession that cost the Soviet leader little; he rejected the suggestion of international supervision over the elections. The Declaration on Liberated Europe, promising sovereign rights of democratic self-determination, provided a false sense of agreement; there were to be no free elections in Soviet-controlled eastern Europe.

A number of territorial changes were also accepted, pending final settlement at a postwar peace conference. The Russian-Polish, or eastern, boundary of Poland would be set roughly at the so-called Curzon line, the frontier contemplated by the Allies in 1919 before the Poles conquered territory to their east. The Poles would be compensated, in the north and west, at the expense of Germany (see map, p. 859). On this and on other matters relating to Germany there was a large area of accord; the three were united in their hatred of German Nazism and militarism. Germany was to be disarmed and divided into four occupation zones under the administration of the Big Three powers and France—the latter at the insistence of Churchill. There was vague talk, at Yalta and earlier, of dismembering Germany, of undoing the work of Bismarck, but the difficulties of such an undertaking were understood and the proposal was eventually discarded. The Americans and British rejected as excessive the Soviet proposals for reparations, a sum of $20 billion to be paid in kind, half to the Soviets. It was agreed, however, that reparations would go to those countries that had borne the main burdens of the war and suffered the heaviest losses. The Soviet Union was to receive half of whatever total sum was set.

The United Nations

To the satisfaction of everyone, the participants agreed on plans for a postwar international organization, to be called the United Nations. Roosevelt believed it essential to win the Soviets over to the idea of an international organization. He was convinced that the Great Powers, cooperating within the framework of the United Nations and acting as international police, could preserve the future peace and security of the world. No less than Stalin or Churchill, he emphasized the importance of the Great Powers in the new organization, although he accepted a dignified role for the smaller nations as well. All agreed that each of the Great Powers, the permanent members of the new organization's Security Council, would have a veto power on important decisions. The Soviets pressed for 16 votes in the General Assembly of the new organization, arguing that their constitution gave sovereign rights to each of their then 16 constituent republics and that the British dominions would each have a seat. In the interests of harmony, at Churchill's behest, they were given three.

Critical agreements were reached on East Asia. Here political and military decisions were inextricably linked. The Soviets had remained neutral in the Pacific war despite their

The final meeting of Roosevelt, Churchill, and Stalin took place in the Crimean resort city of Yalta in February 1945. Roosevelt's position here between the other two leaders suggests his mediating position at the conference. The agreements reached at Yalta shaped the postwar organization of eastern Europe, laid the foundation for the United Nations, and eventually brought the Soviet Union into the war against Japan, but some critics in the West later complained that the Yalta accords made too many concessions to Stalin and opened the way for Soviet expansion into central Europe.

(Courtesy Franklin D. Roosevelt Library)

historic interests in that part of Asia. Given the magnitude of the war effort on the European front, no one had pressed them to enter the Pacific war earlier. It was agreed to wait at least until the Germans were on the verge of defeat. At Yalta, Stalin agreed to enter the war against Japan, but Soviet "public opinion," he averred, would demand compensation. The U.S.S.R. would enter the war against Japan "two to three months" after Germany had surrendered. In return, the Soviets would receive territories and rights that tsarist Russia had lost to Japan 40 years before in the Russo-Japanese war of 1904–1905 (see map, p. 652), with the addition of the Kurile Islands, which had never been Russian before.

Roosevelt made concessions at Yalta because he believed he needed Soviet support in the last phase of the war against Japan and because he wished to preserve the Western-Soviet coalition until final victory was guaranteed. He believed also that wartime cooperation would produce postwar harmony. Churchill, less sanguine about the future and about "diplomacy by friendship," would have preferred a franker definition of spheres of influence. Such ideas were ruled out as the thinking of a bygone era. Yet the spirit of the Atlantic Charter, so closely identified with the American president, the pledge of sovereign self-determination for all peoples, was already being contravened.

At Potsdam, in July 1945, after the German collapse, the Big Three met again. A new American president, Harry S Truman, represented the United States; President Roosevelt had died in April, on the eve of final victory. Churchill, in the midst of the conference, was replaced by a new *The Potsdam Conference* British prime minister, Clement Attlee, after the Labour party's victory at the polls. Stalin still represented the Soviet Union. By now, disagreements between the Western Allies and the Soviets had deepened, not only over Soviet control in Poland, eastern Europe, and the Balkans, but over German reparations and other matters. Yet the Western leaders were still prepared to make concessions in the hope of establishing harmonious relations. Agreements were announced on the postwar treatment of Germany, on German disarmament, demilitarization, "denazification," and the punishment of war criminals. Each power could take reparations in kind from its occupation zone and the Russians would get substantial additional deliveries from the Western zones so that the original $10 billion Soviet demand was virtually met.

Pending the final peace treaty, German territory east of the Oder-Neisse rivers was committed to Polish administration. The details of this decision had earlier been postponed; the Polish-German boundary was now set at the western Neisse, even further west than originally envisaged. Poland thus extended its territorial boundaries about a hundred miles westward as compensation for Russian westward expansion at Polish expense. German East Prussia was divided between the Soviet Union in the north and Poland in the south. Königsberg, founded by the Teutonic Knights, for centuries the ducal seat of Prussian dukes and the coronation city of Prussian kings, became the Russian city of Kaliningrad. The ancient German cities of Stettin and Breslau became the Polish cities of Szczecin and Wroclaw. Danzig became Gdansk. The de facto administration of these areas hardened into permanent rule. The transfer of the German population in these eastern areas was supposed to be effected in an orderly and humane fashion; but millions of Germans were driven from their homes or fled within a few months. For them (and for the Germans who were expelled from Czechoslovakia) it was the final consummation of the war that Hitler had unleashed.

Germany divided

The Potsdam participants agreed that peace treaties would be signed as soon as possible with the former German satellite states; the task of preparing them was entrusted to a council of foreign ministers representing the United States, Britain, France, the Soviet Union, and China. In the months that followed, the widening chasm between the Soviets and the West manifested itself in stormy meetings in London, Paris, and New York, as well as in a peace conference held in Paris in 1946, at which were represented the 21 states that had contributed substantial military forces to the defeat of the Axis powers. In February 1947 treaties were signed with Italy, Romania, Hungary, Bulgaria, and Finland, all of which paid reparations and agreed to certain territorial adjustments. In 1951 a peace treaty was signed with Japan, but not by the Soviets, who signed their own treaty in 1956. The years went by, but no final treaty was signed with Germany, a Germany that long remained divided. For the wartime Western-Soviet coalition had fallen apart, shattering the dreams and aspirations for a lasting peace of those who had fought the Second World War to a triumph over one kind of aggression and totalitarianism, and now found themselves confronted with a new age of crisis.

Chapter 22

THE POSTWAR ERA:

COLD WAR AND

RECONSTRUCTION

A cataclysm, according to Webster's dictionary, is "any violent change involving sudden and extensive alterations of the earth's surface; hence, any upheaval, especially a social or political one." The human world witnessed such a cataclysm in the twentieth century. The First World War, the collapse of the old European dynasties, the Russian Revolution, the Fascist and Nazi dictatorships, the Second World War, the nuclear bomb, the end of the European colonial empires, the rise of Communist China—all are part of the changes that have altered the coastlines of modern human society, and for which cataclysm is not too strong a word.

It is difficult to do justice to the complexities of contemporary history and to keep current with the onrushing events of our own times. The chapters that follow can only sketch the most memorable developments of the postwar era and the years that have followed.

109. THE COLD WAR: THE OPENING DECADE, 1945–1955

Certain issues that had confronted humankind for over a century became even more complex and more urgent in the second half of the twentieth century. Three can be singled out: science, the organization of industrial society, and national sovereignty.

Chapter emblem: Hungarian protestors burning a picture of Joseph Stalin in 1956.

The atomic bomb   The atomic bomb dramatized the problem of science. The world shuddered at the instantaneous destruction of Hiroshima. The postwar contest to produce more sophisticated nuclear weapons spurred the realization that a third world war would be unthinkable. Human beings possessed the means to annihilate not only civilization but even human existence on the planet, a thought especially shocking to a world that set one of its highest values on scientific progress.

Science, and its partner, invention, had for a long time transformed both industry and war. It had conquered many of the dreaded plagues and diseases of the world. Everyone had long known that science could be applied either constructively or destructively. It was the magnitude of destructive possibilities that now made thoughtful people worry. Scientists themselves, after the first atomic explosion, affirmed the need for a moral regeneration. They insisted that science was neutral, free from blame for the horrors of Hiroshima and Nagasaki, that the trouble lay not with science but with the uses to which scientific knowledge was put.

Organizing industrial society   The problem of organizing industrial society was also unresolved after 1945. There were in theory two opposite social poles. At one, best represented by the Union of Soviet Socialist Republics (until its demise in 1991), all capital was owned by the state and supplied to managers and workers as needed, and all production and interchange were planned in advance by public authorities. In the Soviet form of socialism (as well as in the People's Republic of China after 1949), which the outside world called communism because it had come about through revolution and been maintained through dictatorship, the government's role was all-encompassing. At the other pole, best exemplified by the United States, capital was owned by private persons, who chose the channels of investment and hence determined the availability of jobs, and interchange took place through the mechanism of the market. Neither the socialist nor the capitalist system was pure in practice, and even in capitalist countries mixed economies became the rule, with varying degrees of government intervention. The chief drawback in the Soviet system was the lack of freedom, political and economic, and its stifling of initiative; in the American system, its periodic economic crises. In the years after the Second World War, Americans expended a good deal more effort trying to correct the lack of security than the Soviets did to correct the lack of freedom.

Another postwar question hinged on the unity of the modern world. It was indisputably one world in the sense that there existed a close-knit, interdependent economy, that political events and environmental changes affected the whole globe, and that world cultures and religions interacted as never before. But it was far from homogeneous. All admired the steam turbine and stood in awe of nuclear fission, but beyond the material level schemes of values diverged. No people wished to be subordinated to another, or to an international body, or to lose its way of life in a uniform world civilization.

The United Nations   After the Second World War, as after the First, an international organization was set up to prevent war in the future. A conference of all anti-Axis powers, held at San Francisco in 1945, founded the United Nations (UN) and drew up its charter. The new organization was designed to maintain international peace and security and to encourage cooperative solutions to international social, economic, and cultural problems. Although it was widely acknowledged that peace would depend primarily on the Great Powers, all states, regardless of size, would be represented. Two agencies were central. The General Assembly was a deliberative body in which all member states, however small, had an equal vote. The Security Council, whose primary responsibility was to preserve peace, consisted of the five Great

Powers, who were to be permanent members, and ten rotating members chosen for two-year terms. Apart from the two superpowers, the United States and the U.S.S.R., it was not easy to define the Great Powers in 1945, but the permanent seats were assigned to the United States, the Soviet Union, Great Britain, France, and China.[1]

Each permanent member had a veto power. Thus the Security Council could act on important matters only if the Great Powers were unanimous. Although widely criticized, the veto was accepted as necessary. In major crises the agreement of the Great Powers would be needed to maintain world peace. The U.S.S.R. demanded the veto most frankly, but the United States would not have joined without this safeguard. In the following years, however, even small countries refused to abide by judgments of the United Nations. No nation, large or small, was willing to forgo its independence or subordinate itself to an international body with the authority to put down violence, but the hope was strong that the authority and prestige of the UN would grow with time.

The United Nations had 51 original members. To symbolize the American commitment, its headquarters was located in New York. The charter provided for the admission of new members, including the former Axis countries and their satellites, and also wartime neutrals, so that it could be truly international. From 1947 to 1955 a few additional states were admitted; in 1955, 16 more; and in the next several decades, after decolonization and other changes, the organization expanded so that by 2000 it counted 189 members. In 1948, in good part because of the persuasive powers of the American delegate Eleanor Roosevelt, it adopted a sweeping Declaration of Universal Human Rights, but left unanswered the means of implementing it.

Membership expands

The United Nations and its Security Council failed to fulfill the role projected for it in the early postwar era because of the tensions between the American-led Western powers and the Soviets. Although the UN remained one of the few arenas where the Americans and Soviets could meet and debate, it was powerless to prevent the two superpowers from drifting further and further apart. On the other hand it helped from the beginning to mediate regional disputes and to play a role in peacekeeping missions. The office of the secretary general grew in importance. With the expansion of the UN to include the nations of the Third World—a term devised to describe the developing countries, mostly former colonial countries, not directly aligned with either the Western or Soviet camp—the General Assembly became a forum for debate in which the developing nations, critical of the wealthier West, vehemently voiced their social and economic grievances.

The Cold War: Origins and Nature

The Second World War left only the United States and the Soviet Union still standing in any strength. The United States emerged physically unscathed from the war, its economy stronger than ever before. Although it demobilized much of its wartime military force, it alone possessed the atomic bomb. The Soviet Union had been devastated by the war, in which over 20 million of its population had perished, but it was still a formidable military power, with four million soldiers under arms and in control of populations and territories in central and eastern Europe well beyond its pre-1939 boundaries. It became common to speak of the two countries as superpowers—continental land giants, possessing enormous

---

[1]Nationalist China (the Republic of China, or Taiwan) occupied the seat until 1971, even though the People's Republic of China (Communist China) governed the Chinese mainland after 1949.

The United Nations was established to resolve international conflicts and to foster peaceful exchanges between nations, but it also adopted a Declaration of Universal Human Rights. This picture of an early UN meeting shows a representative of the Philippines, Pedro Lopez, calling for the establishment and protection of a free press in all nations of the world.

(Hulton-Deutsch Collection/Corbis)

resources, overshadowing all other states, including the nations of western Europe long dominant in the modern centuries.

The characteristic of a two-state system is that each power knows in advance who its only dangerous enemy can be. In such a situation a diplomatic equilibrium is more difficult to sustain. Each views measures taken by the other power for what it considers its security as aggression or as provocation; and each, ignorant of the other's strength, exaggerates it. After the war the United States and the U.S.S.R. fell into this unhappy dual relationship. It was compounded by a deep-seated ideological tension between capitalist democracy and Marxist-Leninist communism that dated back to the Bolshevik Revolution of 1917. A widening diplomatic, geopolitical, and ideological clash of interests came to be known as the Cold War, so called because the antagonisms and rivalries, intense though they were, always fell short of open or direct military hostilities between the two powers.

The Cold War

It was not possible for anyone to know what Stalin, who dictated all decisions, or his lieutenants in the Kremlin, really believed or intended at the end of the Second World War. Probably they considered a clash between the U.S.S.R. and the Western capitalist powers as inevitable at some point in the future. Probably they were disturbed by the ambitious goals of American capitalism, which sought markets in eastern Europe and elsewhere, and by the American monopoly of the atomic bomb. They themselves undoubtedly saw an opportunity to consolidate their hold over territories gained during the war (or regained, since some of these had been lost at the end of the First World War), and to create an outer buffer zone for Soviet national security. Undoubtedly they also saw in the aftermath of the Second World War, as of the First, an opportunity to promote the international Communist cause.

Whether the Soviets were acting to protect their national security, fulfill old Russian territorial ambitions antedating communism, or promote communism on a world scale, President Truman and his advisers, and a great majority of the American people, became convinced that the Soviets were bent not only on consolidating their grip on central and eastern Europe but were also embarking on a worldwide Communist offensive. It was therefore the responsibility of the United States, as the only power in the West able to act effectively, to "contain" this offensive. Although the United States government would take military steps mainly in reaction to Soviet expansion or threats of expansion, many Americans came to ascribe almost all of the complex social and political unrest on the globe to initiatives launched by the Kremlin.

Containment

In Europe, at the close of hostilities, Soviet armies occupied eastern Europe and Germany as far west as the Elbe River. American, British, and French armies held the remainder of Germany, most of Austria, and all of Italy. During the war, the armed forces liberating an area exercised political authority. In that way, the sweep of the Red Army gave the Soviets political control over much of central and eastern Europe; 100 million people passed under Soviet domination. On the other hand, the United States excluded the Soviets from any active role in its occupation of Italy (and, in Asia, of Japan). For the Soviet Union, occupation meant full control over the political, economic, and social institutions of countries and the right to shape them in its own image. The Western powers, on the other hand, had hoped for pluralist and democratic societies, which would have been open to Western trade and influence. During the war the Americans and British had conceded Soviet predominance in eastern Europe, which the Soviets had liberated, but they soon resented the transformation of Poland and other East European countries into Soviet-dominated Communist states.

For Stalin, however, this kind of transformation was the only way to guarantee "friendly regimes" on his borders. From the Potsdam conference in July 1945 on, Truman denounced the Soviets for violating their pledge of free elections for the East European states and for failing to cooperate in the joint occupation of Germany. To the Americans Soviet control over eastern Europe seemed like the first step in a plan for unlimited expansion in Europe and elsewhere—not unlike the Nazi and Fascist aggression of the 1930s, to which Truman frequently compared it. Stalin may have been acting more as a Russian nationalist bent on protecting Russian national security than as a champion of worldwide Communist revolution, but his stubbornness and paranoia about capitalist encirclement, and lack of concern for world public opinion, made it difficult for the West to deal with him in the Cold War or to distinguish between what might have been legitimate Soviet security needs and expansionist missionary zeal.

Concerns about Soviet expansion

A series of Soviet actions fed the belief that Stalin's ambitions transcended eastern Europe. In Asia, as pledged at Yalta, the Soviets had declared war on Japan in August 1945 and moved into Manchuria, where they were well positioned to help the Chinese Communists. In Korea, once the Japanese were defeated, the Soviets by agreement occupied the northern part of the country but also took steps to consolidate their occupation zone into a

Communist government. Iran was another trouble spot. The Americans, British, and Russians had jointly occupied Iran during the war to forestall a Nazi takeover, but the Soviets refused to evacuate their troops at the stipulated time and pressed for oil concessions (such as the British and Americans already enjoyed).

The Soviets sought a trusteeship over the former Italian colonies in North Africa, within easy reach of the Suez Canal, and they massed troops on the Turkish border, pressing for joint control over the Black Sea straits and for naval access to the Mediterranean through the Dardanelles—an old tsarist goal. The British, acting as the guardians of the Mediterranean and Middle East, bolstered the Turkish defenses despite their own financial weakness. In Greece, in a civil war which raged from 1946 to 1949, Communist guerrillas battled the British-supported royalist, or nationalist, army. Stalin, as if recognizing his wartime commitment to Churchill that Greece remain in the Western sphere of influence, lent little aid to the Communists, but Tito's new Communist regime in Yugoslavia helped the Communist guerrillas. The Communist pressures on Turkey, Greece, and Iran aroused deep British and American concerns about Soviet strategic designs on the eastern Mediterranean and on the oil reserves of the Middle East.

Mutual mistrust

One casualty of the tension was a plan for international supervision of nuclear weapons. The United States knew that it was only a matter of time before the Soviets (and other nations) could build the atomic bomb, since the scientific basis for it was known. At the moment the British alone shared the secret. The United States proposed in 1946 that atomic energy be controlled by an international authority and that its use be limited to peaceful purposes. Such an international body would have the right to send inspectors into any country to check violations and enforce sanctions that would not be subject to veto in the Security Council. The Soviets objected and would not give up their veto. The idea of foreigners freely examining their society was repugnant to them. They questioned the good faith of the United States, which would not destroy its atomic bombs or halt further testing and production until the proposed international authority was established (many Americans also opposed international controls on their own nuclear arms). The British, in turn, fearful of an American relapse into isolationism, undertook to become a nuclear power on their own. The plan for international control foundered on mutual suspicion and mistrust. The Soviets proceeded with their own atomic research (and efficient espionage), which yielded results even sooner than expected. In 1949 the Soviets successfully tested an atomic bomb, and the nuclear arms race, universally dreaded, began.

The political conflicts had meanwhile deepened in 1946 and 1947. The American policy of containment, as formulated by the State Department, postulated that the Russians would expand wherever a power vacuum existed. Advocates for the strategy of containment argued that the West should show both patience and firmness, and in time Soviet society itself might change. In the meantime, however, the West needed to maintain its military strength and use economic and other counterpressures to resist the Soviets. Containment, the cornerstone of American policy, came to be interpreted in more rigorously military terms than some of its proponents had intended, and it was accompanied by a tendency of some Americans to blame all global unrest on a monolithic Moscow-controlled communism. Meanwhile Churchill, even before the Soviets had fully completed the transformation of eastern Europe into Communist satellites, made an eloquent speech in March 1946 in which he described the "iron curtain" that had descended between eastern and western Europe—"from Stettin in the Baltic to Trieste in the Adriatic." That spring the United States turned down a pending Soviet request for a reconstruction loan, Congress having decided that Lend-Lease should end with the war, and also cut off reparations deliveries to the Soviets from the American occupation zone of Germany.

In 1947 financially strained Great Britain, forced to cut back on its commitments in the Mediterranean, informed Washington that it could no longer aid the anti-Communist forces in Greece or support Turkey in its resistance to Soviet pressures. The United States quickly moved to fill the vacuum. Truman not only agreed to provide the necessary assistance in the Mediterranean but at the same time also formulated in March 1947 a broad national policy to contain communism everywhere—"to assist free peoples who are resisting attempted subjugation by armed minorities or by outside pressures." The Truman Doctrine committed the United States to unprecedented involvement in global military and economic affairs. The Marshall Plan, designed to hasten European economic recovery and hence check Communist expansion, was also announced in the spring of 1947.

The Truman Doctrine

The American national security state began to take shape. A National Security Council was created to advise the president on security matters and a Central Intelligence Agency (CIA) was created to coordinate the gathering of intelligence. The CIA soon received authorization to conduct covert operations as well. The authority of the executive branch to conduct foreign policy grew. In 1948 the United States adopted its first peacetime military draft.

The Soviets in their turn denounced the American capitalist and imperialist "warmongers." With the United States arming Greece and Turkey, American air bases established in the Middle East, American armed forces in occupation of Japan, Okinawa, and South Korea, and the Americans possessing the atomic bomb, the Soviets felt threatened and encircled. Soviet suspicions, dating from Western intervention in the Russian Revolution and civil war in 1917–1920, their exclusion from the Munich Pact, the delay in opening up a second front in the Second World War, the cessation of Lend-Lease at the end of the war, and the rejection of a requested postwar loan, mounted.

Soviet suspicions

In 1947 the Soviets, to exert closer control over all Communist parties, reestablished in new form the old Communist International, or Comintern, which had been abandoned in 1943 as a gesture of wartime cooperation and goodwill, renaming it the Communist Information Bureau, or Cominform. The Soviets also replaced coalition governments in central and eastern Europe, in which the Communists had formerly shared power, with regimes dominated by Communist parties. In Czechoslovakia, where President Benes's democratic coalition had been viewed as a possible bridge between East and West, the Czech Communist party, faced with defeat in a forthcoming election, seized power in February 1948. A serious crisis next arose over Berlin.

Germany: The Berlin Blockade and the Airlift of 1948–1949

The key to the rebuilding of Europe, and the most critical area of Soviet-Western contention, was Germany, divided by Allied agreement into four zones and occupied by the United States, the Soviet Union, Britain, and France. The Allies had agreed to joint Allied policies for a defeated Germany, even though each of the four powers was to occupy its separate zone. Berlin also was divided into four separate Allied sectors, with joint administration for the city as a whole. All had agreed that Germany should pay reparations, both in capital equipment and current production, mainly to the Soviet Union, which had suffered most from German military destruction, and that limits should be placed on German productive capacity.

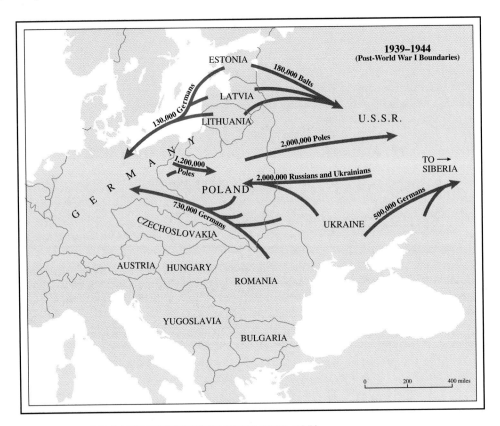

DEPORTATION AND RESETTLEMENT, 1939–1950

The age-old distribution of nationalities in central and eastern Europe was radically transformed between 1939 and 1950. About 6 million Jews died in the Holocaust, with over 300,000 survivors emigrating to Israel by 1950, and millions of Germans, Poles, and others were forcibly uprooted.

Left panel: **The first stage began with the Nazi–Soviet Pact of 1939, after which the Germans occupied western Poland, while the Russians annexed eastern Poland and the three Baltic republics. Western Poland received Poles expelled from Germany, while in eastern Poland about 2 million Poles were deported to Siberia, being replaced by about the same number of Russians and Ukranians. Many Estonians, Latvians, and Lithuanians were moved to other parts of the Soviet Union. Thousands of Germans were "returned" to Germany from the Baltic republics and from places such as Romania, where they had long formed German enclaves. The "Volga Germans," Tatars, and others in south Russia were sent to Siberia.**

Two Germanys emerge

At the war's end the Americans, supported by the British, quickly came to favor the economic reconstruction of Germany to accelerate European recovery and to reduce European dependence on American financial aid. The Ruhr, in the western zone, was still Europe's industrial heartland. The Soviets, on the other hand, were determined to use German resources to repair the devastation in their own country. They removed large amounts of food and stripped entire plants of machinery in their zone. The Western Allies refused to permit the dismantling of factories in their zones and insisted that the Soviets take their share of current production only from their own zone. By May 1946 joint administration of Germany

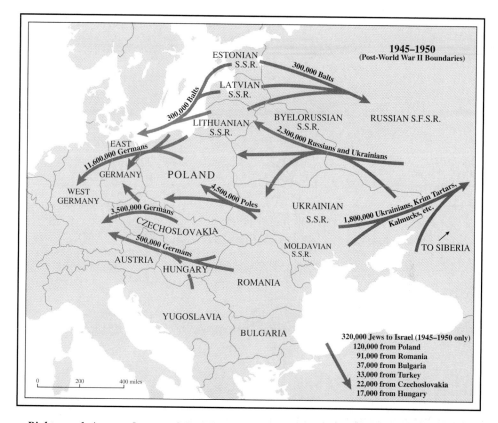

1945–1950
(Post-World War II Boundaries)

ESTONIAN S.S.R.

300,000 Balts

LATVIAN S.S.R.

300,000 Balts

LITHUANIAN S.S.R.

BYELORUSSIAN S.S.R.

RUSSIAN S.F.S.R.

2,300,000 Russians and Ukrainians

EAST GERMANY

11,600,000 Germans

POLAND

WEST GERMANY

3,500,000 Germans

4,500,000 Poles

UKRAINIAN S.S.R.

1,800,000 Ukrainians, Krim Tartars, Kalmucks, etc.

CZECHOSLOVAKIA

500,000 Germans

AUSTRIA

HUNGARY

MOLDAVIAN S.S.R.

TO SIBERIA

ROMANIA

YUGOSLAVIA

BULGARIA

320,000 Jews to Israel (1945–1950 only)
120,000 from Poland
91,000 from Romania
37,000 from Bulgaria
33,000 from Turkey
22,000 from Czechoslovakia
17,000 from Hungary

0   200   400 miles

Right panel: **A second stage of displacements came with the Soviet victory and collapse of Hitler's Reich. The German–Polish frontier was now moved westward to the Oder River. Millions of Germans from east of the Oder, along with other millions from the Sudeten regions of Czechoslovakia, from Hungary, and from Romania, were thrown back into what remained of Germany, most fleeing to the Western zone. Poles streamed into what had been Germany east of the Oder; others came into Poland from Ukraine. Russians moved into what had been eastern Poland and the Baltic states. Ukranians and various non-Russian minorities were sent to Siberia. Some Balts escaped to the West; others were redistributed to various places in the Soviet Union.**

Amid all of these movements of people, the most conspicuous, long-term changes, in addition to the virtual disappearance of East European Jews, were the expulsion of the Germans from Eastern Europe and a westward movement of Poles and Russians.

(Westermanns Atlas zur Weltgeschichte)

had all but broken down. Early in 1947 the United States and Britain united their two zones (which they called "Bizonia"); the French, overcoming their initial reluctance to see a revived Germany, soon merged their zone as well. The Western powers encouraged the reconstruction of governments in the individual German states and the convening of a constituent assembly to set up a federal republic. The Soviets, in their zone, took steps to establish a Communist-dominated government. Two Germanys were emerging.

In June 1948 the Western powers, recognizing the need for drastic currency reform to cope with inflation and encourage West German economic revival, suddenly revoked the old worthless currency and at a 1-to-10 ratio issued a new German mark, the Deutsche

The Soviet closure of the railways and roads into Berlin provoked one of the most dramatic events of the early Cold War: the Berlin Airlift. For almost a year (1948–1949) the Americans and their Western allies flew supplies into the isolated city on military aircraft such as the plane in this picture. Images of the airlift became part of the evolving Cold War struggle for international public opinion and an enduring symbol of the links between West Berlin and the Western Allies.

(Hulton-Deutsch Collection/Corbis).

Berlin blockade and airlift

mark. The Soviets, who had not been consulted, objected to this violation of the wartime agreement to treat Germany as a single economic unit. In retaliation they blockaded all road and rail access to Berlin, which lay 100 miles deep within the Soviet zone. The blockade was a sharp challenge and test of will. If the West abandoned Berlin, it could lose authority in all Europe and open the way for Soviet westward expansion, and perhaps expansion elsewhere. Knowing that they could not resort to military measures against the much stronger Soviet ground forces, the Allies responded with a massive air lift. For close to a year, American and Western aircraft flew in thousands of tons of food and other supplies to the occupation forces and to the three million inhabitants of West Berlin. The Soviets harassed the planes but avoided direct confrontation and, finally, in May 1949 lifted the blockade.

Each side proceeded with the formation of a German government. The Federal Republic of Germany, its capital in the small Rhineland city of Bonn, came into existence in September 1949; the German Democratic Republic, its capital in the eastern sector of Berlin, one month later. There were now two Germanys. The division of Europe had hardened.

The Atlantic Alliance

In 1948 Britain, France, Belgium, the Netherlands, and Luxembourg formed a West European Union for collective self-defense, but it remained at the time of only nominal importance. In 1949 the United States took the lead in creating a larger military alliance and collective security system. The United States, Canada, and ten European nations met in Washington and agreed to military arrangements for the joint defense of western Europe. The Atlantic Pact was a military alliance of unlimited duration and broad scope: "an armed attack against one or more" was to be considered "an attack against all." The United States formally committed itself to the security of western Europe and agreed to supply funds and equipment for European rearmament. It was the first such military alliance of its kind in American history.

The North Atlantic Treaty Organization (NATO) emerged with a network of military arrangements and a chain of command headed by General Eisenhower. Because West Germany remained the most vulnerable target for Soviet expansion, large numbers of American troops (eventually over 300,000) were stationed there as the nucleus of the NATO armed forces. With overwhelming Soviet superiority in ground forces, the NATO defense strategy was based primarily on American air power rather than on ground troops alone. The treaty solemnly affirmed American determination not to abandon the Continent. In later years the West Europeans became restive with American leadership, or, alternatively, feared an American decoupling from Europe, but NATO remained western Europe's shield against Soviet aggression. The Truman Doctrine, the Marshall Plan, and the North Atlantic Treaty Organization were the three prongs of the American and Western response to a potential Soviet challenge.

NATO

Meanwhile the West European countries, with the aid of the Marshall Plan, were making an impressive economic recovery and cooperating with each other. In a few short years after the most devastating war in history western Europe had reconstructed itself politically, recovered economically, and was rearming. The Soviets could not be expected to view with equanimity the revival and growing unity of western Europe. American financial and military assistance, NATO, the containment policy, all defensive in Western eyes, and indeed provoked by Soviet expansionism, were hostile acts from the Soviet perspective. The Soviet Union drew its six satellite or client states, variously styled people's republics or people's democracies, closer to it. It formalized economic ties by creating in 1949 a Council for Mutual Economic Aid and a few years later coordinated the existing network of military alliances in the Warsaw Pact of 1955. The Soviets added to their military and air power and continued their nuclear research.

By 1949 Stalin's postwar expansion seemed contained and Truman could claim success for his policies. The Soviets had dropped their demands on Turkey and departed from

Iran. Insurrectionary strikes launched by Communist parties in western Europe had failed, as did a Communist bid for power in Italy in the elections of 1948, in which the Vatican and the United States strongly supported the anti-Communist camp. Marshal Tito in 1948 successfully defied the Cominform and Yugoslavia went its separate Communist way. In Greece the American- and British-backed Greek royalists triumphed in 1949 against the Communist guerrillas. The Soviet blockade of Berlin had failed to drive the West from the city.

Stalemate in Europe

The rivalry over Europe ended in stalemate. The Soviet threat to western Europe diminished. The continent remained divided into a western and eastern Europe (the term central Europe tended to drop from use), Germany into two Germanys, Berlin into West and East Berlin. After the failure of the Soviet blockade of Berlin, there was no such overt conflict in Europe. Despite renewed threats to Berlin, each side recognized the strength and security concerns of the other. But any thoughts that the world might settle into peace, no matter how uneasy, were shattered in June 1950. The Western-Soviet struggle shifted to Asia.

The Revival of Japan

In Asia events also moved rapidly in the early postwar years. In China the Chinese Communists triumphed over the Nationalists and Mao Zedong proclaimed the People's Republic of China in 1949. In Japan the United States used its military occupation from 1945 to 1952 to foster parliamentary institutions and revive the Japanese economy.

The occupation of Japan

Rejecting Soviet demands for a share in the occupation of Japan, the United States, with British and French approval, lodged full authority in General Douglas MacArthur as supreme commander of the occupation forces. In good part in response to Cold War tensions the American occupation encouraged economic revival and political reconstruction, not vindictiveness, and the Japanese, stunned by their disastrous defeat, cooperated. In the interests of stability the emperor received special status and was shielded from trial or even criticism. A new constitution in 1946 ended divine-right rule, transferred sovereignty from the emperor to the people, established machinery for parliamentary government, gave women the vote, and encouraged local self-government. The constitution "forever" renounced war and the threat or use of force as a means of settling international disputes; the small Japanese armed forces were to be restricted to defensive purposes. Although trials of Japanese war criminals were held, there were no extensive purges. The Japanese paid reparations to Asian nations that had been the victims of Japanese conquest but did not even years later fully acknowledge the brutality that had accompanied these conquests.

Efforts at social and economic reform under the occupation were less sweeping than originally planned. The large family holdings in heavy industry and banking were dissolved, but within a short time new forms of economic concentration replaced them. Labor unions were reinstituted but their powers were curtailed. When the occupation inaugurated a program of land redistribution, with a limit on large landholdings, small farmers lacked the means to purchase the land offered them. Although a moderate Socialist party emerged, and militant activists in later years frequently demonstrated their discontent, political control remained in the hands of conservatives drawn from the upper social classes.

By the end of the occupation the Liberal Democratic party (a conservative party) dominated the government and long continued to do so.

Economic recovery

The conservative-led political consensus had a strong commitment to economic recovery and growth. Like western Europe, Japan, too, recovered rapidly. In 1945 it had been prostrate, a fourth of its housing destroyed, agricultural and industrial output reduced to half its prewar level, its shipping and financial reserves gone. Under the occupation, and with American help, the economy revived and expanded; by 1954 its gross national product reached prewar levels. Labor self-discipline and social patterns of deference and loyalty kept industrial unrest to a minimum. Close cooperation between government and business encouraged savings, investment, research, and economic growth. The very need to rebuild and renovate the economy from the bottom up proved an advantage.

Beginning in the early 1950s the economy grew at an amazing rate of nearly 10 percent each year; manufacturing output, at 14 percent. Despite the repatriation of millions of Japanese from Manchuria, Korea, and other parts of Asia and the addition of large numbers of rural workers to the labor force, Japan still had a labor shortage. The response was an intense level of automation. Japan became a pioneer in advanced high technology and came to depend on technological innovations to sustain its growth. Its consumer products soon entered the world economy, and its exports came to rival those of the Americans and the Europeans. Because a large military establishment was forbidden, expenditures that might have gone into the military, as in the past, were now plowed into industrial investments. By the 1950s Japan was once again a major economic power, a bastion of social stability, and a major new element in the global economy. For the Soviets the revival of Japan under American auspices, which they saw as a counterweight to Soviet influence and as a bulwark against revolution in Asia, loomed as still another threat.

Containment in Asia: The Korean War

In June 1950 the Korean War broke out. The Western Allies and the Soviet Union had agreed that Korea, once an object of imperialist rivalry between Japan and tsarist Russia, but under Japanese rule since 1910, would become free and independent after Japan's defeat. In 1945 the United States, for reasons of military expediency, proposed that Soviet troops temporarily occupy the northern part of the country down to the thirty-eighth parallel; United States troops would temporarily occupy the southern half. But postwar negotiations for a unified Korea foundered. The U.S.S.R. established a satellite government in its occupation zone under the Communist leader Kim Il Sung and built up North Korean military strength. The United States developed its own client state in the south and lent economic and military assistance. In 1947 a UN commission sought to sponsor nationwide elections, but the Soviet Union would not permit supervision of elections in the north. The elections in the south in May 1948 resulted in the presidency of Syngman Rhee, who, despite superficial forms of democracy, governed autocratically. Anticommunism in Korea and elsewhere did not necessarily equate with democracy. After the elections the United States withdrew its occupation forces but continued military and economic support. The Soviet Union also removed its occupation forces but left behind a well-trained and well-equipped North Korean army. Despite the original intention, two Koreas had come into existence.

By 1950 the situation in East Asia, as we have seen, had altered dramatically. Japan had revived. The United States through its postwar occupation had helped to create a stable Japan, friendly to the West and with a prospering economy. In addition, the Chinese Communists, with only limited and grudging Soviet support, had triumphed over the Nationalists in a long civil war and in 1949 had proclaimed the Chinese People's Republic. Although relations between the Chinese Communists and the Soviets were neither warm nor cordial, the two countries,

East Asia in 1950

out of mutual concern over the revival of Japan and the growth of American influence in East Asia, drew together in a mutual defense pact in February 1950. The U.S.S.R. meanwhile campaigned to have the People's Republic of China replace Nationalist China in the United Nations. When the effort failed, the Soviets in protest boycotted the Security Council meetings.

Although border skirmishes between North and South Korea had been frequent, the full-scale North Korean invasion of the south came as a surprise. In the West it was seen as an open act of military aggression, the first such clear-cut military aggression of the Cold War. Because of the boldness of their initiative and their superior forces, the North Koreans expected a quick victory. They gambled that the United States would not intervene and that the outside world would lodge no more than a moral protest.

The precise inspiration for the invasion remains somewhat unclear. North Korea, concerned over the south's avowed ambition to unite the country on pro-Western terms, seems to have taken the initiative on its own. It is known, however, that Stalin was aware of the North Korean intentions and even allowed the Soviet military to help plan aspects of the invasion, counting on a quick victory and a limited international response. Yet the timing of the invasion seems to have surprised the Soviets who, as noted, were boycotting the Security Council, unable to exercise their veto when the Council condemned the invasion and authorized military countermeasures. The Chinese, recovering from their civil war, barely established in power, and still facing a challenge from the Nationalists in Taiwan, could scarcely have helped initiate it. Meanwhile the sweeping initial successes of the North Koreans offered the Soviets and the Chinese an opportunity to check the growing American influence in Japan and East Asia. The Soviets quietly furnished military aid to North Korea and denounced the United States for intervening in Asian affairs—on the very doorsteps of the U.S.S.R. and the People's Republic of China.

For the American government, and for most Americans, it was difficult to believe that the attack had not been engineered in Moscow or that the North Koreans were capable of independent action. The assumption was that the Soviets, probing in Asia for weak spots, as they had elsewhere, had found one and now must be halted. Korea, like Berlin, became another test of American and Western will. Truman, already concerned about the "loss of China" (the formula used at the time by his political critics for the Chinese Communist victory in 1949) saw it as a test of the "free world's commitment to liberty." The attack challenged the entire system of collective security and containment built to stem the tide of Soviet communism. The Soviets, he said, had passed "beyond the use of subversion" to "armed invasion and war." Without asking for an American declaration of war because it was deemed to be a "police action," Truman, in conformity with the Security Council resolution, ordered American combat troops to Korea and called for air strikes above the thirty-eighth parallel. General MacArthur, the wartime hero of the Pacific who had successfully presided over the occupation of Japan, was named commander of the UN multinational forces, of which the Americans made up the major part.

A test of will

In the early fighting in the summer of 1950 the American-led United Nations forces were driven south to the very water's edge, where they faced expulsion from the peninsula. But in September MacArthur made a remarkable amphibious landing on the western side of the peninsula, drove the North Koreans back above the thirty-eighth parallel, and then rapidly moved north toward the Yalu River, the boundary between Korea and the People's Republic of China. Mao, incensed, took action to assert China's international importance. In late October, a large Chinese "voluntary" army suddenly appeared and within two

The Korean War was a key test for President Harry Truman's policy of containing communism, yet, like all modern wars, it disrupted the lives of millions of civilians, including those who knew little about the larger political issues at stake. This Korean girl and her baby brother were photographed near an American tank in the summer of 1951, but their expressions convey some of the timeless, local struggle to survive amid the violent international conflicts of governments and global powers.
(R. V. Spencer/TimePix)

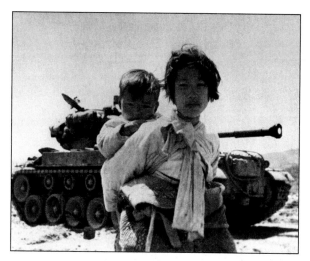

weeks drove the advancing UN armies back below the thirty-eighth parallel. It was an entirely new war, to which China was now committed. The European allies, at first gratified by the American show of determination, grew worried that the war could escalate into a global, possibly nuclear, conflict.

Meanwhile the battle lines seesawed. MacArthur forced the Chinese and North Korean troops to retreat, again crossed the thirty-eighth parallel, and demanded unconditional surrender. He proposed to blockade the Chinese coast, bomb Chinese cities, encourage the Chinese Nationalists to attack the Chinese mainland, and even seal off Korea from China by a field of radioactive waste. Truman, alarmed, recognized that MacArthur's threats could lead to full-scale war with China, to Soviet intervention, and to a wider war in which the United States would lack the full support of its European allies. When the general publicly flouted the president's authority, Truman relieved him of his command and replaced him.

In July 1951 a cease-fire agreement brought large-scale fighting to a halt, but armistice negotiations dragged on, deadlocked over the repatriation of North Korean prisoners who did not wish to return home. In July 1953 under General Eisenhower's presidency an armistice was signed, the line of partition drawn roughly where the fighting had begun three years *Cease-fire and armistice* earlier, at the thirty-eighth parallel, with provision for a demilitarized buffer zone. The partition hardened into a long-term division. North Korea became a Communist state and a full-fledged ally of the Soviet Union. South Korea, unable to achieve political democracy under Syngman Rhee or for a long time under his successors, nonetheless developed a dynamic capitalist economy, far outstripping North Korea in economic strength. At the end of the century, many decades later, over 40,000 American troops remained stationed in South Korea to police the demilitarized zone, but negotiations were beginning to reduce some of the tensions between the two Koreas.

The United States spent over $15 billion on the war. Because it could not by itself supply all its military needs, the war vastly stimulated the eco- *Results of the Korean War* nomic growth of western Europe and Japan. It also quickened the pressures for German rearmament. Although 15 countries participated in the fighting, it was largely an American military operation. The United States furnished half the ground forces and close to all the naval and air power. The Americans suffered over 54,000 battle deaths in the undeclared war, close to half as many as in the First World War; the American wounded were estimated at over 100,000. But the South Koreans suffered over one million casualties in dead, wounded, and missing; the North Koreans and the Chinese, each an equal number. In all some three to four million lives may have been lost. The Soviets had fought by proxy.

In American eyes a flagrant act of aggression had been checked, and a precedent for a containment strategy in Asia had been established. In western Europe, despite the anxiety over MacArthur's recklessness, the show of American firmness was reassuring. As seen in the Communist world, however, and indeed in many of the nonaligned countries in Asia such as India or Indonesia, the United States, the great capitalist power, had been prevented from reasserting Western imperialist supremacy in the East. In its efforts to create regional security pacts in Asia, the United States found little enthusiasm among the larger non-Communist Asian powers who disliked communism but also distrusted the West. Although the United States had been the least involved of all the Great Powers in nineteenth-century territorial imperialism in Asia, its new leadership of the Western world made it a symbol of Western oppression, buttressed by the suspicion that its free-world rhetoric only masked a drive to create world markets for American capitalism—an image assiduously cultivated by the Soviets and, even more aggressively, by the Chinese Communists.

On the other hand, its success in checking the North Korean act of aggression by force of arms reinforced the American belief that military strength and decisiveness could check Communist expansion anywhere in the world; containment would be global. The Korean War inaugurated an era of deep American involvement in Asia and served as prelude to an even longer and more costly conflict, the war in Vietnam in the following decade. In late 1952 the United States successfully tested its first thermonuclear or hydrogen bomb, hundreds of times more powerful than the atomic bomb used at Hiroshima; the Soviets at almost the same time, in 1953, did the same.

American involvement in Asia

The Korean War had its political repercussions in Europe. Despite continuing misgivings in France and in other parts of Europe over a revival of German military strength, the Americans pressed for West German rearmament. When a French proposal for a European Defense Community (with a "European army," in which the Germans were to serve as "European soldiers") failed to pass the French legislature in 1954, West Germany was authorized to create an army of its own under the overall command of NATO. Concern over a resurgent German militarism was receding. The West German constitution guaranteed civilian control over the military, and a strong antimilitarist movement had emerged in the country itself. In 1955 the Federal Republic of Germany became a full member of NATO.

Peace with Japan

The Korean War hastened a peace treaty with Japan. In the peace treaty signed in 1951 in San Francisco by 50 nations, but without Soviet participation, no general reparations were exacted, but individual countries were to work out their own reparations agreements. In a separate security pact the United States retained military rights in Japan and occupied nearby islands, where, under agreement, the United States would remain as long as necessary for peace and security. A year later the American occupation of Japan formally ended. The Soviets made no move to return the Kurile Islands, which they had occupied at the end of the Second World War. The United States meanwhile signed security pacts with Australia, New Zealand, and the Philippines, reinforcing its global commitments.

The decades that followed the troubled international relations of the early Cold War brought new confrontations and crises—over Berlin, Cuba, Vietnam, the Middle East, and

Africa, to name only the most important—and above all, a mounting nuclear arms race between the two superpowers and the stockpiling of the most formidable weaponry ever assembled. But before continuing with the Cold War, we must examine in this and the following chapter many other developments of these years—the remarkable economic recovery and political reconstruction of western Europe, the reshaping of the global economy, the world of the Communist countries, and the emergence of new nations from the old Western colonial empires.

110. WESTERN EUROPE: ECONOMIC RECONSTRUCTION

The Second World War had left Europe in a worse state of disorder than the First. It had ruined one of the world's chief industrial areas and brought its economic system to collapse. Even when the worst local devastation was repaired, suffering and distress persisted. With problems of transportation and exchange unresolved, western Europe was cut off from the areas with which it had traded. It could no longer pay for the imports that it needed. During the war the West Europeans, and especially the British, had used up their overseas investments and lost a good share of the shipping services they had once provided. Overseas countries had built up their own industries and needed those of Europe less, and the United States had taken over markets once in European hands.

At the same time, western Europe was not to be written off. Its population exceeded that of either of the superpowers. Even in ruins, it still possessed one of the world's leading industrial plants and the skills needed to rehabilitate and run it. The Europeans did not wish to be rescued by either of the superpowers. Most rejected communism as a form of slavery. Yet they feared excessive dependence on the United States. Memories of the stock-market crash of 1929, the economic collapse of Europe after the withdrawal of American capital, and the Great Depression bred skepticism about American capitalism. Europeans were also sensitive to a persistent strain of American isolationism.

The Marshall Plan and European Recovery

For the non-Communist world, the single most important factor in the early postwar years was the productivity of the American economic system. The American economy had expanded enormously during the war. At the war's end the United States accounted for two-thirds of the world's industrial production and held two-thirds of the world's gold. Its gross national product was two and a half times higher than in 1939; its exports were three times greater. Despite predictions about postwar economic collapse, its economy grew at unprecedented rates in the 1950s and 1960s.

U.S. economic strength

When Lend-Lease ended after the war, the United States sent billions of dollars worth of goods to western Europe to relieve distress and made loans to individual states, especially to Britain. But the Europeans themselves quickly set about to rebuild their economies. Within two years, by 1947, the economies of western Europe were approaching prewar levels of production. American aid was still desperately needed, however, to continue the purchase of food, fuel, raw materials, and industrial parts essential to full recovery. By the spring of 1947 that recovery appeared at risk. The poorest harvest in a century was feared. With Cold War tensions mounting, Communist parties in France and Italy, which had earlier cooperated in postwar reconstruction, launched strikes. Even if the Soviet Union was not actively promoting revolution in western Europe, understanding perhaps that the West would not tolerate overt revolution there, the Americans were concerned about European stability. Between the two superpowers the Soviets had more to gain by chaos in western Europe and the United States had more to gain by its rebuilding.

The Marshall Plan

American economic aid so far had been improvised and piecemeal. In June 1947 Secretary of State George C. Marshall used the occasion of his Harvard commencement address to invite the Europeans to cooperate in drawing up blueprints for a broad program of reconstruction, for which the United States would provide the financial support. The plan, as formulated, was "directed not against country or doctrine, but against hunger, poverty, desperation, and chaos." To reinforce its nonpolitical character, the United States extended the invitation to all European governments, including the Soviet Union and the East European states. The Soviet Union rejected the proposal and forbade the participation of its East European satellites, some of which had evinced interest, denouncing the plan as "a new venture in American imperialism."

The West European countries responded eagerly. Under the Marshall Plan, or European Recovery Program, as enacted by Congress, American aid was coordinated with each country's needs and with joint European priorities to maximize the benefits. The Office for European Economic Cooperation (OEEC) in Paris, with which the Americans worked closely, identified projects, coordinated the planning, and allocated the funds.

Results of the Marshall Plan

The results of the Marshall Plan exceeded the boldest anticipations of its American sponsors. The West Europeans utilized their technical and managerial skills to improve transportation facilities, modernize their infrastructure, and expand their productive capacity. They reduced trade barriers among themselves and facilitated trade by setting up a payments union. Hard currency, now available for imports, reduced financial pressures and the need for further austerity. The Marshall Plan accelerated the recovery already under way, smoothed the recovery process, and encouraged the economic cooperation of the European countries with each other.

While the United States thus used its economic resources to help revive its competitors, the Marshall Plan also served American interests by restoring a world market, of which the United States would be a principal beneficiary. By creating markets for American exports, it helped fuel the postwar economic boom in the United States. The Americans satisfied their humanitarian impulse, served their economic needs, and reduced the drift of Europeans into the Communist camp. At the same time the Marshall Plan sharpened the division between the Soviet bloc and the West.

Economic Growth in Western Europe

For West Germany the currency reform of 1948, Marshall Plan aid, and the economic opportunities opened up by the Korean War ignited a stunning economic revival and expansion, the *Wirtschaftswunder,* or "economic miracle." By 1950 the Federal Republic of Germany by itself exceeded prewar Germany's production levels before embarking on an even more spectacular economic boom. By 1958 it was the leading industrial country of western Europe. But France, Italy, and other West European countries experienced an "economic miracle" also. For two and a half decades, from 1948 to 1974 (when a global recession set in), the western European economies grew at unprecedented and uninterrupted rates of growth. The West Europeans basked in prosperity and rising living standards. Europeans

The silver '50s and golden '60s

The European "economic miracle" of the 1950s and 1960s brought new jobs and wealth to workers throughout Europe. This picture of British workers in 1957 shows women assembling circuit panels for television sets, one of the important new consumer products in post–World War II economies and social life.

(Hulton Archive)

would later speak of the "silver '50s" and the "golden '60s"; the French would speak also of the "30 glorious years." Although Britain's economy, burdened by older industries and the loss of overseas markets, lagged, it too grew faster than at any time in the interwar years. Japan, as we have seen, from the 1950s on also experienced a remarkable expansion.

The prosperity of western Europe derived from a competitive, capitalist, free-market and private-enterprise economy, but it was accompanied almost everywhere by varying degrees of extensive economic planning, systematic government intervention, and a network of social services to help cope with the instability of competitive capitalism and the business cycle. No one anywhere wished to repeat the hard times and suffering of the Great Depression. Keynes's theories, first formulated in the 1930s but without many adherents

Economic planning and government intervention

at that time, took hold in the postwar era and dominated government policy in the 1950s and 1960s even when conservative governments were in control. Governments kept their economies under close surveillance and used their fiscal and monetary powers to promote investment, production, and employment, and to control inflation. They took "counter-cyclical" measures; that is, at signs of decline in the business cycle they increased government spending. Full employment was accepted as a goal. Improved statistical techniques and economic forecasting, although far from precision instruments, made economic planning and "fine-tuning" feasible. Such planning, however, took the form of guidance and direction, not coercion, and differed markedly from the rigid, detailed, and doctrinaire centralized planning of the Soviet Union and Soviet bloc.

In Britain, France, and Italy (less so in West Germany, which had lived through state control under the Nazis), the postwar governments also nationalized a number of the key sectors of the economy to bring them under government control. But even in these mixed economies, the private capitalist sector represented the major share of economic activity. In all western Europe economic growth became virtually an obsession. Governments and people came to expect growth rates far exceeding those of the past. It was as if western Europe was catching up, compensating for the lost time of the interwar years and the Second World War, and for the economic stagnation of a generation.

A steady stream of immigrants

When the sustained economic growth of the next two decades led to a labor shortage, West Germany and other countries invited foreign workers to join their labor force. Turks, Greeks, Yugoslavs, Spaniards, Portuguese, and Italians (mostly from southern Italy) were invited in as "guest workers." Four and a half million workers arrived in the Federal Republic of Germany alone, over half of them Turks, who did not return home but formed large unassimilated enclaves. After the postwar collapse of the European colonial empires, immigrants from the former European colonies in Asia, Africa, and the Caribbean also arrived in western Europe in large numbers. From the 1950s on a steady stream of immigrants came to Britain from India, Pakistan, the West Indies, and Africa. France drew large numbers from its former North African colonies, especially Algeria. The Netherlands became home for many Indonesians. Later political refugees also arrived in Europe from Vietnam and other parts of Asia. The new Europeans were often of different cultures, religion, racial composition, or skin color. Mosques became a common sight in European cities. The influx of guest workers and immigrants by the millions later created new social conflicts and resentments, especially in less affluent times. The presence of the new Europeans led to friction, often overtly racial, testing the flexibility and tolerance of a European society becoming increasingly multiethnic and multicultural.

With a postwar baby boom and an influx of at least 13 million immigrants and refugees the population of western Europe grew by 25 percent between 1945 and 1970. But by the 1960s the birth rate of the West Europeans, as we shall see, began to level off and western Europe's population began to show a continuing decline.

Growth of the welfare state

In these same postwar years the welfare state grew, going well beyond its pre-1914 origins or its expansion in the interwar years. The postwar governments gave a high priority to social objectives, to what the French Resistance charter had called "a more just social order": the right to a suitable job, government compensation in the event of unemployment or disability, social security in old age, free or subsidized health care, and the redistribution of wealth and income through progressive taxation. The protection of the welfare state was intended to be universal, not confined, as in earlier times, to the poor and disadvantaged. Its social objectives could be achieved in the 1950s and 1960s because of a salutary interplay of government, management, and labor, which all shared in the consensus about investment and growth. Only later, from the late 1970s on, did the argument gather strength that all these entitlements had become excessive and an impediment to economic growth and competitiveness.

111. WESTERN EUROPE: POLITICAL RECONSTRUCTION

Western Europe also confronted overwhelming challenges of political reconstruction at the end of the war. Britain was economically exhausted and in the process of liquidating its empire. France, recovering from the collapse of 1940, the occupation, and the wartime Vichy regime, found itself engaged in colonial wars in Indochina and Algeria. Italy had to renew its political life after two decades of fascism. Germany, after the Nazi rout, was divided and under military occupation. Nevertheless political reconstruction went forward. Britain resumed its role as the world's oldest parliamentary democracy; France and Italy adopted new constitutions; out of the western zone of occupied Germany the Federal Republic of Germany emerged in 1949.

The smaller states of western Europe also resumed their parliamentary democracies. Only Spain and Portugal remained under prewar dictatorships until those regimes also came to an end in the mid 1970s. The memories of dictatorship receded. The suffrage was broadened. Women finally received the vote in France and Italy as the war drew to a close; in Switzerland, in 1971. And in a suffrage reform that went almost unnoticed, the legal voting age in most countries was quietly reduced to 18 in the 1970s.

A renovating spirit swept western Europe, fueled by the memories of 1914–1918, the economic dislocations of the 1920s, the miseries of the Great Depression of the 1930s, and the human toll of the Second World War. The wartime Resistance movements called for a federal union of Europe to prevent future wars and emphasized economic and social rights as well as political freedom. Liberal democracy, though crucial, was not sufficient; postwar governments were asked to provide protection against the insecurities of old age, disability, ill health, and unemployment.

A renovating spirit

The earliest elections confirmed the strength of the new reform spirit, but before long politics reverted to older ways. The welfare state idea persisted, as did the impulse for an integrated Europe, but politics became more pragmatic and less ideological. Socialists, following the Scandinavian model, became Social Democratic reformists, accepting capitalism but insisting that they could manage capitalist economies more effectively than liberals, centrists, or conservatives. In France and Italy the presence of large Communist parties, with strong attachments to the Soviet Union in the early postwar years, complicated matters. In the Federal Republic of Germany, Italy, and France, the Christian Democrats, drawing inspiration from Roman Catholic religious and ethical precepts, played a key role in shaping and governing the new regimes. They accepted the welfare state but backed away from the egalitarianism of the socialists and, over time, became increasingly representative of conservative and business interests.

Great Britain: Labour and Conservative

In Great Britain, the first parliamentary elections in ten years, in July 1945, unseated Winston Churchill and the Conservative-led wartime coalition and voted in a Labour government. For the first time in its history Labour had a majority of its own. Governing from 1945 to 1951, with Clement Attlee as prime minister, it set a new course for Britain.

Once the center of high capitalism, Britain for a time became the world's chief exemplar of parliamentary socialism and the modern welfare state. On the premise that the country's basic industries could not be left to the unplanned anarchy of capitalism and unregulated competition, the Labour government nationalized the Bank of England, the coal mines, electricity and gas, iron and steel, and other parts of the economy. Because four-fifths of industry remained in private hands, it was a mixed economy that emerged. At the same time Labour greatly expanded and revamped the social insurance program inherited from the Liberal reforms of 1906–1914. All parties had committed themselves during the war to an extension of these welfare services. The wartime Beveridge Report of 1942 had sketched a program to guarantee "full employment in a free society" and social security for all "from the cradle to the grave." Labour now extended insurance coverage for unemployment, old age, and other contingencies; inaugurated a comprehensive national health service; and increased income and inheritance taxes.

Labour government

In the elections of 1951 Labour lost its majority in Parliament. The Conservatives returned to office and governed for the next 13 years under a succession of prime ministers. After 1964 the two parties alternated in office. The shifting electoral fortunes stemmed from disagreement within the country over the welfare state, dissatisfaction with the performance of the economy, and frustration at Britain's diminished global status.

During their years in office, the Conservatives restored some nationalized industries to private control and modified the national health insurance program but did little else to dismantle the welfare state. Both parties recognized, however, that the social reforms of the welfare state could be absorbed only if the economy prospered. But there were nagging economic problems. After the Second World War Britain was much weaker than after the First. The liquidation of its investments to pay for the war, the loss of export markets, and its reduced income from shipping and other services adversely affected its balance of payments and undermined the pound. With American financial aid, an intensified export drive, an austerity program that reduced imports, and a curtailment of military and imperial commitments, the economy improved and the country began to experience a modest prosperity. But the British failed at the time to rebuild their obsolescent capital equipment and infrastructure as effectively as their West European neighbors across the Channel.

A modest prosperity

British industry was outstripped even in its own domestic market. Its economy grew more slowly than that of western Europe and Japan. When out of power, Labour argued that the Conservatives lacked economic dynamism and were responsible for the lagging economy. But Labour in office did no better and was forced to devalue the pound and extend austerity measures. When inflation set in during the late 1960s, and intensified in the 1970s, the trade unions demanded wage increases to match rising prices. Strikes and prolonged work stoppages troubled the economy and divided British society. Until the late 1970s, when a new era opened, the question was whether Labour or the Conservatives could better manage British decline, not how they could overcome it.

Meanwhile troubles in Northern Ireland persisted. After the partition in 1922, the six counties of Northern Ireland, predominantly Protestant, had remained part of the United Kingdom. The Catholic minority, about one-third of the population, protested militantly that they were victims of political and economic discrimination and pressed for annexation to the Republic of Ireland.

Troubles in Northern Ireland

Open violence broke out in 1969, inflamed by the Irish Republican Army on the one hand and Protestant extremists on the other. In the sectarian violence that followed, over 3,000 persons lost their lives. At the end of the century a compromise was in sight, but serious troubles persisted.

The French Republic: Fourth and Fifth

After the liberation of France, General Charles de Gaulle, the very incarnation of the Resistance, became provisional president. Because no one wished to return to the Third Republic after its ignominious collapse in 1940, nor to the stalemate society of the interwar years, elections were held for a Constituent Assembly. With the parties of the Right discredited by their role in Vichy, the Left emerged enhanced in strength and prestige. The Communists, the Socialists, and the Popular Republican Movement (*Mouvement Républicain Populaire,* or MRP), a Catholic progressive party akin to Christian Democrats elsewhere on the Continent, formed the provisional government. The Left pressed for a systematic purge of collaborators, despite the difficulties in determining levels of guilt. The purge, which had begun as soon as the army reached French soil, initially took the form of angry drumhead trials and executions. Gradually, the process was brought under more orderly judicial procedures. Even so, the trials of Marshal Pétain and Pierre Laval were impassioned showpieces. The debate over collaboration and trials of collaborators continued to divide the country in later decades. Not all the French had been part of the Resistance, and some of the most egregious acts of violence against the French Jews and others had originated with the French Vichy government and not the Nazi occupiers.

Purging collaborators

The Fourth Republic in its machinery of government differed in only a few details from the Third. Once again the presidency was only ceremonial and the premier and cabinet were responsible to an all-powerful National Assembly. De Gaulle made no secret of his dislike for the constitution being prepared in 1946, the return of party rivalries, and the dominant role of the legislature, all of which interfered with his vision of a strong France ready to resume a leadership role in world affairs. He resigned in protest in December 1946. The Communists, Socialists, and MRP continued their tripartite coalition under Socialist leadership until the Communists, in the heightened tensions of the Cold War, fomented a series of strikes and were expelled from the cabinet in May 1947.

Parliamentary division and ministerial instability grew more acute. The Socialists and the MRP formed unstable coalitions with each other and with the reviving smaller parties. Periodically de Gaulle returned to the political scene, heading a movement called the "Rally of the French People," which he described as "above parties." Except for the brief reform ministry of Pierre Mendès-France in 1954–1955, governmental ineffectiveness in the midst of domestic and foreign crises filled the public with cynicism and hostility.

"Rally of the French People"

Yet despite its record of political instability—25 cabinets from 1946 to 1958—the Fourth Republic enacted significant legislation. The provisional government had nationalized several key industries, and as in Britain a mixed economy had emerged. The existing social security legislation was expanded. An economic plan, drawn up by Jean Monnet, a farsighted economist and public official who later played a large role in the creation of the European Economic Community, enlarged and modernized the country's economic base and paved the way for industrial expansion. A flexible form of economic planning, inspired by Monnet, in which government, management, and labor played mutually reinforcing roles, became an accepted part of French economic life. By 1952 production levels were one and a half times those of 1938, and industrial output was growing at an annual rate of over 5 percent. From 1946 to 1966 production tripled. (In the half-century from 1889 to 1940, it had no more than doubled.) Meanwhile Monnet and the MRP premier, Robert Schuman, took the lead in promoting European economic integration in the 1950s and in tightening ties with the other West European countries. The country also displayed a demographic vitality for a time that confounded pessimists who had long worried about France's low birth rate.

Colonial wars

What finally brought down the Fourth Republic was the strain of trying to preserve the old French colonial empire. France alone, of all the major powers, was almost continuously at war for close to 15 years, fighting colonial wars. It could envy the lot of Germany, Italy, and Japan, the losers in the Second World War, with no restless colonies to subdue. The constitution of 1946 provided representation in Paris for the colonies, but limited reforms did not satisfy nationalists pressing for independence. From 1946 to 1954 the French forces unsuccessfully fought against independence movements in Indochina until they finally had to withdraw. Then, within a matter of months, the Algerian war broke out, which drained the material resources, morale, and self-esteem of the French even more. The European settlers in Algeria and army leaders adamantly opposed French withdrawal and staged an insurrectionary coup in Algiers in May 1958. When civil war threatened, the country turned to the one man it believed could save the situation—Charles de Gaulle, then living quietly in self-imposed retirement. The army leaders, the settlers in Algeria, and the parties of the Right were convinced, given de Gaulle's solicitude for the army and French national pride, that he would keep Algeria French. De Gaulle accepted the summons. In June 1958 the National Assembly invested him as premier, giving him emergency powers for six months, including the authority to prepare a new constitution.

In that way the Fifth Republic was born. In the autumn of 1958 the new constitution was overwhelmingly accepted in a popular referendum, and de Gaulle was shortly thereafter elected president. The presidency, as de Gaulle had long urged, became the fulcrum of power. The president was the final authority in foreign affairs and national defense. The president named the prime minister (as the premier was now called) and had the right to dissolve the National Assembly, call for new elections, submit important questions to popular referendums, and assume emergency powers, all of which de Gaulle did in his years in office. Political instability disappeared; in the first 11 years of the Fifth Republic there were only three cabinets.

France under De Gaulle

DeGaulle settled the Algerian crisis in his own way. Sensitive to the revolution sweeping the colonial world, he step by step evolved a policy of independence for Algeria, which the country approved in a referendum in July 1962. Even earlier he granted independence to all of the French colonies in sub-Saharan Africa. With peace, governmental stability, and economic prosperity, the French reconciled themselves to the loss of empire and took pride in their heightened importance on the world scene under de Gaulle. France became the world's fifth industrial power in the 1960s, behind only the United States, the U.S.S.R., West Germany, and Japan. In 1960 France became the fourth nation, along with the United States, the U.S.S.R., and Britain, to develop a nuclear capacity. De Gaulle even created an independent nuclear strike force. France also became western Europe's largest producer of nuclear energy for peacetime energy needs.

After the settlement of the Algerian crisis, de Gaulle built a kind of plebiscitary democracy by direct appeals to the electorate. Although civil liberties were preserved and

Demonstrations and strikes swept across France in May 1968, evoking memories of nineteenth-century revolutionary battles in the barricaded streets of Paris, but President de Gaulle was more successful than earlier French kings in quelling crowds and protests. As this photograph suggests, however, clashes between the police and student demonstrators produced strong reactions among all groups in French society during the weeks before de Gaulle and his followers consolidated their power by winning new national elections.

(Dalmas-SIPA Press)

free speech and free elections were maintained, the old democratic ferment disappeared. The older political parties were paralyzed or impotent, skilled technicians ran the affairs of state, and de Gaulle, an uncrowned republican monarch, presided as arbiter over the nation's destinies.

The nation grew restless. A reorganized Socialist party took the lead in uniting the Left and reaching out to the middle classes. There was increasing skepticism about de Gaulle's extravagant posturing in world affairs. Suddenly, in May 1968, grievances in the overcrowded universities sparked a revolt that led to demonstrations by hundreds of thousands of students and then brought 10 million workers out on strike, paralyzing the economy and threatening the regime itself. De Gaulle survived the revolt but only after assuring himself of army support. Holding out the threat of communism and chaos, he won an overwhelming majority for his party in new elections. The country seemed to forget the outburst of radical political agitation, which was similar to other revolts of students and young people all over the

May 1968

globe in 1968. Educational changes were introduced, but the economic disruption of the spring hurt the economy. In 1969 de Gaulle chose to make a referendum on a series of constitutional and regional reforms a vote of confidence in himself. When it lost by a small margin, he resigned and retired to his country estate, where he died a year later, an august, heroic, austere, and always controversial figure, whose exploits in war and peace assured him a lasting place in France's history. The stability of the Fifth Republic was one of his major contributions.

The Federal Republic of Germany

The Nuremberg Trials

To communicate to the German people and to the entire world the enormity of the Nazi crimes, the four wartime Allies convened an international trial in 1945–1946 at Nuremberg. Hitler, Himmler, and Goebbels were already dead, but 22 other Nazi leaders and the major Nazi organizations were indicted for crimes against peace, that is, plotting and waging a war of aggression; war crimes, which were defined as violations of the accepted laws and conventions of warfare; and crimes against humanity, that is, acts of mass murder and genocide. The evidence of evil deeds, massive and incontrovertible, was set down for posterity in many volumes of recorded testimony. Despite the high moral purpose of the trials and an honest effort to establish fair judicial procedures for the accused, some critics, at the time and later, questioned their appropriateness, especially the decision to try the leaders of a defeated sovereign nation for planning and waging war and to indict an agency like the General Staff. Some questioned the propriety of the Soviet Union, which had itself contributed to the outbreak of the war, shared in the partition of Poland, and incorporated the Baltic states into its borders, sitting in judgment on the Nazis. Others dismissed the trials as victors' justice. Yet the Nuremberg trials contributed in a singular way to reinforcing international standards of civilized behavior. The court condemned 12 of the defendants to execution. Seven received prison terms of varying length, including life sentences; three were acquitted. The last of the Nuremberg prisoners, Rudolf Hess, serving a life sentence, died in prison in 1987.

Denazification

On a lesser scale a "denazification" program, carried out by the four occupation authorities, each in its own way, and later by German courts, produced mixed results. Because so many technically trained and professional Germans had been members of Nazi organizations, it became difficult to exclude them from public life if the normal processes of government were to resume. Some individuals guilty of the more heinous crimes associated with the Third Reich and who had fled the country were still being apprehended and tried many decades after the war's end by the Germans themselves or in French or Israeli courts. But not until the end of the century did efforts succeed to make financial restitution to the survivors or families of the Nazi victims.

Divided Germany (and Berlin) became a central arena of the Cold War. The German Democratic Republic became one of the most loyal client states of the Soviet Union. The Federal Republic of Germany became a prosperous parliamentary democracy, a full partner of the West. It faced up to and made efforts to atone for the horrors of the Nazi regime.

A "social market economy"

The West German government, although it shaped overall economic policies, encouraged private industry and a capitalist, competitive economy; but it also provided broad social services so that West Germany emerged with what became known as a "social market economy." The guar-

GERMANY AND ITS BORDERS, 1919–1990

Upper panel: the boundaries established after the Treaty of Versailles. Note the Free City of Danzig and the Polish Corridor. *Middle panel:* Germany's borders at the height of the Second World War in 1942. The Reich proper had then annexed (1) Luxembourg, (2) Alsace and Lorraine from France, (3) Carniola from Yugoslavia, (4) Austria, (5) the Sudeten regions and a Bohemian–Moravian protectorate from Czechoslovakia, (6) the Free City of Danzig, and (7) Poland. *Lower panel:* Germany after Hitler's defeat. East Prussia was divided between Poland and the U.S.S.R., and Poland reached westward almost to Berlin. A Communist East Germany (the German Democratic Republic) and a democratic West Germany (the Federal Republic of Germany) grew out of the zones occupied respectively by the Soviets and the West. After the fall of the Communist regime in East Germany, Germany was reunited in 1990.

anteed benefits came to exceed those of other major industrial Western countries. The Federal Republic also pioneered in bringing labor and capital together. The labor unions accepted a role as social partners in the expanding economy, moderating wage demands to avoid inflation. A "codetermination" law gave workers seats on the boards of directors of larger firms.

After independent state governments had been set up in each state (or *Land*) in West Germany with the encouragement of the occupying powers, a constitutional convention representing the ten German states met in 1948–1949 in Bonn. The convention produced a Basic Law (or *Grundgesetz*) and officially established the Federal Republic of Germany. The Basic Law, by design not called a constitution, was to be temporary, valid only until at some future date the two parts of Germany could be reunited. An extensive bill of rights was one of its most prominent features. Power was decentralized under a federal system.

The founders deliberately set out to avoid the weaknesses of the Weimar Republic. The president, elected indirectly and not by popular vote, was a ceremonial figure with limited political power; a president of stature could, however, as the years revealed, exercise substantial moral authority. The head of government, or real executive, was the chancellor, responsible, along with the cabinet, to the majority in the popularly elected lower house, the *Bundestag*. To avoid instability, a chancellor could be overthrown only when a new majority was ready with an immediate replacement. Proportional representation guaranteed that each party would be apportioned seats equivalent to its share of the popular vote, but to prevent splinter parties and political fragmentation, a party received seats in the legislature only if it won at least 5 percent of the national vote. The Christian Democratic Union and the Social Democrats emerged as the two chief parties and shared between them a large proportion of the popular vote. The Free Democrats, a small liberal centrist party, played a lesser role but formed coalitions, when necessary, with one or the other of the two major parties.

The power of the chancellor

The Christian Democratic Union governed uninterruptedly for 20 years, from 1949 to 1969. In reaction to the Nazi barbarism, it sought to infuse politics with a moral idealism and ethical purpose. Not a confessional party, it appealed to Protestants and Catholics alike, who were almost equally represented in West Germany, and received strong support from the business community and large segments of the middle classes. The dominating figure in the party and government in the early years was the Christian Democratic leader, Konrad Adenauer, who had begun his career in the pre-1914 imperial era. A patriarchal, strong-willed personality, his ambition was to regain for Germany a position of dignity and international respect. He became chancellor in 1949 at the age of 73 (with only a slim majority) and governed for 14 years. Opponents criticized *der Alte* ("the old man") for creating a "chancellor's democracy," but he provided the resolute leadership, stability, and continuity that made possible the remarkable economic expansion of the 1950s and the regaining of full West German sovereignty. His economics minister, Ludwig Erhard, succeeded him as chancellor in 1963.

Christian Democrats and Konrad Adenauer

Adenauer successfully integrated the Federal Republic of Germany into the emerging political, economic, and military structures of western Europe, strengthening ties with France, cooperating in the movement for European economic integration, and winning the support and confidence of the United States and the other Western powers. The major opposition party, the Social Democrats, heirs to the Social Democratic party founded in the 1870s, criticized him for his overly close identification with the United States and the West and for ignoring the issue of national reunification. But the Social Democrats abandoned their Marxist ideology at a party congress in 1959 and broadened their appeal to the middle classes and younger voters.

In 1965 the Social Democrats, who had softened their neutralist stand in foreign affairs, joined the Christian Democrats and the Free Democrats in a "grand coalition," with Willy Brandt as foreign minister. Brandt, for many years the Social Democratic mayor of West Berlin, launched his "Eastern policy," or *Ostpolitik,* a policy that encouraged building bridges to

Willy Brandt's "grand coalition"

The new spirit of international cooperation in postwar Europe was expressed in the collaboration of French President Charles de Gaulle and German Chancellor Konrad Adenauer (standing next to de Gaulle here and waving to a crowd). The two leaders met often to create a partnership that became the foundation for a new Europe. After fighting three major wars in the heart of Europe over a period of 75 years, Germany and France established a peaceful alliance that brought stability to the continent and eliminated the traditional problem of warfare between two former enemies.

(Dalmas/Sipa Press)

the Soviet Union and eastern Europe, including East Germany. In 1969, with the support of the Free Democrats, he became chancellor of a new coalition that ended the 20-year tenure of the Christian Democrats. Brandt negotiated treaties with the Soviet Union and Poland in 1971, formally accepting the German eastern frontier at the Oder and West Neisse River line. His government officially recognized the German Democratic Republic and promoted close economic ties with it and other countries of eastern Europe. When a spy scandal cut short his chancellorship in 1974, his Social Democratic colleague Helmut Schmidt took over and continued his policies. Not until 1982 would the Christian Democrats return to office with Helmut Kohl as chancellor.

Within a decade after the disastrous military defeat that had left a shattered and occupied country, West Germany was a major economic and political power, a coveted ally of the West in the Cold War, an equal member of the North Atlantic Treaty Organization. Those who had lived through the Nazi years tried to forget them. Inflammatory issues faded, material progress seemed triumphant over ideology, and democracy seemed assured. Reunification with East Germany remained unlikely, only a remote possibility.

The Italian Republic

During the struggle to oust the German armies from the Italian peninsula after the fall of Mussolini in 1943, the Italian political parties, repressed for over two decades under Fascism, sprang to life. All supported the provisional governments in postwar reconstruction and committed themselves to democratic renewal. In 1946 the country voted by a narrow margin to abolish the Savoy monarchy, never very distinguished, and now tarnished by its cooperation with the Fascist regime. A constitution for the new Italian Republic established a ceremonial presidency, cabinet government, and legislative supremacy. Proportional representation guaranteed equitable representation for all political parties, large and small.

The Christian Democrats quickly became the dominant party. More than a successor to the Popular party, the old clerical Roman Catholic party, it appealed to all classes and sectors of Italian society, successfully blending support for democratic political principles, a moderately regulated free-enterprise economy, and the labor tenets of social Catholicism.

Alcide De Gasperi's Christian Democrats

Although the party maintained its independence of the church, it remained close to the hierarchy. In Alcide De Gasperi, who had survived the Fascist years as a librarian in the Vatican, it found an effective leader. For seven formative years from 1946 to 1953 he presided over a series of coalition governments, which made possible postwar economic reconstruction and expansion. In the Cold War he kept Italy firmly in the Western camp. The Communist party successfully publicized its role in the Resistance, capitalized on the fact that much of the country's social elite had cooperated with Fascism, and exploited existing grievances to become and long remain the second leading party. As in France, the Communists at first held seats in the cabinet and cooperated in economic reconstruction, but when they fomented politically inspired strikes in 1947, De Gasperi dismissed them from his ministry. In 1948, in the early years of the Cold War, the United States intervened openly for the first time in its history to influence a European election, throwing its weight behind the Christian Democrats to thwart the Communists. The Christian Democrats for the first and only time won an absolute majority in the legislature. The Communists, despite their continuing parliamentary strength and support by a third to a fourth of the electorate, remained excluded from the cabinet.

After De Gasperi's disappearance from the political scene in 1953, the Christian Democrats governed under a succession of short-lived coalition cabinets formed with small centrist parties. Although the party could not form stable parliamentary coalitions or durable ministries, it clung to power. Over the years the Christian Democrats became faction-ridden and less interested in reform than in patronage. Abandoning their initial idealism, they catered to propertied and narrow interests, and many in the party profited from business connections. In the early 1960s the Socialists became part of the governing coalition, but this "opening to the Left" did not alter political rigidities. Although prospering economically, the country grew impatient with the uninterrupted tenure of the Christian Democrats.

The Communists gained further strength in the 1960s. They weakened their ties with Moscow, renounced such tenets of Marxist-Leninist orthodoxy as the dictatorship of the proletariat, and tempered their assault on religion. Architects, with the French party, of what came to be known as "Eurocommunism," they declared that each nation, without deferring to Moscow, must find its own way to a new society through parliamentary democracy and national consensus.

Eurocommunism

The Italian Communists condemned the Soviet military intervention in Hungary in 1956 and in Czechoslovakia in 1968 (soon to be described) and even endorsed Italian membership in NATO. The strongest Communist party in the Western world, the Italian party counted 1.8 million members at its peak in the mid-1970s and won the support of 35 percent of the electorate. Communist mayors and municipal councils governed in many major cities, including Rome. But the Christian Democrats continued to reject the Communist bid for seats in the national government.

A prosperous economy

The unstable political scene did not interfere with unprecedented economic growth and prosperity. The industrial triangle of Genoa, Milan, and

Turin in northern Italy provided the nucleus for recovery and expansion. A prosperous economy emerged. By 1949 industrial production reached 1939 levels. From 1953 on Italy's rate of industrial growth rivaled that of West Germany and France. Italy was transformed from the primarily agricultural country it had been before the Second World War into one of the world's leading industrial nations. Only the underdeveloped south remained a troubled area, even in times of advancing prosperity.

Despite one-party domination, cabinet instability, hints of corruption in high places, and periodic social turbulence (Aldo Moro, a former prime minister, was kidnapped and murdered in 1978), the Italian republic in these postwar decades seemed to show flexibility and resilience, an ability to absorb a large Communist party into its parliamentary democracy, and a commitment to civil rights and individual freedoms. Fascism seemed forgotten, like a bad dream of the interwar years, a hiatus in history. An economic revolution had elevated living standards for most, if not all, Italians.

112. RESHAPING THE GLOBAL ECONOMY

Even before the close of hostilities the United States, with British support, developed a bold initiative to reshape the postwar world economy. Determined to avoid the economic nationalism, trade restrictions, and currency instability of the interwar years, the planners sought to restore the free flow of trade and the stable currencies of the pre-1914 era. In 1944 the United States convened an international conference of 44 nations at Bretton Woods, New Hampshire. The participants pledged to reduce trade barriers and work for stable currencies in the postwar world.

An effort to establish a formal world trade organization to oversee international commerce foundered, as did attempts to curtail or abolish all preferential systems, trade restrictions, and protectionism. Britain, for one, refused to end its "imperial preferences." But an alternative strategy proved successful. The United *GATT* States had earlier negotiated bilateral trade agreements with a number of countries to reduce tariffs on a reciprocal basis, with each agreement carrying a "most-favored nation" clause whereby concessions to one country were extended to all. These piecemeal arrangements led in 1948 to a broader arrangement, the General Agreement on Tariffs and Trade (GATT), embodying the same negotiating principle. Subscribed to initially by 23 nations, GATT became the foundation of postwar global commerce.

The General Agreement laid down rules to prevent discrimination in international trade, set up procedures for handling complaints, and provided a framework for continuing negotiation through lengthy bargaining sessions, or "rounds," designed to lower tariffs and remove nontariff barriers. By the 1990s over 100 countries were participating. GATT was only a partial substitute for a formal international trade organization, but it contributed remarkably to the vast expansion of world trade beginning in the 1950s. Not until 1997 was a formal World Trade Organization (WTO) established, with enlarged powers to mediate agreements and settle trade disputes. The WTO in its turn faced new problems and recurring controversies as it tried to resolve the conflicting claims of different nations in the global economy.

The "world economy" in the early postwar years meant the world's non-Communist or free-market economies. The strategic centers were North America and western Europe, with the addition of Japan, which doubled its share of world trade between 1951 and 1960. Integrated into the world economy were Latin America, Asia, the Middle East, Australasia,

Japan's dynamic new influence in the postwar global economy grew out of the nation's willingness and ability to develop technological innovations in the 1950s and 1960s. This super-express train, which went into service between Tokyo and Osaka in 1964 and is shown here passing Mount Fuji, became one of the well-known symbols of modern Japanese society. Reaching speeds of over 150 miles per hour, these trains set a standard for the later development of other very high-speed trains in Europe.

(George Gester/Photo Researchers)

and Africa, so that it was truly an economy of global dimensions. The Soviet Union played no part in any of the postwar trade negotiations and restricted its commerce principally to its East European bloc of satellites. In the late 1960s the Soviets and the East European countries opened up trade and economic relations with the West, but not until the late 1980s did they seek integration into the global economy.

Currency Stability: Toward the "Gold-Dollar" Standard

If the first objective of the wartime Bretton Woods conference was to liberalize trade, the second was to stabilize the world's currencies. The chaos of the interwar years when nation after nation abandoned the gold standard and competed in currency devaluations to gain trade advantages haunted everyone. The Bretton Woods conference sought to restore the equivalent of the pre-1914 gold standard, which had provided for fixed exchange rates and the convertibility of all currencies into gold or into the equivalent at the time, British pounds sterling.

Currency stabilization, however, turned out to be more difficult than anticipated. Not until the end of 1958, by which time western Europe and Japan had expanded their trade and doubled their dollar reserves, was convertibility into gold or dollars at fixed exchange rates possible. For about a dozen years, until 1971, each major currency had a par value in gold and in dollars. For that same short time the American dollar, like the British pound before 1914, was accepted as the equivalent of gold itself. But the postwar economic scene changed rapidly; the era of the "gold-dollar standard" proved short-lived, and a system of "floating currencies" and fluctuating exchange rates took its place.

Currency stabilization

Meanwhile two important agencies established after the war helped in international financial settlements. The International Monetary Fund (IMF) provided loans to governments to manage temporary balance of payments difficulties and to help reduce the need for currency devaluations. The International Bank for Reconstruction and Development (or World Bank) made long-term loans to governments for economic development. Both agencies played a larger role in later years than in the immediate postwar era, and both became controversial when critics complained that their policies did not really benefit the world's poorer nations or people. Both were located in Washington, their major funding provided by the United States. The economic center of gravity for the West, like the political and the military, lay after 1945 on the American side of the Atlantic.

The IMF and the World Bank

European Integration: From the Common Market to the European Community

As western Europe expanded economically, it also drew closer together. There had been numerous proposals in the interwar years for a European federation. The war, the wartime Resistance movements, the Marshall Plan, European cooperative recovery efforts, and the threat from the Soviet Union in the Cold War all reinforced the idea that western Europe's future lay in unity. A number of European leaders pressed for the creation of a "United States of Europe." In 1949 delegates representing the parliaments of ten countries met in Strasbourg to establish a Council of Europe with the hope that it might become a legislative body for a federated Europe. The British, interested in cooperation but not integration, opposed any form of supranational authority. Although the Council of Europe grew in membership over the years and continued to support the idea of federation, it never became an important political force. It confined itself to humanitarian, cultural, and social issues. In 1958 it set up a European Court of Human Rights to protect the rights of individuals in its member nations against arbitrary government actions. It banned corporal punishment in the schools and the death penalty for convicted criminals.

Expansion and unity

European integration itself took a different path, beginning in the economic area. In 1948 Belgium, the Netherlands, and Luxembourg created a customs union, called Benelux, which provided the benefits of a sizable free trade area for the three small countries. At the same time the visionary but pragmatic French administrator Jean Monnet, who had helped reorganize the postwar French economy, recognized at an early date that the first steps to unity had to develop along modest economic lines and begin with specific objectives. Political leaders like Schuman in France, Adenauer in West Germany, De Gasperi in Italy, and Paul-Henri Spaak in Belgium responded warmly to the initial proposals for integration.

In 1952, under a plan designed by Monnet, six West European countries—France, the Federal Republic of Germany, Italy, and the three Benelux nations—placed their coal and steel industries under a form of supranational authority. They established the European Coal and Steel Community, its headquarters in Luxembourg. Initially the plan was designed to allay anxiety about the revival of German heavy industry and to guarantee access for all to the coal and steel resources of the Ruhr, but it went further. The six nations not only agreed to eliminate import duties and quotas on coal and steel but also placed production under a common High Authority with decision-making powers. A council of ministers represented the six governments, but the High Authority carried out major administrative functions.

The European Coal and Steel Community

Monnet was the first president of the European Coal and Steel Community, which paved the way for economic integration that would extend far beyond a single sector of the West European economy. In a momentous second step, the same six nations on March 25, 1957, signed the Treaty of Rome, creating a large free-trade area or customs union, the European Economic Community, or Common Market, its headquarters in Brussels, with the goal of moving toward full economic and even political integration. The six nations pledged to eliminate tariff barriers, develop a common tariff with respect to the outside world, harmonize social and economic policies, and work toward the free movement of capital and labor. Under a separate treaty the member countries also agreed to coordinate their nonmilitary atomic research and technology in a European Atomic Community.

The Common Market

The six-nation Common Market, encompassing 175 million people in 1958, quickly became one of the thriving economic aggregates of the expanding world economy. By 1968, even earlier than anticipated, the last internal tariff was dropped and trade among the six nations grew at a rate double that of trade with outside countries. Its influence spread to the former European colonies, with which it worked out preferential trade arrangements. Through the Common Market, western Europe set about to recapture a key role in the new configuration of global affairs; without it, Europe faced being dwarfed by the two superpowers. It helped further absorb a revived democratic West Germany into western Europe and to nurture reconciliation between France and Germany, ending the internecine rivalries between the two that had devastated the European continent in the first half of the twentieth century.

In 1967 the three "Communities" consolidated themselves into what was now designated the European Community. Their high commissions became the European Commission and their assemblies became the European Parliament, meeting in Strasbourg. The members of the European Parliament took seats by party affiliation and not by nation. In 1979, for the first time, they were not chosen by their respective governments but were elected by a Europeanwide electorate. The Parliament enjoyed only limited legislative authority, but it supervised the budget and the European Commission and kept alive the idea of unity. Final decision making still rested with the council of ministers representing each of the member nations, whose decisions on important matters had to be unanimous.

The European Community

Great Britain initially refrained from joining the Common Market. Its economic ties to the Commonwealth, its dependence on low-priced food imports, and its unwillingness to accept any supranational authority kept both Labour and Conservative governments from joining. As an alternative, Britain helped create in 1960 a more limited customs union of seven states to reduce tariff barriers but with no larger ambitions for economic or political integration. While it achieved some limited success, it was no match for the Common Market. When Britain, whose economy was lagging behind that of the major West European nations, eventually sought membership in 1963, its request was vetoed by President de Gaulle, who regarded Britain and its admittedly "special relationship" with the United States as a threat to French leadership on the Continent. Not until after de Gaulle retired from the political scene in 1969 did Britain gain admission.

If the years 1958–1968 showed remarkable gains in economic integration, the advance toward political unity was slower. Although de Gaulle understood the contribution of the Common Market to the prosperity of western Europe, as well as the importance of a strong western Europe as a counterpoise to the two "hegemonic superpowers," he opposed political or supranational authority for the Community. Europe had to be a Europe of sovereign states, a *Europe des patries*. The more dedicated Europeanists were disappointed. Yet the supranational economic and political machinery of the Community, the day-to-day cooperation of the European civil servants or bureaucrats (inevitably called "Eurocrats") in Brussels and Strasbourg, and the close consultation on common interests were favorable signs for unity, even apart from the military and defense ties that brought the western Europeans together in NATO. French-German friendship, cemented by de Gaulle and Adenauer and reinforced by their successors, remained the linchpin of cooperation within the Community.

Advance toward political unity

The likelihood of political union, a "United States of Europe," remained remote. The Europeans showed no haste to surrender their national sovereignty and independence, but the European Community created a strong sense of common destiny, a shared faith in democratic institutions and market economies, and a concern for human rights and social needs. It not only contributed immeasurably to the economic and political strength of western Europe but also helped restore it to a larger role in world affairs; and by the beginning of the twenty-first century the European Community was projecting its own transnational military force.

Western Europe accounted in the 1960s for one-fourth of all imports and one-fifth of all exports in the world economy; for a time its exports equaled those of the United States and Japan combined. One-third of the largest multinational corporations, that is, corporations which set up subsidiaries outside their own country for manufacturing or sales, were European. London, Frankfurt, and Paris were again important financial centers. In 1971 West European steel production surpassed that of the United States. European (and Japanese) automobiles cut sharply into American domestic and foreign markets. Self-sufficient in food, western Europe became the world's largest exporter of dairy products, even though 10 million people left the farms for the cities in the 1950s and 1960s. The Federal Republic of Germany enjoyed a gross national product exceeded only by the economies of the United States and the U.S.S.R., even though it had only one-fourth the population of each; it accounted for one-third of the Common Market's gross national product. Western Europe and Japan were whittling away at the American economic lead in production and trade and bringing to a close the era of the dollar's supremacy.

West European competition

End of the Gold-Dollar Standard, 1971

The new trading patterns created monetary problems. Because America's exports no longer exceeded its imports, the American trade balance and its balance of payments shifted unfavorably. The United States spent more

Trade imbalances

The global economy of the 1970s and the "floating" of national currencies gave an ever-growing importance to the world's leading stock exchanges and financial markets. Governments in all parts of the world found their money, debts, and economic stability significantly affected by the speculations or judgments of influential investors and financial traders. This picture of the New York Stock Exchange in 1979 suggests the scale of the modern financial systems and the bustling activity of a typical trading day.

(Bettmann/Corbis)

abroad than it earned abroad. The postwar dollar shortage in other countries gave way to a "dollar glut." Western Europe accumulated large dollar reserves (or "Eurodollars"), some $50 billion by 1971; oil-rich Arab states held "petrodollars." The number of dollars held abroad exceeded American gold reserves.

The shift in the American economic position undermined confidence in a dollar which many now viewed as overvalued. De Gaulle, resentful of American political and economic power, demanded an end to the gold-dollar standard and a return to gold itself. In 1965 France redeemed hundreds of millions of its dollar holdings for gold. Even though other central banks in Europe and Japan did not follow suit, private investors speculated against the dollar. American gold and foreign currency reserves dropped precipitously.

In 1971 President Nixon unilaterally suspended gold convertibility and thus devalued the dollar, with a second devaluation in 1973. The monetary system projected at Bretton Woods ended. Despite many proposals, there was no formal reform. Instead, on a day-to-day basis, and with considerable success, the world's major currencies were allowed to "float," that is, to fluctuate daily against each other and against the dollar. Gold itself fluctuated freely and official gold prices were abolished. Although the American dollar remained the world's principal reserve currency, the West German mark and the Japanese yen took their place beside the dollar as key currencies.

Floating
currencies

The breakdown of the postwar monetary arrangements did not seriously affect the world economy. Currencies did not collapse because they were no longer exchangeable for gold. For currency stability the world learned to rely mainly on international consultation and rapid exchange of information, but governments found their currencies and economic policies vulnerable to a global financial system that crossed all national boundaries.

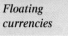 113. THE COMMUNIST WORLD: THE U.S.S.R. AND EASTERN EUROPE

Stalinism in the Postwar Years

In March 1953 Russia's twentieth-century Peter the Great died. Stalin had a massive impact during his close to 30 years in power. He was responsible for industrialization in the 1930s, the rallying of the country in the Great Patriotic War, the expansion of the nation's borders, the consolidation of Communist regimes in eastern Europe, and the emergence of the Soviet Union as a nuclear power. But the human costs of the Stalinist transformation of the country were staggering. Millions had fallen victim in the 1930s to his forced collectivization of the countryside and the ensuing famine, and additional millions had fallen as a result of his purges. Western and Soviet scholars alike have estimated the total figure of Stalin's victims at least as high as 20 million, quite apart from the millions of lives lost in the Second World War. Because the civil war and war communism earlier, under Lenin, had also consumed millions of lives, the Communist regime from its emergence in 1917 to its demise in 1991 must be counted among the costliest experiments in social engineering in all history.

The Stalinist terror had continued during the war. Entire ethnic groups like the Crimean Tatars and the Volga Germans, suspected of collaboration with the Nazis, were forcibly moved east to Siberia. Mass deportations took place from Estonia, Latvia, and Lithuania, the three Baltic republics that had been formally annexed in 1940. At the war's end, returning Soviet soldiers who had been prisoners of war and civilian deportees forced to work for the Nazis in Europe were sent off to labor camps because their exposure to the West made them suspect. The network of forced labor camps grew in size. Ideological restrictions tightened. Stalin's personal suspicions, growing sharper with the passage of the years, filled even his closest associates with dismay. The unbridled authority of the NKVD (later the KGB), the secret political police who did Stalin's bidding, continued in power, gaining ascendancy over the party itself. In later years, in a freer atmosphere, the country debated whether Stalin's dictatorship represented a logical outgrowth of the Bolshevik Revolution itself and of many of Lenin's policies or was his own personal distortion.

Stalinist
terror

Controls over intellectual life in the postwar years took on a vehemently nationalistic and xenophobic tone; deviations from Stalin's "line" in economics, music, genetics, history, and linguistics were forbidden. An officially inspired anti-Semitism, thinly disguised as anti-Zionism, emerged; Jewish intellectuals were accused of being "rootless cosmopolitans." Party purges and massive arrests continued into the last years of Stalin's life. The political police meanwhile fabricated conspiracies to justify the terror. In the fictitious "doctors' plot," officially announced in early 1953, a score of Jewish doctors were arrested for plotting to poison Stalin and other Kremlin leaders; one month after Stalin died, his successors withdrew the charges and freed the imprisoned physicians.

Khrushchev: The Abortive Effort at Reform

After Stalin's death the party leaders resolved to exercise collective control, determined that no single leader should again dominate party and government. To thwart a coup by Lavrenti Beria, who had headed the secret police since 1939, the new leaders arrested and executed him. In the struggle for power, authority gradually shifted to Nikita S. Khrushchev. Outwardly jovial and ebullient, Khrushchev was a tough and hardened party stalwart who had enforced Stalin's purges in Ukraine and had long been a member of the Central Committee and Politburo, but he was shrewd enough to recognize the need for change.

Khrushchev's "thaw"

In part to win allies against those in the party who were opposed to change, Khrushchev encouraged a greater measure of cultural and intellectual freedom—a "thaw." He put restraints on the still formidable powers of the political police. He surprised many with an attack on Stalin's record. In a speech to the twentieth party congress in 1956, he officially revealed or corroborated the "crimes of the Stalin era," making partial but nonetheless startling disclosures of the Stalinist terror, confirming the worst speculations of Western critics over the years. Stalin had been personally responsible for the purges and executions of the 1930s and millions of victims had been innocent of the charges against them; his most intimate colleagues had lived in fear for their lives. Khrushchev also revealed Stalin's initial loss of nerve and ineptitude at the time of the German invasion in June 1941.

Although Khrushchev criticized Stalin, the thaw in Soviet society was never systematic or thorough. In 1958 Boris Pasternak was forbidden to accept the Nobel Prize in literature because his novel, *Dr. Zhivago,* by stressing individual freedom, implicitly condemned the oppressiveness of Soviet society. But in 1962 Alexander Solzhenitsyn was permitted to publish his *One Day in the Life of Ivan Denisovich,* a depiction of human suffering in the world of the forced labor camps. Khrushchev continued the de-Stalinization campaign. Cities named in Stalin's honor were renamed: Stalingrad, the most famous, became Volgograd. Stalin's body was removed from the mausoleum on Red Square, where it had lain next to Lenin's, and buried outside the Kremlin Wall.

Decentralization

For the economy Khrushchev pressed decentralization, attempting to loosen tight central economic controls by creating regional economic councils and offering factory managers greater autonomy and incentives for efficiency and profitability. Meanwhile the country successfully tested the hydrogen bomb, launched its first space satellite, Sputnik, in 1958, and built its first intercontinental ballistic missiles. The Soviet economy was second only to that of the United States in gross national product. Within a decade, Khrushchev boasted in the early 1960s, the Soviet economy would surpass the American. The stress on heavy industry and on military expenditures meant, of course, continuing privation for the ordinary citizen, and the emphasis on quantity to the neglect of quality concealed deep flaws in the system as a whole.

The Cold War did not end after the death of Joseph Stalin, but the new Soviet leader Nikita Khrushchev spoke of "peaceful coexistence" with Western nations and traveled to the United States. Wearing his Soviet medals, Khrushchev appears in a congenial mood during a White House meeting in 1959 with the American President Dwight Eisenhower and Vice President Richard Nixon.

(RIA-Novosti/Sovfoto)

Khrushchev's most ambitious effort lay in agriculture, the weakest sector of the economy ever since Stalin's forced collectivization. He sought to bring under cultivation the "virgin lands" of Soviet Central Asia, in Kazakhstan and elsewhere, but crop failures thwarted the experiment. His reforms did little to alter the bureaucratized system of collective and state farms inherited from Stalin or inspire the collective farmers to increase their output. For the party itself he unsuccessfully sought fixed terms of office for important party posts. Few of his reforms were acceptable to the government and party bureaucrats, the *apparatchiki*, who saw their privileged positions threatened and who mustered opposition to his "hare-brained" schemes.

Khrushchev pursued a truculent foreign policy. Proclaiming that war was not inevitable with the United States and other capitalist countries, he spoke of "peaceful coexistence," and relations for a time improved. But in 1960 he scuttled a summit meeting with Allied leaders and in 1962 overreached himself in the confrontation with the United States during the Cuban missile crisis. He also clashed openly with Communist China. His boastfulness and recklessness, his retreat in Cuba, the failure of his agricultural and other economic policies, and his attempt to reform the party itself led to his downfall. In 1964 the party leadership ousted him from office. He lived quietly in Moscow until his death in 1971. In the post-Stalin era,

Khrushchev's fall

a reformer did not necessarily have to fear for his life, but there were clear limits to the reforms the party and bureaucracy would tolerate. Leonid I. Brezhnev, who had helped engineer Khrushchev's downfall, soon emerged as the new Soviet leader.

Eastern Europe: The Decades of Dictatorship

Although nothing like the Russian Revolution of 1917 erupted in Europe after the Second World War, communism made dramatic advances in central and eastern Europe through the Red Army's military presence and the support given to local Communist leaders. Eleven European states and 100 million Europeans fell under Communist-style governments. The areas considered in 1919 to be a protective buffer against Bolshevism were now under Communist domination.

Soviet satellites

The three Baltic states, Estonia, Latvia, and Lithuania, came under Soviet control under the terms of the Nazi-Soviet pact, and in 1940 they were incorporated into the U.S.S.R. as Soviet socialist republics. Later, in the sweep of military operations during the last months of the war, Poland, Hungary, Romania, Bulgaria, and Czechoslovakia fell into the orbit of Soviet influence. East Germany, initially part of the joint Allied occupation of Germany, was shaped into a sixth Soviet satellite as the German Democratic Republic. Yugoslavia and Albania, liberated by their own partisan leaders rather than by the Red Army, were governed by Communist regimes but with looser ties to the Soviet Union and soon broke with the Soviets. Despite its defeat in the Soviet-Finnish War in 1940, Finland escaped Communist domination. Accepting its wartime territorial losses, it maintained its independence by a cautious neutrality in foreign policy and a discreetly correct relationship with the Soviets. Austria, after a decade of joint occupation by the four Allied powers, gained independence as a neutral state in 1955.

Consolidation of Communist Control

The Soviets consolidated control in eastern Europe in stages. Soviet military occupation made it possible for local Communist leaders, many returning from exile in Moscow, to dominate Left coalition governments. In the case of Poland, Western pressure at Yalta and Potsdam forced the Soviets to give representation to the government-in-exile in London; the leader of the agrarian party returned to Poland to serve for a time as deputy premier. In the early coalition governments everywhere, the Communists shared power but held the key ministries of interior, propaganda, and justice, and controlled the police, the army, and the courts. Individuals alleged to have been "fascist" or to have collaborated with the Nazis were barred from public life and from voting; the loose definition of "fascist" and "reactionary" barred many who were only anti-Communist. In the first elections, in Poland and elsewhere, purges and disfranchisement made a mockery of Stalin's pledge at Yalta to hold "free and unfettered elections" in eastern Europe. Protests by the United States and Great Britain only hardened the Soviet position.

Agrarian reform and nationalization

The new regimes confiscated and redistributed large estates and put uncultivated land to use, so that three million peasant families acquired about six million acres of land; the agrarian reforms were the final blow to the landed aristocracy that had once ruled in eastern Europe. They also nationalized the economy. As they struggled with postwar reconstruction, the new regimes had lent a sympathetic ear to the American invitation in 1947 to accept Marshall Plan aid. But Stalin was not disposed to permit the East European countries to drift into the Western economic orbit. After the summer of 1947, wherever non-Communists were still strong, the Communists ousted their political rivals and banned or reduced to impotence all other political parties. In Czechoslovakia the coalition government lasted longer than elsewhere but fell victim to a Communist coup in February 1948.

With the Communists in control, the leaders of the opposition political parties were forced into flight, imprisoned, or in other ways silenced. The new regimes, notably in Poland and Hungary, clashed also with the Roman Catholic church; high-ranking prelates were brought to public trial and imprisoned, and church property was confiscated. The Communist leaders themselves soon became Stalin's victims. From 1949 to 1953, reflecting the repression in the Soviet Union in Stalin's last years, purges, arrests, trials, confessions, and executions occurred in the highest ranks of each party. Leaders were accused of nationalist deviations and of conspiring with Tito, the independent-minded Communist leader of Yugoslavia.

The new "people's democracies" took steps to collectivize agriculture. In Bulgaria, the most docile of the satellites, over half the arable land was collectivized; but in Hungary, only about a third. In Poland, where resistance was strongest, collectivization was halted after a short time. Agriculture in the people's republics, as in the Soviet Union, remained the weakest part of the economy. Peasants diligently cultivated their individual plots of land but worked reluctantly on the large collectives.

Collectivization

Industry made headway. Poland and Hungary, agricultural before the war, became industrial states; Czechoslovakia and the German Democratic Republic expanded their manufacturing base. But the emphasis on heavy industry to the neglect of consumer goods and pressures to complement the economy of the Soviet Union severely limited the improvement of East European living standards.

The Soviets formalized their economic relationship with East Europe through the Council for Mutual Economic Assistance established in 1949, but it never worked as cooperation among equals. The Soviets provided low-cost raw materials and oil and provided a large market for East European goods, regardless of their quality, but much of the economic cooperation principally benefited the Soviet Union. Militarily, the Warsaw Pact, signed in 1955, brought the six East European countries together into a mutual defense alliance, and Soviet troops remained stationed in eastern Europe in large numbers.

Economic and political cooperation

Yugoslavia, freed from the Nazis largely by its own partisan armies, made a remarkable show of resistance to the Soviets. The Yugoslav Communist leader, Marshal Tito, kept a tight grip on the multinational state but loosened centralized controls over the economy and abandoned collectivization of agriculture. He pursued an independent foreign policy, openly defied Moscow, and took his stand with the neutralist nonaligned nations of Asia and Africa. The first major Communist figure to declare his independence from Moscow, Tito established a model of national autonomy for other Communist leaders and parties to follow.

Ferment and Repression in East Germany, Poland, and Hungary, 1953–1956

The changes in the Soviet Union after Stalin's death directly affected the Soviet satellites. The East Europeans chafed at collectivization, forced industrialization, austere living standards, subservience to the Soviets, and harsh rule by Stalinist-type leaders who remained in power for years after Stalin disappeared. An initial outburst, riots in East Berlin in June 1953, was quickly suppressed. New ferment rose to the surface, however, after Khrushchev denounced the brutal character of the Stalin dictatorship and, in an attempt to win back Yugoslavia, made the official concession that "different roads to socialism" were possible. This concession and his de-Stalinization speech in 1956 opened a Pandora's box; undermining Stalin's infallibility undermined Soviet infallibility as well.

Revolt in Poland and Hungary

In 1956 open revolt broke out in Poland and Hungary, led by the East European Communist party leaders themselves. In Poland, where national sentiment and church attachments ran deep, pressures for internal freedom and for independence from Moscow led to riots and demonstrations. The Communist leader Wladyslaw Gomulka relaxed political and economic controls, halted collectivization, improved relations with the church, and took steps to loosen the bonds to Moscow. The country welcomed an alternative to direct Soviet control. Khrushchev threatened military action but backed down. For a few years, Gomulka curbed police terror and created a freer atmosphere, but the reform era was short-lived.

In Hungary, in 1956, events took a tragic turn. When news of Gomulka's success in Poland reached Budapest, demonstrations broke out; young rioters even toppled a statue

The demand for reforms spread rapidly in Hungary during the fall of 1956. Emboldened by changes in Communist Poland and by the policies of Hungarian reformer Imre Nagy, the people of Budapest protested the repressive policies of the Soviet Union, destroyed statues of Communist leaders, and (like the group in this picture) defiantly burned portraits of Joseph Stalin. The Soviets soon intervened with decisive military force. Nagy was executed, and the new Soviet-supported Hungarian regime crushed all forms of anti-Communist dissent.

(Hulton-Deutsch Collection/Corbis)

of Stalin. The reform-minded Communist leader Imre Nagy, who had earlier been driven from the premiership, returned to power. His reform program and release of political prisoners ignited pressures not only for democratization and parliamentary government but also for the severance of ties to Moscow. Alarmed, the Soviets forced the party leadership to remove Nagy from power and to replace him with the more subservient János Kádar, who accepted Soviet intervention. Khrushchev dispatched troops, tanks, and artillery to suppress the "counterrevolution" and forcefully reestablished Communist rule. Severe reprisals followed. Nagy himself was imprisoned, then tried and hanged, and his body was thrown into a mass grave. In the wake of the repression, 200,000 Hungarians fled into exile, mainly to the United States, a larger number than at any time since the crushing of the European revolutions of 1848–1849. The Soviet tanks in Budapest weakened any remaining illusions about the benevolence and liberalism of Stalin's successors and shook the Communist faithful in western Europe and elsewhere.

114. THE COMMUNIST WORLD: MAO ZEDONG AND THE PEOPLE'S REPUBLIC OF CHINA

The Civil War

The proclamation on October 1, 1949, of the People's Republic of China by Mao Zedong and the Chinese Communist party, the final episode in the long civil war between the Guomindang, or Nationalists, and the Communists, was among the most momentous of events shaping the world after 1945.

Nationalists and Communists

The civil war had gone on intermittently since 1927. In 1937 Nationalists and Communists entered into an uneasy alliance to fight the Japanese. Mao agreed to place the People's Liberation Army under the command of Chiang Kai-shek and the Nationalists, but Mao actually waged a separate guerrilla war against the Japanese from the northern bases he controlled and over which he imposed his own Communist regime, winning peasant support through land reforms. The Nationalists, cut off by the Japanese from the urban centers of eastern China, suffered from chaotic economic conditions and severe inflation and became increasingly corrupt, authoritarian, and repressive.

The victory over Japan in 1945 set the stage for renewed civil war. Nationalist troops, with American aid, returned to eastern China. The Communists, moving out from their guerrilla bases, poured into the northern provinces and made contact with the Russians in Manchuria. When Mao refused to surrender the northern provinces, disband his army, and accept Nationalist political control, the civil war resumed. An American-sponsored truce temporarily halted hostilities, but when the U.S.S.R. withdrew from Manchuria in the spring of 1946 (after removing Manchurian industrial assets as reparations), Nationalists and Communists clashed over control of Manchuria.

Taiwan

In the fighting from 1946 to 1949, the Nationalists, despite substantial American support, lost ground steadily. By the autumn of 1949 the Communists had routed the demoralized Guomindang armies. Chiang withdrew his shattered forces to the island of Taiwan (and to the lesser islands of Matsu and Quemoy), where he established a small but soon prospering Republic of China in Taiwan. The mainland regime never gave up its claim to Taiwan, and the fate of Taiwan remained an unresolved international legacy for later generations. In 1971 Taiwan had to surrender to the People's Republic of China the seat set aside for China in the United Nations.

Mao: The New Regime

Mao Zedong

For the next 27 years, until his death in 1976, Chairman Mao, as uncontested head of the party, molded the destinies of China. Much more is known about him now than at the time. He had earlier imposed his iron rule on the party and on the populations under his control. He had ruthlessly eliminated all party rivals in periodic purges. Now nothing but the total transformation of backward, agrarian China, long the hapless victim of foreign powers, would satisfy him. He had earlier formed his vision of a new proud China in which the social order of domineering landlords and oppressed peasants would be reversed, the country would be industrialized and modernized, and China would be internationally respected. In many ways he personified the Chinese resentment of Western imperialism, which had humiliated China and all but carved the country to pieces in the nineteenth century. He was resolved to set China on the path to modernity, no matter what the cost.

In 1949, for the first time since the revolution of 1911, and indeed for generations before that, a unified central government controlled China, able to direct and mobilize the most populous nation in the world. Even before the Communist triumph Chairman Mao, despite his modest title, already saw himself as something of a successor to the ancient Chinese emperors. He could link Marx's world view, which since 1920 he had adopted as the instrument for Chinese liberation, to the 4,000-year-old imperial tradition of an all-powerful emperor ruling together with mandarin scholar-officials. The emperor was to rule with the mandate of Heaven in accordance with Confucian moral precepts, as interpreted by his learned officials. They were obligated to criticize the emperor, but if they went too far they could meet a grim end—in ancient times buried alive. The new regime inherited also an ancient tradition of Chinese preeminence in the East Asian world. With traditional ways of life disrupted by decades of revolution, civil struggle, and the war against Japan, Mao's communism in some ways provided a surrogate for the older Confucian values.

The Soviet example

Mao leaned heavily on Soviet experience. The Communist party controlled and policed each level of government and manipulated all organs of information and political indoctrination. The party also added "thought control" and "rectification" labor camps, and it inaugurated a reign of terror. In the first six months of 1950, by Mao's own estimate, some 700,000 "local bullies and evil gentry" labeled "counterrevolutionaries" lost their lives. In the next two years, from 1950 to 1952, a campaign directed against the "landlords" as a class meant that some half million more men, women, and children lost their lives or were sent to labor camps. The purges then took a different turn. In 1956, in what seemed to be a burst of enthusiasm for greater diversity and toleration in the country, Mao proclaimed: "Let a hundred flowers bloom, let a hundred schools of thought contend." But as soon as critics were encouraged to come forward, he quickly instituted a new period of repression, an "antirightist" campaign that sent more than a half million "rightists," and "class enemies" to prisons or forced labor camps, many never to return.

Mao relentlessly mobilized the nation to rebuild the war-devastated economy and then to transform the country into an industrial power. Eliminating the old land regime in the countryside, the party established agricultural cooperatives as a prelude to collectivization. The country's initial Five-Year Plan, launched in 1953 with Soviet economic and technical assistance during a period of initial friendly relations, concentrated on heavy industry, with significant results even if all targets were not reached. In agriculture the same floods and droughts that had troubled China for centuries refused to obey government decrees.

Impatient with what he considered the slowness of progress, Mao in 1957 launched the "Great Leap Forward," designed to transform the country's industry and agriculture more rapidly. The program adopted by the party proclaimed that China would "catch up with Britain" in a few years' time. The cooperatives in the countryside were amalgamated into larger "people's communes." Tightly organized in military fashion as production brigades, they were responsible for mechanizing production on the farms and developing local rural industry. Communal kitchens, nurseries, and schools left women freer to work on an equal basis in the fields and factories. Borrowing from some of the discredited Soviet experiments of Stalin, the government ordered farmers to abandon their traditional farming and to plant grain and rice everywhere, whether in suitable soil or not, and to crossbreed crops. Farmers were also encouraged to set up metallurgical furnaces in their backyards and learn to make steel.

The Great Leap Forward

The Great Leap Forward turned into disaster. Despite the image Mao had cultivated as the champion of the peasantry, he miscalculated on its ability to resist change. The persistent opposition of the peasants, severe crop failures, and the more bizarre experiments brought a disastrous famine. Up to 30 million died of hunger in what may have been the most disastrous agricultural experiment of all time. The outside world knew little of what was going on. Visitors to China were shielded from the disaster, which later scholars call "Mao's secret famine." Eventually moderates within the party curbed Mao's excessive zeal. Although the land remained collectivized, the party suspended the more rigid aspects of the communal experiment. Farmers were even permitted to sell or barter a portion of their crops.

But the industrial sector made progress. In the years before the Communist regime, annual steel production had never reached 1 million tons; by 1960 it exceeded 18 million. By 1960 China's industrial output ranked among the top ten powers in the world, and its factories had created a base for further expansion. The government also marshaled the country's scientific and technological talents for the new technological age. It successfully tested an atomic bomb in 1964 and a hydrogen bomb in 1967, and it orbited space satellites in the 1970s.

Industrial gains

The regime transformed life in many ways. Road, rail, and air transport physically unified the country. Public sanitation and public health received a high national priority. Labor gangs systematically drained and filled snail-infested canals, curbing the spread of diseases like schistosomiasis. Progress was made in overcoming illiteracy. The government reformed and simplified the written Chinese language and moved toward a single spoken tongue. It also adopted a new transliteration system for spelling Chinese names and words in the Latin alphabet. Women, encouraged to reject traditional Confucian virtues of obedience and deference, received legal equality with men and could count on new opportunities, even if few entered the higher ranks of political power. Old abuses such as child marriage and concubinage were outlawed; foot-binding had been eliminated earlier in the century. More profoundly than the Russian, the Chinese Revolution refashioned the habits and ethos of a gigantic population, reaching remote villages and hamlets untouched for centuries. Within a generation an agrarian, semifeudal country was developing into a modern industrial society. Mao's transformation was succeeding—at tremendous cost, to be sure.

Suddenly, beginning in 1966, the country was convulsed by the Cultural Revolution unleashed by Mao. Fearful that the revolution would not

The Cultural Revolution

The Cultural Revolution in China was led by millions of young "Red Guards" who—with the encouragement of Mao Zedong—sought to rekindle the revolutionary fervor of the Communist revolution and to disrupt or overthrow the bureaucratic order in Chinese society. These young people in Shanghai demonstrated their militant support for Chairman Mao during a typical Red Guard rally at the height of the Cultural Revolution in early 1967.

(Bettmann/Corbis)

survive him and that its purity was endangered, he called for a purge of the highest ranks of government and party and for the removal of those who had succumbed to bureaucratic routine or lacked the zeal to push on with the social revolution. For his cause he mobilized millions of teenage students and other young people as Red Guards, or armed shock troops. Converging on Beijing and other cities, they denounced bourgeois ways, attacked Western imperialist culture, and brutally harassed and humiliated government and party officials as well as cultural and educational leaders. The worst of the brunt fell on intellectuals. Men and women of all backgrounds were arrested, marched through the streets in dunce caps, beaten, and maimed. When fanatical mobs threatened to tear the country apart, army leaders finally intervened and received Mao's authorization to restore order.

A turbulent sequence followed. Because Mao proclaimed the virtues of the land, white-collar workers, teachers, students, and party officials were forcibly sent off to the countryside to labor in the fields and experience rural life. The economy and the entire educational system broke down. By the time the worst disturbances were over in 1969, hundreds of thousands of lives had been lost. Three million persons had been sent to labor camps or to work in the fields. Thousands of high-ranking officials in the government and party, including two-thirds of the party's central committee, had been purged. The impact of the Cultural Revolution lingered on in an authoritarian pall that settled over the country. Mao himself retreated after 1971 into a kind of self-indulgent isolation in Beijing.

The pragmatic and moderate Zhou Enlai, who had little influence in restraining Mao's more radical experiments, faithfully served him for many years as premier and foreign minister. Had he outlived Mao, he might well have been his successor, but Zhou Enlai died in early 1976. Later that same year, Mao died. The Great Helmsman was widely mourned as the towering father of the revolution for over half a century and as one of the giant figures in the history of China. He had forged a revolutionary party and a revolutionary army, fought the Japanese, defeated the Nationalists, and presided over a revolution that had unified, revitalized, and modernized the country. His theoretical teachings on the struggle against imperialism and on the vanguard role of the peasantry, and his practical successes in guerrilla warfare, influenced revolutionaries all over the world. His most famous precept, that "political power grows out of the barrel of a gun," reinforced revolutionary zeal everywhere. His homilies, published in a little red book called *The Living Thoughts of Chairman Mao*, were widely quoted and assiduously studied. Mao's revolution had brought self-respect and self-confidence, industrialization, technological progress, unity, and pride to the country.

The Great Helmsman

But his radical experiments and the uncontrolled violence he had repeatedly unleashed also did irreparable harm. His experiments in social engineering in some ways outdid Stalin's and must also be counted among the most costly in all history. By any criteria he ranks among the most brutal of dictators. His successors a few years later tempered their praise for Mao, still lauding his monumental achievements as a revolutionary leader but criticizing him for his "grave blunders."

Foreign Affairs

The emergence of China as a second major Communist power undermined the ideological leadership of the Soviet Union. Stalin, playing his own game, had not always wholeheartedly supported the Chinese Communists in their civil war with the Guomindang. But once the Communist regime was established the U.S.S.R. surrendered to it the concessions acquired in Manchuria under the Yalta agreement. For a time relations remained cool but correct, although Mao always resented being treated as a junior partner. In the 1950s the Chinese received military aid, capital loans, and technical assistance from the Soviets. The Korean War, in which Chinese troops fought the Americans as alien intruders who threatened their very borders, for a time drew them closer to the Soviet Union. Western leaders were even more firmly convinced that a monolithic world Communist movement existed. The Chinese Communists resented American support for the regime in Taiwan and the American effort over two decades to bar the People's Republic of China from the United Nations.

Although professing peace, the People's Republic pursued an aggressive foreign policy. In 1950, pressing old Chinese claims of suzerainty over Tibet and in the guise of liberating the country from clerical, that is, Buddhist, despotism, China occupied Tibet and forcibly maintained its rule there over the years. Monasteries were closed; the Dalai Lama, the country's ruler, was forced into exile; and large numbers of Chinese arrived as settlers. Unresolved tensions continued to affect the people of Tibet and the Tibetan borders. In 1962 China clashed with India in border disputes along India's northeastern frontier, although India from the beginning had been one of the staunchest defenders of the Chinese Revolution.

An aggressive foreign policy

In the 1960s relations with the Soviet Union became strained. The two states hurled polemics at each other in their rivalry for ideological leadership and for control of the lands of inner Asia into which Russia had expanded in the age of the tsars. Mao, undaunted by nuclear arms, accused Khrushchev of pusillanimous behavior in the Cuban missile crisis of 1962. In 1972 the two countries clashed over border territory that divided Manchuria and Russia's maritime provinces, and they continued to confront one another with large armies in other areas. Although both countries supported North Vietnam in the Vietnam War, China after the war opposed the Soviet-backed intervention by Vietnam in Cambodia. Not until the 1980s was there a rapprochement and the promise of troop reductions along the Chinese-Soviet borders.

With time, relations with the United States improved. In 1971, when the United States withdrew its objections, the People's Republic of China replaced Taiwan in the United Nations, including its permanent seat on the Security Council. The following year Mao welcomed President Nixon on a dramatic visit to China. Diplomatic channels opened and relations were normalized. The United States conceded that one day in the indefinite future Taiwan would be reunited with the mainland, with its different social and economic system respected.

Mao meets Nixon

The Chinese People's Republic had emerged as one of the great potential centers of global power. And in 1976 it was about to embark on an impressive new era of more peaceful modernization under Mao's successor. But we must first turn to those other parts of the colonial world that after the Second World War also entered a new stage in their history.

Chapter 23

EMPIRES
INTO NATIONS:
THE DEVELOPING
WORLD

Of all the political changes in the history of the modern world, affecting hundreds of millions of people, nothing was more revolutionary, more dramatic, or more unexpected than the end of the European overseas colonial empires. In 1945 the British, the French, the Dutch, the Belgians, and the Portuguese still governed large parts of the world's population, but within 30 years each of these colonial empires disappeared. Europe's world supremacy came to an end.

The Second World War reinforced nationalist agitation for independence and freedom. It was difficult to wage war in the name of self-determination and democracy, often with the colonial countries as allies, without encouraging the idea of freedom among subject peoples. The Japanese conquests in Asia had also undermined the image of European invincibility. After the war the Europeans, economically exhausted, learned that they could rule only at prohibitive military cost and in embarrassing contradiction to their professed ideals of self-government.

Contradictions of empire

In some instances the colonial powers, bowing to agitation for independence, liquidated their colonial holdings without armed struggle, as in the British withdrawal from the Indian subcontinent in 1947. Elsewhere the European powers withdrew only after protracted bloody wars, as in the case of the Dutch in Indonesia, the French in Indochina and Algeria, and the Portuguese in Angola and Mozambique. The United States also played a part in the transformation. It gave independence to the Philippines, granted Puerto Rico commonwealth status, took in Alaska and Hawaii as equal members of the federal union, and surrendered its privileges in the Panama Canal. The last vestiges of the European empires in Asia ended when Britain surrendered Hong Kong to China in 1997 and Portugal transferred Macao to China in 1999. The second half of the twentieth century witnessed the largest liberation of colonial peoples and transfer of power in all history.

Chapter emblem: Farmers harvesting barley in Ecuador in the 1990s.

New nations

The end of the colonial empires and the emergence of over 100 new nations must count among the most far-reaching consequences of the two World Wars, and especially of the Second. But many of the new nations were nations only in a limited sense. They were now sovereign territorial entities, with definite boundaries, internationally recognized, with seats in the United Nations, but many of them lacked the internal coherence and shared experience of nations in the older sense of the word. Nor did nationhood for the most part carry with it democracy, civil rights, or the rule of law, nor alleviate deep-seated social and economic problems.

The imperialist colonial experience left these regions of the world underdeveloped economically. In an uneven exchange they had depended on the industrial nations for capital, technology, and manufactures, while they in turn furnished the industrial countries with raw materials, foodstuffs, minerals, oil, and other primary commodities. With assistance from the industrially developed world, they now undertook modernization programs—against many obstacles and with mixed results. The winning of political independence in Asia and Africa, the mixed record of democratic self-government after independence, the effort to share in the earth's advanced technology and financial riches, and the struggle to reconcile older cultural values with modernization—all in the context of unprecedented population growth, colonial and regional wars, and international tensions—contributed to the saga of the developing world in the years after 1945. The Latin American nations, despite their more than a century of political independence by 1945, shared in many of the same experiences. Despite advances, many were still groping their way to constitutional government, social stability, and industrialization.

The Third World

In the years after the Second World War the term "Third World" came to describe the less economically advanced, or developing, nations of Asia, Africa, the Middle East, and Latin America. It was coined originally to distinguish the "developing" world from the two "industrial" worlds—the American-led bloc of nations and the Soviet-led Communist bloc. The term "Third World" carried the additional political meaning of nonalignment, the intention of many of the formerly colonial countries to remain uncommitted in the Cold War. Although that political meaning was rendered obsolete by the disintegration and collapse of Soviet communism in 1991, the term in its economic sense has persisted and seems destined to survive as a synonym for the developing world.

The present chapter examines the historical record of the new nations in their first half-century of independence, extending the time span in some cases beyond the chapters that follow. Although the peoples in diverse European colonial empires differed in their struggles for independence, they faced similar postcolonial challenges as they sought to establish the political, economic, and cultural foundations for stable, modern nation-states.

115. END OF THE EUROPEAN EMPIRES IN ASIA

End of the British Empire in Asia

The end in 1947 of British rule in India, the largest and most populous of all colonial areas ruled by Europeans, was epoch-making. Unfortunately, it fueled an explosion of ethnic and religious conflicts on the Indian subcontinent. The Indian National Congress, founded in 1885, had developed strength in the interwar years under the leadership of Gandhi and Nehru. The Congress party leaders demanded independence but also wished to avoid social revolution in the complex multiethnic country. Along with the British-trained Indian civil service, they considered themselves well prepared to govern an independent state. But the Muslim League, founded in 1906, claimed to speak, under Muhammad Ali Jinnah's leadership, for millions of Muslims unwilling to live in an India dominated by the Hindus and the Congress party. The Muslims insisted on their own national state, rooted in Islam. The Congress leaders, in contrast, pressed for a unified, secular India, with religion separated from politics and with freedom of worship for all religions.

During the Second World War India supported the British, but at the same time the Congress party and the Muslim League stepped up a "quit India" campaign. To retain Indian support for the war effort and to counter Japanese anti-Western propaganda, the British pledged independence. At the war's end, the British under Labour party leadership were poised to honor their pledge, but the differences between the Congress party and the Muslim League continued to be irreconcilable. To end the impasse the British decided on partition. In 1947 Britain granted independence to two *Partition* nations: to India, predominantly Hindu, with a population of 350 million at *of India* the time, which became the Republic of India; and to Pakistan, mainly Muslim, with a population of 75 million, which became the Islamic Republic of Pakistan. Because of the Muslim demographic concentration in Britain's former Indian empire, Pakistan was established in two disconnected parts, West and East Pakistan, separated by a thousand miles of Indian territory. About 60 million Muslims were also left in India, which helped keep India the multireligious secular state that Gandhi and Nehru desired. Ceylon (later renamed Sri Lanka) and Burma (later called Myanmar) in South Asia also received independence from Britain at this time.

The partition, overly hasty and ill-conceived, led to tragedy. Independence in August 1947 brought with it terrible communal riots between the Hindu and Muslim communities costing at least a million lives in a matter of weeks; some 17 million Hindus and Muslims were caught up in mass expulsions and turbulent migrations. In the worst of the tragedies, in the northern province of Punjab, Hindu and Sikh religious zealots ambushed and slaughtered trainloads of Muslim refugees fleeing east to Pakistan and Muslim fanatics did the same to Hindus and Sikhs migrating west to India. Gandhi, while praying for civil peace, was himself assassinated in 1948 by a Hindu extremist protesting his program for religious toleration. Only after the uglier features of the communal warfare subsided could the tasks of governing begin.

With his Congress party dominant, Nehru governed India as prime minister from 1947 until his death in 1964, setting the country on the path of British-style parliamentary democracy and even a kind of Fabian socialism. With no effective opposition, Nehru's program was more paternalistic than democratic. The masses *Nehru's* looked to him to resolve the country's enormous problems of poverty, rap- *paternalism* idly growing population, and ethnic, religious, and linguistic diversity. In addition to Hindi and English, 16 other languages received official recognition. In economic matters Nehru, a moderate socialist, understood the need for private capitalist enterprise but believed that economic planning, government controls, and the nationalization of key industries were also necessary. Under his leadership a modern industrial India with a mixed economy began to take shape and in many ways grew impressively in the years that followed.

But from independence on, the former princely state of Kashmir (officially, Jammu and Kashmir) in the Himalayas remained a trouble spot. Although three-fourths of the population were Muslim, the Hindu maharajah after procrastinating opted to join India. Open fighting between India and Pakistan broke out in 1948, and tense relations and

The British partition of its South Asian colonial empire into mostly Muslim Pakistan and pre-ponderantly Hindu India led to chaotic mass migrations and expulsions as people fled across the new borders in all directions. These trains in Amritsar, India, were swamped with Indian refugees who were trying to move to other Indian cities after fleeing from West Pakistan in October 1947.

(Bettmann/Corbis)

intermittent conflicts have continued ever since. War again broke out over Kashmir in 1965–1966, ending in an uneasy truce. In 1971 India went to war with Pakistan, but this time to support Bangladesh in its bloody war of secession from Pakistan.

Neutralism and nonalignment

In international affairs Nehru's defense of neutralism and nonalignment in the Cold War, which he forcefully articulated at a milestone conference of emergent Asian and African nations in 1955 in Bandung, struck a responsive chord in many parts of the Third World. Although firmly committed to democracy, Nehru retained a deep antagonism toward Western imperialism and capitalism, which reinforced his neutralism in the Cold War. As to China, although Nehru championed the right of the People's Republic of China to pursue its own path of social development, he condemned the Chinese occupation in 1950 of Tibet and, as we have seen, actual hostilities broke out over border disputes between India and China in 1962.

Nehru's Successors

When Nehru's immediate successor died in office in 1966 the Congress party leaders chose Nehru's daughter Indira Gandhi to be prime minister. Gandhi was her name through marriage, not through any kinship to the famous founder of Indian nationalism. She turned out to be a strong-willed *Indira Gandhi* political leader in her own right, but subordinated some of her father's more idealistic principles to political opportunism. More than Nehru, she looked for support to the masses, who idolized her for her carefully publicized pledges to abolish poverty. To win continuing support at the polls she made deals with Hindu nationalists, Muslims, and Sikhs. Corruption, already common, became even more fully entrenched.

In 1975 Gandhi, fearing losses in a coming election, proclaimed emergency rule, suspended constitutional government, and had hundreds of opponents arrested. After close to two years an outraged parliament drove her from office. But still popular, she returned to office as prime minister in 1980 and then governed constitutionally. Confronting a Sikh secessionist movement in the Punjab, she misguidedly sent army troops to invade their sacred Golden Temple at Amritsar. A few years later, in 1984, she was assassinated by Sikh soldiers of her own personal security guard.

The Congress party turned to her older son, Rajiv Gandhi, who had shown little interest in politics; his more politically minded younger brother, whom his mother had groomed for leadership, had been killed in an airplane crash in 1980. Governing not very effectively over the next five years, from 1984 to 1989, he seemed at times out of touch with the country's pressing social problems. By now the long-entrenched Congress party was in decline, and in 1989 it lost its parliamentary majority.

The very concept of a tolerant secular India came under siege. A strong *Hindu revivalism* Hindu revivalist movement grew in strength in the 1990s, preaching "Hindu values" and pledging to restore India to a Hindu "golden age" antedating the Muslim conquests and British colonial rule. A right-wing political party, the Indian People's party (the Bharatiya Janata, or BJP) used the movement for its own political ends, and through it Hindu revivalism entered the mainstream of Indian politics. The consequences were hostility, suspicion, and outright violence directed against the country's now 120 million Muslims.

Successfully exploiting widespread dissatisfaction with the Congress party, the BJP continued to increase its strength. Nonetheless, when in a new tragedy the following year Rajiv Gandhi was assassinated at a campaign rally, a sympathetic backlash helped the Congress party to win the new elections.

For the next five years, from 1991 to 1996, the Congress party held office, but the Nehru-Gandhi dynasty had come to an end. The veteran reform-minded party leader V. Narasimha Rao took steps to reform the *Congress party reforms* party, reduce bureaucracy, and curb widespread corruption. Rao also relaxed the economic controls that had become obstacles to economic growth in a country that was now a major economic power, restoring several nationalized industries to private ownership. He encouraged foreign investment and reduced or eliminated excessive protectionist barriers. In the 1990s India was demonstrating a facility for the new computer technology and was more fully integrated into the world economy than ever before.

While the economic results were impressive, the political scene grew more troubled. In December 1992 Hindu extremists clashed with Muslims over religious sites sacred to

Islam, and riots erupted in major cities. The Congress party, itself divided, was on the defensive. For the 1996 elections, invoking again a magic name, it called upon Rajiv Gandhi's Italian-born widow, Sonia Gandhi, to lead the party, but the party met with an even worse electoral setback. Short-lived unstable coalition governments followed. The Janata party, which had mobilized its strong Hindu base to replace the splintered Congress party, moved to fill the political vacuum and in 1999 headed a fragile coalition. Unstable governments did not, however, interfere with continuing economic reforms nor with firmness toward Pakistan.

Nuclear concerns

Although Nehru had worked for a non-nuclear India, his successors took a different path. In May 1974, after refusing to sign nonproliferation or comprehensive test ban treaties, India tested an underground nuclear device and became the world's sixth nuclear nation. Two decades later, in 1998, Pakistan demonstrated its nuclear prowess by test detonating a nuclear bomb. India responded with nuclear tests of its own. At the end of the century tensions and open hostilities again flared up over the perennial issue of Kashmir, when India repulsed Pakistani armed incursions supporting Islamic rebels in Kashmir. The presence of nuclear arms in both countries made the armed conflict even more alarming. South Asia was one of the most serious of the world's trouble spots.

Fifty Years of Independence

In 1997 India celebrated 50 years of independence. After over a half-century India remained a land of many contradictions. It could boast of a large, well-educated, ambitious middle class benefiting from an increasingly modern economy. Although the caste system had undergone many changes, it still persisted. But many born into the lower castes had moved into the mainstream of the business and professional world. In 1997 India elected its first president born an "untouchable," President V. R. Narayan.

A land of contradictions

Through medical advances, better nutrition, and a decline in infant mortality, death rates had declined and population almost tripled in the first 50 years, passing the one billion mark in 1999. But economic growth and rising consumer standards for some classes hardly affected village India—nine-tenths of the population. Poverty, illiteracy, disease, and malnutrition remained widespread. Over half the country was illiterate; for women and girls the number was higher and they labored under additional disadvantages as well. Over 200 million people were without safe drinking water and 650 million were without basic sanitation. Population growth continued to threaten economic advances. A sporadic but ineffective family planning program was still widely resisted. Although poverty had declined in the past 50 years, over 40 percent of the population remained impoverished by internationally accepted standards. The cities were congested and slum-ridden, swollen by millions who had left the villages to find jobs. India, despite its economic and technological advances, remained a Third World country.

The status of women

Much remained to be done to improve the status of women. Old forms of discrimination persisted, accompanied at times by outright violence in matters of dowries, divorce, and inheritance, and in the plight of widows who were thrown on the mercy of their husbands' families for survival. The highly visible presence of women in high political ranks in India and elsewhere in South Asia belied their lower status in general. In India, as in Pakistan, Burma, Indonesia, Bangladesh, Sri Lanka, the Philippines, and elsewhere, women became presi-

THE INDIAN SUBCONTINENT, 2000

The map shows nations that emerged from the dissolution of the British Empire in South Asia. East Pakistan was part of Pakistan until its war of secession in 1971 led to the establishment of an independent Bangladesh; Pakistan and Bangladesh are predominantly Muslim. India is predominantly Hindu, but large Muslim and Sikh minorities live there. The political ascendancy of a Hindu nationalist party in the 1990s altered India's pluralistic political culture and also changed the names of cities that have long been known as Bombay, Calcutta, and Madras (Mubai, Kolkata, and Chennai). Political movements have changed other colonial-era names in the region, including the name of the country now called Myanmar, which was known as Burma throughout the era of British control and early independence. The island once called Ceylon is now Sri Lanka. The dispute between India and Pakistan over the status of Jammu and Kashmir has remained unresolved. Conflicts in this disputed territory, intensified by the development of nuclear weapons in India and Pakistan, as well as continuing internal conflicts in Sri Lanka and Myanmar, make South Asia one of the world's politically volatile regions at the beginning of the twenty-first century.

dents, prime ministers, or opposition leaders, but invariably they came to office as daughters or widows in leading political families similar to the Nehru-Gandhi "dynasty."

The Congress party, in power for most of the years since independence, had undoubtedly provided the stability needed for survival of the diverse country as a united nation. Parliamentary democracy, the rule of law, a free press, and an effective judiciary prevailed, and at the end of the century over 600 million people exercised their right to vote (on ballots still marked by party symbols because of the widespread illiteracy). Yet bribery, venality, and corruption continued to be pervasive at all levels of government and the country's "invisible majority"—its needy millions— remained neglected. Nehru's appeal at the time of independence for India's

The invisible majority

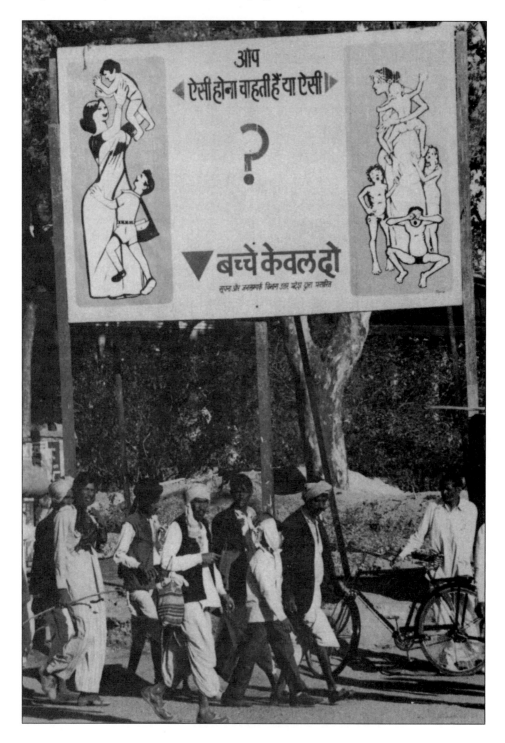

"tryst with destiny" had to be postponed. And rising ethnic and religious tensions, graver in the 1990s than at any time since independence, threatened to undermine India's democracy and destroy the multireligious tolerance that India's founders had originally envisaged.

The Islamic Republic of Pakistan

Pakistan's independence leader, Jinnah, a British-educated lawyer, was by no means an Islamic militant and might have made a significant difference in the country's history, but he died shortly after independence, and his successor was assassinated. Despite the machinery of parliamentary democracy, the Islamic Republic of Pakistan soon succumbed to military rule, and over the years oscillated between periods of military rule, restoration of constitutional government, which generally meant civilian misrule, and the return of military dictatorship. By the end of the century military dictators had run the country for half of its years of independence. It remained predominantly agricultural, and was still one of Asia's poorest and least developed nations.

Even the awkward postcolonial territorial arrangement had not lasted. In East Pakistan, carved out of the old state of Bengal, more than half the population lived in a congested area and in 1971 political and social resentments exploded into secession. When East Pakistan proclaimed independence as the new state of Bangladesh (or "Bengali nation"), the Pakistani government dispatched a large army to suppress the rebellion and hundreds of thousands *Bengali secession and war*
were killed in the unequal civil war. At that point, however, India massively intervened and compelled the recognition of independence. Bangladesh remained impoverished, one of the poorest and most densely populated countries in the world, subject not only to floods, drought, and famine but also to political violence, assassinations, and military coups.

Civilian rule was restored in Pakistan for a short time after the war over Bangladesh, but in 1977 the now familiar Pakistani political pattern continued. The military took power and executed President Ali Bhutto. Even when civilian rule was restored the army kept a watchful eye on the political scene. In 1988 Benazir Bhutto, the Western-educated daughter of the former president, returned from exile and in new elections became the first woman prime minister of a major Islamic nation. Promising liberalization and reform, she provoked opposition from militant Muslim groups and members of the military, who used evidence of corruption to discredit her leadership and eventually force her from office. Meanwhile the Islamic religious movements grew larger and more militant, bolstered by Muslim refugees and guerrilla fighters fleeing Afghanistan after the Soviet Union invaded that country in 1979. Muslim extremism continued to grow, and by the early 1990s the government ruled that Islamic law should take precedence over the constitution.

The steady increase of the population in India—more than 1 billion people at the end of the twentieth century—continued to affect the status of women and the economic conditions of the nation's impoverished classes. Seeking to reduce the rate of population growth, the Indian government has promoted a campaign for family planning. This large sign in New Delhi portrays a woman, but its question seems to be directed at men and women alike: Do you want joy and comfort with two children, or destitution with four?

(François Lochon/Liaison Agency)

When the Soviet Union invaded Afghanistan in 1979 Pakistan became caught up in the contest between the superpowers in the Cold War. The United States used Pakistan as a conduit for arms being shipped to the Muslim guerrillas fighting the Soviets, and over two million Afghan refugees fled to Pakistan.

Political disarray and financial straits

In 1997 Benazir Bhutto's successor and chief opponent so thoroughly undermined the authority of parliament, the judiciary, and the provincial legislatures that the country was in political disarray and in financial straits. Relations with India, as we have seen, deteriorated. The military suffered a humiliating defeat when it crossed the border into Indian territory in Kashmir in 1999. Later that year, as economic matters worsened and renewed political instability threatened, the army leader General Musharraf staged a military coup. The new government included a number of civilian leaders and promised future elections. The coup was not unpopular because the Pakistani people were desperate for change, but the nation's political record of military rule aroused skepticism about the return to civilian government, let alone to parliamentary democracy.

The presence in South Asia at the end of the century of two nuclear powers nursing old grievances was of more than regional significance. Tensions over Kashmir (or over other matters) could escalate, and the strength of Hindu chauvinist parties in India and of Islamic militancy in Pakistan added to uncertainties.

The Union of Burma (Myanmar)

Burma, India's neighbor to the east, embarked on a unique path of isolation and repression after gaining independence in 1948. In 1989 its military leaders renamed it Myanmar. After annexing the country in 1885 to its Indian empire, Britain built a railway network, developed the country's mining and forest resources, and encouraged rice cultivation, so that for a time Burma was the world's largest exporter of rice. In the interwar years the British encouraged limited self-government but at the same time imprisoned nationalist leaders like Aung San who pressed for immediate independence. After the Japanese invasion of Burma in the Second World War the nationalist leaders took up arms against the Japanese but also took advantage of the Japanese conquest to advance Burma's independence from Britain.

Burmese independence

After the war the British recognized Burma's independence, but Aung San, who was to become prime minister, was assassinated and his associate, U Nu, a devout Buddhist and a somewhat doctrinaire socialist, became the first prime minister. To the new leaders of the nation anti-imperialism meant anticapitalism and the new government was determined to socialize the country rapidly. With little money, however, it was difficult to import machinery and to train workers; "the Burmese path to socialism," as it was styled, became impossible. In addition to economic chaos, Burma faced armed rebellion from insurgent separatist minorities, many of them reinforced after 1949 by the new Communist regime in China. Ethnic minorities made up about one-third of the country's population. Many of these minorities were incensed by Nu's plan to make Buddhism the official state religion.

Despite the political framework of a multiparty parliamentary democracy, the military exercised a parallel power with the civilian authorities. As the ethnic insurgencies became more threatening in 1962, the army head General Ne Win staged a military takeover. He would retain power for the next 26 years in a one-party state still dedicated to pursuing the "Burmese path to socialism," but in effect a military regime.

As economic difficulties and ethnic turbulence steadily worsened, the country retreated into deeper isolation. By the early 1970s insurgent groups controlled one-third of the country. Popular discontent mounted and in the 1980s a new opposition party emerged, the National League for Democracy, headed by Aung San Suu Kyi, the daughter of the country's martyred founder. Educated in India, she also spent some 20 years at Oxford where she was a graduate student and married an Oxford don. An immensely popular and charismatic figure, she incorporated in her person the nonviolence of traditional Buddhism with Western democratic values. When in 1988 the military dictator resigned, she addressed large crowds of supporters and proclaimed that Burma's "second struggle for independence" was under way. But in the end a repressive military junta took power and placed her under house arrest.

Isolation and repression

Confronted with continuing massive demonstrations, the military agreed to open elections in 1990, the first in 30 years. But when the democratic opposition won 90 percent of the popular vote and over four-fifths of the parliamentary seats, the stunned military declared the elections null and void and took reprisals against the party leaders. Aung San Suu Kyi remained under strict surveillance, her movements and visitors severely restricted. But she became an international symbol of democratic aspirations; in 1991 she received the Nobel Peace Prize. Meanwhile military repression thwarted the popular desire for democratic self-government and civilian rule, and the leaders of the democracy movement remained virtually imprisoned.

Malaysia

In the Malayan peninsula British plans for independence were delayed because of tensions between the country's Muslim Malay majority and its sizable Chinese and Indian minorities, who had lived there since the nineteenth century when the British had imported workers from China and India to work in the tin and rubber mines. The Chinese had come to play a dominant role in the economy. At the same time a militant Communist movement had emerged, and the British for several years fought a Communist insurgency. In 1957, with the rebellion mostly subdued, Britain granted independence. Five years later Malaya joined with Singapore and other former British dependencies to create the Federation of Malaysia. Singapore withdrew in 1965 to become a small island-nation with a flourishing modern economy and high living standards but governed by a semi-authoritarian, paternalistic regime. Singapore, Taiwan, and South Korea made striking economic advances in East Asia without establishing full-fledged democracies. There was no absolute repression, but no genuine democracy either. Under more or less authoritarian regimes, the ruler or ruling group brought all political parties under the umbrella of "national unity" and discouraged militant opposition or open dissent. Not until late in the century did democracy make headway in Taiwan and South Korea.

Ethnic conflicts flared up again in Malaysia in 1969, and riots led to the suppression of parliamentary rule for about two years. After that difficult period, although the Malay political dominance remained clear, multiethnic coalitions gradually helped to ease tensions. Already prospering because of tin, oil, rubber, and lumber resources, Malaysia in the 1980s developed new high-technology industries, and its economy became one of the fastest growing in Asia, attracting foreign investment as well. The economic program included ambitious construction projects. Although at the end of the 1990s the country was hurt by financial and currency crises that interrupted its spectacular growth and led to political instability, Malaysia had climbed out of Third World status.

Economic growth

Malaysia's growing role in the global economy is reflected in the soaring, contemporary office buildings of the capital city, Kuala Lumpur. The Petronas Towers, which rise to a height of almost 1,500 feet and loom over the other offices in this picture, were the tallest buildings in the world at the beginning of the twenty-first century.
(John Dakers; Eye Ubiquitous/Corbis)

As this brief survey demonstrates, the British surrendered all but small outposts of their vast empire within a decade or so after the end of the Second World War. However, most of its former colonies in Asia (as well as in Africa, the Caribbean, and the Pacific) agreed to retain a voluntary association with Britain and each other in a new Commonwealth of Nations, far different from the old "white" Commonwealth of Australians, New Zealanders, Canadians, and white minority South Africans. The new Commonwealth grew into an association of over 50 independent nations, which agreed to consult, though not necessarily act in concert, on matters of common interest. It helped to promote Western and non-Western interchange between Britain and the diverse far-flung parts of the world that had once constituted the British empire.

End of the Dutch Empire: Indonesia

Another great empire in the East, the Dutch East Indies, also came to an end. Agitation for independence, as in India, went back to pre-1914 days, but the Indonesian Nationalist party, founded in 1927, and a growing Communist party had met with little success in the interwar years. The Japanese, as elsewhere in Asia, exploited anti-Western sentiment during the Second World War and found Indonesian nationalist leaders to use as collaborators in their military occupation. At the same time a broad resistance movement emerged in which the Communists played a major part. Once the Japanese were ousted at the war's end in August 1945, before the Dutch could return, the Indonesian Nationalist leader Sukarno (Indonesians often use only their family name in public life) proclaimed the country's independence. For four years the Dutch stubbornly fought the nationalist movement, but at the end of 1949 they finally ceded independence.

A large, multi-ethnic country

By the end of the twentieth century Indonesia's population exceeded 215 million, making it the fourth most populous country in the world. An archipelago situated along the equator with thousands of islands strung together over 3,000 miles, it is rich in oil, natural gas, timber, and other resources. A modified form of Malay is the official language, but over 300 languages and dialects are used. With some 88 percent of the population Muslim, it has the largest Islamic population in the world. The first and continuing task was to establish and maintain a sense of national identity in so large and multiethnic a country.

Sukarno began with a parliamentary constitutional program and a democratic ideology derived from the struggle against the Dutch, but the democratic phase did not last. In 1959 he dissolved the Constituent Assembly and governed in the following years under a populist dictatorship that he called "guided democracy"; before long he insisted upon being elected "president for life."

Sukarno's "guided democracy"

Sukarno became one of the chief spokesmen for the developing nations of Asia and Africa. He hosted the meeting in Bandung in 1955 at which leaders of 29 of the new nations rejoiced in their new sovereignty, condemned Western imperialist and capitalist exploitation, and pledged neutralism and nonalignment in the Cold War. Sukarno cultivated friendship with the Soviet Union and Communist China and loosened economic ties with the West. Meanwhile the Indonesian Communist party, backed by the People's Republic of China, had quietly grown into the third largest Communist party in the world with some two million members.

For a time Sukarno managed to work with and control the large Communist party, but in 1965 leftist army officers attempted a coup. A relatively unknown army leader, General Suharto, quickly moved to suppress what was alleged to be a Communist rebellion and ousted Sukarno. What ensued, as the army stood by, was the dreadful slaughter by Islamic militants of hundreds of thousands of Communists and leftists in a bloodbath that could rank among the major atrocities of the twentieth century. A half million Communists and leftist suspects were murdered, two million were arrested, and thousands were imprisoned. The

Suharto's war on the Communists

Indonesian President Sukarno became a leader of the world's new and developing nations during the era of decolonization. He is shown here in 1955, addressing the international meeting at Bandung, where representatives of nonaligned nations affirmed their independence, pledged to remain neutral in the Cold War, and condemned the legacies of Western imperialism.

(Lisa Larsen/TimePix)

violence also took a racial turn when many ethnic Chinese fell victim. The repression destroyed the Indonesian Communist party.

Over the next 32 years General Suharto retained power, running his island empire from the capital in Jakarta under a system of controlled elections in which he was dutifully reelected president every five years. Without him, the message went out, Indonesia would fall apart or succumb either to a revived communism or Islamic extremism. The military presence, a shadow presence ever since independence, was pervasive. A single governing party ruled.

An impressive economy

Suharto's anti-Communist credentials brought him Western support in the Cold War and attracted foreign investment to the country. He presided over an impressive economy, which showed annual growth rates that became another of the success stories of the developing world. The economy expanded sixfold over 30 years, and Indonesia ranked as one of the ten strongest emerging markets of the world. New construction changed the face of the nation, especially of the capital. A few in Indonesia became very rich; the middle classes grew in number and comfort; and there was a general decline in poverty throughout the country.

Spread of corruption

At the same time a culture of corruption grew. Suharto, his family, his political entourage, and an inner circle of bankers, business leaders, and technocrats enriched themselves, to the growing resentment of people outside the ruling elite. Suharto aroused opposition in other ways. In 1975, when Portugal withdrew from East Timor, an enclave it had long ruled adjacent to Indonesian territory, Suharto in an ill-advised move annexed it. The population of almost one million, many of whom were Christian, wanted independence and resisted the brutal annexation. Close to 100,000 lives were lost in the repression that followed and brought worldwide denunciation of Suharto. Not until international intervention at the end of the century was East Timor's independence recognized.

Much of Indonesia's economic success depended on foreign loans, and its foreign debt mounted. With capital pouring in, no one adequately supervised the financial structure of the country. Risky loans and overexpansion of credit took their toll. In the latter half of 1997 a financial panic swept Indonesia (and other parts of southeast Asia as well). In 1997–1998 the currency lost four-fifths of its value and the poverty rate tripled.

Suharto ousted

The economic collapse brought Suharto's downfall. When he insisted on reelection for a seventh term as president and the servile parliament permitted it, riots and demonstrations broke out. Suharto was forced to relinquish power in May 1998, naming as his successor his vice president and protege H. J. Habibie. He pledged free elections and sweeping reforms, but no one could count on him to square accounts for the years of dictatorship and corruption. The country was in economic chaos but also in political ferment. The press was freed, political parties reemerged, and new elections were organized.

In the midst of these events the demand for independence in East Timor came to a head. The new government's proposal for a UN-supervised referendum met with violent opposition from the military. When the pro-independence results were announced, armed militia forces sought to retain Indonesian control by unleashing a campaign of terror and revenge. An international peacekeeping force was needed to help restore order.

President Wahid, a Muslim political and intellectual figure, took office in 1999. As a concession to the opposition, Megawati Sukarnoputri, the daughter of the country's independence leader and first president, who had emerged as leader of the popular protests against Suharto, became vice president. Two years later she succeeded Wahid when the legislature removed him from office. The prospects for stability and democracy remained clouded. There was concern whether the country would remain a tolerant multireligious society or succumb to Muslim extremism and fear that separatist pressures could cause the large country to disintegrate.

Steps toward democracy

The economy was unsettled, foreign capital was slow in returning, and corruption had reached to the presidency, while the role of the army, still seeing itself as the "protector of the nation," remained unpredictable.

End of the French Colonial Empire: Indochina

The French colonial empire also fell apart, not, however, without a struggle. The first of France's postwar colonial wars, as noted in the previous chapter, was fought over Indochina. When France offered autonomy to the states of Indochina at the end of the Second World War within a continuing French federation, Cambodia and Laos accepted, but Vietnam (as Cochin-China, Tonkin, and Annam jointly came to be called) demanded full independence. Open warfare broke out in 1946, and French armies and Communist-led Vietnamese forces fought each other for $7^1/2$ years.

The Communist leader Ho Chi Minh, who headed the independence movement in Vietnam, had spent many earlier years in London, in Paris (where he was present at the founding of the French Communist party in 1920), and in Moscow. He returned to Vietnam in 1941, organized a Vietnamese independence movement (the Viet Minh), and mobilized guerrilla armies to fight the Japanese. At the war's end he proclaimed Vietnam's independence. The French tried to reassert control by using an ineffectual former emperor of Annam as a puppet. When negotiations failed, Ho turned his armies against the French. Because the Communists led the independence movement, the French could claim that they were fighting to stem the tide of world communism, not to preserve nineteenth-century colonial privileges.

Communism and imperialism

Yet communism here, as often in Asia, was linked to nationalism, anticolonialism, anti-Westernism, and genuine popular discontent.

Under President Eisenhower the United States, anticolonial but ready to champion anti-Communist causes in the Cold War, aided the French financially but refrained from open military intervention. The war drained French morale and resources. In the spring of 1954 at the very time that an international conference was meeting in Geneva to arrange a settlement in Indochina, the French army after a long, costly siege suffered a severe defeat at the battle of Dien Bien Phu. The conference, with French acquiescence, recognized the independence of Vietnam, as well as of Cambodia and Laos. The colonial empire in French Indochina came to an end.

Vietnam was provisionally partitioned at the seventeenth parallel into a northern and southern sector until elections could be held for the entire country, but the elections never took place. Neither Ho nor the Western-backed regime in the south was satisfied with the settlement of 1954, and a civil war of increasing intensity soon began. The United States, as we shall see, became deeply involved in the war by the early 1960s, seeing the struggle in Vietnam as part of the global Communist challenge that had to be contained.

The Americans and the Philippines

The Americans, too, shared in the liquidation of colonial empires in Asia. In the Philippines a strong independence movement had emerged in the late nineteenth century directed against the decaying Spanish empire. Revolution under the leadership of Emilio Aguinaldo was well under way when the Spanish-American War broke out in 1898. With American encouragement Aguinaldo joined the war against Spain and unilaterally declared independence, promulgating the first democratic and republican constitution in Asia. But disappointment followed when Spain transferred the islands to the United States at the end of the war. Aguinaldo and his followers rebelled and took up arms against the United States. The suppression of the Filipino independence movement over the next three years cost the United States more money and more lives than the war against Spain itself.

*Transition
to independence*

Independence remained a pressing issue both in the islands and in the United States, which after semimilitary rule in the 1920s proposed a transition to self-rule and eventual independence. An act of Congress in 1934 granted self-governing commonwealth status with a pledge of full independence in the near future. Delayed by the Second World War, independence was finally granted in July 1946.

In the early years of independence a succession of governments did little to help the impoverished peasants or even maintain political order. Communist-led guerrilla movements pressing for land redistribution added to instability.

*Marcos
as president*

Ferdinand E. Marcos, president after 1965, governed as a dictator, the Americans acquiescing because of his staunch anticommunism. Throughout the 1970s poverty and government corruption steadily increased while Marcos and his family grew wealthy and spent money extravagantly.

After the assassination in 1983 of the popular opposition leader Benigno Aquino upon his return to the islands from exile, his widow Corazón Aquino spearheaded the opposition and contested Marcos in the 1986 presidential elections. When Marcos, despite clear evidence of fraud, attempted to declare himself the winner, the country turned decisively against him, and his support eroded even in the United States. The ensuing popular upheaval forced him into exile.

*American
withdrawal*

President Aquino faced continuing pressures from Right and Left, but restored democratic elections and civil rights. She also slowly inaugurated land and other reforms, setting an example for those who followed her. In the early 1990s the Filipino legislature opposed the renewal of leases for America's military bases, and the United States agreed to withdraw. Another chapter of Western imperialism came to an end, but the future of domestic peace and government stability on the islands, as in so many other parts of Asia, was far from assured in the opening years of the new century.

116. THE AFRICAN REVOLUTION

Africa is a large continent, considerably larger than North and Central America combined. With an estimated population of 220 million in 1950 and some 870 million in 2000, it has

*North and sub-
Saharan Africa*

had one of the fastest growing populations in the world, although the ravages of AIDS have taken a serious toll since the 1980s. A distinction may be made between North Africa and sub-Saharan Africa. North Africa, stretching from Mauritania and Morocco to Egypt, mostly Muslim and Arab, belongs as much to the Mediterranean world (and even more to the Islamic Middle East) in ethnic composition, culture, geography, and history. In sub-Saharan Africa, to the south, below the Sahara Desert, lives a population of over 600 million people, where Islam, Christianity, and traditional African animist faiths are found and where the population is predominantly black. An ethnographic and linguistic map of Africa would reveal hundreds of different ethnic groups and some 800 African languages, of which about 50 are spoken by a half million people or more. A large number of Africans since the colonial era also speak English or French, and English or French is one of the official languages of many of the newly independent nations. There are also numerous descendants of European and South Asian settlers and immigrants, most notably in South Africa.

In 1945 the map of Africa was scarcely different from what it had been in 1914. All of Africa was European-governed with the exceptions of Egypt, Liberia, and Ethiopia (the latter had regained its independence from Italy during the war). By the early 1960s, however, there were 35 independent states, and most of Africa was either independent or close to achieving independence. By the early 1990s with the addition of Eritrea, there were 53 independent African states, making up close to a third of the membership of the United Nations. Of the 53 states, 48 were in sub-Saharan Africa.

Independence movements

The new states differed from older nations in many ways. African geographical boundaries had been drawn by the European colonial powers in the late nineteenth century, often arbitrarily, and the new states contained within their borders diverse ethnic and linguistic groups. These groups often lived together uneasily, while ethnically related peoples were frequently distributed over two or more countries. With independence, the African states rapidly assumed the full panoply of national sovereignty, but the people in these states had a less unified national heritage than those in most older nations of Europe and Asia, and the new African governments faced the daunting challenge of welding their disparate ethnic groups into nationhood. The age of imperialism had left the African states economically underdeveloped, dependent on world markets, and with little experience in self-governing institutions; the very rapidity of the transition to independence added to their difficulties. Ethnic and civil wars and regional conflicts marked much of the first half-century of independence. The following survey of important developments in postcolonial Africa can only sketch the broad outlines of African history in these years.

French North Africa

During the Second World War the Allied leaders had made various commitments to self-determination. With Italy defeated, the wartime Allies in 1951 granted independence to the former Italian colony of Libya, and the British took steps to end what was left of their privileged position in Egypt. These events galvanized all of French North Africa, where Arab nationalist leaders, often French-educated, had pressed for independence since the 1920s. In Morocco, Tunisia, and Algeria—the Maghreb, as these Arab states of northwest Africa are called—they mounted a vigorous campaign. Morocco and Tunisia were not outright colonies but protectorates under their traditional rulers, the Moroccan sultan and the Tunisian bey. The French in 1956 granted independence to both countries. The Moroccan sultan became king as a constitutional monarch, but as the years went by the monarchy enlarged its powers. Tunisia became a republic and was governed for its first 30 years by Habib Bourguiba, who introduced many democratic reforms (including rights of divorce for women) but insisted on being named president for life. In both countries modernization and pressures for liberalization continued, often against counterpressures from Muslim traditionalists.

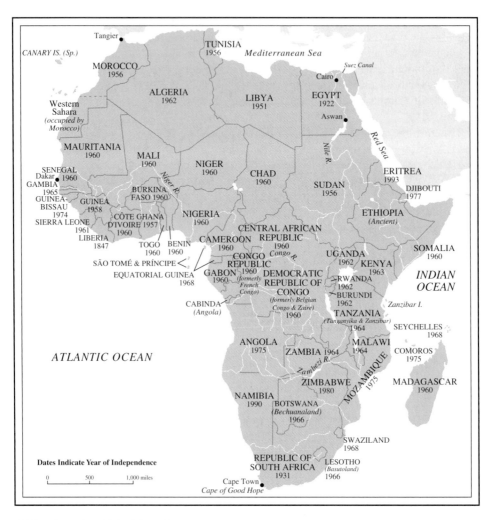

CONTEMPORARY AFRICA

This map shows the emergence of independent African states and may be compared with earlier maps for precolonial Africa (p. 637) and for Africa in 1914 at the height of European imperialism (p. 640). The first of the new sub-Saharan states was Ghana, which gained independence from Britain in 1957 and took its name from a medieval African kingdom that had been located further north. The more recently established states include Zimbabwe (1980) and Namibia (1990) in southern Africa and Eritrea (1993) in northeastern Africa. By the end of the twentieth century all of the European colonial empires had disappeared and the white-controlled apartheid regime in South Africa had given way to a nonracial, democratic political system.

Algeria

Algeria's story was very different. In the early nineteenth century the French conquered Algeria, part of the decaying Ottoman Empire, and it became a full French colony by mid-century. Later in the century French and other Europeans settled there in substantial numbers and soon dominated the political and economic life of the country and its Arab population. The French provided limited measures of self-rule and representation along with

a promise that further concessions could be made when the country became fully assimilated to French and European ways. Some political concessions were made in the interwar
years, but Algerian nationalists now pressed for full independence. Algeria was represented in the French legislature in Paris, but the suffrage in Algeria was heavily weighted
in favor of the European settlers to the distinct disadvantage of the Arab majority. Of the
nine million or so inhabitants, about one million were Europeans. The
colons, mostly French, like the family of the French writer Albert Camus,
had lived there for generations. Because the Europeans controlled the economy and owned most of the land and industry, they feared for their political and economic privileges if Algeria were cut loose from France and gov-

*French colons
in Algeria*

erned by an Arab Muslim majority smarting from years of unequal treatment. The French
military suppressed initial postwar uprisings, but the nationalist movement grew, and in the
autumn of 1954 the National Liberation Front (FLN) began a fierce guerrilla war against
the French.

The French-Algerian war lasted $7^1/2$ years, involving at its peak
500,000 French troops and provoking sharp political divisions within
France. The FLN received aid and support from Egypt and other Arab
states. Torture and cruelty became common on both sides. In the spring of

*The French-
Algerian War*

1958, during a French cabinet crisis in which the *colons* in Algeria feared that a negotiated
settlement might be arranged, an insurrection by army leaders and diehard settlers in Algiers brought political changes in Paris and General Charles de Gaulle's return to power.
To the dismay of the army leaders, however, de Gaulle arranged a cease-fire and soon
spoke of autonomy and self-determination for the Algerians. In 1961 he won the backing
of the French electorate for full independence. Army leaders rebelled, and some of his
closest former associates helped form a secret army of terrorists who bombed and killed,
and even attempted his assassination. Nevertheless, in 1962 French rule ended. The struggle for independence had cost the lives of 10,000 French and 100,000 Algerian combatants
and of additional thousands of Algerian civilians.

After independence there was a mass exodus of Europeans from Algeria, but most of
the French and Algerians were grateful that de Gaulle had ended the ordeal. The French
accepted the loss of Algeria, and of other parts of their empire, and with a prospering economy in the 1960s turned their attention to other matters. Although staunchly anti-Western,
the Algerians accepted French technical assistance for the development of Algeria's extensive oil and natural gas resources.

The FLN retained power and governed the country under a military-
dominated one-party regime for the next 30 years. The party became increasingly corrupt, and it mismanaged the cumbersome state-owned

The FLN

planned economy, which survived only through the country's oil and gas revenues. When oil
prices declined, the result was widespread unemployment. In the 1980s about three-fourths
of all young Algerians were without jobs and many were homeless as well. An additional two
million Algerians migrated in search of jobs, mainly to France. In 1988 general frustration
with the political and economic situation in Algeria exploded into urban riots.

In its effort to cement ties with other Arab states, the FLN had allowed Islamic fundamentalists to teach and to grow in political influence. Among the parties that emerged
was an extremist Islamic Salvation Front. It organized itself into a mass political movement, offered itself as a substitute for the FLN, and won broad support from
many segments of the disenchanted population. It vehemently opposed
the Western-style secularization that had emancipated women from Islamic rules in dress and other matters and pressed for the reimposition of

*Islamic
fundamentalism*

The Algerian war for independence from France was one of the most bitter, protracted struggles for decolonization, in part because a large French population had lived in Algeria for several generations. France had about 500,000 soldiers in Algeria, including these troops in the city of Oran, but the French army could not defeat the Algerian National Liberation Front or regain control of the Algerian countryside. Algeria became an independent nation in 1962.

(Hulton Archive)

fundamentalist rules of dress and comportment. In late 1991 the Islamic party overwhelmingly won the first multiparty parliamentary elections ever held in the country, but the army leaders peremptorily canceled the election results and declared the Islamic party illegal.

After 1992 the social and political life of Algeria entered a violent phase. The armed movement of the Islamic extremists unleashed a reign of terror, attacking whole villages and settlements, killing even children. Moderate Islamic leaders were helpless. The military responded with brutal terror of its own. Tens of thousands lost their lives. By the beginning of the new century the Algerian government was belatedly checking the assaults, but new forms of ethnic unrest were emerging.

End of British Rule in West Africa

In North Africa nationalist agitation for independence, already under way in the interwar years, might have been expected, but south of the Sahara the movement for liberation was never as far advanced. Yet the pace of independence after the Second World War was unexpectedly rapid. Here black African populations lived in colonial empires that Europeans had carved out either in the colonial age that opened in the fifteenth century or in the "scramble for Africa" in the brief decade and a half of European imperialist competition after 1885.

Independence movements, barely in existence earlier, announced their presence. The British first resisted the mounting nationalist pressures, imprisoning or exiling nationalist leaders, but then yielded. They first provided broader African representation in the colonial legislative assemblies, then granted autonomy and independence to the colonies as dominions, and in short order the dominions became independent republics.

From colonies to independent republics

For many years the postcolonial republics were mostly ruled by authoritarian governments more interested in sustaining their own power than in developing democratic societies. Although there was a trend toward democratization across parts of the continent in the 1990s, serious economic challenges persisted almost everywhere, and African economies remained dependent on development assistance and on the fluctuating price of commodities in the global economy.

The Gold Coast (Ghana) became the first British colony to win independence. The British initially resisted a militant civil disobedience movement led by the nationalist leader Kwame Nkrumah and even imprisoned him. But in 1951 they freed Nkrumah and conceded self-government. Nkrumah's party overwhelmingly won the elections that followed and he became prime minister. In 1957 the colony won full independence with dominion status, and in 1960 Nkrumah transformed it into a republic with himself as president. With independence, the country shed the name of Gold Coast, which was too closely identified with the centuries of imperialist exploitation and the slave trade. It called itself Ghana, recalling an African kingdom somewhat to the north which had flourished from the sixth to the eleventh centuries. Nkrumah quickly gathered extensive power into his own hands, banned opposition parties, governed autocratically, and declared himself president for life. In Africa (and in Asia) the charismatic nationalist leaders who led the struggles for independence repeatedly turned into personal dictators once independence was won, and the party of the independence movement often became the sole legal party.

Nkrumah's Ghana

Nkrumah adopted an anti-Western stance, championed a nonalignment policy in the Cold War, and sought a leading role in a pan-African movement, hosting in 1958 the first All-African People's Congress in Ghana's capital, Accra. He cultivated ties with the Soviet Union and the People's Republic of China. Nkrumah introduced, and his successors continued, a program of "African socialism," placing the economy under rigorous state control. In these new forms of socialism in Asia, Africa, and the Middle East, the state ran the economy, the ruling elite accumulated power and wealth, and there was little of the egalitarianism promised by traditional socialism. The Ghanaian economy, prosperous at independence with abundant natural resources, the world's largest producer of cocoa and the source of a tenth of the world's gold, declined in the years after independence and became heavily dependent on foreign loans, in large part because of ill-conceived development projects.

Fed up with Nkrumah's arbitrary rule, unbridled public and private extravagances, and cult of personality, military leaders ousted him in 1966. There then followed a series of new military coups in the country with brief sporadic efforts to return to constitutional and civilian rule. Finally, in 1979 a junior air force officer, Flight Lieutenant Jerry John Rawlings, seized

Power of the military

control. He introduced a program of self-sufficiency and austerity and curbed state social-ism. With financial assistance from the World Bank and market reforms the economy in the late 1980s began to show significant growth. By the early 1990s Rawlings was offer-ing the promise of a more liberal political regime, including free, multiparty elections. At the opening of the new century he even voluntarily surrendered power and made way for an elected successor. There was reason to hope that Ghana might be moving toward democracy.

Nigeria

Nigeria, the largest British-governed colonial territory in Africa, became the most popu-lous country in postcolonial Africa, with a population of over 110 million by the opening of the twenty-first century, and with 250 ethnic groups. The four largest, the Hausa and Fu-lani in the north and the Yoruba and Ibo in the south, all of which had had distinctive im-portant cultures, trading economies, and city-state organizations in precolonial times, com-prised two-thirds of the population. Britain had established its hold over the country through conquests and treaties in the mid–nineteenth century, but it had governed "indi-rectly" through local traditional rulers, thereby providing Nigerians with little or no role in self-government at higher levels.

Western-educated Nigerians, who had pressed for political representation in the 1920s, stepped up pressure after the Second World War. In 1960 Britain granted Nigeria independence and in 1963 it became a republic, with the respected nationalist leader Nnandi Azikewe as its first president. To cope with the country's ethnic diversity, the con-stitution established three large geographical regions and 21 federal states. With a constitution, democratic machinery, a federal structure, political par-ties, and guarantees of civil rights the Nigerian republic held the promise of serving as a democratic model for the rest of the continent.

The promise of democracy

Unfortunately, regional and ethnic tensions, civil war, and a succession of military coups thwarted that promise. Only six years after independence a brutal civil war broke out. Because the northern region had come to dominate the government, the ed-ucated and economically advanced Ibos in the south, mostly Christian, saw themselves as excluded from an appropriate national role. In 1966 Ibo army officers staged a coup, but a Hausa-led military takeover almost immediately followed and became the signal for a widespread slaughter of Ibos. Large numbers fled to the east, where in 1967 they pro-claimed an independent state of Biafra. A terrible civil war and blockade lasted $2^1/2$ years, from 1967 to 1970, and resulted in close to a million deaths from the blockade and star-vation. The Ibo secession collapsed. After the war the federal government followed a pol-icy of reconciliation, reintegrated the Ibos into national life, and sought, with some suc-cess, to overcome other regional and ethnic differences.

Coups and assassinations

But more coups and assassinations took place and the military re-mained in control. In 1979 General Olusegnu Abusanjo after three years of military rule restored civilian government, but in 1985 a new coup returned the military to power. Although they promised to restore free elections, they did not do so until eight years later.

For a time, in the early 1970s, Nigeria enjoyed a booming economy, based on its large oil resources, which made it the world's sixth largest oil producer. Lagos, the Nigerian cap-ital at the time, quadrupled in size. But in the 1980s, when the world market experienced an oil glut, petroleum prices plummeted. The oil wealth had failed to stimulate broader

Nigeria has become one of the world's most important producers and exporters of crude oil since the 1970s. This oil derrick in the delta of the Niger River is part of the booming petroleum industry, which accounts for much of Nigeria's income from international trade but also makes the economy vulnerable to rapid, global fluctuations in the price of oil.

(Liaison Agency)

economic development and corruption was endemic. Severe drought and a growing population forced dependence on food imports, which led to inflation and debt.

The 1990s brought important political changes. When the military eventually permitted presidential elections in 1993, the popular opposition leader Moshood Abiola clearly won, but the ruling general nullified the results and imprisoned Abiola. His death in prison five years later, allegedly of a heart attack, sparked nationwide protests that eventually brought a restoration of civilian government. In the 1999 elections the voters turned to General Obesanjo, who 20 years earlier had been the first Nigerian military ruler to give up power voluntarily to a civilian regime. Nigeria's early promise of parliamentary democracy, repeatedly frustrated over the past four decades, received a new chance. Nigeria was moving also toward a leading regional peacekeeping role in the affairs of the African continent.

Shift to a civilian regime

End of British Rule in East Africa: Kenya, Tanzania, Uganda

In East Africa, especially in Kenya, the independence movement after 1945 encountered obstacles. European settlers, who had arrived early in the century in considerable numbers, dominated economic and political life. They had dispossessed the Kikiyu and Maasai peoples to create large coffee and tea plantations on the most desirable land. Many Indians had also arrived from South Asia as merchants and traders. Africans, restricted to working as subsistence small farmers, agricultural laborers, and unskilled workers in the cities, resented their own economic and social status.

In the 1920s young nationalist leaders, many of whom, like Jomo Kenyatta, had studied abroad, agitated for land reform and African representation in government. After the Second World War a movement for independence led by

Kenyatta and Kenyan independence

Kenyatta and his party gathered momentum. When the European settlers stubbornly resisted pressures for independence, the militants responded with violence and acts of terrorism. The settlers retaliated, and as the violence mounted the British declared a state of emergency and imprisoned or removed from the troubled area many of the nationalist leaders. Eventually, however, the British faced up to the inevitable. They ended the state of emergency, released Kenyatta, and in 1963 granted Kenya independence. Over 55,000 Europeans left the country.

Kenya became a republic in 1964 with Kenyatta as its first president. Until his death 14 years later he completely dominated political life. Despite a constitution and a facade of parliamentary government, he permitted only one legal party and imprisoned ethnic and political opponents. He followed the all-too-familiar pattern of the independence leader turning dictator after independence. Like other new African leaders he championed pan-Africanism and neutralism in the Cold War.

When he died in office in 1978, Daniel arap Moi, who had been his vice president, governed under the same kind of authoritarian one-party regime, rejecting pressures for liberalization. The economy deteriorated and unemployment ran high. Riots and ethnic violence cost thousands of lives. International lending agencies refused to provide aid until reforms were undertaken. At the opening of the new century, despite some political changes, Kenya was still far from practicing democracy or introducing needed economic reforms.

Tanzania

Tanzania came into existence as a result of a union between two former colonial states in East Africa. In 1961 the British granted independence to Tanganyika, where they had exercised a UN trusteeship over what in 1914 had been part of German East Africa, and to Zanzibar, a British island protectorate since 1890. After a leftist revolution in Zanzibar that pitted black Africans against the Arab sultan, the two states united in 1964 to form Tanzania.

Here, too, the nationalist leader dominated the government after independence. Julius Nyerere allowed only one party, and relinquished power to a successor in 1985 only after holding office for 25 years, but his rule in many ways was progressive. By promoting literacy and establishing Swahili along with English as the official language of public life, he helped unite the country's ethnic and linguistic groups. His economic policies were less successful and the country remained impoverished. Also a champion of "African socialism," he nationalized much of the economy, including agriculture. In the Cold War he drew close to the Soviet Union and to China, and for a time Tanzania served as a principal bridgehead for Chinese Communist influence on the African continent. Under Nyerere's successors, the government denationalized many state industries, sought to end overly rigid economic controls, and restored collective farms to family cultivation. In 1995 it held its first multiparty elections. Meanwhile the country's problems were aggravated by a flood of hundreds of thousands of refugees from civil wars in neighboring states.

Uganda

Uganda, which Winston Churchill once described as the "pearl of Africa" because of its natural beauty, won independence in 1962. It, too, encompassed many ethnic groups. In the late nineteenth century Britain had come to dominate the kingdom of Buganda and the territories that bordered it, and in 1894 the East African area became officially a British protectorate known as Uganda. It was the scene of much missionary activity. Both Protestantism and Roman Catholicism made many converts so that the population became two-thirds Christian. While some permanent European settlers established large plantations, small African farmers cultivated cotton, tea, and coffee, and South Asians arrived to play a leading role as merchants. In 1921 Britain established a legislative council, but the first African members were admitted only in 1945, and not until several years later did they receive a substantial number of seats. As Britain prepared to grant independence, the kingdom of Buganda unsuccessfully demanded a separate state.

With independence near, political parties emerged and ethnic rivalries sharpened. Political organizations that were resentful and suspicious of Bugandan intentions coalesced into the leading party and Milton Obote, its leader, became prime minister. In 1963 a constitution transformed Uganda into a republic. As a compromise, the king of Buganda, the kabaka, was elected ceremonial president. But in 1966 Obote, bent on centralizing authority, forced the kabaka to flee the country. Obote promptly concentrated more and more power into his own hands, and over the next five years alienated many in the country. In 1971 a flamboyant, ruthless soldier, Idi Amin, rose from the ranks to become commanding general, seized power, and for eight years brutalized the country, shocking Africa and the world with executions, massacres, and torture. As many as 300,000 Ugandans may have lost their lives; *Idi Amin's reign of terror* entire ethnic groups were singled out for destruction. A once prosperous agricultural economy with thriving coffee, tea, and cotton exports lay in ruins. Professionals and intellectuals fled. In 1972 he expelled some 60,000 Asians, mostly Indians, who had been a strong presence in the country's commerce and industry. In 1976 he declared himself president for life. At last, in 1979, after he had invaded northern Tanzania over disputed border territory and devastated the area, a Tanzanian army, accompanied by Ugandan exiles, moved into Uganda and overthrew the dictator.

Obote, returning with the Tanzanian army, regained power and crushed all opposition forces to restore unity and authority. Additional tens of thousands lost their lives or fled to neighboring states. Eventually a guerrilla army under Yoweri Museveni, which had fought a guerrilla war against Idi Amin, now helped to overthrow Obote, and in 1986 Museveni took power. He moved to end what he deplored as the "massive hemorrhage" of Ugandan lives, set about to restore a measure of constitutional government, and with international assistance took the first steps to rehabilitate the devastated country. Economic production in Uganda in 1989 was one-fifth what it had been at the time of independence, but a measure of political stability, international financial assistance, and foreign investment made economic growth once again possible. The political atmosphere became freer. The government pioneered in aggressive steps to check the spread of the AIDS epidemic that was ravaging the country.

At the beginning of the new century Uganda still faced continued guerrilla warfare in the countryside led by a fanatical Christian religious leader. Museveni meanwhile became involved in the complicated and shifting warfare in Congo, disappointing some of his international supporters.

Southern Africa

In southern Africa the British peacefully transferred power in the early 1960s to black majority governments in Zambia (formerly Northern Rhodesia), Malawi, and Botswana. But elsewhere in this part of the African continent a white colonial minority held out against yielding or even sharing power.

Zimbabwe

In Southern Rhodesia (now Zimbabwe) the British government in London tried to negotiate political rights for the black majority before granting independence, but the small white community resisted, and in 1965 it unilaterally proclaimed independence from Britain. After 15 years of escalating guerrilla warfare and international political and economic pressure, the white leaders yielded. In 1980 Southern Rhodesia became Zimbabwe, with a black majority government. Within a few years the independence leader Robert Mugabe, combining the posts of president and prime minister, created a one-party state, which he continued to govern for the next two decades. Frustrated by the country's continuing economic difficulties, he allowed and even encouraged armed Africans to seize land that had long been in the hands of white fellow Zimbabweans; violence erupted in many parts of the country, creating alarming episodes of unrest and lawlessness at the opening of the new century.

The Union of South Africa

In the extreme south of the continent, in the Union of South Africa, a very special drama unfolded. In the late 1980s in a population of just over 40 million, about 6 million whites lived uneasily with 30 million blacks, 3 million people of mixed background (denominated "coloureds"), and 1 million Asians; both of the latter groups were classified as nonwhites. The whites, though a minority, were far more numerous than elsewhere in Africa south of the Sahara and had lived there for a long time. They were numerous enough to constitute a social and cultural outpost of European civilization and to develop the most prosperous economy of the continent, but they were greatly outnumbered, and many feared losing their dominant status. About half the whites, the Afrikaners, were mainly descendants of Dutch Calvinist immigrants from as far back as the founding of Cape Town in 1652; the other half represented immigration from Great Britain since the 1820s. The two halves did not easily mix. The Afrikaners, during their long isolation from Europe, developed a new language of their own, Afrikaans, derived from Dutch, and they retained unpleasant memories of British expansion, especially of the Boer war in the late nineteenth century.

In 1948 the Afrikaner-controlled Nationalist party came to power for the first time, campaigning for racial separation and the preservation of a white-dominated society. It legislated a sweeping policy of *apartheid* (the Afrikaans word for separation or segregation). The new laws excluded blacks from political life and imposed blatant forms of racial discrimination in housing, transportation, land ownership, and employment. Between 1950 and 1980 well over one million nonwhites in the cities were forced to leave white areas of residence and to relocate. Permits to blacks for urban jobs were granted only as industry required workers. Under a program of "separate development," the government also established four of a projected ten autonomous homelands *(bantustans)* for various black ethnic groups, but they met with little favor or outside acceptance. The land was poor and movement to the rest of the country was strictly regulated. The practices of apartheid and the racist laws enforcing it were internationally condemned. Finding itself increasingly isolated from the rest of the world, the South African government in 1961 broke all official ties with Britain and the Commonwealth and proclaimed itself the Republic of South Africa.

Apartheid and separate development

Opponents, black and white, of the restrictive laws encountered police brutality, torture, preventive detention, and prison sentences. Nelson Mandela, the black leader of the African National Congress, was sentenced to life imprisonment. The black leadership of the African National Congress turned to armed struggle, strikes, riots, and demonstrations, which the regime forcefully suppressed. There were tragic clashes at Sharpeville in 1960 and at Soweto in 1976, among others, costing the lives of hundreds of black protesters. By the 1970s increasing numbers of whites were protesting apartheid, and the United Nations had imposed sanctions. The United States, which had gone through its own civil rights movement in the 1960s to overcome the legacy of slavery and racism and had its own black heroes like Martin Luther King, Jr., joined in the economic sanctions and encouraged business corporations to withdraw or withhold investments.

The international political and economic pressures began to have an impact on the regime. A more enlightened wing of the Nationalist party attempted to moderate the apartheid laws, but initial reforms aroused opposition from Afrikaner diehards. In 1989 President F. W. de Klerk, anxious to defuse the explosive situation and sensitive to international opinion as well as the threatened deterioration of the economy, accelerated the reform program. In 1990 the

Countdown to democracy

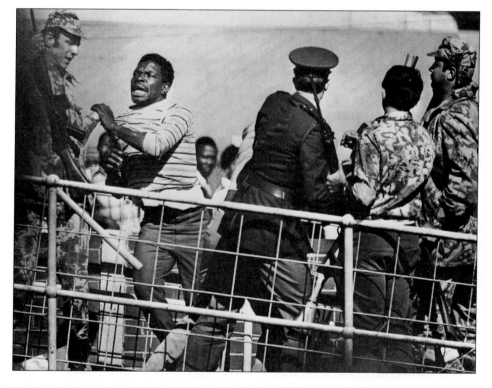

Black protestors often clashed with the police during the long era of official racial segregation under South Africa's apartheid laws. This picture shows one such clash in 1976 in Soweto, where numerous demonstrations were violently repressed and several hundred people were ultimately killed.

(Hulton-Deutsch Collection/Corbis)

government freed Nelson Mandela, who had become an internationally hailed hero and martyr after his more than 27 years in prison. In 1991 the government repealed all of the apartheid laws, ending over a half-century of enforced legal segregation. A year later the white electorate voted overwhelmingly in a referendum to end white minority rule. In Mandela's words, the "countdown to democracy" had begun.

In 1994 the first democratic nonracial elections, in which 22 million voters participated, brought Mandela and the African National Congress to power with provisions for a multiparty government of national unity during the period of transition. In 1996 the country adopted a constitution with the broadest bill of rights to be found anywhere in the world. It not only guaranteed political freedoms, but it also proclaimed social and economic entitlement to adequate food, housing, education, and health care. Meanwhile a Truth and Reconciliation Commission held hearings that disclosed the former government's full panoply of cruel abuses and acts of violence. In what many considered a model worthy of imitation in other post-autocratic regimes, amnesty was guaranteed to all who came forward with confessions of wrongdoing.

Freedom and challenges

After its long travail, and with enormous challenges, South Africa at last had the opportunity to create a nonracial democratic political system. The government in its first five years brought electricity and clean water to millions. During the country's second post-apartheid elections, in 1999, the African National Congress party came under heavy criticism for not accomplishing more but again won a sweeping victory and Thabo Mbeki replaced Nelson Mandela, who was voluntarily retiring, as the country's president. South Africa still faced poverty, unemployment, and a high crime rate, all heightened by the spread of AIDS. Land ownership remained predominantly in white hands; 85 percent of the population was black, but they owned only about 20 percent of the land. The standard of living for white South Africans, it was estimated, ranked 24th in the world; that of black South Africans, 126th. But the battle for the most elementary political and social freedoms had been won.

The political transformation affected other people in the region because the white-dominated earlier regime had intervened to oppose black-led independence movements in other African countries. At the same time it had refused to surrender its international trusteeship over what had once been German Southwest Africa. The black leadership there, with the support of the United Nations, sought independence as the new state of Namibia, but it required a long guerrilla war before Namibia's independence was officially recognized in 1990.

The French Sub-Saharan Empire

The French, largely as a consequence of the bloody war in Algeria, dissolved their vast colonial empire in sub-Saharan Africa peacefully. After the Second World War they had hoped that a French-educated and assimilated African elite would maintain ties to France in a loosely organized French Union. They gave the African colonies representation in the French National Assembly and promised self-governing institutions, but control remained centralized in Paris and by the mid-1950s the African colonies, inspired by nationalist movements elsewhere, pressed for independence. De Gaulle recognized the inexorable pressure for independence and offered the black sub-Saharan colonies their freedom of choice. By 1960 all 15 colonies had chosen independence.

French aid and cooperation

Many, however, retained close ties with France for economic aid and cultural cooperation. France remained a strong presence among the African francophone nations (and indeed the strongest presence of all the Western countries on the African continent), training the armies of the new states, lending financial assistance, and taking a leading role in economic development.[1] On almost a dozen occasions after 1960 the French intervened with military force. In 1979 they helped overthrow a brutal dictator who had seized power in the Central African Republic in 1966 and for 13 years ruled as head of a self-proclaimed Central African Empire. In Chad, they intervened when rebels in the north backed by Libya threatened to overthrow the government. The French organized the African Financial Community, helped stabilize African currencies, and became the largest donor of aid to the continent. While some African leaders criticized the French presence as neocolonialism, others viewed it more as a partnership than an intrusion. As elsewhere in Africa, the promise of democratic government in the former French colonies turned for the most part into civilian or military dictatorships, even if the degree of repression varied. Here too the independence party often became the sole legally recognized political party. Presidents concentrated power in their own hands, often holding office for 20 years or more. As late as 1998 in Senegal, by no means the worst example of repression, the parliament passed a law allowing its second president to become president for life. In 1999 Ivory Coast experienced its first military coup since independence in 1960.

The Belgian Congo: From Mobutu's Zaire to the Democratic Republic of Congo

The Belgian Congo was a byword for European imperialist exploitation in the late nineteenth century. The most abusive features were remedied before 1914, but political control remained concentrated in Brussels and little was done to prepare the large colony (it was 80 times the size of Belgium) for self-government. Agitation for independence intensified when the French African colonies, including the French Congo, its capital at Brazzaville, won independence in 1960 and became the Republic of Congo.

Faced with pressure for independence, the Belgian government, which had first proposed a transition period of 30 years, decided against gradualism and in 1960 announced its withdrawal in six months' time. Chaos followed. The two key nationalist leaders, one of them the leftist leader Patrice Lumumba, were at odds with one another. Ethnic and regional antagonisms ran deep, and no one was prepared to carry out governmental responsibilities. The army mutinied, and the soldiers turned against their European officers. Meanwhile the copper-producing province of Shaba (then called Katanga) attempted to secede. Belgian paratroopers hastily flew back, and a United Nations international military force attempted to restore order. When Lumumba was assassinated in 1961, the troubled situation became even more volatile because of a threatened Soviet-Western confrontation. The Soviets charged the Europeans and their American supporters with deliberately creating the chaos so that the Europeans might return.

Cold War entanglement

---

[1]The francophone, or French-speaking, sub-Saharan African states emerging from the French colonial empire in 1960 were Benin (until 1975 called Dahomey), Cameroon, Central African Republic, Chad, Republic of Congo (Brazzaville), Gabon, Guinea, Ivory Coast, Madagascar (or Malagasy Republic), Mali, Mauritania, Niger, Senegal, Togo, and Burkina Faso (until 1984 called Upper Volta). Comoros became independent in 1975; Djibouti, in 1977. Morocco, Algeria, and Tunisia, in North Africa, are also part of francophone Africa as former French protectorates, as are the Democratic Republic of Congo (once the Belgian Congo, and from 1971 to 1997 called Zaire), and Burundi and Rwanda (once Belgian trusteeships).

**Mobutu
and Zaire**

The Shaba secession was halted, but the government with Belgian and American support continued to battle leftist rebels. Eventually, in 1965, Colonel Joseph Désiré Mobutu established a dictatorship that would last for the next 32 years. He at once nationalized the large mining enterprises and other parts of the economy. To symbolize the new era, all geographical and personal names were Africanized. He himself took the name Mobutu Sese Seko. The country became Zaire, as did the famous river. The capital city of Leopoldville and the second largest city, Stanleyville, both carrying names reminiscent of European imperialism, became Kinshasa and Kisangani; Lake Albert became Lake Mobutu.

Zaire, the third largest country in size in Africa (second only to Sudan and Algeria), its cities widely separated and with poor, overgrown roads, had vast copper, diamond, cobalt, and other mineral resources, but its potential riches remained undeveloped and Mobutu's extravagances over the years drove the country to the brink of economic ruin. By his last years it had fallen heavily into debt, was dependent on imported food, and had become increasingly corrupt. The United States, to prevent the expansion of Communist influence, continued its financial assistance and used the country as a base for operations against neighboring countries like Angola, where leftist regimes were fighting to establish themselves.

**Democratic
Republic
of Congo**

When in 1987 Mobutu could no longer count on American support, he met his mounting domestic opposition by agreeing to multiparty elections, but he ignored the results and continued his dictatorial rule over the next several years. Meanwhile guerrilla forces, the principal one led by Laurent Kabila, with support from Zaire's neighbors Rwanda and Uganda, gathered strength and in 1996 swept through the country in a seven-month campaign, meeting little resistance. Kabila's forces gained control of the capital in 1997 and forced Mobutu to flee. Zaire took back its old designation Congo and officially became the Democratic Republic of Congo. One of the most repressive, corrupt, and ruthless dictatorships of postcolonial Africa came to an ignominious end and Mobutu died in exile a few months later.

But the country's troubles were not over. Satisfaction over Mobutu's downfall faded when Kabila, assuming a dictatorial role himself, banned all political parties except his own, arrested rival opposition leaders, and refused to permit a UN-sponsored human rights investigation into the brutal acts of his army. Because he relied on troops from neighboring countries and made no effort to build a national army, many in the country came to view him as a puppet of neighboring states who were eager to pillage Congo's vast resources. Because Kabila's weak hold on power disturbed his former allies, Rwanda and Uganda opened a military campaign to overthrow him and soon controlled half the country. By 2000 five separate nations had armed forces warring in Congo, supporting or opposing Kabila, and Rwanda and Uganda were fighting each other. The following year Kabila was assassinated and a hasty effort was made to provide stability by swearing in his son as his successor. But further turmoil and even disintegration threatened.

**An unrealized
renaissance**

In the 1990s many observers hoped for an "African renaissance"—an end to dictatorships or at least to their liberalization, to economic progress, and to the cessation of ethnic, civil, and regional wars. But in many parts of the continent democratization or peace remained unrealized in the opening years of the twenty-first century.

Burundi and Rwanda

Belgium, which had governed colonial Congo directly, had also administered under a League mandate and a UN trusteeship two small territories that had been part of German East Africa before 1914. In 1962 they became the independent states of Burundi and Rwanda. Both were predominantly Christian, divided between Roman Catholics and Anglicans. Although the two states went their separate ways, there were many parallels. Long-standing tensions between the dominant Tutsi minority and a resentful Hutu majority, partly a legacy of colonial policies, had led to power struggles and internecine warfare over the years but nothing comparable to the tragic events that took place in the mid-1990s.

The Hutu, a Bantu people, the original settlers, were agricultural farmers. The Tutsi (or Watusi) arrived, possibly from Ethiopia, in the late fifteenth century. A tall warrior people who were cattle herders, they came to dominate the more numerous Hutu who worked the land for them in a kind of semifeudal relation. The German and later the Belgian colonial administrators favored the Tutsi, treating them as an elite group and enlisting their assistance in governing. After the Second World War, however, a new generation of Belgian administrators shifted to the view of redressing the balance in favor of the Hutu majority. When independence came the Tutsi were still in control of the army and government, but the Hutu saw an opportunity to avenge themselves for the years of subjugation.

The Hutu and the Tutsi

In Burundi an army captain in 1966 overthrew the traditional monarchy and declared the country a republic. Six years later when the exiled king returned under a safe-conduct guarantee, he was seized and executed by the Tutsi-controlled government. The Hutu rebelled and set off one of the worst ethnic conflicts in Africa to that time, massacring some 10,000 Tutsi; this in turn led to Tutsi reprisals and the deaths of thousands of Hutu. Tutsi military regimes succeeded one another. In 1987 one such regime pledged itself to work for ethnic reconciliation and in 1993 allowed presidential elections. A Hutu, the first ever, was elected president. His efforts to form a stable, ethnically balanced government proved difficult. In Rwanda, meanwhile, similar efforts at reconciliation had led to the election of a Hutu president who proceeded to show good faith by appointing Tutsi ministers to the cabinet. In April 1994 an unexpected catastrophe occurred. A plane carrying the presidents of Burundi and Rwanda returning from a conference was shot down under mysterious circumstances, killing both presidents.

In Rwanda the event set off a wild outburst of revenge by Hutu extremists, who broadcast radio calls for a wholesale massacre of Tutsi. In a few weeks' time over a half million Tutsi were killed, along with Hutu moderates who refused to go along. The killings were accompanied by all kinds of atrocities. Men, women, and children seeking refuge in churches were tracked down and slain, at times with the complicity of Hutu Roman Catholic and Anglican clergy. The international community, meanwhile, stood aside while the massacres went on unchecked. The worst carnage ended when Tutsi armed exiles, many of whom had been living in Uganda, swept back into the country, subdued the Hutu extremists, and reestablished a government pledged to work out some form of reconciliation.

Outburst of revenge

But armed Hutu extremists in considerable numbers had fled to the eastern borderlands of neighboring Congo, and Rwanda became enmeshed in Congo's civil war, which soon turned into a regional multinational war.

Regional warfare

The brutal violence of Hutu extremists in Rwanda sent a flood of refugees into the neighboring countries of central Africa in 1994. Hundreds of thousands of people in Tutsi communities were massacred, along with many thousands of Hutu moderates. Both Tutsi and Hutu families fled from the atrocities and joined other refugees in places such as this makeshift "camp" in the Congolese city of Goma. The people in this group were mostly Hutus, but the violence and displacement tragically affected everyone in Rwanda.

(Mark Peters/Sipa Press)

All these events posed problems for the international community. It could not intervene in all cases of civil war to prevent human rights atrocities, but there was wide agreement that some middle ground had to be found between international intervention and the almost complete failure to act during the racist brutality and wholesale slaughter in Rwanda in 1994.

End of the Portuguese Colonial Empire

Of all the colonial powers Portugal, itself under authoritarian dictatorship until 1974, clung longest to its colonies, symbols of grandeur from the days of Vasco da Gama's explorations and the early age of European expansion. To retain Angola, on the southwestern African coast, and Mozambique, on the southeastern, both of which at one time had been flourishing centers of the slave trade and had been under Portuguese rule for over 400 years, the Portuguese dictatorship stubbornly suppressed anticolonial revolts which broke out in 1961 and lasted 13 years. It was in the course of the fighting that disaffected officers and soldiers in the army, radicalized by the prolonged colonial war, turned against the regime and overthrew it in 1974. The following year Portugal granted independence to Angola, Mozambique, and its smaller African colonies. Hundreds of thousands of Portuguese fled.

In Angola independence touched off a struggle for power by competing groups in which outside powers intervened, the Soviet Union and Cuba on the one side, the United States and South Africa, still under its apartheid regime, on the other. The Soviet bloc provided weapons and advisers to a Marxist faction, and the Cuban dictator Fidel Castro, who projected himself as a Marxist-Leninist defender of oppressed colonial peoples everywhere, dispatched 50,000 troops. Although the leftist group won out, proclaiming a "people's republic" in 1976, anti-Communist rebel groups with the support of the United States and South Africa continued the struggle. The war dragged on and cost hundreds of thousands of lives. Not until the early 1990s did the outside powers withdraw, the arduous task of economic reconstruction begin, and UN-supervised elections take place, but with renewed strife still threatening.

Angola

Mozambique, also a "people's republic," became engaged for the next 16 years in warfare with a militant rightist insurgency. The continuing wars and such natural disasters as drought and famine cost the small country over half a million lives and created one and a half million refugees. In the early 1990s both Angola and Mozambique abandoned Marxism, loosened economic controls, and turned to the West for desperately needed economic assistance.

Mozambique

Ethiopia, Eritrea, Somalia, and Sudan

Ethiopia, Eritrea, and Somalia, on the Horn of Africa, the northeastern part of the continent, had all been part of Italy's short-lived East African empire. Ethiopia, conquered by Mussolini in 1936, was the last European colonial annexation in Africa. After the Italian armies were routed by British and Ethiopian forces in 1941, Haile Selassie returned as emperor. But a Soviet-backed military coup in 1974 deposed him, established a Marxist, vehemently anti-Western regime, and transformed the country into a client state of the Soviet Union. Eventually the Soviets lost interest in supporting Ethiopia, partly because of its costly war against Eritrean secessionists, and Ethiopia turned to the West. Eritrea, which Ethiopia had annexed, had launched a military campaign for independence in the early 1960s. In 1993 a new regime in Ethiopia finally recognized its independence, but this did not prevent a deadly war over border disputes from breaking out between Eritrea and Ethiopia later that decade, which was not settled until the spring of 2000.

Somalia, partly under Italian control before 1914, and eventually placed under a postwar UN trusteeship, won independence in 1960. An army coup brought a Soviet-backed military dictatorship to power. But when Somalia in 1977 invaded Ethiopia, laying claim to a region where many Somalis lived, the Soviets chose to support Ethiopia. Soviet military aid (and 17,000 Cuban troops airlifted from Angola) assured Ethiopia's victory. Somalia shifted its allegiance to the West but soon fell under dictatorship. War broke out between competing warlords after the fall of the dictatorship, and by the early 1990s Somalia had fallen into virtual anarchy. Neither American nor UN peacekeeping troops were able to restore order and stability.

Somalia

Sudan, on the very eve of independence in 1956, when joint Anglo-Egyptian rule ended, fell into a long civil war. The black population in the south, who were mainly Christian but also followers of traditional African animist faiths, rose in rebellion against the Arab government in the north, which was intent on imposing Islamic law on the entire country. After the government put down the rebellion, which lasted 17 years and cost over a million and a half lives, it granted a

Sudan

measure of autonomy to the south. But the stubborn efforts in later years to extend Islamic law by force provoked renewed violence and resistance.

The casualties of the wars, famine, and drought from which Ethiopia, Eritrea, Somalia, and Sudan suffered in the postwar years numbered in the millions, and the turmoil displaced a flood of some two million refugees.

Liberia and Sierra Leone: Civil War

Civil war also devastated Liberia, the only country in Africa that had not formed part of a European colonial empire. Founded in the early nineteenth century in West Africa as a home for emancipated American ex-slaves, it became an independent republic in 1847. The black American settlers and their descendants, although never more than a small percentage of the population, dominated the country's business and political life. After years of relative stability, Liberia fell victim to the postcolonial ferment in Africa. In 1980 an army sergeant, alleging misrule and corruption on the part of the ruling settler group, staged a bloody coup and held power for the next ten years. His overthrow by a former aide in 1989 precipitated a brutal $3^{1}/2$-year civil war in which tens of thousands of lives were lost, civilians were massacred, and half the population was left homeless. African peacekeeping forces finally ended the violence in the early 1990s, but Liberians continued to face the uncertainties of an unstable government and the threat of renewed political violence.

Black American settlers

Sierra Leone, whose capital, Freetown, had once been the principal British base for enforcing the international ban on the slave trade, also became the scene of deadly civil war in the 1990s and of human rights atrocities. A rebel leader used the country's rich diamond mines to purchase unlimited arms for his followers. His forces killed or deliberately mutilated thousands of civilians, including children, sparking outrage in international circles. Kofi Annan, the Ghanaian-born UN secretary general, remarked in 1998 that the challenge was "a matter of defending humanity itself." Nigeria and other West African nations organized regional intervention to restore order, with some success.

Human rights atrocities

The African Revolution

For Africa one age came to a close after the Second World War and a new era opened. The map of contemporary Africa shows the vast political transformation, the emergence of 53 states, 48 of them in sub-Saharan Africa (see map, p. 898). One unfinished item on the political agenda, the extension of democratic rights to the black majority in South Africa, was resolved with the momentous transfer of power in 1994, and democratic movements also gained power in several other African nations during the last years of the same decade.

Uhuru and négritude

Independence provided a deep source of self-esteem. The word *uhuru,* freedom, rang through the continent in the heady days of decolonization. Léopold Senghor, the poet-president of the formerly French colony of Senegal, gave voice to the idea of *négritude,* a powerful far-reaching black self-consciousness, a pride in ancient cultural roots, which also struck a responsive chord in Americans of African descent whose ancestors had been brought in chains from lands like Senegal that were now modern sovereign states. Black Africa exulted when the Nigerian playwright, poet, and novelist Wole Soyinka, who blended Yoruba and Western traditions in his writings, received the Nobel Prize for literature in 1986. Meanwhile Chinua Achebe's novel about Nigeria during the early years of European colonialism, *Things Fall Apart* (1959), entered the canon of world literature.

The African revolution ended Western colonialism and ushered in a new era of independence and national sovereignty, but it did not automatically bring democratic government, civil and human rights, the resolution of ethnic and regional antagonisms (some of which were the residue of Europe's colonial policies and arbitrary boundary divisions), or a meaningful improvement in the quality of human lives. Ethnic hatreds, civil wars, regional conflict, and brutal internal repression cost the lives of millions. Africans killed Africans in the years of independence, mainly in civil wars within the borders of the new states. In the countryside ethnic loyalties often transcended national loyalties. Natural disasters, drought and floods, eroding soil, and diseases added to the continent's tribulations. At the opening of the twenty-first century African refugees from wars and repressive regimes made up over 6 million or close to one-fourth of the world's 22 million refugees; many more were uprooted and displaced in their own country. African agriculture and other economic activities remained hostage to world price fluctuations.

A new era

The social and economic situation was grim. In the late 1990s close to one-half of sub-Saharan Africa's population of 600 million survived on less than $1 a day. The continent's debt burdens amounted collectively to $200 billion. Many of the world's older infectious diseases such as malaria were still prevalent. The death toll from AIDS and the rate of infection from the HIV virus was devastating. Of the 36 million people in the world living with HIV, the virus that causes AIDS, over two-thirds were in sub-Saharan Africa. Some 15 million Africans had already died from it and 11 million had been left orphans. Scientists and others agreed that AIDS could well be the most serious infectious disease in recorded human history. For Africa it was described as the worst social disaster since the slave trade. All the hard-won gains in development, economic growth, and quality of life were in danger of reversal.

The new states began independence with constitutions, elected parliaments, independent judiciaries, and formal guarantees of civil liberties. But under the pressure of ethnic conflict, economic burdens, and political instability, the machinery of constitutional government quickly succumbed to dictatorship, generally military. In country after country, generals, admirals, colonels, majors, and officers of lesser rank pushed aside the civilian rulers. The warrior caste, often a law unto themselves, became the accomplices and tools of the new rulers, tyrannizing the population. Nigeria, which at least made sporadic efforts to preserve constitutional government (and its federal system for the multiethnic state), counted six military coups in the years from 1966 to 1985. At the very outset, charismatic independence leaders—like Kwame Nkrumah in Ghana, Jomo Kenyatta in Kenya, and Julius Nyerere in Tanzania—transformed themselves into virtual dictators under varying forms of authoritarianism, becoming presidents for life. Of over 150 African heads of state in the first three decades of independence, only six voluntarily relinquished their offices. In Zambia and Ivory Coast, leaders like Kenneth Kaunda and Félix Houphouet-Boigny governed under a milder authoritarianism. But mainly the dictatorships were repressive, corrupt, and tyrannical. Until the late 1980s there were few examples of free elections, multiparty systems, political pluralism, orderly changes of government, or freedom from censorship.

Constitutional governments fall

Spread of democracy

But in the late 1980s and in the 1990s the spread of democracy world-wide caught up in Africa as well. By 1999, 32 of 53 African states had free or partly free elections of some credibility. The orderly election and presidency in South Africa of Nelson Mandela and the transition to his successor provided reassurances of South Africa's democratic progress. Nigeria ended years of repressive and corrupt military rule when the country was restored to civilian rule. A new generation of leaders paid increasing attention to health care, education, and women's needs and rights. In the 1990s more than 30 sub-Saharan countries adopted economic reforms liberalizing trade and investment, stabilizing currencies, and privatizing cumbersome and wasteful state enterprises. A small group of states showed economic growth rates of over 6 percent. The Organization of African Unity pledged to punish with economic sanctions any African government that came to power by military coup.

Yet talk of an African renaissance could not ignore the continent's continuing social and economic crises. At the opening of the twenty-first century sub-Saharan countries still filled all the bottom ranks in global tables of economic growth. Fewer than half of young Africans were attending schools, and the economic gap between Africa and the rest of the world was widening.

Africa's problems

No single theory could explain African problems. Some pointed to nineteenth-century European imperialist rule and exploitation as the root cause. Colonial rule lasted only a few generations but perhaps long enough to undermine African societies and institutions and yet not long enough to replace them with new ways of life. Above all, it had undeniably eroded African confidence and experience in self-governing institutions. On the other hand, postcolonial failure seemed to be largely a failure of leadership. When the European colonial rulers departed, they left highly centralized authoritarian states in the hands of small elite groups with little political experience. Europeans had established colonies like the Belgian Congo to be exploited for profit, and their postcolonial African successors often followed in the same path. The new rulers transformed the independence party into the sole or dominant government party. Although ostensibly opposed to ethnic separatism, the political leaders manipulated ethnic rivalries to enhance their own power. The Cold War also contributed to the setback of democracy in that the Western-Soviet competition for client states led to the support of dictators. American policy was designed to win and retain reliable allies in the fight against communism, and the Americans applied no litmus tests of democracy before giving financial aid. In the 1980s the four largest African recipients of American economic aid were the rightist dictators in Liberia, Somalia, and Zaire, and the anti-Communist rebel leader in Angola.

The key question for the African continent was how to anticipate and prevent crises leading to war, a goal that required institutional safeguards to ensure that the military remained subordinate and accountable to civilian authority. For the outside world the question was how to provide economic assistance that would be used constructively and improve the quality of life for all.

"No-party democracy"

Some Africans argued that to counter separatist ethnic and regional forces, cope with economic underdevelopment, and provide the cohesion necessary for national unity, strong, single-party governments were more effective than multiparty democratic systems. President Museveni, who had accomplished so much in Uganda to overcome the chaos and torment of the early years of independence, put his concept of a "no-party democracy" to a referendum in 2000, and voters accepted his recommendation that what he called "the Movement" be the sole governing party. Western-style democracy was still an alien concept for many Africans, difficult to nurture in societies with high illiteracy, a small middle class, and cultural traditions of lifetime tenure for chiefs and kings. But other Africans rejected such arguments and maintained that they should choose and control their rulers, and the governments they lived under, and one day would do so.

Many of the African states for a time were professedly Marxist. They spoke of "African socialism" and styled their regimes "people's democratic republics." In Mozambique the main avenues were named for Lenin and Mao Zedong; the flag of the People's Republic of the Congo (in colonial times the French Congo) flying in Brazzaville displayed a hammer and sickle. Such regimes turned away from free enterprise, which they identified with the profit-making, exploitation, and racial humiliation of Western colonialism. They looked to government, public ownership, and centralized planning to oversee new economic structures that would hasten development and provide a more egalitarian society. They nationalized their industries and collectivized agriculture. In the years of the Cold War many of these countries received technical and material assistance from the U.S.S.R., the Soviet bloc, and the People's Republic of China. But rigid state control and overly centralized planning (as in the Communist countries themselves) led to economic stagnation and corruption.

African socialism

Once self-sufficient in food, Africa after 1964 became an importer of food. Wars and preparations for wars were costly, so that expenditures on arms often exceeded the international financial assistance received for economic development. Yet in spite of the painfully slow progress in improving the quality of life, Africans in the first generations of independence felt a new sense of control over their own destiny. They were not eager to cast themselves in the Western democratic image or simply to follow Western economic models, although it increasingly appeared that globalization might well preclude other options. Nonetheless, economic growth was a prerequisite to survival and to the improvement of human lives, as were political stability and peace. All of these were still proving elusive, close to a half-century after independence.

117. FERMENT IN THE MIDDLE EAST

The Islamic and the Arab World

In the Islamic, or Muslim, world, the age of colonial domination also ended, and a powerful renewed sense of identity emerged. Much of the Islamic world was determined to share in modernization and Western material advances, but many parts of it resisted Western cultural patterns. Religious and cultural traditions slowed the pace of modernization or influenced emerging new institutions. An elitist organization of society, traditional obstacles to full equality for women, and widespread illiteracy presented powerful obstacles to social change. The 40 or so identifiable Islamic countries, Arab and non-Arab, differed vastly from each other so that the Islamic world had no single sense of identity. Although the pace of transformation was uneven, older life styles were undermined everywhere. In many cases strong tensions developed as Islamic traditionalists resisted secular changes. Turkey made a concerted effort to protect the secular society decreed by its founder, Kemal Atatürk, but elsewhere, in Saudi Arabia, Iran, Afghanistan, Sudan, and other countries, Islamic fundamentalism created virtual theocracies.

Islamic identity

The heartland of Islam was the Arab world and the Arabian peninsula, where the Muslim religion was founded by Muhammad in the seventh century. The Muslim calendar dates from the Hegira, or Muhammad's flight in 622 from Mecca to Medina (both of which are now part of Saudi Arabia). In Islamic belief the divine revelation to Muhammad and his message of redemption through Allah are accepted as a link to the ancient Hebrew prophets and to Jesus and the Christian Bible, with Muhammad held to be the last and greatest of the prophets. One of the great expansionist religions, Islam led to conquest in the name of Allah. So effective in spreading the faith were Muhammad's earliest followers that by the time of his death in 632 most of the Arabian peninsula had been brought under Islamic rule, as was nearby Palestine a few years later. Under the caliphs who succeeded Muhammad and who commanded both religious and secular authority, Islam swept from the Arabian peninsula into non-Arab lands. Turks and other non-Arab peoples who were converted to Islam continued the expansion. The Ottoman Empire, founded by the Ottoman Turks, ruled at its height in the sixteenth century over Arab and non-Arab peoples and included Palestine, with sites holy to Judaism, Christianity, and Islam. When the empire gradually disintegrated in the modern centuries, the Europeans expanded their economic and political influence in the Middle East. From the Ottoman Empire emerged many of the states of the contemporary Muslim world, Arab and non-Arab, at first as international trusteeships and mandates, and then as independent nations.

The Middle East

The term Middle East itself is imprecise but widely used. For the Europeans who coined the term it meant the geographic area midway between Europe and East Asia. The Near East, a term which has all but disappeared, was long used for the states bordering on or close to the eastern Mediterranean and was at one time also called Asia Minor. The Middle East is used now to designate that part of the world that is predominantly Islamic in religion and culture stretching from the states of North Africa to Western Asia. The major non-Arab Muslim states include Indonesia (with the world's largest Islamic population), Malaysia, Pakistan, Bangladesh, Afghanistan, and Iran (the only country where the Shiite rather than the Sunni branch of Islam prevails).[2] The Islamic world also includes a half-dozen states in central Asia in the former Soviet Union. Millions of Muslims, non-Arab and Arab, also live in India, in Africa, in the Balkans, and increasingly in western Europe and the United States. At the opening of the twenty-first century there were about 1.1 billion Muslims, or close to one-fifth the world's population, second in numbers only to Christianity in all its branches.

About one-fifth of the world's Muslims, or some 200 million, are Arabs, that is, people whose primary language is Arabic. Because the language of the Koran (Qur'an), used in the religious practices of Muslims worldwide, is Arabic, it is in a sense the second language of non-Arab Muslims as well. The Arab states stretch from the Atlantic coast of North Africa to the Persian Gulf, from Morocco to Iraq.[3] In that part of the Middle East lies a large part of the world's petroleum reserves on which the economic activity of the industrial world depends, and the region has been one of the modern world's most troubled areas.

The Arab states

The Arab states that emerged from the collapse of the Ottoman Empire at the end of the First World War became League of Nations mandates under British or French administration, with the expectation of one day re-

---

[2]The schism originated in an armed struggle over the succession to Muhammad after the prophet's death in 632, in which the Shiite faction supported Ali, Muhammad's son-in-law, and the Sunni favored another line of succession. The schism became permanent. There are also differences in doctrine and ritual between the two important divisions. The Shiite form of Islam became the state religion in Persia (Iran) in the sixteenth century and has remained dominant in Iran, but there are important Shiite communities in Iraq, Pakistan, Yemen, and elsewhere.

[3]The principal Arab states are Morocco, Algeria, Tunisia, Egypt, and Libya, in North Africa; Lebanon, Syria, Jordan, and Iraq (Israel's neighbors), close to the eastern Mediterranean; and Saudi Arabia, Yemen, Oman, the United Arab Emirates, Qatar, Bahrain, and Kuwait, in the Arabian peninsula.

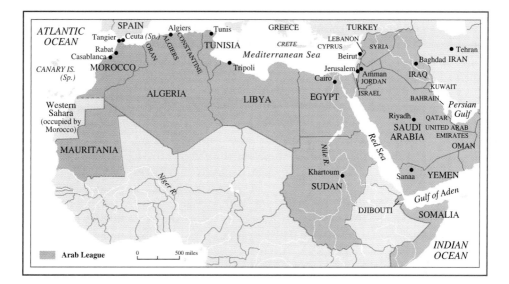

THE MODERN ARAB WORLD

The Arabic language zone is one of the most extensive in the world, reaching from the Atlantic Ocean to the Persian Gulf. In 1945 the Arab states formed a League, which came to have 22 members, including the Palestine Liberation Organization (PLO). The League proved to be rather loose and its members often disagreed, but after 1948 all Arab nations expressed varying levels of suspicion and hostility toward the Israeli state in the midst of an otherwise predominantly Arab world.

ceiving independence. Egypt became nominally independent in 1922 and Iraq, in 1932, although the British retained treaty rights in each until after 1945. The other Arab states became independent during or after the Second World War, when the British and French ended their mandates. In 1945 Egypt, Iraq, Lebanon, Saudi Arabia, Syria, and Jordan formed the influential League of Arab States, or Arab League. Libya, after gaining independence in 1951, also became a member. In the decades that followed, newly independent Arab states as well as the Palestine Liberation Organization (PLO) joined so that it grew to have 22 members by the 1970s.

The unity of the Arab world is more fragile than often thought. Divisive rivalries persist. The pan-Arabism advocated by Egypt's Colonel Nasser in the 1950s and Libya's Colonel Qaddafi in the 1980s failed to rally lasting support. A United Arab Republic joining Egypt and Syria in 1958 *Arab rivalries* was short-lived. After the Second World War, however, the Arab states found common cause in their opposition to the state of Israel, which itself emerged as a new sovereign state in the Middle East in 1948. The Arab states viewed Israel as a Western-backed intrusion into their land, and the result has been a series of continuing tensions and conflict since 1945 that brought even wider international forces into play.

The Emergence of Israel

Zionism, evolving in the late nineteenth century as a response to European anti-Semitism, became a movement to establish (or reestablish) a Jewish homeland in Palestine, then part of the Ottoman Empire. A small number of Jewish pioneers from Russia and eastern

Europe made their way to Palestine before 1914. During the First World War, while at war with the Ottoman Empire, the British by the Balfour Declaration of 1917 voiced support for "a Jewish homeland in Palestine" but in other ways supported emergent Arab nationalism. In 1923, after the demise of the Ottoman Empire, the British received a League of Nations mandate for Palestine, and a growing number of Jewish settlers arrived in the 1920s and 1930s.

The question of Palestine

The whole question of Palestine poignantly reemerged at the end of the Second World War when the homeless survivors of the Nazi Holocaust, which had all but wiped out central and eastern Europe's Jews, sought out Palestine as a place of refuge. But in deference to Arab protests the British limited immigration and turned away whole shiploads of refugees. The Jewish leaders pressed their cause with the United Nations and sympathetic American political circles and contested the British restrictions, at times resorting even to terrorist activities directed against the British. In 1947 the United Nations in a vote supported by both the United States and the Soviet Union adopted the recommendations of a UN committee which recommended partition of Palestine into two parts: a Jewish sector and an Arab sector, with the area around Jerusalem under international control.

The Arabs, who had boycotted the committee hearings, rejected the partition, complaining that they were being asked to make sacrifices for Europe's persecution of the Jews. Both sides prepared for conflict. On May 14, 1948, when the Zionist leaders proclaimed the Republic of Israel, Israel's five Arab neighbors, Syria, Lebanon, Jordan, Egypt, and Iraq, refused recognition and invaded the new state. The Israelis (as the citizens of the new republic called themselves) not only defended themselves but also counterattacked. In the course of the fighting at least 600,000 Palestinian Arabs fled, or in many cases were forced to flee, to Jordan, Lebanon, Syria, and other Arab states. During the war Jordan took over the West Bank of the Jordan River and part of Jerusalem and Egypt took the Gaza Strip, but elsewhere Israel gained territory.

By the end of hostilities and the armistice of 1949 Israel had increased its originally allotted land by about half. Jerusalem came under divided control. The plan for international control was abandoned. Jordan now governed East Jerusalem, but Israel retained control of West Jerusalem. The Arab states, unwilling to negotiate peace or even recognize the existence of Israel as a sovereign state, made little effort to absorb the Palestinian refugees who had fled to the Arab states and who continued to live in overcrowded, squalid refugee camps for decades to come.

The New State of Israel

A Jewish homeland

The Israelis saw themselves as creating a Jewish homeland after the Holocaust, so that persecuted Jews would never again be without a refuge. Under a Law of Return Jewish immigrants from anywhere in the diaspora were automatically entitled to citizenship. Secular-minded founders of the state like David Ben-Gurion did not define the role of religion too closely. Freedom of religion and freedom of conscience were equally to be protected, but rabbinical authorities controlled such matters as marriage and divorce, definitions of Jewishness, and observance of the Sabbath. Ultra-Orthodox Jews eventually came to exert influence out of proportion to their numbers and to create a larger political voice for themselves than originally envisaged.

After independence Israel built a modern, Western-style, urban, industrial society with a democratically elected parliament, the Knesset, and a lively political culture. For many years the moderately socialist Labor party governed. The country provided a large role for labor unions and agricultural cooperatives (famous as *kibbutzim*) and extensive health and educational services. About half the economy was government-controlled until a later shift to privatization.

Economic development took off swiftly. Through ingeniously engineered irrigation schemes the Israelis reclaimed vast stretches of the Negev *Economic growth* desert. The amount of land under cultivation more than doubled. In 1948 Israel produced only one-third of its food; by the early 1970s it was producing enough to meet almost all of its domestic needs and began to export. Industry expanded. Before long the Israelis exported electronic products, precision instruments, and military hardware. Extensive foreign investment, especially from the United States, further stimulated economic development. Living standards exceeded those of other countries in the Middle East and compared favorably to those of western Europe.

Over 2 million immigrants arrived in the decades after 1948. Many Jews arrived from the Arab states in North Africa and from Arab and non-Arab Muslim states in Asia, forced to abandon established communities where their families had lived for centuries but where Jews were now persecuted. From 1989 to 1992 about 400,000 Soviet Jews, finally permitted by the Soviet government to migrate, reached Israel. The population of 870,000 in 1948 reached about 5,750,000 by the opening of the twenty-first century. In the 1990s problems of unemployment, housing shortages, and a lack of skilled jobs surfaced, especially for the former Soviet Jews. At great financial strain, but benefiting from American foreign aid, the Israelis also developed powerful modern military forces and air power. They built nuclear reactors for the production of electric power and quietly created a nuclear military capacity.

The Arab-Israeli Wars after Independence

Four more Arab-Israeli wars were fought after 1948–1949, one in each of the next four decades, in 1956, 1967, 1973, and 1982. Israel, with Britain and France as allies, went to war with Egypt in 1956 when Egypt nationalized the Suez Canal and attempted to bar Israeli shipping. In 1967 Israel waged the Six-Day War against Egypt, Syria, and Jordan, when Egypt moved to close the Gulf of Aqaba to Israel, which would have strangled the Israeli economy. The outcome of the brief fighting in 1967 was momentous. After defeating the three Arab armies, Israel took from Jordan the West Bank of the Jordan River and East Jerusalem; from Syria the Golan Heights (from which the Syrians had been able to shell Israeli settlements); and from Egypt the Sinai Peninsula and Gaza Strip. Israel emerged with territory four times its original size; over one million additional Arabs came under Israeli rule.

The next conflict broke out in 1973 when Egyptian and Syrian forces attacked the Israelis on the Jewish holy day Yom Kippur. Israel recovered from the surprise attack, defeated the Syrian army, and trapped the Egyptian forces in the Sinai Peninsula. With the Israelis near victory and in control of additional Arab territory, the League of Arab States suddenly introduced a new strategic weapon in support of Egypt and Syria, an embargo on oil shipments. Although the embargo was lifted a few months later, early in 1974, the oil-producing nations had quadrupled the price of oil, with global economic consequences far beyond the conflict in the Middle East. Meanwhile, the war ended with an American-mediated settlement. Israel withdrew from the west bank of the Suez Canal, but continued to occupy most of the Sinai Peninsula.

In 1982 Israel invaded war-torn Lebanon, where virtual anarchy prevailed. Israel had become the target of repeated raids from Lebanese territory organized by the PLO and by guerrilla forces of Islamic sects armed by Islamic states, including Syria, Iraq, and Iran. Israeli forces pushed as far north as Beirut, forced the expulsion of the PLO, and then withdrew, although continuing for many years to hold a narrow security zone in southern Lebanon. No brief summary of these wars can convey the grief and suffering that each brought to the Israelis and to their Arab neighbors, and with no end in sight to the continuing tensions.

The Middle East became a theater of Cold War rivalries as well. The United States had disapproved of the Suez Canal intervention in 1956, but after that crisis it supported Israel even when it tried to prevent the flow of arms to the Middle East. France, originally a staunch ally, for a time turned against Israel when de Gaulle in the 1960s decided he needed to help restore a balance of power in the region by supporting the Arab states. The U.S.S.R., one of the original backers of the Jewish state, reversed itself and armed Egypt and other Arab states. The United States, following its Cold War strategy of containment, remained determined to prevent Soviet influence from expanding in the Middle East. The Eisenhower Doctrine pledging American support to countries in the Middle East resisting communism met with favor by Israel, while many of the Arab states, looking to the Soviets for support, resented it.

Middle East and the Cold War

The Palestinian Arabs became a highly volatile element and grew steadily more militant, conducting guerrilla warfare against Israel and engaging in terrorist activities within Israel and in other parts of the world. In 1964, under the leadership of Yasir Arafat, the PLO became a full member of the Arab League and received recognition in many quarters as a government-in-exile for the Palestinian Arabs. The PLO professed to speak for all Palestinians, not only the 1.5 million under Israeli occupation but also those who had fled as refugees and who by this time numbered as many as 3 million. The PLO demanded the evacuation of all territories occupied by Israel since 1967 and called for the establishment of a sovereign independent Palestinian state in the West Bank of the Jordan River and the Gaza Strip.

The PLO

The Arab states, Syria in the lead, continued to reject any settlement. In 1975 the Arab states persuaded the UN General Assembly, where the former colonial states of Asia and Africa now held a majority, to adopt a resolution condemning Zionism as a form of racism, even though Zionism had originated as a defense against anti-Semitism and Israel, as a response to the Nazi Holocaust. The resolution remained in effect until it was repealed in 1992.

Palestinian terrorist attacks within Israel and elsewhere altered the political scene in Israel itself. In 1977 Labor for the first time lost control of the government to a conservative, nationalist party of the center-right, Likud, founded by religious groups. Likud, too, could govern only through coalitions, but it generally received the support of the religious parties. The Israeli posture

Israelis vs. Palestinians

In one of the recurring cycles of Middle Eastern violence, Israel responded to attacks from guerrilla bases in Lebanon by sending its army as far north as Beirut in 1982. These Israeli troops were patrolling streets in the Muslim sector of the Lebanese capital during the military operation that drove the Palestine Liberation Organization out of Beirut. Although the Israeli army soon withdrew to southern Lebanon, Israel retained control over a small "security zone" within Lebanese territory until 2000.

(Nackstrand/Sipa Press)

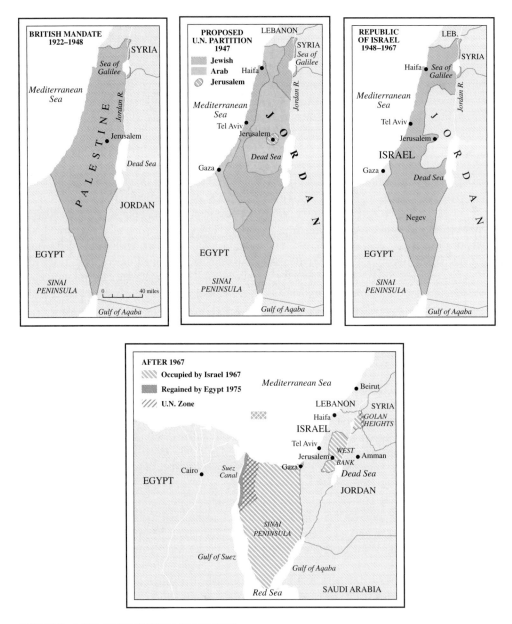

ISRAEL AND ADJOINING REGIONS

"Palestine" is the term by which Europeans long designated a small region of predominantly
Arab population on the east coast of the Mediterranean. The area belonged to the Ottoman
Empire until the end of the First World War. In 1922 the League of Nations made the territory
a mandate of Great Britain, which soon responded to Arab dissatisfactions by placing restrictions on the migration of European Jews, who had been moving into Palestine since the rise of
Zionism in the late nineteenth century. After the deaths of millions of Jews in the Holocaust
during the Second World War, the Zionist aspiration for an independent Jewish state won new
international support. In 1947 the United Nations proposed a partition of Palestinian lands to
create a new Jewish state and a division of the city of Jerusalem in a separate zone. The Arabs

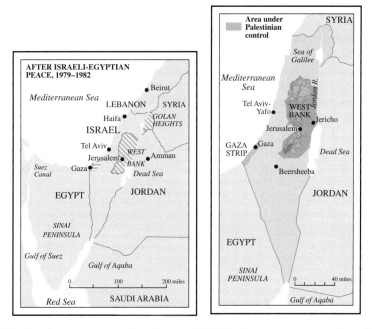

rejected this plan, but in the Arab–Israeli war of 1948 the Israelis won control of wider boundaries than those first proposed. The Arab states still refused to recognize Israel. In the Six-Day
War of 1967 the Israelis occupied additional territory, as shown in the fourth panel, labeled
AFTER 1967. In 1973, in the Yom Kippur War, Egypt and Syria attacked to regain their lost
lands, but Israel defeated them and continued to occupy the Sinai Peninsula and other territories, although Egypt eventually won control of the east bank of the Suez Canal. Under a peace
treaty that Israel and Egypt negotiated in 1979, Israel returned the Sinai to Egypt, but retained
the small area known as the Gaza Strip. In 1993 Israel agreed to begin withdrawing from some
areas of the occupied territories and allow the first steps toward self-government for the Palestinians. A new Palestinian Authority emerged to govern the autonomous Palestinian communities, but a long series of later conflicts and negotiations had still not led to a final peace settlement or an independent Palestinian state by the beginning of the twenty-first century.

toward the Palestinians became more intransigent. Menachem Begin as Likud prime min-
ister encouraged Israelis to make permanent settlements in the occupied West Bank of the
Jordan River (for which he even used the Biblical names of Judea and Samaria) and the
Gaza Strip, and he rejected negotiations with the PLO. In 1980 the government unified the
Israeli capital by unilaterally annexing East Jerusalem, which it had occupied since 1967.

Without a settlement new and even deadlier conflicts threatened to break out. At issue
were the disposition of the territories occupied by Israel since 1967, the demand of the
Palestinian Arabs for an independent national state, assistance to the Palestinian Arab
refugees, and the recognition and guarantee of Israel's legitimacy and security. The Egyptian president Anwar al-Sadat, recognizing the impasse and eager to recover lost Egyptian
territory, broke the united Arab front against Israel when in 1978 he visited Israel and addressed the Knesset in Jerusalem. In 1979, with the United States acting as mediator, Sadat and Begin signed a milestone peace treaty in Washington in the presence of President
Carter. Israel agreed to withdraw from the Sinai Peninsula except for the Gaza Strip and

was guaranteed the free use of the Suez Canal. Outraged at Sadat's recognition of Israel's legitimacy as a sovereign state, the other Arab states expelled Egypt from the Arab League. Sadat himself was later assassinated by Islamic extremists in his own army. His successor, President Mubarak, remained cautiously friendly to Israel, as did King Hussein of Jordan. Syria, Libya, and Iraq assumed the lead in rejecting any wider settlement. To thwart Iraq's growing nuclear capacity Israel in 1982 took the bold step of bombing a nuclear facility near Baghdad but meanwhile continued to build up its own unannounced nuclear capacity.

Israel, the Occupied Territories, and Peace Negotiations

In the 1980s over 1.5 million Palestinian Arabs lived in the West Bank and Gaza Strip, occupied by Israel since the 1967 war. At the end of 1987 nationalist agitation by young Palestinians flared up into a sustained uprising, the *intifada*, as it was called in Arabic. The Israeli military met the stone-throwing, fire-bombing, and civil disobedience with armed force, and casualties mounted. The suppression of the rebellion polarized Israel politically, hurt its economy, and threatened to undermine its democracy. The PLO exploited the popular uprising to press for recognition of an independent Palestinian state.

The intifada

As the Cold War wound down in the late 1980s, the Arab states could no longer be certain of Soviet support, and the United States continued to encourage negotiations. Any genuine settlement would have to revolve around the formula "land for peace": Israel to give up some or all of the territory occupied since 1967 in return for Arab recognition of Israel's legitimacy and existence. The status of the Palestinians would have to be resolved in favor of some form of self-government or statehood. Israel's continuing insecurity lay rooted in the fact that its small population lived in a hostile Middle East. A divided Israel, still haunted by Holocaust memories, feared for the nation's security and the safety of its citizens. For some, territorial expansion was one answer. Begin's successors continued the Likud party's support for increased Jewish settlement in the occupied territories. Many other Israelis recognized the legitimate grievances of the Palestinian Arabs, accepting the fact that Jews and Arabs had to find ways to live together in the small land.

"Land for peace"

In 1992 the possibilities of peace negotiations with the Arabs revived when a Labor coalition returned to office headed by Yitzhak Rabin and Shimon Peres. Rabin halted additional settlements in the West Bank and reopened peace talks. Although official negotiations continued, it was secret talks carried on between Israelis and Palestinians in Oslo, Norway, outside all regular diplomatic channels, that led in 1993 to an extraordinary agreement climaxed in a ceremonial signing by Prime Minister Yitzhak Rabin and Yasir Arafat in Washington in the presence of President Clinton. Under the Oslo accords Israel recognized the Palestine Liberation Organization as the representative of the Palestinian people and agreed to initial steps for Palestinian self-government, including its own security forces. The PLO in turn recognized Israel's legitimate existence as a sovereign state and agreed to abjure acts of violence. Despite many unresolved issues, Arab-Israeli relations seemed to be moving toward a settlement with the PLO, in which Jordan, Syria, and other Arab states might join. In accordance with the agreement Israel withdrew its armed forces from most of the Gaza Strip and from Jericho in the West Bank and took steps to allow Palestinian self-rule in the West Bank and in Gaza.

A fragile agreement derailed

But intransigent groups on both sides began to derail the fragile agreement. Violence erupted again, and in 1995 a fanatical Jewish extremist as-

Israeli Prime Minister Yitzhak Rabin and PLO Chairman Yasir Arafat signed the Oslo accords in Washington in September 1993. This diplomatic event marked the first official agreement between Israel and the Palestinians, and it set the agenda for later, inconclusive negotiations throughout the 1990s. Radicals on both sides condemned the terms of the Oslo agreement, however, and they soon turned to violence. Rabin became one of the victims when he was assassinated by a Jewish extremist in 1995. In this picture, Chairman Arafat is standing next to President Clinton as they both observe the Israeli prime minister signing the accords.

(Cynthia Johnson/TimePix)

sassinated Prime Minister Rabin. In 1996 Peres and the Labor coalition lost the elections to the hard-line Likud leader Benjamin Netanyahu, who immediately relaxed the freeze on new Jewish settlements in the West Bank and Gaza Strip. Even so, Netanyahu, yielding to pressure from the United States, met with Arafat in 1998 and agreed to carry out the Oslo agreement calling for surrender in stages of the occupied West Bank. Even these moderate concessions cost Netanyahu conservative and rightist support. Ehud Barak, a military man and former Israeli chief of staff, representing Labor, centrist, and some religious parties, campaigned on a pledge to move forward with peace negotiations and defeated Netanyahu. Under continuing American brokering, negotiations resumed. Israel began its withdrawal from the West Bank, and Barak, as he had promised, withdrew Israeli armed forces from its southern Lebanon security zone. Barak also made overtures to Syria over the return of all or part of the Israeli-held Golan Heights. His concessions alarmed many Israelis and he lost his majority in the Knesset. Still determined to represent what he considered the popular will for peace, he nonetheless met once again with Arafat in Washington in July 2000, but the new talks foundered, principally over the status of Jerusalem. Despite all that had been offered him, Arafat insisted on his obligation to the entire Arab and Muslim world to claim sovereignty over East Jerusalem and its Muslim holy places and make it the capital of the Palestinian state. Violence erupted again. Arafat, the Israelis protested, seemed unable to control his people. A new *intifada* broke out in the streets of Jerusalem and rapidly spread, provoked initially by an unannounced visit to Muslim sites in East Jerusalem by the hard-line Ariel Sharon, a former top military commander in earlier wars, a determined opponent of Barak's concessions, and now seeking to replace him. As Palestinian violence escalated, public opinion turned against Barak, and in early 2001 Sharon became prime minister by a sweeping popular vote. Many Israelis remained troubled. Some were willing to support

A new intifada

the surrender of the occupied territories to the Palestinian Arabs and to work out compromises on the Israeli settlements and other issues. But many more believed that the concessions had gone too far. They too wanted peace but with firmer guarantees of security. The opportunity for a peace settlement on the basis of the Oslo accords seemed to have slipped away and the troubled region faced renewed guerrilla warfare, Israeli reprisals, and new casualties on both sides.

Libya and Syria

Libya and Syria both added to the explosiveness in the Middle East. The discovery of oil in Libya in 1959 transformed a country of 4 million people into a leading petroleum producer. In 1969 Colonel Muhammar al-Qaddafi ousted the existing monarchy, established a personal dictatorship, and agitated for an extremist Arab nationalism. Using his country's oil wealth for political purposes, he projected himself as a spokesman for pan-Arabism and aspired to a leadership role in African affairs as well. Libya became headquarters for terrorist activities in Europe and elsewhere. Neither economic sanctions nor even military reprisals deterred Qaddafi. In 1997 the United States officially included Libya on its short list of states actively sponsoring international terrorism.

Muhammar al-Qaddafi

The early years of the Syrian Arab Republic were marked by extreme political instability and a succession of military coups. In 1963 one such coup brought the pan-Arab Socialist Baath party to power and banned all other parties. In 1971, in the tenth coup of its kind, Hafez al-Assad, a former defense minister, took power and ruled dictatorially for close to 30 years until his death in 2000. Assad ruthlessly suppressed all opposition, including an insurrection of the Muslim Brotherhood in 1982, in which his air force killed tens of thousands.

Hafez al-Assad

Assad remained one of the most resolute enemies of Israel, intent on recovering all the Arab territory lost since 1967, especially Syria's strategic Golan Heights. In the chaotic civil war in Lebanon he had supported radical Arab militant sects and sent some 35,000 troops as a "peacekeeping force." In the end, to the resentment of many Lebanese, he was virtually in control of Lebanon. At his death Assad's son was quickly named the new president in a carefully prearranged succession and seemed bent on continuing his father's intransigent policies.

The Revolution in Iran

Where change occurred rapidly in the Middle East, it was clear that traditionalists often resented the Westernizing influence of modern economic and cultural forces. They opposed secularism and the disruption of older religious and cultural institutions as a Western subversion. Yet the outside world was not prepared for the fierce anti-Westernism of the Islamic revolution that erupted in 1979, not in an Arab state, but in Iran, where the language was not Arabic but Persian. Iran was also a Shiite state, whereas nine-tenths of the Islamic world adhered to the Sunni branch of Islam. Yet Shiite revolutionary leaders in Iran helped to foment a new religious revivalism everywhere in the Muslim world.

Foreign domination

Over the centuries Persia (its name was changed to Iran in 1935) had a long history of foreign domination. At the opening of the twentieth century Britain and Russia, coveting its newly discovered oil resources, divided it into spheres of influence. After the First World War the British tried to retain control, but in 1921 an army officer, Reza Khan, seized power, assumed the title of shah, or hereditary ruler, in 1925, and embarked on a program of modernization. He abolished extraterritorial rights for foreigners and curtailed the powers of the Muslim clergy, the mullahs. During the Second World War, however, in 1941, when some of his machinations brought him threateningly close to the Axis, the British and Russians occupied the country and forced him to abdicate in favor of his son, Muhammad Reza. The young shah identified with the West.

After the war American influence became dominant. When Prime Minister Mossadegh and a leftist parliament moved to nationalize and control the oil industry in the early 1950s, the shah, with clandestine support from the American CIA, ousted him and blocked the attempt. With oil wealth, and extensive American military and economic aid, the shah embarked upon an ambitious development program. He broke up estates controlled by feudal landowners and the Islamic clergy, reorganized the armed forces, and sent students in large numbers to study abroad. The pace and breadth of secularization and modernizing reforms pleased urban business interests but alienated others, especially in the countryside. Moreover the shah presided over an increasingly authoritarian regime, crushing opposition and dissent with his secret police. His huge wealth also did not go unnoticed. The United States, pleased with the modernization of its anti-Soviet ally in a strategic part of the world, ignored the swelling internal restlessness. In 1978 religious-inspired protests and strikes and riots broke out as the opposition coalesced. A tidal wave of demonstrations forced the shah to flee the country in January 1979.

In February the aged leader of the religious community, Ayatollah Ruhollah Khomeini (ayatollah is the highest rank in the Shiite religious hierarchy) returned from exile in Paris, where for the past 15 years he had been denouncing the shah's pro-Western, anticlerical, and irreligious regime. He quickly assumed leadership of the revolution and proclaimed an "Islamic republic." His newly formed revolutionary guards routed the shah's troops. Supreme control rested with the ayatollah and his council of religious guardians, appointed to guarantee the new regime's strict commitment to Islam and to ensure control of the revolution through a network of mosques.

Ayatollah Khomeini's "Islamic republic"

The revolutionary authorities forcefully restored traditional Islamic ways of life. Women were ordered to wear the chador, the traditional long black dress covering them from head to toe. The necktie was outlawed for men, who were also encouraged to grow beards. The authorities banned Western music, classical and popular, from radio and television and enforced the Islamic prohibition on alcohol. Islamic law, to be interpreted by the clerics, took precedence over secular law. Soon revolutionary justice, in the form of drumhead trials and public execution for religious, moral, or political offenses, cost the lives of thousands. The ayatollah's theocracy pushed aside moderate leaders, even those who had welcomed the overthrow of the shah. The first president was forced to flee into exile; the foreign minister was executed. The new regime imposed tight state control over the economy and nationalized many industries. In the chaos, oil production and revenues fell.

Militants, many of them university students, aroused to frenzied heights by the ayatollah's fervid denunciations of the United States as "the great Satan," took action on their own. Reacting to the admission of the ailing shah to the United States in the autumn of 1979, revolutionary guards and students seized the American embassy in Tehran in retaliation and held 50 American hostages for close to 15 months, demanding the return of the shah and his wealth

"The great Satan"

The revolution in Iran brought on a wave of militant, anti-Western demonstrations. These Iranian women, wearing the chador to assert their strong Islamic values, show their determined support for Islamic religious traditions and the new political order by wielding powerful, modern weapons.

(Spengler/Corbis Sygma)

to Iran. The hostage crisis weakened the administration of President Carter, and the failure of an ill-conceived rescue mission added to American humiliation.

The War between Iran and Iraq

Iran made no secret of its desire to establish a position of leadership in the Muslim world, non-Arab and Arab, and to project its theocracy as a model for others. In 1980 war broke out when Iraq, its Arab neighbor to the west, launched an attack on Iranian territory. Iraq, also rich in oil, was an aggressively nationalistic Arab state under a military-backed secular regime headed by Saddam Hussein, who ruled as a dictator. His party, the Arab Baath Socialist party, was dedicated to Arab revival. A competing branch of the movement ruled in Syria. But ideology was less important to Hussein than the concentration of political power at home and the use of military power for national ends abroad.

The ayatollah had denounced Iraq both for persecuting its large Shiite community and for abandoning Islamic principles. The war itself erupted over a long-smoldering border dispute between the two states concerning a waterway that served as a vital outlet for Iraq to the Persian Gulf. Once awarded to Iraq by an international commission, it had since fallen under Iran's control. Iraq, seizing an opportunity to exploit the revolutionary turmoil in Iran, and gambling on a quick victory, bombed Iranian oil fields in 1980, invaded Iran, and occupied the disputed territory. Iran rallied after the initial invasion, expelled the Iraqi forces from its borders in 1982, and pushed deep into Iraq, hoping to overthrow Hussein and his regime. When Iraq stiffened its defenses, Iran dispatched assault waves of young conscripts, with small gains at huge human costs, reminiscent of trench warfare during the First World War. In one of the rare instances since that war both sides also used poison gas on the battlefield. Iraq used it as well against its Kurdish minority, accused of collaborating with Iran.

Long-smoldering border dispute

As the war dragged on, it assumed a larger international dimension. The land war became a tanker war in the Persian Gulf, involving Saudi Arabia, Kuwait, and other Arab Gulf states dependent on trade with the West and unsympathetic to Iran's Shiite fundamentalism. Both Iran and Iraq attacked neutral shipping in the Persian Gulf to prevent arms deliveries. When the attacks threatened the flow of oil, the United States, supported by the British and French, stepped up its naval presence. The Western navies kept oil shipments flowing and reinforced the continuing strategic objective of preserving Western influence in the Gulf.

By 1987 the Iranian counteroffensive had failed. In August 1988 Iran accepted a cease-fire. The eight-year war had cost tens of thousands of lives on both sides. The Iranian economy was in shambles; its armed forces were exhausted and depleted. The ayatollah's appeal for a holy war had gone unheeded by other Muslim states and had alienated the Arab Gulf states. But he retained a dedicated following in Iran and still sought to assert his authority in the Islamic world. His call to the Islamic faithful for the assassination of the novelist Salman Rushdie for allegedly blaspheming Muhammad in one of his novels shocked the international community.

Cease-fire

After Khomeini's death in 1989 moderate and pragmatic elements urged economic reconstruction and the reestablishment of the country's ties to the outside world. In 1992 supporters of a new president and his moderate economic and foreign policies won a parliamentary majority. President Rafsanjani was able to restrain the most radical excesses of the revolution, but the nation's new spiritual leader and ayatollah, Ali Khameini, still retained paramount power.

Iran in the 1990s became a land of paradoxes and contradictions. A dual power structure existed and the country was no longer a completely closed society or theocracy as in the revolutionary decade. The middle classes assumed an active economic life. There was outspoken criticism of clerical power. In 1997, when the religious authorities gave voters an even freer choice of presidential candidates, 70 percent of the voters (the voting age was 15) chose an even more reform-minded president, Muhammed Khatami. He was a cleric himself and a descendant of religious leaders, but he had a broad intellectual outlook and had studied and written on Western political philosophy. Khatami committed himself to political and economic reform, a civil society,

Changing Iran

the rule of law, and a freer atmosphere, including a free press. He and others like him believed that Islam and democracy were not incompatible. Yet he had to work within the religious system established by the revolution.

The religious authorities controlled the military, the police, the courts, and much of the media, and even held a veto power over the eligibility of candidates for office. While the president called for dialogue with the outside world, the religious leaders kept up their denunciations of the West, America, and Israel. The president moved and spoke cautiously.

A new generation

Meanwhile a new generation of liberal-minded clerics loosened their stranglehold. The stringent dress and behavior codes were relaxed. Globalization had its effect. Western consumer products were in demand, alcohol became available, and music from the outside world could now be heard. Women dressed as they wished in private circles even if they still wore head scarves and cloaks in public. President Khatami and his program received wide support. Many Iranians, especially young people, recognized that without change the country faced economic stagnation and political isolation, and they resented the social and moral straitjacket in which they found themselves. Iranian theologians were themselves arguing that believers in Islam had to be free in their private lives from outside coercion and pressure. The more conservative clerics still retained a strong following in the country, however, and many of them would have liked to reimpose the Islamic orthodoxy of the revolutionary decade.

The population at large, envious of the economic growth and prosperity of the outside world, increasingly supported the relaxed political order. Education, available only for the urban rich before 1979, was now widespread and included wide opportunities for women. In the 1990s the number of young women entering universities and training themselves for modern skills tripled. Meanwhile the population grew from 34 million in 1976 to over 65 million in 2000.

Traditional vs. modern

The Iranian revolution raised the larger question of whether traditional Islamic values, rigidly enforced as they were in the revolutionary decade, could accommodate modernization, democracy, and a pluralist society. The revolution in Iran had unsettled the entire Islamic world. If Iran were to succeed in its moderate course, it could temper Islamic extremism elsewhere as well.

Iraq and the Persian Gulf War of 1990–1991

Iraq, for its part, emerged from the war with Iran with battle-seasoned armed forces but without real victory and with a troubled economy. Saddam Hussein was resolved to recoup his country's economic fortunes. Unable to persuade the other oil-producing states, particularly Kuwait, to curb production and raise oil prices, he denounced his small Arab neighbor to the south, pressed vague territorial claims (going back to the Ottoman Empire and the British protectorate), and in August 1990 invaded and annexed Kuwait. Many in the West feared that he might move next against Saudi Arabia, expand his influence over the Persian Gulf, and acquire a stranglehold over the world's oil resources.

President George Bush took the lead in winning support from the international community, including several Arab nations, and from the UN Security Council for economic sanctions against Iraq and for military measures if necessary. Over the next few months the United States with the support of a multinational Western and Arab coalition pursued a massive buildup in the deserts of Saudi Arabia. When Iraq refused to withdraw from Kuwait, the Americans and their

Operation Desert Storm

allies unleashed in early 1991 a crushing air attack and followed with a ground assault, which quickly forced Iraq's withdrawal. Operation Desert Storm was remarkably successful, but no effort was made to continue on to Baghdad to dislodge Hussein from power. In defiance of the cease-fire terms, Iraq over the next several years repeatedly challenged the UN-imposed ban on the manufacture of nuclear, chemical, and other weapons of mass destruction and obstructed international inspection. The evidence mounted that Iraq was developing such weapons and could one day deploy them.

The maintenance of stability in this vital area of the Middle East with its many rivalries and competing interests remained critical not only for the states of the Persian Gulf, the Arab nations, and Israel but also for the international community as well. Hussein's removal from power, desirable though that might be, could create a vacuum in the region and generate further instability. Meanwhile the sanctions imposed on Iraq after the war caused suffering for the population but did little to weaken the dictator.

Changes in the Middle East

The Islamic world in the Middle East was in the midst of flux and ferment, caught between traditional social and religious beliefs and modern economic and cultural changes. Beginning with the Iranian revolution of 1979, a wave of religious radicalism had accelerated across the region. Islamic fundamentalists rejected such ideas as separation of religion and state and challenged secular tenets. Many sought Islamic theocracies. Women were often the chief targets. Ostensibly to protect them from the dangers of the modern world, religious radicals demanded their segregation and deprived them of educational and vocational opportunities. During the 1990s, for example, Afghanistan fell victim to the extremist Taliban movement, which had emerged in control of the country after the long war against the Soviet Union. The Taliban government imposed the strictest forms of repression, refusing women the right to attend schools or work outside the home and enforcing rigid dress codes. For the population as a whole, they wished to mete out punishments in accordance with the sharia, the centuries-old Islamic legal code.

Islam in flux and ferment

In Egypt the government responded to religious extremism by outlawing the Muslim Brotherhood, which it held responsible for assassinations and other acts of violence. Yet Islamic leaders could rally thousands of young people in Cairo to force the secular government to drop the sponsorship of books considered blasphemous to Islam. In Turkey the army, guardians of the Turkish secular state, took measures against attempts to undermine its secular tradition. In Algeria, as we have seen, the military's nullification of the Islamic party's victory at the polls in 1991 led to the formation of armed militant groups that fell upon parts of the population with wholesale massacres. In Sudan the Islamic regime in the north continued its military campaign to enforce Islam on the entire country.

But cultural changes were also transforming many Islamic nations, as in Iran. Many Muslims favored an Islamic framework for society, but not a rigid Islamic state. Sentiment grew for more flexible interpretations of ancient Koranic law. In Saudi Arabia, where women could not drive cars or eat unaccompanied in public in the presence of men and where the authorities decreed ancient punishments like amputation for theft and beheading for more serious crimes, a new generation urged the modification of such practices. Egypt saw a remarkable breakthrough for women in 2000, when it enacted one of the Muslim world's most far-reaching reforms of family law. Under the new law in Egypt a woman was henceforth free to divorce a

Cultural changes

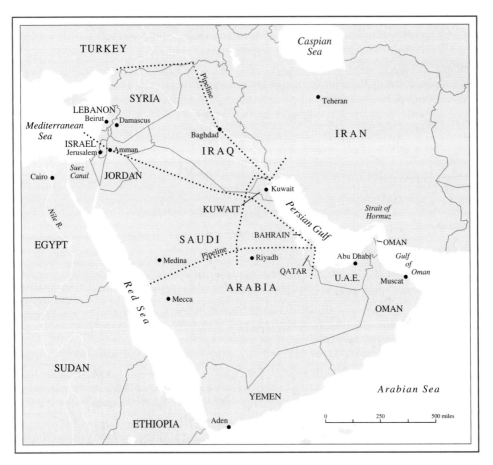

THE PERSIAN GULF AND THE MIDDLE EAST

The map shows important pipelines that move oil across this strategically important region of the world. The oil is exported both by sea from the Persian Gulf and by pipelines that connect the oil-producing centers to the Mediterranean and to the Red Sea. To protect the flow of this vital commodity, the Western oil-consuming countries sent naval forces to the Gulf during the Iran–Iraq war of 1980–1988 and reacted to a later Iraqi assault on its neighbors by driving Iraq's army out of Kuwait in 1991.

husband with or without his consent. Reformers successfully argued that such reforms should be viewed as a modern updating of the equal rights accorded women by the Koran. When in Kuwait the emir decreed that women were eligible to vote and compete in elections, the courts and the legislature blocked the decree, but it was only a matter of time before it would take effect. Many of the cultural changes in law and social patterns were taking place in the smaller Arab states like Kuwait.

The nations of the Middle East often lacked independent political parties and credible parliaments, and the region remained a stronghold of authoritarianism. Although elections were held, their outcomes were generally predictable. What did make a social and political difference, however, was the greater access to the outside world. Satellite television, the Internet, electronic

Impact of the outside world

The city of Jiddah, a thriving port on the Red Sea, is one of the rapidly growing urban centers in contemporary Saudi Arabia. These men have stopped along one of the city's busy streets to engage in one of the daily prayers prescribed by Islam. Surrounded by high-rise apartments, automobiles, and modern traffic problems, they show how people in Islamic societies are blending important religious traditions into the patterns of contemporary social life.
(Liaison Agency)

communications, and close commercial interactions with the rest of the world had a powerful impact. The newest era of globalization was opening horizons, and the world of Islam, from its heartland in the Arab countries to the far reaches of Africa and Asia, remained heterogeneous and diverse yet was evolving in new ways.

118. CHANGING LATIN AMERICA

Unlike the new nations that emerged after the Second World War in Asia, Africa, and the Middle East, most of the Latin American nations had been independent for well over a century by 1945. Yet the legacy of colonialism had left the region, like other parts of the Third World, with unbalanced economic development, heavily dependent on the outside world, and burdened with unresolved political, social, and economic problems.

A region of over 7 million square miles stretching from the Rio Grande to the southern tip of Argentina and Chile, Latin America includes Mexico, Central America, South America, and the islands of the Caribbean. It is mainly Spanish in language and culture, but Portuguese is the language of Brazil, the continent's largest and most populous country. English and French are spoken in some islands of the Caribbean, and a variant of French is spoken in Haiti. The many indigenous Indian languages and dialects, though still widely used in many rural areas, are generally submerged in the majority cultures.

Latin America

It is a region of great racial diversity and mixture. Argentina, because of the flood of immigration in the nineteenth century, is overwhelmingly European in composition, but in Bolivia over half the population is of indigenous Indian origin. In Brazil, the population consists of whites of European background, indigenous Indians, blacks, and mainly an amalgam of mixed peoples. Because of the once flourishing slave trade and slavery half the Brazilian population is wholly or in part of West African ancestry. Almost everywhere, however, European whites and mestizos (that is, people of mixed European and Indian ancestry) tend to dominate. With high growth rates, the population of Latin America more than tripled after 1945, increasing from 160 million in 1950 to over 500 million by the end of the century. Of the ten most populous cities in the world Latin America could claim four: Mexico City, São Paulo and Rio de Janeiro in Brazil, and Buenos Aires in Argentina.

The Colonial Experience and the Wars for Independence

Spanish colonialism

The three centuries of colonial rule after the Spanish *conquista* left an ineradicable mark. Wherever the Spanish found large Indian populations, as in Mexico and in the area then known as Peru, they incorporated them into their colonial system and imposed upon them the hierarchical social structure of the home country. To encourage settlement the crown granted (or "entrusted") large estates to Spanish nobles sent out from Spain to the New World. The Roman Catholic church, also the recipient of large land grants, systematically carried out its holy mission to convert the infidels in the name of Catholic Spain. The Indians were put to work on the large estates with some modest protection provided by the crown and church, but they labored also in underground silver mines under oppressive working conditions.

The arrival of the Europeans led in many places to demographic disaster. In the first generation the new diseases brought by the Europeans decimated the indigenous Indian populations. To work on the sugar plantations in the lowland areas in South America and throughout the Caribbean, the Europeans imported black slave laborers from Africa, eventually in the millions. Slavery was nominally abolished in most areas by the 1850s (although in Brazil not until 1888), but more or less disguised forms of servitude, like peonage, persisted. Indians and blacks remained at the bottom economic rung of society.

The wealth of the colonies flowed out to the mother country, and Spain in turn provided the needed finished goods or arranged for their shipment from other European coun-

The colonial economy

tries. Although Spain did not develop a strong commercial class either at home or in the colonies, ranching and mining became large-scale colonial operations, and a variety of commercial enterprises sprang up. The proud status-oriented nobles in Spain disdained commercial, banking, and business activities, as did the creole (American-born Spanish) elite in the New

World. The church, tightly integrated into the colonial system, employed hundreds of thousands of laborers on its extensive holdings and by 1800, toward the end of the colonial period, owned one-half the productive land.

As the years passed, the American-born creole elite grew wealthy and chafed at European control. They found an opportunity to break away when Napoleon occupied Spain and Portugal and displaced the two royal houses. Although touched by Enlightenment and French revolutionary ideas about the "rights of man," the creole leaders were also frightened by the popular violence of the French Revolution. They intended to control their struggle for independence and protect their privileged social positions and landed wealth. From 1808 to 1826 they fought and won a series of bitterly contested wars for independence; in Brazil members of the Portuguese royal family led the country peacefully into independence. The wars for independence scarcely improved the status of the lower classes who fought the battles, or prepared the way for a more fluid society. Independence, in effect, allowed local elites to wield political power commensurate with their wealth. From the wars for independence and from the subsequent conflicts among the new republics there emerged a large military establishment, a powerful military class, and a succession of caudillos, or dictators, emerging from the military.

Latin American independence

With the withdrawal of the Spanish and Portuguese, dependency on the outside world took a new turn. It was the British, as pioneers in the Industrial Revolution, who moved into Latin American markets. The creole landowners wanted low-priced manufactured imports. British-manufactured goods met with little resistance or competition. British capital also financed the infrastructure, the docks, the roads, and eventually the railroads, to support the expanding trade. Economic penetration by Britain (and soon by the United States) represented a new form of colonialism, or neocolonialism, an economic domination that did not require the acquisition of territory. In the late nineteenth century European and American investments and a flood of European immigration further tied Latin America to the outside world.

Dependency

The Colossus to the North

Independence left the region politically fragmented and unstable, and many of the new republics became mired in civil and national wars. European political control might have been reimposed except for the American Monroe Doctrine (with British support) opposing Continental interference with the independence of the new states. Later in the century the United States also made clear that in cases of civil disorder anywhere in the hemisphere it would not permit the Europeans to intervene to restore stability, protect investments, or collect debts, as was their custom in the era of expansive European imperialism. In what came to be known as the corollary to the Monroe Doctrine, President Theodore Roosevelt announced in 1904 that the United States alone would assume the responsibility of intervention for such purposes. Over the next quarter of a century the United States followed a policy of active armed intervention, or "dollar diplomacy," mainly in Central America and the Caribbean, until gradually modifying its more overt interventionism in the mid-1930s.

The Monroe Doctrine

In the opening years of the twentieth century the United States began to rival the British as the dominant trading partner of Latin America, exporting its manufactures and purchasing many of the region's primary agricultural and mineral products. After the First World War it gradually displaced Britain as the leading source of loans and capital investment. Although centers of manufacturing emerged, Latin America remained industrially underdeveloped, in part because of its dependency on the industrial world and in part because its impoverished masses provided a weak consumer base for industrial expansion. Meanwhile prices of the region's agricultural and mining products became increasingly hostage to the world's markets.

Economic Growth and Its Problems

Latin America suffered heavily when commodity prices plummeted in the dismal years of the Great Depression of the 1930s and foreign investment also dried up. The economic crisis encouraged the Latin Americans to look to their own resources and to attempt to industrialize, as Brazil did under the populist dictator Getulio Vargas in the years 1930 to 1945. When during the Second World War the region was cut off from traditional foreign sources of consumer goods, industrialization received additional stimulus.

Alliance for Progress

Only after 1945 did the economic structure of the region undergo significant transformation. It benefited from the increased demand for its raw materials and agricultural products and from an influx of foreign investment. The Alliance for Progress, sponsored by the United States in the early 1960s under President Kennedy, signaled a new North American commitment to the economic development of the region, even though Latin Americans repeatedly complained of being slighted in favor of other parts of the developing world. In the three decades from 1945 to 1975, Latin American economies grew steadily at impressive rates; steel production multiplied twenty times and electrical energy, metals, and machinery multiplied ten times.

Mexico, Argentina, Brazil, and Chile, despite many internal problems, could justifiably be classified among the newly industrialized countries of the world. Latin Americans manufactured industrial products in larger volume than ever before and no longer relied heavily on foreign imports for their industrial needs. The presence of American and European multinational corporations further stimulated economic progress. Much of this new industrialization, however, developed within a network of protective tariffs, subsidies, and state-controlled enterprises. Moreover, the region had only begun to utilize advanced technology, and low mass-purchasing power continued to impede growth. Economic expansion mostly benefited social elites, increasing the gap between rich and poor.

Debt and inflation

To support economic development the major Latin American governments borrowed heavily in the 1970s from Western (mainly American) banks and international lending agencies, thereby becoming the most heavily indebted nations in the world; for many countries foreign debt nearly quadrupled. By the 1980s the failure to meet debt payments posed a serious financial threat to international creditors, and foreign banks and lending agencies took steps to ease interest payments. The austerity measures imposed by the lending agencies, however, threatened to reduce already depressed living standards. Even in better times many of the Latin American governments assigned a low priority to funding for schools, hospitals, roads, and public health facilities. Large military establishments and bureaucracies also consumed considerable resources. Driven by development ambitions and burdened by other expenditures, many governments simply printed paper money, debasing the currency and promoting extraordinary price rises. In the 1980s several countries suffered "quadruple-digit" annual inflation rates of over 1,000 percent.

Most Latin American nations became steadily more industrialized during the decades after 1945. The workers in this picture are assembling cars at a Volkswagen factory in São Paulo, Brazil. Such factories exemplify the growing role of Latin American cities in the global economy and also the transnational operations of the contemporary world's large industrial corporations.

(Camera Tres/Black Star)

The social difficulties of these unstable economies were compounded when agricultural commodity prices collapsed in the hyperinflation during the 1980s. Economic growth in Latin America slowed to below one percent, or even at times turned negative. As in other developing areas, the 1980s were in many ways a "lost decade." In 1989 production per capita was lower than in 1980. But growth gradually resumed. Many of the Latin American countries abandoned state controls, encouraged freer market economies, introduced sounder public finances, and brought inflation under control. With renewed confidence in the region's economic prospects, foreign bankers and investors once again provided capital for Latin American companies and governments.

A lost decade

Despite economic advances, population growth rates remained a source of concern. As elsewhere in all of the developing world, death rates declined dramatically after 1945 and population growth surged. In Latin America it was even more difficult to cope with rising growth rates because of the Catholic church's prohibition of artificial birth control, although such prohibition was often circumvented or ignored by the upper and middle classes. Growing in many years at three percent annually, the population tripled between 1950 and the 1990s, and the increase all but canceled economic and social gains for the masses of people. On the positive side, population appeared to be stabilizing in the more industrialized Latin American countries.

Population growth

The region remained overwhelmed by the acute needs of its depressed classes, urban and rural. Over the years landless rural workers fled the impoverished countryside, settling in the slums of the congested and polluted cities. A privileged upper-class minority kept many of its financial assets safely abroad but monopolized land and wealth at home. It was estimated in the 1990s that about 180 million people, or about 40 percent of the population of Latin America, lived in poverty. Haiti and Honduras ranked among the poorest countries in the world. Bolivia, whose mineral wealth had once enriched the Incas and the Spanish, had the lowest per capita income of all the South American republics. Beginning in the 1960s, many priests and nuns, touched by the plight of their compatriots, preached "liberation theology," or "the church of the poor," not without opposition from the Vatican, and threw themselves into efforts to improve the lot of the impoverished. Other reformers showed renewed interest in the economic problems and cultural traditions of the indigenous peoples.

Mexico

In Mexico, one of the most developed countries, a large proportion of its more than 100 million people lived at subsistence levels at the opening of the new century and wealth remained highly concentrated in the upper echelons of society. Yet Mexico could look back upon episodes of social revolution beginning in 1910, during which the power of the church and the military was curbed and a land redistribution program was introduced.

The dominant political organization, the Institutional Revolutionary Party (PRI), heir to the Revolution of 1910, was now revolutionary in name only. Opposition parties existed, but the PRI and a small business elite protected their own privileges and interests. The government promoted modernization but slighted social needs; nepotism and corruption flourished. As elsewhere, the human cost of social neglect was malnutrition, disease, infant mortality, limited schooling, illiteracy, and lower life expectancy for all but the elite. The armed revolt in 1994 of an Indian-led peasant movement in the poor southern state of Chiapas dramatized Mexico's broader social problems. The PRI had retained the allegiance of the poor through subsidies and handouts, but its notorious corruption and its tight grip on power through years of controlled elections had left citizens distrustful of all politicians. Despite industrialization and expanding international trade, the economic gulf between rich and poor, and between north and south, increased in Mexico during the 1990s. In the presidential election of 2000 the PRI candidate was defeated by a centrist business leader, Vincente Fox, whose victory ended the 71-year era of PRI control and promised changes in future government and social policies.

End of Yankee Imperialism?

Did the second half of the twentieth century change relationships with the economic colossus to the north? In its "good neighbor" policy in the 1930s the United States appeared to adopt an important step toward surrendering its interventionist prerogatives. Military interventions before 1933 in Mexico, Nicaragua, Panama, Cuba, the Dominican Republic, and Haiti were part of the historical record, and such actions had aroused resentment throughout Latin America. But American marines and troops continued to land in Latin America even after 1945, especially in Central America and the Caribbean, in such countries as Guatemala in 1954, the Dominican Republic in 1965–1966, Grenada in 1983, and Panama in 1989. At times the interventions were tied to American Cold War policies designed to contain communism.

American interventions

As a goodwill gesture after the Second World War, the United States promoted the establishment in 1948 of the Organization of American States (or OAS). In the OAS 35 nations of the Western Hemisphere, including the United States and Canada, joined together to provide a mechanism for settling disputes among the republics. The OAS provided a more dignified alternative than United States interventionism. Another step signaling a new era was the agreement by the United States in 1977 to hand over the Panama Canal to Panama, which took place in 1999.

Among the signs of change in the Western Hemisphere was a growing sense of economic interdependence. The United States needed a stable and prospering Latin America for its own economy. In 1994, at American initiative, the United States, Canada, and Mexico subscribed to a North American Free Trade Agreement, which over a period of time would eliminate all trade barriers among the three countries. Meanwhile large numbers of immigrants from Mexico, the Caribbean, and other parts of Latin America streamed northward, changing the ethnic composition of the United States itself and tightening the bonds among the nations in this region of the world.

Growing sense of interdependence

The Political Record

Politically, the Latin American record in the twentieth century was mostly a history of insecure constitutional regimes and repressive military dictatorships, civil wars and social revolutions, ethnic tensions and labor unrest, coups and countercoups, and agitation against foreign, notably American, interests. There were also episodes of broad-based populist dictatorships with wide mass support, as in Brazil under Vargas, mentioned earlier, and in Argentina under Juan Perón from 1946 to 1955 (with *peronismo* exerting a continuing influence in later years). Disheartening cycles of reform and repression recurred. Central America reflected even greater volatility. Instability from the 1950s to the 1980s was intensified by American anti-Communist commitments in the Cold War and by American support for rightist elements in Central America, particularly in Nicaragua and El Salvador.

Cycles of reform and repression

When leftist regimes were overthrown in Latin America in those years, frequently with unofficial United States help, as in Guatemala in 1954, Brazil in 1964, Chile and Uruguay in 1973, Argentina in 1976, and El Salvador in 1980, harsh repression often followed. Political opponents simply "disappeared"—they were imprisoned, tortured, and often executed, as the later record showed. Two of the most extreme examples occurred in Argentina and Chile. Argentina's "Dirty War," against leftists, claimed over 30,000 lives between 1976 and 1983. Even under democratic regimes in later years those responsible long went unpunished, although the misdeeds were openly acknowledged. A second striking example of military repression occurred in Chile, where a Left coalition elected in 1970, and committed to land reform as well as the nationalization of American-owned copper mines, was toppled three years later by a military coup with the involvement of the United States. The country's democratically elected leftist president, Salvador Allende, and thousands of his supporters lost their lives, and brutal repression followed under a military regime headed for many years by General Augusto Pinochet. The Pinochet era, unlike many dictatorships, left a substantial record of economic growth but also produced bitter memories and a divided country. Arrested in later years while traveling abroad, Pinochet narrowly escaped trial on human rights charges in Europe and in Chile after he returned to his home in 2000.

The most sweeping attempt at social revolution in Latin America in the second half of the twentieth century occurred in Cuba. In 1933 Cuba had fallen under the heavy-handed repressive dictatorship of Fulgencio Batista. In 1959 Fidel Castro and a small band of leftist guerrillas returning from exile succeeded in overthrowing the Batista dictatorship. Castro pledged to institute land reform and end economic dependence on the United States. When his government confiscated American corporate investments and landholdings, the United States retaliated with a trade embargo. Castro, not initially a Moscow-oriented Communist, moved into the Soviet orbit, and tensions over Cuba in 1962 in the context of the Cold War, as we shall see in the chapter that follows, brought the United States and the Soviet Union to the brink of nuclear war.

Cuba and Castro

Cuba became the only professedly Marxist state in the Western Hemisphere. Castro championed anti-imperialism worldwide, aided leftist movements in Bolivia and in Central America, and sent troops across the Atlantic to support anticolonial guerrilla armies in Africa. At home he created an advanced network of social services, promoted public health and literacy, and improved life for the rural masses, but economic failures and totalitarian coercion overshadowed these achievements. He became increasingly dependent on the Soviet bloc for economic aid, receiving favorable terms for the export of sugar and the import of oil. Castro, first secretary of the Cuban Communist party, the only party permitted, ruled as a dictator. Political opponents fled into exile or were imprisoned. His militarized regime and global adventurism cost him support among the reform-minded in Latin America and elsewhere. When Soviet communism collapsed in 1989–1991, Castro, who by then had been in power for over 30 years, lost the economic subsidies on which he depended and became an isolated figure in international affairs. It was difficult to remember that *fidelismo* had once represented a threat to the United States and an opening wedge to communism in the Western Hemisphere.

A diverse region

In the early years of the twenty-first century, Latin America continued to be a diverse region economically and politically. Many Latin American countries were moving toward more stable constitutional government, trying to soften ideological conflict, and working to loosen rigid state controls over their economies. Inflation, heavy debt, currency crises, and population growth, however, still made it difficult to meet the fundamental social needs of the region's impoverished lower classes.

The constitutional democracies often remained fragile. In the 1990s military insurrections broke out in Argentina, Ecuador, and Venezuela, and the civilian president of Peru trampled on the constitution before he eventually was forced from office. In Colombia large-scale drug trafficking disrupted orderly government. In Central America the military again sought power. In many countries the crime rate mounted. Poverty and deep-seated social inequities remained legacies of the region's history.

Democracy emergent and receding

Democracy continued to emerge and recede and to develop unevenly on into the twenty-first century. In 1960 virtually every nation in South America had an elected civilian leader, yet by 1976 all but a few countries in Central and South America had fallen under the control of military or rightist dictatorships. In the 1980s and into the 1990s, however, the trend shifted to democracy. For most of the 1990s no elected civilian president was overthrown by the military, but toward the end of the decade democracy was again being eroded. Electorates seemed frustrated and angered by the ineptitude and corruption of democratic political parties unable to cope effectively with social and economic issues.

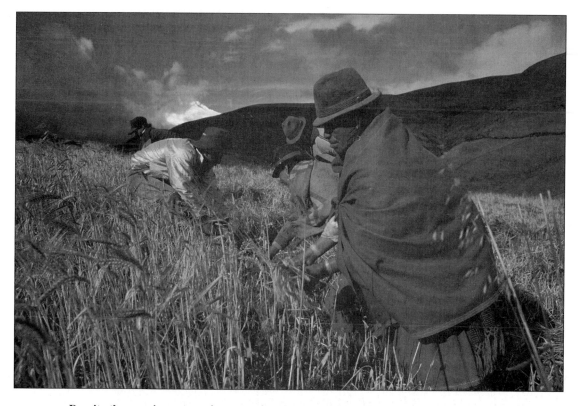

Despite the growing economic connections between all Latin American nations and the modern, international trading system, many people on the continent continue to live and work in long-established, agricultural communities. Like generations before them, these people were harvesting barley in rural Ecuador during the late 1990s, but their economic lives were also linked to a global economy that profoundly affected the price of their crops as well as the value of their wages.

(Pablo Corral V/Corbis)

Venezuela was an especially significant such case because since 1958 it had been a leader in civilian democratic rule and orderly government. Two major parties shared patronage and political spoils for over 40 years, but despite the country's oil wealth did little to relieve poverty and inequality. The election of Hugo Chavez in 1998 as president caused alarm in both of the traditional political parties. Chavez, a former colonel and paratrooper who in 1992 had led a bloody but unsuccessful military coup, won a landslide electoral victory, called for a "peaceful social revolution," convened an assembly to write a new constitution, and after 18 months, in the summer of 2000, stood for reelection. Chavez's regime evoked past memories and fears of populist demagogues, military juntas, and caudillos.

By the early years of the new century Latin America had followed the lead of other industrial countries in moving toward privatization, free trade, open markets, and globalization. Despite periodic setbacks, democracy was growing to be the prevalent pattern of government. But integration into the global economy had not yet brought prosperity or a more balanced distribution of wealth for the vast

A mixed record

majority of Latin Americans. The region was also subject to severe financial crises, such as those that struck Mexico in 1994 and Brazil in 2000. Older leftist movements in Mexico and elsewhere still made their presence felt, and a rising generation of younger activists angrily criticized the new global economy, which they attacked for benefiting only the wealthier nations and wealthier classes.

119. THE DEVELOPING WORLD

At the beginning of the twentieth century, or even in 1945, the sweeping nature and extent of the anticolonial revolution was unanticipated. At best the Western leaders of the colonial empires expected their colonies to evolve slowly toward self-government. The rapid and complete dissolution of the colonial systems was therefore astounding. The age of imperialism had been accompanied by exploitation, brutality, and degradation, and it left an enduring scar on subject peoples all over the globe. Yet paradoxically Western imperialism was also the instrument whereby many of the scientific, material, intellectual, and humanitarian achievements of the West spread to the rest of the world. The West no longer dominated these areas politically, but its culture, technology, and institutions carried a lasting impact. Industry, science, secularization, social mobility, the rule of law, the idea of individual freedom, and other new values or institutions created dislocations and tensions throughout much of the decolonized world. In some instances, as in Iran's Islamic revolution and in outbursts of Islamic extremism elsewhere, resentments at the Western intrusion exploded, but mostly there was hope that some amalgam could be forged of modernization and traditional values.

In few parts of the formerly colonial world did Western-style liberal and democratic institutions prevail in the early years of independence. Economically, neither the newly independent nations nor the international assistance programs were able to raise per capita levels of agricultural and industrial production significantly. Illiteracy and disease persisted, and living standards still lagged behind those of the industrialized nations. Independence brought a new sense of dignity, but it did not automatically bring freedom, self-government, human rights, and the improvement of the human condition. Not until the 1980s did pressures for political and economic liberalization begin to show results.

The Development Experience

After the Second World War the United States took the lead in assisting the developing countries with money and technical aid. Other industrial countries once recovered from the war also committed growing shares of their annual gross national product to development assistance. International agencies provided additional funding and expertise. With modern science, technology, and financial assistance, it was believed that the developing countries could look forward to modernization, economic growth, and social progress. Many of the new leaders of the postcolonial nations, however, believed that central planning, nationalized economies, and government controls would accomplish these ends more rapidly. Nehru's moderate socialism and economic planning in India provided one model. Others turned to the Communist models of the Soviet Union or China. Still others followed the Japanese example of private capitalism in partnership with government. South Korea, Taiwan, Singapore, and Hong Kong in Asia, adopting the Japanese pattern, industrialized and created remarkably successful export economies, with high living standards for their people.

In the postwar decades international agencies helped finance projects for agriculture, industry, health, and education. The 1960s were the "development decade." President Kennedy spoke of raising the "banner of hope" for the poor and hungry. Dams and wells, irrigation schemes, hydroelectric projects, factories and processing mills, and education at all levels became part of the program. Industrialization could end or reduce excessive dependence on imports. In agriculture a "Green Revolution" pioneered by agricultural scientists in the United States, involving the use of chemical fertilizers, new high-yield hybrids, and modern planting and harvesting techniques, enabled farmers to increase productivity. The initial results were promising. Many of the developing countries experienced significant progress, achieving targets of 5 to 6 percent growth annually; per capita income rose; infant mortality rates fell. In the 1960s it seemed possible to speak of "a revolution of rising expectations."

The development decade

But advances in the poorer nations did not bring much change in their relative global economic position. They still did not share proportionately in the industrial world's spectacular postwar economic expansion, in the course of which per capita income in the wealthier nations tripled. The gap between richer and poorer nations widened rather than narrowed. Using the United Nations and other organizations as a forum, the developing nations in the late 1960s argued for a reshaping of the international economy—a "new international economic order"—to offer them greater access to the investment funds, technology, and markets of the West and to shift international financing from Western-dominated agencies like the World Bank to wider international control.

In the tensions of the Cold War the developing nations had formed a bloc of neutralist, nonaligned states. Beginning with 25 states in 1961, the Third World bloc steadily increased in numbers, and although it was non-aligned, it was always more critical of the wealthier West than of the Soviet Union. Because the states were situated mainly in the southern parts of the two hemispheres, their challenges to the wealthiest nations also assumed the configuration of a "north-south" contest.

The "nonaligned states"

The recession that began in 1974 brought a decline in international trade and a shrinkage of international assistance funds. In the 1980s, the developing countries staggered under heavy debts incurred during the earlier optimistic years. Oil-producing countries, particularly, had overcommitted themselves because they calculated on a continuing rise in oil prices. Debt, principally to private commercial banks, soared, one-third of it owed by the Latin American countries, Argentina, Brazil, Mexico, and Venezuela.

After five decades of the development experience, per capita income in the poorest countries had scarcely risen. Almost everywhere the agricultural sector had received a lower priority than the industrial. Agricultural production, even when it increased, often failed to keep up with explosive population growth. To earn the foreign exchange needed to finance the development of an industrial infrastructure, governments encouraged export crops and neglected the production of food for their own people—an agricultural economy was considered a sign of inferiority. Although the developing countries began building their own industries, many of their products failed to compete successfully either at home or in the world market. Much of the economic aid and foreign investment had been channeled to industrial projects in the capitals or other large cities, sometimes to nonproductive and extravagant showpieces.

Development's impact

In the rush for development, government control frequently led to clumsy bureaucracies, extravagance, and corruption. Many governments used development funds to boost national prestige and pride rather than to improve the economic conditions of their people. Inadequate assistance failed to help the rural poor, who sank into deeper poverty. Millions meanwhile fled the countryside for the presumed attractions of city life, only to face joblessness, live in congested shantytowns or slums, and breathe polluted air. Some industrial projects in the Third World were undertaken at enormous cost to the environment.

Changing Worlds and Persistent Problems

In the 1980s economic growth regressed. Forty-three developing countries finished the decade with a decline in per capita real income. The percentage of the world's population living in poverty, slowly shrinking in earlier decades, rose again. Because of population growth, the numbers of the impoverished were far larger than before. As the twentieth century drew to a close well over one billion human beings lived in poverty, mainly in sub-Saharan Africa, Asia, Latin America, and the Middle East. Hundreds of millions suffered from disease and malnutrition.

One billion impoverished

The developing countries, of course, were far from homogeneous. The People's Republic of China (generally not included as part of the Third World but occupying a separate and unique category of its own) continued to industrialize and modernize in its own way. The "little tigers" in East Asia built powerful export economies and raised living standards. In South Korea per capita income rose spectacularly in the years 1970 to 1990 from $270 to $5,400. India, Indonesia, Malaysia, and Thailand as well as Argentina, Brazil, Chile, and Mexico were all industrializing and modernizing. These nations and others seemed to be leaving the Third World behind and forming an intermediate category of their own as "newly industrialized countries." The oil-rich states of the Middle East and elsewhere had the potential to turn their national wealth into the further modernization of their economies and societies. Meanwhile at the very bottom of the economic performance scale were the "least developed countries," among them a number of sub-Saharan African states, Bangladesh in South Asia, and Haiti in the Western Hemisphere. Together they formed a kind of "Fourth World," an impoverished group of hundreds of millions of people lacking bare necessities.

The countries with the greatest success in development had progressed within a framework of market economies, but the debate continued over the role of government in stimulating economic development. Even in the successful market economies, governments played a significant supporting role, and government support for schools, transportation, and infrastructure remained essential for all developing economies. In many of the poorer developing countries, however, the overriding presence of the state, government ownership and controls, bureaucratic interference, and imprudent fiscal policies had choked off growth and progress.

Market economies and the state

The maldistribution of wealth was particularly acute in nations where there were fewer goods and services to distribute and where they were often distributed with gross inequity between the elite who cultivated ever higher standards of luxury and the impoverished masses. Despite some success stories the rising expectations and hopeful visions of the early postwar decades at times turned into ever deeper frustrations for many of the world's peoples. In point of fact at the opening of the twenty-first century there was no Third World. There were only two worlds, one relatively rich, one poor. And the relations between these worlds remained critically important in the evolving global economy.

Reappraising Development

In the closing years of the twentieth century a spirited debate emerged in development circles and international donor agencies about the nature and direction of development assistance. The discussions and criticisms attracted broad public attention and at times ignited confrontational street demonstrations. The major international lending agencies admitted the disappointing progress in reducing poverty and accepted their share in the blame. The number of people living in extreme poverty in the world, that is, surviving on $1 a day, fell only slightly, from 1.3 billion in 1990 to 1.2 billion at the end of the decade. In sub-Saharan Africa it had barely changed.

The two major international agencies, the World Bank and the International Monetary Fund (IMF), both under new leadership, acknowledged a need to shift from "growth and development" to a more explicit commitment to "poverty reduction." Over the years the World Bank had generously financed the building of roads, dams, bridges, and power plants, judging their success solely in quantitative terms, asking only, to cite one example, how much new electricity a project had generated but failing to ask how it had improved lives, reduced poverty, or affected local cultures. The catalogue of inappropriate projects was long and sometimes bizarre. Electrical equipment arrived in villages where no electricity was available, recycled clothing was sent to areas where it hurt local weavers, grain shipments were sent to countries where they adversely affected local growers. Historically, foreign aid had gone to central governments, but it was now apparent that local governments and communities would have to play a larger role than in the past. Human development indexes were to be prepared, focusing not on per capita income alone but on literacy, life expectancy, health, nutrition, and the status of women and children. Donor governments meanwhile agreed to cancel the debt of many of the world's poorest countries in Africa, Asia, and Latin America and to help Third World countries gain freer access to the markets of the industrial world.

Reduction of poverty

The IMF came under heavy criticism. It had intervened in many currency crises over the years, generally pressuring governments to reduce spending and imposing overly rigid austerity measures that ignored the nation's social needs. Exceeding its original mission, it had reoriented development policies in directions it considered economically desirable but with little recognition of the social or political consequences. Agreement emerged that the IMF should restrict itself to resolving currency and other short-time financial crises, no small task in itself, and leave development policies to the World Bank.

Another large and contentious issue was the impact of the global economic integration rapidly making headway in the 1990s. To its most extreme critics global trading systems and financial markets increased poverty, sharpened social divisions, hurt the environment, exploited local working people, used child labor shamelessly, and shifted control over people's lives to multinational corporations and the pursuit of profit. Although economic evidence did suggest that globalization had accomplished far less to relieve poverty and inequality than originally predicted, others maintained that free trade and information technology stimulated economic growth and would in time help the poor to improve their lives.

Impact of global integration

The vigorous debates on development policies may have shaped new priorities for future governmental and international development aid. A related debate explored the extent to which the developing countries might be left behind by the new information

technology. The world of computers and the Internet, like other technological innovations, further widened the economic gap between rich and poor nations and raised new questions about how best to reduce the growing digital divide. All such debates about the development experience reflected the linkage between the historical legacy of the former colonial empires, the rapid process of decolonization, and the emergence in the second half of the twentieth century of the largest number of independent nation-states that the world had ever seen.

Postcolonial nations in Africa and Asia have sought to develop the new technologies and communication systems that are essential for contemporary economic and cultural life, in part because a growing "digital divide" threatens to widen other economic differences between wealthy and poor nations. These young men were working on computer problems at Ibadan University in Nigeria during the early years of computer technology, but their concentration and perplexity reflect the universal effort to comprehend and manage new information technologies in modern societies around the world.

(Marc and Evelyne Bernheim/Woodfin Camp & Associates)

Chapter 24

A WORLD ENDANGERED: COEXISTENCE AND CONFRONTATION IN THE COLD WAR

By the late 1950s many of the early postwar issues had been transformed. Western Europe and Japan had rebuilt themselves with American aid. Western Europe had joined more closely together economically in the evolving European Community and buried many of its old antagonisms. Regions of the world that formerly were part of European colonial empires were asserting their independence. China was positioning itself as another major Communist power. The global economy grew increasingly interdependent and the vicissitudes of economic expansion and contraction reverberated worldwide. Older distinctions became blurred. The emergence of Japan made it impossible to identify industrial and financial might with the West. The Soviet bloc traded with and borrowed from the West.

Yet the Cold War continued to manifest itself in an escalating nuclear arms race and in the confrontation of the two superpowers in many parts of the globe, each attempting to prevent the other from gaining the ascendancy. The stockpiling of nuclear arms and the development of sophisticated long-range delivery systems led to the accumulation of unparalleled destructive power. The nuclear missiles supposedly were built for deterrence and not for use, and a new kind of balance of power emerged that preserved the peace. The world nonetheless lived in the shadow of nuclear catastrophe.

As time passed, the phenomenon of "bipolarity," or the predominance of the two superpowers, the United States and the Soviet Union, gradually gave way to new global configurations. But while the charged atmosphere lasted, despite periods of détente, the world was forced to live with repeated crises. As late as 1985 no one could foresee how or when the Cold War would end.

Chapter emblem: Chinese pro-democracy crowds surround a statue of the "Goddess of Liberty" in Beijing's Tiananmen Square in the spring of 1989.

ꙮ 120. CONFRONTATION AND DÉTENTE, 1955–1975

The Soviet leaders who succeeded Stalin after 1953 seemed at times more conciliatory and willing to acknowledge the need for arms control and cooperation in the nuclear age. An alternative of peaceful coexistence and competing world systems promised to open up, and there were even recognizable periods of détente, or formal relaxation of tensions. But dangerous confrontations recurred, the nuclear arms buildup assumed unprecedented forms and dimensions, and relations seesawed over the next several decades between conciliation and crisis.

Periods of détente

By 1955 the Cold War had stabilized. In Asia the Korean War was over. In Europe the North Atlantic Treaty Organization (NATO), strengthened by the West German armed forces, faced the Warsaw Pact nations. The iron curtain still divided Europe, but the threat of direct military confrontation receded. The Western powers and the Soviet Union were able to agree in 1955 on a treaty with Austria, ending the joint Allied occupation and leaving Austria independent and neutral.

We have seen how Khrushchev had emerged as the dominant Soviet leader. Sharp-tongued, volatile, boastful, he announced that the Soviets would abandon their revolutionary principles only "when shrimp learn to whistle" and pledged that the Soviets would "bury" Western capitalism. Nonetheless he rejected the inevitability of war and emphasized the "possibility and necessity of peaceful coexistence." President Eisenhower, in office from 1953 to 1961, continued the policy of containment and the American military buildup. Eisenhower's secretary of state, John Foster Dulles, who saw the Cold War in almost apocalyptic terms as a Manichean contest between good and evil, at one point urged a "rollback" of Soviet power. Despite his rhetoric, and despite active American military support for anti-Communist forces in Central America, Asia, Africa, and elsewhere, American policy remained limited to containment. Both superpowers recognized the need for coexistence in the nuclear age.

Pressures for coexistence

In 1955 President Eisenhower, along with the British and French, met at Geneva with Soviet leaders in a friendlier atmosphere than any since the Second World War. Although they reached no new agreements, the American president could speak of "a new spirit of conciliation and cooperation." But tensions mounted over Berlin. The Soviets, incensed that East Germans were fleeing in large numbers to West Berlin and then to the Federal Republic of Germany, demanded that the Western powers end their occupation of West Berlin, but Eisenhower forcefully rejected the ultimatum, and the crisis passed. In 1959, when Khrushchev visited President Eisenhower at his weekend retreat in Camp David, they spoke of peaceful coexistence and even of mutual disarmament.

At a second summit conference in Paris, the superpowers continued to recognize their common interests in preserving stability and peace. But by then Khrushchev, under criticism at home and from Mao in China for being too conciliatory toward the West, produced evidence, irrefutable to be sure, of American reconnaissance flights over Soviet territory and broke up the conference. By the summer of 1960 the "spirit of Geneva" and the "spirit of Camp David" had faded. When Khrushchev spoke before the United Nations, he boasted of Soviet arms production and denounced the United States. Crises over Berlin and elsewhere were far from settled.

Cooperation fades

The United States, unwavering in its resolve to maintain the defense of western Europe, accepted Soviet hegemony east of the iron curtain. The Americans protested but did not intervene when in 1953 the Soviets put down antigovernment riots in East Berlin, or when in 1956 the Soviets exerted pressure on Poland to curb its reform movement, or when the Soviets, even more dramatically, sent troops and tanks that year to crush the Hungarian revolt, or later, in 1968, the Czech uprising. The United States offered little more than moral encouragement to dissident groups in all of these eastern European states.

At the same time one part of the world after another was being brought into the American strategic defense system. In the Suez crisis in 1956 (which broke out simultaneously with the troubles in Hungary) the United States deterred Britain, France, and Israel from pressing military action against Egypt, at least in part because it might have encouraged Soviet intervention. The three countries were frustrated, but the Soviets were kept out. The "Eisenhower Doctrine" asserted American primacy in the defense of the Middle East and pledged protection to any government in that region against "international Communism." Under that policy, Eisenhower dispatched marines to Jordan and Lebanon in 1958 when their pro-Western governments were threatened. In the Western Hemisphere the United States rallied the Latin American republics to resist domination or control of any American state by the "international Communist movement." American foreign policy in the Cold War remained based on the premise that unrest on every continent was Soviet-inspired. That premise sometimes prevented Americans from understanding the complex local causes of regional conflicts around the world.

American Cold War policy

The nuclear arms race continued. In October 1957 the Soviets, to the world's astonishment, demonstrated their prowess in the new era of rocket technology when they successfully launched *Sputnik,* the first artificial satellite to orbit in outer space. A few months later the United States launched its own space satellite, *Explorer I.* The space age had opened. The military implications of space rocketry quickly became apparent. The same principles of propulsion could launch armed missiles over long distances. In 1958 the Soviets developed the first intercontinental ballistic missile (or ICBM) capable of delivering nuclear warheads to North America and elsewhere thousands of miles away. The United States in turn developed its own intercontinental ballistic missiles and proceeded to build an arsenal of nuclear weapons far larger than that of the Soviets.

A new kind of arms race, based on "mutual deterrence," emerged; it was useless to speak of "massive retaliation." Now that American cities were vulnerable to nuclear destruction, anxiety spread in western Europe that the United States might not so readily defend it. De Gaulle, the French president, voiced these and other misgivings in the 1960s and called for a more independent role for the West Europeans. Rejecting the rigid patterns of the Cold War and viewing postwar international relations as a traditional struggle between great powers rather than as a conflict of ideologies, he called for a return to a more open recognition of spheres of national interest and for Europe's reunification—"from the Atlantic to the Urals." He declined to follow the American lead in foreign policy in Europe or elsewhere. Although he kept France in the Atlantic alliance, in a gesture of independence he withdrew France from the integrated NATO military command in 1966 and pressured NATO into moving its headquarters from French soil. His aspirations for a leadership role for France troubled many Europeans, but he nevertheless articulated European uneasiness with American hegemony over the West in world affairs.

A new kind of arms race

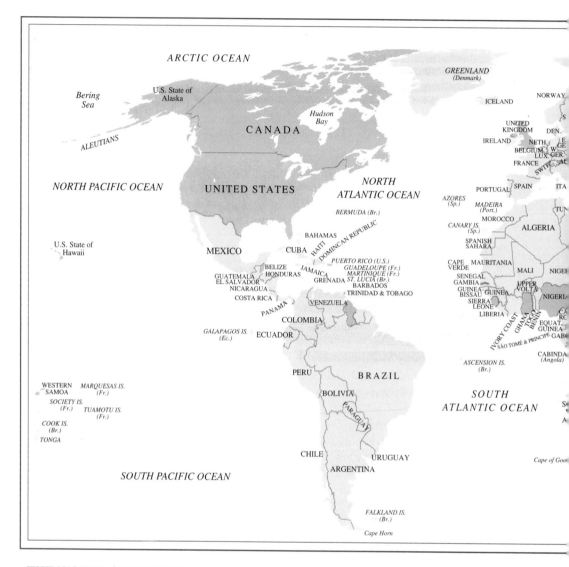

THE WORLD ABOUT 1970

This political map of the world about 1970 shows a number of important changes after the end of the Second World War: the breakup of the European colonial empires in Asia and Africa, the emergence of some 50 independent republics in Africa and of several new states in Asia, the emergence of the People's Republic of China, and the peripheral expansion of the Soviet Union.

The Kennedy Years, 1961–1963

The gravest direct Soviet-American confrontations came during the Kennedy presidency. President Kennedy heightened the rhetoric of the Cold War. The United States "had to pay any price, bear any burden, meet any hardship, support any friend or oppose any foe in order to assure the success and survival of liberty." He took steps to close what was termed

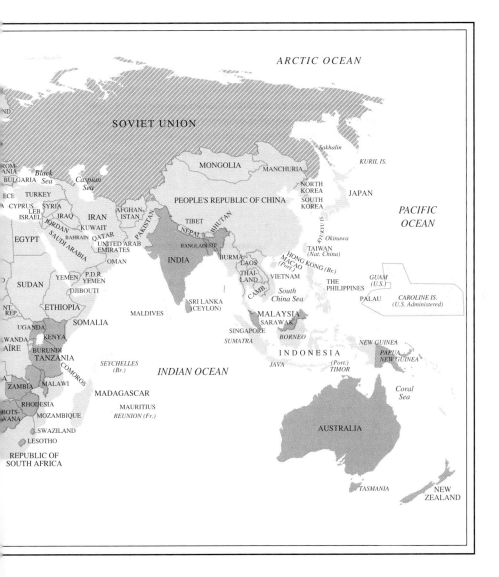

the "missile gap." Alarmed by Soviet successes in space, he pledged that the Americans would reach the moon before the end of the decade and encouraged large expenditures for space exploration. At the same time Kennedy increased foreign aid to the developing countries and sponsored the Peace Corps, which took young Americans to Latin America, Asia, and Africa to aid in social and economic development programs designed to improve life and reduce the attractions of communism. For Latin America, which resented the large sums that had gone to Europe, he organized the Alliance for Progress to encourage investment and growth.

In Cuba, Kennedy inherited an explosive situation. Many in the United States and elsewhere had initially regarded Fidel Castro as a progressive leader favorably disposed to democracy and committed to much needed

Kennedy and Cuba

change in a country where a dictatorship had long kept the population impoverished and repressed. But Castro, no simple reformer, inaugurated a sweeping agrarian program, expropriated large American corporate holdings, and imprisoned or executed political opponents. Thousands of Cubans fled to the United States, settling in large numbers around Miami. Although Castro originally kept his movement aloof from the Cuban Communist party, he now openly joined ranks with the Communists. President Eisenhower, who dealt with Castro's leftist regime before Kennedy came to office, was alarmed by the threat of communism in the Western Hemisphere and had imposed a strict embargo on imports from Cuba. Castro for his part moved closer to the Soviet Union. Within a short time, four-fifths of Cuban trade was with the Soviets and eastern Europe. The United States broke off diplomatic relations, and the CIA secretly trained a small group of Cuban refugees for an armed invasion of the island.

Kennedy inherited the plans for the invasion and, without seriously reassessing the Castro threat, resolved to go forward with it to end the Communist menace 90 miles from the American mainland. The invasion at the Bay of Pigs in April 1961, without adequate air protection, turned into a failure; most of the 1,500 invaders were captured. Castro now inflated his revolutionary rhetoric, openly projected himself as a Marxist-Leninist, affirmed the country's ties with the Soviet Union, and championed the cause of international revolution throughout Latin America and elsewhere. The United States tightened its embargo.

The Bay of Pigs

At a meeting with Kennedy in Vienna that year, the Soviet leader delivered a new ultimatum for the Western powers to leave Berlin. Kennedy, smarting over the Bay of Pigs defeat, reaffirmed the Western resolve to remain in Berlin. He asked Congress to expand American military forces, inaugurated a civil defense program, and made plans for fall-out shelters in the event of nuclear war. The Atlantic alliance backed him. The immediate crisis passed. But in the summer of 1961 the Soviets, still exasperated at the continuing exodus from East Berlin (over three million East Germans had already fled), constructed the Berlin Wall, a 28-mile rampart of concrete and barbed wire, with armed sentry stations. The Wall stood as a grim physical reminder of the Cold War; hundreds of East Germans who attempted to cross the barrier met their deaths. The Soviet Union also ended a three-year moratorium on nuclear testing; both countries resumed tests underground and in the atmosphere.

The Berlin Wall

The Cuban Missile Crisis of 1962

The most dangerous Western-Soviet confrontation did not occur in Berlin, but in Cuba, where in the fall of 1962 Khrushchev showed an unanticipated recklessness. Announcing his intention to defend Cuba against a second American invasion (plans for which existed), he dispatched Soviet soldiers and technicians to the island to construct missile sites that would have brought the American mainland within target range. For the United States this Soviet intrusion on America's own doorstep was unthinkable; moreover, it could inalterably change the nuclear balance between the two superpowers.

During 13 tense days in October President Kennedy and his advisers resolved not to take any hasty military action but to stand firm against the Soviet military presence in Cuba, fully aware that the showdown could lead to nuclear war. Kennedy imposed a blockade (or quarantine) of the island, forbidding further deliveries of arms and supplies. The launching of any nuclear missile from Cuba, he made clear, would lead to a "full retaliatory response upon the Soviet Union." At the height of the emergency American planes carrying nu-

An eyeball-to-eyeball confrontation

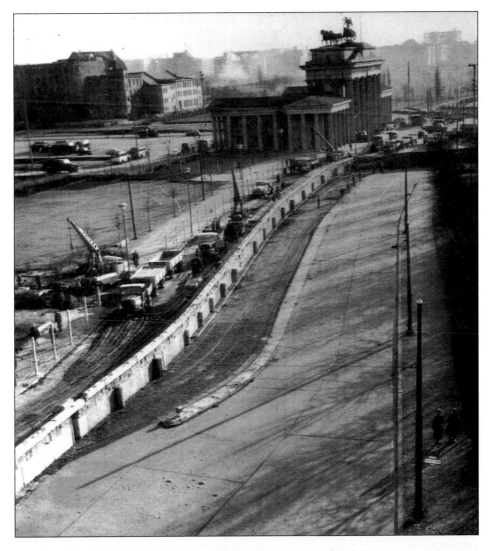

The bleak, concrete Berlin Wall became both a physical and symbolic expression of the bitter divisions in Europe during the Cold War. This picture, which shows a section of the newly constructed Wall near the famous Brandenburg Gate, illustrates the stark separation between East and West Berlin that the Soviets sought to establish when they built the Wall in 1961. Although the Wall accomplished the Soviets' short-term political objective by stopping the exodus of East Germans, it also confirmed the repressive character of Soviet-controlled states in eastern Europe.

(AKG/Sipa Press)

clear bombs were airborne. Although Khrushchev blustered that the blockade was illegal, he backed down; on October 24 two Soviet ships and their submarine escort turned back. In one note Khrushchev agreed to remove the missile sites in return for an American pledge not to invade Cuba. In a second note, more aggressive in tone, he demanded the removal of American missile sites in Turkey. Kennedy replied only to the first message, but privately let it be known that the United States would eventually remove its missiles in Turkey. By October 28, the most ominous crisis of the Cold War, an "eyeball-to-eyeball" confrontation, as the American Secretary of State Dean Rusk described it, was over.

Khrushchev had lost face; he was weakened still further at home, and in 1964 he was ousted from power. The People's Republic of China, which was assuming the role of spokesman for the Third World, ridiculed his capitulation. Even though tensions once again eased, and the Soviet leaders would never again show such recklessness, the Cuban crisis had a direct effect on the arms race. Both the Soviet Union and the United States moved to expand their nuclear arsenals, and the Soviets under Khrushchev's successors were determined to achieve nuclear parity.

The United States and the Vietnam War

The resolve to contain Communist expansion entangled the United States in deepening hostilities in Southeast Asia. In Vietnam, as we have seen, the Communist leader Ho Chi Minh led an anticolonial war against the French that lasted over eight years, from 1946 to 1954. After France acknowledged its military defeat, an international conference at Geneva in 1954, it will be recalled, formally recognized the independence of Vietnam, as well as of Laos and Cambodia, all part of former French Indochina.

Vietnam divided

But in Vietnam Communists and anti-Communists now confronted each other in a divided country. In the north Ho Chi Minh consolidated his Communist regime in its capital at Hanoi. A Western-backed regime under Ngo Dinh Diem governed the south, its capital in Saigon. Neither regime wanted a divided country, but the Geneva conference had partitioned Vietnam at the seventeenth parallel until general elections for a unified country could be held in 1956. In the interval the armies of the rival regimes were to withdraw behind the stipulated boundary, across which there was to be free movement of peoples. In the months that followed, close to one million Vietnamese fled southward. In South Vietnam a referendum in 1955 established an independent republic.

The government in South Vietnam, already aware that the Communists had acquired a large popular following in the wars against the Japanese and French, refused to participate in the scheduled countrywide elections. Communist guerrilla forces, known as the Viet Cong, who had stayed behind when the main army withdrew under the 1954 Geneva agreement, began a campaign to undermine the South Vietnamese government. The National Liberation Front emerged as a rival civil authority. Skilled in insurgent warfare, the Viet Cong won popular support by distributing land and by denouncing South Vietnam as a puppet of the West. Regular army units from North Vietnam soon reinforced the Communist guerrilla units. Ho Chi Minh, while never sacrificing his political independence, received generous aid for his regime from the U.S.S.R. and from the People's Republic of China. South Vietnam, hard-pressed despite technical advice and assistance from the United States, appealed for more and more American aid.

"Like a tumbling row of dominoes"

The United States, from President Eisenhower on, saw a need to fill the vacuum created by the French withdrawal and to check Communist expansion in Indochina. To prevent the other states in Southeast Asia from toppling one by one—"like a tumbling row of dominoes," in his phrase—Eisenhower sent some limited aid and military advisers, but Kennedy further bolstered the Diem regime with additional military advisers, financial backing, and arms. The United States acted on the premise that this was not a civil war among the Vietnamese but a war between two independent states, one anti-Communist and therefore to be supported, and the other Communist, receiving aid and support from the Soviet Union and Communist China. Vietnam was seen as part of the global struggle between communism and democracy. While the repressive character of the regime in the north was apparent, the southern regime's authoritarian practices, ineptitude, corruption, and acts of coercion, especially against its large Buddhist population, became increasingly embarrassing to its American sponsors.

American involvement deepened and spanned the administrations of five presidents, Eisenhower, Kennedy, Johnson, Nixon, and Ford. Under Eisenhower a few hundred military advisers were present, and military and economic aid began; as early as 1959 two military advisers were killed in an attack north of Saigon. In 1961, under Kennedy, additional military advisers and American support troops arrived; a year later 4,000 military personnel were on hand, and the first battle deaths were reported. The Kennedy administration, through the CIA, intervened in South Vietnamese politics; the Americans first propped up and then in 1963 helped to overthrow the increasingly repressive government of Diem, in the course of which Diem and his brother were murdered.

After Kennedy's assassination in November 1963, and the succession of Lyndon B. Johnson to the presidency, American intervention to achieve a military victory in Vietnam gained added momentum. In 1964, on the alleged ground that North Vietnamese torpedo boats in the Gulf of Tonkin had attacked United States destroyers, Johnson ordered immediate air strikes against North Vietnam and secured support for a joint congressional resolution empowering him to take "all necessary measures" to defend the United States and its ally. The Gulf of Tonkin resolution was the only explicit congressional sanction for the deepening American involvement. In 1965 American marines arrived. After 1965 heavy air raids on supply bases in the north and on Communist-controlled areas in the south became an almost daily occurrence. American bombers attacked as far north as Hanoi.

Gulf of Tonkin resolution

To root out the elusive Viet Cong in the countryside, American soldiers conducted "search and destroy" missions among the villagers, and American planes dropped incendiary materials and chemicals, burning whole villages, defoliating hundreds of thousands of acres of land, and turning the survivors into homeless refugees. The bombing raids, the commitment of American ground troops, and the casualties mounted. In 1966 there were close to 200,000 American troops in Vietnam; by 1969 at their maximum there were close to 550,000. In addition to the South Vietnamese army, military forces came from Thailand, the Philippines, Australia, and New Zealand, but it was an American war. In the massive bombings from 1965 to 1969 the Americans dropped more tons of explosives than against the Axis powers in the Second World War.

The large-scale American military intervention was unable to overcome the persistence of the North Vietnamese, aided by the Soviet Union, which never directly intervened with combat troops but lent assistance of other kinds. American military reports about the "pacification" of the countryside and about the number of enemy casualties (or "body counts") were confounded by the Communists' Tet, or New Year's, offensive at the opening of 1968. Although unsuccessful, the scale of the Communist offensive shook American complacency about the outcome of the war. To many it was clear that a negotiated settlement would be necessary.

The Tet offensive

America's allies in western Europe were critical of the deepening American involvement. De Gaulle, a moralizer when it suited his purposes, called it "detestable" for "a great nation to ravage a small one." In the United States the war became a root cause of disorders and protests on college campuses and in the cities. Criticism of American policy added fuel to

Critics of American involvement

Peace and Communist victory

intervened—peace had finally come to the country, and with it Communist victory. Reunification and reorganization of the country proceeded quickly. The new regime launched a "political reeducation" campaign, nationalized property, and forcibly moved large numbers of the population from the cities to the countryside. Thousands, mostly ethnic Chinese, tried to flee in makeshift, overcrowded boats, many perishing in the attempt or discovering that the countries which they reached would not offer them a haven.

In the wake of North Vietnam's victory, Cambodia and Laos also fell under Communist control. Thirty years after the end of the Second World War, all that had once been French Indochina was in Communist hands, and a reunified Vietnam emerged as a new military power in Southeast Asia.

The costs of war

The Vietnam War was extremely costly for the Vietnamese people; 1.3 million Vietnamese died in the fighting and bombings. For the United States the war was a searing experience. Battle and battle-related deaths exceeded 58,000, higher than in the Korean War. The impact of the military expenditures was heightened by the failure to place taxes on a wartime basis, contributing to inflationary pressures. The political and moral costs were enormous. The war created a mistrust of

This photograph of terrified children fleeing from the bombing of their village in South Vietnam suggests how the disturbing pictures and television images of the Vietnam War raised painful moral questions and contributed to the development of a strong antiwar movement in the United States.

(AP/Wide World Photos)

presidential power in the United States—of an "imperial presidency." In 1973 Congress adopted legislation to curb presidential initiatives that could lead to future episodes like the war in Vietnam. The war had left Americans with a disturbing series of painful images and memories: the deadly bombings, the gruesome battle scenes visible in the first war reported in detail on television, the revelation of atrocities and war crimes committed by American troops (as at My Lai in 1968, first covered up and then made the subject of a public inquiry and trial), and the demoralization of veterans, who were convinced that their sacrifices in the unpopular war had brought them little recognition. America's giant industrial and military power had failed to bring victory. Technological superiority in armaments and air power proved inadequate against an enemy skilled in insurgent warfare and imbued with a revolutionary zeal.

The travail of Southeast Asia did not end. During the war North Vietnam had infiltrated border areas of Cambodia and helped arm Communist insurgents, the Khmer Rouge, who, after a lengthy civil war, overthrew the Cambodian government. In 1975 the leader of the Cambodian Communists, the ruthless Pol Pot, subjected Cambodia to brutal dictatorship and grisly terror; an unknown number, but over two million people, died in the small country from 1975 to 1978 as a result of mass executions, forced labor, and famine.

The Khmer Rouge turned out to be more pro-Chinese than suited Vietnam or the Soviet Union. In 1979 Vietnam invaded Cambodia and overthrew the Pol Pot regime: China took retaliatory steps, but could not force Vietnam to withdraw from Cambodia until the Soviets themselves encouraged the Vietnamese withdrawal in the late 1980s. Ancient rivalries between China and Vietnam, and between Vietnam and Cambodia, as well as tensions between the Soviet Union and China prolonged the agonies of Southeast Asia. There was no monolithic communism in this part of the globe, where nationalism was as important as Communism in shaping the violent conflicts of the postcolonial era.

Communism and nationalism

Brezhnev: The "Prague Spring"

Leonid I. Brezhnev, who emerged as the dominant Soviet leader after Khrushchev's fall from power in 1964 and came to head both party and state, was intent, with reckless disregard for the costs to the economy, on building the country's military and naval strength to compete with the United States. Yet he avoided direct confrontation and saw political and economic advantages in a relaxation of tensions and arms negotiations. The open rift with Communist China made détente with the West even more important. But the two superpowers continued to vie with each other for influence in the Middle East, Africa, and other strategic areas of the world, and the Soviets consolidated their hold on eastern Europe.

Despite the failure of the Hungarian uprising in 1956, the longing for freedom and independence in eastern Europe refused to be suppressed. When, in 1968, the reforms of Alexander Dubček threatened the one-party state in Czechoslovakia, Brezhnev and the party leadership ruthlessly crushed the "Prague spring." They dispatched 250,000 troops, including token Polish, Hungarian, and East German contingents, to suppress the incipient revolution and remove Dubček and his reformist allies from power. The "Brezhnev Doctrine" that year proclaimed the Soviet right to intervene in the name of "proletarian internationalism" in any Communist country to protect "socialism" against "internal or external forces" and prevent the "restoration of a capitalist regime." It was in its own way a kind of

The Brezhnev Doctrine

The citizens of Prague responded angrily to the Soviet military forces in their city in August 1968, but they could do little against the 250,000 well-armed troops. These young people celebrated the destruction of a Soviet tank; elsewhere in the city, however, the Soviets were destroying the reformist government of Alexander Dubcek and suppressing the movement that had attempted to create a more democratic political system in Czechoslovakia.

(Hulton Archive)

mirror image of the Truman Doctrine. Czechoslovakia returned to a tight dictatorship ruled by party bosses with close ties to Moscow. The United States did no more than protest the armed intervention in Czechoslovakia, demonstrating once again that it would not openly challenge Soviet control over eastern Europe in what was tacitly accepted as a sphere of Soviet influence. But the invasion of Czechoslovakia, even more than the suppression of the 1956 Hungarian uprising, alienated the Communist faithful in many parts of the world and undermined the Soviet leadership of Western Communist parties, which strongly denounced the brutal intervention.

Brezhnev and Nixon

Although President Nixon, who took office in 1969, continued and even intensified the war in Vietnam, he introduced greater flexibility into the American policy of containment and pursued a policy of systematic détente in the Cold War. With Kissinger (and somewhat like de Gaulle) he believed in the balance of power diplomacy of an earlier age and that each country's long-range national self-interest and geopolitical concerns should count more than ideology. The growing importance of the People's Republic of China had to be recognized. The

Nixon and détente

United States would be unable to curb Soviet expansion altogether, but it could offer economic concessions and other inducements for cooperation and peace.

Under the Nixon-Kissinger policy the United States linked Western technology, trade, and investment to Soviet cooperation in international affairs. The economic inducements were important because the Soviet Union's economic difficulties were aggravated by its growing arms burden. Khrushchev's earlier boast of surpassing the West economically had proved hollow. The Soviets badly needed Western technology, Western investment credits, and, because of their persistent agricultural crises, Western grain. In the new atmosphere American and West European private bankers made large loans to the East European nations, which benefited even more than the Soviets from détente. The two Germanys moved closer together in economic relations, recognized each other diplomatically, and were admitted to the United Nations in 1973 as two separate sovereign states.

The Nixon-Kissinger policies developed out of a reassessment of global realities. Unlike the bipolar situation in 1945 when there were only two superpowers, there were now other emergent power centers, and the most important of them was the People's Republic of China. In 1971 the United States withdrew its objections to the entry of the People's Republic of China into the United Nations as a replacement for Taiwan, although it would still recognize "two Chinas" and work toward their peaceful reunification one day as "one country, two systems." Then in an unannounced move in 1972, after careful secret preparations, Nixon, who had built his domestic political career on anticommunism, took the dramatic step of visiting Mao in Beijing and initiated diplomatic and economic relations with China.

The opening to China

The American opening to China increased pressure on the Soviets to pursue détente. The Soviet arms buildup under Brezhnev signified that the Soviets were approaching nuclear parity, and both the United States and the Soviet Union found it to their advantage to negotiate arms reduction. The Strategic Arms Limitation (or SALT) talks begun under President Johnson were resumed. In 1972 Nixon and the Soviet leaders reaffirmed the goal of "peaceful coexistence" and signed the SALT I treaty. Each nation agreed to reduce its antimissile defense system to make it possible to work toward equality in offensive weapons. They agreed also to hold offensive weapons to a fixed number for a period of five years. The treaty did not halt the arms race, but it reduced fears on both sides of a preemptive strike and promised continued negotiations. After Nixon resigned from the presidency in 1974 following the Watergate scandal, détente continued under his successor, President Ford.

SALT I

Détente offered an opportunity to settle or phase out some unresolved issues of the Second World War. In 1975, in what resembled a peace conference for Europe, three decades after the Second World War had ended, 35 nations—the 16 members of NATO, the 7 Warsaw Pact states, and 12 European countries not formally members of either alliance—met at Helsinki over a period of two years in a Conference on Security and Cooperation in Europe. They pledged to work for peace, economic and cultural cooperation, and the protection of human rights. The Helsinki accords, although not a formal treaty, ratified the European territorial boundaries established after the Second World War and set up "Helsinki watch committees" for the surveillance of human rights in nations that signed the agreements. The U.S.S.R. considered the commitment to human rights a small price to pay in exchange for the economic and other benefits of détente. It still expected to keep strict limits on dissent within its own country and in the East European states, but it failed to see how much the Helsinki accords would encourage dissenters to

The Helsinki accords

defy repression. The Helsinki conference was the high point of Cold War détente; not long thereafter, in 1979, Soviet-Western relations took another downward turn. But we must first turn to the changing world economy, to which the Soviet Union and the Eastern bloc were now more closely tied than ever before.

121. COLLAPSE AND RECOVERY OF THE GLOBAL ECONOMY: THE 1970S AND 1980S

Interdependence is a form of dependency, and the expansion of the global economy after the Second World War made each country more vulnerable to events in distant places. In 1974, after two and a half decades of spectacular growth, the Western economic boom wound down abruptly. Signs of economic slowdown and inflationary pressures were already visible in the late 1960s and recession might have occurred in any event, but it was the oil embargo growing out of the Arab-Israeli war in the autumn of 1973 that precipitated the crisis.

Oil had replaced coal as a major source of energy. Readily available at low prices, it came primarily from the vast reserves of the Middle East and was transported easily and economically by tanker through the Persian Gulf and Suez Canal. The major international oil companies, mostly American, for a long time controlled prices and production, and purchasers paid for the oil in dollars. The Western economies, the Japanese, and others in

OPEC

Asia had come to depend on cheap oil. In 1960, 14 of the oil-exporting countries in the Middle East, Africa, and Latin America formed the Organization of Petroleum Exporting Countries (or OPEC) to curb the monopoly concessions enjoyed by foreign companies and to assume a larger share of authority over production and prices.

Within OPEC the Arab states of the Middle East were the most assertive. The oil issue turned intensely political during the Arab-Israeli war of October 1973 when the Arab oil-producing states embargoed the shipment of oil to states accused of supporting Israel. The OPEC cartel cut back production and quadrupled oil prices. Apprehension spread in western Europe and Japan, and in the United States, which needed foreign oil to supplement its domestic resources. Never had an essential commodity risen in price so rapidly; the entire global industrial complex seemed vulnerable. The oil shortage and the price escalation, coming on the heels of the international monetary difficulties and devaluations of the dollar in 1971–1973, sharply increased the balance of payment deficits for all oil-importing countries, undermined currencies, accelerated an inflationary spiral already underway, and seriously interrupted the spectacular growth of the West European economies.

Dependence on oil

The immediate panic caused by the oil embargo passed, but prices remained at a much higher level. Later in the decade, in 1979, a second oil crisis occurred when Iran, in the midst of its revolution, halted oil exports and the OPEC cartel again doubled prices. In the 1980s the Iran-Iraq War once more reduced global oil supplies and threatened the free movement of tankers through the Persian Gulf, prompting the United States and other Western countries to take naval action. Eventually, however, the oil cartel proved less cohesive and intimidating than originally feared. Additional energy resources became available. After the discovery of oil in the North Sea, Britain and Norway became exporters of oil. The Netherlands and other countries turned to natural gas; France, to nuclear energy. Many countries initiated energy conservation measures. When prices declined in the 1980s as a result of falling demand, oil-producing countries like Nigeria and Mexico found themselves deeply in debt because they had geared their economies and government expenditures to the sale of high-priced oil. The decline in oil revenues led to restlessness in the Arab states. The Persian Gulf War, precipitated by the American and international response to Iraq's invasion of oil-producing Kuwait in August 1990, made clear the critical role that oil continued to play in international affairs.

The Recession: Stagnation and Inflation

The recession that began in 1974 was the most severe since the 1930s, although it never approximated the depths of the Great Depression. What set it apart from previous economic declines was the accompanying inflation, which raced on in major industrial countries at double-digit annual figures.

In some European countries the annual rate of inflation rose to over 20 percent; it reached 27 percent in Britain in 1975. In the United States prices doubled over the course of the decade. For a time economic growth ground to a standstill in western Europe. By the late 1970s the recession was worldwide. Bankruptcies shook several countries; production declined; economic growth slowed or even halted. In the 24 non-Communist industrial countries the number of jobless was estimated at 15 million in 1975 and over 32 million in 1983. Over 10 percent of the American and West European labor force was unemployed. From a low point of 3.4 percent in 1969 unemployment in the United States rose to 10.8 percent in 1982. American factories operated at two-thirds their capacity. Unemployment once more became the bane of industrial capitalism.

The bane of industrial capitalism

The economic troubles were somewhat cushioned for the unemployed in industrial countries. Labor unions were still active, although declining in membership and influence, and welfare benefits were more advanced than they had been in the 1930s. Workers in Essen, Turin, Liverpool, or Detroit could count on severance pay, trade union benefits, and government unemployment compensation far beyond the welfare payments and dole of earlier generations. These benefits reduced human suffering and also limited the decline in consumer purchasing power. The recession, however, aggravated the problem of "structural unemployment." Because of automation, high technology, and the dwindling importance of older, less efficient sectors (such as coal mining, shipbuilding, and other so-called smokestack industries), many workers would never return to their old jobs or use their old skills again.

Structural unemployment

The combination of stagnation and inflation (dubbed "stagflation" by journalists) created unprecedented problems for governments. Keynesian theory, which had gained a wide following after 1945, called for government spending and deficit financing in slow times to buoy demand and keep employment stable. With inflation rampant, such measures became questionable. The dilemma centered on whether curbing inflation or reducing unemployment should claim the highest priority. Efforts to fight inflation by tight money and high interest rates would discourage investment, aggravate the business slowdown, and swell the ranks of the unemployed. Government spending to prime the pump or reducing interest rates to facilitate private borrowing could feed inflation.

Stagflation

With the American economy also troubled, the Western industrial countries looked to the Federal Republic of Germany and its powerful economy and trade surpluses to take the lead in expanding investment and production. Germany, however, mindful of the hyperinflation of the 1920s, set its highest priority on controlling inflation; it kept interest rates high and rejected expansionist policies. Other countries followed the same policies. By the early 1980s inflation was brought under control in the United States and in western Europe, but in Europe unemployment continued at levels unheard of in the early postwar decades.

Faith in Keynes shaken

Faith in Keynesian prescriptions of government spending to combat recessions when private investment had dried up was now seriously shaken. In addition, the post-1945 welfare state had also spent freely for social purposes in keeping with the precepts of progressive liberalism. From 1950 to the mid-1970s the percentage of gross national product expended on social measures in the industrial countries had more than doubled.

The established tenets of Keynesian economics were now challenged as never before. The British Conservative party leader Margaret Thatcher, who became prime minister in 1979, led the campaign against the welfare state and was soon joined by Ronald Reagan, the American Republican president from 1981 to 1989. Both leaders attacked the welfare state as costly, wasteful, paternalistic, and bureaucratic and blamed it for eroding individual initiative and responsibility. Nationalized industries, where they existed, also came under criticism.

Although conservative governments continued heavy expenditures for national defense, they curbed government spending on social measures. Meanwhile to stimulate production they offered numerous incentives to private enterprise, including tax reductions, deregulation, and restraints on unions that interfered with technological innovation. "Supply side" economics, as these ideas were labeled, emphasized increased production rather than the hitherto prevailing notion of increased consumer demand as most important for economic growth. The results were then expected to "trickle down" for everyone's benefit, with a safety net in place for the truly disadvantaged.

Supply side economics

The gradual return of prosperity, especially in the United States from about 1982 on, reinforced faith in the free-market economy, despite uneasiness about the continuing vicissitudes of the business cycle. Conservative economic theories and policies appeared to be confirmed by a worldwide movement toward market economies and away from centralized planning, which in its rigidly Marxist form had manifestly failed in the Soviet Union and eastern Europe. Defenders of the welfare state, however, continued to stress the importance of supplementing market economies with direct action by governments to meet individual and social needs. The welfare, or interventionist, state still served important social needs and seemed destined to survive, even if in modified form. A new generation of liberal, labor, and socialist leaders came to preach the virtues of a "new middle way" that leaned heavily on market economies as the key to economic growth but without surrendering the prerogatives of government in confronting the social and economic problems of modern societies.

Economic and Political Change in Western Europe

Britain was especially hard hit by the recession of the 1970s. Of all the industrial nations, it suffered the highest rate of inflation. Unemployment climbed, and the pound dropped to a new low in global financial markets. To avert collapse, the country depended on foreign loans. The trade unions refused to accept the sacrifices that even their own Labour party believed necessary, and disruptive strikes in coal and transportation weakened and exasperated the country. Radical factions in the Labour party pressed for increased nationalization of

Conservatives sought to dismantle or reduce the social programs of the modern welfare state after they won control of the national governments in Great Britain and the United States during the 1980s. Prime Minister Margaret Thatcher and President Ronald Reagan, shown here at a meeting of Western government leaders in 1984, became close political allies and friends in these years. They both promoted conservative policies by reducing the government's participation in domestic economic life, though they increased national spending for military forces and believed that their governments should play a strong, activist role in international affairs.

(Hulton Archive)

industry and for nonalignment in the Cold War. Alienated by the economic confusion and collapse of moral authority, which they blamed on Labour governments that had been in power since 1974, the voters in 1979 turned to the Conservatives.

Margaret Thatcher

Margaret Thatcher, the first woman prime minister in any major Western country, headed a Conservative government resolved to change matters. She immediately and decisively cut government expenditures, reduced imports, and resisted trade union wage demands. The focus shifted to investment, productivity, and economic growth. Inflation was curbed, but unemployment rose. The Thatcher government in its early years seemed headed for political trouble, but in 1982 Thatcher stirred old patriotic and imperial memories by dispatching a small armada 8,000 miles to the coast of South America, thwarting the attempted takeover of the Falkland (or Malvina) Islands by Argentina. The Conservatives won a sweeping parliamentary majority the following year.

For a time in the 1980s the Thatcher policies were successful. The government curtailed the power of the unions, returned over one-third of the nationalized industries to private enterprise, and made credit more readily available for business and for home buyers. Britain could soon point to the highest economic growth rate of all the European countries, rising productivity, low inflation, a stronger pound, a higher standard of living for most people, widened home ownership, and buoyant self-confidence. Unemployment, however, remained high; fiscal retrenchment hurt education, especially the universities; and pockets of deep depression persisted, especially in the north of England and in Scotland and Wales where traditional industries such as coal mining and shipbuilding faced difficulties competing in the new global economy. The south and southeast enjoyed a bustling prosperity, especially in the high-technology industries around London and Cambridge. Meanwhile London reinforced its position as a world financial center and the United Kingdom became once again a leading creditor nation. Decades of economic decline and demoralization seemed to have been reversed. The opposition was disunited and in disarray. In the elections of 1987, Labour's popular vote dropped to its lowest point in decades, and union membership declined.

But when economic growth slowed after the stimulus of privatization and deregulation wore off, Thatcher introduced a number of fiscal measures that led to her fall in 1990. Her

New Labour

successor as prime minister, John Major, had to cope with a new recession that set in after 1990, a weakened pound, and unemployment. Labour, meanwhile, under new leadership that abandoned older ideas of class struggle and attracted a broad range of middle-class support, continued to challenge the Conservatives, arguing that the Thatcher era had favored the rich and fostered a less equitable society. Finally, under the moderate "New Labour" leadership of Tony Blair, the Labour party won the parliamentary elections in 1997 and regained control of the government for the first time since 1979.

In France, politics in the 1980s veered Left earlier. The austerity program adopted in the 1970s by the conservative parties to combat inflation was unpopular, and the government's aloofness, elitism, and seeming unconcern with social issues under de Gaulle's successors helped the Socialist-led opposition grow in strength. In 1981 François Mitterrand achieved the goal he had set for himself and the Socialist party. He himself had had a varied career, some aspects of which were unknown until the last years of his life, including his association with right-wing causes in the early 1930s and his service to Vichy in wartime before joining the Resistance movement. He was known as a moderate Socialist, whose socialism owed more to liberal idealism than to Marxism. A consummate politician, he revitalized the Socialist party, persuaded it to drop its class-struggle rhetoric, successfully relegated the still strong Communists to a subordinate place among the parties of the Left, and reached out to many who chafed at the social insensitivities of the Gaullists and Conservatives. "Changer la vie"—change life for everyone—was his campaign slogan. Not only did he win the presidency, but his Socialist party triumphantly gained an unprecedented absolute majority in the National Assembly.

Mitterrand and "Changer la vie"

Labor reforms were immediately introduced, reducing the workweek from 40 to 39 hours and adding a fifth week of annual paid vacation. Following up on the nationalizations of 1945, Mitterrand nationalized the remaining large banks as well as several leading industrial corporations. One of the few European leaders still faithful to Keynesian precepts in the 1980s, he expected government pump priming and labor reforms to raise purchasing power, stimulate the economy, and thus absorb the costs of the expanded welfare state. But increased labor costs reduced French competitiveness abroad, and private investment also dried up. The immediate consequences were slow economic growth, trade deficits, inflation, unemployment, and a weakening franc. Within two years Mitterrand abruptly changed course. He halted further nationalization and other reforms, insisted on retrenchment and austerity to cope with inflation, and placed a strong emphasis on modernization. Cutting off subsidies to decaying industries, he shifted government support to high technology. The new policies encouraged economic growth but contributed little to reducing unemployment. His Socialist followers were disenchanted and frustrated. Others in the country, however, were relieved to see him concentrate on strengthening the nation's economy rather than on sectarian politics.

Politically, Mitterrand had isolated the Communists, hitherto the largest party of the Left, and dramatically reduced their electoral strength. Without a dynamic competitor, the French Socialists could act more like Socialists and Social Democrats elsewhere, campaigning for moderate reform, looking to middle-class support, and seeking to "manage" capitalist economies. Renewed economic problems, however, cost the party popular support. It lost its parliamentary majority in 1986 and Mitterrand was forced to govern with a Conservative prime minister. The term "cohabitation" entered the language to signify a popularly elected president of one party governing with a prime minister who represented the opposing parliamentary majority. It was a precedent that de Gaulle never foresaw. But as an established practice that was repeated over the years to come, it became a legacy of Mitterrand that demonstrated the resiliency of the Fifth Republic. In the Gaullist tradition the president continued to determine defense and foreign policy.

"Cohabitation"

When in 1988 Mitterrand was reelected president, the Socialists regained a small plurality in the National Assembly. But unemployment, scandals involving Socialist ministers, and inroads by environmental and other groups led to their rout in 1993 and the return of a large conservative majority. Cohabitation resumed under the conservative Gaullist Prime Minister Jacques Chirac, who was then elected to the presidency in 1995, and the seesaw pattern of French politics continued in his administration. While the French economy strengthened impressively in the 1990s, unemployment remained a problem, especially for young people. One measure, adopted by the Socialist prime minister, Lionel Jospin, reduced the workweek from 39 to 35 hours to create new jobs, but met with strong opposition from most employers. During these years women played a much larger role in French government and public institutions than ever before, occupying key ministries and high-level posts in business and professional life. A new law, to be implemented in stages, provided that women were to be candidates in elections for representative bodies in equal numbers with men. A few women writers and scholars were even admitted to the French Academy, a male bastion since 1635.

West European Socialists

Socialists holding office in western Europe now championed modernization, market economies, and economic growth as the path to the good society, and their policies won broad support. Moderation and pragmatism succeeded in overshadowing if not entirely replacing older ideologies. Helmut Schmidt, the Social Democratic chancellor in West Germany from 1974 to 1982, was one leading exemplar. In Italy, Bettino Craxi and a Socialist coalition in 1983 ended the long tenure of the Christian Democrats, who had formed 40 consecutive cabinets since 1945. The Italian Socialists governed for an unprecedented four years but were barely distinguishable in policies and practices from the long-entrenched Christian Democratic establishment. In Spain the popular Socialist party leader, Felipe Gonzalez, in 1982 headed the first Left government since the Spanish Civil War of the 1930s and governed on into the mid-1990s. In Portugal, after the revolutionary turbulence of 1974, a Socialist and a Social Democratic party competed with each other on moderate platforms.

In West Germany Helmut Schmidt's Social Democratic government moved to control inflation, its chief concern, through policies of retrenchment and fiscal conservatism, but the industrial slowdown of the late 1970s brought unemployment to a country which for years had known only labor scarcity. Even after recovery, unemployment persisted at about 8 percent. The doors once open to guest workers closed; bonuses were offered to those who would return home; extremist groups (as in Britain, France, and Austria) alarmingly exploited antiforeign sentiment. In 1982 the Christian Democrats were returned to office with Helmut Kohl as chancellor; he would remain in office for the next 16 years. Economic growth resumed, although at more modest rates, and the mark maintained itself as one of the world's strongest currencies. The German Federal Republic remained the most productive nation in western Europe, accounting for a third of the combined output of the European Community. But heavy labor costs, resulting from high wages and generous social

"One nation and two states"

benefits, burdened the economy and reduced its competitiveness in world markets. Meanwhile the prospects in the 1980s for reunification of the two Germanys still seemed remote—Germany would apparently remain "one nation and two states," in Willy Brandt's phrase.

The American Economy

The United States recovered from the post-1974 recession sooner and more completely than the Europeans. The American economy suffered business slowdowns and serious inflation from 1974 to 1982. But once inflation was brought under control the economy began to grow in the 1980s. Deregulation of industry, encouraged under the Reagan and Bush presidencies, and corporate streamlining or restructuring (often called downsizing) produced greater profits and stimulated economic growth, as did the beginnings of the computer revolution. Continuing interventions by the Federal Reserve Board, which raised or lowered interest rates, helped to protect against inflation. The stock market began to rise, as did real estate values. In the 1980s unemployment dropped below 6 percent, and the labor force grew at a time when unemployment was still a persistent problem in Europe, though many of the newly employed in the United States were entering lower-paying service industries. There were setbacks, including a dramatic, temporary fall in stock prices in 1987 and a notorious failure of savings and loans banks, which had overextended their credit. A more general economic slowdown again set in after 1989, and unemployment rose to 7.8 percent. Campaigning on the poor performance of the economy, the Democratic candidate Bill Clinton was able to defeat President Bush in the election of 1992. At the time few recognized that by the spring of 1991 the economy was already embarking on an extraordinary expansion that would continue throughout the decade and into the opening of the new century.

There were still many areas of economic concern in the 1980s. The trading strength of the United States accentuated some of its economic problems. The oil crisis of the 1970s had ultimately reinforced the dollar (oil profits were invested in dollars), and the dollar's value rose steadily in the early 1980s, raising the cost of American goods in global markets. American exports also faced strong competition from western Europe and Japan, and *Economic concerns* from the newly industrialized small states in the Pacific, where labor costs were low and newer highly mechanized plants provided a competitive edge. The strong dollar made it difficult for the United States to sell its products and aggravated its already heavy trade deficit. The United States therefore sought to bring down the high value of the dollar by 1985, and over the next three years the dollar lost almost 50 percent of its value in relation to foreign currencies, declining to its lowest level since 1945 and creating a new challenge for the American economy. Japanese, West Europeans, Canadians, Arabs, and others seized the opportunity to buy into American corporations, banks, brokerage houses, and real estate. By the late 1980s foreign holdings of American assets totaled $1 trillion.

Meanwhile the Japanese economy reached such giant dimensions that corporations like the Fujita Bank and the Toyota Corporation were valued at five to ten times the market value of the largest American companies. The Nomura Securities Corporation of Tokyo became the largest brokerage firm in the world. Not one of the world's ten largest banks in the 1980s was American. From 1985 on, for the first time since 1914, the United States was a debtor nation. Foreign interests owned more assets in the United States than Americans owned abroad, which meant a steady outflow of interest, dividends, and rents. Even when American exports expanded, imports continued to grow and the trade balance remained unfavorable. The annual budget deficit mounted and the national debt soared from less than $1 trillion in 1981 to well over $4 trillion by 1990. Foreign capital financed the American debt and profited from the interest on loans.

Concern mounted, even as the American economy was recovering, over the weakness in exports, the balance-of-payments deficits, the burden of defense expenditures, the growing national debt, the large annual budget deficits, and the foreign acquisition of American assets. Analysts pointed to inadequate American savings *Relative decline in growth* and investment, a relative slowdown in productivity gains since the 1960s, a lag in industrial research and development, and shortcomings in American education for an increasingly competitive world. The American economy was still the largest in the world; in the early 1990s its gross domestic product exceeded $5 trillion, far ahead of Japan and Germany. But it had shown a relative decline in growth in relation to the other major industrial nations. Between 1970 and 1990 American economic output dropped from five times that of Japan to less than twice as much; the gap between American and German output also shrank. Deep pockets of poverty and racial tensions persisted within the country. It was debated at the time whether the United States, still the premier political, economic, and military power, might lose its primacy because of economic weaknesses—as Spain, the Netherlands, France, and Britain had in the modern centuries.

The prospects that opened up in the late 1980s of an end to the Cold War and of a measure of relief from the burden of arms expenditures brought some reassurances. In the short-lived recession that began in 1990 the United States recovered faster than other countries. Japan itself in 1989, its prosperity based on overinflated stock market and real estate values, entered on a long period of economic difficulties that persisted throughout and beyond the following decade. Meanwhile, American productivity, economic growth, technological innovation, and international competitiveness during the 1990s made most of the earlier jeremiads seem hollow or short-sighted.

The Financial World

The world's largest stock exchanges and financial markets were centered in New York City. Deregulation in the 1980s brought with it a sharp increase in financial acquisitions and mergers. New forms of trading in options and futures and widening participation by small investors contributed to the stock market's growth and volatility. Once again, as in the 1920s, the lines between speculation and investment became blurred. In October 1987, a tremor ran through the United States and world markets when stocks on the New York Stock Exchange in one day lost close to one-fourth their value, conjuring up memories of the October 1929 crash and the ensuing Great Depression. But the market recovered, and in the following decade it went on to reach new heights—and to experience new periods of extreme volatility. The episode clearly demonstrated the interdependence of the world's financial markets. Reverberations of the 1987 shock in New York were felt instantly in London, Frankfurt, Tokyo, Hong Kong, Singapore, Taipei, Sydney, and elsewhere. The financial markets, like the currency markets, were decentralized but more interwoven than ever before. With new systems of telecommunications and other advanced computer technology, a single financial market operated around the world and around the clock.

Speculation and investment

The sense of mutual interdependence in the global economy came to be widely shared. The United States, western Europe, and Japan recognized that the prosperity of each depended on the smooth functioning of the world economy. The heads of state of the seven largest industrial powers with market economies (the "Group of Seven"—the United States, Britain, France, the Federal Republic of Germany, Italy, Canada, and Japan) met from the 1970s on in annual economic summits to consult on the state of the economy. The leading central banks made efforts to stabilize interest and exchange rates. The Organization for Economic Cooperation and Development (OECD) brought together the 24 leading industrial nations of the world, and GATT continued its "rounds" of negotiations to reduce tariffs. The integration of the Soviet Union and eastern Europe into the world economy, initiated in the 1970s in the first period of détente, and the rapid political changes taking place in that part of the world after the late 1980s provided further opportunities for international cooperation. The developing nations, however, remained somewhat on the economic periphery, their heavy debt and slow economic growth intensifying their dependence on the industrial world. They remained critical of a globalization that seemed to ignore or pay inadequate attention to their needs.

Mutual interdependence

The Enlarged European Community: Problems and Opportunities

After de Gaulle passed from the political scene in 1969, the way opened for enlarging the six-nation European Community (EC). In 1973 Britain, Denmark, and Ireland were admitted; the six became nine. In the next decade, with the admission of Greece in 1981 and

Japan's financial markets developed into an important component of the international economy, attracting investments from all parts of the world. These traders at the Tokyo Stock Exchange in the early 1990s use advanced technologies to manage the sale of stocks and to keep track of the information that flows constantly through such markets and the international economic networks that they support.

(Charlie Cole/Sipa Press)

Spain and Portugal in 1986, the 9 became 12. In 1995, with the admission of Austria, Finland, and Sweden, the numbers would grow to 15, with many other countries actively seeking membership.

Enlargement brought new difficulties, aggravated by the economic slowdown of the 1970s. A food importer, Britain objected to the "common agricultural policy" agreed upon in 1968, whereby countries such as France and Italy received large subsidies for their farmers, whose products were *Growing pains* withheld from the open market and stored at great expense to keep prices artificially high. The British complained of paying a disproportionate share of the EC budget without receiving commensurate benefits. The admission of the less industrially advanced southern Mediterranean states in the 1980s introduced serious regional differences. Despite the original promise and accomplishments of the Community as a whole, the free trading area remained far from complete. Countries still placed quotas on agricultural imports; France kept out Italian wines. Burdensome administrative regulations at the borders persisted.

Except for a limited circle of Europeanists, the enthusiasm for close political integration seemed to have dimmed. With enlargement and greater diversity, the Community became even more intergovernmental and less supranational. Britain was always reluctant to support additional supranational authority for the Community. In periods of economic slowdown and monetary instability the national governments themselves had to cope with the problems. In 1973 the government leaders began meeting on a regular basis, the presidency rotating among the member states. The first elections to the European Parliament in 1979 were more symbolic than substantial, and the Parliament's role as a legislature failed to grow significantly. While the more ambitious dream of a United States of Europe went unrealized, the Community, for all its problems, remained an important institution, poised for further growth.

Toward a "Single Europe": the European Union

Even during the prosperous 1960s, the European economy did not maintain its growth in all areas. But in the 1970s the world itself was entering a new phase of industrialism, a "third industrial revolution," marked by the introduction of automation, computers, and other forms of advanced technology. Progress would no longer be measured in coal and steel or in ships and textiles but in nuclear reactors, microelectronics, telecommunications, computers, robotics, and space technology. In the "postindustrial" age data processing, information storage and retrieval, and more and more sophisticated communications capabilities were the keys to competitive success. In 1977 the first personal computer was produced for what would become a mass market, with rapid improvements to follow in speed and capacity. More workers were employed in the service sector than in the older basic industries, and the service economy was growing faster than either agriculture or industry. It was widely noted that the global economy was eroding the economic and political autonomy of the nation-state. Using new technologies, the multinational corporations of the industrial world invested capital and set up shop across the globe, independent of all national boundaries.

The postindustrial age

In the new forms of technology, the Europeans found themselves for a time outdistanced by the Americans and the Japanese. American multinational corporations controlled most of the high-technology industries in Europe—before the Japanese arrived to compete. Trade competition from Japan and the rapidly developing industrial countries of the Pacific Rim grew. The post-1974 recession made it difficult for the Europeans to promote research and development. Western Europe lagged behind other parts of the world in recovering economically after 1974 or in coping with unemployment. On into the 1980s journalists spoke of "Eurosclerosis" and "Europessimism."

The European Community set about to reinvigorate itself. Although internal tariffs had disappeared, nontariff obstacles still impeded the flow of trade. Nationally dictated, and therefore varying, standards of production and quality prevailed. In 1987, by the "Single European Act," the 12 member-nations agreed to establish common production standards, remove impediments to the flow of capital, seek uniform tax rates, recognize each other's professional and commercial licensing, and honor a common charter of labor rights. They would create a truly integrated "single Europe," a "Europe without borders." A unified European currency and central banking system were projected for the end of the 1990s, and a common defense and foreign policy were envisaged for the future. The arrangements were confirmed in a Treaty of European Union signed at Maastricht in the Netherlands at the close of 1991, and ratified after protracted debate by the parliaments or electorates of the member states by the end of 1992. Opponents in several countries raised objections to the loss of national control in so many areas, but the treaty was adopted. The European Community became the European Union. The way was open to closer integration.

The Single European Act

The European Union represented a domestic market of 345 million people (one-third larger than that of the United States) and was the largest trading bloc in the global economy, accounting for 40 percent of all international trade. With the new steps toward integration, Europeans hoped to enlarge investment, develop high technology, stimulate productivity, end the lagging rate of economic growth, and reduce an unemployment rate that was still distressingly high.

For the world as a whole, a return to protectionism was always a lurking danger. The advanced industrial nations might divide into large regional trading blocs—a North American or Western Hemisphere bloc led by the United States, a Pacific bloc, the European Union, and possibly others. New competitive barriers could interfere with the free trade that had contributed so much to post-1945 prosperity.

Dangers of protectionism

122. THE COLD WAR REKINDLED

We must go back in time to pick up the flow of international affairs. In the summer of 1974 President Nixon resigned his office to avoid impeachment over his role in the Watergate scandal. His vice president, Gerald Ford, succeeded him. But in the next election the Democratic candidate, Jimmy Carter, won and took office in 1977. More than any American president since Woodrow Wilson, President Carter sought to infuse American foreign policy with moral idealism. Human rights, he declared, must be "the soul of our foreign policy." Détente with the Soviet Union was more closely linked than before to respect for human rights; economic aid would be forthcoming only if the Soviets permitted freedom to dissenters, the right of emigration for Soviet Jews and others, and an end to the coercion of Poland. The Soviets did not take kindly to these public pressures. Both sides meanwhile reinforced their military and nuclear strength.

Human rights

On the other hand both countries continued strategic arms talks and after tortuous negotiations signed a SALT II treaty in January 1979. They agreed to parity in strategic, or long-range, nuclear missiles. Although the number of powerful missiles remained high and nothing prevented the development of new sophisticated weapons, the agreement might have been an important breakthrough in arms control. But before it could be ratified by the Senate, the Soviet Union moved troops into the neighboring state of Afghanistan to bolster a weak pro-Soviet leftist regime. It was the first Soviet military intervention of that kind outside eastern Europe.

Soviet invasion of Afghanistan

Condemning the act as invasion and aggression, Carter denounced it as a new phase of expansion by the Soviets threatening the entire Middle East—"a stepping stone in their possible control over much of the world's oil supplies." He warned that an attempt by any outside force to gain control of the Persian Gulf region would be regarded as "an assault on the vital interests of the United States" and would be repulsed "by any means necessary, including military force." He withdrew the SALT II treaty from the Senate, embargoed sales of grain and high technology to the Soviets, took measures to increase the military budget, and set up procedures at home for a renewal of the draft.

The invasion of Afghanistan, Carter informed the U.S.S.R., was the most serious threat to world peace since 1945. The European allies were not as convinced. Some argued that the Afghanistan episode was a regional matter, that the Soviet Union was acting to prevent instability on its borders, and that détente should continue. Unwilling to disturb commercial relations with the Soviets and eastern Europe, they refused to support the economic embargo which, among other consequences, would have interfered with the completion of a Soviet natural gas pipeline to western Europe. As it developed, Afghanistan turned out to be the U.S.S.R.'s Vietnam. Some 100,000 troops fought for over 8½ years before withdrawing ignominiously in 1989. Like the Americans in Vietnam, the Soviets were unable to use their overwhelming military power to defeat the Muslim guerrillas who, armed with American weapons and supported by Pakistan, fought stubbornly from their mountain strongholds.

Hostages in Iran

At the very time of the Soviet intervention in Afghanistan, as we have seen, the United States became preoccupied with the Iran hostage crisis, the seizing of American hostages by Iranian revolutionary militants in Tehran. It was a heavy blow to American prestige, compounded by the failure of an ill-fated rescue attempt. To add to Carter's humiliation, the hostages were freed on the day that his Republican successor, Ronald Reagan, took office in January 1981.

The Reagan Years: From Revived Cold War to New Détente

Reagan and the "evil empire"

There was no doubt of the new president's commitment to a hard line in the Cold War. The Soviet Union, Reagan asserted in 1983, represented "the focus of evil in the modern world." It was "an evil empire" with "dark purposes." After the humiliation of the hostage crisis, he pledged to restore America's lost prestige. Despite the strain on its economy, the Soviet Union during the 1970s had built up its military strength, modernized its conventional fighting forces, created a powerful navy, and achieved nuclear parity. With congressional support Reagan substantially increased defense appropriations, sponsored the largest peacetime military spending in the nation's history, and took a confrontational stand against communism everywhere. In Afghanistan, he stepped up arms shipments to the Muslim guerrillas and to Pakistan, which was backing the rebels. Against the Communist government in Poland he applied economic sanctions when, under pressure from the Soviets, it imposed martial law in 1981 to suppress the Solidarity trade union movement. He reinforced the embargo on the sale of high technology to the Soviets and to eastern Europe, but the embargo on grain sales was dropped because of opposition from American farmers.

In Central America and the Caribbean, Reagan accused the Soviets of using Castro's Cuba and the leftist Sandinista regime in Nicaragua as proxies to spread communism in the Western Hemisphere. The United States armed anti-Communist opponents of the regime in Nicaragua and reinforced anti-Communist regimes in neighboring states and other parts of Latin America. In 1983 American forces invaded the small Caribbean island of Grenada to overthrow a leftist government that was permitting the Cubans to build an airport of potential military use.

Even more than his predecessors, Reagan and his foreign policy advisers supported repressive authoritarian regimes so long as they were anti-Communist on the theory that one day such regimes might be liberalized; Communist governments, they believed, transformed their societies irreversibly. Critics, on the other hand, argued that revolutionary movements in Latin America and elsewhere sprang not from the Cold War but from older systems of privilege and exploitation; they opposed military solutions and support to repressive regimes as inappropriate responses.

In Libya, the administration demonstrated the American willingness to take unilateral military action. American planes bombed military installations in retaliation for what it was convinced were Libyan-sponsored terrorist activities. Some European allies, alarmed by the president's belligerence, opposed the operation and refused to permit air passage to the American bombers. In Lebanon, in the throes of civil war, the United States organized a multinational peacekeeping force in 1982. The American fleet landed marines, and terrorists retaliated by blowing up the American embassy and the American and French command centers, killing hundreds of American marines and French soldiers. The peacekeeping force withdrew.

Cold War allies

In the war between Iran and Iraq that broke out in 1980, described earlier, in the course of which attacks on tankers in the Persian Gulf threatened the flow of oil from the Arab Gulf states, the United States escorted a selected number of tankers under the protection of the American flag. There were some armed clashes and loss of lives, but the oil deliveries went through. The United States was intent on asserting American leadership in world affairs and on keeping the Soviets, insofar as possible, out of the Middle East.

Asserting American leadership

Nuclear Arms Control

No nuclear weapons were used in any conflict in the years after 1945, yet over every crisis hung the ultimate threat of a nuclear clash. We have seen how the earliest negotiations on nuclear disarmament, at a time when the United States alone possessed the atomic bomb, were broken off in 1947; how in 1949 the Soviets successfully tested their first atomic bomb, ending the American monopoly; and how the United States in 1952 and the Soviet Union shortly thereafter developed the hydrogen or thermonuclear bomb, which by its chain reaction had vastly more destructive capacity than the mere 20,000 tons of TNT of the Hiroshima bomb. By the 1960s both superpowers were building strategic long-range missiles, that is, intercontinental ballistic missiles, capable of delivering their nuclear warheads accurately and swiftly to targets in each other's homeland. They could be launched from land (from either stationary or mobile sites), from sea (from ships or submarines), or from bombers in the air. The world had entered a new age of military technology. Guided missiles were the key strategic weapons of the modern age. Because of their immense destructive power, the nuclear weapons could not be used without unleashing unspeakable damage; they were different and distinct, it was agreed, from conventional weapons. Arms experts insisted that nuclear arms were built not for use but for deterrence.

The ultimate threat

Because nuclear testing threatened to poison the earth's atmosphere, and perhaps even damage the genetic endowment of present and future generations, controls were imperative. In 1963, despite Cold War tensions, the United States and the U.S.S.R. initiated a partial test-ban treaty, which banned testing in the atmosphere and permitted only underground testing. Concern over the spread of nuclear weapons prompted the two superpowers to propose a nonproliferation treaty, which was endorsed by the UN General Assembly in 1968 and eventually signed by over 130 states. It lacked binding force, however, and was ignored by countries bent on developing nuclear power.

The United States had led the way in the development of nuclear weapons, with Britain also participating from the beginning. The Soviet Union had then followed. France in 1960 became a fourth nuclear power, China in 1964 became a fifth, India in 1974 a sixth. By the late 1990s the list of countries that had achieved or were seeking to achieve a nuclear capacity included Israel, Pakistan, Iran, Iraq, Libya, and North Korea, and perhaps

Concerns about nuclear proliferation

others. The fear that terrorist organizations as well as states that had demonstrated a flagrant disregard for international law might come to possess nuclear materials prompted even greater concerns.

So long as the peaceful use of nuclear energy was encouraged, it was difficult to prevent proliferation. Nations purchasing nuclear power plants from industrial countries, ostensibly for peaceful purposes, could reprocess the plutonium from the spent fuel and build nuclear bombs, as India did. The search for alternative energy sources in the 1970s to replace oil stimulated many nations to build nuclear power plants that could easily be transformed for nonpeaceful purposes. Accidents at nuclear power plants, the most notorious of which were at Three Mile Island, Pennsylvania, in 1979 and, even more serious, at Chernobyl in Ukraine in 1986, did not deter the building of nuclear power plants but underscored the need for safer construction. From Chernobyl, radioactive materials in the atmosphere traveled as far as western Europe.

From the 1960s on debate continued in the United States about the missile gap, about the comparative numbers of the American and Soviet missile systems deployed on land and sea and in the air, and about the vulnerability of the American land-based missile systems. Following the Soviet missile buildup after the Cuban crisis of 1962, the two superpowers had achieved a rough parity by the 1970s. Although both recognized superiority as an elusive goal, nothing restrained them from adding more and more strategic arms. Strategists on each side supported the buildup. Using advanced computer programs, they calculated the potential casualties in a nuclear exchange between the superpowers in millions of deaths (or "megadeaths") and evaluated the effects of deterrents and counterdeterrents and of "first strikes" and "counterstrikes" on each nation's ability to wage and survive nuclear war. The balance of power was spoken of as a "balance of terror"; experts referred to "mutually assured destruction" (the acronym for which, ironically, was MAD). Deterrence was the accepted formula.

MAD: mutually assured destruction

Each side amassed huge stockpiles of arms, capable of destroying each other many times over, in what was described as "overkill." The two superpowers were also under continuing pressure to modernize their systems competitively—at exorbitant cost. When the Soviets developed defense systems, that is, antiballistic missiles, which undermined deterrence, the American response was to build its own defense systems and more powerful offensive weapons—such as the MIRV (a "multiple independently targeted reentry vehicle"), a delivery system carrying up to 10 nuclear warheads, each independently guided to separate targets, each warhead many times more powerful than the Hiroshima bomb. The Russians developed their own multiwarhead systems—all leading to an even higher level of armaments and greater uncertainty. Both sides had satellite reconnaissance systems, but for a time neither could determine the number of warheads on the other side and hence know with accuracy the other's capability. After the first SALT treaty, signed in 1972, each side developed new weapons outside the classes that were limited. The United States developed cruise missiles, designed to fly low to the ground and hence protected from defense systems; the Soviets, supersonic bombers. SALT II, signed in 1979 but not ratified until later, produced tentative agreement on equality in the total number of strategic long-range weapons, but protracted discussions continued.

Overkill

At the close of the 1980s each superpower possessed about 25,000 nuclear weapons, of which 12,000 on each side were strategic, that is, long-range, or intercontinental. Together the two arsenals exceeded 500,000 megatons (millions of tons) of explosive power,

The rapid development of intercontinental missile systems in the 1960s led finally to a "balance of terror" or system of deterrence called "mutually assured destruction." According to this theory, all nations would be deterred from launching nuclear assaults because they could expect a retaliatory attack that would destroy their own cities and people. This is the prototype of a Titan Intercontinental Ballistic Missile (ICBM), which the United States began to store in underground silos during the Cold War arms race. Since the 1960s missiles with nuclear weapons have been kept ready for immediate launching as part of the strategic deterrence plan.

(Hulton Archive)

dwarfing the total explosive power used in all previous wars. If only a small number of these nuclear arms reached their targets, the two countries could destroy each other's major cities and countryside and kill millions in the attack and in the radioactive after-effects, which would spread to neighboring areas. In the "nuclear winter" that might follow, human survival itself was at risk. There was always the dread possibility also of accident, miscalculation, or failure of communication. So deliberately suspended over the human race was the nuclear sword of Damocles that a direct communication link, or "hot line," was installed between the Kremlin and the White House in 1963, soon after the Cuban missile crisis, and in the following decades it was modernized and improved. It was designed to prevent the accidental outbreak of a nuclear war because of political misunderstanding, human error, or mechanical slipup; direct communication between the tribal chieftains was necessary in the nuclear age. No more than a 20-minute warning might be available.

The debate over security in the Cold War went beyond that of the defense strategists. Many pointed to the danger, the paradox, and even the immorality of building vast nuclear arsenals to prevent nuclear war; some (in the West) even urged unilateral disarmament. Others argued that without a high level of armaments a nation could be subject to nuclear blackmail. They maintained that the nuclear balance between the two opposing camps, and the principle of deterrence, had protected the peace. Everyone, to be sure, affirmed the need to reduce the political tensions and insecurity that fed the arms competition. Yet in the rekindled Cold War tensions of the early 1980s there seemed to be no solution to the impasse. Reluctantly, the world reconciled itself to the existing "balance of terror," except for piecemeal negotiations on arms limitations. It was only the unanticipated changes in the Soviet Union, its break-up, and the ending of the Cold War that brought unprecedented opportunities for nuclear arms reduction. But the altered situation would raise different dangers, leave proliferation a continuing threat, and still require constant reassessments of global safety.

Security debates

123. CHINA AFTER MAO

After Mao died in 1976 moderates and radicals competed for leadership. Mao's widow Jiang Qing, one of the firebrands of the Cultural Revolution, together with a small group of Maoist radicals, sought to win control and purge the moderates, but the attempt failed and she and her three associates—the so-called "gang of four"—were arrested and imprisoned. From behind the scenes Deng Xiaoping, the leader of the moderates, emerged by 1977 to become the most powerful figure in the country. Deng was a veteran party leader who had fallen out of favor with Mao in 1956–1957, was purged and humiliated in 1967 during the Cultural Revolution for having taken the "capitalist road," and purged for a third time in 1976 by the Maoist radicals. To counteract the Maoist cult of personality Deng over the years declined to accept the leading post in either government or party, and instead placed his protégés in top positions, but everyone knew who was in command.

Deng's Reforms

By late 1978 Deng won the party over to a sweeping reform program designed to curb the radical and utopian phases of the revolution, de-emphasize Marxist ideology and class struggle, and focus on economic growth and modernization. Deng proposed to transform the central economic planning, nationalized industry, and collectivized agriculture inherited from Mao—and indirectly from the Soviet Union. Without abandoning socialism as the eventual goal, he sanctioned numerous capitalist practices; he encouraged private enterprise, production for profit, and a competitive marketplace, at first in limited areas of the country and then more extensively. For state-owned industries he demanded profitability and accountability. The new system would be "a marriage," he said, "between a planned and a market economy." Dismantling the collectivized farms and communes, which had proved disastrous for agriculture, he allowed cultivation of the land by individual farmers and their families.

Both a planned and a market economy

He opened the country to foreign investment and welcomed Western science, technology, and management techniques. Although heavy industry was not neglected, Deng placed a new emphasis on consumer goods; factories that once manufactured military hardware began to produce refrigerators, washing machines, bicycles, and motorcycles.

Deng's reforms transformed Chinese society. Their most striking success was in the countryside, where farmers sold a significant portion of their product on the open market. Within a decade output doubled; more food became available for the cities, and even for export. In other parts of the economy retail outlets, repair shops, and other small businesses were in private hands. Special economic enclaves were established along the southern coast to encourage foreign enterprise and investment, much of it from Hong Kong. Foreign capital flowed in; a stock exchange was introduced. Gross domestic product, which had never risen by more than 2 or 3 percent annually under Mao, grew at an average 9 percent annually in the 1980s and then at even higher rates. By the calculations of some international agencies China's economic output was the third largest in the world. Many of the new entrepreneurs (and some farmers) became wealthy. The big cities took on aspects of a consumer society. Temporary joblessness was tempered by a state network of social services—an "iron rice bowl." The country enjoyed an unprecedented rise in living standards. The People's Liberation Army was reduced in size, but was modernized and made more professional, and the government bureaucracy was trimmed down. State-owned industries still accounted for a major share of production, but the growing private sector, flourishing in the coastal regions, represented the most vigorous part of the economy.

China transformed

Even if China remained a one-party state, a "people's democratic dictatorship" in one of the official phrases, and individual human rights (especially freedom of religion) were frequently violated, a more open and relaxed cultural and intellectual atmosphere prevailed. People tuned in on radio and television programs from the outside world. Students traveled and studied abroad. Many Western books (including this one, in its 1978 edition) were translated into Chinese. At no time since the Communist triumph in 1949 were the people so free to absorb ideas from the outside world. Foreign tourists visited in large numbers to see the new China. What earlier patriots and reformers like Sun Yat-sen had dreamed of, and Mao had failed to achieve because of his revolutionary excesses, Deng seemed to be accomplishing. Ideology was edged out by material advance, by the idea of a "rich and strong China."

Deng wished to provide an orderly succession. He therefore dislodged veterans of the older generation (many, like him, survivors of the Long March of 1934–1935) who clung to older Maoist ways, resisted Western political and economic ideas, and tried to block reform. The old guard retained a network of influence, and the country deferred to Deng as a central authority figure, but younger leaders began to emerge.

As the decade progressed, Deng's reform program, for all its accomplishments, showed serious imperfections. The rapid economic growth fueled inflation (a 20 to 30 percent annual rate in the late 1980s). The emphasis on rising levels of consumption strained resources. Despite its avowals, the government did not liquidate its unprofitable state-owned industries, one-fifth of which operated at a loss. An erratic system of price controls encouraged a black market. Even agricultural production slowed down. The consumer society bred extravagance, conspicuous consumption, and wastefulness. Corruption, endemic in China, became widespread because government and party leaders were closely tied to business enterprises, government and private. Idealistic critics voiced dissatisfaction with the corruption and with growing inequalities and inequities in a socialist society. In response to these cumulative problems Deng in 1988 called for retrenchment and a pause in further reform.

Economic difficulties

With time and vigilance the economic difficulties in the transitional economy might have been overcome. What interrupted Deng's memorable decade of reform was

*Rejection
of democracy*

the refusal to permit political reform and democratization to accompany the economic changes. Deng and others in the party believed that the country, for all its social advances, was unprepared for political democracy, which in their opinion would only breed chaos and confusion, as it had in the Cultural Revolution, and interfere with the order and stability necessary for economic growth and modernization. Further, nothing could be permitted to weaken the stewardship of the party, the heir to the old imperial dynasties, over the country's destiny.

Yet in the freer atmosphere that Deng had encouraged, many of the country's intellectual leaders, and younger people destined to be its future leaders, pressed for a loosening of the party's political controls, a freer press, and the right to criticize the corruption and other shortcomings of the system. Political liberalization and democratic advances elsewhere in the world in the 1980s reinforced the restlessness in China.

The "Democracy Movement"

When at the end of 1986, Hu Yaobang, general secretary of the party and at the time the 82-year-old Deng's designated successor, encouraged the belief that greater political freedom might be permitted, students took to the streets to show their support. Hu vacillated in suppressing the demonstrations and the party summarily replaced him.

*Tiananmen
Square*

Two years later the democratic ferment came to a head. Hu's death in April 1989 set off a series of student demonstrations in the huge central square in Beijing–Tiananmen Square, or Gate of Heavenly Peace. The demonstrators demanded democratization. Students from other parts of the country arrived to join what came to be called the "democracy movement," and ordinary citizens lent their support. The demonstrations mounted in intensity. At one point a statue of the Goddess of Liberty (its name and Phrygian cap recalling both the American and French revolutions) appeared. For seven weeks the demonstrators brought the capital and other parts of the country to a standstill. At the height of the ferment as many as a million people were massed in and around Tiananmen Square.

For a time the party seemed likely to accede to some demands. Zhao Ziyang, who had succeeded Hu as party leader, pressed for conciliation. But Deng, who took the side of the hard-liners, would not tolerate a recurrence of anarchy and turmoil as in the Cultural Revolution, nor permit the continuing embarrassment and humiliation of the party, army, and government. The government imposed martial law. Although their numbers had somewhat declined, the students refused to abandon the square. In the predawn hours of June 4, the army moved in with tanks, trucks, and armored cars and opened fire, with hundreds of victims. Perhaps no government could have tolerated such defiance of law and order and loss of prestige, but even modest concessions, patience, or the exhaustion of the demonstrators might have brought the demonstrations to a peaceful end. The army and the Deng regime now had the people's blood on their hands. Deng's enormous popularity plummeted.

*A "Western-
inspired
conspiracy"*

In the repressive atmosphere that followed, Deng and the party attributed the "counterrevolutionary" rebellion to a "Western-inspired conspiracy." For his conciliatory stance Zhao was dismissed from his posts. The new party and government leaders, echoing Deng, alleged that counterrevolutionaries "had attempted to install capitalism in China and make it dependent on certain foreign countries." While the nation still urgently needed Western technology and foreign investment and wished to continue with its "socialist market economy," the party vowed to supervise the private sector closely, reinforce Marxist ideology and political education, and determine the pace and timetable of change. Thou-

Enormous crowds gathered in Beijing's Tiananmen Square in the spring of 1989 to demand democratic reforms in the Chinese political system. The "democracy movement" drew students and others from many parts of the country. It also generated new political publications and popular symbols, including this statue of a Goddess of Liberty. The statue evoked memories of earlier political revolutions and became a prominent image of the democracy movement. The Chinese government ultimately suppressed the demonstrations by imposing martial law and dispersing the protestors, many of whom were killed or injured when the army opened fire.

(Peter Turnley/Corbis)

sands remained political prisoners, and the government resisted, and resented, all international pressures for their release.

Forty years after its founding in 1949, the People's Republic of China could look back upon a quarter-century of revolutionary transformation and turmoil under Mao, a brief transitional interlude after Mao's death, and a decade under Deng of economic progress, stability, openness to the West, and a freer intellectual atmosphere—until the yearning for greater freedom led to the massive demonstrations in the spring of 1989 and their repression. In the euphoria of the Deng years, many forgot the intense suspicion of the West that Deng shared with Mao, derived from the years when a weak China had lain open to exploitation.

In the distant past Confucian scholars, trained to enter the emperor's service, accepted the right of the emperor to rule autocratically but reserved the right to criticize harsh or incompetent rule. A ruler governed not by force alone but by moral example, virtue, and rectitude—or risked losing the "mandate of Heaven." The democracy movement brought into question the right of the party to rule in the old way, especially when authoritarianism was itself in decline in other parts of the world. The democracy movement demonstrated how deeply liberal values—"bourgeois liberalism," as it was denounced—had penetrated China and how powerful were the pressures for

Pressures for political change

political change. Continuing economic modernization, even under authoritarian control, could still lead to political liberalization. Fortunes were fickle in China, as Deng's own career demonstrated; moderate leaders might reemerge. After the passing of Deng and his aged contemporaries, a new generation was preparing to come to power.

Deng, a shadow of his former self, died in 1997, or as he had said earlier, he "went to meet Marx." His successor Jiang Zemin in some ways proved surprisingly moderate. He had been mayor of Shanghai and hence could distance himself from the events of 1989. He pursued Deng's goals of modernization even more vigorously and sought reconciliation with the West and closer integration into the global economy. But as the new century opened China had to balance its desire for closer economic ties with the West, including membership in the World Trade Organization, against Western criticisms of its continuing poor record on human rights, its assault on religion, and its belligerent stance on reunification with Taiwan.

Population Growth

On a less dramatic front (beneath the surface of mere "events") the pressure of the expanding population on the economy remained serious. Not irrelevantly, the character for "population" in the Chinese language depicts a mouth. Of all the larger developing countries, however, China was the most successful in coping with population growth. Through a system of central and local control, including forms of outright coercion that Western societies would find difficult to accept, a one-child-per-family rule, massive education programs, and social pressures, the birth rate declined significantly. In the years of relative prosperity under Deng and his successors the government found it difficult to enforce the one-child rule because affluent families, both in the city and countryside, were willing to risk fines for having more than one child. Nor were contraceptive devices always the most modern or most efficient. Yet on balance the program was effective.

Population policies

In 1982 the Chinese population passed the 1 billion mark and in 2000 the population, over 1.25 billion, was growing at the rate of 15 million annually. The need to feed, clothe, and house this immense population at rising consumption levels made enormous demands on the economy, no matter how modernized, and on the country's natural resources. China at the turn of the new century was a regional superpower and a nuclear power with a rapidly growing economy and rising living standards, but it was still under a tight authoritarian and Marxist regime—in sharp contrast to changes elsewhere, where the Communist regimes of the Cold War era were disappearing from the societies they had once controlled.

Chapter 25

A WORLD
TRANSFORMED

The world was astonished in the mid-1980s to see some of the basic structures of Soviet communism, as they had evolved since the Russian Revolution of 1917, begin to come apart. It was equally surprised by a series of extraordinary events in 1989 in central and eastern Europe, where the existing Communist regimes collapsed one by one and were replaced with virtually no violence. In an even more epochal event in 1991, the Communist regime of the Soviet Union itself, in power for 74 years, ended, and the U.S.S.R. disintegrated into Russia and its other component republics.

In a strict sense there was no actual revolution in 1989–1991, and indeed it was a source of wonder and satisfaction that such sweeping change could occur without armed struggle. The older regimes disappeared less by explosion than by implosion—a breakup from within. The "revolution" could remain peaceful because it faced no strong internal resistance or threat of foreign intervention. Yet the upheavals were revolutionary in that they demolished existing repressive authorities and brought abrupt, radical change. They reasserted ideals that were revolutionary when proclaimed in America in 1776, in France in 1789, throughout Europe in 1848, and in the West in 1919 and 1945, and were now called human rights and civil society. These ideals had been incorporated into the American Declaration of Independence and the French Declaration of the Rights of Man, and they had become the guiding ideals for democracies in most of the modern world. Democracy meant representative and constitutional government and freely contested elections; and freedom and independence meant guarantees against repression by one's own government and dictatorial foreign rule.

Chapter emblem: View of the planet Earth, photographed from Apollo 17 in December 1972.

With the Revolution of 1989 the people of central and eastern Europe could decide their own destiny. With the collapse of the U.S.S.R. one of the two superpowers that had dominated international affairs disappeared. The Cold War, as the world had known it since 1945, ended. A new global political era opened, understandably with new challenges and frustrations.

The dramatic political and economic changes in formerly Communist societies, however, were but one of the "revolutions" changing the world at the end of the twentieth century. New computer technologies and communications systems moved information around the globe with virtually instantaneous speed; a global "culture industry" spread the same music, films, and fashions throughout the world; rapidly evolving conceptions of knowledge and scientific research reshaped intellectual debates as well as artistic creativity; and long-existing barriers to the education, professional careers, and political rights of women continued to fall in every modern nation. The pace of change seemed to be increasing in all spheres of modern life, creating a "global village" that was both united and divided in new ways by the processes of contemporary globalization.

124. THE CRISIS IN THE SOVIET UNION

Neither the transformation of central and eastern Europe nor of the Soviet Union could have taken place as they did without the changes in the U.S.S.R. that began in 1985. It is not easy to explain how the reformist Soviet leader Mikhail S. Gorbachev could have risen to supreme power from within the Soviet system except that the country was in dire straits and the party leadership itself was desperate. As a young man Gorbachev studied at the university in Moscow and at the agricultural institute in Stavropol, his home city in southwestern Russia. After working as an agricultural researcher, he received a full-time party assignment in the region and came to the attention of Yuri V. Andropov (soon to be the party general secretary) and other party leaders in Moscow. His appointment to the party secretariat in Moscow in 1978, with special responsibility for agriculture, afforded him a privileged view of the country's deep economic troubles. By 1980 he was a member of the Politburo, and by 1984 he was being groomed by Andropov for top party leadership. After the frustrating experience of an incapacitated Brezhnev clinging to power and of Andropov and Konstantin U. Chernenko, his two successors, dying in office after only brief terms, the Politburo in March 1985 decided that it was time for change. At 54, Gorbachev was by far its youngest member. Andrei Gromyko, for many years foreign minister of the U.S.S.R. but too closely identified with the Stalin era to be chosen general secretary himself, ultimately endorsed Gorbachev and is said to have reassured those with doubts: "He has a nice smile but he has iron teeth."

Gorbachev at once demonstrated a dynamism and vigor absent from the leadership for years. His first task was to convince the party and country of the need for fundamental economic restructuring if economic stagnation was to be overcome—*perestroika* he called it. By *perestroika* he meant a drastic modification of the centrally planned command economy inherited from Stalin and carried forward with only minor changes since. However well the older system had served the industrialization of the country, the test of the Second World War, and postwar reconstruction, it was ill-suited for the contemporary industrial world. Industry and agriculture urgently needed freedom from restraints to release creative energies, provide incentives for productivity, raise quality levels, and satisfy consumer needs. Gorbachev's proposed remedies were decentralization; self-management for industry and agriculture;

Perestroika

an end to the rigidity imposed by the *apparat,* or party and government bureaucracy; and incentives for productivity. He moved cautiously, believing that exhortation and a sense of urgency would bring results, but his appeals and initial moderate reforms quickly clashed with the vested interests of the entrenched bureaucrats.

For his economic restructuring to succeed, Gorbachev had to have the support of the country, which he hoped to win through political change. Thus he also called for *glasnost,* or "openness," which he closely linked to economic reform. By *glasnost* he meant the right to voice the need for change, the freedom to criticize the existing system, and the willingness even to reexamine past mistakes and wrongdoings. Even if it originally had a more limited objective, *glasnost* soon took on a dynamic of its own. It led to a totally unprecedented liberalization of Soviet society, a freer press, and an end to the decades of totalitarian control over political, cultural, and intellectual life. The ferment choked off after Khrushchev's "thaw" was reborn. Newspapers, theater, the arts, and political discourse opened up as at no time before. Books and plays written in the 1960s or earlier but never permitted publication or performance made their appearance, including Pasternak's *Dr. Zhivago* and eventually even Solzhenitsyn's *Gulag Archipelago,* the novel that gave the outside world the name for Stalin's network of forced labor camps. Gorbachev permitted the physicist Andrei Sakharov, a leading dissenter and committed opponent of the regime, to return to Moscow from exile and take an active part in political life. Soviet Jews, who had earlier been refused permission to leave the country, were allowed to emigrate in larger numbers. The atmosphere changed visibly. People became freer and less fearful. The legal codes were revised to encompass a measure of civil liberties, allow freedom of expression, and reduce police abuses. The KGB itself came under public and legislative scrutiny. Gorbachev even spoke of freedom of conscience and tolerance for religion, negotiating a rapprochement with the Orthodox church.

Glasnost

In 1987, on the very occasion of the seventieth anniversary of the Bolshevik Revolution, Gorbachev spoke openly of "Stalin's enormous and unforgivable crimes." The courts rehabilitated Stalin's political opponents and victims; early Bolshevik leaders like Bukharin, Zinoviev, and Kamenev were restored to their places in history. A monument to Stalin's victims was planned, while the press openly discussed their total number, clearly in the tens of millions. New history textbooks were prepared, as well as a revised history of the party. Gorbachev told the country that there should be "no forgotten names or blanks in history or literature."

Although Gorbachev did not challenge the role of the Communist party as the directing agent of Soviet society, he was clearly introducing changes that would curb its monopoly on power. Remembering how Khrushchev had been dislodged after only a few years, he set out to mobilize a wide popular base for himself. Reform could not simply be imposed from above. The people, he said, needed more than a "good tsar." Constitutional reforms in 1988 created a new national legislature, and multicandidate elections were to replace the traditional one-party slate of nominees. What began as a technocratic vision of a more efficient economy was moving the country to a sweeping transformation of Soviet life and society.

Gorbachev's constitutional reforms

In the freer atmosphere the government released information suppressed for years, of poor grain harvests, of inefficient state enterprises, and even of nuclear accidents before the disaster at Chernobyl in 1986. At party meetings and at the new Congress of People's Deputies the public heard for the first time outspoken critiques of Soviet society:

descriptions of poverty, corruption, crime, alcoholism, and drugs; of serious shortcomings in medicine, health, and housing; of environmental decay. Tens of millions, perhaps one-fifth the population, lived in poverty.

Gorbachev soon recognized that the country's economic problems were more intractable than he had thought, but he persisted with his gradualist reform program. For the first time since Lenin's New Economic Policy, when Lenin had liberalized the economy in the early 1920s, individuals were encouraged to start up businesses on their own or form cooperatives, and even hire workers. Private enterprise and state industries were one day to be integrated into a market-based economy, linked to the outside world. Foreign capital for trade and investment and joint ventures with foreign firms were welcomed. Soviet managers were encouraged to travel abroad to learn advanced (sometimes elementary) business and accounting practices. But many of these reforms remained paper decrees only; party officials and government bureaucrats helped checkmate others. The older economic system remained virtually unchanged. Gorbachev shrank from moving more rapidly to a market-oriented competitive economy. His concerns about painful short-term dislocations and political unrest reinforced his commitment to reform rather than abandon the older system.

Limited economic reforms

Gorbachev's reforms in agriculture fell far short of what was needed. Accepting the existing structure of state and collective farms, he did little more than allow them greater managerial autonomy. Production did not rise. Belatedly, he launched a more extensive agrarian policy. Farmers and farm families would be permitted to work with state and collective farms on a share-crop basis, or farm their own land. They could lease land for their lifetime and even bequeath this right to their children. But the state remained the legal owner of the land—not as in China, where Deng had at the very beginning of his reforms dismantled the collective farms, returned the land outright to the farmers, and reaped the benefit in increased production. Despite Gorbachev's overtures to small independent farmers, little more than one percent of the land shifted to private hands.

The party's grip loosened

But the constitutional and political changes he had initiated significantly loosened the monopoly grip of the party. In March 1989 openly contested, multicandidate elections were held, the first since 1917, though well over half the seats were reserved for the party and various state-sponsored associations. Voters elected a Congress of People's Deputies, which in turn chose a smaller standing legislative body to meet more frequently. Both were empowered to initiate legislation and freely debate issues. In 1990, under another constitutional reform, the Congress of People's Deputies created a presidency with broad executive powers modeled on the American and French examples. The Congress elected Gorbachev president.

Gorbachev brought about stunning political changes, unprecedented in the years since the revolution. Western political leaders in the era of the Great Depression had sought to save capitalism by reforming it. Gorbachev was likewise bent on saving the Communist system by reform, yet the country remained divided and disoriented. It was torn between the old guard, who resisted the Gorbachev changes, and a growing group of democratic reformers in the central legislature and in the newly elected parliaments of the restless component republics, who believed that Gorbachev had not gone far enough in either political or economic matters. As time went by, praise for his policies gave way to criticism for the continuing dismal economic record and for his indecisive, sometimes contradictory, steps in shaping a market economy

Criticisms of Gorbachev

Mikhail Gorbachev advocated economic and cultural reforms that came to be known in general terms as the call for *glasnost,* **or "openness," and** *perestroika,* **or "structural reforms." Gorbachev expected the reforms to benefit agriculture as well as the industrial sector of the Soviet economy, and he campaigned for his program among both farmers and workers. He is shown here (smiling, on the left) during a meeting with potato farmers near Moscow in 1987. Such contacts with people in the countryside affirmed the spirit of** *glasnost,* **but the reforms on state-owned farms did not go far enough to bring about a rise in agricultural production.**

(Tass/Sovfoto)

and his reluctance to revamp the collectivized agricultural system. He also seemed determined to repress ethnic unrest and was rejecting the demands of the constituent republics for greater freedom from central control. The military, the industrial bureaucrats, and the party were still in command.

The loosening of totalitarian controls unleashed long-suppressed ethnic tensions in the country. Azerbaijan and Armenia fought over a disputed enclave within Azerbaijan where the majority of the inhabitants were Armenian; violence also flared up in Georgia and elsewhere. Every one of the 15 federated constituent republics of the Soviet Union began to raise demands for independence. Secessionist pressures understandably went furthest in the three Baltic republics. People in Latvia, Lithuania, and Estonia remembered their 20 years of independence between the two world wars; how they had fallen victim to the Nazi-Soviet pact of 1939; and how one-third of their population had been killed, deported, or driven into exile in the war and postwar years. In the freer atmosphere of *glasnost,* the constituent republics, which had come to consider themselves trapped within the Soviet empire, were able to denounce Soviet control. For his part Gorbachev was willing to create a federation council to advise on matters relating to the republics but would not risk the wrath of the old guard by going beyond that.

Gorbachev and the West

As the new era evolved, Communist ideology and the view of world affairs that had helped to create and prolong the Cold War were also transformed. Gorbachev repudiated ideological struggle. He cited the progress of science and technology as requiring "a different road to the future." In an interdependent globe besieged by nuclear, ecological, and economic dangers, the highest concern must be "universal human interests" and the "universal human idea." Since Marx and Lenin had taught their followers to reject "universal" ideals as a smoke screen for class rule and oppression, the turnabout was startling.

Encouraging détente

Gorbachev changed the image of the Soviet Union as a military threat and promoter of world revolution. He became a familiar and popular figure in Western capitals as a negotiator, diplomat, and often Western-style politician. He followed his conciliatory words with deeds. He removed troops and weapons from eastern Europe, negotiated nuclear arms reduction agreements with the United States, ended the war in Afghanistan, and helped to resolve Cold War regional conflicts. And he accepted, even encouraged, reforms in eastern Europe, probably not foreseeing how far they would go. He spoke up for human rights, paid tribute to the standards embodied in the Helsinki accords, and called for a "common European home" for western and eastern Europe. The Cold War of the post-1945 years, which had been brought on, or intensified, by Soviet revolutionary ideology and expansionism—which in turn had led to the American containment policy and countercrusade—gave promise of ending. For Gorbachev, as a matter of policy, détente and arms reduction were essential to relieve the intolerable military burden on the Soviet economy; détente went hand in hand with domestic reform. From their low point in the early 1980s Soviet–United States relations abruptly changed after 1985. A new and more genuine spirit of détente emerged, holding out higher expectations for peace and disarmament than at any time since 1945.

Early in the Reagan administration, in 1981, during the Brezhnev era, discussions had resumed on strategic arms limitations (now called START), but in an atmosphere of mistrust, suspicion, and continuing arms buildup. Especially disturbing was the deployment in eastern Europe in the late 1970s of new Soviet intermediate-range nuclear missiles capable of reaching targets within a radius of 600 to 1,500 miles. Together with its European allies the United States had reinforced existing defenses in western Europe with equally modern American nuclear missiles while simultaneously pressing the Soviets to reduce or remove theirs. The construction of the American missile sites touched off large protest demonstrations in western Europe, but the West European governments remained firm in their support. In Reagan's first term of office he did not meet with the incapacitated Brezhnev or with either of the two ailing Soviet leaders who in quick succession followed him. But in 1985, after the emergence of Gorbachev, who was anxious to reduce the strain on the troubled Soviet economy, the possibilities for arms limitation opened up. Unlike his predecessors, Gorbachev seemed to view détente not as an alternate way of pursuing revolutionary goals but as essential to avoid catastrophe in the nuclear age. For his part, Reagan, confident that the United States had rebuilt its own military strength, held four summit meetings with Gorbachev over the next two and a half years.

End of the Cold War

At their third meeting, in Washington in December 1987, the two presidents made a remarkable breakthrough by consenting to remove the intermediate-range missiles each had installed in Europe. Gorbachev agreed also to reduce the number of short-range nuclear missiles. The Soviets were willing to destroy over four times as many missiles as the United States. Even more unprecedented was the willingness to permit the United States to verify the destruction of the weapons—the on-site verification which had long been a stumbling block to arms reduction. Finally, the two leaders agreed to continue negotiations on the reduction of strategic, or long-range, nuclear weapons.

In summit meetings in Washington and Moscow, the two presidents had closer contact with each other's people than ever before. Gorbachev mingled with throngs in crowded Washington streets. Reagan, in the shadow of Lenin's tomb in Moscow, spoke openly about the Soviet repression of dissidents, the refusal to permit Jews to emigrate, religious persecution, and the ongoing war in Afghanistan. Gorbachev in turn committed his country to the withdrawal of Soviet troops from Afghanistan—a "bleeding wound" he called it. The Soviets were eager to cut their commitments and abandon their adversarial stance all over the globe. Meanwhile Gorbachev lent encouragement to the vast changes taking place in eastern Europe. In 1990 Gorbachev and President George Bush, Reagan's successor, could jointly hail the end of the Cold War. In 1991 they signed a strategic arms treaty pledging each nation to scale down by about a third its arsenal of long-range nuclear missiles.

125. THE COLLAPSE OF COMMUNISM IN CENTRAL AND EASTERN EUROPE

Meanwhile in the mid-1980s central and eastern Europe remained under Stalinist-type party bosses, some in office for over 30 years, impervious to pressure for reform. But cracks and fissures were already apparent even before Gorbachev's reforms in the Soviet Union. The years of détente had already opened up the East European states to Western loans and investments and to closer contacts with the West. Dissidents called for a recognition of the human rights guaranteed by the Helsinki accords in 1975, to which the Soviet Union and the East European bloc had subscribed. They wrote about ending party-state dictatorships and the restoration one day of a "civil society," in which people could live their lives free from the dictates of the state.

As in the Soviet Union itself, East Europeans discussed the shortcomings of their centrally planned economies, which had stagnated since the 1970s. Initiative and productivity were stifled, and large subsidies propped up inefficient state-run monopolies unchallenged by competition. The older plants and industrial infrastructure were decaying; the environment was deteriorating. A scarcity of investment capital prevented the growth of new industries. Only in Hungary had decentralizing reforms and tentative steps toward a market economy been adopted. In East Germany, the showcase for achievements under central planning, economic growth had slowed and consumer goods were scarce. Even if state-run planned economies were to continue, many argued for new market competition, incentives for entrepreneurs and workers, and encouragement of joint ventures with the outside capitalist world. *Economic stagnation*

The East European countries were also overwhelmed by the billions of dollars of debt incurred to Western banks in the 1970s, of which Poland owed close to half. To pay the interest alone on these huge sums and simultaneously control inflation demanded austerity and reduced living standards.

Poland: The Solidarity Movement

In the 1970s and 1980s demands for economic reform and political liberalization surfaced almost everywhere, but nowhere so forcefully as in Poland. Gomulka, who governed Poland for 14 years after 1956, disappointed the reformers. He used troops to put down strikes, persecuted church leaders, and in 1968 permitted an anti-Semitic campaign against the small number of Jews still living in Poland. In 1970, after riots over food prices, the party replaced him with the reform-minded Edmund Gierek, who embarked on an ambitious economic development program, financed by heavy borrowing from the West. The initial results were promising, but to meet its debt obligations, the country expanded exports at the expense of domestic consumption. Economic conditions steadily deteriorated.

In 1980 the rise in food prices led to widespread strikes, which began in the Lenin shipyards in Gdansk and spread rapidly. A somewhat freer political atmosphere made it possible for workers to create an aggressive independent trade union federation, Solidarity, the first of its kind in any Communist country. It found a militant leader and national symbol of protest in Lech Walesa. Before long Solidarity claimed a national membership of 10 million industrial and agricultural workers. With church backing, its leaders called for free elections and a role for Solidarity in government. The Soviets, still in the Brezhnev era, once again saw a socialist regime threatened. They put heavy pressure on the Polish government and party to curb Solidarity, oust Gierek, and install the steely General Jaruzelski as party head and premier. When strikes and demonstrations continued, raising the threat of Soviet military intervention, Jaruzelski in 1981 imposed martial law, banned Solidarity, and arrested its leaders.

Lech Walesa

But once the power of Solidarity was curbed and the Soviet threat of intervention passed, Jaruzelski himself took a different tack. To placate labor he lifted martial law and initiated a reform program of his own. International pressure also contributed to liberalization. John Paul II, the first Polish pope to head the Roman Catholic church, elected in 1978, inspired huge demonstrations for freedom during his visits to Poland. Lech Walesa was honored with a Nobel Peace Prize in 1983. President Reagan imposed economic sanctions against Poland when martial law was declared.

Jaruzelski's efforts at economic reform failed to improve the economy or mollify widespread resentments. Gorbachev's liberalizing reforms in the Soviet Union after 1985 further encouraged reform. His example and the sense that the Soviets would not intervene to check liberalization in eastern Europe—that the "Brezhnev Doctrine" was dead—encouraged a movement for reform within the Polish Communist party itself.

Reforms within the party

In 1989 Jaruzelski and the party leadership permitted parliamentary elections, in which Solidarity and other groups were free to put forward candidates, although the Communist party was guaranteed a fixed number of seats. The first open elections in Poland in over 40 years gave Solidarity a landslide victory in all contested seats. A Solidarity-led coalition cabinet was formed in which the Communists were a minority. The party took steps to transform itself into a Western-type socialist party, but many of its members drifted away. The party-state dictatorship ended without bloodshed. The dike in eastern Europe was breached.

The new government moved at once to restructure the economy along free-market lines. Sharp differences emerged between Lech Walesa, elected president in 1990, and his one-time political allies, and former Communists soon returned to the political scene, but Poland was in charge of its own destiny.

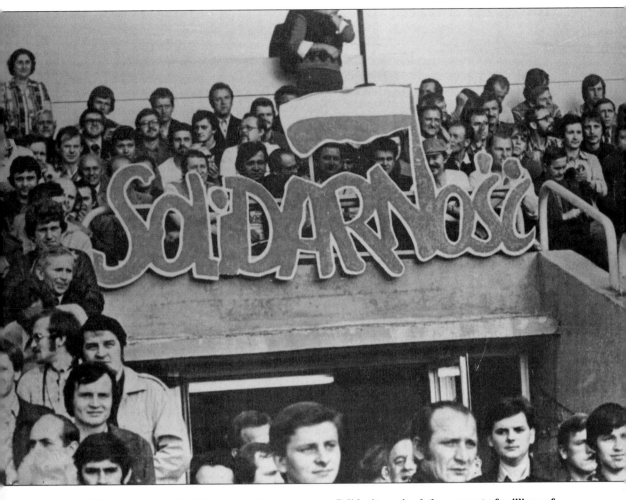

The independent Polish trade union movement, Solidarity, gained the support of millions of workers in the early 1980s. Solidarity organized strikes and demonstrations, demanding better wages for workers and major reforms in the Communist political system. These demonstrators gathered to support Solidarity at a rally outside the court buildings in Warsaw in November 1980. The Solidarity movement was suppressed after martial law was imposed the following year, but the Polish Communist party could never destroy the movement's popular appeal. Solidarity eventually won control of Poland's first new government in free elections that took place at the end of the decade.

(Hulton Archive)

Hungary: Reform into Revolution

In Hungary the attempt at reform in 1956, initiated by the Communist party leadership itself, was brusquely interrupted when the Soviets intervened with troops and tanks to suppress the "counterrevolution." Imre Nagy, the party leader, and other leaders of the revolt were hanged. For the next 32 years, hard-liner János Kádár ran the country. But even under Kádár the party, without relinquishing its monopoly on political control, moved away from an inflexible centrally planned economy, encouraged a degree of private enterprise, and turned to the West for capital investment. For a time the economy expanded and standards of living rose, but the limited reforms accomplished no fundamental change. After 1985, in the wake of Gorbachev's reforms in the Soviet Union, some of which were modeled on the Hungarian example itself, a new drive for reform surfaced.

Party initiatives

In 1988 the party, eager to encourage change and still maintain power, eased Kádár out of office. The new leadership opened the way to opposition parties and multiparty elections and began to dismantle the older party-state apparatus. It dissolved the Communist party, reconstituting it along socialist and social democratic lines, and a wide range of independent political groups came forward. Reform, initiated by the party itself, had turned into revolution, and without bloodshed. The new leaders reclaimed the 1956 uprising as a progressive movement and formally condemned those who had invited Soviet intervention. Nagy's body was exhumed from a mass grave and given a hero's reburial. By sweeping aside the humiliation of 1956, the country reasserted its national independence, restored self-government and civic freedom, and opened the way to a market-oriented economy and a pluralist democracy.

The developments in Hungary precipitated even more dramatic events in eastern Europe. The new Hungary, looking westward, symbolically demolished a portion of the barbed-wire barrier on its Austrian border. A few months later, in September 1989, when large numbers of East Germans vacationing in Hungary sought to emigrate to the West, Hungary opened its border with Austria and allowed the Germans to exit. For the first time since 1961 East Germans found a safe way to leave their country.

The German Democratic Republic: Revolution and Reunification

Given Gorbachev's positive attitude toward reform, it was understandable that the pace of change in eastern Europe would accelerate, but neither he nor anyone else could have anticipated its full dimensions. In the four hard-line dictatorships—the German Democratic Republic, Czechoslovakia, Bulgaria, and Romania—there still appeared to be little chance for a Communist sharing of power in the spring of 1989, let alone a revolutionary transformation. Yet by the end of that year the Communist regimes had fallen in all of these countries.

In the German Democratic Republic Erich Honecker, in power since 1961, stubbornly held the line against reform. Although the country boasted the strongest economy and highest per capita income in eastern Europe, its citizens enjoyed far fewer amenities than the West Germans. The Berlin Wall built in 1961 still barred their exodus to the West. Even though Honecker had agreed after 1970 to the closer economic and political relations with West Germany initiated by Willy Brandt's *Ostpolitik* in 1969, he refused to relax controls at home. But the East Germans excitedly watched the Gorbachev changes in the Soviet Union and the rush of events in Poland and Hungary. When in the autumn of 1989 Hungary opened the way for them to leave, thousands seized the opportunity. The trickle soon became a flood. The East Germans, many of them skilled workers and professionals, fled the repression and drabness of the German Democratic Republic for the Federal Republic of Germany, where as Germans they were entitled by law to receive citizenship and assistance in finding homes and jobs. By the end of 1989, 350,000 of East Germany's population of 17 million had left, and many more emigrated in the early months of 1990.

Flight from Honecker's rule

When demonstrations against the East German government mounted, Gorbachev clearly signaled that Honecker could not expect the Soviet troops stationed in East Germany to save the regime, and he even warned against the use of force to prevent reform. In Leipzig, over 100,000 demonstrators, assembling in churches, marched in solemn procession with lighted candles, calling for the resignation of party and government leaders and for an end to the police state. The party forced Honecker to resign.

The new leadership promised elections and confirmed the right of free and unrestricted travel. On November 9, 1989, when the government opened up the hated symbol of confinement itself, the Berlin Wall, excited Berliners on both sides of the barrier tore it down. The exodus to West Germany continued. By now even the new freedom of movement, the end of censorship, the new parliamentary supervision over the state security police, and the pledge of free elections did not suffice. Many East Germans were infuriated by public disclosure of the corruption and luxurious living that Honecker and the party elite had enjoyed while ordinary people suffered over the years. Economic conditions had worsened in the last years, and even the party leadership had been kept ignorant of the extent of the government's soaring debt. The entire party structure came crashing down. The Politburo and Central Committee resigned. Honecker and other leaders were arrested on charges of corruption and embezzlement, and younger reformers assumed control. Delegates from a wide variety of opposition groups, exultant over their "gentle" revolution, met with reform-minded representatives of the former Communist party to oversee the transition to a new constitutional regime, which many still envisaged as a socialist but democratic society.

Corruption within the party

Once the German Democratic Republic was no longer Communist, however, pressure for reunification began to build, especially in West Germany, at the initiative of Helmut Kohl, the Christian Democratic chancellor. For many of the wartime Allies the prospect of a reunified Germany of close to 80 million people, possessing one of the world's most powerful economies, stirred grim ghosts of the past. The "German question" resurfaced. The entire postwar settlement stood at issue. Since no final peace treaty had ever been signed, reunification required the approval of the four major Allied powers of the Second World War. There was hesitation, especially in France and Britain, but it was difficult, as the Americans argued, to deny the German people the right of self-determination 45 years after the end of the war. Moreover, the Federal Republic of Germany had demonstrated its commitment to democracy. There was confidence that a reunified Germany could integrate East Germany and remain part of democratic western Europe and the European Community. Despite the unspeakable crimes of the Nazi era, it seemed unreasonable to insist upon unalterable traits of national character or to punish future generations for atrocities in the past.

The "German question" revived

Reunification moved forward swiftly. The four Allied powers, including the U.S.S.R., gave their approval and relinquished their occupation rights. Germany confirmed the earlier cession of territories in the east to the U.S.S.R. and Poland and pledged the inviolability of the German-Polish border. The two German states merged their economies and the West German mark became the common currency. On October 3, 1990, the two states formally united to become an enlarged Federal Republic of Germany, its capital to be reestablished within a few years in Berlin. In the first nationwide elections, Chancellor Kohl and his Christian Democrats, who played a key role in the reunification, won a sweeping victory. Although the postelection exhilaration was soon tempered by the gigantic problems of modernizing and absorbing the thoroughly decayed East German economy, Germany had been reunited under democratic auspices.

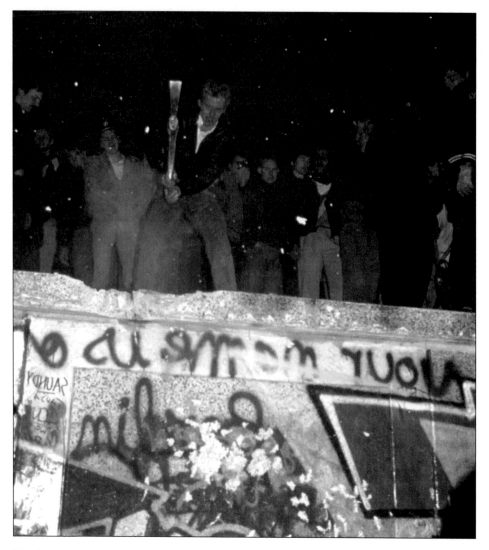

The destruction of the Berlin Wall in November 1989 provided dramatic physical and symbolic evidence of the collapse of Communist regimes in eastern Europe. Young people shattered the Wall in a great celebration that released long-suppressed political anger and marked the culmination of a nonviolent revolution in East Germany. Within a year, the two postwar German states were united in a new, enlarged Federal Republic of Germany, which faced the social and economic challenges of bringing two different societies into an integrated national political system.

(Robert Wallis/Sipa Press)

Czechoslovakia: "'89 is '68 Upside Down"

In Czechoslovakia the ruling hard-liners, who took power after Soviet military forces had ruthlessly crushed the "Prague spring" in 1968, disapproved of Gorbachev's reforms in the Soviet Union and stifled dissent at home. But the dissidents quietly grew in numbers and influence. Charter '77, an organization of intellectuals formed after the Helsinki accords of 1975, became a rallying point for the struggle against the dictatorship. The Czech public followed with intense interest the disintegration of Communist power in Poland, Hungary, and East Germany. When demonstrations broke out in the autumn of 1989, the government arrested the dissident leaders, but thousands of demonstrators in Prague called for the release of the imprisoned dissidents and for the government's resignation. The reform movement gained added momentum when the Soviet Union and other Warsaw Pact nations voted to express "regret" for the military invasion of 1968. Reformers came together in a loose coalition and found inspiring leadership in the dissident writer Vaclav Havel, an outspoken opponent of the regime who had repeatedly suffered persecution and imprisonment for his views.

The demonstrations grew in intensity. When 350,000 demonstrators in Prague on November 24 furiously demanded an end to the party-state dictatorship and a general strike threatened to bring the country to a standstill, the government and party leaders all at once resigned. Alexander Dubček, the hero of 1968, dramatically appeared on a balcony alongside a new reform-minded Communist prime minister, who appointed opposition leaders to his cabinet, pledged a free press and free elections, dissolved the secret police, and abolished the compulsory teaching of Marxism-Leninism in the universities. The party's 41 year monopoly on power ended. Havel became provisional president and led a new cabinet in which the Communists were a minority. Gorbachev took steps to withdraw the 75,000 Soviet troops stationed in the country since 1968. In the excitement someone exultantly observed: "'89 is '68 upside down." The people had wrested control without bloodshed in a "velvet" revolution that liberated the country.

A "velvet revolution"

Of all the nations in the Eastern bloc Czechoslovakia had the strongest democratic tradition. Despite long-standing ethnic tensions and resentment at Czech domination, it had developed a genuine parliamentary democracy in the interwar years and was the last of the East European states to fall under Communist dictatorship after the Second World War. Even though its economy was one of the strongest of the Eastern bloc, it lagged far behind the West and required large infusions of capital to modernize its older technology. It moved rapidly toward a market-oriented economy and a pluralist democracy—the civil society that Havel, now elected president of the republic, and others had sought. But an unexpected political sequel followed within three years. The country came apart when Slovak political leaders pressed for an independent Slovakia, which some had wanted since 1918. A negotiated settlement arranged for the peaceful division of the country in January 1993 into two independent and sovereign nations—the Czech Republic and Slovakia.

Bulgaria's Palace Revolution, Bloodshed in Romania

Even Bulgaria, considered the most docile of the Soviet client states, succumbed to the revolutionary contagion. Mass demonstrations in Sofia demanded an end to the Communist dictatorship, and pressure from within the party forced the resignation of the party chief who had run the country for 35 years. His foreign minister, who replaced him, pledged parliamentary elections, economic reforms, and an end to the party's monopoly on power. New political groups emerged, fragmented yet strong enough to press for reform.

The revolution in Bulgaria was essentially a palace coup within the party, but it, too, arose in response to deep mass resentments. In a country that had known little freedom even in the pre-Communist years, the question was whether the reform-minded former Communists who, like many others elsewhere, renamed themselves Socialists, could work together with the new opposition to create a true democracy.

Only in Romania did events take a violent turn in 1989. It seemed at first as though the revolution would not reach Bucharest. Since 1965, the dicta-

The Ceausescu regime

tor Nicolae Ceausescu had firmly controlled party and government, ruling with the help of his wife and family and building a cult of personality around himself. He remained isolated in a rigid autocracy with a large private security force, which he favored over the regular army. His Stalin-like ambition was to transform a backward agrarian society into a modern industrial society regardless of the human cost. For his modernization program he borrowed heavily from the West, but to remain independent of the outside world he insisted that the country regularly pay the interest on its debt despite the sacrifices this required from an already suffering population. He used state resources to build an enormous presidential palace. All dissent was kept under tight surveillance and control. What was distinctive about Ceausescu was his break from Moscow and his independent position in foreign and military affairs. Unlike the other members of the Warsaw Pact, he supported Israel in the Arab-Israeli wars and refused to join the invasion of Czechoslovakia in 1968.

Throughout the revolutionary autumn of 1989 Ceausescu ignored the upheavals in central and eastern Europe. But in December protest riots broke out in Timisoara, a key provincial capital. The military refused to fire on the demonstrators, but the

Ceausescu's security forces

dictator's security forces took over, killing hundreds. Word of the brutality spread, sparking new protests. When the security forces attempted to suppress demonstrators in Bucharest, angry crowds forced the dictator to flee the capital.

For days a battle raged between the security forces and regular army units supporting the revolutionists until the security forces were routed. Ceausescu and his wife were apprehended in the provinces and executed by a firing squad. A National Salvation Front, consisting of former officials of the Ceausescu regime and emergent opposition leaders, took control. Although former Communists dominated the new regime and the strength of the democratic forces remained unclear, the party's authority ended and the most repressive dictatorship of the Eastern bloc came to an ignominious end.

The Revolutions of 1989 in Central and Eastern Europe

Except in Romania, the revolution was carried out everywhere by placards and candles, not by rifles. Solidarity's early struggle in Poland and Gorbachev's liberalization in the Soviet Union made it possible for revolutionary changes in central and eastern Europe to take place as they did. With a suddenness that took even the closest observers by surprise, smoldering discontents flared up all at once. Gorbachev, committed to curtailing economic and military obligations for the sake of the Soviet economy, accepted the end of the Communist regimes imposed by Stalin after the Second World War.

The groundwork for change had been prepared by the growing economic ties and contacts with the West during the years of détente, the Helsinki accords, the

Gorbachev's decisive role

stubborn challenge of Solidarity, and the courage of the dissidents. But it was Gorbachev's clear signal that the Soviets would not intervene outside their own borders that made the stupendous chain of events possible, toppling one regime after another. The dramatic flight of the East Germans symbolized the desire of all eastern Europe to escape from behind the iron curtain. The revolutionists, armed only with a moral cause, would have found it difficult to prevail if any of their own governments had chosen to use the full power of the army and police. The repression at Tiananmen Square in China in June 1989 might have been repeated in eastern Europe. But the ruling elites, without Soviet support to bolster them, yielded; they simply lacked the will to govern under what was for them, too, an alien system.

126. THE COLLAPSE OF THE SOVIET UNION

Before the stunning developments in eastern Europe could be fully absorbed, an even more epochal event occurred. An all but bloodless revolution brought the collapse of communism in 1991 in the very epicenter of world communism, undoing the Russian Revolution of 1917 and ending three-quarters of a century of Communist party rule. The Union of Soviet Socialist Republics itself, heir to the one-time tsarist empire, dissolved into its component republics. Russia reemerged.

How did this collapse of a seemingly impregnable regime with a heavy apparatus of military and police security occur? We have already seen how Gorbachev in the years after 1985 opened up Soviet society to revitalize the system but avoided the more decisive measures that might have ended the hegemony of the Communist party. Gorbachev vacillated between the reformers and the hard-line conservatives. A superb political tactician—no one could have brought the party and the system as far as he had—he nonetheless gave the impression that he did not know where he was taking the country or how thorough a transformation he would permit. The old guard became further embittered as they witnessed the loss of Soviet control over eastern Europe. Meanwhile the economy worsened, and by 1990 production was in steep decline. Gorbachev tried plan after plan, but the economic structure remained virtually unchanged. In addition, not only the Baltic republics, as might have been expected, but the Russian republic itself and all the other component republics of the U.S.S.R. were pressing for sovereignty—self-government and control over their political and economic fortunes.

The "Creeping Coup d'État"

In the autumn of 1990 Gorbachev again was maneuvering. He replaced reform-minded ministers and other key officials with old-guard appointees unsympathetic to his reform program. He summarily abandoned an important "500-Day" economic plan that would have freed prices and moved more swiftly to a market economy. The plan would also have curtailed the military budget and given broad economic powers to the republics. It now appeared that military force was to be deployed against the secessionist Baltic republics, which in the spring of 1990 had proclaimed their independence. Edward Shevardnadze, Gorbachev's foreign minister and closest political associate, resigned with ambiguous and pessimistic allusions to the future of democratic reform in the country and to the threat of a coming dictatorship. In January 1991 Soviet troops, apparently taking matters into their own hands without Gorbachev's prior approval, used military force against demonstrators in Lithuania, with a loss of lives, and there was anxiety about where the military might move next.

The democratic reformers grew alarmed by the turn of events. Some spoke of "six wasted years of reform communism" and of a "creeping coup d'état." They had concluded that the country's economic problems could not be resolved short of demolishing the entire central planning structure, and also that each republic must be allowed to work out its own destiny. To the reformers Gorbachev seemed a barrier to further change, and he in

Uneasiness of reformers

turn grew increasingly hostile to them, convinced that he alone knew the proper pace of reform.

The democratic reformers turned to a political figure who on the surface seemed an unlikely choice as their leader. Boris N. Yeltsin was blunt and outspoken, not by any definition an intellectual. His personal style made a striking contrast to the suave, smooth, and urbane Gorbachev, but Yeltsin knew the Communist party well, and all its secrets. He had been party boss in Moscow and a member of the Politburo. When in 1987 he openly attacked the privileges, perquisites, and downright incompetence of the party officials, he had been dismissed from his posts, vilified in the press, and sent off into the political wilderness. Humiliated by Gorbachev and the party, he found allies among the democratic reformers, who saw in him a populist figure around whom they could rally public support. They helped polish some of his rough edges, undertook his political reeducation, and converted him into an opposition leader of stature.

Yeltsin becomes opposition leader

Elected to the Soviet legislature in March 1989, he played a key role in the opposition. With the encouragement of his political allies, however, he turned to a new, and seemingly unpromising, power base, the Russian legislature, that is, the legislature of the Russian constituent republic. Elected to it in 1990, he became chairman and used his position to step up his attacks on Gorbachev, the party, and the central government. Then, benefiting from a Gorbachev concession permitting the constituent republics to choose their presidents in direct popular elections, he won election in June 1991 as president of the Russian republic in an overwhelming victory over his Communist opponents—the first president in Russian history to be elected by popular vote. It was a distinction that Gorbachev, elected president of the U.S.S.R. solely by the Soviet Congress, could not claim. (It was at the time of Yeltsin's election that Russia's second largest city voted to change its name from Leningrad back to St. Petersburg, as it had been called before 1914.) From his new position of strength Yeltsin demanded immediate independence for the three Baltic states and self-government for Russia and the other Soviet constituent republics. Relations between Yeltsin and Gorbachev grew more tense.

Gorbachev, intent on keeping the country and the union intact, began negotiations with the presidents of the republics. He agreed to surrender considerably more autonomy to the 15 republics, including substantial control over the economic and financial resources that Moscow had always tightly guarded. The three Baltic republics, insisting on full independence, refused to participate in the negotiations, as did Georgia, now embroiled in its own internal turmoil. But in August the Russian republic and ten other constituent republics agreed to sign Gorbachev's "union treaty."

The Failed August Coup

For the old-guard hard-liners in the party, the military, and the secret police the treaty was the final straw—the end of the union as originally created by Lenin in 1922 after the Bolshevik Revolution of 1917 and the ensuing civil wars. Despite lip service to the sovereignty of the republics and the federal structure set forth in the Soviet constitution, the Soviet Union was from the beginning, and increasingly under Stalin, a Russian-dominated centralized nation, virtually the successor to the empire of the tsars. To abandon the union was more than many of the old guard could tolerate. The day before the treaty was to be signed, a small coterie of eight hard-liners acted to seize power. They included high-ranking party and government functionaries, among them, the head of the KGB and the commander of the Soviet land forces. All key figures were Gorbachev appointees. Several of the plotters, including the chief of Gorbachev's personal cabinet, arrived at Gorbachev's summer home in the Crimea, possibly hoping to win him to their side. When under forced detention he refused to cooperate or yield to pressure, they proclaimed a Committee of State Emergency, headed by the country's vice president, to replace him.

The *putschists* expected the coup to be a simple operation. Resistance in the country, they were convinced, could be overcome by a simple show of military strength. But they miscalculated, underestimating the new political forces alive in the country. Gorbachev disavowed the plotters. In Moscow Yeltsin gained additional stature when he rallied the Russian legislature in defense of Gorbachev, warned that anyone supporting the coup would be subject to grave criminal charges, and appealed for popular support against any military show of force. But the assault never came. At least one KGB unit disobeyed orders to attack; other tank units advanced only half-heartedly. There was some sporadic street fighting, and three civilian deaths. The coup failed, over in four days. The plotters turned out to be feckless and irresolute bunglers. The Central Committee of the party did not speak out during these events, but its silence seemed to sanction the attempted coup.

The failed coup

Gorbachev, his ordeal over, returned to Moscow. He had demonstrated with courage that he was not the prisoner of the old guard and now went further. Because of the party's complicity in the affair, he resigned as general secretary. Yet he still failed to comprehend how far matters had gone. He believed it sufficient only to replace the traitors and "return to the business of reform." Once again he defended "socialism" as "the choice made in 1917" and stressed the need to preserve the unity of the U.S.S.R., so that the country would not fall apart.

Yeltsin acted immediately and decisively on an entirely different agenda. As president of the Russian republic, he issued a series of decrees, describing the Communist party as "not a political party but an unlawful apparatus that took over the Soviet state" and denouncing it as "one of the principal villains" in the attempted coup. Suspending its activities throughout the Russian republic, he transferred to the state the party's vast property, along with its files and archives. The Soviet Congress of People's Deputies meeting in Moscow soon validated the decrees for the entire country before voting itself out of existence. In all this Gorbachev could take satisfaction, even if he was in Yeltsin's debt. In many ways what happened in the aftermath of the failed coup was the culmination of the Gorbachev six-year reform era. But the dissolution of the party-state regime, at Yeltsin's hands, was the revolution.

Yeltsin dissolves the regime

All that remained of the earlier framework was a federation council consisting of the presidents of the constituent republics, over which Gorbachev continued to preside. It immediately recognized the independence of the three Baltic republics. For the country as a whole Gorbachev still hoped to salvage his older idea, a "union of sovereign states," which, while granting self-government to the republics, would retain a central authority. But the republics pressed for full independence; hostility toward central authority had intensified after the bungled coup. The very party leaders, as in the Ukrainian S.S.R., who themselves once suppressed separatist movements, had by now taken over the leadership of nationalist independence movements.

The Ukrainian S.S.R. proclaimed itself independent as Ukraine (no longer to be referred to as *the* Ukraine) immediately after the August coup. In December, Yeltsin announced that Russia would not remain in the union

The U.S.S.R. dissolves

Boris Yeltsin's firm resistance to an attempted coup against the government of Mikhail Gorbachev by old-guard Communists in August 1991 confirmed Yeltsin's stature as the most popular political figure at the time. He is shown here waving to the huge crowd that gathered outside the Parliament building to show its support for the political reforms that were transforming the Soviet Union. Yeltsin was the first popularly elected president of Russia when it was still part of the U.S.S.R., a position he continued to occupy after the formal dissolution of the Soviet Union in December 1991.

(Michael Samojeden/Archive Photos)

without Ukraine. Thereupon the three Slavic states—Russia, Ukraine, and Belarus (the new name for Byelorussia), the states that had originally created the Union of Soviet Socialist Republics in December 1922—dissolved it. Gorbachev resigned as president. Yeltsin at once occupied his office in the Kremlin.

The other republics of the Soviet Union also agreed to its dissolution. A loose organization called the Commonwealth of Independent States (CIS) consisting of Russia and ten other republics came into existence.[1] The Baltic states had already gone their separate

---

[1]The 11 republics affiliating themselves with the Commonwealth of Independent States, created December 25, 1991, as successor to the U.S.S.R. in order of population (with their capitals in parentheses) were as follows: Russian Federation (Moscow), Ukraine (Kiev), Uzbekistan (Tashkent), Kazakhstan (Alma-Ata), Belarus (Minsk), Azerbaijan (Baku), Tajikistan (Dushanbe), Moldova (Chisinau), Kyrgyzstan (Bishkek), Turkmenistan (Ashkhabad), and Armenia (Yerevan). Georgia (Tbilisi) joined in 1994.

ways. Georgia, still in turmoil, did not join until a few years later. The Union of Soviet Socialist Republics, for close to seven decades the world's largest multinational state, stretching over one-sixth the earth's surface and 11 time zones, with close to 300 million people, one of the world's two superpowers for over 40 years after the Second World War, simply disappeared from the map as a geographic entity. Russia, still the world's largest nation in area and itself a mixture of many peoples, succeeded to the Soviet Union's permanent seat on the UN Security Council.

Gorbachev for the moment returned to private life, declaring "the main task" of his life to have been accomplished. He has to be counted as one of the great reformers in history. The "Gorbachev factor," as it has been called, made an immeasurable difference. His tragedy was that he failed to build a new system to replace the communism that he had undermined. He unleashed powerful winds of change that ultimately he could not direct or control. He *Gorbachev's legacy* drastically altered a totalitarian system yet refused to recognize that the demolition of the entire structure was necessary. Eventually he became a danger to the old order and an impediment to the new. Yeltsin, who took undisguised satisfaction in the fall of his once all-powerful rival, said of him: "We, like the world, respect him for what he did, especially in the first years of *perestroika* beginning with 1985 and 1986." After that, he said, the "errors" began. Russia, predicted George Kennan, one of America's preeminent diplomat-historians and Russian specialists, would eventually regard Gorbachev as the "person who led it out of bondage" even if "he was unable to reach the Promised Land." But it was not yet time to render final historical judgments. For the vast lands and peoples that had once been the Soviet Union, and for Russia and Yeltsin himself in 1991, the future held many uncertainties, a future in which the entire world had an enormous stake.

127. AFTER COMMUNISM

Marxist-Leninist ideology as the undergirding for one-party dictatorship still persisted at the opening of the twenty-first century in the People's Republic of China, the world's most populous country, and in the smaller states of North Korea, Vietnam, and Cuba. Albania, the last of the Communist regimes in Europe, and the most impoverished, threw off Communist rule in 1991. Yugoslavia's disintegration after the end of communism, as we shall see, unfolded separately. In western Europe, most notably in France, Italy, Spain, and Portugal, once strong Communist parties reexamined their beliefs, at times abandoned the party name, and adapted to changed circumstances. Marxism, born in the mid–nineteenth century in response to the instability and inequities of industrial capitalism, would survive as a scholarly, analytical tool, but it held little broad appeal as a political philosophy or program of political action, at least in the distorted form given it by Lenin and the Russian Revolution of 1917. Proletarian internationalism likewise lost much of its appeal because it had been used to support an ill-concealed Soviet hegemony.

The revolutions of the late twentieth century in the Soviet Union and central and eastern Europe seemed to herald the international triumph of the historic political liberalism of Western societies. The democratic reformers sought free elections, political and civil rights, and respect for human dignity. Their people had too long been the pawns of totalitarian party-state *Triumph of liberalism* regimes which self-righteously demanded sacrifice and subservience in the name of an ultimate utopia. The reformers objected to the centrally planned bureaucratic command economies, which had deprived almost everyone of decent living standards. They envied the immeasurably more prosperous economies of the United States, western Europe, and elsewhere, even if they, too, had their inequalities and social problems. The official formula that all citizens enjoyed the rights and privileges of an egalitarian "socialist" society had only concealed political repression, economic stagnation, and social immobility. For many, the public revelation of the Communist party elite's special privileges and luxuries proved the final shock.

The revolutionary changes made possible, but did not guarantee, democratic and pluralist societies in which the citizens themselves through responsible government could shape their political and economic future. The road to democracy and free economies was not an easy one. If democratic governments failed to take root, new authoritarian political parties and repressive governments could reemerge. The revolutionary changes released many ugly currents, ominous for the future—anti-Semitism, xenophobia, chauvinistic nationalism, irredentism—all easily mobilized when discontented people seek scapegoats for their frustrations.

Difficult economic and political transitions

Russia, the other former Soviet republics, and the countries of central and eastern Europe entered a period of difficult transition. In principle, they were transforming their political systems into representative democracies and their centrally planned economies into competitive market economies. But bureaucrats and managers of the old order often remained in control under new labels. Many used the knowledge and networks of privileged positions in the older regimes to benefit financially from the newly privatized enterprises. Despite infusions of international aid, the new regimes struggled to cope with the disorienting challenges of a free market, capitalist economy, new technologies, and a global financial system.

The market economy could take many forms. The state had always played a large role in central and eastern Europe. It was unlikely that the new regimes would turn to a pure laissez-faire model of private enterprise, any more than Western economies had. Governments would remain actively engaged, seeking to ensure a protective network of social services. As for socialism, marginal as it was in American life, democratic socialism and social democracy still had considerable appeal in Europe. The Soviet experience had tarnished, even poisoned, the image of socialism, but its egalitarian message retained an attraction when linked to respect for democracy and individual rights as propounded by British Labour and other European Socialist and Social Democratic parties. Meanwhile all countries with capitalist market economies and democratic political systems, in the West and elsewhere, were challenged to create societies that could overcome economic instability, individual insecurity, unemployment, and gross social and economic injustices. Democracies and market economies offered a means toward desired ends, not final goals in themselves. Yet prosperity and productivity could do more to overcome social inequities than would-be utopias.

Russia after 1991

At the close of 1991 the Russian flag replaced the Soviet hammer and sickle over the Kremlin. As of January 1, 1992, the Union of Soviet Socialist Republics ceased to exist. The 15 Soviet republics were independent states. Officially, the Russia that emerged from the Soviet Union was the Russian Federation, with 21 "federated republics" of its own and with numerous additional ethnic-based territorial units. With almost twice the land area of the United States and a population of close to 150 million, Russia, even if in desperate economic straits, was still a great power.

The most pressing international concern was the nuclear weaponry of the former U.S.S.R. Yeltsin had worked out an agreement with the other former Soviet republics whereby Russia alone was to retain nuclear weapons. Although four-fifths of the nuclear weapons were located on Russian soil, nuclear arms were positioned in Ukraine, Kazakhstan, and Belarus. The United States mediated an agreement under which the three republics consented to dismantle their weapons in return for generous financial reimbursement. Russia for its part soon began the initial stage of dismantling its vast arsenal of strategic weapons in accordance with the arms reduction treaty that had been signed with the United States in 1991.

Nuclear arms

The new Russia, like the Soviet Union in its final stages, faced separatist threats. Several of its "federated republics" adopted their own constitutions, flags, and anthems and before long enjoyed considerable de facto independence from Moscow. Only in the southern Chechen Republic did the secessionist threat become reality, and before long Russia was involved in a brutal, draining war to prevent secession by Chechnya. Meanwhile 25 million Russians who had long made their home in other parts of the former Soviet Union came to be regarded in those places as foreigners and in some instances were treated with hostility. Violence and civil war also persisted or flared up in several of the former Soviet republics in the Caucasus, especially in Georgia, and in the predominantly Muslim republics in central Asia.

Separatist pressures

In domestic affairs Yeltsin faced severe economic problems. He and his succession of prime ministers met with little success in making the transition to a market economy. In the first four years of Yeltsin's presidency production declined, the ruble fell in value, and standards of living sank. Life at times seemed more trying for the average citizen than before the collapse of communism. The regional and local governments tended to ignore Moscow and even withheld tax collections. The erosion of government authority contributed to widening corruption and crime throughout the country.

Despite large infusions of capital from the United States and international lending agencies, the Russian economy and financial institutions remained in deep disorder. After temporizing at first, Yeltsin turned to a Western-oriented economist as his key adviser and economics minister in the belief that a swift transition to a market economy would be the least painful course. From late 1991, a flood of decrees deregulated prices, ended or cut subsidies to state-owned industries, and moved forward with privatization. But most Russians suffered a serious decline in living standards by the spring of 1992 while privatization enriched others who bought into former state industries at bargain prices. An industrial and financial oligarchy of "robber barons" developed a system of "crony capitalism"; and a "shadow" economy run by mafia-type gangsters appeared on the borderlines of the legal system.

The failure of the economic program intensified Yeltsin's struggle with the legislature, where a mixed group of Communists and nationalists rejected the austerity program and attacked the "elite theorists" who had allowed prices to rise. All this time the value of the ruble kept declining. In the spring of 1993 a frustrated Yeltsin appealed to the country to support a new constitution that would provide for "a strong presidential republic." That September Yeltsin dissolved the legislature and called for new elections as well as for a referendum on his proposed constitution. For two weeks the lawmakers, denouncing the dissolution as "a coup d'État," refused to leave the parliament building. Demonstrators, incited by the legislative leaders, threatened insurrection. Yeltsin felt bound to act. On October 4 tanks fired on the building and set it ablaze. The legislators were evacuated and the leaders

Yeltsin's new constitution

RUSSIAN FEDERATION IN 2000

The map shows the territories of the Russian Federation, the largest and most important of the republics to emerge from the breakup of the former Soviet Union (U.S.S.R.) in 1991. The hatched lines indicate the lands of the other former Soviet republics, which are clustered to the south and west of the Russian Federation. The Federation itself consists of some 21 "federated units," including Chechnya, where the Russians have waged a military campaign to suppress a Chechen independence movement. The vast lands of the Russian Federation make it territorially the largest nation in the world. Although much of this land is sparsely populated, the Federation's 147 million people ranked seventh on the list of the world's most populous nations in 2000.

were arrested. Over 100 persons died in the confrontation and many more were injured. In point of fact, both sides shared in the blame for the conflict, but the violence showed that Russia was still going through its revolution.

The new constitution, approved in December 1993, gave broad political authority to the president, including the right to dissolve the legislature. A popularly elected lower house, the State Duma, the old name deliberately chosen because of its pre-Soviet roots, replaced the former Congress of People's Deputies. The elections to the new Duma proved a setback for the candidates of the reform parties, who had underestimated popular discontent. The Communist party and its political allies won a good share of the seats. The top popular vote winner, an ultranationalist, Vladimir Zhirinovsky by name, spoke openly in inflammatory rhetoric of reuniting the old Russian empire and reviving Russia's military might.

In a stinging rebuke to Yeltsin, the new Duma in one of its first acts voted amnesty to the legislative leaders arrested in October—and to the hard-line old-guard plotters against Gorbachev in the failed coup of August 1991. Lacking the necessary political support, Yeltsin's ministers abandoned many of the economic reforms and restored government controls on wages, prices, and profits. Yeltsin himself as president now possessed greatly expanded executive powers but diminishing authority. He was showing physical and emotional strain. Erratic and impulsive, with worsening health problems and given to excessive drinking, he was frequently absent from his Kremlin office over the remaining years of his presidency, and at times vanished from public view.

Yeltsin's problems

Meanwhile, Yeltsin's political troubles continued in the Chechen Republic. Chechnya, in the oil-rich Caucasus, its population mostly Islamic, had a long tradition of rebellion and stubborn resistance to Russian domination. In 1991, as the Soviet Union was collapsing, the Chechens had demanded independence, or at least equal partnership with Russia. Militant guerrilla forces now proclaimed independence, but Russia was intent on retaining control of its southern borderlands and the links to central Asia as well as strategic oil resources and pipelines. The threat of a precedent for other federal republics was also an ongoing concern.

For three years Yeltsin did nothing except to support covert efforts to overthrow the rebel regime. Suddenly, toward the end of 1994, at the urging of his entourage who saw an opportunity to make political capital out of a quick victory, Yeltsin gave orders to invade Chechnya. In a grievous failure of military intelligence the invasion led to disastrous results. For close to two years the Russian army sank into a frustrating guerrilla war for which its poorly trained conscript army was ill-prepared and ill-equipped. When the army failed to take the capital city of Grozny, the military resorted to air bombing and rockets, killing thousands of civilians. In April 1996 Yeltsin, admitting that the military action in Chechnya was "the greatest mistake" of his first four years as president, withdrew the army. Chechen cities, towns, and villages had been destroyed and some 20,000 to 40,000 of Russia's Chechen citizens had been killed. The war was widely criticized at home and abroad.

Chechnya invaded

In the presidential elections of June 1996 Yeltsin, agile politician that he was, won reelection but only after he was forced into a run-off with the Communist party's candidate. The Chechen war cost Yeltsin some support, but the weak state of the economy was his most serious handicap.

The economic stagnation and draining budgetary deficits continued well into Yeltsin's second term. In March 1998 Yeltsin appointed a new cabinet of young reformers who in turn met with opposition. Economic difficulties assumed enormous proportions: a deep slide in the ruble, currency devaluation, and default in payments on the country's foreign debt. The International Monetary Fund (IMF) and Western banks stepped in to prevent utter bankruptcy.

The deteriorating economy brought further political instability. Yeltsin made a whole series of short-lived cabinet appointments and changed his prime minister five times in 18 months. Finally, in August 1999, he appointed as his prime minister Vladimir V. Putin, a former intelligence operative who had been stationed in East Germany and then served as head of the domestic security agency, the reorganized KGB. It was transparent that Yeltsin was choosing his successor to run in the presidential elections in 2000. Despite his recurrent illnesses and growing evidence of corruption in his family and inner political circle, he rejected all calls for his resignation.

Putin chosen as successor

Suddenly trouble broke out anew in Chechnya. Chechen guerrillas crossed over into the neighboring republic of Dagestan in an unsuccessful effort to agitate support. In the fall of 1999 mysterious explosions in Moscow and nearby cities took the lives of some 300 civilians. Prime Minister Putin at once blamed the explosions on Chechen terrorists and the government proceeded to take drastic military measures. Intent on avoiding the costly mistakes of the earlier war, the army launched large-scale air and artillery attacks on the Chechen cities and countryside. The results for the Chechen population were deadly, with a minimal loss of Russian troops. Over 4,000 deaths were reported and over 200,000 refugees were forced to flee their homes. The Chechen capital was destroyed. The United States and its allies condemned the Russian response, but the government's decisive action was popular in Russia and Putin's decisiveness enhanced his political stature.

On the last day of December 1999 Yeltsin dramatically announced his resignation and, in accordance with the constitution, appointed Putin acting president. The date of the presidential elections was advanced by three months. Yeltsin had found his successor. In the elections that followed in the spring of 2000 Putin readily won election.

An ambiguous legacy

Yeltsin left a mixed record. He had not been a pioneering champion of reform in the U.S.S.R., as Gorbachev had been in 1985, but once ousted from the inner circles of the party he allied himself with the reformers.

He was the first democratically elected president of the Russian republic while it was still part of the U.S.S.R. and he supported the independence movements of the other Soviet republics. He rallied the population to reject the hard-liners' coup against Gorbachev and became the chief architect of the Soviet Union's dissolution. His efforts to introduce Western-style market reforms met with only limited success. He had supported the disastrous intervention in Chechnya in 1994–1996, which exposed the incompetence of the army and alienated international opinion, and the renewed assault on Chechnya a few years later. In his second term it seemed possible that reforms might turn the economy around, but within two years his economic program was in shambles. Yeltsin enjoyed the trappings of power, but he was uninterested in the details of government. Power in the country had shifted to a group of industrial tycoons allied with a coterie of Kremlin insiders. Toward the end Yeltsin was increasingly an object of derision, saved only by the domestic popularity of the Chechen campaign and the vigor and decisiveness of his new prime minister. His two terms as president disappointed his Western sympathizers and democratic reformers within Russia as well. Yet he left the country with a constitutional system intact, and the way was still open for democracy to take root.

Yeltsin's historical legacy would depend in part on the policies and democratic commitments of his successor. Putin's newfound reputation was based largely on his vigorous prosecution of the war in Chechnya. Yet he knew how to pledge commitment to democracy, pay his respect to the reformers of the 1980s, and hail the protection of private property as one of the "hallmarks of civilization." To some, however, his proclaimed dedication to a "strong state" aroused concerns.

Over a decade after the collapse of the Soviet Union, the old Leninist-Stalinist communism was gone. No one expected Russia to return to a command economy and the rigidities of central planning or to put together the pieces of the old Russian empire of the tsars or the Soviets. The country had a constitution, civil rights, freedom of religion, and free, contested elections. That more was not accomplished in Russian economic and political life after the disappearance of the Soviet Union had to be balanced against the seven decades of twentieth-century dictatorship.

The Resurgence of Nationalism: the Breakup of Yugoslavia

Of all the explosive issues that confronted Europe after the downfall of communism in 1989, ethnic nationalism proved the most intractable. Nationalist passions, suppressed or permitted only limited cultural outlets during the decades of Communist rule, resurfaced. Czechoslovakia, as we have seen, divided peacefully in 1993 in response to Slovak pressures. But in Yugoslavia, the large multiethnic, multinational federation created at Versailles in 1919, politically ambitious leaders stirred up old national and even religious tensions which tore the state apart and confronted Europe and the international community with violence, armed combat, atrocities, floods of refugees, and civilian suffering not seen in Europe since the Second World War.

What happened in Yugoslavia was deeply rooted in historical animosities that were awakened and exploited for selfish political purposes by nationalist political leaders in the wake of communism's collapse in eastern Europe. To go back in time, the Balkan peninsula had been conquered by the Ottoman Turks in the fourteenth century. Serbia, once a powerful medieval kingdom attached to the Eastern Orthodox church, fell under Ottoman rule in 1389 and remained under Turkish rule for close to 500 years. In 1878 it broke away from the decaying Ottoman Empire and with the backing of the European Great Powers regained its status as an independent kingdom. Its neighbors Croatia and Slovenia had also been ruled by the Ottomans, but Croatia and Slovenia rejoined the Austrian Habsburg empire in the late seventeenth century and reaffirmed their ties with Roman Catholicism and central Europe. Bosnia (more precisely Bosnia and Herzegovina) long had a mixed population of Serbs, Croats, and Muslims; many Bosnians of Slavic blood in the long years of Turkish rule had adopted Islam. It too was freed from Ottoman rule in 1878 but was taken over by the Habsburg empire.

Political leaders and historical animosities

Serbia found a patron in tsarist Russia with which it shared its Orthodox faith. In the years before 1914 the Serbs with Russian encouragement agitated for an enlarged Slavic nation-state for all people speaking the Serbo-Croatian language, which was directed at the Croats and Slovenes within the Habsburg empire. It was this nationalist agitation that led to the assassination in Sarajevo, Bosnia's capital, of the heir to the Habsburg throne in 1914, and coupled with the alliance systems of the Great Powers led to the First World War.

When both the Austrian and Ottoman empires collapsed at the end of the First World War, Serbia together with other South Slav nationalists in 1918 proclaimed a "Kingdom of the Serbs, Croats, and Slovenes." At the Paris Peace Conference in 1919 it was permitted also to annex Bosnia, Montenegro (also ethnically Serb), and other formerly Ottoman territories. All were now joined together under the Serb monarchy in a large multinational federation. For many years the nationalities held together in a somewhat uneasy alliance under a kind of royal dictatorship. In 1929 King Alexander in a symbolic effort at achieving greater unity changed the country's name to Yugoslavia (or South Slav state). Croat separatism remained alive and a Croat nationalist assassinated King Alexander in 1934. Yet many people spoke of themselves as Yugoslavs and regarded Belgrade as their capital, and the outside world accepted a Yugoslav national identity.

During the Second World War, after the Nazis invaded Yugoslavia in 1941, the internal tensions in the Serb-dominated country reemerged. Croatia proclaimed its independence and for a time was governed as a separate Nazi puppet state. A Croat fascist organization, the Ustachi, collaborated with the Nazis in rounding up and brutally mistreating

NATIONALITIES IN CENTRAL AND EASTERN EUROPE

The map shows national boundaries and the location of various peoples at the end of the twentieth century. East Germany has been reunited with the rest of Germany. Czechoslovakia has broken into the Czech Republic and Slovakia. The state of Yugoslavia has lost control over Slovenia, Croatia, Bosnia, and Macedonia, all of which are now independent nations. Yugoslavia consists now of only Serbia and Montenegro. A numerous Serbian population remains in Bosnian territory, along with Croats and a large number of Slavic-speaking Muslims. The population in Macedonia includes many Albanians. The region of Kosovo, though officially part of Serbia, has a preponderantly Albanian Muslim population; it remained under the control of NATO military forces after the Balkan war in 1999. There are many Hungarians in the countries that surround Hungary, and about 1 million Turks live in Bulgaria. Moldova has been an independent nation since 1991 (it was part of the Soviet Union from 1940 to 1991), but much of its population speaks Romanian. Although the region's diverse ethnic groups have often lived together peacefully for long periods of their history, the modern nationalist emphasis on cultural differences and identities, at times inflamed by political leaders, has produced strong ethnic hostilities and recurring cycles of violence.

Serbs, Jews, and others. For the country as a whole the Yugoslav military resistance to Hitler turned divisive and eventually evolved into a civil war between the royalist (mostly Serb) army and guerrilla forces (mainly non-Serb) led by the prewar Communist leader Marshal Tito. By his greater effectiveness against the Nazis, Tito won the support of Churchill and Roosevelt and triumphed in the civil war.

After its wartime ordeal, with some two million of its people dead, Yugoslavia emerged in the postwar years under a Communist regime headed by Tito, who soon broke with Moscow. In 1946 he set up a federal republic with six component "republics" (Serbia, Croatia, Slovenia, Bosnia, Montenegro, and Macedonia), along with two "autonomous provinces," one of which was Kosovo. Although himself a Croat, he suppressed all separatist movements with an iron hand, but allowed each of the republics a degree of autonomy. In Bosnia he recognized the Bosnian Muslims as a distinct "national group" and gave them equal status with the Serbs and Croats. So long as he lived Yugoslavia retained its national unity and identity. It was when he died in 1980 that latent separatist movements reemerged. His successors in the next several years, who had to struggle with a troubled economy also, tried various solutions, including a rotating federal presidency, but with little success. When in 1989 communism collapsed all over eastern Europe, the regime in Yugoslavia collapsed as well. Yugoslavia's reform Communists (now calling themselves Socialists) relaxed the party's authoritarian grip on the country, faced up to its nationalities problem, and held elections on the country's future. Only Serbia and Montenegro (the two Serb states were always closely allied) voted to maintain the federal republic. Croatia, Slovenia, Macedonia, and Bosnia all voted for parties committed to independence.

Marshal Tito

Former Communist leaders, like Slobodan Milosevic in Serbia and Franjo Tudjman in Croatia, seeing power slip away, placed themselves at the head of nationalist crusades. Milosevic, the Serbian president and former Communist party leader, rallied Serbs in Bosnia, Croatia, and Slovenia to fight to remain under Serb control whenever secession took place. His fiery speeches and tactics backfired. Alarmed by Serb militancy, Croatia and Slovenia held referenda and in 1991 proclaimed their independence. They received immediate recognition from the international community, which was persuaded that prompt recognition would forestall Serb military action.

Nationalist secessions

In Bosnia, the Serbs and Croats together comprised over half the population, but the Muslims, as the largest single national group, dominated the government and, over the opposition of the Serb and Croat representatives, the Muslim nationalist leaders declared Bosnia's independence. The secession of Croatia, Slovenia, and Bosnia and their immediate international recognition infuriated Milosevic, who now governed the former Yugoslavia as a rump state consisting of only Serbia and Montenegro.

Open warfare broke out in mid-1991. Local Serb paramilitary forces, reinforced by army units from Belgrade, proceeded to carve out enclaves in the secessionist states where Serbs lived in significant numbers and to drive out non-Serbs. In the fighting in Croatia and Slovenia Serb forces seized territory in each. After months of heavy fighting, a temporary cease-fire was arranged.

Meanwhile Tudjman goaded the Croat nationalists into action. The worst violence occurred when both Serbs and Croats attempted to create enclaves for themselves in Bosnia. For years the mixed population there, despite ethnic and religious differences, had lived peacefully side by side and had even intermarried. In the war that ensued, the Serb military forces brutalized the Muslim population. The barbaric deeds, labeled "ethnic cleansing," included large-scale expulsions, wholesale civilian slaughter, pillage, and rape. A prolonged siege of Sarajevo took place. At Srebenica in eastern Bosnia Serb militia executed some 8,000 Muslim men and buried them in mass graves. A shocked world could scarcely believe such events were occurring in civilized Europe in the closing decade of the twentieth century.

The international community could not agree on measures to cope with the situation. United Nations contingents were unable even to deliver food and medical supplies. Given the historical complexity of the Balkans and the memories of earlier ferocious conflicts, neither the European powers, which might have been expected to take the lead, nor the United States would intervene with any meaningful show of force. The Security Council, however, imposed economic sanctions against the former Yugoslavia (which consisted now of only Serbia and its historical ally, Montenegro), embargoed the shipment of arms, and made plans for war crimes trials at The Hague.

UN and U.S. mediation

In 1994, to end the siege of Sarajevo the United Nations (UN), the United States, and the North Atlantic Treaty Organization (NATO) mediated a cease-fire and threatened air strikes if it were violated. For Bosnia a partial diplomatic settlement was negotiated. Croats and Muslims agreed to create a Croat-Muslim federation in what remained of Bosnian territory after the Serb conquests. The Serbs now occupied two-thirds of Bosnia and one-third of Croatia, with no intention of surrendering their gains. By 1994, 200,000 people were dead or missing, mostly in the fighting in Bosnia since 1991; there were about 4.4 million displaced persons. And still the fighting went on. In 1995 the Croatian army repulsed the Serb military and recovered most of the territory it had lost to the Serbs four years earlier. The Croats undertook their own "ethnic cleansing" program, expelling over 200,000 Serbs. In Bosnia the Serb offensive failed as well. In 1996 Serbia agreed to terms mediated by the United States at a meeting in Dayton, Ohio, accepting the new boundaries of Croatia and Bosnia and agreeing that UN peacekeepers would supervise the settlement in Bosnia.

New troubles soon ensued, this time within Serbia itself in its province of Kosovo, where a growing separatist movement alarmed the Serbs. As early as 1989 Milosevic, as part of his initial pro-Serb agitation throughout Yugoslavia, had rescinded the province's autonomy. Ethnic Albanians, Muslim in religion, had long lived in Kosovo; through immigration from Albania and with large families, they had grown in such numbers that they now made up 90 percent of the population of two million. The Kosovars, as they were known, considered themselves related in religion, language, and culture to fellow Albanians in Albania. The Serbs were especially concerned because they themselves viewed Kosovo as a kind of holy land, where their ancestors had fought and lost the famous battle of Kosovo in 1389 to the Ottoman Turks.

Kosovar separatism repressed

The separatist movement grew at first under moderate leadership, but the Kosovars soon turned to their small but militant liberation army. In 1998 Milosevic launched a military offensive aimed at wiping out the Kosovar forces. Serb military and police units blasted villages and towns to root out the rebels, killing civilian men, women, and children as well. International efforts to mediate failed. In 1998 the United States and NATO, acting not only because of the egregious human rights violations but because of the threat to the stability of the wider Balkan region, warned Milosevic that it would not allow the Serbs to do in Kosovo what they done in Bosnia a few years earlier. Milosevic nonetheless continued the wholesale Serb offensive, with mandates for "ethnic cleansing" that seemed intended to destroy the Kosovars or drive them into exile. By that time over 800,000 Kosovars had been forced to flee; at least 10,000 were dead.

In March 1999 NATO, for the first time in its 50-year history, undertook a military offensive, launching large-scale air attacks against Serbia. The bombing, led by the United States, continued for 78 days with severe damage in Belgrade and elsewhere before Milosevic yielded. It was, to be sure, an attack upon a sovereign European state, not charged with external aggression, and it seemed to violate a fundamental principle of national sovereignty. But the egregious abuses by Serbia and the violations of human rights against its own citizens made it difficult to argue against the need for what President Clinton described as "humanitarian intervention." New international law was being made. The United States and its European allies were compensating for the failure of the international community to act against the mass killings in Bosnia a few years earlier.

The NATO air offensive

The refusal of the American leadership in the bombing offensive to commit ground troops, as some of its NATO allies urged, or even to announce it as an option, may have prolonged the bombing, but made it easier for the American president to retain political support at home. In the end Milosevic had to yield, but a Russian-backed UN Security Council resolution confirmed Yugoslav sovereignty over Kosovo even if Milosevic had to accept 50,000 armed NATO troops as peacekeepers there.

That summer Kosovars returned under international protection. The UN forces now faced the difficult task of relief and reconstruction and of providing security for both Kosovars and Serbs. The indictment of Milosevic as a war criminal by the international court at The Hague and his international isolation added to his unpopularity, but he did not give up power until he unexpectedly lost an election in the fall of 2000. Refusing at first to accept the election results, he was forced to resign after massive demonstrations demanded the recognition of his opponent, a respected law professor who had kept aloof from the regime, as president. Vojslav Kostunica took office with broad popular and international support, but he faced enormous economic problems as well as the unsettled future of Kosovo. Under international pressure, Milosevic was handed over in 2001 to the war crimes tribunal to face trial at The Hague.

Milosevic ousted

Central and Eastern Europe after 1989

But we must return to central and eastern Europe, where developments took place more peacefully than in Yugoslavia. With the revolutionary changes of 1989 in the former Soviet bloc communism was gone and the Cold War was over. No longer was Europe divided into East and West. The liberated nations were moving toward democracy, the rule of law, and a free economy. But as in Russia, law and government had fallen into disrepute during the more than four decades of Soviet control; crime, corruption, and cynicism toward authority had become a method of survival. The success in open elections of former Communists, who had helped reconstruct their parties under various names and with varying degrees of success along reform lines, resulted from the hard times associated with the traumas of transition; but the new reform Communists, it must be said, learned to live and work with the democratic parties. Virtually every country in the former Soviet bloc for a time had either a head of state or head of government who once was a Communist political leader. Poland in 1993 had its first ex-Communist prime minister and in 1995 an ex-Communist president. Many of the post-Communist societies experienced a repetition of the greed and rapaciousness of early Western capitalism. As in Russia, the former ruling and managerial elites profited personally from the newly privatized state industries, accumulating economic power and wealth.

Economic sanctions, military setbacks, and Serbia's isolation from other European societies helped fuel the growing opposition to Serbian president Slobodan Milosevic. This crowd in the streets of Belgrade was part of a massive protest movement that demanded Milosevic's resignation after he lost an election in the fall of 2000. The protests forced Milosovic to accept the electoral victory of his opponent, Vojslav Kostunica, thus demonstrating again the important influence of popular mobilization in the former Communist states of central and eastern Europe.

(Spasa Dakic/Sipa Press)

The 1989 revolution assessed

Some observers judged the "revolution" of 1989 harshly, arguing that despite its significance in overthrowing a failed system and casting off foreign domination the new regimes were bent mainly on emulating the material successes of the West. The goal of a democratic, civil society to supplement the organized state seemed to have faded. Party politics and party maneuvering became the rule. Because the revolution was peaceful, some speculated, a revolutionary catharsis may have been missing.

Confronting the past

Yet there was a partial effort to reckon with the past. The former German Democratic Republic conducted trials and purges and opened the files of the East German secret security police (the Stasi), dramatically revealing wide networks of informers. The Czechs tried to ban men and women accused of serving as informers or collaborators from participation in political life for stipulated time periods, but that led to excessive abuses and was abandoned. The Poles at first sought to draw a "thick line," as they described it, between past and present, but then they too conducted purges and opened police files. Some said the Europeans might have benefited from "truth commissions," as in Latin America or South Africa before which past offenders against human rights could come forward to admit their misdeeds without necessarily expecting forgiveness.

Poland, Hungary, and the Czech Republic took the lead in the transition to democratic freedoms, market economies, the rule of law, and pluralist societies, closely followed by the three Baltic states, Estonia, Latvia, and Lithuania. They all looked forward to early admission to the European Union. From 1995 on economies in central and eastern Europe were growing. The most prosperous countries were those that early on took the most drastic economic measures, even though the initial social consequences at the time were painful. Poland was the best example of a country that benefited from such "shock therapy" and from the mid-1990s enjoyed a vigorous expanding economy. Despite persistent problems, the overall economic balance sheets showed progress throughout central and eastern Europe.

Western Europe after the Cold War: Economic and Political Uncertainties

It was generally expected that the nations of central and eastern Europe would suffer in the transition to market economies. What was unanticipated was the burden of economic and political troubles that western Europe found itself confronting. Buoyant and self-confident because of continuing prosperity during the 1950s and 1960s, it was first jolted by the recession of the 1970s that combined economic stagnation with inflation. By the mid-1980s the European democracies had recovered, although with lower growth rates than in the past and with discomfiting levels of unemployment.

In Germany the economic situation after 1989 was complicated by the reunification with East Germany. The steep costs of absorbing East Germany's decayed economy and the decision to convert the East German mark on an equal basis with the West German made inflation a threat. To combat it the German Bundesbank kept interest rates high. But tight money choked off credit and investment when downturns occurred as in the early 1990s, delaying economic recovery for itself and its European neighbors and leading to currency devaluations and instability.

Costs of German reunification

Despite recovery, many West Europeans had remained unemployed. By the early 1990s unemployment rose to postwar highs. For the members of the European Union the unemployment figure approached 19 million, or more than 12 percent of the workforce; including the European countries not members of the European Union, the total was 23 million. Long-term unemployment became a recognized phenomenon, as well as the disconcerting corollary that many workers would never again be employed at their old skills. Young people especially were hurt by shrinking job prospects.

The Europeans slowly came to realize what had only been suspected in the earlier recession, that the problem of unemployment was not temporary, limited to the business cycle, but was deep-seated and structural. High labor costs that included generous welfare-state benefits for unemployment, disability, retirement, and extended paid vacations undercut western Europe's ability to compete globally. Many corporations, like their American counterparts, began to restructure, sharply reducing employment rolls and introducing other economies. American and European multinational corporations shifted manufacturing operations to areas like Southeast Asia where labor costs and benefits were lower. For the first time in the years since 1945 the West European nations, echoing the British example under the Thatcher government, took steps to roll back the welfare state as it had evolved by consensus since the end of the Second World War.

Persistent unemployment

Western Europe: Political Crises and Discontents

Meanwhile there was widespread dissatisfaction with the governing political parties of the center and center-left, which were judged to have held office too long and seemed incapable of providing fresh vision for the future. Shocking revelations of scandal and corruption tarnished the Christian Democratic and Socialist parties in several major countries.

Italy's Christian Democrats

Nowhere did dissatisfaction with the political system reach the proportions that it did in Italy. For years the Christian Democrats had dominated the political scene, forming successive coalition governments, with the Right in the 1950s and with the Socialists and other parties in the 1960s. By the 1970s in the midst of economic setbacks their popular support shrank rapidly. In the 1980s the Socialists replaced them, heading a cabinet for a record four years. Meanwhile the country's second strongest party, the Italian Communist party, which had earlier demonstrated its independence from Moscow, was excluded from government at the national level but won numerous mayoralties and control of municipal councils. In 1989, with the collapse of communism and end of the Cold War, the party renamed itself the Democratic Party of the Left and began a new quest for participation in the national government.

Over the years the Christian Democrats kept a tight grip on power and patronage and maintained close ties both to state-owned enterprises and private business. In good part because the Christian Democrats projected themselves as Italy's defenders against communism they were shielded from scrutiny or criticism. But in the early 1990s evidence surfaced of bribes, kickbacks, and payoffs for government contracts up to the highest political levels. There had been illegal payments to the political parties and widespread collusion with organized crime. Soon the government was charged with a failure to provide adequate protection for the investigating magistrates, some of whom had been assassinated. Former prime ministers, cabinet ministers, and parliamentary deputies of all political parties as well as top business executives were implicated. So tainted was the Christian Democratic party that it renamed itself the Popular Party. The aroused electorate in 1993 approved a new electoral system, one feature of which was to abandon proportional representation.

New parties

In the elections in 1994 both the former Christian Democratic party and the Socialist party were routed. Three new parties won and formed a Center–Right coalition. But the new parties inspired little confidence and their political leaders were unable to provide stability or serve as civic models. All the governments inherited public deficits, economic slowdown, unemployment, social tensions, and the continuing corruption inquiries. In 1998 the Popular Party joined with the Democratic Party of the Left to form a cabinet, and Massimo d'Alema, the head of the former Communist party, became prime minister. The reconstructed Communists were committed to financial stability, private enterprise, and economic growth as the best means of advancing social needs. But this cabinet lasted only briefly. In 2001 the media magnate Silvio Berlusconi headed a coalition that won the elections; its Center–Right majority promised stability but also aroused misgivings about the ambitious prime minister and his assertive *Forza Italia* party.

Europe's Immigrants and Refugees

We have already seen how the influx of millions of immigrants and refugees since the 1960s was altering the nature of European societies. In the 12 years from 1980 to 1992, 15 million new immigrants arrived to make their home in western Europe. Some sought po-

The populations of all modern nations have become increasingly diverse as immigrants and mobile workers stream across national borders in search of better jobs, education, cultural freedom, and basic human rights. These children at a primary school in contemporary London exemplify the diverse racial, ethnic, and cultural backgrounds of the people who now live in contemporary multicultural nations. Immigration is constantly changing the workforce, schools, food, music, and neighborhoods of modern cities; it also at times provokes anti-immigrant political movements and affects the political culture of every nation.

(Christine Osborne/Corbis)

litical asylum, but mainly they came in search of wider economic opportunities than could be found in their own impoverished countries. They were usually willing to fill the lower paid, less desirable jobs that the Europeans did not want. When the Cold War ended and Communist barriers came down, a flood of refugees left eastern Europe, and additional refugees streamed in from war-torn Yugoslavia.

The steady flow of immigrants visibly changed the ethnic composition of Europe. In Germany the Turkish workers settled in with their families as permanent residents; many reared their children as Muslims. In France in a population of 57 million in the mid-1990s, 4 million, or 7 percent, were foreign-born—mainly Arabs from Algeria and immigrants from other former French African colonies but also Vietnamese from Southeast Asia. In Britain, with a population of 56 million, at least 2.5 million could be counted as "ethnic minorities," mainly from various parts of Asia, Africa, and the Caribbean. Nations that had long sent emigrants to all parts of the world now found themselves absorbing large new populations from abroad.

Shifts in Europe's ethnic composition

The hostility which had manifested itself earlier in western Europe again flared up. In Germany there were physical assaults on Turks, firebombings, and other acts of violence.

Neo-Nazis in Germany, "skinheads" in Britain (who dated from the 1950s), neo-Fascists in Italy, and followers in France of Jean-Marie Le Pen's National Front agitated the immigrant issue and even resorted to racist violence. Governments adopted laws to reduce or eliminate further immigration. Germany in 1993 repealed a constitutional provision that had offered asylum to "all persecuted on political grounds," but it became virtually impossible to distinguish between political and economic refugees. France moved toward "near-zero" immigration and abandoned a tradition going back to the Revolution of granting citizenship to any child born on French soil. Unemployment and troubled economies made the social tensions potentially explosive and fed prejudices of all kinds, including anti-Semitism. But western Europe was only one outpost of a global crisis of refugees and migrants on the move.

Western Europe seemed enveloped in gloom and pessimism during the early 1990s. The end of the Cold War had not automatically ushered in peace, prosperity, and harmony. Unemployment, especially for the young, marred the economic scene. In the euphoria following the collapse of communism, few had anticipated the resurgence of the kind of explosive nationalism that brought bloodshed to the Balkans. Western Europe, for all its announced commitment to democratic institutions and for all its military strength, feared the entanglements of intervention so much that until the Kosovo bombing offensive it refrained from decisive action. On the political scene conservative and centrist political leaders offered few new initiatives, and the Left seemed in disarray. On the other hand, many were still confident that western Europe would reach out to central and eastern Europe, continue to work toward a united Europe, and reassume a central role in the world's economy and international affairs.

Post-Cold War gloom

Economic Recovery and Boom: A "Third Way" in Politics

In the 1990s President Clinton set the tone for a new type of democratic politics. Taking his lead from Republican pro-business policies, Clinton promoted a program that favored economic growth and productivity but combined it with such social issues as health care and education and concern for the disadvantaged and minorities. He was favored by an upturn in the business cycle. In 1992, the American economy began to embark on a peacetime expansion that exceeded the previous nine-year record of the 1960s. Unemployment dropped to an all-time low, trade and production expanded, the stock market rose to unprecedented heights. The economy benefited from earlier corporate cost-cutting and restructuring and from the emergence and growth of the revolutionary new computer industries and information economy. Before long the global economy, buoyed by American prosperity, followed suit despite financial crises in Asia, Latin America, and elsewhere. Clinton also pursued an activist foreign policy, especially in the Middle East. His second term as president was marred, however, when his denial of sexual indiscretions in the White House with a young woman intern led to a vote of impeachment by the House of Representatives; the Senate after a trial came short of the two-thirds vote needed for his removal from office.

Clinton and Blair

Clinton found a kindred political spirit in the buoyant British Labour Party leader Tony Blair, who also adopted many conservative pro-business policies. Blair persuaded his party to abandon what still remained of its earlier socialist and welfare-state platform. Neutralizing the party's older trade union and left-wing bastions, he projected an image of the party as "New Labour." The best prescription for prosperity was to encourage economic growth and industry but without satisfying "pure selfish individualism" or neglecting social needs, which he accused Thatcher and the Conservative party of doing. A market economy and private enterprise would unleash productive forces that would benefit everyone. After four Conservative electoral victories since 1979 and 18 years of Conservative leadership, the country was ready for change. Labour in 1997 won with a huge majority and with its largest margin of victory since 1945.

As in the United States, the economy turned upward in Britain. Blair's political strength and popularity enabled him to institute a number of constitutional changes, measures that some called "a constitutional revolution." The United Kingdom had long had a highly centralized government, with all power emanating from the Westminster Parliament in London. The Labour party with its large majority in the House of Commons took unprecedented steps toward a devolution of power to a new parliament in Scotland, where the reform was intended to defuse a strong separatist movement, and to a new legislative assembly in Wales. Each gained broad jurisdiction over its internal affairs. Voters in Scotland for the first time since the Act of Union of 1707 went to the polls to elect their own parliament, and in Wales voters elected an assembly for the first time ever. Critics saw the devolution of authority as the "undoing of Britain" and an erosion of parliamentary sovereignty. Others recognized that stability did not necessarily mean resistance to change. No one wished to repeat the mistakes of earlier years when Britain's resistance to home rule for Ireland had led to continuing violence, partition, and prolonged strife.

In Northern Ireland matters seemed to be taking a more peaceful turn. The Protestant and Catholic parties reached an agreement in 1998, moving to end a violent conflict that over the past 30 years had cost the lives of over 3,000 people. The new arrangements authorized a legislative council of representatives from Britain, Northern Ireland, and the Republic of Ireland, and a sharing of power in a joint cabinet. That the solution would satisfy the die-hards on both sides was questionable.

The settlement in Northern Ireland

In another momentous break with tradition a reform bill in 1998 stripped the hereditary peers in the House of Lords of their parliamentary seats. The hereditary seats, it was widely recognized, represented a political anachronism, untenable in a contemporary democracy. A reorganized House of Lords would consist only of lifetime peers. Many in Britain were opposed, but others placed the reform in the long tradition of broadening the suffrage and other democratic innovations.

In Germany and in France political leaders also represented the new politics of the Left and Left-Center. In Germany the Social Democratic Chancellor, Gerhard Schröder, replaced Helmut Kohl in 1998 after the Christian Democratic chancellor's 14 years in office. Schröder, whose party's moderate wing had triumphed over its more radical elements, was committed to curbing the generous provisions of the postwar welfare state, which had driven up labor costs and made it difficult to hire new workers. He too spoke of his program as a "middle way."

Schröder

In France Daniel Jospin, a long-time moderate Socialist leader, who hoped to continue President Mitterrand's reformist policies, became prime minister in 1997. Two years earlier he had lost the presidential elections to his conservative, Gaullist opponent Jacques Chirac, but the Socialists soon won a majority in the legislature; under the now established practice of "cohabitation" the president appointed Jospin prime minister. Jospin, too, though still resolutely committed

Jospin

to a large role for government on social issues, believed in moderation and pragmatism and favored a market economy and the continuing privatization of state-owned industries. The constitution meanwhile was amended to curtail the powerful role of the presidency by reducing the term of office from seven to five years.

In 1999 political leaders representing a "middle" or "third" way between conservatism and radical progressivism agreed to an "agenda" for contemporary democracy that recognized an essential role for governments in dealing with social problems but also called for reduced public spending, budget balancing, limits on regulation, and a climate of opportunity for business enterprise. Pragmatism and moderation seemed to be triumphant over older socialist views and the older welfare-state ideology that had prevailed in the years after the Second World War.

Japan in the 1990s

The 1990s were an economic and political watershed for Japan. Its economy had expanded almost uninterruptedly since the postwar years. In the 1970s and 1980s capital investment in industry, and especially in advanced technology, grew at times at twice the rate of American and West European investment. Between 1981 and 1989 stock market values and property prices each more than quadrupled. But in the summer of 1991 Japan suffered a severe financial crisis and sank into a deep and stubborn recession.

The downturn signaled a problem that was more than a swing in the business cycle. The country was paying the price for years of uncontrolled speculation at home and abroad. Investors, including the largely unregulated banks, had made risky forays into real estate and financial markets. Government control over monetary policy had been lax. A "bubble economy" had emerged, not unlike the economy of the 1920s in the United States that led to the Great Depression. When the bubble burst in 1991, Japan suffered bank failures and bankruptcies, and as the downturn continued the government unsuccessfully tried to revive the economy with belated and ineffective fiscal and monetary policies. Japan's export economy added to its difficulties. Over the years the country exported freely while sharply restricting imports, and other nations finally rebelled. New low-cost competition was now invading its own markets. Japan also was forced to deal with social pressures. Although wages, educational opportunities, and living standards remained high, housing was scarce and expensive and the country's infrastructure suffered from neglect.

The price of speculation

In the midst of its economic troubles a political crisis, unprecedented in the years since the Second World War, shook the country. Cumulative evidence mounted of bribery, corruption, and ties to organized crime among high-ranking political and business leaders. In 1993 the Liberal Democratic party, which had dominated political life and served as the political pillar of Japan's prosperity and stability, for the first time lost its parliamentary majority in the Diet and fell from office. New faces and new parties emerged to replace the old guard, even though the country's bureaucracy remained entrenched. The recession dragged on and currency and financial crises in much of Asia in 1998 set recovery back, but toward the end of the decade the economy showed some signs of renewed growth. The crisis and prolonged recession transformed the country. Japan was not to be counted out as one of the world's leading political and economic powers. Efforts at political reform stimulated a reexamination of the past and aroused hopes for a revived economy, a more democratic future, and a more flexible society. But in the 1990s Japan faded as the model of postwar industrial and financial success and served instead as an example of a "bubble economy" that had burst.

The European Union: Widening and Deepening

By the opening of the twenty-first century European integration had made remarkable progress. The European Economic Community, established in 1957, became the European Community in 1965, and it in turn became the European Union (EU) under the Treaty of Maastricht signed in 1991. With the admission of Austria, Finland, and Sweden in 1995, the EU membership increased from 12 to 15 nations, with more than a dozen additional countries, mostly but not all from the former Soviet bloc in central and eastern Europe, about to be admitted. The EU was an economic superpower, the world's largest single market with over 370 million people, closely bound together in ways other than economic as well.

As agreed under the Maastricht treaty, the EU embarked in the 1990s on one of its most ambitious enterprises, the voluntary adoption of a common currency. Of the 15 EU members, Britain, Sweden, and Denmark chose not to join the currency union immediately, and Greece failed to meet the stringent budgetary and fiscal requirements for admission. But 11 member-states agreed to substitute for their own currency a new common currency designated as the "euro." In use at the beginning of 1999 by banks, brokerages, and other businesses, the euro was to be in general circulation for the public as bills and coins in 2002, taking the place of the mark, the franc, the lira, the peseta, and the other historic currencies of the participating nations. Relative to the American dollar, the euro's initial value was about $1.17, but its value, like any other currency, would fluctuate (and it fell steadily in its early years). In another unprecedented step a European Central Bank was established in Frankfurt with the authority to set monetary policy for the member countries. The full implications for each country's social and economic policies remained to be seen.

A common currency

Meanwhile the requirements for admission to the European Union remained firmly attached to liberal political and economic models. An applicant nation had to demonstrate its commitment to "liberty, democracy, respect for human rights and fundamental freedoms, and the rule of law." A functioning free market economy was also required. The EU acted briskly when an outspoken apologist for Nazism became a member of the Austrian cabinet in 1999. In contrast to its slow expansion earlier, the EU now welcomed all European nations meeting its specifications. At the opening of the new century it had invited applications from 12 candidates, 10 from central and eastern Europe. Cyprus, Estonia, Hungary, Poland, the Czech Republic, and Slovenia were poised for early admission. The EU was widening well beyond western Europe.

The EU was also "deepening" in additional ways. The Maastricht treaty had called for the continued development of common foreign and defense policies. The failure of the Europeans to prevent or halt the bloody events in Bosnia in the early 1990s and the later failure to thwart more quickly Serbia's assault on Kosovo had embarrassed the Europeans. The American-led NATO intervention in Kosovo also demonstrated how far the Europeans lagged behind the Americans in modern military technology. In June 1999 the EU foreign ministers resolved to develop a capacity for collective military action of their own. The EU would move toward creating an armed force supplementary to but not supplanting NATO. The Atlantic alliance would remain firm, but the Europeans signaled their intention to end their long-term dependence on the United States, rejecting the status of "an American protectorate." The decision both pleased and disturbed American policy makers who wanted Europe to play an independent role, especially in European matters, but did not wish to see resources drained off from NATO.

Common foreign and defense policies

Structurally, the EU changed only in small ways. The European Commission, with an extensive civil service bureaucracy in Brussels, served as its executive and administrative branch and had the right to initiate proposals for legislation. The European Parliament, elected by a Europeanwide electorate, supervised the budget and debated Commission proposals. It never aroused much enthusiasm, and voter turnout in the member nations at election time remained small. Although the heads of government held regularly scheduled meetings, the foreign ministers of the member-nations meeting as a council convened frequently to discuss and vote on matters of common interest. It had not been anticipated that the ministers would evolve into the chief policy-making body, but in some ways it tied the EU to democratic support in a way that the European Commission had failed to do.

Cooperation or supranationalism?

The early impetus for supranationalism in the Union faded, but what remained was the close pragmatic cooperation of the ministers representing the member-states and their people, discussing and making decisions on the basis of a half-century of common values and experience and a body of jurisprudence and legal principles under the jurisdiction of the Union's Court of Justice. Each nation saw its stability, prosperity, and security enhanced by membership in the Union and recognized that the loss of sovereignty had been less than feared. Even if the European Union had not developed as the more visionary advocates of an earlier generation had anticipated, it could rightly be called a political success story. No one could predict how it would further evolve in its enlarged form.

French-German cooperation, which had been the original driving force behind the success of integration, still remained critical. It had suited France and Germany alike in the early years for France to lead on behalf of both countries. But after 1989, with reunification, Germany was more populous and in some ways richer and stronger than all other countries in western Europe. The return to Berlin as its capital in 1999 was symbolic of a new era of German strength and national pride. On the other hand, Germany's integration into the democratic European Union was crucial to its own future and to the future of Europe. Germany seemed clearly destined to play an ever larger role in European and world affairs.

Uneasiness over American-led globalization

In Europe the older strategic threat from the Soviet Union was gone, but many Europeans now saw a threat to the European way of life in American-led "globalization," which Europeans criticized as a worship of mass consumerism and a materialistic abandonment of social and cultural values. To Europeans, even among admirers of American accomplishments, the EU provided an essential balance to American hegemony in world affairs.

The "New Economy": The 1990s and Beyond

The global economy that reemerged after the Second World War seemed to enter a new phase in the 1990s. Globalization was the key word. It meant the more rapid and efficient movement of capital and technology worldwide across all geographical and political boundaries. The United States took the lead in globalization and in the development of what came to be known as the "new economy," but large multinational corporations were also based in all regions of the world.

An information economy

The new economy was an information economy. At its base was the computer revolution and the Internet, a word scarcely known at the decade's beginning. By the late 1990s it was in everyone's vocabulary, and at the disposal of tens of millions in offices and homes worldwide. It provided instant access to information of all kinds. It was as if a new industrial revolution was setting in and at an accelerated speed exceeding all previous industrial changes. Meanwhile world output grew steadily, driven by rapid growth in the United States. Trade expanded. The flow of private investment capital from the industrial nations to the developing countries quickened. Living standards in many parts of the world rose, all tied to growing trade and investment. Globalization, driven by the profit motive, arguably held greater potential for Third World countries than foreign aid or loans from governments and international agencies.

The United States was the driving force in the new global economy. The American economy began an initial period of quiet growth and expansion in 1982. The inflation of the 1970s had been brought under control by high interest rates imposed by the Federal Reserve Board, the nation's politically independent central bank, which continued its periodic interventions to adjust to economic changes. There were setbacks and brief recessions, but by 1992 the economy began a period of uninterrupted growth that surpassed in length the 1960s. Unemployment declined to 4 percent, the lowest since the 1960s. Government revenues were available for many purposes, and some were used to reduce the national debt. American productivity, aided by computer technology, rose. Inflation with respect to consumer prices, although not for equities and real estate values, was kept in check. Consumer confidence and purchases, buoyed by the rising values of stocks and homes and the availability of credit, remained high. Only at the beginning of the new century did signs of a declining stock market and an economic downturn begin to appear. By that time the country had experienced the longest period of uninterrupted economic expansion in its history.

But there were troubled areas elsewhere in the industrial world. Japan, still suffering from a long severe recession after its financial collapse in 1989, was only beginning to recover at the end of the 1990s. Mexico experienced financial difficulties in 1994, Brazil in 1998, and there were continuing crises in Russia's unsettled economy, including the drastic devaluation of the ruble in 1998.

Troubled areas

This office of International Business Machines stands near a mosque in Istanbul, Turkey, suggesting a cultural and economic juxtaposition of the new and the old that also often appears beside Gothic cathedrals in Europe and Buddhist temples in Thailand—wherever modern technologies enter into long-established societies. The international economy now depends upon computers and digital information systems that link East and West as well as the newest and oldest forms of human cultural expression.

(IBM Archives, Somers, New York)

Especially serious were currency and financial crises in 1997–1998 in several of the hith-erto golden economies of Asia. The troubles there began with a loss of confidence and col-lapse of the currency in Thailand and led to a withdrawal of foreign investment that sent currencies tumbling in Malaysia, South Korea, Indonesia, Hong Kong, and Singapore—the same countries that had helped create the "Asian miracle." Speculation in real estate and equities in these countries had gone wild. Imprudent business practices came home to roost.

Along with the Japanese recession, these crises shattered the thesis that "Asian val-ues," meritorious though many were, would guarantee continued economic progress. Among the envied values were disciplined work habits, rigorous educational standards, worker dedication to employers, reciprocal obligations by employers (including a com-mitment to lifetime employment for their workers), and a close partnership between gov-ernment and business in research and development. When the American and West Euro-pean economies sagged in the 1970s and 1980s the Japanese and other Asian economic models had been held up as object lessons for the United States and the West.

Political crises followed the Asian economic collapse and opposition parties grew in strength. The IMF made multibillion-dollar loans but imposed austerity measures that brought social hardships. We have seen how Japan, with the second largest economy of the world, sank into deep recession in 1989 after the collapse of its stock market. In magnitude and duration it turned into the most pro-longed economic crisis the post-1945 industrial world had seen. Just as the recession was beginning to lift, the economy suffered additional setbacks as a result of the more general Asian crisis. Japan's industrial skills and infrastructure were still sound, but the country found fundamental changes difficult to undertake.

Japan's difficulties

To enhance competitive power in the global marketplace large corporations in the United States, Europe, and Asia were buying other companies to become even larger, within and across national lines. Multinational corporations grew in numbers and size everywhere, and there seemed to be little concern, as previously, over foreign companies taking over domestic corporations. London regained much of its financial prestige and strength as the financial center for European mergers and amalgamations, which acceler-ated as never before.

As the American stock market boomed in the 1990s, and new computer technology companies soared in value, some observers recalled the prosperity and speculative ex-cesses of the 1920s and the American stock market crash in October 1929. Despite warn-ings against "irrational exuberance," stock values kept climbing. Some saw warnings in the collapse of the Japanese bubble after 1989. Still others recalled past speculative fever and manias in history: tulips in the seventeenth century; colonization schemes in the eighteenth; canals, railroads, gold, and silver in the nineteenth.

The computer technology revolution

The computer revolution and the emergence of the new computer tech-nology companies created a new economy in many ways. They helped the economy to grow through greater productivity and helped fuel the rising prices in global stock markets. Computer wizards as well as brokers, finan-cial executives, and entrepreneurs of all kinds became wealthy, often at an early age. Inventions in makeshift garage workplaces by obscure individuals, backed by ven-ture capital, led to the establishment of multibillion-dollar corporations. The president of Mi-crosoft, Bill Gates, became the richest man in the world, counting a fortune in the billions.

Through all this period of economic growth the Federal Reserve Board kept a vigilant eye on inflation and intervened periodically to raise interest rates to keep the economy from succumbing to inflation. To all Cassandras the response was that this was a "new economy" and that market prices would be sustained on a new high plateau. But some economists had made somewhat similar predictions in 1929. There were indeed grounds for believing that the market did reflect profound changes in the American and global economy closely related to computer technology and increased productivity, but there were warning signs in the early years of the new century that speculative fever here too had gone too far. Shock waves reverberated throughout the economy when high technology computer stocks, which had risen in price all out of proportion to their earnings, faltered and were on the brink of collapse in the early years of the new century.

The two most important developments in the computer revolution of the 1990s were the Internet and the World Wide Web. The Internet began from modest beginnings in the late 1960s in the United States as a government-sponsored project to enhance communications. Computer scientists around the world enlarged its scope and made it easier for individuals and companies to utilize in their daily work. The World Wide Web was first developed in 1980 at a nuclear physics research center near Geneva when the young English physicist Tim Berners-Lee developed a program to process information through electronic associations and linkages. For a time it remained neglected, but by 1990 he and others had revived and perfected it. By means of the Internet, the World Wide Web became a mass medium navigated by millions around the world, and its users continued to multiply. It revolutionized communications; people could send electronic mail to each other, negotiate financial transactions, make purchases, tap all kinds of sources for information and education, and use the Web for entertainment as well. Many compared the significance of the new computer technology to the invention of the printing press in the fifteenth century. So rapidly was the new technology developing in speed, efficiency, and versatility that new computer models would become available almost immediately after earlier ones first came into use.

The Internet

Nearly half of the world's Internet users at the turn of the new century were to be found in the United States, more than double the percentage in Germany or Britain. English became the dominant language of the Internet. Some Europeans and Asians expressed concern that the Internet represented not only an immense step toward globalization but also toward Americanization. However, global competition continued. A Finnish company held the lead in the cellular phone market, computer specialists developed innovative software programs in India, and companies in Taiwan manufactured many of the most advanced computer chips. But a serious gap opened up meanwhile between those who had the opportunity and means to avail themselves of the new computer technology and those who did not. A "digital divide" existed both within countries and between the wealthy and poorer countries of the world.

It was possible to raise questions about the spectacular American economy of the 1990s and its impact on American society. The economic boom seemed to have left those at the bottom of the economic ladder falling behind. The gap between rich and poor was widening. In the years from 1988 to 1998 the income of the wealthiest fifth of American families rose by 15 percent as against less than 1 percent for the poorest fifth. The incomes of the poor and of many working-class and middle-class families fell or stagnated even when entire families worked. The gap grew wider between those who could save, invest, and build more wealth and those who could not. More Americans were living below the poverty line in 1999 than in 1969. Lack of opportunity for education and training in the new skills presented a new kind of challenge for many.

Gap between rich and poor

The new worldwide faith in the market and market forces presented other challenges as well. Faith in a kind of vulgarized or oversimplified laissez-faire market economy spread globally, a kind of "market fundamentalism," not unlike a religious faith. The invisible hand would make it all right for everyone in the end, its supporters said, and a rising tide would lift all boats. Globalization and the world's market economy, its advocates claimed, made government intervention unnecessary. The argument found critics everywhere. In France, where unemployment was still high, some argued that it was immoral for corporations to earn large profits while at the same time laying off workers in what were described as "abusive job cuts."

The founding of the WTO

Meanwhile the growth in world commerce led to the creation in 1994 of a more formal World Trade Organization (WTO) to replace the General Agreement on Tariffs and Trade (GATT) in effect since 1948. GATT had been immensely successful in lowering tariffs and enlarging world trade through informal bargaining procedures and agreements. By 1986 it had grown to include 92 nations. In 1995 the United States succeeded in creating a permanent, more formal organization. The WTO was authorized to draw up and oversee agreements, enforce trade rules, and settle disputes. It grew to 135 participants but at its first new-style open bargaining sessions in Seattle, it met with opposition and demonstrations in the streets, as would soon become the pattern at other international meetings elsewhere. Such negotiated free trade agreements, the critics protested, paid little attention to environmental and labor conditions, or even to the exploitation of child labor in large parts of the developing world. The developing nations, for their part, saw themselves at risk of losing out on cheaper labor costs, one of their chief competitive advantages, and they pointedly underscored the large share of ecological damage for which the industrial nations were responsible. The initial public meetings of the WTO exposed obstacles to agreement on the international regulation of the global economy. Opponents refuted arguments for free trade as a means of enhancing living standards for all. The violence of the protests offended many, but they aroused new sensitivities to social issues worldwide.

Globalization, already visible in earlier periods of the world's history, and especially so in the nineteenth and twentieth centuries, seemed to be the defining social and economic theme for the new century. National boundaries, though not disappearing, were increasingly transcended by cross-boundary transactions and global exchanges in the world of communications, industry, culture, travel, food, popular entertainment, even apparel. To some globalization was still thought of as "Westernization" or "Americanization." By the beginning of the twenty-first century, however, it defined only the latest phase of modernization, shared by many more of the world's people than ever before.

Critics of globalization

The giant multinational corporations, no longer exclusively European or American but home-based in nations all over the world, depended as never before on the movement of capital, goods, trained personnel, technology, and ideas that flowed across traditional national boundaries.

128. INTELLECTUAL AND SOCIAL CURRENTS

Although much of twentieth-century culture had its origins in the years 1871 to 1914, science, philosophy, the arts, and religion crossed new frontiers or took new directions in the course of the twentieth century. Even to single out a few of these developments will suggest the vast changes of the contemporary era.

One sign of globalization—or what some critics have called "Westernization"—is the growing popularity of similar foods and consumer products in different societies and national cultures. This Chinese child is enjoying a famous American beverage as he sits on the Great Wall of China. Most of the present wall dates from the seventeenth century, but some parts were built 2,000 years ago to protect Chinese culture from the foreign intrusions of that day. Although such walls no longer impede the flow of cultures, fashions, or products across national borders, different societies still find distinctive ways to use the consumer goods and ideas that reach them through the global economy.

(Andanson/Corbis Sygma)

The Advance of Science and Technology

Science and technology expanded rapidly in the half-century before the First World War, but the pace quickened in the following years. Scientific discovery advanced more rapidly in the years after 1919 than in all previous human history. For one thing, more scientists were at work. At the opening of the twentieth century, about 15,000 scientists were exploring scientific problems; in the latter half of the century, over a half-million scientists were engaged in research, more than in all previous centuries combined. Over 85 percent of all scientists who had ever lived were at work in our own age.

The average person experienced the triumphs of science most dramatically in medicine and public health. Nothing in previous medical discovery could equal the contributions of sulfa drugs, antibiotics, cortisone, and other substances used to combat formerly crippling or deadly diseases, including pneumonia and tuberculosis; hormones, adrenaline, and insulin

Medicine and public health

were also available to promote health or relieve suffering. Vaccines combated a number of dread diseases, including, after 1955, poliomyelitis; by 1975 smallpox had been eradicated worldwide. Remarkable accomplishments in surgery included the transplanting of vital organs. Apart from the advances in medical science, people benefited from modern technology in almost every aspect of their daily lives. For entertainment, radio and the motion picture were available and, after the Second World War, television. Washing machines, freezers, frozen foods, and microwave ovens lightened household duties. After 1947 airplanes could fly faster than the speed of sound; giant aircraft could traverse huge distances in a few hours; tourist travel to distant parts of the earth became commonplace. A world of electronics, robotics, rocketry, and space technology opened, and a new industrial age based on computer technology was emerging. Many people came to believe that technological solutions could be found for every problem.

It was therefore a shattering experience when the fatal disease AIDS (Acquired Immuno-Deficiency Syndrome) appeared in the early 1980s and by the 1990s was assuming global epidemic proportions. The first case was reported in the United States in mid-1981, but the disease seems to have originated earlier and elsewhere. Deaths from the disease mounted, and it was estimated that tens of millions had the disease or were infected with HIV, the human immunodeficiency virus that caused it. While medical scientists worked to devise a vaccine or to prolong or ease the life of its victims, educational efforts to prevent its spread focused on sexual practices, intravenous drug use, and the protection of blood supplies. Uncertainty and anguish increased as time went by without a cure for what loomed as the greatest threat since the Black Death of the fourteenth century.

Nuclear Physics

In pure, or theoretical, science the transformation of physics in the twentieth century could be compared only to the scientific revolution of the sixteenth and seventeenth centuries. Early in the twentieth century scientists had discovered the natural radioactivity of certain elements, physicists like Max Planck and Albert Einstein had developed quantum physics and relativity theory, and Einstein had propounded his now famous formula for the conversion of mass into energy ($e = mc^2$). After 1919 a series of discoveries led to a deeper understanding of the atom. The cyclotron, developed in 1932 at Cambridge University, made it possible to penetrate or "bombard" the nucleus of the atom at high speed. The nucleus, scientists learned, consisted not only of protons but of other particles like neutrons as well. In 1938 the German chemist Otto Hahn discovered that when he bombarded the atomic nucleus of the heavy radioactive element uranium with neutrons it became unstable and split into two, which meant that energy trapped within the atom could be released. Additional scientists, including Lise Meitner, a German-Jewish scientist who had been forced to flee Nazi Germany, expanded upon these findings. In 1939 Nils Bohr, a Danish physicist, brought word of these developments to American scientists.

The implications of this breakthrough in theoretical science were clear. If the atoms in a large amount of uranium were split in a chain reaction, enormous amounts of energy would be released. In the troubled atmosphere of 1939 the possibility arose of its use for military purposes. When the war came, scientists in the United States, including Einstein, who had fled the Nazis in 1934, prevailed upon the American government to explore its military use before the Germans succeeded in doing so. In 1942 American and British scientists and European refugee scientists like the Italian Enrico Fermi brought about the first sustained nuclear chain reaction. This in turn led to the secret preparation of the atomic bomb at Los Alamos, New Mexico, its testing at Alamagordo in the New Mexican desert in July 1945, and its use by the United States against Japan at Hiroshima and Nagasaki in August 1945. The bomb tested at Alamagordo and the bombs dropped on Japan heralded the atomic age.

The first atomic bomb

After the war even more staggering technical developments followed. The hydrogen or thermonuclear bomb was built independently by the Americans and by the Soviets in 1952–1953; it involved nuclear fusion, or the joining together of hydrogen and other elements at great heat, using the atomic or fission bomb as a detonator with a stupendous chain reaction. Such thermonuclear fusion is responsible for the energy of the sun itself.

The first use of nuclear energy was for military purposes, but it held constructive peacetime potential; a tiny grain of uranium (or plutonium, another radioactive element) could produce power equal to almost 3 tons of coal. In the 1990s over 15 percent of the world's electricity was generated by nuclear power plants; in a country like France, over 65 percent. At the same time the awesome explosive powers unleashed by the scientists and the dangers of radioactivity were alarming. Accidents in nuclear power plants threatened the surrounding population and environs with the release of radioactive gases; nor could nuclear meltdowns be ruled out. Popular opposition to the building of nuclear power plants grew, as did concern over their proper design and the disposition of nuclear waste.

In military affairs a true nuclear clash of arms could mean apocalypse. Scientists who had prepared the first atomic bomb believed it to be so awesome a weapon as to make its future use unthinkable and in that way bar future major wars. In part they were correct; a balance of terror emerged so that over the years since August 1945 no nuclear weapon has been used in warfare. But nuclear bombs became part of the world's arsenal, an ever-present threat to human life and to the planet itself. The nuclear powers possessed missiles and warheads in the thousands, representing an accumulation of explosive power unparalleled in history.

The nuclear danger

In later years scientists used linear accelerators like the cyclotron and even more powerful colliders and supercolliders as atom smashers to explore the nature of the atom and the behavior of its subatomic particles. Building upon the work of Einstein and others, the theoretical physicists searched for an overarching theory that would explain the interrelationship of gravity, electromagnetism, and nuclear force, all of which were to be found in the subatomic world and in the cosmos as a whole.

Social Implications of Science and Technology

As in the case of nuclear physics, science in the contemporary age was closely allied with technology and the organized effort to exploit new scientific findings. Government and industry subsidized most scientific research. Laboratory equipment was expensive, and complex investigation required large-scale collaborative efforts; the solitary scientific investigator virtually disappeared. The subsidization of research for national purposes raised fears that scientific discoveries might serve political and not human goals.

Science had always affected the way people thought about themselves and their universe. The Copernican revolution had removed the earth from its central position in the scheme of things; Darwinian evolution had demonstrated that *Homo sapiens* was biologically a species that had evolved and survived. The philosophical implications of contemporary physics were only vaguely understood, yet they reinforced theories of relativism in all spheres. Ironically, at the very time that the average person was awed by the capabilities of science, scientists themselves recognized that they did not possess a magic key to the nature of things. Generally they claimed no more than the ability to determine, or guess at, relationships, which in the world of the atom (as in the cosmos itself) were mysterious and uncertain.

Questioning scientific advances

Some thoughtful persons questioned scientific and technological advance and asked whether modern technology had grown beyond human control. Ecologists pointed to the wastage and despoliation of natural resources and the threat to the environment. In another way the life-preserving features of medicine and public health could result in overpopulation and in perhaps unmanageable pressure upon the limited resources of the globe. The techniques developed to save or prolong human life also raised ethical and legal issues, including new definitions of life and death, and the rights in such matters of patients, families, hospitals, and physicians. Questions arose over test-tube fertilization and other forms of artificial conception made possible in the late 1970s, and later over stem-cell research using human embryos. Those who condemned modern technology extolled the virtues of a prescientific and preindustrial age; others called for sharper awareness of present and future dangers. In an age of destructive weaponry and threats to the environment, no longer was the advance of science and technology unequivocally equated with the idea of progress.

Meanwhile, in the quest to understand nature the old divisions between the sciences broke down and new sciences appeared. Biochemistry, cell and molecular biology, biophysics, astrophysics, geophysics, and other subdisciplines arose, and all made intensive use of mathematics. In biology genetics made striking advances. While physicists discovered new atomic particles, biochemists isolated the organic substance found in the genes of all living cells, the chemical carriers of all hereditary characteristics. When scientists deciphered the genetic "code" and synthesized the basic substance of heredity (DNA), it became possible by splicing genes to alter the characteristics of plant and animal species and to clone or reproduce in the laboratory an animal such as a frog or a sheep with desired hereditary characteristics. The implications for the possibility of even human cloning at some remote future date were staggering. Meanwhile biotechnologists were revolutionizing food production by genetically engineering new varieties of crops, which provoked strong objections in various quarters. Medical scientists could also hope to conquer inherited diseases, a goal that moved closer to reality when researchers announced in 2000 that they had decoded the human genome—the more than three billion chemical units of DNA that control the human body and also contribute to genetic-based illnesses.

The other life sciences and social sciences also grew in importance. Psychological exploration of human behavior, as well as the treatment of mental and emotional disorders through psychiatry and psychoanalysis, expanded rapidly. Freud, who had first developed his theories of psychoanalysis before 1914, became more widely known in the 1920s. His emphasis on the human sex drive and sexual repression was much modified. Many students of human behavior argued that his contributions were not universally or scientifically valid but reflected the values of pre-1914, middle-class, male-dominated Viennese society. New schools emerged with different interpretations and techniques, and new drugs were developed to treat psychological depression and other mental illnesses. But the search, initiated by Freud, for the unconscious sources of individual and collective human conduct remained a hallmark of contemporary thought and culture.

Impact of Freud

Anthropologists and other social scientists increasingly stressed the relativism of all culture. They denied notions of cultural superiority or hierarchies of cultural values, or even that there were objective criteria of historical progress. If Western society, they noted, made notable progress in science and technology, other cultures accomplished more in self-discipline, individual integrity, and human happiness. The adjective "primitive," as opposed to "civilized," tended to disappear, and a new cultural humanism emerged that recognized and esteemed values distinct from the Western tradition.

Space Exploration

Among the most dramatic developments in science and technology in the second half of the twentieth century was space exploration. In the 1950s the Soviets and the Americans competed with each other as part of the Cold War; each made important advances in rocket research. Even before 1914 the significance of rocketry had been grasped by pioneers in aerodynamics, and toward the end of the Second World War the Germans first used rockets in warfare. Both the U.S. and the U.S.S.R. now mastered multistage rocket launching. The Soviets opened the space age when in 1957 they launched *Sputnik,* the world's first artificial satellite; in 1961 they sent the first human, Yuri A. Gagarin, in orbital flight around the earth. The Americans sent their own astronauts into space in 1961 and 1962. In the 1960s both countries launched unmanned automated spaceships to probe and explore the moon and then the planets of the solar system and their satellites. Early in the 1960s President Kennedy pledged that Americans would land on the moon before the end of the decade. In 1969 three American astronauts, as planned in Project Apollo, made the quarter-million-mile journey to the moon, and millions around the globe watched on television as Neil Armstrong took his first steps on the moon. The Americans made five additional trips to the moon over the next three years. Automated robot spaceships were launched in the 1960s and later on long journeys to explore the planets of the solar system. The American spaceships approached or orbited the planets and soft-landed instrument packages, which

U.S.-Soviet competition

Exploration of outer space marked an important new phase in the modern search for knowledge about the Earth and other planets of the solar system. In contrast to earlier explorations such as the European voyages to the New World, millions of people were watching on television when the first human beings walked on the surface of the moon. The American astronaut Neil Armstrong took this picture of Edward E. Aldrin, Jr., as the two men made one of their "moonwalks" in July 1969. Although this dramatic event was a famous milestone in the history of human exploration, later space programs focused principally on unmanned space exploration and on orbiting space stations.

(NASA)

over a period of years sent back a rich harvest of data, providing more knowledge than ever before possessed about the nature and origins of the planets and about the earth itself. The later space probes explored the more distant planets. *Voyager 2*, launched in 1977, traveling close to 4.5 billion miles over 12 years' time, reached the outermost planets before flying into interstellar space. In 1990 the United States placed in orbit the Hubble space telescope, capable of seeing light years away into distant galaxies and reporting back its findings.

The Soviets also conducted impressive space probes, to the moon, to Mars, and to Halley's comet, whose behavior had been predicted in the seventeenth century and which once again returned close enough for observation in 1986. The Soviets also built a permanent space station and set records in testing human endurance in weightless space.

As time went on, Cold War rivalries played less of a role in space exploration, but military objectives were never completely absent. The U.S. and U.S.S.R., and later other countries, launched spy satellites for reconnaissance and information gathering. The United States initiated research in the 1980s into an enormously costly strategic defense initiative that would deploy laserlike weapons in outer space (hence called "Star Wars") as a defensive shield against nuclear missile attacks. The project was abandoned in 1990 but was revived again in the following decade, with ardent champions and equally vehement critics.

International cooperation

In the 1980s space enterprise showed promise of international cooperation and was no longer confined to the military superpowers. France, China, Japan, and other countries became spacefaring nations, planning and launching satellites and space probes of their own. The European Space Agency carried out its own operations. A multinational human expedition to Mars sometime in the twenty-first century was discussed. After the Cold War the Americans and the Russians began to cooperate in space, most notably in the development and joint use of a Russian-built space station. On the other hand, the need for human expeditions came under serious scrutiny. Dismayed by a number of serious accidents and impressed by the accomplishments of the robot spaceships, some critics contended that unmanned space flights might accomplish more, at less cost, and at less risk to human life. Many objected to the enormous expense of space exploration when acute social needs at home remained unfulfilled. But its champions defended it as part of the continuing human effort to cross new frontiers, expand horizons, and explore the unknown. The twentieth century may be remembered, apart from the destructiveness of its terrible wars, as the century in which humans first set foot on the moon and with robot spaceships devised and guided by human intelligence began to explore the universe.

Philosophy: Existentialism in the Postwar Years

In the early years after the Second World War, a loosely organized body of ideas called "existentialism" grappled with the human predicament. The existentialists formed no one school of thought and held no coherent body of principles. There were religious and atheist existentialists. Yet all held some beliefs and attitudes in common. All reflected a troubled civilization, a world disturbed by war and oppression, a civilization of material progress and moral uncertainty in which the individual could be crushed by the very triumphs of science and technology.

Existentialist thought owed a debt to Pascal, Nietzsche, and others who had underscored the tragic element in human existence and the limitations on the power of human reason. More directly it owed a debt to Søren Kierkegaard, the nineteenth-century Danish religious philosopher. But it was French writers, and espe-cially Jean-Paul Sartre, who after the Second World War developed exis-tentialist thought in literature and philosophy in a form that for a time gave it a wide popular following. In a hostile world, the existentialists contended, human beings had to make choices and commitments on their own. They were "condemned to be free" and were alone responsible for the choices and actions that defined their very existence; for most existentialists, there was no inherent human nature. The authentic existentialist could not be contemplative only but had to be committed to belief and action, even though aware that human action might fail to change the world. Albert Camus, influenced by the existentialists, drew upon the myth of Sisyphus, who was condemned continuously to roll his stone uphill even though it rolled back down again, his very humanity growing out of courage and perseverance at a hopeless and absurd task. Existentialism emphasized the an-guish of human existence, the frailty of human reason, the fragility of human institutions, and the need to reassert and redefine human freedom. Although its popular following waned, and Sartre himself was dislodged from his earlier lofty eminence, existentialism never completely disappeared from contemporary philosophy or religion.

Jean-Paul Sartre

Philosophy: Logic and Language; Literary Criticism; History

Professional philosophy in the twentieth century seemed to contribute less to an under-standing of contemporary problems than in the past. Always concerned with the origins and nature of knowledge, it had also shared an interest in metaphysics and ethics. In the early twentieth century it became highly analytical, focusing especially on the limits and criteria of knowledge. In the formal study of logic, mathematical symbols replaced the use of traditional language. On the eve of the First World War Bertrand Russell and Alfred North Whitehead explored logic and mathematics in their monumental *Principia Mathe-matica.* In the 1920s an influential group of philosophers and mathematicians in Vienna, among them Ludwig Wittgenstein, sought to introduce the methodology and precision of mathematics into the study of philosophy as a whole, in what they called logical posi-tivism. They rejected the ambiguities of language used in traditional speculation on morals and values, turning away from the nondemonstrable—that is, "God, death, what is higher," in Wittgenstein's phrase. The Vienna group disintegrated in the 1930s, but logical posi-tivism remained influential. Most professional philosophers continued to emphasize sci-entific rigor and linguistic analysis. A smaller but growing number, responsive to contem-porary ethical concerns, devoted themselves to unresolved human and social dilemmas.

New studies in philosophy, linguistic analysis, and semiotics (that is, the study of signs and symbols in communication) drew attention to the complex relation between lan-guage and reality. Philosophers also challenged many of the dualisms taken for granted in Western thought. In literary studies "deconstruction" theory emerged to offer new methods of analysis and criticism. Its proponents sought to analyze, or "deconstruct" a body of writing or "text" (which could be a painting or other kind of cultural object as well) to examine its implicit cultural as-sumptions and its indebtedness to its cultural traditions. No single valid meaning was to be attached to any individual work. According to its advocates, deconstruction made it possi-ble to reveal the philosophical, class, racial, ethnocentric, or sexual assumptions hidden in the language of a work. It also contested older hierarchical standards of literary quality, blurred distinctions between elite and popular culture, made less of a dichotomy between

Deconstruction

fact and fiction (and other dualisms), and broadened the existing canon of writings studied in literature, history, law, religion, and other disciplines.

The work of the critic was said to be as much a creative enterprise as literary or artistic creation itself. Propounded originally in the late 1960s in broad philosophical terms by the French philosopher Jacques Derrida, and developed further by other writers and scholars of various disciplines and nationalities, deconstruction won its largest following in the United States. Its opponents viewed it as abandoning traditional literary history and rejecting standards that had shaped modern thought since the Enlightenment.

The writing of history also underwent a profound change. A group of French historical scholars (called the *Annales* school, from a journal with which they were associated) gained wide influence after the Second World War. They

New interests among historians

focused on long-term elements in historical change such as population, economy, climate, and natural resources, relegated politics to a lesser role, and avoided the traditional narrative of "events." They studied also the lives of ordinary people in the past and tried to reconstruct the collective outlook of social classes. The newer social history in France, England, and the United States also paid special attention to the inarticulate and illiterate and to all those with strong oral traditions, such as the American slaves in the antebellum South, the English working classes, and the peoples of Africa, reconstructing their culture and lives despite scarce written sources. Another new emphasis greatly expanded the historical study of women from antiquity to the present, leading, among other results, to cultural and social reassessments of entire historical eras. A variety of social themes also received new historical attention: marriage, divorce, the family, childhood, sexuality, even insanity and death through the ages. For their part, many traditional historians, who had not been wholly insensitive to these concerns, widened their own narratives.

The Creative Arts

The revolution against older traditions in the creative arts assumed new dimensions. Ever since the Renaissance visual artists had followed certain norms of representation and space perspective. But much of twentieth-century art prided itself on being nonobjective; it rejected the idea of imitating or reconstructing nature, or mirroring it with realism or photographic fidelity. The artistic revolution inaugurated in France before 1914 accelerated in the interwar years and after 1945. It seemed to mirror the political turbulence of the times and the disillusionment with rationalism and optimism. It reflected the influence of Freudian and other schools of psychology and the emphasis on the unconscious and irrational, as well as the relativity of the new physics and its uncertainties about the nature of matter, space, and time.

Artists continued the pre-1914 experimentation in color, form, and use of materials, but went well beyond, seeing the world around them in new

Seeing the world in new ways

ways. The Spanish artist Pablo Picasso systematically distorted and deformed the objects in his cubist paintings to convey his image of human and nonhuman figures. Some artists expressed themselves through geometric form; others left reality behind and tried to represent their own unconscious fears or desires. The results were fascinating but frequently baffling. After the Second World War, the United States took over from Europe the leadership role in the visual arts and evolved new forms of abstract art.

Contemporary art resulted in original and striking expressions of form and color, but the conscious subjectivism widened still further the gap between artist and public. The

INVASION OF THE NIGHT

By Roberto Sebastian Matta Echaurren (Chilean, lived in France, United States, Italy, 1911–)

This work is an example of the modern trend toward abstract art, though it also shows the influence of European surrealism. Painted in New York in 1941 by a Chilean artist who worked in Europe during the 1930s and later lived mostly in Italy, this picture suggests the sense of dread or dislocation that creative artists often expressed during and after the Second World War. The figures in this painting cannot be identified, but the artist uses forms, colors, and shapes to convey the chaos and disorder of a world that is falling into darkness. Matta's artistic abstractions as well as his migratory life on three continents represent recurring tendencies in both the work and personal experiences of many twentieth-century artists.

(San Francisco Museum of Modern Art, Bequest of Jacqueline Marie Onslow-Ford)

artist, painter, and sculptor (and the poet, musician, playwright, and novelist, who were also rejecting the older conventions) were conveying their own visions of the world, not an objective reality that could easily be understood by others. Perhaps the greatest innovation was that the public, baffled as it was by much of contemporary art, came to accept the avant-garde as normal, even if on occasion it rebelled against it. Democratic societies accepted the need for artistic experimentation and innovation, which had been frowned upon or banned as degenerate or socially dangerous in totalitarian societies like Nazi Germany or the Soviet Union. Representational art, of course, never completely disappeared anywhere, and many artists reaffirmed it, contributing to a growing pluralism in contemporary art.

Subjectivism and the unconscious in literature

The focus on subjectivism and the unconscious was reflected in literature too. The reconstruction of lost time and the unfolding of the individual's innermost experience through a stream of consciousness and flood of memories, which had appeared first in the work of Marcel Proust and James Joyce before and shortly after the First World War, remained important for a new generation of novelists after 1945. Not only writers but also cinematographers experimented with probing the unconscious in evocative but mystifying ways. All of this cultural experimentation contrasted with the popular entertainment provided through the mass media, especially movies and daily diets of television, and hardly touched the average citizen.

Postmodernism

Sometime in the early 1970s the phenomenon of postmodernism emerged in architecture, literature, and other art forms. In all areas the postmodernists borrowed from the past and mixed the old and new, and the popular and elite, to suit their tastes. Unlike modernists from the late nineteenth century on, the postmodernists did not reject the commercialization and materialism of contemporary culture but embraced it and incorporated it in new ways, often with humor. The American architect Robert Venturi and his collaborators wrote a book called *Learning from Las Vegas* (1972). Composers introduced street noises (and silences) into their music. Repetition,

TWINNED COLUMN

By Antoine Pevsner (Russian, then French, 1886–1962)

Antoine Pevsner left his native Russia after the Soviet regime began to disapprove of "modern" art. This picture shows one of his sculptures, a bronze piece about 40 inches high, constructed in 1947. The symmetry and the column recall the classical tradition, but the work also conveys the technological interests of the twentieth century and a concern with the meanings of abstract space. Pevsner's sculptural space is not the familiar medium in which human beings ordinarily live and move, yet it provokes reflection on the objects and physical senses through which people experience their daily lives.

(Solomon R. Guggenheim Museum, New York)

as in the commercial world of packaging, marketing, and television advertising, was adopted as an artistic technique. The artist Andy Warhol painted serial pictures of Coca-Cola bottles and of the film star Marilyn Monroe. In fiction the postmoderns mingled actual events and fantasy. A play by Harold Pinter, Samuel Beckett, or Eugène Ionesco was very different from a play by Shakespeare, Molière, Ibsen, or Shaw. The postmoderns also rejected traditional ideas of structure, seeing no need in literature or art for a beginning, a middle, and an end. Postmodernism was both a phase of the modernist rebellion against traditionalism and a fragmented sequel to it with new messages. Where modernism typically sought to convey an artist's unique personal vision, postmodernists insisted that writers inevitably expressed the language and values of their culture rather than a distinctive individual consciousness. Because the writer and the subject were now less important, it was possible to speak metaphorically of the "death of the author."

Religion in the Modern World

Religion was in flux in the modern world. With the continuing inroads of secularism, the challenges of science, and the post-1945 advances of communism in eastern Europe, China, and elsewhere, organized religion encountered many obstacles. But the churches survived Marxist regimes and retained their vitality. Statistics on religious affiliation are never exact, but some figures on the religions with the largest number of adherents in the opening years of the twenty-first century were clear. Islam, with well over one billion adherents, was the fastest growing faith; it made large inroads in postcolonial Africa. There were close to 800 million Hindus and 350 million Buddhists in the world. Christianity, if all branches are added together, remained the largest religion, counting close to two billion adherents, of which more than half were Roman Catholic, a fourth were Protestant, and a fourth were Eastern Orthodox.

The ecumenical movement in Christianity, that is, the organized effort to unite the many branches of Protestantism, and eventually all Christianity, which began in the nineteenth century, made headway throughout the half-century after the Second World War. A World Council of Churches was founded in 1948. In historic breakthroughs toward the end of the century Lutheran churches announced a reconciliation and alliance with the Episcopalian churches, and Lutherans and Calvinists resolved theological differences over Luther's definition of salvation, "justification by faith." When in the 1960s the Roman Catholic church abandoned its insistence on a privileged position in Christianity, it too encouraged ecumenicism. All Christian churches moved toward a closer dialogue with non-Christian world faiths as well.

The ecumenical movement

As in the late nineteenth century, tensions between modernism (in its religious sense) and fundamentalism continued. Many of the Protestant churches in the twentieth century for the most part reconciled their traditional teachings with science and Biblical scholarship, minimized the supernatural and dogmatic aspects of their faith, and sought to adapt the teachings of the gospel to the social needs of the contemporary world. But the two world wars and the troubled century dealt a blow to theological modernism and to the inherent optimism of the social gospel. In the 1920s, not only did fundamentalism revive but an intellectual reaction also set in among Protestant theologians who emphasized revealed religion and elements of faith. The Swiss theologian Karl Barth in his writings from 1919 to the 1960s endeavored to lead Protestantism back to the root principles of the Reformation. There was

Religious tensions

much interest in Kierkegaard who, like Luther, had resolved his own deep anguish by a personal commitment to religious experience. After the Second World War, as a result of the work of Barth, Paul Tillich, and others, a powerful movement in Protestantism reasserted its dependence on revealed religion and denied that human reason could ever properly judge divine revelation. Some church writers, unable to explain the wrenching experience of the Second World War and the Holocaust, spoke of "post-Auschwitz theology" and of "God's removal from history." Evangelical Protestantism, with its literal adherence to the gospel, spellbinding preachers, and revivalist emotional appeal also flourished, especially in the United States, and conducted a continuing crusade against the teaching of evolution in the schools. But Protestantism generally accepted religious scholarship and the intellectual validity of modern scientific knowledge.

The Roman Catholic church was passing through one of its great historic phases beginning in the second half of the century. Although the church no longer actively suppressed all forms of modernism, the Vatican in the early postwar years reaffirmed dogmatic training in the seminaries. In 1950 Pius XII (1939–1958), who headed the church during the Second World War (and was criticized in some quarters for insufficiently opposing the terrible Nazi atrocities against the Jews), proclaimed the Assumption, the literal, or bodily ascent of the Virgin Mary into heaven, the only new Roman Catholic dogma to be promulgated in the entire twentieth century.

Pius XII was succeeded in 1959 by John XXIII. Although elected at the age of 77, and reigning for only 4½ years until his death in 1963, John proved to be one of the most innovative popes of modern times, working to bring the church and its teachings into greater harmony with the contemporary world. His powerful encyclicals gave a global emphasis to the older social teachings of the church and called upon the wealthier nations to share their resources with the less favored. *Pacem in Terris* (1963), the first encyclical ever addressed to Catholics and non-Catholics alike, appealed for peace and human rights. A champion of ecumenism, he opened dialogues with other faiths. In 1962, against the advice of his own theologians, he convened the Second Vatican Council, the first such council since 1870, and as it turned out, the most important since the sixteenth-century Council of Trent. Vatican II reshaped contemporary Catholicism.

Vatican II

John did not live to see the Council's labors completed, but was the principal inspiration for its reforms. His successor Paul VI (1963–1978) shared John's social concerns and encouraged ecumenism, but was more conservative in other ways. The Council completed its work in 1965. Accepting the principle of religious pluralism, it abandoned the older insistence on a Catholic monopoly on religious truth. It affirmed the principle of collegiality, which had gone into eclipse in the modern centuries, the view that the pope must share his authority with the prelates of the church, thus strengthening the authority of the national churches on substantive matters. It revised the liturgy and various church practices. The Mass, henceforth, would be conducted in vernacular tongues instead of in Latin, which had been the rule for centuries. The Council relaxed restrictions on dress for priests and nuns. In one historic declaration, the Council explicitly absolved the Jewish people from the charge of deicide that had fed and inflamed anti-Semitism over the ages. John XXIII's goal—the revitalization and updating of church teachings and practices—was amply fulfilled by the Council. There were limits to the changes, to be sure. The Council reaffirmed celibacy for the clergy and refused to sanction the ordination of women as priests. Paul VI, meanwhile, upheld papal supremacy and took a firm conservative stance on moral issues, especially against all artificial means of birth control.

After Paul VI's death in 1978 (and when a successor died after only 34 days in office), John Paul II, the archbishop of Cracow, became the new head of the church, the first Polish pope ever elected, and the first non-Italian pontiff in over 450 years. Robust, earthy, energetic, versatile in languages, and with a keen sense of pageantry and papal majesty, he brought an added dynamism to the church. Not only did he encourage the Christian ecumenical movement, but he also reached out to non-Christians as well, traveling widely in Asia, Africa, and Latin America. During the Cold War years he entered into diplomatic negotiations with the Soviet Union and the Communist countries of eastern Europe to improve the status of the church and contributed much to the revolutionary transformation of his own country and eastern Europe in the 1980s.

John Paul II

In his indefatigable global travels John Paul presided over Mass for millions of Roman Catholics, and he offered apologies for past wrongs going back to the Crusades and including the abuses of the Inquisition, whose archives he opened to historians. He apologized for the Inquisition's condemnation of scientists like Galileo. In formal statements and documents he offered specific apologies to the Jews for abuses they had suffered over the centuries and especially for the ordeal of the Holocaust, and in a historic visit to Jerusalem he prayed at the Western Wall.

Although on global, social, and economic issues John Paul held progressive views and was sharply critical of unbridled capitalism and irresponsible materialism, in matters of church doctrine and governance he favored orthodoxy and papal supremacy. He appointed conservative archbishops, bishops, and cardinals, silenced dissenting theologians, and curbed the growing assertiveness of national churches. He would not countenance marriage for the clergy, the ordination of women as priests (an innovation accepted by the

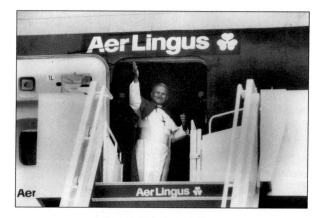

Pope John Paul II combined his defense of the traditional values of Roman Catholic Christianity with a reliance on the most advanced forms of travel and communications. He is shown here on an airplane during the early years of his pontificate. Traveling more widely than any of his predecessors, John Paul II contributed to the growth and visibility of the Roman Catholic church throughout the world. The rapidly growing number of Roman Catholics in Asia, Africa, and Latin America (along with the many adherents in Europe and North America) gave the Roman Catholic church and its pope a wider global presence than at any time in history.

(Hulton Getty/Archive Photos)

Church of England in 1994), rights of divorce (or of remarriage for the divorced), or homosexuality.

Objections to Vatican centralism

John Paul's stance on many issues engendered protest against the "new Roman centralism," the failure to modernize the church more thoroughly, and the unwillingness to respect the spirit of shared authority promised by the Council. His defenders argued that in upholding tradition he was restoring a balance upset by overly rapid changes in the church introduced by Vatican II.

Judaism

Judaism, the third important faith of the Western world, was haunted in the years after 1945 by the traumatic experience of the Holocaust. At the close of the twentieth century, of the world's 14 million Jews, 5.8 million lived in the United States, 4.6 million in Israel, and 2.4 million in Europe. The earlier trend to secularism persisted, but more striking was the vitality of all its branches, Orthodox, Conservative, and Reform. Jews everywhere, and especially in the United States, many not Zionists, lent moral and financial support to the state of Israel, although many were troubled by Israeli militancy and intransigence and by the role in domestic politics of ultra-orthodox religious groups that refused to accept a secular state. Anti-Zionism, not only in the Arab world but elsewhere as well, at times served as a thin screen for anti-Semitism. In the former Soviet Union (as in several Islamic states in the Middle East), Jews insistent on practicing their faith had met harassment and persecution and, when permitted, emigrated in large numbers. The collapse of communism reignited older currents of anti-Semitism in eastern Europe.

The major non-Western religions, Islam, Hinduism, and Buddhism, also made efforts to adjust millennia-old doctrines to the secular tendencies of the contemporary age, but in some instances such changes were adamantly rejected. Eastern religions attracted adherents in the West: the Nation of Islam among African Americans; Buddhist meditative teachings and practices among students, intellectuals, and others. The large numbers of African and Asian immigrants to western Europe, and of Asian immigrants to the United States, brought their religious faiths with them.

Spread of fundamentalism

The latter part of the twentieth century saw the rise and spread of militant religious reform movements (often called "fundamentalist" by outsiders), especially in the Islamic world. All such movements rejected the secularism of the modern world and turned to the literal reading of ancient texts for their own guidance and to impose rules of conduct on others. Nowhere did popular frenzy and the adulation of a religious leader reach such heights as in Iran in 1979, but Muslim activists were also at work in Egypt, Algeria, Nigeria, and elsewhere seeking to subvert secular regimes, impose theocracies, and use state power to enforce religious views. In several states, as in Sudan and Afghanistan, militant regimes attempted to impose Koranic law on nonbelievers.

The fundamentalists in all societies typically demanded an unswerving adherence to the sacred texts regardless of changing times and circumstances; an identification of religion with political and moral values; and a strict moral code extending to diet, dress, and the relationship of the sexes; all interpreted and enforced by messianic religious leaders who mobilized mass followings to accomplish these ends. Muslim fundamentalism had a counterpart in an extremist Hindu movement in India, which unleashed violence against the Muslims in the country and threatened the secular state.

Fundamentalism could be found in evangelical Christian sects and in extremist Orthodox Jewish quarters as well. It easily bred intolerance and separatism, and ran counter to the blending of cultures in the contemporary world. In the West the separation of political and religious authority had become so widely accepted that it became difficult to understand the strength and appeal of the new religious ferment.

Activism: The Youth Rebellion of the 1960s

In the second half of the twentieth century young people seemed to acquire a collective identity that historically youth did not possess earlier. It was possible to speak of a youth market, a youth culture, youth movements. In part the phenomenon was demographic in origin, the result of the extraordinary number of births in the decade and a half after the Second World War—the "baby boom." A large cohort grew up in a rapidly changing world, and they developed a generational identity through a new popular culture that appeared in music, fashion, films, and advertising. Youth culture became a key component of modern global culture.

In the 1960s a youth activism made a startling appearance, marked by a widespread student rebellion. A generation came to college age and attended institutions of higher learning in larger numbers than ever before. It *Youth activism* was a generation that knew nothing firsthand of the turbulence of the 1930s or the Second World War. Young people grew up in an era of global change and scientific breakthroughs, to which their elders were no certain guides. They took for granted the scientific, technological, and other accomplishments of their world and concentrated on its deficiencies—the flagrant contradictions of wealth and poverty within and among nations, racial injustice, discrimination, colonialism, the impersonal quality of mechanized society and bureaucratized institutions (including colleges and universities), the violence that destroyed human beings in continuing wars, and always the threat of nuclear destruction. The rebelliousness extended beyond the traditional generation gap; it was directed at all established society and reiterated romantic or utopian themes that had influenced social criticism since the beginnings of modern history.

The revolt burst forth in the late 1960s in widely separate parts of the world. The cultural revolution in China, although in an entirely different context, was not unrelated and indirectly inspired it. At the peak of the movement in 1967–1968 students demonstrated and rioted on campuses and battled po- *1968* lice all over the world; American, Canadian, Mexican, West German, French, Italian, and Spanish universities were heavily involved.

France was at the center of the storm. Demonstrations there reached near-revolutionary dimensions in the spring of 1968 and threatened to overthrow the regime when 10 million workers also went out on strike, partly in sympathy and partly for their own grievances. But the militancy of the students alienated many, and the government restored order. Such initial grievances as inadequate physical facilities in the overcrowded universities and impersonal and remote instruction were almost forgotten in the upheavals in France and elsewhere.

Some of the earliest and largest demonstrations took place in the United States, sparked by the struggle for civil rights for American blacks and heightened by resistance to American involvement in the unpopular Vietnam War. The assassinations in 1968 of the dedicated black leader of the civil rights movement, Martin Luther King, Jr., and of Robert Kennedy, brother of the slain president, fueled further anger in the ranks of the young.

The rebelling students made heroes of the sworn foes of the established order: Fidel Castro and his martyred Lieutenant Che Guevara, Ho Chi Minh, Mao Zedong, militant

American black leaders like Malcolm X, the heralds of the colonial revolution such as Frantz Fanon (the West Indian author of *The Wretched of the Earth*), and others. They read the neo-Marxist philosopher Herbert Marcuse, who warned that the very tolerance of bourgeois society was a trap to prevent true protest against injustice; they learned from him that the industrial working class, co-opted by the existing system, was no longer a revolutionary force. A "New Left" dismissed older revolutionaries in the Soviet Union as stodgy bureaucrats and affirmed that revolutionary leadership would come from Maoist China and the Third World. They attacked materialism, affluence, and conformity, and the power structure of contemporary society. Many believed in confrontation and action for the sake of action, recalling an older anarchism and nihilism. They called on each other to destroy in order to purify, assuming that their generation could overcome the social hierarchies and injustices in modern democratic societies.

Emergence of the New Left

The rebellion in its mass phase faded by the early 1970s. In the United States it helped bring the Vietnam War to an end. Only a small number of extremists continued a kind of urban guerrilla war through underground terrorist organizations. Mostly, the rebels of 1968 moved on to places in established society. While many people shuddered at the attack on traditional institutions and orderly processes, others were shaken out of their complacency about social and racial inequities. Efforts were made to reform university administration and to provide more adequate teaching facilities. The youth movement, even after its political radicalism subsided, had a continuing effect on all age groups in loosening older standards of language, dress, and sexual mores.

The Women's Liberation Movement

The feminist, or women's liberation, movement was another, but more enduring, manifestation of twentieth-century and contemporary social ferment. From the time of the French Revolution, as noted earlier, a few thinkers in France and England had raised the question of equal rights for women, and a women's political movement had also developed in the United States by the mid–nineteenth century. Elizabeth Cady Stanton and a small group of associates in 1848, inspired in part by revolutionary developments in Europe that year, proclaimed a declaration of independence for women, demanding the right to vote, equal compensation for work, legal equality in property and other matters, and expanded educational opportunities. In Britain, later in the century, the suffragettes raised similar demands in their militant campaign for the vote. Women won the right to vote before the First World War in a few American states and in a few of the smaller countries; after 1918, in many more nations, including the United States and Britain; and after 1945, in almost all other countries. But other objectives went unrealized.

The militant twentieth-century phase of the women's movement began in the United States in the mid-1960s, partly as a parallel to the civil rights movement on behalf of the African-American population. The women's liberation movement, inspired by such books as Simone de Beauvoir's *The Second Sex*, published in France in 1949, and Betty Friedan's *The Feminine Mystique*, which appeared in the United States in 1963, contended that women, half or more of the human race, had always been and continued to be oppressed by a male-dominated society and that women were systematically denied access to positions of authority, leadership, property, and power. Although the more blatant forms of legal discrimination, in such matters as property rights for example, had been or were being

Inspirations and demands

The French writer Simone de Beauvoir, shown here in 1947, wrote about the social position of women in her widely read book *The Second Sex* (1949). Beauvoir analyzed the constraints and myths that affected women in what she described as patriarchal societies and called for the independence or liberation of women in contemporary social and political life. Her work became an influential statement of themes and ideas that helped shape a new international women's movement in the 1960s and 1970s.

(Hulton-Deutsch Collection/Corbis)

removed, twentieth-century feminists demanded an end to all barriers to equal participation in the economy and society. Betty Friedan's influential book appealed to women to give up traditional lives devoted mainly to the home and family and utilize their education, skills, and abilities in the outside world as well. Large numbers of women entered the job market for the first time in the 1970s. Between 1970 and 1990 the ratio of women to men working in the economy in the United States or actively seeking employment rose from 37 women per 100 men to 62 per 100 men. The new role for women required adjustments in family responsibilities not always easily arranged.

The campaign for equal rights called upon a different agenda in the poorer, less developed countries of the world, where women generally had to overcome centuries-old neglect, abject repression, abuse, and disregard of the most elementary human rights. The United Nations from the time of its founding had committed itself to equal political, economic, and educational rights for women. But in many parts of Africa, Asia, and Latin America adult illiteracy rates were still significantly higher for women and were declining more slowly. In 2000 it was estimated that of 110 million children worldwide not attending schools two-thirds were female. Yet in the developing world, where a majority of the world's women lived, opportunities for women, especially in education, could accelerate social advances for the entire population.

At UN sponsored international conferences government delegates and representatives from nongovernmental organizations affirmed the "universal rights of women" and insisted on their right to decide freely on *UN support for women* matters relating to all aspects of their lives free from "coercion, discrimination, or violence." Discrimination, it turned out, was not confined to capitalist societies. Despite Communist verbal promises, the advance to equality, or even to equality of opportunity, in the former Soviet Union and in the People's Republic of China was disappointing.

Some women, more so than in the past, when authority resided only with reigning women sovereigns, held positions of the highest authority in their countries at various times in the years after 1945. Among them were Indira Gandhi in India, Golda Meir in Israel, Corazón Aquino in the Philippines, Benazir Bhutto in Pakistan, Margaret Thatcher in Britain, and a growing list of other women presidents or prime ministers in such widely differing countries as Sri Lanka, Portugal, Norway, Iceland, Nicaragua, Ireland, Bangladesh, France, Poland, Turkey, Finland, Canada, and Indonesia. Many women occupied key cabinet or high judicial posts in a number of countries, including the United States, or headed opposition movements, as in Myanmar.

Meanwhile the development of advanced contraceptive technology, especially of the birth control pill in the early 1960s, and the legalization and greater access to safer abortion procedures if desired, provided a new biological freedom and autonomy for women. Changing social patterns tolerating sexual freedom and new and more equal forms of relationships between the sexes in marriage also contributed to social liberation. In the last decades of the twentieth century women were filling a larger share of places in higher education and in professional schools than ever before. In the United States women students made up more than half the number of undergraduate students in colleges and universities and were close to that ratio in law and medical schools. As more women became part of the labor force at all levels, the demand arose not only for equal compensation for equal work, still far from realized, but also for better pay for jobs that were poorly compensated because they had been traditionally filled by women. Although there were disagreements in and outside the women's liberation movement on the methods and tempo of change, and more radical feminist activists emerged, wide agreement existed on the need to utilize fully all of society's human resources in every part of the globe. If that could be accomplished, it would count among the most memorable of the revolutionary changes of the contemporary era.

129. FACING THE TWENTY-FIRST CENTURY

The end of the Cold War and the demise of the U.S.S.R. in 1991 transformed the foundations on which international relations had rested since 1945. The Western campaign to contain communism, for which there had been a broad consensus in American public opinion, was over. The United States was now the sole superpower, the leading economic and military power of the globe. The key question was whether it could handle this power with restraint and with consideration for its allies and other nations. International stability in good part depended on how it conceived of its responsibilities in world affairs and how it shaped its relationships with the UN, its European allies, Russia, China, and the developing world. A new configuration of world affairs was emerging, but its outlines, and the American role, were only roughly apparent. Peace and security remained the world's most pressing problems. One new challenge was the eruption of conflicts more frequently within nations than between nations.

The twentieth century, heralded in its opening years for its promise of peace and progress, had seen more than 200 million people perish as victims of wars and brutal regimes. The last decade alone had seen five million deaths resulting directly or indirectly from armed conflict. The early years of the twenty-first century witnessed a more tempered optimism. It was clear that the end of the Cold War had not brought peace to the world.

Religious divisions could shape conflicts

Some close analysts of international affairs maintained that the future world order might best be understood in the context of rivalries and conflicts between religion-based civilizations, not between nation-states. There was already some evidence of this. The Russian offensive against Chechnya had anti-Islamic overtones, as did the Serb and Croat attacks on Muslims in Bosnia and the Yugoslav war against the Albanian Muslims in Kosovo. In turn, Orthodox Christian church leaders in Russia and Greece condemned the Western air offensive against Serbia. India, once intended as a haven for a tolerant secularism, was now increasingly Hindu-oriented, and its clashes with Islamic Pakistan over Kashmir and other matters were sharpened by religious tensions. The conflicts between Israel and its Arab neighbors in the Middle East had religious overtones. The extremist Muslim Taliban rulers in Afghanistan willfully destroyed ancient Buddhist sculptures as offensive to their faith. Chinese communism displayed something of the older Confucian and imperial traditions hostile to the outside world and was intolerant of religious threats to its rule.

But nonreligious factors remained preponderant in international affairs, and even in religion-based civilizations there was marked diversity. A common faith in Islam did not prevent Iran and Iraq from their bloody war in 1980–1988 or protect Kuwait from invasion by Iraq in 1990. The world's religions were far from homogeneous, and all had been touched to some degree by secularism and globalization. The two great wars of the twentieth century had originated in conflicts between nations in the Christian West itself.

It was nevertheless important to call attention to the global diversity of traditions, cultures, and religions if only to shed any illusions in the West that it was destined to spread its ideas and values across the world unchallenged. Western civilization, with its Judeo-Christian heritage, had been enriched by interaction with other civilizations. By the twenty-first century its global influence was undeniable, but people in the West needed to recognize the existence of deep-seated cultural allegiances in every part of the world and to understand the enduring importance of cultural differences in diplomatic affairs, economic exchanges, and political conflicts.

Recognizing global diversity

The much used term "international community" was indispensable but defied precise definition. The closest approximation to it was the United Nations. Here the Security Council was the dominant institution. The original roster of five permanent members of the Council, the victors in the Second World War, was modified only in 1971 when the People's Republic of China replaced Nationalist China and in 1991 when Russia succeeded to the seat of the dissolved U.S.S.R. The political and economic changes in the world spurred proposals for giving other powers permanent seats, so that they might exercise international responsibilities commensurate with their economic and military resources. Even the veto power of the five permanent powers came into question.

The United Nations counted 51 members at its inception in 1945. It grew dramatically from the 1960s on, beginning with the admission of the states emerging from the former European colonial empires. After the breakup of the U.S.S.R., the disintegration of Yugoslavia, and the addition of several former colonies, the UN counted 189 members at the opening of the new century and was expected to add a few more soon. When small colonies achieved independence, as in the case of former Caribbean or Pacific island dependencies, many had populations no larger than those of a small city. St. Kitts and Nevis, a former British colony in the Caribbean, admitted to the UN in 1983, had a population of 40,000. Tuvalu in the South Pacific, once part of the British-held Gilbert and Ellice Islands, admitted in 2000, had only 10,500. The 80 or so smallest members of the UN represented less than 10 percent of the world's population.

UN membership expands

It was in the General Assembly that the new states mainly exercised their authority. Regardless of size, each member deliberated and voted in full equality. As we have seen, the General Assembly frequently served as a forum for the grievances of the developing nations against the wealthier industrial world. Several of the UN's agencies played significant roles in dealing with population, health, social welfare, and humanitarian issues. After the Cold War, the developing nations somewhat tempered their anti-Westernism, but they continued to demand a high priority for their enormous economic needs, including debt relief. Their earlier complaints against the West increasingly took the form of resistance to an economically driven globalism that many considered insensitive to social needs.

Debate went on in the United Nations, the European Union, and elsewhere over the interpretation of human rights. The Universal Declaration of Human Rights, adopted by the UN in 1948, had focused on political and civil rights, emphasizing protection from arbitrary arrest, imprisonment, and torture. Pressure later mounted to broaden the largely political definition to include economic rights, the necessity of meeting human needs within each country, and the right to international development assistance for those purposes.

Defining human rights

An even more complex issue troubled the United States, the UN, and the broader international community: The developing nations at times contended that even the political and civil rights generally described as universal were really Western and should be modified to fit the culture, history, and religions of other parts of the world. Equality for women or the rights of children, in this interpretation, could have different meanings in countries whose cultural traditions differed from those of the West. But many across the globe continued to maintain that human rights, no matter how difficult to define, of Western origin or not, represented a common core of values that should protect every individual human being against enslavement, violation, or discrimination. Respect for cultural pluralism or local traditions should not cover or excuse any form of human indignity.

Implications of Western definitions

The practical implications of such debates were significant. In many Islamic countries there were fewer opportunities for women to attend school, work outside the home, drive cars, or vote. The governing regime in Sudan was still sanctioning slavery and forcibly converting its non-Islamic population in the south to Islam. Polygamy was still widely practiced and sanctioned by some religions and cultures. Some African peoples still practiced the centuries-old practice of female genital mutilation. In many parts of the world young children, boys and girls, were forced to serve in combat by guerrilla military units. To abolish cruel and unusual punishments many nations would have to ban flogging, mutilation, and maiming as punishments. The United States itself promoted extensive incarceration practices and retained capital punishment, the latter now banned in the European Union. The dilemma continued. There was little desire to meddle in the internal affairs of other peoples, but it was difficult to ignore egregious violations of human rights or to accept the argument that Western values were being imposed on others.

Politically, the explosion of virulent ethnic and religious-based nationalism after the end of the Cold War confronted the UN with new issues of humanitarian assistance and intervention. The distinction between peacemaking and peacekeeping was still unresolved. Both functions seemed destined to grow, and peacekeeping meant help in the reconstruction of devastated countries and peoples as well as providing a protective military presence. Supporters of the UN's expanding role urged advanced planning for troubled areas to prevent the escalation of conflict. They projected rapid deployment forces, as once envisaged, with contingents drawn from the member states. Much depended on the support of the United States, which while maintaining its leadership role in the Security Council, for a long time refused to place any of its own troops in UN-controlled peacekeeping forces and repeatedly criticized the UN's large bureaucracy.

The UN's role was still evolving. Its goals remained as formulated in 1945: to prevent the scourge of war, advance human rights, promote equality, protect the independence of nations, encourage social progress, raise living standards, and work for peace and security. But the world's nations, large and small, were not ready to subordinate their national interests or sovereignty to any international organization. Without armed power of its own, the United Nations was powerless in large conflicts.

The United States, as the sole superpower after 1991, was called upon to exercise the leading role in international affairs, even if in concert with its European allies and other major powers. At times it took initiatives that made it difficult to distinguish between American unilateralism and international action. The Security Council in 1990 condemned Iraq's aggression against Kuwait, but it was the United States that assembled a formidable multinational military force, including over a half-million American troops, and in 1991 forced the Iraqi withdrawal from Kuwait. Years later, with the Iraqi dictator Sadam Hussein still in power, the United States continued to oversee and enforce the military terms of the cease-fire with sanctions, the inspection of sites thought to be producing forbidden chemical and biological weapons of mass destruction, and other measures.

U.S. leadership in international affairs

In 1992, toward the close of President George Bush's administration, American troops were used for the first time to reinforce UN peacekeeping forces in Somalia, in northeast Africa, where warring militias had made it impossible to deliver food and other supplies to the starving population. President Clinton in the next administration continued the policy, calling for an "assertive multilateralism." But peace had not yet been achieved and more than peacekeeping was required. In a failed military mission in October 1993, American military units under American command were attacked by Somali paramilitary groups and 18 American soldiers were killed. Publicly televised scenes of corpses dragged through the streets incited Congress to sweep "assertive multilateralism" away and for a time restrict similar interventions.

Recommendations to enlarge the authority and functions of the UN seemed doomed for a time and even threatened the peacekeeping role that the UN had successfully pursued for some 40 years in places like Zaire (now Congo), southern Lebanon, Cyprus, Cambodia, Angola, and elsewhere. In part the new attitude explained the failure of the UN or the United States and its allies to act in Bosnia in 1992–1993. The Security Council had imposed economic sanctions on the rump Yugoslav government, provided humanitarian aid to Sarajevo and other besieged cities in Bosnia, and laid plans for war crimes trials, but neither the UN nor the United States nor the European powers intervened effectively enough to prevent the terrible atrocities against Bosnia's Muslim population. The same misgivings were behind the failure to take timely action to prevent the massacre of the Tutsi people in 1994 in Rwanda, in which some 800,000 Tutsi were killed and hundreds of thousands were driven into exile.

In later crises the international community did take action. As we have noted earlier, the massive American-led air offensive by NATO against the former Yugoslavia in 1999 set a precedent for multinational "humanitarian intervention" within a sovereign state, although no ground troops were used. The UN did not join the war, but it participated in postwar peacekeeping in Kosovo. International war crimes trials under UN jurisdiction were held or were projected for political and military leaders charged with war crimes and crimes against humanity in Rwanda and in the former Yugoslavia. An international

Multinational humanitarian intervention

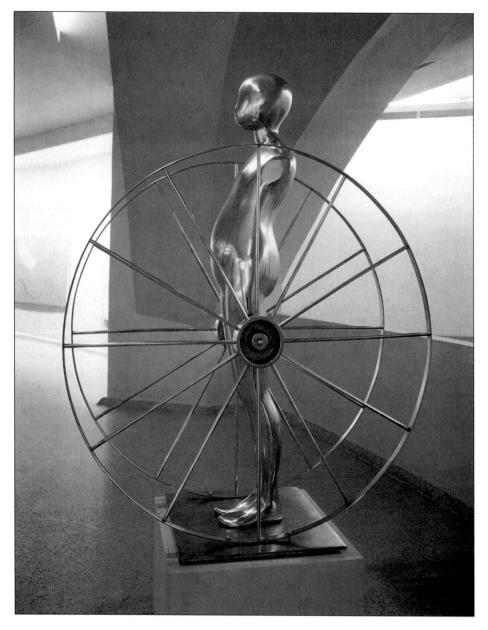

WHEEL MAN

By Ernest Trova (American, 1927–   )

Trova has created a dehumanized, life-size bronze figure of no particular sex, age, race, culture, or environment. Compressed between the two wheels, it seems to present humanity as the victim of its own complicated inventions. The wheels may also symbolize the rolling vicissitudes of human fortune. The date 1965 is inscribed on the base, and the whole faceless assemblage suggests that the wheels of human progress and civilization have not exactly carried human beings to the happy condition that an earlier, more optimistic age had expected.

(Solomon R. Guggenheim Museum, New York, John G. Powers Fund) force intervened to protect the people of East Timor after they voted in a UN-sponsored referendum for independence from Indonesia and then faced virtual butchery by Indonesian paramilitary forces. Intervention in Sierra Leone also protected many from brutalization by extremist rebels. Although regional peace forces were evolving, the UN still had an important role to play.

It was a formidable challenge to decide on the legitimate use of international force against sovereign nations to protect threatened or abused populations. As President Clinton noted, the UN's mission from the time of its charter was to protect the world from the scourge of war. "If so," he announced in 2000 to a special planning and celebratory millennium meeting of the United Nations, "we must respect sovereignty and territorial integrity but still find a way to protect people as well as borders." UN Secretary General Kofi Annan strongly endorsed his plea.

Many in the United States understood the need for intervention when American national interests were involved and supported the American role in mediation as pursued by successive administrations in troubled areas, as in the Middle East. Unresolved was the definition of national interests and whether the United States would accept the risks of military casualties in repeated interventions. The new American president, elected in late 2000, George W. Bush, son of the former President Bush, was expected to reassess the concept of "humanitarian intervention." Meanwhile the Europeans took steps to strengthen an independent military and defense role for the European Union. The French, not unlike de Gaulle in the Cold War years, called for recognition of a "multipolar world," in which the EU would be a more equal partner, and they objected, if only in rhetoric, to the hegemony of the "American hyperpower."

Russia's role undefined

The role of Russia in the new world order was critical but not yet precisely defined. That it was still a major power and not ready to abandon aspirations to an important role in world affairs and especially in areas of its own historic and strategic interest was evident in its pro-Serb stance in the Balkans. How to deal with an assertive Russia still armed with thousands of nuclear weapons was a major challenge. NATO, meanwhile, at American initiative, admitted Hungary, Poland, and the Czech Republic as full members in 1999 and planned the admission in the near future of other countries of formerly Soviet-controlled central and eastern Europe. The Central and East European nations, who believed that their admission was necessary and appropriate, not only wished to be full partners in Europe but also saw their membership in NATO as the best guarantee of their future security. The admission of these states up to the very borders of Russia, however, was regarded by many in Russia as a provocation. On the other hand, Russia's president now met regularly with the heads of government of the seven leading industrial nations.

Nuclear disarmament loomed as another key issue in the post–Cold War international order. The collapse of the U.S.S.R. promised to end the "balance of terror" that had resulted from the nuclear buildup of the two superpowers. Despite initial obstacles, the United States and Russia confirmed and broadened their commitment to the mutual reduction of long-range nuclear arms under the SALT treaties. The voluntary reduction of nuclear arms by both countries proceeded in good faith. The number of nuclear warheads in the world, of which the largest number were held by the U.S. and the U.S.S.R., was reduced from 7,000 to fewer than 3,500, or by about 50 percent, in the 15 or so years between the mid-1980s and 2000.

The threat of nuclear proliferation, of course, persisted, keeping the issue high on the international agenda. By the end of the century 187 nations had signed the 1968

Non-Proliferation Treaty. At one of the periodic meetings held to review the status of the treaty, in May 2000, the five major nuclear powers—the United States, Russia, Britain, France, and China—in the first such declaration ever made pledged themselves "unequivocally" to the eventual elimination of all nuclear weapons. There was satisfaction and reassurance also that since August 1945 no nuclear bomb had been exploded in warfare. That additional nations were or might be developing nuclear arms, as India and Pakistan had recently demonstrated, gave cause for continuing concern, as did clandestine nuclear arms efforts by such states as Libya and Iraq. A major setback to the progress of nuclear arms control was the refusal of the United States Senate in late 1999 to ratify the Comprehensive Nuclear Test Ban Treaty on the grounds that the nation's security and the security of other states required periodic testing of the American nuclear arsenal. Almost all other countries had ratified this treaty, which would have prohibited all nuclear weapons testing. In addition, President George W. Bush's proposal to build a missile defense shield against nuclear attack threatened to upset existing arms control policy, which at least since the Antiballistic Missile Treaty of 1972 had focused on the reduction of offensive weapons and banned the building of defensive ones. The proposal especially disturbed Russia and China.

Relations with the People's Republic of China

If relations with Russia were important, so also were relations with the People's Republic of China. Some saw engagement with China through trade and other forms of peaceful interchange as the path to take. Others insisted that the West could not keep silent in the face of human rights violations, the suppression of religious groups, and the mistreatment of Tibet. The United States was committed to a two-China policy that recognized the continuing existence of a non-Communist Taiwan until peaceful union could take place, but there were some alarming threats of future forcible annexation. China could be expected to make its considerable weight felt in world affairs and was opposed to international interventions for human rights abuses.

Meanwhile the world's trouble spots continued to grow. Where new eruptions would occur, whether in the Middle East, Asia, Africa, or elsewhere, was a matter of conjecture. The UN, NATO, the European Union, and all other nations constituting the international community could hope only to limit conflict and tensions, respond to extreme violations of human rights, and explore all possible avenues of international cooperation.

The Population Explosion

Of all the social developments in the second half of the twentieth century one of the most spectacular was the growth of the world's population. From about 1950, as a result of medical discoveries, improved health and sanitation measures, declining infant mortality, and more efficient food production and distribution, death rates declined dramatically while birth rates rose. In India the death rate in 2000 was half the 1950 figure and its population rose from 350 million in 1950 to close to 1 billion 50 years later. Globally, the number of human beings grew so rapidly that demographers spoke of a population explosion. In 1950, when the contemporary takeoff began, world population totaled 2.5 billion; at the end of the century it exceeded 6 billion. Never before had human beings lived through a doubling of the world's population in their own lifetime.

Growth in the late twentieth century

It took the world millions of years for its human population to reach the quarter-billion mark some 2,000 years ago. Not until about 1650 did the population double to a half-billion. It then doubled in less than two centuries to reach its first billion about 1830. By about 1930, in only one century, it again doubled to reach two billion. By 1960, in a little over 30 years, it grew to three billion; 14 years later, in 1974, to four billion; 13 years later, by 1988, to five billion; and in 1999 after only 11 years, it passed the six billion mark. The time required to add a billion people to the world's population, and for the population to double in size, had grown shorter than ever before in history. The annual growth rate for much of this time, close to 2 percent, meant the addition of well over 80 million people annually.

Although predictions were never certain, demographers did not expect the unprecedented acceleration to continue into the twenty-first century, and there were already indications of a slowdown. Sometime between 1965 and 1970 the global annual growth rate seems to have peaked at about 2 percent and then began to decline, unevenly and irregularly, to about 1.5 percent. Nonetheless, because of the huge population base demographers still pushed well into the future the time and estimated figure at which stabilization might be achieved. Even with a reduced growth rate, the world population figure was projected for 2050 at a range of from 8 to 12.5 billion, with some thought that it could peak at just over 11 billion. A debate continued over the "carrying capacity" of the earth, the maximum number of humans that the earth's resources could sustain.

The population growth rate after about 1965 was showing signs of decline not because of wars, the global AIDS epidemic, periodic famines, or the poverty, malnutrition, illiteracy, and disease that afflicted so many in the less developed parts of the world but apparently because of declining birth rates, a pattern manifesting itself not only in the industrial world but in the developing world as well. The population increase in the second half of the twentieth century, it will be recalled, was largely a phenomenon of the developing world in Asia, Africa, and Latin America, where three-fourths of the world lived and where birth rates were highest. By contrast, in North America and in Europe birth rates were already lower. Industrialization, urban life, education, and social pressures for smaller families had begun to reduce birth rates ever since the late nineteenth century. In many industrially developed countries in Western Europe as well as in Japan, Canada, Australia, and elsewhere growth rates were now below the population replacement rate of 2.1 children. Italy and Spain had the lowest rates with an average of 1.2 children per woman of childbearing age, and Italy was expected to decline from a population of 57 million to 51 million in the next 25 years unless considerable immigration took place. In the United States the population was still growing, in good part because of immigration and immigrant families. Measured against the dramatic rise in global figures and in the developing world, Europe and North America were experiencing a shrinking share of world population.

Changing birth rates

A new factor was that after earlier resistance to Western calls for control over family size, the developing countries were now accepting the need to limit population growth. A striking decline in birthrates and in family size in the developing countries was now taking place. In 1970 women in the less developed countries were having an average of six children, but by the opening of the new century, only 30 years later, women in these countries were having an average of four children. Whether the decline was due to voluntary control over family size, the availability of family planning counseling, or a greater empowerment of women over their lives and access to education and employment was still under discussion.

Population and economic growth

Even when fertility rates began to decline and population growth slowed in the developing countries, population growth still threatened to cancel economic advances. No ready solution was in sight. Even with lower

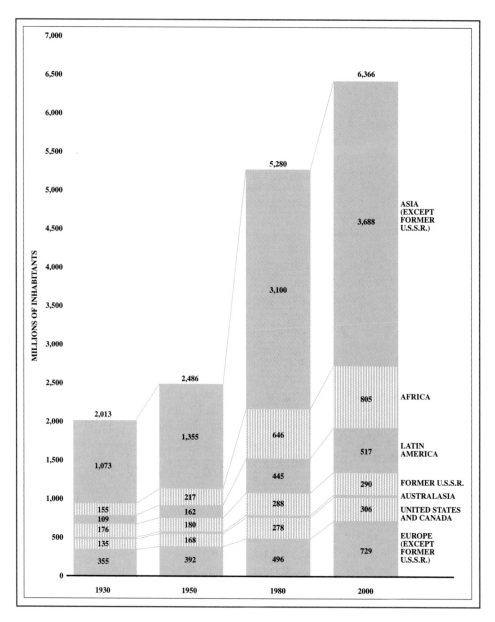

THE POPULATION EXPLOSION

The world's population has more than tripled in size since 1930, but the growth has been most rapid over the last five decades, especially in Latin America, Africa, and Asia. Before the twentieth century, world population had never before doubled in any half-century, so the recent increase can truly be called an "explosion." The world's population passed the 6 billion mark in 1999. Although wealthy societies have lower growth rates than most poor nations, the wealthy societies consume the largest portion of the world's resources. Future population growth is expected to occur mainly in the less industrialized regions of the globe, but demands on the earth's limited resources will continue to grow in both the wealthy and poor nations. The question is whether the growth of population and the growing demand for resources can be slowed in ways that will protect the earth's increasingly overstrained environment.

(United Nations Demographic Yearbook)

birth rates the total number of births annually cannot decline sharply because of the large population base. Contraceptive technology, with its many advances, was increasingly accessible but still not available to everyone. The number of couples in the developing world with access to family planning is judged to have grown from 10 percent to 60 percent in recent decades. But at least 100 million women of child-bearing age, it has been estimated, still lacked access to fertility control. Several of the world's major religions continued to forbid artificial birth control measures, numerous societies restricted educational and vocational opportunities for women, and traditional patterns of life in many parts of the world, especially the poorest, encouraged large families for the sustenance and support of the elderly. The impact of the population explosion of the second half of the twentieth century would be felt far into the future.

The Environment

As serious a threat as growing numbers posed for the world's resources, the planet also faced other dangers. From 1950 to 2000 world industrial production grew more than fivefold, burning coal, oil, and natural gas, and consuming a variety of synthetic chemicals, all of which emitted heat-trapping gases into the atmosphere. Although the full implications remained controversial, many scientists and aroused citizens were convinced that these emissions were eroding the protective upper ozone layer in the atmosphere that shields the earth from excessive solar heat and harmful radiation, and that the resulting warming of the climate could have serious consequences. One troubling sign was that the decade of the 1990s was the warmest globally in 600 years. The ongoing debate prompted governments worldwide to convene periodic conferences to try to agree on regulatory measures.

Environmental pollution and damage

Industrial pollution also caused the acid rain that laid waste to many forests, lakes, and rivers in the industrial nations. Severe environmental damage in the former Soviet Union and the Soviet-bloc nations confirmed that pollution was not confined to any single economic system; central planners there had pressed development with little regard for the ecological consequences. Developing nations also paid little attention to their environment. Under the pressure of expanding population and rapid urbanization, they permitted the slashing and burning of tropical forests for ranching, timber exports, and resettlement. Arable acreage declined; pasture land turned into desert. From 1950 to 2000 the world lost over one-fifth of its topsoil and one-fifth of its tropical rain forests. Plant and animal species were endangered. Nowhere was this more striking than in Latin America and Africa. The partial loss of the Amazon Forest in Brazil before preventive measures were taken dramatized the extent of the damage.

Sustainable economic growth

From the 1970s on a newly sensitized world began to speak of sustainable growth rates, growth that could be maintained without the destruction of humanity's natural habitat. Alternative forms of energy, some as old as the sun and the wind, others new, like nuclear energy (with proper safeguards, to be sure) were proposed. Emissions from industrial factories and from vehicles came under stricter controls. The United States Environmental Protection Agency came into existence in 1970. In 1973 representatives of 80 nations signed an agreement to protect endangered species. In 1989 a number of industrial nations agreed to stop production of chlorofluorocarbons, which released dangerous amounts of chlorine into the upper atmosphere and were widely used in air-conditioning and in aerosol propellants. Other meetings and treaties followed. In 1992, at the first "Earth Summit" meeting in Rio de Janeiro, representatives of 178 countries pledged to protect plant and animal species and to take steps to halt global warming. In

1997 representatives from 150 countries met at Kyoto, where they agreed to reduce the emission of so-called greenhouse gases by 50 percent by 2010.

As awareness of ecological dangers grew, grass-roots environmental organizations multiplied, and in several countries emerged as "Green" political parties. Despite the numerous pledges and measures to counter the threat of environmental deterioration, opposition on economic grounds in the industrial countries, including the United States, and conflicts with plans for economic growth in the developing nations trying to catch up with the industrial world slowed their adoption and enforcement.

Population growth and the threat to the environment added to the world's concerns as it entered the twenty-first century and the new millennium. Many of the most pressing were older concerns: the implications for society of contemporary science and technology, the sovereignty of nations, peace among nations, and the quest within nations for freedom, dignity, and economic well-being. All were aspects of one overriding problem. How could human beings in each generation on earth, regardless of sex, color, creed, religion, nationality, or ethnic background—beings said by some to be made in the image of God, by others to have a natural right to liberty and happiness, by still others to have the freedom to create meaning in a meaningless universe—live out their lives in peace, fulfill their destiny, and pass on their heritage to future generations?

These concluding chapters began with the analogy of a cataclysm. The analogy is still pertinent. A cataclysm, as already observed, is not a time of downfall only. Mountains crumble, but others are thrust up. Lands vanish, but others rise from the sea. So it is with the political and social cataclysm of our times. Old landmarks are worn down. Empires pass away; new nations arise in their place. Subjugated peoples regain independence; rigid ideologies collapse. The ascendancy of Europe, the West, and the European nations closes; they learn to negotiate with others, not to rule them. There is a greater fluidity in social relationships. Women and minorities struggle for equal places in society. But social justice and peace remain elusive goals. The gap between rich and poor among nations, and within nations, is not easily overcome. Old and new diseases, natural catastrophes, and armed conflicts exact their toll. Resurgent nationalism feeds on intolerance and hatred. Never has war been so potentially destructive; the menace of a nuclear war that would blight much of civilization wanes but does not disappear. Uncontrolled economic development threatens the environment, and population growth presses on natural resources. International cooperation and intervention are needed to protect human rights, prevent wars, and sustain the earth's billions.

But there is a growing global recognition of all these concerns. To close this long history on a note of placidity would indeed be inappropriate, but it would also be wrong to close on a note of doom. The history of the modern world shows the astonishing range of human imagination and ingenuity, and there are good historical reasons to believe that people will continue to confront future problems and challenges with determination and creativity.

APPENDIX,
SUGGESTIONS FOR
FURTHER READING,
INDEX

RULERS AND REGIMES

In Principal European Countries since 1500

HOLY ROMAN EMPIRE

Habsburg Line

Maximilian I, 1493–1519

Charles V, 1519–1556

Ferdinand I, 1556–1564

Maximilian II, 1564–1576

Rudolph II, 1576–1612

Matthias, 1612–1619

Ferdinand II, 1619–1637

Ferdinand III, 1637–1657

Leopold I, 1658–1705

Joseph I, 1705–1711

Charles VI, 1711–1740

Charles VI was succeeded by a daughter, Maria Theresa, who as a woman could not be elected Holy Roman Emperor. French influence in 1742 secured the election of

Bavarian Line

Charles VII, 1742–1745

On Charles VII's death the Habsburg control of the emperorship was resumed.

Lorraine Line

Francis I, 1745–1765 (husband of Maria Theresa)

Habsburg-Lorraine Line

Joseph II, 1765–1790 (son of Francis I and Maria Theresa)

Leopold II, 1790–1792

Francis II, 1792–1806

The Holy Roman Empire became extinct in 1806.

AUSTRIAN DOMINIONS

The rulers of Austria from 1438 to 1740, and at least titular kings of Hungary from 1526 to 1740, were the same as the Holy Roman Emperors. After 1740:

Habsburg Line (through female heir)

Maria Theresa, 1740–1780

Joseph II, 1780–1790

Leopold II, 1790–1792

Francis II, 1792–1835

In 1804 Francis II took the title of Emperor, as Francis I of the Austrian Empire. Austria was declared an "empire" because Napoleon proclaimed France an empire in that year, and because the demise of the Holy Roman Empire could be foreseen.

Ferdinand I, 1835–1848

Francis Joseph, 1848–1916

Charles I, 1916–1918

The Austrian Empire became extinct in 1918.

BRITISH ISLES

Tudor Line

Kings of England and Ireland

Henry VII, 1485–1509

Henry VIII, 1509–1547

Edward VI, 1547–1553

Mary I, 1553–1558

Elizabeth I, 1558–1603

In 1603 James VI of Scotland, a great-great-grandson of Henry VII, succeeded to the English throne.

Stuart Line

Kings of England and Ireland, and of Scotland

James I, 1603–1625

Charles I, 1625–1649

Republican Interregnum

The Commonwealth, 1649–1653

The Protectorate

Oliver Cromwell, 1653–1658, Lord Protector

Richard Cromwell, 1658–1660

Restored Stuart Line

Charles II, 1660–1685

James II, 1685–1688

In 1688 James II was forced out of the country, but Parliament kept the crown in a female branch of the Stuart family, calling in Mary, the daughter of James II, and her husband William III of the Netherlands. Mary died in 1694.

William III and Mary II, 1689–1702/1694

Anne, 1702–1714

In 1707, through the Union of England and Scotland, the royal title became King (or Queen) of Great Britain and Ireland. The Stuart family having no direct Protestant heirs, the throne passed in 1714 to the German George I, Elector of Hanover, a great-grandson of James I.

Hanoverian Line

Kings of Great Britain and Ireland

George I, 1714–1727

George II, 1727–1760

George III, 1760–1820

George IV, 1820–1830

William IV, 1830–1837

William IV having no heirs, the British throne passed in 1837 to Victoria, a granddaughter of George III. Though the British family has continued in direct descent from George I, it has dropped the Hanoverian designation and is now known as the House of Windsor. From 1877 to 1947 the British rulers bore the additional title of Emperor (or Empress) of India.

Victoria, 1837–1901

Edward VII, 1901–1910

George V, 1910–1936

Edward VIII, 1936

George VI, 1936–1952

Elizabeth II, 1952–

FRANCE

Valois Line

Louis XI, 1461–1483

Charles VIII, 1483–1498

Louis XII, 1498–1515

Francis I, 1515–1547

Henry II, 1547–1559

Francis II, 1559–1560

Charles IX, 1560–1574

Henry III, 1574–1589

In 1589 the Valois line became extinct, and the throne passed to Henry of Bourbon, a remote descendant of French kings of the fourteenth century.

Bourbon Line

Henry IV, 1589–1610

Louis XIII, 1610–1643

Louis XIV, 1643–1715

Louis XV, 1715–1774

Louis XVI, 1774–1792

The Republic

Convention, 1792–1795

Directory, 1795–1799

Consulate, 1799–1804

The Empire

Napoleon I, 1804–1814, Emperor of the French and King of Italy

Restored Bourbon Line

Louis XVIII, 1814–1824

(Royalists count a Louis XVII, 1793–1795, and date the reign of Louis XVIII from 1795.)

Charles X, 1824–1830

The Revolution of 1830 gave the throne to the Duke of Orleans, descendant of Louis XIII.

Orleans Line

Louis-Philippe, 1830–1848

Second Republic

1848–1852

Second Empire

Napoleon III, 1852–1870, Emperor of the French

Third Republic

1870–1940

Vichy Regime

1940–1944

Provisional Government

1944–1946

Fourth Republic

1946–1958

Fifth Republic

1958–

PRUSSIA (AND GERMANY)

A continuous Hohenzollern line ruled until 1918.

Electors of Brandenburg and Dukes of Prussia

George William, 1619–1640

Frederick William, 1640–1688, the "Great Elector"

Frederick III, 1688–1713

In 1701 Frederick III was permitted by the Holy Roman Emperor to entitle himself King in Prussia, as Frederick I.

Kings of Prussia

Frederick I, 1701–1713

Frederick William I, 1713–1740

Frederick II, the "Great," 1740–1786

Frederick William II, 1786–1797

Frederick William III, 1797–1840

Frederick William IV, 1840–1861

William I, 1861–1888

In 1871 William I took the title of German Emperor.

German Emperors

William I, 1871–1888

Frederick III, 1888

William II, 1888–1918

The German Empire became extinct in 1918. It was succeeded by the

Weimar Republic

1919–1933

(The Weimar Republic is an unofficial title for what was still called the Deutsches Reich, a phrase not easy to translate accurately.)

The Third Reich

1933–1945

(The Third Reich is an unofficial title for the Deutsches Reich under Adolf Hitler.)

Allied Military Government in 1945 was followed by

German Federal Republic (West Germany)

1949–1990

German Democratic Republic (East Germany)

1949–1990

The two Germanys were united in 1990.

German Federal Republic

1990–

SARDINIA (AND ITALY)

In 1720 Victor Amadeus II, Duke of Savoy, took the title of King of Sardinia, having acquired the island of that name. The kingdom was often called Piedmont because of the king's older mainland domain.

Kings of Sardinia

Victor Amadeus II, 1720–1730

Charles Emmanuel III, 1730–1773

Victor Amadeus III, 1773–1796

Charles Emmanuel IV, 1796–1802

Victor Emmanuel I, 1802–1821

Charles Felix, 1821–1831

Charles Albert, 1831–1849

Victor Emmanuel II, 1849–1878

In 1861 Victor Emmanuel II took the title of King of Italy.

Kings of Italy

Victor Emmanuel II, 1861–1878

Humbert I, 1878–1900

Victor Emmanuel III, 1900–1946

Humbert II, 1946

In1946 the Kingdom of Italy became extinct and was succeeded by the

Italian Republic
1946–

SPAIN

Ferdinand and Isabella, 1479–1504/1516

Isabella died in 1504, but Ferdinand lived until 1516, whereupon the Spanish thrones were inherited by their grandson Charles, who became Charles V of the Holy Roman Empire, but was known in Spain as Charles I.

Habsburg Line
Charles I, 1516–1556

Philip II, 1556–1598

Philip III, 1598–1621

Philip IV, 1621–1665

Charles II, 1665–1700

With Charles II the Spanish Habsburg line became extinct, and the throne passed to the French Bourbon grandson of Louis XIV of France and great-grandson of Philip IV of Spain.

Bourbon Line
Philip V, 1700–1746

Ferdinand VI, 1746–1759

Charles III, 1759–1788

Charles IV, 1788–1808

Bonaparte Line
Joseph, 1808–1813 (brother of Napoleon)

Restored Bourbon Line
Ferdinand VII, 1813–1833

Isabella II, 1833–1868

In 1868 Isabella abdicated; after a regency, and a brief reign by Amadeus I (Savoy), 1871–1873, there was a short-lived First Republic, 1873–1874, succeeded by

Alfonso XII, 1874–1885

Alfonso XIII, 1885–1931

In 1931 a republican revolution unseated Alfonso XIII.

Second Spanish Republic
1931–1936

Spanish Civil War
1936–1939

Regime of General Francisco Franco
1939–1975

Upon the death of Franco the Bourbon family was restored.

Juan Carlos I, 1975–

RUSSIA (AND U.S.S.R.)

Grand Dukes of Moscow
Ivan III, the "Great," 1462–1505

Basil III, 1505–1533

Ivan IV, the "Terrible," 1533–1584

In 1547 Ivan IV took the title of Tsar of Russia.

Tsars of Russia
Ivan IV, the "Terrible," 1547–1584

Theodore I, 1584–1598

Boris Godunov, 1598–1605

Time of Troubles
1604–1613

Romanov Line
Michael, 1613–1645

Alexis, 1645–1676

Theodore II, 1676–1682

Ivan V and Peter I, 1682–1689

Peter I, the "Great," 1689–1725

Catherine I, 1725–1727

Peter II, 1727–1730

Anna, 1730–1740

Ivan VI, 1740–1741

Elizabeth, 1741–1762

Peter III, 1762

Catherine II, the "Great," 1762–1796

Paul, 1796–1801

Alexander I, 1801–1825

Nicholas I, 1825–1855

Alexander II, 1855–1881

Alexander III, 1881–1894

Nicholas II, 1894–1917

In 1917 the tsardom became extinct.

Provisional Government

1917

Communist Revolution

1917

Union of Soviet Socialist Republics

1922–1991

In 1991 the Communist regime ended and the U.S.S.R. dissolved into its component republics (Russia, Ukraine, Belarus, etc.), loosely associated with each other in a Commonwealth of Independent States.

Russian Federation

1991–

Suggestions for Further Reading

The following bibliographical guide is intended for the convenience of students, teachers, and general readers. Although professional students of history may also find it useful, no attempt has been made to provide comprehensive coverage of special areas or topics, or to include specialized monographs. Although many older volumes have been included, the aim throughout has been to call attention to recent historical works, to which the reader may turn for additional bibliographical guidance. Classification follows the plan of chapters in the present book. For reasons of space, untranslated works in foreign languages have been excluded, as have been general textbooks, articles in periodicals, and (with a few exceptions) primary source materials. When a second date of publication for a book is given without further specification, it is generally the date of reprinting or reissue.

Many of the titles are available in paperback; up-to-date listings may be found in *Books in Print* and in the *Paperback Book Guide for Colleges.*

INTRODUCTION

Guides, Reference Works, and Special Topics

An invaluable bibliographical tool for historical works published prior to 1992 is the American Historical Association's *Guide to Historical Literature* (3rd ed., 2 vols., 1995). Much expanded since its second edition in 1961, the *Guide* consists of 48 sections organized into regional, national, chronological, and topical categories, with coverage from prehistory to the present. It provides annotated entries for thousands of books and articles as well as an introductory essay for each section, all carefully indexed. The *Guide's* first section, "Theory and Practice in Historical Study," provides a convenient introduction to historical method, historiography, philosophy of history, demography, the many varieties of history, and other important subjects. To keep up with the outpouring of historical books, however, it is important to read the book reviews and listings of new books in the *American Historical Review,* the *Journal of Modern History, The Journal of World History,* the (London) *Times Literary Supplement,* the *New York Review of Books,* and other periodicals, and the book reviews in the daily and weekend press. A valuable source of information on relevant articles is *Historical Abstracts,* now available in an electronic database. Many historical resources are now accessible on the Internet, though readers must use such materials with careful assessments of their reliability. For a helpful guide to history on the Internet, organized by thematic categories, readers may consult D. A. Trinkle and S. A. Merriman (eds.), *The History Highway 2000: A Guide to Internet Resources* (rev. 2000).

Brief descriptions of major events and historical figures as well as a chronology of world history may be found in the *Oxford Encyclopedia of World History* (1998); there are also chronologies in S. H. Steinberg, *Historical Tables, 58 B.C.–A.D. 1990* (rev. 1991); and in similar works. Of the many multivolume encyclopedias, the *Encyclopedia Britannica* (15th ed., with periodic updates) remains the most valuable, and articles may now be found electronically at www.britannica.com. Convenient one-volume reference tools are the *Cambridge Encyclopedia* (rev. 1997), the *Columbia Encyclopedia* (5th ed., 1993), and the Concise Columbia Encyclopedia (3rd ed., 1994).

Among historical atlases that place European history in its world setting, G. Parker (ed.), the (London) *Times Atlas of World History* (rev. 1993) and N. Grove (ed.), *National Geographic Society Atlas of World History* (1997) are impressive. Also useful, and periodically updated, are the *Rand McNally Atlas of World History,* Hammond's *Historical Atlas of the World,* and the Penguin Historical Atlas series. Of many geographical atlases one of the best is the *National Geographic Atlas of the World* (7th ed., 1999).

Of multivolume historical series, the *New Cambridge Modern History* (14 vols., 1957–1979) remains useful. The volumes, which will be referred to in the chapters below, contain outstanding contributions by specialists from all over the world. For European history, *The Rise of Modern Europe* (20 vols., 1936–1985), known as the "Langer series" for its general editor W. L. Langer, provides three to four volumes for each of the modern centuries, but many are now outdated. There are other series, to which reference will be made below, under the auspices of various publishers.

Geographical influences on European history are discussed in E. A. Freeman and J. B. Bury, *The Historical Geography of Europe* (1974); N.J.G. Pounds, *An Historical Geography of Europe* (3 vols., 1973–1985); and the essays in E. Genovese and L. Hochberg (eds.), *Geographic Perspectives in History* (1989). The case for new conceptualizations in geography is made in M. W. Lewis and K. E. Wigen, *The Myth of*

Continents: A Critique of Metageography (1997). J. G. Simmons, *Changing the Face of the Earth: Culture, Environment, and History* (1989) traces the human impact on the planet over the centuries; E. Le Roy Ladurie examines an important subject in *Times of Feast, Times of Famine: A History of Climate since the Year 1000* (trans. 1971).

For the impact of famine, disease, and the movement of peoples, one may read W. H. McNeill, *Plagues and Peoples (1976) and The Global Condition: Conquerors, Catastrophes, and Community* (1992); T. McKeown, *The Origins of Human Disease* (1988); A. Crosby, *Germs, Seeds and Animals: Studies in Ecological History* (1994); and K. F. Kiple (ed.), *The Cambridge World History of Human Disease* (1992), a valuable reference work. On cultural advantages and disadvantages in the encounters between peoples, J. Diamond, *Guns, Germs, and Steel: The Fate of Human Societies* (1997), is rewarding.

Of the many books on military history treating war as a social and human phenomenon, three outstanding studies ranging from earliest times to the present are A. Jones, *The Art of War in the Western World* (1989); R. L. O'Connell, *Of Arms and Men: A History of War, Weapons, and Aggression* (1990); and J. Keegan, *A History of Warfare* (1993); the latter, like others of Keegan's books, is especially noteworthy. Of interest in a related category is M. Walzer, *Just and Unjust Wars* (1977). The importance of technology is stressed in B. Brodie and F. Brodie, *From Crossbow to H-Bomb* (rev. 1973); W. H. McNeill, *The Pursuit of Power: Technology, Armed Force, and Society since A.D. 1000* (1982); and M. van Creveld, *Technology and War: From 2000 B.C. to the Present* (1988).

A few books of special interest deserve mention here: W. H. McNeill, *The Rise of the West: A History of the Human Community* (rev. 1991), a notable effort to recount the human experience in a global setting; E. R. Wolf, *Europe and the People without History* (1983), by an anthropologist, which portrays Western history as seen by non-Western societies in Asia, Africa, and the Americas; P. Kennedy, *The Rise and Fall of the Great Powers: Economic Change and Military Conflict from 1500 to 2000* (1987), which examines the political and economic fortunes of the European nations that successively played the leading role in world affairs in the modern centuries; and J. Barzun, *From Dawn to Decadence: 500 Years of Cultural Life, 1500 to the Present* (2000), a provocative study of Western thought since the sixteenth century. Two recent efforts at a synthesis of European history are N. Davies, *Europe: A History* (1997), a highly idiosyncratic but challenging work; and J. M. Roberts, *A History of Europe* (1996), a more conventional, thoughtful account. F. Fernando-Armesto, *Millennium: A History of the Last Thousand Years* (1995), is

an imaginative, not completely successful, attempt at global history. K. A. Appiah and H. L. Gates, Jr., *The Dictionary of Global Culture* (1998) is a pioneer effort to integrate the contributions of Western and non-Western cultures.

Changing Directions in Historical Writings

For a sampling of insights into recent trends in historical writing, one may turn to M. Kammen (ed.), *The Past before Us: Contemporary Historical Writing in the United States* (1980); T. K. Rabb and R. I. Rotberg (eds.), *The New History: The 1980s and Beyond* (1982); P. Burke (ed.), *New Perspectives on Historical Writing* (1992); J. Appleby, L. Hunt, and M. Jacob, *Telling the Truth about History* (1994); G. Iggers, *Historiography in the Twentieth Century: From Scientific Objectivity to the Postmodern Challenge* (1997); and B. Southgate, *History, What and Why? Ancient, Modern, and Postmodern Perspectives* (1996).

One of the major contemporary interests of historians has been social history. Stimulated by the *Annales* school of historical writing in France (the name derived from the French periodical *Annales: économies, sociétés, civilisations,* which in 1994 was renamed *Annales: histoire, sciences sociales*), and by newer kinds of working-class history in England, in which E. P. Thompson, *The Making of the English Working Class* (1963), was a pioneer, historians have concerned themselves increasingly with a social history distinct from traditional interests in social classes and labor and laboring conditions. They have been examining such subjects as the history of the family, women, sexuality, marriage, the everyday lives and outlook (or *mentalité*) of the urban and rural poor, and popular culture—all studied as history "from the bottom up." Many such works are listed below in the appropriate chapters. An introduction to the newer social history and to popular culture is provided in O. Zung (ed.), *Reliving the Past: The Worlds of Social History (1985); P. Burke, Popular Culture in Early Modern Europe* (rev. 1994); C. Mukerjee and M. Schudson (eds.), *Rethinking Popular Culture* (1990); and L. Berlanstein (ed.), *Rethinking Labor History: Essays on Discourse and Class Analysis* (1993). A useful collection of recent contributions to the newer social history is available in R. M. Goldin (ed.), *The Social Dimension of Western Civilization* (4th ed., 1999).

Although the *Annales* historians have contributed a good deal to the newer social history, they have also been important for their emphasis, often quantitative and interdisciplinary, on long-term factors that influence the course of historical change, such as geography, environment, resources, climate, population, diet, and disease, which in their view often merit closer attention than "events." Here F. Braudel, *The Mediterranean and the Mediterranean World in the*

Age of Philip II (2 vols., 1949; trans. 1974; rev. and abridged 1 vol. ed., 1992), was a pioneering work; his other books are described in the chapters below.

There has been much attention in recent decades to the history of women. Many of the writings call for reassessments of various historical eras from the viewpoint of women's status in the era and for the fuller integration of the history of women into general history. Contributions to the history of women in Europe and the West may be sampled in R. Bridenthal, S. Stuard, and M. Wiesner (eds.), *Becoming Visible: Women in European History* (rev. 1998), with essays covering ancient times to the twentieth century; M. J. Boxer and J. H. Quataert (eds.), *Connecting Spheres: European Women in a Globalizing World, 1500 to the Present* (rev. 2000), case studies with informative overview chapters; B. S. Anderson and J. P. Zinsser, *A History of Their Own: Women in Europe from Prehistory to the Present* (2 vols.; rev. 2000), thematically organized; and B. G. Smith, *Changing Lives: Women in European History since 1700* (1989), a helpful narrative account. G. Duby and M. Perrot (gen. eds.), *A History of Women in the West* (trans. 1992–1994), is a multivolume history from ancient times to the present. Important theoretical perspectives on the role of gender in historical understanding can be found in *Women, History and Theory: The Essays of Joan Kelly* (1984); and J. W. Scott, *Gender and the Politics of History* (rev. 1999). G. Lerner provides many insights into women and history in *The Creation of Patriarchy* (1986) and *The Creation of Feminist Consciousness: From the Middle Ages to 1870* (1993). Four documentary histories available are J. C. Fout and E. Reimer (eds.), *European Women: A Documentary History, 1789– 1945* (1980); J. O'Faolain and L. Martines (eds.), *Not in God's Image: Women in History from the Greeks to the Victorians* (1973); E. O. Hillerstein, L. P. Hume, and K. M. Offen (eds.), *Victorian Women: Women's Lives in England, France, and the United States* (1981); and S. G. Bell and K. M. Offen (eds.), *Women, the Family, and Freedom: The Debate in Documents* (2 vols.; 1983).

Psychological approaches to the writing of history are explored in S. Friedländer, *History and Psychoanalysis* (trans. 1978); P. Loewenberg, *Decoding the Past: The Psychohistorical Approach* (1982); and P. Gay, *Freud for Historians* (1985). For an introduction to the quantitative analysis of historical data, one may turn to K. H. Jarausch and K. A. Hardy, *Quantitative Methods for Historians: A Guide to Research, Data, and Statistics* (1991). Of special interest also is R. G. Hawks, *Economics for Historians* (1980). Two useful introductions to a crucial component of contemporary historical work are J. L. Reiff, *Structuring the Past: The Use of Computers in History* (1991) and D. I. Greenstein, *A Historian's Guide to Computing*

(1994). There is much practical information on historical research and writing in J. Barzun and H. F. Graff, *The Modern Researcher* (rev. 1992).

The tapping of neglected sources through the methods of oral history is examined in P. Thompson, *The Voice of the Past: Oral History* (1978); D. Henige, *Oral Historiography* (1982); D. K. Dunaway and W. K. Baum (eds.), *Oral History: An Interdisciplinary Anthology* (1984); and K. Howarth, *Oral History* (1999). A contemporary medium is explored in P. Sorlin, *The Film in History: Restaging the Past* (1980); J. E. O'Connor (ed.), *Image as Artifact: The Historical Analysis of Film and Television* (1990); R. Rosenstone (ed.), *Revisioning History: Film and the Construction of a New Past* (1995) and *Visions of the Past: The Challenge of Film to our Idea of History* (1995).

Changing assessments of cultural and intellectual history, borrowing from philosophy, linguistics, anthropology, and literary criticism, which may remain elusive for many readers, may be sampled in L. Hunt (ed.), *The New Cultural History* (1989); V. E. Bonnell and L. Hunt (eds.), *Beyond the Cultural Turn: New Directions in the Study of Society and Culture* (1999); D. LaCapra, *Rethinking Intellectual History: Texts, Contexts, Language* (1983); and C. Ginzburg, *Clues, Myths, and the Historical Method* (trans. 1992).

Some books critical of the trends in historical writing that have emerged since the 1960s and 1970s include J. Barzun, *Clio and the Doctors: Psychohistory, Quantohistory, and History* (1974); J. H. Hexter, *On Historians: Some of the Makers of Modern History* (1979); T. S. Hamerow, *Reflections on History and Historians* (1987); G. R. Elton, *Return to Essentials: Some Reflections on the Present State of Historical Study* (1993); G. Himmelfarb, *The New History and the Old* (1987) and *On Looking into the Abyss: Untimely Thoughts on Culture and Society* (1994); and E. Fox-Genovese and E. Lasch-Quinn (eds.), *Reconstructing History: The Emergence of a New Historical Society* (1999). Two probing accounts of the historical profession in the United States, with insights into past and present historiographical debates, are J. Higham, *History: Professional Scholarship in America* (rev. 1989); and P. Novick, *That Noble Dream: The "Objectivity Question" and the American Historical Profession* (1988).

On the relationship of history to other disciplines and its own distinctive role one may turn to such varied explorations as E. H. Carr, *What Is History?* (1962); A. Nevins, *The Gateway to History* (rev. 1962); P. Gay, *Style in History* (1974); L. Gottschalk, *Understanding History* (rev. 1969); A. Marwick, *The Nature of History* (rev. 1989); L. Gossman, *Between History and Literature* (1990); D. LaCapra, *History and Criticism* (1985); and H. V. White, *Metahistory:*

The Historical Imagination in Nineteenth-Century Europe (1973). Of special interest for the relationship of the discipline to the social sciences are P. Burke, *History and Social Theory* (1993); T. J. McDonald (ed.), *The Historic Turn in the Human Sciences* (1996); and J. Elster, *The Cement of Society: A Study of Social Order* (1991) and *Nuts and Bolts from the Social Sciences* (1991).

Among thoughtful reflections by historians who have themselves made notable contributions to the writing of history, the following may be suggested: B. Lewis, *History-Remembered, Recovered, Invented* (1975); F. Gilbert, *History: Choice and Commitment* (1977); W. H. McNeill, *Mythistory and Other Essays* (1986); C. Vann Woodward, *Thinking Back: The Perils of Writing History* (1986) and *The Future of the Past* (1989); L. Stone, *The Past and the Present Revisited* (1987); D. Cannadine, *The Pleasures of the Past* (1989); W. J. Bouwsma, *A Usable Past* (1990); M. Beloff, *An Historian in the Twentieth Century* (1992); G. Lerner, *Why History Matters: Life and Thought* (1997); and C. E. Schorske, *Thinking with History* (1998). Other interesting historical reflections appear in two collections of interviews with contemporary historians: H. Abelove (ed.), *Visions of History* (1984), and R. Adelson, *Speaking of History: Conversations with Historians* (1997).

Finally, there are numerous anthologies, collections of source materials, and problems series in historical interpretation. A few titles in these categories will be cited at the end of each chapter.

11. REACTION VERSUS PROGRESS, 1815–1848

The resettling of Europe institutions after the French Revolution and Napoleon in many ways marked the opening of a new historical era. There are numerous general, national, and topical histories accordingly that take their starting point around 1815.

Nineteenth-Century Europe

Helpful guides to all aspects of nineteenth-century history include M. S. Anderson, *The Ascendancy of Europe, 1815–1914* (rev. 1986); T. S. Hamerow, *The Birth of a New Europe: State and Society in the Nineteenth Century* (1983); and R. Gildea, *Barricades and Borders: Europe, 1800–1914* (rev. 1996). There are informative chapters also in Vol. V of the UNESCO *History of Mankind:* C. Morazé (ed.), *The Nineteenth Century, 1775 to 1905* (1977). Useful discussion of European politics, society, and economic life is available in T.C.W. Blanning (ed.), *Short Oxford History of Europe: The Nineteenth Century* (2000); and the first half of the century may be surveyed in J. Sperber, *Revolutionary Europe, 1780–1850* (2000).

Important works on the social history of the nineteenth century include Vol. IV of the *History of*
Private Life: M. Perrot (ed.), *From the French Revolution to the Great War* (1987). Numerous other works on social and on women's history in these years are cited in chapter 15. For social classes one may turn to J. Kocka and A. Mitchell (eds.), *Bourgeois Society in Nineteenth-Century Europe* (1993); P. M. Pilbeam, *The Middle Classes in Europe, 1789–1914: France, Germany, Italy, and Russia* (1990); and for the upper classes, D. Lieven, *The Aristocracy in Europe, 1815–1914* (1992). For rural change in the late eighteenth and nineteenth centuries, there are J. Blum, *The End of the Old Order in Rural Europe* (1978) and A. Moulin, *Peasantry and Society in France since 1789* (trans. 1991). For religion one may read H. Vidler, *The Church in the Age of Revolution* (1961); H. McLeod, *Religion and the People of Western Europe, 1789–1970* (1981); and O. Chadwick, *The Secularization of the European Mind in the Nineteenth Century* (1976). On women in the nineteenth century, in addition to general works already cited, useful books are P. Branca, *Women in Europe since 1750* (1978); S. Delamont and L. Duffin (eds.), *The Nineteenth-Century Woman: Her Cultural and Physical World* (1978); and P. S. Robertson, *An Experience of Women: Patterns and Change in Nineteenth-Century Europe* (1982).

Europe, 1815–1848

General guides to the reorientation after 1815 include G. de Bertier de Sauvigny, *Metternich and His Times* (trans. 1967) and W. L. Langer, *Political and Social Upheaval, 1832–1852* (1969). There are valuable chapters in Vol. IX of the *New Cambridge Modern History,* C. W. Crawley (ed.), *War and Peace in an Age of Upheaval, 1793–1830* (1965); and in Vol. X, J.P.T. Bury (ed.), *The Zenith of European Power, 1830–1870* (1960). E. J. Hobsbawm has written one of his provocative interpretive histories on this era, *The Age of Revolution: Europe, 1789–1848* (1962), the first volume of a trilogy on what he calls the "long nineteenth century," 1789–1914. For the papacy in the revolutionary ferment of the age, one may read O. Chadwick, *The Popes and European Revolution* (1981).

Industrial Revolution

One of the best introductions to economic history during and since the Industrial Revolution is D. S. Landes, *The Unbound Prometheus: Technological Change and Industrial Development in Western Europe from 1750 to the Present* (1969). Other informative accounts are C. M. Cipolla (ed.), *The Emergence of Industrial Societies* (1973); S. Pollard, *Peaceful Conquest: The Industrialization of Europe, 1760–1970* (1981); C. Trebilcock, *The Industrialization of the Continental Powers, 1780–1914* (1981); and T. Kemp, *Industrialization in Nineteenth Century Europe* (rev. 1985).

There are thoughtful essays in P. Mathias and J. A. Davis (eds.), *The First Industrial Revolutions* (1990). The social and political implications of an industrial civilization are examined in J. McManners, *European History: Men, Machines, and Freedom* (1967); P. N. Stearns, *The Impact of the Industrial Revolution* (1971); and E. A. Wrigley, *People, Cities, and Wealth: The Transformation of Traditional Society* (1987).

The complexities surrounding the emergence of industrialism in England are examined in numerous books. Brief informative accounts include T. S. Ashton, *The Industrial Revolution 1760–1830* (1948), still useful; P. Deane, *The First Industrial Revolution* (rev. 1979); and P. Mathias, *The First Industrial Nation: An Economic History of Britain, 1700–1914* (rev. 1983). P. Mantoux, *The Industrial Revolution in the Eighteenth Century* (1906; reissued 1983 with forewords by T. S. Ashton and by J. K. Galbraith) may still be read with profit. Additional interpretive accounts include M. Berg, *The Age of Manufactures, 1700–1820: Industry, Innovation, and Work in Britain* (1985); E. A. Wrigley, *Continuity, Chance, and Change: The Character of the Industrial Revolution in England* (1988); and P. Hudson, *The Genesis of Industrial Capitalism* (1986) and *The Industrial Revolution* (1992).

Insights into the nineteenth-century manufacturers are provided in A. Howe, *The Cotton Masters, 1830–1860* (1984); F. Crouzet, *The First Industrialists* (1985); L. Davidoff and C. Hall, *Family Fortunes: Men and Women of the English Middle Class, 1780–1850* (1987); and R. S. Fitton, *The Arkwrights: Spinners of Fortune* (1989). Changes in British agriculture and the impact on the countryside may be studied in D. B. Grigg, *English Agriculture* (1989); and K.D.M. Snell, *Annals of the Labouring Poor: Social Change and Agrarian England 1660– 1900* (1985).

Social Consequences of Industrialism

There is a large and controversial literature on the effects of industrial change on the British working classes. F. Engels, *The Condition of the Working Class in England* [1844; reissued, D. McLellan (ed.), 1993] and A. Toynbee, *Lectures on the Industrial Revolution in England* (1884, 1969), were classic descriptions of such exploitation. Meanwhile J. L. Hammond and B. Hammond in several vehement books, such as *The Town Labourer, 1760–1832: The New Civilization* (1919) and *The Age of the Chartists* (1930), also stressed the economic abuse of the common people. For somewhat modified views one may read J. T. Ward, *The Factory System, 1830–1855* (1962); M. I. Thomis, *Responses to Industrialization: The British Experience 1780–1850* (1976); and R. Gray, *The Factory Question and Industrial England, 1830–1860* (1996). P. Laslett, *The World We Have Lost: England before the Industrial Age* (rev. 1973), contrasts the new age with what he saw as the stability of the early mod-

ern centuries. E. P. Thompson, *The Making of the English Working Class* (1963), in a highly influential book presents the picture of a militant working-class culture emerging to resist industrial society. For a helpful synthesis the reader may turn to two books by J. Rule: *The Experience of Labour in Eighteenth-Century English Industry* (1984) and *The Labouring Classes in Early Industrial England, 1750–1850* (1986).

Working-class experiences are depicted in E. R. Pike, *Human Documents of the Industrial Revolution in Britain* (reissued 1988); D. Vincent, *Bread, Knowledge and Freedom: A Study of Nineteenth-Century Working Class Autobiography* (1981); I. Pinchbeck, *Women Workers and the Industrial Revolution, 1750–1850* (1930, 1969); and I. Pinchbeck and M. Hewitt, *Children in English Society* (2 vols., 1969–1973). In a very different vein G. Himmelfarb, *The Idea of Poverty: England in the Early Industrial Age* (1984) and *Poverty and Compassion: The Moral Indignation of the Late Victorians* (1991) examine the writings of these years to demonstrate the complexities involved in defining poverty and social responsibilities.

For protest movements of the age, D. G. Wright, *Popular Radicalism: The Working Class Experience, 1780–1880* (1988) is helpful as a summary. Special studies include M. I. Thomas, *The Luddites: Machine-Breaking in Regency England* (1979); D. Rend, *Peterloo: The Massacre and Its Background* (1958); R. Reid, *The Peterloo Massacre* (1989); E. J. Hobsbawm and G. Rudé, *Captain Swing* (1969), a study of the rural poor and agrarian unrest; and J. Knott, *Popular Opposition to the 1834 Poor Law* (1986).

For the Chartists recommended books include T. Ward, *Chartism* (1973); D. Jones, *Chartism and the Chartists* (1975); and D. Thompson, *The Chartists: Popular Politics in the Industrial Revolution* (1984). The creation in England and Ireland of a modern police system to suppress popular protest is studied in S. H. Palmer, *Police and Protest in England and Ireland, 1780–1850* (1988).

An overall view of social policy and reform is available in S. G. Checkland, *British Public Policy, 1776–1939* (1985). For the pressures to repeal the tariffs on grain, one may read N. McCord, *The Anti-Corn-Law League 1838–1846* (1958); and B. Hilton, *Corn, Cash, Commerce: The Economic Policies of the Tory Governments, 1815–1830* (1978). On the Reform Bill of 1832, M. Brock, *The Great Reform Act* (1973), is an outstanding study; and N. D. LoPatin, *Political Unions, Popular Politics, and the Great Reform Act of 1832* (1999), discusses the popular political mobilizations of this period.

Several books study the antislavery movement as part of this age of protest. Slavery as an institution is masterfully explored in several books by D. B. Davis, including for these years, *The Problem of Slavery in* the Age of Revolution, 1770–1823 (1975). The final phases of slavery in the Atlantic world are examined in R. Blackburn, *The Overthrow of Colonial Slavery* (1989); D. Eltis, *Economic Growth and the Ending of the Transatlantic Slave Trade* (1988); R. Anstey, *The Atlantic Slave Trade and British Abolition, 1760–1810* (1975); and S. Drescher's three books: *Econocide: British Slavery in the Era of Abolition* (1977), *Capitalism and Anti-Slavery: British Mobilization in Comparative Perspective* (1988), and *From Slavery to Freedom: Comparative Studies in the Rise and Fall of Atlantic Slavery* (1999). Other useful books on the antislavery movement include D. Turley, *The Culture of English Antislavery, 1780–1860* (1991) and J. Walvin, *Making the Black Atlantic: Britain and the African Diaspora* (2000), which provides a concise description of both the slave trade and the movement to abolish it.

For Britain after 1815 and the Victorian age that opened in 1837, the most informative synthesis is N. Gash, *Aristocracy and People: Britain, 1815–1865* (1979). A. Briggs, *The Age of Improvement, 1783–1867* (rev. 2000), and his other books on social history are also useful. Of special importance are J. W. Osborne, *The Silent Revolution: The Industrial Revolution in England as a Source of Culture Change* (1972); and H. Perkin, *The Origins of Modern English Society, 1780–1880* (1969, 1985).

Among the many biographies of the political leaders and reformers of the age, one may read F. A. Smith, *Lord Grey, 1764–1845* (1990); J. W. Derry, *Charles, Earl Grey: Aristocratic Reformer* (1992); N. Gash's outstanding study of Peel: *Mr. Secretary Peel and Sir Robert Peel* (2 vols.; rev. 1985); G.F.A. Best, *Shaftesbury* (1964); J. Pollock, *Wilberforce* (1978); J. Dyck, *William Cobbett and Rural Popular Protest* (1992); and N. C. Edsall, *Richard Cobden: Independent Radical* (1986). There are biographies of Robert Owen by G.D.H. Cole (rev. 1966) and M. I. Cole (1953, 1969). Radical social criticism is also studied in W. Stafford, *Socialism, Radicalism, and Nostalgia, 1775–1830* (1986). For women in the era one may turn to J. Perkin, *Victorian Women* (1993); and J. H. Murray, *Strongminded Women and Other Lost Voices from Nineteenth-Century England* (1982), a useful anthology of writings by and about women.

France, 1815–1848

Among accounts that begin in this era are A. Jardin and A.-J. Tudesq, *Restoration and Reaction, 1815–1848* (1973; trans. 1983); R. Magraw, *France, 1815–1914: The Bourgeois Century* (1983); J.P.T. Bury, *France, 1814–1940* (rev. 1986); R. Price, *A Social History of Nineteenth-Century France* (1988); W. Fortescue, *Revolution and Counter-Revolution in France, 1815–1852;* and R. Tombs, *France, 1814–1914* (1996). A helpful work of reference is E. L. Newman (ed.), *Historical Dictionary of France from the 1815 Revolution to the Second Empire* (2

vols.; 1987). Of special interest is F. Furet, *Revolutionary France, 1770–1880* (trans. 1992), which describes the struggle in the nineteenth century to absorb the changes introduced by the Revolution. For economic developments one may turn to F. Caron, *An Economic History of Modern France* (trans. 1979) and R. Price, *An Economic History of Modern France, 1730–1914* (1981). An insightful monograph illuminating the sexual division of labor in French rural industry is G. L. Gullickson, *The Spinners and Weavers of Auffray* (1986). The essays in K. S. Vincent and A. Klairmont-Lingo (eds.), *The Human Tradition in Modern France* (2000), covering the years 1789 to the present, seek to restore the human and personal element in French historical writing for these years.

For the years 1815–1830 G. de Bertier de Sauvigny, *The Bourbon Restoration* (trans. 1966) remains valuable, while S. Mellon, *The Uses of History: A Study of Historians in the French Restoration* (1958) and A. B. Spitzer, *The French Generation of 1820* (1987) add special insights. The evolving liberal movements of this era are discussed in L. Kramer, *Lafayette in Two Worlds* (1996), which also describes the links between France and America. Conservative ideas and activities are examined in P. Spencer, *Politics of Belief in Nineteenth-Century France* (1954); D. Porch, *Army and Revolution: France, 1815–1848* (1974); and R. Rémond, *The Right Wing in France: From 1815 to de Gaulle* (trans. 1966), useful for this period on into the twentieth century. An insightful study of an important conservative thinker is available in O. Bradley, *A Modern Maistre: The Social and Political Thought of Joseph de Maistre* (1999). For religion A. Dansette, *The Religious History of Modern France* (2 vols.; trans. 1961), may be supplemented by R. Gibson, *A Social History of French Catholicism, 1789–1914* (1989) and N. Ravitch, *The Catholic Church and the French Nation, 1685–1985* (1990).

The July Monarchy

For the revolutionary events of 1830 one may read D. H. Pinkney, *The French Revolution of 1830* (1972); P. Pilbeam, *The 1830 Revolution in France* (1991), an insightful analytical study rather than a narrative; and C. H. Church, *Europe in 1830: Revolution and Political Change* (1983), which places the revolution in its Europeanwide setting. For Louis Philippe's reign one may read H.A.C. Collingham, *The July Monarchy* (1988), a detailed political account, and D. H. Pinkney, *Decisive Years in France, 1840–1847* (1986), which presents the years of the July Monarchy as a watershed in French social and economic development. Labor and popular stirrings are examined in R. J. Bezucha, *The Lyon Uprising of 1834* (1974) and E. Berenson, *Populist Religion and Left-Wing Politics in France, 1830–1852* (1984).

An impressive study in cultural and social history focusing on the importance of the Revolution in the political culture and lives of the people is M. Agulhon, *The Republic in the Village: The People of the Var from the French Revolution to the Second Republic* (1971; trans. 1982). Newer approaches to social history are found also in W. H. Sewell, Jr., *The Language of Labor from the Old Regime to 1848* (1980) and two books by W. M. Reddy, *The Rise of Market Culture: The Textile Trade and French Society, 1750–1900* (1984) and *The Invisible Code: Honor and Sentiment in Postrevolutionary France, 1814–1848* (1997). P. N. Stearns explores class relationships in *Paths to Authority: The Middle Class and the Industrial Labor Force in France, 1820–1848* (1978). Studies in urban history include J. M. Merriman, *The Red City: Limoges and the French Nineteenth Century* (1985) and the *Margins of City Life: Explorations of the French Urban Frontier, 1815–1851* (1991); and W. H. Sewell, Jr., *Structure and Mobility: The Men and Women of Marseille, 1820–1870* (1985). L. Kramer, *Threshold of a New World: Intellectuals and the Exile Experience in Paris, 1830–1848* (1988), conveys the cultural vitality of the city as it appeared to exiles like Marx and others. An older study of importance is L. Chevalier, *Laboring Classes and Dangerous Classes in Paris during the First Half of the Nineteenth Century* (trans. 1973).

Biographical accounts of two historians who became important political leaders in these years are J.P.T. Bury and R. P. Tombs, *Thiers, 1797–1877* (1986) and D. Johnson, *Guizot: Aspects of French History, 1787–1874* (1963, 1975). For the last Bourbon king one may read V. D. Beach, *Charles X of France* (1971); and for Louis Philippe, T. Howarth, *Citizen-King* (1961).

Germany, 1815–1848

J. J. Sheehan, *German History, 1770–1866* (1990), is invaluable for these years. Also informative are W. Carr, *A History of Germany, 1815–1990* (1991) and H. James, *A German Identity, 1770–1990* (1990), perceptive on economic and other matters. Two important inquiries into the failure of German liberal democracy before 1914 are J. J. Sheehan, *German Liberalism in the Nineteenth Century* (1978) and J. L. Snell and H. A. Schmitt, *The Democratic Movement in Germany, 1789–1914* (1976). There are thoughtful essays in L. E. Jones and K. H. Jarausch (eds.), *In Search of a Liberal Germany: German Liberalism from 1789 to the Present* (1990).

Austria, Russia, Poland, Greece, Spain, Italy, and Other Countries

On the Habsburg monarchy after 1815, C. A. Macartney, *The Habsburg Empire, 1790–1918* (1969) is a masterful survey with full treatment of the nationalities. Recommended also are A. Wandruszka, *The House of Habsburg* (trans. 1964); R. A. Kann, *A History of the Habsburg Empire, 1526–1918* (1974); and

A. Steed, *The Decline and Fall of the Habsburg Empire 1815–1918* (1989). Foreign affairs are emphasized in B. Jelavich, *The Habsburg Empire in European Affairs, 1814–1918* (1969) and F. R. Bridge, *The Habsburg Monarchy among the Great Powers, 1815–1918* (1991). All aspects of Austrian history on into the twentieth century are ably treated in B. Jelavich, *Modern Austria: Empire and Republic, 1815–1986* (1987).

For Europe from the Baltic to the Aegean, R. Okey, *Eastern Europe, 1740–1985* (rev. 1987) covers these years. For Russia, two outstanding accounts are H. Seton-Watson, *The Russian Empire, 1801–1917* (1967) and D. Saunders, *Russia in the Age of Reaction and Reform, 1801–1881* (1993). On the life of the early nineteenth-century tsar, there is the work of J. M. Hartley, *Alexander I* (1994). A major study of Alexander's successor is W. B. Lincoln, *Nicholas I: Emperor and Autocrat of All the Russias* (1978). For these years, one may also read M. Zetling, *The Decembrists* (1985) and M. Raeff, *The Decembrist Movement* (1966), a narrative with documents. For Poland, one may turn to the second volume of N. Davies, *A History of Poland: God's Playground* (2 vols.; 1981); his briefer *Heart of Europe: A Short History of Poland* (1986); and P. Wandycz, *The Lands of Partitioned Poland 1795–1918* (1974).

For the Balkans in these years, informative volumes are B. Jelavich, *History of the Balkans* (2 vols.; 1983); B. Jelavich and C. Jelavich, *The Establishment of the Balkan National States, 1804–1920* (1980); and S. Pavlowitch, *A History of the Balkans, 1804–1945* (1999). For Greece, a balanced authoritative study is R. Clogg, *A Concise History of Greece* (1992). Stirrings in this period are described in C. M. Woodhouse, *The Greek War of Independence* (1952); D. Howarth, *The Greek Adventure* (1976); and R. Clogg (ed.), *The Struggle for Greek Independence* (1973), a collection of essays.

For the initial phases of the ferment in Italy good introductions are D. Beales, *The Risorgimento and the Unification of Italy* (1971); H. Hearder, *Italy in the Age of the Risorgimento, 1790–1870* (1983); S. Woolf, *A History of Italy, 1700–1860* (1986); and C. M. Lovett, *The Democratic Movement in Italy, 1830–1876* (1982).

For Belgium and the Dutch Netherlands in these and subsequent years, a discerning account by an eminent Dutch historian is E. H. Kossman, *The Low Countries, 1780–1940* (1978). The emerging importance of Belgium in international affairs is traced in J. E. Helmreich, *Belgium and Europe: A Study of Small-Power Diplomacy* (1976). For Spain, a balanced, comprehensive account is R. Carr, *Spain, 1808–1975* (rev. 1982).

Nineteenth-Century Thought

Two overall surveys carrying cultural and intellectual history forward to the twentieth century are

G. L. Mosse, *The Culture of Western Europe: The Nineteenth and Twentieth Centuries* (rev. 1988) and R. N. Stromberg, *European Intellectual History since 1789* (rev. 1994). A special theme is skillfully explored in O. Chadwick, *The Secularization of the European Mind in the Nineteenth Century* (1976). Older general works include P. Roubiczek, *The Misrepresentation of Man: Studies in European Thought in the Nineteenth Century* (1947); M. Peckham, *Beyond the Tragic Vision: The Quest for Identity in the Nineteenth Century* (1962); and M. Mandelbaum, *History, Man, and Reason: A Study of Nineteenth-Century Thought* (1971).

Among the many books on Hegel and Hegelian thought one may turn to L. Dickey, *Hegel: Religion, Economics, and the Politics of Spirit, 1770–1807* (1987); T. Pinkard, *Hegel: A Biography* (2000); and J. E. Toews, *Hegelianism: The Path toward Dialectical Humanism 1805–1841* (1985).

The "Isms"

On the nature of ideology, the best introduction is D. McLellan, *Ideology* (1986). Also helpful are G. Rudé, *Ideology and Popular Protest* (1980); and for political alignments, D. Caute, *The Left in Europe since 1789* (1966); and H. Rogger and E. Weber (eds.), *The European Right: A Historical Profile* (1965).

The vast literature on nationalism, including many older studies by C.J.H. Hayes and H. Kohn, may be approached through B. C. Shafer, *Faces of Nationalism* (1972); E. J. Hobsbawm, *Nations and Nationalism since 1780* (rev. 1992); E. Gellner, *Nations and Nationalism* (1983); A. D. Smith, *The Ethnic Origins of Nations* (1986) and *National Identity* (1991); and L. Kramer, *Nationalism: Political Cultures in Europe and America, 1775–1865* (1998). A useful collection of essays is available in G. Eley and R. G. Suny (eds.), *Becoming National: A Reader* (1996). B. Anderson's book, *Imagined Communities: Reflections on the Origin and Spread of Nationalism* (rev. 1991), has contributed an influential conceptual framework for much of the recent scholarship on nationalist movements. An impressive comparative work on nationalism, studying England, the United States, France, Germany, and Russia, is L. Greenfeld, *Nationalism: Five Roads to Modernity* (1992).

Political and other meanings of romanticism are examined from diverse political perspectives in J. Barzun, *Classic, Romantic, and Modern* (rev. 1961, 1975) and *Berlioz and the Romantic Century* (1950, 1982); M. H. Abrams, *Natural Supernaturalism: Tradition and Revolution in Romantic Literature* (1971); J. McGann, *The Romantic Ideology: A Critical Investigation* (1983); N. Rosenblum, *Another Liberalism: Romanticism and the Reconstruction of Liberal Thought* (1987); and N. V. Riasanovsky, *The Emergence of Romanticism* (1992).

For classical liberalism, a thoughtful introduction is J. Gray, *Liberalism* (rev. 1995), which may be read along with A. Arblaster, *The Rise and Decline of Western Liberalism* (1984); J. G. Merquior, *Liberalism, Old and New* (1991); and J. Rawls, *Political Liberalism* (1992), a searching philosophical inquiry. An influential earlier account was H. J. Laski, *The Rise of European Liberalism* (1936). An insightful collection of essays by Isaiah Berlin, *The Crooked Timber of Humanity* (1990, 1998), stresses a liberal's suspicion of utopian schemes to change human beings in revolutionary ways. Two useful anthologies are A. Bullock and M. Shock (eds.), *The Liberal Tradition* (1957) and D. Sidorsky (ed.), *The Liberal Tradition in European Thought* (1970).

Among books on the leading exemplar of classical liberalism, one may read R. J. Halliday, *John Stuart Mill* (1976), a brief introductory account; G. Himmelfarb, *On Liberty and Liberalism: The Case of John Stuart Mill* (1974); B. Semmel, *John Stuart Mill and the Pursuit of Virtue* (1984); D. F. Thompson, *John Stuart Mill and Representative Government* (1976); and the unsympathetic M. Cowling, *Mill and Liberalism* (rev. 1990). Other useful works include J. Skorupski, *The Cambridge Companion to Mill* (1998), an excellent collection of essays, and W. Stafford, *John Stuart Mill* (1998), a concise analysis of Mill's life and thought. In an area where Mill and his wife pioneered, A. Rossi has edited *John Stuart Mill and Harriet Taylor Mill, Essays on Sex Equality* (1970). Mill and others are studied in S. R. Letwin, *The Pursuit of Certainty: David Hume, Jeremy Bentham, John Stuart Mill, Beatrice Webb* (1963). Bentham is also studied in a biography by M. Mack (1963) and in a brief appraisal by J. Dinwiddy (1989). For the French setting an admirable study is G. A. Kelly, *The Humane Comedy: Constant, Toqueville, and French Liberalism* (1992), which may be supplemented by B. Fontana, *Benjamin Constant and the Post-Revolutionary Mind* (1991).

For the persistence of conservatism one may read P. Viereck, *Conservatism Revisited: The Revolt against Revolt, 1815–1949* (rev. 1965); J. Weiss, *Conservatism in Europe, 1770–1945* (1977); R. A. Nisbet, *Conservatism: Dream and Reality* (1986); and T. Honderich, *Conservatism* (1991).

Good starting places for the study of the socialist and revolutionary tradition are F. E. Manuel, *The Prophets of Paris: Turgot, Condorcet, Saint-Simon, Fourier, Comte* (1962), which stresses the link between Enlightenment ideas and nineteenth-century social thought, and J. H. Billington, *Fire in the Minds of Men: Origins of the Revolutionary Faith* (1980), which focuses on the more conspiratorial revolutionaries. F. E. Manuel and F. P. Manuel masterfully trace an important theme in *Utopian Thought in the Western World* (1979), which may be supplemented with K. Kumar, *Utopia and Anti-Utopia in Modern Times* (1987).

Books on Marx and Marxism will be cited in the following chapter. The best one-volume introduction to the origins and evolution of socialism is A. S. Lindemann, *A History of European Socialism* (1983). Informative also are L. Derfler, *Socialism since Marx: A Century of the European Left* (1973) and W. Lerner, *A History of Socialism and Communism in Modern Times* (rev. 1994). G. Lichtheim, *The Origins of Socialism (1969), A Short History of Socialism* (1970), and his other writings are especially valuable. Two large-scale comprehensive studies are G.D.H. Cole, *A History of Socialist Thought* (4 vols.; 1953–1956), covering the years 1789–1939; and C. Landauer and others, *European Socialism* (2 vols.; 1960), which covers about the same years. Utopian socialists are studied in two excellent books by J. F. Beecher: *Charles Fourier: The Visionary and His World* (1987) and *Victor Considérant and the Rise and Fall of French Romantic Socialism* (2001). Other early socialists are examined in F. E. Manuel, *The New World of Henri Saint-Simon* (1956); G. G. Iggers, *The Cult of Authority: The Political Cult of the Saint-Simonians* (1958); and R. B. Carlisle, *The Proffered Crown: Saint Simonianism and the Doctrine of Hope* (1987).

Early feminist thought is discussed in J. Rendall, *The Origins of Modern Feminism: Women in Britain, France and the United States, 1780–1860* (1985); M. LeGates, *Making Waves: A History of Feminism in Western Society* (1996); and C. G. Moses and L. W. Rabine, *Feminism, Socialism, and French Romanticism* (1993), a valuable book that includes long excerpts from the texts of early feminist authors. Recent biographies on important women writers in this era include S. Grogan, *Flora Tristan* (1998); B. Jack, *George Sand* (2000); R. Bolster, *Marie d'Agoult: the Rebel Countess* (2001); and P. Stock-Morton, *The Life of Marie d'Agoult, alias Daniel Stern* (2001).

On the link between socialism and women activists, one may read M. J. Boxer and J. H. Quataert (eds.), *Socialist Women: European Socialist Feminism in the Nineteenth and Early Twentieth Centuries* (1978), and other books to be cited in Chapter 15. A. Fried and R. Sanders, *Socialist Thought: A Documentary History* (rev. 1993) and I. Howe (ed.), *Essential Works of Socialism* (1976) are handy anthologies.

Economic Thought

An innovative and rewarding book is M. Berg, *The Machinery Question and the Making of Political Economy, 1815–1848* (1980). J. K. Galbraith, *The Age of Uncertainty* (1977) is a sprightly series of essays on economic thinkers from Adam Smith to the present; and R. Heilbroner, *The Worldly Philosophers* (rev. 1999) is useful on the economic liberals. For Adam Smith's moral and economic ideas, an especially thoughtful overview is J. Z. Muller, *Adam Smith in His Time and Ours: Designing the Decent Society* (1992); informative also are D. A. Riesman, *Adam Smith's Sociological Economics* (1976); D. Winch, *Adam Smith's Politics* (1978); and P. H. Werhane, *Adam Smith and His Legacy for Modern Capitalism* (1991). For Malthus, a useful biographical account is P. James, *Population Malthus: His Life and Times* (1979), while S. Hollander, *The Economics of Thomas Robert Malthus* (1996) analyzes his ideas.

International Affairs after the Congress of Vienna

For diplomacy and international affairs, two valuable surveys are F. R. Bridge and R. Bullen, *The Great Powers and the European States System, 1851–1914* (1980) and N. Rich, *Great Power Diplomacy, 1815–1914* (1980). An important reevaluation is P. W. Schroeder, *The Transformation of European Politics, 1763–1848* (1994), which sees the era after 1815 not as a restoration but as a revolutionary transformation of international relations; Schroeder has also written *Metternich's Diplomacy at Its Zenith, 1820–1823* (1962). H. Kissinger, the former American Secretary of State, author of *A World Restored: Metternich, Castlereagh, and the Problem of Peace, 1812–1822* (1957), revisits the post-1815 years in his more recent *Diplomacy* (1994). In addition to older studies by C. K. Webster and other historians of the era of Castlereagh and Palmerston, one may turn to C. J. Bartlett, *Castlereagh* (1967); J. Derry, *Castlereagh* (1976); W. Hinde, *George Canning* (1989); D. Southgate, *"The Most English Minister": The Policies and Politics of Palmerston* (1966); and K. Bourne, *Palmerston: The Early Years* (1982). American foreign policy in these years is assessed in B. Perkins, *The Creation of a Republican Empire, 1776–1865* (1993).

The involvement of the European powers and the United States in Latin America is studied in R. Miller, *Britain and Latin American in the Nineteenth and Twentieth Centuries* (1993); D. Perkins, *A History of the Monroe Doctrine* (1941, 1963); and E. R. May, *The Making of the Monroe Doctrine* (1975). A special perspective is provided in J. J. Johnson, *A Hemisphere Apart: The Foundations of United States Policy toward Latin America* (1990), which focuses on the years 1815–1830. For all aspects of the colonial revolutions one may turn to J. Lynch, *The Spanish American Revolutions, 1808–1821* (rev. 1986); M. P. Costeloe, *Response to Revolution: Imperial Spain and the Spanish American Revolutions, 1810–1840* (1986); and the chapters in Vol. III of L. Bethell (ed.), *The Cambridge History of Latin America* (1988). Biographical studies are available in J. B. Trend, *Bolívar and the Independence of Spanish America* (1968); J. L. Salcedo-Bastardo, *Bolívar: A Continent and its Destiny* (trans. 1977); and J. Kinsbrunner, *Bernardo O'Higgins* (1968).

Problems and Readings

P. N. Stearns (ed.), *A Century for Debate: Problems in the Interpretation of European History, 1789–1914* (1969) and G. Rudé, *Debate on Europe, 1815–1850* (1972), summarize historiographical debates on many issues. A stimulating examination of one such issue in the American and British setting is T. Bender (ed.), *The Antislavery Debate: Capitalism and Abolitionism as a Problem in Historical Interpretation* (1992).

Specialized pamphlets include G. A. Cahill (ed.), *The Great Reform Bill of 1832: Liberal or Conservative?* (1969); J. M. Merriman (ed.), *1830 in France* (1976); J. B. Halsted (ed.), *Romanticism: Definition, Explanation, and Evaluation* (1965); H. F. Schwarz (ed.), *Metternich: The "Coachman of Europe": Statesman or Evil Genius?* (1962); M. Walker (ed.), *Metternich's Europe, 1815–1848* (1968); and E. E. Kraehe (ed.), *The Metternich Controversy* (1971).

Social and economic themes are explored in P.A.M. Taylor (ed.), *The Industrial Revolution in Britain: Triumph or Disaster?* (rev. 1970); A. J. Taylor (ed.), *The Standard of Living in Britain in the Industrial Revolution* (1975); L. R. Berlanstein (ed.), *The Industrial Revolution and Work in Nineteenth Century Europe* (1992); M. L. McDougall (ed.), *The Working Class in Modern Europe* (1975); and A. Lees and L. Lees (eds.), *The Urbanization of European Society in the Nineteenth Century* (1976). P. N. Stearns, *Interpreting the Industrial Revolution* (1991), helps place the changes in comparative perspective. Many of the readings in the Anvil series and their introductory essays remain useful: H. Kohn, *Nationalism: Its Meaning and History* (1965, 1982); P. Viereck, *Conservatism: From John Adams to Churchill* (1956); J. S. Schapiro, *Liberalism: Its Meaning and History* (1958); J. H. Stewart, *The Restoration Era in France, 1814–1830* (1968); and P. Beik, *Louis Philippe and the July Monarchy* (1965). On Latin American subjects, two titles in the same series are R. A. Humphreys and J. Lynch, *The Origins of the Latin Americans Revolutions, 1808–1826* (1967) and J. J. Johnson, *Simón Bolívar and Spanish-American Independence, 1783–1830* (1968, 1992).

12. REVOLUTION AND THE REIMPOSITION OF ORDER, 1848–1870

A useful synthesis for the revolutions of 1848 is W. L. Langer, *Political and Social Upheaval, 1832–1852* (1969). Other informative studies include P. N. Stearns, *1848: The Revolutionary Tide in Europe* (1974); J. Sigman, *1848: The Romantic and Democratic Revolutions in Europe* (trans. 1973); J. Sperber, *The European Revolutions, 1848–1851* (1994); and the essays in R.J.W. Evans and H. P. Von Strandmann, *The Revolutions in Europe, 1848–1849* (2000). Of special interest is L. B. Namier, *1848: The Revolution of the*

Intellectuals (1946, 1992), which sees the events in central and eastern Europe as ushering in an age of nationalism, not of liberalism. E. J. Hobsbawm continues his provocative triology for the years 1789–1914 with *The Age of Capital, 1848–1875* (1976). A.J.P. Taylor, *The Struggle for Mastery in Europe, 1848–1918* (1954), remains unequalled as a study of international affairs for these years.

Revolutions in Various Countries

FRANCE. General histories include G. Duveau, *The Making of a Revolution* (trans. 1968); F. A. De Luna, *France under Cavaignac* (1969); and R. Price, *The French Second Republic: A Social History* (1972). Informative also are the essays edited by R. Price, *Revolution and Reaction: 1848 and the Second French Republic* (1976), while M. Agulhon, *The Republic Experiment, 1848–1852* (1983) subtly examines republican and revolutionary symbolism.

Studies offering insights into popular militancy include P. H. Amann, *Revolutions and Mass Democracy: The Paris Club Movement in 1848* (1976); M. Traugott, *The Armies of the Poor* (1985); J. W. Merriman, *The Agony of the Republic: The Repression of the Left in Revolutionary France, 1848–1851* (1978); and T. W. Margadant, *French Peasants in Revolt: The Insurrection of 1851* (1979).

HABSBURG LANDS. For Austria there are several volumes on the Habsburg empire cited in Chapter 11, but for more specific studies of Francis Joseph and his long reign from 1848 to 1916 one may read A. Palmer, *Twilight of the Habsburgs: The Life and Times of Emperor Francis Joseph* (1995) and S. Beller, *Francis Joseph* (1996).

For the empire in revolt one may read R. J. Rath, *The Viennese Revolution of 1848–49* (1957); S. Z. Pech, *The Czech Revolution of 1848–1849* (1979); B. K. Kiraly, *Ferenc Deák* (1975); and I. Deák, *The Lawful Revolution: Louis Kossuth and the Hungarians, 1848–1849* (1979), a vivid account. The end of the revolution is described in A. Sked, *The Survival of the Habsburg Empire* (1979) and I. W. Roberts, *Nicholas I and the Russian Intervention in Hungary* (1991).

ITALY. Books on the beginnings of the Risorgimento have been cited in Chapter 11; others on unification will be described in the chapter that follows. Studies relevant to 1848 are G. M. Trevelyan's classic account, *Garibaldi's Defense of the Roman Republic, 1848–1849* (1907, 1949); and P. Ginsborg, *Daniele Manin and the Venetian Revolution of 1848–49* (1979). There is also useful information on the people and events of this era in J. A. Davis (ed.), *Italy in the Nineteenth Century: 1796–1900* (2000).

GERMANY AND THE FRANKFURT ASSEMBLY. In addition to L. B. Namier, *1848: The Revolution of the Intellec-*

tuals (1946, 1992), cited earlier, which is sharply critical of the Frankfurt Assembly, informative studies include E. Eyck, *The Frankfurt Parliament, 1848–1949* (1968), a detailed account of the assembly itself; and J. Sperber, *Rhineland Radicals: The Democratic Movement and the Revolution of 1848–1849* (1991), which focuses on the more radical elements in the revolution.

ENGLAND AND IRELAND. The confrontations with both Chartism and Irish nationalism are recounted in J. Saville, *1848: The British State and the Chartist Movement* (1987). A special subject is graphically treated in C. B. Woodham-Smith, *The Great Hunger: Ireland 1845–1849* (1962).

Marx and Marxism

D. McLellan, *Karl Marx: A Biography* (rev. 1995), is an outstanding account of Marx's life and thought; other insightful studies include J. Seigel, *Marx's Fate: The Shape of a Life* (1978, 1993); I. Berlin, *Karl Marx: His Life and Environment* (rev. 1996); S. K. Padover, *Karl Marx: An Intimate Biography* (1978); and B. Mazlish, *The Meaning of Karl Marx* (1984). An amusing but overly flippant account is F. Wheen, *Karl Marx: A Life* (2000). Helpful for the life and thought of Engels are studies by S. Marcus (1974); D. McLellan (1978); T. Carver (1990); J. D. Hunley (1990), and S. H. Rigby (1992).

On Marxism and the theoretical foundations of socialism, there is an enormous and controversial literature, to which the books cited for the beginnings of socialism in Chapter 11 and for the years after 1870 in Chapter 15 may offer some additional guidance. Recommended studies include J. Elster, *An Introduction to Karl Marx* (1986); R. N. Hunt, *The Political Ideas of Marx and Engels* (2 vols.; 1976–1984); R. Tucker, *The Marxian Revolutionary Idea* (1969) and *Philosophy and Myth in Karl Marx* (rev. 1972); G. Lichtheim, *Marxism: An Historical and Critical Study* (1961); and S. Avinieri, *The Social and Political Thought of Karl Marx* (1968, 1990). The intellectual context that shaped Marx's early work is examined in W. Breckman, *Marx, The Young Hegelians and the Origins of Radical Social Theory* (1999).

E. Wilson's older book, *To the Finland Station: A Study in the Writing and Acting of History* (1940), is an imaginative discussion of the use of history by socialists and non-socialists. Insights into the Marxist interpretation of history are provided in G. A. Cohen, *Karl Marx's Theory of History: A Defense* (1978), an especially cogent analysis; W. H. Shaw, *Marx's Theory of History* (1978); and M. Rader, *Marx's Interpretation of History* (1979). R. Williams, *Marxism and Literature* (1977), demonstrates one aspect of the wider applicability of Marx's theories.

For Auguste Comte and positivism there are available A. R. Standley, *Auguste Comte* (1981), the best brief introduction; M. Pickering, *Auguste Comte: An Intellectual Biography* (1992); W. M. Simon, *European Positivism in the Nineteenth Century* (1963); D. G. Charlton, *Positivist Thought in France during the Second Empire* (1959); and T. R. Wright, *The Religion of Humanity: The Impact of Comtean Positivism on Victorian Britain* (1986). G. Lenzer has edited *Auguste Comte and Positivism: The Essential Writings* (1975).

Napoleon III and Bonapartism

The best overview is A. Plessis, *The Rise and Fall of the Second Empire, 1852–1871* (trans. 1985). Other informative accounts are J. M. Thompson, *Louis Napoleon and the Second Empire* (1954, 1967); G. P. Gooch, *The Second Empire* (1960), a collection of judicious essays; J.P.T. Bury, *Napoleon III and the Second Empire* (1964); B. D. Gooch, *The Reign of Napoleon III* (1969); and W.H.C. Smith, *Second Empire and Commune: France, 1848–1871* (rev. 1996), which emphasizes the regime's disastrous foreign policy and collapse. A useful reference tool is W. E. Echard (ed.), *Historical Dictionary of the French Second Empire* (1985).

Biographical treatments include T.A.B. Corley, *Democratic Despot: A Life of Napoleon III* (1961); W.H.C. Smith, *Napoleon III* (1973); J. F. McMillan, *Napoleon III* (1991); and F. Bresler, *Napoleon III* (1999). There are three evocative explorations of the age by R. L. Williams: *The World of Napoleon III* (1957), *The Mortal Napoleon III* (1971), and *Manners and Murders in the World of Louis Napoleon* (1975); and a study by D. Bagley, *Napoleon III and His Regime: An Extravaganza* (2001). On the reconstruction of Paris in these years, one may read D. H. Pinkney, *Napoleon III and the Rebuilding of Paris* (1958) and D. P. Jordan, *Transforming Paris: The Life and Labors of Baron Haussmann* (1995). A scholarly effort to rehabilitate the empress is H. Kurtz, *The Empress Eugénie, 1826–1920* (1964), which may be supplemented by N. N. Barker, *Distaff Diplomacy: The Empress Eugénie and the Foreign Policy of the Second Empire* (1967). Tendencies in later years to praise Napoleon III for presiding over political stability and material progress are explored in S. L. Campbell, *The Second Empire Revisited: A Study in French Historiography* (1978).

Problems and Readings

Useful booklets include M. Kranzberg (ed.), *1848: A Turning Point?* (1959); S. M. Osgood (ed.), *Napoleon III and the Second Empire* (1973); and D. G. Gooch (ed.), *Napoleon III, Man of Destiny: Enlightened Statesman or Proto-Fascist?* (1963, 1976). In the Anvil and other series, there are G. Bruun, *Revolution and Reaction, 1848–1852* (1958); W.H.C. Smith, *France, 1848–1871* (1985); G. Fasel, *European*

Upheaval: The Revolutions of 1848 (1970); and P. Jones, *The 1848 Revolutions* (1992). R. Price (ed.), *Documents on the French Revolution of 1848* (1996), provides useful sources. R. Tucker has edited *The Marx-Engels Reader* (rev. 1978), an anthology with thoughtful introductions, while J. Elster (ed.), *Karl Marx: A Reader* (1986), is organized thematically.

13. THE CONSOLIDATION OF LARGE NATION-STATES, 1859–1871

J.P.T. Bury (ed.), *The Zenith of European Power, 1830–1871* (1966), cited in Chapter 11, offers many informative chapters; and N. Rich, *The Age of Nationalism and Reform, 1850–1890* (1970), provides a balanced synthesis. Analytical books on nationalism have been cited in Chapter 11.

The Crimean War

For the war itself and its complexities one may read A. Palmer, *The Banner of Battle, The Story of the Crimean War* (1987); T. Royle, *Crimea: The Great Crimean War, 1854–1856* (2001); and earlier accounts by L.F.V. Blake (1972) and P. Warner (1973). The diplomatic aspects are studied in W. Baumgart: *The Peace of Paris, 1856* (1981); N. Rich, *Why the Crimean War? A Cautionary Tale* (1985); D. Wetzel, *The Crimean War: A Diplomatic History* (1985); and D. M. Goldfrank, *The Origins of the Crimean War* (1993). An impressive book rehabilitating Austrian policy is P. W. Schroeder, *Austria, Great Britain, and the Crimean War: The Destruction of the European Concert* (1972), while J. S. Curtiss, *Russia's Crimean War* (1979), sees the Western powers as more responsible than Russia for the outbreak. The famous "Charge of the Light Brigade" is skillfully recounted in C. B. Woodham-Smith, *The Reason Why* (1953); and the same author has written a biography of Florence Nightingale (1951). For the founding spirit behind modern nursing two more recent biographies are available by H. Small (2000) and by B. Dossey (2001), the latter stressing her spiritual qualities.

Unification of Italy

To the books on unification that have already been cited should be added F. J. Cappa, *The Origins of the Italian Wars of Independence* (1992) and the concise account by L. Riall, *The Italian Risorgimento* (1994). For the unification leaders, D. Mack Smith has written the most informative studies: *Cavour and Garibaldi in 1860* (1954, 1985); *Giuseppe Garibaldi* (1956); *Cavour* (1985), which is critical of the Piedmontese stateman's opportunism; and *Mazzini* (1994). One may also read C. Hibbert, *Garibaldi and His Enemies* (1966), a vivid popular account; and J. Ridley, *Garibaldi* (1975), a detailed, authoritative study. An outstanding history of Italy after unification is D. Mack

Smith, *Modern Italy* (rev. 1997). The same author's *Italy and Its Monarchy* (1990) is an unflattering portrait of the House of Savoy.

Bismarck and the Founding of the Second Reich

G. A. Craig, *Germany, 1866–1945* (1978) is a masterful account covering the years from Bismarck to Hitler, with many insights into German society and culture; a companion volume, *The Germans* (1982), equally perceptive, is a series of thematic essays; and the same author's *The Politics of the Prussian Army, 1640–1945* (1956, 1964) is as useful for the nineteenth and twentieth centuries as for the earlier years.

For Bismarck two comprehensive accounts are O. Pflanze, *Bismarck and the Development of Germany* (3 vols.; 1990), demonstrating how Bismarck controlled the dynamic social and economic forces of his day; and L. Gall, *Bismarck: The White Revolutionary* (2 vols.; trans. 1986–1987). E. Eyck, *Bismarck and the German Empire* (1950, 1984), summarizes this German historian's larger critical work. Other biographical accounts include A. Palmer, *Bismarck* (1976), a judicious, well-balanced account; A.J.P. Taylor, *Bismarck: The Man and the Statesman* (1955, 1987), less judicious but provocative; and J. E. Rose, *Bismarck* (1987). W. N. Medlicott, *Bismarck and Modern Germany* (1965) and D. G. Williamson, *Bismarck and Germany, 1862–1890* (rev. 1998) are useful brief introductions. B. Waller, *Bismarck* (rev. 1997) is an informative essay. G. O. Kent, *Bismarck and His Times* (1978) is especially useful for the historiographical debate on Bismarck.

Social and economic aspects of unification are studied in W. O. Henderson, *The Rise of German Industrial Power, 1834–1914* (1976) and T. S. Hamerow, *The Social Foundations of German Unification, 1858–1871* (2 vols.; 1969–1972). An interesting account of Bismarck's Jewish financial adviser, illuminating much of German history during these years, is F. Stern, *Gold and Iron: Bismarck, Bleichröder, and the Building of the German Empire* (1977). W. J. Mommsen, *Imperial Germany, 1867–1918* (trans. 1995) is a collection of essays by an influential German historian.

For the events of 1870–1871, recommended studies include W. Carr, *The Origins of the Wars of German Unification* (1991); L. D. Steefel, *Bismarck, the Hohenzollern Candidacy, and the Origins of the Franco-German War of 1870* (1962); and M. Howard, *The Franco-Prussian War: The German Invasion of France, 1870–1871* (1967, 1981), a major study of the war and related events.

Austria-Hungary

For the Compromise of 1867 and the creation of the Dual Monarchy, the volumes by C. A. Macartney and other studies cited in Chapter 11, will be helpful. W. S. Johnston, *The Austrian Mind: An Intellectual and Social History* (1976) covers broad aspects of Austrian life, while Jewish contributions to Habsburg culture and society are sympathetically assessed in R. S. Wistrich, *The Jews of Vienna in the Age of Franz Joseph* (1989); S. Beller, *Vienna and the Jews* (1989); and W. O. McCagg, Jr., *A History of Habsburg Jews, 1670–1918* (1993). For the military, there are studies by G. E. Rothenberg, *The Army of Francis Joseph* (1976); and I. Deák, *Beyond Nationalism: A Social and Political History of the Habsburg Officer Corps, 1848–1918* (1990), which illuminates the Dual Monarchy in many other ways. For Hungary, G. Szabod, *Hungarian Political Trends between the Revolution and the Compromise, 1849–1867* (1977) provides insights into Magyar politics and society, while J. K. Hoensch, *A History of Modern Hungary, 1867–1994* (1996) carries the story forward in time.

The Russia of Alexander II, 1855–1881

An authoritative treatment for these years is provided in D. Saunders, *Russia in the Age of Reaction and Reform, 1801–1881* (1992), cited in Chapter 11, and R. Pipes, *Russia under the Old Regime* (1974). On the reign of the last five rulers from Alexander I to Nicholas II, S. Harcave has written *Years of the Golden Cockerel: The Last Romanov Tsars, 1814–1917* (1968), a subject covered also in the latter portions of W. B. Lincoln, *The Romanovs: Autocrats of All the Russias* (1981).

On the reforms of Alexander II, one may turn to W. E. Mosse, *Alexander II and the Modernization of Russia* (1958) and D. Lieven, *Russia's Rulers Under the Old Regime* (1989), which describes Alexander's efficient bureaucracy. The peasant emancipation may be studied in J. Blum, *The End of the Old Order in Rural Europe* (1978); G. T. Robinson, *Rural Russia under the Old Regime* (1930, 1980); and T. Emmons, *The Russian Landed Gentry and the Peasant Emancipation of 1861* (1968).

For the activist world of nineteenth-century Russia and the world of the Russian exiles there is a helpful synthesis: F. Venturi, *A History of the Populist and Socialist Movements in Nineteenth-Century Russia* (trans. 1983); and many special studies, among them E. H. Carr, *The Romantic Exiles: A Nineteenth Century Portrait Gallery* (1933, 1949) and *Michael Bakunin* (1937); M. A. Miller, *The Russian Revolutionary Emigrés 1825–1870* (1986); A. P. Mendel, *Michael Bakunin: Roots of Apocalypse* (1982); M. E. Malia, *Alexander Herzen and the Birth of Russian Socialism* (1961); V. Broido, *Apostles into Terrorists: Women and the Revolutionary Movement in the Russia of Alexander II* (1977); and I. Berlin, *Russian Thinkers* (1978), which is especially rewarding.

United States

The Civil War and Reconstruction have been the subject of many histories, but two books present each with remarkable narrative skill and analytical insight: J. M. McPherson, *Battle Cry of Freedom: The Civil War Era* (1988) and E. Foner, *Reconstruction: America's Unfinished Revolution, 1863–1877* (1988). The essays in S. Forster and S. Nagler (eds.), *On the Road to Total War: The American Civil War and the German Wars of Unification, 1861–1871* (1997), model studies in comparative history, demonstrate the origins of twentieth-century warfare in these two conflicts.

Books by D. B. Davis and others on slavery and the slave trade as a Western institution have been cited earlier. To them may be added O. Patterson, *Slavery and Social Death: A Comparative Study* (1982), which examines the institution and practice in various cultures and eras. A large literature has developed on the slave experience in North America, which P. Kolchin, *American Slavery, 1619–1877* (1993), skillfully synthesizes; the same author has also written an outstanding comparative study, *Unfree Labor: American Slavery and Russian Serfdom* (1987). Two leading examples of the literature on American slavery are E. D. Genovese, *Roll, Jordan, Roll: The World the Slaves Made* (1974) and H. G. Gutman, *The Black Family in Slavery and Freedom, 1750–1925* (1976). Two informative surveys of African-American history are J. H. Franklin and A. A. Moss, Jr., *From Slavery to Freedom: A History of African Americans* (rev. 2000) and M. F. Berry and J. Blassingame, *Long Memory: The Black Experience in America* (1982).

Canada, Australia, New Zealand

Informative introductions to the history of Canada include M. Conrad and others, *History of the Canadian Peoples* (2 vols.; 1993), the volumes dividing at 1867; G. Woodcock, *A Social History of Canada* (1988); J. L. Granatstein and others, *Nation: Canada since Confederation* (rev. 1991); and J. L. Finlay and D. N. Sprague, *The Structure of Canadian History* (2 vols.; 1992), which is especially insightful. The growth of Canadian self-government within an imperial framework is described in J. M. Ward, *Colonial Self-Government: The British Experience, 1759–1856* (1976); and the emergence of the dominion idea, beginning in these years, is comprehensively treated in W. D. McIntyre, *The Commonwealth of Nations: Origins and Impact, 1869–1971* (1977). *The Encyclopedia of Canada* (4 vols.; 1988) is a valuable reference tool. The Australian story is ably recounted in S. Macintyre, *A Concise History of Australia* (1999); G. Blainey, *A Shorter History of Australia* (1994); and J. Rickard, *Australia: A Cultural History* (rev. 1996). A valuable reference tool is J. Bassett, *The Oxford Illustrated Dictionary of Australian History* (1993).

The wider regional history is discussed in D. Denoon, P. Mein-Smith, and M. Wyndham, *A History of Australia, New Zealand and the Pacific* (2000). An excellent introduction to New Zealand is G. W. Rice (ed.), *The Oxford History of New Zealand* (rev. 1992).

Japan and the West

Two books by C. Totman provide comprehensive overviews of Japan before and during the modern era: *Early Modern Japan* (1993) and *A History of Japan* (2000). Other informative histories include E. O. Reischauer, *Japan: The Story of a Nation* (rev. 1989); W. G. Beasley, *The Rise of Modern Japan* (rev. 1995); and M. B. Jansen, *The Making of Modern Japan* (2000).

The best account of the Meiji era is W. G. Beasley's *The Meiji Restoration* (1972), but it may be supplemented by K. B. Pyle, *The Making of Modern Japan* (rev. 1996) and C. Gluck, *Japan's Modern Myths: Ideology in the Late Meiji Period* (1985). For the Japanese occupation of Korea, P. Duus, *The Abacus and the Sword: The Japanese Penetration of Korea, 1895–1900* (1998) is rewarding.

Problems and Readings

For an overall perspective, H. Kohn (ed.), *Nationalism and Realism, 1852–1879* (1968) is still useful, as is B. D. Gooch (ed.), *The Origins of the Crimean War* (1969). For Italy there are available C. F. Delzell (ed.), *The Unification of Italy, 1859–1861* (1965); M. Morrogh, *The Unification of Italy* (1991), with key documents; and M. Clark, The Italian Risorgimento (1998). For Germany one may turn to T. S. Hamerow (ed.), *Otto von Bismarck: A Historical Assessment* (rev. 1994); O. Pflanze (ed.), *The Unification of Germany, 1848–1871* (1979); and M. Gorman (ed.), *The Unification of Germany* (1989). For Austria-Hungary, H. J. Gordon and N. M. Gordon, *The Austrian Empire: Abortive Federation?* (1975), is helpful.

14. EUROPEAN CIVILIZATION, 1871–1914: ECONOMY AND POLITICS

Books on cultural and social history are mainly described in Chapter 15, but many titles overlap. Two older volumes that help to provide a synthesis for these years are C.J.H. Hayes, *A Generation of Materialism, 1871–1900* (1941, 1983), portraying the dual nature of the age as climax of enlightenment and seedtime of future turmoil; and O. J. Hale, *The Great Illusion, 1900–1914* (1971), exploring the many accomplishments of the early twentieth-century years and the widespread belief in continuing peace and progress. E. J. Hobsbawm completes his books on the years 1789–1914 with *The Age of Empire, 1875–1914* (1988), useful also for the two chapters that follow. The early chapters of J. Joll, *Europe Since 1870* (rev. 1990) are helpful for this period. G. Barraclough, *An*

Introduction to Contemporary History (1964), a provocative essay, emphasizes the need for a global approach to the years since 1890, a theme developed at length in J. Romein, *The Watershed of Two Eras: Europe in 1900* (trans. 1978). Also of interest is N. Stone, *Europe Transformed, 1878–1919* (rev. 1999).

There are informative chapters in F. H. Hinsley (ed.), *Material Progress and Worldwide Problems, 1870–1898* (1962) and C. L. Mowat (ed.), *The Shifting Balance of World Forces, 1898–1945* (rev. 1968). C. Nicholls (ed.), *Power: A Political History of the Twentieth Century* (1990) and S. Pollard (ed.), *An Economic History of the Twentieth Century* (1990) begin with these years.

The European and World Economy

For Europe, economic and social development is studied in F. B. Tipton and R. Aldrich, *An Economic and Social History of Europe, 1890–1939* (1987), with a sequel volume for later years. For industrial growth on the Continent, one may also turn to A. S. Milward and S. B. Saul, *The Development of the Economies of Continental Europe, 1850–1914* (1977); C. P. Kindleberger, *Economic Growth in France and Britain, 1851–1950* (1963); and W. O. Henderson, *The Rise of German Industrial Power, 1834–1914* (1976), cited earlier.

For the global economy during these years, W. W. Rostow, *The World Economy: History and Prospect* (1978) is an ambitious effort to study industrial growth from its origins in eighteenth-century Britain to its global diffusion. Other useful works include W. Ashworth, *A Short History of the International Economy since 1850* (rev. 1987); W. Woodruff, *The Impact of Western Man: A Study of Europe's Role in the World Economy, 1750–1960* (1966); and A. G. Kenwood and A. L. Lougheed, *The Growth of the International Economy, 1820–2000* (rev. 2000). K. Pomeranz, *The Great Divergence: Europe, China, and the Making of the Modern World Economy* (2000) discusses European colonialism in a comparative study of the evolving world economic system.

International finance is examined in C. P. Kindleberger, *A Financial History of Western Europe* (rev. 1992), cited earlier; M. DeCecco, *Money and Empire: The International Gold Standard, 1890–1914* (1974); R. S. Sayers, *The Bank of England, 1891–1944* (2 vols., 1985); and R. C. Michie, *Capitals of Finance: The London and New York Stock Exchanges, 1850–1914* (1987). The role of foreign capital in the economy of the United States is analyzed in M. Wilkins, *The History of Foreign Investment in the United States to 1914* (1989).

Demography and Migration

Several books on population growth, also useful here, have been cited earlier. C. M. Cipolla, *The Eco-*

nomic *History of World Populations* (1962) and T. H. Hollingsworth, *Historical Demography* (1969), are good guides. Recommended studies include T. McKeown, *The Modern Rise of Population* (1977); E. A. Wrigley, *Industrial Growth and Population Change* (1961); D. Grigg, *Population Growth and Agrarian Change* (1980); and C. Tilly (ed.), *Historical Studies of Changing Fertility* (1978).

For the movement of peoples, two collections of essays are helpful: W. H. McNeill and R. S. Adams (eds.), *Human Migration; Patterns and Politics* (1978), and I. Glazier and L. deRosa (eds.), *Migration across Time and Nations: Population Mobility in Historical Contexts* (1986). Additional Informative works include L. P. Moch, *Moving Europeans: Migration in Western Europe since 1650* (1993); M. L. Hansen, *The Atlantic Migration, 1607–1860* (1940); and P. Taylor, *The Distant Magnet: European Migration to the United States* (1971). On the absorption of America's immigrants, S. Thernstrom and others (eds.), *Harvard Encyclopedia of American Ethnic Groups* (1980) is a valuable work of reference.

France, 1871–1914

For France in this era the reader may turn to J. M. Mayeur and M. Rebérioux, *The Third Republic from Its Origins to the Great War, 1871–1914* (trans. 1984); and M. Agulhon, *The French Republic, 1879–1992* (trans. 1993), a challenging interpretive study. A concise synthesis is R. D. Anderson, *France, 1870–1914: Politics and Society* (1977). A provocative Marxist analysis is provided in S. Elwitt's two-volume study: *The Making of the Third Republic* (1975) and *The Third Republic Defended* (1988). An older account, D. Brogan, *The Development of Modern France, 1870–1939* (rev. 1967) remains valuable. The most recent treatment of the revolutionary uprising that ushered in the Third Republic is R. Tombs, *The Paris Commune, 1871* (1999).

A valuable guide to major themes in French history and to writings on France beginning with these years is J. F. McMillan, *Twentieth-Century France: Politics and Society in France, 1898–1991* (1992), while two works of reference are P. Hutton (ed.), *Encyclopedia of the French Third Republic* (2 vols.; 1986) and D. Bell and others (eds.), *A Biographical Dictionary of French Political Leaders since 1870* (1990).

Outstanding biographies include J.P.T. Bury's three-volume study (1936–1981) of Gambetta; D. R. Watson, *Georges Clemenceau* (1974), on the Radical parliamentarian and premier; and H. Goldberg, *The Life of Jean Jaurès* (1962), on the Socialist tribune. Informative studies of the Dreyfus affair may be found in D. Johnson, *France and the Dreyfus Affair* (1967); J. D. Bredin, *The Affair: The Case of Alfred Dreyfus* (trans. 1986); E. Cahm, *The Dreyfus Affair in French*

Society and Politics (1996); and M. P. Johnson, *The Dreyfus Affair* (1999).

Great Britain, 1871–1914

E. J. Feuchtwanger, *Democracy and Empire: Britain, 1865–1914* (1985) places the period in broad context. Other useful surveys include N. McCord, *British History, 1815–1906* (1991) and D. Read, *The Age of Urban Democracy: England, 1868–1914* (rev. 1993). The economy is studied in F. Crouzet, *The Victorian Economy* (trans. 1982); S. Pollard, *British Economy, 1870–1914* (1989); E. Hobsbawm, *Industry and Empire* (rev. 1999); and B.W.E. Alford, *Britain in the World Economy since 1880* (1996). Special insights are added in A. L. Friedberg, *The Weary Titan: Britain and the Experience of Relative Decline, 1895–1905* (1989) and B. Porter, *Britain, Europe, and the World, 1850–1986* (rev. 1987). Two valuable bibliographical guides are H. J. Hanham (ed.), *Bibliography of British History, 1851–1914* (1977) and A. F. Havighurst, *Modern England, 1901–1984* (rev. 1988).

The patterns of urban and rural life and the shift to an urban society are examined in two outstanding collaborative histories: H. J. Dyos and M. Wolff (eds.), *The Victorian City* (2 vols.; 1973) and G. E. Mingay (ed.), *The Victorian Countryside* (2 vols.; 1918); the shift to an urban society is examined in detail in G. E. Mingay, *The Transformation of Britain, 1830–1939* (1986). The changing fortunes of the landed aristocracy are studied in F.M.L. Thompson, *English Landed Society in the Nineteenth Century* (1989) and D. Cannadine, *The Decline and Fall of the British Aristocracy* (1990), which focuses with telling detail on the 1870s to the present.

In addition one may read G. M. Young, *Portrait of an Age: Victorian England* (2 vols.; 1934, 1977); three books by A. Briggs: *Victorian People* (1954), *Victorian Cities* (1963), and *Victorian Things* (1989); and G.S.R. Kitson Clark, *The Making of Victorian England* (1967). Of the many biographies of Victoria, one may still turn to L. Strachey's adulatory *Queen Victoria* (1921), but one should also read E. Longford, *Queen Victoria* (1965), a sympathetic yet balanced account, and S. Weintraub's two books: *Victoria* (rev. 1996), a reappraisal with interesting insights, and *Uncrowned King: The Life of Prince Albert* (1997).

In addition to many older studies of Gladstone, there are available biographies by E. J. Feuchtwanger (1975), P. Stansky (1979), and R. Jenkins (1997); there is also a brief account by E. F. Biagini (2000). For Disraeli, older biographies have been superseded by R. Blake, *Disraeli* (1967, 1998), a biography of distinction; there are other studies by G. Bradford (1983), J. Vincent (1990), and S. Weintraub (1993); and one may also read R. Shannon, *The Age of Disraeli, 1868–1881: The Rise of Tory Democracy* (1992). In addition to older biographies, useful works on Joseph

Chamberlain include R. Jay, *Joseph Chamberlain* (1981) and M. Balfour, *Britain and Joseph Chamberlain* (1985). There is a comprehensive three-volume biography of David Lloyd George by J. Grigg (1973–1985); briefer accounts are available by M. Pugh (1988), S. Constantine (1991), C. Wrigley (1992), and I. Packer (1998). For Asquith one may read S. Koss, *Asquith* (1976); and for Balfour, R. F. Mackay, *Balfour: Intellectual Statesman* (1985).

On the extension of the suffrage in 1867 one may read M. Cowling, *1867: Disraeli, Gladstone, and Revolution: The Passing of the Second Reform Bill* (1967) and F. B. Smith, *The Making of the Second Reform Bill* (1966). The transformation of the Liberals in the early twentieth century is studied in R. Richter, *The Politics of Conscience* (1964); G. L. Bernstein, *Liberalism and Liberal Politics in Edwardian England* (1986); and D. Powell, *The Edwardian Crisis: Britain, 1910–1914* (1996). An important account of a critical event is B. K. Murray, *The People's Budget, 1909–1910: Lloyd George and Liberal Politics* (1980). The emergence of the "new liberalism" in the early twentieth century is clarified in D. Roberts, *Origins of the British Welfare State* (1960); P. Clarke, *Liberals and Social Democrats* (1978); M. Freeden, *The New Liberalism: An Ideology of Social Reform* (1978); and J. Brown, T*he Welfare State in Britain* (1993). J. Gray, *Isaiah Berlin* (1996), and Berlin's own writings exemplify the later evolution of twentieth-century liberalism.

The Irish question is discussed in J. C. Beckett, *The Making of Modern Ireland* (rev. 1981), cited earlier; K. T. Hoppen, *Ireland since 1800: Conflict and Conformity* (1989); and in two books by D. G. Boyce: *Ireland, 1828–1923* (1992) and *Nationalism in Ireland* (rev. 1995). There is a remarkable study focusing on the years 1912–1921 by G. Dangerfield, *The Damnable Question: A Study of Anglo-Irish Relations* (1976). The same author's *The Strange Death of Liberal England* (1935, 1997) remains provocative as a searching study of the tensions in English society between 1910 and 1914. For informative essays on Britain's global influence in this era, one may turn to Vols. 3 and 4 of *The Oxford History of the British Empire*: A. Porter (ed.), *The Nineteenth Century* (1999) and J. M. Brown and W. R. Louis (eds.), *The Twentieth Century* (1999).

The German Empire, Italy

To books for Germany in the nineteenth century already cited may be added: H. U. Wehler, *The German Empire, 1871–1918* (1973; trans. 1985), reflecting the thinking of an influential generation of German historians; V. R. Berghahn, *Imperial Germany, 1871–1918* (1995) and *Modern Germany: Society, Economy, and Politics in the Twentieth Century* (rev. 1987); the concise survey by M. S Seligmann and R. R. McLean, *Germany from Reich to Republic, 1871–1918* (2000);

and the important, comprehensive study by M. L. Anderson, *Practicing Democracy: Elections and Political Culture in Imperial Germany* (2000).

Other influential works on imperial Germany and class relationships include D. Blackbourn and G. Eley, *The Peculiarities of German History: Bourgeois Society and Politics in Nineteenth-Century German History* (1984); G. Eley, *From Unification to Nazism: Reinterpreting the German Past* (1986); D. Blackbourn, *Populist and Patricians: Essays in Modern German History* (1987); R. J. Evans, *Rethinking German History: Nineteenth Century Germany and the Origins of the Third Reich* (1990); and the essays in two useful collections: J. C. Fout (ed.), *Politics, Parties, and the Authoritarian State: Imperial Germany, 1871–1918* (2 vols.; 1986), and G. Eley (ed.), *Society, Culture, and the State in Germany, 1870–1930* (1996).

For developments in the immediate post-Bismarckian years one may read J.C.G. Röhl, *Germany without Bismarck: The Crisis of Government in the Second Reich, 1890–1900* (1968). Two outstanding biographies of William II are M. Balfour, *The Kaiser and His Times* (1964) and L. Cecil's two-volume work: *William II: Prince and Emperor, 1859–1900* (1989) and *Emperor and Exile, 1900–1941* (1996). T. A. Kohut, *Wilhelm II and the Germans* (1991) is an insightful study, as is J.C.G. Röhl, *The Kaiser and His Court: Wilhelm II and the Government of Germany* (1996). The universities in this era are examined in K. H. Jarausch, *Students, Society, and Politics in Imperial Germany: The Rise of Academic Liberalism* (1982); and the same author has also written an illuminating biographical study of Bethmann-Hollweg (1973). Of special interest for pre-1914 German society are R. Gay, *The Jews of Germany* (1992) and F. Stern, *Einstein's German World* (1999).

The best narrative accounts of Italy since unification are D. Mack Smith, *Modern Italy* (rev. 1997), cited earlier, and M. Clark, *Modern Italy, 1871–1995* (rev. 1996). For the years after unification, an illuminating account is C. Seton-Watson, *Italy from Liberalism to Fascism, 1870–1925* (1967), which may be supplemented by J. A. Thayer, *Italy and the Great War: Politics and Culture, 1870–1915* (1964); S. Saladino, *Italy from Unification to 1919* (1970); and R. A. Webster, *Industrial Imperialism in Italy, 1908–1915* (1976).

Problems and Readings

Pamphlets and collections of documents relating to this chapter include R. L. Williams (ed.), *The Commune of Paris, 1871* (1969); R. Gildea, *France, 1870–1914* (rev. 1996); M. Burns, *France and the Dreyfus Affair: A Documentary History* (1999); P. Adelman, *Gladstone, Disraeli and Later Victorian Politics* (rev. 1996); T. S. Hamerow (ed.), *The Age of*

Bismarck: Documents and Interpretations (1974); J. J. Sheehan (ed.), *Imperial Germany* (1976); and I. Porter and I. D. Armour, *Imperial Germany, 1890–1918* (1991).

15. EUROPEAN CIVILIZATION, 1871–1914: SOCIETY AND CULTURE

Many books on the social, cultural, and intellectual history of the nineteenth century have been listed in earlier chapters, beginning with Chapter 11.

Labor, Social Democracy, Socialism

Overall introductions include H. Mitchell and P. N. Stearns, *Workers and Protest: The European Labor Movement, the Working Classes, and the Origins of Social Democracy, 1890–1914* (1971); A. Przeworski, *Capitalism and Social Democracy* (1985); H. Pelling, *A History of Trade Unionism* (1963); and D. Sassoon, *One Hundred Years of Socialism: The West European Left in the Twentieth Century* (1996), taking its start in 1889.

There are many specific studies of Socialist parties in each country. For Germany, informative books include C. E. Schorske, *German Social Democracy, 1905–1917* (1955); P. Gay, *The Dilemma of Democratic Socialism: Eduard Bernstein's Challenge to Marx* (rev. 1962); M. B. Steger, *The Quest for Evolutionary Socialism: Eduard Bernstein and Social Democracy* (1997); S. Pierson, *Marxist Intellectuals and the Working Class Mentality in Germany, 1887–1912* (1993); W. M. Maehl, *August Bebel: Shadow Emperor of the German Workers* (1980); and V. L. Lidtke, *The Outlawed Party: Social Democracy in Germany, 1878–1890* (1966). Lidtke has also written an outstanding study of the working-class culture that developed around the German Socialist movement: *The Alternative Culture: Socialist Labor in Imperial Germany* (1985).

For Britain, N. MacKenzie and J. MacKenzie, *The Fabians* (1977) skillfully combines biography and social and intellectual history, while two leading Fabians, Sidney and Beatrice Webb, are studied in R. J. Harrison, *The Life and Times of Sidney and Beatrice Webb* (2000) and P. Beilharz and C. Nyland (eds.), *The Webbs, Fabianism, and Feminism* (1998). Recent works on George Bernard Shaw include biographies by M. Holroyd (1998), which condenses a comprehensive, multivolume study; and L. Hugo (1999). The origins of British socialism are probed in S. Pierson, *Marxism and the Origins of British Socialism* (1973) and *British Socialists: The Journey from Fantasy to Politics* (1979); and a related subject is studied in R. Moore, *The Emergence of the Labour Party, 1880–1924* (1978), a thoughtful synthesis.

For France, for an overall view with many interesting insights, one may read T. Judt, *Marxism and the*

French Left: Studies in Labour and Politics in France, 1830–1981 (1986); R. Magraw, *A History of the French Working Class* (2 vols.; 1992), the first volume studying the years 1815–1870, the second, 1871–1939; and R. Stuart, *Marxism at Work: Ideology, Class, and French Socialism during the Third Republic* (1992). There are informative biographical studies of Socialist leaders, among them H. Goldberg on Jean Jaurès (1962), cited earlier; L. Derfler (1977) and M. M. Farrar (1991) on Alexandre Millerand; L. Derfler on Paul Lafargue (2 vols.; 1991, 1998); and K. S. Vincent on Pierre-Joseph Proudhon (1985) and Benoît Malon (1992). The spiritual precursor of Christian social democracy is studied in H. A. Schmitt, *Charles Péguy: The Decline of an Idealist* (1967).

On the Socialist international organization, J. Joll, *The Second International, 1889–1914* (rev. 1974) is a concise survey; and J. Braunthal, *History of the International* (3 vols.; trans. 1961–1980) is a detailed study. The breakup of the International is described in G. Haupt, *Socialism and the Great War: The Collapse of the Second International* (1972). The most comprehensive introduction to anarchism is G. Woodcock, *Anarchism: A History of Libertarian Ideas and Movements* (1962), but also useful are J. Joll, *The Anarchists* (rev. 1981) and R. D. Sonn, *Anarchism* (1992).

Labor History in Cultural Context

Recent labor history has attempted to convey the experiences of laboring men and women apart from organized labor movements and to integrate labor protest into a broader cultural context. Here E. P. Thompson's works have been cited earlier. Another exemplar, E. J. Hobsbawm, has written, among other books, *Primitive Rebels* (rev. 1971), *Labouring Men* (1964), and *Workers: Worlds of Labour* (1985). A successful study of the English experience in these years is S. Meacham, *A Life Apart: The English Working Class, 1890–1914* (1977). Other interesting works for British labor are J. Benson, *The Working Class in Britain, 1850–1939* (1989); D. M. MacRaild and D. E. Martin, *Labour in British Society, 1830–1914* (2000); and J. Bourke, *Working-Class Cultures in Britain, 1890–1960: Gender, Class, and Ethnicity* (1994).

For France, examples of the newer labor history include J. W. Scott, *The Glassmakers of Carmaux: French Craftsmen and Political Action in a Nineteenth-Century City* (1974); B. H. Moss, *The Origins of the French Labor Movement, 1830–1914: The Socialism of Skilled Workers* (1976); L. R. Berlanstein, *The Working People of Paris, 1871–1914* (1984); M. P. Hanagan, *The Logic of Solidarity: Artisans and Workers in Three French Towns, 1871–1914* (1980); D. Reid, *The Miners of Decazeville* (1986) and *Paris Sewers and Sewermen* (1991); J. G. Coffin, *The Politics of Women's Work: The Paris Garment Trades,*

1750–1915 (1996); and N. L. Green, *Ready-to-Wear and Ready-to-Work: A Century of Industry and Immigrants in Paris and New York* (1997), an excellent study of twentieth-century labor that exemplifies the new comparative social history. A comprehensive study is G. Noiriel, *Workers in French Society in the 19th and 20th Centuries* (trans. 1990); and the strike as a social phenomenon in these years is studied in M. Perrot, *Workers on Strike: France, 1871–1890* (trans. 1987). The importance of syndicalism is examined in several older books and in S. Milner, *French Syndicalism and the International Labor Movement, 1900–1914* (1990).

For Germany books providing broad insights into politics, society, and class include D. Crew, *Town in the Ruhr: A Social History of Bochum, 1860–1914* (1979); D. Blackbourn, *Class, Religion, and Local Politics in Wilhelmine Germany* (1980); M. Nolan, *Social Democracy and Society: Working Class Radicalism in Düsseldorf, 1890–1920* (1980); and S.H.F. Hickey, *Workers in Imperial Germany: The Miners of the Ruhr* (1985).

Women's History, Women's Rights, Feminism

Books on recent themes in women's history have been cited in the introductory section and in earlier chapters. For the background to women's history in modern Europe, one may turn to K. Offen, *European Feminisms, 1700–1950: A Political History* (2000); P. Branca, *Women in Europe since 1750* (1978); S. Delamont and L. Duffin (eds.), *The Nineteenth-Century Woman: Her Cultural and Physical World* (1978); and P. S. Robertson, *An Experience of Women: Patterns and Change in Nineteenth-Century Europe* (1982). Women's lives and activities are documented in E. O. Hellerstein, L. P. Hume, and K. M. Offen (eds.), *Victorian Women: A Documentary Account of Women's Lives in Nineteenth-Century England, France, and the United States* (1981). S. Rowbotham, *A Century of Women: The History of Women in Britain and the United States* (1997) begins with chapters on the era before The First World War.

For Britain in this era a sampling of the many studies that examine the status and role of women of various backgrounds would include M. Vicinus, *Suffer and Be Still: Women in the Victorian Age* (1973), and the volume she has edited, *A Widening Sphere: Changing Roles of Victorian Women* (1977); P. Branca, *Silent Sisterhood: Middle Class Women in the Victorian Home* (1975); E. Longworth, *Eminent Victorian Women* (1981); and B. Caine, *Victorian Feminists* (1982). J. Giles, Women, *Identity and Private Life in Britain, 1900–50* (1995), describes the experiences of women in the early twentieth century.

Working-class women are studied in N. C. Solden, *Women in British Trade Unions, 1874–1976* (1978) and E. Roberts, *A Woman's Place: An Oral History of Working Class Women* (1985). A key social problem is thoughtfully examined in J. R. Walkowitz, *Prostitution and Victorian Society: Women, Class, and the State* (1980); the same author has also written *City of Dreadful Delight: Narratives of Sexual Danger in Late-Victorian London* (1992). One may also read P. McHugh, *Prostitution and Victorian Social Reform* (1980).

The struggle for women's suffrage is studied in J. Kamm, *Rapiers and Battleaxes: The Women's Movement and Its Aftermath* (1966); C. Rover, *Women's Suffrage and Party Politics in Britain, 1866–1914* (1967); D. Morgan, *Suffragists and Liberals: the Politics of Woman Suffrage in England* (1975); A. Rosen, *Rise Up Women!: The Women's Social and Political Union, 1903–1914* (1974); and J. Liddington and J. Norris, *One Hand Tied Behind Us: The Rise of the Women's Suffrage Movement* (rev. 2000). D. Mitchell's popular account, *The Fighting Pankhursts: A Study in Tenacity* (1967), may be supplemented by P. W. Romero, *E. Sylvia Pankhust: Portrait of a Radical* (1987); and B. Winslow, *Sylvia Pankhurst: Sexual Politics and Political Activism* (1996). In addition, S. Holton, *Feminism and Democracy: Women's Suffrage and Reform Politics in Britain, 1900–1918* (1986) focuses on less known provincial suffragists, and S. K. Kent, *Sex and Suffrage in Britain, 1860–1914* (1990) sees the suffrage campaign as part of a broader movement for a reformed society.

The history of women in the Third French Republic is examined in J. F. McMillan, *Housewife or Harlot: The Place of Women in French Society, 1870–1940* (1981), the title derived from a remark by Proudhon, and in the same author's excellent *France and Women, 1789–1914: Gender, Society, and Politics* (2000). S. C. Hause with A. R. Kenney, *Women's Suffrage and Social Politics in the French Third Republic* (1984) explores the failed movement in these years to extend the suffrage to women.

Other works on French women in this age include B. G. Smith, *Ladies of the Leisure Class: The Bourgeoises of Northern France in the Nineteenth Century* (1982); C. G. Moses, *French Feminism in the Nineteenth Century* (1984); J. W. Scott, *Only Paradoxes to Offer: French Feminists and the Rights of Man* (1996); and E. A. Accampo and others, *Gender and the Politics of Social Reform in France, 1870–1914* (1995). An informative comparative study is T. McBride, *The Domestic Revolution: The Modernization of Household Service in England and France, 1820–1920* (1976). The essays in J. B. Margadant (ed.), *The New Biography: Performing Femininity in Nineteenth-Century France* (2000) discuss the complex roles that women played in French society.

On the activist role of women in the Socialist movement one may turn to R. J. Evans, *Comrades and Sisters: Feminism, Socialism, and Pacifism in Europe,*

1870–1945 (1987); and M. J. Boxer and J. H. Quataert (eds.), *Socialist Women: European Socialist Feminism in the Nineteenth and Early Twentieth Centuries* (1978), cited earlier. For the German Socialists there is J. H. Quataert, *Reluctant Feminists in German Social Democracy, 1865–1917* (1979); and for the French, C. Sowerwine, *Sisters or Citizens: Women and Socialism in France since 1876* (1982); and P. Hilden, *Working Class Women and Socialist Politics in France: A Regional Study, 1880–1914* (1986). For Rosa Luxemburg and her contributions to German and international socialism, J. P. Nettl, *Rosa Luxemburg* (2 vols., 1966; abridged 1 vol., 1969), is an admirable biography. Other studies include books by N. Geras (1976); E. Eltinger (1987); R. Abraham (1989); S. E. Bronner (1990); D. E. Shepardson (1996); and J. Mathilde (trans. 2000).

The role of women in German society is examined in R.F.B. Joeres and M. J. Maynes (eds.), *German Women in the Eighteenth and Nineteenth Centuries* (1986); J. C. Fout (ed.), *German Women in the Nineteenth Century: A Social History* (1984); and U. Frevert, *Women in German History: From Bourgeois Emancipation to Sexual Liberation* (1989).

R. J. Evans provides a comparative study in *The Feminists: Women's Emancipation Movements in Europe, America, and Australia, 1840–1920* (1977), and focuses on a single country in *The Feminist Movement in Germany, 1894–1933* (1976). On the transatlantic and international campaign in the nineteenth century one may turn to B. S. Anderson, *Joyous Greetings: The First International Women's Movement, 1830–1860* (2000). The scene in Russia is studied in R. Stites, *The Women's Liberation Movement in Russia: Feminism, Nihilism, and Bolshevism, 1860–1930* (rev. 1991). On the two pioneer women leaders of emancipation in the United States, one may read G. C. Ward, *Not for Ourselves Alone: The Story of Elizabeth Cady Stanton and Susan B. Anthony* (1999).

Cultural and Intellectual History

Two surveys of cultural and intellectual history are G. L. Mosse, *The Culture of Western Europe: The Nineteenth and Twentieth Centuries* (rev. 1988); and R. N. Stromberg, *European Intellectual History Since 1789* (rev. 1994), both cited earlier. A few special books on this period also deserve mention. R. Wohl, *The Generation of 1914* (1979) relates the restlessness of the postwar generation to the prewar ferment; B. W. Tuchman, *The Proud Tower: A Portrait of the World before the War, 1890–1914* (1966) is an older, popular account with colorful vignettes, and E. R. Tannenbaum, *1900: The Generation Before the Great War* (1976) offers a potpourri of insights into the social history of the times. A. J. Mayer, *The Persistence of the Old Regime: Europe to the Great War* (1981) contends that aristocratic values dominated European society

and culture down to 1914. A positive assessment of the closing years of the nineteenth century emerges from the essays in M. Teich and R. Porter (eds.), *Fin de Siècle and Its Legacy* (1990).

In a special category and a major contribution to social and cultural history of this era is P. Gay, *The Bourgeois Experience: Victoria to Freud* (5 vols.; 1984–1998); the five volumes illuminate in fascinating detail how Victorian men and women in their emotional life were not inhibited by social restraints. One should also read D. Newcome, *The Victorian World Picture* (1997), on how the world perceived the Victorians and how they perceived themselves.

For France an unconventional social history with absorbing details and insights is T. Zeldin, *France, 1848–1945* (2 vols.; 1973–1977, 1992): Vol. I, *Ambition, Love and Politics,* and Vol. II, *Intellect, Taste and Anxiety.* Other aspects of French social and cultural history are studied in E. Weber, *France, Fin de Siècle* (1986), which offers vignettes and anecdotal insights into French society and life; the same author demonstrates that French national unity was accomplished only belatedly by such agencies as the schools and army in *Peasants into Frenchmen: The Modernization of Rural France, 1870–1914* (1976). The arts and cultural life are examined in R. Shattuck, *The Banquet Years: The Arts in France, 1885–1918* (1958); T. J. Clark, *Image of the People* (1973) and *The Painting of Modern Life: Paris in the Art of Monet and His Followers* (1984, 1999); and J. Seigel, *Bohemian Paris: Culture, Politics, and the Boundaries of Bourgeois Life, 1830–1930* (1986).

Three introductions to the origins of modern art in France and subsequent developments are H. H. Arnason, *History of Modern Art* (rev. 1998); C. Naylor (ed.), *Contemporary Artists* (rev. 1989); and R. R. Brettell, *Modern Art, 1851–1929: Capitalism and Representation* (1999), which relates the major avant-garde innovations to the rapid social, economic, and political changes of the age. S. Kern, *The Culture of Time and Space, 1880–1918* (1983) also stresses the cultural responses to changing modern technologies.

C. E. Schorske, *Fin de Siècle Vienna: Politics and Culture* (1979) is a remarkable study of political, artistic, and intellectual responses to the failures of late-nineteenth-century liberalism in central Europe. Important also is A. Janik and S. Toulmin, *Wittgenstein's Vienna* (1973), while an evocative portrait of life and creativity in the second city of the empire is J. Lukacs, *Budapest 1900* (1989).

New Movements in Science

A general introduction to science in the nineteenth and early twentieth centuries is available in D. Knight, *The Age of Science* (1986). On biology, evolution, and Darwinism there is a considerable literature, much of it published in recent years. One may turn to

A. Desmond, *The Politics of Evolution* (1989); A. Desmond and J. Moore, *Darwin* (1991); and D. l. Hull, *Darwin and His Critics* (1993). Desmond has also written an extraordinary biography of Darwin's forceful champion, *Huxley: From Devil's Disciple to Evolution's High Priest* (1997). The ongoing debate about Darwin's theories may be sampled in N. Eldridge, *Reinventing Darwin* (1995); the same author's *The Triumph of Evolution and the Failures of Creationism* (2000); and D. J. Depew and B. H. Weber, *Darwinism Evolving* (1995). S. Jones, *Darwin's Ghost: "The Origins of the Species" Updated* (2000) is a remarkable rewriting of Darwin in light of the evolutionary biology that has developed since his day. Other books on evolution written by M. Ruse (1979), P. J. Bowler (1990), J. Bowlby (1991), and D. Young (1993) also merit attention.

Brief biographical accounts of two other key biologists of this era are L. J. Jordanova, *Lamarck* (1985) and V. Orel, *Mendel* (1985). The breakthrough in geology and its cultural impact may be studied in C. C. Gillispie, *Genesis and Geology* (1951); R. Porter, *The Making of Geology* (1977); D. R. Dean, *James Hutton and the History of Geology* (1992); and S. J. Gould, *Time's Arrow, Time's Cycle: Myth and Metaphor in the Discovery of Geological Time* (1987).

For the impact of these scientific developments on religion, the classic account is A. D. White, *A History of the Warfare of Science and Theology* (1896, many eds.); informative studies include W. Irvine, *Apes, Angels, and Victorians* (1955, 1983); J. R. Moore, *The Post-Darwinian Controversies* (1979); D. C. Lindberg and R. L. Numbers (eds.), *Historical Essays on the Encounter between Christianity and Science* (1986); and H. J. Brooke, *Science and Religion: Some Historical Perspectives* (1991). On the famous Scopes trial of 1925 in the United States, an even-handed scholarly account is E. J. Larson, *Summer for the Gods: The Scopes Trial and America's Continuing Debate over Science and Religion* (1998).

Debates on the nature of scientific discovery still refer often to the influential work of T. S. Kuhn, *The Structure of Scientific Revolutions* (1962, 1989). On the emergence of modern physics and the transformation of Newtonian concepts one may turn to V. F. Weisskopf, *Physics in the Twentieth Century* (1972) and B. L. Cline, *Men Who Made a New Physics* (1965, 1987). Einstein may be approached through two major biographies: A. Pais, *"Subtle is the Lord" The Science and the Life of Albert Einstein* (1982); and A. Folsing, *Albert Einstein* (1993, trans. 1997), excellent both for Einstein's science and his personal life. There are informative accounts also by H. Cuny (1962), brief and concise; R. W. Clark (1971); J. Bernstein, *Einstein* (1973); M. White and J. Gribbon (1994); and D. Brian (1996). Recommended biographies of two other contributors to the new physics are S. Quinn, *Marie Curie*

(1995) and R. L. Sime, *Lise Meitner: A Life in Physics* (1997).

For Freud, there is an older biography by E. Jones, an English co-worker (1 vol. abridged; 1974), and many other studies including the thoughtful work by P. Gay, *Freud: A Life for Our Time* (1988). A. Storr, *Freud* (1989) is a good brief assessment. To sample the large literature critical of Freud, one may read A. Esterson, *Seductive Mirage: An Exploration of the Work of Sigmund Freud* (1993) and the essays in M. S. Roth (ed.), *Freud: Conflict and Culture* (1998).

Social Thought

Outstanding works are H. S. Hughes, *Consciousness and Society: The Reorientation of European Social Thought, 1890–1930* (1958); G. Masur, *Prophets of Yesterday: Studies in European Culture, 1890–1914* (1961); M. Biddis, *Age of the Masses: Ideas and Society Since 1870* (1977); W. R. Everdell, *The First Moderns: Profiles in the Origins of Twentieth-Century Thought* (1997); and J. W. Burrow, *The Crisis of Reason: European Thought, 1848–1914* (2000). Virtually a history of thought from Herbert Spencer to the present is W. W. Wagar, *Good Tidings: The Belief in Progress from Darwin to Marcuse* (1972); on that theme one may also read R. Nisbet, *History of the Idea of Progress* (1980); and a thoughtful collaborative volume, G. Almond and others (eds.), *Progress and Its Discontents* (1982).

The best studies of Nietzsche are W. A. Kaufmann, *Nietzsche: Philosopher, Psychologist, Antichrist* (rev. 1974); R. Hayman, *Nietzsche: A Critical Life* (1980); R. J. Hollingdale, *Nietzsche: The Man and His Philosophy* (rev. 1999); and T. B. Strong, *Friedrich Nietzsche and the Politics of Transfiguration* (rev. 2000). There are other biographical studies by C. Brinton (1941, 1965), J. P. Stern (1979), R. Schacht (1983), and G. Clive (1984). Useful anthologies are R. N. Stromberg (ed.), *Realism, Naturalism, and Symbolism: Modes of Thought and Expression in Europe, 1848–1914* (1968); and E. Weber (ed.), *Movements, Currents, Trends: Aspects of European Thought in the Nineteenth and Twentieth Centuries* (1991).

Religion since 1871

The relationship between secularized European civilization and its Christian origins is ably treated in O. Chadwick, *The Secularization of the European Mind in the Nineteenth Century* (1976), and H. McLeod, *Religion and the People of Western Europe, 1789–1970* (1981); both were cited in Chapter 11. For religious thought, J. Pelikan, *Christian Doctrine and Modern Culture: Since 1700* (1990), may be read along with C. Welch, *Protestant Thought in the Nineteenth Century* (2 vols.; 1985), the second volume studying the years 1870–1914. For the Roman

Catholic reactions to the changes in science and religious scholarship one may read T. M. Loome, *Liberal Catholicism, Reform Catholicism, and Modernism* (1979); and L. R. Kurtz, *The Politics of Heresy: The Modernist Crisis in Roman Catholicism* (1986).

For Judaism, H. M. Sachar, *The Course of Modern Jewish History* (rev. 1990) and *A History of Israel: From the Rise of Zionism to Our Time* (rev. 1996) relate the nineteenth-century background. The fullest account of Zionism's emergence as an ideology is the impressive three-volume study by D. Vital: *The Origins of Zionism* (1975), *Zionism: The Formative Years* (1982), and *Zionism: the Crucial Phase* (1987), which carries the story to 1919. Another insightful work is S. Avinieri, *The Making of Modern Zionism: The Intellectual Origins of the Jewish State* (1981).

The Assault on Liberalism: Racism, the Cult of Violence

Many of the books cited earlier in this chapter under Social Thought examine the undermining of liberal values in the late nineteenth century, with implications for the years that followed. Two key studies are H. Arendt, *The Origins of Totalitarianism* (rev. 1973), an influential, far-reaching work; and J. Barzun, *Darwin, Marx, Wagner: Critique of a Heritage* (rev. 1981), which stresses similarities as the author sees it in the way each of these figures undermined classical liberalism. These books may be supplemented by J. W. Burrow, *The Crisis of Reason: European Thought, 1848–1914* (2000), cited earlier.

For racism and anti-Semitism in these years one may read P. Pulzer, *The Rise of Political Anti-Semitism in Germany and Austria* (rev. 1988); L. Poliakov, *The Aryan Myth: A History of Racist and Nationalist Ideas in Europe* (trans. 1974); J. Katz, *From Prejudice to Destruction: Anti-Semitism, 1700–1933* (1980); G. L. Mosse, *Toward the Final Solution: A History of European Racism* (1978); and two books by P. L. Rose, *Revolutionary Anti-Semitism in Germany from Kant to Wagner* (1991) and *Wagner: Race and Revolution* (1992). Anti-Semitism is placed in broad historical perspective in R. S. Wistrich, *Anti-Semitism: The Longest Hatred* (1992), a remarkable account ranging from pre-Christian times through the twentieth century; G. I. Langmuir, *History, Religion, and Anti-Semitism* (1990) and *Toward a Definition of Anti-Semitism* (1991); and A. S. Lindemann, *Esau's Tears: Modern Anti-Semitism and the Rise of the Jews* (1997). Books on anti-Semitism in France relating to the Dreyfus Affair include S. Wilson, *Ideology and Experience: Anti-Semitism in Modern France at the Time of the Dreyfus Affair* (1982), which is especially insightful; books on the affair itself have already been cited. A. S. Lindemann, *The Jew Accused: Three Anti-Semitic Affairs: Dreyfus, Beilis, Frank, 1894–1915* (1991) skillfully compares the French affair with episodes in tsarist Russia and the United States. For comparative insights in other frameworks, one may read G. Fredrickson, *The Comparative Imagination: On the History of Racism, Nationalism, and Social Movements* (1998). J. J. Roth, *The Cult of Violence: Sorel and the Sorelians* (1980) is illuminating on the inspiration behind syndicalism. The origins of twentieth-century fascist ideology are studied in Z. Sternhell, *Neither Right Nor Left: Fascist Ideology in France* (1986) and, in collaboration with others, *The Birth of Fascist Ideology: From Cultural Rebellion to Political Revolution* (trans. 1994); these two much debated books find the roots of fascist thought in the ideas and ideology of the Left. A precursor of fascism is studied in C. S. Doty, *From Cultural Rebellion to Counterrevolution: The Politics of Maurice Barrès* (1976) and R. Soucy, *Fascism in France: The Case of Maurice Barrès* (1972).

Problems and Readings

Two useful anthologies are I. Howe (ed.), *Essential Works of Socialism* (1976) and A. Fried and R. Sanders, *Socialist Thought: A Documentary History* (rev. 1993), cited earlier. Helpful on other subjects for these years are H. Schultz (ed.), *English Liberalism and the State: Individualism or Collectivism* (1974); E. C. Black (ed.), *Victorian Culture and Society* (1974); and P. Stansky (ed.), *The Victorian Revolution: Government and Society in Victoria's Britain* (1973). There are valuable collections of documents in F. Gordon and M. Cross (eds.), *Early French Feminisms, 1830–1940* (1996) and J. Waelti-Walters and S. C. Hause (eds.), *Feminisms of the Belle Epoque: A Historical and Literary Anthology* (1994). Also useful are R. S. Levy (ed.), *Anti-Semitism in Modern Times: An Anthology of Texts* (1991), and two works cited in Chapter 11: M. L. McDougall (ed.), *The Working Class in Modern Europe* (1975), and A. Lees and L. Lees (eds.), *The Urbanization of European Society in the Nineteenth Century* (1975). M. J. Maynes, *Taking the Hard Road* (1995) brings together autobiographical documents by German workers in the era of industrialization. Materials on science and intellectual developments are available in H. Vanderpool (ed.), *Darwin and Darwinism* (1974); and L. P. Williams (ed.), *Relativity Theory: Its Origins and Impact on Modern Thought* (1968). Zola's writings on the Dreyfus Affair are available in A. Pagès (ed.), *The Dreyfus Affair: "J'accuse" and Other Writings* (1996).

16. EUROPE'S WORLD SUPREMACY

Many of the general accounts for the years 1871–1914 cited in the two previous chapters will also be helpful here. Informative introductions, some moving on into the twentieth century, include H. Gollwitzer, *Europe in the Age of Imperialism, 1848–1917* (1974); W. D. Smith, *European Imperialism in the Nineteenth* and *Twentieth Centuries* (1982); V. G. Kiernan, *From Conquest to Collapse: European Empires from 1815 to 1960* (1982); and J. N. Pieterse, *Empire and Emancipation* (1980). W. L. Langer, *The Diplomacy of Imperialism, 1890–1902* (2 vols.; 1935, 1951, 1965), remains valuable; it may be supplemented by R. Shannon, *The Crisis of Imperialism, 1865–1915* (1974). The role played by Western technology in European expansion is examined in D. R. Headrick, *The Tools of Empire* (1981) and *The Tentacles of Progress* (1988); and M. Adas, *Machines as the Measure of Men: Science, Technology, and Ideologies of Western Dominance* (1989). The role played by disease is examined in S. Watts, *Epidemics and History: Disease, Power, and Imperialism* (2000). A long-range view of European imperialism is provided in D. B. Abernathy, *The Dynamics of Global Dominance: European Overseas Empires, 1415–1980* (2001).

Imperialism in General

Debate about the nature of imperialism has in part been stimulated by the seminal study of R. Robinson and J. Gallagher, *Africa and the Victorians: The Official Mind of Imperialism* (1961, 1981), comparing political and economic motives; it is summarized in W. R. Louis (ed.), *Imperialism: The Robinson-Gallagher Controversy* (1976). Informative studies include D. Fieldhouse's two books, *Economics and Empire, 1830–1914* (1973) and *Colonialism, 1870–1945* (1981); and P. J. Cain and A. G. Hopkins, *British Imperialism: Innovation and Expansion, 1688–1914* (2 vols.; 1993). Motives and justifications for nineteenth-century imperialism are also analyzed in R. Koebner and H. D. Schmidt, *Imperialism: The Story and Significance of a Political Word, 1840–1960* (1964); A. P. Thornton, *Doctrines of Imperialism* (1965); G. Lichtheim, *Imperialism* (1970); C. Reynolds, *Modes of Imperialism* (1981); T. Smith, *The Pattern of Imperialism* (1982); and W. J. Mommsen, *Theories of Imperialism* (trans. 1980).

Provocative discussions of the confrontation between Europeans and non-Europeans include R Maunier, *The Sociology of Colonies: An Introduction to the Study of Race Contact* (2 vols.; 1949); D. Mannoni, *Prospero and Caliban: The Psychology of Colonization* (1956), which stresses the psychological impact on both rulers and the governed; T. Geiger, *The Conflicted Relationship: The West and the Transformation of Asia, Africa, and Latin America* (1967); G. W. Goug, *The Standards of "Civilization" in International Society* (1984); V. G. Kiernan, *The Lords of Human Kind: Black Man, Yellow Man, and White Man in the Age of Empire* (1987); and P. D. Curtin, *The World and the West: The European Challenge and the Overseas Response in the Age of Empire* (2000). E. Said, *Culture and Imperialism* (1994), explains how imperialism affected European culture itself; and the

issue of gender in European empires is examined in N. Chaudhuri and M. Strobel (eds.), *Western Women and Imperialism: Complicity and Resistance* (1992).

British and other European Imperialisms

Recommended studies for British imperialism include B. Porter, *The Lion's Share: A Short History of British Imperialism, 1850–1995* (rev. 1996), a lively and informative account; R. Hyam, *Britain's Imperial Century, 1815–1914* (1976); and C. A. Bayly, *The Imperial Meridian: The British Empire and the World, 1780–1830* (1989). Critics of imperialism are discussed in A. P. Thornton, *The Imperial Idea and Its Enemies* (1959); and B. Porter, *Critics of Empire: British Radical Attitudes to Colonialism in Africa, 1895–1914* (1968). Excellent discussions of British colonial expansion may be found in W. R. Louis (ed.), *The Oxford History of the British Empire* (5 vols.; 1998–1999), of which the relevant volumes for this period are A. Porter (ed.), *The Nineteenth Century* (1999), and J. M. Brown (ed.), *The Twentieth Century* (1999).

The imperial activities of the other European powers are described in W. O. Henderson, *Studies in German Colonial History* (1963); W. D. Smith, *The German Colonial Empire* (1978); H. Brunschwig, *French Colonialism, 1871–1914* (1960; trans. 1966); and M. Kuietenbrouwer, *The Netherlands and the Rise of Modern Imperialism* (trans. 1991). On both the theory and practice of imperialism an important comparative study is W. Baumgart, *Imperialism: The Idea and Reality of British and French Colonial Expansion, 1880–1914* (trans. 1982). Cross-cultural and interracial interactions are studied in J. Clancy-Smith and F. Gouda (eds.), *Domesticating the Empire: Race, Gender, and Family Life in French and Dutch Colonialism* (1998).

The Americas

For all aspects of relationships with Latin America, the essays in the first five volumes of L. Bethell (ed.), *The Cambridge History of Latin America* (1988) are valuable: Vols. I and II, *Colonial Latin America;* Vol. III, *From Independence to c. 1870;* and Vols. IV and V, *From 1870 to 1930.* D. Bushnell and N. Macaulay, *The Emergence of Latin America in the Nineteenth Century* (rev. 1994) is a helpful survey; it may be supplemented by E. B. Burns, *The Poverty of Progress: Latin America in the Nineteenth Century* (1980) and by chapters on this period in J. Chasteen, *Born in Blood and Fire: A Concise History of Latin America* (2001).

D. Dawson, *The Mexican Adventure* (1935), is a careful account of Napoleon III's fiasco during the 1860s, and may be read along with N. N. Baker, *The French Experience in Mexico, 1821–1861* (1979). Two informative histories of Mexico are R. E. Ruiz, *Triumphs and Tragedy: A History of the Mexican People*

(1992); and E. Krauze, *Mexico, Biography of Power: A History of Modern Mexico, 1810–1996* (trans. 1997). The nineteenth-century Mexican leader Benito Juárez is studied in B. Hamnett, *Juárez* (1993); and the Indian revolutionary leader Emiliano Zapata, in biographies by J. Womack (1968) and R. Parkinson (1980). The last Brazilian monarch and his attempts at modernization are studied in R. J. Barman, *Citizen-Emperor: Pedro I and the Making of Brazil, 1825–1891* (2000).

For the imperialist activities of the United States in these years, one may consult J. W. Pratt, *America's Colonial Empire* (1954); W. LaFeber, *The New Empire* (1963); F. Merk, *Manifest Destiny and Mission in American History* (1963); and J. Dobson, *America's Ascent: The United States Becomes a Great Power, 1880–1914* (1978). Interpretive studies include W. A. Williams, *The Tragedy of American Diplomacy* (rev. 1988), highly critical of American imperialism; and E. R. May, *Imperial Democracy* (1961) and *American Imperialism: A Speculative Essay* (1968), which are balanced assessments of American motives.

For the Spanish-American War one may read D. F. Trask, *The War with Spain in 1898* (1981); I. Musicant, *Empire by Default: The Spanish American War and the Dawn of the American Century* (1998); and the provocative analysis by L. Perez, Jr., *The War of 1898: The United States and Cuba in History and Historiography* (1998). Other studies of American expansion include P. Stanley, *A Nation in the Making: The Philippines and the United States* (1974); S. Karnow, *In Our Image: America's Empire in the Philippines* (1989); M. Tate, *The United States and the Hawaiian Kingdom* (1965); D. McCullough, *The Path between the Seas: The Creation of the Panama Canal, 1870–1914* (1977); and W. LaFeber, *The Panama Canal* (rev. 1989).

The Ottoman Empire, the Middle East, and the Balkans

An informative synthesis for the years since the founding of Islam is S. N. Fisher and W. Ochsenwald, *The Middle East: A History* (rev. 1997). An excellent study of late Ottoman history is available in D. Quataert, *The Ottoman Empire, 1700–1922* (2000). For the role of the Ottoman Empire in European diplomacy and for national stirrings in the Empire, the books cited in Chapter 11 by M. S. Anderson (1966) and M. E. Yapp (1988) are instructive.

S. Deringil, *The Well-Protected Domains: Ideology and the Legitimation of Power in the Ottoman Empire, 1876–1909* (2001), describes the positive aspects of the often maligned Empire. J. Haslip, *The Sultan: The Life of Abdul Hamid II* (1958), is a vivid scholarly biography. The attempts at reform are discussed in R. H. Davison, *Reform in the Ottoman Empire, 1856–1876* (1963) and D. Kushner, *The Rise of Turkish Nationalism, 1876–1908* (1977). For Egypt, there

are available D. S. Landes, *Bankers and Pashas: International Finance and Economic Imperialism in Egypt* (1958); R. L. Tignor, *Modernization and British Colonial Rule in Egypt, 1882–1914* (1966); and T. Mitchell, *Colonising Egypt* (1988), a cultural history of European attitudes and policies. Carrying the story toward the present is P. J. Valikiotis, *The History of Modern Egypt: From Muhammad Ali [Mehemet Ali] to Mubarek* (rev. 1991). The diplomacy surrounding the construction of the Suez Canal may be studied in J. Marlowe, *World Ditch: The Making of the Suez Canal* (1964); J. Pudney, *Suez: De Lesseps' Canal* (1969); and J. P. D. Balfour [Patrick Kinross], *Between Two Seas* (1969). The French experience in Lebanon is examined in J. F. Spagnolo, *French and Ottoman Lebanon, 1861–1914* (1977); and the Italian occupation of Libya is studied in C. G. Segrè, *Fourth Shore: The Italian Colonialization of Libya* (1975).

For the rivalries in the Balkans and the emergent nationalist movements, in addition to books cited in Chapter 11, one may turn to B. H. Sumner, *Russia and the Balkans, 1870–1880* (1974) and B. Jelavich, *Russia's Balkan Entanglements, 1806–1914* (1991).

Africa

Three excellent introductions to African history are R. Oliver, *The African Experience: From the Olduvai Gorge to the 21st Century* (2000); J. Iliffe, *Africans: The History of a Continent* (1995); and J. Reader, *Africa: A Biography of the Continent* (1998). Other valuable introductions include B. Davidson, *Africa in History* (rev. 1991); R. Hallett, *Africa to 1875* (1970) and *Africa since 1875* (1974); R. W. July, *A History of the African People* (rev. 1998); and P. D. Curtin and others, *African History* (rev. 1995). A new generation of African historians, including A. E. Afigbo, E. A. Ayandele, and others study the continent over the past two centuries in *The Making of Modern Africa* (2 vols.; rev. 1986). The years of colonial domination and the African response are also studied by African scholars in J.F.A. Ajayi (ed.), *Africa in the Nineteenth Century until the 1880s* (1989) and A. A. Boahen (ed.), *Africa under Colonial Domination, 1880–1935* (1985; abridged ed. 1990). The use of oral histories in the reconstruction of African history is elucidated in J. Vansina, *Oral Tradition: A Study of Historical Methodology* (1963), and is demonstrated by the same author in *Kingdoms of the Savanna* (1966).

P. Duignan and L. H. Gann, *Burden of Empire: An Appraisal of Western Colonialism South of the Sahara* (1967), and their other writings emphasize a "benevolent imperialism." In the same tradition, T. Pakenham has written a detailed narrative, *The Scramble for Africa: The White Man's Conquest of the Dark Continent from 1870 to 1912* (1992). These books may be compared with A. A. Boahen, *African Perspectives on Colonialism* (1989) and F. McLynn,

Hearts of Darkness: The European Exploration of Africa (1993).

Available also are H. S. Wilson, *The Imperial Experience in Sub-Saharan Africa since 1870* (1977), a well-balanced synthesis; and for the French experience, W. B. Cohen, *Rulers of Empire: The French Colonial Service in Africa* (1971) and *The French Encounter with Africans: White Response to Blacks, 1530–1880* (1980). On the slave trade and its abolition, in addition to works cited in Chapters 3 and 11, one may read B. Davidson, *Black Mother: The Years of the African Slave Trade* (1961); and on the Brussels Conference of 1889, S. Miers, *Britain and the Ending of the Slave Trade* (1975).

There are biographical studies of Livingstone by, among others, T. Jeal (1973) and O. Ransford (1978). Other leading figures are examined in R. Hall, *Stanley: An Adventurer Explored* (1976), highly informative; F. J. McLynn, *Stanley* (2 vols.; 1989, 1991); J. Bierman, *Dark Safari: The Life Behind the Legend of Henry Morton Stanley* (1990); J. H. Waller, *Gordon of Khartoum* (1988); J. Pollock, *Gordon: The Man Behind the Legend* (1993); and M. F. Perham, *Lugard* (2 vols.; 1956, 1960), an impressive older work. J. Pollock, *Kitchener: Architect of Victory, Artisan of Peace* (2001), and P. Warner, *Kitchener: The Man behind the Legend* (1986), somewhat adulatory, may be compared with T. Royle, *The Kitchener Enigma* (1986), which is more critical. The brief biography of Cecil Rhodes by J. Flint (1976) merits reading, but R. I. Rotberg, *The Founder: Cecil Rhodes and the Pursuit of Power* (1988, 1990) is an outstanding study enriched by psychological insights. For a biography of the African leader who defeated the Italians at Adowa, one may read H. G. Marcus, *The Life and Times of Menelik II: Ethiopia, 1844–1913* (1975).

The best studies of the European atrocities in the Congo are R. Slade, *King Leopold's Congo* (1962); N. Ascherson, *The King Incorporated* (1963); R. Anstey, *King Leopold's Legacy* (1966); and the vivid A. Hochschild, *King Leopold's Ghost: A Story of Greed, Terror, and Heroism in Colonial Africa* (1998).

For the emergence of the Union of South Africa, and later events, L. Thompson, *A History of South Africa* (rev. 2000), is a superb synthesis; also available is R. Ross, *A Concise History of South Africa* (1999). The South African War of 1899–1902 is recounted in B. Farwell, *The Great Boer War* (1999) and T. Pakenham, *The Boer War* (1979). A thoughtful biographical account relating to these years is K. Ingham, *Jan Christian Smuts: The Conscience of a South African* (1986).

Asia

Among informative general surveys of the European impact on Asia are K. M. Pannikar, *Asia and Western Dominance: The Vasco da Gama Epoch of Asian His-* *tory, 1498–1945* (rev. 1959); E. S. Dodge, *Islands and Empires: Western Impact on the Pacific and East Asia* (1976); and R. Murphey, *The Outsiders: The Western Experience in India and China* (1977). Case studies of European expansion in Asia are provided in I. Copeland, *The Burden of Empire: Perspectives on Imperialism and Colonialism* (1991). A number of recent books have argued that the economic and social institutions of Asian societies should be studied for their own importance and should not be viewed simply as a response to the arrival of the Europeans. These arguments are developed in R. B. Wong, *China Transformed: Historical Change and the Limits of European Experience* (1997); A. G. Frank, *Reorient: Global Economy in the Asian Age* (1998); and K. Pomeranz, *The Great Divergence: Europe, China, and the Making of the Modern World Economy* (2000).

For India, one may read W. Golant, *The Long Afternoon: British India, 1601–1947* (1975); M. E. Chamberlain, *Britain and India: The Interactions of the Peoples* (1974); C. A. Bayly, *Indian Society and the Making of the British Empire* (1990); J. M. Brown, *Modern India: The Origins of an Asian Democracy* (rev. 1994); and L. James, *Raj: The Making and Unmaking of British India* (1999). The revolt of 1857 is studied in S. Sen, *Eighteen Fifty Seven* (1957); C. Hibbert, *The Great Mutiny: India, 1857* (1978); E. Stokes and C. A. Bayly, *The Peasant Armed: The Indian Rebellion of 1857* (1986); and T. R. Metcalf, *The Aftermath of Revolt: India, 1857–1870* (1964). The contest between Britain and Russia for remote parts of central Asia is recounted in K. E. Meyer and S. B. Brysac, *Tournament of Shadows: The Great Game and the Race for Empire in Central Asia* (2000).

One of the best introductions to East Asia is J. K. Fairbank, E. O. Reischauer, and A. M. Craig, *East Asia: Tradition and Transformation* (1989, with periodic revisions); and for China, J. K. Fairbank and M. Goldman, *China: A New History* (rev. 1998). Other overviews of Chinese history include C. O. Hucker, *China's Imperial Past* (1975); N. F. Sizer, *China: A Brief History* (1981); and I.C.Y. Hsu, *The Rise of Modern China* (rev. 2000). J. E. Wills, Jr., *Mountain of Fame: Portraits in Chinese History* (1994) provides a valuable biographical approach to Chinese history. J. D. Spence, *The Search for Modern China* (rev. 1999), goes back over four centuries with perceptive insights into China's relations with the West. The same author's *The Gate of Heavenly Peace: The Chinese and Their Revolution, 1895–1980* (1981) links earlier history to twentieth-century revolutions, the subject also of J. K. Fairbank, *The Great Chinese Revolution, 1800–1985* (1986).

A detailed authoritative study of the mid-nineteenth century Taiping upheaval is Jen Yu-wen, *The Taiping Revolutionary Movement* (1973), but one may also read S. Y. Teng, *The Taiping Rebellion and* the *Western Powers* (rev. 1977); and on its Christian leader, J. D. Spence, *God's Chinese Son: The Taiping Heavenly Kingdom of Hong Xiuquan* (1996). The Opium Wars are studied in J. K. Fairbank, *Trade and Diplomacy on the China Coast: The Opening of the Treaty Ports, 1842–1854* (2 vols.; 1953); and in books by J. Beeching (1976), P. W. Fay (1975, 1997), and B. Inglis (1976). The antiforeign upheaval of 1898–1900 is examined in J. W. Esherick, *The Origins of the Boxer Uprising* (1987); D. Preston, *Besieged In Peking: The Story of the 1900 Boxer Rising* (1999); and P. A. Cohen, *History in Three Keys: The Boxers as Event, Experience, and Myth* (1997), which describes both Chinese and European interpretations of the events at the time and in historical memory.

On the American role in the Far East and the Open Door policy one may read W. Cohen, *America's Response to China* (rev. 2000); J. C. Thomsen, Jr., P. W. Stanley, and J. C. Perry, *Sentimental Imperialists: The American Experience in East Asia* (1981); and A. Iriye, *Pacific Estrangement: Japanese and American Expansion, 1897–1911* (1972). The confrontation between Russia and Japan is studied in I. Nish, *The Origins of the Russo-Japanese War* (1985); J. A. White, *The Diplomacy of the Russo-Japanese War* (1964); and D. Walder, *The Short Victorious War: The Russo-Japanese Conflict, 1904–1905* (1975). The Japanese occupation of Korea is recounted in P. Duus, *The Abacus and the Sword: The Japanese Penetration of Korea* (1998).

Problems and Readings

Relevant titles include H. M. Wright (ed.), *The "New Imperialism": An Analysis of the Late Nineteenth Century Expansion* (rev. 1975); R. Owen and B. Sutcliffe (eds.), *Studies in the Theory of Imperialism* (1972); A. L. Conklin and I. C. Fletcher (eds.), *European Imperialism, 1830–1930: Climax and Contradiction* (1999); W. R. Louis (ed.), *Imperialism: The Robinson-Gallagher Controversy* (1976); R. F. Betts (ed.), *The Scramble for Africa: Causes and Dimensions of Empires* (1966); M. E. Chamberlain (ed.), *The Scramble for Africa* (rev. 1999), R. I. Rotberg (ed.), *Africa and its Explorers* (1970); T. C. Caldwell (ed.), *The Anglo-Boer War* (1965); and R. A. Austen (ed.), *Modern Imperialism: Western Overseas Expansion in the Age of Industrialization* (1969). On the nineteenth-century conflicts in India, there is A. T. Embree (ed.), *1857 in India: Mutiny or War of Independence?* (1963). Two studies exemplifying newer approaches to the study of imperialism, both in the AHA Pamphlet series, are M. Adas, *"High" Imperialism and the "New" History* (1994); and M. Strobel, *Gender, Sex, and Empire* (1994).

17. THE FIRST WORLD WAR

Accounts of international relations emphasizing the shift in the twentieth century from a European to a global balance of power include G. Ross, *The Great Powers and the Decline of the European States System, 1914–1945* (1983); C. J. Bartlett, *The Global Conflict: The International Rivalry of the Great Powers, 1880–1990* (rev. 1994); J. Joll, *Europe since 1870: An International History* (rev. 1990); and W. R. Keylor, *The Twentieth-Century World: An International History* (rev. 2001).

Diplomatic Background, Origins, Responsibilities

The most judicious account of the war's complex origins, assessing both the evidence and divergent interpretations, is J. Joll, *The Origins of the First World War* (rev. 1992). Two attempts to synthesize the continuing debate over war responsibility are J. W. Langdon, *July 1914: The Long Debate: 1918–1990* (1991) and R.J.W. Evans and H. P. Van Strandmann (eds.), *The Coming of the First World War* (1989).

The controversy reopened after 1945 when the West German scholar Fritz Fischer, on the basis of new archival materials, argued the case for German culpability in *Germany's Aims in the First World War* (1961; trans. 1967) and in several later books. He argued that Germany had to grasp for "world power" or face decline and that elite groups in Germany pressed this objective to thwart democratization.

On diplomacy in the decades after 1870, there are the important older studies by W. L. Langer: *European Alliances and Alignments, 1871–1890* (1931, 1950) and *The Diplomacy of Imperialism, 1890–1902* (2 vols.; 1935, 1951, 1965), cited earlier. A masterful diplomatic account is available in two volumes by G. F. Kennan: *The Decline of Bismarck's European Order: Franco-Russian Relations, 1875–1890* (1979) and *The Fateful Alliance: France, Russia, and the Coming of the First World War* (1984). A colorful reconstruction of the era for the general reader, focusing on monarchs, military leaders, and diplomats is available in R. K. Massie, *Dreadnought: Britain, Germany, and the Coming of the First World War* (1992). N. Ferguson, *The Pity of War* (1999), despite many striking insights into diplomatic and military matters, argues, not convincingly, that there was no compelling reason for Britain to become involved.

D. E. Lee's careful study, *Europe's Crucial Years: The Diplomatic Background of World War I, 1902–1914* (1974), reaffirms the argument that each state acted out of desperate concern for its own presumed interests. Domestic and foreign considerations are linked in a British series of books that includes V. R. Berghahn, *Germany and the Approach of War in 1914* (rev. 1993); Z. S. Steiner, *Britain and the Origins of the First World War* (1977); R.J.B. Bosworth, *Italy, the Least of the Great Powers: Italian Foreign Policy before the First World War* (1980); J.F.V. Keiger, *France and the Origins of the First World War* (1984);

D.C.B. Lieven, *Russia and the Origins of the First World War* (1984); and S. R. Williamson, Jr., *Austria-Hungary and the Origins of the First World War* (1991). Three volumes in another British series on foreign policy are also valuable for these years: J. Néré, *The Foreign Policy of France from 1914 to 1945* (trans. 1975); F. R. Bridge, *From Sadowa to Sarajevo: The Foreign Policy of Austria-Hungary, 1866–1914* (1972); and C. J. Lowe and F. Marzari, *Italian Foreign Policy, 1870–1940* (1975).

For prewar diplomacy and strategic planning, readers will find especially useful three books by P. Kennedy: *The Rise of the Anglo-German Antagonism, 1860–1914* (1980), *Strategy and Diplomacy, 1870–1945* (1984), and a collaborative volume he has edited, *War Plans of the Great Powers, 1880–1914* (1979). The Balkan antecedents of the war are examined in R. C. Hall, *The Balkan Wars, 1912–1913: Prelude to the First World War* (2000).

The involvement of the United States in the war is studied in E. R. May, *The World War and American Isolation, 1914–1917* (1959), an outstanding study; R. Gregory, *The Origins of American Intervention in the First World War* (1971); P. Devlin, *Too Proud to Fight: Woodrow Wilson's Neutrality* (1974); R. H. Ferrell, *Woodrow Wilson and World War I* (1985); and M. Harries and S. Harries, *The Last Days of Innocence: America at War, 1917–1918* (1997).

The War

For the war there are informative narratives, among many others, by B. H. Liddell Hart (1934), C.R.M. Cruttwell (1934, 1990), M. Gilbert (1995), and J. Keegan (1999). Books focusing on the social impact of the war include M. Ferro, *The Great War, 1914–1918* (trans. 1973); K. Robbins, *The First World War* (1984); B. E. Schmitt and H. C. Vedeler, *The World in the Crucible, 1914–1919* (1984); and J. M. Winter, *The Experience of World War I* (1989).

Books that seek to convey the ordeal of trench warfare on the western front include E. J. Leed, *No Man's Land: Combat and Identity in World War I* (1979); T. Ashworth, *Trench Warfare, 1914–1918: The Live and Let-Live System* (1980); and J. Ellis, *Eye-Deep in Hell: Trench Warfare in World War I* (1989). J. Keegan, *The Face of Battle* (1976), in one memorable chapter evokes the horrors of the Somme. For the American military experience, one may read E. M. Coffman, *The War to End All Wars* (1968, 1998).

The Home Front: Social, Economic, and Cultural Impact of the War

For the impact of war and of preparations for war on European society, one should read B. Bond, *War and Society in Europe, 1870–1970* (rev. 1998); A. Marwick, *War and Social Change in the Twentieth Century*

(1975), a comparative examination of five countries; and G. Hardach, *The First World War, 1914–1918* (1977), focusing on the economic aspects of the war and its consequences. There are many informative studies in the multivolume Carnegie Endowment *Economic and Social History of the World War* (J. T. Shotwell, gen. ed., 1924–1940), of which over 100 volumes were published.

For the war on the home front one may turn to F. Chambers, *The War behind the War, 1914–1918* (1939), an older but still valuable account; J. Williams, *The Other Battleground: The Home Fronts—Britain, France and Germany, 1914–1918* (1972); and the essays in R. Wall and J. Winter (eds.), *The Upheaval of War: Family, Work, and Welfare in Europe, 1914–1918* (1989). For Britain, one may read J. M. Winter, *The Great War and the British People* (1986), an outstanding volume; A Marwick, *The Deluge: British Society and the First World War* (1965); T. Wilson, *The Myriad Faces of War: Britain and the Great War, 1914–1918* (1968); B. Waites, *A Class Society at War: England, 1914–1918* (1988); and J. Bourne, *Britain and the Great War, 1914–1918* (1989). For Germany: J. Kocka, *Facing Total War: German Society, 1914–1918* (trans. 1984); L. V. Meyer, *Victory Must Be Ours: Germany in the Great War, 1914–1918* (1995); and R. Chickering, *Imperial Germany and the Great War, 1914–1918* (1998). For France: J. J. Becker, *The Great War and the French People* (trans. 1986) and P. J. Flood, *France, 1914–1918: Public Opinion and the War Effort* (1989). For the United States: D. M. Kennedy, *Over Here: The First World War and American Society* (1980).

The contributions of women to the war effort are examined in A. Marwick, *Women at War, 1914–1918* (1977); G Braybon, *Women Workers in the First World War: The British Experience* (1981); M. W. Greenwald, *Women, War, and Work: The Impact of World War I on Women Workers in the United States* (1980); and D. Schneider and C. Schneider, *Into the Breach: American Women Overseas in World War I* (1991).

The dictatorial powers that the German generals preempted is examined with telling detail in M. Kitchen, *The Silent Dictatorship: The Politics of the German High Command under Hindenburg and Ludendorff, 1916–1918* (1976). On the human costs of the war, one may consult T. J. Mitchell and G. M. Smith, *Medical Services: Casualties and Medical Statistics of the Great War* (1931); and for the devastating worldwide influenza epidemic that doubled the combat toll, A. W. Crosby, *America's Forgotten Pandemic: The Influenza of 1918* (1976, 1990) and G. Kolata *The Story of the Great Influenza Pandemic of 1918* (2000).

One of the lesser-known tragedies of the war, the forced deportation of the Armenians by the Turkish authorities, and the ensuring mass deaths, is recounted in C. J. Walker, *Armenia: The Survival of a Nation* (rev. 1990); D. M. Lang, *The Armenians: A People in Exile* (1989); and R. Melson, *Revolution and Genocide: On the Origins of the Armenian Genocide and the Holocaust* (1993), which sees the episode as the first chapter in twentieth-century ethnic destruction.

The cultural meaning of the war is examined in P. Fussell, *The Great War and Modern Memory* (1975, 2000), a moving account of how the miseries of the war became part of contemporary literature and culture, and S. Hynes, *A War Imagined: The First World War and English Culture* (1992). Other studies of the war's impact on intellectual life are R. Wohl, *The Generation of 1914* (1979); R. N. Stromberg, *Redemption by War: The Intellectuals and 1914* (1982); J. Cruickshank, *Variations on Catastrophe: Some French Responses to the Great War* (1982); F. Field, *British and French Writers of the First World War* (1991); M. Ecksteins, *The Rites of Spring: The Great War and the Birth of the Modern Age* (1989, 2000), an inquiry into the shaping of a new cultural consciousness; and G. Mosse, *Sites of Mourning: The Great War in European Cultural History* (1996).

Wartime Diplomacy

For wartime diplomacy one profits from D. Stevenson, *The First World War and International Politics* (1988) and Z.A.B. Zeman, *The Gentlemen Negotiators: A Diplomatic History of the First World War* (1971). Two provocative studies focusing on the diplomatic duel between the United States and Russia are V. S. Mamatey, *The United States and East Central Europe, 1914–1918* (1975) and A. J. Mayer, *Wilson vs. Lenin: The Political Origins of the New Diplomacy* (1959). The fate of the German colonial empire is explored in W. R. Louis, *Great Britain and Germany's Lost Colonies, 1914–1919* (1967).

For Allied activities in the Middle East, and on the revolt of the Arabs against the Turks, one may begin with T. E. Lawrence, *Seven Pillars of Wisdom* (1926, 1935), fascinating but to be read with caution, and J. Wilson, *Lawrence of Arabia: The Authorized Biography of T. E. Lawrence* (1990), the fullest account. Focusing on the Middle East and the end of the Ottoman Empire are C. E. Dawn, *From Ottomanism to Arabism* (1973); H. M. Sachar, *The Emergence of the Middle East, 1914–1924* (1969); P. C. Helmreich, *From Paris to Sèvres: The Partition of the Ottoman Empire at the Peace Conference of 1919–1920* (1974); D. Fromkin, *A Peace to End All Peace: Creating the Modern Middle East, 1914–1922* (1989), especially informative; and E. Karsh and I. Karsh, *Empires of the Sand: The Struggle for Mastery in the Middle East, 1789–1923* (1999), providing the background to the postwar settlement.

The emergence of the British mandate for Palestine is studied in impressive detail in L. Stein, *The Balfour Declaration* (1961) and R. Sanders, *The High Walls of Jerusalem: A History of the Balfour Declaration and the Birth of the British Mandate* (1984).

The Peace

For the armistice, one may turn to S. Weintraub, *A Stillness Heard Round the World: The End of the Great War, November 1918* (1987), a colorful evocation of the war's end, and B. Lowry, *Armistice 1918* (1996), a thorough diplomatic analysis. The postwar revolutionary mood is described in G. Schulz, *Revolution and Peace Treaties, 1917–1920* (trans. 1972); F. L. Carsten, *Revolution in Central Europe, 1918–1919* (1972); and the essays in C. L. Bertrand (ed.), *Revolutionary Situations in Europe, 1917–1922* (1977). The end of the Dual Monarchy is studied in A. J. May, *The Passing of the Habsburg Monarchy, 1914–1918* (2 vols.; 1966) and Z.A.B. Zeman, *The Breakup of the Habsburg Empire, 1914–1918* (1961).

On the Paris peace conference, the best introduction is A. Sharp, *The Versailles Settlement: Peacemaking in Paris* (1991). Valuable older accounts include P. Birdsall, *Versailles Twenty Years After* (1941), sympathetic to Wilson; and H. Nicholson, *Peacemaking, 1919* (1933, 1939). The decision-making process itself is studied in H. Elcock, *Portrait of a Decision: The Council of Four and the Treaty of Versailles* (1972). The debates are available in P. Mantoux (ed.), *The Paris Peace Conference, 1919: Proceedings of the Council of Four* (1955; trans. 1964).

On Wilson's role, the best study is A. Walworth, *Wilson and His Peacemakers: American Diplomacy at the Paris Peace Conference, 1919* (1987); also helpful are K. A. Clements, *The Presidency of Woodrow Wilson* (1992), a concise appraisal; A. Heckscher, *Woodrow Wilson* (1992), a detailed full-length biography; L. Auchincloss, *Woodrow Wilson* (2000), an insightful brief biography; and two studies by Wilson's major biographer, A. S. Link: *Wilson the Diplomatist* (1957) and *Woodrow Wilson: War, Revolution, and Peace* (1979). Biographies of Clemenceau by D. R. Watson (1974) and D. S. Newhall (1991), and of David Lloyd George by J. Grigg (1973–1985) and others have been cited in Chapter 14; to them should be added J.F.V. Keiger, *Raymond Poincaré* (1997).

A study arguing that the major preoccupation underlying decisions at Versailles was the threat of Bolshevism and domestic radicalism is A. J. Mayer, *Politics and Diplomacy of Peacemaking: Containment and Counter-Revolution at Versailles, 1918–1919* (1967); it may be compared with J. M. Thompson, *Russia, Bolshevism, and the Versailles Peace* (1966), which views the revolutionary threat as important but not dominating. Important balanced reappraisals, many based on new archival materials, may be found in the contributions to M. F. Boemeke, G. D. Feldman, and E. Glaser (eds.), *The Treaty of Versailles: A Reassessment After 75 Years* (1998).

In addition to S. Bonsal, *Suitors and Suppliants: The Little Nations at Versailles* (1964), there are also monographs on many of the smaller countries: F. Deák on Hungary (1942), D. Perman on Czechoslovakia (1962), D. Spector on Romania (1962), T. Komarnicki on Poland (1957), I. J. Lederer on Yugoslavia (1963), and S. Marks on Belgium (1981). The Polish question is carefully examined by a Danish historian, K. Lundrgreen-Nielsen, *The Polish Problem at the Paris Peace Conference* (trans. 1979). On the disputed issue of reparations, J. M. Keynes, *The Economic Consequences of the Peace* (1920), became the single most influential book, vehemently critical of the entire peace settlement. E. Mantoux, *The Carthaginian Peace—or the Economic Consequences of Mr. Keynes* (1946), is a vigorous reply to Keynes written many years later. The first volume of a valuable three-volume study, R. Skidelsky, *John Maynard Keynes: A Biography:* Vol. I, *Hopes Betrayed, 1883–1920* (1986), carries Keynes through the peace conference.

Problems and Readings

Conflicting interpretations of the war's origins are presented in D. E. Lee (ed.), *The Outbreak of the First World War* (rev. 1976); J. Remak (ed.), *The First World War: Causes, Conduct, Consequences* (1971); H. W. Koch (ed.), *The Origins of the First World War: Great Power Rivalry and German War Aims* (rev. 1984); I. Geiss (ed.), July 1914 (1969); and H. H. Herwig (ed.), *The Outbreak of World War I* (1997). For the peace settlement there are N. G. Levin (ed.), *Woodrow Wilson and the Paris Peace Conference* (1972); R. A. Stone (ed.), *Wilson and the League of Nations: Why America's Rejection?* (1967, 1978); and W. R. Keylor (ed.), *The Legacy of the Great War: Peacemaking, 1919* (1998). Documents on the American role in the war may be found in J. D. Keene, *The United States and the First World War* (2000). The impact of the war is assessed in R. Albrecht-Carrié (ed.), *The Meaning of the First World War* (1965) and J. J. Roth (ed.), *World War I: A Turning Point in Modern History* (1967). For the twentieth-century world in general a useful anthology of interpretive readings is L. Derfler, *An Age of Conflict* (1990).

18. THE RUSSIAN REVOLUTION AND THE SOVIET UNION

With the collapse of the Soviet Union in 1991 new archival materials have made it possible to confirm, modify, or refute earlier works and to rethink Russian history. Recent histories include O. Figes, *A People's Tragedy: A History of the Russian Revolution* (1997); G. Hosking, *Russia and the Russians* (2001), now the best one-volume narrative available. The same author's *Russia: Empire and Nation* (1997) may be compared with D. Lieven, *The Russian Empire and Its Rivals* (2001). M. E. Malia, *The Soviet Tragedy: A History of Socialism in Russia, 1917–1991* (1993), maintains that the utopian goals were doomed from the beginning; the same author's *Russia Under Western Eyes: From the Bronze Horseman to the Lenin Mausoleum* (1999), argues that Russia at least since Peter the Great was always more Western-oriented than most observers believed. Additional accounts will be listed in later chapters.

Russia before 1917: Late Tsarist Russia

A number of books on nineteenth-century Russia have been cited earlier. For late tsarist Russia one may read L. Kochan, *Russia in Revolution, 1890–1918* (1966) and H. Rogger, *Russia in the Age of Modernization and Revolution, 1881–1917* (1983).

Political thought and ferment may be studied in F. Venturi, *Roots of Revolution* (trans. 1983), cited earlier; A. Vucinich, *Social Thought in Tsarist Russia* (1976); and P. Pomper, *The Russian Revolutionary Intelligentsia* (rev. 1993). Two books stressing the non-revolutionary progressive views of many pre-1914 Russian intellectuals are I. Berlin, *Russian Thinkers* (1978), cited earlier, and A. H. Kelly, *Toward Another Shore: Russian Thinkers between Necessity and Choice* (1998). The world of labor is examined in V. E. Bonnell, *Roots of Rebellion: Workers' Politics and Organizations in St. Petersburg and Moscow, 1990–1914* (1983) and in the volume she has edited of workers' autobiographical accounts, *The Russian Worker: Life and Labor under the Tsarist Regime* (1983).

Political leaders who served the tsar are studied in R. F. Byrnes, *Pobiedonostsev: His Life and Thought* (1968), an exemplar of tsarist obscurantism; and R. Pipes, *Struve* (2 vols.; 1970–1980), informative on the fate of liberalism. Right-wing extremism linked to anti-Semitic pogroms is explored in W. Laqueur, *Black Hundred: The Rise of the Extreme Right in Russia* (1993). For the emergent revolutionary leaders, one may read D. W. Treadgold, *Lenin and His Rivals: The Struggle for Russia's Future, 1898–1906* (1955); L. Haimson, *The Russian Marxists and the Origins of Bolshevism* (1955); I. Getzler, *Martov* (1967); S. H. Baron, *Plekhanov* (1963); and A. Ascher, *Pavel Axelrod and the Development of Menshevism* (1972). On the anarchists, there are P. Avrich, *The Russian Anarchists* (1967) and on a leading exemplar, M. A. Miller, *Kropotkin* (1976) and C. Cahm, *Peter Kropotkin and the Rise of Revolutionary Anarchism* (1989).

The events of 1905 are narrated and analyzed in a valuable two-volume account by A. Ascher: *The Revolution of 1905:* Vol. I, *Russia in Disarray* (1988) and Vol. II, *Authority Restored* (1992), carrying the story to 1907. Also informative is A. M. Verner, *The Crisis of Russian Autocracy: Nicholas II and the 1905 Revolution* (1990).

Explorations of the ill-fated effort to establish a constitutional monarchy after 1905 include A. E. Healy, *The Russian Autocracy in Crisis, 1905–1907* (1976); and G. Hosking, *The Russian Constitutional Experiment: Government and Duma, 1906–1914* (1973). The Russian wartime experience is vividly described in W. B. Lincoln, *In War's Dark Shadow* (1983) and *Passage through Armageddon* (1986). The confusion at the court graphically emerges from R. K. Massie's *Nicholas and Alexandra* (1967, 1985). For the last Romanoff one may also read M. Ferro, *Nicholas II: The Last of the Tsars* (1993) and R. D. Warth, *Nicholas II: The Life and Reign of Russia's Last Monarch* (1998). E. Radzinsky, *The Last Tsar: The Life and Death of Nicholas II* (trans. 1992) reconstructs the execution of the royal family in 1918; the same author has also used a newly available dossier on Rasputin to write a vivid biography of the mad monk who became the royal family's close adviser, *The Rasputin File* (trans. 2001).

The Revolutions of 1917

The best account of the earlier revolution is T. Hasegawa, *The February Revolution: Petrograd, 1917* (1981); there are other informative studies by G. Katkov (1967), M. Ferro (1971), and E. N. Burdzhalov (1987). The ill-fated Kerensky is studied in R. Abraham, *Alexander Kerensky: The First Love of the Revolution* (1987).

For the fullest and most comprehensive account of the revolutionary years one turns to R. Pipes, *The Russian Revolution* (1990) and *Russia Under the Bolshevik Regime* (1994), the latter carrying the story through Lenin's death in 1924. Available also is C. Read, *From Tsar to Soviets: The Russian People and the Revolution, 1917-1921* (1996). Focusing on the social breadth and depth of the revolution are two books by M. Ferro: *The Fall of Tsarism and the Origins of Bolshevik Power* (trans. 1967) and *October 1917: A Social History of the Russian Revolution* (trans. 1980).

The best introductions to the civil war, the formation of the Soviet state, and foreign intervention are E. Mawdsley, *The Russian Civil War* (1987); W. B. Lincoln, *Red Victory: A History of the Russian Civil War* (1990); and V. N. Brovkin, *Behind the Front Lines of the Civil War: Political Parties and Social Movements in Russia, 1918–1922* (1994). The reconquest of Ukraine and of other parts of the tsarist empire that for a time had become independent is described in an earlier book by R. Pipes, *The Formation of the Soviet Union: Communism and Nationalism, 1917–1923* (rev. 1964). For the withdrawal from the war and the subsequent Allied intervention one may turn to G. F.

Kennan, S*oviet-American Relations, 1917–1920* (2 vols.; 1956–1958) and R. H. Ullman, *Anglo-Soviet Relations, 1917–1921* (3 vols.; 1961–1972). The best study of the peace imposed by Germany remains J. W. Wheeler-Bennett, *The Forgotten Peace: Brest-Litovsk, March 1918* (1939, 1966); the stormy relations of the Soviet Union with newly independent Poland are described in P. S. Wandycz, *Soviet-Polish Relations, 1917–1921* (1969). A helpful reference guide for all these events is H. Shukman (ed.), *The Blackwell Encyclopedia of the Russian Revolution* (1988).

The U.S.S.R.

For the early years one should read R. Pipes, *Russia under the Bolshevik Regime* (1994), cited earlier, which examines in detail the consolidation of the dictatorial regime by 1924. P. Avrich, *Kronstadt, 1921* (1970, 1991), describes the leftist uprising and its suppression. An institution that was destined to endure is studied in L. D. Gerson, *The Secret Police in Lenin's Russia* (1976) and G. Leggett, *The Cheka: Lenin's Political Police* (1981).

For the years under Lenin and the early years of Stalin's rule one may consult E. H. Carr's synthesis of his massive 14-volume study (1950–1979), *The Russian Revolution from Lenin to Stalin* (1979), in which Carr seeks to make the best possible case for the reconstruction of Soviet society in the years 1917–1929. Focusing on sociological and cultural aspects of this period are R. Stites, *Revolutionary Dreams: Utopian Vision and Experimental Life in the Russian Revolution* (1988); V. Brovkin, *Russia after Lenin: Politics, Culture and Society, 1921–1929* (1998); G. Hosking, *The First Socialist Society: A History of the Soviet Union from Within* (rev. 1993), which carries a comprehensive social history through to the end of the Soviet experiment; and S. Fitzpatrick's three books: *The Russian Revolution, 1917–1932* (1982), *The Cultural Front: Power and Culture in Revolutionary Russia* (1992), and *Everyday Stalinism: Ordinary Life in Extraordinary Times* (1998). For all aspects of economic developments from 1917 on, one may turn to A. Nove, *An Economic History of the U.S.S.R.* (rev. 1992).

Stalin's collectivization of agriculture may be studied in M. Lewin, *Russian Peasants and Soviet Power* (trans. 1975) and R. Conquest, *The Harvest of Sorrow: Soviet Collectivization and the Terror-Famine* (1987), which graphically reconstructs the ruthlessness of collectivization and the accompanying famine of 1932. Conquest, one of the earliest critics of the Stalinist terror, has also written numerous other books.

For the political terror in the Stalin era the most revealing studies are R. Medvedev, *Let History Judge: The Origins and Consequences of Stalinism* (trans. 1989), by a Soviet dissident historian; and for the party purges and terror of 1936–1938, stressing the enormity of the now officially conceded blood bath,

R. Conquest, *The Great Terror: A Reassessment* (1968, 1990). Some of the corroborative new evidence surfacing in the years after 1985 is discussed R. Pipes, *The Unknown Lenin: From the Soviet Archives* (1997) and W. Laqueur, *Stalin: The Glasnost Revelations* (1990). The origins of the party purges are examined in R. Conquest, *Stalin and the Kirov Murder* (1989), and from a different perspective in the controversial J. A. Getty, *Origins of the Great Purges: The Soviet Communist Party Reconsidered, 1933–1938* (1986). An insightful general account of the years from the Revolution to Stalin's death is H. Carrère d'Encausse, *A History of the Soviet Union, 1917–1953* (2 vols.; trans. 1982).

Biographical Accounts

Among older biographical accounts for these years are B. D. Wolfe, *Three Who Made a Revolution: A Biographical History* [Lenin, Trotsky, Stalin] (1948, 1964); H. Shukman, *Lenin and the Russian Revolution* (1987); and A. B. Ulam, *Lenin and the Bolsheviks* (1965, 1969). There are also lives of Lenin by D. Shub (1948, 1966), L. F. Fischer (1964), M. C. Morgan (1971), R. Conquest (1972), R.H.W. Theen (1973), and M. Lewin (1978). Lenin's wife and her fate in the Stalin years are ably studied in R. H. McNeal, *Bride of the Revolution: Krupskaya and Lenin* (1972).

I. Deutscher's overly sympathetic three-volume life of Trotsky (1954–1963), and R. Segal, *Leon Trotsky* (1979), also sympathetic, may be compared with the more balanced appraisals by R. S. Wistrich, *Trotsky: Fate of a Revolutionary* (1979) and I. Howe, *Leon Trotsky* (1979). S. F. Cohen, *Bukharin and the Bolshevik Revolution: A Political Biography, 1888–1938* (1973, 1980) is an outstanding study of a leading Old Bolshevik who helped shape Lenin's New Economic Policy and had he prevailed, might have averted Stalin's dictatorship.

For an outstanding study of Stalin in the years before the Second World War one may read R. C. Tucker, *Stalin as Revolutionary, 1879–1929* (1973) and *Stalin in Power: The Revolution from Above, 1928–1941* (1990). Other biographical accounts are A. B. Ulam, *Stalin: The Man and His Era* (1973); the imaginative but uncritical I. Deutscher, *Stalin: A Political Biography* (1967); and R. H. McNeal, *Stalin: Man and Ruler* (1988).

In a special category, a series of recent biographies by D. Volkogonov has appeared in English translation. Volkogonov was for many years a top-ranking Soviet military intelligence official with unique access to key archival sources and his books provide indispensable special information. Among them are *Stalin: Triumph and Tragedy* (trans. 1992), *Lenin: A New Biography* (trans. 1995), *Trotsky: The Eternal Revolutionary* (trans. 1996), and for his overall review of Soviet history, *Autopsy for an Empire: The Seven*

Leaders Who Built the Soviet Regime [Lenin to Gorbachev] (trans. 1998).

Among thoughtful earlier efforts to assess the Russian experience from the revolution on into the interwar years and beyond are T. H. Von Laue, *Why Lenin? Why Stalin? A Reappraisal of the Russian Revolution, 1900–1930* (rev. 1993); E. Acton, *Rethinking the Russian Revolution* (1990); A. Nove, *Was Stalin Really Necessary?* (1965); S. F. Cohen, *Rethinking the Soviet Experience: Politics and History since 1917* (1985); and two books by M. Lewin: *The Making of the Soviet System: Essays in the Social History of Interwar Russia* (1985) and *The Gorbachev Phenomenon: A Historical Interpretation* (rev. 1991). Books on the last years of the Soviet regime and on its collapse in 1991 will be described in Chapter 25.

Other Themes and Institutions

On other subjects and institutions one may read R. Kolkowitz, *The Soviet Military and the Communist Party* (1967); L. R. Graham, *Science and Philosophy in the Soviet Union* (1972), and his other writings; and C. V. James, *Soviet Socialist Realism* (1973), on the arts and literature. For religious policies one may read S. P. Ramet (ed.), *Religious Policy in the Soviet Union* (1992); and N. Davis, *A Long Walk to Church: A Contemporary History of Russian Orthodoxy* (1995). The Jewish question is thoughtfully explored in Z. Gitelman, *The Jews of Russia and the Soviet Union* (1988); A. Vaksberg, *Stalin Against the Jews* (1994); and G. Kostyrchenko, *Out of the Red Shadows: Anti-Semitism in Stalin's Russia* (1996).

The role of women in the prerevolutionary and postrevolutionary years may be studied in R. Stites, *The Women's Liberation Movement in Russia: Feminism, Nihilism, and Bolshevism, 1860–1930* (rev. 1991); L. Engelstein, *The Keys to Happiness: Sex and the Search for Modernity in Fin-de-Siècle Russia* (1992), on the late nineteenth century; G. W. Lapidus, *Women in Soviet Society: Equality, Development, and Social Change* (1978); B. E. Clements and others (eds.), *Russia's Women: Accommodation, Resistance, Transformation* (1990); and L. Edmondson (ed.), *Women and Society in Russia and the Soviet Union* (1992).

Soviet Foreign Relations and World Communism

Still useful for Soviet foreign policy are A. B. Ulam, *Expansion and Coexistence: The History of Soviet Foreign Policy, 1917–1973* (rev. 1974), and his other writings; and the volumes by L. F. Fischer: *The Soviets in World Affairs, 1917–1929* (rev. 1960) and *Russia's Road from Peace to War: Soviet Foreign Relations, 1917–1941* (1969).

On the transformation of earlier socialism and Marxism into communism, a number of studies have been described in Chapters 11, 12, and 15. Recommended also are A. B. Ulam, *The Unfinished Revolution: An Essay on the Sources of Marxism and Communism* (1960); A. G. Meyer, *Leninism* (1957) and *Communism* (1960); and O. A. Narkiewicz, *Marxism and the Reality of Power* (1981). Personal testimonies about the impact of communism may be found in A. Balabanoff, *My Life as a Rebel* (1938) and R. H. Crossman (ed.), *The God that Failed* (1950), an insightful series of autobiographical essays on faith and disillusionment.

On the Comintern, one may turn to H. Seton-Watson, *From Lenin to Khrushchev: The History of World Communism* (1953, 1960), K. E. McKenzie, *Comintern and World Revolution, 1928–1943* (1964); and K. McDermott and J. Agnew, *The Comintern: A History of International Communism from Lenin to Stalin* (1997). The clash of Bolshevism with French, Italian, and German socialism is ably explored in A. S. Lindemann, *The "Red Years": European Socialism vs. Bolshevism, 1918–1920* (1974), while R. Wohl examines the French experience with insight and depth in *French Communism in the Making, 1919–1924* (1966).

Problems and Readings

Available are R. H. McNeal (ed.), *Russia in Transition, 1905–1914: Evolution or Revolution?* (1969); M. McCauley (ed.), *Octobrists to Bolsheviks: Imperial Russia, 1905–1917* (1984); R. G. Suny and A. E. Adams (eds.), *The Russian Revolution and Bolshevik Victory* (rev. 1990); V. D. Medlin (ed.), *The Russian Revolution* (1979); B. M. Unterberger (ed.), *American Intervention in the Russian Civil War* (1969); S. W. Page (ed.), *Lenin: Dedicated Marxist or Pragmatic Revolutionary?* (1969); R. V. Daniels (ed.), *The Stalin Revolution* (rev. 1997); R. C. Tucker and S. F. Cohen (eds.), *The Great Purge Trials* (1965); and G. F. Kennan, *Soviet Foreign Policy, 1917–1941* (1960, 1979).

19. THE APPARENT VICTORY OF DEMOCRACY

A number of general histories of the twentieth century begin with the First World War and the revolutionary changes that accompanied it. Among these are E. J. Hobsbawm, *The Age of Extremes: A History of the World, 1914–1991* (1994), an insightful book on the years between the First World War and the collapse of the Soviet Union, which he calls the "short twentieth century"; J.A.S. Grenville, *A History of the World in the Twentieth Century* (1994), a detailed narrative; and H. Evans and others, *The American Century* (1999), an interpretive account of major developments and issues. Informative also are the essays in R. W. Bulliet (ed.), *The Columbia History of the Twentieth Century* (1998) and M. Howard and R. Louis (eds.), *The Oxford History of the Twentieth Century* (1998, 2000). A useful reference book for twentieth-century world history is

The Longman Handbook of World History since 1918 (1991).

For Europe in the twentieth century one may read J. Joll, *Europe since 1870* (1990), cited earlier; R. O. Paxton, *Twentieth Century Europe* (1994), especially informative; and M. Mazower, *Dark Continent: Europe's Twentieth Century* (1999), a thoughtful book which sees more negative than positive features in Europe's history during these years.

The attempt in the interwar years to put together a shattered polity in Europe is described in R. J. Sontag, *A Broken World, 1919–1939* (1971) and M. Kitchen, *Europe Between the Wars* (1988). Two efforts to examine the pattern of reconstruction in Europe after the war are C. S. Maier, *Recasting Bourgeois Europe: Stabilization in France, Germany and Italy in the Decade after World War I* (1975), stressing the link between interest groups and conservative governments, and D. P. Silverman, *Reconstructing Europe after the Great War* (1982). Additional books for the interwar years, including works on the new states of central and eastern Europe, are described in the chapter that follows.

International Relations in the 1920s

Introductions to international affairs in this era are P. Renouvin, *War and Aftermath, 1914–1929* (1968); S. Marks, *The Illusion of Peace: International Relations in Europe, 1918–1933* (1976); and A. Adamthwaite, *The Lost Peace: International Relations in Europe, 1918–1939* (1981). The high point of reconciliation with Germany is ably treated in J. Jacobson, *Locarno Diplomacy: Germany and the West, 1925–1929* (1972). For American foreign policy encompassing the interwar years and the two world wars, A. Iriye, *The Globalizing of America, 1913–1945* (1993) is illuminating.

B. Kent, *The Spoils of War: The Politics, Economics, and Diplomacy of Reparations, 1918–1932* (1989) synthesizes the considerable literature on the complex reparations question, on which related studies include M. Trachetenberg, *Reparations in World Politics: France and European Economic Diplomacy, 1916–1923* (1980); S. A. Schuker, *The End of French Predominance in Europe* (1976); and B. F. Martin, *France and the Après Guerre, 1918–1924* (1999). The American role in these years is also studied in M. P. Leffler, *The Elusive Quest: America's Pursuit of European Stability and French Security* (1979), and on a broader scale in F. Costigliola, *Awkward Dominion: American Political, Economic, and Cultural Relations with Europe, 1919–1933* (1984). On the British role one may read A. Orde, *British Policy and European Reconstruction after the First World War* (1990). The response of the United States and Britain to the revolutionary events of the era, and not only to the revolution in Russia, is examined critically in L. C. Gardner,

Safe for Democracy: The Anglo-American Response to Revolution, 1913–1923 (1984).

The cooperation between the Soviet Union and Weimar Germany is studied in G. Freund, *Unholy Alliance* (1957); K. Rosenbaum, *Community of Fate: German-Soviet Diplomatic Relations, 1922–1928* (1965); and H. L. Dyck, *Weimar Germany and Soviet Russia, 1926–1933* (1966).

For the League of Nations one may read F. S. Northedge, *The League of Nations: Its Life and Times, 1920–1946* (1986), which notes that despite its shortcomings it helped to transform the older diplomacy. A special problem in which the League played an important role is discussed in a wide-ranging study, M. R. Marrus, *The Unwanted: European Refugees in the Twentieth Century* (1985). Books on efforts at disarmament include R. H. Ferrell, *Peace in Their Time: The Origins of the Kellogg-Briand Pact* (1952); R. Dingman, *Power in the Pacific: The Origins of Naval Arms Limitation, 1914–1922* (1976); and E. W. Bennett, *German Rearmament and the West, 1932–1933* (1979).

Anticolonialism in Asia: East Asia

For China in the early part of the twentieth century, in addition to books cited in Chapter 16, the best introductions are H. Z. Schiffrin, *Sun Yat-sen and the Origins of the 1911 Revolution* (1969); F. Wakeman, *The Fall of Imperial China* (1975); and the essays in M. C. Wright (ed.), *China in Revolution: The First Phase, 1900–1913* (1968). The story of the last Manchu (or Qing) ruler (later appointed by the Japanese to rule in conquered Manchuria) is recounted in B. Power, *The Puppet Emperor: The Life of Pu Yi, Last Emperor of China* (1988).

Biographical studies for Sun include L. Sharman, *Sun Yat-sen and Communism* (1961); C. M. Wilbur, *Sun Yat-sen: Frustrated Patriot* (1976); and M. C. Bergère, *Sun Yat-Sen* (trans. 1998). On the resentments stirred by the Chinese treatment at Versailles, one should read V. Schwarcz, *The Chinese Enlightenment: Intellectuals and the Legacy of the May Fourth Movement of 1919* (1986). The era of Chiang Kai-shek and Guomindang rule is studied in L. Eastman, *The Abortive Revolution: China under Nationalist Rule, 1927–1937* (1974, 1990); and J. C. Strauss, *Strong Institutions in Weak Polities: State Building in Republican China, 1927–1940* (1998). On the emergent Communist movement one may read A. Dirlik, *The Origins of Chinese Communism* (1988), and the accounts of the Long March of 1934–1935 by D. Wilson (1972), H. Salisbury (1984), and B. Yang (1990).

General books on Japan have been cited in Chapter 13. On the rise of militarism in Japan one should read J. B. Crowley, *Japan's Quest for Autonomy: National Security and Foreign Policy, 1930–1938* (1966).

Japanese-American relations and the failure to arrive at an international settlement in East Asia is traced in A. Iriye: *Pacific Estrangement: Japanese and American Expansion, 1897–1911* (1972) and *After Imperialism: The Search for New Order in the Far East, 1921–1931* (1965). M. Harries and S. Harries, *Soldiers of the Sun: The Rise and Fall of the Japanese Imperial Army* (1992), carries its subject from 1904 to military collapse in 1945.

A general account of the Japanese intervention in China during the 1930s is available in M. Dryburgh, *North China and Japanese Expansion, 1933–1937* (2000). The brutal Japanese assault on Nanjing in 1937 is described in I. Chang, *The Rape of Nanking* (1997) and H. Katsuichi, *The Nanjing Massacre* (trans. 1999); its continuing effects on national memories in China and Japan are analyzed in J. A. Fogel (ed.), *The Nanjing Massacre in History and Historiography* (2000).

Anticolonialism in Asia: The Middle East and South Asia

An introduction to the nationalist ferment is provided in J. Romein and J. E. Romein, *The Asian Century: A History of Modern Nationalism in Asia* (trans. 1962). In addition to books cited in Chapters 16 and 17, introductions to the Middle East and the continuing importance of the "Eastern question" include P. Mansfield, *The Ottoman Empire and Its Successors* (1973); A. Hourani, *The Emergence of the Modern Middle East* (1981); E. Monroe, *Britain's Moment in the Middle East, 1914–1971* (rev. 1981); and M. E. Yapp, *The Near East since the First World War* (1996).

For the Turkish Revolution, B. Lewis, *The Emergence of Modern Turkey* (rev. 1968) remains the outstanding account. Among other useful studies are E. J. Zürcher, *Turkey: A Modern History* (1993); W. F. Weiker, *The Modernization of Turkey* (1981); and F. Ahmad, *The Making of Modern Turkey* (1993). Biographical accounts of the Turkish statesman-reformer include J.P.D. Balfour [P. Kinross], *Atatürk: A Biography of Mustafa Kemal* (1965, 1992) and A. Mango, *Atatürk: The Biography of the Founder of Modern Turkey* (2001), a balanced, comprehensive account that distributes both praise and criticism. An insightful book carrying the story to the end of the century is N. Pope and H. Pope, *Turkey Unveiled: A History of Modern Turkey* (1999).

Arab stirrings in the Middle East in these years are discussed in G. Antonius, *The Arab Awakening* (1965); Z. B. Zeine, *Struggle for Arab Independence* (1986); J. E. Kedourie, *Islam and the Modern World* (1980); J. Jankowski and I. Gershoni (eds.), *Rethinking Nationalism in the Arab Middle East* (1997); and B. M. Nafi, *Arabism, Islamism and the Palestine Question, 1908–1941* (1998). The response of the

European powers is described in A. Williams, *Britain and France in the Middle East and North Africa, 1914–1967* (1969).

For the Indian subcontinent, two histories that try to understand developments in Indian terms and not as reactions to the West are P. Spear, *The Oxford History of Modern India* (rev. 1979) and S. Wolpert, *A New History of India* (rev. 2000). Recommended also is S. Sarkar, *Modern India, 1885–1947* (rev. 1989). The origins of Indian nationalism are discussed in A. Seal, *The Emergence of Indian Nationalism* (1968); R. J. Moore, *The Crisis of Indian Unity, 1917–1940* (1974); and Ian Talbot, *India and Pakistan* (2000), which describes the development of both Hindu and Muslim national identities.

Of many existing studies of Gandhi one may turn to J. M. Brown's impressive trilogy: *Gandhi's Rise to Power in Indian Politics* (1972); *Gandhi and Civil Disobedience* (1977), carrying the story to 1934; and *Gandhi: Prisoner of Hope* (1990). Informative also are S. Wolpert, *Gandhi's Passion: The Life and Legacy of Mahatma Gandhi* (2001); A. Copley, *Gandhi* (1987), a good brief account; and M. B. Steger, *Gandhi's Dilemma: Nonviolent Principles and Nationalist Power* (2000), which thoughtfully examines Gandhi's complex ideas. For Nehru, among many studies there are S. Gopal, *Jawaharlal Nehru: A Biography* (1 vol. abridged ed.; 1993); S. Wolpert, *Nehru: A Tryst with Destiny* (1996); and J. M. Brown, *Nehru* (1999). Nehru's autobiography, *Toward Freedom* (1941), and his other writings provide insights into the anticolonial mind. For the career and life of Nehru's daughter, his successor in office, one may read K. Frank, *The Life of Indira Nehru Gandhi* (2001).

The Depression: Collapse of the World Economy

Books on the impact of the depression on politics and society in various countries will appear in the following chapter.

The economy of the post-1919 world may be studied in D. N. Aldcroft, *From Versailles to Wall Street: The International Economy in the 1920s* (1977) and G. Ziebura, *World Economy and World Politics* (trans. 1990). For the stock market collapse, J. K. Galbraith, *The Great Crash, 1929* (1955, 1988) is a vivid account, while a comprehensive analysis of the worldwide depression is C. P. Kindleberger, *The World Depression, 1929–1939* (rev. 1986). Informative too are P. Fearon, *The Origins and Nature of the Great Slump, 1929–1932* (1979) and G. Rees, *The Great Slump: Capitalism in Crisis, 1929–1933* (1972).

Still useful older surveys include H. V. Hodson, *Slump and Recovery, 1929–1937* (1938); H. W. Arndt, *The Economic Lessons of the Nineteen Thirties* (1944), especially insightful; G. Haberler, *Prosperity and De-*

pression (rev. 1941); and W. A. Lewis, *Economic Survey, 1919–1938* (1948). There are helpful essays in W. Laqueur and G. L. Mosse (eds.), *The Great Depression* (1970) and K. Brunner (ed.), *The Great Depression Revisited* (1981). An often neglected subject is examined in A.J.H. Latham, *The Depression and the Developing World, 1914–1939* (1981). Two informative International studies are E. W. Bennett, *Germany and the Diplomacy of the Financial Crisis, 1931* (1962) and A. Schubert, *The Credit-Anstalt Crisis of 1931* (1992), on the Austrian bank failure.

For Keynes, there is the illuminating second volume of the three-volume biography by R. Skidelsky, *John Maynard Keynes: The Economist as Saviour, 1920–1937* (1993). There are also biographical accounts by D. E. Moggridge (1992), the editor of Keynes's papers, and by C. Hession (1989). One may also read P. Clarke, *The Keynesian Revolution in the Making, 1924–1936* (1989) and R. Lekachman, *The Age of Keynes* (1960), which focuses on the post-1945 years when Keynesian influence was stronger.

There are useful descriptions of modernist literature in R. J. Quinones, *Mapping Literary Modernism* (1985) and M. Levenson (ed.), *The Cambridge Companion to Modernism* (1999). For examples of the social themes in interwar literature readers may turn to the relevant chapters of W. B. Rideout, *The Radical Novel in the United States, 1900–1954: Some Interrelations of Literature and Society* (1956, 1992).

Problems and Readings

Two titles in the Heath problems series are relevant here: M. D. Lewis (ed.), *Gandhi: Maker of Modern India?* (1965) and R. F. Himmelberg (ed.), *The Great Depression and American Capitalism* (1968). J. M. Laux, *The Great Depression in Europe* (1974), is a thoughtful, brief account.

20. DEMOCRACY AND DICTATORSHIP

Some general accounts for the interwar years and the Great Depression have been described in the previous chapter, and books on the international crisis of the 1930s will appear in the chapter that follows. Helpful introductions to the democracies and dictatorships in this era are E. Wiskemann, *Europe of the Dictators, 1919–1945* (1966, 1980); S. J. Lee, *The European Dictatorships, 1918–1945* (1987); and D. C. Large, *Between Two Fires: Europe's Path in the 1930s* (1990).

The United States and the New Deal

The interwar years, the impact of the depression, and the New Deal may best be approached through W. E. Leuchtenburg, *The Perils of Prosperity, 1914–1932* (rev. 1993) and *Franklin D. Roosevelt and the New Deal, 1932–1940* (1963); T. H. Watkins, *The Great*

Depression: America in the 1930s (1993); and a more recent, impressive account, D. M. Kennedy, *Freedom from Fear: The American People in Depression and War, 1929–1945* (1999).

Several biographical accounts of Roosevelt offer insights into his presidency and the bold but pragmatic efforts to cope with the Great Depression. Among the most illuminating are A. M. Schlesinger, Jr., *The Age of Roosevelt* (3 vols.; 1956–1960); J. M. Burns, *Roosevelt: The Lion and the Fox* (1956); and F. Freidel, *A Rendezvous with Destiny* (1990). The effect on those who lived through the economic crisis is vividly portrayed in C. Bird, *The Invisible Scar* (1966); S. Terkel, *Hard Times: An Oral History of the Great Depression* (1970); R. J. Simon (ed.), *As We Saw the Thirties* (1967); and R. S. McElvaine (ed.), *Down and Out in the Great Depression* (1983). The growth of the labor movement in these years may be studied in I. Bernstein, *The Turbulent Years* (1970), and the impact on women in W. D. Wandersee, *Women's Work and Family Values, 1920–1940* (1981). Two informative comparative studies are S. Salter and J. Stevenson, *The Working Class and Politics in Europe and America, 1929–1945* (1989) and J. A. Garraty, *The Great Depression* (1986), which examines diverse national responses to the crisis in the United States and Europe.

Britain between the Wars

General accounts for Britain, some extending beyond the interwar years, are C. L. Mowat, *Britain between the Wars, 1918–1940* (1955), an older but still valuable synthesis; A.J.P. Taylor, *English History, 1914–1945* (1965), written with the author's usual verve; A. Marwick, *Britain in the Century of Total War: War, Peace, and Social Change, 1900–1967* (1968); W. N. Medlicott, *Contemporary England, 1914–1964* (1967); and M. Beloff, *Wars and Welfare: Britain, 1914–1945* (1984). An overview of the British economic scene is provided in S. Pollard, *The Development of the British Economy, 1914–1990* (rev. 1992).

An outstanding account of changes in British life is provided in J. Stevenson, *British Society, 1914–1945* (1984). Other suggested studies include S. Glynn and J. Oxborrow, *Interwar Britain: Social and Economic History* (1976); N. Branson and M. Heinemann, *Britain in the Nineteen Thirties* (1971); J. Stevenson and C. Cook, *The Slump: Society and Politics during the Depression* (1978); S. Hynes, *The Auden Generation: Literature and Politics in the 1930s* (1977); and R. Blythe, *The Age of Illusion: Some Glimpses of Britain between the Wars, 1919–1940* (rev. 1984). The postwar lot of the British wartime women workers is portrayed in D. Beddoe, *Back to Home and Duty: Women between the Wars, 1919–1939* (1989), and women activists are described in B. Harrison, *Prudent Revolutionaries: Portraits of British Feminists between the Wars* (1987).

On the decline of the Liberal party and the rise of Labour, one may read W. Wilson, *The Downfall of the Liberal Party, 1914–1935* (1966); and M. Freeden, *Liberalism Divided: British Political Thought, 1914–1938* (1986). For the general strike of 1926 and the cabinet crisis of 1929 the best synthesis is P. Williamson, *National Crisis and National Government: British Politics, the Economy, and the Empire, 1926–1932* (1992).

Among many biographies, there are studies of Ramsay MacDonald by D. Marquand (1977) and by A. Morgan (1987); of Arthur Henderson, MacDonald's rival for Labour party leadership, by F. M. Leventhal (1989); and of Stanley Baldwin by K. Middlemas and J. Barnes (1969). K. Rose, *King George V* (1984), is a scholarly biography of the monarch.

On British relations with the dominions one may turn to D. Hall, *Commonwealth: History of the British Commonwealth of Nations* (1971) and N. Mansergh, *The Commonwealth Experience* (1969). An outstanding study of Ireland in this era is J. M. Curran, *The Birth of the Irish Free State, 1921–1923* (1980) and on a broader time scale, J. J. Lee, *Ireland, 1912–1985: Politics and Society* (1990). The thorny issue of Northern Ireland is examined in N. Mansergh, *The Unresolved Question: The Anglo-Irish Settlement and Its Undoing, 1912–1972* (1991).

France between the Wars

Two general accounts for these years are P. Bernard and H. Dubief, *The Decline of the Third Republic, 1914–1938* (trans. 1985) and J. P. Azéma, *From Munich to the Liberation, 1938–1944* (trans. 1985), somewhat more probing. There are incisive essays in S. Hoffmann and others, *In Search of France: The Economy, Society, and Political System in the Twentieth Century* (1963). An illuminating study of government planning, which was less successful in the interwar years than later, is R. F. Kuisel, *Capital and the State in Modern France: Renovation and Economic Management in the Twentieth Century* (1981). The political and social divisions within France are colorfully conveyed in E. Weber, *The Hollow Years: France in the 1930s* (1995).

The response to the depression and the threat to the Third Republic are explored in two books by J. Jackson: *The Politics of Depression in France, 1932–1936* (1985) and *The Popular Front in France: Defending Democracy, 1934–1938* (1988). For the Socialist leader of the Popular Front one may read J. Colton, *Léon Blum: Humanist in Politics* (1966, 1987) and J. Lacouture, *Léon Blum* (1977; trans. 1982). Other studies of the political left in the Popular Front era include P. J. Larmour, *The French Radical Party in the 1930s* (1964); N. Greene, *Crisis and Decline: The French Socialist Party in the Popular Front Era* (1969); D. Caute, *Communism and the French In-*

tellectuals, 1914–1960 (1965); and D. R. Brower, *The New Jacobins: The French Communist Party and the Popular Front* (1968). For right-wing and fascist-type movements, in addition to books cited in Chapter 15, one may read R. Soucy, *French Fascism: The First Wave, 1924–1933* (1985) and *French Fascism: The Second Wave, 1933–1939* (1995). French national identity is examined in H. Lebovics, *True France: The Wars over Cultural Identity, 1900–1945* (1992). Studies of the countryside include G. Wright, *Rural Revolution in France: The Peasantry in the Twentieth Century* (1964) and R. O. Paxton, *French Peasant Fascism: Henry Dorgères' Greenshirts and the Crisis of French Agriculture, 1929* (1997).

Still valuable for the 1930s are the perceptive accounts, as journalist and observer, of A. Werth, of which *The Twilight of France, 1933–1940* (1942) is a condensation of his earlier volumes.

Italy: The Fascist Experience

Introductions to the Italian experience include A. Cassels, *Fascist Italy* (1968); E. Wiskemann, *Fascism in Italy* (1969); F. Chabod, *A History of Italian Fascism* (1963), concise but perceptive; and an impressive book on the early years, A. Lyttelton, *The Seizure of Power: Fascism in Italy, 1919–1929* (1973). Mussolini's flamboyant precursor is studied in J. Woodhouse, *Gabriele d'Annunzio: Defiant Archangel* (1998).

On the nature of the Fascist state, H. Finer, *Mussolini's Italy* (1933, 1965) and G. Salvemini, *Under the Axe of Fascism* (1936, 1970) remain informative but should be supplemented by R. Sarti, *Fascism and the Industrial Leadership in Italy, 1919–1940* (1971) and M. Gallo, *Mussolini's Italy: Twenty Years of the Fascist Era* (1973). The impact on Italian society is comprehensively examined in E. R. Tannenbaum, *The Fascist Experience: Italian Society and Culture, 1922–1945* (1972); V. de Grazia, *The Culture of Consent: Mass Organization of Leisure in Fascist Italy* (1981) and *How Fascism Ruled Women: Italy, 1922–1945* (1991); and E. Gentile, *The Socialization of Politics in Fascist Italy* (1994), portraying fascism as a civic and political religion.

The compromise with the church is explored in R. A. Webster, *The Cross and the Fasces: Christian Democracy in Italy* (1960) and J. F. Pollard, *The Vatican and Italian Fascism, 1920–1932* (1985). Mussolini's racial policy, moving on into the war years, is studied in M. Michaelis, *Mussolini and the Jews: German-Italian Relations and the Jewish Question in Italy, 1922–1945* (1978); S. Zucotti, *The Italians and the Holocaust: Persecution, Rescue, and Survival* (1988); and A. Stille, *Benevolence and Betrayal: Five Italian Jewish Families under Fascism* (1993), a poignant portrayal.

On Il Duce, the best study is D. Mack Smith, *Mussolini* (1982), straightforward and comprehensive,

but there are also informative biographies by I. Kirkpatrick, *Mussolini: Study of a Demagogue* (1964); and J. Ridley, *Mussolini* (1997). Other useful studies include A. J. Gregor, *Young Mussolini and the Intellectual Origins of Fascism* (1979) and Z. Sternhell, *The Birth of Fascist Ideology: From Cultural Rebellion to Political Revolution* (1993), a controversial but outstanding study cited earlier.

Foreign and colonial policy is examined in G. Barclay, *The Rise and Fall of the New Roman Empire: Italy's Bid for World Power, 1890–1943* (1973) and D. Mack Smith, *Mussolini's Roman Empire* (1976). The last phase of the dictator's career is narrated in detail in F. W. Deakin, *The Brutal Friendship: Mussolini, Hitler, and the Fall of Italian Fascism* (1962), the final chapters of which are available as *The Six Hundred Days of Mussolini* (1966).

Germany, 1919–1933: The Weimar Republic

For the collapse of the Weimar Republic and the emergence of Hitler, several of the longer-range histories of Germany by G. A. Craig and others, cited in Chapters 13 and 14, will also be helpful. For accounts of Weimar one may turn to A. J. Nicholls, *Weimar and the Rise of Hitler* (rev. 2000); S. Taylor, *Revolution and Counter-Revolution in Germany 1918–1933* (1984); E. Kolb, *The Weimar Republic* (trans. 1988); H. Heiber, *The Weimar Republic: Germany, 1918–1933* (1986); and H. Mommsen, *The Rise and Fall of Weimar Democracy* (trans. 1996).

The most informed inquiry into German efforts to cope with the depression is H. James, *The German Slump: Politics and Economics, 1924–1936* (1986). The inability of the political parties and diverse interest groups to cooperate is critically analyzed in D. Abraham, *The Collapse of the Weimar Republic* (rev. 1986) and L. E. Jones, *German Liberalism and the Dissolution of the Weimar Party System, 1918–1933* (1989). W. L. Guttman, *The German Social Democratic Party, 1875–1933* (1981) examines a major party of the Left. The resort to extraparliamentary tactics receives attention in J. M. Riehl, *Paramilitary Politics in Weimar Germany* (1977); P. Fritzsche, *Rehearsals for Fascism: Populism and Political Mobilization in Weimar Germany* (1990); and E. Rosenhaft, *Beating the Fascists? The German Communists and Political Violence, 1929–1933* (1984). The question of army loyalties is examined in depth in F. L. Carsten, *The Reichswehr and Politics, 1918 to 1933* (trans. 1966); J. W. Wheeler-Bennett, *The Nemesis of Power: The German Army in Politics, 1918–1945* (rev. 1964); and G. A. Craig, *The Politics of the Prussian Army, 1640–1945* (1956, 1964), cited earlier.

Among thoughtful efforts to explore the ideological roots of Weimar's failure are F. Stern, *The Politics of Cultural Despair: A Study in the Use of the Germanic Ideology* (1961) and G. L. Mosse, *The Crisis of*

German Ideology: Intellectual Origins of the Third Reich (1964). Cultural history in these years is examined in P. Gay, *Weimar Culture: The Outsider as Insider* (1968); W. Laqueur, *Weimar: A Cultural History, 1918–1933* (1974); and D. J. K. Peukert, *The Weimar Republic: The Crisis of Classical Modernity* (trans. 1992). A helpful discussion of key political figures is available in P. Stachura, *Political Leaders in Weimar Germany: A Biographical Study* (1993).

Germany, 1933–1945: The Third Reich

A valuable introduction to the vast literature on the Third Reich is I. Kershaw, *The Nazi Dictatorship: Problems and Perspectives of Interpretation* (rev. 2000), while P. Ayçoberry, *The Nazi Question: An Essay on the Interpretation of National Socialism, 1922–1975* (trans. 1981) and J. Lukacs, *The Hitler of History* (1997) are helpful historiographical studies. Two successful recent efforts to provide a thoughtful overview of the Nazi era are K. P. Fischer, *Nazi Germany* (1995) and M. Burleigh, *The Third Reich* (2000).

On the coming to power of the Nazis one may first turn to M. Broszat, *Hitler and the Collapse of Weimar Germany* (trans. 1987), focusing on the years 1929–1933. An informative study is H. A. Turner, *German Big Business and the Rise of Hitler* (1985), which may be supplemented by his *Hitler's Thirty Days to Power: January 1933* (1997). Two studies illuminate the Nazi appeal to diverse segments of the population: W. S. Allen, *The Nazi Seizure of Power: The Experience of a Single German Town, 1922–1945* (rev. 1984) and J. H. Grill, *The Nazi Movement in Baden, 1920–1945* (1984). Two efforts to assess the Nazi appeal at the polls are R. F. Hamilton, *Who Voted for Hitler?* (1982) and T. Childers, *The Nazi Voter: The Social Foundations of Fascism in Germany, 1919–1933* (1983) which both tend to confirm that Nazi support came from all segments of the population, not only from the lower-middle class. How the movement's "populist nationalism" rallied wide support is recounted in P. Fritzsche, *Germans Into Nazis* (1998).

M. H. Kater, *The Nazi Party: A Social Profile of Members and Leaders, 1919–1945* (1983) is an exhaustive sociological analysis of those who joined and led the party, while D. Orlow, *The History of the Nazi Party* (2 vols.; 1969–1973) is a comprehensive organizational history. There are many studies of such key Nazi institutions as the SS, the Gestapo, and the courts, too numerous to cite here. For the military one may read O. Bartov, *Hitler's Army: Soldiers, Nazis, and War in the Third Reich* (1991).

Religion and related matters are examined in E. C. Helmreich, *The German Churches under Hitler* (1979); J. S. Conway, *The Nazi Persecution of the Churches, 1933–1945* (1968); D. Bergen, *Twisted Cross: The German Christian Movement in the Third Reich* (1996); G. Lewy, *The Catholic Church and Nazi Germany* (1964); and S. Friedländer, *Pius XII and the Third Reich* (1966). Books on Hitler's persecution of the Jews, and on the death camps and the Holocaust, will be described in the next chapter, but one should mention here L. S. Dawidowicz, *The War against the Jews, 1933–1945* (1976); S. Gordon, *Hitler, Germans, and the Jewish Question* (1984); and S. Friedländer, *Nazi Germany and the Jews: The Years of Persecution, 1933–1939* (1997), the first of a projected two volumes.

On the Nazi state four outstanding analyses are K. D. Bracher, *The German Dictatorship* (trans. 1970); M. Broszat, *The Hitler State* (trans. (1981); K. Hildebrand, *The Third Reich* (1984); and M. Burleigh and W. Wippermann, *The Racial State: Germany, 1933–1945* (1992). D. Schoenbaum, *Hitler's Social Revolution: Class and Status in Nazi Germany, 1933–1939* (1966) sees a leveling effect not accomplished by earlier German regimes. Studies exploring new avenues to understanding popular responses include I. Kershaw, *The "Hitler Myth": Image and Reality in the Third Reich* (1987); D.J.K. Peukert, *Inside Nazi Germany: Conformity, Opposition, and Racism in Everyday Life* (trans. 1987); and P. Ayçoberry, *The Social History of the Third Reich* (trans. 2000). There are also perceptive insights into life under the Nazis in R. Bessel (ed.), *Life in the Third Reich* (1987) and G. L. Mosse, *Nazi Culture: Intellectual, Cultural, and Social Life in the Third Reich* (1966).

The best study of women in the Third Reich, with special attention to those who supported and those who resisted the regime, is C. Koonz, *Mothers in the Fatherland: Women, the Family, and Nazi Politics* (1987). It may be supplemented by J. Stephenson, *Women in Nazi Society* (1976) and *The Nazi Organization of Women* (1981); and the essays in R. Bridenthal and others, *When Biology Became Destiny: Women in Weimar and Nazi Germany* (1989).

That there was no mass resistance but opposition only from resolute individuals and small groups emerges from two comprehensive accounts: P. Hoffmann, *German Resistance to Hitler* (rev. 1988) and M. Balfour, *Withstanding Hitler in Germany 1933–1945* (1989). These accounts may be supplemented by T. Prittie, *Germans against Hitler* (1964); H. Rothfels, *The German Opposition to Hitler* (rev. 1962); and J. Fest, *Plotting Hitler's Death* (trans. 1997). One may also consult D. C. Lodge (ed.), *Contending with Hitler: Varieties of German Resistance in the Third Reich* (1992) and on the Resistance legacy, M. Geyer and J. W. Boyer (eds.), *Resistance Against the Third Reich, 1933–1990* (1994).

Of the many biographies of Hitler the two volumes of I. Kershaw are undoubtedly now the most authoritative: Hitler, *1889–1936: Hubris* (1998) and

Hitler, 1936–1945: Nemesis (1999), a remarkable study explaining how Germans identified with Hitler and how his arrogance and pride brought him initial success and then disaster. Two other biographies are outstanding: A. Bullock, *Hitler: A Study in Tyranny* (1952, 1964), and J. C. Fest, *Hitler* (trans. 1975). Bullock has also written a remarkable in-depth comparative study, *Hitler and Stalin: Parallel Lives* (1992). Hitler's early years in Vienna have been reexamined in B. Hamann, *Hitler's Vienna: A Dictator's Apprenticeship* (1999). R. Binion, *Hitler among the Germans* (1976), uses psychoanalytical methods to explain the inner wellsprings of the obsessed leader, while R. L. Waite, *The Psychopathic God: Adolf Hitler* (1977), effectively combines psychoanalytical and more conventional techniques. Two interpretive essays that raise pertinent questions are S. Haffner, *The Meaning of Hitler* (trans. 1980) and W. Carr, *Hitler: A Study in Personality and Politics* (1979). The end of the leader and his regime is vividly recounted in H. R. Trevor-Roper, *The Last Days of Hitler* (rev. 1966).

Some of Hitler's associates are studied in J. C. Fest, *The Face of the Third Reich: Portraits of the Nazi Leadership* (trans. 1977); B. F. Smith, *Heinrich Himmler: A Nazi in the Making, 1900–1926* (1971); R. Smelser, *Robert Ley: Hitler's Labor Front Leader* (1989); R. G. Reuth, *Goebbels* (trans. 1994); and D. Irving, *Göring* (1989) and *Goebbels: The Mastermind of The Third Reich* (1996), both of which, as in this author's widely criticized books on the Third Reich, make the best possible case for his subjects. Hitler's foreign minister is studied in M. Bloch, *Ribbentrop* (1993), a detailed diplomatic account, and J. Weitz, *Hitler's Diplomat: The Life and Times of Joachim Ribbentrop* (1992). G. Serenz, *Albert Speer: His Battle with Truth* (1995) is highly critical of Hitler's wartime economic planner. Two convenient handbooks on the institutions and personalities of the regime are R. S. Wistrich, *Who's Who in Nazi Germany* (1982) and C. Zentner and F. Bedürftig, *The Encyclopedia of the Third Reich* (2 vols.; 1991).

Defining Totalitarianism and Fascism

The origins and nature of twentieth-century ideologies are explored in many books, notably in K. D. Bracher's comprehensive *A History of Political Thought in the Twentieth Century* (trans. 1984). Among efforts to examine totalitarianism, Left and Right, are C. J. Friedrich and Z. K. Brzezinski, *Totalitarian Dictatorship and Autocracy* (rev. 1965); H. Arendt, *Origins of Totalitarianism* (rev. 1966), cited in Chapter 15; H. Bucheim, *Totalitarian Rule* (trans. 1967); and S. P. Soper, *Totalitarianism: A Conceptual Approach* (1985). An important comparative study is the collection of essays in I. Kershaw and M. Levin (eds.), *Stalinism and Nazism: Dictatorships in Comparison* (1997).

For the most comprehensive and insightful study of fascism as a phenomenon of the interwar years one must turn to S. G. Payne, *A History of Fascism, 1914–1945* (1996). Informative also are F. L. Carsten, *The Rise of Fascism* (rev. 1980); H. R. Kedward, *Fascism in Western Europe, 1900–1945* (1969); R. De Felice, *Fascism* (1976), by the Italian biographer of Mussolini; and W. Laqueur, *Fascism: Past, Present, Future* (1996). Readers will find E. Nolte, *Three Faces of Fascism: Action Française, Italian Fascism, National Socialism* (trans. 1966), provocative but difficult.

Other European Developments in the Interwar Years

Spain and the Spanish Civil War are discussed in the following chapter. The most informative volumes on central and eastern Europe are H. Seton-Watson, *Eastern Europe between the Wars, 1918–1941* (rev. 1967); J. Rothschild, *East Central Europe between the Two World Wars* (1975); A. Palmer, *The Lands Between: A History of East-Central Europe since the Congress of Vienna* (1970); and I. T. Berend, *Decades of Crisis: Central and Eastern Europe Before World War II* (1998). A special subject is ably explored in E. Mendelsohn, *The Jews of East Central Europe between the World Wars* (1983).

A few titles may be suggested for some of the successor states. For Austria: C. A. Gulick, *Austria from Habsburg to Hitler* (2 vols.; 1948); C. E. Edmondson, *The Heimwehr and Austrian Politics, 1918–1936* (1978); M. Kitchen, *The Coming of Austrian Fascism* (1980); F. L. Carsten, *Fascist Movements in Austria: From Schönerer to Hitler* (1977); B. F. Pauley, *Hitler and the Forgotten Nazis: A History of Austrian National Socialism* (1981) and *From Prejudice to Persecution: A History of Austrian Anti-Semitism* (1998). For Hungary: C. A. Macartney, *October Fifteenth: A History of Modern Hungary, 1929–1945* (2 vols.; rev. 1962); R. L. Tönes, *Bela Kun and the Hungarian Soviet Republic* (1967), on the short-lived Communist regime of 1919; and T. Sakmyster, *Hungary's Admiral on Horseback: Miklós Horthy, 1918–1944* (1999). For Czechoslovakia: J. Kolvoda, *The Genesis of Czechoslovakia* (1985); Z.A.B. Zeman, *The Masaryks: The Making of Czechoslovakia* (1976, 1991); R. W. Seton-Watson, *A History of the Czechs and Slovaks* (1943, 1965); E. Wiskemann, *Czechs and Germans* (rev. 1967); V. Olivova, *The Doomed Democracy: Czechoslovakia in a Disrupted Europe, 1918–1938* (1972); and C. S. Leff, *National Conflict in Czechoslovakia: The Making and Remaking of a State, 1918–1987* (1988), which carries the story toward the present. For Yugoslavia: I. Banac, *The National Question in Yugoslavia* (1985), an informative inquiry into the genesis of the multiethnic state, for which other books will be cited in Chapter 25;

F. Singleton, *A Short History of the Yugoslav Peoples* (1985); and R. West, *Black Lamb and Grey Falcon* (1941, 1992), a gifted journalist's older insightful account. For Poland: M. K. Dziewanowski, *Poland in the Twentieth Century* (1977); A. Polonsky, *Politics in Independent Poland, 1921–1939* (1972); H. Roos, *A History of Modern Poland* (1966); and the volumes of N. Davies cited in Chapter 11. For Finland and the Baltic states: J. H. Wuorinen, *A History of Finland* (1965); D. G. Kirby, *Finland in the Twentieth Century* (1979); and G. von Rauch, *The Baltic States—Estonia, Latvia, and Lithuania: The Years of Independence, 1917–1940* (trans. 1974, 1995).

Problems and Readings

For the American New Deal: M. Dubofsky (ed.), *The New Deal: Conflicting Interpretations and Shifting Perspectives* (1992) and D. E. Hamilton (ed.), *The New Deal* (1999). For Britain: J. A. Thompson (ed.), *The Collapse of the British Liberal Party: Fate or Self-Destruction?* (1969) and A. Thorpe, *Britain in the 1930s* (1992), a brief narrative essay. For Italy: S. W. Halperin, *Mussolini and Italian Fascism* (1964) and R. Sarti (ed.), *The Ax Within: Italian Fascism in Action* (1974). For Weimar Germany: R. N. Hunt (ed.), *The Creation of the Weimar Republic: Stillborn Democracy?* (1969); F. K. Ringer (ed.), *The German Inflation of 1923* (1969); and I. Kershaw (ed.), *Weimar: Why Did German Democracy Fail?* (1990). For the Nazi era: F. Stern (ed.), *The Path to Dictatorship* (1967); H. A. Turner (ed.), *Nazism and the Third Reich* (1972); A. Mitchell (ed.), *The Nazi Revolution* (rev. 1997); R.G.L. Waite (ed.), *Hitler and Nazi Germany* (rev. 1969); J. Noakes and G. Pridham (eds.), *Documents of Nazism, 1919–1945* (1975); and W. Simpson, *Hitler and Germany* (1991), also a collection of documents. For Eastern Europe: G. Augustinos (ed.), *The National Idea in Eastern Europe* (1996). On fascism and totalitarianism, there are available P. T. Mason, *Totalitarianism: Temporary Madness or Permanent Danger?* (1967); E. Weber, *Varieties of Fascism: Doctrines of Revolution in the Twentieth Century* (1964, 1982); N. Greene (ed.), *Fascism: An Anthology* (1968); C. F. Delzell (ed.), *Mediterranean Fascism* (1970); W. Laqueur (ed.), *Fascism: A Reader's Guide* (1976); H. A. Turner, Jr., (ed.), *Reappraisals of Fascism* (1975); R. de Felice (ed.), *Interpretations of Fascism* (trans. 1977); and G. L. Mosse (ed.), *International Fascism: New Thoughts and New Appraisals* (1979).

21. THE SECOND WORLD WAR

Spain and the Spanish Civil War

The most comprehensive narrative account of the Spanish conflict, including the international ramifications, is H. Thomas, *The Spanish Civil War* (1961, 1986), in which Franco's skill as a manipulator and survivor clearly emerges. But other recommended accounts are G. Jackson, *The Spanish Republic and the Civil War, 1931–1939* (1965; abridged ed., 1974); B. Bolloten, *The Spanish Civil War: Revolution and Counterrevolution* (1991); P. Broué and E. Témime, *The Revolution and the Civil War in Spain* (trans. 1972); and histories by P. Wyden (1983), A. Beevor (1983), and S. M. Ellwood (1991). H. Browne, *Spain's Civil War* (rev. 1996) and F. Ribeiro de Meneses, *Franco and the Spanish Civil War* (2001) provide brief overviews; G. Esenwein and A. Shubert, *Spain at War: The Spanish Civil War in Context, 1931–1939* (1995) and R. Carr, *The Spanish Tragedy: The Civil War in Perspective* (1977) add broader analytical insights. The turbulent background is ably conveyed in R.A.H. Robinson, *The Origins of Franco Spain: The Right, the Republic, and the Revolution, 1931–1936* (1971); E. E. Malefakis, *Agrarian Reform and Peasant Revolution in Spain: Origins of the Civil War* (1970); and P. Preston, *The Coming of the Spanish Civil War: Reform, Reaction, and Revolution in the Second Republic, 1931–1936* (1978).

Studies of the American response to the war include A. Guttman, *The Wound in the Heart: America and the Spanish Civil War* (1962) and R. P. Traina, *American Diplomacy and the Spanish Civil War* (1968). The emotions stirred by the events are evoked by S. Weintraub, *The Last Great Cause: The Intellectuals and the Spanish Civil War* (1968). The volunteers who fought for the Republic are studied in C. Geiser, *Prisoners of the Good Fight: The Spanish Civil War, 1936–1938* (1994); M. Jackson, *The International Brigades in the Spanish Civil War, 1936–1938* (1994); and P. N. Carroll, *The Odyssey of the Abraham Lincoln Brigade: Americans in the Spanish Civil War* (1994). A large-scale, critical study of Franco is P. Preston, *Franco: A Biography* (1995), but one may also read J.J.W. Trythall, *El Caudillo* (1970) and S. Ellwood, *Franco* (1994). S. G. Payne has written a comprehensive study, *Fascism in Spain, 1923–1977* (1999) and, on Franco's years in power, *The Franco Regime, 1936–1975* (1987).

Background to the Second World War

Although there is no one comprehensive treatment taking into account all the sources now available for the diplomacy of the interwar years and the background to the Second World War, there are a number of important books on the subject. Among the most informative general inquiries into the coming of the war are P. Renouvin, *World War II and Its Origins: International Relations 1929–1945* (trans. 1969); M. Baumont, *The Origins of the Second World War* (trans. 1978); P.M.H. Bell, *The Origins of the Second World War in Europe* (rev. 1997); R. Overy with

A. Wheatcroft, *The Road to War* (1999); and A. J. Crozier, *The Causes of the Second World War* (1997).

On the 11 months between Munich and the outbreak of the war, D. C. Watt, *How War Came: The Immediate Origins of the Second World War, 1938–1939* (1989), is a masterful study. One may also read S. Aster, *1939: The Making of the Second World War* (1973) and M. J. Carley, *The Alliance That Never Was and the Coming of World War II* (1999), on the failure to create a Western-Soviet alliance at the time. A.J.P. Taylor's *The Origins of the Second World War* (1961) depicts Hitler as one who did not desire war but took advantage of his opponents' uncertainty. On the Taylor thesis one may read the evaluations in G. Martel (ed.), *"The Origins of the Second World War" Reconsidered: The A.J.P. Taylor Debate after Twenty-Five Years* (1986) and R. Boyce and E. M. Robertson (eds.), *Paths to War: New Essays on the Origins of the Second World War* (1989).

A major study of German foreign policy based on exhaustive use of the documents and strongly emphasizing Hitler's responsibilities and initiatives is G. L. Weinberg, *The Foreign Policy of Hitler's Germany:* Vol. I, *Diplomatic Revolution in Europe, 1933–1936* (1970), and Vol. II, *Starting World War II, 1937–1939* (1980, 1994). A second study with similar conclusions is N. Rich, *Hitler's War Aims* (2 vols.; 1973–1974). For assessments of German foreign policy, one may also read E. M. Robertson, *Hitler's Pre-War Policies and Military Planning, 1933–1939* (1967); K. Hildebrand, *The Foreign Policy of the Third Reich* (1974); J. Hiden, *Germany and Europe, 1919–1939* (rev. 1993); E. Jäckel, *Hitler's World View* (1981); and the essays in V. R. Berghahn and M. Kitchen (eds.), *Germany and the Age of Total War* (1981).

British policy in the 1930s, including the economic and political constraints on a more assertive policy, is examined in M. Cowling, *The Impact of Hitler: British Politics and British Policy, 1933–1940* (1975); R. P. Shay, Jr., *British Rearmament in the Thirties: Politics and Profits* (1977); G. C. Peden, *British Rearmament and the Treasury, 1932–1939* (1979); and F. McDonough, *Neville Chamberlain, Appeasement, and the British Road to War* (1998), which shows the links between domestic and foreign policies. The opposition to appeasement is examined in A. L. Rowse, *Appeasement: A Study in Political Decline, 1933–1939* (1961); M. Gilbert and R. Gott, *The Appeasers* (1963); and M. George, *The Warped Vision: British Foreign Policy, 1933–1939* (1965); W. R. Rock, *Appeasement on Trial: British Foreign Policy and Its Critics, 1938–1939* (1966); N. Thompson, *The Anti-Appeasers* (1971); and R.A.C. Parker, *Chamberlain and Appeasement* (1993). K. Robbins, *Appeasement* (rev. 1997) provides a brief overview of the debate.

For the 1930s, Winston Churchill's *The Gathering Storm* (1948), covering his years in the opposition, the first volume of his six-volume history, described below, is indispensable. Biographical studies focusing on British foreign policy include two studies of Anthony Eden, one highly critical, by D. Carlton (1981), the second more defensive, by R. Rhodes James (1987); and a study of Sir Samuel Hoare by J. A. Cross (1977). For Neville Chamberlain there are studies by K. Feiling (1946), I. MacLeod (1961), and J. Charmley (1990), all somewhat defensive, and a balanced assessment by W. R. Rock (1969).

Among the several impressive studies that examine British foreign policy in long-range perspective are F. S. Northedge, *The Troubled Giant: Britain among the Great Powers, 1916–1939* (1966); W. N. Medlicott, *British Foreign Policy since Versailles, 1919–1963* (rev. 1968); P. Kennedy, *The Realities behind Diplomacy: Background Influences on British External Policy, 1865–1980* (1983); and C. J. Bartlett, *British Foreign Policy in the Twentieth Century* (1989).

For French foreign policy in these years the fullest accounts are by A. Adamthwaite, *France and the Coming of the Second World War, 1936–1939* (1977) and *Grandeur and Misery: France's Bid for Power in Europe, 1914–1940* (1995). They may be supplemented by R. J. Young, *France and the Origins of the Second World War* (1996). The limited options of the Popular Front are carefully examined in N. Jordan, *The Popular Front and Central Europe: The Dilemmas of French Impotence, 1918–1940* (1992).

There are many books on specific episodes and subjects. The German militarization of the Rhineland is examined in J. T. Emerson, *The Rhineland Crisis, 7 March 1936* (1977). On the annexation of Austria, one may read J. Gehl, *Austria, Germany and the Anschluss, 1931–1938* (1963) and D. Wagner and G. Tomkowitz, *Anschluss: The Week Hitler Seized Vienna* (1971). For Munich, the best detailed account is T. Taylor, *Munich: The Price of Peace* (1980), but also informative are J. W. Wheeler-Bennett, *Munich: Prologue to Tragedy* (1948, 1963); K. Eubank, *Munich* (1963); H. Noguères, *Munich: "Peace for Our Time"* (trans. 1963); and K. Robbins, Munich 1938 (1963). G. A. Craig and F. Gilbert (eds.), *The Diplomats, 1919–1938* (1953, 1994) includes valuable chapters on the individuals who helped make foreign policy in the era.

Studies focusing on eastern Europe include A. Cienciala, *Poland and the Western Powers, 1938–1939* (1968); S. Newman, *March 1939: The British Guarantee to Poland* (1976); and A. J. Prazmowska, *Britain, Poland, and the Eastern Front, 1939* (1987). The origins and subsequent history of the German-Soviet Pact of August 23, 1939, are recounted in A. Read and D. Fisher, *The Deadly Embrace: Hitler, Stalin and the Nazi-Soviet Pact, 1939–1941* (1989).

The role of the United States in these years is traced in two comprehensive volumes by W. L. Langer and S. E. Gleason, *The Challenge to Isolation, 1937–1940* (1952) and *The Undeclared War, 1940–1941* (1953). Other important studies include C. A. MacDonald, *The United States, Britain, and Appeasement, 1930–1939* (1981); D. Reynolds, *The Creation of the Anglo-American Alliance, 1937–1941* (1982); and W. R. Rock, *Chamberlain and Roosevelt: British Foreign Policy and the United States, 1937–1940* (1989). The most informative study of Roosevelt's foreign policy, sympathetic yet critical, is R. Dallek, *Franklin D. Roosevelt and American Foreign Policy, 1932–1945* (1979, 1995). For the war years it may be supplemented by J. M. Burns, *Roosevelt: The Soldier of Freedom* (1970); F. Marks, *Wind over Sand: The Diplomacy of Franklin Roosevelt* (1988); and W. F. Kimball, *The Juggler: Franklin Roosevelt as Wartime Statesman (1991)* and *Roosevelt, Churchill, and the Second World War* (1997).

For the widening of the Japanese invasion of China in 1937 and the later expansion of the European conflict into a global war one may read A. Iriye, *The Origins of the Second World War in Asia and the Pacific* (1987); D. J. Lu, *From the Marco Polo Bridge to Pearl Harbor* (1961); R. Butow, *Tojo and the Coming of the War* (1961); and W. Carr, *Poland to Pearl Harbor* (1985). The attack of December 7, 1941, is studied in R. Wohlstetter, *Pearl Harbor: Warning and Decision* (1962); G. W. Prange, *At Dawn We Slept: The Untold Story of Pearl Harbor* (1981); and H. C. Clausen and B. Lee, *Pearl Harbor: Final Judgment* (1992), an updating of an official inquiry first published in 1946.

The War: Military Aspects

Of the numerous narrative histories of the war, the most comprehensive and up-to-date syntheses are J. Keegan, *The Second World War* (1989) and G. L. Weinberg, *A World at Arms: A Global History of World War II* (1994). Also available are M. Gilbert, *The Second World War* (rev. 1991); H. P. Willmott, *The Great Crusade* (1990); P. Calvacoressi, G. Wint, and J. Pritchard, *Total War: Causes and Courses of the Second World War* (rev. 1989); R.A.C. Parker, *The Second World War: A Short History* (rev. 1997); and A. W. Purdue, *The Second World War* (1999), a concise overview of the main events. An older insightful account focusing on Europe is G. Wright, *The Ordeal of Total War, 1939–1945* (1968), in the Langer series. *The Oxford Companion to World War II* (1995) helps provide encyclopedic coverage of all aspects of the war, and D. Flower and J. Reeves, *The War: A Documentary History* (1960, 1997) is also helpful. J. Keegan has edited the superb *Times Atlas of the Second World*

War (1989), and he analyzes historical and other writings on the war, including the myths and controversies surrounding it, in *The Battle for History: Re-fighting World War II* (1996). W. S. Churchill, *The Second World War* (6 vols.; 1948–1953; 1 vol. abridged, 1959), already mentioned, is an indispensable, full-dress history by the historian-statesman written in the grand style, but it should be read in conjunction with other studies now available. M. Gilbert, *Churchill: A Life* (1992) synthesizes Gilbert's monumental official biography (8 vols.; 1966–1989). Of many other biographies K. Robbins, *Churchill* (1992), is a balanced brief study.

Many volumes of the detailed official histories of the United Kingdom, Canada, and the United States have appeared. Of special note is S. E. Morison, *The Two-Ocean War* (1963), which summarizes the multivolume U.S. Navy official history. On naval warfare, R. Hough, *The Longest Battle: The War at Sea, 1939–1945* (1986) is also available. Another important aspect is examined in R. J. Overy, *The Air War, 1939–1945* (1980), and the greatest air battle is described in R. Hough and D. Richards, *The Battle of Britain* (1989). C. K. Webster and N. N. Frankland, *Strategic Air Offensive against Germany, 1939–1945* (1961) demonstrates that Allied strategic bombing was less effective than thought at the time.

The Allied penetration and use of the highest secret German military code in Operation Ultra, not revealed or utilized in writing the history of the war until the 1970s, is recounted in F. Winterbotham, *The Ultra Secret* (1974) and R. Lewin, *Ultra Goes to War* (1979). A comprehensive account of cryptography covering all theaters of the war is S. Budiansky, *Battle of Wits: The Complete Story of Codebreaking in World War II* (2000).

The military aspects of France's defeat in 1940 may be approached through A. Horne, *To Lose a Battle: France, 1940* (1969), the most detailed account; G. Chapman, *Why France Fell: The Defeat of the French Army in 1940* (1969); A. Beaufre, *1940: The Fall of France* (trans. 1968); A. Shennan, *The Fall of France, 1940* (2000); and E. R. May, *Strange Victory: Hitler's Conquest of France* (2001), a provocative in-depth study, which concludes that the German victory was far from inevitable. The background to the defeat is explored in P.C.F. Bankwitz, *Maxime Weygand and Civil-Military Relations in Modern France* (1967); R. F. Young, *In Command of France: French Foreign Policy and Military Planning, 1933–1940* (1978); and M. S. Alexander, *The Republic in Danger: General Maurice Gamelin and the Politics of French Defence, 1938–1940* (1993). The relationship with Britain is studied in E. M. Gates, *End of the Affair: The Collapse of the Anglo-French Alliance, 1939–1940* (1981). W. L. Shirer, *The Collapse of the Third Republic: An Inquiry into the Fall of France in 1940* (1969) is a thoughtful account by a reflective journalist; and M. Bloch, *Strange Defeat* (1940) is an incisive memoir by the eminent medievalist later executed as a member of the Resistance. J. Blatt (ed.), *The French Defeat of 1940: Reassessments* (1997) is a valuable set of recent essays.

The Russo-Finnish conflict of 1939–1940 is narrated in R. W. Condon, *The Winter War* (1972); F. Chew, *The White Death* (1971); and M. Jacobson, *The Diplomacy of the Winter War* (1961). For the war in eastern Europe after the German invasion one may read A. Clark, *Barbarossa: The Russian-German Conflict, 1941–1945* (1965); A. Seaton, *The Russo-German War* (1971); and two works by J. Erickson, *The Road to Stalingrad* (1975, 1999) and *The Road to Berlin* (1984, 1999). A. Seaton, *Stalin as Military Commander* (1976) is a careful study. A. Paul, *Katyn: The Untold Story of Stalin's Polish Massacre* (1991) recounts the early episode of the war in which over 4,000 Polish officers and soldiers captured in 1939 were executed at Stalin's orders, as confirmed by recently opened archives.

The war in the Pacific is ably presented in C. Bateson, *The War with Japan* (1968); S. Ienaga, *The Pacific War: World War II and the Japanese, 1931–1945* (trans. 1978), by a distinguished Japanese historian; and A. Iriye, *Power and Culture: The Japanese-American War, 1941–1945* (1981), offering some new insights. M. Harries and S. Harries, *Soldiers of the Sun* (1992), cited earlier, recounts the story of the imperial army in conquest and collapse, while H. T. Cooke and T. F. Cooke, *Japan at War: An Oral History* (1992) provides unusual eyewitness testimony to Japanese military conduct. A far-reaching study examining the impact of the war on Asia is C. Thorne, *The Far Eastern War: States and Societies, 1941–1945* (1985, 1988). On the last phase in the Pacific, R. Butow, *Japan's Decision to Surrender* (1954) and W. Craig, *The Fall of Japan* (1968) help illuminate controversies over how inevitable or imminent Japan's surrender was.

On the development of the atomic bomb and its first use, one may read W. L. Laurence, *Dawn over Zero* (1946) and R. Rhodes, *The Making of the Atomic Bomb* (1986), a remarkably comprehensive account; and on the German effort to create the bomb, M. Walker, *German National Socialism and the Quest for Nuclear Power, 1939–1949* (1990).

The War: Social and Economic Impact

For the social and economic impact of the war the best one-volume synthesis is A. S. Milward, *War, Economy, and Society, 1939–1945* (1977). For the British wartime scene, A. Calder, *The People's War: Britain, 1939–1945* (1969) is highly informative, while A. Marwick, *The Home Front: The British and the Second World War* (1977) is a graphic documentary

and photographic account. E. S. Beck, *The European Home Fronts, 1939–1945* (1993) is a useful brief synthesis. The wartime Soviet scene is studied in detail in J. Barber and M. Harrison, *The Soviet Home Front, 1941–1945* (1992). Various phases of the American domestic scene are treated in D. M. Kennedy, *Freedom from Fear* (1999), already cited; A. R. Buchanan, *The United States and World War II* (2 vols.; 1964); and A. M. Winkler, *Home Front U.S.A.* (1986). A spirited treament of the GI's, civilians-turned-soldiers, appears in various books by S. E. Ambrose, which are synthesized in *The Victors: Eisenhower and His Boys, the Men of World War II* (1998). The American troops stationed in Britain are studied with good humor in D. Reynolds, *The American Occupation of Britain, 1942–1945* (1995). On the other hand, W. L. O'Neill, *America's Fight at Home and Abroad in World War II* (1993), M.C.C. Adams, *The Best War Ever: America and World War II* (1994), and P. Fussell, *Wartime: Understanding and Behavior in the Second World War* (1989) deflate military and civilian leadership.

The entry of women into the wartime labor force is examined in K. Anderson, *Wartime Women: Sex Roles, Family Relations, and the Status of Women during World War II* (1981); L. J. Rupp, *Mobilizing Women for War: German and American Propaganda, 1939–1945* (1978); and the essays in M. R. Higonnet and others, *Behind the Lines: Gender and the Two World Wars* (1987). Women's wartime experiences are also described in N. A. Dombrowski (ed.), *Women and War in the Twentieth Century* (1999); H. Diamond, *Women and the Second World War in France, 1939–1948* (1999); and J. B. Litoff and D. C. Smith (eds.), *American Women in a World at War* (1997), which includes writings by numerous women who served in the military or worked in war industries.

Many aspects of the home front in Germany are covered in books cited in the previous chapter. That Hitler did not prepare for war in depth because he expected a quick victory emerges clearly from B. H. Klein, *Germany's Economic Preparations for War* (1959); B. A. Carroll, *Design for Total War: Arms and Economics in the Third Reich* (1968); and A. S. Milward, *The German Economy at War* (1965).

Hitler's New Order: Collaboration and Resistance

The first attempt to study the German occupation of Europe as a whole was in a *Survey of International Affairs* volume covering the years 1939–1946: A. Toynbee and V. Toynbee (eds.), *Hitler's Europe* (1954). Numerous studies have since appeared on individual countries, many on the French experience.

Among the most informative books on the French accommodation to the Nazi occupation are P. Burrin, *France Under the Germans: Collaboration and Compromise* (trans. 1997); I. Ousby, *Occupation:*

The Ordeal of France (1997); J. Jackson, *France: The Dark Years* (2001); and R. O. Paxton, *Vichy France: Old Guard and New Order, 1940–1944* (1972). Paxton and M. R. Marrus, *Vichy France and the Jews* (1981, 1995) first demonstrated the French initiative for many actions against the Jews, on which one should also read S. Zucotti, *The Holocaust, the French, and the Jews* (1993). J. F. Sweets, *Choices in Vichy France: The French under Nazi Occupation* (1986) poignantly demonstrates the complexities of collaboration and resistance in an industrial city. A. S. Milward, *The New Order and the French Economy* (1970) surveys the economic aspects of the regime, while cultural aspects may be approached through A. Kaplan, *Fascism, Literature, and French Intellectual Life* (1986); G. Hirshfeld and P. Marsh (eds.), *Collaboration in France: Politics and Culture during the Nazi Occupation, 1940–1944* (1989); and M. C. Cone, *Artists under Vichy* (1992). For the French postwar struggle to face up to the Vichy trauma one should read H. Rousso, *The Vichy Syndrome: History and Memory in France since 1944* (trans. 1991); E. Conan and H. Rousso, *Vichy: The Ever-Present Past* (trans. 1998); and R. J. Golsan, *Vichy's Afterlife: History and Counterhistory in Postwar France* (2000).

American relations with Vichy are studied in W. L. Langer, *Our Vichy Gamble* (1947), a somewhat defensive account; and British relations, in R. T. Thomas, *Britain and Vichy: The Dilemma of Anglo-French Relations, 1940–1942* (1979). There is a biography of Laval by H. Cole (1963), and a detailed study focusing on diplomatic events by G. Warner, *Pierre Laval and the Eclipse of France, 1931–1945* (1968), while H. R. Lottman, *Pétain, Hero or Traitor* (1985), focuses on the ambivalent role played by the marshal.

The Resistance in France may be studied in D. Schoenbrun, *Soldiers of the Night: The Story of the French Resistance* (1980); M.R.D. Foot, *SOE in France* (1966, 1984), on British intelligence operations; J. F. Sweets, *The Politics of Resistance in France, 1940–1944* (1976); H. R. Kedward, *Resistance in Vichy France* (1978) and *In Search of the Maquis* (1993); and M. L. Rossiter, *Women in the Resistance* (1985). The liberation is dramatically described in R. Aron, *France Reborn* (trans. 1964); related events, in P. Novick, *The Resistance versus Vichy: The Purge of Collaborators in Liberated France* (1969) and H. R. Lottman, *The Purge* (1986). The divisions in France over the purge are studied in M. Koreman, *The Expectation of Justice: France, 1944–1946* (1999). On the trials of collaborators, some of them years later, one may read R. J. Golsan (ed.), *Memory, the Holocaust, and French Justice: The Bousquet and Touvier Affairs* (1996) and A. Kaplan, *The Collaborator: The Trial and Execution of Robert*

Brassillach (2000). For the years from the 1930s to liberation, Charles de Gaulle's *War Memoirs* (3 vols.; trans. 1958–1960) are indispensable. De Gaulle's wartime difficulties with London and Washington are described in M. Viorst, *Hostile Allies: FDR and Charles de Gaulle* (1965); F. Kersaudy, *Churchill and de Gaulle* (1982); and R. Aglion, *Roosevelt and de Gaulle: Allies in Conflict* (trans. 1988), by one of de Gaulle's diplomats. For de Gaulle, J. Lacouture's biography (2 vols.; trans. 1992) is the outstanding account: Vol. I, *The Rebel, 1890–1944,* and Vol. II, *The Ruler, 1945–1970.*

A sampling of studies of other countries under the German occupation include W. Warmbrunn, *The Dutch under German Occupation, 1940–1945* (1963); G. Hirschfeld, *Nazi Rule and Dutch Collaboration, 1940–1945* (trans. 1988); A. S. Milward, *The Fascist Economy in Norway* (1972); R. L. Braham, *The Hungarian Labor Service System, 1939–1945* (1977); J. Gillingham, *Belgian Business and the Nazi New Order* (1977); and M. Mazower, *Inside Hitler's Greece: The Experience of Occupation, 1941–1944* (1993). The Polish experience is recounted in J. T. Gross, *Polish Society under German Occupation* (1979) and R. C. Lukas, *The Forgotten Holocaust: The Poles under German Occupation, 1939–1944* (1986). In its Norwegian setting, collaborationism is illustrated in detail in O. K. Hoidal, *Quisling: A Study in Treason* (1989). The Nazi purloining of Europe's art treasures is described in L. H. Nicholas, The *Rape of Europa: The Fate of Europe's Treasures in the Third Reich and the Second World War* (1994). The role of the Swiss banks in concealing the looted gold used for the Nazi war effort is disclosed in I. Vincent, *Silent Partners: Swiss Bankers, Nazi Gold, and the Pursuit of Justice* (1998).

For the Europewide Resistance, there is the informative study by H. Michel, *The Shadow War: The European Resistance, 1939–1945* (trans. 1972); the useful M.R.D. Foot, *Resistance: European Resistance to Nazism, 1940–1945* (1977); and J. Haestrup, *European Resistance Movements, 1939–1945* (rev. 1981), a comprehensive account. The renovative spirit of the Resistance and its message for the postwar world are captured in J. D. Wilkinson, *The Intellectual Resistance in Europe* (1981). The ethical aspects of collaboration and resistance are explored in R. Bennett, *Under the Shadow of the Swastika: The Moral Dilemmas of Resistance and Collaboration in Hitler's Europe* (1999). Books on the German Resistance have been cited in Chapter 20.

The Holocaust

There is a large literature on the grim subject of the Nazis' systematic, willful, mass slaughter of the European Jews during the war years. The most informative and comprehensive study is R. Hilberg, *The Destruction of the European Jews* (3 vols.; rev. 1983; 1 vol. abridged, 1985), which may be supplemented by the same author's *Perpetrators, Victims, Bystanders: The Jewish Catastrophe, 1933–1945* (1992). Other important studies are M. Gilbert, *The Holocaust: The History of the Jews of Europe during the Second World War* (1986); L. S. Dawidowicz, *The War against the Jews, 1933–1945* (1976), cited earlier; Y. Bauer, *A History of the Holocaust* (1982) and *Rethinking the Holocaust* (2001); and L. Yahil, *The Holocaust: The Fate of European Jewry, 1932–1945* (trans. 1990). A provocative interpretive account is A. J. Mayer, *Why Did the Heavens Not Darken? The "Final Solution" in History* (1989), which sees the root cause in earlier twentieth-century destructiveness. An exhaustive reference work, with contributions by many scholars and with bibliographies in many languages, is I. Gutman (ed.), *Encyclopedia of the Holocaust* (4 vols.; 1990), while the best one-volume coverage is in W. Laqueur (ed.), *The Holocaust Encyclopedia* (2001). M. Gilbert has edited an *Atlas of the Holocaust* (1993).

H. Fein, *Accounting for Genocide: National Responses and Jewish Victimization during the Holocaust* (1979) examines the diversity of the experience in different countries, while R. L. Braham, *The Politics of Genocide: The Holocaust in Hungary* (2 vols.; 1981) is an outstanding study of one country. A key episode of Jewish resistance is recounted in I. Gutman, *The Jews of Warsaw, 1939–1943: Ghetto, Underground, Revolt* (trans. 1982).

Among many studies of the concentration and death camps one should read Primo Levi's moving accounts of his experience, *Survival in Auschwitz* (trans. 1947; 1958) and *The Drowned and the Saved* (trans. 1986). One may also read E. Kogon, *The Theory and Practice of Hell* (1950); T. Des Pres, *The Survivor: An Anatomy of a Life in the Death Camps* (1976); T. Segev, *Soldiers of Evil: The Commandants of the Nazi Concentration Camps* (trans. 1989); and W. Sofsky, *The Order of Terror: The Concentration Camp* (trans. 1997). On the link between the medical profession and the killings R. J. Lifton, *The Death Doctors: Medical Killing and the Psychology of Genocide* (1987) may be read along with H. Friedlander, *The Origins of Nazi Genocide* (1995), focusing on its prewar program of euthanasia for the sick and the handicapped.

For the debate over the origin of the Holocaust, that is, between "intentionalists," who see the genocidal destruction as motivated from the beginning by Hitler and his ideology, and "functionalists," who see it as developing incrementally once the Nazis controlled eastern Europe, the best synthesis is C. Browning, *The Path to Genocide: Essays on Launching the Final Solution* (1992). Hitler's fundamental responsibility is described in G. Fleming, *Hitler and the Final Solution* (1984) and R. Breitman, *The Architect of Genocide: The Final Solution* (1991).

The subject of much discussion and controversy, D. Goldhagen, *Hitler's Willing Executioners: Ordinary Germans and the Holocaust* (1996) argues that ordinary Germans, not only Nazi extremists, participated in the brutal killings because they shared a German legacy of "eliminationist anti-Semitism." On the other hand, C. Browning, *Ordinary Men: Reserve Police Battalion 101 and the Final Solution in Poland* (1992, 1999) demonstrates that peer pressures on the German participants seemed to be more important than any historical legacy of anti-Semitism.

How historians have written about the subject is explored in L. S. Dawidowicz, *The Holocaust and the Historians* (1981) and M. R. Marrus, *The Holocaust in History* (1987). A much discussed essay on the question of responsibility and guilt is H. Arendt, *Eichmann in Jerusalem: A Report on the Banality of Evil* (1963), written at the time of the trial of the high-ranking bureaucrat who carried out much of the operation. Y. Bauer, *The Holocaust in Historical Perspective* (1978) argues the uniqueness of the episode and disputes later misuses of the word "genocide"; on that issue, one may also read L. Kuper, *Genocide: Its Political Use in the Twentieth Century* (1982).

The acrimonious debate among German historians in the mid-1980s, in which E. Nolte and others sought to mitigate the evils of the Holocaust by comparing it to other twentieth-century atrocities such as those of Stalin, is thoughtfully explored in C. S. Maier, *The Unmasterable Past: History, Holocaust, and German National Identity* (1988) and R. J. Evans, *In Hitler's Shadow: West German Historians and the Attempt to Escape from the Nazi Past* (1989). On a related subject one may read J. Kramer, *The Politics of Memory: Looking for Germany in the New Germany* (1996). Broader efforts to deny or minimize the Holocaust are critically scrutinized in two persuasive books: D. E. Lipstadt, *The Growing Assault on Truth and Memory* (1993), and P. Vidal-Naquet, *Assassins of Memory: Essays on the Denial of the Holocaust* (trans. 1992).

There is a large literature on the failure of the authorities in the United States, Britain, and the Vatican to rescue the doomed European Jews; among the more searching inquiries are B. Wasserstein, *Britain and the Jews of Europe, 1939–1945* (1979); M. Gilbert, *Auschwitz and the Allies* (1981); and R. Breitman, *Official Secrets: What the Nazis Planned, What the British and Americans Knew* (1998). On the role of the Vatican in these years one may read J. F. Morley, *Vatican Diplomacy and the Jews during the Holocaust, 1939–1945* (1980) and M. Phayer, *The Catholic Church and the Holocaust, 1930–1965* (2000), a comprehensive account. Two studies indicting the wartime pope for failure to take more decisive action are J. Cornwell, *Hitler's Pope: The Secret History of Pius XII* (1999) and S. Zucotti, *Under the Very Windows: The Vatican and the Holocaust in Italy* (2001).

For the Nazi atrocities against other ethnic groups in Europe, including Russians, Poles, Gypsies, and others, one may read B. Wytwycky, *The Other Holocaust: Many Circles of Hell* (1986), a brief introduction; and the essays in M. Berenbaum (ed.), *A Mosaic of Victims: Non-Jews Persecuted and Murdered by the Nazis* (1992). For the fate of the Gypsies, or Roma, one may read I. Fonseca, *Bury Me Standing: The Gypsies and Their Journey* (1995).

The proceedings of the Nuremberg trials were published by the postwar International Military Tribunal as *Trial of the Major War Criminals before the International Military Tribunal, 1945–1946* (42 vols.; 1947–1949) and *Nazi Conspiracy and Aggression* (8 vols., 2 supplements; 1946–1958). B. F. Smith's two books, *Reaching Judgment at Nuremberg* (1977) and *The Road to Nuremberg* (1981) argue that the trials prevented an anarchic bloodbath and should not be dismissed as merely "victor's justice." Other thoughtful discussions are found in E. Davidson, *The Trial of the Germans: Nuremberg, 1945–1946* (1966); W. Maser, *Nuremberg: A Nation on Trial* (1979); R. E. Conot, *Justice at Nuremberg* (1983); J. E. Persica, *Nuremberg: Infamy on Trial* (1995); and T. Taylor, *The Anatomy of the Nuremberg Trials* (1993), by a chief prosecutor who analyzes deficiencies in the procedures and questions the effectiveness of the trials as a deterrent to later wrongdoing. The trials of the Japanese war leaders are critically analyzed in R. Minear, *Victor's Justice: The Tokyo War Crimes Trial* (1979), which should be supplemented by P. R. Piccigallo, *The Japanese on Trial: Allied War Crimes Operations, in the East, 1945–1951* (1979) and A. C. Brackman, *The Other Nuremberg: The Untold Story of the Tokyo War Crimes Trials* (1987). On national responses in later years to these events one may read an insightful study by I. Buruma, *The Wages of Guilt: Memories of War in Germany and Japan* (1994).

Wartime Diplomacy and Origins of the Cold War

A large literature has emerged stressing the origins of the Cold War in Soviet-American wartime relations. The volumes of H. Feis, sympathetic to the Western leaders, are indispensable as an introduction: *Churchill, Roosevelt, Stalin: The War They Waged and the Peace They Sought* (1957), covering the years from 1941 to the collapse of Germany; *Between War and Peace: The Potsdam Conference* (1960); and on the last phase, *The Atomic Bomb and the End of the War in the Pacific* (1961, 1966). Of special value are

G. Smith, *American Diplomacy during the Second World War, 1941–1945* (1965); J. L. Gaddis, *The United States and the Origins of the Cold War, 1941–1947* (1972); V. Mastny, *Russia's Road to the Cold War* (1979); and R. V. Daniels, *Russia: The Roots of Confrontation* (1985).

On the American use of the atomic bomb, one may read M. J. Sherwin, *A World Destroyed: The Atomic Bomb and the Grand Alliance* (1975), an impressive, balanced study, and G. Herken, *The Winning Weapon: The Atomic Bomb in the Cold War, 1945–1950* (1980, 1988). For the debate over the dropping of the bomb, a debate that was renewed on its 50th anniversary, one may read G. Alperowitz and others, *The Decision to Use the Atomic Bomb and the Architecture of an American Myth* (1995), highly critical; while R. V. Maddox, *The Hiroshima Decision Fifty Years Later* (1995) defends the use of the bomb. The continuing moral dilemma is ably presented in R. J. Lifton and G. Mitchell, *Hiroshima in America: Fifty Years of Denial* (1995). A concise survey and bibliographical guide is J. S. Walker, *Prompt and Utter Destruction: Truman and the Use of the Atomic Bomb against Japan* (1997). Two older books criticizing the use of the bomb are G. Alperowitz, *Atomic Diplomacy: Hiroshima and Potsdam* (rev. 1985); and B. J. Bernstein, *The Atomic Bomb: The Critical Issues* (1975).

On population movements during and following the war there are available J. B. Schechtman, *European Population Transfer, 1939–1945* (1946); E. M. Kulischer, *Europeans on the Move: War and Population Changes, 1917–1947* (1948); M. J. Proudfoot, *European Refugees, 1939–1952* (1957); M. R. Marrus, *The Unwanted: European Refugees in the Twentieth Century* (1985), cited earlier; and M. Wyman, *DP: Europe's Displaced Persons, 1945–1951* (1989, 1998).

Problems and Readings

For prewar diplomacy and the war there are available: H. W. Gatzke (ed.), *European Diplomacy between Two Wars, 1919–1939* (1972); L. F. Schaefer (ed.), *The Ethiopian Crisis: Touchstone of Appeasement?* (1961); G. Jackson (ed.), *The Spanish Civil War: Domestic Crisis or International Conspiracy?* (1967); A. Forrest, *The Spanish Civil War* (2001), a useful collection of readings from the period; K. Eubank, *The Origins of World War II* (rev. 1990); A Guttmann (ed.), *American Neutrality and the Spanish Civil War* (1963); A. P. Adamthwaite, *The Making of the Second World War* (1979), a brief survey with documents; F. L. Loewenheim (ed.), *Peace or Appeasement: Hitler, Chamberlain, and the Munich Crisis* (1965); and D. E. Lee (ed.), *Munich: Blunder, Plot, or Tragic Necessity?* (1969).

Other episodes and debates are explored in S. M. Osgood (ed.), *The Fall of France, 1940* (rev. 1972);

I. Morris (ed.), *Japan, 1931–1945: Militarism, Fascism, Japanism?* (1963); H. L. Trefousse, *Pearl Harbor: The Continuing Controversy* (1982); K. W. Eubank (ed.), *World War II: Roots and Causes* (rev. 1991); L. S. Dawidowicz (ed.), *A Holocaust Reader* (1976); D. Niewyk (ed.), *The Holocaust* (1991); and N. Levin *The Holocaust Years* (1990). The debate among German historians over the uniqueness of the Holocaust may be sampled in G. Thomas (ed.), *The Unresolved Past: A Debate in German History* (1991). M. R. Marrus has edited *The Nuremberg War Crimes Trial, 1945–1946: A Brief Documentary History* (1997).

22. THE POSTWAR ERA: COLD WAR AND RECONSTRUCTION

The Cold War

Informative narratives for the global history of the post-1945 years include P. Calvacoressi, *World Politics, 1945–2000* (rev. 2001) and D. Reynolds, *One World Divisible: A Global History since 1945* (2000); and for the twentieth century as a whole, J. M. Roberts, *Twentieth Century: The History of the World, 1901 to 2000* (2000); C. Pointing, *The Twentieth Century: A World History* (1999); and E. J. Hobsbawm, *The Age of Extremes, 1914–1991* (1994), cited earlier. Studies examining the Cold War with new historical perspectives after the collapse of the Soviet Union include M. Walker, *The Cold War: A History* (1994); R. Crockett, *The Fifty Years' War: The United States and the Soviet Union in World Politics, 1941–1991* (1995); and S. J. Ball, *The Cold War: An International History, 1947–1991* (1998). In addition to books on the wartime origins of the Cold War, cited in the previous chapter, thoughtful works include H. Feis, *From Trust to Terror: The Onset of the Cold War, 1945–1950* (1970), a sequel to his earlier volumes; D. Sharnik, *Inside the Cold War* (1987); W. LaFeber, *America, Russia, and the Cold War, 1945–1990* (1991); and W. I. Cohen, *America in the Age of Soviet Power, 1945–1991* (1993). J. L. Gaddis has helped to evaluate interpretations of the Cold War on the basis of archival evidence now available from the Soviet files in *We Now Know: Rethinking Cold War History* (1997), much of which confirms many earlier interpretations. For a judicious assessment of the Cold War compromises in Europe one may read M. Trachtenberg, *A Constructed Peace: The Making of the European Settlement, 1945–1963* (1999).

Two early efforts to examine the tensions in broader historical perspective, going back to 1917, are L. Halle, *The Cold War as History* (1967) and A. Fontaine, *History of the Cold War* (2 vols.; trans. 1968–1969). A large revisionist literature blamed American postwar political and economic ambitions or miscalculations for the Cold War. One of the most cogent of such interpretations is W. A. Williams, *The Tragedy of American Diplomacy* (rev. 1988), cited earlier. For guidance to the literature as a whole, including the revisionist accounts, one may turn to J. L. Black, *Origins, Evolution and Nature of the Cold War: An Annotated Bibliography* (1986) and J. W. Young, *The Longman Companion to America, Russia, and the Cold War, 1941–1998* (rev. 1999).

The transition from the Second World War to the postwar years is explored in R. Douglas, *From War to Cold War, 1942–1948* (1981); J. L. Gormly, *The Collapse of the Grand Alliance, 1945–1948* (1987); H. Thomas, *Armed Truce: The Beginnings of the Cold War, 1945–1946* (1986) and F. J. Harbutt, *The Iron Curtain: Churchill, America, and the Origins of the Cold War* (1986). D. McCullough, *Truman* (1992), is a colorful, carefully researched biography; Secretary of State Dean Acheson is studied in biographies by D. Brinkley, *Dean Acheson: The Cold War Years, 1953–1971* (1992) and J. Chace, *Acheson* (1998), a detached and comprehensive treatment. On the diplomat who helped shape the American containment policy and later regretted the heavy emphasis on military force that it came to assume, one should read G. F. Kennan, *American Diplomacy* (rev. 1984), among his several other books. Kennan, Acheson, and other key American foreign policy figures are studied in W. Isaacson and E. Thomas, *The Wise Men* (1986). On the "Munich syndrome," the resolve by Truman and others not to repeat the appeasement of the 1930s, one may read G. Rystad, *Prisoners of the Past* (1982); E. R. May, *The Lessons of the Past: The Use and Misuse of History in American Foreign Policy* (1973); and D. Halberstam, *The Best and the Brightest* (1972), principally on the war in Vietnam.

Two informative volumes on the nuclear dangers confronting the postwar world are D. Holloway, *Stalin and the Bomb: The Soviet Union and Atomic Energy, 1939–1956* (1994) and R. Rhodes, *Dark Sun: The Making of the Hydrogen Bomb* (1995), a sequel to his book on the atomic bomb cited in the previous chapter. The revolutionary implications of nuclear weapons for the post-1945 world are discussed in M. Mandelbaum, *The United States and Nuclear Weapons, 1946–1976* (1979) and *The Nuclear Revolution: International Politics before and after Hiroshima* (1981). Additional books on nuclear arms and disarmament will be suggested in later chapters.

The origins, founding, and subsequent history of the United Nations are studied in T. Hoopes and D. Brinkley, *FDR and the Creation of the UN* (1998) and S. Meisler, *United Nations: The First Fifty Years* (1998). The limitations of international cooperation are astutely assessed in T. M. Franck, *Nation against Nation* (1985) and A. Roberts, *United Nations, Divided World* (1988).

Economic Reconstruction and the Reshaping of the World Economy

Informative studies of postwar economic reconstruction and of the economic growth that followed for close to three decades are H. van der Wee, *Prosperity and Upheaval: The World Economy, 1945–1980* (1986) and P. Armstrong, A. Glyn, and J. Harrison, *Capitalism since World War II: The Making and Breakup of the Great Boom* (1984). They may be supplemented by the essays in S. A. Marglin and J. B. Schor (eds.), *The Golden Age of Capitalism: Reinterpreting the Postwar Experience* (1990).

The Bretton Woods monetary arrangements and their evolution are examined in R. Solomon, *The International Monetary System, 1945–1981* (1982) and, in a sequel volume, *Money on the Move: The Revolution in International Finance since 1980* (1999). More general studies, which include valuable information on the postwar era, include S. Pollard, *The International Economy since 1945* (1997); J. Mills, *Managing the World Economy* (2000), a useful survey of the twentieth century as a whole; and R. K. Schaeffer, *Understanding Globalization* (1997).

Thoughtful surveys of Europe for the first several decades of the postwar era include W. Laqueur, *Europe in Our Time: A History, 1945–1992* (rev. 1992); F. Tipton and R. Aldrich, *An Economic and Social History of Europe, 1939 to the Present* (1987); D. Urwin, *A Political History of Europe since 1945* (rev. 1997); and M. Fulbrook (ed.), *Europe since 1945* (2001), which includes helpful essays on politics, social history, economic changes, and culture.

For the American role in reconstruction, M. J. Hogan, *The Marshall Plan: America, Britain, and the Reconstruction of Western Europe, 1947–1952* (1987) is outstanding. Other books that merit attention are A. S. Milward, *The Reconstruction of Western Europe, 1945–1951* (1984), which credits European initiative and skills as much as American aid; J. Gimbel, *The Origins of the Marshall Plan* (1976); C. L. Mee, *The Marshall Plan and the Launching of the Pax Americana* (1980); and D. W. Ellwood, *Rebuilding Europe: Western Europe, America, and Postwar Reconstruction, 1945–1955* (1992). An impressive synthesis on postwar reconstruction in all aspects is P. Duignan and L. H. Gann, *The Rebirth of the West: The Americanization of the Democratic World, 1945–1958* (1992). The same authors have extended their analysis of transatlantic relations in *The USA and the New Europe, 1945–1993* (1994).

Some of the social consequences of the economic changes in Europe are also explored in S. Rothman, *European Society and Politics: Britain, France, and Germany* (1976) and A. Sampson, *The New Europeans* (rev. 1971). An important social issue receives attention in two books by S. Castles: *Here for Good:* *Western Europe's New Ethnic Minorities* (1984) and *Migrant Workers in European Societies* (1989). Other works on the growing multiculturalism of European societies include G. Dale and M. Cole (eds.), *The European Union and Migrant Labour* (1999) and S. Castles and A. Davidson, *Citizenship and Migration: Globalization and the Politics of Belonging* (2000).

The postwar welfare state is examined in D. E. Ashford, *The Emergence of the Welfare States* (1987). On Keynes and Keynesianism, influential in the managed economies of the early postwar decades, one may read R. Lekachman, The *Age of Keynes* (1966) and books on Keynes cited in Chapter 20. R. Skidelsky, *John Maynard Keynes: Fighting for Britain, 1937–1946* (2000) concludes his three-volume biography. On the role of government one may also read A. Shonfield, *Modern Capitalism: The Changing Balance of Public and Private Power* (1969); S. Lieberman, *The Growth of the European Mixed Economies, 1945–1970* (1977); and the essays in A. Graham with A. Seldon (eds.), *Government and Economies in the Postwar World* (1990).

On western European economic integration, A. S. Milward, *The European Rescue of the Nation-State* (1992) is an outstanding study that explores and interprets the origins of the European Community, while J. Lukacs, *Decline and Rise of Europe* (1965) provides additional historical background. Informative also for these years are J. Gillingham, *Coal, Steel, and the Rebirth of Europe, 1945–1955: The Germans and the French from Ruhr Conflict to Economic Community* (1991) and D. W. Urwin, *The Community of Europe: A History of European Integration since 1945* (rev. 1995). A good brief introduction is F. Lewis, *Europe: Road to Unity* (1992). For a key architect of European unity, one may turn to M. Bromberger and S. Bromberger, *Jean Monnet and the United States of Europe* (trans. 1969) and D. Brinkley and C. Hacket (eds.), Jean Monnet: *The Path to European Unity* (1991). Additional books on European integration will be cited in Chapter 24.

The Western Countries and Japan after 1945

Britain. K. O. Morgan, *The People's Peace: British History since 1945* (rev. 1999) and D. Childs, *Britain since 1945* (rev. 1997) provide good overviews. Britain's loss of primacy and world power is discussed in M. W. Kirby, *The Decline of British Economic Power since 1870* (1981); R. Blake, *The Decline of Power, 1915–1964* (1985); B. Porter, *Britain, Europe, and the World, 1850–1986: Delusions of Grandeur* (1987); and in two incisive analyses by C. Barnett: *The Collapse of British Power* (1986) and *The Pride and the Fall: The Dream and Illusion of Britain as a Great Nation* (1987). That the reasons for decline remained controversial, however, emerges from the debate and discussion in A. Sked, *Britain's Decline: Problems and Perspectives* (1987) and from the essays in B. Collins and K. Robbins (eds.), *British Culture and Economic Decline* (1990).

The best account of the postwar Labour governments and the emergence of the welfare state is K. O. Morgan, *Labour in Power, 1945–1951* (1984), a balanced study with in-depth portraits of Clement Attlee and other key figures; informative also is H. Pelling, *The Labour Governments, 1945–1951* (1984). The creation and consolidation of the welfare state is studied in P. Gregg, *The Welfare State* (1969); S. H. Beer, *British Politics in the Collectivist Age* (1965); and T. O. Lloyd, *Empire, Welfare State, Europe: English History, 1906–1992* (rev. 1993). For the social impact one may read A. Marwick, *British Society since 1945* (rev. 1996) and A. Sampson, *The Changing Anatomy of Britain* (rev. 1983). Special subjects are explored in two books by Z. A. Layton-Henry: *The Politics of Race in Britain* (1984) and *The Politics of Immigration: "Race" and "Race" Relations in Post-war Britain* (1992).

FRANCE. Fourth and Fifth Republics. A useful reference tool is W. Northcutt (ed.), *Historical Dictionary of the French Fourth and Fifth Republics, 1946–1991* (1991). The best syntheses for the short-lived Fourth Republic are J.-P. Rioux, *The Fourth Republic, 1944–1958* (trans. 1987) and F. Giles, *The Locust Years: The Story of the French Fourth Republic, 1946–1958* (1996). I. M. Wall's two books, *The United States and the Making of Postwar France, 1945–1954* (1991) and *France, The United States, and the Algerian War* (2001), and R. Kuisel, *Seducing the French: The Dilemma of Americanization* (1993) are insightful on American political and cultural influences. Kuisel's *Capitalism and the State in Modern France* (1981), cited in Chapter 20, places government direction of the postwar economy in historical perspective. The reform minister Mendès-France's reform efforts in the early 1950s are sympathetically portrayed in J. Lacouture, *Pierre Mendès-France* (trans. 1984). Incisive on the cultural and political scene are T. Judt, *Past Imperfect* (1992), a critique of the political influence of Sartre and other intellectuals in the early postwar years, and *The Burden of Responsibility: Blum, Camus, Aron and the French Twentieth Century* (1998), on three influential figures whom he believes made more positive contributions.

Of the colonial wars that helped bring down the Fourth Republic, the war in Indochina is graphically portrayed in B. B. Fall, *Street without Joy: Indochina at War, 1946–1954* (rev. 1964) and *Hell in a Very Small Place: The Siege of Dien Bien Phu* (1967). Other books on Vietnam and Indochina will be cited in Chapter 24. The ill-fated effort to retain Algeria is described in A. Horne, *A Savage War of Peace: Algeria, 1954–1962* (1978), a comprehensive account and J. Talbott, *The War without a Name: France in Algeria, 1954–1962* (1980). Subsequent relationships with Algeria are traced in J. Reudy, *Modern Algeria: The Origins and Development of a Nation* (1992). For the Fifth Republic there are available S. Berstein, *The Republic of de Gaulle, 1958–1969* (trans. 1993), an excellent synthesis; S. Hoffmann's informative *Decline or Renewal? France since the Popular Front: Government and People, 1936–1986* (1988); J. Ardagh, *The New France, De Gaulle and After* (rev. 1977); and M. Larkin, *France since the Popular Front: Government and People, 1936–1996* (rev. 1997). J. Lacouture's authoritative biography of de Gaulle (2 vols.; trans. 1992) has been mentioned in Chapter 21; there are also biographical accounts by B. Crozier (1973), B. Ledwidge (1983), D. Cook (1984), and A. Shennan (1993).

GERMANY. For West Germany during the years of partition an impressive comprehensive narrative is D. L. Bark and D. R. Gress, *A History of West Germany* (2 vols.; rev. 1993). A briefer account is M. Balfour, *West Germany: A Contemporary History* (rev. 1982). For the West German "economic miracle" one may read H. C. Wallich, *Mainsprings of the German Revival* (1955) and A. Kramer, *The West German Economy, 1945–1955* (1991); and for the powerful economy that emerged, E. Hartrich, *The Fourth and Richest Reich* (1980). Of special interest is V. R. Berghahn, *The Americanization of West German Industry, 1945–1973* (1986). Konrad Adenauer's accomplishments are assessed in R. Hiscocks, *The Adenauer Era* (1966); and T. Prittie has written biographies of Adenauer (1972) and of Willy Brandt (1974).

For West and East Germany, including the relationship of the two states over the four postwar decades of partition, two informative accounts are H. A. Turner, Jr., *Germany from Partition to Reunification* (rev. 1992) and M. Fulbrook, *The Divided Nation: A History of Germany, 1918–1990* (1992), cited earlier. T. Garton Ash, *In Europe's Name: Germany and the Divided Continent* (1993) incisively reassesses Willy Brandt's efforts to improve East-West relations. For the formation and early years of the German Democratic Republic one should read N. M. Naimark, *The Russians in Germany* (1995). The East German Communist leader is examined in C. Stern, *Ulbrecht: A Political Biography* (1965), and the effort to prevent the flight of the East Germans after 1961 is studied in P. Galante and P. Miller, *The Berlin Wall* (1965).

There are provocative insights into the German search for self-understanding in R. Dahrendorf, *Society and Democracy in Germany* (1967); F. Stern, *Dreams and Delusions: The Drama of German History* (1987, 1999); and two books cited earlier:

G. A. Craig, *The Germans* (1982) and H. James, *A German Identity, 1770–1990* (1990).

ITALY AND SPAIN. Three insightful studies of Italian political life are F. Spotts and T. Wieser, *Italy: A Difficult Democracy* (1986); J. LaPalombara, *Democracy, Italian Style* (1987); and R. Putman, *Making Democracy Work: Civic Traditions in Modern Italy* (1993). All three describe the paradox whereby the country has known remarkable social and economic progress despite political difficulties. For the postwar years one may also read D. W. Ellwood, *Italy, 1943–1945* (1985); N. Kogan, *A Political History of Postwar Italy* (2 vols.; 1966–1981); P. Ginsborg, *A History of Contemporary Italy: Society and Politics, 1943–1988* (1990); and the essays in P. McCarthy, *Italy since 1945* (2000). The American role in the early years is assessed in J. L. Harper, *America and the Reconstruction of Italy, 1945–1948* (1986). The special role of the Italian Communist party from liberation to the mid-1980s is examined in J. B. Urban, *Moscow and the Italian Communist Party: From Togliatti to Berlinguer* (1986) and A. De Grand, *The Italian Left in the Twentieth Century: A History of the Socialist and Communist Parties* (1989).

For Spain, changes under Franco are well conveyed in J. Grugel and T. Rees, *Franco's Spain* (1997); the transition to a modern democracy after Franco is described in K. Maxwell and S. Spiegel, *The New Spain* (1994) and V. Pérez-Diaz, *Spain at the Crossroads* (1999).

JAPAN. One of the best introductions to contemporary Japan is E. O. Reischauer and M. B. Jansen, *The Japanese Today: Change and Continuity* (rev. 1995). Books that analyze Japanese changes after the wartime defeat and occupation include J. W. Dower, *Embracing Defeat: Japan in the Wake of World War II* (1999), an insightful account of the American occupation, and *Japan in War and Peace* (1993); D. Irokawa, *The Age of Hirohito: In Search of Modern Japan* (1998), for the years 1926–1989, a remarkable social history of transition from an agrarian to an industrial society; P. Smith, *Japan: A Reinterpretation* (1997); and H. P. Bix, *Hirohito and the Making of Modern Japan* (2001). For the postwar years one may also turn to P. J. Bailey, *Postwar Japan, 1945 to the Present* (1996), an excellent, brief narrative account. Of special interest are C. Johnson, *MITI and the Japanese Miracle: The Growth of Industrial Policy, 1925–1974* (1982), on the government research and development agency and W. W. Lockwood, *State and Economic Enterprise in Japan* (1986). A critical assessment of the troubled Japanese economy in the 1990s is C. Wood, *The Bubble Economy* (1992).

The Soviet Union: From Stalin to Brezhnev

Of the many volumes for the Stalin years listed in Chapter 18, one of the best assessments is A. B. Ulam, *Stalin: The Man and His Era* (1987). The postwar years and the evolution of the Soviet system after Stalin are explored in A. Nove, *Stalinism and After: The Road to Gorbachev* (rev. 1989); S. Bialer, *Stalin's Successors: Leadership, Stability, and Change in the Soviet Union* (1980) and *The Soviet Paradox: External Expansion, Internal Decline* (1986); and A. Nove, *The Soviet Economic System* (rev. 1986). Foreign policy is studied in R. Edmonds, *Soviet Foreign Policy: The Brezhnev Years* (1983) and V. Mastny, *The Cold War and Soviet Insecurity* (1996); and the origins and nature of the involvement in Afghanistan are studied in M. Urban, *The War in Afghanistan* (rev. 1990).

For the Soviet dissenters one may turn to R. Conquest, *The Politics of Ideas in the USSR* (1967); P. Reddaway, *Russia's Underground Intellectuals* (1970); A. Rothberg, *The Heirs of Stalin: Dissidence and the Soviet Regime, 1953–1970* (1972); and R. T. Tökes (ed.), *Dissent in the U.S.S.R.: Politics, Ideology, and People* (1975). M. Scammell, *Solzhenitzyn* (1984), provides a balanced assessment of the controversial novelist. A. Knight, *The KGB: Police and Politics in the Soviet Union* (rev. 1990) carries the story of the secret police to the mid-1980s. Anti-Semitism in these years may be studied in L. Rapoport, *Stalin's War against the Jews: The Doctors' Plot and the Soviet Solution* (1990); B. Pinkus, *The Soviet Government and the Jews, 1948–1967* (1985), cited earlier; and R. O. Freedman (ed.), *Soviet Jewry in the Decisive Decade, 1971–1980* (1987). For the international Communist movement in the postwar years, A. Westoby, *Communism since World War II* (rev. 1989), provides in-depth coverage. An initial effort to assess Soviet archival material now becoming available is V. Zubak and C. Pleshakov, *Inside the Kremlin's Cold War: From Stalin to Khruschev* (1996).

Eastern Europe under Soviet Domination

How communism was imposed on eastern Europe is explored in H. Seton-Watson, *The East European Revolution* (rev. 1956). The years of Communist domination and the mounting restiveness in eastern Europe are studied in J. Rothschild and N. M. Wingfield, *Return to Diversity: A Political History of East Central Europe since World War II* (rev. 2000) and G. Schöpflin, *Politics in Eastern Europe, 1945–1992* (1993).

For Hungary and the uprising of 1956 one may read P. C. Zinner, *Revolution in Hungary* (1962); B. Kovrig, *Communism in Hungary from Kun to Kádár* (1979); and C. Gati, *Hungary and the Soviet Bloc* (1988). Czechoslovakia as victim, first of Hitler then of Stalin, is examined in E. Toborsky, *President Eduard Benes: Between East and West, 1938–1948* (1981). The crisis of 1968 is studied in G. Golan, *The Czechoslovak Reform Movement: Communism in Crisis, 1962–1968* (1971); K. N. Skoug, Jr., *Czechoslova-*

kia's Fight For Freedom, 1967–1969 (1999), by a former American diplomat who was in Prague at the time; and books by V. Kusin (1971), Z.A.B. Zeman (1969), and K. Dawisha (1984).

For the emergence of communism in Yugoslavia, A. Djilas, *The Contested Country: Yugoslav Unity and Communist Revolution, 1919–1953* (1991) is an outstanding study. Informative on Tito's efforts to govern the multinational state are D. Rusinow, *The Yugoslav Experiment, 1948–1974* (1977); D. Wilson, *Tito's Yugoslavia* (1979); and H. Lydall, *Yugoslavia in Crisis* (1989). Additional books for the former Yugoslavia and for other East European countries after communism will be described in Chapter 25.

China under Mao

As background to the emergence of communism, and for a sense of the continuing revolution in China in modern times, books cited in Chapters 16 and 19 will also be helpful. One of the best overall histories is J. K. Fairbank and M. Goldman, *China: A New History* (rev. 1999), cited earlier. For the years after 1949 informative overviews are M. Meisner, *Mao's China and After* (rev. 1999) and L. Ditmer, *China's Continuous Revolution: The Post-Liberation Era, 1949–1981* (1987). There are authoritative chapters in the collaborative *Cambridge History of China*, R. MacFarquhar and J. K. Fairbank (eds.), Vol. 15: *The People's Republic*, published in two parts for the years 1949–1982 (1987, 1992). J. Becker, *Hungry Ghosts: Mao's Secret Famine* (1996) carefully reconstructs the three terrible years of famine 1959–1961 precipitated by Mao's Great Leap Forward. For the upheaval of 1966–1969, R. MacFarquhar, *The Origins of the Cultural Revolution* (3 vols., 1974–1997) is indispensable. Two biographies of Mao are rewarding: P. Short, *Mao: A Life* (2000), detailed, colorful, and comprehensive, and J. D. Spence, *Mao Zedong* (2000), a concise, insightful account. They may be supplemented by Mao's personal physician's revealing memoir, Li Zhisui, *The Private Life of Chairman Mao* (trans. 1994).

The Korean War

For background, J. Matray, *The Reluctant Crusade: American Foreign Policy in Korea, 1941–1950* (1985) is helpful. The fullest inquiry into the origins of the Korean War, openly revisionist, is B. Cumings, *The Origins of the Korean War* (2 vols.; 1981–1990); it may be compared with P. Lowe, *The Origins of the Korean War* (1986). There are narrative accounts by B. I. Kaufman (1986), M. Hastings (1987), C. Blair (1989), and J. Merrill (1989). The Chinese role is studied in S. G. Zhang, *Mao's Military Romanticism: China and the Korean War, 1950–1953* (1995). The military aspects are emphasized in A. Bevin, *Korea* (1987) and J. B. Toland, *In Mortal Combat: Korea, 1950–1953* (1992). An interesting biographical study is D. S. Suh,

Kim Il Sung: The North Korean Leader (1988). For the two Koreas after the war one may read B. Cumings, *Korea's Place in the Sun* (1997), critical of both Koreas, and D. Oberdorfer, *The Two Koreas: A Contemporary History* (1997).

Problems and Readings

The background to the Cold War may be examined in N. A. Graebner (ed.), *The Cold War: A Conflict of Ideology and Power* (rev. 1976); T. G. Paterson and R. J. McMahon (eds.), *The Origins of the Cold War* (rev. 1991); E. R. May (ed.), *American Cold War Strategy: Interpreting NSC* [National Security Council] *68* (1994); R. H. Miller (ed.), *The Evolution of the Cold War: From Confrontation to Containment* (1979); and C. S. Maier (ed.), *The Cold War in Europe: Its Origins and Consequences* (rev. 1990). E. H. Judge and J. W. Langdon (eds.), *The Cold War: A History through Documents* (1999), provides an excellent selection of key documents. The movement toward European unity is examined in H. A. Schmitt (ed.), *European Union: From Hitler to de Gaulle* (1969) and F. R. Willis (ed.), *European Integration* (1975). For the Communist triumph in China there is P.P.Y. Loh, *The Kuomintang Debacle of 1949: Conquest or Collapse?* (1965).

23. EMPIRES INTO NATIONS: THE DEVELOPING WORLD

End of the European Empires

Many of the books mentioned in Chapters 16 and 19 should also be consulted. For the background to the post-1945 colonial revolutions, there are useful introductions in R. F. Betts, *Uncertain Dimensions: Western Overseas Empires in the Twentieth Century* (1985) and in two older works: R. Emerson, *From Empire to Nation: The Rise to Self-Assertion of Asian and African Peoples* (1960) and T. Hodgkin, *Nationalism in Colonial Africa* (1956). The end of colonial rule is comprehensively treated in F. Ansprenger, *The Dissolution of Colonial Empires* (1989), while informative briefer accounts are available in R. F. Betts, *Decolonization* (1998), M. E. Chamberlain, *Decolonization: The Fall of the European Empires* (rev. 1999), and J. Springhall, *Decolonization since 1945* (2001). Books that examine colonial administration in the final phases before independence include M. Perham, *Colonial Sequence, 1930–1949* (1976) and R. F. Holland, *European Decolonization, 1918–1981* (1985). American responses to the breakup of empires are examined in D. Ryan and V. Pungong (eds.), *The United States and Decolonization* (2000). There are vignettes of selected Asian and African nationalist leaders in H. Tinker, *Men Who Overturned Empires: Fighters, Dreamers, and Schemers* (1987). A widely read, impassioned brief for anticolonialism was F. Fanon, *The Wretched of the Earth* (trans. 1963).

On nationalism and the emergent nations, many of the books cited in Chapter 11 on the older nationalism should also be consulted. To them should be added E. Kedourie, *Nationalism in Asia and Africa* (1971); A.D.S. Smith: *Nationalism in the Twentieth Century* (1979), *The Ethnic Origins of Nations* (1986), and *Nations and Nationalism in a Global Era* (1995); and B. Anderson, *Imagined Communities: Reflections on the Origin and Spread of Nationalism* (rev. 1991), cited earlier.

End of the British Empire, Changes in Asia

The disintegration of the British empire is studied in J. Darwin, *Britain and Decolonization: The Retreat from Empire in the Post-War World* (1988) and his briefer account, *End of Empire* (1991); D. A. Low, *Eclipse of Empire* (1991); and D. Judd, *Empire: The British Imperial Experience from 1765 to the Present* (1996). There are valuable essays in Vol. 5 of the *Oxford History of the British Empire: J. M. Brown* (ed.), *The Twentieth Century* (1999). Wartime controversies between Churchill and Roosevelt are skillfully analyzed in W. R. Louis, *Imperialism at Bay: The United States and the Decolonization of the British Empire 1941–1945* (1978). Of special interest for Britain's continuing global role is P. J. Cain and A. G. Hopkins, *British Imperialism: Crisis and Deconstruction, 1914–1990* (1993). British and French reactions to the loss of empire are compared in M. Kahler, *Decolonization in Britain and France* (1984).

The Indian nationalist struggle, the British withdrawal from the Indian subcontinent, and the early years of independence are examined S. Sarkar, *Modern India, 1885–1947* (rev. 1989); H. V. Hodson, *The Great Divide: Britain-India-Pakistan* (rev. 1985); J. M. Brown, *Modern India: The Origins of an Asian Democracy* (rev. 1994); and A. Read and D. Fisher, *The Proudest Day: India's Long Road to Independence* (1998). For India, and the politics and culture of South Asia in general, one may turn for guidance to S. Wolpert, *A New History of India* (rev. 1997). Biographies of Gandhi and Nehru have been cited in Chapter 19. For the years of independence after August 15, 1947, one may turn to P. Brass, *The Politics of India since Independence* (rev. 1994) and S. Tharoor, *India from Midnight to the Millennium* (2000). Among the thoughtful assessments of contemporary India are A. T. Embree, *Utopias in Conflict: Religion and Nationalism in Modern India* (1990); B. Crossette, *India: Facing the Twenty-First Century* (1993); and S. Khilnani, *The Idea of India* (1998). The resurgence of Hindu nationalism is studied in P. Van der Veer, *Religious Nationalism: Hindus and Muslims in India* (1994); C. Jaffrelot, *The Hindu Nationalist Movement in India* (1997); and T. B. Hansen, *The Saffron Wave: Democracy and Hindu Nationalism in Modern India* (1999). For an introduction to cultural

debates in which Indian theorists have had an important global influence, readers may turn to B. Moore-Gilbert, *Postcolonial Theory: Contexts, Practices, Politics* (1997).

For Pakistan and its founder informative studies are A. Jalal, *The Sole Spokesman: Jinnah, the Muslim League, and the Demand for Pakistan* (1985); S. Wolpert, *Jinnah of Pakistan* (1984); and A. S. Ahmed, *Jinnah, Pakistan, and Islamic Identity* (1997). The failure to integrate East Pakistan with the new state and the secession of Bangladesh are studied in R. Jakan, *Pakistan: Failure in National Integration* (1972). Informative for India, Pakistan, and South Asia in general is S. Bose and A. Jalal, *Modern South Asia: History, Culture, Political Economy* (1998).

For all East Asia the best introduction is J. K. Fairbank, E. M. Reischauer, and A. M. Craig, *East Asia* (rev. 1989). For developments in Southeast Asia, the best introduction is D. R. SarDesai, *Southeast Asia, Past and Present* (rev. 1997). A brief thematic survey of culture and politics in the region may be found in M. S. Heidhues, *Southeast Asia, A Concise History* (2000). The war fought by the British in the Malay peninsula is described in R. Jackson, *The Malayan Emergency: The Commonwealth Wars, 1948–1966* (1990). For the British success in attracting the newly independent states to membership in the transformed Commonwealth of Nations one may read R. J. Moore, *Making the New Commonwealth* (1987).

The struggle against the Dutch in Indonesia and the years of independence may be approached through two biographical accounts: J. D. Legge, *Sukarno* (1972, 1984), and D. Jenkins, *Suharto and His Generals* (1984).

A New Africa

To the histories of Africa cited in Chapter 16 should be added the informative J. Iliffe, *Africans: The History of a Continent* (1996). For decolonization, two indispensable volumes are P. Gifford and W. R. Louis (eds.), *The Transfer of Power in Africa: Decolonization, 1940–1960* (1982) and *Decolonization and African Independence: The Transfer of Power, 1960–1980* (1988). Good overviews are provided in J. D. Hargreaves, *Decolonization in Africa* (rev. 1996) and H. S. Wilson, *African Decolonization* (1994). An insightful survey for the years 1914 to the present is available in B. Davidson, *Modern Africa: A Social and Political History* (rev. 1994). Important additional perspectives by African historians are provided in A. A. Mazrui (ed.), *Africa since 1935* (1993). Assessments of the years of independence include B. Davidson, *The Black Man's Burden: Africa and the Curse of the Nation-State* (1992), which sees the Western model of the nation-state as an artificial importation into the continent; C. Young, *The African Colonial State in Comparative Perspective* (1995), stressing the harmful legacy bequeathed by colonialism; J. Harding, *The Fate of Africa: Continent on the Brink of Ruin* (1993), which graphically portrays ethnic conflicts; and G.B.N. Agittey, *Africa in Chaos* (1998), an angry critique of African governments and economic policies by a writer from Ghana. Francophone Africa is studied in E. Mortimer, *France and the Africans, 1944–1960* (1969) and J. F. Clark and D. E. Gardinier (eds.), *Political Reform in Francophone Africa* (1997). The career of the poet-statesman of Senegal is portrayed in J. G. Vaillant, *Black, French, and African: A Life of Léopold Sédar Senghor* (1990).

The best historical account of South Africa and its peoples is L. Thompson, *A History of South Africa* (rev. 2000), cited in Chapter 16, while a good brief introduction is N. Worden, *The Making of Modern South Africa* (rev. 2000). One may also read F. Welsh, *South Africa: A Narrative History* (1998), informative but somewhat Eurocentric, and R. Ross, *A Concise History of South Africa* (1999). Thoughtful accounts of two brutal episodes are R. R. Lemarchand, *Burundi: Ethnic Conflict and Genocide* (1996) and G. Prunier, *The Rwanda Crisis: History of a Genocide* (1996). Among the many studies of the struggle against apartheid are J. Lelyveld, *Move Your Shadow: South Africa Black and White* (1986); D. Ottoway, *Chained Together* (1992); M. Meredith, *In the Name of Apartheid: South Africa in the Postwar Period* (1989); A. Sparks, *The Mind of South Africa* (1990) and *Tomorrow is Another Country: The Inside Story of South Africa's Road to Change* (1995); and H. Adam and K. Moodley, *The Opening of the Apartheid Mind: Options for the New South Africa* (1993). A. Sampson, *Mandela: The Authorized Biography* (2000) also merits reading.

The Middle East

For good introductions one may turn to two brief, illuminating books by B. Lewis: *The Middle East: A Brief History of the Last 2000 Years* (1995, 1997) and *The Multiple Identities of the Middle East* (1998, 1999).

Books that examine the variety and complexity of Islam and its political manifestations include H. Munson, Jr., *Islam and Revolution in the Middle East* (1988); E. Swan, *Radical Islam: Medieval Theology and Modern Politics* (1985) and *Interpretations of Islam* (1988); B. Lewis, *The Political Language of Islam* (1988) and *Islam and the West* (1993); J. I. Esposito, *The Islamic Threat: Myth or Reality?* (1992); and B. B. Lawrence, *Shattering the Myth: Islam Beyond Violence* (1998). Two books that examine the ideologies of contemporary religious movements are B. Tibi, *The Challenge of Fundamentalism: Political Islam and the New World Disorder* (1998) and R. S. Appleby, *Spokesmen for the Dispossessed: Fundamentalist Leaders of the Middle East* (1997).

For Iraq informative studies include P. Marr, *The Modern History of Iraq* (1985); M. F. and P. Sluglett, *Iraq since 1958: From Revolution to Dictatorship* (1990); and S. al-Khalil [K. Makiya], *Republic of Fear: The Politics of Modern Iraq* (rev. 1998) and *Cruelty and Silence: War, Tyranny, Uprising, and the Arab World* (1993). The Iraqi dictator and the Baath party dictatorship are also studied in E. Karsh and I. Rautsi, *Saddam Hussein: A Political Biography* (1991).

Two introductions to the history of modern Israel are H. M. Sachar, *A History of Israel* (2 vols.; rev. 1996) and M. Gilbert, *Israel A History* (1998). Two biographies that help explain the early idealism of Zionism are J. Reinharz, *Chaim Weizmann* (2 vols.; 1985–1993), and S. Teveth, *Ben-Gurion: The Burning Ground, 1866–1948* (1987); there are studies also of Golda Meir by E. Ayres (1969) and P. Mann (1971). Two books that examine conflicting ideals of labor Zionism, nationalism, and religious conservatism are M. Cohen, *Zion and State: Nation, Class, and the Shaping of Modern Israel* (1987) and Z. Sternhell, *The Founding Myths of Israel: Nationalism, Socialism, and the Making of the Jewish State* (trans. 1998). Insights into ultra-Orthodox pressures are provided in D. Landau, *Piety and Power: The World of Jewish Fundamentalism* (1994).

The Arab-Israeli wars from 1948 to 1973 are traced in R. Ovendale, *The Origins of the Arab-Israeli Wars* (rev. 1999) and S. D. Bailey, *Four Arab-Israeli Wars and the Peace Process* (1990). Two moving accounts of Israeli-Palestinian tensions are T. L. Friedman, *From Beirut to Jerusalem* (1989) and D. K. Shipler, *Arab and Jew: Wounded Spirits in a Promised Land* (1989). Thoughtful studies focusing on the Palestinians are B. Kimmerling and J. S. Migdal, *Palestinians: The Making of a People* (1993); C. P. Smith, *Palestine and the Arab-Israeli Conflict* (rev. 2001); and two books by Israeli revisionist historians: A. Shlaim, *The Iron Wall: Israel and the Arab World since 1948* (1999) and B. Morris, *A History of the Zionist-Arab Conflict, 1881–1999* (1999), synthesizing his earlier books on Arab-Israeli relations and the Palestinian refugees.

The Revolution in Iran

The revolutionary events in Iran may be studied in N. R. Keddie, *Roots of Revolution: An Interpretive History of Modern Iran* (1981, 1990); D. Wilber, *Iran Past and Present: From Monarchy to Islamic Republic* (rev. 1981); S. Bakhash, *The Reign of the Ayotollahs: Iran and the Islamic Revolution* (rev. 1990); and R. Mottahedeh, *The Mantle of the Prophet: Religion and Politics in Iran* (1985). R. Wright's three books carry the story toward the present: *In the Name of God: The Khomeini Decade* (1989), *Sacred Rage: The Wrath of Militant Islam* (1989), and *The Last Great Revolution: Turmoil and Transformation in Iran*

(2000). An informative biography is B. Moine, *Khomeini: Life of the Ayotollah* (2000). For the American involvement one may read J. A. Bill, *The Eagle and the Lion: The Tragedy of American-Iranian Relations* (1988). The eight-year war between Iran and Iraq is described in D. Hiro, *The Longest War: The Iran-Iraq Military Conflict* (1991) and E. Karsh (ed.), *Iran-Iraq War: Impact and Implications* (1990).

Changing Latin America

Changes in Latin America are examined in T. E. Skidmore and P. H. Smith, *Modern Latin America* (rev. 2001); L. Bethell (ed.), Latin America since 1930 (1991); and R. Thorp, *Progress, Poverty, and Exclusion: An Economic History of Latin America in the Twentieth Century* (1998). A helpful reference work is S. Collier and others, *The Cambridge Encyclopedia of Latin America and the Caribbean* (rev. 1992).

The vicissitudes of American policies toward Latin America are explored in L. Langley, *America and the Americas* (1989); R. A. Pastor, *Whirlpool: United States Foreign Policy toward Latin America and the Caribbean* (1992); and W. LaFeber, *Inevitable Revolutions: Reflections on American Equality and Foreign Liberation* (rev. 1993). An excellent guide, including cultural interactions, is R. H. Holden and E. Zolov, *Latin American and the United States: A Documentary History* (2000).

Modernization and Development in the Third World

The impact of modernization is examined historically and comparatively in I. R. Sinai, *The Challenge of Modernization* (1964) and *In Search of the Modern World* (1968); L. S. Stavrianos, *Global Rift: The Third World Comes of Age* (1981); T. H. Von Laue, *The World Revolution of Westernization: The Twentieth Century in Global Perspective* (1987), which stresses the destabilizing effects of modernization; and D. K. Fieldhouse, *The West and the Third World: Trade, Colonialism, Dependence, and Development* (1999).

For development models followed in the post-1945 years, one may read A. Bagchi, *The Political Economy of Underdevelopment* (1982), an important study; H. W. Arndt, *Economic Development: The History of an Idea* (1987); W. W. Rostow, *Theorists of Economic Growth from David Hume to the Present* (1990); B. L. Billet, *Modernization Theory and Economic Development: Discontent in the Developing World* (1993); M. Wolfe, *Elusive Development* (1996); B. Hettne, *Development Theory and the Three Worlds* (rev. 1995); L. E. Harrison, *Underdevelopment Is a State of Mind* (rev. 2000); R. D. Stone, *The Nature of Development* (1992); and A. Sen, *Development as Freedom* (2000). Many of these are critical of efforts to introduce Western-style development in different cultural contexts or without adequate preparation.

For the development experience in Africa one may turn to R. Dumont, *False Start in Africa* (1966); C. Young, *Ideology and Development in Africa* (1982); D. K. Fieldhouse, *Black Africa, 1945–1980: Economic Decolonization and Arrested Development* (1986), which studies both British and French former colonies; L. Cockcroft, *Africa's Way: A Journey from the Past* (1990); and J. Iliffe, *The African Poor: A History* (1987).

For Asia one may read R. A. Scalapini, *The Politics of Development: Perspectives on Twentieth-Century Asia* (1989), an insightful small book, and A. Richards and J. Waterbury, *A Political Economy of the Middle East* (rev. 1996). Available also are J. Mayall and A. Payne (eds.), *The Fallacies of Hope: The Post-Colonial Record of the Commonwealth Third World* (1991) and T. Kemp, *Industrialization in the Non-Western World* (rev. 1989).

The best introduction to the North-South debate over a new international economic order was the report by the Independent Commission on International Development chaired by Willy Brandt: *North-South: A Program for Survival* (1980). It may be supplemented by W. A. Lewis, *The Evolution of the International Economic Order* (1978); A. Fishlow and others, *Rich and Poor Nations in the World Economy* (1978); B. Nossiter, *The Global Struggle for More: Third World Conflicts with the Rich Nations* (1986); and J. W. Warnock, *Politics of Hunger: The Global Food System* (1987). Other themes of the debate emerge in C. Thomas and P. Wilkin (eds.), *Globalization and the South* (1997), which argues that new global economic patterns are adding to global social inequalities, and M. Waters, *Globalization* (rev. 2001), a concise, balanced survey of contemporary international social and economic relations.

Problems and Readings

For background there is a helpful anthology, G. Nadel and P. Curtis (eds.), *Imperialism and Colonialism* (1964), cited earlier. Two relevant pamphlets are J. Baird (ed.), *The End of the European Empires: Decolonization after World War II* (1975) and T. W. Wallbank (ed.), *The Partition of India: Causes and Responsibilities* (1966). For the Middle East one may turn to T. E. Farah (ed.), *Pan-Arabism and Arab Nationalism: The Continuing Debate* (1987) and A. Hourani, P. S. Khouri, and M. C. Wilson (eds.), *The Modern Middle East: A Reader* (1993). For Latin America there are D. Rock (ed.), *Latin America in the 1940s: War and Postwar Transitions* (1994) and R. Salvucci (ed.), *Latin America and the World Economy* (1996). Two comparative studies in the Anvil series are illuminating for different parts of the world: L. L. Snyder (ed.), *Contemporary Nationalisms* (1992) and W. Connor, *Ethnicity, Ethnocentrism, and Ethnonationalism* (1993).

24. A WORLD ENDANGERED: COEXISTENCE AND CONFRONTATION IN THE COLD WAR

International Relations: Confrontation and Détente

To the books described in Chapters 21 and 22 that focus on the postwar decades of Soviet-American relations may be added R. Levering, *The Cold War* (1994); S. R. Ashton, *In Search of Détente: The Politics of East-West Relations since 1945* (1989); S. Brown, *The Faces of Power: United States Foreign Policy from Truman to Clinton* (rev. 1994); and G. A. Craig and F. Loewenheim (eds.), *The Diplomats, 1939–1979* (1994), a valuable set of essays.

How the developing world became involved in the Soviet-Western confrontation is explored in R. J. Barnet, *Intervention and Revolution: The United States in the Third World* (1968); G. Kolko, *Confronting the Third World: U.S. Foreign Policy, 1945–1980* (1988), critical of U.S. policies; B. D. Porter, *The U.S.S.R. in Third World Conflicts: Soviet Arms and Diplomacy in Local Wars, 1945–1980* (1984); and G. Lundestad, *East, West, North, South: Major Developments in International Politics since 1945* (rev. 1999), by a Norwegian historian.

For the background and nature of Castro's revolution in Cuba, one may read L. A. Perez, Jr., *Cuba: Between Reform and Revolution* (rev. 1995); J. M. del Aquila, *Cuba: Dilemmas of a Revolution* (rev. 1994), which includes an account of Castro's military activities in Africa; and M. Merez-Stable, *The Cuban Revolution: Origins, Course, Legacy* (1993). R. E. Quirk, *Fidel Castro* (1993) is a critical biographical assessment, and there are good biographies of Che Guevara by L. L. Anderson (1997) and J. Castañeda (1997).

The best introduction to the Kennedy years is M. R. Beschloss, *The Crisis Years: Kennedy and Khrushchev, 1960–1963* (1992). The Bay of Pigs episode is described in T. Higgins, *The Perfect Failure* (1987) and the essays in J. G. Blight and P. Kornbluh (eds.), *The Politics of Illusion: The Bay of Pigs Invasion Reexamined* (1998). The missile crisis of 1962 is studied in L. Brune, *The Missile Crisis* (1985); G. T. Allison and P. D. Zelikow, *Essence of Decision: Explaining the Cuban Missile Crisis* (rev. 1999); and A. Fursenko and T. Naftali, *"One Hell of a Gamble": Khrushchev, Castro, and Kennedy, 1958–1964* (1997), by a Russian and an American scholar with access to Khrushchev's papers. The deliberations of Kennedy and his advisers are available in E. R. May and P. D. Zelikow, *The Kennedy Tapes: Inside the White House during the Cuban Missile Crisis* (1998).

On the American relationship with its NATO allies in the Cold War years, one may read R. J. Barnet, *The Alliance* (1983); D. P. Calleo, *Beyond American Hegemony* (1987); and L. S. Kaplan, *NATO and the United States* (rev. 1994).

The Vietnam War

Two studies that place post-1945 events in Vietnam in historical perspective are A. B. Woodside, *Community and Revolution in Modern Vietnam* (1976) and W. J. Duiker, *The Rise of Nationalism in Vietnam, 1900–1941* (1976). The struggle for independence is recounted in J. P. Harrison, *The Endless War: Vietnam's Struggle for Independence* (1989); A. Short, *The Origins of the Vietnam War* (1989); D. R. SarDesai, *Vietnam: The Struggle for National Identity* (rev. 1992); M. B. Young, *The Vietnam Wars, 1945–1990* (1991), a valuable synthesis; and W. J. Duiker, *The Communist Road to Power in Vietnam* (rev. 1996). Duiker has also written a scholarly biographical account of the Vietnamese leader, *Ho Chi Minh* (2000).

The American involvement is skillfully explored in G. McT. Kahin, *Intervention: How America Became Involved in Vietnam* (1986), which perceives the United States as ignoring the nationalist aspects of the war and seeing it as Communist aggression only. American miscalculations are heavily emphasized in D. Halberstam, *The Best and the Brightest* (1972), cited in Chapter 22; L. Berman, *Lyndon Johnson's War* (1989); and D. Kaiser, *American Tragedy: Kennedy, Johnson, and the Origins of the Vietnam War* (2000). R. S. McNamara, *In Retrospect: The Tragedy and Lessons of Vietnam* (1995) looks back with regret on his role as defense secretary from 1961 to his resignation in 1968. A defense of the American involvement as essential to its global containment policy is M. Lind, *Vietnam: The Necessary War: A Reinterpretation of America's Most Disastrous Conflict* (1999).

American military actions are studied in G. Herring, *America's Longest War: The United States and Vietnam, 1950–1975* (1979); S. Karnow, *Vietnam: A History* (rev. 1994, 1997); R. D. Schulzinger, *A Time for War: The United States and Vietnam, 1941–1975* (1997); and L. H. Addington, *America's War in Vietnam* (2000), a concise, informative narrative. On the extension of the war under Nixon and Kissinger one may read W. Shawcross, *Kissinger, Nixon, and the Destruction of Cambodia* (1979) and S. Hersh, *The Price of Power* (1983). For Cambodia there are three valuable studies by D. P. Chandler: *The Tragedy of Cambodian History: Power, War, and Revolution since 1945* (1991), *A History of Cambodia* (rev. 2000), and *Brother Number One: Pol Pot* (rev. 1999). M. van Creveld, *The Transformation of War* (1991) is a searching reassessment of guerrilla warfare and other patterns of modern conflict.

The Nuclear Arms Buildup

There are numerous books on the nuclear arms buildup, the apocalyptic dangers the world has learned to live with, and the contributions of strategic deterrence to the armed peace in the Cold War years. An outstanding exhaustive study is McG. Bundy, *Danger and*

Survival: Choices about the Bomb in the First Fifty Years (1988); only gradually, he notes, was it recognized that the bomb could not be thought of as an instrument of war like other weapons. Other counsels on strategy, accepting deterrence but calling for continuing efforts at nuclear arms control, are R. McNamara, *Blundering into Disaster: Surviving the First Century of the Nuclear Age* (1987); G. F. Kennan, *The Nuclear Delusion: Soviet-American Relations in the Atomic Age* (1983); S. Zuckerman, *Nuclear Illusion and Reality* (1982); G. Gasteyer, *Searching for World Security* (1987); M. Mandelbaum, *The Fate of Nations: The Search for National Security in the Nineteenth and Twentieth Centuries* (1988); and J. Newhouse, *War and Peace in the Nuclear Age* (1989). Another kind of literature has called for a fundamental rethinking about nuclear arms. Representative are J. Schell's two books, *The Fate of the Earth* (1982) and *The Abolition* (1984), both now available in a one-volume edition (2000); the same author's *The Gift of Time: The Case for Abolishing Nuclear Weapons Now* (1998); and F. Dyson, *Weapons and Hope* (1984), by an eminent physicist. A thoughtful contribution to the discussion is J. Finnis, J. M. Boyle, Jr., and G. Grisez, *Nuclear Deterrence, Morality, and Realism* (1987). The worldwide movement for nuclear disarmament is examined in A. Carter, *Peace Movements: International Protest and World Politics since 1945* (1992).

Books that illuminate the successes and failures of détente include R. L. Garthoff, *Détente and Confrontation* (1985); R. W. Stevenson, *The Rise and Fall of Détente* (1985); and W. Bundy, *A Tangled Web: The Making of Foreign Policy in the Nixon Presidency* (1998), an in-depth critical assessment. Also available are R. D. Schulzinger, *Henry Kissinger: Doctor of Diplomacy* (1989); W. Isaacson, *Kissinger: A Biography* (1992); R. C. Thornton, *The Carter Years: Toward a New Global Order* (1991); and T. G. Patterson, *Meeting the Communist Threat: Truman to Reagan* (1989). For assessments of American foreign policy and the search for security in the perspective of over four decades one should read J. L. Gaddis, *The Long Peace: Inquiries into the History of the Cold War* (1987), a thoughtful appraisal; T. J. McCormick, *America's Half-Century: United States Foreign Policy in the Cold War and After* (rev. 1995); and N. Friedman, *The Fifty Years' War: Conflict and Strategy in the Cold War* (2000). The collapse of the Soviet Union in 1991 and the altered international scene have brought additional books, cited in the final chapter.

The World Economy: Global Recession

To books on the global economy as it developed in the first four decades after 1945 may be added W. W. Rostow, *The World Economy: History and Prospect* (1978), W. M. Scammell, *The International Economy since 1945* (rev. 1983) and A. G. Kenwood and A. I.

Lougheed, *The Growth of the International Economy, 1820–1980* (1983). For the multinational corporations as they evolved in this era, one may turn to M. Wilkin, *The Maturing of Multinational Enterprise* (1974); R. Vernon, *Storm over the Multinationals* (1977); and R. J. Barnet and J. Cavanagh, *Global Dreams: Imperial Corporations and the New World Order* (1994).

The role of oil in the economy and in global politics is admirably described in D. Yergin, *The Prize: The Epic Quest for Oil, Money, and Power* (1991) and P. R. Odell, *Oil and World Power* (rev. 1986). The impact of the oil embargo of 1973–1974 on Europe is studied in R. Lieber, *Oil and the Middle East: Europe in the Energy Crisis* (1976).

The historic link between economic strength and political and military hegemony is traced masterfully in P. Kennedy, *The Rise and Fall of the Great Powers: Economic Change and Military Conflict from 1500 to 2000* (1987), cited earlier; it may be read along with M. Olson, *The Rise and Decline of Nations* (1982). Kennedy's volume and other books in the 1970s and 1980s raised the question of America's relative decline in economic leadership. The Japanese challenge, in particular, was described in E. F. Vogel, *Japan as Number One: Lessons for America* (1979) and C. V. Prestowitz, Jr., *Trading Places: How We Allowed Japan to Take the Lead* (1988). On the challenge from more than one source, one may read L. Thurow, *Head to Head: The Coming Economic Battle among Japan, Europe, and America* (1992), which describes the "geo-economic" struggle. The phenomenal economic growth of Hong Kong, Taiwan, Singapore, and South Korea is described in E. F. Vogel, *The Four Little Dragons* (1991). The decline of older American industry is examined in B. Bluestone and B. Harrison, *The Deindustrialization of America* (1982), but the continuing importance of the American economy emerged from M. Feldstein (ed.), *The United States in the World Economy* (1988); H. R. Nye, *The Myth of American Decline* (1990); and J. S. Nye, *Bound to Lead: The Changing Nature of American Power* (1990).

The impact of the global recession that began in 1974 and the dilemmas it posed for policymakers are studied in several of the books on the global economy cited in Chapter 22; to them should be added L. Anel, *Recession, the Western Economies, and the Changing World Order* (1981); E. S. Einhorn and J. Logue, *Welfare States in Hard Times* (1982); and R. Skidelsky (ed.), *The End of the Keynesian Era* (1977).

In addition to books cited in Chapter 22, the operations, accomplishments, and problems of the European Community may be studied in D. Swann, *The Economics of the Common Market* (rev. 1988) and *European Economic Integration* (1996), and H. Brugmans (ed.), *Europe: Dream, Adventure, Reality* (1987), assessing the first 30 years of West European integration. On progress toward closer unity and the transformation of the European Community (EC) into the European Union (EU) under the Maastricht treaty, good guides are available in J. Pinder, *European Community: The Building of a Union* (rev. 1995) and *The European Union: A Very Short Introduction* (2001).

Western Europe: Politics and Society since 1974

For Britain, Margaret Thatcher's conservative leadership and the changes in Britain in the decade after 1979 are assessed in P. Jenkins, *Mrs. Thatcher's Revolution: The Ending of the Socialist Era* (1988); P. Riddell, *The Thatcher Era and Its Legacy* (rev. 1991); and H. Young, *The Iron Lady: A Biography of Margaret Thatcher* (1989). Two comparative studies of the conservative efforts in the United States and Britain in the 1980s to curb the welfare state, encourage entrepreneurial spirit, and revive national pride are J. Krieger, *Reagan, Thatcher, and the Politics of Decline* (1986); A. Gamble, *The Free Economy and the Strong State* (rev. 1994); and P. Pierson, *Dismantling the Welfare State? Reagan, Thatcher, and the Politics of Retrenchment* (1994).

For France, Mitterrand's leadership of the Socialist party and his presidency are assessed in J. W. Friend, *Seven Years in France: François Mitterrand and the Unintended Revolution, 1981–1988* (1989) and *The Long Presidency: France in the Mitterrand Years, 1981–1995* (1998); and M. Mclean (ed.), *The Mitterrand Years: Legacy and Evaluation* (1998).

For the evolution of socialism one may read M. Harrington, *Socialism: Past and Future* (1989); S. Padgett and W. Patterson, *A History of Social Democracy in Postwar Europe* (1991); and D. Sasson, *One Hundred Years of Socialism: The West European Left in the Twentieth Century* (1997), cited earlier.

On developments in Spain one may read R. Carr and J. P. Fusi-Azpurúa, *Spain: Dictatorship to Democracy* (rev. 1981); P. Preston, *The Triumph of Democracy in Spain* (1986); and K. Maxwell and S. Spiegel, *The New Spain: From Isolation to Influence* (1994). F.J.R. Salvadó, *Twentieth-Century Spain* (1999) places recent events in a wider historical context. For Portugal, the revolution of 1974 and the gradual emergence of political stability are studied in H. G. Ferreira and M. W. Marshall, *Portugal's Revolution: Ten Years On* (1986); T. Gallagher, *Portugal: A Twentieth Century Interpretation* (1983); and the later chapters of D. Birmingham, *A Concise History of Portugal* (1993).

The Communist World: China after Mao

Several of the volumes cited for the Mao era also describe Deng's program of modernization and liberalization. To these may be added H. E. Salisbury, *The New Emperors: China in the Era of Mao and Deng*

(1992), by an insightful journalist; H. Harding, *China's Second Revolution: Reformation after Mao* (1987); and M. Goldman, *Sowing the Seeds of Democracy: Political Reform in the Deng Xiaoping Era* (1994).

Assessments providing balanced judgments on Deng's reforms, the post-Deng years, and the prospects for democratization since the setbacks at Tiananmen Square are J. B. Starr, *Understanding China: A Guide to China's Economy, History, and Political Structure* (1997); J. Miles, *The Legacy of Tiananmen: China in Disarray* (1997), A. J. Nathan, *China's Transition* (1998); and B. Gilley, *Tiger on the Brink: Jiang Zemin and China's New Elite* (1999). Informative also are the essays in R. MacFarquhar (ed.), *The Politics of China: The Eras of Mao and Deng* (1997) and D. Shambaugh (ed.), *Deng Xiaoping: Portrait of a Chinese Statesman* (1997). One of the most detailed accounts of the setback to democracy at Tiananmen Square in 1989 is J. Wong's colorfully entitled *Red China Blues: My Long March from Mao to Now* (1996).

Problems and Readings

For the confrontation over Cuba and other subjects, one may turn to D. B. Kunz (ed.), *The Diplomacy of the Crucial Decade: American Foreign Relations during the 1960s* (1994) and R. A. Divine (ed.), *The Cuban Missile Crisis* (rev. 1990), cited earlier. For Vietnam there are J. P. Kimball (ed.), *The Reason Why: The Debate about the Causes of American Involvement in the Vietnam War* (1991); D. W. Levy, *The Debate over Vietnam* (1993); and J. S. Olson and R. Roberts, *My Lai: A Brief History with Documents* (1998). The origins of nuclear arms and efforts at arms control are examined in K. Eubank, *The Bomb* (1991), in the Anvil series. O. Schell and D. Shambaugh (eds.), *The China Reader: The Reform Era* (1999) is an excellent collection of documents and commentaries on recent Chinese politics, society, and economic change.

25. A WORLD TRANSFORMED

It is difficult to assess the durable value of the literature dealing with the events and developments of recent years. For new books the reviews and bibliographies published in the periodical and daily press and in the professional journals should be consulted.

The Soviet Union: Crisis, Reform, and Collapse

Efforts to assess the Gorbachev reforms in their historical context include A. Nove, *Glasnost in Action: Cultural Renaissance in Russia* (1989); A. Aslund, *Gorbachev's Struggle for Economic Reform* (rev. 1991); B. Kerblay, *Gorbachev's Russia* (1989); G. Hosking, *The Awakening of the Soviet Union*

(1991); and A. Brown, *The Gorbachev Factor* (1996), a convincing assessment. Especially valuable also is J. B. Dunlop, *The Rise of Russia and the Fall of the Soviet Empire* (1993), while M. E. Malia, *The Soviet Tragedy: A History of Socialism in Russia, 1917–1991* (1994), cited earlier, critically evaluates the more than seven decades. F. Furet, *The Passing of an Illusion* (trans. 1999), by a distinguished French historian, assesses the ending of an era in which many in the West and elsewhere were attracted to communism.

The Collapse of Communism and the Dissolution of the Soviet Union

For the events of 1991 and the dissolution of the U.S.S.R., one may turn to D. Remnick, *Lenin's Tomb: The Last Days of the Soviet Empire* (1993), by a perceptive journalist-observer; J. F. Matlock, Jr., *Autopsy of an Empire* (1995), a compelling contribution by the American ambassador at the time; and R. V. Daniels, *The End of the Communist Revolution* (1993). On the ethnic and national tensions that led to the dissolution of the union one may read H. Carrère d'Encausse, *The End of the Soviet Empire: The Triumph of the Nations* (trans. 1993); G. I. Mirsky, *On Ruins of Empire: Ethnicity and Nationalism in the Former Soviet Union* (1997); and R. G. Suny, *The Soviet Experiment: Russia, the U.S.S.R., and the Successor States* (1997).

Assessments of the Yeltsin presidency and efforts at economic reform may be found in R. W. Davies, *Soviet History in the Yeltsin Era* (1997); D. Remnick, *Ressurrection: The Struggle for a New Russia* (1997); T. Gustafson, *Capitalism Russian Style* (1997), especially informative for the economy; and A. Shleifer and D. Treisman, *Without a Map: Political Tactics and Economic Reform in Russia* (2000). The suppression of the Chechen rebellion is studied in J. Dunlop, *Russia Confronts Chechnya* (1998).

The Transformation of Central and Eastern Europe, 1989

Several books have already been cited in Chapter 22 for central and eastern Europe in the post-1945 years. The growing restiveness under Soviet domination also emerges from M. Charlton, *The Eagle and the Small Birds: Crisis in the Soviet Union from Yalta to Solidarity* (1984) and G. Schöpflin and N. Woods (eds.), *In Search of Central Europe* (1989).

T. Garton Ash, a British journalist-historian, vividly describes the collapse of the Communist regimes in central and eastern Europe in 1989 as he witnessed and reflected on these events in *The Uses of Adversity: Essays on the Fate of Central Europe* (1989) and *The Magic Lantern* [a theater in Prague]: *The Revolution of '89 Witnessed in Warsaw, Budapest, Berlin, and Prague* (1990). Other informative studies include Z.A.B. Zeman, *The Making and Breaking of Communist Europe* (1991); the essays in I. Banac

(ed.), *Eastern Europe in Revolution* (1992); G. Stokes, *The Walls Came Tumbling Down: The Collapse of Communism in Eastern Europe* (1993); and V. Bunce, *Subversive Institutions: The Design and the Destruction of Socialism and the State* (1999). Of special interest is J. Lévesque, *The Enigma of 1989; the U.S.S.R. and the Liberation of Eastern Europe* (1997), an effort to assess the Soviet Union's reactions.

Careful assessments of the events leading to German reunification are T. Garton Ash, *In Europe's Name: Germany and the Divided Continent* (1993), cited in Chapter 22; K. H. Jarausch, *The Rush to German Unity* (1993); E. Pond, *Beyond the Wall: German's Road to Unification* (1993); C. S. Maier, *The Crisis of Communism and the End of East Germany* (1997), with special insights into the decayed East German economy; and P. Zelikow and C. Rice, *Germany Unified and Europe Transformed: A Study in Statecraft* (1997), with early access to key documents.

A few additional books on the Revolution of 1989 in the central and eastern European countries merit citing. For Poland one may read A. Kemp-Welch, *The Birth of Solidarity* (1991) and J. Harrison, *The Solidarity Decade: Poland, 1980–1991* (1993). For Czechoslovakia there are available B. Wheaton and Z. Kavan, *The Velvet Revolution* (1992); two biographical accounts of its leader, communicating the playwright-statesman's thought and influence: E. Kriscova, *Vaclav Havel: The Authorized Biography* (1993), somewhat uncritical; and J. Keane, *Vaclav Havel* (2000), exploring in depth his political career both as dissident activist and as president. An informative survey of Czech history carrying the story toward the present is D. Sayer, *The Coasts of Bohemia: A Czech History* (1999), while E. Stein, *Czecho/Slovakia: Ethnic Conflict, Constitutional Fissure, Negotiated Breakup* (1997) helps explain the peaceful separation of the Czech Republic and Slovakia in 1993. For the revolt against the Romanian dictator one may read N. Ratesh, *Romania: The Entangled Revolution* (1992), the best brief account; E. Behr, *"Kiss the Hand You Cannot Bite": The Rise and Fall of the Ceausescus* (1992); and T. Gilberg, *Nationalism and Communism in Romania: The Rise and Fall of Ceausescu's Personal Dictatorship* (1990).

The Baltic states, where the independence movements helped catalyze the dissolution of the U.S.S.R., are studied in A. Lieven, *The Baltic Revolution: Estonia, Latvia, Lithuania and the Path to Independence* (1993) and R. J. Misiunas and R. Taagepera, *The Baltic States: Years of Dependence, 1940–1991* (1993), a detailed account of the years under Soviet rule.

The Disintegration of Yugoslavia

To books cited earlier on Balkan history one should add M. Glenny, *The Balkans: Nationalism, War, and* the Great Powers, 1804–1999 (2000) and M. Mazour, *The Balkans: A Short History* (2000) an insightful distillation of the complex story. For the background and nature of the Tito years one should read A. Djilas, *The Contested Country: Yugoslav Unity and Communist Revolution, 1919–1953* (1991), cited earlier; R. West, *Tito and the Rise and Fall of Yugoslavia* (1995); and J. R. Lampe, *Yugoslavia as History: Twice There Was a Country* (1996), focusing on the years 1918–1941, the Second World War, and the years 1945–1991.

The events of the 1990s may be followed in T. Judah, *The Serbs: History, Myth and the Destruction of Yugoslavia* (2000), which graphically demonstrates that the breakup was the consequence of demagogic incitement of ethnic animosities, not the ethnic differences themselves; L. Silber and A. Little, *Yugoslavia: Death of a Nation* (1999); and M. Glenny, *The Fall of Yugoslavia: The Third Balkan War* (rev. 1996). The Serb dictator and his regime are studied in R. Thomas, *Serbia Under Milosovic: Politics in the 1990s* (1999), and additional biographical details are provided in D. Dodier and L. Branson, *Milosovic: Portrait of a Tyrant* (2000). Secession and the wars that followed are studied in M. Tanner, *Croatia: A Nation Forged in War* (1997) and N. Malcolm, *Bosnia: A Short History* (rev. 1996).

For the international reactions to the ethnic warfare one may turn to J. Gow, *Triumph of the Lack of Will: International Diplomacy and the Yugoslav War* (1997); W. Bert, *The Reluctant Superpower: United States Policy in Bosnia, 1991–1995* (1997); D. Rohde, *Endgame: The Betrayal and Fall of Srebrenica: Europe's Worst Massacre since World War II* (1997), on the mass slaying of Bosnian Muslims; and R. Holbrooke, *To End a War* (1998), by the American diplomat who helped negotiate the Dayton accords. M. Ignatieff, *The Warrior's Honor: Ethnic War and the Modern Conscience* (1998), reflects on the moral dilemmas the events posed to the international community.

For the suppression of the rebellion in Kosovo one may read N. Malcolm, *Kosovo: A Short History* (1998) and M. Vickers, *Between Serb and Albanian: A History of Kosovo* (1998); and for the American-led NATO air offensive against Serbia, M. Ignatieff, *Virtual War: Kosovo and Beyond* (2000) and T. Judah, *Kosovo: War and Revenge* (2000).

After Communism: Central and Eastern Europe

Insightful books include R. Dahrendorf, *Reflections on the Revolution in Europe* (1991); T. Rosenberg, *The Haunted Land: Facing Europe's Ghosts after Communism* (1995); and R. Skidelsky, *The Road from Serfdom: The Economic and Political Consequences of the End of Communism* (1996). There are also well-informed analyses of central European societies in

T. Garton Ash, *History of the Present: Essays, Sketches, and Dispatches from Europe in the 1990s* (1999). The efforts to establish stable democracies are assessed in R. Rose and others, *Democracy and Its Alternatives: Understanding Post-Communist Societies* (1998); P. Juviler, *Freedom's Ordeal: The Struggle for Human Rights and Democracy in Post-Soviet States* (1997); and V. Tismaneanu, *Fantasies of Salvation: Democracy, Nationalism and Myth in Post-Communist Europe* (1998). Some unsavory aspects of the postliberation era are described in P. Hockenos, *Free to Hate: The Rise of the Right in Post-Communist Eastern Europe* (1993).

Europe in the 1990s

Books that examine the new configuration of European relationships and the evolving European Union include A. E. Stent, *Russia and Germany Reborn: Unification, the Soviet Collapse, and the New Europe* (1999); E. Pond, *The Rebirth of Europe* (1999); M. Keens-Soper, *Europe in the World: The Persistence of Power Politics* (1999); and M. Emerson, *Redrawing the Map of Europe* (1999). T. Judt, *A Grand Illusion? An Essay on Europe* (1996) expresses pessimism on the future of European unity. A fresh overview of Britain in the postwar half-century is presented in H. Young, *This Blessed Plot: Britain and Europe from Churchill to Blair* (1999); and Tony Blair's "new Labour" program is examined in A. Giddens, *The Third Way: The Renewal of Social Democracy* (1998). For Italy three books that examine the unseating of the Christian Democrats in the 1990s and the attempts to deal with the corruption that tarnished the regime include A. Stille, *Excellent Cadavers: The Mafia and the Death of the Italian Republic* (1995); M. Frei, *Getting the Boot: Italy's Unfinished Revolution* (1995); and P. McCarthy, *The Crisis of the Italian State* (1995).

Culture, Science, and Thought

Many of the books described in Chapter 15 should be consulted, including H. S. Hughes, *Consciousness and Society: The Reorientation of European Social Thought, 1890–1930* (1958), which examines post-Enlightenment ways of looking at positivism, science, and the social sciences, and G. L. Mosse, *The Culture of Western Europe* (rev. 1988). An informative survey, focusing especially on the twentieth century, is J. Winders, *European Culture since 1848* (2001).

For distinctions between "modernism" and "postmodernism" in various contexts, one may read S. Toulmin, *Cosmopolis: The Hidden Agenda of Modernity* (1989); Z. Bauman, *Legislators and Interpreters: On Modernity, Post-Modernity, and Intellectuals* (1987); J. McGowan, *Postmodernism and Its Critics* (1991); M. Sarup, *An Introductory Guide to Poststructuralism and Postmodernism* (rev. 1993); and E. Heartney, *Postmodernism* (2001). Newer trends in historical writing are assessed in J. Appleby, L. Hunt, and M. Jacob, *Telling the Truth about History* (1994), cited in the Introduction, and W. Thompson, *What Happened to History?* (2000). A postmodern critique of historical studies is developed in K. Jenkins, *Why History?* (1999); while K. Windschuttle, *The Killing of History* (1998) strongly objects to the assault by literary critics, social theorists, and others on more traditional conceptions of historical knowledge.

A helpful introduction to intellectual trends after the Second World War is R. N. Stromberg, *After Everything: Western Intellectual History since 1945* (1975); the same author has written *Makers of Modern Culture: Five Twentieth-Century Thinkers* (1991), exploring Freud, Einstein, Wittgenstein, Joyce, and Sartre. N. E. Cantor, *Varieties of Culture in Modern Times* (1988, 1998) is vehemently critical of contemporary cultural trends. A very different critical view appears in the Marxist analysis in F. Jameson, *Postmodernism, or the Cultural Logic of Late Capitalism* (1991) and T. Eagleton, *The Idea of Culture* (2000).

Useful introductions to the professional philosophers are available in J. Passmore, *Recent Philosophers* (rev. 1985) and A. J. Ayer, *Philosophy in the Twentieth Century* (1982). Two recommended biographical accounts of twentieth-century philosophers are C. Moorehead, *Bertrand Russell: A Life* (1993) and R. Monk, *Ludwig Wittgenstein: The Duty of Genius* (1990). Of special interest is J. Maritain, *On the Use of Philosophy* (1961), by an influential Roman Catholic philosopher. The origins and nature of existentialism may be studied in M. Warnock, *Existentialism* (1970); G. Brée, *Camus and Sartre* (1972); A. Cohen-Salal, *Sartre* (trans. 1987); and T. R. Koenig, *Existentialism and Human Existence* (1992). For Michel Foucault, several of whose influential historical works have been cited in the Introduction, an unflattering personal portrait emerges from D. Eribon, *Michel Foucault* (trans. 1991) and J. Miller, *The Passion of Michel Foucault* (1993). The debate on Freud, referred to in Chapter 15, continues with numerous books, among them P. Robinson, *Freud and His Critics* (1993), which defends Freud but explores the challenges to his influence. The interpretation of Nietzsche as precursor to postmodernism is rejected in L. Ferry and A. Renaut (eds.), *Why We Are Not Nietzscheans* (1997).

Introductions to the complexities of contemporary art are provided in A. Neumeyer, *The Search for Meaning in Modern Art* (trans. 1964); G. Woods, *Art without Boundaries, 1950–1970* (1972); and S. Hunter, *Modern Art from Post-Impressionism to the Present* (rev. 1985). A. Appel, Jr., *The Art of Celebration: Twentieth-Century Painting, Literature, Sculpture, Photography, and Jazz* (1982), stresses the vitality of contemporary culture, including popular culture; while R. Templin (ed.), *The Arts: A History of Expression in the Twentieth Century* (1991), is informative on both the visual arts and literature.

Western religious thought is explored in J. Macquarrie, *Twentieth-Century Religious Thought: The Frontiers of Philosophy and Theology, 1900–1960* (1963) and J. C. Livingston, *Modern Christian Thought: From the Enlightenment to Vatican II* (1971). R. N. Bellah, *Beyond Belief: Essays on Religion in a Post-Traditional World* (1991) explores the major world religions and society in diverse cultural contexts. The rise and growing strength of religious fundamentalist movements in Judaism, Christianity, and Islam is studied in K. Armstrong, *The Battle for God* (2000).

The continuing debate between science and religion is studied in S. L. Jaki, *The Road of Science and the Ways to God* (1978) and J. H. Brooke, *Science and Religion: Some Historical Perspectives* (1991). For the profound doctrinal and social changes in contemporary Roman Catholicism one may turn to L. Gilkey, *Catholicism Confronts Modernity* (1975); J. D. Holmes, *The Papacy in the Modern World, 1914–1978* (1981); and E. O. Hanson, *The Catholic Church in World Politics* (1987). For the recent popes there are biographies of John XXIII by M. Trevor (1967) and L. Elliott (1973); of Paul VI by P. Hebblethwaite (1993), a detailed and documented account; and a valuable assessment of John Paul II in J. Kwitny, *Man of the Century: The Life and Times of John Paul II* (1998).

Books on Einstein and early twentieth-century physics have been cited in Chapter 15. Two good introductions are B. L. Cline, *Men Who Made a New Physics* (1965, 1987), cited earlier, and B. Greene, *The Elegant Universe* (1999). A. Pais has followed up his biography of Einstein (1982) with *Niels Bohr's Times: In Physics, Philosophy, and Polity* (1992). For contemporary physics one may turn also to H. C. Von Baeyer, *The Taming of the Atom: The Emergence of the Visible Microworld* (1992) and J. Bernstein, *Quantum Profiles* (1991) and *Cranks, Quarks, and the Cosmos* (1993). Of special interest to the general reader will be L. M. Krauss, *Fear of Physics: A Guide for the Perplexed* (1993).

On the biological revolution, an excellent introduction is S. Jones, *The Language of the Genes: Biology, History and the Evolutionary Future* (1994), while E. F. Keller, *The Century of the Gene* (2000), is informative but somewhat technical. One may also read R. Clowes, *The Structure of Life* (1967); R. Olby, *The Path to the Double Helix* (1974); H. F. Judson, *The Eighth Day of Creation: The Makers of Revolution in Biology* (1979); and B. Wallace, *The Search for the Gene* (1993). In J. Watson, *The Double Helix: A Personal Account of the Discovery of the Structure of DNA* (rev. 1980), a scientist describes himself and other biologists at work. On the need for communication between scientists and nonscientists, an indispensable book remains C. P. Snow, *The Two Cultures and the Scientific Revolution* (1959; new critical ed., with introduction by S. Collini, 1993). It may be supplemented by B. Appleyard, *Understanding the Present* (1993), on the links of science, philosophy, and society; and F. J. Dyson, *The Sun, the Genome, and the Internet* (1999), by a renowned physicist.

To study modern medicine in perspective one should turn to R. Porter, *The Greatest Benefit to Mankind: A Medical History of Humanity* (1998). The setback to medical science and the challenges to society posed by the appearance of AIDs are studied in M. D. Grmek, *History of AIDs: Emergence and Origin of a Modern Pandemic* (trans. 1990); E. Fee and D. Fox (eds.), *AIDS: The Making of a Chronic Disease* (1991); V. Berridge and P. Strong (eds.), *AIDS and Contemporary History* (1993); and K. R. Hope, Sr. (ed.), *AIDS and Dvelopment in Africa* (1999), which examines the pandemic's social effects on the continent that has been most affected by the disease. Of special interest for health matters is L. Garrett, *Betrayal of Trust: The Collapse of Global Public Health* (2000).

For space exploration in all its aspects, one should read W. A. McDougall, . . . *the Heavens and the Earth: A Political History of the Space Age* (1985) and W. J. Walter, *Space Age* (1992). Special dimensions are added in V. Cronin, *The View from Planet Earth: Man Looks at the Cosmos* (1981) and J. S. Lewis and R. A. Lewis, *Space Resources: Breaking the Bonds of Earth* (1987).

Activist Movements: 1968

A comprehensive account of the student upheaval of 1968 as a worldwide phenomenon is D. Caute, *The Year of the Barricades: A Journey through 1968* (1988); it may be supplemented by G. Katsiafacis, *The Imagination of the New Left: A Global Analysis of 1968* (1987); T. Gitlin, *The Sixties* (1987); A Marwick, *The Sixties: Cultural Revolution in Britain, France, Italy, and the United States* (1998); and the essays in C. Fink and others (eds.), *1968: The World Transformed* (1999). The turbulent French scene in 1968 is studied in R. Aron, *The Elusive Revolution* (trans. 1969); B. E Brown, *Protest in Paris: Anatomy of a Revolt* (1974); and A. Touraine, *The May Movement: Revolt and Reform* (trans. 1979). K. Reader, *The May 1968 Events in France* (1993) includes documents from the period as well as a wide range of historical interpretations.

The Women's Liberation Movement

For the background to the women's liberation movement, the books on the history of women described in the Introduction and in Chapter 15 will also serve as a guide. A thoughtful survey is O. Banks, *Faces of Feminism: A Study of Feminism as a Social Movement* (1981, 1986); J. S. Chafetz and A. G. Dworkin, *Female Revolt: The Rise of Women's Movements in World and Historical Perspective* (1986); and D. Dahlerup (ed.), *The New Women's Movement* (1986). I. Whelehan, *Modern Feminist Thought: From the Second Wave to 'Post-Feminism'* (1995) describes the historical development of feminist theories that shaped the modern women's movement. An anthology of early feminism is A. S. Rossi (ed.), *The Feminist Papers: From [Abigail] Adams to [Simone] de Beauvoir* (1974). The links in the United States between feminism and the civil rights movement and the changing status of American women are studied in W. R. Chafe, *The Paradox of Change: American Women in the 20th Century* (rev. 1992). For the European context, good introductions are J. Lovenduski, *Women and European Politics: Contemporary Feminism and Public Policy* (1986) and G. Kaplan, *Contemporary Western European Feminism* (1992); while J. Gelb, *Feminism and Politics* (1990) compares American and European experiences. The British scene is studied in S. Rowbotham, *The Past Is before Us: Feminism in Action since the 1960s* (1989) and in her impressive comparative study, *A History of Women in Britain and the United States* (1998). For the United States a recent synthesis with helpful bibliographical guidance is R. Rosen, *The World Split Open: How the Modern Women's Movement Changed America* (2000). For France one may turn to C. Duchen, *Feminism in France: From May '68 to Mitterrand* (1986) and *Women's Rights and Women's Lives in France, 1944–1968* (1994); D. M. Stetson, *Women's Rights in France* (1987); and a selection of readings in E. Marks and I. De Courtivron (eds.), *New French Feminisms: An Anthology* (1980). A convenient anthology for the German scene is H. Altbach and others (eds.), *German Feminism: Readings in Politics and Literature* (1984); for Italy one may read L. C. Birnbaum, *Liberazione della Donna: Feminism in Italy* (1986).

On women's changing role in various settings and cultures a sampling of additional books would include N. J. Hafkin and E. C. Bay (eds.), *Women in Africa: Studies in Social and Economic Change* (1976); N. R. Keddie and B. Baron (eds.), *Women in Middle Eastern History: Shifting Boundaries in Sex and Gender* (1991); L. A. Brand, *Women, the State, and Political Liberalization: Middle Eastern and North African Experiences* (1998); J. Nash and H. I. Safa (eds.), *Women and Change in Latin America* (1986); and F. Miller, *Latin America: Women and the Search for Social Justice* (1991), an impressive study. Valuable comparative assessments are I. Tinker (ed.), *Persistent Inequalities: Women and World*

Development (1990) and the insightful A. Sen, *Inequality Reexamined* (1996), by a leading development economist and social philosopher. The failure to achieve promised equality in socialist societies is examined in books on the Soviet Union cited in Chapter 18; to them may be added F. du P. Gray, *Soviet Women: Walking the Tight Rope* (1990). For China one may read E. Croll, *Feminism and Socialism in China* (1978); J. Stacey, *Patriarchy and Socialist Revolution in China* (1983); and the essays in T. E. Barlow (ed.), *Gender Politics in Modern China* (1994) and C. K. Gilmartin (ed.), *Engendering China: Women, Culture and the State* (1994).

Population, Resources, Environment

One of the best introductions to the global demographic explosion of our times and the pressure on natural resources is J. E. Cohen, *How Many People Can the Earth Support?* (1997), a provocative demographic analysis relating population numbers to living standards. The "fertility collapse" in the West and its social and political implications are studied in M. S. Teitelbaum and J. M. Winter, *A Question of Numbers: High Migration, Low Fertility, and the Politics of National Identity* (1998). The growing proportions of the elderly in the population, especially in industrial countries, is the subject of P. G. Peterson, *Gray Dawn: How the Coming Age Wave Will Transform America—and the World* (1999).

Good introductions to environmental issues are J. T. Hardy, *Science, Technology, and the Environment* (1975); D. Worster (ed.), *The Ends of the Earth: Perspectives on Modern Environmental History* (1988); A. Gore, *Earth in the Balance: Ecology and the Human Spirit* (1992); and J. R. McNeill, *Something New Under the Sun: An Environmental History of the Twentieth-Century World* (2000). Environmentalism is also examined in R. C. Paehlke, *Environmentalism and the Future of Progressive Politics* (1989); C. O. Paepke, *The Evolution of Progress: The End of Economic Growth and the Beginning of Human Transformation* (1993); and C. Ponting, *A Green History of the World: The Environment and the Collapse of Great Civilizations* (1992).

The Post–Cold War Era

The end of the Cold War brought a number of thoughtful studies on the changing international scene, among them W. G. Hyland, *The Cold War Is Over* (1991); J. L. Gaddis, *The United States and the End of the Cold War* (1992) and *We Now Know: Rethinking Cold War History* (1997), both cited earlier; and J. Chace, *The Consequences of the Peace: The New Internationalism and American Foreign Policy* (1992). Additional insightful studies include M. Mandelbaum, *The Dawn of Peace in Europe* (1996); S. Hoffmann, *World Disorder: Troubled Peace in the Post-Cold War Era*

(1999) and *The Ethics and Politics of Humanitarian Intervention* (1996); and M. Howard, *The Invention of Peace: Reflections on War and International Order* (2001). H. Kissinger, *Diplomacy* (1994), and in his three volumes of memoirs, offers historical and other perspectives on international relations. A vehemently critical view of the legacy of Kissinger's global policies may be found in C. Hitchens, *The Trial of Henry Kissinger* (2001).

For the United States the tensions between American national interests and the assumption of international leadership in the contemporary era emerge from these books and from G. Bush and B. Scowcroft, *A World Transformed* (1998), by the former president and his national security adviser. These themes are explored for the Clinton administration in R. W. Haass, *The Reluctant Sheriff: The United States after the Cold War* (1998) and D. Callahan, *Unwinnable Wars: American Power and Ethnic Conflict* (1998). G. Kennan, *At a Century's Ending: Reflections, 1982–1995* (1996), remains critical of "neo-Wilsonian" idealism but is sensitive to America's global responsibilities.

China's role in the new era is studied in C. Patten, *East and West: China, Power, and the Future of Asia* (1998), written by the last British governor of Hong Kong, while American relationships with China are studied in J. H. Mann, *About Face: A History of America's Curious Relationship with China, from Nixon to Clinton* (1999).

The continuing nuclear threat is explored in McG. Bundy, W. J. Crowe, Jr., and S. D. Drell, *Reducing Nuclear Danger: The Road Away from the Brink* (1993); M. van Crevel, *Nuclear Proliferation and the Future of Conflict* (1993); and W. E. Burrows and R. Windrem, *The Dangerous Race for Superweapons in a Fragmenting World* (1994). For terrorism and its implications for contemporary society one may turn to R. E. Rubinstein, *Alchemists of Revolution: Terrorism in the Modern World* (1987); P. Wilkinson, *Terrorism in the Modern World* (1987); and B. Hoffman, *Inside Terrorism* (1998), a concise but comprehensive, historically informed account. There are insightful essays in W. Gutteridge (ed.), *The New Terrorism* (1986) and W. Reich (ed.), *Origins of Terrorism: Psychologies, Ideologies, Theologies, States of Mind* (1990). American vulnerability is studied in R. A. Falkenrath and others, *America's Achilles Heel* (1998), examining nuclear, biological, and chemical threats.

For the Persian Gulf War of 1990–1991 one may read E. Sciolino, *The Outlaw State: Sadam Hussein's Quest for Power and the Gulf Crisis* (1992); D. Hiro, *Desert Shield to Desert Storm: The Second Gulf War* (1992), excellent on the military aspects; and L. Freedman and E. Karsh, *The Gulf Conflict, 1900–1991: Diplomacy and War in the New World Order* (1993), a comprehensive account. The dictator's continued hold on power is examined in A. Cockburn and P. Cockburn, *Out of the Ashes: The Resurrection of Sadam Hussein* (1994).

The explosive ethnic tensions in the contemporary world are thoughtfully examined in D. P. Moynihan, *Pandemonium: Ethnicity in International Politics* (1993); W. Pfaff, *The Wrath of Nations: Civilization and the Furies of Nationalism* (1993) and A. D. Smith, *Myths and Memories of the Nation* (2000). Of interest also are M. Juergensmeyer, *The New Cold War? Religious Nationalism Confronts the Secular State* (1993) and M. Ignatieff, *Blood and Belongings: Journeys into the New Nationalism* (1994). Books on the Balkan crises have been listed earlier.

A much-discussed, controversial book, S. P. Huntington, *The Clash of Civilization and the Remaking of World Order* (1996), sees future conflicts among civilizations shaped by the world's major historic religions and warns against Western "universalist" missions in international affairs. The complex historical nature of Western culture as opposed to simplistic notions of democracy and market capitalism is well conveyed in D. Gress, *From Plato to NATO: The Ideas of the West and Its Opponents* (1998). J. Lukacs, *The End of the Twentieth Century and the Passing of the Modern Age* (1992) warns of resurgent nationalism overshadowing liberal democracy and rational humanism. Two books exposing the failures of twentieth-century regimes that sought to reshape human society are R. Conquest, *Reflections on a Ravaged Century* (1999), describing the human costs of war and totalitarianism, and J. C. Scott, *Seeing Like a State: How Certain Schemes to Improve the Human Condition Have Failed* (1998). Both may be read in conjunction with Isaiah Berlin's rejection of utopianism and social engineering in *The Crooked Timber of Humanity* (1990, 1998), cited earlier, and his other writings in defense of pluralist liberalism.

Human Rights

On the increasing importance of human rights issues in international affairs readers may find informative historical studies in P. G. Lauren, *The Evolution of Human Rights: Visions Seen* (1999); J. Morsink, *The Universal Declaration of Human Rights: Origins, Drafting, and Intent* (1999); and the essays in Y. Danieli and others (eds.), *The Universal Declaration of Human Rights: Fifty Years and Beyond* (1999). An eloquent statement by a Roman Catholic philosopher is J. Maritain, *The Rights of Man and Natural Law* (1986), cited earlier. W. T. de Bary, *Asian Values and Human Rights* (1998) makes clear that cultural relativism should not affect universal human rights.

A key study examining past and present efforts to judge and punish crimes against humanity and human rights abuses is Y. Beigbeder, *Judging War Criminals: The Politics of International Justice* (1999); other informative books, inspired by events in Bosnia,

Rwanda, and elsewhere, include W. Shawcross, *Deliver Us from Evil: Peacekeepers, Warlords, and a World of Endless Conflict* (2000); A. Neier, *War Crimes: Brutality, Genocide, Terror, and the Struggle for Justice* (1999), strongly supportive of international jurisdictions; and M. Minow, *Between Vengeance and Forgiveness: Facing History after Genocide and Mass Violence* (1999), less convinced of the efficacy of international tribunals.

On the question of political justice and retribution by postdictatorial regimes in Europe and elsewhere a large-scale multivolume study is under way: N. J. Kritz (ed.), *How Emerging Democracies Reckon with Former Regimes* (1998–). For Europe, informative books on the subject are J. McAdams, *Judging the Past in Unified Germany* (2000); J. Borneman, *Settling Accounts: Violence, Justice, and Accountability in Postsocialist Europe* (1997); and the essays in I. Deák, J. T. Gross, and T. Judt (eds.), *The Politics of Retribution in Europe: World War II and Its Aftermath* (2000).

Modern Society, Information Technology, Globalization

The present and future impact of information technology on contemporary society may be studied in M. Dertouzos, *What Will Be: How the New World of Information Will Change our Lives* (1997); and F. Cairncross, *The Death of Distance 2.0: How The Communications Revolution Will Change Our Lives* (rev. 2001), an updated edition to keep pace with rapid technological changes.

On the much discussed issue of globalization helpful introductions include T. L. Friedman, *The Lexus and the Olive Tree* (1999), on the gap between modernization and traditional values as well as on attempts to narrow the gap by such instruments as the Internet. The debate on globalization continues in P. Kennedy, *Preparing for the Twenty-First Century* (1993); J. N. Rosenau, *Along the Domestic-Foreign Frontier: Exploring Governance in a Turbulent World* (1997), touching on such questions as the erosion of sovereignty; R. Gilpin, *The Challenge of Global Capitalism* (2000), an especially helpful, balanced study; and R. Heilbroner, *Twenty-First Century Capitalism* (1999). Highly critical of efforts to remake the world on Western economic models are W. Greider, *One World, Ready or Not: The Manic Logic of Global Capitalism* (1997); J. Gray, *The Delusions of Global Capitalism* (1999); and E. Luttwak, *Turbo-Capitalism: Winners and Losers in the Global Economy* (1999), the title referring to unregulated market economies. Other illuminating books include D. Yergin, *The Commanding Heights: The Battle Between Government and the Marketplace That Is Reshaping the Modern World* (1998); J. H. Mittleman, *The Globalization Syndrome: Transformation and Resistance* (2000), informative on the opposition to international lending agencies and the World Trade Organization; and J. Micklethwaite and A. Wooldridge, *A Future Perfect: The Essentials of Globalization* (2000), which sees the benefits of present trends outweighing the disadvantages. In G. Soros, *The Crises of Global Capitalism* (1998) an investment banker–philanthropist argues that the emphasis on free markets has overshadowed social responsibilities.

On the related question of the role played by cultural values in economic development thoughtful analyses include H. De Soto, *The Mystery of Capital: Why Capitalism Triumphs in the West and Fails Everywhere Else* (2000); D. S. Landes, *The Wealth and Poverty of Nations* (1998), an important book cited earlier; and the essays in L. E. Harrison and S. P. Huntington (eds.), *Culture Matters: How Values Shape Human Progress* (2000).

The lessons of financial history from the seventeenth century to the present are ably conveyed in E. Chancellor, *Death Take the Hindmost: A History of Financial Speculation* (1999), while financial markets in the United States and elsewhere at the turn of the twenty-first century are shrewdly scrutinized in R. J. Shiller, *Irrational Exuberance* (2000). Studying the financial crises of the 1990s in various parts of the world and the prolonged recession in Japan, P. R. Krugman in *The Accidental Theorist: And Other Dispatches from the Dismal Science* (1998) and *The Return of Depression Economics* (1999) argues for neo-Keynesian expansionist government policies. One of the most discussed books in recent years, F. Fukuyama, *The End of History and the Last Man* (1992), perceptive in some ways, proved to be overly optimistic about the triumph of liberal democracy after the fall of Soviet communism. On predictions in general, R. Heilbroner, *Visions of the Future: The Distant Past, Yesterday, Today, Tomorrow* (1995) explores the expectations of earlier generations about their future and the fate of those expectations.

Problems and Readings

Helpful collections on events in the recent past include H. R. Huttenbach, *Nationalities in the Soviet Union* (1993), in the Anvil series; R. V. Daniels (ed.), *Soviet Communism from Reform to Collapse* (1995); and L. H. Legters (ed.), *Eastern Europe: Transformation and Revolution, 1945–1991* (1992). E. Weber (ed.), *Movements, Currents, Trends: Aspects of European Thought in the Nineteenth and Twentieth Centuries* (1992) brings together key materials from modern European cultural history. L. E. Cahoone (ed.), *From Modernism to Postmodernism: An Anthology* (1996) is a collection of readings from key figures in modern and contemporary cultural and intellectual movements. Readings on feminism are available in S. E. Cooper (ed.), *Western Feminism in the Twentieth Century* (1993), in the Anvil series. R. D. Germain (ed.), *Globalization and Its Critics* (2000) provides useful writings by economists on current debates about the international economy.

Dates given after names of rulers and popes are the years of reigns or pontificates; those given for all others are the years of birth and death.

Pronunciation is indicated where it is not obvious. With foreign words the purpose is not to show their exact pronunciation in their own language but to suggest how they may be acceptably pronounced in English. Fully Anglicized pronunciations are indicated by the abbreviation *Angl.* Pronunciation is shown by respelling, not by symbols, except that the following symbols are used for vowel sounds not found in English:

ø   indicates the sound of ö as in Göttingen. To form this sound, purse the lips as if to say *o,* and then say *ay* as in *ate.*

U   indicates the sound of the French *u,* or of German *ü.* To form this sound, purse the lips as if to say *oo,* and then say *ee* as in *eat.*

aN,   oN, uN, iN indicate the sounds of the French nasal vowels. Once learned, these are easily pronounced, roughly as follows: For aN, begin to pronounce the English word *on,* but avoid saying the consonant *n* and "nasalize" the *ah* sound instead. For oN do the same with the English *own;* for uN, with the English prefix *un-;* for iN, with the English word *an.*

The sound of *s* as in the word *treasure* is indicated by *zh.* This sound is common in English, though never found at the beginning or end of a word. *igh* always indicates the so-called long *i* as in *high.* The vowel sound of *hoot* is indicated by *oo,* that of *hood* by *ŏo.*

Compared with English, the European languages are highly regular in their spelling, in that the same letters or combinations of letters are generally pronounced in the same way.

Index